WITHDRAWN

WITHDRAWN

Architecture and Construction in Steel

is the Steel Construction Institute. Its overall objective is to promote and develop the proper and effective use of steel. It achieves this aim through research, development of design aids and design approaches, publications and advisory and education services. Its work is initiated and guided through the involvement of its members on advisory groups and technical committees. The Institute is financed through subscriptions from its members, revenue from research and consultancy contracts and by sales of publications.

Membership is open to all organizations and individuals that are concerned with the use of steel in construction, and members include designers, architects, engineers, contractors, suppliers, fabricators, academics and government departments in the United Kingdom, elsewhere in Europe and in countries around the world. A comprehensive advisory and consultancy service is available to members on the use of steel in construction.

Further information on membership, publications and courses is given in the SCI prospectus available free on request from:

The Membership and Council Secretary, The Steel Construction Institute, Silwood Park, Ascot, Berkshire SL5 7QN.
Telephone: (0344) 23345, Fax: (0344) 22944

British Steel sponsored the preparation of this book by The Steel Construction Institute and this support is gratefully acknowledged. The different divisions of British Steel produce and market a comprehensive range of steel products for construction. Advisory Services are available to help specifiers with any problems relevant to structural steelwork and to provide points of contact with the sales functions and technical services. A series of publications is available dealing with steel products and their use. A list of addresses and telephone numbers is given in the Appendix.

Architecture and Construction in Steel

Edited by

Alan Blanc
Consultant Architect

Michael McEvoy
Senior Lecturer in Construction
Department of Architecture and Engineering,
University of Westminster

Roger Plank
Senior Lecturer in Structures,
School of Architectural Studies,
University of Sheffield

The Steel Construction Institute

E & FN SPON
An Imprint of Chapman & Hall
London · Glasgow · New York · Tokyo · Melbourne · Madras

Published by
E & FN Spon, an imprint of Chapman & Hall, 2–6 Boundary Row, London SE1 8HN

Chapman & Hall, 2–6 Boundary Row, London SE1 8HN, UK

Blackie Academic & Professional, Wester Cleddens Road, Bishopriggs, Glasgow G64 2NZ, UK

Chapman & Hall Inc., One Penn Plaza, 41st Floor, New York, NY 10119, USA

Chapman & Hall Japan, Thomson Publishing Japan, Hirakawacho Nemoto Building, 6F, 1-7-11 Hirakawa-cho, Chiyoda-ku, Tokyo 102, Japan

Chapman & Hall Australia, Thomas Nelson Australia, 102 Dodds Street, South Melbourne, Victoria 3205, Australia

Chapman & Hall India, R. Seshadri, 32 Second Main Road, CIT East, Madras 600 035, India

---

First edition 1993

Typeset in 9/11pt Bembo by Type Study, Scarborough, North Yorkshire
Printed and bound in Great Britain at the University Press, Cambridge

ISBN 0 419 17660 8

A catalogue record for this book is available from the British Library

Library of Congress Cataloging-in-Publication data

Architecture and construction in steel/edited by A. Blanc, M. McEvoy, R. Plank.
p. cm.
Includes bibliographical references and indexes.
ISBN 0-419-17660-8
1. Building, Iron and steel. 2. Building, Iron and steel—case studies. I. Blanc, A. (Alan) II. McEvoy, M. (Michael) III. Plank, R. (Roger)
TH1611.A73 1992
691′.7—dc20 92-6490
CIP

Contents

Contributors

Professor W. D. Biggs OBE, AMET, BSc, PhD, CEng, FIStructE, FCIOB
Following a period in industry was appointed lecturer and tutor in engineering at Cambridge University. From 1978 he was Head of the Department of Construction Management at Reading University. He is now retired and is a consultant to Buro Happold, Bath.

Bryn Bird BSc, CEng, MICE, FIStructE, MConsE
Graduated from Queen Mary College, London in 1968 and gained contracting experience on roads, river works and bridges. Has extensive experience of large foundations and transfer structures and has a particular interest in masonry and new high strength materials. Since establishing Whitby and Bird with Mark Whitby in 1984, he has been responsible for a wide range of new structures and large scale refurbishments in Docklands and London, including Jubilee Hall, Covent Garden, and the Port of London Authority headquarters. High security projects have included the British Embassy in Dublin.

Alan Blanc RIBA, DipArch (PNL)
Alan Blanc is a chartered architect in private practice in London, a writer, lecturer, traveller and bon vivant. He has lectured at the Universities of London, North London and Westminster, UK and was Fulbright Scholar at Washington State University, USA in 1986. Since 1987 he has been a consultant to the Steel Construction Institute. He is author of 'Landscape Construction', 'Stairs, Steps and Ramps' and Mitchell's 'Building Construction: Components'.

Peter Brett DIC, CEng, FIStructE, FCIOB, MConsE
Senior Engineer with Ove Arup and Partners for ten years followed by architectural practice in Stockholm for a year. Formed Peter Brett Associates in 1965. He has been involved in BSI committees responsible for all Codes of Practice for steel and composite structures in Britain. He has been a Council member of the Institution of Structural Engineers since 1983 and was Vice President in 1991/92.

Ken Chandler BSc (Eng), CEng, FIM, ARSM, FICorr
Formerly Head of Corrosion Advice Bureau, British Steel Corporation, he at present runs a consultancy practice. Chairman of various BSI Committees, including BS 5493 and also of ISO group on surface preparation of steel. Joint author with D. A. Bayliss of 'Steelwork Corrosion Control' published in 1991 by Elsevier Applied Science.

David J. Cochrane IEng, MIMechIE
A mechanical and aeronautical engineering background was followed by 18 years with British Steel, Stewart and Lloyds, Constrado and the SCI. He has served on several BSI Committees. He formed his own consultancy, Technical Publication Services, in 1987. He has been a consultant engineer to the Nickel Development Institute since 1987, on the market development and use of stainless steel in building. He has served on several BSI Committees, and has written numerous articles and lectured on stainless steel.

Yvonne Dean BA Arch (Newc), BA (Open), RIBA
Architect and principal lecturer in materials and construction, senior subject tutor in technology and Director of the Low Energy Architecture Research Unit in the Department of Architecture and Interior Design at the University of North London.

Anthony Gregson MSc, DipArch, DipTP, RIBA, MRTPI, FRSA
Qualified as an architect in 1959 and practises as an architect and town planner and as consultant to GMW Partnership. Has extensive experience in UK, USA, Hong Kong, Malaysia, East Africa, the Middle East and Europe.

David Harriss AA Dip, RIBA
Educated at the Architectural Association 1966–72. Professional career has included working for Foster Associates 1970–71 (year out) and 1972–75, Michael Hopkins 1977–81 and Nicholas Grimshaw and Partners 1981 to present.

Eric Hindhaugh
Structural engineer specializing firstly in steel and then in timber design. Involved with publishing work for the Steel Sheet Trade Association from 1965–70 and then editor for 'Building with Steel'. Since 1975, manager responsible for market development and construction at Strip Products, Newport for British Steel. Retired from British Steel in 1992 and now acts as a consultant in matters related to metal roofing and cladding, publications and market research.

Hal Iyengar BA, MA, FIStructE, FASCE
Obtained a BA in civil engineering in 1955, and MA in structural engineering in 1959. He was a partner at Skidmore, Owings and Merrill in Chicago from 1975 until 1992, where he was responsible for many tall structures including the Sears Tower and John Hancock Center. He now works

for Structural Design International Inc. in Illinois. He has written over 100 technical articles concerned with tall building design.

Ian Liddell MA, DIC, CEng, MICE, FIStructE
A partner in Buro Happold since the firm started in 1974, he has been responsible for a wide range of special structures around the world. These include the State Mosque of Sarawak, fabric and tensile structure roofs for the Diplomatic Club Riyadh, the Hyperion Air Ship for Euro Disneyland and the Imagination HQ roof, London. He has published a number of papers on tension and fabric structures, which have been presented at symposia and colloquia around the world and he was the convenor of an IABSE Colloquium on this subject in May 1992. Currently he is responsible for the firm's New York joint company FTL/Happold.

John Le Good MPhil (Soton), FIStructE, MICE, AIWSc
John Le Good worked at F. J. Samuely and Partners in the early 1960s on analysis and testing of the London Zoo Aviary, and on the Sangamo factory, Felixstowe, followed by three years on the advanced structures course and research on timber columns at Southampton University. From 1966 to 1987 he taught in the Portsmouth Polytechnic Architecture Department, where his interests included building design, windflow, and the work of Frei Otto, Robert Maillart, Walter Segal and H. Isler. His book 'Principles of Structural Steelwork for Architectural Students' was published by Constrado in 1983. Since taking early retirement in 1987, he still teaches at Portsmouth and Southampton, and is involved with general design and research with Barron and Partners.

Michael McEvoy MA, DipArch (Cantab), M Arch (Cornell), RIBA
Michael McEvoy trained as an architect at the Cambridge School of Architecture, UK and at Cornell University, USA. He practised and taught architecture in the USA and Canada for five years and worked at Arup Associates in London from 1979–1988. He is currently senior lecturer and Co-ordinator of Technical Studies in the Department of Architecture and Engineering at the University of Westminster, London, UK.

Keith Moores CEng, FIStructE, MSAICE, MConsE
A Partner with S. B. Tietz and Partners, consulting, civil, structural and traffic engineers. Keith Moores spent the early part of his career with specialist steelwork contractors initially as a design engineer. He has been in private practice in the United Kingdom, South Africa and Rhodesia for the last 20 years and served as Chairman of the Zimbabwe Association of Consulting Engineers in 1979/80.

Patrick Morreau BA(Cantab), CEng, FIStructE
Educated at Cambridge in 1955, and has practised as a structural engineer in California and Massachusetts and, since 1972, with Ove Arup and Partners in London. He has also taught structural design at UC Berkeley, MIT and elsewhere.

Roger Plank BSc (Eng), PhD, CEng, MICE, MIStructE
Roger Plank is a qualified structural engineer and senior lecturer in structures at the School of Architectural Studies, University of Sheffield, UK. From 1973–76, he worked as a design engineer, and lectured in civil engineering at the University of Sheffield from 1976–87. He has very close links with the steelwork industry – in his research into fire-resistant design of steel structures, in developing teaching material for designing in steel, and in his role as chairman of the ECCS Commission on architectural aspects of steel construction.

Jef Robinson BSc, CEng, MIM, MCIM
Graduated in metallurgy at Durham University in 1962 and undertook research for the NASA space programme. Moving to the steel industry, he designed steel for special applications including supertankers, offshore drilling rigs and long span bridges. Since 1976 he has been Market Development Manager, British Steel, General Steels – Sections, responsible for identification and development of new products for the construction industry. He chaired the BS 5950 Part 8 committee on fire-resistant design and is closely involved in formulating the equivalent European Standards.

Julian Ryder-Richardson DipArch, RIBA
Julian Ryder-Richardson is a chartered architect, and was elected a member of the British Academy of Experts in 1992. He joined GMW Partnership in 1960, becoming a partner in 1971, and has been a senior partner since 1981. Among key buildings he has been associated with are the Commercial Union HQ and Banque Belge (both steel framed) and Barings Bank in the City of London. He wrote 'An Integrated Approach to the Design of Steel Framed Office Buildings of Medium Height' for Constrado, published in 1972

Richard Saxon BArch (Hons), MC, RIBA
An Architect Partner of Building Design Partnership since 1977 and author of 'Atrium Buildings' (Architectural Press, 1986), the definitive work on the subject. His next book 'The Atrium Comes of Age' will be published in 1993. Recent designs include the J. P. Morgan headquarters (1991) and plans for Paddington Basin, the All England Lawn Tennis Club at Wimbledon, and Glaxo at Greenford.

Tom Schollar MA (Cantab), CEng, MIStructE
A partner of consulting engineers F. J. Samuely and Partners. He graduated from Cambridge in 1973 with a double first in engineering, and has worked on a number of building projects, including the refurbishment of Michelin House and the Design Museum in London. Teaches structural engineering at the AA and the Bartlett School of Architecture.

Dennis Sharp MA, AA Dip, RIBA
Trained at the Architectural Association and Liverpool University. Professional work has included periods with the Civic Trust, the multi-disciplinary Atelier St Albans, and his own practice Dennis Sharp Associates. He has taught at the AA since 1969. Well known as a writer, critic and editor, his books include 'Twentieth Century Architecture: A Visual History' (1990), 'Sources of Modern Architecture' (1981), and 'Illustrated Dictionary of Architecture' (1991). He was editor of *AA Quarterly* (1969–82) and *World Architecture* (1988–92). He is currently RIBA Vice President: Architecture Centre and Chairman of DOCOMOMO UK. In 1987 he was made Professor of the International Academy of Architecture and in 1991 he received the Medaille d'Argent of the French Academie d'Architecture.

Derek Sugden CEng, MICE, MIStructE, MWeldI, MIOA
Studied civil and structural engineering at Westminster Technical College. After working for contractors and consultants joined Ove Arup and Partners 1953 and became an Associate in 1957. Founder partner in 1963 of the multi-disciplinary team Arup Associates, Chairman 1984 to retirement in 1987. Founder Principal of Arup Acoustics 1980 and now consultant to that practice. Visiting Professor, University College London, Bartlett School of Architecture and Planning and also at the School of Architecture, Polytechnic of the South-West. Visiting lecturer at various architectural schools in the USA, UK, Germany and the Netherlands.

Robert Taggart CEng, MIStructE
Gained his experience on the design of a wide range of steel framed buildings initially within the fabrication industry and subsequently in a consultancy role. He is presently an Advisor for British Steel, General Steels Division.

John Thornton BSc, CEng, MIStructE
John Thornton joined Ove Arup and Partners in 1968, where he is now a director. He was an associate at Whicheloe Macfarlane Partnership 1977–8. Projects for which he has been responsible include Fleetguard and Saint Herblain in France, The Mound, Compton and Edrich Stands at Lord's Cricket Ground, and Bracken House in London, and the visitors' towers at the Reina Sofia Gallery in Madrid. Current projects include Glyndebourne Opera House and the New Parliamentary Buildings in Westminster, London. He has written articles and prepared educational and CPD material on tension structures.

Stefan Tietz BScEng, FEng, FICE, FIStructE, MConsE
A partner with S. B. Tietz and Partners, consulting civil, structural and traffic engineers. Recent projects include the winning scheme for the National Gallery and a major office development in Watford. He is a past President of the Société des Ingenieurs et Scientifiques de France, serves on several technical committees of the Institution of Structural Engineers and also acts extensively as an expert at public inquiries and legal disputes.

Bjorn Watson BSc, MSc, CEng, MICE
Early experience with Trollope and Colls, followed by ten years in Africa and Middle East. Returning to the UK working for Mott Hay and Anderson. Joined YRM in early 1980, starting the Civil and Structural Division.

Mark Whitby BSc, CEng, FICE
Graduated in civil engineering from Kings College London and subsequently worked for contractors on major civil engineering projects and as a consultant on a wide range of civil and building designs. projects include Southampton Docks, M4 Motorway bridges, the Saudi Arabian parliament buildings, the British Antarctic survey base at Halley Bay and the African Aviary at London Zoo. He set up the consultancy of Whitby and Bird with Bryn Bird in 1984, and has developed this into a multi-disciplinary engineering practice with a particular emphasis on elegant, easily constructed structures. Notable competition successes include the design for Bracken House with Michael Hopkins, and the Stock Exchange and Chamber of Commerce in Berlin with Nicholas Grimshaw. Mark Whitby is a member of the Council of the Institution of Civil Engineers and of the Joint Committee on Structural Safety.

Peter Wright BA, CEng, MIStructE, AMICE
Spent 14 years with consulting engineers in south east England working on new buildings and refurbishment. Joined British Steel in 1981 and subsequently manager of Structural Advisory Service.

Preface

The genesis of this book stems from British Steel's architectural teaching programme, released in January 1990. Many of the authors engaged in that project have participated in preparing this textbook with the continued benefit of Professor Derek Sugden as honorary editor. My role has been to weld together the disparate elements and to expand the architectural content. The discipline of reducing turgid prose and guarding against repetition has been the role of my co-editors Dr Roger Plank and Michael McEvoy. The end result would never have been completed without the constant advice on content and style by Derek Sugden. The day-to-day work of editing the various contributions has led my colleagues to rewrite some sections to bring matters fully into line with the 1990s. The gestation time of five years is a long one but is needed when running a stable of around 30 writers.

Earlier periods that followed a building boom have seen the publication of books that attempt to summarize the state of the art of steel construction. The present time is perhaps similar to the early 1970s which saw such classics as *Multi-storey Buildings in Steel* (by F. Hart, W. Henn and H. Sontag), and *Buildings for Industry* (by W. Henn). Both were published originally in West Germany to cover post-war construction in the 1950s and 1960s, and English language editions were subsequently published by Granada and Iliffe respectively. This new book is intended to address current developments and to discuss ways of building that are now commonplace in Britain and North America.

Encyclopaedic volumes like *Fundamentals of Building Construction Materials and Methods* by Edward Allen, published by John Wiley and Sons in the USA are excellent teaching manuals but fail to provide a really wide range of up to date case studies to interest the general practitioner. The editing team for *Architecture and Construction in Steel* have aimed at a collation of writing which delves into contemporary practice but provides sufficient historic reference to interest the conservationist whether architect or engineer.

The main readership is seen as practitioner or student from architectural and design disciplines related to building. Engineering concepts of design differ from those cherished by architects, and the texts that follow may help to resolve the misunderstandings. Derek Sugden's introduction seeks to build many bridges to the 'art of construction'. This latter description is perhaps the most valuable concept that the editing team have developed.

The warmest appreciation needs to be expressed for the valuable support from British Steel plc and in particular for the funding granted to The Steel Construction Institute that enabled writers to be commissioned. British Steel also furnished specialist advice from their Structural Advisory Service and from Strip Products, whilst staff, both present and retired, contributed to a number of key chapters.

The personal enthusiasm engendered by Robert Latter, Marketing Manager for British Steel (Structural Steels Division) and by Dr Graham Owens, Acting Co-director of The Steel Construction Institute ensured that the momentum was maintained despite the lengthy process of satisfying a critical editorial board. That board was drawn from the writers involved and reinforced by outspoken outsiders like Dr Bill Addis and Chris McCarthy.

The penultimate thankyous must be awarded to the fellow writers that have given of their expertise and time to ensure success to the venture. . . Professor Bill Biggs, Bryn Bird, Peter Brett, Ken Chandler, David Cochrane, Yvonne Dean, Anthony Gregson, David Harriss, Eric Hindhaugh, Hal Iyengar, Ian Liddell, John Le Good, Michael McEvoy, Keith Moores, Patrick Morreau, Dr Roger Plank, Jef Robinson, Julian Ryder-Richardson, Richard Saxon, Tom Schollar, Dennis Sharp, Professor Derek Sugden, Robert Taggart, John Thornton, Stefan Tietz, Bjorn Watson, Peter Wright and Mark Whitby.

The final words of appreciation are for the work of Ruth Lush and Sylvia Blanc in converting unruly scripts into the tidy realm of computer discs. Special thanks are also due to Susan Boobis, the lively copy-editor engaged by E. & F. N. Spon who grappled with awry spelling, last minute corrections and wild captions to convert all and sundry into printable and readable format. To E. & F. N. Spon, John Saunders and to everyone else involved my heartfelt thanks for a task well done and for the patience of the SCI since Easter 1987.

Alan Blanc, April 1993

Acknowledgements

We have tried as far as possible to trace the holders of copyright material and sources of previously published material. The illustrations would never have been completed without generous help from all the architects and engineers in lending their drawings, photographs and slides and it has not been feasible to list each individual. Our warmest thanks are given to everyone who furnished material.

Anthony Leitch must be warmly acknowledged as the illustrator who converted many diagrams and the roughest of sketches into figures with a clear and consistent style of presentation.

ILLUSTRATION CREDITS

Aldington, Craig and Collinge 35.10
Alsop and Stormer 38.6
Arup Associates 21.7, 37.7a–e
Blanc, A., 1.2 to 1.5, 1.9, 1.14 to 1.16, 1.18 to 1.21, 1.25, 1.28, 1.29, 2.8, 2.9, 2.11, chapter 3 lead-in, chapter 6 lead-in, 6.4, 6.5, 6.12, 6.24, chapter 7 lead-in, 7.1 to 7.5, 10.7, 10.9, 10.10, 10.13, 10.14, 12.23, 12.24, 15.17a, 16.16, 16.20, 16.22, 21.6a, 21.39, chapter 22 lead-ins, 23.5, 24.13, 24.17, 24.21b, 25.9, 25.10, 25.15, 25.19, 25.21, 25.22, 25.27, 25.33, 26.18, 27.1, 27.2, 27.18, 27.21, 28.6, 28.7, 29.7, 30.1, 30.16, 31.1 to 31.3, 31.5 to 31.8, 31.17, 31.20, 31.22 to 31.28, 31.31, 31.37, 31.38, chapter 32 lead-in, 32.1, 33.1, 33.3, 33.4, 33.9, 33.10, 33.14, 33.18, chapter 34 lead-in, 34.4, 34.9, 34.11, 35.1a–h, 35.3 to 35.7, 35.11, 35.12, 35.15, 35.17, 36.21a, 38.1, 38.5
Book Art 2.5
Brick Development Association 25.11, 25.12, 25.31, 26.16, 26.17
British Gypsum 30.2, 30.3, 30.4, 30.5, 30.6
British Steel 4.1, 4.5, 4.6, 4.7, 4.8, 4.10, 4.12, 5.1, 5.3, 5.4, 5.7, 5.11, 5.12, 9.1 to 9.13, 12.31, chapter 16 lead-in, 16.10, 16.11, 16.18, 16.21, 24.20, 26.3, 27.14
Brookes, A., 26.9
Bryant, R., 35.9
Building Design Partnership 24.12
Buro Happold 20.1, 20.71
Carl Fisher Partnership, The 24.15, 24.16
Charles, M., 12.6b and c, 12.7c, 12.7d
Chorley and Handford 37.13c,e
CLASP Development Group 12.21, 12.22, 12.23, 12.24
Clestra Hauserman 30.8
Cochrane, D. J., chapter 6 lead-in (a), 6.6, 6.7, 6.11, 6.17, 6.18, 6.19, 6.20, 6.21, 6.22, 6.23, 6.25, 6.26
Coopers & Lybrand 10.11, 17.14
Couturier, S., 36.16d
Damplaat Ltd 26.5
de Maré, E., 1.8
Dennis Sharp Architects 1.27, 2.6
Design Group, Cambridge 12.7a, 12.7b
Dexion Ltd 29.10
Donat, J., chapter 26 lead-in
Dorchester Hotel 26.11
Drawn Metal Ltd 6.13–6.15
Dubosc, E., and Landowski, M., 30.15
Dupain, M., 5.2, 36.24d–f
E. J. Studios 16.22a
ECD Partnership 12.5a
Edward Mills and Partners 12.26
Einzig, R., 12.32
EPR 24.18, 24.19
Erisco Bauder plc 25.28
Eternit UK Ltd 27.15
FaulknerBrowns 12.29d
Fitch and Co., 12.9
Fitzroy Robinson 24.22b
Sir Norman Foster and Partners, chapter 2 lead-in, chapter 12 lead-in, 12.15, 12.17, 16.17, 21.29, 32.7, 36.11a–g, 37.2b
Fullflow Systems Ltd 28.8
Gail Ceramics 30.13, 30.14
GMW chapter 23 lead-in
Greenwood Airvac Ventilation Ltd 31.40
Grimshaw, N., 12.33
Grozier Building Systems 26.6
Hambourg, S., 36.16a
Hanisch, M., 31.29
Harris and Edgar Ltd 27.20, 29.8, 29.9
Harry Seidler and Associates 36.23a,c
Horden, R., 25.29, 25.30, 25.31
Hunter, A., 12.8c, 12.8d
Hursley, T., chapter 10 lead-in
Institut für Leichte Flachentragwerke Fritz Dressler 38.3
Jansen VISS AG 25.5, 25.6, 25.7, 25.8, 27.13, 31.13, 31.14
Jiricna, E., chapter 33 lead-in, 33.25a, 33.25b
John Winter and Associates 36.1a–c

Lambot, I., 10.15, 37.8b, 37.8g
Le Good, J., 11.1, 11.2, 11.6, 11.11, 11.15, 11.16, 11.27, 11.28, 11.34
Leslie, R., and Turner A., chapter 5 lead-ins
Levitt Bernstein Associates 10.17
London Brick Co., 26.21
Michael Hopkins and Partners 27.12
Museum of Modern Art, New York, The 10.6, 25.23
Newby, F., 17.10
Outram, J., 35.18
Ove Arup & Partners, Intro 1–14, 16–21, 12.5b, 12.10, 17.11, 17.15, 17.16, 17.18, 17.19, 17.20, 17.21, 19.18, 19.19
Paternoster Associates 38.4
Pentagram 35.2
Pei Cobb Freed and Partners 36.16b, 36.16c
Pilkington Glass Ltd 27.9, 27.11
Plank, R., chapter 21 lead-in (a)
Plannja 11.53
Preston, J., 12.29c
Reid, J., and Peck, J., 36.4a,c,d, 36.22b,c,d, chapter 37 lead-in
Richard Quinnell Ltd 35.19
Richard Rogers Partnership 33.24, 35.13, 35.14
Riedinger 26.7
Ritchie, I., 27.8
Ritz Hotel 2.4
Royal Botanic Gardens, Kew 12.12a
Saxon, R., 19.1–19.17, 19.20–19.42
Schollar, T., 21.4, 21.10–21.12, 21.20, 21.21, 21.30, 21.31, 21.36–21.38, 21.43–21.47
Selfridges Ltd 26.22
Shafler, A., 36.10a–d
Steel Framing Systems Ltd 30.9
Steinkamp, J. R., 36.7d
Soar, T., 11.12
Sologlass Architectural Systems 32.2, 32.8, 32.9
SOM chapter 15 lead-in, 17.12
Stoller, E., © Esto 10.12, 15.4, 15.10, 15.13, 15.17c
Tate Access Floors 13.11
Thermalite plc 26.15
Tietz, S., chapter 18 lead-ins, 18.1 to 18.8
Trent Concrete Structures 26.14
Turpin, R., 35.16
Welland Grating Ltd 33.11
Wendker-Gail 27.19
Whitby and Bird 38.2b
Wilkinson, R., chapter 11 lead-in, 11.8
YRM International chapter 14 lead-in, 14.1 to 14.30

PUBLICATION CREDITS

Bancroft, J., and Rogers, P., (1986) *Structural Steel Classics*, Cleveland, UK, British Steel, 1.10, 2.4, 10.16, 16.19, 17.8, 36.6b, 36.12a
Burt *et al.*, (1945) *House Construction*, HMSO, 30.10, 30.11, 30.12
Cantacuzino, S., (1975) *New Uses for Old Buildings*, London, The Architectural Press, 24.1
de Maré, E., (1948) *New Ways of Building*, London, The Architectural Press, 26.20
Guise, D., (1985) *Design and Technology in Architecture*, USA, John Wiley and Sons Inc, 16.14
Hart, F., Henn, W., Sontag, H., (1978) *Multi-storey Buildings in Steel*, Crosby Lockwood Staples, Blackwell Scientific Publications 1.13, 16.23, 16.24, 16.25, 16.26, 25.18, 25.20
Henn, W., (1965) *Buildings for Industry*, London, Iliffe Books Ltd 27.10
Highfield, D., (1991) *Construction of New Buildings Behind Historical Facades*, London, E & FN Spon 24.2, 24.4, 24.5, 24.14
Insall, D., (1972) *Care of Old Buildings Today*, The Architectural Press, 24.24
Layson, J. F., *Great Engineers*, London, Walter Scott, chapter 1, lead-in
Le Good, J. P., (1983) *Principles of Structural Steel Work for Architecture Students*, Constrado, 12.1, 12.2
Lyall, S., (1991) *Designing the New Landscape*, London, Thames and Hudson, 36.19e
Ogg, A., (1987) *Architecture in Steel*, Red Hill, Australia, The Royal Australian Institute of Architects, 1.6, 1.7, 1.17, 2.8, 2.10, 2.14, 2.15, 10.4, 10.8, 36.2a, 36.8d,e,g, 36.24b
Pracht K. (1986) *Treppen*, Stuttgart, Deutsche Verlags-Anstalt GmbH 33.19–33.21
Saxon, R., (1986) *Atrium Buildings*, London, The Architectural Press, 36.7a
Sharp, D., (1984) *Bossom's American Architecture*, London, Book Art, 2.3
Sharp, D., (1981) *Sources of Modern Architecture*, London, Book Art, 1.11
Stillman, C. G., and Castle Cleary, R., (1949) *The Modern School*, London, The Architectural Press, 28.1
Thorne, R., (1980) *Covent Garden Market*, London, The Architectural Press, 24.3
Walker, D., (1987) *Great Engineers*, London, Academy Editions, 1.23, 24.6

Whittick, A., (1974) *European Architecture in the 20th Century*, Aylesbury, Leonard Hill Books, International Textbook Co Ltd, 26.8
Yorke, F. R. S., Gibberd, F., (1948) *The Modern Flat*, London, The Architectural Press, 26.10

Journals

AJ Focus, 12.6a, 12.8a and b, 12.27, 12.28
Architects' Journal The chapter 9 lead-in, 12.13, 12.20, 12.27, 12.29a, 12.29b, 13.15, 17.17, 22.1a, 22.10, 29.1 to 29.6, 30.7, 33.12
Architecture Today chapter 27 lead-in
Architectural Forum 26.12, 27.4, 27.5
Architectural Review 1.26, 2.12, 2.13, 26.1, 27.6, 36.3a,b
Arup Journal, Ove Arup & Partners, (Winter 1988/1989) 12.5b, 12.10a to d
Arup Journal, Ove Arup & Partners, (Summer 1987) 17.15, 17.16
Arup Journal, Ove Arup & Partners, (Winter 1985) 17.18, 17.19. 17.20, 17.21, 37.8d
Arup Journal, Ove Arup & Partners, (Spring 1989) 36.15b
Structural Steel Design Awards Scheme, Steel Construction, (November 1987) 37.10a and b
Structural Steel Design Awards Scheme, (1986) Steel Construction 12.19
Institution of Structural Engineers, (September 1985) The Structural Engineer, Vol 63A, No 9, 17.4

Introduction

Derek Sugden

From the early days of the iron and steel frame there have been manuals, treatises and text books written primarily for the engineer and constructor. For the UK and the English speaking worlds they stretch from William Fairbairn's classic of 1854, *On the Application of Cast Iron and Wrought Iron to Building Purposes* (second edition 1857–8 to which is added 'A Short Treatise on Wrought Iron Bridges') to the *Steel Designers' Manual* of 1955 by Gray, Kent, Mitchell and Godfrey. The last edition of the manual appeared in 1972 and a new edition was published in 1993. Since the first edition of the *Steel Designers' Manual* there have been many books and pamphlets ranging from the erudite, analytical paper to those publications verging on the 'coffee table genre' on the subject of the steel frame in building, but they are invariably written for the engineer. One of the most successful was the book prepared for the Deutscher Stahlbau-Verband *Multi-Storey Buildings in Steel* by the three Profs Dr-Ings Hart, Henn and Sonntag. An excellent book in every way but predominantly a German/American view of the multi-storey steel frame and its development.

Following the publication and success of the *British Steel Teaching Programme* for Engineering students in 1985 and its subsequent publication in the book *Structural Steel Design* (Dowling, Knowles, Owens, 1988) A British Steel Teaching Programme for architectural students was prepared and issued to the architectural departments of all the UK universities and polytechnics in January 1990. The Architectural Teaching programme has some 28 authors, many of whom prepared more than one paper. The editorial work and organization of the whole enterprise was carried out by Dr Roger Plank, Dr Brenda Vale and Robert Vale at Sheffield University with an overview from Dr Graham Owens and Alan Blanc of the SCI. The teaching programme is divided into six sections, the 'History of Iron and Steel', 'Steel Technology', 'Design and Analysis in Steelwork', 'Element Behaviour and Design', 'Non-Structural Uses of Steel' and 'Architecture of Steel'. The lectures are supported by slides, videos and software and are structured in such a way as to provide a continuous teaching programme, although each section and unit is a complete discrete teaching package and may be selected in any order. *Architecture and Construction in Steel*, like *Structural Steel Design*, is a natural consequence of the teaching programme. Because of its unique nature, this first text book on steel construction, aimed specifically at architects, was expanded to cover every aspect of the use of steel and iron in building construction.

The iron and steel frame had a radical, if not revolutionary effect on the way designers thought about buildings. The skeletal frame could be described as the 'armature' of the modern movement because it released building from the inhibitions of the loadbearing wall and trabeated construction. As a natural consequence it changed the way that architects and engineers thought about building and was a great influence on the development of architectural theory. There were historical precedents for thinking and theorizing about an architecture based on a skeletal frame. The two outstanding examples are the Sung Dynasty Building Standards or 'Ying-Tsao Fa-Shih' which dominated Chinese official building for nearly 1000 years and was last defined in an official publication of 1078 pages (Figs 1 and 2)

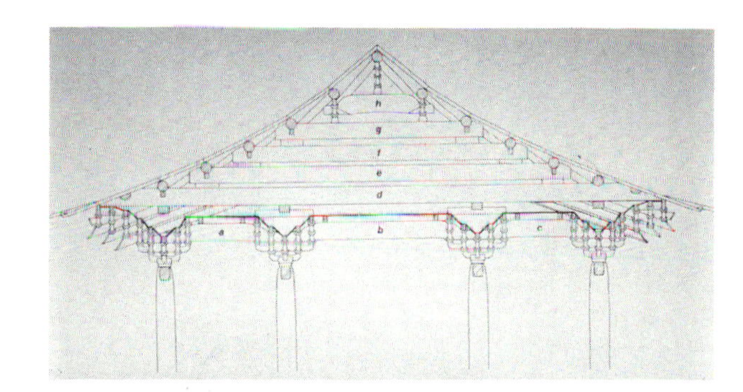

Fig. 1 *Six tiers of beams in Chinese Temple.*

Fig. 2 *Temple gateway, Canton (three tiers of beams).*

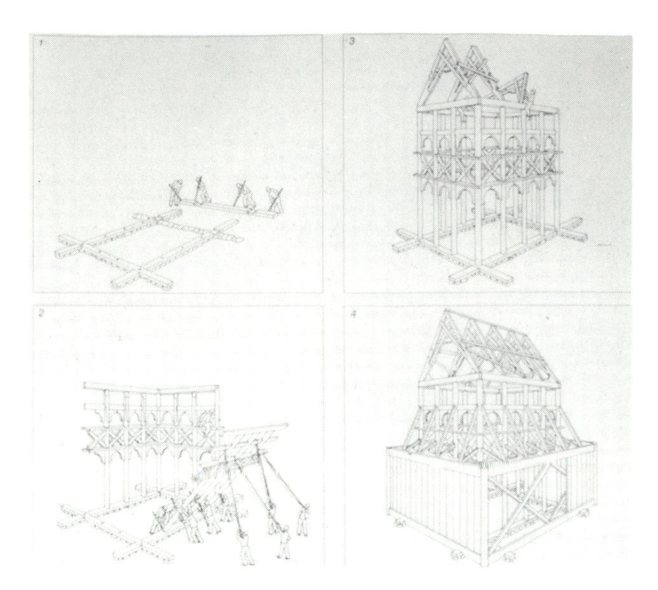
Fig. 3 *Construction of a small stave church, Norway (11th century).*

presented to the throne in 1100 AD; and the 11th century stave churches of Norway, perhaps the first European prefabricated industrialized building system (Figs 3 and 4). They are isolated examples, however, and had little effect on the development of building technique and architectural theories which remained rooted in the trabeated tradition for the vast majority of buildings with the exception, of course, of the arches, vaults and buttresses of the Gothic tradition and the domes of the Byzantine and the Romanesque tradition.

If there is one system that has revolutionized our thinking about ways of building it is the skeletal frame, and if there is one material that has dominated frame construction it is mild steel. It is also the material on which, following the example of Mies van der Rohe, many architects have continuously developed their own philosophy of building. These architectural ideas are still very potent and in the last 20 years have become the driving force behind some of the world's most distinguished buildings.

There are examples of timber skeletal frame construction in the early silk mills and frame and cross wall construction in the buildings of the Hanseatic League, but fire soon became the dominant factor in the design of these timber frames. The first person to tackle the problem in a vigorous way was William Strutt, son of Arkwright's partner Jedediah Strutt. William Strutt's first essay in fireproof building was the Derby Cotton Mill 1792–3 (Fig. 5). This mill had brick arches spanning between heavy timber cross beams supported by cast iron columns. The exposed soffits of the beams were protected against fire by plaster. It was Charles Bage, however, who first introduced cast iron beams into the frame of the Shrewsbury Mill (Fig. 6) of 1796. This followed a correspondence between Strutt and Bage on the suitability of cast iron for beams, William Strutt being rather

Fig. 4 *Fantoff Stave Church, Norway (c. 1200).*

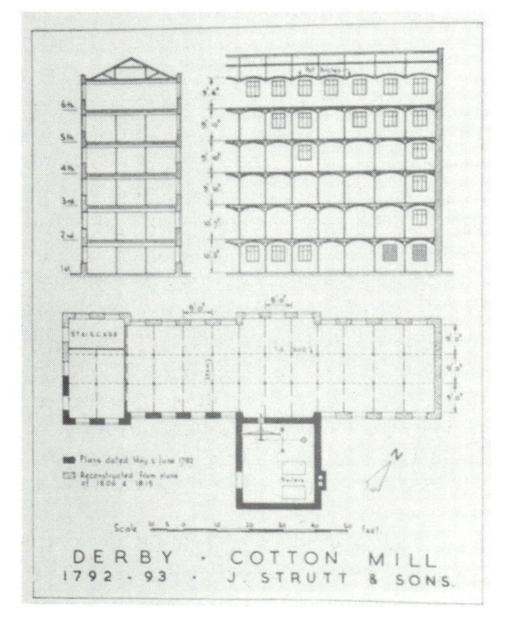

Fig. 5 *Derby Cotton Mill 1792–3 (engineer William Strutt).*

Fig. 6 *Shrewsbury Mill 1796–97 (engineer Charles Bage).*

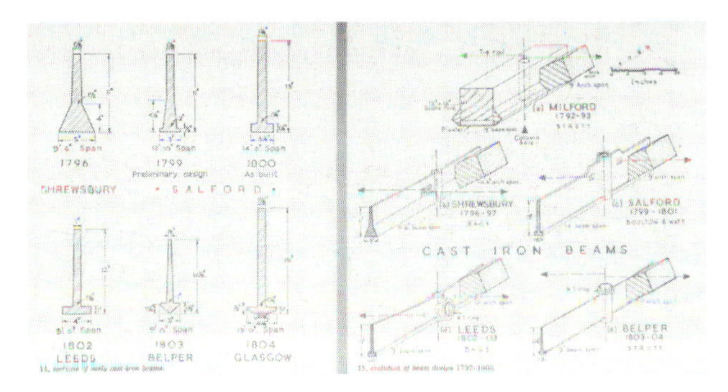

Fig. 7 *Evolutional cast iron beam design 1792–1803.*

cautious because of the brittle nature of the material. Bage however, carried out tests and produced calculations to support this development and after the Shrewsbury Mill cast iron beams became almost standard. Figure 7 shows the development of the cast iron beam section for the early mills. Boulton and Watt made a great contribution to this development but one of the most outstanding examples was William Strutt's Belper North Mill (Fig. 8), a brilliant early example of the rigorous integration of an industrial structure with its energy distribution system. Following this early 'structural revolution' the evolution of the mill and warehouse building was slow; cast iron was gradually replaced by riveted wrought iron. From the middle of the century the style was dominated by the Fairbairn-type wrought iron frame (Fig. 9) with the columns remaining in cast iron but with the development of main beam and secondary beam construction.

The external stabilizing walls were retained throughout the 19th century, together with the cast iron columns. There was one notable exception, and that was the Boat Store, Sheerness 1858–60 in cast and wrought iron described in

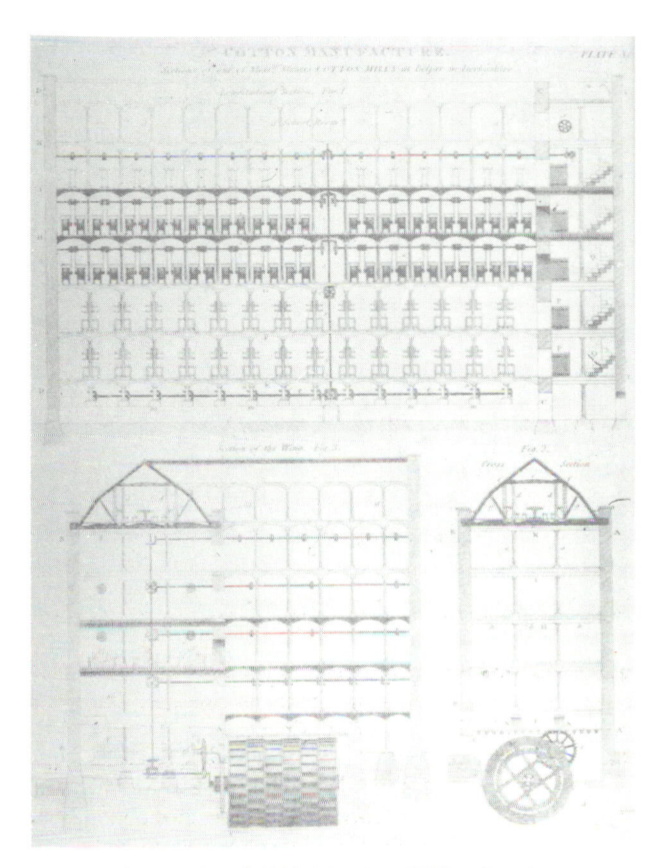

Fig. 8 *Belper North Mill 1803–4 (engineer William Strutt).*

Fig. 9 *Fairbairn-type wrought iron frame LNWR warehouse, Manchester, 1869 interior after conversion (engineers LNWR company).*

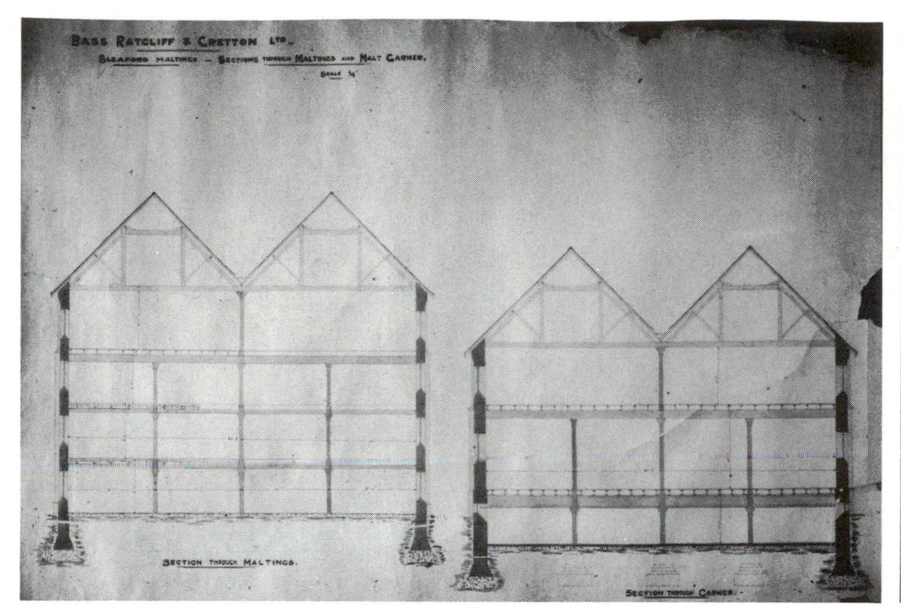

Fig. 10 *Sleaford Maltings 1897–1903.*

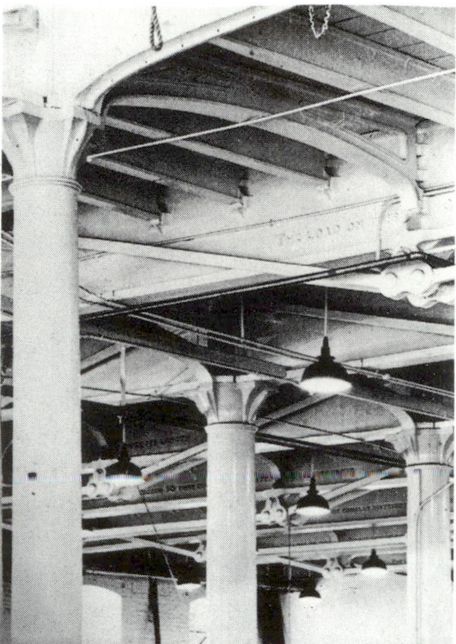

Fig. 12 *Royal Navy Dockyard, No. 6 Boathouse Portsmouth 1843–5.*

Fig. 11 *Albert Dock, Liverpool 1848 (architect Philip Hardwick: engineer Jesse Hartley).*

detail by Dennis Sharp in the first chapter of this historical survey. For me it is perhaps the UK's most seminal building of the modern movement. Its influence at the time seems to have been very small. The heavy loadbearing and stabilizing external walls remained and an example as late as the turn of the century, Sleaford Maltings 1897–1903 (Fig. 10) shows how, despite the adoption of the mild steel frame, the cast iron columns and the external wall are retained in a virtually identical cross section to the 'Fairbairn' frame of 50 years earlier.

It was not until the London County Council (LCC) by-laws of 1909 that the presence of a steel frame in the external wall allowed for panel construction as opposed to a traditional loadbearing wall. The first public building in England to use a fully framed steel frame was the Ritz Hotel of 1906. The facade, however, did not indicate or even suggest the underlying steel frame. The external wall was still carrying its own weight from the roof to the ground. The frame was still not recognized as a loadbearing element in the facade as exploited by Green at Sheerness over 40 years before. The first major building to do this and to exploit the new LCC regulations was Kodak House of 1911 where Sir John Burnet made an innovative attempt to express the underlying steel frame.

Alongside the development of the iron frame in the UK, the new materials of cast iron and wrought iron were used for many building elements and building types, from Gothic revival churches of the early 19th century, prefabricated cast iron churches and sunday schools for export, to the cast iron clad frames of Liverpool and Glasgow. Despite these early developments in the UK of the frame, roof and cladding systems, the potential of the skeletal frame was only fully realized in the USA and particularly Chicago, and well documented under 'Chicago style' in Dennis Sharp's historical review.

During the development of the skeletal frame in the 19th century tensions grew between the architect and the engineer. On many occasions this was supremely well resolved as in Jesse Hartley's Albert Dock (Fig. 11) where he worked very closely with the architect Philip Hardwick using cast iron doric columns to support the great warehouses and cast iron doric columns for the Dock office. When wrought iron

Fig. 14 *Standard structural columns in various styles from catalogue of Abraham Derby and Co 1875.*

began to replace cast iron and the I-section and H-section developed, cast iron was still the preferred material for the column. They were invariably of circular section and influenced by architectural precedents. A Royal Navy Dockyard boathouse (Fig. 12) at Portsmouth shows this influence very clearly. An extreme case of these architectural precedents, particularly prevalent in railway architecture where the engineer's work finished at the eaves level and the architect took over at the head of the column, is the decorated platform column at Malvern Station, 1860 (Fig. 13). It is interesting to look at the standard catalogue of the great iron foundry, Abraham Darby and Co., who built the

Fig. 13 *Architectural design applied to column capital: Malvern Station, 1860.*

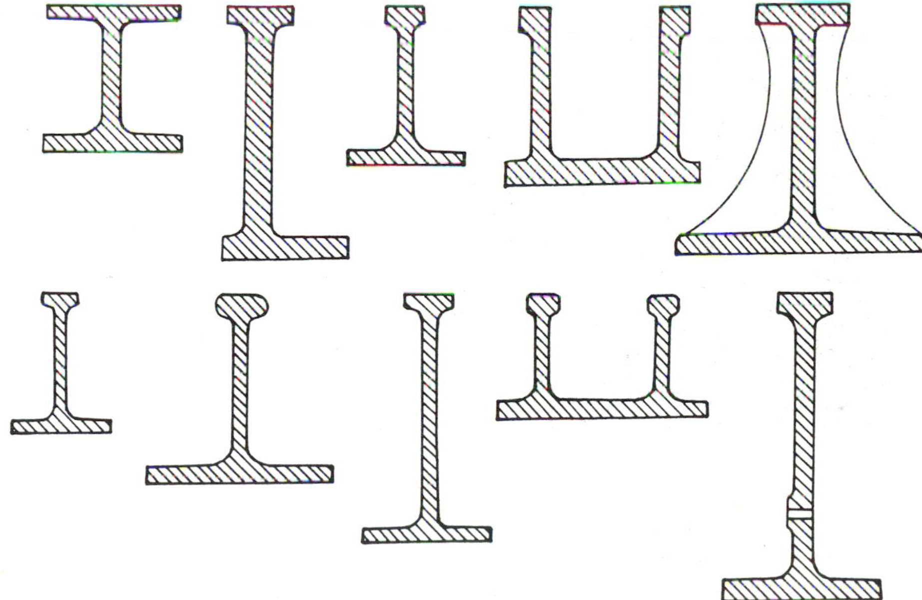

Fig. 15 Early cast iron beam sections.

Fig. 16 *Bibliothèque Nationale Paris 1865–1868 (architect Henri Labrouste).*

first cast iron bridge at Coalbrookdale. In 1875 it showed standard columns (Fig. 14) all decorated in various styles, whilst standard beams were all the result of rigorous testing and calculation and available in forms produced by engineers and constructors alone (refer to Fig. 1.1).

The use of modern materials within established architectural styles contrasts with allowing the architectural form to be influenced by the nature of the material and its construction. There is no better example of this than in the work of a single architect, Henri Labrouste. Twenty years separates his two great libraries in Paris. The first, St. Généviève, 1843–1850 (Fig. 17), is of cast iron throughout, the barrel vaults of prefabricated sections in cast iron reflecting faithfully the Gothic tradition; the second, the Bibliothèque National, 1865–1868 (Fig. 16), is of wrought iron with the domes constructed of plates and flats riveted together in the new tradition, creating a totally new style springing from the material and the process. The columns remain in cast iron inhibited as usual by the Classical tradition.

There are four great examples spanning the 19th century in England which illustrate the theme of engineers working alone and following the disciplines of the nature of the new material and its potential and working in close collaboration with the architect who is still carrying the cultural baggage of previous centuries applying their styles to modern materials and structures. In Telford's magnificent Pont-y-Cysylte aqueduct, built between 1795 and 1803 (Fig. 18) the concept and detailing of the structure springs entirely from the nature of the materials cast iron and stone, the process of their manufacture and of the construction of the great structure. This elegant simplicity is even more surprising when considering that Telford was born in 1757, 13 years before Beethoven, Hegel and Wordsworth. He was

Fig. 17 *Bibliothèque St Généviève, Paris 1843 (architect Henri Labrouste).*

Fig. 18 *Pont-y-Cysylte Aqueduct detail view of cast iron elements.*

Fig. 19 *The Great Stove, Chatsworth 1836–40 (designer Joseph Paxton assisted by Decimus Burton).*

also apprenticed to a stone mason and would have been influenced in his most formative years by the architects of the eighteenth century, and yet this great structure is free from all architectural precedents. The Great Stove at Chatsworth (Fig. 19), built between 1836 and 1840, was the work of Paxton but assisted by the London architect, Decimus Burton. It was one of Paxton's most innovative structures in its combination of cast iron, timber and glass. The portico however, designed by Burton, large enough to take Queen Victoria's carriage, is influenced by Classical and Gothic precedents which would please many of our present day 'post-modernists'. A work of real collaboration, however, was the great tubular bridge over the Menai Strait by Robert Stephenson and the architect, Francis Thompson (Fig. 20). Here this vast engineering concept is cloaked with Thompson's Egyptian architectural style which in no way detracts from the impact of the great structure. The fourth example is Benjamin Baker's Forth Bridge of 1890 (Fig. 21), a masterpiece in the new material of structural steel, totally uncompromising in its 'functional design'. It was attacked by William Morris who claimed that 'there never would be

Fig. 20 *Tubular Bridge, Menai Strait 1846–1850 (architect Francis Thompson: engineer Robert Stephenson).*

Fig. 21 *Construction of cantilevers to the Firth of Forth railway bridge (refer also to lead-in picture to chapter 7).*

an architecture of iron, every improvement in machinery being uglier and uglier until they reach the supremest specimen of all ugliness – the Forth Bridge'. Less than 100 years separates the Forth Bridge from Pont-y-Cysylte. Sir Walter Scott called Telford's cast iron aqueduct 'the greatest work of art he had ever seen' but since his day a gulf had opened up between the arts and the sciences, between architects and engineers who sadly no longer spoke the same language. The gulf is still with us today.

From these few examples it is possible to generate a thesis that architects and engineers differ fundamentally in their approach to design, with architects working from precedent and engineers working intuitively. Throughout the book the reader will see many examples which both support and question this thesis. No one can escape from his own particular 'cultural baggage' and due to our specialist, numerate and literary dominated educational system the cultural baggage of architects and engineers usually differs very widely indeed. It is hoped that many aspects of this book will introduce architects not only to the intuitive way which engineers work but to some of the precepts developed through their intuitive and analytical techniques. In addition we hope it will appeal to many engineers who should profit by an introduction to the logic behind so many architectural precedents which they will find illustrated and explained within the text.

Architecture and Construction in Steel is in six parts.

Part One 'History of Iron and Steel Construction' by Dennis Sharp, is divided into chapters on the 19th and 20th centuries. *Chapter 1* 'The 19th Century' opens with a general discussion on the influence of materials and techniques on architecture, on iron and steel in particular and the influence of the work on the 19th century engineers. It moves to Chicago, Eiffel and Paris and Vienna, it describes some of the great engineering structures, particularly bridges and railway stations and encompasses the influence of such diverse persons from Abraham Darby and Telford to Loos and Taut and many others. *Chapter 2* 'The 20th Century' is concerned with the scene after 1900. It begins with statistics on steel production and another quote from Adolf Loos. It touches on the inhibiting effect of the by-laws on the development of the steel frame in the UK and describes how the Modern Movement arrived in England 'by the back door'. It traces the development of the Modern Movement and its love affair with technology, engineering and the steel and glass aesthetic, an indivisible trio. It is concerned with the enormous influence which the dialectic of Mies van der Rohe had on the way architects thought about buildings and how strong that influence still is on many of the most outstanding buildings of the last decade.

Part Two 'Materials' has seven chapters which cover all aspects of the properties of steel, its fundamental characteristics, the current techniques of processing, using and protecting the material, particularly within the building industry. *Chapter 3* by Professor Bill Biggs, one of the world's leading experts on materials in the construction industry, is concerned with the basic properties of steel and *chapters 4, 5 and 6* are concerned with 'Structural Steel Components for Buildings', 'Sheet and Strip' and 'Stainless and Related Steels' respectively. *Chapter 4* by the engineer Keith Moores describes the manufacturing process of all the current sections including circular and rectangular hollow sections, cables, ropes, couplings and wire. It also includes a section on components and wire rope fittings which are so widely used in contemporary cable stayed roofs. *Chapter 5* by engineer Eric Hindhaugh includes all those building elements which are processed from strip-steel – a wide range of products, from profiled sheeting to the anchors, connectors and truss plates of the timber trade. The chapter describes their strength, treatment, processing, coating and protection for various applications and environments. *Chapter 6* is a discourse by the engineer D. J. Cochrane on the properties and applications in the building industry of stainless and related steels. The chapter covers their application to structural work, roofing, wall cladding and masonry fixings. *Chapters 7, 8 and 9* are concerned with corrosion and protection. *Chapter 7* 'Nature of Corrosion' by the architect Yvonne Dean, is a survey of the nature of corrosion with particular respect to carbon steel. *Chapter 8* 'Anti-corrosion Measures' by Ken Chandler, includes a review of preparation techniques, painting systems and modern metallic coating systems. In addition, it makes references to design techniques to minimize corrosion. *Chapter 9* 'Fire Protection' by the engineer J. T. Robinson, covers the whole field of fire engineering including design techniques and the full range of passive and active protection systems.

Part Three 'Principles of Steel Framing' could be described as the core of the book. The eleven chapters cover all those aspects of steel frame design which within an architectural concept are concerned with 'choosing'. Choice is at the centre of design, as it is at the centre of all human creativity, and these eleven chapters are essential reading for the student and practising architect in guiding those choices, which are so necessary in evolving a frame which will support and sustain the essential idea of an architectural concept. *Chapter 10* 'The Architecture of Steel' by the engineer Patrick Morreau, sets the steel frame within an architectural perspective. *Chapters 11–14*, all written by practising engineers and one leading academic, are concerned with framing in all its aspects. *Chapter 11* by engineer John Le Good, a practitioner with a wide experience of teaching structures to architects, is concerned with the 'Basic Theory of Framing'. *Chapter 12* by engineer Roger Plank, one of the leading teachers of structures in our schools of architecture writes together with engineer Peter Brett and architect David Harriss on 'Multiple Bay Single Storey Buildings'. *Chapter 13* 'Floor Framing and Services', one of the most important choices in developing the anatomy of a building in these days of complex services, is written by engineer Tom Schollar with architect Anthony Gregson. *Chapter 14* 'Multi-Storey Frames' is the work of engineer Bjorn Watson and is based on his wide experience in Scandinavia, the UK and the USA. *Chapter 15* by Hal Iyengar, one of America's leading structural engineers, is all about 'Tall Structures', an essential primer for a generation of architects who may be involved in the UK's move to the development of buildings over 30 storeys, after the precedent of Canary Wharf. *Chapter 16* by the engineer Roger Plank and architect Anthony Gregson, describes the design and application of 'Composite Floors and Structures' such as the use of reinforced concrete shear walls in combination with a skeletal frame, a knowledge so essential to the emergence of the modern steel frame. *Chapter 17* 'Transfer Structures' by engineer Bryn Bird is concerned not with one of the major elements of the frame, but with a species or offshoot made necessary by the creation of so many multi-storey buildings which exploit the air rights over sites which are usually developments of main line railway termini in our urban centres. These developments create particular problems of transferring the loads of a space divided structure to a space enclosing structure. From these constraints the collaboration of a gifted architect and an innovative engineer may create a dominating and exciting image. *Chapter 18* 'Foundation Structures' by Stefan Tietz makes some necessary references to simple footings and deep basements, but is mainly concerned with all aspects of piling which is invariably necessary for multi-storey steel framed building construction. *Chapter 19* by the architect Richard Saxon is concerned with the design of atria which are now associated with any and every office development within the last 10 years. In addition to covering every aspect of the anatomy of atria it also addresses the problems of climate, fire protection, thermal movement and all the physical problems of this demanding structure. Part Three is brought to a brilliant conclusion in *chapter 20* by the two engineers John Thornton and Ian Liddell who take us through 'Tensile Structures' with all their attendant complications and contradictions.

Part Four 'Steel Construction' has four chapters and is concerned with the detailed aspects of designing, making and erecting a steel frame. *Chapter 21* 'Structural Connections for Steelwork' by Tom Schollar is a review of that part of a steel structure which receives a great deal of 'lip service' but often scant attention. The chapter includes a classification of connections, the type and magnitude of loads, the important separation of exposed and hidden connections and the ever recurring question of bolting versus welding. It expands on welding techniques which includes a short historical review of the subject. *Chapter 22* covers the subject which is invariably a closed book to the professional side of the industry, 'Fabrication and Erection', a subject which is difficult to teach within the academic tradition and is rarely attempted. Bob Taggart's chapter, well and simply illustrated, is an essential guide to techniques of shop and site. *Chapter 23* 'Tolerances and Movement in Building Frames' by the architect Julian Ryder-Richardson quite rightly describes it as an 'emotive subject'. He develops a clear approach to tolerances and separates out the confusion that exists with allowances for movement due to elastic deflection and other deformations. The chapter also puts the whole problem within the context of the changing pattern of contracting and how this reflects back into our approach to the specifying of tolerances. *Chapter 24* 'Insertion and Strengthening of Frames and Upgrading Facades' by engineer Peter Wright and architect Alan Blanc is a response to that somewhat pejorative term 'Facadism' which, due to the pressures of the conservation lobby, has been the catalyst for engineers to develop techniques for supporting and strengthening some very and some not so very distinguished facades while the entire building is demolished and rebuilt behind them, often in a manner and style totally foreign to the architecture of the facade.

Part Five 'Secondary Steel Elements' includes eleven chapters by Alan Blanc which cover all those elements of building where steel in all its various forms dominates or is among the main materials available. *Chapters 25–27* are concerned with cladding systems and facades. 'Decking and Built up Roofing' are covered in *Chapter 28*: 'Fastenings' and 'Metal Studwork and Laths' in *Chapters 29 and 30*. The four important categories of Windows, Door Frames, Staircases and Balustrades and Gutters and Fittings are included in *Chapters 31–34*. There is a final *Chapter 35* written from the heart by Alan on 'Decorative Iron and Steel'.

Part Six 'Outstanding Contemporary Steel Architecture' is a coda in sonata form. *Chapter 36* 'Oustanding Steel Buildings Worldwide' by Dennis Sharp is an interesting and erudite selection of buildings from the 'Centre Le Corbusier' in Zurich and Arup Associates' Stockley Park to Philip Johnson's 'The Garden Church' in California and Philip Cox, Richardson and Taylor's Football Stadium in Sydney. There are always certain buildings another contributor would choose or exclude. Some well known icons of the last few years have been overexposed and this perhaps persuaded Dennis Sharp quite rightly that other lesser known but important buildings should be included. His examples with their individual analyses will make us all look more carefully at the way architecture is made and what it has to fulfil rather than for the current obsession with its surface appeal. *Chapter 37* 'Structural Steel Design Awards' by Alan Blanc speak for themselves but are additionally illuminated by Alan Blanc's commentary. All the examples are by definition by UK designers and are a striking example of the architectural quality of so many recent British buildings and particularly the outstanding contribution being made by the current generation of British structural engineers. *Chapter 38* 'Futures' is by Mark Whitby and Alan Blanc. Mark is one of Britain's most distinguished and inventive young engineers who typifies the current generation's concern with the primacy of design in their approach to building engineering. He has contributed a broad brush view about the social and technological influences which he sees in the shaping of man's creativity in the future with Alan Blanc providing the 'last word' in his own inimitable way.

Mark Whitby's chapter is a grand overview which begs the question 'but what about the next generation of buildings?' Perhaps we should try and look a little closer at architecture and steel construction over the next few years. During the 1940s when, following the Second World War, the building industry began to be revitalized, the steel frame was again the preferred solution for the single and multi-storey building. It followed the pattern involved in the early days of the 20th century and apart from the development of welding techniques and lip service to plastic design theories, the approach to design and construction was very static. The 1950s and 1960s saw the rapid development of in situ and precast concrete for building frames, accelerated by architectural theories, local and central government policies and the rise of industrial building with its closed and open building systems.

The late 1970s saw a return to the steel frame stimulated by an overall improvement in service from the constructional steel industry combined with the emergence of new forms of management contracting and construction management. On a visit to Finsbury Avenue during the erection of the steel frame, nearly 40 years since my first involvement with steel frames, I felt 'just where I came in'. The only explicit difference was the use of composite construction for the floors, universal beams replaced rolled steel joints and there were more sophisticated drylining fire protection systems. What of the next generation? For the multi-storey frame there will be more sophisticated holistic analyses which will be integrated into the CAD systems for the architecture and building services. More attention arising from the holistic analysis will be paid to composite construction with a more sophisticated approach to dealing with lateral forces and elastic and thermal movement. The frame and floors acting with the cladding and partition system will be part of the total energy analysis and physical analysis of the building in its creation, life span and demolition.

The single storey building will give even greater scope for the innovative engineer working with a creative architect to use structural steel and steel products in the most radical and one hopes 'outrageous' ways which are yet integrated in a realistic way with the building physics. The opportunity is there to design and build stunning buildings which may also be described as 'Triumphs of Technology' rather than 'Triumphs over Technology'.

Part One

History of Iron and Steel Construction

Isambard Kingdom Brunel, 1806–59

George Stephenson 1781–1848

Gustave Eiffel, 1832–1923

Sir William Fairbairn, 1789–1874

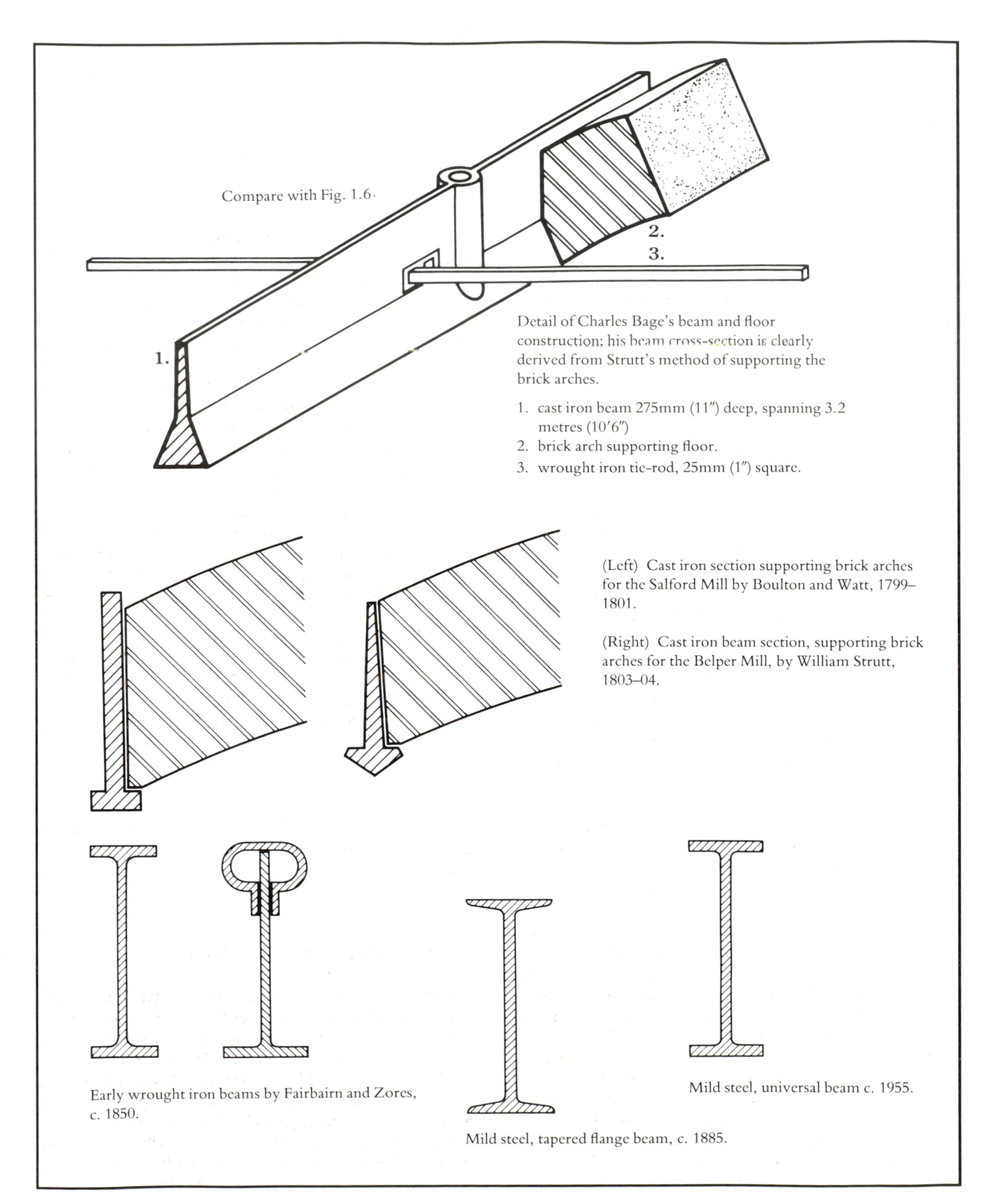

The development of cast iron and wrought iron beams in the 18th and 19th century. By kind permission of Alan Ogg.

1

The 19th century

Dennis Sharp

1.1 INTRODUCTION

It has often been claimed that the new spirit in building of the 19th century had little to do with architecture. Architects, it has been argued, were in the main preoccupied with stylistic matters rather than technical ones, producing architectural cloaks for public buildings such as the new town halls, opera houses, theatres, libraries and museums. The less stylistically inclined engineer was conversely building (and often inventing) new systems of construction and the structural shapes of bridges, furnaces, warehouses, derricks, workshops and factories as well as other utilitarian structures of the time.

Although this myth is not entirely true, substantially it remains a valid summary. The exceptions, it is now more readily acknowledged, provided the 'contact points' in the growth and development of new techniques, skills and means of expression in the construction industry. Having previously enjoyed both creative and technical freedoms in the construction of cathedrals, churches, cloth halls, towers and barbicans, architects and master masons had never really experienced the coincidence of untrammelled possibilities for a series of new materials, unprecedented social, political, economic and speculative opportunities. The lack of a consistent architectural style for a whole panoply of new building types was a constant embarrassment, even in the early years of the 19th century: 'Architects harangued each other, laymen harangued architects, and the only point on which almost everyone . . . agreed was that the architecture of the immediate past, of the first years of the century was at the best boring and at the worst common' [1].

It is perhaps too easy to chart the course of innovation and speculative prototypes as if they were themselves part of some great Darwinian scheme, as if a casual plan was at work in which an inevitable course was gradually being uncovered by curious, brilliant and inventive people. It was hardly that. Revolutionary yet simple means brought about the rapid growth of events that led to the introduction of lighter materials into the building industry. The industry had taken centuries to master the weightiness of stone, the massive nature of brick and the solidity of the surface volumes that result from the combination of these natural materials. Iron offered a multitude of new possibilities in a constructional sense, not the least of which was the desire to prefabricate and site assemble complex structures. To create wide spans and to form simply supported but transparent envelopes as shelters for activities and as protections against nature were somewhat simple minded design aims, they formed but the basis on which the new technology got underway. In the later medieval period stained glass windows were often strengthened by wrought iron framing members. Wrought iron cramps were also later introduced to reinforce masonry.

As designers reached for the sky in their efforts to create bigger and larger structures they pushed the possibilities of wrought iron to the known limits of the material. The 19th century saw some of the boldest experiments in comprehensive constructional techniques since the introduction of the arch. The experiments began with revisions to the simple elements of building. In Europe, iron roofing members were introduced in the 18th century in buildings for fire reasons also, particularly for theatres and warehouses. Victor Louis constructed a wrought iron roof for his *Théâtre Français* in 1786; other designers followed his methods with interest.

It is, however, bridges that provide a key introduction to the topic of historic cast and wrought iron. The earliest known examples that employed iron in their construction seem to be the Chinese chain bridges which are represented in the famous 'Bridge (magic) myths'. An 'iron bridge' on a suspension principle crossed the Kin-Sha river in China in the 8th century. Chain bridges were common in Yunnan much earlier [2]. Iron was also employed in Pagoda construction certainly from the Sung period and perhaps earlier. Later examples are better known and significant advances in the early use of iron can be illustrated by reference to such famous British engineers as Brunel, Telford, the Stephensons and Rennie.

1.2 CAST AND WROUGHT IRON

The modern story in fact starts with the work of the Darby Brothers at Coalbrookdale. They brought the new smelting process into common use, forming rough bars of 'pig' iron. However, cast and wrought iron had been used in a number of Gothic buildings. The concurrence of coal and iron ore measures at Coalbrookdale led to the most rapid advances in iron casting culminating in 1777–9 with the construction of the famous clear span 'Ironbridge' at Coalbrookdale over the River Severn (Fig. 1.1). The assembly of the cast iron components for this semi-circular bridge resembled the spokes of a gigantic wheel, with the elements put together using pins and bolts rather in the manner of an oak truss assembly with metal fastenings. There were technical limitations in making long lengths of cast iron, so the bridge comprises a whole series of short compression elements. The technical ingenuity in putting together the components to achieve a 100 ft span (30 m) was a remarkable achievement in terms of accuracy and workmanship. The designers understood the compression attributes of cast iron which, coupled with its low corrosion risk, achieved a viable arched bridge structure in the new material. It still stands today, the noble father of a family of cast iron bridges that covers the elegant Mythe Bridge at Tewkesbury (1823–6) to the climax of wrought iron suspension bridge construction over the Menai Straits (1819–26), both by Thomas Telford (1757–1834).

The reputation of West Midlands ironfounders was enhanced by their collaboration with the canal engineer Telford in developing solutions for wide span cast iron aqueducts, such as Pont-y-Cysyllte (1795–1805), carried on masonry piers. Flanged castings were used in this project, bolted together to form a box-like channel to support the water trough with flange arched elements below. The combined span of the 19 arches was 1001 ft (302 m) with a height of 120 ft (36 m) above the valley floor; each arch spanned 45 ft (13.5 m).

Telford saw the great potential of iron as a structural material but his background was that of a skilled stonemason. His approach was therefore largely empirical in the constructional use of cast iron, although he was one of the first engineers, together with John Smeaton (1724–92), to appreciate the scientific basis of structures and their European origins [3]. His confidence, however, was such that a proposal for a 600 ft (180 m) clear span bridge was made for London in 1800, a simple development of the arched span components used on canal bridges.

The engineering achievements in the early 19th century were fuelled by the post-Waterloo boom in Britain's economy and led to extensive road construction, many fine bridges, and finally to even greater engineering works linked with the expansion of the railway which included viaducts, railways sheds and stations as well as more bridges of a revolutionary design.

The engineering practice of Isambard Kingdom Brunel (1806–59) and his father Sir Marc Brunel (1769–1849) brought scientific principles to bear on engineering construction. Besides introducing mathematical calculations into structure, the skill of the Brunel partnership was also directed to the use of forged wrought iron using steam hammers to achieve structural sections with a wide range of applications such as bulbous 'I-bars' for ships and tees for rail tracks. These former were developed for building beams with extended webs and additional forged members to the lower flange.

The inventiveness of Brunel can be seen in the first

Fig. 1.1 *Ironbridge, Coalbrookdale 1777–9 (engineer Abraham Darby).*

proposals for the Clifton Suspension Bridge (1831 but completed 1864, five years after his death) (Fig. 1.2). It had a 702 ft span and a width of 31 ft. Wrought iron chains and suspenders carry the cross framed road deck between the masonry towers. It is anchored back to the cliff abutment 245 ft above water level. The great Royal Albert, Saltash railway bridge, by contrast, was a tubular arched girder bridge raised off masonry towers, with a slung lattice for the rail deck below. It was partly built with ironwork reserved for Clifton but made up of 17 land spans and having a total length of 2220 ft (Fig. 1.3). Another wrought iron tubular bridge was constructed by Brunel over the Wye at Chepstow.

Another remarkable advance made by the Brunels was in ship construction (Fig. 1.4). Here they developed the first screw propeller driven iron ship capable of crossing the Atlantic. The ship's construction comprised iron rib and deck beams and iron plating and rivets which were used for the first time in its construction instead of conventional timber planking. The *Great Britain* made her maiden crossing in 1845 and was followed within 10 years by a ship that was 680 ft (204 m) long and not exceeded in size until the launching of the *Titanic*. The wrought iron used by the pioneer engineers was produced in relatively small furnaces and prepared and worked to achieve specific shapes and strengths.

1.3 FORTH RAILWAY BRIDGE: FIRST STEEL STRUCTURE

The production of mild steel followed the adoption of the converter process from 1856 onwards. The first large scale use of modern day steel in Britain was in the construction of the Forth Railway Bridge (Fig. 1.5), a fine, elegant tubular cantilever structure designed by Benjamin Baker and completed in 1890. Here the work embodied the latest technology with steel tubular trusses put together by riveted and

Fig. 1.2 *Clifton Suspension Bridge, Bristol 1831–64 (engineer I. K. Brunel).*

Fig. 1.5 *Forth Railway Bridge under construction, late 1880s (engineer Benjamin Baker).*

Fig. 1.3 *Royal Albert Railway Bridge, Saltash 1852–9 (engineer I. K. Brunel).*

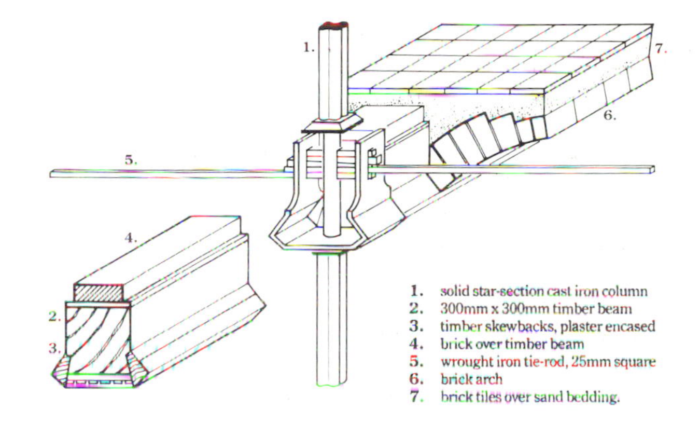

Fig. 1.6 *Strutt's use of wooden beams and brick arches with cast iron columns. Courtesy Alan Ogg:* Architecture in Steel.

Fig. 1.4 *SS Great Britain 1845 (engineer I. K. Brunel).*

bolted work to achieve the tapered cantilevered trusses with multiple spans, max: 1710 ft (523 m). The advance to modern day steels meant that bridge designers finally had a mass produced material available of proven strength. Like wrought iron, it had the ability to be bolted, riveted or forged together to form the composite elements needed in this kind of large scale bridge construction.

1.4 MILL BUILDINGS IN BRITAIN

Cast iron was extensively used in mill buildings in Britain from 1780 onwards with the growing need to protect premises and stored goods from fires. The early mills however had wood beams carried by cast iron columns as detailed in Fig. 1.6. The cotton mill for Phillips, Wood and Lee was erected in Salford in 1801 and, according to Giedion, 'surpasses all others of its time in the boldness of its design'. Considerable refinement took place at the end of the 18th century under the influence of Charles Bage and William Strutt; as shown in the lead-in illustration. Salford represents the first experiment in the use of iron pillars and beams for the whole interior framework of a building [4]. It set the precedent until William Fairbairn turned his attention to more sophisticated fireproof methods at mid-century (Fig. 1.7).

The Industrial Revolution saw the development of new types of buildings for manufacturing and assembly purposes, many of which demanded new technical solutions for their construction. These technical requirements led to innovations that in turn had a significant effect on the determination of the architectural result. But, it has to be said, that up to the 1840s '. . . builders, engineers, and more rarely architects (were) constructing mills according to the structural and architectural traditions that had developed in the latter part of the 18th century' [5]. This meant following, often quite crudely in some of the early mills, the Palladian pattern books of the period, for the main facades of these new buildings. But coincidentally the buildings themselves were growing to awesome sizes, and minor emphatic facades became of less importance in the face of large repetitively patterned walls of brick and iron framed windows and the vast interiors that had to provide large uninterrupted spaces for the vast new machines and the hundreds of workers employed in them. Light had to be provided internally and, increasingly, the need for overall fire protection became a critical issue. The technical part of this story, particularly as it becomes more concerned with ferrous metals, takes on a special significance: first cast iron, then the growing awareness of the better structural strength characteristics of wrought iron emerged, and then steel, the full architectural possibilities of which were not grasped until the end of the 19th century. Thus the rise of iron as a prime building material can be traced sequentially in its initial partial application in mill buildings such as those erected by William Fairbairn, the Manchester based engineer, in the northern industrial cities [6]. An interesting side issue in Britain was the adoption of a neo-classical vocabulary for some of the exteriors of mill, works and dock buildings. Stuart and Revett had drawn the attention of connoisseurs and collectors to the virtues of the pure Greek

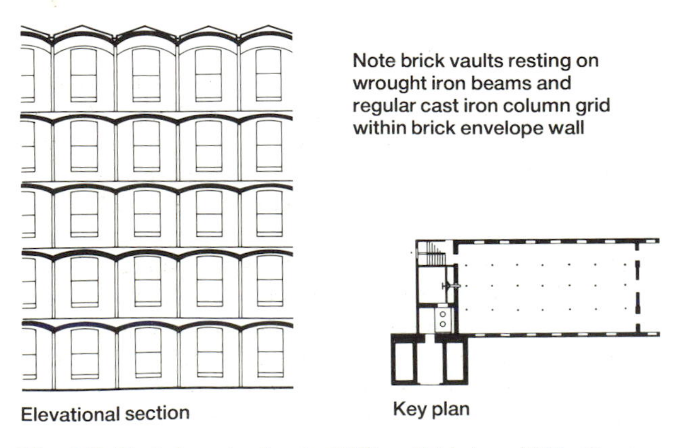

Fig. 1.7 *Typical construction by William Fairbairn c.1845. Courtesy Alan Ogg:* Architecture in Steel.

Fig. 1.8 *Boat Store, Sheerness 1858–66 (engineer Col. G. T. Green).*

Fig. 1.9 *Menier Chocolate Factory, Noisiel-sur-Marne 1869–74 (engineer Jules Saulnier).*

Fig. 1.10 *Iron vaulted construction (architect Viollet-le-Duc). From Entretiens sur l'Architecture 1863–72.*

style through their magnificent delineations of the Attic monuments in their five volume work, *Antiquities of Athens* (1762–1830).

The fully framed Boat Store erected for the Royal Navy in the Naval Dockyard at Sheerness in 1858–66 and designed by the Admiralty Engineer Col. G.T. Green (1807–86) was the first of a long line of multi-storey iron structures (Fig. 1.8). It was a mixture of cast and wrought iron and four storeys in height. It served as a foundry, a fitting out shop and boat store. It had a single storey central nave some 210 ft long and transverse cast iron columns and beams supported timber joists whilst wrought iron longitudinal plate girders spanned the 30 ft between. It is claimed to be the first 'portal action' structure. Externally the striated bands of windows were separated by surface panels of corrugated iron, thus completing a simple and very 'functional' looking facade. This simple elevational treatment of the innovative cast iron structure fascinated the apologists of the Modern Movement in architecture [7].

William Fairbairn's faith in the structural nature and ability of cast and wrought iron was maintained well into the second half of the 19th century. Sir Henry Bessemer's conversion process of 1855 took a long time to develop, although it eventually heralded the introduction of mild steel as a constructional material. It possessed many of the same properties as iron but as a 'new' material required some adaptation in its use both by architect and engineer. Essentially it was a better quality material and much more consistent in its manufacture. It was more ductile and could withstand considerable deformation before failure and was equally strong in tension and compression. It exhibited great inherent qualities as a skeletal framing material for high buildings, although it was not necessarily an easier material to erect than iron. Side by side with other technical developments, methods of analysis, constructional regulations and new inventions – including most importantly the refinement of the earlier invention of the lift or elevator – steel construction was soon to provide the basic bones for a generation of new glazed and framed buildings onto which were fastened a whole variety of building cloaks.

Initially steel framed construction was introduced to replace iron for increasingly higher public and commercial buildings in rapidly expanding town centres, largely in the US. Later it did become economical for use in the construction of tall residential blocks there. In Europe it was used extensively for railway stations and factories. Its first extensive use there was as a large scale multi-framing material at Saulnier's Menier Chocolate Factory at Noisiel-sur-Marne near Paris, 1869–74 (Fig. 1.9).

This building is considered to be the first one in Continental Europe to have been composed in its entirety of a wrought iron frame with non-loadbearing masonry external walls. In reality, it was like a great bridge resting on piled foundations driven deep into the River Marne which it used for hydraulic power purposes. It was indeed an industrialized Old London Bridge with its lightweight framework above infilled with decorative brickwork and tiles which caused the great French architect and archaeologist Eugene Viollet-le-Duc to eulogize in his *Entretiens* (Fig. 1.10) on its 'progressive medieval appearance'. The repeated frame was so arranged that the uppermost floor was suspended from the roof structure, leaving the floor below completely free of columns.

Otherwise the material was only slowly introduced into the building industry during the following 25 years. As it became cheaper to make, its use was more widely accepted in the 1890s. In London it was not introduced until the early part of the new century and then for the new steel-framed Ritz Hotel in 1904 and two years later the east wing of Selfridges in Oxford Street.

1.5 CHICAGO STYLE

In Chicago after the great fire of 1871 an opportunity arose to rebuild most of the central area of the old city. The great 'garden city' of the American mid-west – the grain centre of the world at the time – was rebuilt with grand boulevards, huge lakeside parks and promenades and later grew up the tall stone clad and iron – later, steel – framed blocks characteristic of this great regional centre. For a time Chicago was a cauldron of ideas for these new materials. Apart from one or two significant and notable exceptions, the use of ferrous metals for high building was *de rigueur*. However, there is the 16 storey high brick masonry-bearing Monadnock Block of 1891, erected when complete skeletons were becoming standard practice. Indeed, there is evidence to show that it was intended originally to be built entirely in steel but John Wellborn Root (1851–91), the energetic architectural partner of Daniel Burnham, who was largely responsible for the planning of Chicago, decided upon a tapering brick slab with such subtle refinements that the eminent 19th century American critic Montgomery Schuyler pronounced it 'the best office building of the day'. It still remains a much admired landmark. Its walls, however, were some 6 ft thick at their base. Elegant it may have been from an architectural point of view, but it was overtaken by events.

There was a certain degree of inevitability it seems about skeleton construction developments in America. Certainly in Chicago it was seen as a positive response to the city's unstable soil conditions and many of the early skyscrapers were supported on isolated pier foundations before caisson foundations were introduced in 1894 at the Stock Exchange in North LaSalle.

Larger window sizes, of course, were another inevitable outcome of the new framed construction aesthetic, although architects were still keen to shower ornament and decoration onto their unacceptably simple functional and economic steel frames. By the turn of the century it was claimed that Chicago had more tall buildings – many artistically considered – than all the other cities of the world put together! The initiative with the new high building was to stay with Chicago for many years. New York was not to lag too far behind in terms of individual building examples, although the great boom in high-grade skeletal structures in the centre of Manhattan was to take place between the wars. For a time New York was even to take the lead as the city with the highest building in the world when the Empire State Building was topped-out in 1921, but what was high in those days can hardly be considered so today. When the Sears Tower, Chicago, designed by SOM, reached its epoch-making 1700 ft it reduced its neighbours to mere pygmies, although it could not hold a candle to the quality of architecture, engineering and urban comparability of its earlier relatives. One example is the Adler and Sullivan Auditorium Building, completed in 1889, which now accommodates Roosevelt University as well as the great 4000 person plus auditorium from which it derives its name. Perhaps this building demonstrates more clearly than any other Chicago structure of the end of the 19th century an effort to bring about a unity between uses and materials. The brick-built theatre auditorium was entered from street level, whilst the hotel was situated at the top of the building, served by a bank of lifts and looking out across the lake and, at the time, enjoying a unique view of the Columbian World Exposition. Sullivan, whose masterpiece the Auditorium most certainly was, modelled its exterior to a very large extent on the earlier Marshall Field store (built in 1884 but demolished in 1929), designed by his mentor H.H. Richardson (1838–86). A similar rough textured finish was given to the stonework of the lower storeys to the Auditorium and a consistent Romanesque motif used for the windows on the great facades. The iron structure situated on the edge of the lake soared to a height of 270 ft (17 storeys to the top of the tower) above ground level; it reputedly weighed 110 thousand tonnes deadweight. In 1888, the year it opened, it was the tallest structure in the city.

Fig. 1.11 *Portrait of Louis Sullivan 1856–1924.*

The Auditorium block differed materially in many respects from other commercial buildings of the time. It was one of the first major custom designed multi-purpose buildings on the new American skyscraper pattern. Although it housed an auditorium of sumptuous proportions with clubrooms and hotel, it also served as a central location business address, thus providing theatre patrons with places to stay and dine as well as to work. The idea had been conceived by the building's owner Mr Ferdinand Peck, who, developing his profit opportunities as they arose, altered his requirements and the architect's plans time and time again. Sullivan (Fig. 1.11) brought about a cultural masterpiece with decorative patterns the like of which the mid-west had only seen before in the swirling patterns made by nature on the waters of the Lake or on the wind-swept prairies. But it was his engineer-trained German Jewish architect partner Dankmar Adler (1844–1900) who was responsible for tying this unique iron structure together from an engineering point of view and for introducing complex steel elliptical trusses to span the 117 ft across the Auditorium (Fig. 1.12).

Burnham and Root's Reliance Building was designed in 1890 but completed in 1894 some three years after John Root's death and still remains an important articulate example of the sheer glass, open-walled skeletal building (Fig. 1.13). In its general treatment it anticipated by decades the Modern Movement glass tower and in the detail treatment of its flat cornice (removed c.1948) also seems to anticipate Frank Lloyd Wright's bold oversailing roofs.

The building had an unusual constructional history. It has been referred to as perhaps the ultimate refinement of the 19th century skeletal frame skyscraper. Its site was hemmed in by existing leases: the leases on the lower floors ran out in 1890 and the upper storeys in 1894. The first stage – designed by Root – saw the demolition of the ground floor and the construction of the beam and rail foundations for the high-rise tower, whilst the upper floors were supported on screwjacks.

Charles B. Atwood, a New York architect, entered Burnham's office after Root's death to redesign the upper storeys. He put the screwjacks back temporarily in order to support the old building before its final destruction and then added 13 bay-windowed floors over the present ground floor shop.

The steel skeleton went up in just over a fortnight and the whole exterior was completed in less than six months. The beautiful full length bays were totally incorporated into the body of the building and are today still the building's most characteristic feature. Set close to the surface (cf Belluschi's Equitable Savings and Loan Association Building, Portland, Or., 1948, see chapter 27) the full width 'Chicago Windows' give the building the appearance of a tightly sealed yet transparent membrane. All structural support is provided by the internal skeleton, and the window walls as well as the floors were contained within the building envelope.

How high, how far, how big? That was the numbers game. Just how far could these extraordinary new materials go? Prior to the great engineering monuments of the 19th century, there had been many exceptional wonders in the world of an engineering kind, many of which had exploited the use of materials; some defied gravity.

The psychology of size has always held a fascination for mankind. Today, books set out the league tables of the well known – and even the more obscure – items in this record breaking world. In a sense they show the same sort of enthusiasm that the builders of the Colossus of Rhodes must have felt, or the constructors of the colossal Qutub Minar in Delhi or even for that matter the designers of the great obelisks of Egypt and Washington, DC. It is a puzzling but

Fig. 1.12 *Interior of the Auditorium Theatre, Chicago 1887–89. The two upper galleries and much of the first balcony could be closed off to reduce the capacity to 2574 seats (architects and engineers: Adler and Sullivan).*

Fig. 1.13 *Reliance Building, Chicago 1890–94 (architects and engineers Burnham and Root).*

compulsive tendency to achieve great structural and engineering feats, and iron and steel offered almost limitless opportunities, it would appear.

Sometimes the creative existentialism operates on a more mystical plane and record breaking desires are subordinated to spiritual or symbolical goals. Who knows, for example, where the ideas and the technical knowhow came from that produced the massive iron Ashoka columns of North India, the great rebuilt (1835) iron trusses at Chartres of the 1870s (370 ft high above the floor) or the interwoven and interlocking patterns of the stonework lintels of the chief Cairo mosques? Perhaps it is that atavistic spirit that is part of one's make-up that motivates the creative process to seek the ultimate answer.

In the modern steel age Frank Lloyd Wright had no doubts at all that his design for a 1 mile high tower could be built, and, lest we forget it too easily, engineers have more recently flung a great bridge across the Bosphorus achieving success where before such a structure was considered to be a complete impossibility. Konrad Wachsmann's enormous tubular steel projects for aircraft hangers and Buckminster Fuller's great dome constructions are all part of this exciting story.

1.6 IRON'S GREAT SYMBOL: THE EIFFEL TOWER

It is no wonder sensing the challenges of the Modern Age that Gustav Eiffel (1832–1923) – a man in his late 50s and an engineer who had grown increasingly confident of his abilities with the use of iron – should seek the judicious use of the new material to create a world record. Through the use of special techniques and innovative methodologies he created the tallest structure in the world – 300 m (or 986 ft) – to crown the 1889 Paris Exposition (Fig. 1.14). It took 2 years to complete. It was prefabricated and site riveted. His tower exemplified the 'new' industrial age of the second half of the 19th century. In a sense too the tower brought to a head the results of his experiments in straight girder bridge construction, for the kind of iron framed rigidity he had developed for Bartholdi's New York *Statue of Liberty* and for inventing ways of conveying heavy materials on a slope. Le Corbusier called it the 'Fruit of intuition, of science, of faith, daughter of courage and of perseverance' [8].

Erecting the world's tallest *structure* – it can hardly be described as a building in any conventional sense – was a challenge as big as walking on the craggy surface of the moon was in the mid-20th century. Certainly at the time no-one got a closer view of the moon than from the top of Eiffel's own prefabricated iron tower. Although of hard iron, it became a romantic dream. His detractors claimed he was mad and that the tower would surely topple within a short period of time. It was described as 'unrealisable, useless and senseless'.

Fig. 1.14 *Eiffel Tower, general view of 300 m shaft 1887–89 (engineer Gustav Eiffel).*

Fig. 1.15 *'The real strength of the Eiffel Tower is in its voids as much as in its iron'.*

One eminent French writer, who abhorred it, dined there every day in order that he should not see it! Wind forces had proved a big problem and to solve it the supporting elements were reduced to a minimum. As Joseph Harriss has written: 'The real strength of the Eiffel Tower is in its voids as much as in its iron!' (Fig. 1.15) [9]. With the accurate pre-punched rivetting the whole structure was assembled on site in a smooth straightforward manner. Even so it was also described at the time as 'a colossus of iron' and compared favourably with the Washington Obelisk (555 ft high), the Great Pyramid of Egypt and Cologne Cathedral (512 ft high). Today the structure has itself become the very symbol and principal marker of the city of Paris; perhaps even of France itself. It has been used as the subject of films, paintings, sculpture and more recently an elegant essay by Roland Barthes [10].

1.7 KINGS CROSS/ST PANCRAS STATIONS

Kings Cross Station, the largest station in London at the time of its construction (1852), was a plain-fronted brick building designed by the architect Lewis Cubitt with the collaboration of engineers Sir William and Joseph Cubitt. It was erected in one of the most dilapidated, squalid and poverty ridden areas of London and opened in 1852, bringing a new kind of elegance into the area. Its plain brick bipartite facade presented two identical semi-circular arches to the road surmounted by a squat clock tower. Its original appearance was not a great deal different from the frontage that can be seen today. Its importance, however, at the time was as one of the more functionally designed train shed structures. Its lengthy arrival and departure platforms were arranged on either side of an arched brick wall topped by two great laminated timber roofs. These proved unsatisfactory and were soon replaced by iron ribbed roofs in 1869–87. It still retains its long, low character, presenting a great contrast to the great open train shed next door at St Pancras built for the Midland Railway Company by their engineers W.H. Barlow and R.M. Ordish. This building represents a peak in iron railroad construction both in terms of its structural ingenuity, with iron ties supporting its single parabolic iron roof under the platforms, and its direct expression of architectural space. Motivated by a desire to express and, one expects, create an ornamental arrival venue for the new noble iron 'horses', this great railway stable was erected to cover a multitude of noisy, hot, sweaty and steamy activities. Long lines of railway coaches discharged their passengers onto simple platforms. They were led from these at one side to a busy road and on the other through elegant doors to the luxurious *Midland Hotel*, a fairytale confection dreamed up by Sir George Gilbert Scott for the delectation of the exhausted traveller, thus providing an entry into the genteel but expensively upholstered world of London business and society. To professional eyes it seemed that these two related but unconnected worlds, of the functional rail shed and the posh hotel, symbolized the division between public decorated architecture and simple mechanical functional engineering. Indeed, it is worth noting that there is a decisive structural gap even today between the last of the train shed's arch bow trusses and the ornamental brick facade of the former hotel's private walls.

For a time, in Europe at least, traditional architectural and innovative engineering solutions did not mix. Unlike the Romanesque and Gothic method of accepting and co-existing side-by-side with alterations, the implementation of stylistic improvements and changes, at St Pancras the lines of demarcation were clearly drawn. More consistent design relationships were to be found in many European railway station examples in places like Paris, Hamburg and, some years later, in Stuttgart and Helsinki. Some of these were the result of architectural competitions that had purposefully sought out new and original solutions for combining all the various elements of great station termini.

Fig. 1.16 *Bibliothèque de Sainte-Généviève, Paris 1843–50 (architect Henri Labrouste).*

Fig. 1.17 *Galerie des Machines, Paris 1889 (engineers Dutert and Contamin). Courtesy Alan Ogg:* Architecture in Steel.

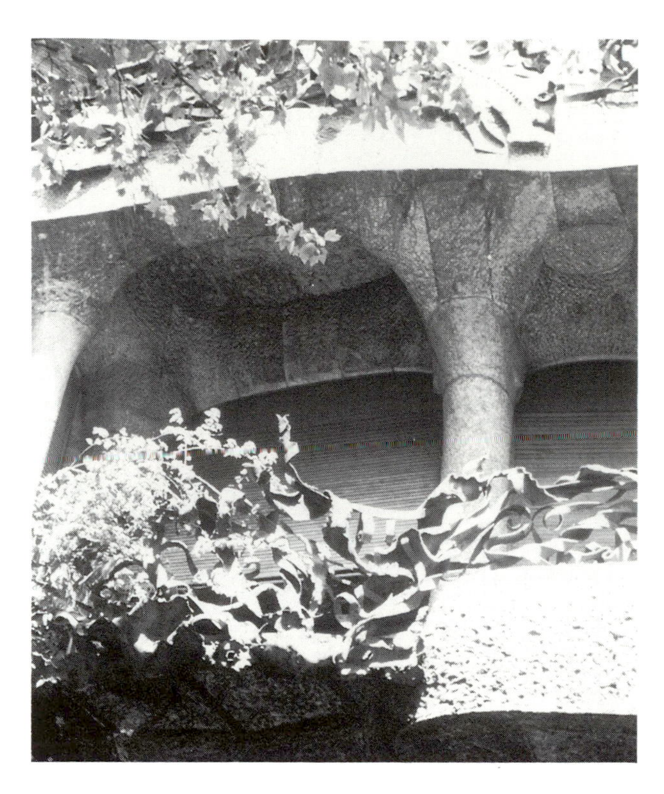

Fig. 1.18 *Wrought iron balconies of Casa Milà, Barcelona 1905–10 (architect Antoni Gaudi).*

1.8 EUROPEAN PIONEER IRONWORK

Much earlier than Eiffel's epoch making landmark tower, Henri Labrouste's *Bibliotheque de Sainte-Genevieve*, Paris, 1843–50 used cast iron internally in a thoroughly imaginative and sympathetic manner (Fig. 1.16). His building – what Hitchcock has called '. . . the finest structure of the forties in France' [11] – combined two architectural languages, the restrained classical for the facades and the new lightweight, filigree construction for the interior. With the *Sainte-Généviève Library* Labrouste left its metal frame exposed in an audacious gesture towards the Vitruvians. Without such a brave act, Frantz Jourdain wrote in a well known essay on August Perret 'Baltard would probably have not built the *Halles Centrales* or the dome of St-Augustin in iron'; without him it seems unlikely that Sedille would have used this outcast material in the *Au Printemps* department store. He went on to indicate the abhorrence the establishment felt towards the material: 'The Institut treated iron with a pious terror that might have been appropriate for a shameful disease'. In effect it was not until a succession of exemplary world expositions had taken place in Paris culminating in the Exposition 1889 – which of course included Eiffel's Tower as well as Dutert and Contamin's *Galerie des Machines* (Fig. 1.17) – that the virus was eventually killed and then only after a struggle to take land height and width records. At roughly the same time the incursion of craftsmen and artists into the field of ornamental casting led eventually to the establishment of what was to become known as the art nouveau, a playful and highly naturalistic decorative style that was to sweep through France. It reached its apotheosis as a style at the Paris Exposition of 1900. Here iron and wood took on an entirely new significance. They were used in their most original forms in the shaping of sinewy, elegant and often quite beautiful shapes as armatures for furniture, lamp standards, metro entrances – as with the work of Hector Guimard – as well as gable ends and balconies. In the worst possible taste both materials were also employed to outline curves and evocative shapes as if they had been squeezed from a toothpaste tube instead of cast or cut from root or branch. Iron had a particularly important role to play too in its use as a framing material for stained and clear glass used in laylights or for impressive domes of light above grand stairs such as in the brilliant work of Baron Victor Horta in Brussels or Antoni Gaudi in Barcelona. They took advantage of the material, setting it up architecturally to create a filigree effect or as a firm support for a translucent screen.

The curving, flowing linearity of the early art nouveau, seen in building interiors, in furniture design, book illustrations and graphics as well as in the flowing robes and bodily movements of celebrated dancers like Loie Fuller – herself a minor sensation at the 1900 Paris Expo – was soon followed by an apparent rationalization, a *massen regie* that was to prepare the world for the kind of geometric definitions that produced the early signs of artistic cubism on the one hand and 'functional' architecture on the other.

Around the turn of the century the new materials that had been introduced and ridiculed and attacked as insubstantial and unevocative of cultural values – cast, wrought iron, steel and concrete – were becoming *de rigueur*, at least among the European avant-garde. As well as Baron Victor Horta in Belgium and the individualistic Antoni Gaudi in Barcelona (Fig. 1.18) – the virtual leaders of the *fin de siècle* movement – Hector Guimard and Frantz Jourdain in France, Otto Wagner, Josef Hoffmann and J.M. Olbrich in Vienna and, to a degree, C.R. Mackintosh in Glasgow all saw the potential of the new adaptable materials. They began to use them structurally, decoratively and most certainly organically in their designs. Horta's experiments are among the most interesting. He often introduced lightweight materials to facilitate his supporting problems for complicated building sections. The inventive light wells he designed with domes and laylights were essential for the deep sites of his Brussels apartment blocks (Fig. 1.19). But it was as an adjunct to the new transportation systems then under construction in many European cities that both cast and wrought iron really came into their own. Earlier cast iron had been a feature in the Baroque palaces and town centres for the ornamental gates and park fences, the garden monuments, fountains and balconies (from Versailles, Bath and Nancy to New Orleans and Liverpool). It had all the festive feel of a world fair pavilion, yet as a material it was hard wearing and ductile. It could easily be fashioned to imitate natural forms, and decorated. It offered untold opportunities to an original designer. Numerous permutations of the materials were possible for rolling stock, rails, bridges, entrances, pavilions and canopies for the new Paris Metro around 1900, by Hector Guimard and the new *Bahnhofen* by Otto Wagner for Vienna (Fig. 1.20).

After this peculiarly eclectic art nouveau phase in the 19th century cast and wrought iron began to be employed on a much wider basis in structural and architectural contexts. It was no longer necessary to mimic past stylistic motifs, as Hardwick had done with his cast iron Doric style dockside buildings in London and Liverpool, in order to appear up-to-date and 'modern'. No, that had come about by the application of the age-old mimetic and nationalistic motifs and devices that had given birth originally to the language of architecture – from primitive hut to reed temple – and which, for a time at least, caught Europe eventually in a creative and fashionable storm. It forced to a head the all-important issue of the machine and art, of craft and skill, and, ultimately of quality and inventiveness in architecture. The acceptability, respectability and usefulness of the new

Fig. 1.19 *Staircase in Hotel Solvay, 224 Avenue Louise, Brussels, Belgium 1894–90 (architect Victor Horta).*

Fig. 1.20 *Karlsplatz Station, Vienna 1894–98 (architect Otto Wagner).*

Fig. 1.21 *Post Office Savings Bank, Vienna 1904–6 (architect Otto Wagner).*

materials was soon established. A whole new propagandist literature emerged in Europe, including Wagner's *Moderne Architektur* (1896) and Loos's early essays, *Spoken into the Void* (1897–1900) and in particular his later attack on 'Ornament and Crime' (1908) which, building on the work of Viollet-le-Duc and others, confirmed the importance and applicability of the new materials as a part of 'Modern' architecture.

The public hall of Wagner's Post Office Savings Bank building in Vienna, 1904–6, is an astonishingly successful amalgamation of iron and glass design (Fig. 1.21). It is a piece of inventive architecture that followed the tradition of the *Länderbank*, with their courtyard-like banking halls as well as the great railway shed tradition (admittedly somewhat scaled down and refined in its aesthetic treatment). Its pure shapes and plastic forms were integrated with the surface elements of the building into a unified and harmonious whole. In the original competition entry design of 1903 Wagner had shown a three-part glazed roof for the banking hall suspended from cables. However, the final design incorporated a kind of double roof with both the actual roof members and the glass ceiling supported on iron beams.

Here in Vienna, whilst Germany was still absorbed with the decorative excesses of the Jugendstil and Muthesius's continuing flirtation with the English Arts and Crafts, the distinctly new: 'Modern' architecture had emerged in the Austrian capital. Wagner had successfully discarded his earlier reference to the French decorative ironwork tradition which was to be seen in the subway buildings for the Hof Pavillion and the Karlsplatz Station, both of 1898. His new architecture was characterized by its flat planes and its restrained detailing.

1.9 THE CRYSTAL PALACE AND ITS SIGNIFICANCE

The 1851 Crystal Palace by Joseph Paxton is often referred to as one of the most important innovative iron buildings in the history of architecture. Paxton's design was unique, as was the way it was selected for construction. Some 233 designs were submitted for the competition for the Crystal Palace, none of which were adopted. However, designs by Hector Horeau, whose design for an earlier adventurous iron and glass market hall for Paris also remained unbuilt, was awarded a special mention. But Paxton came in from the outside, a persuasive horticultural engineer with a flair for getting his own way. He produced his own design (originally sketched on a piece of paper) (Fig. 1.22) in nine days. It was drawn out quickly in Manchester and built in less than four months on the Hyde Park site by Fox and Henderson and Co.

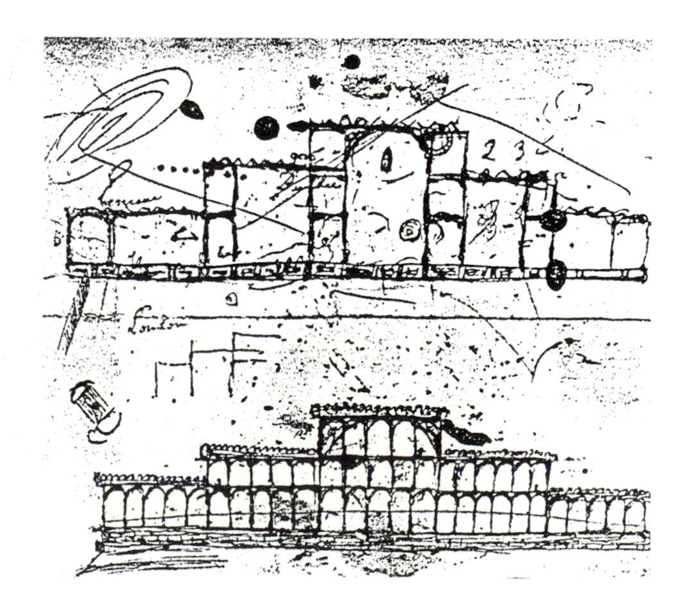

Fig. 1.22 *Paxton's first rough sketch for Crystal Palace 1850.*

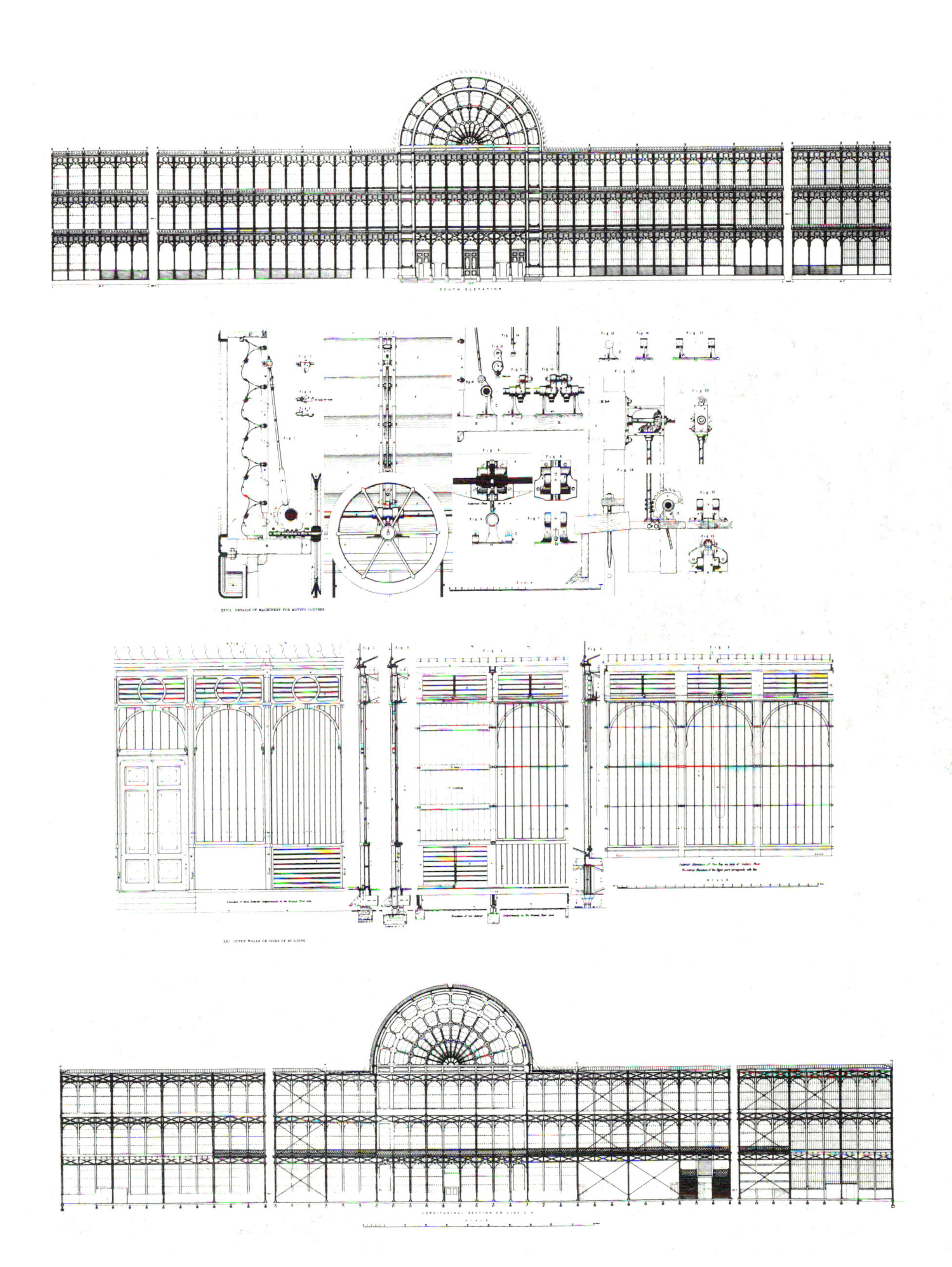

Fig. 1.23 *Crystal Palace elevations, sections and details, Hyde Park, London 1851 (designer Joseph Paxton).*

Fig. 1.24 *Interior of Crystal Palace 1851.*

The ground plan was a vast rectangle, sized approximately 1851 ft along the long axis. It was 450 ft wide (with 72 ft broad transepts) and the highest transepts reached 104 ft. The building covered 18 acres. Its magnitude can be appreciated when it is stated that it was four times the size of St Peter's at Rome, and six times that of St Paul's, London. Prefabricated out of moulded cast iron, it set the tone for iron buildings of the next 50 years (Figs 1.23 and 1.24). It employed 3300 cast iron columns, 2220 girders, 1128 girder bearers and 34 miles of guttering tubes as well as 250 miles of wooden sash-bars.

In Britain the use of iron as an 'architectural' material was not exactly popular. Few architects really knew how to use it from a technical point of view. There was at the time no architectural language in iron which could be adopted. What was learnt came from earlier prototypes, principally from timber and stone sources as we have already seen at Ironbridge as well as experiments like those of Horeau and the 'genius' or 'magician' Paxton. However, it was extensively used by Dean and Woodward for their Oxford Museum of 1854–60 (Fig. 1.25). This building came under the close critical eye of contemporary Gothicists such as John Ruskin, who claimed that they could only use new materials such as iron fashioned into some kind of medieval frame. The building eventually went up against a barrage of ridicule and the material used was considered quite unsuitable for its purpose as a museum. Nevertheless, the use of iron and glass construction at the Oxford Museum was singularly innovative. It may well now be assessed as part of a new architectural sensibility. Certainly at the time it must have been viewed as part of a growing new convention of ideas that took into account large scale stores and shops, arcades, galleria, winter gardens, palm houses and floral halls. These sorts of buildings were beginning to appear in fashionable cities throughout Europe, from Gothenberg to Genoa.

As building types, arcades were splendid examples of the everyday commercial application of iron and glass construction. They took up the baton handed on by Paxton's prefabricated iron and glass parts and like the Crystal Palace they offered ease of erection and connection as well as volumetric economy.

Indeed, the arcades of the 1870s and 1880s provided inspiration in other areas of design as both spatial and social structures. Ebenezer Howard, for example, in his diagram for the 'ideal Garden-city' envisaged a wide glazed shopping 'arcade' ring all around his central park fashioned in a kind of circular boulevard plan. Significantly, it was to be called 'The Crystal Palace'. More modest experiments were undertaken such as the remarkably original contribution of architects such as Peter Ellis in Liverpool (Fig. 1.26). His

Fig. 1.25 *Oxford Museum 1854–60 (architects Deane, Son and Woodward: metalwork Skidmore).*

Fig. 1.26 *Oriel Chambers (left), Liverpool 1864–5 (architect Peter Ellis).*

Oriel Chambers (1864–5) located in Water Street has been described as 'the most significant office building in Liverpool' [12]. An impressive iron framed building, it brought together an inventive constructional methodology and a unique means of architectural expression. It relied largely for its effect on a shallow oriel bay elevational treatment. The building's iron frame was clad in stone on the main elevations and the oriel bay window effect also took into account the reflective quality of Liverpool's evening sunlight [13]. The oriel windows seem to be a refined outcome of the great tradition of decorative and structural cast iron that grew out of the early experiments of architects like Thomas Rickman, with his iron framed prefab churches at Everton and Aigburth [14].

Tower Bridge (1894) was a totally different proposition. Built to the design of Sir Horace Jones with J.W. Barry as engineer it epitomized the confusion that existed between architecture and engineering. Here a naked utilitarian steel structure was overhung with a heavy cloak of Scottish style castellated architectural decoration. This effect, as a fairytale fiction, clearly outdid even Sir George Gilbert Scott's earlier Midland Hotel at St. Pancras. It provoked a critic in *The Builder* to write that it was 'The most monstrous and preposterous architectural sham that we have ever known'! In its construction no foundations were required for the great facades as these 'side walls' were hung off gigantic stirrups of steel. *The Builder* critic went on that it was 'a discredit to the generation that has erected it . . . one of the worst and most ludicrous failures we know of' [15].

Such a view, of course – although genuinely shared at the time – palls into insignificance today when one realises the bridge's huge general public popularity. Perhaps this is what was meant by the 19th century phrase 'romancing the stone'? Tower Bridge, with all its stylistic inconsistencies, is certainly an example of the continuing concoction of structural brilliance and architectural exuberance that was to blossom in England around the turn of the century – in this case based on the notion of a national gateway to the capital – when the rest of Europe was beginning to come to terms with the architectural opportunities of the new material.

There are few buildings in Britain which actually fall into the art nouveau category, many of which used iron in order to portray natural forms. The great exception is the work of Charles Rennie Mackintosh, particularly in the two stages of the development of the Glasgow School of Art (1896–1908) along Renfrew Street, Glasgow. In Mackintosh's building there was a close identification with iron as a material, the adoption of natural form metaphors and its structural importance. In the new Library wing the design of the high feature windows in particular indicates the architect's mature understanding of the potentiality of materials like iron. 'Shapes are always derived from the character of the materials', one writer remarked of Mackintosh's building. The famous curvilinear brackets beneath the great studio windows to the main Renfrew Street elevation also provide lateral bracing. Furthermore, they give lateral support to the window cleaner's ladders! Thus the brackets are given a role both as ornamental decoration and as a utilitarian one. In this they share a similar visual interest to that displayed by architects like Antoni Gaudi in Barcelona (Fig. 1.18), with the great swirling iron balcony decoration of the Casa Milà and the much more formal ornamental use of ironwork as it was used by Josef Maria Olbrich at the Artists' Colony in Darmstadt (1901–3). Here the material was converted into repetitive design motifs by local blacksmiths under the careful scrutiny of the architect.

For architects iron and steel offered the opportunity to develop a new means of expression that they largely thought of as a component-based trabeated form of construction and structural innovations like the Eiffel Tower which, as we have noted, had an open framework for wind resistance, provided inspiration both for new spatial compositions with filigree effects and much later for a concern with transparent and translucent building envelopes.

One of the first major experiments in this area was carried out by the young Bruno Taut in his so-called 'Monument of

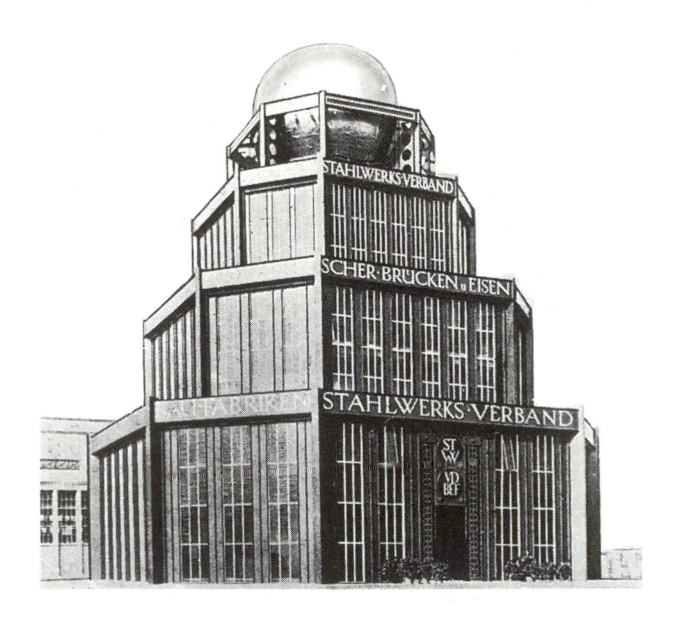

Fig. 1.27 *Steel Pavilion, Leipzig Fair 1913 (architect Bruno Taut).*

Iron' which was designed for the Träger-Verkaufskontor, Berlin in 1910, with its open freestanding metal framework straddling a small, almost classical, *tempieto*. A couple of years later Taut designed his memorable steel pavilion for the Stahlwerks Verband at the Leipzig Fair, 1913 (Fig. 1.27) which had a gold coloured sphere surmounting a steel framed octagonal pyramid with obvious echoes of J.M. Olbrich's Secession House, Vienna of 1896 whose own giant filigree domed structure was dubbed 'the golden cabbage'.

At around the same time the eminent architect/teacher Hans Poelzig also produced his own multi-purpose and monumental water tower site in Posen (now Wroclaw, Poland). This too had an elemental steel frame with huge open filigree columns in its interior. This structure was virtually contemporary with Peter Behrens' turbine hall for the AEG Company situated on the Huttenstrasse, Berlin, a three pin metal arched building which for many people is the first significant example of the new architecture (Figs 1.28 and 1.29).

This first phase of modern architecture saw many efforts to create a valid new means of structural expression and, contrary to the mythology that has built up over the years that it was an episode entirely dominated by white, smooth faced surfaces of reinforced concrete, many architects employed steel construction. Some mixed steel with brick, others with glass panels. Erich Mendelsohn designed his Rudolf Mosse Pavilion for the Cologne Press Show in 1928 in steel and glass and his more permanent Bexhill Pavilion in Sussex, won in competition with Serge Chermayeff, also had a steel frame designed by the London based Austrian engineer Felix Samuely. Arthur Korn's Fromm Rubber

Fig. 1.28 *AEG Building, turbine factory, Berlin 1909. Facade showing vertical legs of portal frames (architect Peter Behrens).*

Fig. 1.29 *AEG Building, turbine factory, Berlin 1909. Detail view of base to portal frame.*

Factory of the early 1920s also had a steel frame. Rudolf Schindler, who emigrated to the west coast of the US from Austria in the early 1920s, summed up the contemporary feeling about steel and architecture as follows: 'Architectural forms symbolize the structural functions of the building material. The final stage of this development was the architectural solution of the steel skeleton: its framework is no longer a symbol. It has become form itself.' This 'functional' philosophy was at the root of the developments we call the 'Modern Movement' in architecture. It spread through its 'International Style' phase from 1929 to 1939 but lost its impetus in Europe in the postwar phase due to steel shortages and restriction on the use of the material in housing schemes, as the following chapter indicates.

REFERENCES

1. Steegman, J. *Victorian Taste: A study in the Arts and Architecture from 1830–70*, London 1970, p. 102.
2. Robins, F.W. *The Story of the Bridge*, London n.d. p. 91. See also Needham, J., (Ed) *Science and Civilization in China*, Vol IV, Pt. 3. Sects. 28–9, London 1965, Cambridge University Press.
3. See Mainstone, R. Introduction to Collins, A.R. (Ed.) *Structural Engineering – two centuries of British Achievement*, London 1983, p. 15 ff.
4. Giedion, S. *Space Time & Architecture*, London 1967 (1941) p. 191.
5. Jones, E. *Industrial Architecture in Britain 1750–1939*, London 1985, p. 52. Batsford.
6. *Op. cit.*, pp. 56–8. See also the chapter 'Building with Iron and Glass 1790–1855' in Hitchcock, H-R, *Architecture: Nineteenth and Twentieth Centuries*, Harmondsworth, 1958, pp. 115–130.
7. Although considered now as *the* utilitarian cast iron building of the 19th century the Sheerness Boat Store was re-discovered in the late 1950s by Eric de Maré who featured it in an article in the *Architectural Review*, CXXII, 1957. See also Skempton, A.W. 'The Boat Store, Sheerness (1858–60)', *Transactions of the Newcomen Society*, XXXII, 1959–60. Giedion did not mention it and Pevsner in his *Pioneers of Modern Design* referred to it only in the 1960 Penguin edition. The building however does form part of the 'functional tradition' outlined by J.M. Richards.
8. Harriss, J. *The Tallest Tower*, Boston, 1975.
9. *Op. cit.*, p. 63.
10. Barthes, R. *The Eiffel Tower and other essays*, London.
11. Hitchcock, H-R. *Architecture: Nineteenth and Twentieth Century*, Harmondsworth, 1958, p. 51. See also p. 123 for a description of the ironwork barrel roofs.
12. See, Hughes, J.Q. *Liverpool*, London 1969, p. 60.
13. See, Hughes, J.Q. *Seaport*, London, 1964.
14. See, Hughes, J.Q. *op. cit.* p. 24.
15. *The Builder*, 30 June 1894.

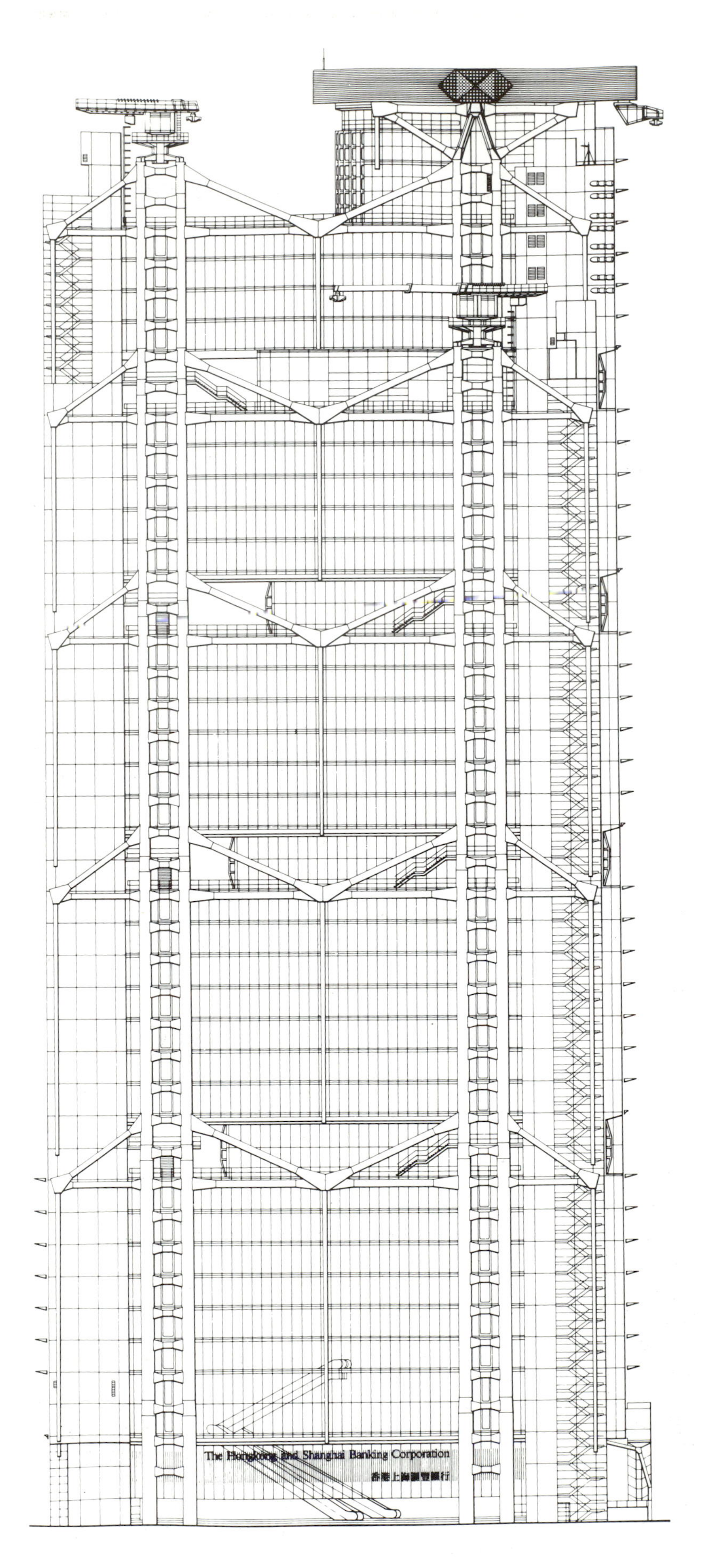

Elevation of Hongkong and Shanghai Bank 1986 (architects Foster Associates: engineers Ove Arup and Partners)

2

The 20th century

Dennis Sharp

2.1 INTRODUCTION

The last quarter of the 19th century saw a meteoric growth in the total world output in steel to around 28 million tonnes. The United States produced almost twice as much steel as Britain, with Germany nearer the US total with 8 million tonnes per year. However, British engineering experience in combination with this plentiful supply of iron and steel enabled the country to gain an unprecedented lead in areas such as shipbuilding. In the 1890s four-fifths of the world's new shipbuilding was in British hands; in 1913 her share was still more than three-fifths [1]. Between 1898 and 1899 some 98.8% of the ships launched were made of steel [2].

Urban life too greatly benefited from the new steels. From lamps, street lights, telephones and typewriters to the startling effects of the flickering projectors of the new cinematography, to the wide use of overground and underground railways the new world welcomed the industrialization and mechanization that steel had brought. It had arrived. Adolf Loos, a prophet of the new architecture from Vienna, soon dubbed the American plumber 'the quartermaster of culture' – at least that culture that was decisive for the modern world. The new machine age was fashioned in steel: the great airship hangars were some of the early symbols of the era.

Fig. 2.1 *Pictures of war work by Joseph Pennell.*

Artists, writers, photographers and poets were creatively stimulated by the potentialities of the new age and its materials. Joseph Pennell and Frank Brangwyn recorded the excitement of steel armament manufacturing processes during the period of the First World War with their atmospheric and evocative pictures of war work in Britain and the USA (Fig. 2.1). Fernand Léger, the architect trained Parisian artist of the Purist Group, made a series of drawings and paintings of steel constructors (Fig. 2.2). Robert Delauney depicted the interpenetrating planes of Eiffel's tower in a succession of canvases. Carl Sandburg, the American poet and writer, saw the publication of his 'Smoke and Steel' in 1921. It included such verses as:

Oh, the sleeping slag from the mountains, the slag-
heavy pig-iron will go down many roads.
Men will stab and shoot with it, and make butter and
tunnel rivers, and mow hay in swaths, and slit
hogs and skin beeves, and steer airplanes across
North America, Europe, Asia, round the world.
Hacked from a hard rock country, broken and baked
in mills and smelters, the rusty dust waits
Till the clean hard weave of its atoms cripples and
blunts the drills chewing a hole in it.
The steel of its plinths and flanges is reckoned, O, God,
in one-millionth of an inch. [3]

But above all iron and steel made the skyscraper possible, heralding a new architectural era.

What for some men was seen as poetry to others became a structural and constructional challenge. Having already seen how the use and employment of the new framing materials had precipitated a high building boom in great centres such as Chicago and New York, smaller towns were to share in the new building art throughout the United States. Among the many pioneering advocates of the efficient systematic use of steel was Alfred C. Bossom (later, Lord Bossom of

Maidstone and one of Churchill's aides on postwar prefabrication) who had migrated, temporarily as it turned out, to the USA as a young, promising architect to work on the steel towns designs in and around Pittsburgh for Andrew Carnegie. Bossom did well in the States, marrying advantageously into a banking family. In towns like Galveston, Houston and Buffalo his new tall bank buildings (often the tallest structures) demonstrated the architect's growing organizational skill in producing fast-track, efficient and economic tall buildings (Fig. 2.3). After his return to England Bossom published his own poetic, but essentially practical, eulogy to the new universal building type, the skyscraper, bearing the romantic title *Building to the Skies* (1934). In this book he recorded the sense of adventure he shared with the pioneers of the high building art and emphasized the difference in attitude between North American and British practice. When he was building his 23-storey Liberty Bank in Buffalo, a question arose as to the strength of its steel skeleton. 'It was above the New York City standard of strength, but, oddly enough, below that called for by the local building laws', he wrote, 'I had little difficulty in persuading the authorities that their rules . . .

Fig. 2.2 *Les Constructeurs, by Fernand Léger.*

Fig. 2.3 *Liberty Bank, Buffalo, NY mid-1920s (architect Alfred Bossom).*

were obsolete. I was not only allowed to build to my own plans, but was virtually invited to rewrite the structural steel building code for the entire city . . . In Britain . . . I should probably have been run in by the police as a public danger.' It was the immense adaptability of the skyscraper 'by virtue of the simplicity of its steel framework' and its concentration of functions and services that Bossom so admired in the 1930s [4]. Structural steel made the skyscraper possible for a number of practical reasons, but it must be remembered too that it had a profound effect on building economics. The cost of a steel frame ranged from 8% to 15% of total building costs in the 1920s [5].

Fig. 2.4 *Ritz Hotel, Piccadilly, London 1903–6 (architects Mewès and Davis).*

In London in 1905 one of the first steel framed buildings (probably the first in the capital) was the Ritz Hotel, Piccadilly (Fig. 2.4), by Mewès and Davis, although the frame itself was not expressed externally, as the reduction of thickness of external walls was not permitted until 1909 in London.

Steel soon became the commonest structural material in Britain. It took on many shapes in its manufactured states but its main form was as a constructional framework with supports laid out on a grid pattern with trussed or with flat roofs. During the interwar period steel framed single storey factories and warehouses consisting of rows of supporting steel columns carrying sawtooth north light roofs or simply open trussed pitched roofs were to be found along many of the new arterial highways. Gradually, welded portal frames were introduced and as the new high tensile steels were made available longer spans, and north–south monitor roof lights, became possible.

Modern architecture entered British life largely by the backdoor. It was an expatriate movement. In the late 1920s the Russian Berthold Lubetkin arrived from Paris to work in Hampstead. Soon afterwards the German émigrés arrived, fleeing Hitler's purges. Gropius came with his wife Ilse directly from Rome, where he had been giving a paper on theatre design; Erich Mendelsohn arrived with his wife, having fled Berlin in haste. He took up practice with Chermayeff, a Harrow-educated Englishman originally from the Caucasus. Later Breuer, Frankel and Korn arrived (Fig. 2.5). I mention this for one reason only – they were all men committed to the architecture of steel and glass that I mentioned earlier when referring to Otto Wagner. They worked in close collaboration with engineers like Arup and Samuely who knew German but, importantly, were well acquainted with the new techniques of building associated with the modern architectural movement. One of the most successful buildings to emerge from this influx of foreign architects and engineers was the De La Warr Pavilion (Fig. 2.6) won in competition by Mendelsohn and Chermayeff in 1934 for the exceedingly dull geriatric seaside resort of Bexhill-on-Sea. It was the first all welded steel construction building in the UK and part of the plastic design revolution of the 1930s.

The structure was calculated by Felix Samuely, who had known Mendelsohn in Berlin and who, on the strength of this collaboration set up his practice with Cyril Helsby, a New Zealander; Conrad Hamann joined them a little later. Writing in 1935 Samuely remarked that welding had been adopted for economical reasons 'but it also had the advantage of permitting the fabrication of such structural units which left unaltered the lines and overall dimensions of sections desired by the architects' [6]. The building was described at the time as 'a welded steel skeleton with curtain walls of reinforced concrete'. It was meticulously detailed and at times daringly complicated from a structural point of view as the great north staircase cantilever still testifies today. It remains the greatest German building in Britain and one of modern architecture's finest achievements anywhere.

Fig. 2.5 *Fromm Contraceptives Factory, Berlin, 1928–30 (architects Artur Korn and Sigfried Weitzmann).*

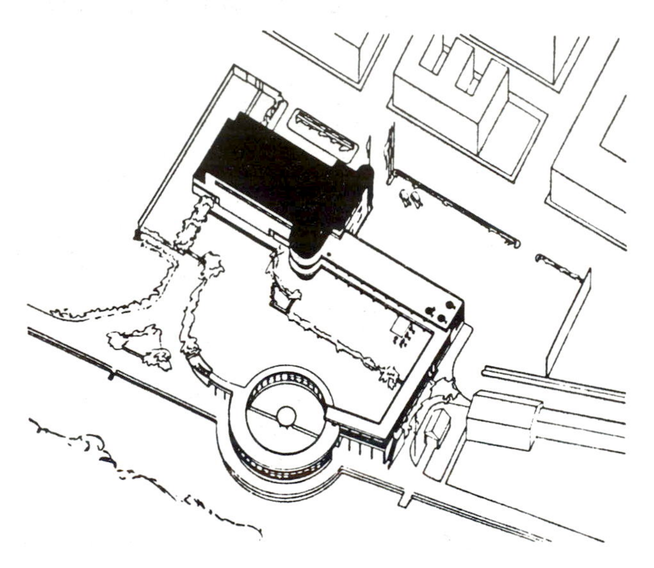

Fig. 2.6 *De la Warr Pavilion, Bexhill-on-Sea 1933–35 (architects Mendelsohn and Chermayeff: engineer Felix Samuely).*

In the postwar period, particularly for industrial and factory buildings, welded tubular construction was used to create even larger spans, give economy in the use of material, accelerate erection, and give added ability to support simple roof coverings. Such developments were of immense importance in the development of new prefabrication techniques. Those designers who were interested in standardization and industrialized components in the years immediately after the Second World War built on this earlier knowledge to forge ahead of other European countries [7].

During the war years in Britain the Government had issued an order to prohibit the use of steel for building except under licence by private merchants (contractors); steel licences were already required for the general sale and purchase of steel [8]. Few public, and even fewer private buildings were produced anywhere in the world during the war years. Automation progressed considerably, as did the growing awareness of the advantages of lighter weight metals and plastics. These too were to be absorbed into the programme for industrialized buildings that got underway in the early 1950s. All this activity was supported by a growing awareness internationally of a need for a philosophy of architecture and for new principles of design.

In the immediate postwar period the tenets of the Modern Movement in architecture's white cubic concrete phase were even more closely adhered to than in the 1930s. However, there was also an awareness of the potential of transportable buildings and lightweight components manufacturing. These technologies were transferred from the wartime aeronautical and destruction industries into the peacetime needs of rebuilding industry and society. The Portal Committee in Britain provided the Government of the day with essential information on the applicability of prefabrication closely following American practice [9].

All of this may be seen as part of that formal tradition in architecture and with a firm place in the intellectual apparatus of postwar design theory. In Britain too there was also a quasi-intellectual group of Neo-Georgians whose influence extended well into the public housing programmes whose strong lobbying after the war ensured their preferences were absorbed into postwar reconstruction proposals. Another group, The Empiricists (if one dares to use that term to describe the socially conscious reformers whose legacy derives from Robert Owen via Henry George and Ebenezer Howard) seized the new opportunities offered by an optimistic government to create New Towns and to revert to the informal picturesque tradition and vernacular materials albeit to see their designs set in prairie-like environments. In such places steel as a building material only played a small part in design considerations as the chief component for the prefabricated schools put up in Hertfordshire and Essex in places like Hatfield, Stevenage, Hemel Hempstead and Basildon.

One event certainly stands out as a major statement on architecture: the 1951 Festival of Britain (Fig. 2.7), an experiment in aesthetic values as well as in materials, technologies and supportive national psychology. However it did, at the time, appear somewhat trivial. The completion of the solid Royal Festival Hall at the same time allowed a restatement of architectural values to be made at the Festival. It was a strong building whose imagery earned the title of the New Empiricism.

The Festival Hall was somewhat despised by those who recognized the directness of Mies van der Rohe's cold steely aesthetic. It was seen as relevant and appropriate to the postwar age. Thus the emphasis swung back to Chicago. The city underwent a Teutonic renaissance and Mies, with Holabird and Root and others, erected a series of minimalist structures in steel (with brick panels) between 1940 and 1953 for the Illinois Institute of Technology campus (Fig. 2.8). These buildings were based on a standard bay grid of 24 ft by 24 ft × 12 ft high and expressed externally by an exposed

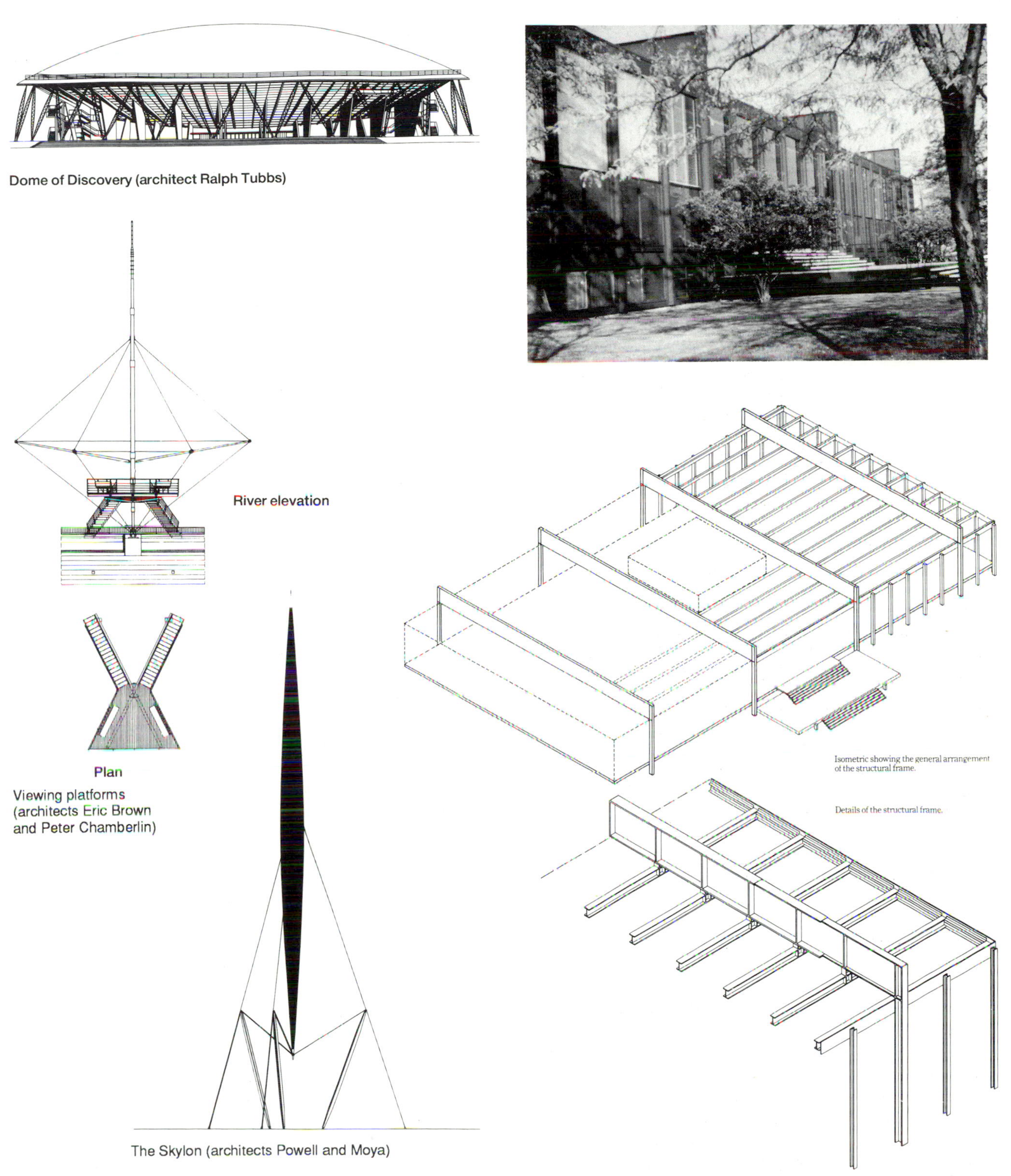

Fig. 2.7 *South Bank designs for various buildings, Festival of Britain, London 1951.*

Fig. 2.8 *Alumni Memorial Hall, IIT Campus, Chicago 1945–46 (architect Mies van der Rohe). Courtesy Alan Ogg:* Architecture in Steel.

Fig. 2.9 *Lake Shore Drive apartments, Chicago 1948–51 (architect Mies van der Rohe).*

steel structure. H.P. Berlage's structural honesty argument was taken literally. Mies's structural elements, at IIT, were as clear in their architectural intentions as those admired by Goethe at Strasbourg Cathedral. They had been conceived, as his disciple Philip Johnson wrote, 'in terms of steel channels and angles, I-beams and H-columns, just as medieval design is conceived in terms of stone vaults and buttresses' [10]. Mies's Lake Shore Drive apartments were built at the same time, with planted I-beams to act as stiffeners on the outside as well as columnar devices (Fig. 2.9). The Mannheim Theatre Project, the uniquely beautiful Farnsworth House (Fig. 2.10), the Berlin National Gallery and a succession of well disciplined, if somewhat plagiarized, examples of the Miesian mode followed. The best examples include the Smithson's school at Hunstanton (1954), Eiermann's fine German Pavilion at the Brussels Exposition, 1958 (Fig. 2.11), and John Winter's 'Cor-Ten' house in London's Hampstead (see section 36.2.1). As his legatees soon discovered, a Mies van der Rohe design exhibited many concerns about unity, organic principles, order and the *Zeitgeist* but also, as he reminded an IIT audience: 'everything depends on how we use a material, not on the material itself' [11]. The Smithson's school was important too in its innovative use of 9 inch RSJs as H frames frames welded on site into beams and stanchions, the whole based on the use of plastic theory as a stressing discipline (Fig. 2.12).

Steel may well have worked well for Mies van der Rohe as an appropriate material for apartment construction in Chicago and Detroit. It was not so readily available or acceptable in Europe, or in Britain in the postwar years. The Smithson's school was a notable exception [12]. Concrete construction had largely taken over. Steel was retained for single storey buildings, farms and factories or large complex public buildings dependent on composite construction. It was in the area of single storey lightweight structures that it was to make its most telling advances in the hands of revolutionary designers like Buckminster Fuller, Jean Prouvé and Frei Otto. Before examining their contribution it is useful to examine the influential climate of opinion that grew up as part of modern architectural design theory.

2.2 MECHANIZATION AND NATURE

In his seminal work, *Mechanization takes Command* (New York, 1948) [13], Sigfried Giedion referred to the growth of mechanization as 'a contribution to anonymous history'. In this extensive study he looked at not only a hidden tradition but also at something rather more specific: a collection of ideas that when brought together would show that a fundamental split, in 'our period', as he called it, between thought and feeling came about by mechanization. Whereas his earlier polemical work [14] *Space, Time and Architecture* (1941) attempted to show how a new phase of engineering and architecture had emerged at the end of the 19th century, *Mechanization takes Command* opened up a much larger field of enquiry. Mechanization was viewed from a human standpoint and how far 'mechanization corresponds with and to what extent it contradicts the unalterable laws of human nature' was the theme. He saw questions about the *limits* of mechanization (as far as the human aspect was concerned) as fundamental tenets which should under no circumstances be disregarded. Its subtle effects and influences made it difficult to isolate, thus he dubbed his study an 'anonymous history'. Giedion rightly felt that it was a neglected and under-researched area.

Mechanization has affected all aspects of life and has had an impact on most designed objects, including cities, factories, houses and furniture. His concern was that the reader should understand the tools of mechanization but not merely in a technical sense. With such an understanding we can then begin to assess the wider significance of the mechanized culture into which Giedion's own pioneer generation was born.

Mechanization, as a phenomenon, is marked in its beginning by the elimination of the 'application of handicraft'. This process had begun in the United States during the second half of the last century. This 'assembly line' displays 'the symptom of full mechanization' in Giedion's view. Further, he argued, the problems of mechanization have a typological aspect and that, 'the history of styles follows its theme along a horizontal direction; the history of types along a vertical one'. Such a viewpoint remains valid today and was one recognized by Nikolaus Pevsner in his *A History of Building Types* (1976) [15] where he argued that buildings 'have a use before they have a style'. Also, he wrote that it is pointless to evaluate the second without understanding the first, an attitude that was adopted in the work of the British architectural historian the late Reyner Banham in his book *The Architecture of the Well-tempered Environment* [16]. Banham examined mechanization in a building services 'performance' context. He adopted a somewhat different method of analysis to Giedion, looking at the efficiency and purpose of a work of architecture in relation to its wider environmental considerations, to structure, to form and cultural conditioning factors as well as a technological context.

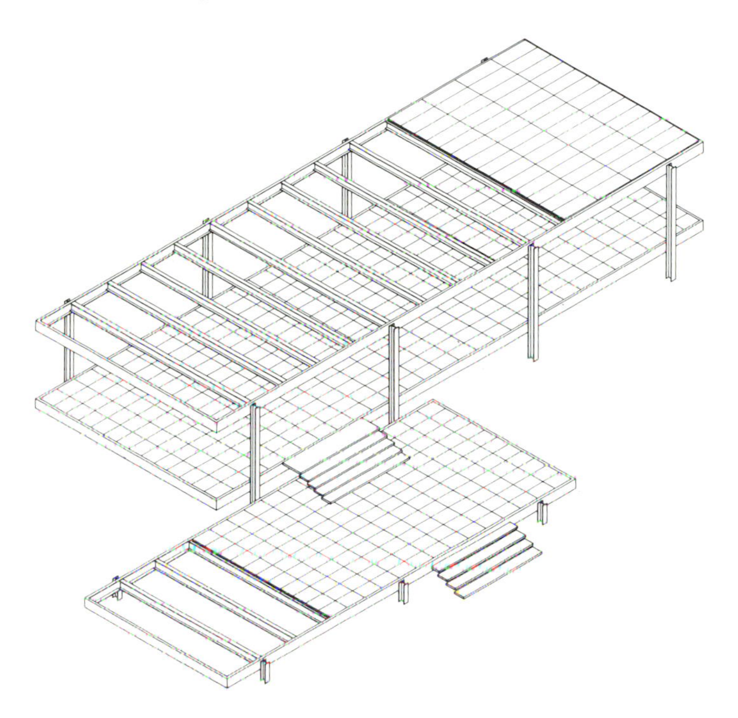

Fig. 2.10 *Farnsworth House, Illinois (diagram of frame) 1946–49 (architect Mies van der Rohe). Courtesy Alan Ogg:* Architecture in Steel.

Fig. 2.11 *German Pavilion, Brussels Exposition 1958 (architect Egon Eiermann).*

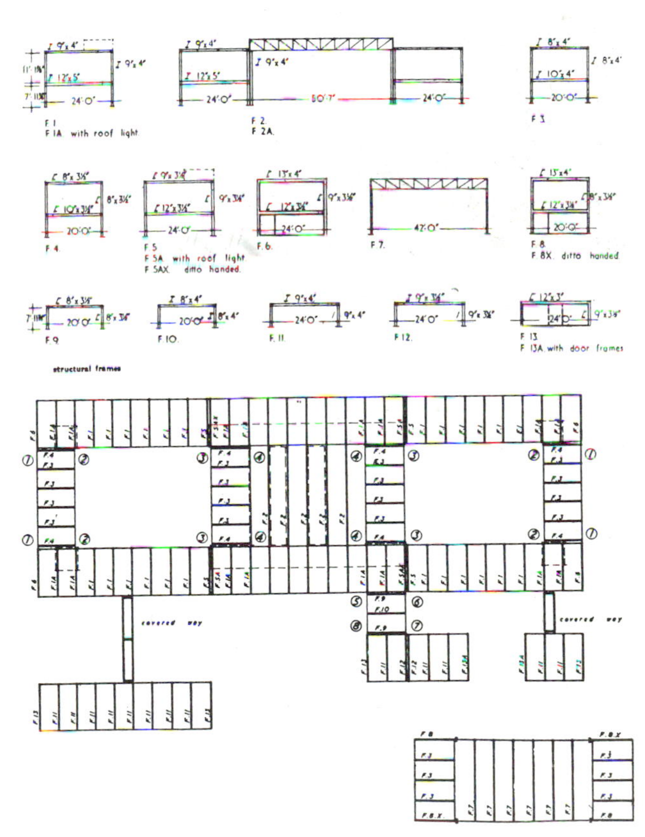

Fig. 2.12 *Hunstanton School, Norfolk 1950–54, diagram of welded frame (architect Alison and Peter Smithson: engineers Ove Arup and Partners).*

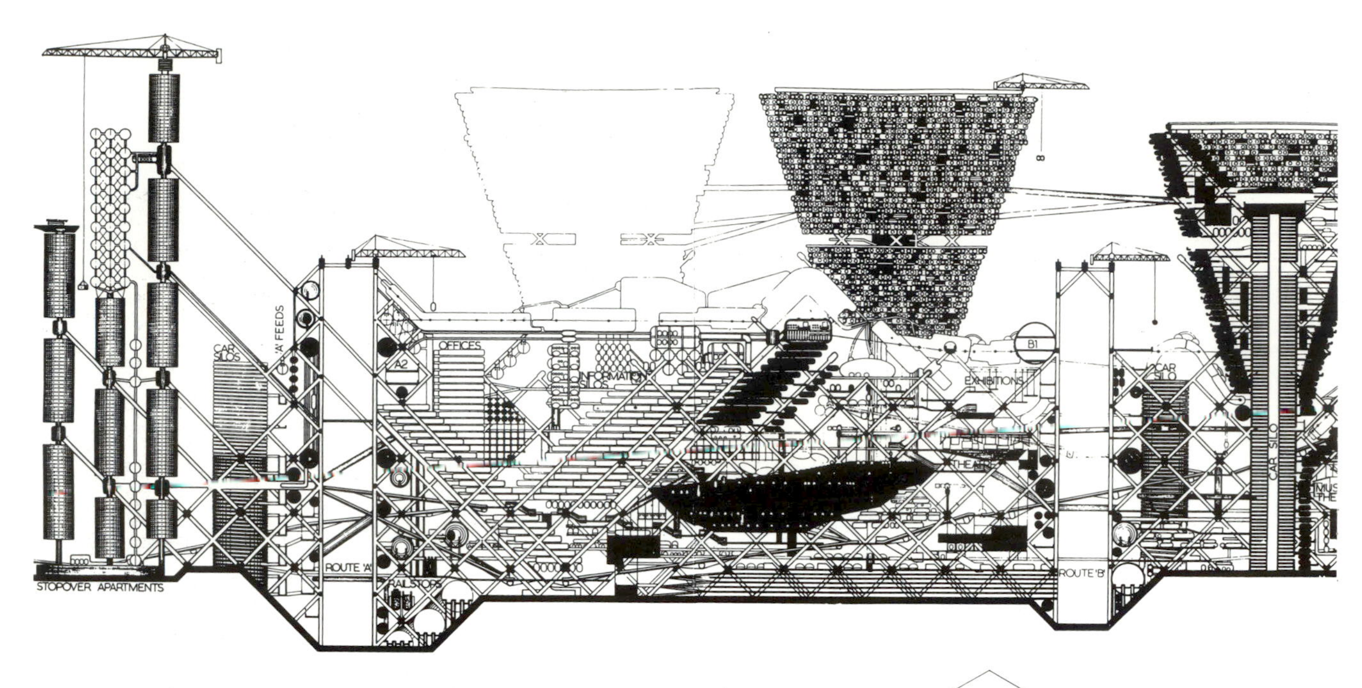

Fig. 2.13 *Plug-in City, 1967 (Archigram).*

Surely it is from these deeply rooted attitudes to cultural and architectural history that the current 'Hi-Tech' architectural attitudes have gained a renewed effectiveness and credibility? Whilst this term 'Hi-Tech' itself is a meaningless and only a currently fashionable stylistic label, the astonishing persistence of this attitude – perhaps one might call it a 'mechanical' or systemic industrially designed architecture – is remarkable. Metal construction has always provided the framework for this approach, from Paxton to Grimshaw. Today it is no longer anonymous but systematic, rationalized high profile design suitable for the fast-track, economic one-off structures required by today's clients.

There are many buildings and structures in the world which owe much to the persistence of this engineering approach and its aesthetic formulation into a 'style' has been one of the most welcome and surprising developments of the past two decades. It has swung the emphasis away from concrete and its attendant solidity.

Recently, architecture has gone through periods of formalism, historicism, so-called 'Post-Modernism', Beaux-Arts and Classical Revivalism, even what the French term 'graphic terrorism', all under the general term of pluralism in current design. Pastiche, and historically referenced remodelling, have dated far quicker than anyone

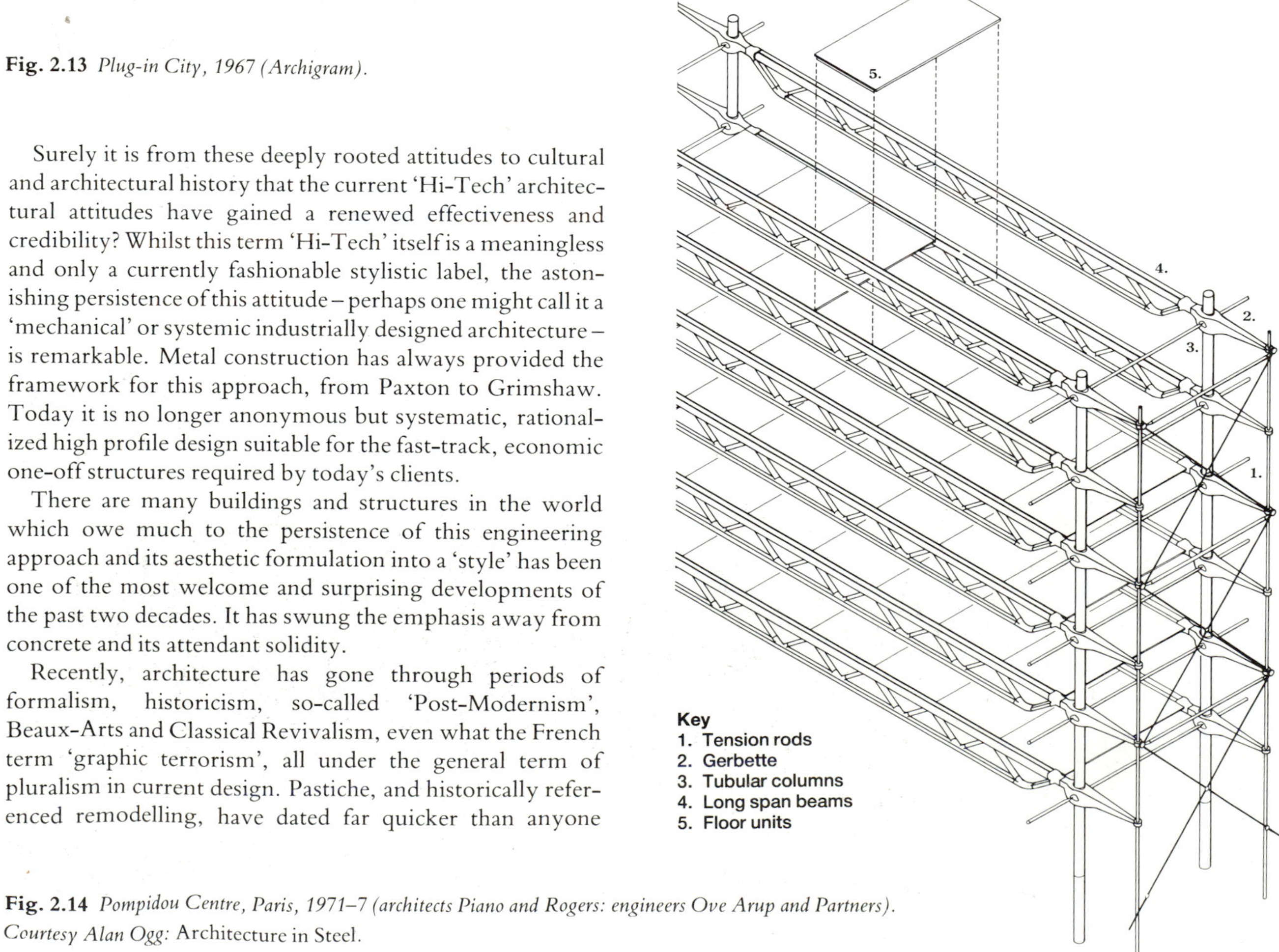

Fig. 2.14 *Pompidou Centre, Paris, 1971–7 (architects Piano and Rogers: engineers Ove Arup and Partners). Courtesy Alan Ogg:* Architecture in Steel.

expected and seem to be as empty as many had predicted. However, those architects who have consistently pursued a line that accepted rational engineering principles and the logical use of structural systems in steel, concrete and glass have created a potent new vocabulary of forms. In some cases techniques from industry have been borrowed and materials have been employed in a way that is entirely consistent with a modern architecture freed from current stylistic clichés. It would perhaps be absurd to suggest that these trends dropped out of the blue. Rather, they have evolved in parallel with major technological advances in the fields of mechanization, engineering and industrial design aided, and indeed only made possible, by the many new computer techniques available to its designers. Whilst many of the architects and designers responsible for the new metal architecture may well view themselves as direct inheritors of the 19th century engineering legacy and of such innovations as dirigibles, lightweight bridges and aircraft construction, there is little doubt that the new techniques have played their part in enabling entirely new structural types to be calculated. This is true for complex roofs like the great concrete sails of the Sydney Opera House as well as for complicated lightweight tensile structures as developed by Frei Otto and others. Their historic pedigrees, however, are unquestionable.

Otto, in the foreword to his first volume of *Tensile Structures* (1967) recorded that: 'The primary impulse for engineering projects employing tensile structures was provided in the past century by Roebling and his suspension bridges followed by those of Ammann, Leonhardt, Steinman and Strauss'. But whereas these pioneers provided the

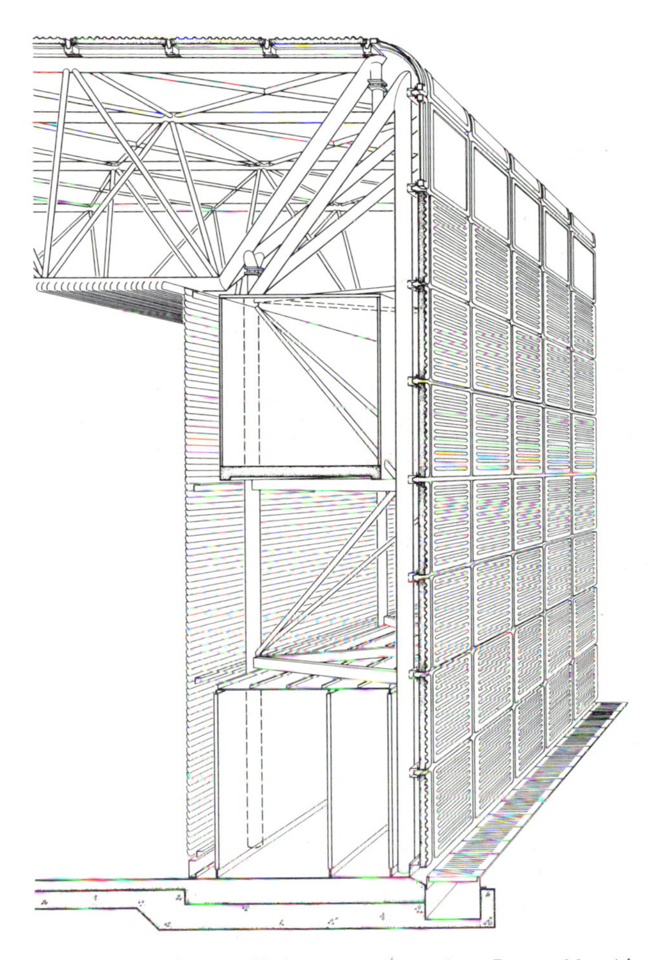

Fig. 2.15 *Roof and wall frames Sainsbury Arts Centre, Norwich, 1974–8 (architects Foster Associates: engineers Anthony Hunt Associates). Courtesy Alan Ogg:* Architecture in Steel.

Fig. 2.16 *Gallery end, Sainsbury Arts Centre, 1974–8 (architects Foster Associates: engineers Anthony Hunt Associates).*

fundamental theories the new techniques, new forms and new expressions required for such structures were nearly all developed by later designers. Indeed, in the area of lightweight structures greater possibilities of flexibility occurred in the late 1950s when aerodynamic shapes and light, transportable structural elements were adopted to form a variety of new structural forms and coverings.

In the early 1960s the German architect Rudolph Doernach developed a deformed metal skin into a single curvature structure and Buckminster Fuller continued to develop his extremely lightweight domes of pneumatic sandwich panels. At about the same time new types of air and bubble structures were also being developed.

Parallel to these new engineering inventions ran a series of theoretical, polemical ideas about architecture and the 'spatial city'. Developed by architects, teachers and idealists such as the London-based 'Archigram' group (Fig. 2.13), Otto and the Paris-based Hungarian designer Yona Friedman. A graphic portrayal of a new architecture was depicted requiring unusual methods of engineering and architectural assemblage. These ideas were without issue at the time, but by the mid-1970s buildings like the Pompidou Centre on the Place Beaubourg, Paris, erected to a design won internationally by Renzo Piano and Richard Rogers (Fig. 2.14), bore a close resemblance to the visionary Archigram work and the work of Eames, Ehrenkrantz, Fuller, Wachsmann and to some extent Prouvé. In this kind of architecture the advantages of modern metals were explored, as were the expressive and technical advantages of separating structural supports from services. Foster's Faber building, with its totally transparent facade and mechanized interior, at Ipswich (1975) and the Sainsbury Arts Centre (1978) (Figs 2.15 and 2.16), an industrial shed at University of East Anglia, Norwich, also by Foster, as well as some of the early work of Farrell and Grimshaw were also part of the genre. In such projects as Cesar Pelli's large 'Blue Whale' design store in Los Angeles and the series of industrial capsule projects by Japanese architects such as Kisho Kurokawa and other 'Metabolists' the rapid extension of these experimental ideas took root internationally.

Gradually, these designs and the innovations they represent have led to a whole new line of rational, Hi-Tech, steel framed and finished buildings. British architects and engineers, acknowledging their obvious debt to the pioneering work of 19th century engineers as well as to the anonymous designers of airship hangars and aircraft now clearly lead the world with buildings like 'Lloyds' and 'Inmos', Gwent, by Rogers, Foster's Renault Centre, Swindon and the Hongkong and Shanghai Bank with its great 'coathanger' structure. In Australia, too, with the experience and knowledge of engineers from Arup's working in close collaboration with firms like Cox, Richardson and Taylor, the steel tradition is enthusiastically continued [18]. But it is not just a matter of good, even smart, fashionable, design that expresses technological excitement in the use of materials that have lain dormant for far too long. It provides speedy construction, on and off site, prefabrication and assembly, economy of detailing, finer tolerances and good value for the client.

REFERENCES AND TECHNICAL NOTES

1. Knapton, E.J. and Derry, T.K. (1965) *Europe 1815–1914*, London, 1965, p. 283.
2. *Op. cit.*, p. 284.
3. Published in *Smoke and Steel* by Carl Sandburg, New York: Harcourt, Brace and Co., (1921).
4. See Bossom, A.C. (1984) *Building to the Skies: The Romance of the Skyscraper*, London: Studio, 1934 and also Sharp, D. (Ed) *Alfred C. Bossom's American Architecture* London: Book Art.
5. See the chapter 'The Economic Argument' in Clark, W.C. and Kingston, J.L. *The Skyscraper*, New York: Am. Inst. of Steel Construction. n.d. (c.1924).
6. Quoted in the special issue of the *AA Journal* on F. J. Samuely, June 1960, p. 7.
7. *A Survey of Prefabrication* produced for the Ministry of Works in 1945 by D. Dex Harrison, J.M. Albery and M.K. Whiting was a worldwide investigation of prefabricated methodologies, types and materials which examined many pressed and framed (sheets in pan form) steel examples and saw that 'cast iron was the precursor of all prefabricated metals . . .'
8. Kohan, C.M. (1952) *Works and Buildings*, London: HMSO, pp. 45–8.
9. The report of Lord Portal's mission (largely compiled by Sir Alfred Bossom, ibid.) was published as *Methods of Building in the USA*, London: HMSO (1944).
10. Johnson, P. (1947) *Mies van der Rohe*, New York: MOMA, p. 138.
11. *Op. cit.*, p. 198.
12. A full description of the design considerations of the Hunstanton School is to be found in *The Architectural Review* issue for September, (1954), pp. 148–62.
13. Giedion, S. (1948) *Mechanization Takes Command*, Harvard University Press.
14. Giedion, S. (1941) *Space, Time and Architecture*, Harvard University Press.
15. Pevsner, N. (1976) *A History of Building Types*, Penguin Books.
16. Banham, R. (1969) *The Architecture of the Well-Tempered Environment*, Architectural Press.
17. Otto, F. (1967) *Tensile Structures*, Volume 1, MIT Press.
18. See Ogg, A. (1987) *Architecture in Steel: The Australian Context*, Sydney. Royal Australian Institute of Architects.

Steel production at British Steel, Redcar, UK.

Part Two | Materials

Symbolic molecule of iron. The Atomium, Brussels 1958 (architects A. and J. Polak: engineer A. Waterheys).

3

Properties of steel

W. D. Biggs

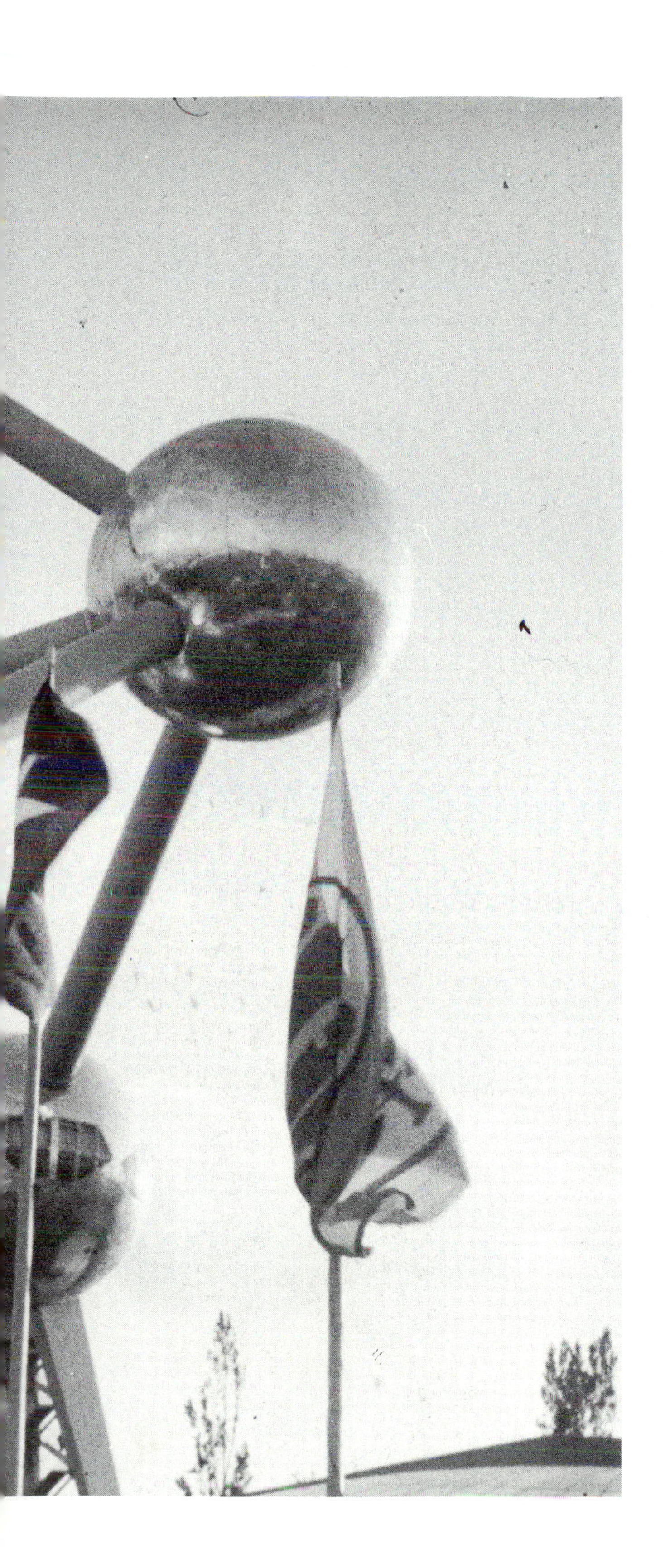

3.1 INTRODUCTION

Steel is essentially an alloy of iron and carbon but, despite this apparent simplicity, it is one of the more complex and interesting of all materials. In this chapter the manufacturing process is described briefly. This will enable steel to be distinguished from its close relatives – wrought iron, cast iron and cast steel – and also explain some terms found in specifications. Note that the descriptions are based upon traditional steelmaking practice – nowadays there are many variations. The chemistry, however, remains the same.

Like all metals iron is extracted from naturally occurring ores. These are complex chemical compounds but, for simplicity, it can be assumed that the basic source material is iron oxide (FeO) even though these ores have long since been worked out. Historically iron was late upon the scene – this was largely due to the high temperatures needed (c. 1600°C or 3000°F) to reduce the oxide to the metal. A forced air blast (e.g. a blacksmith's bellows) solved this and the addition of a reducing agent (carbon) achieved the reaction

$$FeO + C \rightarrow Fe + CO$$

the carbon monoxide gas being released into the air. This first reaction produces *pig iron*. This contains a considerable amount of carbon which exists in the form of the hard, brittle carbide of iron (Fe_3C) and pig iron is only useful for further processing.

By remelting the pig, sometimes with scrap, and by controlled oxidation, again using an air blast, the carbon content is reduced to between 2.4% and 4.0%. This is *cast iron* which, as its name implies, is cast directly into shape in sand or metal moulds. Because of its high fluidity at iron-making temperatures it produces a sharp impression of the mould, and for many purposes no further machining is required. Depending on the composition the carbon can now exist in two different forms – as graphite (grey cast iron) or as iron carbide (white cast iron). Both impart brittleness to the material, although this can be ameliorated by reheating white cast iron to produce *malleable* iron. Its use in structural engineering is therefore limited – manhole covers, pipes etc. Its earlier widespread use for rainwater goods has now largely given way to polymeric materials. Nonetheless it was the predominant structural material in the 19th century and will be found as beams and columns in many rehabilitation and refurbishment projects. For all practical purposes it should be regarded as unweldable and should be handled with great care.

Steelmaking requires even closer control of the oxidation process, since it is now necessary to reduce the carbon content to rather less than 1%, indeed to around 0.2% for most structural steels. This is achieved in one of two ways: by remelting a charge of pig, possibly with scrap iron and steel, in a large open furnace and using relatively pure iron oxide (open hearth process) or by transferring a molten charge into a converter and blowing air (nowadays often oxygen) through the melt (Bessemer or converter process). In order to maintain the reaction a considerable excess of oxygen must be added and the melt is sampled periodically to check the carbon content. When the desired value is reached the reaction is stopped by the addition of elements which 'fix' the surplus oxygen as oxides. After a period of resting, these rise to the surface and may be skimmed off as slag. The elements used for this are generally manganese and silicon, and steels treated in this way are known as killed steels. The addition of manganese is important for another reason. One of the commonest – and most deleterious – impurities in steel is sulphur, originating from the ore or the coke. It causes a defect known as hot shortness in which the steel cracks disastrously and irremediably if it is subjected to any stresses (including cooling stresses) whilst hot. Apart from any other beneficial effects, manganese neutralizes this and specifications often require a minimum content of manganese even in the most pedestrian of steels.

Not all steels are treated in this way, however. Some steels are poured into moulds without 'killing' – in this case the carbon/oxygen reaction continues in the mould and a line of blowholes (the result of carbon monoxide formation) appears just below the outer skin. These are rimming steels and are quite acceptable for some purposes such as steel plate, sheet and strip according to BS 1449 [1], since the rolling needed to produce these products closes up the blowholes and a fully coherent product emerges.

In between killed and rimming steels lie the so-called balanced steels. These contain just enough deoxidizer to suppress the formation of blowholes but are not fully 'killed': BS 4449 permits these to be used for reinforcement bars [2].

In the traditional manufacturing process, steel is cast into ingots which are then subjected to further processing by forging or rolling to produce engineering sections such as angles, I-beams, plate, sheet etc. Some engineering components are, however, cast directly to shape – *cast steel*. The production process is not significantly different but cast steels, in general, contain a higher carbon content than wrought steels of equivalent properties, and this has some consequences if welding is to be used.

Continuous casting (concast) is a rather different process; it is a recent development which combines several of the operations associated with rolled steel products. This, together with other advances such as vacuum degassing, has led to considerable improvements in efficiency and quality.

The traditional terminology for the different types of steel is far from precise – steels with up to, say, 0.3% carbon are described as mild steels, from 0.3% to about 0.6% carbon as medium carbon steels (or often simply carbon steels) and thereafter as high carbon steels. If alloying elements are added (see section 3.5 below) they then become alloy steels.

Wrought iron is a variant of the basic material. Traditionally this was produced by 'puddling', in which pig iron is remelted and oxidized until the carbon content is reduced to about 0.05% and allowed to cool until it is a pasty mass. This is then removed from the furnace and hammered or rolled into bars. The impurities, mostly manganese sulphides, are stretched into longitudinal threads giving wrought iron its characteristic fibrous texture. Although not much is used now except for decorative purposes, wrought iron, with its excellent ductility and toughness and good resistance to corrosion, was the main competitor to cast iron before the introduction of cheap steel (c. 1870). It is still to be found in structures dating from Victorian times, such as the Eiffel Tower (1889) which was contemporaneous with the Queensferry Bridge (1890) of steel construction.

3.2 MECHANICAL PROPERTIES

3.2.1 Introduction

Before attempting to classify the various alloys of iron it is necessary to consider the properties which are important to the designer. In fact, these are not specific to steels but apply generally to all metallic materials.

Metallurgists tend to divide properties into two groups: *structure insensitive* and *structure sensitive*. Structure insensitive properties are wholly invariant – they are associated with the properties of the atoms themselves and the primary forces between them. They do not depend on the arrangement of the atoms. The principal properties here are the *elastic modulus*, the *density* and some chemical, electrical and thermal characteristics. As the name implies, the structure sensitive properties are wholly dependent upon the past history – whether hot-rolled or cold-rolled, whether heated and cooled and if so how. All of these processes disturb the atomic arrangement and these disturbances are reflected in changes in properties. From the designer's point of view the most important structure sensitive properties are the *yield strength* and the *fracture strength*.

3.2.2 Tensile properties

In a tensile test steel behaves substantially as shown in Fig. 3.1 from which the following properties can be defined.

Elastic moduli. These are commonly defined in terms of the relationship between stress, σ, and strain, ϵ, in that region

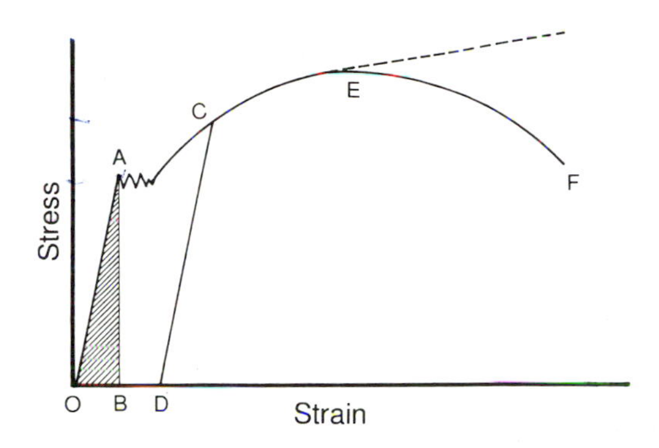

Fig. 3.1 *Stress/strain curve for steel (schematic).*

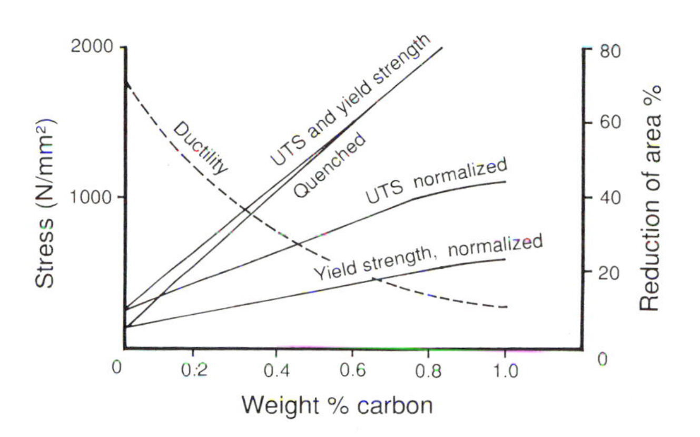

Fig. 3.2 *Effect of carbon on the strength and ductility of plain carbon steel.*

where the curve is linear (OA). The most frequently used is the modulus in tension:

$$\text{Young's modulus } E = \frac{\text{tension stress}}{\text{tension strain}}$$

$$\text{Also used is the shear modulus } G = \frac{\text{shear stress}}{\text{shear strain}}$$

Note that since strain is simply a ratio, the units of modulus are the same as those of stress i.e. N/mm^2 (ksi). The two moduli are mathematically related and, if the stress is reversed, the same values apply. Since the modulus is a structure insensitive property the normal design values $E = 205$ kN/mm^2 (30×10^6 psi or 30 000 ksi) and $G = 81$ kN/mm^2 (11×10^6 psi or 11 000 ksi) may be used with confidence for all steels, regardless of composition, origin, prior history etc.

An important property deriving from the modulus is the *elastic resilience* or stored energy. The area under the linear portion of the curve, shown shaded, has the dimensions of energy per unit volume, which for the region OAB is $\sigma^2/2E$. Stored energy is well exemplified by a clock spring which is loaded by winding the clock and which then releases the energy stored to drive the mechanism. It is of some importance in highly stressed structures (especially post-tensioned and cable structures) where, if the cable fractures, the considerable energy released causes the cable to whip violently with consequent danger to surrounding people and property. It is also an important consideration in connection with brittle fracture (see section 3.2.3 below).

Yield strength. Beyond the point A in Fig. 3.1 further stressing produces permanent deformation, i.e. if the material were stressed from A to C and then unloaded it would have increased in length by OD. On reloading, however, the stress/strain curve is linear until stress C is reached when permanent (plastic) extension recommences. Comparing this with the original, unstrained sample the yield stress has increased. This is known as work-hardening or strain-hardening and is the commonest (and oldest) way of increasing the yield strength of metals and alloys generally. Commercially, strain hardening is achieved by *cold working*, that is by rolling, drawing, extrusion etc. at, or only slightly above, room temperature. The yield stress is also affected by composition, especially by carbon content as shown in Fig. 3.2.

Some steels do not exhibit a clearly defined transition from elastic to plastic behaviour, and instead the stress-strain relationship follows a smooth continuous curve. It is nevertheless necessary to specify a stress which corresponds to a definite amount of permanent extension. This is called the proof stress and can be considered as the equivalent of the yield stress.

Tensile strength. At point E in Fig. 3.1 the stress falls away. This occurs because, as the material starts to deform locally, a waist or neck is produced at which fracture will eventually occur. Because of the reduction in diameter less force is needed to sustain a given stress, hence the drop. However, stress is conventionally defined as load/*original* area so the net result is that the *breaking stress* (F) appears to be lower than the maximum. In the early days of testing the change in behaviour at E was readily observed and was described as the *ultimate tensile strength* (*UTS*), a term which is still, regrettably, in use. Its value is of little concern in design.

If the reduction in area is measured and the *true* stress (i.e. load/actual area) calculated the dashed curve is obtained, which looks more intelligible. This value is rarely determined except for research purposes. Figure 3.2 shows that the *UTS* is affected by carbon content in the same way as yield strength.

Ductility. The reduction in area and the total elongation at fracture are both conventionally used as measures of ductility. Figure 3.2 shows that as yield and tensile strength increase ductility decreases. Clearly the same will apply to cold worked materials – as the yield strength is raised ever closer to the tensile strength the reserve of ductility diminishes and, in the limit, the material will snap under heavy cold working. This is familiar to anyone who has broken a piece of wire by continually bending and rebending it.

3.2.3 Fracture toughness

The classic theory of fracture in brittle solids such as glass was put forward by A. A. Griffith in 1923–4. Basically Griffith postulated that such solids contain minute defects (microcracks) which raise the stress locally to the level where the breaking stress is exceeded. Here is not the place for mathematics, but there are two principal conclusions which are worth noting. Firstly the stress to cause fracture (σ) is inversely proportional to the length of the crack c: actually

$$\sigma \propto \sqrt{E/c}$$

where E is the elastic modulus. This explains why glass will break along a line scribed with a diamond – the scribed line is deeper than the largest internal crack and determines the fracture path.

Secondly, once the crack has started to run it soon propagates at high speed – in the limit, the speed of sound in the material. For glass this is about 500 m/s (1650 ft/s) and we may assume that, once started, the crack cannot be arrested even if the load is removed.

For many years it was thought that these considerations applied only to materials having properties akin to glass (brick, tile, concrete etc.). However, catastrophic fractures in welded ships early in World War II revealed that, for all its apparent ductility, steel could also behave in a similar way (brittle fracture). The precise mechanisms are, even now, a matter for discussion but certain observations can be made:

(a) Brittle fracture always starts at a discontinuity such as a notch (e.g. a screw thread), an incompletely fused weld or, in extreme cases, a design discontinuity such as a hole or a corner where the stress is locally increased.
(b) For a steel of given composition the onset of brittle, rather than ductile, behaviour is affected both by temperature and rate of loading.

Table 3.1 Weldable Structural Steels (BS4360: 1986, Section 6)

Grade	*Chemical composition*							*Normal supply condition*	*Tensile strength*
	C max	Si	Mn max	P	S	Nb	V		
	%	%	%	%	%	%	%		N/mm^2
40A	0.22	0.50 max	1.60	0.050	0.050	–	–	As rolled	340/500
40B	0.20	0.50 max	1.50	0.050	0.050	–	–	As rolled	340/500
40C	0.18	0.50 max	1.50	0.050	0.050	–	–	As rolled	340/500
40D	0.18	0.50 max	1.50	0.050	0.050	–	–	As rolled or normalized	340/500
40E	0.16	0.10/0.50	1.60	0.040	0.040	–	–	As rolled or normalized	340/500
43A	0.25	0.50 max	1.60	0.050	0.050	–	–	As rolled	430/580
43B	0.22	0.50 max	1.50	0.050	0.050	–	–	As rolled	430/580
43C	0.18	0.50 max	1.50	0.050	0.050	–	–	As rolled	430/580
43D	0.18	0.50 max	1.50	0.040	0.040	0.003/0.10	0.003/0.10	As rolled or normalized	430/580
43E	0.16	0.10/0.50	1.50	0.040	0.040	–	–	As rolled or normalized	430/580
50A	0.23	0.50 max	1.60	0.050	0.050	0.003/0.10	0.003/0.10	As rolled	490/640
50B	0.22	0.50 max	1.50	0.050	0.050	0.003/0.10	0.003/0.10	As rolled	490/640
50C	0.22	0.50 max	1.50	0.050	0.050	0.003/0.10	0.003/0.10	As rolled	490/640
50D	0.20	0.50 max	1.50	0.040	0.040	0.003/0.10	0.003/0.10	Normalized	490/640
50E	0.20	0.10/0.50	1.50	0.040	0.040	0.003/0.10	0.003/0.10	Normalized	490/640
55C	0.22	0.60 max	1.60	0.040	0.040	0.003/0.10	0.003/0.20	As rolled	550/700
55EE	0.22	0.10/0.60	1.60	0.040	0.040	0.003/0.20	0.003/0.20	Normalized or quenched and tempered	550/700

(c) The chemical composition of the steel (especially the carbon/manganese ratio) and the grain size affect the ductile-brittle transition.

Nowadays it is customary to rewrite the Griffith equation in the form:

$$\sigma\sqrt{\pi c} = \sqrt{EG_c}$$

where c is the crack length, E is the elastic modulus and G_c is a stress intensity factor related to the size and shape of the controlling discontinuity. The critical value of the stress intensity factor is given the symbol K_c and is known as the fracture toughness and is a property of the material [3]. Typical values are shown below.

Material	Fracture toughness $(\text{MNm}^{-3/2})\{\text{kips in}^{-3/2}\}$
Mild steel	140 (5300)
High carbon steel	20–50 (750–1900)
Cast iron	6–20 (225–750)
Aluminium alloys	20–70 (750–2640)
Concrete	0.5 (20)
Glass	0.8 (30)
Polymers	0.5–5 (20–200)

So far as structural engineering is concerned, fracture toughness is not used directly in design. An assessment of the capacity of a steel to behave in either a ductile or a brittle manner involves a test which combines the observations in (a) and (b) above. This is the *notch impact* test in which a specimen, notched in a specified way, is subjected to a hammer blow of specified energy. If a series of tests are carried out at different temperatures a curve such as that shown in Fig. 3.3 is obtained indicating the temperature range over which the ductile-brittle transition occurs. Most specifications now require the steel to display a minimum energy absorption at a specified temperature – see, for instance, Table 3.1 where grade 40B steel is required to possess a minimum energy absorption of 27 Joules (20 ft.lb) at room temperature whereas 40D should absorb the same energy at −20°C (−4°F). Note that the grades 40B and 40D refer to BS 4360 [4], which will be discussed in more detail later.

Improvements in notch ductility are obtained by a

Minimum yield strength, for thickness (in mm)				*Minimum elongation, on gauge length of 5.65 $\sqrt{S_o}$*	*Minimum Charpy V notch impact test value*		*Grade*
Up to and including 16	*Over 16 up to and including 40*	*Over 40 up to and including 63*	*Over 63 up to and including 100*		*Temp*	*Energy min value*	
N/mm²	N/mm²	N/mm²	N/mm²	%	°C	J	
235	225	215	205	25	–	–	40A
225	225	215	205	25	20	27	40B
235	225	215	210	25	0	27	40C
235	225	215	215	25	−20	27	40D
260	245	240	225	25	−40	27	40E
275	265	255	245	22	–	–	43A
275	265	255	245	22	20	27	43B
275	265	255	245	22	0	27	43C
275	265	255	245	22	−20	27	43D
275	265	255	245	22	−40	27	43E
355	345	340	325	20	–	–	50A
355	345	340	325	20	20	27	50B
355	345	340	325	20	0	27	50C
355	345	340	325	20	−20	27	50D
355	345	340	325	20	−40	27	50E
Up to and including 16	Over 16 up to and including 25	Over 25 up to and including 40	Over 40 up to and including 63				
450	430	415	–	19	0	27	55C
450	430	415	9	19	−50	27	55EE

reduction in carbon content or an increase in manganese content or both. The result is the 'notch ductile' mild steels with the manganese content raised to around 1.5% and a progressive reduction in carbon content (see Table 3.1 for weldable structural steels and Table 3.2 for alloy steels).

3.2.4 Fatigue

Failure by fatigue occurs as a result of a member or component being subjected to reversing or fluctuating stress even when the maximum applied stress is below that normally required to cause fracture and, indeed, below the yield strength of the material. As with brittle fracture, fatigue always starts from a stress raiser, though here it may be a less obvious focal point – thus in standing machinery subjected to many reversals fatigue starting from one machined groove a little deeper than the rest is not uncommon.

The appearance of a fatigue fracture is quite characteristic, showing a series of ripples spreading from the focal point. These correspond to progress in crack growth and, when the crack is large enough, brittle fracture follows as described in section 3.2.3. above.

In laboratory tests a plot of the stress range versus cycles to failure generally appears as shown in Fig. 3.4(ABC). This would seem to imply a limiting stress below which fatigue failure will not occur. This is, however, an assumption which should be treated with great caution for, even under the most moderately corrosive conditions (e.g. a 'normal' urban atmosphere) the curve of Fig. 3.4(ABD) is more typical.

With much reservation it may be stated that, in most buildings, the designer has little to fear from fatigue in the structure itself. However, such cases as the collapse of the oil rig Alexander Kielland in 1980, due to fatigue failure in one of the legs, cannot be ignored. Certainly individual components may be at risk, and it is still not possible to rule out fatigue at the root of a screw thread as a contributory factor in the collapse of the overhead walkway across the atrium of the Kansas City, Hyatt Regency Hotel in 1981 which killed 114 people and injured almost 200 more [5].

3.3 SPECIFICATIONS FOR STRUCTURAL STEELS

With these definitions in mind it is now possible to review the requirements of a typical specification for structural steel. Until recently the relevant document was BS 4360: 1986 Weldable Structural Steels [4]. With the harmonization of standards throughout Europe, this is being replaced with a European Standard EN 10 025 [6], although this will incorporate the provisions of BS 4360. The following notes therefore relate to the current British Standard, in which sections 1 and 2 refer to general requirements and for tolerances. Section 3 specifies test requirements. Section 4

Table 3.2 Typical Alloy Steels – BS970:1983, Part I

	C	*Mn*	*Cr*	*Mo*	*Others*	*Conditions*	*Ruling section (mm)*			*Tensile strength (N/mm^2)*	*Yield strength (N/mm^2)*	*Min elong (%)*	*Impact (J min)*
530M40	0.36–0.44	0.60–0.90	0.90–1.20			Hardened and tempered	R	> 63	≤ 100	700–850	525	17	50
						+ turned or ground	S	≥ 6	≤ 63	775–925	585	15	50
							T	≥ 6	≤ 29	850–1000	680	13	50
						Hardened and tempered	R	> 63	≤ 100	700–850	540	12	–
						+ cold drawn or	S	> 13	≤ 63	775–925	600	11	–
						hardened and tempered	T	≥ 6	≤ 29	850–1000	700	9	–
						+ cold drawn + ground							
604M36	0.32–0.40	1.30–1.70		0.22–0.32		Hardened and tempered	R	>150	≤ 250	700–850	495	15	28
						+ turned or ground	R	> 29	≤ 150	700–850	525	17	50
							S	> 13	≤ 100	775–925	585	15	50
							T	≥ 6	≤ 63	850–1000	680	13	50
							U	≥ 6	≤ 29	925–1075	755	12	42
							V	≥ 6	≤ 19	1000–1150	850	12	42
						Hardened and tempered	R	> 29	≤ 150	700–850	540	12	–
						+ cold drawn or	S	> 13	≤ 100	775–925	600	11	–
						hardened and tempered	T	≥ 6	≤ 63	850–1000	700	9	–
						+ cold drawn + ground	U	≥ 6	≤ 29	925–1075	770	9	–
							V	≥ 6	≤ 19	1000–1150	865	9	–
606M36	0.32–0.40	1.30–1.70	0.22–0.32		P. 0.060 max	Hardened and tempered	R	> 13	≤ 100	700–1150	525	15	50
					S. 0.15–0.25	+ turned on ground	S	≥ 6	≤ 63	775–925	585	13	42
					Si. 0.25 max		T	≥ 6	≤ 29	850–1000	680	11	35
						Hardened and tempered	R	> 29	≤ 100	700–850	540	11	–
						+ cold drawn or	S	≥ 6	≤ 63	775–925	600	10	–
						hardened and tempered	T	≥ 6	≤1000	850–1000	700	8	–
						+ cold drawn + ground							

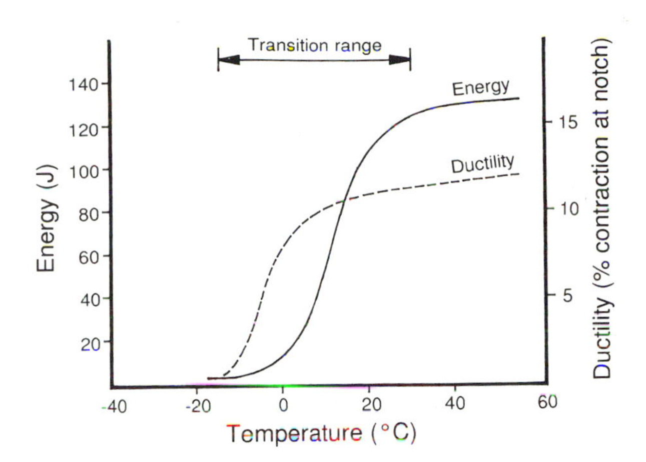

Fig. 3.3 *Typical ductile-brittle transition range for mild steel.*

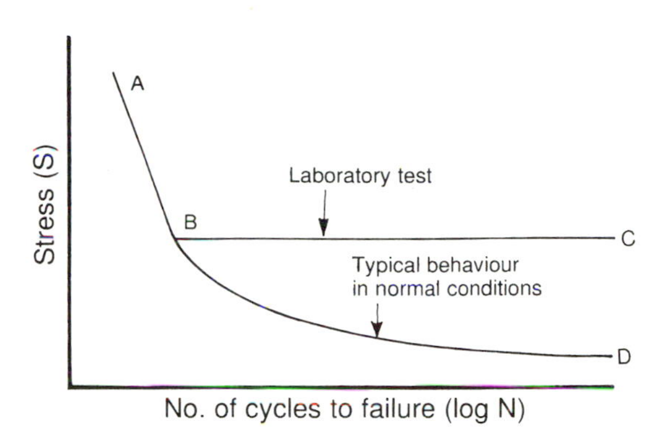

Fig. 3.4 *Typical fatigue curve (schematic).*

covers the specification of four grades of steel – 40, 43, 50 and 55; these numbers are related to the tensile strength (400, 430, 500 and 550 N/mm^2 respectively – 58, 62, 72 and 80 ksi).

Table 3.1 reproduces some parts of the specification and the following comments can be made:

(a) In both grades 43 and 50 the minimum specified yield strength can be achieved by various combinations of carbon and manganese. With additional alloying, some permissible deviations from the chemical composition are permitted. These are listed elsewhere in the specification.
(b) Sulphur and phosphorous are both 'tramp' elements. In excess they are deleterious but to try to remove them completely would be totally uneconomical. The values specified are maxima for safety in all steels but especially for weldable steels.
(c) With few exceptions structural steels are delivered either slowly cooled in a furnace (*annealed*) or after somewhat faster cooling in air (*normalized*). The term '*as rolled*' simply implies that no special treatment was given, and the bars were simply left to cool where they lay: this is fairly close to, but a little slower than, normalizing. Note, however, that the surface of a member delivered 'as rolled' requires special preparation before protective coatings are applied (see chapter 8).
(d) Table 3.1 shows that as the steel thickness increases the specified yield strength is lowered. This is one manifestation of the *size effect* and arises from the fact that thicker sections cool more slowly than thinner sections and thus cause the carbon to be redistributed in a different way which results in a lower yield.

Within each strength grade there are several subgrades from the lowest, A, to the highest, F. Weather resistant steels are denoted by the prefix WR (Table 3.3). Higher subgrades indicate stricter defect tolerance and amended chemical composition, in particular reduced carbon content. The latter results in improved mechanical properties, including increased tensile strength and toughness, improved weldability and lower transition temperatures. The improved performance is particularly appropriate for structures subject to low temperature, fatigue or impact loads or for site welding where conditions are not as easy to control.

As the specification improves there is normally a cost penalty. In addition, rolling mills may require a minimum ordered tonnage to comply with delivery requirements. These aspects should be checked prior to specifying higher subgrades.

3.4 COLD WORKED STEELS

As noted earlier, stressing a steel beyond its yield point leads to an increase in the yield strength on subsequent reloading. In a simple tension test a limit is reached at the *UTS* when localized necking occurs. However, if the cross-sectional area of the steel is reduced uniformly by rolling or drawing then very high strains are achieved with consequent increases in yield strength. In general this increase in yield strength is not accompanied by a marked decrease in ductility unless the amount of cold working is excessive.

In contrast, if a cold worked steel is reheated the benefits of cold working are lost and the steel begins to revert to its original, softer state. Softening starts to become noticeable after reheating to around 500°C (932°F) – higher temperatures cause faster and more complete softening. It follows that cold worked steel should not be welded, although one exception to this rule is found in BS 4461 [7], where cold-rolled reinforcement bars may be joined by flash welding. In this process the bars, each carrying an electric current, are forced together under pressure, and the arc formed as they meet produces the weld. There is, of course, softening in the bar adjacent to the weld but the process is so

Table 3.3 Weather Resistant Steels (BS4360:1986, Section 8)

Grade	Chemical composition (%)									
	C max	Si	Mn	P	S max	Cr	Ni max	Cu	Al	V
WR50A	0.12	0.25/0.75	0.30/0.50	0.070/0.15	0.050	0.50/1.25	0.65	0.25/0.55	–	–
WR50B	0.19	0.15/0.65	0.90/1.25	0.040 max	0.050	0.50/0.65	–	0.25/0.40	0.01/0.06	0.02/0.10
WR50C	0.22	0.15/0.65	0.90/1.45	0.040 max	0.050	0.50/0.65	–	0.25/0.40	0.01/0.06	0.02/0.10

fast that the soft zone is highly localized and has a negligible effect upon the load carrying characteristics.

3.5 HEAT TREATED STEELS

One particular attraction of steel is the way in which its mechanical properties can be controlled by heat treatments. If steel is cooled rapidly (quenched) the distribution of carbon is wholly different from that attained by annealing and/or normalizing, which involve slow cooling. Rapid cooling causes the steel to become intensely hard and brittle and, for most engineering purposes, it is of little use. As the carbon content increases, the effects of this treatment on the mechanical properties are more noticeable (Fig. 3.2). However, controlled reheating (tempering) allows the carbon (actually iron carbide) to be redistributed in a uniform, finely divided state – the uniformity of distribution and the size of the distributed particles being *solely a function of the tempering temperature*. Figure 3.5 shows the general effect of tempering upon a plain carbon steel.

Heat treatable steels usually contain additional alloying elements, notably manganese (Mn), chromium (Cr), nickel (Ni), and molybdenum (Mo). The effects of these are not, as is often wrongly supposed, primarily to increase the yield strength or tensile strength, but rather to reduce the 'size effect' noted earlier. Thus a heat treated steel containing, say, 0.3–0.45% carbon and no significant alloying elements will only develop the specified properties in bars up to a certain diameter. A steel of the same carbon content (and remember that the carbon content is essentially the determinant of strength) but with added nickel and chromium will develop the specified properties right through a bar of much larger diameter. This is the '*limiting ruling section*' i.e. the maximum cross-sectional area which, after the specified heat treatment, will yield the specified properties.

It must be remembered that heat treatment is a carefully controlled operation and that any process which involves reheating the steel (e.g. welding, flame cutting etc.) will counteract the effects. This is considered further in section 3.6 below.

In structural engineering the most widespread use of heat

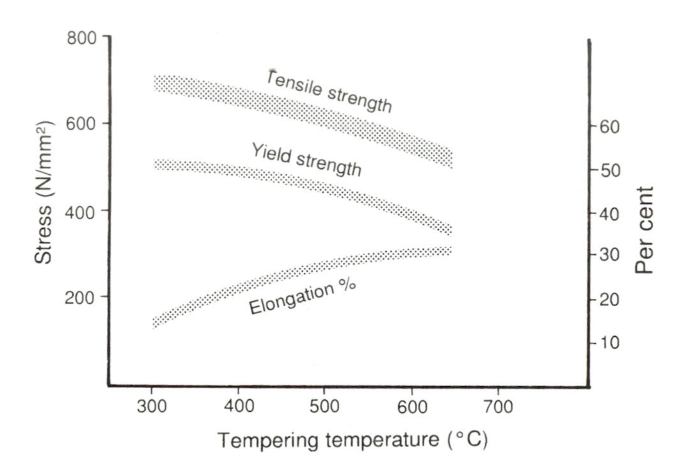

Fig. 3.5 *The effect of tempering on tensile strength, yield strength and ductility for carbon-manganese steel, oil-quenched and tempered for 60 min at temperatures shown.*

treated steels is for HSFG (high strength friction grip) bolts. Table 3.2 contains an extract from BS 970 [8]. It can be seen that, for steels of the same ruling section, maximum notch toughness is associated with lower yield strength – the trade-off problem again.

3.6 WELDING

The various welding processes that are available are not listed here: for details of these see [9]. All welding involves essentially the same sequence of operations – the temperature of the steel is raised, locally, to its melting point when additional metal may, or may not, be supplied. It is then allowed to cool naturally, the cooling rate being affected by the size and shape of the parent components.

Whatever the process, all welds should comply with two requirements:

(a) Ideally there should be complete continuity between the parts to be joined and every part of the joint should be indistinguishable from the parent material. In practice,

Normal supply condition	Minimum tensile strength (N/mm²)	Minimum yield strength (N/mm²), for thickness (in mm)				Minimum elongation (%)	Minimum Charpy V-notch impact test value			Grade
		Up to and including 12	Over 12 up to and including 25	Over 25 up to and including 40	Over 40 up to and including 50		Temp (°C)	Energy min value (J)	Thickness max (mm)	
As rolled	480	345	325	325	–	19	0	27	12	WR50A
As rolled or normalized	480	345	345	345	340	19	0	27	50	WR50B
As rolled or normalized	480	345	345	345	340(4)	19	–15	27	50	WR50C

this is rarely achieved, though welds giving satisfactory performance can be made.

(b) The joint materials should have satisfactory metallurgical properties – this is largely the concern of the supplier, though poor welding practice can affect the end result.

During welding, a temperature gradient is created in the plate material, ranging from the melting point at the fusion zone to room temperature at some point distant. The quality of the joint is affected by the structure and properties of both the weld metal and that part of the parent plate which undergoes significant metallurgical changes: this is the heat affected zone (Fig. 3.6). Both are significantly affected by the rate of cooling.

It is a general principle of metallurgy that the slower the rate of cooling the closer the structure is to equilibrium. This was seen earlier in connection with heat treated steels where fast quenching produces an unstable structure which can, however, be stabilized by controlled re-heating or tempering. The heat source in welding is highly localized and, in metal arc welding at least, at a very high temperature. The principal way in which the heat is dissipated is by conduction through the parent plate.

The thermal conductivity of a metal is a fixed property so that, for a given heat input, the major factor influencing the rate of cooling is the thermal mass, i.e. the thickness of the plates to be welded. The greater the thermal mass the faster is the cooling rate. In plates of unequal thickness it is the larger one which dominates.

The weld metal is cooled rapidly from the liquid state and the metal shows all the characteristics of a casting – the metallurgical properties are generally tolerable but less than ideal. However, further superimposed layer(s) of weld metal re-heat and refine the structure and, given no discontinuities (such as unwelded areas, entrapped slag etc.) the properties of a multi-run weld are as good as, and in many ways superior to, those of the parent plate. Multi-run welds should be used wherever possible.

The so-called 'free-cutting' steels contain higher sulphur than is normally permitted. This forms a brittle compound (iron sulphide) which causes the machining chips to break

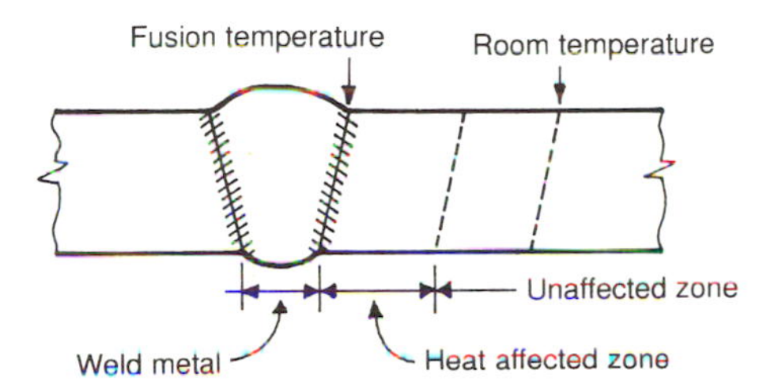

Fig. 3.6 *Schematic section through weld. In the heat affected zone significant changes to the metallurgical structure occur.*

up and allows faster machining speeds. However, an uptake of sulphur into the weld metal produces hot shortness and the weld cracks open while it cools. Free-cutting steels should never be welded.

Metallurgical changes in the heat affected zone are, however, of considerable importance, although in structural steels of grades 40 and 43 of BS 4360 they are generally of little significance provided, as always, that they are welded using good practice and as recommended by the manufacturer of the welding material. Steels to grades 50 and 55, and alloy steels as a whole, require more care. If cooled rapidly, e.g. as with a small weld on a heavy plate, the cooling rate can be similar to that achieved by quenching (section 3.5). In this case the hard, but brittle, quenched steel may be obtained.

The high stresses set up by contraction of the weld metal on cooling, especially in joints where movement is restrained, may lead to cracking. Many failures have been initiated not in the main structure but in small tack welds used to attach ancillary equipment as, for instance in the failure of the oil platform Alexander Kielland. The presence of hydrogen (derived from water vapour in the arc atmosphere) intensifies this tendency. For these steels hydrogen-controlled electrodes should be specified and these must be used strictly in accordance with the manufacturers' recommendations. BS 5135 [10] covers details of accepted practice. For the same reasons flame cutting of grades 50 and 55 should be approved by the supervising officer. The welder's competence to undertake any work specified by the designer is laid down by the tests required in BS 4872 [11].

The weldability of a steel is conveniently expressed by the *carbon equivalent* in which the various elements are grouped in terms of their contribution to the formation of the hard, but brittle, quenched structure noted above and expressed in terms of the amount of carbon to produce the same hardness. BS 4360 gives

$$CE = \mathrm{C} + \mathrm{Mn}/6 + (\mathrm{Cr} + \mathrm{Mo} + \mathrm{V})/5 + (\mathrm{Ni} + \mathrm{Cu})/15$$

and a value of between 0.39 and 0.51 is specified for each steel, taking into account the mass to be welded as well as the composition.

3.7 BOLTING

Bolting and riveting were the only possible ways of making joints in cast and wrought iron. Riveting involved the close hammering of a red hot rivet into prepared holes: as the rivet contracted upon cooling the plates were locked together, essentially, by the tensile stress in the rivet. High strength friction grip (HSFG) bolts work in much the same way. The bolt is tightened to some predetermined stress and it is this prestress which holds the two components together by friction. As noted earlier, HSFG bolts are made from quenched and tempered alloy steel in order to obtain a high yield point combined with good ductility. As with all heat treated steels no heat should be applied or the properties will be affected. The use of HSFG bolts is covered by BS 4604 [12].

3.8 MISCELLANEOUS PROPERTIES OF STEEL

Density	7900 kg/m^3 (492 lb/ft^3)
Thermal conductivity at or near 0°C (32°F)	60 W/mK (35 Btu.ft/ft^2.h.°F)
Coefficient of linear thermal expansion	12×10^{-6}/K (7×10^{-6}/°F)
Poisson's ratio	0.30
Speed of elastic waves	380 m/s (1245 ft/s) longitudinal 240 m/s (790 ft/s) transverse

ACKNOWLEDGEMENT

Extracts from British Standards are reproduced by permission of BSI. Complete copies can be obtained from BSI, Linford Wood, Milton Keynes, MK14 6LE.

REFERENCES AND TECHNICAL NOTES

1. BS 1449 Part 1: 1991 Carbon and carbon manganese plate, sheet and strip.
2. BS 4449: 1978 Hot rolled steel bars for the reinforcement of concrete.
3. Ashby, M.F. and Jones, D.R.H. (1980) *Engineering Materials: an Introduction to their Properties and Applications*, Pergamon Press, Oxford.
4. BS 4360: 1986 Weldable structural steels.
5. Petrowski, H. (1982) *To Engineer is Human*, Macmillan, London.
6. BS EN 10 025: 1990 Hot rolled products of non-alloy structural steels and their technical delivery conditions.
7. BS 4461: 1978 Cold worked steel bars for the reinforcement of concrete.
8. BS 970 Part 1: 1983 Wrought steels for mechanical and allied engineering purposes: carbon, carbon manganese, alloy and stainless steel.
9. Houldcroft, P.T. (1977) *Welding Process Technology*, Cambridge University Press, Cambridge.
10. BS 5135: 1974 Arc welding of carbon and carbon manganese steels.
11. BS 4872 Part 1: 1982 Approval testing of welders. Fusion welding of steel.
12. BS 4604: 1970 The use of high strength friction grip bolts in structural steelwork.

4

Structural steel components for buildings

Keith Moores

4.1 INTRODUCTION TO SHAPING STEEL

The production of molten steel described in the previous chapter is only the first stage in the process of manufacturing raw steel products, such as structural sections, plate and wire, as required by a wide range of industries – for example, motor manufacture, ship building and construction.

In the traditional manufacturing process, steel is cast into ingots typically 600 mm (24 in) square in section and weighing about 20 tonnes. After cooling the moulds are stripped and the steel re-heated before being passed through a sequence of rollers to form a slab of steel typically 1500 mm (5 ft) wide and 250 mm (10 in) thick, the exact size depending upon the intended finished product. These are then subjected to further processing to produce engineering sections such as angles, I-beams, plate, sheet etc. This generally requires considerable heat input in order to soften the steel and is therefore both expensive and inefficient.

Continuous casting (concast) is now superseding much of this process. This involves the molten steel being poured into the top of a water-cooled mould. The solidifying steel is drawn through at the bottom in a continuous operation to form the slab before further cooling and rolling into the final cross-sectional shape (Fig. 4.1). Because this replaces with one operation several steps in traditional steelmaking – ingot casting, mould stripping, heating in soaking pits and primary rolling – considerable savings in energy and production costs have been achieved. In addition, it permits much tighter quality control. There are three basic shaping processes by which the slab is formed into the final product. These are rolling, forging and extrusion.

Rolling is the most common method used for shaping and is particularly suitable for products of simple, constant cross-section such as rods, universal beams and columns, plate, and sheet.

Forging is generally preferred where the end product has a complicated shape. The technology involves either hammer forging, in which shapes are altered by blows from a moving weight, or press forging in which a steady squeeze is applied.

Extrusion implies producing steel close to the final shape, by forcing it through a die. Products of complicated cross-section can be produced by this technique.

The shaping processes for structural steels in buildings are described in more detail below.

4.2 MANUFACTURING METHODS

4.2.1 Rolling mills

Most structural steel products, such as I-beams or channels, are produced in rolling mills. Starting in the form of a slab the steel is reheated before passing through a system of rotating rolls (called the 'Mill Stand'). The re-heating process can be either 'batch' or 'continuous', the latter being typical of modern mills rolling sheet strip, plate and rod.

The rolls are arranged and shaped to change the rectangular cross-section of the slab into the required form. This starts with the reduction of the slab to a smaller profile at a 'roughing stand'. The steel then passes through an 'intermediate stand' which produces a profile close to the finished section. Finally, the finishing stand of rolls produces the finished section.

Universal beam mills use both horizontal and vertical rolls simultaneously (Fig. 4.2). These can be adjusted to modify the profile of the section and hence produce a range of universal beams and columns, identified by serial size and mass per unit length. Each serial size corresponds to a different set of roller sizes, whilst changes in mass per unit length are achieved by opening the rollers to increase the thickness of the flanges (Fig. 4.3).

Light section rolling mills produce both profiled sections (Fig. 4.4) and solids such as rounds and squares which may be the finished shape, or be subject to further processing, for instance in the case of solid round bars from which wire is drawn or modified for use as reinforcement in concrete.

4.2.2 Flat rolled products

Three categories of flat steel products are manufactured by rolling processes - sheet (wide hot strip), strip (narrow hot strip, cold-rolled strip) and plate.

Wide hot strip is produced in thicknesses between 1 and 3 mm (1/32 and 1/8 in), up to 1.8 m (6 ft) wide and is available either coiled or in flat sheets. It frequently undergoes further processing, for instance cold rolling or galvanizing, to form finished products such as cladding (refer to chapter 5 for details).

Narrow hot strip is rolled in thicknesses ranging from 1 mm to 12 mm (1/32 to 1/2 in) and in widths of between 20 mm (3/4 in) and 610 mm (24 in); it is often used for welding into small diameter tubes.

Fig. 4.1 *Continuous casting (a) slab caster; (b) billet casting; (c) billet caster; (d) diagram of process.*

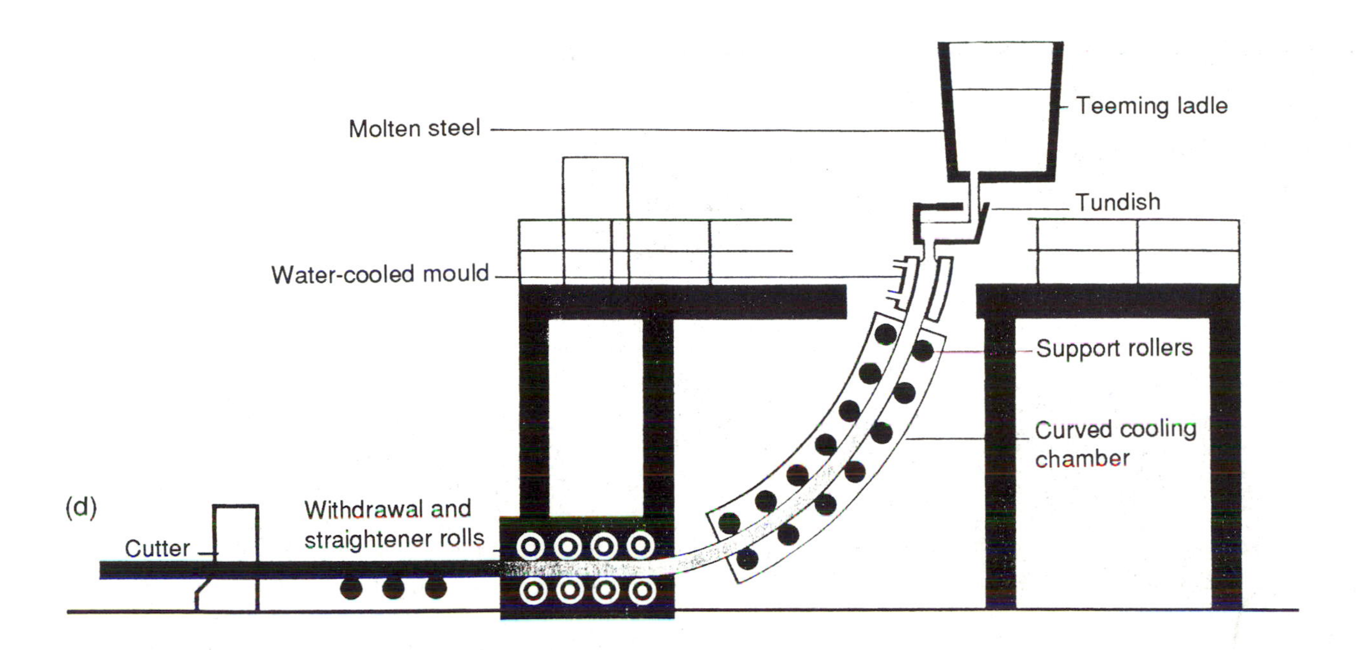

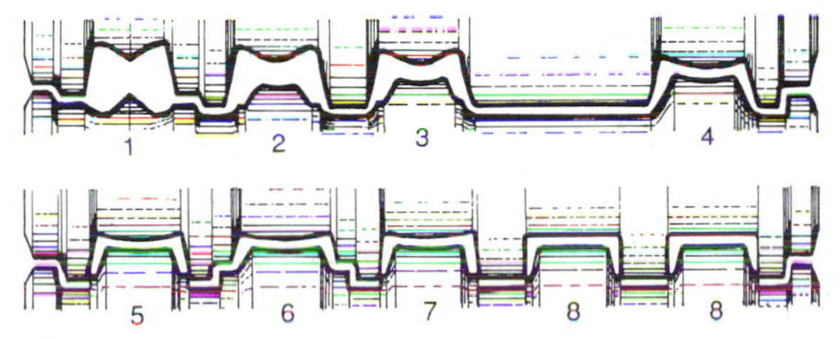

Fig. 4.2 *Model of profile roll.*

Cold-rolled strip is light gauge sheet or strip manufactured to exacting tolerances with regard to thickness and surface finish. The final reduction in hot finished material is carried out using a cold rolling process. This is one of the most complex of rolling operations and is dependent upon a high standard of initial hot-rolled product.

'Temper' mills and 'skin pass' mills are also used in cold-rolling operations. These are mills which reduce the thickness of sheet and strip by a limited amount, eliminate undulations in hot rolled coil and put a controlled amount of hardness or temper into the surface skin of cold-rolled strip which has become softened after annealing. Special equipment is available for maintaining variation of thickness to approximately six microns.

Cold rolling gives a good surface and controlled width to steel strip, although it also increases hardness, which is undesirable in products which have to be reshaped during manufacture. However, this can be relieved by an annealing process in which the steel is heated up to controlled temperatures (which are lower than those required for hot rolling) and allowed to cool again.

Plate making

Plates are rolled up to 3.6 m (12 ft) wide and in thicknesses from 3 mm to 10 mm (⅛ to ⅜ in) (light plate) and 10 mm to 50 mm (⅜ to 2 in) (heavy plate). Tolerances are less strict for plate than for thinner rolled products, although high accuracy can be achieved with vertical rolls as used in 'universal plate mills'. This can lead to significant economies, for instance in avoiding edge machining in welded structures.

During normal rolling the plate is elongated almost wholly in the direction of the roll wheels and this can impair the final mechanical properties. Rolling in two perpendicular directions (or 'broadsiding') minimizes this and improves plate quality. After rolling, the plate is flattened by pressing the plate in either a hot or cold state, and heat treated to improve the properties of the steel.

4.2.3 Forging

The principles of forging are an extension of the original methods employed by blacksmiths (refer to chapter 35). Forging operations are generally carried out on steel which has been re-heated in a gas furnace, although for light forgings electrical heating is occasionally used. Cold forging is restricted to small items due to the considerable force needed to shape the cold steel, but has the advantage that high standards of accuracy can be achieved.

Press forging is a process in which the steel is slowly squeezed to shape under hydraulic pressure, where both the

Universal columns	Universal beams	Joists
Serial/Size mm	Serial/Size mm	Serial/Size mm
356 x 406	914 x 419	254 x 203
356 x 368	914 x 305	254 x 114
305 x 305	838 x 292	203 x 152
254 x 254	762 x 267	152 x 127
203 x 203	686 x 254	127 x 114
152 x 152	610 x 305	114 x 114
	610 x 229	102 x 102
	533 x 210	89 x 89
	457 x 191	76 x 76
	457 x 152	
	406 x 178	
	406 x 140	
	356 x 127	
	305 x 165	
	305 x 127	
	305 x 102	
	254 x 146	
	254 x 102	
	203 x 133	
	203 x 133	
	203 x 102	
	178 x 102	
	152 x 89	
	127 x 76	

Fig. 4.3 *Range of serial sizes for universal columns, beams and joists.*

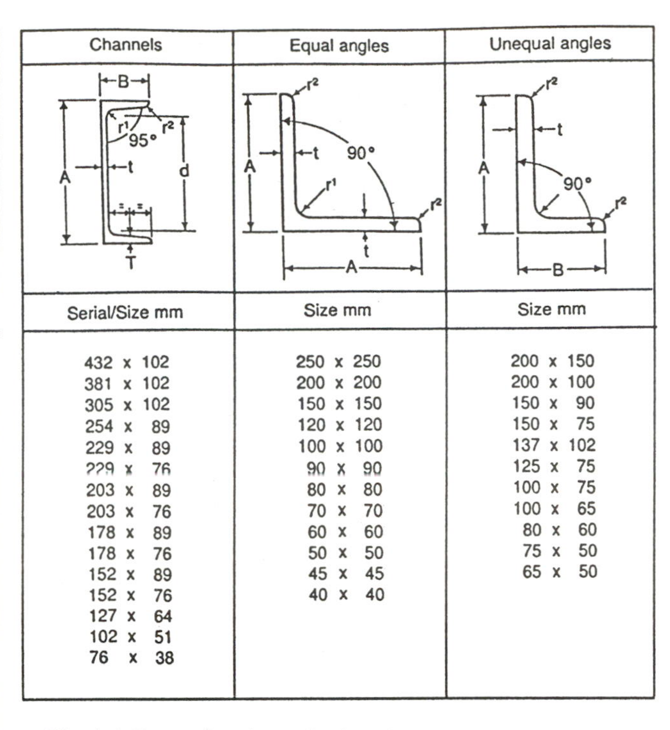

Channels	Equal angles	Unequal angles
Serial/Size mm	Size mm	Size mm
432 x 102	250 x 250	200 x 150
381 x 102	200 x 200	200 x 100
305 x 102	150 x 150	150 x 90
254 x 89	120 x 120	150 x 75
229 x 89	100 x 100	137 x 102
229 x 76	90 x 90	125 x 75
203 x 89	80 x 80	100 x 75
203 x 76	70 x 70	100 x 65
178 x 89	60 x 60	80 x 60
178 x 76	50 x 50	75 x 50
152 x 89	45 x 45	65 x 50
152 x 76	40 x 40	
127 x 64		
102 x 51		
76 x 38		

Fig. 4.4 *Range of serial sizes for channels, equal and unequal angles.*

Fig. 4.5 *Hammer forging using 25T Beche Counterblow hammer.*

Fig. 4.6 *Drop forging.*

pressure and position of the forging head are precisely controlled.

Hammer forging and drop forging (Figs 4.5 and 4.6) employ the impact of a falling weight to squeeze the steel into shape with successive blows. In drop forging dies are positioned on the hammer and anvil; the hammer blow then forces the hot steel to take up the shape of the cavity formed by the dies.

4.2.4 Extrusions

Extruded profiles are formed by squeezing metal through a shaped die. Generally the material is extruded hot but a limited number of products of short length and involving relatively little reduction are also processed cold.

Extruding, like rolling, produces profiles of a constant cross-section but the shapes can be more complex (Fig. 4.7) since the forms can be tubular as well as solid. The actual process depends upon hydraulic cylinders forcing heated billets of steel past a single die, the maximum length currently produced being 12 m (40 ft). Some seamless tubes, including lighting columns, are produced this way.

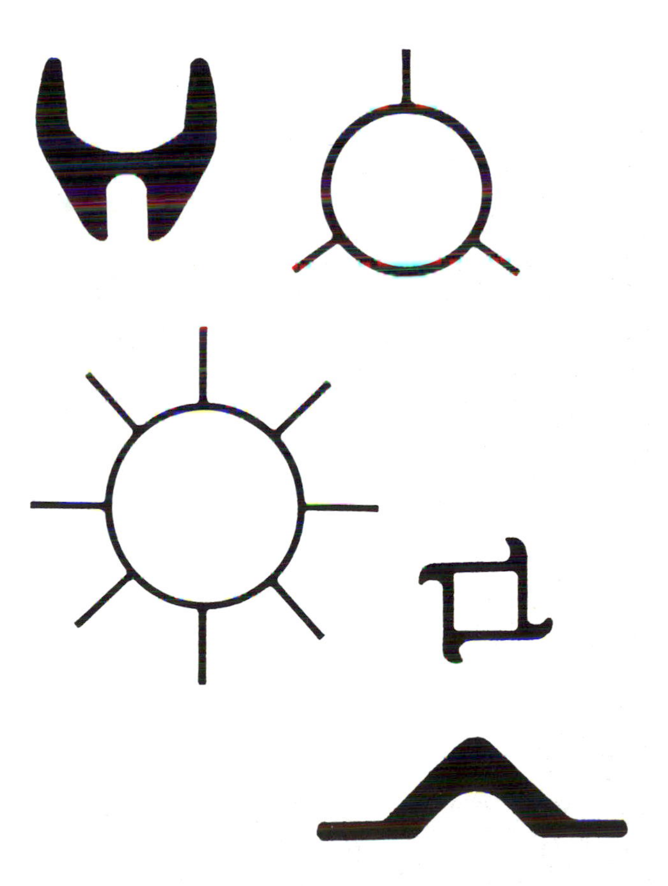

Fig. 4.7 *Typical extruded forms.*

4.3 TUBULAR SECTIONS

4.3.1 Introduction to manufacturing methods

The two principal ways of making structural hollow sections are the seamless method or by welding. Some seamless tube is produced by extrusion as described earlier, but the majority is made by piercing the solid ingot or bar and then elongating it in a rotary forge (termed the Pilger Process).

4.3.2 Seamless hollow sections

Rotary forge manufacture

Traditionally seamless tubes are produced by the rotary forge method from circular or tapered fluted ingots. After re-heating the ingots are pierced with a mandrel using a hydraulic press. The tube is then formed by rolling externally in a helical manner, reducing the thickness and outside diameter to that of the finished tube whilst the bore remains unchanged (Fig. 4.8).

The finished tube length is restricted by the weight of the ingoing billet, and the number of passes required to reduce to the final size is restricted by the billet's size. The development of continuous casting means that a greater range of billet diameter and weight can be produced which can reduce the conversion time and also allow longer lengths to be produced.

After rolling, the tube is cropped and then passed through a set of sizing rolls which control the outside diameter. When controlled bore tubes are required this operation is omitted since the bore of the tube is the prime dimension.

Seamless hollow sections can be produced in circular form in sizes up to 500 mm (20 in) and in thicknesses up to 50 mm (2 in).

4.3.3 Welded hollow sections

Welded hollow sections are produced by a range of processes including butt or continuous weld, electric weld, spiral weld and submerged arc welding.

(a) Butt or continuous weld process

In the butt or continuous weld process, hot-rolled strip is heated almost to welding temperature and bent into a horseshoe shape forming a nearly closed tube. The strip edges are then heated locally and pressed together to make the weld. The hot tube then goes through sizing rolls which reduce the outside diameter to within the specified tolerance. This method is often used for tubes up to 100 mm (4 in) in diameter, but in practice its use for structural hollow sections is limited to 48 mm (2 in) diameter.

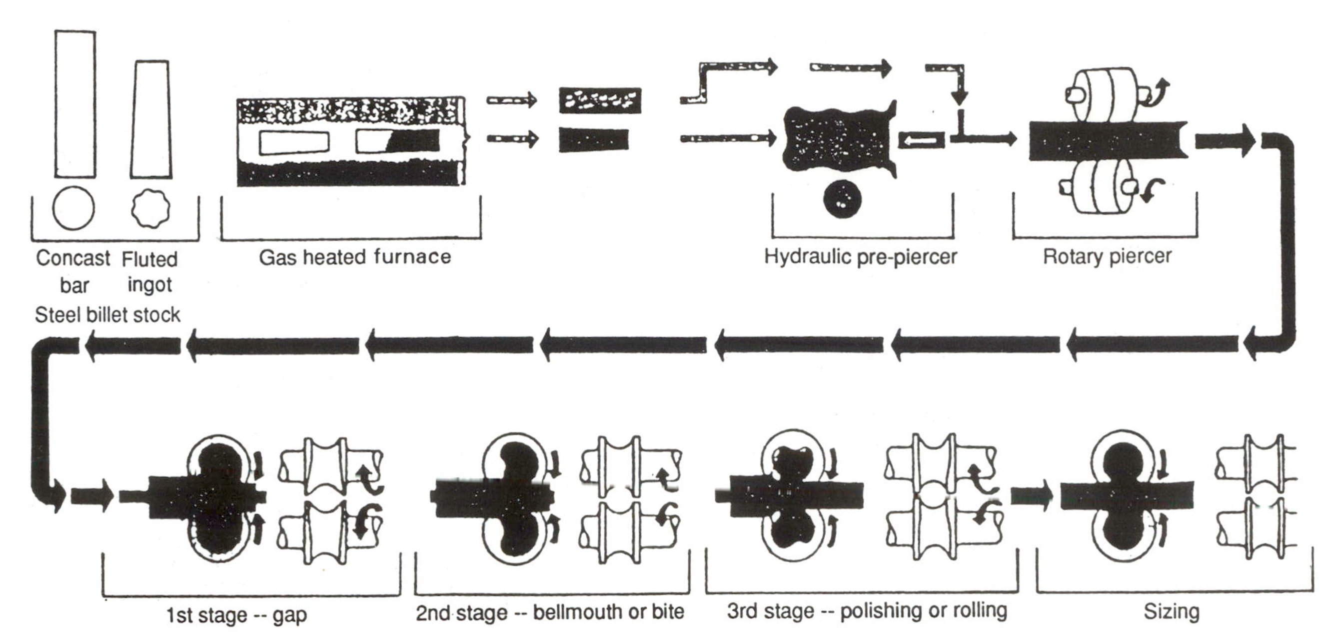

Fig. 4.8 *Rotary forge press.*

(b) Electric weld process

The majority of hollow sections used in buildings are produced by the electric weld method, which can produce circular sections from 48 mm (2 in) diameter up to 508 mm (20 in) diameter, square sections from 40 × 40 mm (1¾ × 1¾ in) up to 400 × 400 mm (16 × 16 in), and rectangular sections from 50 × 30 mm (2 × 1¼ in) up to 500 × 300 mm (20 × 12 in). The thickness produced depends on the size and ranges from 2.5 mm to 6.0 mm (1/10 in to ¼ in) in the small sizes up to 10.0 mm to 16.0 mm (⅜ in to ⅝ in) in the larger sizes.

Electric weld tubes can be produced as hot finished or cold-formed sections. Both processes use hot finished strip as their feedstock and are initially formed into cold round sections and welded. Cold-formed sections are then finished into circular, square or rectangular shapes cold, whilst hot finished sections are heated and formed into circular, square or rectangular shape whilst in the normalizing temperature range.

The finished products are thus different in their mechanical performance and each has its own design code and product standard.

Cold-formed sections are supplied to BS 6363 [1] and designed to BS 5950 Part 5 [2] and hot finished are supplied to BS 4360 [3] and BS 4848 Part 2 [4] and designed (in keeping with most other structural sections) to BS 5950 Part 1 [5]. Substitution on a size for size basis should not be made without checking equivalent strengths.

In the electric weld process the ingoing strip is progressively formed into a round, nearly closed tube shape and then passes through a high frequency induction coil which raises the strip edges to fusion temperature. The edges are then pressed together, forming a weld without the use of any filler (electrode) material. The round hollow is formed to a diameter which will provide the finished section size.

Hot finished sections are then passed into furnaces for heating up to normalizing temperature, after which they are shaped. Cold-formed sections are shaped whilst cold.

The electric weld process is used to produce 'hollows' for processing by the stretch reduction method which is the main method of producing hot finished sections in sizes up to 139.7 mm (55 in) diameter (100 mm (4 in) square, or equivalent rectangle).

(c) Stretch reduction and heat treatment

The 170 mm (7 in) nominal diameter hollow tubes produced by the electric welding process can be stretch reduced to produce other structural hollow section sizes up to the following sizes:

1) Circular hollow sections; 140 mm (5.5 in) nominal outside diameter
2) Square hollow sections; 100 mm (4 in) square
3) Rectangular hollow sections 110 × 80 mm (4.5 in × 7.25 in)

In all cases the maximum wall thickness is 8 mm (0.32 in)

(d) Submerged arc welded process

This process is generally used for tubes over 500 mm (20 in) diameter up to 2134 mm (84 in) diameter. Larger sizes are formed from two semi-circular rolled plates, smaller sizes from single circular rolled plate with the final weld being made by the submerged arc (SAW) process. These sections can be produced as welded or, if required, be heated up to normalizing temperature.

(e) Spiral welded process

Spiral welded tubes are made by helical forming of strip which is then welded by SAW or CO_2 processes. The method is generally used to produce large diameter thin wall tubes that are used in bored foundation piles.

(f) Standard tubes

Most hollow sections used in buildings are required in the shape of circular, square, or rectangular hollow sections (Fig. 4.9). A range of wall thicknesses are produced for each serial size. Hollow section properties and tolerances are given in reference [6].

4.3.4 Tube bending

Limitations on bend radii are frequently not fully appreciated by those using hollow sections in curved work. Bend limitation is dependent upon several factors including:

Physical constraints. Tensile stress, grade, metallurgy, thickness and cross-sectional geometry can affect the minimum radii to which hollow sections can be curved.

Structural design parameters. It is important when dealing with cold-worked sections to maintain 'normal' good practice with regard to detailing, avoiding multi-axial stresses and

Square hollow sections	Rectangular hollow sections	Circular hollow sections
Size D x D mm	Size D x B mm	Outside diameter mm
20 x 20	50 x 25	21.3
25 x 25	50 x 30	26.9
30 x 30	60 x 40	33.7
40 x 40	80 x 40	42.4
50 x 50	90 x 50	48.3
60 x 60	100 x 50	60.3
70 x 70	100 x 60	76.1
80 x 80	120 x 60	88.9
90 x 90	120 x 80	114.3
100 x 100	150 x 100	139.7
120 x 120	160 x 80	168.3
140 x 140	200 x 100	193.7
150 x 150	250 x 150	219.1
180 x 180	300 x 200	244.5
200 x 200	400 x 200	273
250 x 250	450 x 250	323.9
300 x 300	500 x 300	355.6
350 x 350		406.4
400 x 400		457
		508

Fig. 4.9 *Serial sizes for tubes.*

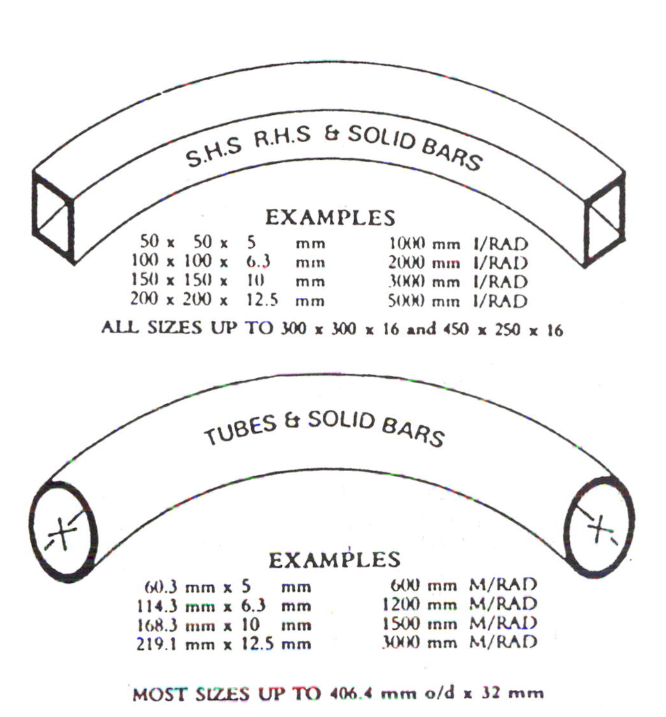

Fig. 4.10 *Typical radius bends for tubes.*

complicated welded joints. Mechanical testing is not normally carried out after bending, although it can be arranged if requested where fatigue, low temperature or other operating conditions call for known ductility or yield/ultimate tensile stress characteristics.

The above factors should be taken into account when determining the minimum radii for curved sections. It will therefore be appreciated why no hard and fast rules are laid down. For guidance, however, Fig. 4.10 shows some examples of bends which can be achieved: they are not necessarily minimum radii.

Generally sections with thick walls can be curved to tighter radii than a similar section with thin walls. Sections without straight ends can be curved to tighter radii then those needed to have straight ends incorporated (without any joint). In the latter case, the straight portion is blended into the curve.

Many specialist bending companies should be able to advise minimum radii with regard to physical constraints. In marginal cases they are usually prepared to experiment with trial bends.

4.4 CABLES, ROPES AND COUPLINGS

Cables and ropes are produced from wire. Their main use in buildings and structures is in guyed and suspended structures, suspension bridges, and lifting equipment (refer to chapter 20).

4.4.1 Production methods for wire

The production of wire from wire rod involves a variety of processes such as patenting, heat treatment/annealing and wire drawing.

Wire drawing is a cold working process which increases the strength and hardness of wire but reduces its ductility. This can be countered by subsequent heat treatment (annealing). The quality of wire produced, the amount of carbon in the steel, the degree of draw reduction, and the applied heat treatments are all inter-dependent. High carbon steels require a heat treatment known as patenting before heavy drawing reduction. During the process, the rod is held in a furnace for a specified time and temperature; this is followed by controlled cooling. High quality wires such as piano wire may also be passed through baths of molten lead. Patenting refines the microstructure of the steel and improves wire properties.

Low carbon content wire rods may not require patenting but they may have to be heated and allowed to cool to complete the annealing process. This is particularly where extensive drawing is used to make heavy reductions in cross-section.

In the drawing process the end of the rolled rod is passed through a tapered hole in a drawing die manufactured from hard tungsten carbide to resist wear. The wire is lubricated before entering the die by passing it through a box containing soap flakes or powder. The rod is gripped and pulled through the tapered die, thus elongating it and reducing its cross-section. It is only possible to reduce the cross-section of a rod passing through a single die to a limited extent. Wire drawing machines are therefore frequently arranged in line with dies of reducing diameter. Using continuous wire rod, thousands of feet of wire can be produced in a minute. Some grades of wire can be reduced by over 90% of the original cross-section, thus producing ten times the length of the original wire rod.

4.4.2 Cable and rope production

Cables and ropes are widely used in tensile structures, such as suspension bridges, as guys or stays to main structural members and for other purposes such as supporting lifts in high-rise buildings.

Cables and wire ropes are made up of a number of individual steel wires which are spun into a strand. A number of strands (usually six) are woven around a central core to form a rope, and a number of ropes, again usually six, form a cable (Fig. 4.11). The largest ropes normally produced are approximately 100 mm (4 in) in diameter and are made up with six strands each containing 52 wires. The largest cables normally produced are made up of six ropes of approximately 70 mm (2¾ in) diameter.

The function of the core is to provide support to the strands and hold them in the correct position under working conditions. Cores may be of fibre or steel composition.

Fig. 4.11 *Typical cable construction. Reprinted by kind permission of British Ropes Ltd.*

Fibre cores are able to withstand mild acids and alkalis, are resistant to rotting and reduce internal corrosion due to non-absorption or retention of moisture. In addition, rope dressing is unnecessary for internal lubrication.

Steel cores provide better support to the outer strands and perform well in severe working conditions; they also have greater crushing resistance against drums and pulleys.

Ropes can be protected by zinc coating/galvanizing which provides sacrificial protection to underlying wires against corrosion. Alternatively, synthetic sheathing can be used to provide a barrier between the rope and the environment. Sheathing can be nylon or PVC which can be coloured. Some ropes are now manufactured using stainless steel wires which are particularly suitable for many corrosive environments.

When ropes are subjected to tensile loads they extend in length due to a number of effects. These include the initial bedding down of wires against each other, normal elastic extension and thermal expansion or contraction. Additional increases in length can also be caused by free rope being allowed to rotate, and wire wear which reduces cross-sectional area.

The initial extension can largely be overcome by pre-stressing or loading the rope until such time as the bedding down process is nearly complete. Prestressing can only be undertaken on wire strands or on wire ropes with steel cores.

Elongation must be considered when specifying ropes and where necessary specialist advice should be sought.

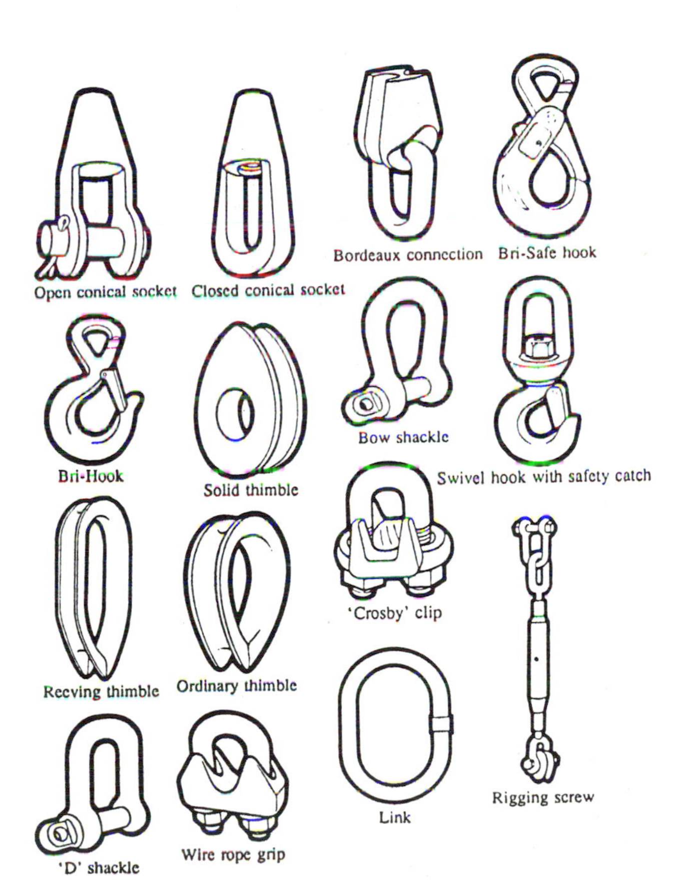

Fig. 4.12 *Typical wire rope fittings. Reprinted by kind permission of British Ropes Ltd.*

4.4.3 Maintenance and inspection

Ropes do not have an indefinite life – rope fatigue and wear normally take place (especially on moving ropes), eventually necessitating replacement or repair. Usual visible signs of rope deterioration are corrosion, excessive wear, broken wires, and distortion. However, the rope's life can be extended considerably by adequate attention to maintenance, regular inspection and lubrication, correct handling and prevention of mechanical damage.

4.4.4 Jointing and coupling

There are several methods of jointing and coupling steel ropes some of which are shown in Fig. 4.12. Readers should turn to chapter 20 (20.7 and 20.8) and chapter 21 (21.4.4) for further references to coupling and jointing in cable structures.

REFERENCES AND TECHNICAL NOTES

1. BS 6363: 1983 Welded cold-formed steel structural hollow sections.
2. BS 5950 Part 5: 1987 Structural use of steel in building Code of Practice for design of cold-form sections.
3. BS 4360: 1990 Weldable structural steels.
4. BS 4848 Part 2: 1991 Specification for hot finished hollow sections.
5. BS 5950 Part 1: 1990 Structural use of steelwork in building. Code of Practice in design in simple and continuous construction: hot rolled sections.
6. *Hot Finished Structural Hollow Sections: Sizes, Properties and Technical Data*, British Steel Technical Manual TD167, July 1991, British Steel, Corby, UK.

FURTHER READING

A Simple Guide to Basic Processes in the Iron and Steel Industry (an excellent book published by British Steel)

Alexander, W.O. and Street, A. (1989) *Metals in the Service of Man*, Penguin.

Single storey unit, Antrim Technology Park, Northern Ireland (architects, BDP). Cladding: finely rubbed composite panels in Silver Colorcoat PvF2.

Architect's house in Delft, Holland. Descapner, Copezed. Cladding with stainless steel wall panels.

Metrodome sports complex, Barnsley. Cladding: Briggs Amasco Perfrisa panels.

Canteen for the gas utility, Emmen, Holland. Cladding: white prepainted Colorcoat HP200.

Dentist's surgery. Veldhoven, Holland. Cladding: Silver Colorcoat Pvf2 complimenting the exposed steel structure.

5

Sheet and strip

Eric Hindhaugh

5.1 INTRODUCTION

Corrugated iron is one of the earliest applications of sheet iron, the patent dating back to 1829. In the last century it became the principal cladding material for the iron building frames and trusses which were exported throughout the world and in many parts it remains a common sight. Corrugated iron has now been largely superseded by steel products, although it still formed a common roofing material in Finland at the beginning of the 1980s. The trends in the total roofing market for that country are shown in Table 5.1.

Profiled steel sheeting has not only taken over from corrugated iron but its use has also increased at the expense of other materials. The changing situation in the UK from 1976 to 1988 is revealed in the changes in market share for corrugated and profiled sheet (Table 5.2).

Clearly, sheet steel products have a role not only as insulated panels but also as a product with excellent decorative qualities. The actual range of products for wall cladding and roofing includes corrugated sheeting, profiled sheeting, composite cladding (with face sheet, insulation

Table 5.1 Recent trends in use of materials for roofing in Finland

	1981	*1987*
Corrugated asbestos	4%	0%
Felt shingles	9%	1%
Felt roofing	20%	19%
Concrete tile	15%	27%
Corrugated iron	40%	5%
Organic coated steel	12%	12%
Steel tiles (strips of moulded sheet that simulate pantiles)	0%	36%

Table 5.2 Increased use of profiled steel sheet in roofing between 1976 and 1988 in the UK

	1976	*1988*
Asbestos/fibre cement	52%	5%
Profiled steel	12%	78%
Profiled aluminium	9%	12%
Flat metal deck	25%	4%

and liner sheet), panel products, and folded trim (parapet capping, fascia and verge trim, gutters, corner flashings and trim for doors and windows at cills, heads and jambs).

There are other related specialized products such as 'moulded tiles', a pressed steel strip which simulates traditional roofing. Another variation is roof decking, where galvanized profiled sheet is used as a structural deck overlaid by insulation and felt/polymer coverings. This latter application is detailed in chapters 27 and 28, the focus here being on the manufacture of strip products for cladding.

5.2 HISTORICAL REVIEW

The use of ferrous metals for roof cladding and framing stems from developments in Paris in the late 18th century. The primary uses were to provide a fireproof system of enclosure for public halls and theatres, an early example being the Théâtre Français in Paris (1786). Coverings were developed which consisted of metal plates and cover battens laid over wrought iron bow string trusses. Another cladding type developed in the 18th century comprised interlocking tiles of copper or zinc, resembling 'fishscales'.

Corrugated iron was first made from wrought iron sheets to form a single lap sheet suitable for purlin spacings of about 1.8–2.1 m (6–7 ft). This simplified subframing for both roof and wall enclosure. The patent was taken out by Henry Robinson Palmer of the London Dock and Harbour Company in 1829. The first manufacturer was Richard Walker, and protection by galvanizing had already become common by the 1830s.

Sheet steel replaced wrought iron as the basis for corrugated iron after the 1860s, and improved finishes were developed which involved bitumen coating and bitumen felt as a weather coat. Another version from the 1920s was a sandwich form with an asbestos core to give fire resistance to roof and wall cladding; the coating was of chlorinated rubber paint.

Fig. 5.1 *75 mm (3 in) corrugated sheeting.*

Fig. 5.2 *The vernacular material of Australasia – house by Glenn Murcutt, 1985.*

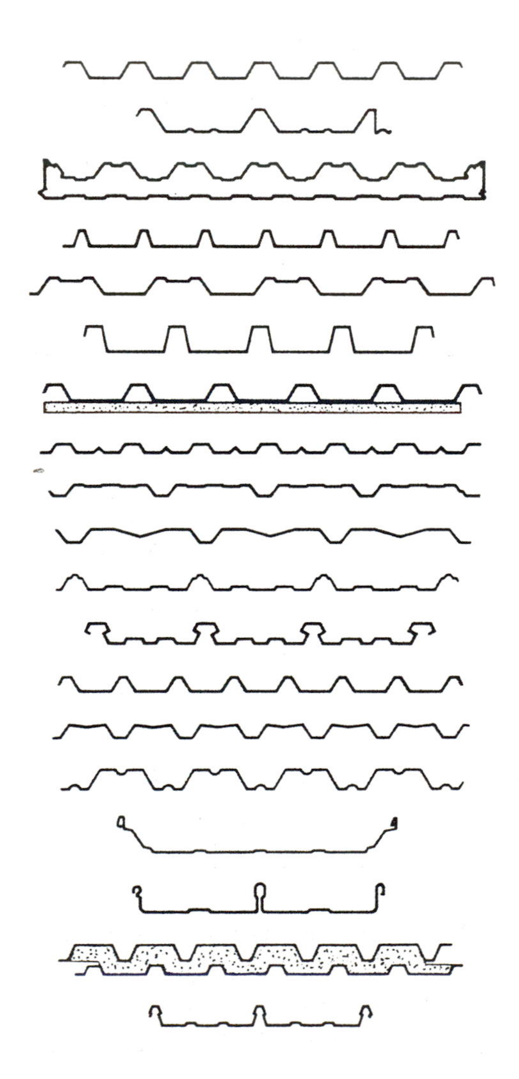

Fig. 5.3 *Selection of trapezoidal profiles.*

Current corrugated products are galvanized with optional coloured coatings and manufactured to BS 3083 [1]. The sinusoidal (double curve) profile is efficient as a weatherproof surface above 15 degree pitch (Fig. 5.1). Sealing is necessary at all edges for lower roof pitches, with bitumen coating as a weather face. The product is still widely used in the tropics and the southern hemisphere and could be called the vernacular material of Australasia (Fig. 5.2). There are limitations regarding strength and security of fixings. While sheets can be formed curved or straight, double curved work is not feasible.

Trapezoidal profiles were first developed for steel floor decks in American skyscraper construction. They were introduced in Europe in the 1920s. An early example was cold formed steel decking used for floors, roofs and walls in the experimental house at Weissenhof, Stuttgart by Ludwig Hilbersheimer (1927). The 'Sunspan' houses devised by Wells Coates had a similar concept with corrugated sheets forming a 'box frame'. This was first shown at the Ideal Home Exhibition in 1934.

Steel cladding and roofing utilizing profiled trapezoidal shapes (Fig. 5.3), though available by the early 1950s, did not become widely used until satisfactory colour coatings could be achieved.

5.3 MANUFACTURE OF STEEL SHEETING

The manufacture of steel sheeting is based on steel strip, treated with some form of protective coating to provide corrosion resistance, and profiled to give strength and stiffness.

The production of steel strip is described in chapter 4. The manufacture of steel sheeting uses hot rolled coil, in widths up to 1650 mm (5 ft 6 in) and a range of thicknesses from 1.6 mm (1/16 in) up to 3 mm (1/8 in). Most steel strip used in building is coated for corrosion resistance. All coating work is carried out prior to profiling and the finishes are therefore tough enough to resist the stresses involved. A guide to the coating types, both metallic and organic, is given below. A more detailed description of the theoretical basis for anti-corrosion measures is included in chapter 8. Fig. 5.4 summarizes the range of specifications (steel grade and coating) in accordance with current European standards.

5.4 METALLIC COATINGS

5.4.1 Zinc coatings

The most common coating for building applications is zinc. This can be applied by two processes. The first – electro zinc coating or electrodeposition – is suitable for very light

Metallic Coating	Zinc	5% Aluminium + zinc	55% Aluminium + zinc
European Standard	EN 10147	EN 10214	EN 10215
Permitted Grades	Fe E 220 G	S 220 GD + ZA	—
	Fe E 290 G	S 250 GD + ZA	S 250 GD + AZ
	Fe E 280 G	S 280 GD + ZA	S 280 GD + AZ
	Fe E 320 G	S 320 GD + ZA	S 320 GD + AZ
	Fe E 350 G	S 350 GD + ZA	S 350 GD + AZ
	Fe E 550 G	S 550 GD + ZA	S 550 GD + AZ

In the above grades the numeric part of the reference represents the yield stress in N/mm^2
eg FeE 280 G has a yield stress of 280 N/mm^2

Coating mass
The recommended minimum coating mass for steel sheet without organic coating is

Steel to EN 10147	350 g/m^2 including both sides
Steel to EN 10214	Not recommended
Steel to EN 10215	185 g/m^2 including both sides

The recommended minimum coating mass for steel sheet with organic coatings is

Steel to EN 10147	275 g/m^2 including both sides
Steel to EN 10214	255 g/m^2 including both sides
Steel to EN 10215	150 g/m^2 including both sides

Fig. 5.4 *Grades of steel in draft European Standard for roofing sheets.*

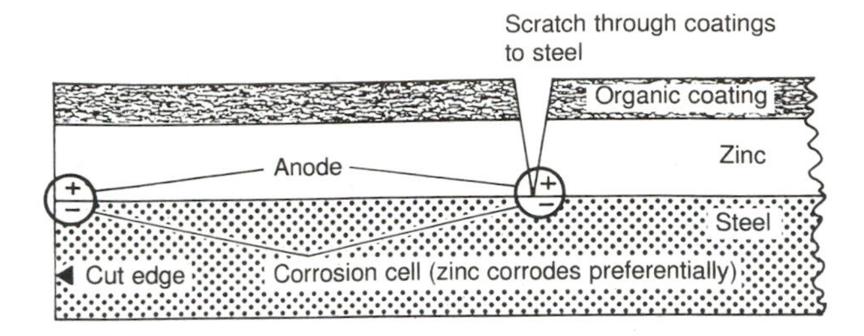

Fig. 5.5 *Zinc coatings protect steel by acting as a barrier and also by corroding preferentially at scratches and cut edges, where the zinc acts as the anode and steel as the cathode in corrosion cells.*

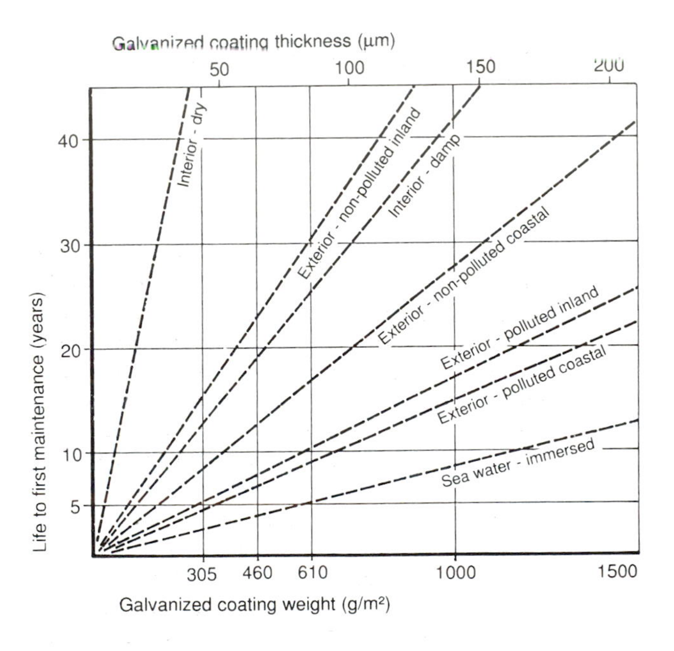

Fig. 5.6 *Relationship between life of zinc coating and its thickness.*

coatings, and protects the steel during storage and fabrication whilst giving some resistance to corrosion in use. It is suitable for internal partitions and other interior applications but is not normally used for exterior components or structural items.

The second process is known as hot-dip coating, usually called galvanizing. The steel strip is cleaned and then passed through a bath of molten zinc. An alloy layer is formed at the steel surface and zinc adheres to this, the thickness being controlled by the speed of the strip, length of submersion and subsequent processes. After emerging from the bath the zinc cools naturally to produce the well-known crystalline or spangle finish. By controlling the cooling process it is possible to change the appearance, and matt finishes are available. The normal commercial grade of coating mass is 275 g/m^2, including both sides (i.e. 137.5 g/m^2 each side. The thickness of this coating is 20 μm or 0.02 mm (80 thou). This grade is not usually recommended for exterior purposes without further protection but is used extensively as a substrate for subsequent organic coating. Other coating masses for zinc include 350 g/m^2, 450 g/m^2 and 600 g/m^2 as well as some lighter grades. Of these 350 g/m^2 may be used without organic coating in benign environments when great durability is not required. It is also used in the substrate for British Steel's Colourfarm AP which is designed to withstand the very aggressive environments in some farm buildings.

Zinc coated steel with a coating mass of 600 g/m^2 is not normally used for roofing and cladding sheets but may be found in some types of lightweight steel lintel, provided that a damp proof membrane is used to protect the lintel.

Zinc protects the steel in two ways. Firstly, it acts as a barrier preventing water and oxygen from attacking the steel surface. Secondly, it corrodes sacrificially before the steel. At a damaged surface or a cut edge, the zinc will corrode before the steel is attacked, and tend to hold off the damage. Only when a substantial amount of zinc has gone will the steel itself corrode (Fig. 5.5). Since zinc has a relatively low corrosion rate, this clearly extends the life of the steel considerably.

In the atmosphere and exposed to direct rainfall the life of the zinc coating is directly proportional to its thickness (Fig. 5.6). When protected from direct rainfall this life can be extended considerably. Field experience has shown that the moisture in the atmosphere (from condensation or dew) will initially generate a similar rate of corrosion to that found on exposed components. The zinc salts which form on the surface are soluble in water, but since there is no appreciable supply of free water they do not dissolve. Instead they steadily build up until they form a very effective barrier to prevent further attack on the zinc. The indications are that under those conditions a coating mass of 275 g/m^2 will have a life in excess of 200 years. For this reason a coating mass of 275 g/m^2 is recommended in British Steel's Galvatite range for cold formed steel framing, now being increasingly used for offices, houses and low rise buildings of all types. Further details can be found in chapter 30.

5.4.2 Aluminium zinc alloys (Zalutite)

These alloys have recently become available, the coatings comprising a combination of aluminium (55%), zinc (43.5%), and silicon (1.5%) (Fig. 5.7). These proportions are by weight; by volume the ratio of aluminium to zinc is about 80/20. The coating was developed by the Bethlehem Steel Corp of the USA under the name Galvalume. It has subsequently been licensed to other steel producers and the product manufactured by British Steel is called Zalutite. Extended field tests and user experience in the USA show that Zalutite will have between two and six times the life of a

plain zinc coating of equal thickness (Fig. 5.8). This means that in some circumstances Zalutite may be used externally without further protection. The coating has a smooth surface and has good bend performance. It is also very suitable as the substrate for some organic coatings.

In general uncoated Zalutite is suitable for cladding farm buildings where the internal environment is not too aggressive, for instance implement stores and dry crop stores. It is not recommended for animal housing and wet crops. Like Galvatite, Zalutite is available in different weights – 150 g/m^2 (0.5 oz/ft^2) for internal uses and as a substrate for organic coating, and 185 g/m^2 (0.6 oz/ft^2) for exposed applications such as roofs. The respective thicknesses are 20 μm and 25 μm (80 and 100 thou).

5.4.3 Terne (lead/tin alloy coating)

Terne is the name given to cold reduced steel sheet and coil when coated with a lead/tin alloy. The coating has a 12% tin content and weighs 120 g/m^2 (0.4 oz/ft^2). Terne can be seam spot welded, soft soldered or brazed. Applications relate to industrial roofing where severe corrosion risks may occur. The external face can have additional protection of thin lead sheet bonded under pressure to the terne panels. The finish is left lead coloured with the inner liner painted.

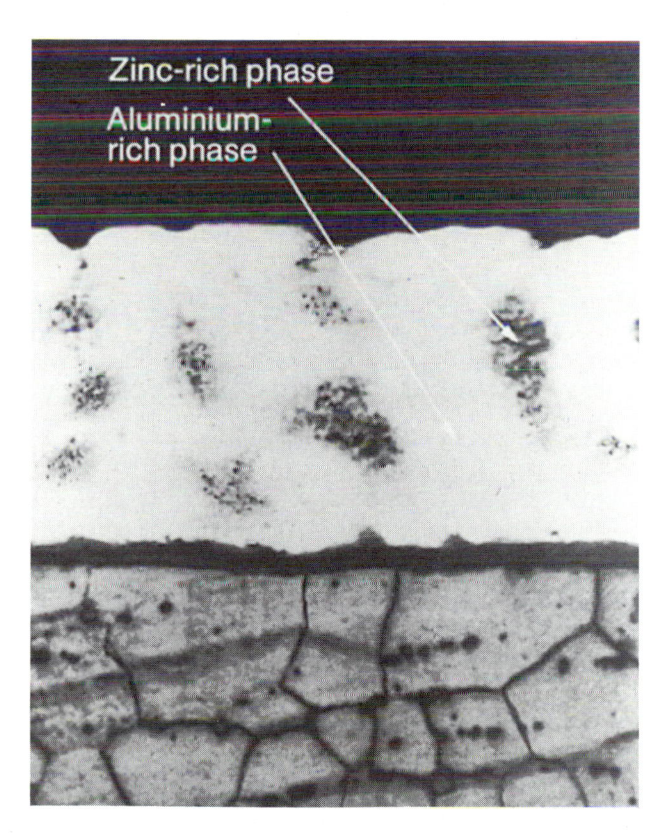

Fig. 5.7 *Micro section of Zalutite surface.*

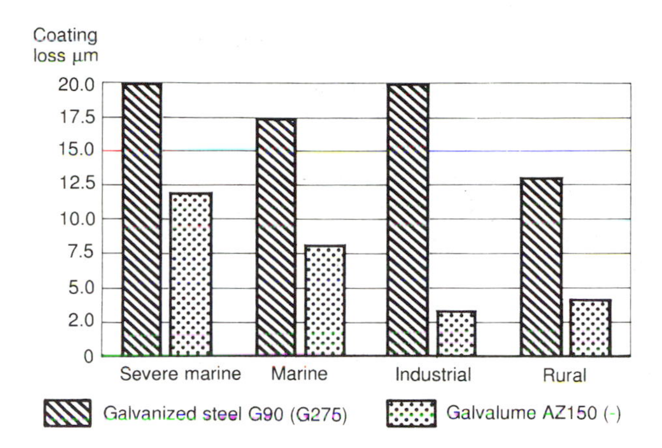

Fig. 5.8 *Bar chart showing the performance of Zalutite compared with conventional galvanizing.*

5.4.4 Tensile strengths of metallic coatings

As can be seen in Fig. 5.4 Galvatite (to EN10147) and Zalutite (to EN10215) are available in a range of tensile strengths and are referred to by their yield stresses which range from 220 N/mm^2 to 550 N/mm^2. All of these are used by profile sheet manufacturers and it is important to note which grade is specified when comparing performance claims from different manufacturers. All structural grades have similar values for Young's Modulus (E) and this must be recognized when deflection is the limiting criterion.

Apart from the chemistry of the steel, which is an important factor in determining the strength of the material, the production processes themselves can work to harden the steel and produce higher strengths than claimed. For instance, it is possible for the yield strength of FeE220G steel (220 N/mm^2) to be over 300 N/mm^2 after it has passed through galvanizing and organic coating lines.

Some types of steel sheet cladding components, such as certain tile designs or panels, require material that can be pressed into shape. Generally, the structural grades discussed above would not be suitable. However steels to EN10142 (zinc coated) EN10214 (5% Al, Zn) and EN10215 (55% Al, Zn) are available with progressively 'softer' properties enabling pressings to be made without risk of damaging the steel.

5.5 ORGANIC COATINGS

The success of steel as a roofing and cladding material since the 1960s is undoubtedly attributable to the use of organic coating as compared with traditional paint finishes (bitumen, oil or rubber based). The term 'organic coating' applies to factory processes in which steel strip is passed

Fig. 5.9 *The Chapman Taylor designed Lakeside Pavilion at Thurrock Lakeside Shopping Centre in Essex features profiled steel cladding in a style that resembles timber store houses. The architect received a certificate of special commendation for it in the sixth British Steel Colorcoat Building Awards.*

Fig. 5.10 *Colorcoat cladding is available in multi radius curved sheets from Dupral (UK) Ltd. It features in the design of the Space Habitat at Huntsville in Alabama, USA.*

through a plant to produce a heat bonded film of PVC, plastisol or polyvinylidene fluoride to the weather face or to both faces of the sheet. The following notes apply to British Steel developments with organic coatings which began with PVC plastisol in 1965 (the trade name is Colorcoat). The range of proprietary coatings has been extended to cover different applications and finishes. The bonding between film and metal is such that all bending and processing can be carried out after the coating process without breakdown of the protective system. There are six principal coating forms and these are described below.

5.5.1 Colorcoat HP200

This coating takes the major share of the UK market for cladding and roofing (Figs 5.9 and 5.10). British Steel has always had a PVC plastisol as part of the Colorcoat range and from 1965 to 1977 this was offered in a limited colour range. From 1977 to 1986 an improved formulation was produced to overcome fading and the colour range completely changed. In 1986 a third improvement was introduced while the appearance of the colour range was little altered. The pigmentation, however, was completely revised to extend further the period to first maintenance. This enabled British Steel to claim performance figures precisely related to the location of the Colorcoat and the actual colour. In 1992 British Steel changed the durability criterion from 'Period to first maintenance' to 'Period to repaint decision'. They also produced a new method of assessing the durability of a building making it possible to consider each plane of the envelope separately. Coupled with this, precise performance data are given for each colour. It is not possible within this book to explain the complete procedure but British Steel's *Roofing and Cladding in Steel: A Guide to Architectural Practice*[2] includes the method. Fig. 5.11 shows the graph which enables the reader to predict the performance of each plane of the building for any colour and in any location.

In addition to the good performance of HP200 in the atmosphere, it also has very good scratch and impact resistance. Pre-finished sheets require careful handling. Damage to the surface can occur, however, during the manufacturing process, transport and erection, with risk of damage to the metal substructure. The success of HP200

Colour			Environment (for code references see matrices on page 49)												
Groups	Specific Colours	Ref. No.	A	B	C	D	E	F	G	H	J	K	L	M	N
A	White	1													
	Goosewing Grey	2													
	Mushroom	3													
	Bamboo	4	19	20	21	22	23	24	25	26	27	28	29	30	
	Moorland Green	5													
B	Merlin Grey	6													
	Black	7													
	Eau de Nil	8													
	Svelte Grey	9													
	Aztec Yellow	10													
	Saffron	11													
	Tangerine	12	16	17	18	19	20	21	22	23	24	25	26	27	28
	Orange														
	Golden Glow	13													
	Burnt Orange	14													
	Poppy Red	15													
C	Acorn Brown	16													
	Dijon Yellow	17													
	Oakleaf Green	18													
	Linden Green	19													
	Verona Green	20	12	13	14	15	16	17	18	19	20	21	22	23	24
	Wedgwood Blue	21													
	Olive Green	22													
D	Ocean Blue	23													
	Jade	24													
	Solent Blue	25													
	Vandyke Brown	26	10		11	12	13	14	15	16	17	18	19	20	
E	Petra	27													
	Terracotta	28													
			A	B	C	D	E	F	G	H	J	K	L	M	N

Fig. 5.11 *Table of HP200 performance.*

rests largely with the thicker coating of 200 μm or 0.2 mm (8 thou). This ensures that the coated sheet is less vulnerable and minimizes time spent on site touching up the scratches.

5.5.2 Colorcoat Pvf2

This coating is primarily for roofing purposes where damage is less likely. The coating is relatively thin −27 μm or 0.027 mm (10 thou). Site work will need to be carefully arranged to prevent damage but the weathering performance is good, particularly with dark colours and with metallic silver. The finish is smooth and self cleaning as compared with the embossed surfaces usual with HP200.

5.5.3 Polyesters

Polyester coatings are a cheap alternative for finishing steel strip, popular in some countries, and are made in a wide colour range. Repainting will be needed after 7–10 years, and this has to be offset against the lower initial cost. It is a common finish for internal sheet steel.

5.5.4 Lining enamel

These enamels were developed for liner panels in roof and walls and for the inner skin of composites. The standard colour is off-white with a tough finish which can be easily cleaned.

5.5.5 Colorfarm AP

This form of coating has been developed for farm buildings, including stock housing. The primer has a 'high build' character with the weather coatings available in six colours to blend with the natural vernacular materials of old farms.

5.5.6 Stelvetite

It is possible to bond various films to steel to give a laminated finish. 'Stelvetite' is a calendered PVC film 2 μm or 0.2 mm (8 thou) thickness which can be bonded to steel strip. There is a good choice of colours, decorative effects and textures. The product, which was first used in the UK in 1957, is only suitable for internal applications such as partitions, panelling and radiator casings.

5.6 MAKING PROFILED SHEET

There are two ways of manufacturing profiled sheet – break press or roll forming. In the first method, sheets of finite length, up to 11 m (36 ft) are shaped using a tool which can perform two bends in each operation. The process is slow but is suitable where specials have to be made or where small orders are involved. Large quantitites or proprietary profiles warrant setting up a roll forming mill. In this case coils of coated sheet are loaded into machines with a series of rolls or stands which gradually shape the sheet into the profile without distressing the finished sheet (Fig. 5.12). The latter process can allow for refinements such as 'indents' to give mechanical bond to concrete for composite floor decks (for details refer to chapter 16) or for perforation where acoustic absorption is needed. The end bay is provided with a flying shear and mechanical equipment for wrapping and stacking. Roll forming is the more common process and is more readily adaptable for complicated shapes.

Fig. 5.12 *Profile roll former.*

5.6.1 Type of profile

The simplest sections are regular trapezoidal forms. These are easy to make and have adequate strength for most purposes. They have reasonable conversion efficiencies, with a high ratio of developed effective width measured against the plain sheet.

Typical profiles most commonly used in the UK have depths of around 34–38 mm (1⁵⁄₁₆–1½ in). The fixings are made through the crown or trough or by spring clips so that the weather surface is not perforated (for details refer to chapter 28). Other types of sheet have been developed which superficially resemble copper roofing and are termed 'standing seam'. The patents stem from the USA. The basis is a trough form on a module of about 600 mm (2 ft). The seaming is mechanical with fixing brackets pressed into the seam joint.

5.6.2 Strength of profile

Profiled sheet is also used for decking. The demand for larger spans requires deeper trapezoidal sections with a risk of instability in the compression zones. Stiffening swages (see Fig. 5.3) are introduced to stabilize these. This allows the designer to use more metal in the working part of the profile and improves the efficiency ratio (metal used to effective girth achieved). Design calculation methods are complicated, and manufacturers generally provide simple tables relating span and load conditions for particular profiles [3].

5.6.3 Composite panels (see chapter 26 for illustrations)

All forms of insulated roof involve a composite construction of outer sheet, insulation and inner lining. Site work with at least three separate components is increasingly replaced by factory made units called 'composite' panels. These are of a sandwich construction with the insulation fitted between inner and outer skins. The insulating core is foamed plastic which is effectively bonded to the envelope of steel strip. The foam takes the shear loads and the composite action enables a 30% longer span for the composite panel than for a simple trapezoidal sheet backed up on site by insulation and inner lining. Laid-up panels offer an alternative. With board-like materials such as glass fibre or mineral wool faced on both sides with coated steel, they form a pre-finished panel for roofing and walling. A detailed review of all forms of cladding and panel construction is set down in chapters 26 and 27.

5.6.4 Flashings and trim

Roof envelopes fall into two categories: water shedding and watertight. The water shedding requirement is satisfied when the sheets and trim are at sufficient pitch to shed rainfall without penetration. A conservative estimate is a minimum of 15 degrees.

Lower roof pitches mean reliance upon mastic, mechanical joints or a combination of both to achieve weather-tightness. The detailing of flashings and trim needs as much care as the joints between roofing components. The range of details shown in chapter 26 illustrates some of the more important aspects. Face fixing may be the only solution for flashings. Buckling due to thermal movement or wind pressures may occur. The stiffening returns or nibs require special details to ensure an accurate line to the crucial edges of roofs, walls and windows.

Curved and double curved sheets are now feasible for a whole range of complex sheets. This has become part of the vocabulary of steel cladding. The usual applications are at ridges and eaves and can also be utilized for external and internal return corners. Omitting gutters to shed-type roofs that will flood doors and windows unless adequate hood flashings are provided. These principles of cladding are outlined in chapters 25 and 26.

High performance from components under heavy rain loading requires high levels of workmanship not normally associated with the cheapest site labour – a good reason to return to nominated subcontracting for such a crucial part of the building envelope.

5.7 DURABILITY AND MAINTENANCE

Good design can extend the life of cladding by ensuring that rainwater is efficiently discharged from the building face. This requires good drainage to roofs and guttering. This is particularly important where low pitches are employed. Many profile manufacturers claim that their roof sheets can be used down to pitches as low as 1 degree. This figure needs to be treated with caution since 2.5 degrees is a realistic pitch in order to ensure 1 degree on site after deflections under load, tolerances sheet to sheet and distortion at bolt positions are taken into account. Making a substructure for 1 degree falls will lead to ponding and considerably shorten the life of finishes and sealants. Minimal pitches also accumulate debris and dust on the roof surface due to the reduced scouring effect of rainwater on near flat surfaces. This also applies to gutters which should always be pitched to adequate falls of 1:100 to 1:120.

5.7.1 Mastic seals

Mastic seals have a life expectancy of around 20 years. This implies regular maintenance of sheeting and/or gutter systems where mastics are used. Sheeting forms which rely on efficient laps without sealant will give lower maintenance costs unless one views building envelopes as expendable items on a 20–25 year cycle.

The high temperature and movement range of sheet steel – 2.5 mm per m (1/32 in per ft) run for a 100°C (180°F) temperature difference – excludes the use of oleoresinous air drying sealants and polysulphides. The customary seal today is 'grease based' and used in soft ribbon form. Foam seals are used for side laps but never at end laps due to the compression needed to guarantee watertight joints.

5.7.2 Cut edges

Trimming sheets at junctions to eaves and verges or other cutting due to site geometry means bare metal at cut edges to cladding and flashings. In traditional work these edges were left untreated since the sacrificial action of the galvanizing continued to provide protection. However, there is much greater risk of corrosion with roof pitches below 4 degrees as these allow water to remain longer on slopes, particularly at the eaves. Here the trough ends should be bent down to a 10 degree slope, or alternatively the cut edge painted to counter wet edge corrosion. The same precaution is taken for all cut edge work below 4 degree pitch. Translucent paints have been developed for this purpose to make the task less daunting on site, although visible paint is more foolproof.

5.7.3 Maintenance for coated sheet

Trade literature for sheeting uses the term 'period to first maintenance'. This refers to the preferred time for site painting. This timescale is not the life of the material but simply the recommended cycle in order to maximize the life of coated sheet. It is difficult to provide precise figures since exposure and pollution levels have such a wide variation. In general terms PVC coatings have a cycle to first maintenance of 10 to 20 years for roofing and 10 to 25 years for walling. Pvf2 has comparative figures of 10 to 15 years whilst aluminium/zinc coating (without paint) will need painting on the same cycle.

Overpainting will clearly extend the life of all these coatings. The estimated life for such overpainting is 10 years. The likely changes in appearance after these periods are loss of gloss, some chalking at water scour points and perhaps a change in intensity of hue. Fading is a characteristic of darker shades, so that the wise designer utilizes lighter tints where changes are less noticeable.

5.7.4 Solar reflection

Another advantage of light coloured sheets is that they are solar reflective and remain cooler than dark coloured material. This causes less thermal movement and less stress on fixings and fixing holes. The temperature difference can be such that white sheets only reach 41°C (115°F) on a hot summer's day while dark brown sheeting will heat up to 76°C (170°F). Multi-coloured sheeting patterns need greater insulation thickness for the dark toned panels. A further disadvantage in roof sheeting which reaches surface temperatures in excess of 70°C (160°F) is that the sacrificial action between zinc coating and steel sheets reverses, with the steel corroding to protect the zinc, and entrapped water at overlap 'cuts' can provide rapid corrosion points.

5.7.5 Marine environments

Coastal exposure implies higher wind speeds and salt laden rainfall. Droplets are forced into sheet crevices below eaves and verge overhangs or into the overlaps on the roof slopes. Evaporation leads to salt deposits in locations which will not be washed with normal rainfall. Salt is hygroscopic and will absorb moisture from the air, thus becoming a very powerful corrosive agent. Precautions should include high quality coatings to backs of sheets and trim. Great care is necessary on site to paint all cut edges. The use of sealants to exclude salt laden deposits at all joints is vital.

5.8 OTHER APPLICATIONS

Strip steel is found in hundreds of components for the building industry, key references being found in the following chapters:

Chapter 25 – Principles of cladding
Chapter 26 – Light and heavyweight cladding
Chapter 27 – Window walls and rain-screen facades
Chapter 28 – Decking and built-up roofing
Chapter 32 – Metal doors

There are other applications such as ducting, flooring trays and suspended ceiling components and which are referred to in chapter 13.

Finally, there is a whole range of cold formed connectors used in the timber trade – anchors, truss plates, herringbone struts, joist connectors and shoes. Space does not permit illustration but the combined virtues of steel and timber in conjunction just shows the ubiquitous role of steel strip in today's building technology. A step forward from the corrugated iron of yesteryear!

REFERENCES AND TECHNICAL NOTES

1. BS 3083: 1983 Hot-dip zinc coated and hot-dip aluminium/zinc coated corrugated steel sheets for general purposes.
2. *Roofing and Cladding in Steel: A Guide to Architectural Practice* (1992), British Steel.
3. BS 5427: 1976 Code of practice for performance and loading criteria for profiled steel sheeting in building.

Stainless steel curtain wall to the Vickers Tower, London 1961–3 (architect Ronald Ward and Partners). Refer to Fig. 6.10 for detail.

6

Stainless and related steels

D. J. Cochrane

6.1 INTRODUCTION

Stainless steel is a most interesting material. It has an unusual combination of properties, being a ductile material which is tough and durable, and requires no added surface protection against corrosion. It is also readily formable; it can be cast, forged and welded, and can be used effectively at temperatures ranging from −200°C to +800°C (−328°F to 1472°F). Its surface can be polished to a highly reflective mirror finish, it can be abraded to a matt or satin appearance, or given a textured pattern such as linen, pearl or mosaic, by the rolling process. Stainless steel presents an image of strength and quality. It is approximately five to eight times as expensive as ordinary steel.

Colour can be added to these surface finishes by a chemical process which colours the inert film on the surface of stainless steel to give a permanent decoration in a range from bronze to blue. In its natural colour, however, stainless steel will reflect the colours which surround it.

Stainless steel is available in plate, sheet, strip and structural sections including I-beams, channels and angles which may be hot-rolled, cold formed, or extruded. Additionally, a range of proprietary fixings, from bolts to door handles are available to complement virtually all building requirements.

Stainless steel is well suited for building applications as it is unaffected by other building materials, and it will not stain other materials – an important architectural consideration. In areas which are inaccessible, such as wall cavities, the durability and integrity of stainless steel enable it to function without maintenance for the lifespan of the building – hence its widespread specification for these areas.

Externally, as roofing and cladding for example, stainless steel can have both a decorative and functional role. Because it is waterproof, the outer skin may be used in thin gauges, providing a saving in weight and hence a possible reduction in structural steelwork and foundation costs.

The maintenance requirements of stainless steel are minimal, which is particularly useful in the facades of high-rise buildings as this cleaning can be carried out simultaneously with window cleaning. Examples include the Millbank Tower, the Post Office Tower, the National Westminster Tower and the Canary Wharf Tower, each in its time the highest building in London.

The special properties of stainless steel are associated with the inclusion of significant amounts of chromium and other alloying elements during the manufacturing process. A wide range of stainless steel material grades is available, 57 in all, although these can be narrowed considerably for building applications. Three basic groups of stainless steel can be distinguished by metallurgical terms: austenitic, ferritic and martensitic. By far the most widely specified, and the most appropriate, are the austenitic steels, and in particular the 300 series in which the dominant specifications, for building applications, are types 304 (17.5/19.0% chromium, 8.0/11.0% nickel) and 316 (16.5/18.5% chromium, 10.0/13.0% nickel, 2.25/3.0% molybdenum). The inclusion of molybdenum increases the material's resistance to corrosion, hence the wide application of type 316 in aggressive marine and industrial environments.

On a limited scale, ferritic stainless steel, particularly type 430 (16.0/18.0% chromium), is also used in building. As this material is a straight chromium steel, it has only moderate corrosion resistance and its application is limited to interior uses where corrosion is not a consideration. Ferritic steels are non-hardenable and magnetic but are weldable and considerably cheaper than the austenitic stainless steels.

Although austenitic stainless steels cannot be hardened by heat treatment, they readily work harden and tensile strengths of the order of 1000 N/mm^2 (145 ksi) may be realized. Advantage can be taken of this feature, in reinforcing bars for instance, where the bars are warm worked in forming the ribs essential for bonding to the concrete.

An early example of the use of stainless steel reinforcement is in the remedial works to supporting piers for the huge dome of St. Paul's Cathedral where, in the 1930s, 120 tonnes of 'Staybrite' bars were used. Tie rods, also in 'Staybrite', were used for securing the inner leaf of the dome to the outer wall.

Demand for stainless steel in the UK has more than doubled over the last 20 years, from 4.04 million tonnes in 1968 to 9.32 million tonnes in 1987. Improved plant and production techniques have been utilized to meet this demand and improve the quality of the product.

Electric arc furnaces are used to produce the molten steel – around 1600°C (3000°F) – which is transferred to and refined in an argon oxygen decarburizing (AOD) vessel. The liquid steel is transferred to a continuous casting (concast) machine which produces the slabs for subsequent hot rolling into plate up to 10 m (33 ft) long and 3.05 m (10 ft) wide, and coils for later use for cold rolling. Extensive plate finishing facilities include shot blasting, descaling and grinding equipment to facilitate a high quality surface product.

For the production of cold rolled flat products the feedstock is hot rolled coils produced from the concast slabs. The feedstock passes through annealing, pickling and coil grinding stages to cold rolling, followed by further annealing and pickling or bright annealing. A final roller sheath pass on highly polished rolls prior to cutting, slitting or coiling ensures a high quality finished product. Coils can be up to a 12 tonnes capacity, 1512 mm (5 ft) wide and range from 0.4 mm to 50 mm (16 thou to 2 in) in thickness. Sheets may be up to 6.0 m (20 ft) in length and range in width from 610 to 1525 mm (2 to 5 ft).

The specialized finishes mentioned in this chapter are produced on patterned rolls.

6.2 APPLICATIONS

6.2.1 Roofing

Stainless steel is widely used as a roofing material in Europe for many categories of building. The key to success is installation, with mechanically seamed sheets utilizing continuous lengths up to 15 m (50 ft) long. In the UK the initial use has been for church roofing in outlying areas as stainless steel is not attractive to thieves, unlike lead, and is cost-effective when compared with super-purity aluminium or copper. Today stainless steel roofing is common for flat and pitched roofing for both public buildings and industrial work, where a corrosion resistant and tough surface is needed. It is common practice in the UK to allow 9 m (30 ft) as a maximum length between weather steps.

The usual specification is for a softened material, preferably with a hardness value of less than 150 Vickers, 28 SWG in thickness (0.4 mm–16 thou) [1]. This is preferred for ease of forming to minimize the 'springback' which occurs with other stainless steels. The finish can be dull matt, similar to that of 2D in BS 1449: Part 2 [2], or 'terne' coated to give an appearance similar to leadwork.

There are two basic patterns for laying: standing seam or batten roll. The former has a less conspicuous profile, whilst the batten roll gives a visually bold line at the batten joints and requires greater care with roof geometry, namely matching pitches at ridge and valley junctions (Fig. 6.1). Batten roll (Fig. 6.2) is employed for pitches up to and including 7 degrees whilst steeper slopes can be clad with the roll or standing seam method (Fig. 6.3). The latest technology from Sweden enables a seam joint to be made on site which is both folded and welded to produce a watertight joint, suitable for flat roofs or as the substrate for roof gardens. The structural deck can be precast concrete, cement fibre slabs, or, most commonly, tongued and grooved boards or plywood with inodorous felt to separate deck and roofing. Composition boards should not be used.

Fig. 6.1 *Stainless steel standing seam roofing at the Swan Theatre, Stratford, UK (architects Norman and Underwood).*

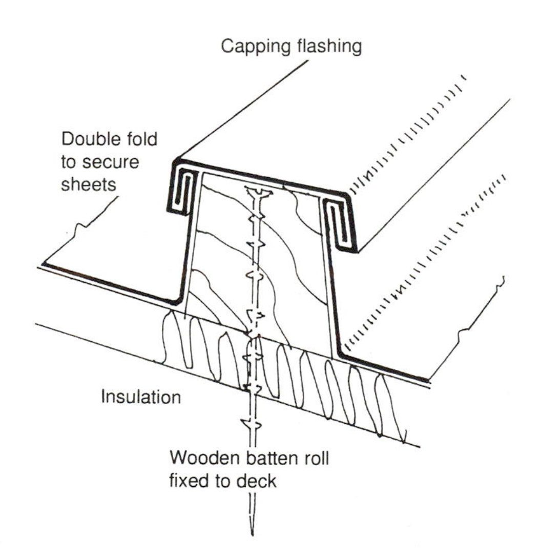

Fig. 6.2 *Formation of batten roll.*

Historically, the most famous example is the roof finial of the Chrysler Building (Fig. 6.4) from 1928–30 (architect William van Alen), which is as bright and shiny today as six decades ago, following a thorough cleansing operation in the late 1970s which revealed no deterioration of the metal cladding or fixings [3]. The original materials were 'Enduro KA2 Rezistal Stainless Steel', known as Nirosta, and developed in Germany. The whole of the upper works were fabricated abroad and shipped to New York for installation.

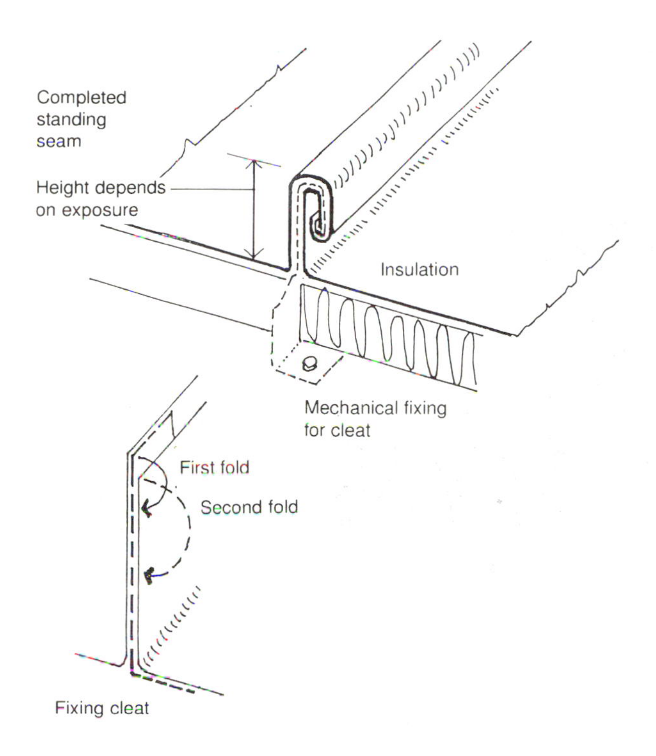

Fig. 6.3 *Formation of standing seam.*

Fig. 6.4 *Roof finial of the Chrysler Building, New York 1928–30 (architect William van Alen).*

Figs 6.5 *Thames Barrier, London, UK: stainless steel roof panels to piers (architects Architects Department, Greater London Council, engineers Rendel Palmer and Tritton).*

Figs 6.6 *Thames Barrier, London, UK: stainless steel roof panels to control tower (architects Architects Department, Greater London Council, engineers Rendel Palmer and Tritton).*

An equally famous modern structure is the Thames Barrier (Figs 6.5 and 6.6). The piers of this familiar landmark are clad with stainless steel type 316, 0.376 mm (15 thou) in thickness, the dimpled appearance created by the flat panels being curved in two directions to accommodate the shape of the timber subframing. The roofs of the adjacent control tower are also clad with stainless sheeting. It is worth noting by comparison that the structural steelwork employed for the main barrier rising gates, which rest within the tidal Thames, is protected from corrosion by 40 tonnes of paint and 20 tonnes of sacrificial anode.

One further example illustrates the way stainless finishes can be used to form 'laid up' panels. The envelope for the Doncaster Bus Workshop required a fire resistance of 2 hours coupled with minimal maintenance for both roofing

Fig. 6.7 *Doncaster Bus Workshop, UK (architect and engineer Barnsley Metropolitan Borough Council).*

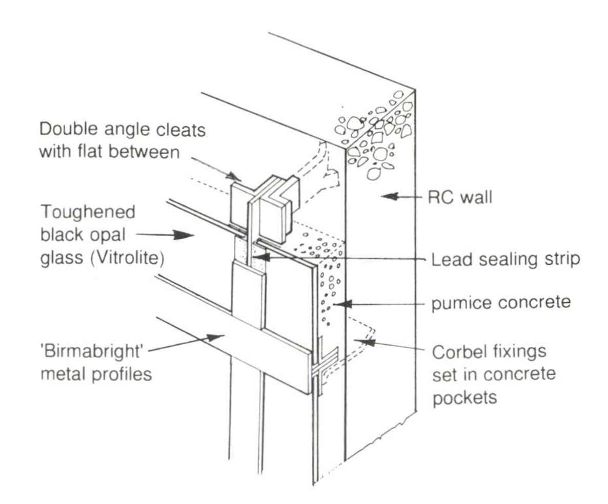

Figs 6.8 *Daily Express, Fleet Street, London 1932: detail of Vitrolite secured by 'Birmabright' components.*

and the inner lining. The panels comprise a liner tray, an insulation core of 80 mm (3¼ in) mineral wool with a roof facing of type 316, 0.7 mm (28 thou) thick profiled stainless sheet. The sheet has a mosaic pattern to soften the visual impact (Fig. 6.7).

6.2.2 Window walls

Stainless components were developed for window walls in the 1930s, the most memorable being the range of 'Birmabright' cover strips developed for the Daily Express facades by Sir Owen Williams, with Ellis and Clarke [4]. Elevations faced with toughened glass (Vitrolite) and stainless steel glazing bars can still be found at the 'Express' buildings in Fleet Street (Figs 6.8 and 6.9), Glasgow and Manchester. Post-war developments departed from the conventional cover bar form and involved a steel core (often a steel flat) with encasement by U-shaped sheaths to give thermal breaks as well as the facility to secure a wide range of panel thicknesses and cleaning gear. The most sophisticated ideas emanated from Morris Singer and Co. in the cladding of the Vickers Tower (Fig. 6.10).

Individual casements are available with external stainless facings (like the Swedish Carda range) or assembled with hollow rolled forms such as the patterns from 'Frametal' (Fig. 6.11). The stainless steel is type 304, 0.8 mm (32 thou) in thickness, providing a smooth profile which is easy to clean and neither oxidizes nor suffers from scale due to weathering.

It is worth noting that stainless steel elements on the Daily Express facades and on the 387 ft (117 m) high Vickers Tower have never been painted – the maintenance amounts to washing on the same cycle as cleaning the adjacent glazing.

Fig. 6.9 *Daily Express, Fleet Street, London (1932): example of Vitrolite secured by 'Birmabright' components (architects Ellis and Clarke: engineer Sir Owen Williams).*

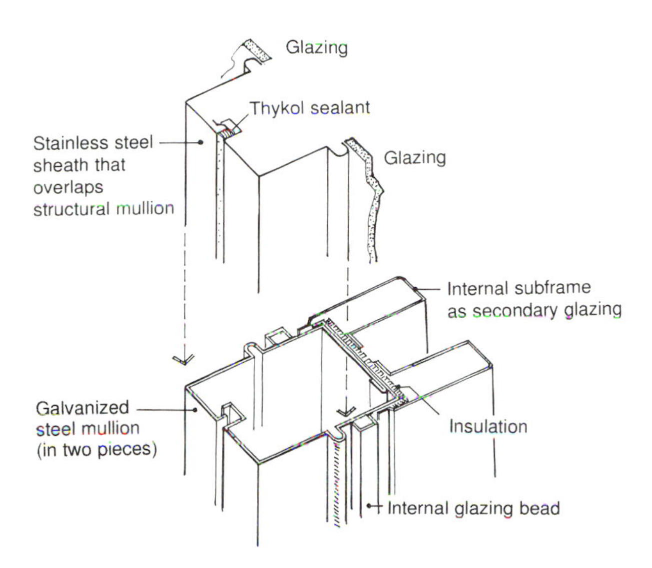

Fig. 6.10 *Vickers Tower, Embankment, London 1961–3 (specialist stainless steel fabricator Morris Singer and Co.: detailer Gordon Wimborne).*

Fig. 6.12 *Lavatory pods clad with composite stainless steel window and wall panels, Lloyds HQ, London 1986 (architects Richard Rogers Partnership: engineers Ove Arup and Partners).*

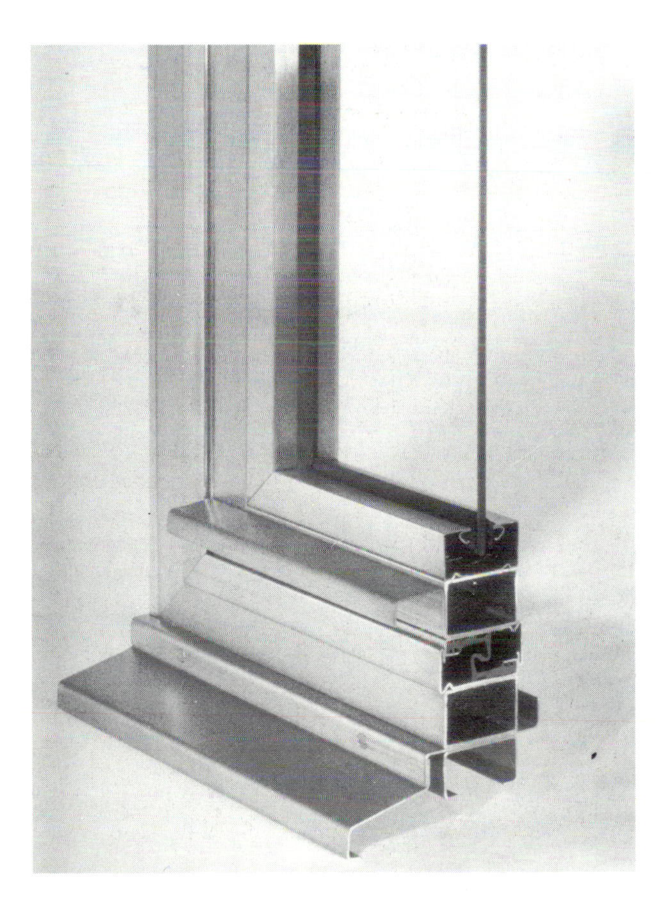

Fig. 6.11 *Roll formed stainless steel sections in window construction, from Frametal, Vitry, France.*

Stainless panels feature within window walls in the USA and Japan, the surface being patterned or shaped to mask rippling. The terms 'oil canning' or 'ponding' are often used to describe this phenomenon relating to difficulties in obtaining true optical flatness. Most patterning is multi-dimensional (curved or pyramid type) or ribbed, all of which help to stiffen the panel skin [1]. The underframe or chassis to such panel walls comprises a bolted or welded steel trellis. The structural combination of mild steel and stainless sheet is operable, since the modulus of elasticity is similar for both metals. At elevated temperatures stainless steel has improved performance over structural steels, hence its application for fire-resisting spandrels and for composite panels which embrace the roof and wall zone (Fig. 6.12).

The inherent resistance to hard wear coupled with high strength is the reason why shopfitting components are often specified in stainless steel. The fabrication involves stainless cladding over aluminium, steel or hardwood cores, the metal thickness being 26 SWG for cladding work and up to 3 mm (⅛ in) for formed sections with welded joints (Figs. 6.13, 6.14 and 6.15).

6.2.3 Building trim

The shopfitting role already described is extended to building interiors, stainless steel being a popular choice for lift finishes, both car and doors (Fig. 6.16), and for trim to railings and staircases. A whole range of interchangeable stainless tubes with mechanical or welded joints is available to suit horizontal and sloping balustrades with infills of toughened glass, rods or wire (Fig. 6.17). Industrial stairs

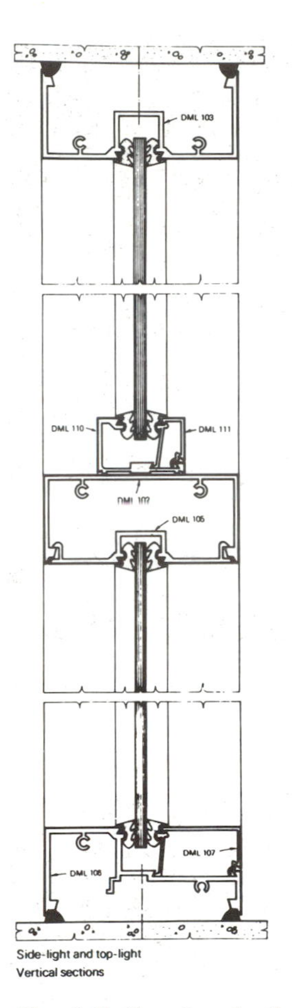

Fig. 6.13 *Shop front detail showing stainless steel cladding over aluminium core – by Drawn Metal Ltd, Leeds, UK.*

Fig. 6.15 *Shopfront using 16 SWG stainless steel pressed to a plywood core – by Drawn Metal Ltd, Leeds, UK.*

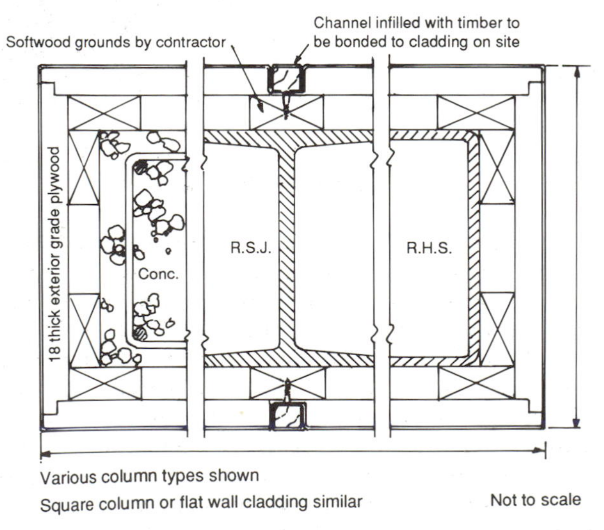

Fig. 6.14 *Stainless steel column casing – by Drawn Metal Ltd, Leeds, UK.*

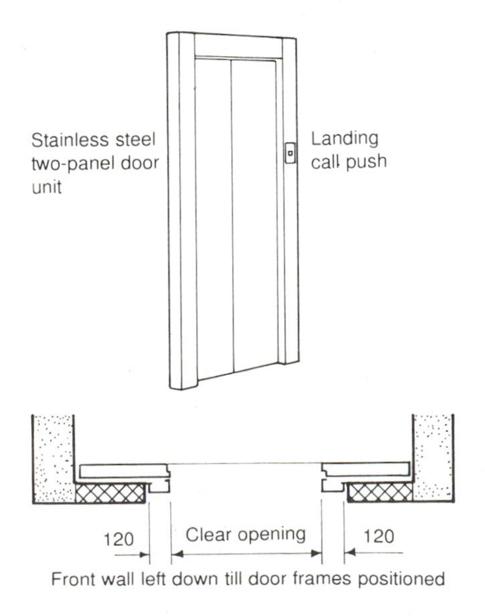

Fig. 6.16 *Lift architraves and doors using stainless steel.*

Fig. 6.17 *Stainless steel handrailing by Krupp, Germany.*

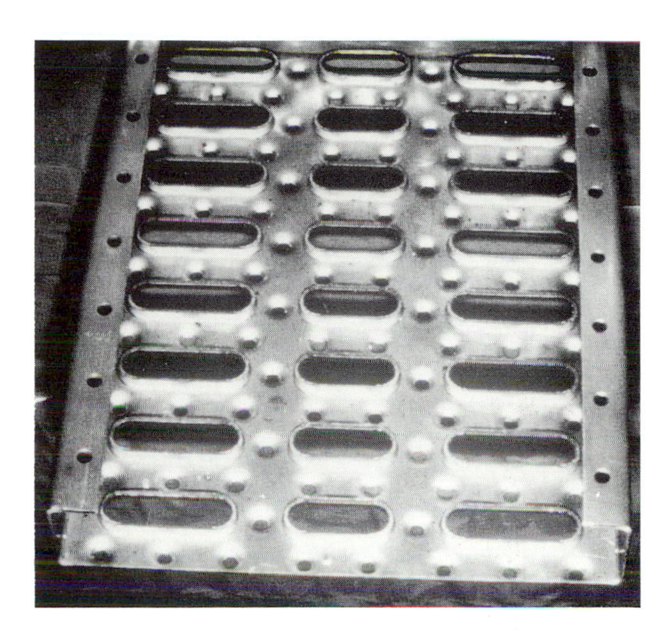

Fig. 6.19 *Plank floor (Wincro Metal Industries Ltd, Fife Street, Sheffield S9 1NJ, UK).*

Fig. 6.18 *Electropolished floor plate (Wincro Metal Industries Ltd, Fife Street, Sheffield S9 1NJ, UK).*

Fig. 6.20 *Grid floor (Redman Fisher Engineering Corp., PO Box 12, Birmingham New Road, Tipton, West Midlands, DY4 9AA, UK).*

have 'Durbar' treads, a further development being 'Durbar' floor plates [5] to give cleanable and non-slip flooring for locations such as dairies, food processing plants or for special industries (chemical and pharmaceutical) where hygiene is a key factor.

Grid and plank flooring can be used for raised floors and walkways. A recent development for renovating factories is a solid floor plate using pressed sheets of 1.5–2 mm (1/16–5/64 in) thickness which can be epoxy bonded to old floors or stairs (Figs. 6.18, 6.19, 6.20 and 6.21).

Street furniture such as lighting and telegraph poles, bus shelters and motorway fencing are exposed not only to the elements but to de-icing salts and traffic pollutants. There is also physical damage from traffic and vandals. Figure 6.22 illustrates base corrosion to carbon steel tube even with regular maintenance, say repainting on a five to seven year cycle. Clearly the eventual consequence is total replacement. Stainless poles and tubes need no maintenance for their lifespan. A current range of street furniture by Stainton Metal Co. Ltd (Fig. 6.23) uses type 316 of thickness 1.6 mm (1/16 in). Another use seen in Switzerland is stainless steel cable net for the central reservation on motorways and as high tensile mesh for roadside fencing (Fig. 6.24).

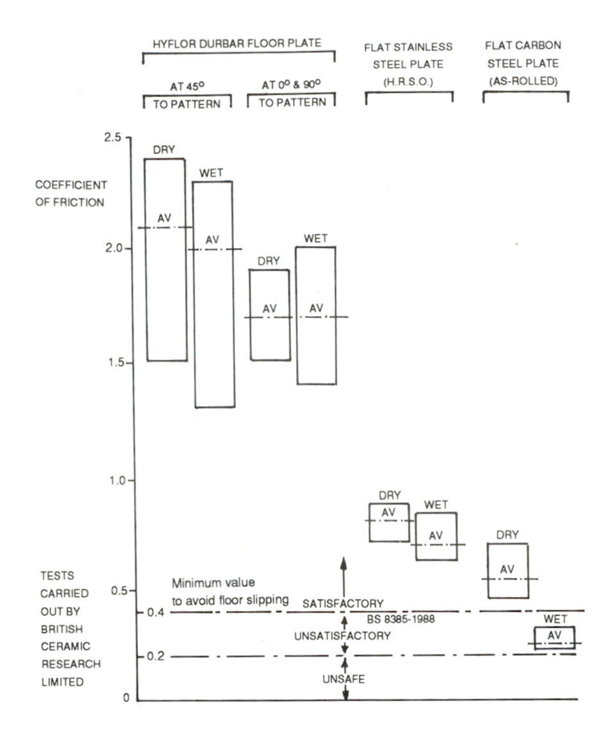

Fig. 6.21 *Slip resistance of floor plate.*

Fig. 6.22 *Corrosion at the base of a plain steel tube.*

6.2.4 Structural work

Stainless steel can be used structurally to perform both an aesthetic and functional role as shown in Figs 6.25 and 6.26. In addition to the commercial applications, it has been specified for industrial areas where conventional materials and protective coatings are inadequate and maintenance is costly and disruptive. It is widely used in the nuclear industry and in very aggressive environments, for instance buildings containing acid baths. In areas such as these, a life

Fig. 6.23 *Stainless steel Telecom distribution pole by Stainton Metal Co. Ltd, Dukesway, Teesside Industrial Estate, Cleveland, TS17 9LT, UK.*

Fig. 6.24 *Use of stainless steel webbing to form a motorway barrier.*

Fig. 6.25 *Stainless steel structural trusses for atrium supporting glass and cleaning trolleys at Stockley House, London (architect A. Bonner: engineers Bunyan Meyer and Partners).*

Fig. 6.26 *Stainless hollow sections and flats, supporting two-storey safety glass screen. Bond Street Station Shopping Mall (architect Chapman Taylor and Partners: engineers Ove Arup and Partners).*

cycle cost comparison can show stainless steel to be very cost-effective.

Bush Lane House in London is an interesting example of a stainless steel structure. The steel frame, which is a diagonal grid of small diameter tubes, is external to the building and is water-filled to provide the required fire protection. Stainless steel was used in this demanding application.

The ductility of stainless steel enables structural sections to be readily formed and cold formed angle sections are widely available, in a general range of sizes up to 250 mm × 250 mm × 16 mm (10 in × 10 in × ⅝ in), but any size of section can be formed to order. Due to the work hardening which takes place when forming austenitic stainless steel, an increase in strength occurs at the bend, and while this can be taken into account in design, it is generally accepted as an additional safety margin.

In designing with stainless steel it should be noted that the material does not, like structural carbon steel, exhibit a yield point and an equivalent value of 0.2% proof stress is provided by manufacturers. Design guidance on the use of cold formed sections is provided in the American Iron and Steel Institute publication [6]. A design study is being sponsored by the Nickel Development Institute, the Chromium Centre and the Department of Energy to develop design rules, in accordance with limit state principles, specifically for the structural use of stainless steel.

Welded and polished hollow sections (square, rectangular and circular) are produced for architectural applications and a range of structural hot rolled and extruded sections such as I-beams, wide flange beams, equal, unequal angles and channels are also available in austenitic grades.

6.2.5 Masonry fixings and supports

Anchors, bolts, corbels and angle cleats are widely used for supporting all forms of masonry and specialist cladding such as GRC and GRP. The standard anchors and bolts are in austenitic stainless steel to BS 6105: 1981 [7]. Three types are classified in Table 6.1 and 6.2 according to their ultimate tensile strength. Design stress levels in stainless bolts can be calculated in accordance with normal structural design rules for bolts in clearance holes.

Many specialist firms provide manuals giving details of cladding fixings [8]. The simplest is a folded plate of angle form to support brickwork (outer leaf) floor by floor. The more sophisticated give individual brick support with sub-fixing devices which provide three-dimensional tolerances using grooved face plates and slotted holes. There are many examples in London (Fig. 6.27) where stone veneer is

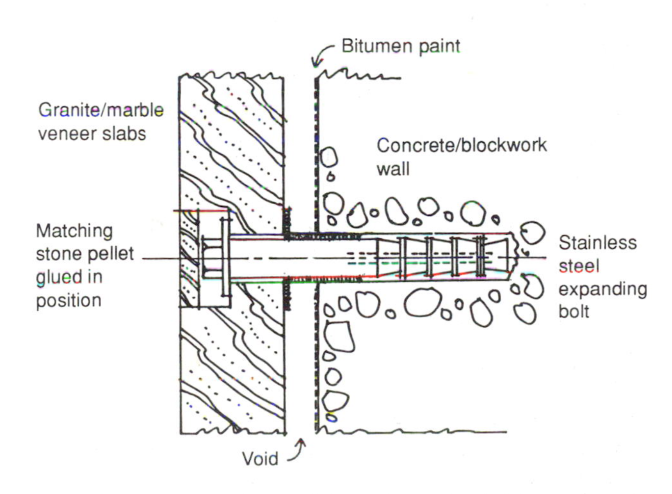

Fig. 6.27 *Stainless steel anchor bolts used as mechanical fixings for each piece of veneer cladding at BP House, Victoria Street, London 1978–9. (architect Elson Pack and Roberts).*

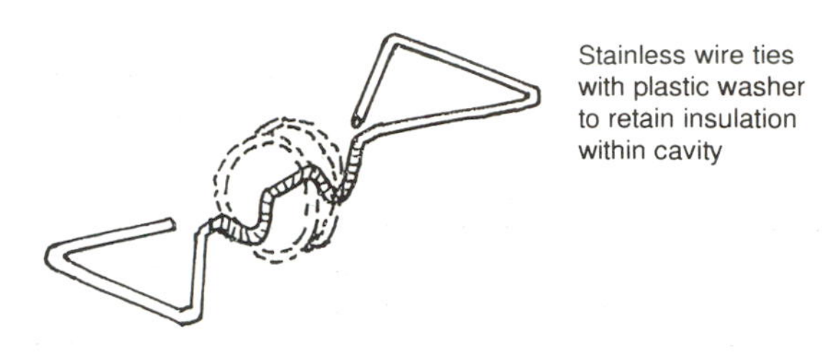

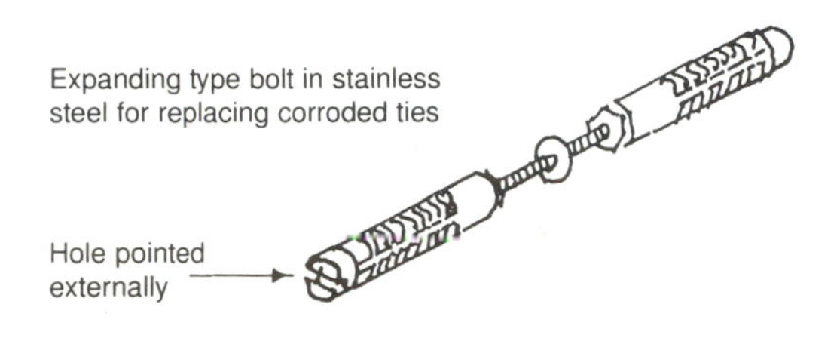

Fig. 6.28 *Stainless steel wall ties by George Clarke of Sheffield, UK.*

face-bolted to stainless inserts, providing a more secure fixing compared with cemented corbels or glued-in-place bolts.

Another critical aspect is the corrosive run-off which occurs within building cavities behind traditional facades. The leached salts from cement mortar, limestone, sandstone and masonry containing sulphates can be a lethal cocktail in terms of corrosion stresses for many metals, including galvanized steel and bronze/copper alloys. The breakdown of galvanized steel cavity ties in a considerably shorter period than the building design life (as reported by the Building Research Establishment [9]) has highlighted this problem and stainless steel is now preferred for new and replacement ties (Fig. 6.28).

6.3 MATERIAL GRADES

Austenitic stainless steel types 304 and 316 – the most appropriate for building applications – in plate, sheet and strip form are produced to BS 1449 Part 2: 1983 [2] from which the mechanical properties shown in Table 6.3 are taken.

Stainless steels with a 0.2% proof stress approximately 30% higher are produced to BS 1501 Part 3: 1973 [10], the higher value being obtained by the inclusion of nitrogen. The corresponding mechanical properties for this plate material are as shown in Table 6.4.

Higher strength steels are also available with Duplex stainless steels, an appropriate building specification being Duplex 2205 (22% Cr, 5% Ni). Widely used in offshore oil platforms, Duplex steels offer high strength and excellent corrosion resistance at less cost than the higher strength nitrogen bearing austenitic steels. It should be noted that the structural members of Bush Lane House were fabricated in a Duplex material, the tubular members being water filled to provide the fire protection to the externally sited lattice framework.

The mechanical properties of Duplex 2205 are given in Table 6.5.

6.4 SURFACE FINISHES

Standard finishes are classified according to Table 6.1 in BS 1449 Part 2: 1983 [2] for both mill and polished finishes. Additionally, producers and fabricators can provide a variety of alternative finishes and it is recommended that samples be obtained and agreed prior to specification.

6.4.1 Mill finish

Mill finish, which is often selected for industrial work and roofing, is available in the following specifications:

2A a bright annealed finish obtained by cold rolling.
2B a smooth finish produced by lightly rolling on polished rolls to give a slightly brighter finish than 2D.
2D a matt finish produced by cold rolling followed by annealing and descaling.

Mill finish is susceptible to finger marking and is seldom used for architectural applications.

6.4.2 Polished finish

Exterior and interior trim such as panelling, stairs and window trim are usually specified as polished with welds and extraneous markings cleaned and matched after fabrication. This implies that working areas are accessible by abrasive polishing wheels, belts or pads.

Standard polished finishes are as follows:

3A a coarse ground finish obtained with abrasives 80–100 grit size.
3B a dull buffed finish produced by abrasive belts 180–220 grit size.
4 a non-directional finish, not highly reflective, treated with abrasives 180–240 grit size.
7 a bright finish, highly reflective, finished with a polishing compound.
8 bright polished or mirror finish, achieved by using successively finer abrasives followed by very fine polishing compounds.

6.4.3 Electro-polishing [11]

An electro-chemical process can be used to provide a finish to shapes which cannot be polished by mechanical means, for instance chequer plate flooring. By immersing the

Table 6.1 Classification of anchors and bolts according to ultimate tensile strength

Type	*Bolts to BS 6105: 1981*		
	Property class	*UTS N/mm² (ksi) (min)*	*Stress at 0.2% permanent strain (min) N/mm² (ksi)*
	50	500 (72)	210 (30)
A1, A2 & A4	70	700 (102)	450 (65)
	80	800 (116)	600 (87)

Table 6.2 Permissible bolt stresses in relation to structural design

Property class	*Permissible bolt stresses*		
	Axial tension N/mm² (ksi)	*Shear N/mm² (ksi)*	*Bearing N/mm² (ksi)*
50	107 (15.5)	71 (10.2)	223 (39.5)
70	230 (33.4)	153 (22.2)	478 (69.3)
80	286 (41.5)	190 (27.6)	596 (86.4)

Table 6.3 Properties of different grades of austenitic stainless steel

Grade	*0.2% Proof stress min. N/mm² (ksi)*	*Tensile strength min. N/mm² (ksi)*	*Elongation %*	*Condition*
*304S11	180 (26.1)	480 (69.6)	40	Softened
304S15 } 304S16 }	195 (28.3)	500 (72.5)	40	Softened
304S31	195 (28.3)	500 (72.5)	40	Softened
*316S11 } *316S13 }	190 (27.6)	490 (71.1)	40	Softened
316S31	205 (29.7)	510 (74.0)	40	Softened
316S33				

* Stainless steels with a low carbon content to avoid intergranular corrosion.

Table 6.4 Properties of higher strength stainless steel plate

Grade	*0.2% Proof stress min. N/mm² (ksi)*	*1% Proof stress min. N/mm² (ksi)*	*Tensile strength min. N/mm² (ksi)*	*Elongation %*
*304S62	250 (36.3)	315 (45.7)	590 (85.6)	35
304S65	250 (36.3)	315 (45.7)	590 (85.6)	35
*316S62	270 (39.2)	340 (49.3)	620 (89.9)	35
316S66	270 (39.2)	340 (49/3)	620 (89.9)	35

* Stainless steels with a low carbon content to avoid intergranular corrosion.

Table 6.5 Mechanical properties of Duplex 2205

Grade	*0.2% Proof stress N/mm² (ksi)*	*UTS N/mm² (ksi)*	*Elongation % min.*
Duplex 2205	450–500 (65–73)	620–880 (90–128)	25–30

Table 6.6 Frequency of washing required for stainless steel architecture

Environment	*Steel type*	
	304	*316*
Coastal		6–12 months
Urban and industrial	3 months	6–12 months
Suburban and rural	Annually for aesthetic purposes	
Internal	As necessary for aesthetic purposes	

stainless steel in vats of hot dense acids and applying an anodic current, a controlled amount of metal is removed from the surface, to leave a smooth finish which facilitates cleaning.

6.4.4 Textured finishes

A wide range of patterned finishes is available. They are achieved by the rolling process to give textured appearances described as linen, pearl and mosaic finish.

Decorative colour in the form of paint, lacquer or vitreous enamel may be applied to stainless steel to produce an attractive combination of steel and colour. Nameplates, with designs etched on the steel and filled with colour, are frequently produced by this method.

6.4.5 Coloured stainless steel [12]

The inert film on the surface of stainless steel can be given colour by means of a chemical process developed by INCO (International Nickel Company, Hereford, UK) in the early 1970s, and a number of companies now manufacture coloured stainless steel under licence. The process, which is time-dependent, involves immersion of the stainless steel in a solution of chromic and sulphuric acids at a temperature a little below boiling point. There is a gradual transition in the colour developed by the film from bronze, through blue, gold, red, purple and finally to green. A water rinse followed by cathodic treatment hardens the film, which is thickened by the process from 0.02 μm (7.8×10^{-8} in) for the light colours, to 0.36 μm (14×10^{-6} in) for the dark.

The final appearance of the stainless steel is dependent upon the starting surface of the steel: bright or polished surfaces will show a high degree of metallic lustre and matt surfaces will result in matt colours. Tests carried out on the film indicate that corrosion resistance is enhanced by the process. Forming of the material after colouring will not affect the colour even on acute bends.

Architecturally there are many applications where coloured stainless steel has been used, including cladding, revolving doors, building entrances and wall panels and lifts (Figs. 6.14–6.16).

6.5 CORROSION RESISTANCE OF STAINLESS STEEL

The corrosion resistance of stainless steel is provided by a stable, inert chromium oxide film at the surface; this passive film is protective in normal or mild aqueous environments and, if damaged, immediately reforms provided that oxygen is present. A level of 10% chromium is theoretically sufficient for protection but increased levels improve the film stability, and the inclusion of nickel and molybdenum further enhances corrosion resistance.

Many atmospheric tests have been carried out on the standard grades of stainless steel, and a study of the data is particularly relevant to architectural applications as it identifies the suitability of the different grades in rural, urban, industrial and marine environments [13]. For the latter two cases, type 316 stainless steel has shown itself to be the most effective; it has also been indicated that polished surfaces are superior to matt finishes and a routine wash to remove contaminants is beneficial.

Although stainless steel performs extremely well in terms of corrosion, there are particular aspects to consider as described in the following sections.

6.5.1 Bimetallic corrosion

Dissimilar metals, when in contact in corrosive environments, require particular attention to design detail. In the electrochemical 'league table' of metals corrosion will occur in the baser of two materials in contact. However, this one fact should not be considered in isolation as the relative mass of material also has an influence. For example, a large mass of carbon steel will not be appreciably affected by contact with a small mass of stainless steel. Similarly, the use of stainless steel glazing clips (type 316) is not deleterious to aluminium with which it is in contact in greenhouses, both materials being protected by oxygen.

This form of corrosion can readily be avoided by preventing the materials from being in direct contact, for instance by using non-metallic washers.

6.5.2 Staining

In order to avoid rust staining, care must always be exercised to ensure that small particles of foreign material such as carbon steel are not lodged on the surface of stainless steel (say from the fabrication workshop).

6.5.3 Intergranular corrosion [14]

When stainless steels are heated in the range of 425–900°C (800–1650°F), as occurs in welding, it is possible for chromium in the steel to react with carbon at the grain boundaries, forming chromium carbides. This results in depletion of chromium close to the boundaries and corresponding loss of corrosion resistance. If heating in this range is to occur then this corrosion risk can readily be avoided by using low carbon grades (0.03%) of stainless steel or stainless steels where the carbon is stabilized with titanium.

6.5.4 Stress corrosion

Austenitic stainless steels, like the majority of other metals and alloys, can be susceptible to this phenomenon under very specific conditions. The problem is critical if austenitic stainless steel is operating under stress in immersed chloride conditions, such as sea water, or in atmospheres where condensation can occur and chloride is present. Typical examples are marine sites (both externally and internally) and where the temperature is in excess of 60°C (140°F). It has also been known to occur at lower temperatures in environments typified by indoor swimming pools. In both cases this type of corrosion can be avoided by proper alloy selection through the advice of a corrosion expert. There have been examples of structural collapse following corrosion of stainless steel components under such conditions, and it is advisable to carry out regular inspections at similar locations.

6.5.5 Crevice corrosion

Crevices, cracks and pockets, where matter can accumulate, can result in crevice corrosion, particularly if chlorides are present in the environment. It is therefore good practice, wherever possible, to avoid crevices or small spaces which cannot be effectively cleared.

6.6 MAINTENANCE

Stainless steel products are commonly protected for delivery by wrapping in self-adhesive plastic sheet which needs to be carefully removed on site. A cleansing agent such as alcohol, paraffin or acetone ether should be used to remove deposits. All weld scale and discolouration must be removed so that the passive surface film can reform for maximum protection, the touching up being by means of proprietary pastes.

In order to retain its pristine appearance, the surface of stainless steel should be kept clean during fabrication, and in particular free of carbon steel particles from forming tools and grinding equipment. Wire wool should never be used for cleaning stainless steel, as particles of the wire will lead to rusting of the wire and unsightly staining [15].

Externally exposed stainless finishes will be effectively cleaned by rain but sheltered areas will collect dirt and need to be cleansed with soap and water followed by water rinse and dry cloth. Dry or dusty climates require more frequent cleansing to keep a bright appearance. Oil-based stains create greater problems and should be treated by adding trichlorethane to the soap wash. If mild abrasives are used they must always be applied in a uni-directional manner, not circular or counter to existing patterning. Table 6.6 provides a guide to the frequency of washing which may be necessary for architectural applications of stainless steel [16].

6.7 SUMMARY

The effectiveness and durability of stainless steel is demonstrated by its performance: the Chrysler Building, where the top 88 m (290 ft) of the towering 320 m (1050 ft) high structure was clad with austenitic stainless steel in 1929, continues to function satisfactorily after 60 years; the Savoy canopy in London, installed four years later in 1933, today exhibits the same brightness as if it had been installed yesterday.

Stainless steel has found many applications [17] since these early days, including the cladding for accommodation modules on oil platforms operating in the North Sea, and in the nuclear industry, where reliability is of paramount importance.

The applications for stainless steel will no doubt increase rapidly with the trend to reduce maintenance and replacement costs, and where building users today have greater expectancy in terms of materials and their performance.

The material presented in this chapter has been prepared for the general information of the reader and should not be used or relied on for specific application without first securing competent advice. The Nickel Development Institute, its members, staff and consultants do not warrant its suitability for any general or specific use and assume no responsibility of any kind in connection with the information herein.

REFERENCES AND TECHNICAL NOTES

1. Smits, B.A. (1986) *Architecture – a Demanding Market for Stainless Steel*. Nickel Development Institute.
2. BS 1449 Part 2: 1983 Stainless steel and heat-resisting steel plate, sheet and strip.
3. Editor's conversation in January 1989 with Myron Wander (director: The Steel Institute of New York).
4. McGrath, R. and Frost, A. C. (1937) *Glass in Architecture and Decoration*, Architectural Press, London.
5. Hyflor Durbar, stainless steel floor plate, safe working load tables. British Steel Stainless, PO Box 161, Shepcote Lane, Sheffield S9 1TR.
6. *Stainless Steel Cold Formed Structural Design Manual*, 1974 edn. American Iron and Steel Institute (distributed by the Nickel Development Institute).
7. BS 6105: 1981 Corrosion resistant stainless steel fasteners.
8. Dier, A. F. *Interim Guide to the Design of Stainless Steel Fixings*. Stainless Steel Advisory Centre (British Steel Stainless). Excellent manuals are also available from George Clarke of Sheffield and Harris and Edgar Ltd.
9. *The Performance of Cavity Wall Tiles*, Building Research Establishment CP3 (1981), Garston, Watford, Hertfordshire, UK.
10. BS 1501 Part 3: 1990 Corrosion and heat resisting steels.
11. *American Society Metals Handbook*, 8th edn.
12. Blower, R. and Evans, T. E. *Introducing Coloured Stainless Steel – A New Product and New Process*, INCO (International Nickel Company).
13. *An Architect's Guide to Corrosion Resistance*, Nickel Development Institute (1990).
14. *Design Guidelines for the Selection and Use of Stainless Steel*, Nickel Development Institute (1987).
15. Tuthill *Fabrication and Post Fabrication Clean Up of Stainless Steel*, Nickel Development Institute.
16. *Cleaning Stainless Steel*, (1988) British Stainless Steel, PO Box 161, Sheepcote Lane, Sheffield, S9 1TR, UK.
17. *Answers for Architects*, Nickel Development Institute.

Forth Bridge – regular inspection and maintenance have helped to keep the bridge fully operational for over 100 years.

7

Nature of corrosion

Yvonne Dean

7.1 INTRODUCTION

The corrosion of ferrous metals is linked to a basic chemical cycle, smelting ores to form iron and steel and thence reversion to rust to complete the cycle. Interrupting this process by design or protective measures requires an understanding of the precise nature of corrosion. This is a topic which must be addressed by designers in any constructional field where iron and steel are employed – by marine architects in ship building, by car designers, by structural engineers in bridge and oil rig construction and by the building team. These notes are aimed at the latter, namely architect, builder, engineer, surveyor and the client, who ultimately bears the cost.

Their purpose is to familiarize designers with the basic chemistry of corrosion, the principles of preventing it, forms of protection, and maintenance, including economic considerations of initial capital costs compared with recurrent costs.

7.2 WORLD ECONOMIC FACTORS

Iron ores are still abundantly available, but the Global 2000 Report predicted that resources would run short in 90 years if consumption was held at 1974 figures [1]. The report also noted that in the mid-1970s 37% of iron production in the USA came from scrap metal, which is more difficult to purify and more prone to corrosion than metals smelted from prime ores.

A key factor in production costs is energy, high grade ores requiring 2000 kWh per tonne compared with 40 000 kWh for low grade material. The cost is even higher where impurities have to be removed from scrap. Anti-corrosion measures must therefore be seen as ways of preserving world resources of both metal and energy.

In 1984 the total annual cost of corrosion in terms of maintenance and replacement was estimated at £6000 million for the UK alone. As stated in the *Corrosion Prevention and Control Report of 1984*, 'We can no longer, either from a national or a world point of view, afford morally or economically to allow metals to revert back to the mineral compounds from which they have been so laboriously extracted' [2]. Worldwide, corrosion is estimated to waste a third of ferrous metal production. Recycling structural steel by using secondhand sections is an obvious way of saving energy. Using scrap iron and steel to replace some of the iron ore in steel production is another alternative, but this needs very careful organization to avoid contaminants which lower working strengths. In consequence, the use of scrap metal is largely restricted to the production of steel for lightweight consumer items such as cans, casings and car body shells, and the recycling of stainless steel. Structural steel is largely made from ore (the cheapest process). Good housekeeping in energy terms should see structural steel as recyclable, whether resmelted or secondhand.

7.3 THE EFFECTS OF CORROSION

The Principles of Modern Building (Vol. 1, 1959) [3] gives an excellent introduction to the topic of corrosion and this is quoted in full.

'The use of metals in building calls for special care in design, in choice of materials and in protection, if serious corrosion problems are not, sooner or later, to arise. Not only is the cost of corrosion alone extremely high, but what is perhaps even more serious is the consequent trouble and expense resulting from it. Thus the steel frame of a building may rust and in so doing crack the external cladding. If the reinforcement in concrete rusts, the surface spalls and disintegration becomes progressive. A galvanized hot-water cylinder or a cold-water cistern is perforated and has to be replaced, while incidental damage is probably caused by water leaking from the cylinder or cistern. Metal piping

Fig. 7.1 *Severe rusting of neglected ironwork at 'Usine Menier', Noisiel-sur-Marne, France, constructed in the 1870s.*

Fig. 7.2 *Corrosion of steel dowel embedded in granite.*

Fig. 7.3 *Damaged travertine blocks at the Colosseum, Rome, where rusting iron cramps, used in the 19th century, have split blocks of Roman masonry.*

and sheeting may corrode to failure in various ways and this may result in serious interruption to services.'

Ferrous corrosion requires the presence of both oxygen and water, and therefore occurs principally under damp conditions. The effects of corrosion concern not only the structural soundness of a component (Fig. 7.1), but can also lead to significant distortions and splitting of materials due to associated increases in volume of more than 100% associated with rusting (Fig. 7.2). Indirect effects, such as water penetration and staining, can be considerable. An illustration of this (Fig. 7.3) is the splitting of travertine building blocks due to corrosion of iron cramps used in the 19th century repairs of the Colosseum, Rome: until then the blocks had survived 1800 years.

7.4 CHEMISTRY OF CORROSION

7.4.1 Introduction

Like many other metals, iron and steel have a natural tendency to corrode in moist air to form oxides and, less commonly, sulphides. These compounds form a surface over the metal, and, in the case of ferrous oxide, will develop from rust spots to pitting. The process continues with wholesale lamination of the surface until the metal is totally decomposed into rust approximately two to three times as thick as the original metal. The type of rust varies according to the type of iron and steel; it is granular with cast iron but in the case of wrought iron and structural steels has a flaky form. It is possible to alloy steels with chromium or copper to produce a film which is protective. The common names for such alloyed steels are 'stainless' and 'weather resistant' steels, respectively, and these are dealt with in more detail in chapters 6 and 8.

7.4.2 Electrochemical corrosion reactions

Iron ores which form the basis of steelmaking are complex oxides, typical examples being haematite ($2[Fe_2O_3]$) and magnetite ($8[Fe_3O_4]$). Considerable energy is used to process these ores to yield molten steel, which as a result is in a thermodynamically unstable state of high energy. As the metal cools, returning to a state of lower free energy, it oxidizes in the atmosphere, combining with air and moisture to form a thermodynamically stable film of rust. It is this process which is the basis of ferrous corrosion.

There are two principal equations explaining how iron dissociates.

Firstly:

(1) $Fe \rightarrow Fe^{2+} + 2e$

Iron → iron ions + free electrons
(positive) + (negative)

Secondly:

(2) $\frac{1}{2} O_2 + H_2O + 2e \rightarrow 2OH^-$

(oxygen + water + free electrons from (1) → hydroxyl ions)

Both of these reactions give products which combine:

$Fe^{2+} + 2OH^- \rightarrow Fe(OH)_2$ (ferrous hydroxide)

This is not the final product, as further oxidation takes place to form ferric hydroxide:

$$Fe(OH)_2 + \tfrac{1}{2}O_2 + \tfrac{1}{2}H_2 \rightarrow Fe(OH)_3$$

This breaks down to a hydrated oxide FeO.OH. Rust is finally a mixture of Fe_2O_3 (ferric oxide) with Fe_3O_4 (magnetite) and the oxide FeO.OH. Rust is predominantly hydrated ferric oxide ($Fe_2O_3.H_2O$).

7.4.3 Electrochemical corrosion

Some metals corrode more readily than others, and this is related to the electrode potential (E/V), measured relative to a known standard. One standard commonly used is hydrogen, which is given a datum value of 0.00. This rates the tendency of a metal to revert back to its more natural state. Precious metals are valued for their durability because they have a low potential to change; indeed they are found in their elemental state as pure silver and gold. They need no refining and are known as noble metals with a positive measured potential. Other metals found in ores in the earth's crust and which need processing have negative potential. All these base metals have a rank order, and the more complex their ore chemistry and the more difficult they are to process, the more likely they are to revert or corrode, and the more negative their electrode potential. Common metals are listed in Table 7.1 in their order of potential.

Different ferrous metals and alloys, in particular stainless steels, have different potentials. However, for mild steel (used for strip and structural products), weather resistant steels, cast iron and wrought iron these differences are small and can be largely ignored.

7.4.4 Bimetallic corrosion

When two dissimilar metals or alloys are adjacent and in contact with moisture or some other medium which allows

Table 7.1 Electrode potential of some common metals

	Electrode potential (V)
Noble metals	
Gold	+1.42
Silver	+0.82
Copper	+0.34
Hydrogen reference	0.00
Base metals	
Lead	−0.13
Iron	−0.44
Chromium	−0.74
Zinc	−0.76
Aluminium	−1.66

the passage of electrons (and hence the flow of an electric current), the difference in potential can generate 'ions' of the metal and 'free' electrons. The metals then form a corrosion couple known as a galvanic cell, the electrons travelling from the more negative metal (anode) to the more positive metal (cathode). This can be explained in a very broad equation:

$$M \rightarrow M^{n+} + e^{n}$$

Metal → metal ions + free electrons

Base metals have this tendency to dissociate. Noble metals have the same reaction but in the opposite direction.

$$M^{n+} + e^{n} \rightarrow M$$

Free metal ions + electrons → Metal

7.4.5 Rates of corrosion

Rates of corrosion are related directly to how fast these electrochemical reactions can proceed, and they increase with higher temperatures, greater humidity and usually a steady oxygen supply – although corrosion can occur in areas that have a limited oxygen supply, such as concealed corners, or under dirt deposits. These are known as differential aeration cells.

In practical terms, real rates of corrosion are affected by climatic conditions. Dry rural areas show a slow rate of corrosion – about 0.25 microns per year in the Sudan for mild steel. This increases in wetter climates and in marine and industrial atmospheres. Average figures for the UK are about 80 μm per year, rising to 100 μm for marine and 150 μm for heavy industrial (polluted) environments. In tropical marine atmospheres such as Nigeria, this can increase to 620 microns (over half a millimetre) which is recognizable as substantial damage to a metal surface. It must be remembered that such severe conditions can be created artificially, for instance in swimming pools.

7.5 EXPOSURE PROBLEMS

Since corrosion, and hence design strategies, are related to exposure conditions, it is convenient to classify these according to whether the steelwork is external, internal, within the building envelope or in contact with other materials (metallic and non-metallic). Particular conditions will dictate whether, or what, corrosion protection will be required.

Structural steelwork in engineering structures such as bridges, cranes, pylons and towers, is normally exposed, the Forth Bridge being perhaps the most famous example. There also many examples of buildings where the structure has deliberately been located outside the building envelope, and corrosion protection is an important feature of both design and maintenance. In the case of the Eiffel Tower,

Fig. 7.4 *Bimetallic corrosion at cable fasteners.*

Fig. 7.5 *Corrosion caused by rain drips from components after seven years.*

Table 7.2 Design factors to be considered for various exposure conditions of steelwork

Exposure condition	*Design factors*	*Exposure condition*	*Design factors*
Corrosion rates for exterior steelwork are affected by rainfall, temperature and atmospheric pollution. The type of rainfall in the UK can be acidic, with typical pH values ranging from 4 to 6 compared with a neutral value of 7.0 [5].	A high standard of corrosion protection and a planned programme of inspection and maintenance is required. Exposed steelwork should be detailed to avoid water traps, promote good drainage and air circulation and provide good access for cleaning and maintenance.	Rainwater splash and snow drifting concentrate corrosion risks in a zone 150–200 mm (6–8 in) above ground in the UK and greater in extreme climate. Road salt and hostile ground salts increase corrosion risks.	Structural and strip steels should be kept clear of the ground to prevent splash reaching end fixing positions. Even structures encased in concrete are best galvanized where below or near ground level.
Different types of steel have differing corrosion resistant properties.	Protection is normally required for all steels, except stainless and weather resistant steels.	Corrosion of steel in wet contact with masonry [6] is a problem which can be intensified by dissolved acids, bases or salts and a supply of air due to porosity. This problem is made worse by rust splitting the masonry and therefore increasing weather penetration. Built-in fixings are most vulnerable. The classic example of this is corrosion of the iron ties buried in the stones of the Colosseum.	Stainless steel should be specified for bolts, masonry fixings and cavity ties. Ragged ends to wrought iron or mild steel balustrading are highly vulnerable. Traditional detailing used molten lead sockets and galvanizing. Alternative designs using face bolted lugs provide less risk and make replacement easier.
Thin material such as strip steel is without sacrificial weight and is particularly vulnerable to the effects of corrosion.	The highest standards of protection are needed and thin components are usually galvanized or manufactured in stainless steel.	Reinforcing bars in concrete are a special case of steel in contact with other materials.	Adequate cover should ensure that the steel is protected.
If steelwork remains dry, as is generally the case within the interior of heated buildings, the risk of corrosion is minimal.	It is now common practice to leave such steelwork unprotected other than the fabrication primer.	Carbonation of concrete can lead to cracking with corrosion risks for reinforcing bars at depths up to 50–60 mm (2–2½ in) in normal conditions, and 100 mm (4 in) in marine environments.	Galvanized steel reinforcement is essential for faced concrete, i.e. concrete without bitumen coating or cladding, and exposed precast work. Its use at the National Theatre has resulted in satisfactory weathering of the concrete externally [7]. Where climates are particularly hostile (industrially polluted and marine), corrosion risks to reinforcement are increased. Stainless steel reinforcement should be used in such cases.
The atmospheric condition within the building, and in particular the likelihood of condensation, is critical for internal steelwork. Lack of heating or ventilation can aggravate the risk of condensation and hence corrosion. This can be a problem in multi-purpose buildings where the uses are not determined at the design stage.	Corrosion protection is needed where moist atmospheres might occur within buildings – perhaps a good reason for leaving the frame fully exposed *internally* so that the building user takes the appropriate precautions. In aggressive conditions such as swimming pools, suspended ceilings, which not only hide steelwork but also enclose areas of potentially high condensation, are best avoided.	Direct contact between dissimilar metals in a potentially moist environment will cause bimetallic corrosion. This is so even if the metals are not very different, for instance mild steel, wrought iron and stainless steel. Pipework services are commonly black iron (heating), galvanized pipe (hot and cold services) and copper (short tails and surface work).	In general metals in contact should be identical, particularly in a moist environment such as in rainwater disposal systems. In practice coatings and insulating washers are used to separate dissimilar metals, although the risk of failure due to damage must be recognized and regular inspection is essential. The use of neutral materials, for instance plastic storage tanks, can help to minimize the problem.
In almost all buildings, some steelwork will be in contact with or penetrate the envelope. The critical zone is the interface between exterior and interior where moisture may penetrate and not be readily dispersed by natural ventilation. In addition, because ferrous metals are excellent conductors, cold bridging occurs, increasing the risk of condensation.	Careful detailing is needed to exclude weather and to avoid corrosion attack behind glands or sealant. Access facilities may be required for inspection in such areas. External coating standards or metal specification should be retained for a buffer zone of a metre or more internally, and where steel penetrates the envelope, it should be insulated for some distance back into the building.	The breakdown of substandard plated screws for exposed work, such as cladding, stairs and windows, will lead to rust spotting. This can attack below coated surfaces at screw holes and break down the protective system.	Considerable care must be taken with the specification of fixing screws.
Where drained cavities or ventilated roof spaces are employed the wet air environment in such voids raises corrosion risks.	Coating specifications need to be upgraded.		
Another critical interface is the point of contact with the ground.	Adequate corrosion protection can be achieved by encasing in 100 mm (4 in) concrete.		

Paris, which is essentially a wrought iron structure, 55 tonnes of paint are used every seven years [4].

Steelwork within buildings is clearly less vulnerable, and bare steel in turn of the century buildings such as the Ritz Hotel (1906) and Selfridges (1908) in London have shown very little corrosion to the internal steelwork. However, this may not necessarily be the case for modern construction methods. The massive masonry envelopes used in the early 1900s (450–1000 mm or 18–39 in) effectively isolated unpainted steel from the atmosphere. Thinner envelopes may not be as effective in this respect and today's thin walled structures, often devised to be rain-screens with drained cavities, constitute greater corrosion risks. Steelwork well within the building is unlikely to be affected, but where it is adjacent to or built into the building envelope some protection will be needed. The flats at Quarry Hill, Leeds, UK (built 1938–9) were constructed with primed steelwork overclad with thin precast slabs using cemented joints. Constant leaking led to corrosion of the steelwork and the flats were finally demolished some 30 years after their construction.

Steelwork in contact with certain other materials poses particular risks, including bimetallic corrosion. This has happened at Renault Swindon, UK where the elegant external stairs and escape balconies are severely corroded due entirely to severe rusting from a few cable fasteners, the run-off collecting at obtuse angles between standards and string and pitting protective coating, spoiling an otherwise perfect detail (Figs 7.4 and 7.5).

The particular design considerations to be given to the various exposure conditions are summarized in Table 7.2.

REFERENCES AND TECHNICAL NOTES

1. *The Global 2000 Report to the President* vol. 1 (1982), Penguin.
2. *Corrosion Prevention and Control Report of 1984.*
3. Fitzmaurice, R. *Principles of Modern Building* (vols 1 and 2) (1959). A useful pair of companion volumes that set down a scientific approach to building performance. HMSO.
4. Harris, J. *The Eiffel Tower* (1976) Elek.
5. *The Effects of Acid Deposition on the Terrestial Environment in the UK* (1988). Terrestial Effects Review Group, HMSO.
6. *Brick Cladding to Steel Framed Buildings* (1986) Brick Development Association, Windsor, and British Steel General Steels, Teesside. Useful analysis of masonry cladding to steelwork.
7. National Theatre Special Issue, *Architectural Review* (January 1977).

FURTHER READING

Steelwork Corrosion Protection Guides for Exterior Environments, Building Interiors. Building Refurbishment and Perimeter Walls. British Steel publication (1986).

BRE Digests
301 Corrosion of metals by wood.
121 Stainless steel as a building material.

British Standards
PD 6484: 1979 Commentary on corrosion at bi-metallic contacts and its alleviation.
BS 7361: 1991 Cathodic Protection, Part 1 Code of practice for land and marine applications.

Books
West, J. *Basic Corrosion and Oxidation* (1986) Ellis Horwood Ltd, Chichester.
Engineering Materials: An Introduction, (Unit 13), Open University Press, Milton Keynes.
Pourbaix, M. *Atlas of Equilibrium Diagrams* (1966) Pergamon Press, Oxford.

8

Anti-corrosion measures

K. A. Chandler, with contribution on weathering steels by A. K. Moores

8.1 INTRODUCTION

In most environments ordinary carbon steels will rust if unprotected. It is therefore usual to take measures to control corrosion, typically by applying some form of coating to the steel. The term 'control' is used deliberately since in most situations it is more economic to control the corrosion, accepting that maintenance will be required, rather than to use expensive methods aimed at preventing rusting completely. There are situations where long-term protection is required, particularly where access for maintenance is difficult. However, even with the best anti-corrosion measures, complete prevention of corrosion is rarely achieved unless a corrosion-resistant alloy is substituted for the normal structural steel.

Two groups of corrosion-resistant ferrous alloys are used in structures and buildings – stainless steels and weathering steels. Stainless steel (described in chapter 6) may be used for cladding, decorative features, fasteners and other specialist applications. In atmospheric environments, the molybdenum-containing stainless steels are virtually corrosion free as regards loss of steel. However, in city atmospheres some rust staining may occur and periodic washing to remove dirt from the surface may be advantageous.

Weathering steels such as Cor-Ten contain a much smaller percentage of the alloying elements used in stainless steel. While stainless steels are virtually rust free, weathering steels rust in a manner similar to that of ordinary structural steels. However, under suitable conditions the rate of corrosion is lower than for non-alloyed steels. More importantly, the rust deposit is stable and inhibits further deterioration of the metal. An economic case can be made for the use of weathering steels in certain structures because of the reduced maintenance required. However, their use in buildings is primarily as an architectural feature. There are many factors which require careful consideration and the notes in section 8.8 provide some guidance. However, designers contemplating the use of weathering steel are advised to seek specialist advice to avoid problems such as rust streaks on other building materials and unacceptable corrosion rates of the steel.

The most common form of corrosion protection for steel is to apply a coating. Specialists prefer the term 'coatings' to 'finishes', since the latter normally refers to the final surface treatments and does not describe the factory preparation or primers which are so important in building up an effective protection. Corrosion occurs because of a reaction between the steel and its environment, in particular moisture and oxygen. The principle of protection by coatings is to form a barrier between the steel and its environment. However, in practice, this is not necessarily a simple matter. Although the coating material is important, it is only one of a number of factors to be considered. Surface preparation and selection of the type, thickness and combination of coatings in relation to exposure conditions are all important aspects and must be considered in relation to cost, both capital and recurrent.

Less common anti-corrosion measures include cathodic protection and the use of chemical water treatments – known as inhibitors – in water systems. The latter method has little application with regard to the structural elements of buildings, except where water-filled tubes are employed to achieve the necessary fire resistance. Inhibitors are then used to control corrosion of the interior surfaces of the tubes.

The principles of electrochemical corrosion, which were described in chapter 7, can be used to protect steelwork. In this process it is the anode which is attacked and the cathode which is protected. In practice this protection can be achieved by deliberately connecting the steel to another less noble metal in the galvanic series, such as magnesium, aluminium or zinc. This will become the anode of the corrosion cell and corrode in preference to the steel (cathode). This is called 'sacrificial protection' since the steel is protected while another metal is sacrificed. An alternative method is to connect the steel to the 'cathode' of a supply of electricity. This is known as an 'impressed current system'.

Cathodic protection is widely used for ships, pipelines and other submerged structures but is not generally applicable to atmospheric situations.

Whatever method of protection is adopted, design details can have a marked effect on its performance. This aspect, together with detailed consideration of coating systems and weathering steel, are discussed in this chapter.

8.2 DESIGN

Sometimes slight changes in design can result in a marked improvement in the life of a coating. Typical design aspects to be considered are:

(a) Access for repainting, in particular the ability to reach all the steelwork for cleaning and coating application.
(b) Avoidance of situations where structural members, for instance channels, might collect water and hence reduce the life of many types of coating. Often suitable drainage holes can be used to overcome the problem.
(c) Avoidance, where practicable, of crevices and similar narrow spaces between members. These are almost impossible to clean and repaint. Where appropriate suitable filling with mastic or welding of cover plates can be used to overcome the problem.

8.3 SURFACE PREPARATION OF STEEL

All materials should be cleaned of surface dirt and grease before painting. In the case of hot-rolled steel, iron oxides, usually called millscale, are present on the surface. The scale is easily cracked and then becomes detached from the steel. Any rusting undermines the scale which, although apparently adherent, is likely to flake off over a period of time. Consequently, if coatings are applied over millscale then flaking may well occur. Rust is also a poor surface on which to apply coatings, so for long-term performance coatings should be applied to clean steel.

8.3.1 Initial preparation

Degreasing is an essential element in the cleaning process of steel and is carried out prior to other cleaning operations. Organic solvents such as white spirit or emulsion cleaners are widely used. Details of the methods used are provided in British Standard CP 3012:1972 'Cleaning and preparation of metal surfaces' [1].

Manual cleaning includes all methods using hand or power operated tools. These include wire brushing, grinding, sanding, impacting and chiselling. They are useful for removing heavy deposits before blast cleaning and may be the only practicable method of cleaning during maintenance. They are not effective in removing tight millscale or adherent rust from the steel surface and are therefore not recommended for new steelwork except possibly where the steel is to be exposed in dry, warm interior situations.

8.3.2 Blast cleaning

Blast cleaning is the method commonly used to clean heavy sections prior to the application of organic coatings. The process consists basically of propelling abrasive onto the surface at a speed sufficient to remove rust and scale. The process results in the roughening of the steel surface. This may be advantageous in improving adhesion of coatings applied to the surface but problems may arise if the steel is roughened too much. The degree of roughness is termed 'surface profile'. Methods of measuring this are available but it is more common to make an assessment using specially prepared comparators, which are available from various suppliers.

There are three general processes for blast cleaning: centrifugal blasting, air blast cleaning and vacuum blast cleaning.

Centrifugal blasting uses a series of impellers placed in a cabinet. Abrasive is thrown by centrifugal force onto the steelwork. This method is particularly suited to relatively simple shapes. The abrasives are commonly steel shot or grit or a mixture of the two. Small portable models are available and these are particularly useful for large flat surfaces.

Air blast cleaning uses compressed air to blow the abrasive onto the surface through a nozzle which may be contained within a cabinet. It can also be used for site work using expendable abrasives such as slags. This method may be adapted to allow water injection so that the abrasive is carried in a jet of water. This has advantages, particularly during maintenance cleaning, because soluble salts are removed more effectively.

Vacuum blast cleaning is carried out with specially designed equipment which collects used abrasive and recirculates it after screening. Although slow, it reduces the hazards of dust and abrasives contaminating the air during on-site cleaning.

8.3.3 Acid pickling

Acid pickling is used to clean steel by immersion in a bath of inhibited acid followed by thorough rinsing. The acid does not dissolve the rust and scale but attacks the steel surface so allowing scale to lift from the steel. The inhibitors in the bath ensure that the attack on the steel is strictly limited. It is used for sheet steel treated in a continuous process and for structural sections prior to hot-dip galvanizing.

8.3.4 Specifications for cleanliness

For some coatings, the steelwork may have to be completely cleaned of all rust and scale. However, this is expensive and a less-than-perfect surface, say 95% of all scale and rust evenly removed, is acceptable for most coatings. The most common method of checking the cleanliness of blast-cleaned steel is to compare the cleaned surface with a series of pictorial standards. These are produced by the Swedish Standards Institution in Swedish Standard SIS 05 59 00:1976 [2]. This is now the basis for an International Standard ISO 8501/1 [3]. A British Standard, BS 4232:1967 [4], which is based on percentages of rust and scale remaining on the surface of steel after blast cleaning, is less widely used.

The Swedish Standard defines various classifications of cleaned surface. For blast cleaning the standard specified is commonly Sa2½, which indicates a near perfect surface. Sa3 is used for some metal coatings and paints but is not commonly specified. Sa2 indicates a surface less clean than Sa2½ and is sometimes specified but generally costs little less than Sa2½.

The standards for manual cleaning are prefixed 'St' in the Swedish Standard but have only limited value.

8.4 PAINT COATINGS

Paints are the most widely used coatings for steelwork. Their basic constituents are binder, pigment and solvent. Other constituents such as driers, extenders and anti-skinning agents are included to modify the properties or to improve application.

The binder forms the film which binds the pigments into the dry coating. It is the main contributor to the durability of the coating and provides the required physical and mechanical proprties. It generally varies from 20% to 50% by weight of the liquid paint. There are various types of binder, such as alkyd or epoxy, and these names are often used to describe the type of paint.

The pigment consists of small particles which provide the colour and opacity of the dry film. It has some effect on reducing permeability. Pigments may be inhibitive, for instance red lead, and these may be included in the coating applied directly to the steel surface. Other pigments, such as micaceous iron oxide (MIO), may consist of particles with a flake or lamellar shape and these may improve the durability of the film. In decorative top coats pigments are usually inert. The pigment typically varies from 15% to 60% in the paint film, although zinc-rich paint containing over 90% of zinc as a pigment is widely used as a primer.

Solvents do not influence the protective value of the paint but are important constituents with regard to application. The amount should be kept low but 5% to 40% by weight may be present. The type of solvent used depends on the binder.

8.4.1 Paint systems

Most paint coatings are applied in a series of separate coats although some thick coatings may be applied in a single application. The total system is made up of three different types of paint coating – primer, undercoat and finishing coat. These are in addition to any blast primer applied immediately after blast cleaning to protect the steel during fabrication. Blast primers are not considered as part of the total coating system, as they are relatively thin – typically 20 microns (less than 1 thou) and add little to the protective value.

The priming coat (or primer) is the coat applied to the steel and may contain inhibitive pigments. Zinc phosphate is now widely used. The function of the primer is essentially to provide an adherent foundation for subsequent coats.

Undercoats are used to build up the total thickness of the coating system. They usually contain inert pigments. In some systems there is no essential difference between priming and undercoats.

The finishing coat, also called the 'top coat' or 'weather coat', serves to protect the whole system. It is often decorative with a gloss finish.

8.4.2 Classification of paints

There are various ways of classifying paints but probably the most useful is by the type of binder. For architectural purposes, the main paints can be classified as follows:

Oil drying type

These are the commonest types of paint and are easily applied. They dry by oxidation processes and contain synthetic resins and oil. Pure drying oil binders are rarely used. Principal paints in the group are: alkyd, silicon alkyd, tung oil phenolic and epoxy ester. The choice from within this group will be determined by cost, decorative requirements and durability. Alkyds can be applied to steel which has not been cleaned to the highest standard, has reasonably good durability, good appearance and can be easily maintained. Silicon alkyds have superior durability and gloss retention but are more expensive than alkyds. All alkyds are available in a range of colours. Tung oil phenolics are not decorative but are somewhat superior to alkyds in durability, particularly when pigmented with micaceous iron oxide.

Epoxy esters, despite their name, are similar to alkyds and are not a cheap form of epoxy coating. Sometimes used as primers with more decorative coatings, they tend to chalk on exterior exposure but form a hard coating with better chemical resistance than alkyds.

From this group of paints, alkyds will most commonly be selected for decorative purposes and tung oil phenolics for situations where appearance is less important than durability. All the paints can be applied by brush, which may be useful for smaller sections, or by spray.

Solvent evaporation type

Unlike the oil drying group which dry by oxidation, paints in this group rely purely on evaporation of the solvent to dry. Basically, the binder is dissolved in a solvent so that when this evaporates a protective dry film is left on the steel surface. The oldest paints of this type are the bituminous, which are used mainly for immersed conditions. For atmospheric use there are three types of paint in this group: chlorinated rubber, vinyl and acrylated rubber. These paints are more durable than the oil drying types and are widely used where chemical resistance is required. They are available in a range of colours but are not as decorative as the alkyds. Although special formulations are available for brush application, they are generally sprayed.

Chemical cured

These paints, unlike those above, are made up of two components, which are mixed before application, and they are generally called two-pack materials. There are two main types, epoxy and urethane. They can be applied to much greater thicknesses than either oil drying or solvent evaporation types and are more expensive. They are used for the most aggressive corrosion situations such as offshore structures but, because of their durability, may be appropriate for some buildings. A high standard of surface preparation is required and, because of the hardness of the coating, they may require abrading before repainting. Epoxies tend to chalk in atmospheric situations and urethanes are much better in this respect.

Cheaper versions containing coal tar or pitch, for instance coal tar epoxy, are widely used for immersed conditions but are rather unattractive and hence unsuitable for most atmospheric situations.

Moisture cured urethane

This particular paint falls into a separate category. Although it is a single pack material, it dries in a different way from oil drying or solvent evaporation paints. It relies on atmospheric moisture to complete the drying reaction, so has something in common with the two-pack materials in that it cures chemically. The dry film retains its gloss well and is hard. This leads to the same problems of overpainting as with the two-pack materials. Because of the way it cures, moisture cured urethane can be applied to surfaces which are slightly damp and is particularly useful for maintenance painting.

8.4.3 Paint application

Paints can be applied by a number of different processes such as dipping, flow coating and rolling. However, for structures and buildings, application is usually by brush or spray. There are two types of spray application, air and airless. With conventional air spray, compressed air is used both to atomize the paint and to carry it to the steel surface. A considerable amount of air is required and this leads to some inefficiency with overspray, particularly when spraying in the open. In airless spraying the paint is forced through a small jet by means of a pump, so it is capable of a faster rate of spray with less loss of paint by overspray. Spraying by this method can produce spray rates up to twice that of air spraying.

Although brush application is slow and may achieve no more than 20% of the rate for spraying it has advantages. It is cheap, allows paint to be worked into crevices and will displace a certain amount of dust and moisture from the steel surface. It is particularly useful for minor touch-up work.

8.4.4 Plastic and powder coatings

Two broad groups of resins or polymers are used for powders to produce what are commonly called plastic coatings. These are thermoplastic polymers which can be heated without chemical change, and thermosetting polymers which, when heated, produce a permanent chemical change. Common polymers in the two groups are:

Thermoplastic – PVC (polyvinyl chloride), nylon and polyethylene.
Thermosetting – phenolics, epoxides and polyesters.

Although fairly large sections of steel can be coated with powder coatings, the most common use of the material is for components and smaller units. They are comparatively expensive to apply and problems arise where welding is required. The welded area, after cleaning, is often coated with an air drying paint, which tends to perform less well than the main plastic coating. Nevertheless, if properly applied, they can provide durable coatings for steel and may well be considered for special features such as balustrades.

8.5 METAL COATINGS

For structures and buildings, the only metal coatings used for anti-corrosion purposes are zinc, aluminium and cadmium. A number of coatings such as chromium, nickel and brass may be used but these are decorative rather than protective coatings.

8.5.1 Zinc coating

Zinc is by far the most commonly used of these coatings and it can be applied in four different ways – hot-dipping, spraying, diffusion (or sheradizing) and electrodeposition.

(a) In the *hot-dipping process*, the steel is first cleaned by acid pickling and then immersed in a bath of molten zinc. A reaction occurs producing a series of iron-zinc (Fe-Zn) layers as a coating with a zinc or zinc-rich surface. This method is used for steel sections, balustrades, fasteners and pipes. Sheet steel is also coated by hot-dipping, in a continuous process.
(b) *Spraying* can be used on steel which has been blast cleaned. Zinc, in the form of powder or wire, is fed through a nozzle of a spray gun with a stream of air or gas and is melted by a suitable gas-oxygen mixture. The melted particles are then sprayed onto the steel surface. The coating is porous but can be applied to a sufficient thickness to provide a coating comparable in protective qualities with the hot-dipped coating.
(c) *Diffusion* is achieved by mixing the components to be coated with zinc powder and heating to just below the melting point of zinc. This process is called sherardizing and produces a thin Fe-Zn coating which exhibits rust

staining if exposed to the atmosphere. It is widely used for nuts and bolts, which are usually subsequently painted.

(d) *Electrodeposition* provides thin coatings to components and fasteners which should be painted if exposed outdoors.

8.5.2 Other metal coatings

Aluminium is usually applied to steelwork by spraying, although there are processes for hot-dipping. However, this is usually carried out on sheet or comparatively small steel items.

Cadmium is sometimes applied as an electrodeposited coating for small items.

8.5.3 Durability of metal coatings

The durability of metal coatings is determined mainly by the thickness of the coating and the environment to which it is exposed. The method of application is important because there is a limit to the amount of zinc which can be applied by a particular mthod. Typical thicknesses are shown in Table 8.1.

The 'life' will be determined by the environment. Typical loss rates for zinc are shown in Table 8.2.

In severely aggressive environments rates will be higher. The figures indicate that, while a hot-dipped coating might well last 50 years in a rural atmosphere, this could be reduced to only 10 years in an industrial environment. Sherardized and electrodeposited coatings will last only a short time in all environments. Aluminium coatings generally last longer than zinc.

Table 8.1 Typical thicknesses of metal coatings

Hot-dip galvanizing	75–125 μm (3–5 thou) 250 μm (10 thou) if steel first blast cleaned (on sheet about 25 μm or 1 thou)
Sheradizing	10–40 μm (0.4–1.6 thou)
Electrodeposited	2–25 μm (0.1–1 thou)
Sprayed	100–200 μm (4–8 thou)

Table 8.2 Loss rates for zinc coatings

Unpolluted (rural)	2 μm (0.1 thou)/year
Marine	5 μm (2 thou)/year
Industrial	10 μm (4 thou)/year

8.5.4 Overpainting metal coatings

Although galvanized steel may be left exposed without further protection, it is often painted to provide a long life coating system. When painting new hot-dip galvanized coatings, problems of adhesion may arise and to prevent premature flaking the following alternative preparations should be considered:

(a) Lightly blast clean the galvanized surface to provide a mechanical key.

(b) Apply a solution of T-wash, a non-proprietary formulation obtainable from many paint companies. The solution, basically phosphoric acid, contains a small quantity of copper carbonate. This provides a method of checking that the wash has reacted properly: if the surface is not black, then further treatment is required.

(c) Two-pack etch primers of a suitable type can be applied to the surface.

(d) Calcium plumbate primer (BS 3698 [5]) may be applied, although this method is not widely used.

If freshly galvanized steel is allowed to weather in the atmosphere for a short period before painting, this usually overcomes the problem of adhesion of the paint.

Sprayed metal coatings can be painted but sealing is generally preferred. The sealer impregnates the pores and produces a smoother surface. A range of materials, for instance epoxies, is available. The sealer is usually applied at the works where the metal spraying is carried out.

8.6 OTHER COATINGS

Various stoved coatings may be used for panels and cladding on buildings. These may be flat or profiled and if correctly applied to well designed components can provide satisfactory protection. They are basically finishes of the type used on cars and domestic appliances and are not suitable for the larger structural members. They are produced in factories and require stoving at 120–150°C (250–300°F).

Vitreous enamel has an almost indefinite life but is expensive and the brittle coating is easily damaged by impact. It is then virtually impossible to repair to the original decorative appearance. The coating is produced by fusing glass onto the steel coating at high temperatures. It is both decorative and scratch resistant and is particularly appropriate for panels etc.

A range of pre-coated steel sheets is available for cladding and roofing of buildings. The most common for corrosion resistant purposes are the PVC plastisols applied to strip and coil and cut into sheets which are generally profiled. Polyvinylidene fluoride coating is corrosion resistant provided it is uniform and non-porous, but it is thin and can be easily damaged. Chapter 5 provides further details.

8.7 PERFORMANCE AND WEATHERING

The life of a metal (particularly zinc) can be predicted with some accuracy based on the considerable number of tests which have been carried out in a range of environments. However, it is far more difficult to predict the life of organic coatings since the coating itself is only one factor. Surface preparation, application procedures, conditions in the workshop and thickness all have significant effects on the life of such systems. Furthermore, most organic coatings do not last for the life of the building or structure and maintenance repainting will be required, possibly a number of times. However, the durability of the air drying paint coatings can be classified as follows:

Most durable – epoxides, urethane, chlorinated rubber, vinyls.
Least durable – alkyds, phenolic-modified.

This does not necessarily take into account appearance. For example, a system pigmented with micaceous iron oxide may be selected but to improve the appearance a decorative alkyd may be applied as a finishing coat. To maintain the high gloss appearance may be more important than the overall durability of the system, so maintenance repainting may be carried out even though the system is still providing adequate corrosion protection.

Few data have been published on the anticipated life of paint coatings and, where it has been, it is necessarily of a general nature. Few British Standards have been produced for paints, so generic descriptions such as chlorinated rubber coatings may not clearly define the material.

BS 5493:1977 [6] classifies the degree of exposure into broad groups. These include exterior conditions categorized as polluted or non-polluted and inland or coastal, and interior conditions categorized as dry or frequently damp. The Standard provides some indication of the performance to be anticipated from different types of paint coating. Although the lives quoted are not accepted by all authorities, they do nevertheless provide some useful information because they indicate the influence of surface preparation, thickness and environment on the life of a coating system. For instance, on blast-cleaned steel, a drying oil type of paint system, such as an alkyd, of about 180 μm (7 thou) is considered likely to last 5–10 years before maintenance in an inland unpolluted environment. To achieve this life in a polluted atmosphere, the thickness must be increased to over 200 μ (8 thou). If the paint system is applied to manually cleaned steel, then the life drops to less than five years.

Although all specifiers of paint systems are naturally interested in the life of such systems, it would be misleading to provide generalized tables of lives for different systems without going into a great deal of further detail. The paint companies are the best source of such information.

8.8 COSTS

The initial costs of various coating systems can be obtained without much difficulty. However, these figures are fairly meaningless unless the performance of the system is related to both the initial and overall costs. If all stages of the application process are carried out correctly, then some broad indication of the potential life can be predicted. A cost comparison can then be made but the costs of maintenance repainting must be taken into account. For many durable coatings the preparation, application and maintenance costs may be higher than for the less durable oil-type drying systems.

Cost comparisons for paint should relate to the dry film thickness/unit area covered rather than the price per unit volume of wet paint. Paints generally have a solid content of 40%–50% (vol/vol) but if it is much lower then more paint will be required to achieve the required thickness.

8.9 MAINTENANCE

Maintenance repainting is carried out for two principal reasons, namely to preserve the structural integrity of the steelwork so that it performs its function satisfactorily over the required life, and to maintain the appearance.

Strictly speaking, only the first is concerned with anti-corrosion measures but the question of appearance cannot be discounted. A considerable amount of rusting can occur before the structural integrity is necessarily affected, so there is often no clear distinction between decorative and anti-corrosion painting. However, where the coating system is protecting the steelwork adequately, but the appearance is poor, additional painting may be required purely for decorative purposes. This should be taken into account when selecting coating systems and estimating costs.

Surveys of buildings and structures have shown that a good deal of maintenance painting is carried out in a fairly haphazard manner. Areas with over 30 coats of paint are found whereas other parts are rusting with only the remnants of the most recently applied coating present. Maintenance repainting is expensive and may be carried out many times on long-life structures. It is therefore advisable to have a clear strategy for repainting. The most expensive part of the maintenance is usually the surface preparation so it is clearly advantageous to carry out repainting before a considerable amount of preparation work is required. It is possible to plan maintenance to take this into account on new structures. On older ones the quality of the repaint will be determined to a large extent by the history of maintenance procedures over the life of the structure.

If the steel is badly rusted and the paintwork is in very poor condition, it may be impossible to bring the steelwork up to standard without removing the whole of the coating, cleaning off the rust and repainting all the steelwork.

8.10 SELECTION OF COATING SYSTEMS

The selection of coating systems is based upon a number of factors, of which the following are usually the most fundamental:

(a) Environment – generally the standard of surface preparation and the coating will be influenced by the severity of the exposure conditions.
(b) Durability – this is important but is not always the determining factor in the choice of coating. The most durable coatings may be considered unnecessarily expensive for many situations.
(c) Access for maintenance is important. Where access is either difficult or impossible, then coatings of the highest durability must be considered.
(d) Type of structure or building will influence the choice of coatings. Metal coatings such as zinc may well be considered for industrial situations.
(e) Appearance – this will influence the choice of the finishing coat, which in turn may have an effect on the overall selection.
(f) Costs are always important. Although lifetime costs should be considered, maintenance may not be the responsibility of the group concerned with the initial protection.
(g) Experience is an important factor and will influence the choice between alternative systems.

8.11 WEATHERING STEELS

Weather resistant steels are structural steels which have better corrosion resistance than ordinary carbon steel due to the inclusion of relatively small quantities of alloying metals, particularly nickel, chromium and molybdenum, typically about 2%–3%. They were first produced in the USA during the 1930s and 1940s under the brand name Cor-Ten. In 1968 a new specification was issued which provided higher strength and enhanced weathering features. In the UK weathering steels are produced in accordance with BS 4360 [7] in grades WR50A, B and C.

8.11.1 Performance and weathering of weathering steels

Under normal conditions weathering steel will initially rust, forming a thin but dense oxide coating. With time, and depending on the environment and degree of exposure, this surface patina becomes tightly adherent to the metal thus reducing the subsequent rate of oxidization. During this development the steel undergoes a progressive darkening from light yellow/brown through to a final colour, normally some shade of brown to dark purplish chocolate, depending upon the exposure conditions. In mild marine atmospheres a grey colour has been observed. There is now sufficient evidence to be able to state that at any particular location the final weathered colour will be consistent throughout, provided adequate precautions have been taken.

During weathering the surface texture of the scale also changes and the appearance of the steel may go through stages where it is loose, unevenly coloured and often marked by salt concentration marks. The time taken for weather resistant steels to develop a stable patina is therefore an important consideration. Where rainfall is light and seasonal, with frequent wetting and drying cycles, it is reasonable to assume that the patina will form in less than two years. In dry, arid areas or in very sheltered conditions, weathering will take place very slowly.

There is no simple way of accelerating consistent patina development, although small concentrations of corrosive material in the atmosphere may help. However, heavier concentrations such as sulphates from flue gases can be a hazard, causing staining and discolouration, and weathering steels immersed in water, exposed to chloride pollution or buried in soil behave in a similar manner to ordinary mild steel.

Steel exposed to differing degrees of exposure, humidity or atmospheric pollution may show inconsistencies in texture and colour. In the northern hemisphere exposed southern and western facades will normally weather and form a patina faster than those on northern and eastern facades. They usually develop a darker even patina, although this does not necessarily occur if the building is extensively sheltered. A heated building can accelerate the wet/dry sequence in the exposed frame due to heat transfer and this can benefit patina colouring. These factors influencing the variability of weathering call for considerable care in design and detailing.

8.11.2 Detailed advice on preparation and protection

Surface preparation requirements are similar to those for normal steel, namely the removal of millscale and grease; in addition, any paint marks must be removed. Weathering steels have to be more carefully handled to avoid scratches. Cleaning is by shot-blasting carried out on site after erection. Acid treatment is not recommended as this may cause severe corrosion in crevices or pockets.

A simple test for the effectiveness of cleaning methods is to wet the steel surface after cleaning. A uniform light yellow oxide should appear within 24 hours on all areas which have been satisfactorily cleaned. Areas which still contain millscale, residual grease, or oily patches will retain the original colour or become mottled.

It is important in the early stages of patina development to prevent scuffing and marking of the steel since even finger marking can delay patina development.

8.11.3 Design details

When weathering steels are used in buildings, the surface should be considered as any other architectural finish, with the same attention to detail. Detailing must allow for weathering. Drips, crevices, ledges, upstands and gutters or areas of steel which are subject to wetting for longer periods than other areas of the work may become streaked and unsightly for some considerable time, inhibit the formation of a stable patina, and cause increased long-term corrosion.

The initial rusting produces a scale containing gelatinous or soluble salts which are washed down with natural weathering. The degree of scale loss depends on the environment. Until such time as a stable rust film has formed, staining can occur on the steel and other materials such as concrete plinths, glazing, sills etc. Selection of compatible materials and attention to detailing are therefore of great importance if staining is to be minimized. Glazed tiles and bricks and some polished stone slabs are less likely to stain than other building elements. Glass is a special case, and wash down of corrosive products onto glass can make the surfaces extremely difficult to clean.

Marking and staining of the steel and other building components can be minimized by an appreciation of the way in which rainwater and dirt wash down the building face. Regular run-off paths should be predicted and dealt with by directing the run-off, particularly at junctions between horizontal and vertical members. Good detailing practice, for instance in avoiding non-draining pockets, should be adopted.

During patina development it is likely that occasional sweeping away of quantities of rust lying at the base of steel structures will be required.

Fasteners, such as bolts and welds, have to be compatible with the weathered steel to ensure consistent corrosion behaviour. Welding presents no difficulty provided the finished work is ground down to remove flux and slag.

8.11.4 Rate of corrosion

The rate of corrosion, as distinct from the initial weathering process to form the patina, varies according to climate and level of atmospheric pollution, particularly sulphur dioxide. It is claimed that serious corrosion of weathering steel only occurs when humidity is above 70% and even then only when the atmosphere is appreciably polluted. However, corrosion can occur at lower humidities when certain salts, particularly chlorides, are present, such as in a marine environment. Air samples should be taken where pollution risks exist, the following being critical zones:

(a) Industrial atmospheres containing high concentrations of corrosive fumes.
(b) Coastal areas subject to salt air, spray or salt laden fog.
(c) Applications where the steel is continuously submerged or buried in soil.

In the USA records of tests on corrosion rates are available over a 25 year period showing corrosion rates for rural, industrial and marine environments. UK tests also exist but for a much shorter period. On this basis it would appear that the corrosion rate would slow down significantly with overall losses of 134 μm (5.28 thou) after 25 years compared with 114 μm (4.5 thou) after the same period in US atmospheres classified on the same basis. These corrosion rates are given for guidance and advice should be sought from steel suppliers on more recent research data.

In view of the above one should be cautious before specifying weathering steel for thin sections, or when steel is not exposed to normal weathering such as steelwork contained in cavity wall construction when the corrosion rate could be high. Cladding in weathering steel appears to be very vulnerable to continued corrosion and has had to be painted after 15 years use in housing at Charleroi (Belgium) and the Transport Museum, Lucerne (Switzerland).

Corrosion can be aggravated by physical abrasion of the surface, for instance by ladders or maintenance cradles that scrape away the patina. Human contact can also wear away the surface of weathering steels, so that colonnades or entries may have to be detailed to isolate pedestrian routes from the structure. In some cases weathering steels have been painted in such situations to prevent complaints from the public and to protect steel at vulnerable locations.

8.11.5 General points relating to weathering steel

Weldable weathering steels are available in structural sections and are only slightly more expensive than for normal grades of structural steel. However, there may be problems of supply since mills will only consider orders over 500 tonnes due to the disruption to standard production. These steels are not suitable for use in all atmospheres and it is essential for designers to obtain expert advice.

Weathered steel has been described as a handsome architectural finish, finely textured, and of earthy colour, blending in well with settings. In order to obtain the best results it is apparent that serious consideration must be given to the environment, location and use of the building or structure. This, together with good planning and detailing, can provide an attractive structure with low maintenance costs.

Amongst the best examples of the use of weathering steel are the Court of Justice, Luxembourg described in chapter 36 (case study 36.2.1), and John Winter's House in Highgate London, UK.

REFERENCES AND TECHNICAL NOTES

1. British Standard CP 3012:1972 Cleaning and preparation of metal surfaces.
2. Swedish Standards Institution in Swedish Standard SIS 05 59 00:1976. Pictorial surface preparation standard for painting steel surfaces. Swedish Standard Institution, Stockholm (available from British Standards Institution, Milton Keynes).
3. International Standard ISO 8501/1: 1988 Preparation of steel substrates before application of paints and related products. Part 1: Rust grades and preparation grades of uncoated steel substrates and of steel substrates after overall removal of previous coverings.
4. British Standard, BS 4232:1967 (now withdrawn) Surface finish of blast-cleaned steel for painting.
5. British Standard, BS 3698: 1964 (1979) Calcium plumbate priming paints.
6. BS 5493:1977, Code of Practice for Protective Coatings of Iron and Steel Structures against Corrosion, British Standards Institution (includes list of relevant standards concerned with the corrosion protection of steelwork).
7. BS 4360: 1990 Weldable structural steels.
8. Technical studies in the *Architects'Journal* (weathering steels).

FURTHER READING

Steel Structures Painting Manual, vols. 1 and 2 (1982) Steel Structures Painting Council, Pittsburgh, USA.

Chandler, K. A. and Bayliss, D. A. (1985) *Corrosion Protection of Steel Structures*, Elsevier Applied Science Publishers, London and New York.

Munger, C. E. (1986) *Corrosion Prevention by Protective Coatings*, National Association of Corrosion Engineers, Houston, USA.

Introduction to Paint Technology (1967), Oil and Colour Chemists Association, London.

The Anti-Corrosion Handbook and Directory (1987), Sawell Publications, London, provides lists of suppliers and contractors for anti-corrosion measures.

Corrosion Protection Guides for Steelwork in Exterior Environments, Building Interiors, Building Refurbishment and Perimeter Walls. British Steel General Steels, Teesside.

The drama of a real building fire.

9

Fire protection

J. T. Robinson

9.1 INTRODUCTION

It is almost impossible to comprehend the awesome horror of a major building fire without personal experience of the speed at which it can spread, the rapid build up of heat, and the panic that is generated by impenetrable choking smoke (Fig. 9.1). It would be a grave moral and ethical error to regard fire safety requirements as an imposition on aesthetic or functional freedom. Indeed fire safety must be regarded as a major priority at the design stage.

Although the objective of this chapter is to illustrate the means of achieving satisfactory performance of structural steel in fire there many aspects of fire safety which must concern the designer. By far the greatest proportion of fatalities in fires is due to inhalation of smoke and so a prime priority must be to minimize the risk of such exposure. Designing buildings so that people can move rapidly away from the site of a fire is an obvious first step, and provisions for means of escape are laid down by regulations. However, designers should ensure that escape routes are easily accessible and clearly signed, particularly in public buildings such as shops, where people may be unfamiliar with the layout. Under these circumstances there is a natural tendency to leave by the same route as was used to enter the building rather than seek alternative, and possibly safer, exits.

Fig. 9.1 *The effect of burning wood and plastic.*

Whenever possible, the internal building space should be divided into compartments by fire resisting floors, walls and fire doors to contain any outbreak of fire which may occur and to limit the spread of smoke and flame.

Responsible building designers should seriously consider additional measures, including sprinklers, smoke control systems, detectors and non-combustible furnishings.

9.1.1 Sprinklers

Sprinklers are a well established means of fire control which come into operation only when fire breaks out. Their action not only helps to extinguish fires, limit fire spread and reduce smoke, but also reduces the ambient temperature, thus limiting structural damage, destruction of contents and consequential losses. Although particularly advisable in large open areas, their installation in almost any building will improve life safety and will attract premium discounts from insurance companies for these reasons.

9.1.2 Smoke control

Serious consideration should be given to smoke control measures in large populated open spaces such as atria and shopping malls. Provision of smoke reservoirs, vertical barriers at ceiling level and heat sensitive vents will limit the spread of smoke, improve visibility and assist escape. Today, computer models are available to assist effective design by predicting smoke movement.

9.1.3 Detectors

Early warning of ignition can be provided by smoke and heat detectors in order to maximize escape time and to help to ensure early intervention of the fire-fighting services. Although detection devices have suffered a somewhat tarnished reputation for false alarms in the past, systems are being developed which have much improved reliability.

9.1.4 Non-combustible furnishings

Unfortunately many modern materials, particularly those used in furnishing, generate large volumes of hot, dense and toxic smoke. Whenever possible, materials chosen for finishes and furnishing should be non-combustible or at least have limited spread of flame characteristics.

All of these measures will help to limit loss in the event of a fire. However, prevention is preferable to containment and any action which reduces the risk is of benefit in this respect. It seems contradictory that smoking is permitted in public areas, even though it is often the cause of the most dreadful fires, such as the Kings Cross Underground disaster in 1987. Although the London Passenger Transport Authority had forbidden smoking on trains they did not extend the ban to the station areas until *after* the catastrophe.

9.2 BUILDING REGULATIONS

Buildings in the UK are generally required to comply with Building Regulations which are mainly concerned with personal safety. The provisions of Approved Document B of the Regulations [1] deal with structural fire precautions and are aimed at reducing the danger to people who are in or around a building when a fire occurs. This is achieved by containing the fire and ensuring the stability of the structure for sufficient time to allow everyone to reach safety.

It is the requirement for structural stability which calls for special attention when steel is used for the structural framework, and it is this aspect which is considered in greater detail in this chapter.

9.2.1 Fire resistance

The strength of all materials reduces as their temperature is increased. Steel is no exception (Fig. 9.2). It is, of course, important that in building fires the structure should not weaken to the extent that collapse occurs prematurely whilst the occupants are seeking to make their way to safety. For this reason it is necessary for designers to provide a degree of 'fire resistance' to the structures that they build.

Fire resistance is expressed in the Building Regulations in units of time, ½ h, 1 h, 1½ h, 2 h and 4 h. It is important to recognize that these times are not allowable escape times for

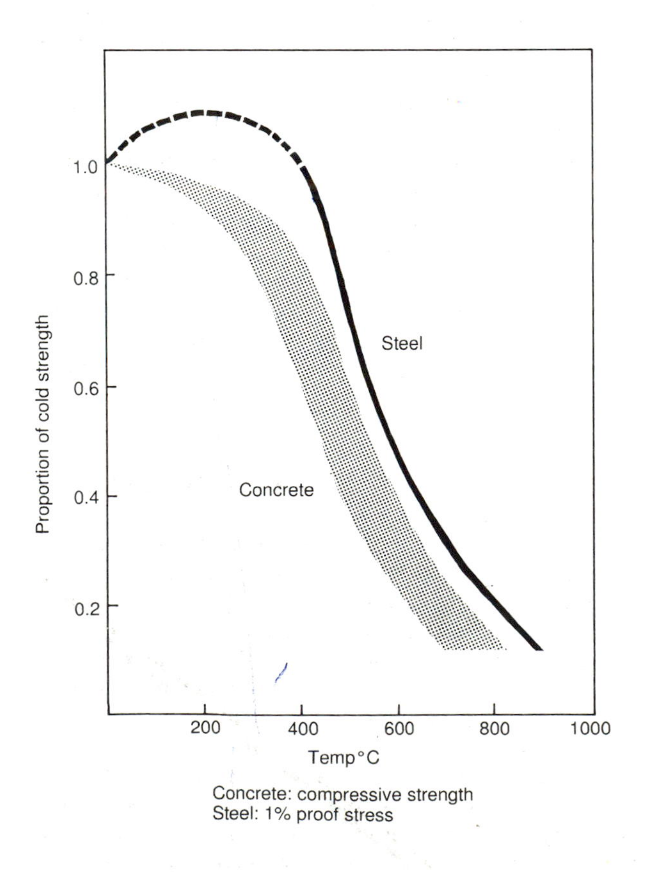

Fig. 9.2 *High temperature structural properties of steel.*

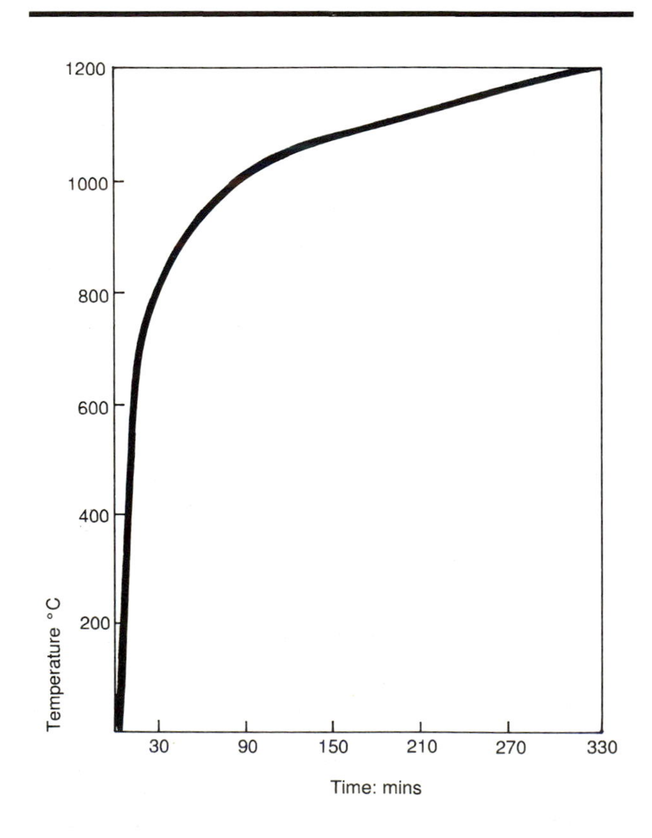

Fig. 9.3 *BS 476 standard fire curve.*

building occupants or even survival times for the structure. They are simply a convenient way of grading different categories of buildings by fire load from those in which a fire is likely to be relatively small (e.g. low-rise offices) to those in which a fire might result in a major conflagration (e.g. a multi-storey library).

The requirements are based largely on the Fire Grading of Buildings Report of 1946 [2] and relate to survival times in a standard fire, defined by BS 476 Parts 20 and 21 [3] and illustrated in Fig. 9.3. The fire resistance periods refer to the time for which an element of structure (a column, beam, compartment wall etc.) should maintain:

(a) Stability: it should not collapse.
(b) Integrity: it should not crack or otherwise allow the passage of flame to an adjoining compartment.
(c) Insulation: it should not allow passage of heat by conduction which might induce ignition in an adjoining compartment.

With steel structural members there is normally little problem in achieving the requirements of integrity and insulation and most attention and cost is directed at satisfying the stability criterion.

9.2.2 Standard fire tests

Structural fire protection systems are typically proved by physical testing. Columns under fire test are exposed to fire on all four sides and loaded axially and the furnace temperature increased according to the standard fire curve (Fig. 9.3) until the design load can no longer be sustained. Beams are loaded in bending and are exposed on three sides, the upper flange being in contact with the furnace roof. The stability limit is deemed to have been reached when the deflection rate reaches $L^2/9000d$ (where L = beam span, d = beam depth), though lower and upper limits of total deflection are set at $L/30$ and $L/20$.

This standard test has been used for many years to evaluate insulation of fire protection materials for use on structural steelwork, and to provide a 'rank order' or comparison of their performance. However, it is only a coarse indication of actual behaviour in real conditions.

9.2.3 Fire resistance requirements

The degree of fire resistance required of a structural member is related to the building function (for instance office, shop or factory), by the building height and by the compartment size in which the member is located (Fig. 9.4). Details are summarized in the Appendix at the end of this chapter.

It should be noted that certain types of building may be exempt, in particular roof structures and single storey structures. However, the latter exemption does not apply where the building is built so close to another property that there would be a risk of fire spread if the structure were to collapse.

Multi-storey shops

Max height	Max floor area (m²)	Max cubic capacity (m³)	Fire resistance (hrs) Ground or upper storey	Basement
7.5	150	No limit	1/2	1
7	500	No limit	1/2	1
15	No limit	3500	1	1
28	1000	7000	1	2
No limit	2000	7000	2	4

Fig. 9.4 *UK Building Regulation requirements for fire resistance for multi-storey shops (1991).*

9.2.4 Achieving fire resistance

Approved Document B [1] requires that adequate provision for fire safety be provided either by fulfilling the requirements prescribed or by suitable alternative methods. These may be termed the 'fire protection' and 'fire-resistant design' approaches, respectively. Both approaches are discussed in this chapter.

In the fire protection approach, which is currently the more common, the structure is designed in the normal manner and the steelwork then insulated so that, in the event of a fire, its temperature remains low. The fire resistant design approach uses calculation methods to predict the performance and survival time of the steelwork based upon its high temperature material properties. This can result in a reduction, or even the complete elimination, of structural fire protection.

9.3 PROTECTION OF STRUCTURAL MEMBERS

For many years the principal method of achieving fire resistance in steel framed structures has been to apply insulation materials which have been deemed to meet Building Regulation requirements as a result of BS 476 standard tests on individual members. The fire protection is applied after erection of the frame and takes the form of an insulating barrier between the steel and the fire to slow down the transfer of heat.

The first protective coatings were made from heavyweight materials such as concrete, brick and plaster and these may still be the optimum solution in some circumstances, for instance where there is a risk of impact damage. However, by the 1920s various forms of asbestos-based sheet and spray coatings had become available. These were almost invariably cheaper than the traditional materials and imposed less load on the structure. The League of Nations HQ at Geneva (1929) is one of the earliest European examples of the use of such lightweight fire cladding.

Asbestos is no longer used for fire protection because of health hazards associated with its use, but other asbestos-free materials have been developed for this purpose. These gain their insulating properties from rock-fibre or exfoliated vermiculite and are available either in the form of a spray for direct application or as boards for mechanical fixing.

9.3.1 Alternative protection systems

Sprays are the cheapest method with costs commonly in the range of £8 to £20/m^2 (£0.75 to £2/ft^2) applied (1991 prices), depending on the fire rating required and the size of the job. Application is fast and it is easy to coat complex shapes or connections (Fig. 9.5). However, they are applied wet, which can create problems in freezing winter conditions. They are messy to apply and the appearance is often poor, so they are most often used in hidden areas such as on beams above suspended ceilings or in plant rooms and basements.

Boards tend to be more expensive, commonly in the range of £11 to £30/m^2 (£1 to £3/ft^2) applied (1991 prices), because of the higher labour content in fixing. The price depends on the rating required and the surface finish chosen but tends to be less sensitive to job size. They are dry-fixed by gluing, stapling or screwing, so there is less interference with other trades on site, and the hollow box appearance is often more suitable for frame elements, such as free-standing columns, which will be in view (Fig. 9.6). A further advantage, particularly at perimeter columns, is that the casing work can house vertical services.

Rockwool can be used to wrap structural sections to provide effective insulation. This can be supported by clipping into place or within a lightweight casing (Fig. 9.7).

Intumescent coatings achieve insulation in a totally different way, the insulating layer only forming by the action of heat when the fire breaks out (Fig. 9.8). The coating is applied as a thin layer, perhaps as thin as 1 mm (40 thou), but it contains a compound in its formulation which releases a gas when heat is applied. The gas inflates the coating into a thick carbonaceous foam, which provides heat insulation to the steel underneath. The coatings are available in a range of colours and may be used for decorative and practical reasons on visible steelwork (Fig. 9.9).

Two types of intumescent coating are currently available. The first, which are water resistant, have a maximum rating of 2 hours, but are expensive, costing £60/m^2 (£5.50/ft^2) at 2 hours rating (1991 prices). Coatings of the second type have a maximum rating of 1.5 hours. These are not so resistant to moisture and not recommended for wet applications such as swimming pools but are satisfactory in dry

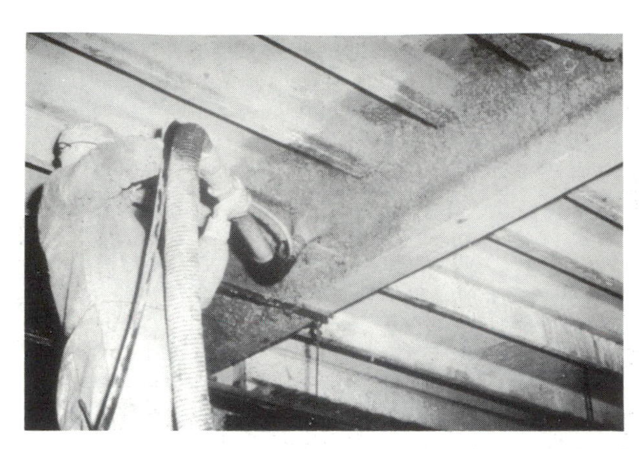

Fig. 9.5 *Application of fire protection spray.*

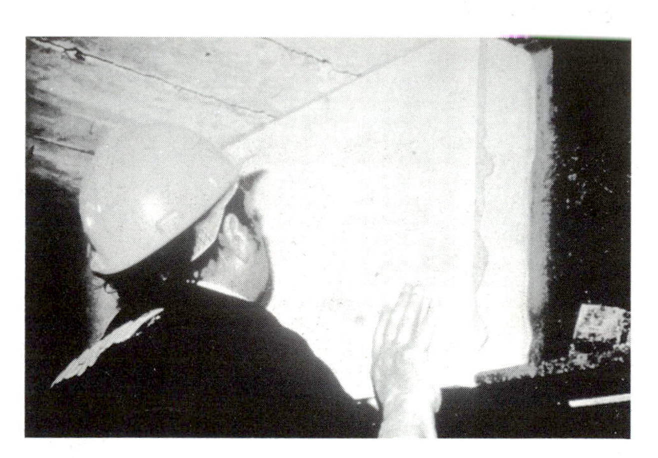

Fig. 9.6 *Example of board protection.*

buildings. Costs range from about £12 to £25/m^2 (£1 to £2.50/ft^2) (1991 prices).

In comparison with these lightweight materials protection by in situ concrete would cost about £20 to £35/m^2 (£2 to £3.25/ft^2) of steelwork encased (1991 prices).

9.3.2 Influence of exposure conditions

The thickness of insulation required to provide a given fire rating depends not only on the thermal conductivity of the insulating material, but also on the dimensions of the steel to which it is applied. The rate of temperature rise of a steel member depends on its mass and its surface area – light members such as purlins or lattice girders heat up much more quickly than heavy columns. The rate of heating of a given section is described by its 'Section Factor' which is the ratio between its surface perimeter exposed to radiation and convection and its mass (which is directly related to the cross-sectional area). This is illustrated in Fig. 9.10 and defined as follows:

Fig. 9.7 *Rockwool wrapping.*

Fig. 9.9 *Example of intumescent coating.*

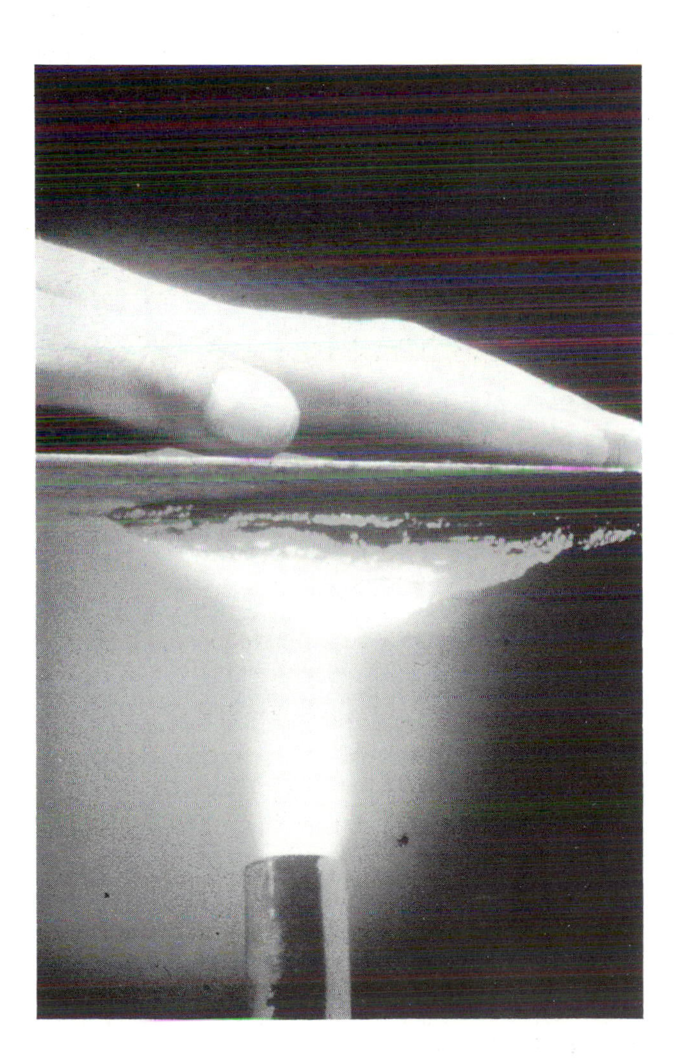

Fig. 9.8 *Effect of heat on intumescent coating.*

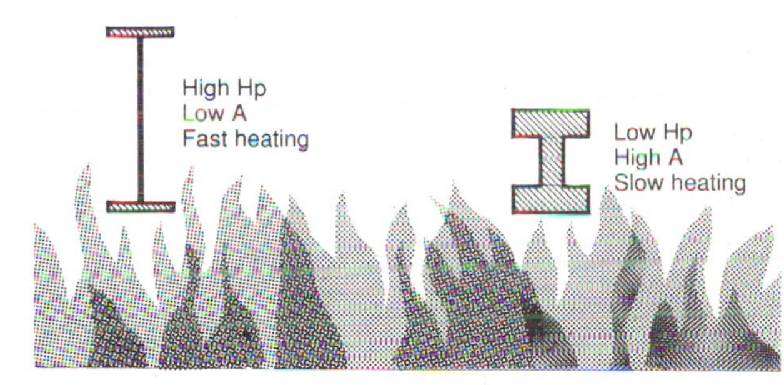

Fig. 9.10 *The section factor – Hp/A.*

Section Factor = Hp/A

Hp = perimeter of the section exposed to fire in m (ft)
A = cross-sectional area of the member in m^2 (ft^2)

A member with a low Hp/A value will be heated at a slower rate than one with a high Hp/A value and will require less insulation to achieve the same fire resistance rating. Standard tables are available listing Hp/A ratios for structural sections and manufacturers of fire protection products now give recommendations relating insulating thickness to this section factor [4]. Some sections at the heavy end of the structural range have such low Hp/A ratios (less than 50 m^{-1} (16 ft^{-1})) and therefore such slow heating rates that failure does not occur within half an hour under standard BS 476 heating conditions, even when they are unprotected.

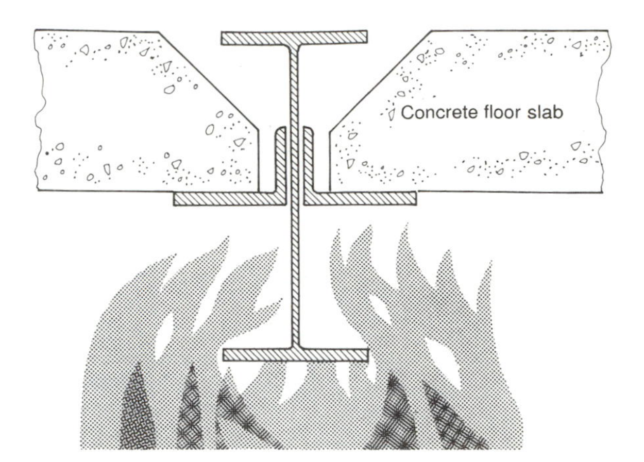

Fig. 9.11 *Shelf angle floor construction providing partial protection to the steelwork.*

In calculating the perimeter of the section exposed to fire, account can be taken of any inherent protection, such as that provided by a floor slab (Fig. 9.11).

9.4 DESIGN FOR FIRE RESISTANCE

The yield strength of steel is known to decrease with increasing temperature (Fig. 9.2), and the lower the applied load on a member, the higher will be the temperature in a fire at which collapse occurs. This clearly implies a longer survival time. Recent research into fire performance has shown that the failure temperature of a member also depends upon its dimensions, stress distribution and the distribution of temperature (sections are rarely heated uniformly). These effects can be quantified to form the basis of a 'fire resistant design' approach, and this has been incorporated into recent design regulations such as the structural design code BS 5950 Part 8 [5] and Eurocode 3 Part 10 [6]. These recognize much more accurately the temperature response of the material and treat fire as a limit state.

BS 5950 Part 8 provides for a variable 'limiting temperature' which depends upon the applied load, the stress distribution and the temperature gradient within a member, and allows two methods of assessing fire resistance of bare steel members, taking account of these parameters. The first, the 'load ratio' method, involves comparison of the 'design temperature', which is defined as the temperature the member will reach in the required fire resistance time, with the 'limiting temperature', which is the temperature at which it will fail. If the limiting temperature exceeds the design temperature, no protection is necessary. The methods allow designers to make use of reduced design stresses and higher strength steels to achieve improved fire resistance times.

The second method, which is applicable to beams only, will give benefits when members are partially exposed and when the temperature distribution is known. The method consists of comparing the calculated moment capacity at the required fire resistance time with the applied moment. When the moment capacity exceeds the applied moment no protection is necessary.

Each of these methods may be used in relation to either standard fire or to natural fire conditions.

Much research is still being carried out, particularly in the UK and Europe, to determine more precisely the behaviour of steel structures at high temperatures and to develop calculation methods which will not only improve the cost-effectiveness of steel structures but will also give designers greater opportunity for expression and innovation.

9.5 TUBULAR STRUCTURES (WITH FILLED TUBES, WATER OR CONCRETE)

The fire resistance of tubular members can be improved by making use of the hollow interior, either for cooling by water-filling, or for load transference by filling with concrete.

Water-filling gives moderate fire resistance when circulation is maintained. This can be achieved by natural convection using a number of interconnecting members (not all of them fire exposed) and a high-level storage tank, by direct connection to water mains and drainage, or by pumps. Research is currently being carried out into static unreplenished systems. Chemicals are added to the water to inhibit corrosion (potassium nitrate) and freezing (potassium carbonate).

The method is expensive, but one water-filled structure has been built in the UK. This is Bush Lane House in Cannon Street, London, by Arup Associates in 1976. The concept was also adopted for the Pompidou Centre, Paris (1972–77) which has water-filled columns (architects Piano and Rogers, engineers Ove Arup and Partners) and there are other examples world-wide. Further information can be found in [7].

The performance of concrete-filled tubular members depends largely on the member size and the tensile and flexural properties of the concrete. Fire resistance is improved markedly by inclusion of reinforcing bars or steel fibre reinforcement, and ratings approaching two hours have been achieved on fully loaded 304 mm (12 in) square columns [8].

9.6 EXTERNAL FRAMES

When the steel framework is placed outside the building shell, the heat transferred to the loadbearing members will depend upon their position in relation to flames escaping from windows and other facade openings. Suitable positioning of members between such openings will allow fire protection to be reduced considerably or even eliminated. Further details may be found in [9].

9.7 FIRE ENGINEERING

The standard BS 476 fire test, and the tables of requirements in Building Regulations which relate to it, have been a simple and convenient means of ensuring satisfactory performance of structures in fire for many years. This classification method will continue to be used for small structures where the expense of more detailed analysis is unjustified. However, it is clear that the conditions during a real fire differ enormously from those during a standard fire test and methods have been developed since the 1960s which enable the behaviour of real structures in real fires to be predicted with greater accuracy. This 'fire engineering' approach, which is now recognized in UK regulations, would normally be carried out by a specialist fire engineering consultant.

The fire engineering design method can be divided into four main stages – determination of fire load, prediction of maximum gas temperature, prediction of maximum steel temperature and assessment of structural stability. These are outlined below.

9.7.1 Determination of the fire load

The fire load of a compartment is the maximum heat that can theoretically be generated by the combustible items of contents and structure, i.e. weight × calorific value. Fire load is usually expressed in relation to floor area, sometimes as MJ/m^2 or $MCal/m^2$ (Btu/ft^2), but more often it is converted to an equivalent weight of wood and expressed as '$kg.wood/m^2$' ($lb.wood/ft^2$). Standard data tables giving fire loads of different materials are available [10].

Examples of typical fire loads are:

Hospital wards	10 kg/m^2 (20 lb/ft^2)
Offices	35 kg/m^2 (70 lb/ft^2)
Textile warehouses	305 kg/m^2 (610 lb/ft^2)

9.7.2 Prediction of maximum gas temperature

The heat that is retained in the burning compartment depends upon the thermal characteristics of the wall, floor and ceiling materials and the degree of ventilation. Sheet steel walls will dissipate heat by conduction and radiation while blockwork will retain heat in the compartment and lead to higher gas temperatures.

It is assumed that window glass breaks in fire conditions and calculations take into account the size and position of such ventilation. Openings near to the ceiling level of a compartment (or disintegrating roofing materials) will tend to dissipate heat whereas the main function of openings near to the floor will be to provide oxygen to feed the fire (Fig. 9.12).

Since a great deal of data has been gathered over the years on the performance of materials in the standard fire test, methods have been sought to relate real fire conditions to standard fire performance in order that the existing data can be used in fire engineering. This is done using the concept of a 'time equivalent', T_{eq}, which is given by:

$$T_{eq} = C.W.Q_f$$

where Q_f = fire load density in MJ/m^2 (Btu/ft^2), i.e. the amount of combustible material per unit area of compartment floor;
W = ventilation factor relating to the area and height of door and window openings;

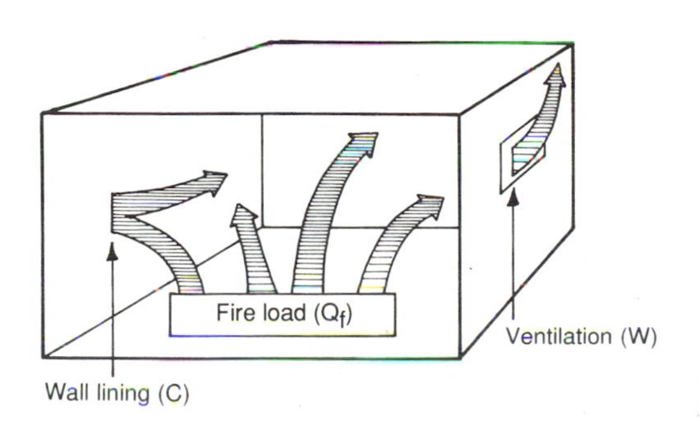

Fig. 9.12 *The major parameters which influence the temperature of natural fires.*

Fig. 9.13 *A fire engineered structure – Ibrox Stadium, Glasgow, Scotland.*

C = a constant relating to the thermal properties of the walls, floor and ceiling.

Studies carried out in the mid 1960s by the Fire Research Station [11] on simulated real fires illustrate the effect of fire load and ventilation on fire temperatures.

9.7.3 Prediction of maximum steel temperature

In a given heating regime the maximum temperature of a steel member will depend upon its size and shape (Hp/A ratio) and its location in relation to the fire – a free-standing column engulfed by flames inside a compartment, for instance, will reach higher temperatures than a column placed outside a window opening.

9.7.4 Prediction of structural stability

The 'limiting temperature' of a structural member, i.e. the temperature at which its loadbearing capacity is exceeded, depends on the applied load and the strength of the steel at high temperatures, factors which have already been discussed. It also depends on structural parameters such as restraint, continuity and composite action. By and large these structural effects are insufficiently quantified for general use at present. It is known that 'structures' have markedly better performance than single elements and much current research is aimed at quantifying these structural influences.

Much of the work on fire engineering has been carried out in Sweden [12], but the concept is being accepted and adopted in other countries. It is not an approach which can be used for buildings which are subject to change of use, such as advance factory units, but many buildings are 'fixed' in terms of their occupancy, for example car parks, hospitals and swimming pools, and in such cases fire engineering is a valid approach.

In the UK a number of buildings have been built using unprotected steel on fire engineering principles. One example is the North Stand at Ibrox football ground in Glasgow (Fig. 9.13). Although in this case a half-hour regulation requirement applied to the building, fire engineering studies showed that a total burn out would not raise steelwork temperatures to the point of collapse. Some £40 000 was saved [13].

APPENDIX

Minimum periods of fire resistance

Purpose group of building	*Minimum periods (minutes) for elements of structure in a:*					
	Basement storey(†) including floor over		*Ground or upper storey*			
	Depth (M) of lowest basement		*Height (M) of top floor above ground in building or separating part of building*			
	more than 10	*not more than 10*	*not more than 5*	*not more than 20*	*not more than 30*	*more than 30*
1. Residential (domestic):						
a. flats and maisonettes	90	60	30*	60**†	90**	120**
b. and c. dwelling-houses	not relevant	30*	30*	60	not relevant	not relevant
2. Residential:						
a. Institutional	90	60	30*	60	90	120
b. other residential	90	60	30*	60	90	120
3. Office:						
– not sprinklered	90	60	30*	60	90	not permitted
– sprinklered(2)	60	60	30*	30*	60	120#
4. Shop and commercial:						
– not sprinklered	90	60	60	60	90	not permitted
– sprinklered(2)	60	60	30*	60	60	120#
5. Assembly and recreation:						
– not sprinklered	90	60	60	60	90	not permitted
– sprinklered(2)	60	60	30*	60	60	120#
6. Industrial:						
– not sprinklered	120	90	60	90	120	not permitted
– sprinklered(2)	90	60	30*	60	90	120#
7. Storage and other non-residential:						
a. any building or part not described elsewhere:						
– not sprinklered	120	90	60	90	120	not permitted
– sprinklered(2)	90	60	30*	60	90	120#
b. car park for light vehicles:						
i. open sided park(3)	not applicable	not applicable	15*+	15*+	15*+	60
ii. any other park	90	60	30*	60	90	120#

Modifications referred to in this table:

† The floor over a basement (or if there is more than 1 basement, the floor over the topmost basement) should meet the provisions for the ground and upper storeys if that period is higher

* Increased to a minimum of 60 minutes for compartment walls separating buildings

** Reduced to 30 minutes for any floor within a maisonette, but not if the floor contributes to the support of the building

Reduced to 90 minutes for elements not forming part of the structural frame

\+ Increased to 30 minutes for elements protecting the means of escape

REFERENCES AND TECHNICAL NOTES

1. The Building Regulations, Approved Document B, HMSO.
2. *Fire Grading of Buildings*, Ministry of Public Building & Works Post War Building Studies No.20. HMSO, 1946.
3. BS 476 Parts 20 and 21: Test methods and criteria for the resistance of elements of building construction. British Standards Institute.
4. Fire Protection for Structural Steel in Buildings, 2nd edn. Steel Construction Institute and Association of Structural Fire Protection Contractors and Manufacturers
5. BS 5950 Part 8: 1990: Structural use of steel in building: code of practice for fire resistant design, British Standards Institute.
6. EC3 Part 10, *Design of Steel Structures. Structural Fire Design*. Commission of the European Communities.
7. Bond, G.V.L. (1975) *Water Cooled Hollow Columns*, Steel Construction Institute.
8. *Design Manual for SHS – Concrete-filled Columns*, British Steel Tubes, Corby, 1984.
9. Law, M. and O'Brien, T. (1986) *Fire Safety of Bare External Structural Steel*, Steel Construction Institute.
10. Gretener, M. (1973) *Evaluation of Fire Hazards and Determination of Protective Measures According to the M. Gretener Method*, Association of Cantonal Institutions for Fire Insurance and the Swiss Fire Prevention Service. Nuschelerstrasse 45 CH 8001 Zurich, Switzerland.
11. Butcher, E.G. *et al.* (1966) *The Temperature Attained by Steel in Building Fires*, Fire Research Station, Technical Paper No. 15, HMSO.
12. Peterson, O., Magnusson S.E. and Thor, J. (1976) *Fire Engineering Design of Steel Structures*, Publication No. 50, Swedish Institute of Steel Construction, Stockholm.
13. *Framed in Steel – 6*, The Ibrox Stadium Redevelopment, British Steel General Steels (1981).

FURTHER READING

Protection materials

Fire Protection of Structural Steel in Buildings, (1992) published by ASFPCM and Steel Construction Institute.

Steel properties

Kirby, B.R. and Preston, R.R. (1988) High temperature properties of hot-rolled structural steels for use in fire engineering studies. *Fire Safety Journal*, Vol 13.

Design for fire

Newman, G.M. (1990) *The Behaviour of Steel Portal Frames in Boundary Conditions*, published by the Steel Construction Institute.

Fire engineering

Thor J. *et al.* (1977) A rational approach to fire engineering design of steel buildings. *Engineering Journal*, American Institute of Steel Construction, Third Quarter.

Fire engineering examples

Thor, J., Pettersson O. and Magnusson, S.E. (1977) A rational approach to fire engineering design of steel buildings. *Engineering Journal*, American Institute of Steel Construction, Third Quarter.

Kirby, B.R. (1986) Recent developments and applications in structural fire engineering design – a review. *Fire Safety Journal*, Vol 11.

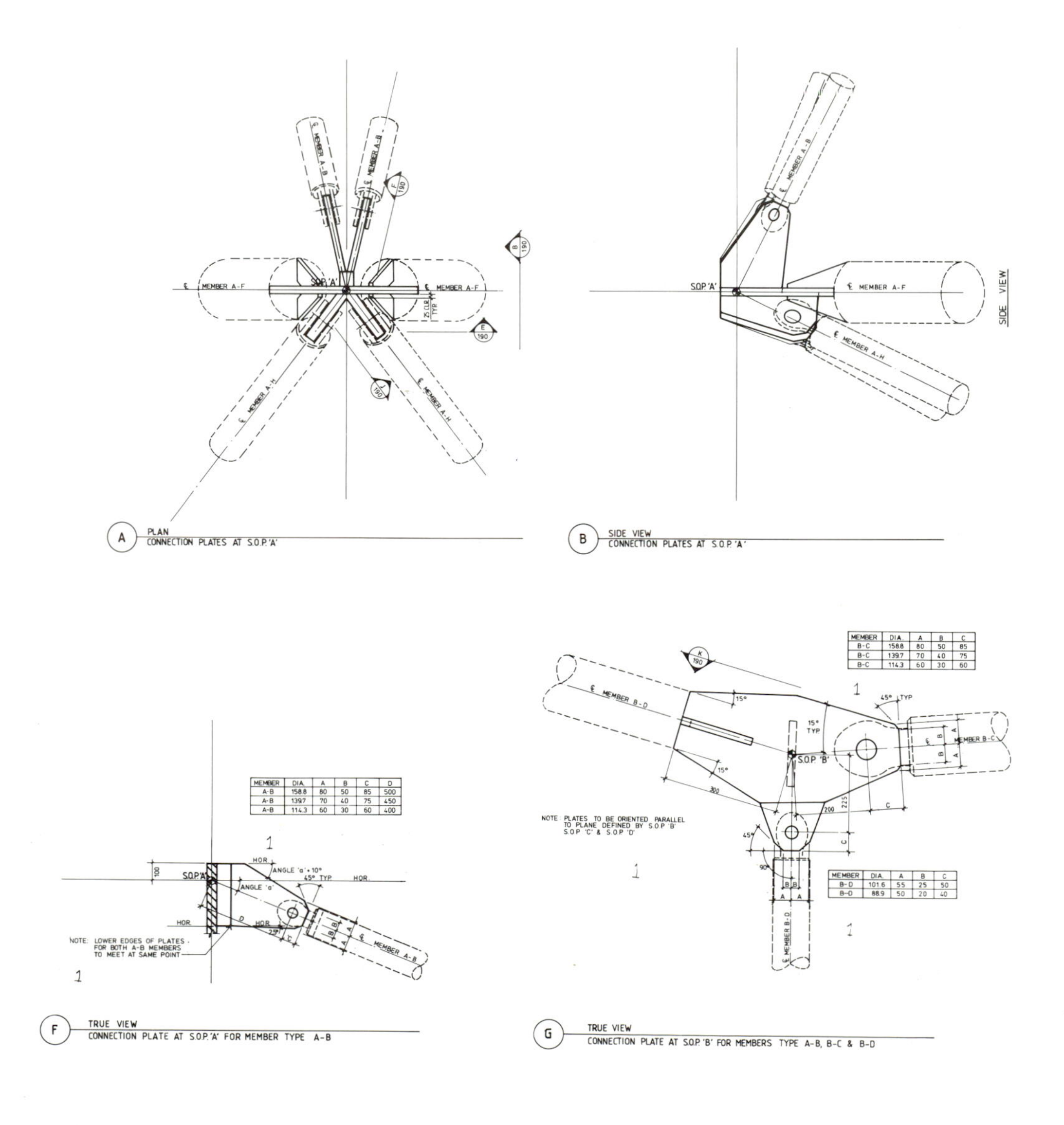

MEMBER	DIA.	A	B	C	D
A-B	158.8	80	50	85	500
A-B	139.7	70	40	75	450
A-B	114.3	60	30	60	400

MEMBER	DIA.	A	B	C
B-C	158.8	80	50	85
B-C	139.7	70	40	75
B-C	114.3	60	30	60

MEMBER	DIA.	A	B	C
B-D	101.6	55	25	50
B-D	88.9	50	20	40

Roof connection details. Sydney Cricket and Sports Ground Trust, Australia (architects Philip Cox and Partners Pty Ltd).

Part Three | Principles of Steel Framing

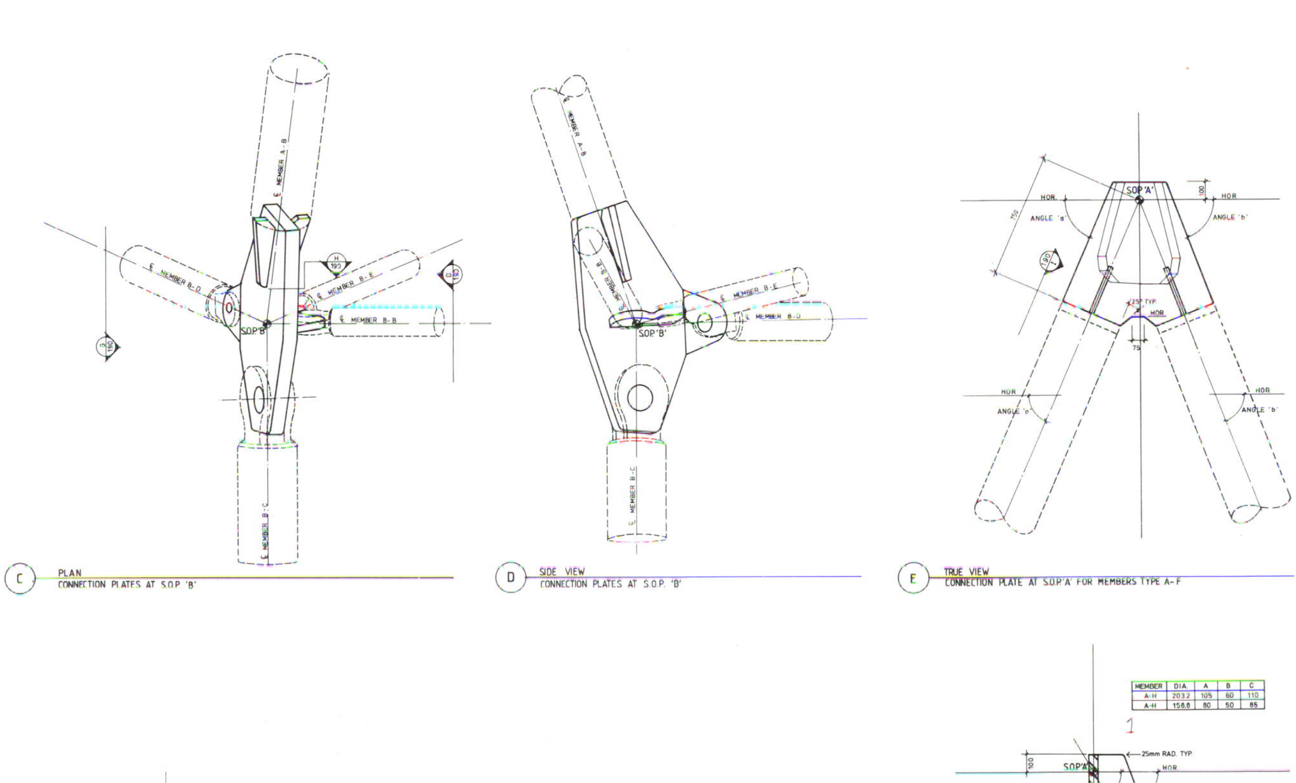

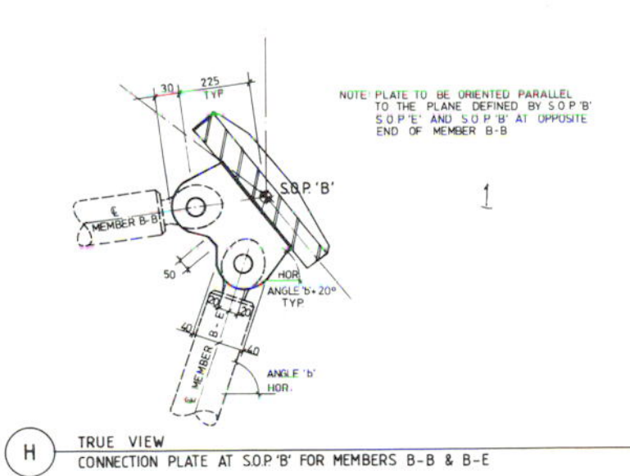

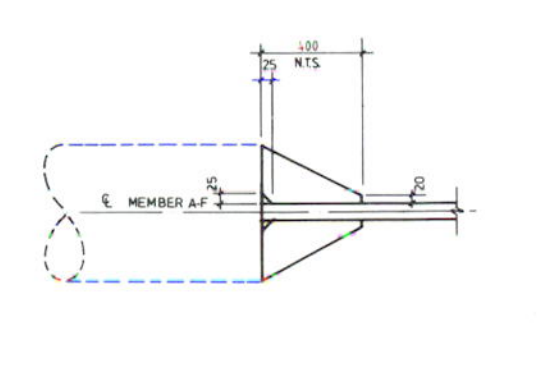

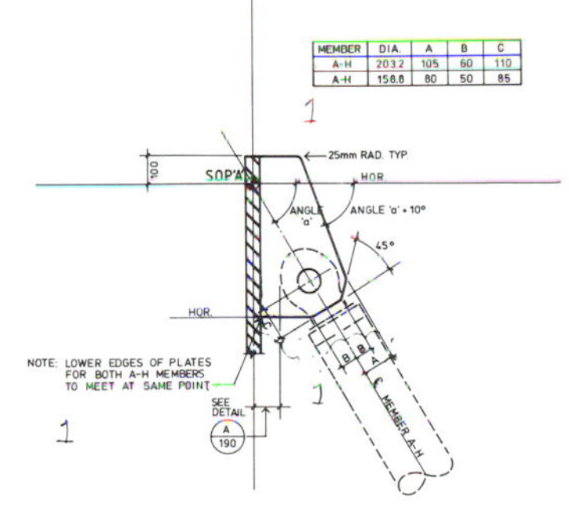

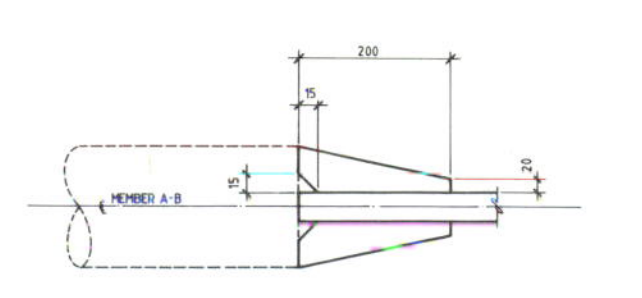

TRUE VIEW
STIFFENER PLATES AT SOP 'B' FOR MEMBER A–B

Chicago, city of steel.

10

The architecture of steel

Patrick Morreau

10.1 INTRODUCTION

This chapter seeks to identify the design opportunities that building in steel offers to architects. It then discusses the functional and economic advantages which can arise from adopting this form of construction, and finally touches on the design approach which is necessary to realize these advantages to their maximum. Other contributors have covered these topics in relation to their subject, sometimes in greater detail: the objective here is to give an overview – a general picture – of the benefits of designing in steel.

10.2 STRUCTURAL STEEL AND ARCHITECTURAL DESIGN

What is the contemporary architectural image of a steel building? Probably: a sense of lightness, both in weight and in transparency; open, but orthogonal in plan and structural arrangement; regular in elevation, with neither set-backs nor overhangs; in fact, the classic Modernist box, now so very much out of fashion. But how true is this image?

For 200 years, steel – and before steel, iron – has been used to realize successfully the architectural objectives of its period. The Théâtre Français (Fig. 10.1), with its forged wrought iron roof structure, and the textile mills of Lancashire and Derby, used metal to achieve longer spans and greater fire resistance. Architecturally more ambitious were the great railway termini in the UK which symbolize so much of the Victorian age: Euston (Fig. 10.2), Paddington (Fig. 10.3) and St Pancras (Fig. 10.4). Paxton's design of the Crystal Palace (Figs 1.23 and 1.24) remains the classic, and near perfect, example of the unity of building design with material and method, while the Oxford Museum (Fig. 1.25) shows us the Gothic Revival interpreted in iron. Throughout the second half of the 19th century, the energy and exuberance of the era was given architectural expression in its iron and steel buildings (Fig. 10.5).

In this century, steel buildings have been the built expression of the machine age. That expression has taken several forms: the careful crafting by Mies van der Rohe at the scale both of the German Pavilion (Fig. 10.6) and the Seagram Building (Fig. 10.7); the continuing exploration of the relationship between structure and cladding; the exploitation of standard steel components in the Eames House (Fig. 10.8) and more recently by Michael Hopkins in his Patera buildings (Fig. 10.9); and the use of steel structure to define an architectural language, represented by the Pompidou Centre (Fig. 10.10) and many buildings since.

The machine age, in architecture characterized by the

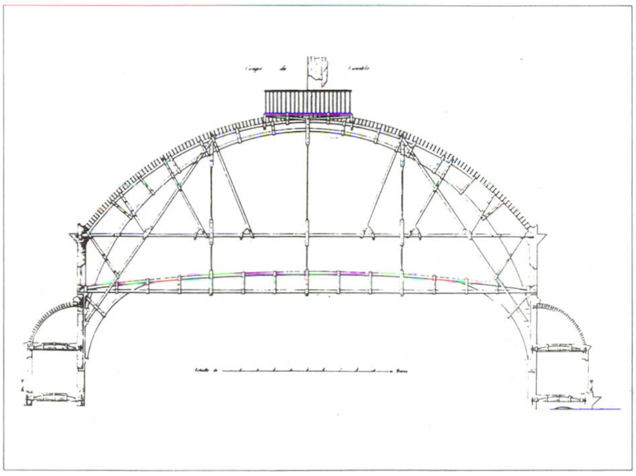

Fig. 10.1 *Théâtre Français, Paris 1786 (architect Victor Louis). Iron truss supporting clay pot vaulting.*

Fig. 10.2 *Euston Station, London, UK 1837 (architect Charles Fox). Wrought iron trusses spanned between cast iron arched girders on cast iron columns.*

Fig. 10.3 *Paddington Station, London, UK 1854 (architect Brunel and Wyatt).*

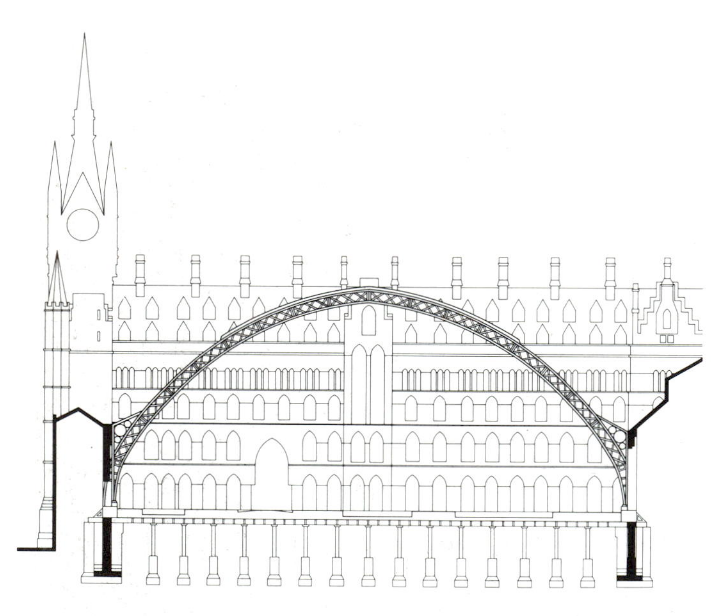

Fig. 10.4 *St Pancras Station, London, UK 1868 (architect/engineer: Barlow and Scott). Detail of trussed arch at the springing with masonry wall and platform shown in outline. Courtesy Alan Ogg:* Architecture in Steel.

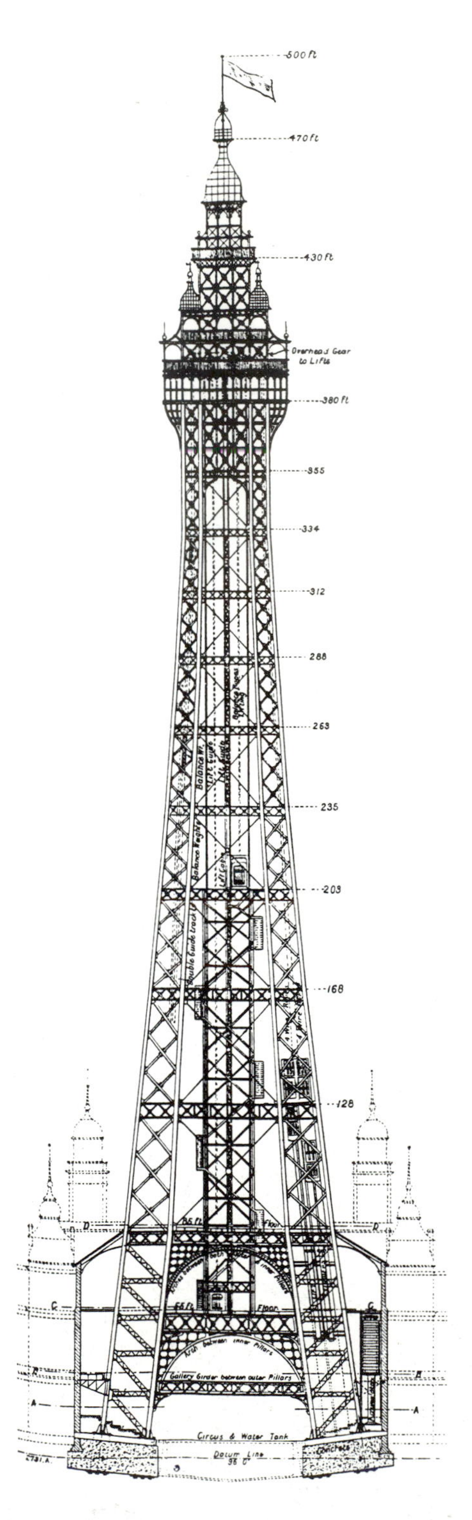

Fig. 10.5 *Blackpool Tower, Lancashire, UK 1889–91 (architect Maxwell and Turkeand). Half-size replica of the Eiffel Tower built as an enthusiastic endeavour.*

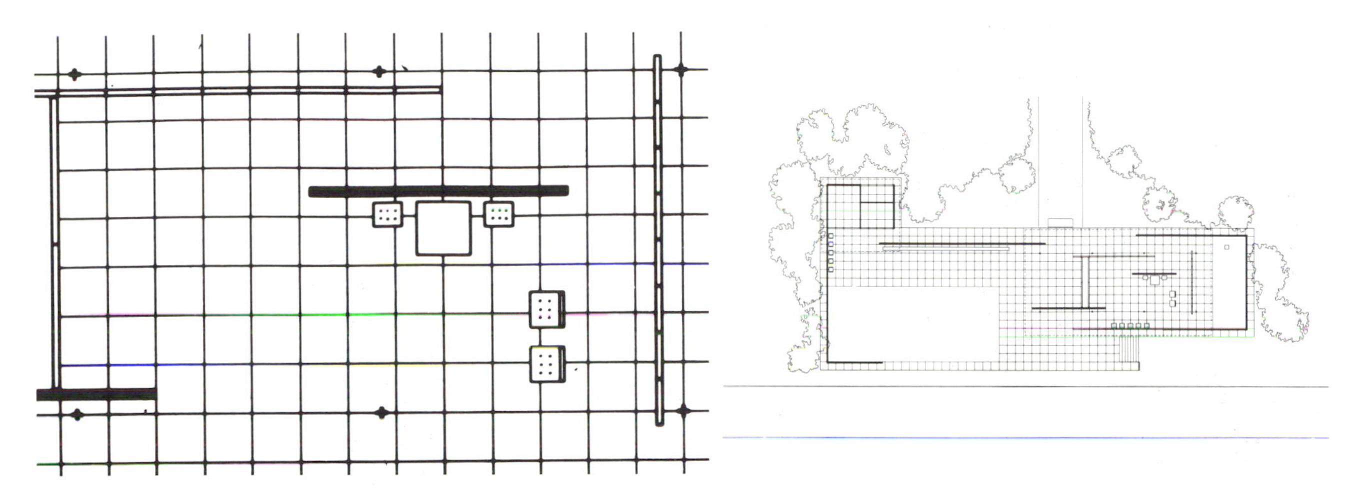

Fig. 10.6 *Mies van der Rohe, Ludwig.* German Pavilion. *Barcelona 1928–29. Floor plan. Drawn by the Mies van der Rohe Chicago office, c. 1964. Ink on illustration board, 30 × 39¾" (76 × 101 cm). Mies van der Rohe Archive, The Museum of Modern Art, New York. Gift of the architect.*

Fig. 10.7 *Seagram Building, New York 1957 (architect Mies van der Rohe).*

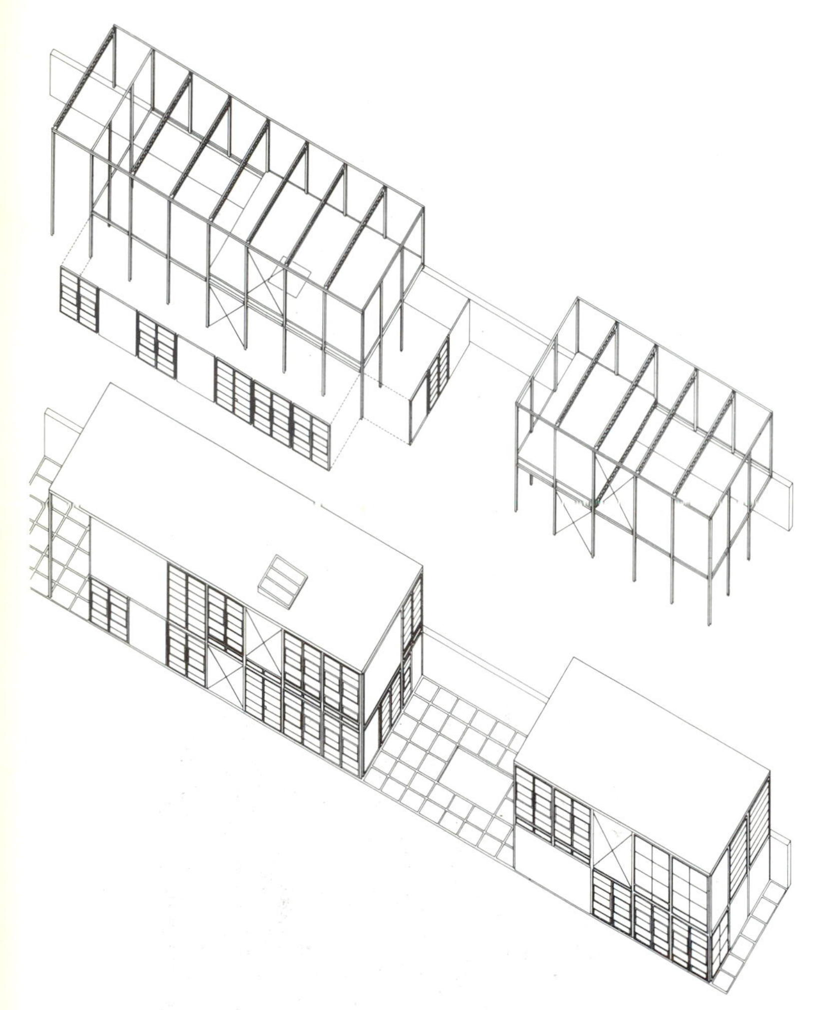

Fig. 10.8 *Eames House, Santa Monica, California 1949 (architect Ray Eames). Courtesy Alan Ogg:* Architecture in Steel.

Fig. 10.10 *Pompidou Centre, Paris 1976 (architect Piano and Rogers: engineer Ove Arup and Partners) (refer to chapter 36 case study 36.4.2).*

Fig. 10.9 *Patera Buildings, London, UK 1982 (architect Michael Hopkins and Partners: engineer Anthony Hunt) (refer to chapter 27, section 27.5.1).*

Modern Movement and structural expression, is today out of fashion. The architectural objectives that generated the architectural image of steel buildings as the classic Modernist box are no longer held by many (perhaps most) architects. Those clean functional lines are now perceived as inhuman and bleakly boring, to be replaced by variety and complexity of form and detail. So how can a steel building respond to demands which seem at odds with an architectural image which is to a great extent derived from the nature of steel buildings?

This can be answered in two parts. First, behind the contemporary Post-Modern facade with its reveals and returns, corners and cornices, is almost always to be found the orderly plan and orthogonal bay so well suited to steel framing. This leaves perhaps only an irregular perimeter strip, which is associated with the second part of the answer: recent advances in fabricating techniques – computer controlled cutting and welding, robotics, bending machines –

Fig. 10.11 *Embankment Place, London, UK. Schematic layout of typical floor plan. Regular grid behind modelled facade 1991 (architect Terry Farrell and Co. Ltd: engineer Ove Arup and Partners) (refer to chapter 17 Fig. 17.14).*

have made special sections, awkward angles, and varying lengths economically viable. What has been lost is what had come to be recognized as the steel aesthetic, out of fashion, for the moment. Still powerfully present are the functional and economic advantages of steel construction (Fig. 10.11).

Before elaborating on those advantages, consider four of the several inherent qualities of steel construction which have enabled it to be used so successfully in the past to realize such a diversity of architectural objectives, and which will continue to offer designers great opportunities in the future.

First, there is the nature of the material itself: stronger than any other used in building, it can be formed into shapes which optimize that strength for specific structural applications – beams for bending, rods for tension, tubes for compression – allowing loads to be carried with the minimum of structural material. Strength, combined with a high modulus of elasticity and efficient shapes, allows long spans with relatively small columns and so, in turn, greater freedom to the designer.

Then, the clarity of the structural function and hierarchy of the components of the steel frame – secondary and primary beams, columns, lateral bracing – is in harmony with architectural objectives which seek to establish a similar clarity in all aspects of the building design.

Third, the functional separation of frame and cladding – the frame as skeleton and the cladding as skin – combines with the attenuation of structure which the strength of steel permits to give the designer great freedom to explore the relationship between the two, both in plan and in elevation. Indeed, the degree of emphasis placed by architects on the external expression of the structure, and since the Pompidou Centre the services, has been one of the most productive areas of architectural-structural design. One has only to compare Lever House (Fig. 10.12) and the John Hancock Tower (refer to lead-in picture and Fig. 10.13) on the one hand with the Sainsbury Centre (Fig. 10.14), the Hongkong

Fig. 10.12 *Lever House, New York 1951 (architect and engineer SOM). (Ezra Stoller © Esto.)*

Fig. 10.13 *John Hancock Tower, Chicago, Illinois 1969 (architect/ engineer SOM) (refer to chapter 36 case study 36.5.1 and chapter 15 for general principles).*

Fig. 10.14 *Sainsbury Centre, Norwich, UK 1978 (architect Foster Associates: engineer Anthony Hunt Associates) (refer to chapter 36 case study 36.3.3).*

and Shanghai Bank (Fig. 10.15) and the Patscenter, New Jersey (Fig. 10.16) on the other to see the range of possibilities that the steel frame opens to the architect.

And, fourthly, there is the accuracy of fabrication and erection which allows, and encourages, the sharpness and precision of architectural detailing compatible with metal and glass cladding as an expression of the clarity of architectural intent and execution.

These, and others, are the qualities of steel construction which transcend the passing fashions in style, while allowing each style to be realized as the designer wishes.

Fig. 10.15 *Hongkong and Shanghai Bank 1986 (architect Foster Associates: engineer Ove Arup and Partners) (refer to chapter 37 case study 37.8).*

Fig. 10.16 *Patscenter, Princeton, New Jersey 1984 (architect Richard Rogers and Partners: engineer Ove Arup and Partners).*

10.3 FUNCTIONAL ADVANTAGES

Many of those qualities of steel construction which enhance the architectural design also enhance the functional performance of the building.

Flexibility of use and adaptability to change are two of the most important requirements imposed on buildings today. They are readily satisfied by steel construction with columns at 10–15 m (30–50 ft) spacing, placing the minimum of constraint on internal planning, and facilitating the frequent re-organization of space so characteristic of modern office and other commercial uses. Change is not limited to single floors: often new stairs or services ducts are needed between floors, with the consequent requirement to cut openings through the structural slab. With the usual concrete topping on metal deck, some 130–150 mm (5–6 in) in thickness, cutting holes between beams is a relatively simple matter. Where the hole does not lie neatly between beams, it is possible to prop, install new beams and remove the old. Since structural steel beams are normally designed as simply supported, the structural effects are limited to the immediate area of the change. Even when changes of use require increased load-carrying capacity, steel frame floors can be strengthened with relatively little difficulty.

Steel framing also provides flexibility in the horizontal distribution of service ductwork and the placing of light fittings, another essential requirement in office buildings. Because the secondary beams are usually spaced 2.5–3.0 m (8–10 ft) apart, the depth of the ceiling void between provides space for duct cross-overs, air-conditioning equipment and so forth. Planned use of this zone can allow a reduction in floor-to-floor height, often an important consideration.

The lateral bracing system in steel frame buildings can provide further flexibility in initial planning and subsequent change. Moment-resisting frames offer no obstacle to the circulation of occupants or services, but are relatively expensive. Diagonally braced frames, usually located at cores, are economical and the configuration of the bracing can be arranged to provide space for doors or ducts. If future change calls for a different configuration, the original bracing can be removed and new installed. Like cutting new openings through floors, structural alterations of this kind are far more easily carried out in a steel frame building than in a concrete one.

Adaptability to change can also mean adding to the building, either vertically or horizontally. Here again, steel framing is advantageous. New columns can be installed and new framing erected above roof level with the minimum of interference; and the separation between frame and cladding makes horizontal extension straightforward, particularly if planned for in the original design.

The relative accuracy of steel frame construction has functional benefits. Because fabrication and erection tolerances are small, and because material properties (strength and modulus of elasticity) are more predictable, less provision needs to be made for construction tolerances and for deflection uncertainties, and so more space can be released for beneficial use. High material strength and smaller columns also release potentially valuable floor area, important in large commercial developments.

One more functional advantage of steel frame construction is its relatively light weight, which can reduce the cost of foundations, and can mean the difference between an expensive piled foundation and cheaper spread footings. On some particular sites, only lightweight steel construction is viable, either because the ground conditions are so bad or, as at the Royal Exchange Theatre in Manchester (Fig. 10.17), where only very limited loads could be added to the existing structure.

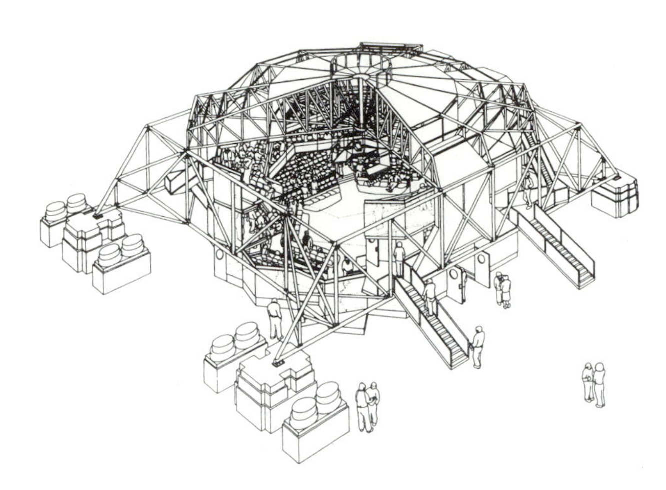

Fig. 10.17 *Royal Exchange Theatre, Manchester, UK 1976 (architect Levitt Bernstein Associates: engineer Ove Arup and Partners) (refer to chapter 36 case study 36.4.6).*

10.4 ECONOMIC CONSIDERATIONS

Most of the arguments in the past about the relative merits of steel and concrete buildings have concentrated on the relative costs of the two methods of construction. Much has been written on the subject, with each side colouring the facts to suit its case. What emerges clearly is that much depends on the greater speed of steel construction.

At the narrowest definition of cost, a steel frame is likely to be more expensive to buy and build than a concrete one. Extend the definition to include the foundations, and the cost difference is smaller. Extend the definition of cost, however, to include the cost of the time taken to complete the building – the contractor's overheads, the interest on the money to finance the project – and then also to include the benefits of earlier completion, either in earlier rental income or earlier use of new facilities, the economic advantages of steel construction can be very real. The challenge to the architect is to design a building which realizes the financial benefits offered by the speed of steel construction.

10.5 DESIGNING FOR STEEL

Earlier sections of this chapter have identified some of the architectural and functional qualities of steel frame buildings, and the previous section concluded that if these qualities were to be economically beneficial, then the potential for rapid completion of steel buildings must be realized to its maximum. In this section – which might appropriately have been called 'Designing for speed' – some of the key elements of the architect's approach to designing in steel are highlighted.

First and foremost is a comprehensive and co-ordinated attitude to the design. Steel frame buildings require that structure, services, cladding and finishes be considered as part of a single design with speed of construction as one of its chief objectives. To achieve that speed, each of the elements mentioned must meet certain requirements.

The structural frame should recognize that, because steel is prefabricated from components in the factory, repetition of dimensions, shapes and details of components will speed up the preparation of shop drawings and the fabrication and erection of the steel. This repetition is most effectively achieved by standardization of bay sizes and the arrangement of beams within bays. Structural components should be selected or designed to satisfy as many variables as possible and so reduce the number of different elements to be fabricated. (It is worth remembering that small savings in material are often negated by additional fabrication or erection time). Temporary propping should be avoided. Decisions which affect the structure must be made before fabrication: late changes can carry heavy cost penalties.

A steel frame building is constructed rapidly on site from components fabricated elsewhere. This approach should be carried through into the other elements of the building: cladding should be prefabricated, whether curtain wall or stone; partitions should be plasterboard on metal studs; ductwork should be prefabricated as much as possible; there should be no wet trades.

Dimensional co-ordination between the various elements is essential. Services, except perhaps for sprinklers, often run in a zone beneath the structural beams, and the various structural and services deflections and tolerances must be taken into account when the depth of that zone is established: tight fit means slow building.

Cladding should be designed and detailed to allow rapid erection, with easy fixing and levelling adjustment, proceeding as soon as possible after the steel frame is in place, and independently of other construction activities.

Structural steel construction, like all building methods which use prefabricated components, imposes a strong discipline on the designer. To gain the maximum benefits that the material offers, the architect must recognize that discipline and, as far as he can, work within it. Design disciplines represent opportunities, as hopefully some of the buildings illustrated in this chapter and elsewhere in the book have shown.

FURTHER READING

Copeland B., Glover, M., Hart, A., Haryott, R. and Marshall, S. (1983) Designing for steel. *Architects' Journal*. Vol. 178. Nos. 34 and 35, pp. 41–57.

Ogg A. (1987) *Architecture in steel, the Australian context*, Royal Australian Institute of Architects.

Leisure Pool, German School, Petersham, 1981 (architects Clifford Culpin and Partners with Kersten Merkinoff and Strunk).

11

Basic theory of framing

John Le Good (with contributions from Peter Brett and David Harriss)

11.1 INTRODUCTION

Choosing an appropriate single storey structural system is a great challenge to the designer and depends on many functional and spatial requirements. There are very many possible structural solutions for creating 'space enclosures' – the basic structural design objectives being to ensure a stiff and stable building of elegant form, for reasonable capital and maintenance cost and construction time. This chapter deals with the basic approach to structural design and outlines the principles of behaviour of simple structural elements. Further discussion of the basis of structural design, with particular reference to steel buildings, is contained in [1]. The various structural forms appropriate to simple single storey buildings are discussed, and some guidance is given with regard to costing. Chapter 12 develops the discussion of alternative forms of construction into multi-span and multi-bay construction, illustrating this with a number of examples.

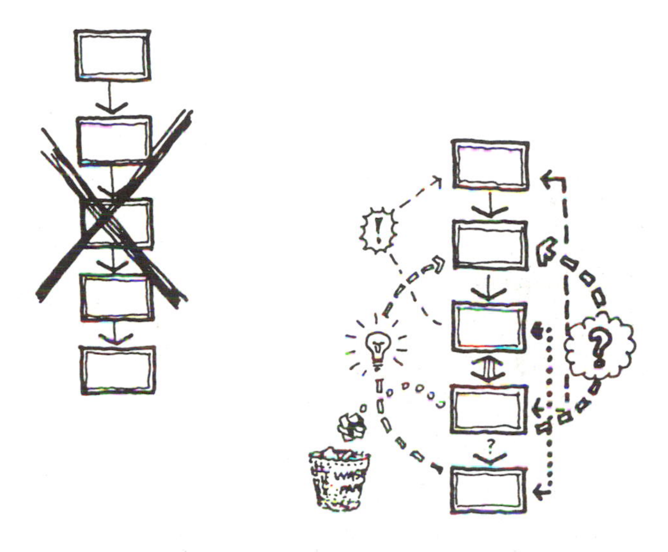

Fig. 11.1 *Design is not a simple linear process.*

11.2 GENERAL STRATEGY

Each fresh task facing the designer will be made easier if a clear overall strategy is adopted as follows:

(a) *Design objectives:* recognize that a problem exists and then clearly define the overall objectives for a design.
(b) *Analysis:* research around the problem and investigate likely relevant information.
(c) *Synthesis:* evolve possible solutions to the problem.
(d) *Evaluation:* decide on and refine the best solution establishing clear priorities for action (in terms of manufacture, construction, operation and maintenance).
(e) *Communication:* communicate decisions to others involved in the problem, including tendering.

This strategy is certainly not a linear sequence of clear questions and answers; it is highly complex as all factors in the design are interdependent to a greater or lesser degree. Hence there will be an immense number of 'steps' and 'loops' within and between the stages (Fig. 11.1). Decisions will often not come easily – some will depend primarily on quantitative factors whilst others will be based on qualitative judgements.

All factors and combinations must be explored comprehensively from idea to detail, with many compromises having to be made and contradictory pressures finely balanced. Qualitative assessment should precede quantitative evaluation. The starting point for 'analysis' may be the designer's current preconceived notion, which may be inspired by other disciplines such as mechanical or aeronautical engineering, or the visual imagination, but the 'synthesis' will reveal the flexibility of the designer's mind to assimilate new ideas critically, free of preconception (Fig. 11.2).

Initially, a rapid pass through stages (a) to (c) above, will indicate the nature and difficulty of the design problem and convince the designer and client that a 'building' is needed. Once this is established, it is wise to start by looking at the basic requirements and the relations between these. This can be assisted by noting individual functions and thence generating a 'bubble' (or flow) diagram of relationships between different functional areas to decide possible interconnections and locations. The next stage is to develop possible plan areas and minimum clear heights for each three-dimensional 'volume of space' (Fig. 11.3).

Suitable layouts should take account of any particular complications of the site, e.g. plan shape, proximity of old buildings, slope or foundation conditions. Many plan

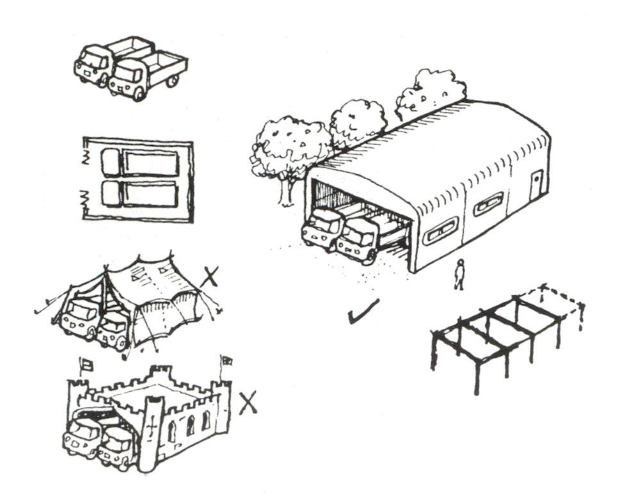

Fig. 11.2 *Arriving at a building solution.*

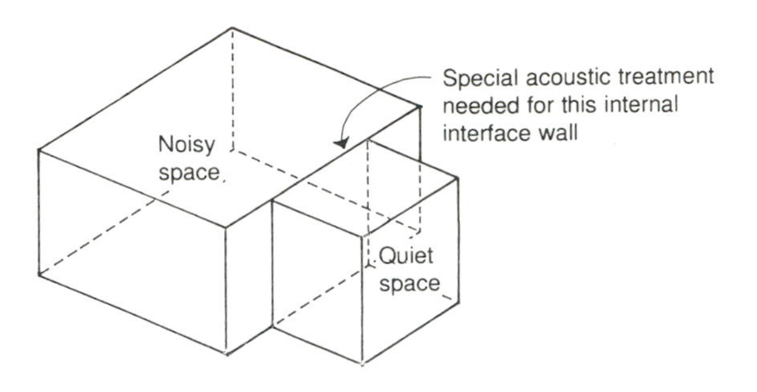

Fig. 11.4 *Special acoustic requirements for adjoining volumes.*

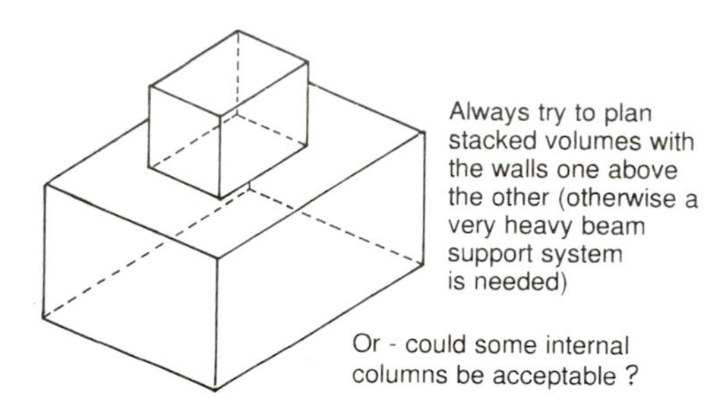

Fig. 11.5 *Vertical relationships between volumes*

arrangements will be possible and should be considered quickly at this stage. The requirements of each 'volume of space' and its interfaces must be examined for all functional, cost and spatial criteria (e.g. what structural loads must be resisted, what heating, ventilating, lighting and acoustic requirements are likely) (Figs 11.4 and 11.5).

The main criteria can be identified and then examined in numerical and economic terms. Incompatibilities may be 'designed out' by rearranging the planned spaces or making other compromises.

It is helpful to set out initial assumptions about possible structural systems ('frame', 'planar' or 'membrane') and materials which might be compatible with the 'volumes of space'. These will be based on previous experience of actual constructions, an understanding of structural and environmental theory, and current availability of materials and craft skills. Initial consultation may be needed with suppliers and fabricators (e.g. for large quantities or special qualities of steel).

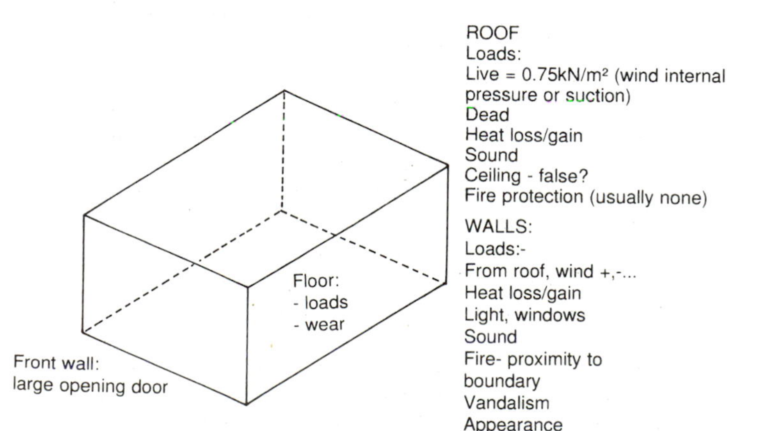

Fig. 11.3 *Volumes of space.*

Steelwork, with its properties of strength, isotropy and stiffness, and linear elements which are straight and compact, lends itself to frame systems; these gather and transfer the major structural loads as directly as possible to the foundations, as a tree gathers loads from its leaves through branches and main trunk to the roots.

A designer should continuously elucidate and test design ideas by making quick three-dimensional sketches, or simple physical models to explore the likely compatibility and spatial impact. It should also be remembered that all principal specialists (architects, engineers for structure and environmental services, quantity surveyors, as well as major suppliers and contractors) must collaborate freely with each other – and also the client – at this conceptual design stage. Poor decisions made now are often difficult and expensive to rectify later. Wise designers think carefully, but work quickly and are readily prepared to modify the concept at this stage.

11.3 ENVIRONMENTAL FACTORS

11.3.1 Lighting

The orientation of a building greatly influences design

through considerations of direct sunlight and daylight (Fig. 11.6). The quantity and quality of light needed internally for the type of building and its use, and the role of artificial light must be examined in relation to solar gain, glare, reflection and distraction to building users [2]. Adjustments to the building form to provide adequate sunshading might be appropriate. Possible solutions (in the northern hemisphere) include north light roofs or north facing fenestration for uniform daylighting. Alternatively, reflective glass, blinds or external sunshades can be used on the southerly facades or the extent of windows simply reduced.

Post-war industrial buildings in the UK have traced the circle from natural daylighting to total reliance upon artificial lighting, with daylight receding from a necessity to an amenity, although with current developments in energy conservation, there are signs that this trend is reversing. The current attitude of 'institutional funding' organizations is to expect 10% roof lighting to buildings whereas a figure of 25% would be needed to provide adequate daylighting at workbench level. Many owners would prefer to omit roof lights altogether, as they can be a considerable source of nuisance with risk of condensation and leaks. They also involve expense in controlling solar gain and maintenance. However, natural daylight is still required in certain processes, for instance where colour matching is an essential aspect of the work. In these cases special monitor lights or window arrangements can be made within the building form (Fig. 11.7).

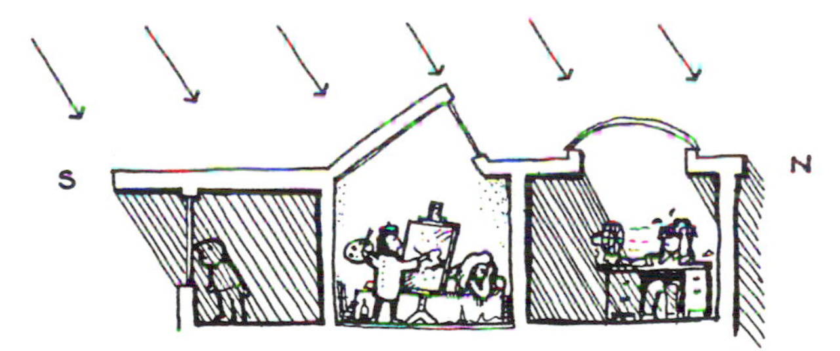

Fig. 11.6 *Daylighting and solar gain.*

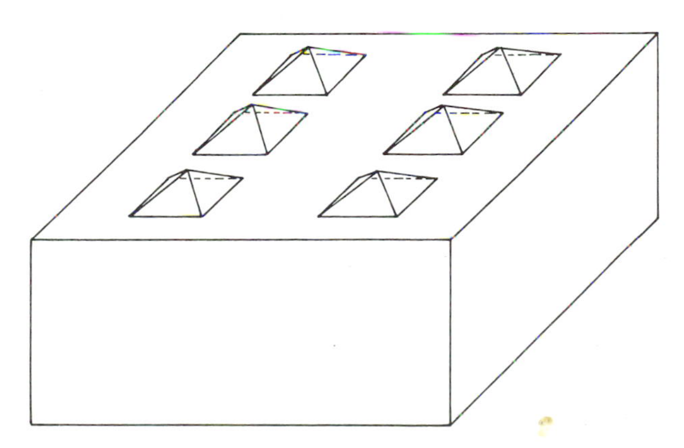

Fig. 11.7 *Rooflights, used as accents or for general lighting.*

Fig. 11.8 *Rooflights and trusses, Leisure Pool, German School, Petersham, 1981 (architects Clifford Culpin and Partners with Kersten Merkinoff and Strunk).*

Where the designer is restricted in the provision of rooflights it is often better to concentrate it on certain aspects of the design – a lightwell or access spine – so as not to imbalance the artificial lighting to the main working area. Leisure facility developments appear less restricted in this respect, although the problem of glare in sports halls must be considered. A variety of solutions is possible, such as monitor lights. These can be supported by triangular or diamond trusses and can combine lighting (artificial and natural) and ventilation within a specific structural feature (Fig. 11.8).

A regular distribution of rooflights at 10% of the area will be of marginal benefit in daylighting terms but will assist with the provision of smoke vents, if required.

Reliance upon artificial illumination has also reduced the importance of clearstorey or side lighting in factory buildings. Windows, if provided, are small for security reasons and devised as vision 'slots' to relieve eyestrain and monotony of view (Fig. 11.9). Another solution is to limit daylighting to communication aisles, the glazing being taken to full height to maximize daylight penetration, the facade having solar screens or recesses to reduce glare and heat gain (Fig. 11.9).

Building zones such as display areas, entry halls, offices and refectories are usually fenestrated to full daylighting standard with window wall or strip glazing in the conventional manner (Fig. 11.10).

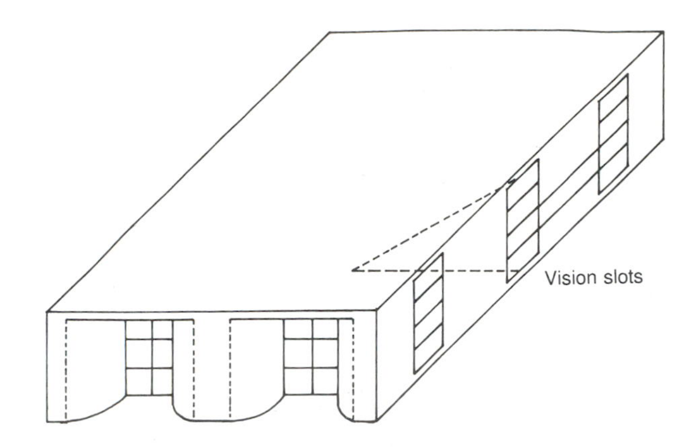

Fig. 11.9 *Vision slots in factory walls.*

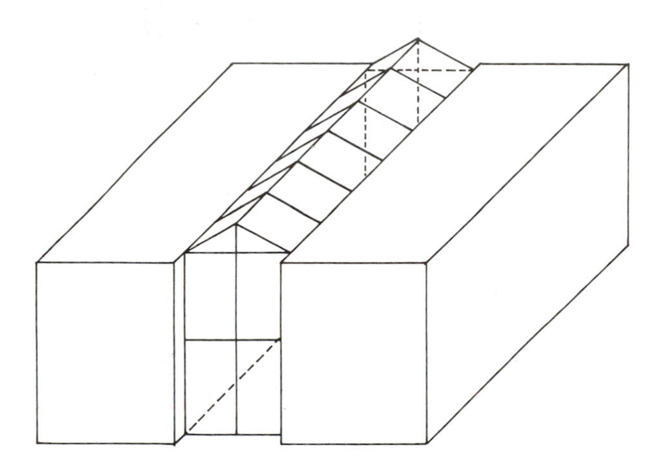

Fig. 11.10 *Full daylighting to specific areas of a building.*

11.3.2 Temperature and humidity control

The basic criteria are the temperature and humidity control needed by building users. Simple storage sheds are the easiest to deal with, since goods instead of people are largely involved. Large office or shop spaces are at the opposite extreme where stale air needs extracting at high level with fresh air introduced evenly at low velocity. Ducts therefore need to be in large sections to contain the air flow from the cooling/heating and humidifying plant (Fig. 11.11). Subdivided office spaces with desk-bound workers will require relatively uniform conditions (Fig. 11.6) with a well insulated envelope free from draughts, extra artificial heat coming from wall radiators or underfloor systems. Large workshops, by comparison, need clear floor and wall spaces, and heating by high-level radiant panels may be the solution.

Large windows cause greater cooling and heating problems (Fig. 11.12). Atria are an extreme example of this, creating a stack effect due to rising internal heat. A wide temperature range for building envelopes or interiors will cause contraction and expansion, this being particularly critical with large buildings (dimensions over 30 m (100 ft)) where such movements present serious problems for building frames and cladding (Fig. 11.13).

Finally, the excellent thermal conduction characteristics of steel can allow cold or heat to track through the structure or cladding rails. Humidity and temperature changes can cause condensation unless envelope materials of roof and wall are correctly installed, with due regard for an adequate 'drying' air flow between building layers or cavities.

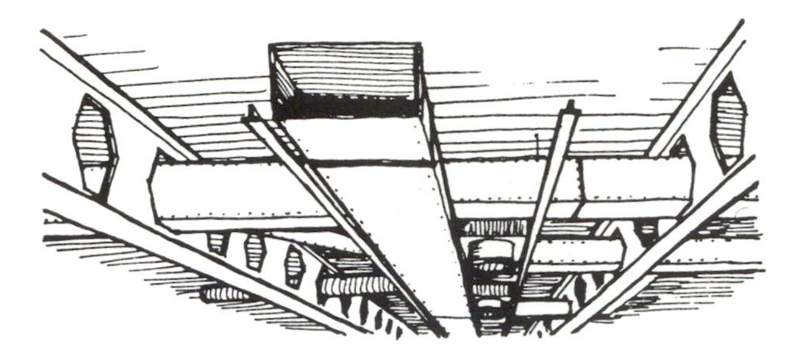

Fig. 11.11 *Air conditioning ducts accommodated within structural zone.*

Fig. 11.12 *Large windows in factory.*

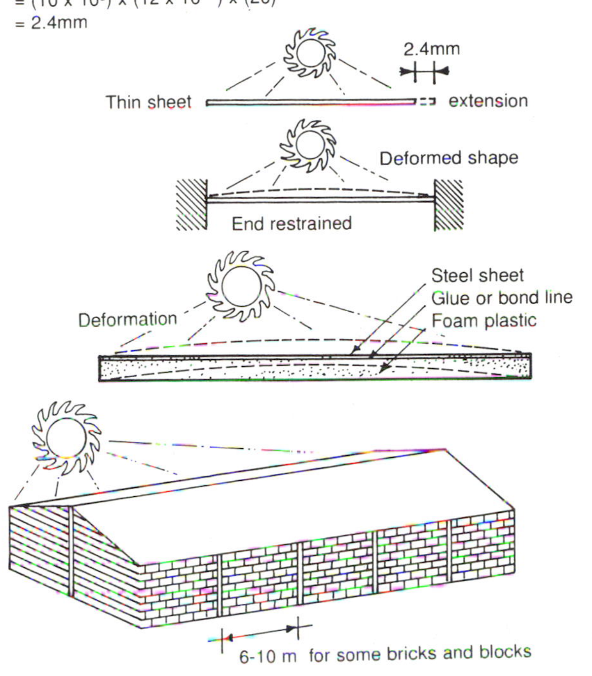

Fig. 11.13 *Typical effects of thermal movements.*

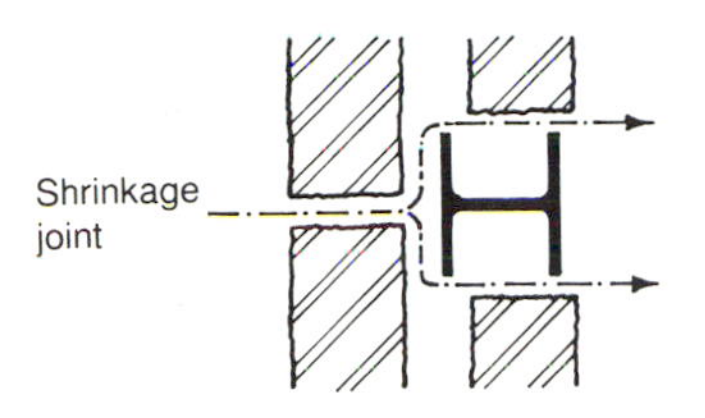

Fig. 11.14 *Inadvertent air movement through small gaps leading to undesirable heat transfer.*

Structural elements bridging cavities are at greatest risk to this cold-bridging (Fig. 11.14).

11.3.3 Precipitation

Rain and snow fall downwards but can also be blown horizontally and upwards, making corner joints and roof edges of building envelopes critical (Fig. 11.15). The simple shed with a face gutter is at far less risk than the parapet form, due to the fact that leaks (if they occur) are external to the fabric. Modern curving forms, without eaves, expose walls to the same degree of risk as roofs, with 100% water run-off affecting wall elements. Guttering and flat roofing must be laid to falls. Typical minimum slopes are 1 in 80 for most gutters with flat roofs at 1 in 40 (felt), 1 in 80 (asphalt) and 5 degrees for most forms of metal sheeting, although some sophisticated systems, such as standing seam roofs, can be laid to shallower pitches.

Fig. 11.15 *Buildings should have an impervious external fabric and coherent jointing system to resist the ingress of water or snow.*

11.3.4 Sound insulation

Unwanted sound can be a considerable irritant in buildings (Fig. 11.16), the conductive quality of steel giving rise to

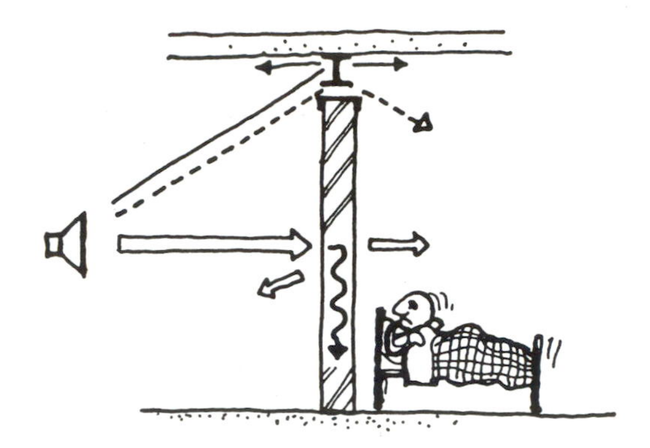

Fig. 11.16 *Sound insulation may be an important design consideration.*

problems with continuous framing of cladding elements or through the main building frame. Natural causes include heavy rain, hail and wind. Human or machine sources are far more troublesome, with the sound transferred through the air and then absorbed by solid barriers, the absorbed energy being transmitted through lightweight floors or thin panel walls and/or around their edges or directly via framing members from one space to the next. Isolating pads may need to be provided for machine bases.

The proportion of building mass to volume is a key factor in determining the acoustic characteristics [3]. At the planning stage, careful consideration should also be given to separating noisy and quiet zones, taking account of the shape and weight of barrier materials for ceilings, floors and walls.

11.3.5 Fire safety

Building legislation to prevent loss of life in case of fire stipulates standards for compartmentation, escape and structural protection. For most single storey buildings these requirements are relaxed and fire protection is not normally required for the structure supporting the roof or the external walls if they are more than 1 m (3 ft) from the relevant boundary and less than 15 m (50 ft) high (Fig. 11.17). However, party wall structures, mezzanines and plant room floors will generally require protection (Fig. 11.18) and, for some uses, insurance requirements relating to loss of goods and trade may be more stringent, including the provision of sprinklers. For portal frame buildings, with fire-protected walls, it is possible to omit fire protection from the roof structure [4,5]. Where needed, lightweight forms of protection as shown in Fig. 11.19. are normally used.

The plan areas for building volumes are limited by length of escape route, affecting plan geometry and development in depth (Fig. 11.20) and by compartment zones [6] defined under the National Building Regulations (part B of schedule 1). In essence, a single exit requires a maximum travel distance of 12 m (40 ft). Once alternative doors are provided, this can be increased to 30 m (100 ft) assuming certain

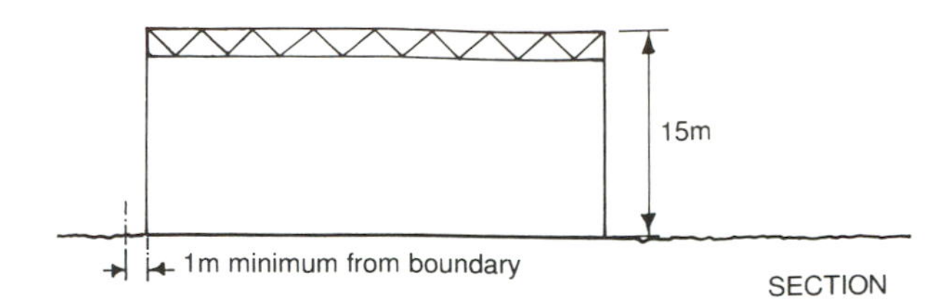

Fig. 11.17 *Single storey buildings for which fire protection is not required under UK legislation.*

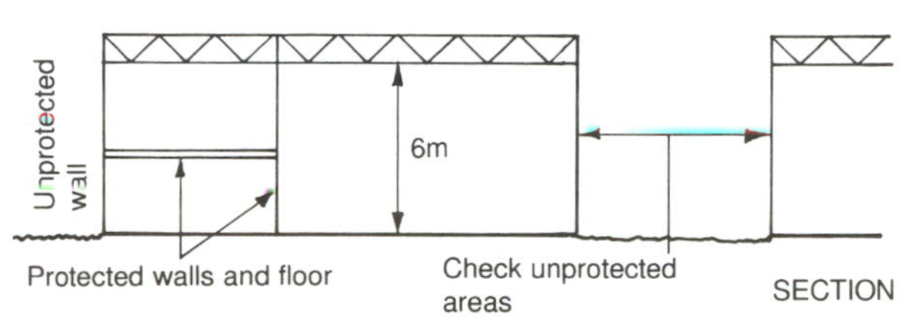

Fig. 11.18 *Areas of single storey buildings requiring protection under UK legislation.*

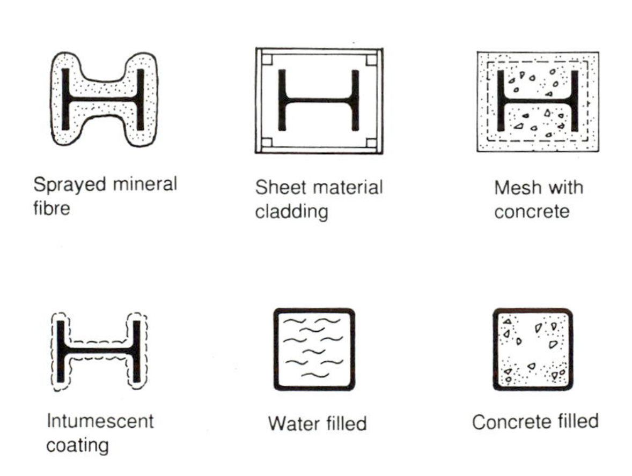

Fig. 11.19 *Alternative forms of fire protection for structural steelwork.*

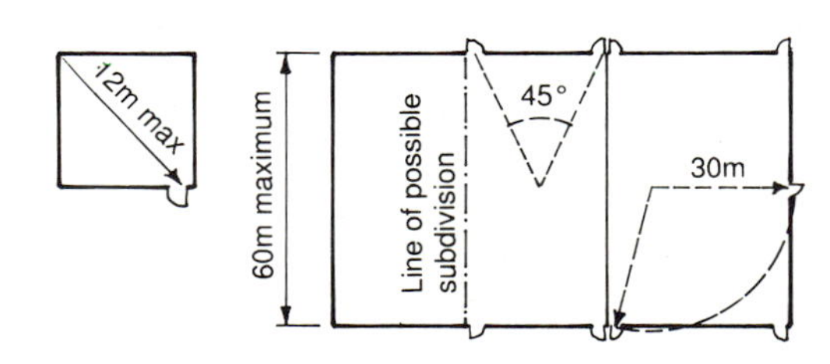

Fig. 11.20 *Escape routes related to plan geometry.*

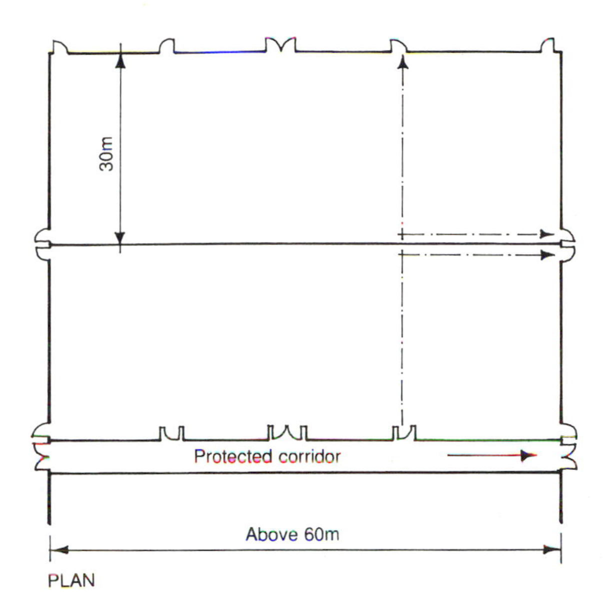

Fig. 11.21 *Escape routes via a protected corridor.*

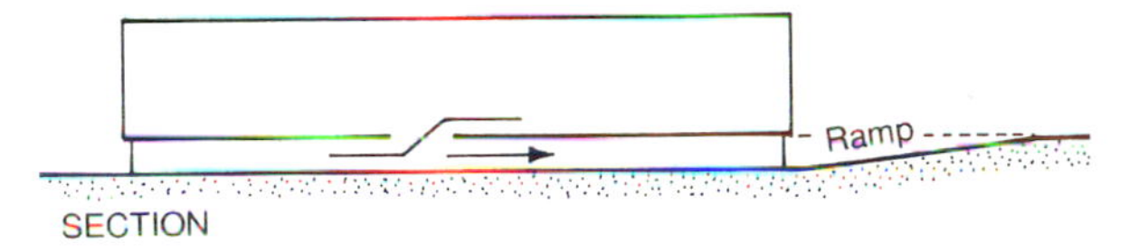

Fig. 11.22 *Basement escape routes.*

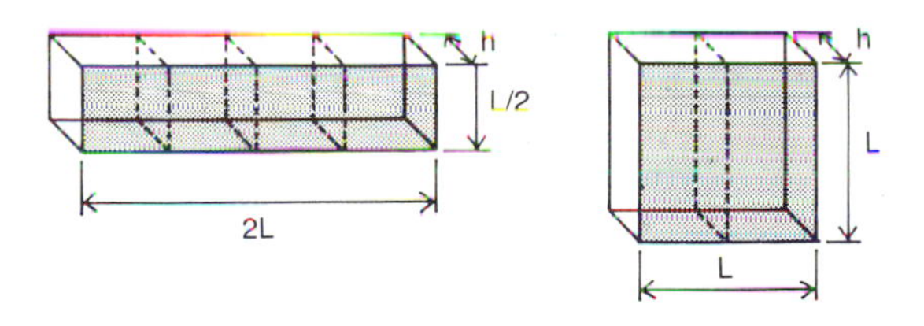

Fig. 11.23 *Comparison of rectangular and square building forms.*

criteria are also satisfied. The 30 m (100 ft) limitation can be eased if exit doors are evenly spaced on the periphery. For full reference refer to BS 5588 for the current Code of Practice for Means of Escape [7].

Multiple occupancy and large buildings with a depth in excess of 60 m (200 ft) need further consideration in terms of fire escape routes. In such cases escape is not permitted through adjoining units but has to be via a protected corridor and thence to the open air (Fig. 11.21). Internal protected routes may be located underground but the specification will be more stringent than protected routes at ground floor; for instance a lobby approach is required (Fig. 11.22). The key advantage of basement routing is the minimal constraint upon ground floor layouts.

11.4 PLAN VARIATIONS

The building shape has a significant effect on the floor-to-wall ratio and the way extension and subdivision can be achieved. Fig. 11.23 illustrates two buildings with the same floor area and with the following advantages and disadvantages:

Square Plan	(+) Provides the least external envelope, with consequent advantage in environmental control (−) Longer span structure (−) Inconvenience with subdivision
Rectangular Plan	(−) Requires 25% more cladding and higher expenditure with cooling and heating (+) Shorter and cheaper span structure is possible (+) Easier subdivision
Compound Forms (Fig. 11.24)	(−) Requires higher expenditure with cladding, cooling and heating (+) Can be related to a square grid for flexibility in planning (+) Bay size proportioned to ideal spans (+) Easy subdivision and extension

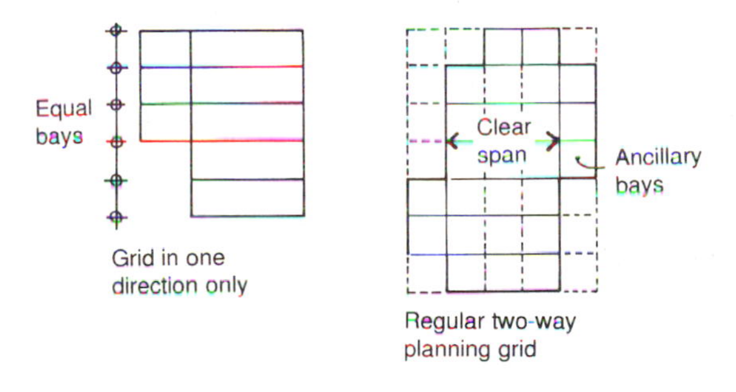

Fig. 11.24 *Compound forms.*

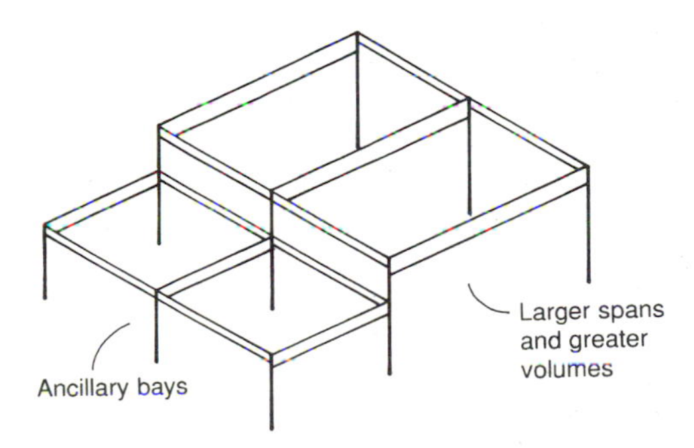

Fig. 11.25 *Structural selection of bay forms.*

Figure 11.24 also reveals the advantage of employing square grid planning in shaping initial studies, which may be developed into rectangular bays as the structure is studied in detail. Fig. 11.25 reveals how Fig. 11.24 might be developed in this fashion with assembly of differing sized volumes.

The principles described above relate to buildings which are essentially rectangular in plan, but they can be applied to buildings with other plan forms. Buildings which are circular in plan in fact require least envelope.

11.5 ROOFS AND ROOFING

A flat roof form of construction provides the most economical building volume and is a form which is most adaptable to change and extension. However, because of the possible need for a more sophisticated waterproofing system flat roofs may not be the most economical solution overall. Pitched roof forms impose discipline in terms of bays and slopes in order to rationalize gutters and the subframing to sloping planes (Fig. 11.26). However, they are less prone to leakage than flat roofs since the water is shed much more efficiently down the sloping plane. Minimum pitches are related to the type of roof covering, common angles being as follows:

Profiled and formed sheets	5 degrees
Felt tiles over ply	12 degrees
Slates	18 degrees (dependent upon size of slate)
Interlocking tiles	22 degrees (dependent upon pattern)
Plain tiles	35 degrees

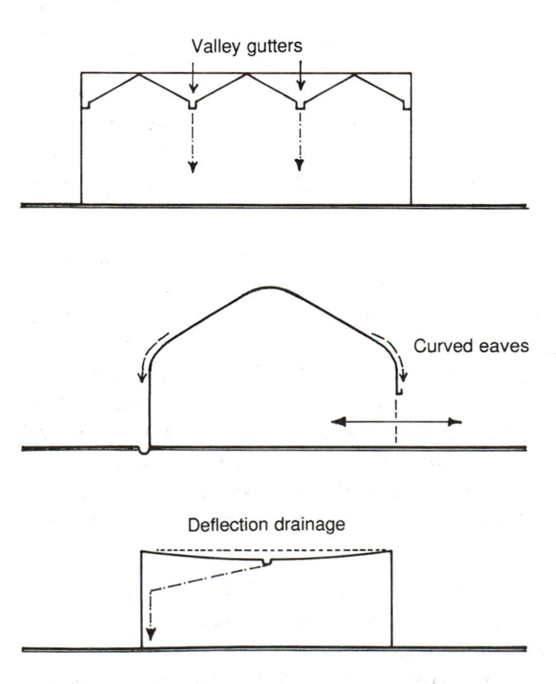

Fig. 11.26 *Alternative roof drainage systems.*

Table 11.1 Cost and maintenance of roofing materials

Form	*Initial cost range*	*First maintenance*
Built-up roofing (felt)	Low	7–10 years
Single layer polymeric	Low	20 years
Coated steel (profiled)	Low	20–40 years (refer to Chapter 5.4)
Interlocking coated steel with standing seam	Medium	20–40 years (as yet unproven) (refer to Chapter 5.4)
Stainless sheeting with standing seam (without mastic joints)	High	At least 60 years (refer to Chapter 6)

The choice of material related to a particular roof slope depends not only upon first cost but also upon the maintenance requirements. It seems appropriate at this stage to set down a summary of key roofing materials and the likely period until first maintenance for systems suitable for shallow pitches (Table 11.1).

Many roof materials will perform equally well on near flat (2½ degrees) and sloping surfaces, the ultimate judgement resting with the roof shape and finish preferred. For detailed appraisal of coverings refer to chapters 26 and 28.

As a general rule the framing construction should suit the economics of the cladding and not the other way about. By example, the designer should seek out the appropriate roof cladding and then size and space the purlins to suit that component. Economizing on purlin design by wider spacing and heavier sizing may well result in a totally uneconomic cladding that is over designed for the particular situation. Similarly roof pitches should be geared to the optimum (lowest pitch) appropriate to the roofing system chosen. Exposure ratings and advice from roofing specialists need to be assessed but architectural taste for 30, 45 or 54 degrees are irrelevant to the technology of fitting pitch to a proprietary cladding. The aim of a roof designer should therefore be to enclose the minimum volume to comply with cladding and design requirements and thus minimize envelope and heating costs.

11.6 STRUCTURAL LOADING

Building structures must be designed to resist the worst combination of applied loads likely to occur during their 'design' lifetime. The principal types of loading are described briefly below.

Dead loads: these are the gravity loads associated with

construction materials, and values can be assessed reasonably accurately from tables of mass density (e.g. the *New Metric Handbook* [8]) or taken from structural engineering tables or manufacturer's data (Fig. 11.27).

Imposed or live loads: the key document is BS 6399: Part 1 [9], which stipulates load values appropriate to different functional activities in buildings. The figures are given as uniformly distributed loads per unit area and are a principal influence on structural design of roofs and floors and their supporting frames and foundations (Fig. 11.27).

Roof loads (Fig. 11.28): these are defined in BS 6399: Part 3 [10] which gives values for loads due to maintenance and snow. In the case of snow loading, the figures vary with roof slope, altitude and geography. Abrupt changes in roof geometry, such as valleys and eaves with parapets, can lead to snow drifts and increased loadings may need to be considered locally. There are examples of such drifting causing roof collapse [11] or damage from falling snow or ice; snow guards are common features at the bottom of roofs in cold climates susceptible to high snowfalls, such as alpine areas.

16 stone man = 1/10 tonf = 102 kgf = approx 1.0 kN

An extreme gale exerts about 0.7- 0.9 kN on an adult (very approximately, as it is dynamic and dependent on size and clothes)

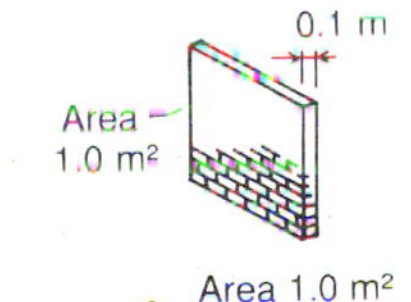

An average brick wall 100 mm thick, weighs (mass density/m³) x (thickness) x (gravity, g)
= 2000 x 0.1 x 9.81/1000
= 1.96 kN/m²

Area 1.0 m²
0.1 m

Concrete floor, 100 mm thick, weighs
= 2400 x 0.1 x 9.81/1000
=2.35 kN/m²

One gallon of water = 10 lbf = 4.54 kg = 0.044 kN
1 m³ water weighs 1000 kg = 0.981 kN

A 203 x 133 UB steel beam weighs 25 kg/m - the strongman could carry a 6 - 8m length

Building usage	U.d.load	Concentrated load on 0.3m²
House	1.5 kN/m²	11.4 kN
Classroom	3.0	2.7
Gymnasia	5.0	3.6
Library, stack room	2.4 kN/m² per m of stack height	7.0

Fig. 11.27 *Applied loadings for buildings.*

Fig. 11.28 *Roof loads.*

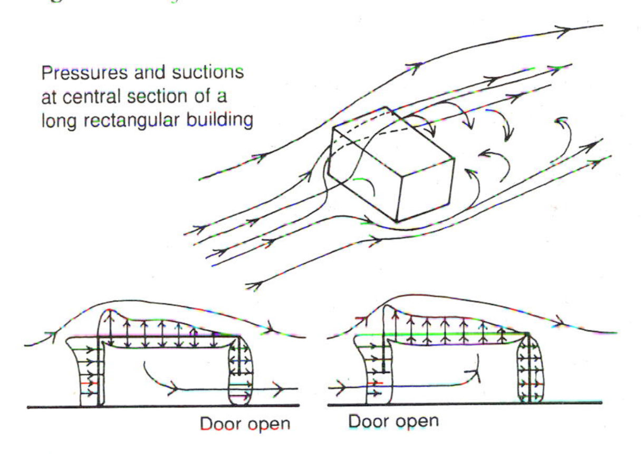

Fig. 11.29 *Wind loads on buildings.*

Wind loads (Fig. 11.29): these are dealt with in CP3 Chapter V Part II [12] (soon to be replaced by a new part of BS 6399), and are related to location and exposure. Pressure distributions can be quite complex. Building walls and roofs may be subject to suction or pressure depending on wind direction and building size and shape. Pressure can also be magnified locally due to turbulence, and individual components, such as cladding panels or glazing, are generally more vulnerable.

Dynamic loads: where load sources are dynamic in nature additional effects may need to be considered [13]. Vibration, due for instance to oscillating machinery, can cause damage unless the structure is designed to be insensitive to the range of frequencies anticipated or absorbent dampers are provided to give structural isolation. Moving loads, such as cranes or traffic, create effects due to acceleration and deceleration. These can often be accounted for by amplifying the effective load on the structure, although in severe cases, the fatigue behaviour of the structure may need to be checked.

Seismic loads: loads due to earthquakes can be particularly onerous with catastrophic consequences. The problem relates to certain areas of the world at the boundaries of slowly moving tectonic plates and requires special consideration [14].

11.7 STRUCTURAL DESIGN SEQUENCE FOR A FRAMED BUILDING

Once a possible fit has been found between the demands of a functional arrangement and a building structure, then a more detailed investigation can proceed, as outlined below.

11.7.1 Form of main structure

Firstly, postulate systems for the main structure, recognizing the need for adequate strength and stiffness to resist the applied loads. Next identify the 'load paths' on the 'structural model' through to the foundations to maintain equilibrium and sketch the likely deflected forms to help understand the load actions. Finally, determine the types of force occurring in the various elements (as shown in Fig. 11.30) – tension T, compression C and bending with shear B + S. These have implications for the size and form of the element, and may therefore influence the design concept.

Element sizes can be estimated on the basis of simple criteria, e.g. 'span/depth' ratios for beams, so that on sketches the elements begin to approximate to their likely final proportions.

11.7.2 Structural design

Figure 11.30 can also be developed as a reference for envisaging joint arrangements and for assessing various loads. Detailed analysis (Fig. 11.31) will enable the calculation of beam and column reactions and those parameters – for example bending, shear and deflection – which affect element sizes.

For a large or complicated structure it is common practice to use a computer program to model the complete structure for all load combinations. However, although such methods can relieve the designer of much of the tedious repetitive calculations at the detailed design stage, they are not a substitute for clear and creative thinking, particularly at the early stages. There is also a tendency to rely too much on computer analysis, both in terms of using oversophisticated

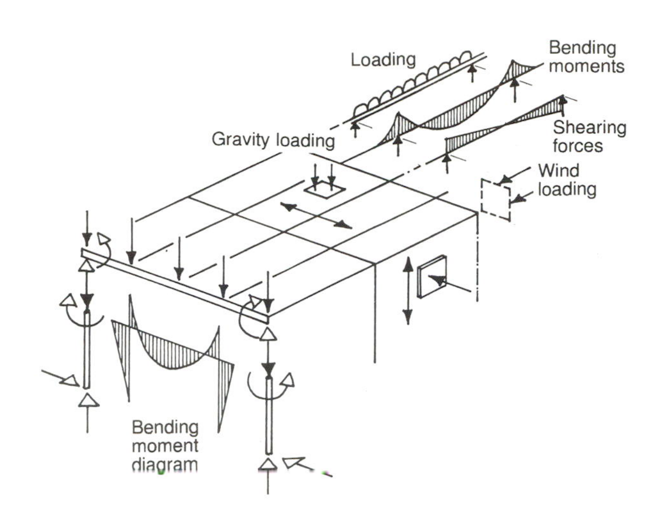

Fig. 11.31 *Structural analysis involves the assessment of loads, and calculation of structural effects such as bending moment, shear force and deflection.*

analysis for simple structures, and accepting results without critical evaluation. However, used in a responsible way, computer-aided design can be a very powerful tool, particularly in analysing structures and sizing individual elements.

11.7.3 Consideration of joints

The process of structural design must eventually develop engineer's line diagrams (Fig. 11.32) into connection 'details' (Fig. 11.33). Where failures in framing have arisen, they are commonly attributed to poor joint design, inadequate detailing of connections and lack of integration in terms of the complete building structure. The detailed examination of joints and the connection of frame to envelope may necessitate a revision of element sizes. Clearly, standardization of elements and simple ways of detailing connections will produce economies and reduce errors during fabrication and erection (refer to chapters 22 and 23).

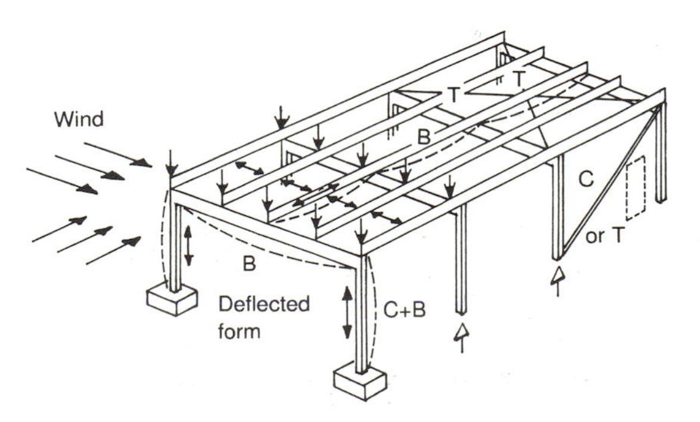

Fig. 11.30 *Typical structural model identifying types of action occurring in the various elements.*

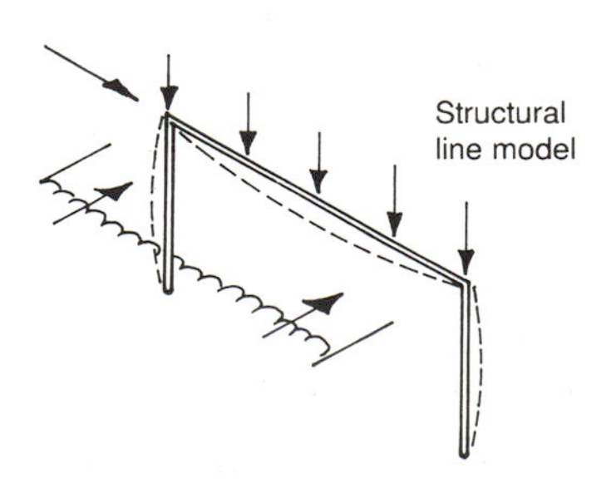

Fig. 11.32 *Line model as a basis for structural element design.*

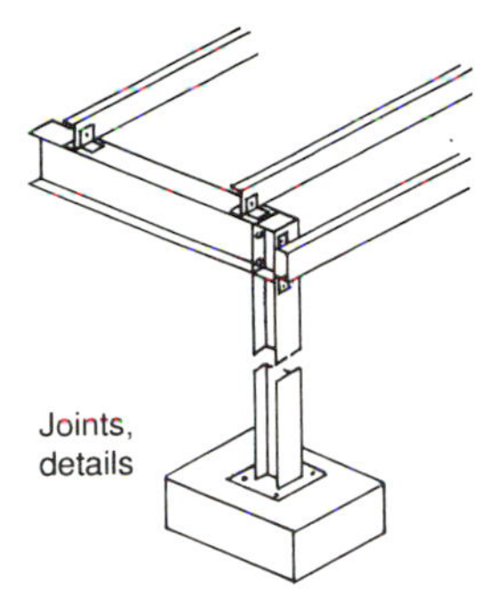

Fig. 11.33 *Detailed structural design involves determining sizes for all elements and joint details.*

11.7.4 Optimum design

Selecting frames by minimizing weight may or may not lead to overall economy. Apart from problems of deflection, sound transmission and vibration, which may be more pronounced in lightweight frames, it is important to recognize that other aspects will influence overall costs. These include the ease with which services can be accommodated, overall floor depth, speed of construction and maintenance. The cost of the structure is often a relatively small proportion of the whole and a well integrated 'simple system' for the structure will often lead to economy overall. However, this may not always equate with visual delight.

In principle, engineers design from the roof downwards whilst constructors think matters through from the foundation upwards; both directions of thought are needed by the designer (Fig. 11.34) since elements and details may also need modification due to the sequence of building operations.

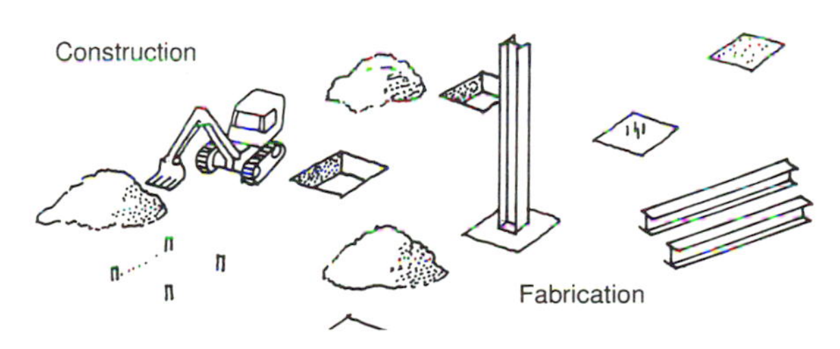

Fig. 11.34 *The building process, starting from foundations and working upwards.*

11.7.5 Communication and integration of ideas

It is of course necessary to communicate the integrity of the system through drawings and work statements to others involved in the construction process. The examples in chapters 36 and 37 reveal how good designers are excellent both in arriving at elegant structures and also in communicating their intentions clearly.

11.8 STRUCTURAL PRINCIPLES RELATED TO STEELWORK

A structural system has to be considered as a complete unit together with the soil below to ensure equilibrium and adequate strength and stiffness to resist any likely loading pattern. However, once the distribution of forces has been established, individual structural elements can be considered largely in isolation in order to determine their form and size. This basic principle is the same whatever the size of structure – small stool or skyscraper.

11.8.1 Structural element types

A simple tension element, such as a cable or chain, with no internal bending stiffness takes up a funicular 'hanging' form (Fig. 11.35), a very large horizontal force being needed to maintain a shallow sag. Deformation involves initial sag due to self weight with further stretching due to applied loads. However, only a modest stiffness is required if bending effects are small, for instance due to self weight only. Although cables have no effective bending stiffness, other types of tension element, such as rods, which are very slender, can be used. Where cables are connected to foundations they can be anchored by mass concrete, piles or rock anchors (Fig. 11.36).

A slender compression element subject to an increasing axial load can deform sideways and eventually buckle laterally. Increasing horizontal loading or the eccentricity of the end loads will make the element deform more easily, and

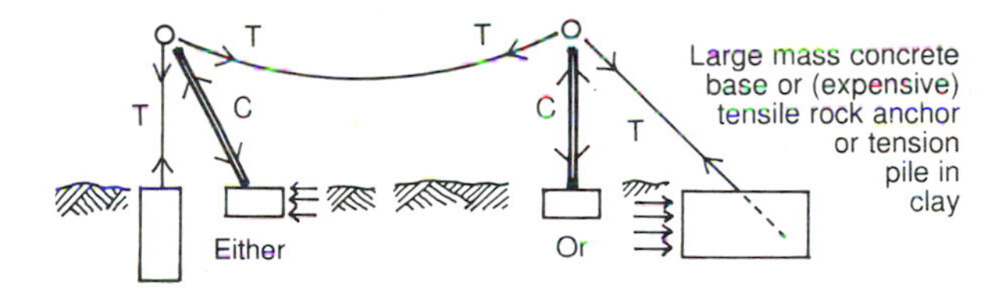

Fig. 11.35 *A simple tension element.*

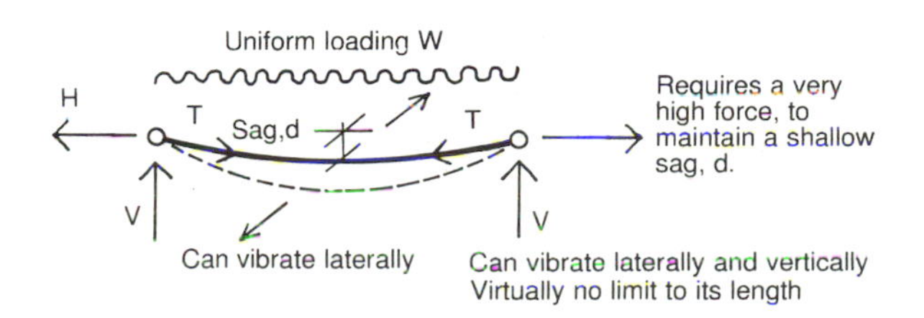

Fig. 11.36 *Anchoring systems for structural cables.*

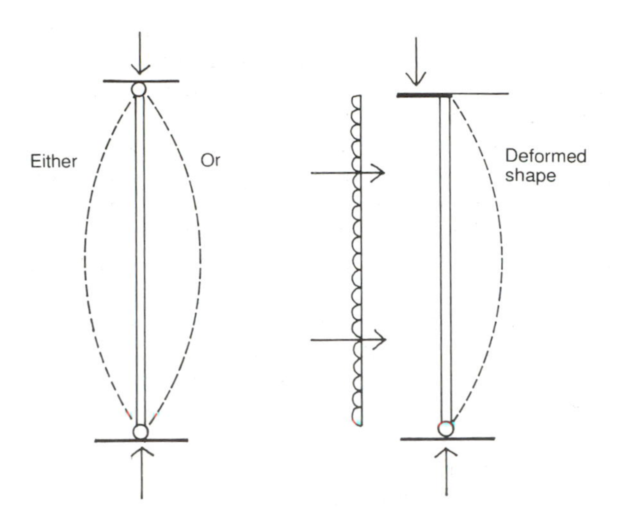

Fig. 11.37 *Simple compression elements may buckle sideways under axial load. This is made worse by horizontal or eccentric loading.*

greater bending stiffness is needed (Fig. 11.37). This can be improved by keeping the column lengths as short as possible or by bracing laterally near mid-height; other alternatives include increasing the size of the cross-section (second moment of area), or increasing restraint at supports thus reducing the effective buckling length. A less common solution for pin-ended columns is to use two-way tapered fabricated columns (cigar shaped), reducing steel towards the joints and increasing it towards the critical central length.

The true arch form is the 'inversion' of a funicular hanging form (but using stiff materials) and is parabolic in shape (Fig. 11.38). Only compression stresses occur, and it is perhaps worth quoting the Persian saying 'that the arch never sleeps' since settlement or spread can be destructive. Other arch geometries, such as circular forms, involve a combination of bending and compression (Fig. 11.39). However, the simpler circular shapes may be cheaper to construct and clad.

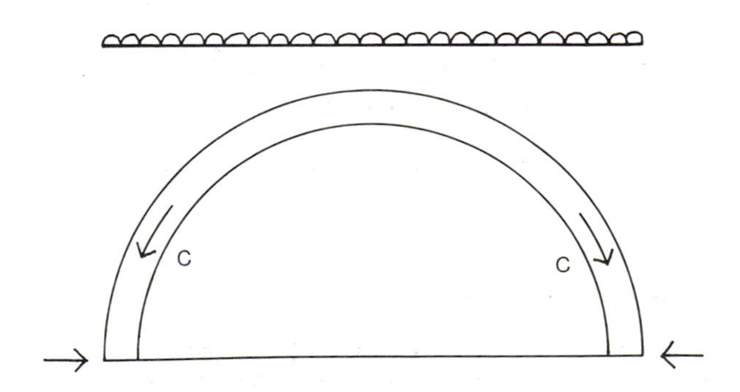

Fig. 11.38 *Basic arch subject to compressive stress only.*

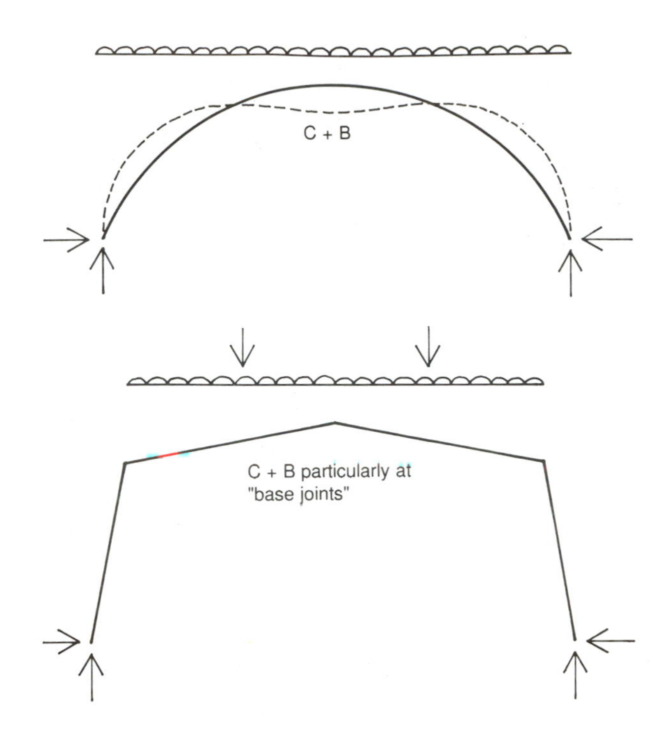

Fig. 11.39 *Non-parabolic arch forms combining compression and bending.*

In common with some other structural forms, notably trusses, size and geometry of arches may present transport difficulties. Arched trusses are only partially assembled before delivery to site. The arch is then completed using bolts or welding before erection. (The same provision is made for trusses in general where the length exceeds 18 m). Cladding to curved structures is usually in the form of corrugated curved sheets with a continuous section placed across the ridge.

Bending elements can take the form of trusses or solid beams. Trusses are a combination of compression and tension (C + T) elements (Fig. 11.40) arranged in a wide variety of shapes. The conventional lattice girder with parallel top and bottom chords provides uniform fixings for services and/or suspended ceilings.

Solid beams combine compression and tension effects within a shallow depth to resist bending (Fig. 11.41). In addition, shearing (S) effects occur. The greatest bending

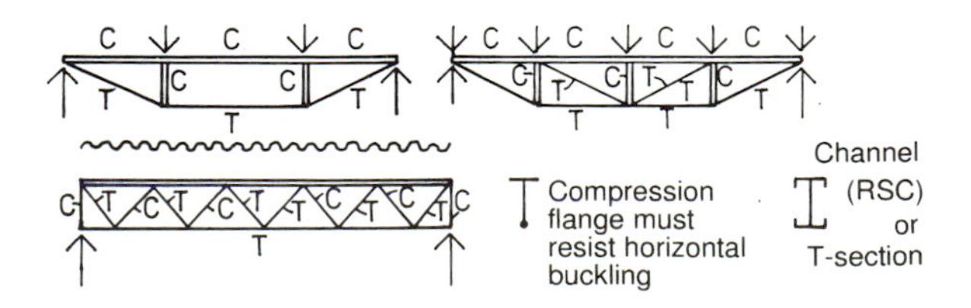

Fig. 11.40 *Truss forms combining compression and tension elements.*

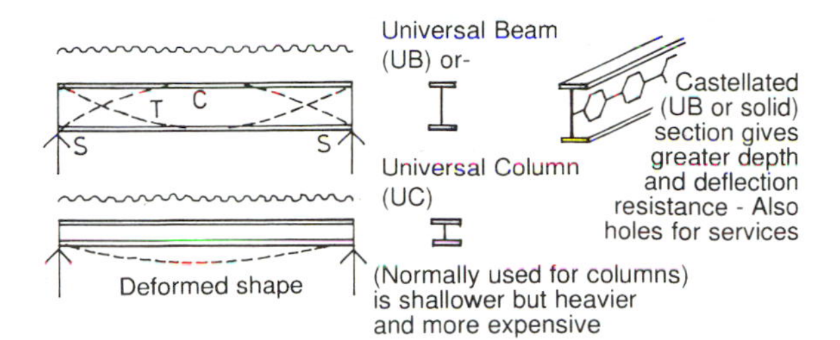

Fig. 11.41 *Solid web and castellated beam.*

Load type	Value of maximum deflection	
W = wL; L	$\delta_{max} = \frac{1}{76.8} \times \frac{WL^3}{EI}$ or $\frac{5}{384} \times \frac{wL^4}{EI}$	
W; L	$\delta_{max} = \frac{1}{48} \times \frac{WL^3}{EI}$	Where:-
W/2, W/2; L/3, L/3, L/3	$\delta_{max} = \frac{1}{56.4} \times \frac{WL^3}{EI}$	W = total load L = span E = Young's modulus
W/3, W/3, W/3; L/4, L/4, L/4, L/4	$\delta_{max} = \frac{1}{60.6} \times \frac{WL^3}{EI}$	I = Moment of inertia
W= wL; L	$\delta_{max} = \frac{1}{8} \times \frac{WL^3}{EI}$	$\delta_{max} = \frac{kWL^3}{EI}$ k is a factor depending on end conditions of beam and load type
W; L	$\delta_{max} = \frac{1}{3} \times \frac{WL^3}{EI}$	

Fig. 11.42 *Deflections related to support and loading conditions.*

		L/D	
Rolled Steel Beams (UB, UC, RSJ)		**= < 20**	**D; Span L**
Trusses: (one way span)	**Heavy Loading**	**= 12 - 15)**	**Use higher values where rigid joints used**
	Medium Loading	**= 15 - 18)**	
	Light (roof) Loading (Max. 3m spacing)	**= 18 - 21)**	
Space Decks and Grids:		**= 20 - 48 bolted/welded joints**	
	'Nodus'	**= 20, with perimeter columns**	
	or	**= 15, only 4 corner columns**	

Limit Column say due to wind force = H/325

Fig. 11.43 *Rules of thumb for estimating the sizes of flexural elements.*

stresses are generally at mid-span whilst the worst shearing effect occurs at the beam ends. Bending and deformation resistance depend on the second moment of area, 'I', a function of the cross-sectional geometry which is closely related to beam depth. A method of increasing load carrying capacity is therefore to use castellated beams which also provide space for services to pass within the structural zone.

Bending is affected by the type as well as the magnitude of the applied loading. A central point load causes double the bending effect of a uniformly distributed load of the same size. Deflections are similarly influenced by load type as well as by support conditions (Fig. 11.42).

Basic rules of thumb (Fig. 11.43) can give the designer guidance as to likely depths for spans using differing forms of roof framing (for example solid beams, trusses or space decks). For columns, notional cross-sectional sizes can be estimated from Safe Load Tables [15].

11.8.2 Structurally continuous elements

Beams or purlins continuous over several spans reduce deformation and even out applied bending moments, reducing maximum stresses and hence allowing shallower sections to be used (Fig. 11.44). However, fabrication may be more complex, and there may be other disadvantages, such as increased transmission of sound and vibrations. Design calculations too are more complicated. Engineers classify such structures as statically indeterminate. Simpler statically determinate structures, such as single span beams, are those for which reactions, forces and moments can be calculated directly from the conditions of equilibrium. By way of contrast, statically indeterminate structures have some degree of 'redundancy', that is some structural actions which are not necessary for maintaining equilibrium. Such cases typically require the solution of simultaneous equations based on assumed member sizes and this can be a complicated process often done now by computer.

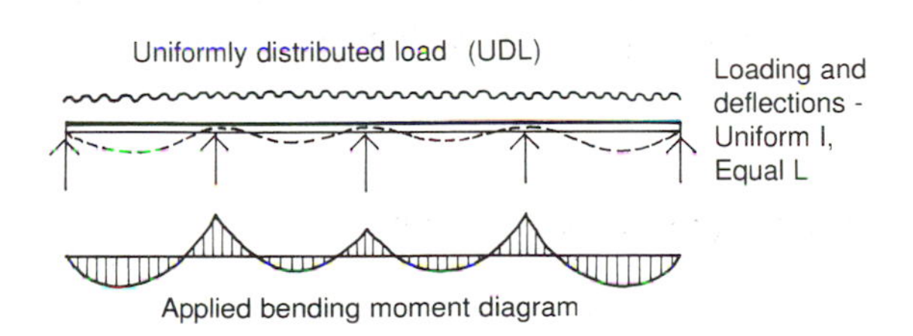

Fig. 11.44 *Reduced bending moments in structurally continuous elements.*

11.8.3 Lateral stability

Figures 11.45 to 11.49 illustrate the principles for resisting sidesway in structures which may be induced by horizontal wind or eccentric vertical loading. Note that combined

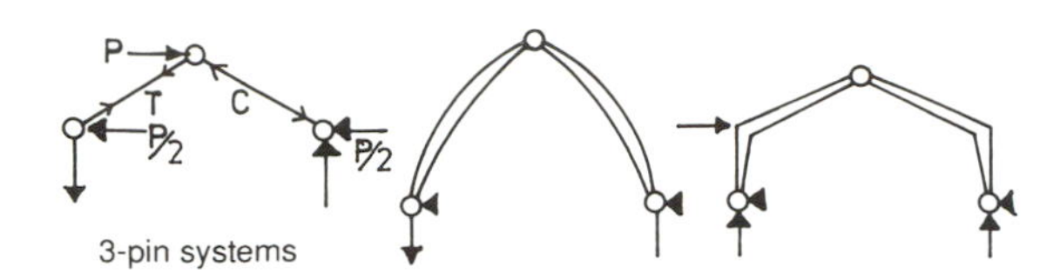

Fig. 11.45 *Triangular tent form developed into cruck frame and inclined rafter portal frame for resisting lateral loading.*

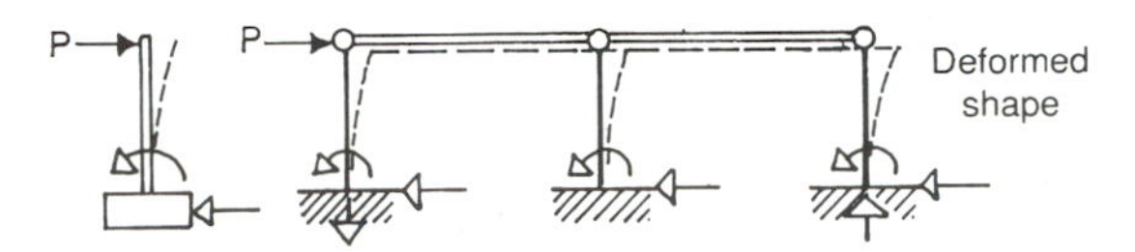

Fig. 11.46 *Fixed base columns providing stability under horizontal load.*

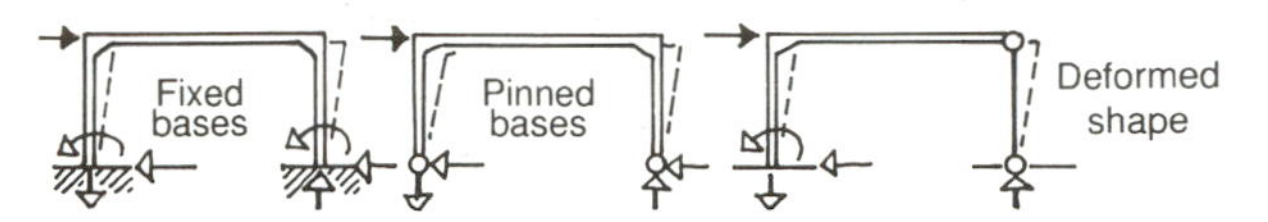

Fig. 11.47 *Rigid beam-column connections providing stability under horizontal load.*

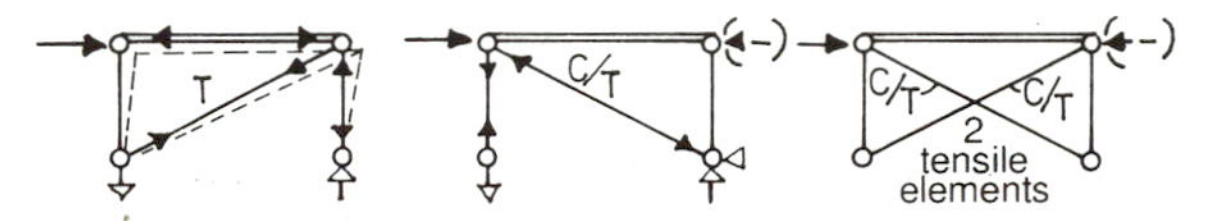

Fig. 11.48 *Diagonal bracing providing stability under horizontal load.*

horizontal and vertical loads will increase this tendency to sway. The simplest form of stable structure in this respect is a triangular 'tent'. Often this form leads to functionally waste space in the bottom corners. From the historical stone arch or timber 'cruck' frame has developed the steel arch and later the inclined rafter portal frame with three-pin, two-pin or 'fixed' joint systems (Fig. 11.45).

Alternative flat roof frames provide the designer with three options. The first is to treat the wall frames as vertical cantilevers, 'rigidly' fixed to the foundation, with simply supported roof beams. Note that the foundation size will be greater than for other alternatives due to the transfer of bending moments to the foundation (Fig. 11.46). Other options are to use a portal frame in which the beam is rigidly jointed to the column (Fig. 11.47) or to brace a pin-jointed structure (Fig. 11.48).

These principles for two-dimensional systems can easily be adopted for three-dimensional buildings, e.g. for a small flat roof framed shed. The minimum requirement for three-dimensional stability is a braced roof and at least three braced connected walls arranged on plan to provide adequate torsional restraint. For deformation and sway control, the fourth wall should also be braced (Fig. 11.49).

Pitched roof structures can use similar methods to achieve lateral stability, with diagonal bracing, possibly in conjunction with the purlins and decking, providing a braced, near

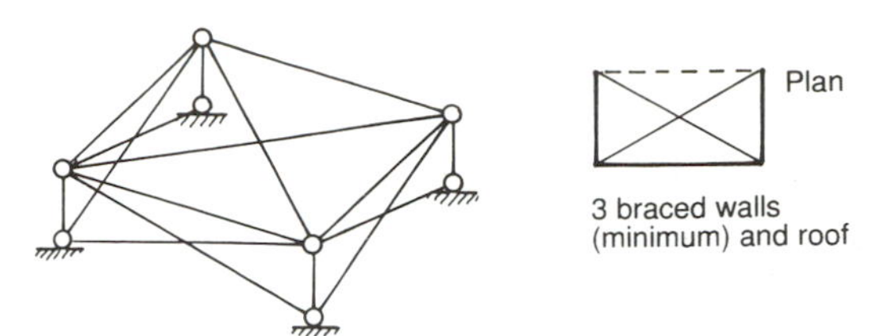

Fig. 11.49 *Bracing requirements for stability in 3-dimensional buildings.*

horizontal, plane. Fixing details must be carefully designed and their installation closely supervised if the roof sheeting is to contribute to this provision .

11.9 STRUCTURAL SYSTEMS FOR SINGLE STOREY FLAT-ROOFED SHEDS

The structure system for a building is usually arranged within or close to the exterior environmental envelope to reduce intrusion into the usable plan area. Planning grids for organizing the layout of spaces should correspond to a suitable structural grid system for compatibility, for example fit of materials, fixed doors and windows. A planning grid may be based on a 100 or 300 mm (4 or 12 in) module, while the main structural grid should be based on some multiple of the former, e.g. 4.8 m or 6.0 m (16 or 20 ft). Further consideration of planning grids is included in chapter 13.

With large span structures, internal columns may have a different spacing from perimeter columns, where a major function of the latter is to stabilize and support the cladding.

11.9.1 Masonry box construction

Figures 11.50 to 11.53 refer to masonry 'box' construction with a flat roof, all primary beams spanning the shortest distance. For modest spans, typically say 5–6 m (16–20 ft), the roof might be formed with timber joists at close centres 400–600 mm (16–24 in) with exterior quality ply deck and felt roofing (Fig. 11.50). If security or increased sound

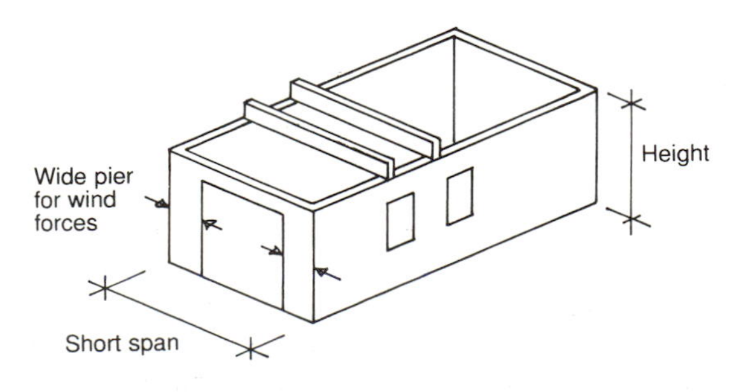

Fig. 11.50 *Masonry box with flat roof consisting of closely spaced timber joists supporting simple deck.*

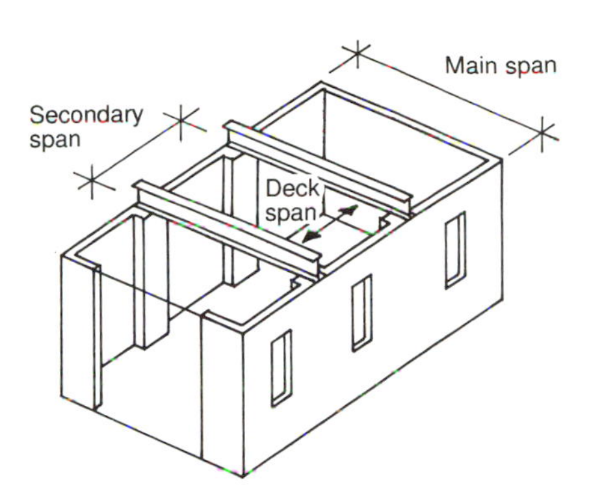

Fig. 11.51 *Roof construction consisting of primary steel beams supporting long span decking.*

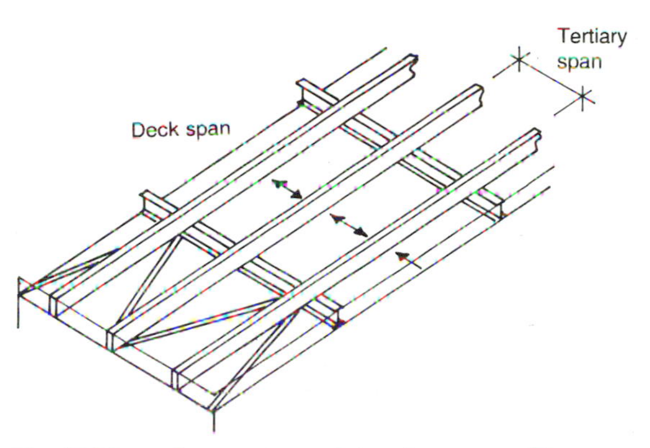

Fig. 11.52 *Roof construction consisting of primary steel beams supporting secondary beams or purlins and simple decking.*

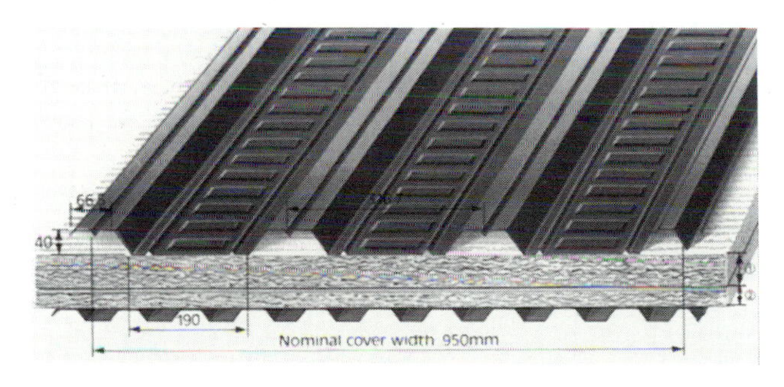

Fig. 11.53 *Long-span deck (Plannja) capable of spanning up to about 10 m (33 ft).*

insulation are design factors then precast concrete planks with insulation and felt may be a more appropriate alternative. The stability of a conventional cavity wall 'box structure' is generally satisfactory if the height is limited to 2.5 m (8 ft) with no expansion joints and a diaphragm roof. Otherwise thicker walls or piers may have to be incorporated to reduce the effective slenderness of the walls. In any

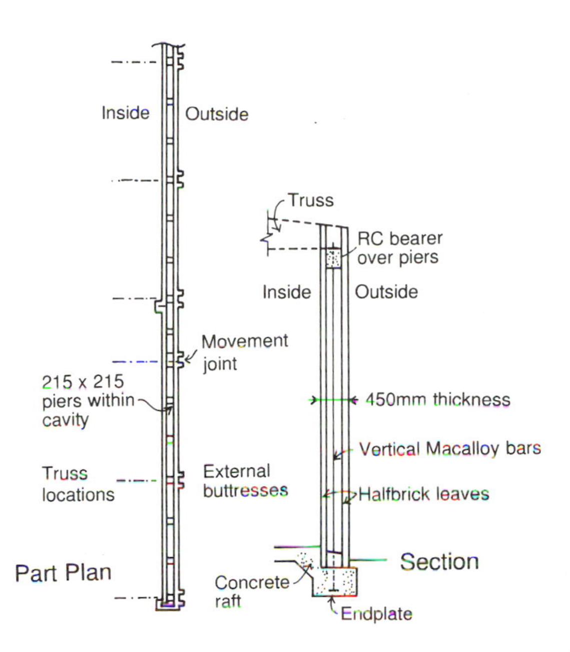

Fig. 11.54 *Diaphragm wall structure.*

case the end walls not providing direct support to the beams must be tied to the roof with straps extending over three joists or roof units.

Wind forces will generally be resisted by end walls unless there is a large opening in the short span wall. Roof decking, when well fixed to beams and walls, can be designed to act as a 'flat plate'. Alternatively, triangular bracing can be used, making a 'horizontal truss'.

Spans over 6 m (20 ft) need primary beams spanning the shortest distance and supporting secondary beams. If these are fixed to the tops of the main beams the economy of beam continuity is maintained, although the overall depth of the roof construction is increased. The main beams might be Universal Beams (UBs), castellated beams or trusses. Secondary members could be cold-formed steel beams or timber joists at about 600 mm (24 in) centres supporting plain woodwool slabs or ply deck. A simpler alternative would be metal decking or reinforced woodwool spanning up to 3 m (10 ft) clear between primary beams (Fig. 11.51). The stability of the main beams can be ensured by close fixings of the decking, by extra bracing tubes or small beams spaced at up to 4 m (13 ft) centres at right-angles to the main beam, with diagonal braces to one full bay.

When main beams span between 8 to 10 m (25 to 30 ft), say, it is probably more efficient to make the decking span onto secondary beams or purlins – possibly cold-rolled lightweight sections – spanning 1.2–2.4 m (4–8 ft) (Fig. 11.52). Although some forms of heavy duty decking (Fig. 11.53) can span 10 m (33 ft) clear, deflections and the need to maintain falls at 1 in 40 to avoid ponding often means that light short deck spans provide the easiest solution. Increasing the spacing of primary beams between 8 and 9 m (27 and 30 ft) not only increases secondary costs (beams or deck) but may also require the walls to be stiffened with piers because of the long distances between supports; it may then be more appropriate to consider a framework.

For larger scale plain box structures, such as sports halls, a masonry diaphragm wall (Fig. 11.54) may provide a suitable envelope. These consist typically of two leaves with a wide cavity – perhaps 400–600 mm (16–24 in) – interconnected with stiffening ribs. Practical structural limitations are a maximum height of 10 m (33 ft) with no large wall openings [16].

11.9.2 Framed construction

Figures 11.55 to 11.57 illustrate steel framed construction for a single storey shed. The main advantages of steel framing are that large clear spans of 40 m (130 ft) or more are feasible; the use of standard structural elements and the erection of prefabricated components on prepared bases means that construction is rapid, with three-dimensional stability ensured at an early stage by the incorporation of diagonal bracing elements to resist wind forces. Totally dry construction methods, even including precast foundations, are possible, the rapidity of construction giving faster occupation and a quicker return on capital. The main frames are often in the form of 'portals' designed to take advantage of continuity and the principles of 'plasticity' to reduce element sizes. Roof decking can be laid rapidly so that a dry platform exists for fitting out and floor laying. The enclosing walls, which can be lightweight cladding, glazing or masonry, are added later. Masonry walling may be particularly required at boundaries for fire protection or for general security, and a common pattern is a standard 2.5 m (8 ft) height to incorporate conventional door and window trim below an imperforate cladding zone. Large openings can be readily created between columns and it is an easy matter to strip out the non-structural envelope for subsequent alterations. The steel frame exposed internally is extremely adaptable for extra fixings (for instance for services or for inner linings).

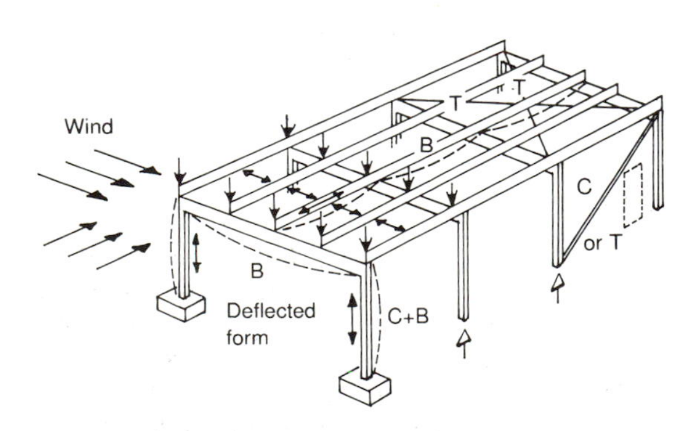

Fig. 11.55 *Isometric of complete steel framed structure.*

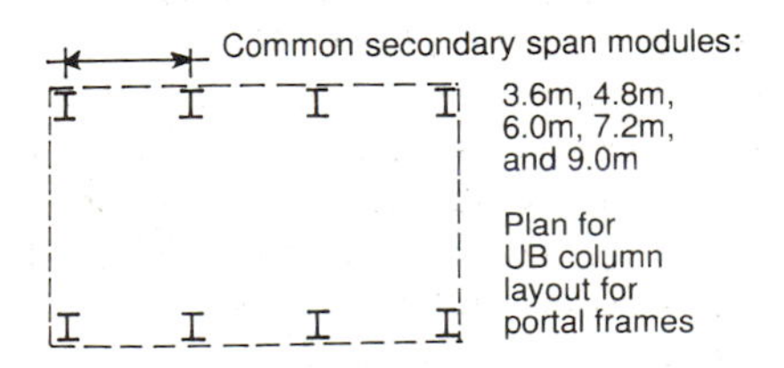

Fig. 11.56 *Plan arrangement for a steel framed building.*

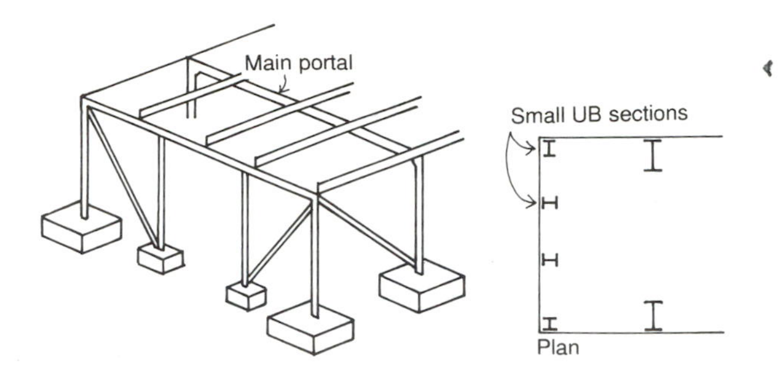

Fig. 11.57 *Gable construction for a steel framed building.*

Referring to Figs 11.56 and 11.57, the main frame sections could be Universal Beams (UBs) or Universal Columns (UCs). Tubular sections could possibly be used for the columns where a clean profile was needed, although tubes are slightly more expensive than rolled open sections.

Wind bracing is typically by means of small diameter rods or flat sections run between columns (for tension only cross-bracing). Bracing can also be formed with angles or, more efficiently and elegantly, with CHS sections (Fig. 11.58) employed as single element diagonal bracing resisting compression or tension stresses. Inevitably such diagonal bracing members are of larger cross-section than the cross-braced elements because of the need to resist compression. End wall cladding requires a subframe for support, with consequently smaller gable beams than the main frames (Fig. 11.57). Wind bracing is often incorporated in the end bay (if without large openings) and the first return bay as these are the first to be erected on site. For very long buildings the erection procedure may be from the centre outwards; with wind bracing at mid-point, two crews can work simultaneously towards the ends, where additional bracing is often included.

Secondary beams at roof level (purlins) were traditionally hot-rolled steel sections – angles, small size Universal Beams or channels at edges. Today's practice is to employ thin cold-rolled galvanized steel sections, called Z or M profiles, for purlins and side wall cladding (refer to chapter 26 for detailing).

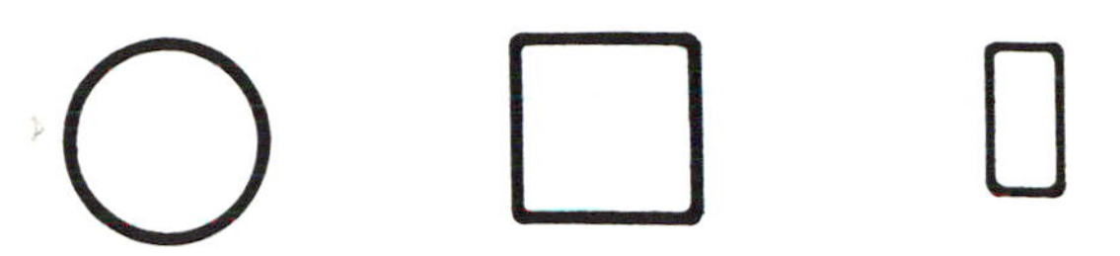

Fig. 11.58 *Structural tubes.*

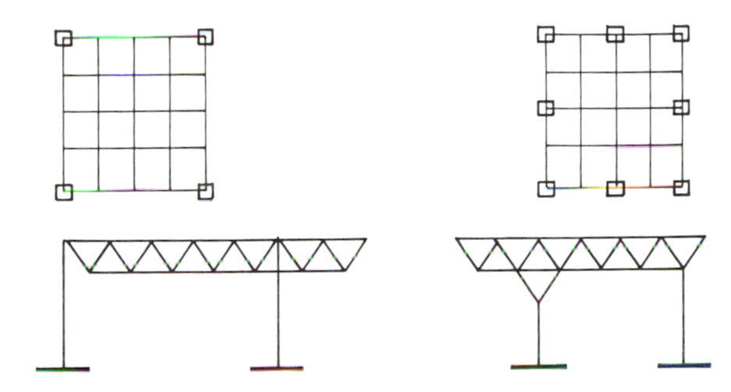

Fig. 11.59 *Space frame structures.*

11.9.3 Space frames (Fig. 11.59)

A sensible solution for a square plan (and up to a ratio of sides of about 1:1.3), might be to use a 2-way spanning 'truss' system or 'space frame' [17]. The principle of a space frame is based on the manufacture of standard small size elements and node joint connections which can be easily transported and erected rapidly. These systems make an interesting internal 'spider web' pattern. The standard systems produced (e.g. Mero and Space Deck) make for deliberate grid planning sizes which must be maintained. Internal wall partitions may need to be stabilized at the top against wind loads and their planning must fit the space frame grid. In economic terms, the joints are expensive to produce and resist less force than a fully welded fabricated joint, leading to deeper overall trusses than linear beam/truss systems. Space frames with one layer set on the diagonal have been found to be between 6% and 17% cheaper than square on square [18]. Space frames should rarely be considered if a false ceiling is to be used below, thus hiding the latticework visually.

The column supports should be distributed regularly around the periphery with the possibility of cantilevers for entrances or loading bays.

11.10 PITCHED AND OTHER ROOF FORMS

Many of the principles discussed above for flat roof structures apply equally well to pitched roofs and other shapes. The simplest cross-sectional shape for steep pitches consists of a sloping roof and vertical columns. This form can be achieved in various ways, and some of the more common systems are described below.

11.10.1 Truss and stanchion construction

The traditional form was a lightweight truss consisting of small angle sections (or angles and tie rods) bolted or riveted together. A slope of about 18 degrees attracted minimum wind loads, but steeper pitches reduced the internal forces within the truss. The compression elements of these trusses were often made of double angles. The gap between could not be repainted and often rusted badly in damp conditions. Smooth tubular elements are preferable in this respect. They are also more elegant and are increasingly common, although more expensive. The design fashion for shallower pitches can still be accommodated using truss forms, but a finite depth of truss must be maintained at the eaves (Fig. 11.60). Knee braces were traditionally used to provide resistance to wind loading (Fig. 11.61) but these are now rare.

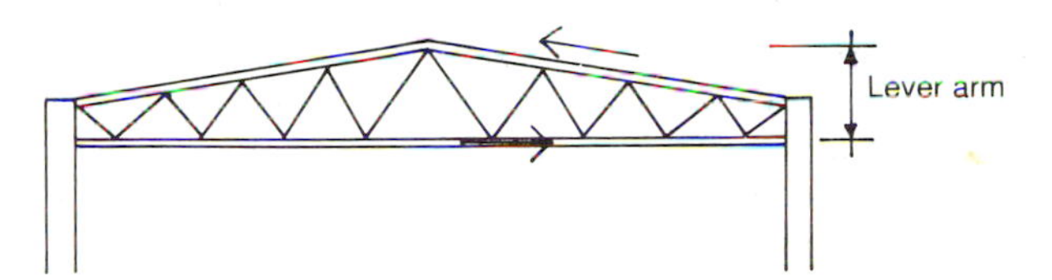

Fig. 11.60 *Tapered truss.*

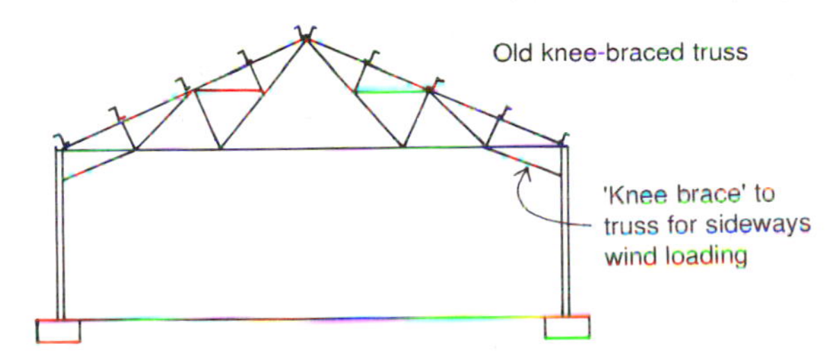

Fig. 11.61 *Knee-braced truss.*

11.10.2 Pitch portal frames

A very efficient form of construction was perfected by Conder using solid Universal Beam sections for column and rafter to form a rigid frame, known as pitch portal frame. The critical point is at the eaves and the introduction of a cut section of UB welded to the underside of the rafter at this point can reduce costs. The greater depth also facilitates a rigid joint between rafters and columns (Fig. 11.62).

These frames are usually designed using the 'plastic' theory. Structural steel is a ductile material which behaves in a 'plastic' manner at high stresses (Fig. 11.63). A section when bent develops a stress pattern which varies from a maximum compression at the top to a maximum tension at the bottom. For stresses up to yield, the variation is linear. However, further bending results in a spread of yield through the beam cross-section until finally all the material above and below the neutral axis is at yield. This condition is referred to as a 'plastic hinge'. Simply supported beams

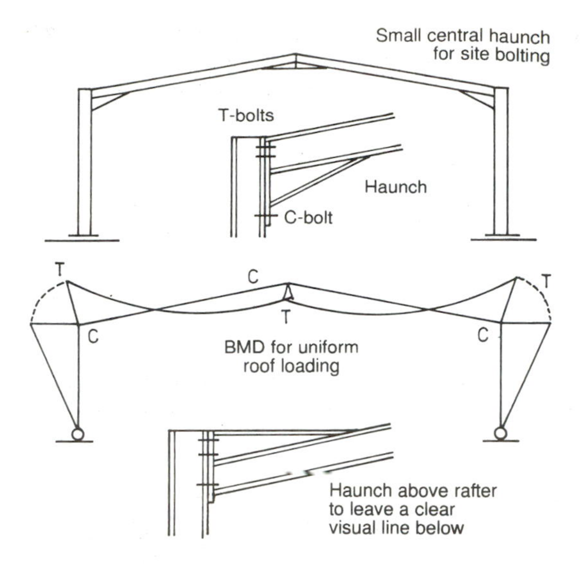

Fig. 11.62 *Portal frame haunch detail.*

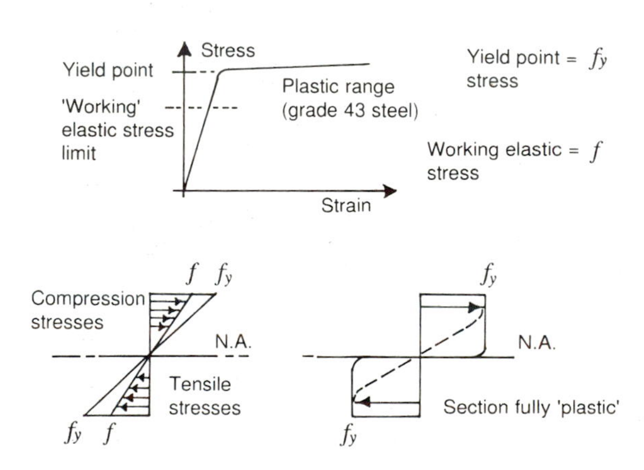

Fig. 11.63 *Plastic behaviour of steel.*

loaded uniformly will fail in this manner at mid-span, the position of maximum moment. However, statically indeterminate structures do not collapse when a single plastic hinge forms. Instead the distribution of stresses throughout the structure changes and additional loads can be carried until sufficient plastic hinges have developed to form a mechanism. In the case of a propped cantilever two 'plastic hinges' are necessary to achieve this condition (Fig. 11.64).

This is a popular approach for designing portal frames and can lead to significant economies. However, deflections at 'working loads' must be checked, for instance to prevent damage to masonry walls, and other failure modes, such as lateral buckling, must be prevented. Thus the rafters and columns are often braced to purlins and sheeting rails at critical points (Fig. 11.65).

Snow and wind loading can cause significant outward deformation and deflections at the eaves must be allowed for, especially for column heights above 4 m and where masonry walls are used.

Variations to standard portals could be more economic but these aspects depend upon relative costs of factory labour, overheads and transport and upon the unit purchase costs enjoyed by the fabricator, volume users obviously buying steel cheaper than one-off specialists. Two alternative structures are shown in Fig. 11.66, firstly a cranked

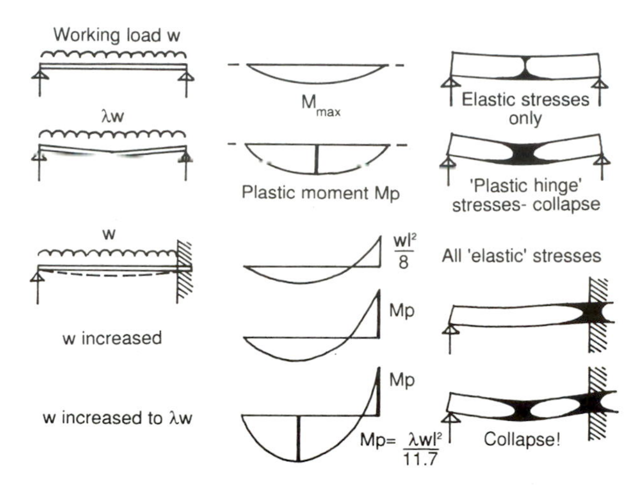

Fig. 11.64 *The development of plastic behaviour in steel beams.*

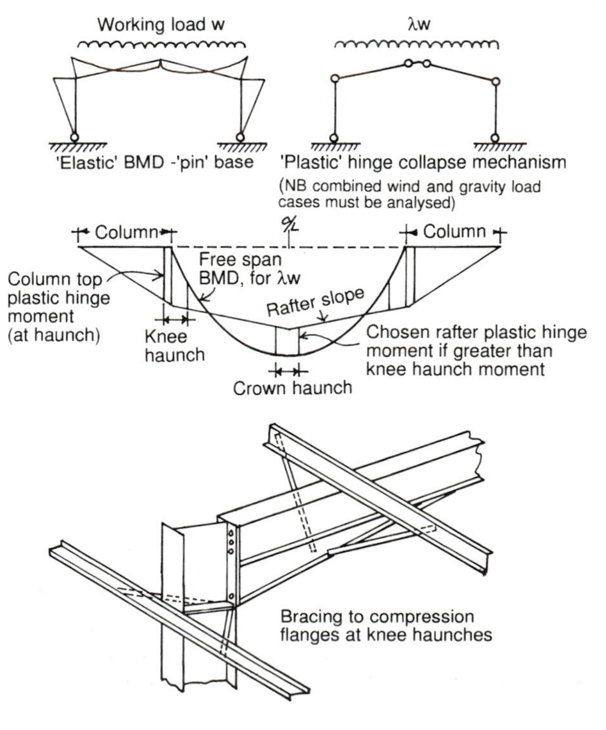

Fig. 11.65 *Portal frame construction showing bracing to critical locations.*

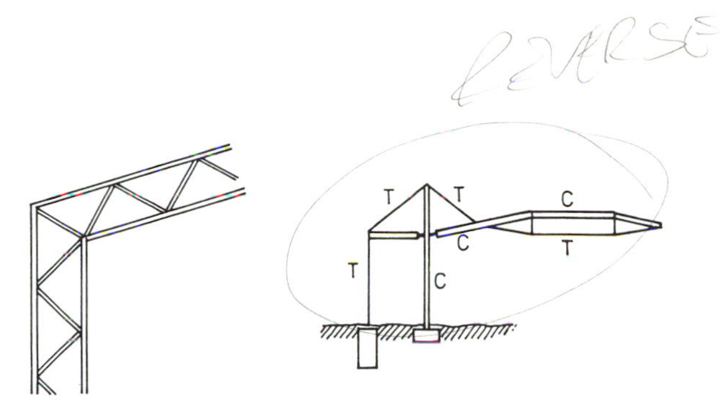

Fig. 11.66 *Cranked truss and cable stayed solutions.*

column truss and an interesting variation with a tensile frame introduced by Ove Arup and Partners for the Renault Distribution building at Swindon, UK (architects Foster Associates). Renault is typical of many commissions where the owners wish to advertise and project a corporate image with unique or innovative forms or silhouettes, another aspect being to provide an environment externally and internally that is a delight to users and visitors. Further details of award winning schemes in chapter 37 show a range of steel framed designs that fulfil this quality.

A more recent development by Wards has been to use I-sections assembled from thin plates welded together and tapered to suit strength requirements.

11.10.3 Curved shapes

An inverted tensile catenary shape is, in principle, ideal for resisting uniform gravity loads (Fig. 11.38). However horizontal and asymmetric loads, for instance due to wind or drifted snow loading, generate bending moments and hence the need for bending stiffness in the arch ribs. This complicates matters and built examples, such as St Pancras Station train shed (1868), are relatively rare. A circular form

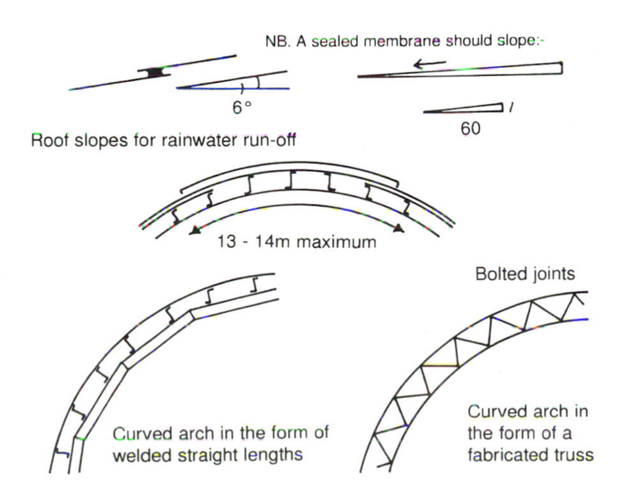

Fig. 11.67 *Alternative steel arch construction.*

is much easier to make by cold bending, or by fabricating from smaller cut sections welded into shape (Fig. 11.67). An excellent example is the Lee Valley Ice Rink in the UK.

11.10.4 Monitor roofs (Fig. 11.68)

Post-war research developed monitor rooflights to provide even daylighting, sometimes with the supporting framework being cranked portals with flat roofed zones (to falls) between and above the monitors [19]. These structural solutions are not ideal and recent developments, such as used at the German School, Petersham [20], demonstrate the way tubular trusses can be combined for roof spans and for monitor light framing where natural lighting is required.

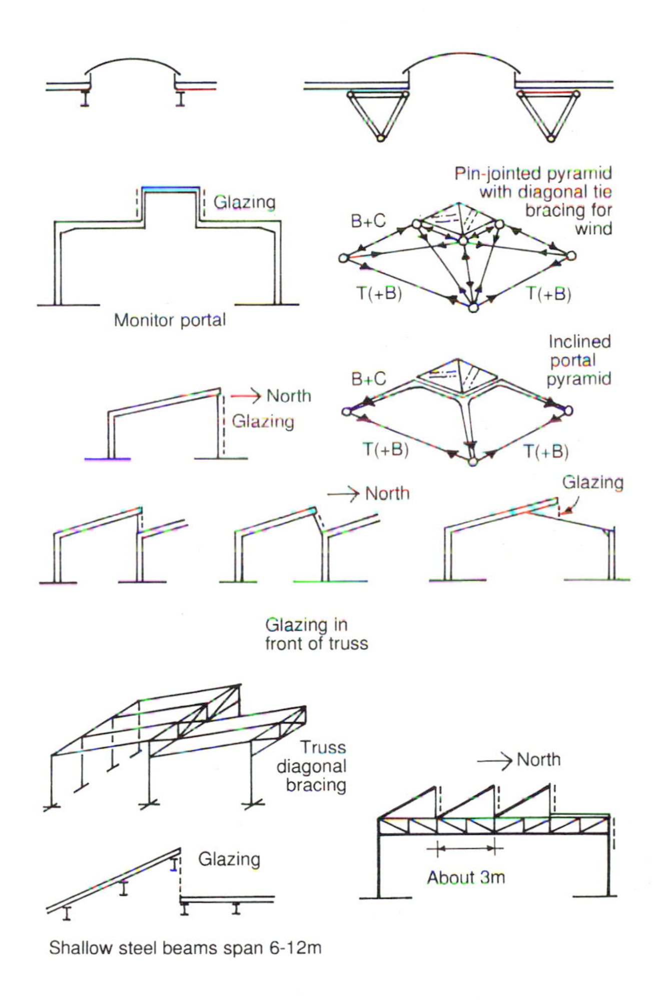

Fig. 11.68 *Monitor rooflights and alternative forms for providing natural rooflighting.*

11.11 RELATIONSHIP BETWEEN PLAN AND ROOF FORM

For rectangular plan areas, the roofing system can be relatively simple. However, even here, there may be complications, and where more complex plan shapes are involved considerable constraints may be placed on the roof design.

11.11.1 Square plan buildings and hipped roofs

If a sloping roof is required for a square plan, then a portal system is a possibility. The dilemma is how to support the cladding over the triangular plan area (Fig. 11.69). If horizontal purlins are used, the purlins are of different lengths and it is the longer which governs the section choice. If rafters are the primary structural element, load is transferred to the edge beam and further columns would be sensible. A variation of this framework was developed by F.J. Samuely [21] – a 'star' structure – and gives an interesting corner possibility as demonstrated at the Leisure Pool, Windsor, UK [22].

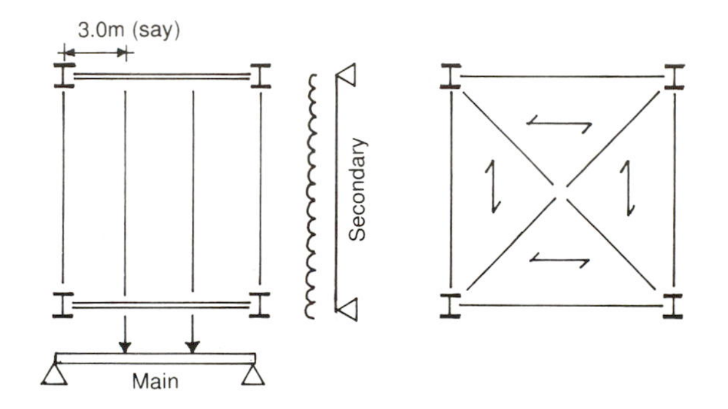

Fig. 11.69 *Alternative structural arrangements for buildings square in plan.*

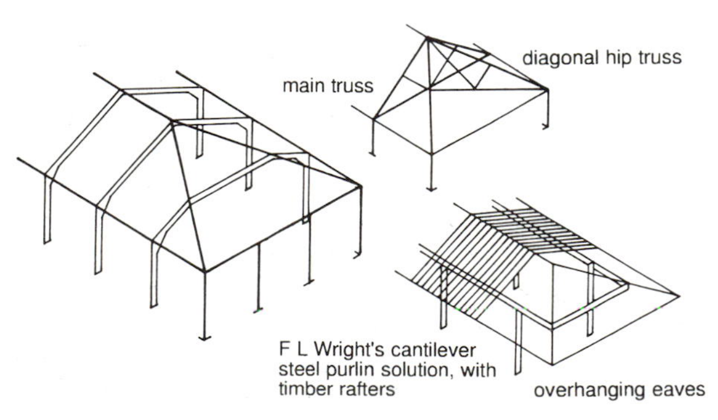

Fig. 11.70 *Alternative structural solutions for hip roofs.*

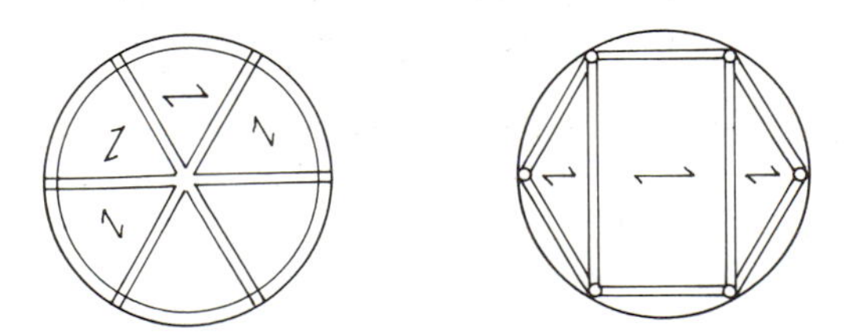

Fig. 11.71 *Alternative structural solutions for flat roofs circular in plan.*

Hip roofs for rectangular shape plans pose the same structural difficulty for which there is no easy elegant solution if the roof shape is to be consistent (Fig. 11.70). End structural frames – portals or trusses – are subject to more severe loading conditions (uniform and point loads) than adjacent frames (uniform loads only) and therefore govern the design.

11.11.2 Circular plan forms (Fig. 11.71)

If the plan shape is circular and a flat roof is to be used, then a radial approach is possible. The edge beams can be pre-bent, but must be torsionally restrained. The length should be kept below 6 m (20 ft). The central joint can be made with top and bottom circular cap plates bolted to the main beams. An alternative, which is less elegant when viewed from within, but easier structurally, is to make the edge beams straight and 'fudge' the curves with additional small bent angles or channels. This is an acceptable solution where a false ceiling is to be used.

If a circular plan with a sloping roof is required the portal approach can be adopted with a direct central joint or a compressive crown ring. For other dome solutions, see [17] or Michael Hopkins' recent workshop at Hathersage [23].

11.11.3 L-shaped plan forms

L-shaped plans also have no simple elegant solutions at the corners. Two possible flat roof solutions are suggested in Fig. 11.72.

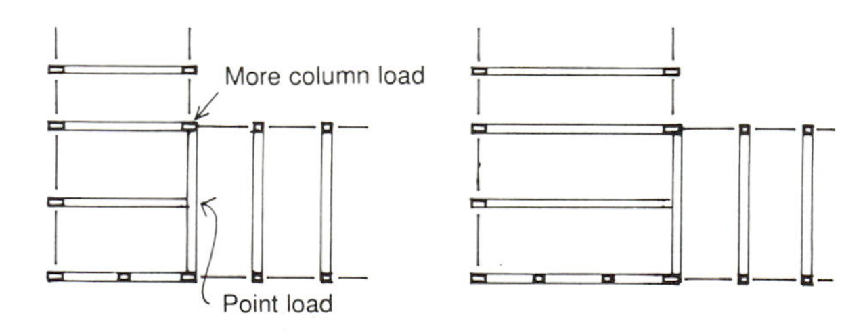

Fig. 11.72 *Corner solutions for flat-roofed buildings L-shaped in plan.*

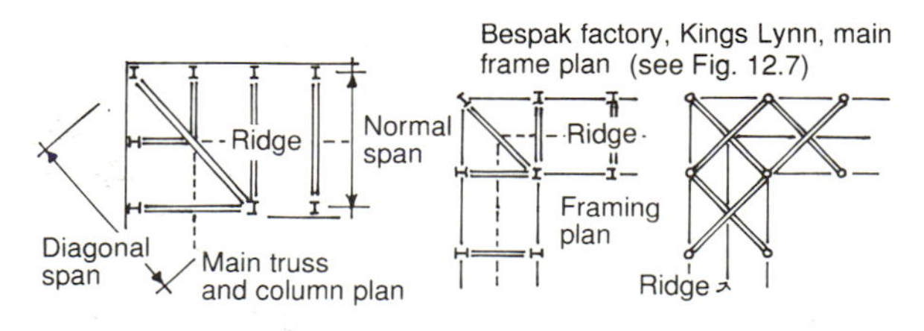

Fig. 11.73 *Corner solutions for pitched roofed buildings L-shaped in plan.*

Sloping roofs must have equal width in plan of the two 'arms', for equal roof slope and ridge height. Two solutions for the framing plan are sketched in Fig. 11.73 for either truss or portal elements.

11.11.4 Irregular plan forms

For unsymmetric shape plans try to arrange the largest area of regular, parallel and almost equal length elements, then support the remainder in the best possible way. A sloping roof is very difficult. A flat space frame roof may be possible subject to the rigorous planning geometry inspired by this type of structure, but it may be better to try and re-plan the building (Fig. 11.74).

11.11.5 Forms to accommodate adjoining spaces of different size

For plans where a larger volume is adjacent to a smaller volume it is probably best to start a suitable structural system for the larger volume, using a grid that is a sub-multiple of the smaller volume's side. The smaller volume's structure can then be developed using the intermediate columns of the larger volume. Sometimes the two grids will not be directly compatible; in this case start again with the larger structure and use a beam to span between the intermediate larger columns. This will provide support for the roof of the smaller structure (see Figs 11.24 and 11.25).

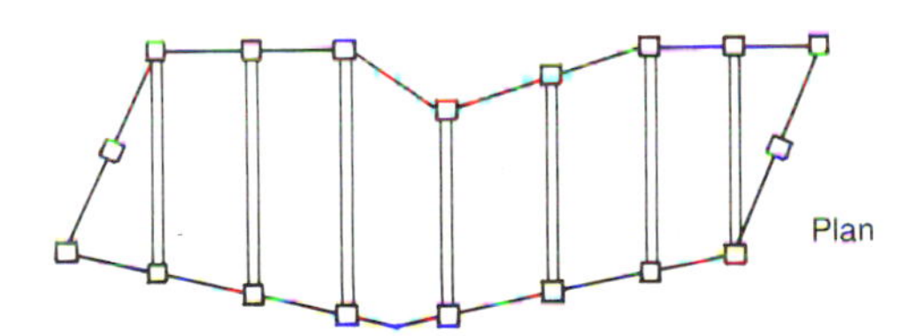

Fig. 11.74 *Accommodating adjacent volumes of different sizes.*

11.12 ADAPTABILITY AND ADDITIVITY

Steel frames can be adapted more easily than any other structural material. Re-drilling or welding on site and even 'clamps' (Lindaptors) bolted to existing sections are a much cheaper alternative to pulling the whole building down and reconstruction. Roofs of portal frames have been raised by cutting the columns and refixing extra sections near the bottom where the bending moment is usually least. Double height 6 m (20 ft) buildings can have mezzanine floors added later, providing foundations are adequate or capable of being strengthened.

If a client anticipates that space requirements will need increasing at a future date, then the initial building should be constructed for easy and non-disruptive extension of

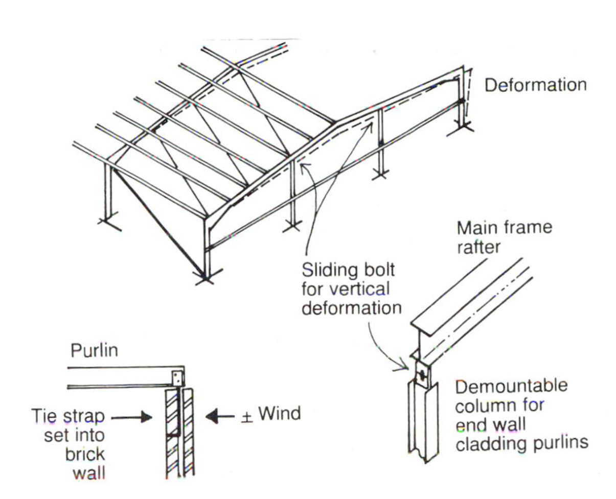

Fig. 11.75 *Use of slotted connections.*

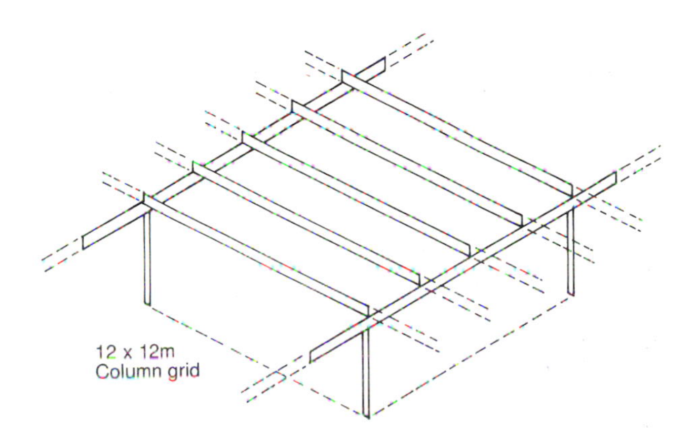

Fig. 11.76 *Provision for two-way extension.*

column-free space, e.g. by using a normal portal in the end wall with gable columns connected to the last portal by slotted connections to allow main portal deflection without transfer of vertical load (Fig. 11.75).

A two-way extension suggests an initial two-way span grid. An example is Foster and Rogers' Reliance Control (later Reliance Spectrol [24]) at Swindon, where projecting stub ends of beams were left for easy welding of new structurally continuous beams (Fig. 11.76).

Walls are more likely to change than roofs and there is a distinct advantage in placing the wall zone clear of the structure, either in front or recessed, to facilitate change; refer to Patera System described in chapter 27. Liner trays (for horizontal or vertical cladding), composite panels and curtain walling have been used in this context. Openings formed at a later stage within clear span cladding will need secondary steelwork framing and costly building work in trimming and weathering.

11.13 GUIDE TO STEELWORK ECONOMICS

This is a notoriously difficult topic as there are so many variables that there are no simple answers; every job has to be considered separately at a particular time and place. Raw materials, sections used, size of job, finish, fabricating shop equipment, labour, overheads, site, state of the order book and politics may all influence costs. It is even hard to identify any 'global basis costs', for example by projecting forward from similar, recently completed jobs, and these should never be taken as gospel. However, some guidance regarding cost-efficient solutions can be given.

The figures presented in Table 11.2 give an indication of the breakdown of costs for a single storey industrial building. The total takes no account of land cost, loan charges, fees, survey or building regulation/planning charges. Even so, it is clear that the structure accounts for a relatively small proportion of overall costs, and this must be remembered when seeking the most cost-effective solution.

In the autumn of 1988 Conder, a major steel construction firm, produced a breakdown of structural costs (excluding cladding to roofs and walls, foundations and other costs and fees) based upon their 'portal' type buildings of 15–35 m (50–110 ft) spans (Table 11.3).

The above figures emphasize that minimizing materials will not necessarily result in the cheapest solution. With regard to the structural frame, a regular overall plan pattern, with equal spans and structural elements at right angles, will lead to greatest economy. Utilize repeated sizes of commonly stocked hot-rolled sections – Universal Beams and Universal Columns and angles – for the main structure, and cheaper cold-rolled sections wherever feasible for secondary structure, such as purlins and sheeting rails.

The structure should be detailed to maximize shop assembly consistent with transport facilities in the shop, to and on the site. Reduce the number of joints and keep the detailing simple, using shop welding and site bolting. (Site welding can be a minimum of five times the cost of shop welding.)

Horridge and Morris [18] have investigated costs around 1980 for commercial steel industrial buildings, comparing alternative structural forms for single bay and multi-bay construction. They considered simple pitched roof trusses, lattice girders, space frames and portal frames for a range of spans. Their findings provide useful guidance with respect to economic span lengths, frame spacings and structural system, and also demonstrated the importance of minimizing the cost of cladding, rather than narrowly focusing on minimum structure, ground floor or foundation costs.

Table 11.2 Percentage element costs for single storey industrial buildings

Structural steelwork	30%
Roof and wall cladding*	30%
Substructure	25%
Services (minimal)	15%

* Cladding costs can rise 5–20 fold depending upon the quality required and type of fenestration.

Table 11.3 Percentage costs for Conder portal frames

Steel	54%
Fabrication	30%
Painting (grit blast priming and one shop coat of paint)*	4%
Transport	1%
Erection	10%
Site touch up for painting	1%

* Galvanizing increases this element 7–8 fold.

11.13.1 Comparison of unit weights and costs

For normal steelwork, the basic cost of unfabricated steel from the rolling mills averaged £344/tonne for grade 43A for loads over 20 tonnes in July 1991. An extra £40/tonne applies for small loads and different grades, and an extra £5/tonne average applies if the steel is obtained from a stockholder. Prices can also vary depending on the rolled section sizes (e.g. +£48/tonne for maximum UB size and −£24/tonne for minimum UB size).

Higher strength grade 50B steel costs an additional £40–50/tonne.

Typical prices for hollow tubes in grade 43A: £369/tonne for 139 mm (5½in) diam; £385/tonne for 139–193 mm (5½–7½ in) diam. and over £400/tonne for the largest diameter.

A summary of approximate guide cost ranges is given in Table 11.4.

Table 11.4 Cost guide for steel sections (July 1991)

Rolled mild steel (43A) I-sections:	from Mills	×1.0–1.14
	Stockholder	×1.04 av.
	fabricated	×1.7–2.1
	fabricated + erected	×1.9–2.3
Trusses:	fabricated	×2.3–6.0*
	fabricated + erected	×2.5–7.0*
Tubes:	from Mills	×1.08–1.25
Castellated beams:		×2.3–3.5
Rolled higher tensile steel (50B) I sections from Mills		×1.14 av.

* The upper end of this range covers high visual appeal fabrications, welded circular tubes, special joints, possibly some curves. Some fabricators are prepared to do this type of work.

11.14 DESIGN LIFE

The above comparisons are concerned with first cost only, and stress the need to consider overall costs rather than isolating and optimizing individual aspects, such as the weight of building structure. Even this is inadequate, since costs of running and maintaining a building should also be included. The differing design life of the various building elements is one of the most important factors to consider at the design stage. A typical breakdown for a large factory unit is shown in Table 11.5.

The design life of the production unit may also be 10–15 years so that it makes good sense to plan replacement of plant runs and services to coincide. Surface installation of services might also be considered to cause minimum disruption.

By comparison, a hypermarket may have an economic life of only 15 years before the building is stripped back to the frame for reuse. These circumstances should be reflected in the design of the external envelope, with short, rather than long, life materials employed. However, there are many examples of short design life solutions, such as the Arcon Prefabs from 1945 or the BSIF Houses from 1946–50 (refer to chapter 30, section 4), which have proved to be remarkably resilient. In both cases it proved an easy matter to replace those elements which had outlasted their design life. Where buildings allow for this, the 'cost in use' can be improved considerably.

Table 11.5 Approximate life expectancy for building elements

Element	*Anticipated life*	*Proportion of first cost*
Structure	50–60 years	15%
External	20–30 years	30–40% (dependent upon window form)
Services	10–15 years	15–20%

Note that external works, foundations, and internal subdivisions are excluded.

REFERENCES AND TECHNICAL NOTES

1. Le Good, J.P. (1983) *Principles of Structural Steelwork for Architectural Students*, SCI (amended 1990).
2. Fitzmaurice, R. (1939) *Principles of Modern Building*, Vol. 1 Chapter 7, HMSO.
3. BRE (1973) Vibration and noise control (Section 3). In *Services and Environmental Engineering*, MTP Construction, 1973.
4. The Building Regulations (1985) now modified by 1991 edition, Part B – Fire, HMSO.
5. Newman, G.M. (1990) *The Behaviour of Steel Portal Frames in Boundary Conditions*, 2nd edition, 1990, SCI.
6. Powell-Smith and Billington (1992) *The Building Regulations Explained and Illustrated*, BSP Professional Books, Oxford.
7. BS 5588 Fire Precautions in the Design Construction and Use of Buildings (published in 7 parts).
8. Tult, P. and Adler, D. (eds.) (1979) *New Metric Handbook*. Architectural Press, London.
9. BS 6399 Loading for Buildings: Part 1: 1984 Dead and imposed loads.
10. BS 6399 Design Loading for Buildings: Part 3: 1988 Code of practice for imposed roof loads (supersedes CP3 Chapter V: Part 2).
11. Pidgeon, N.F., Blockley, D.I. and Turner, R.A. (1986) Design practice and snow loading – lessons from a roof collapse. *The Structural Engineer*, Vol. 64A, No. 3, March.
12. CP3 Chapter V Part 2, 1972 *Wind loads on buildings*, BSI (a forthcoming code will be based on BRE digests).
13. Wyatt, A. (1989) *Design Guides on the Vibration of Floors*, SCI & CIRIA.
14. Dowrick, D. (1988) *Earthquake Resistant Design*, Wiley, New York.
15. Steelwork Design. Guide to BS5950: Part 1 Volume 1 Section Properties and Member Capacities, (1987) SCI.
16. Curtin, W.G. and Shaw, G. (1977) *Brick Diaphragm Walls in Tall Single-Storey Buildings*, BDA.
17. Makowski Z.S. (1965) *Steel Space Structures*, Michael Joseph.
18. Horridge J.F. and Morris L.J. (1986) Comparative costs of single-storey steel framed structures. *The Structural Engineer*, Vol 64A, No. 7, July, pp 177–181.
19. Fitzmaurice, R. (1939) *Principles of Modern Building*, Vol.2, Daylighting pp. 114–119. HMSO.
20. German School, Petersham. Published in *Building* The Building Dossier 30 July 1982.
21. Samuely F.J. (1952) Space frames and stressed skin construction. *RIBA Journal*, March, pp 166–173.
22. Windsor Leisure Pool. F. Newby, private communications.
23. Cruickshank, D. (1988) Rounded design *Architects Journal*, 14th September, pp 26–30.
24. Reliance Control Factory (1967) Architects team 4, Richard and Sue Rogers, Norman and Wendy Foster. Structural engineer Anthony Hunt (*Architects' Journal* 19 July 1967 and Architectural Review July 1967).

Kings Cross Masterplan showing perspective of proposed terminal entrance (architects Foster Associates).

12

Multiple bay single storey buildings

Roger Plank (with contributions from Peter Brett and David Harriss)

12.1 INTRODUCTION

In chapter 11 the principles of framing were discussed in the context of simple single storey buildings. Although there are many examples of such types of construction, buildings of larger scale often require some adaptation of the structural forms. Where overall plan dimensions exceed sensible clear span limitations, some form of intermediate structural support is required in addition to the perimeter columns or loadbearing walls. This intermediate support may be provided by additional internal columns or by some other major structural element, such as a spine girder. There are many different ways of achieving this; some of these are described in the following sections, and illustrated with examples of particular buildings. Attention is again focused on single storey construction, although some of the examples used are low-rise buildings whose roof structures can be considered in the same way.

Multiple bays are normally a repetition of single bay structures (Fig. 12.1). The repetition does, however, offer opportunities to reduce the size of some members if continuity is considered in the structural design. In such cases the plan arrangement need only include two bays to give improved distribution of bending effects. Cantilever bays beyond the perimeter columns will also reduce bending stresses in roof beams (Fig. 12.2).

Where clearer internal space is required, the internal columns must be replaced, at least partly, by some other structural system such as lattice girders or cable supports

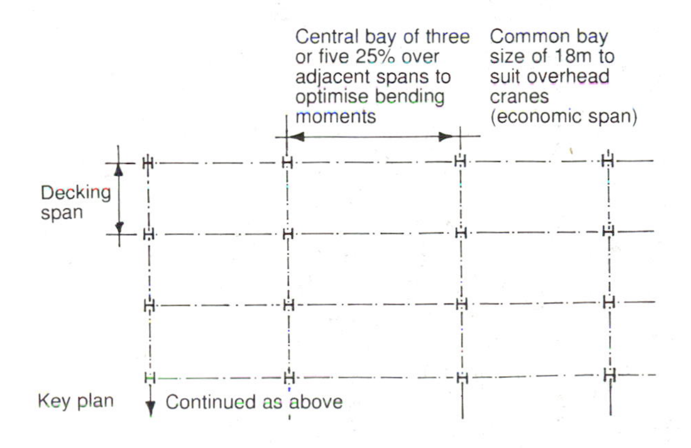

Fig. 12.1 *Typical multi-bay plan layout as a repetition of single bay form.*

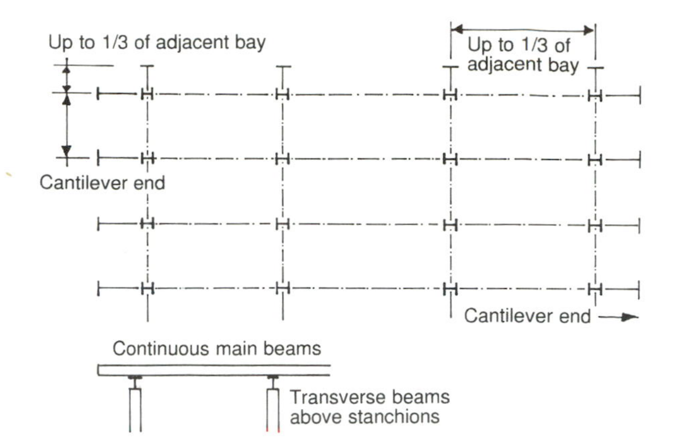

Fig. 12.2 *Cantilever bays beyond the perimeter columns can reduce bending in internal bays.*

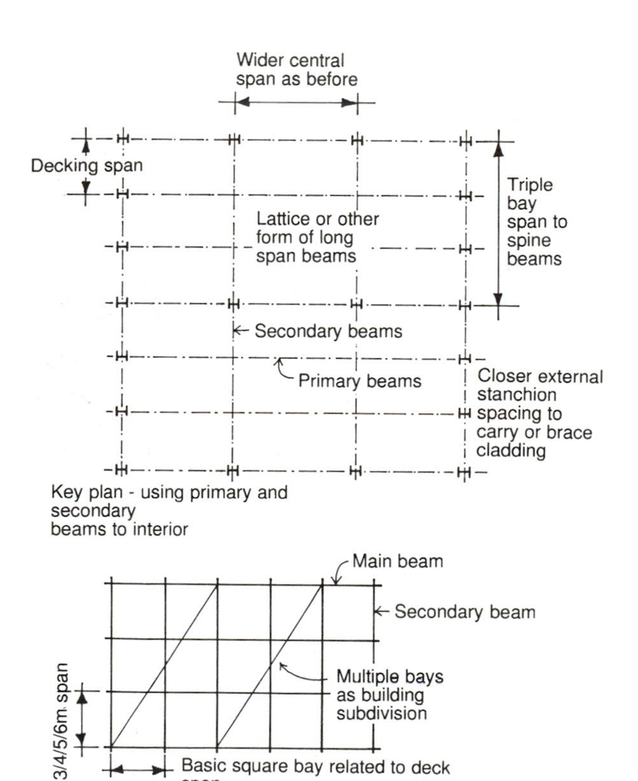

Fig. 12.3 *Internal columns can be minimized by the use of primary beams or trusses to support secondary beams.*

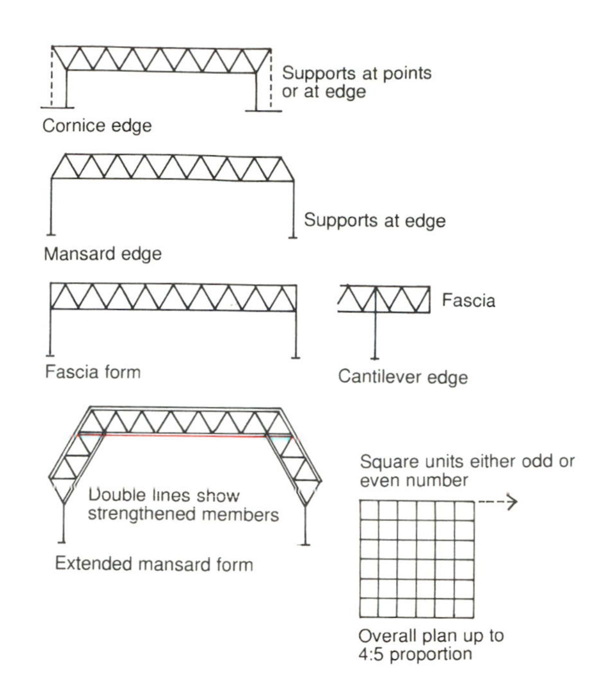

Fig. 12.4 *Space deck construction.*

(Fig. 12.3). Alternative systems such as space frames can be used for large two-way spans without intermediate support (Fig. 12.4).

The requirements of large roof spans can therefore be met in a wide variety of ways. There are very many design possibilities, offering a rich source of architectural expression.

In all cases frame spacing can be varied within a wide range to suit specific requirements. It is normal for the main roof structure to support a system of purlins which in turn support the roof sheeting or decking. The spacing of the purlins is largely dictated by the safe span of the particular roofing system adopted. The purlins are often in the form of lightweight galvanized cold-rolled sections but hot-rolled open sections (angles, channels or small universal beams) can be used for demanding situations, for instance where the purlins are spanning long distances, in excess of 8–9 m (27–30 ft) between main frames. In addition to supporting the roofing, the purlins also have a secondary function of helping to provide the lateral stability to the structural frames.

Trends in the structural layout of industrial buildings have been influenced as much by changes in, for instance, the provision of fork lift trucks and door opening requirements as considerations of structural efficiency. In recent years, main frames have been located at about 6 m (20 ft) centres, with purlins at about 1.5 m (5 ft) centres. As more sophisticated roofing systems become available, it has been possible to increase the purlin spacing. Similarly for both economic and planning reasons the spacing of main frames has also tended to increase.

There is, however, a distinction to be made between different types of building usage, relating to the level of service installation. Warehouses generally have very modest service requirements and the structural arrangement can readily take the form of widely spaced ribs – say 5 m (16 ft) – supporting long span roof decks. In contrast, factories benefit from a more regular beat of the structure, providing easier fixings for services and other attachments. As a result, ribs are more closely spaced – typically 2.5 m (8 ft).

12.2 MULTI-BAY PITCHED TRUSS AND COLUMN CONSTRUCTION

The traditional treatment for multi-bay roof construction was to use a series of pitched roof trusses, simply supported on parallel rows of columns. This precluded the possibility of taking advantage of structural continuity, and the structural treatment is little different from single span buildings of this type. The principal differences are that internal columns carry additional axial load and the provision for bracing may need to be more carefully considered. This is particularly the case where overhead cranes are installed.

Accumulations of snow in the roof valleys can give rise to locally increased loads which should be accounted for, although this may mean little more than using a closer purlin spacing in this region. Valley gutters are also prone to blocking with leaves and other debris, and this could lead to leaks if routine maintenance is neglected.

As for single bay construction, the roof trusses can take a variety of different forms. For instance, north light trusses were commonly used for factory roofs, and shallower pitches can be achieved using a truss with a finite depth at the eaves.

Spectrum 7

The north light form of construction was adopted for the Spectrum 7 building at Milton Keynes [1,2] where the need to reduce energy demand was a dominant consideration (Fig. 12.5). Recognizing lighting as the most significant user of energy in commercial buildings, the designers decided to use natural daylighting wherever possible. The solution was to use rooflights, facing north-east to take account of the need for daylight without sunlight, whilst recognizing the site orientation and internal space planning requirements. Sloping rooflights at an angle of 60 degrees were shown to be more efficient than a vertical sawtooth and the roof geometry therefore comprises two unequal slopes.

The structure is based on a 12 × 8.8 m (40 × 30 ft) grid. It consists of lightweight steel trusses of angle construction spaced at 3.3 m (11 ft) centres and spanning 8.8 m (30 ft) onto the primary beams in the form of simple I-sections. In

(a)

Ventilation air extract
Ventilation air supply
North light strip: daylighting without direct solar gain
Gutter zone
False ceiling zone
Lighting zone
Production
Office
Raised floor
Option for cooling from slab via desk outlet
Forced air movement over slab
Heat absorbed into slab
Heat removed from slab via embedded pipes circulating water through a cooling tower
Passive slab
Option for cooling from slab via fan powered terminal and floor outlet
Power data telecom distribution
Outlet to suit furniture layout

(b)

Fig. 12.5 *Spectrum 7 Milton Keynes (architect ECD Partnership: engineer Ove Arup and Partners) (a) aerial view; (b) typical section.*

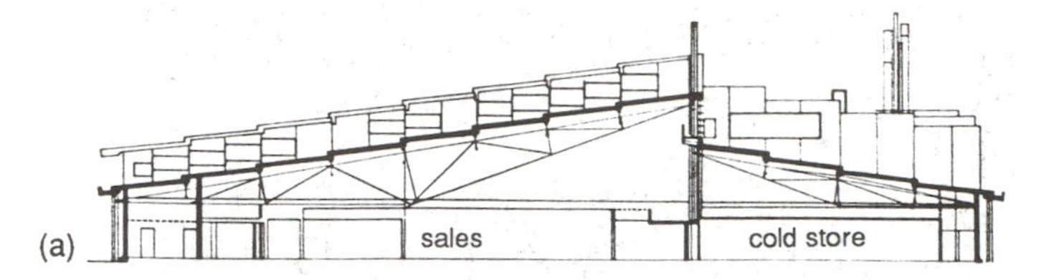

Fig. 12.6 *RAF Alconbury (a) section showing typical 8.8 m (29 ft 4 in) bay; (b) external elevation showing exposed trusses; (c) reversed trusses exposed internally (architect Design Group, Cambridge, UK: engineer Posford Duvivier).*

order to reduce the overall height of the roof, the valley gutters were arranged within the depth of the primary beams. This required a modification to the normally pin-jointed truss construction, with the introduction locally of a more substantial flexural element, but the effect was to reduce the cladding height by 0.5 m (20 in) around the building perimeter. The roof is clad with profiled, insulated steel sheeting supported on continuous cold-rolled purlins, with patent glazing forming the north lights.

A cautionary postscript concerning this well integrated design is the reported installation of a suspended ceiling and extensive artificial lighting by the client [3].

RAF Alconbury, UK

A rather more unusual example of a multi-bay truss solution is the roof by Cambridge Design for the Commissary at RAF Alconbury (Fig. 12.6) [4]. This utilizes inverted trusses spanning two unequal bays of 42 m and 21 m (140 and 70 ft), stepped at their junction to accommodate continuous clerestory north lighting, and provides an attractive solution to the problem of visual bulk. The trusses provide a roof pitch of 10 degrees and are spaced alternately at 10.1 m and 6.06 m (33 ft and 20 ft) and to suit planning considerations. They support lattice purlins at their node points at 5.3 m (17 ft) centres with a Plannja energy roof deck spanning directly between these. The roof panels overlap at purlins to give a stepped appearance. Extensive use is made of circular hollow sections, not only for the truss elements but also the supporting columns and cladding posts. The main columns are set in pockets in the foundations to act as vertical cantilevers in resisting wind loading. The roof drainage system also merits mention. The roof itself overhangs the walls, and gargoyles, again of latticed tubular section, ensure efficient dispersal of the rainwater. The whole structure is protected with a high-quality chlorinated rubber paint system to reduce maintenance requirements.

The structural solution adopted is a dominant feature of the design and is implemented in such a way as to reduce the scale of the building. Internally, the construction provides a dramatic roofscape, yet allows for the efficient integration of services and natural lighting.

Bespak, Norfolk, UK

The Bespak factory extension at Kings Lynn, Norfolk, UK, by Cambridge Design [5] also adopts an unusual multi-bay truss solution (Fig. 12.7). The column grid is 13.5 m (44 ft) in both directions, with the trusses spanning across the diagonals, allowing the roof pitch to return at the corners. Extensive use is made of circular hollow sections, both in the trusses and the columns and in the secondary structural members – rafters, ridge and perimeter beams. This creates a light open space internally and also provides accommodation for the rainwater down pipes within the columns. Conventional purlins spanning between the rafters support the roof sheeting which is simply asbestos cement on the internal slopes since these cannot be seen.

St Enoch Centre, Glasgow, UK

St Enoch Shopping Centre in Glasgow by Reiach and Hall and GMW [6–9] utilizes multi-bay lattice girders to support the glazed roof over the 240 m (800 ft) long mall (Fig. 12.8). The lattice girders, which are inclined to provide a pitched roof form, are 1.8 m (6 ft) deep and span 36 m (120 ft) onto treehead supports. These fan out from columns or the walls of the core buildings and are also of lattice construction. The glazed enclosure provides a headroom of about 9 m (30 ft) at the perimeter, rising to 25 m (80 ft) at the central cores.

Glazing such an enormous and complicated building

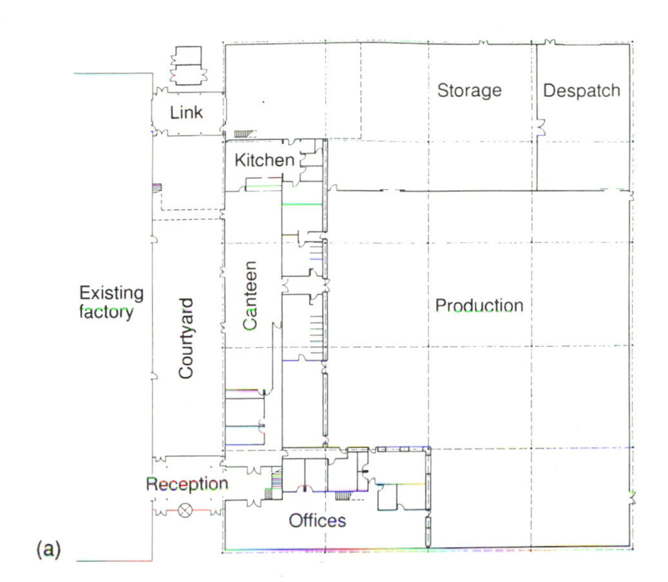

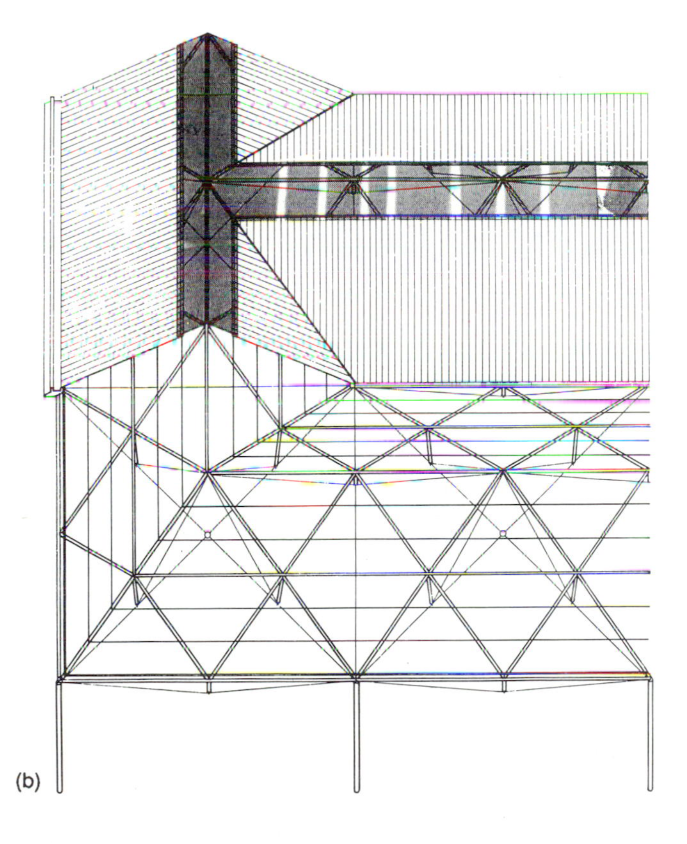

Fig. 12.7 *Bespak Factory extension, Kings Lynn, Norfolk, UK. (a) plan arrangement; (b) roof construction; (c) interior view; (d) exterior view (architect Design Group, Cambridge, UK: engineer Peter Dann and Partners).*

required that careful attention had to be paid to wind load and temperature effects. Structural calculations were performed to predict the movements of the structural steelwork in order that a suitable system of glazing support could be designed. In addition, wind model tests were also conducted to verify the high suction loads anticipated on the glass panels. Testing was also carried out to ensure that the glazing bars would not buckle during wind uplift, and that the system would remain watertight under such conditions. Draining the roof of the largest greenhouse in Europe presented the designers with something of a challenge. The original gutterless sloping wall proposal was abandoned

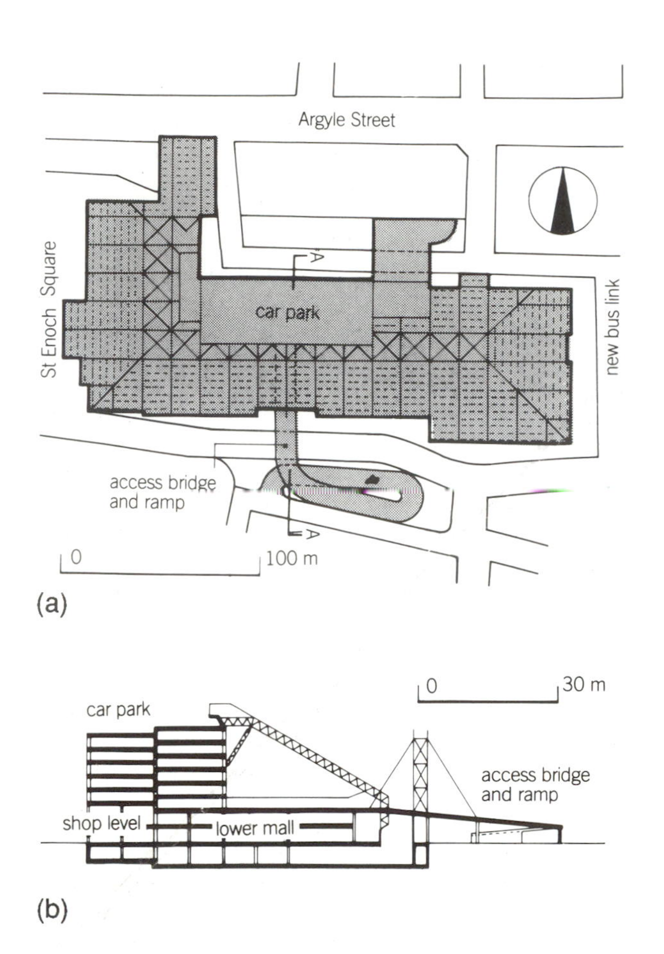

Fig. 12.8 *St. Enoch Centre, Glasgow (a) plan arrangement; (b) typical section; (c) interior view; (d) exterior view (architects GMW and Reiach and Hall; engineer Ove Arup and Partners).*

because of the problem of drips. Instead a concealed perimeter gutter, set back from the edge of the roof, was adopted. The drainage pipework, which utilizes both cast iron and stainless steel, is painted white and is visually lost amid the surrounding structural lattice.

The question of maintenance has been carefully treated, and the brief from the client clearly called for good access internally and externally to enable this. The problem was solved by using a variety of systems, with some gantries sitting on top of the roof, others moving vertically up and down the internal surfaces with hydraulic arms to reach more remote areas, and a further set of gantries to provide access to the external vertical surfaces.

The Pavilions, Uxbridge, UK

The Pavilions shopping centre development at Uxbridge, Middlesex, UK [10–12] was a rehabilitation project which has transformed an outdated and unpopular town centre (Fig. 12.9). The work covered all public areas and included glazed canopies over the malls and squares. Simple forms were chosen for the roof geometry – pitched over the malls and pyramids over the squares – and lightweight, elegant steel structures have been designed to support the glazing. The roof structure over the malls is in the form of aluminium glazing mullions supported on steel purlins and rafters, both of lattice construction. In the square the pyramid roof structure consists of light steel lattice rafters supported on the original buildings around the edge and internally on circular hollow section columns, relieving the perimeter loads. The rafters support purlins, also of lattice construction. These in turn carry a steel subframe to which the aluminium mullions are attached through insulating pads. The steel subframe enables the glazing supports to be visually slender, yet also provide lateral restraint to the purlins. Great care was taken with both design and fabrication and the erection was carried out whilst market trading continued. The effect has been to create a strikingly clean appearance and given a new lease of life to a decaying shopping centre.

Fig. 12.9 *The Pavilions, Uxbridge, UK (architects Fitch and Co: engineer Michael Barclay Partnership).*

Imperial War Museum, London, UK

The roof to the Imperial War Museum, London, UK extension [13,14] is an unusual multi-bay form (Fig. 12.10). Supported on twin tubular columns at 7 m (23 ft) centres, the three-bay roof consists of two monopitch side spans which cantilever 5.5 m (18 ft) beyond the internal row of columns, rather like a crane jib, to support a central barrel vault 12 m (40 ft) wide. This creates a memorable central space 23 m (75 ft) wide, 40 m (130 ft) long and rising to about 23 m (75 ft) high at the top of the barrel. This area is to accommodate five aircraft suspended from the edge beams of the vault using steel cables. The heaviest of these is the World War II Mosquito at 75 kN (7.5 tonnes).

For visual reasons, a single layer diagrid was adopted for the construction of the barrel vault. This was analysed as a complete space frame, with the supporting cantilevers modelled as springs. A single size of tubular member – 139.7 × 10 CHS – was used for all internal members, with a larger section – 219 × 12.5 CHS – for the perimeter members. Grade 50 steel was used throughout. The design was based on unusually low design stresses because many of the welds were to be carried out on site, and, since tubular members were being used, only partial penetration butt welds could be achieved. An extensive programme of non-destructive testing was undertaken for both shop and site welds.

Because of the importance of both close tolerances and visual appearance, trial assemblies were made. This included a full assembly of the barrel vault at the fabricators, prior to its delivery to site in 12 separate pieces. On site the roof was assembled on the ground using the same techniques used during the trial, and then jacked into position at a rate of about 3 m (10 ft) per hour for connection to the cantilever jibs.

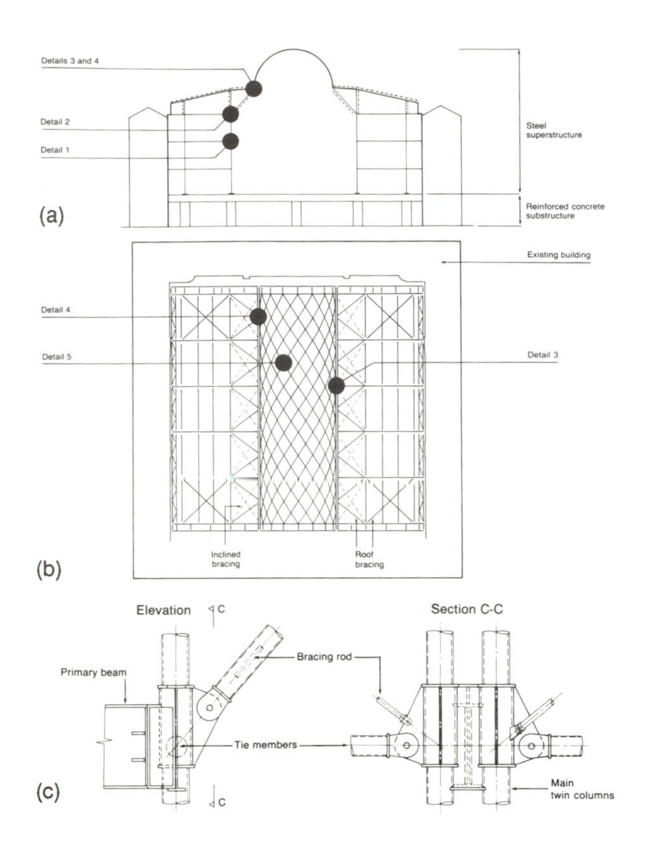

Fig. 12.10 *Imperial War Museum, London (a) typical section; (b) plan arrangement; (c) details; (d) exterior view (architect and engineer Arup Associates).*

12.3 MULTI-BAY PITCHED ROOF PORTAL FRAMES

Pitched roof steel portal frames are now the principal structural form for single bay industrial buildings. This is largely because of economic factors associated with the efficiency of both their construction and structural behaviour. For multi-bay buildings the continuity associated with portal action offers even greater advantages. In many cases the construction is simply in the form of pairs of rafters with equal pitches as this is probably most efficient from a structural point of view, but other shapes such as mansard, monitor or north light can also be used (Fig. 12.11). Pitches are often shallower than for traditional truss forms, helping to minimize enclosed volumes within the roof space, which is in any case more usable. However, problems associated with localized loading conditions and blocking of gutters still need to be considered. The structural performance of tied portal frames can be particularly efficient, but the roof space is obstructed as with trusses.

Princess of Wales Conservatory, Kew

The Princess of Wales Conservatory at Kew, West London, UK [15–18], is an unusual example of multi-bay portal frame construction in that the external rafters, which are of conventional I-section, continue down to ground level (Fig. 12.12). Valleys are propped internally by vertical columns. The frames are spaced at 5.4 m (18 ft) centres and arranged in multiple bays up to five in number. The ridge extends up to a maximum height of 11.4 m (38 ft) and the roof pitch is 26.5 degrees. Longitudinal stability is provided by 144 mm (5½ in) diameter circular hollow sections rigidly connected to the upper flanges of the rafters at intervals. The structure is clad in patent glazing throughout using 6 mm (¼ in) rough cast glass in white powder coated glazing bars supported on purlins. The gable walls are glazed directly to the steel mullions using neoprene gaskets.

The structure has proved an energy efficient solution to the problem of glasshouse construction. The exposed steelwork, which deliberately avoids the use of diagonal bracing, lattice and truss construction, provides easy access for maintenance and is visually pleasing. These aspects were demonstrated in a full size prototype of two bays constructed on site some 18 months prior to the start of the main contract.

The corrosion protection system, in an internal environment which consists of hot humid air, surfaces running with condensation and cleaning with high pressure water spray, was a critical aspect of the design. Design details were carefully developed to avoid water traps and produce clean joints to minimize the possibility of corrosion in unseen crevices and corners, and to facilitate inspection and repainting. The protection system specified was grit blasting, flame sprayed aluminium (100 μm – 4 thou) and chlorinated rubber paint (175 μm – 7 thou).

Stockley Park

The development at Stockley Park, West London, UK, includes a wide variety of different architectural and structural solutions to the same client brief to a shell and core specification. This includes simple fixed geometry constraints related to planning and column grids; floor-to-floor heights and the number of storeys are given, and the type of HVAC system and environmental design criteria are stipulated [19–21]. From this the planners, Arup Associates, developed a building typology, adopting certain characteristics which had been identified for technological industries. These included:

(a) Medium depth, 18 m (60 ft), allowing good levels of outside awareness and natural light, yet providing sufficiently adaptable space for a variety of activities;
(b) Central atria for amenity and efficient layouts;
(c) Pitched roofs to create a distinctive profile and to rationalize positions for mechanical plant.

This typology has permeated throughout the development at Stockley Park, which has justly received wide recognition for the high standards achieved for both the

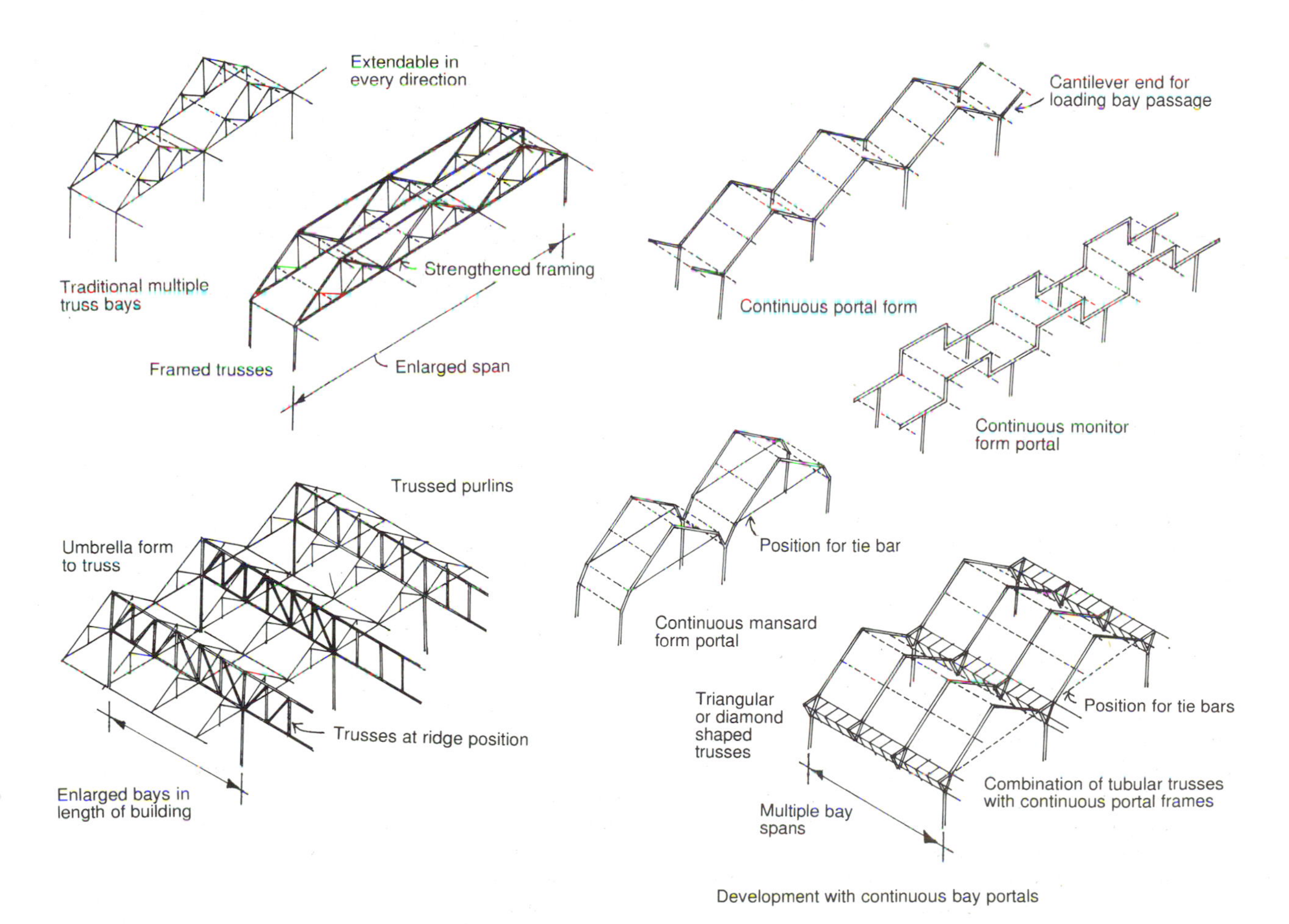

Fig. 12.11 *Multi-bay trusses and portal frames – some alternative forms.*

(a)

(b)

(c)

Fig. 12.12 *Princess of Wales Conservatory, Kew Gardens, London (for plan refer to chapter 37) (a) aerial view; (b) detail; (c) general view (architect and engineer PSA Designer Gordon Wilson).*

buildings and landscape. Yet the construction of the buildings has generally been carried out at prices well below those normally prevailing in the Greater London area. One of the reasons for this is the consistent project team. By maintaining the same specialists, apart from the architect, the team established good relationships with contractors, applied lessons learnt on previous buildings, and improved construction methods, details and servicing concepts. Freshness and challenge has been introduced by using a number of different architects.

The structural solution generally adopted by Arup Associates for buildings in the first phase was a series of pavilion type roofs of portal construction spanning 18 m (60 ft). These are separated by a central circulation space which provides extra daylighting through the roof. The sloping roofs are slated, in dramatic contrast with the white steel frame and panels. Some are of hipped construction, whilst others are based on a series of square plan shapes, creating a pyramidal form (Fig. 12.13). The same form has been adopted for some of the subsequent buildings by Arup Associates [22,23].

The 9 m (30 ft) structural grid either side of an atrium-lit central street was maintained by Troughton McAslan for Apple Computers' new UK headquarters at Stockley Park [24]. Again the roof spans were opened up to 18 m (60 ft), but instead of pavilion roofs, a slightly curving roof form was adopted. The structure consists of main lattice girders supported on circular concrete- encased steel columns. Mild steel struts project from the edge of the building to secure PVC coated polyester sunscreens. These have a black interlayer, allowing only a small proportion of light to pass through and thus providing effective shading to the continuous band of horizontal glazing at first floor level. The translucent cladding system is an innovative feature of the building and provides an attractive diffuse light to internal areas, whilst at night the internal lighting radiates through the walls (Fig. 12.14).

In contrast to its neighbours, Foster's B3 building [25–27] presents a dominant structural form, consisting of three bays of 'Y' frames at 9 m (30 ft) centres forming a canopy roof (Fig. 12.15). The arms of each 'Y' extend 3 m (10 ft) beyond the edge of the building to support aluminium louvre sunscreens. The arms are propped by fin-shaped cladding mullions, reducing edge deflections of the roof. The frames consist of tapered I-sections pinned at the ridges where they connect to the adjacent frame and also at the base. This allows for a graceful form but without undue loss of structural efficiency. The end frames are external to the building and accommodate an entrance canopy on the north elevation. The bays on this elevation are set back, leaving the free end of the 'Y' frames unsupported. These are therefore tied down by vertical stainless steel rods and the frames are stiffened by horizontal ties between the arms of the 'Y'. The structure supports metal roof decking and ridge rooflights above full height atria between each of the bays. The building is clad in structural silicone double glazing finished in a pattern of enamelled dots varying in density; viewed

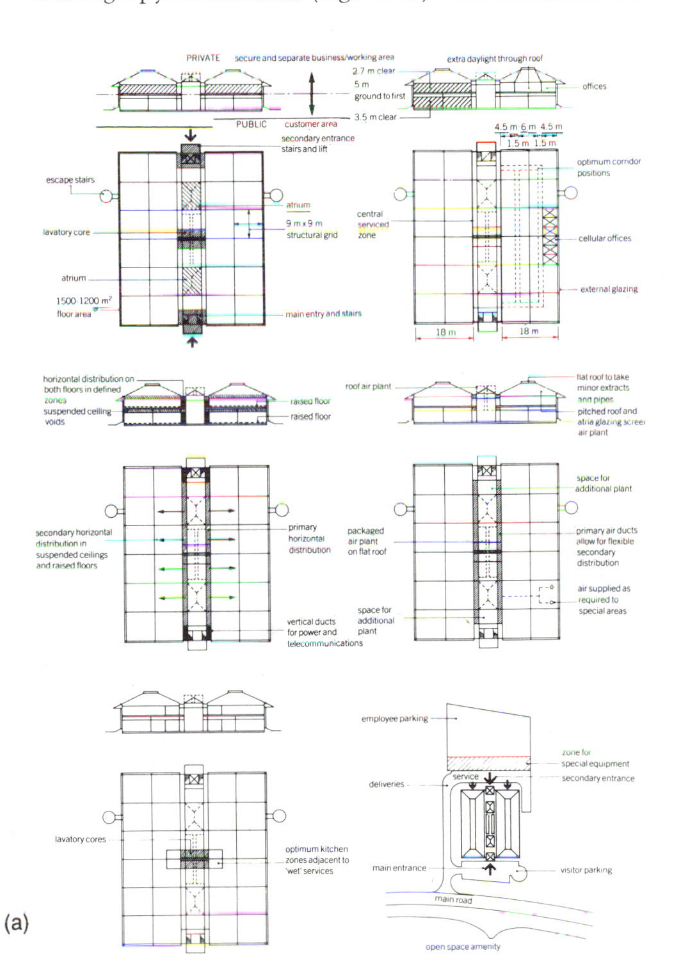

Fig. 12.13 *Stockley Park, UK (a) seed building typology; (b) Control Data, UK building (architect and engineer Arup Associates).*

Fig. 12.14 *Apple Computers UK Headquarters, Stockley Park, London (architects Troughton McAslan: engineer Ove Arup and Partners).*

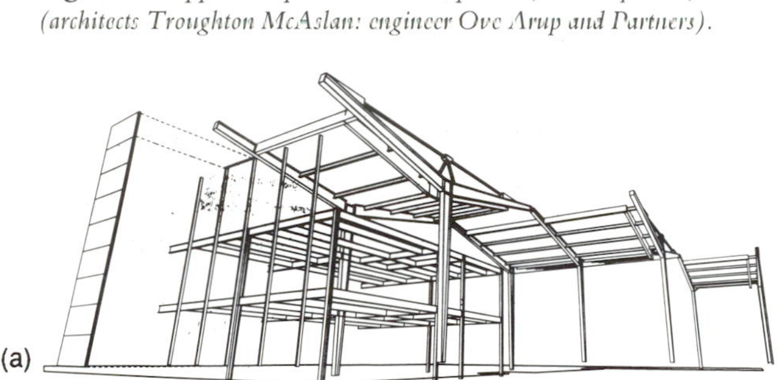

from a distance this gives a shimmering appearance and contributes to a remarkable design.

The B8 building by Ian Ritchie is a three storey multi-span flat roof structure (Fig. 12.16). In this case the basic column spacing of 9 m (30 ft) is extended throughout each floor, enabling a very light form of roof construction. Services are provided from multi-level plant rooms at both ends of the building and distributed within the floor zone either side of the top-lit central atrium.

The development at Stockley Park represents a unique opportunity to compare different solutions, both structural and architectural, to the same basic design brief. The variety and quality of buildings certainly merits detailed study.

Stansted Airport Terminal, UK

The tree-like column style adopted in Foster's Stockley Park B3 building is also used in his terminal building at Stansted Airport, UK [28,29], but in this case in a three-dimensional form. The main structural support is provided by 36 steel 'trees' on a 36 m (120 ft) square grid (Fig. 12.17). Each tree consists of four 457 mm (18 in) diameter circular hollow sections which project vertically 4 m (13 ft) above the concourse level before branching outwards in the form of smaller diameter CHS to reach a height of 12 m (36 ft). The branching structure is braced by an arrangement of tubes

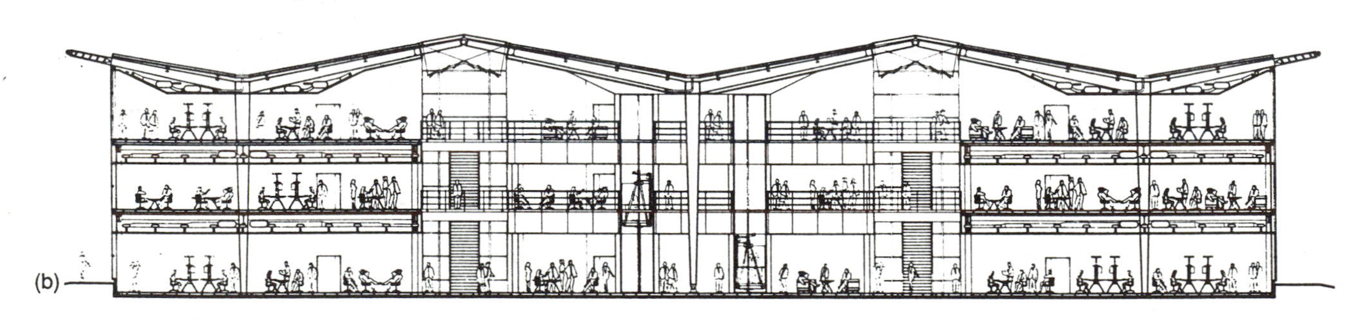

Fig. 12.15 *B3 Building at Stockley Park, London (a) Structural steelwork; (b) typical section (architect Foster Associates: engineer Ove Arup and Partners).*

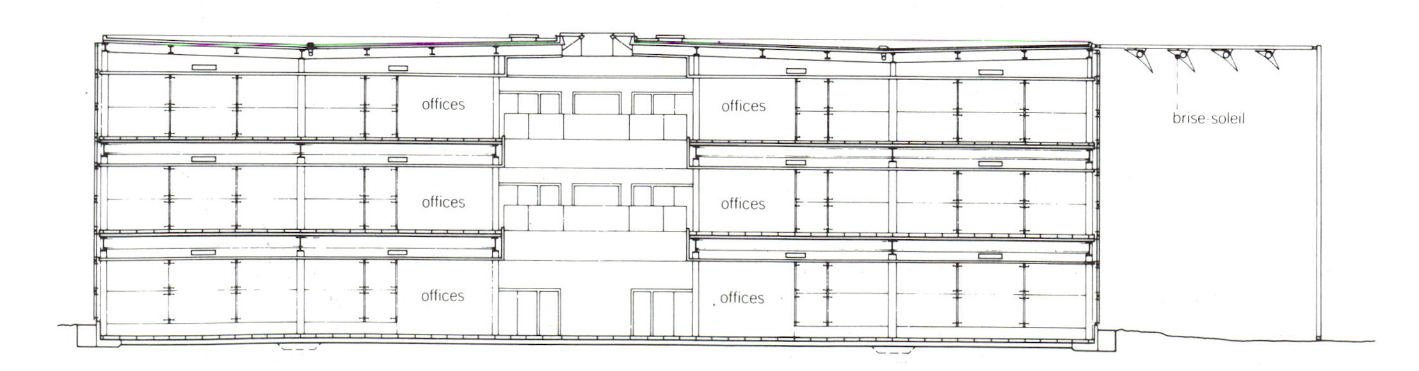

Fig. 12.16 *B8 Building at Stockley Park, London (architect Ian Ritchie: engineer Ove Arup and Partners).*

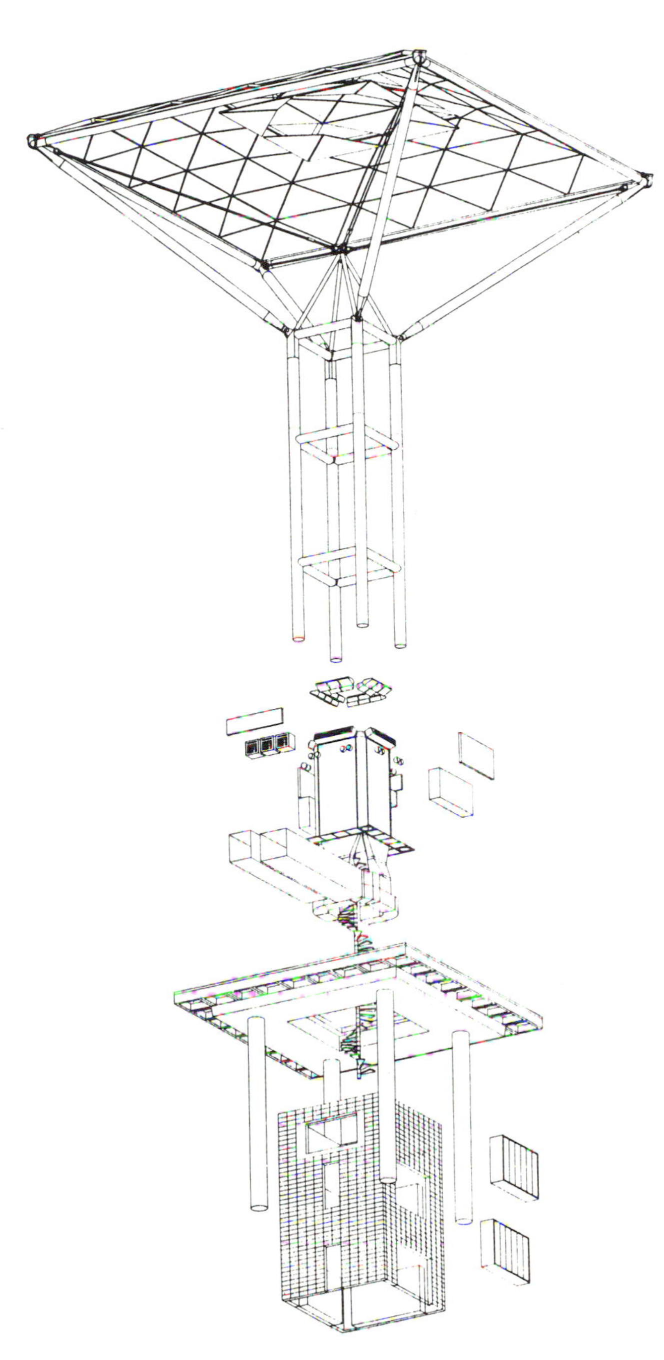

Fig. 12.17 *Stansted Airport, London, UK – column arrangement (architect Foster Associates: engineer Ove Arup and Partners).*

and prestressed rods, with special castings used for the connections. The tips of the branches form a continuous grid 18 m (60 ft) square which provides the support for independent roof panels which are prefabricated at ground level and lifted complete into position. The four legs of each column are connected as a Vierendeel frame, without cross bracing, allowing unobstructed accommodation for the service risers to concourse level.

The roof not only performs a structural function, but also defines the scale of the public space. It was designed to take full advantage of prefabrication and to allow construction to proceed as independently of the weather as possible and simultaneously on a number of fronts across the building. Accordingly, the roof structure was erected at an early stage, some 20 m (66 ft) above ground level. This provided cover to the building work for the concourse and mezzanine levels. The infill panels in the 18 m (60 ft) square bays consist of independent lattice domes in the form of intersecting orthogonal barrel vaults with singly curved sheeting.

The result is a visually stunning building, yet one which has been designed to cost targets below those of comparable terminal buildings (see chapter 36 for details).

12.4 MULTI-BAY FLAT ROOF STRUCTURES

Flat, or nearly flat, roof structures minimize the enclosed volume and avoid problems of valley gutters but clearly

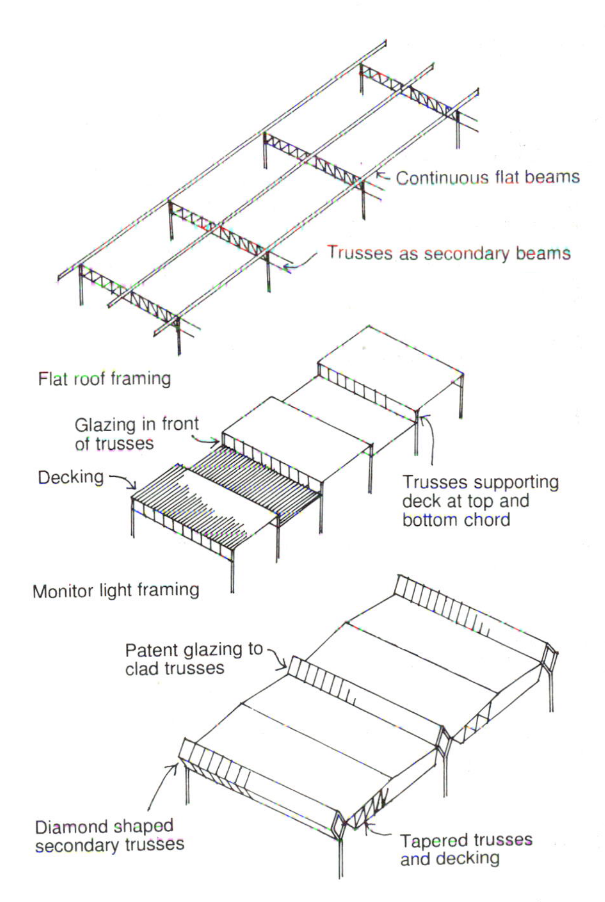

Fig. 12.18 *Multi-bay flat roof structures – some alternative forms.*

require very careful consideration with regard to waterproofing. The structural form could be a series of simply supported beams, which may take the form of Universal Beams, castellated beams or lattice girders (Fig. 12.18). Solid web Universal Beams are often inefficient for supporting roof structures which are typified by long spans and relatively light loading. Under these conditions deflection control is often more critical than bending strength and overall beam depth becomes important. Castellated beams and lattice girders provide this increased depth in a way which minimizes the amount of material used. In addition, the openings within the structural depth provide accommodation for services and diminish the visual bulk of the beam. In the case of lattice girders particularly, advantage can be taken of this last feature to introduce natural lighting within the roof.

Kiln Farm, Milton Keynes, UK

Nevertheless, the use of simple beams can have a striking effect as at the Kiln Farm development at Milton Keynes, UK [30]. The design brief called for light industrial units of a high standard with an appearance more akin to offices than a factory development. The solution was in the form of four rectangular pavilions, each based on a square grid of 10.5 m (35 ft) but with different overall plan form (Fig. 12.19). The main roof beams supported secondary beams at 3.5 m (12 ft) centres and these in turn supported purlins and metal deck roofing. Penthouses are formed in the roof by 1.3 m (4 ft) deep Vierendeel frames. All the structural steelwork to the roof was in the form of conventional I-sections, and simple bolted connections were used throughout. Lateral stability is provided by fixing the columns at foundation level, and providing cross-bracing in the roof. The roof structure extends 1.5 m (5 ft) beyond the external glazed envelope, and is supported on fabricated box columns. The roof deck and internal steelwork are designed to allow for differential movement, with extensive use made of bearing pads, slotted connections and movement joints. The steelwork is exposed both internally and externally, with a required life to first maintenance of 10–15 years. Coatings using a high build epoxy zinc phosphate were therefore used. The excellent detailing and fabrication contribute to the success of this simple, but well designed building, in blurring the distinction between industrial and commercial developments.

Fig. 12.19 *Kiln Farm, Milton Keynes, UK (architect Building Directorate MKDC: engineer F. J. Samuely and Partners).*

JEL factory, Stockport, UK

The JEL factory in Stockport [31] utilizes external trusses of triangular cross-section spanning 18 m (60 ft) and cantilevering a further 6 m (20 ft) (Fig. 12.20). They are supported on RHS columns at 6 m (20 ft) centres longitudinally and the orthogonal frame layout is completed by cold-rolled sections (incorporating gutter supports) and steel purlins on their bottom chords. These in turn support asbestos sheeting, insulation and steel liner panels. The south facing slopes of the trusses are glazed for passive solar gain over the production areas, whilst other triangular roof areas are finished in conventional PVC coated profiled steel sheeting.

CLASP

The CLASP framing system, a unique building method to deal with settlement problems [32], incorporates a system of multi-bay roof trusses (Fig. 12.21). The basis of this structural system is a pin-jointed light steel frame with structural diaphragms at floor and roof level. Horizontal wind loads are transmitted to the ground through a vertical bracing system which, on mining subsidence sites, is unique in that it is spring loaded and allows the whole building to distort with the subsidence movement and then realign itself after it has finished.

The system had its beginnings in the late 1950s when Nottinghamshire County Council, in conjunction with Lister Heathcote of Brockhouse and Co., looked at ways of building on sites affected by mining subsidence, the first school at Bancroft Lane, Mansfield being handed over in 1957. The test came in 1962 when five of the original jobs were subject to significant subsidence. Two suffered trivial damage and the rest remained unscathed. The system was adopted in other mining areas and resulted in a Consortium of Public Sector clients called the 'Consortium of Local Authorities Special Programme' – hence the acronym CLASP (Fig. 12.22). The architectural contribution stemmed from Donald Gibson (lately from Coventry), the group leaders from the famous Hertfordshire School teams, Dan Lacey and Henry Swain, and many other architects whose vision was 'Towards a Social Architecture'.

A critical aspect in designing for settlement (apart from flexibility of framing) is the reduction in building load. Lightweight cold-formed steel members can be used in single storey building to give a minimal loading compared

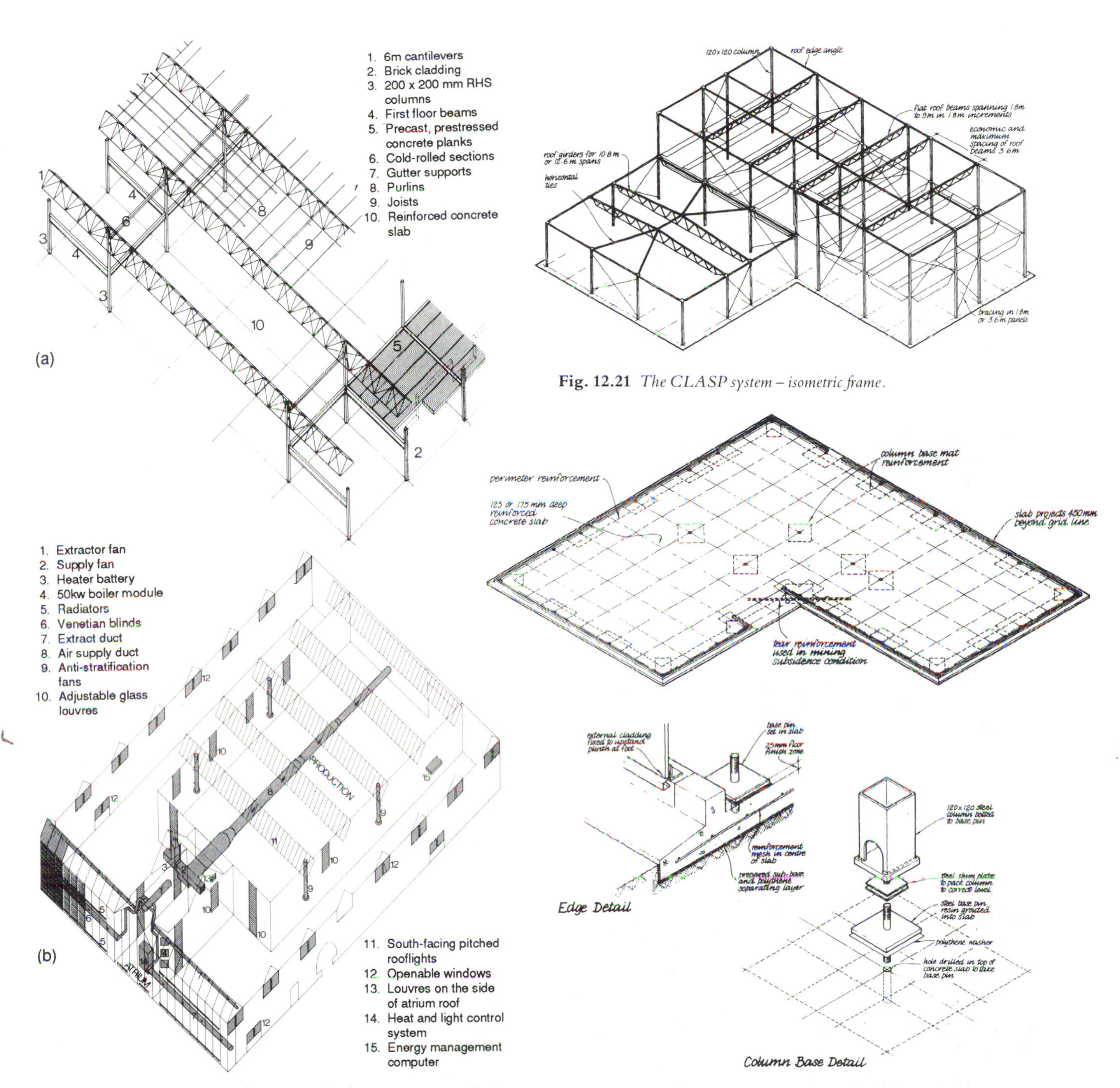

Fig. 12.21 *The CLASP system – isometric frame.*

Fig. 12.20 *JEL Factory, Stockport, UK (architect Dominic Michaelis Associates: engineer Anthony Hunt Associates) (a) structure; (b) performance control elements.*

Fig. 12.22 *The CLASP system – foundation and slab details.*

with traditional construction. This also means that the system is ideally suited for sites with poor ground bearing pressure. The building fabric was also designed to allow mining subsidence movement. Early window systems were timber-framed and designed to distort up to 5 degrees out of square. Later systems in timber and aluminium were designed with slip joints between vertical elements to allow movement without distortion. Early cladding methods tended to be small scale concrete panels or tile-hanging on timber frames. These were superseded by large concrete

Fig. 12.23 *The CLASP system at York University, UK (architects RMJM).*

Fig. 12.24 *Social Services Day Centre in Worksop, UK (architects Nottinghamshire County Architects Department).*

panels with slip joints and the system now incorporates rationalized in-situ brickwork. Up until 1980 roofs were flat and felted but in the current system traditionally tiled pitched roofs are more common.

The large public works programme in the 1960s and 1970s allowed CLASP to maintain the production of specially made components and also develop a system for more heavily loaded buildings such as universities. The most significant of these was the provision of campus architecture for Bath and York Universities under the direction of RMJM with Stirrat Johnson-Marshall and Andrew Derbyshire working on York and Hugh Morris working on Bath (Fig. 12.23). At York in particular the lakeland setting (by the landscape architect Maurice Pickering) showed how system building could be humanized. At both York and Bath the financial impact of using industrialized framing was considerable, since construction was achieved in the inflationary period of the early 1960s without cost overrun and with the jobs finished on schedule.

The CLASP system today has maintained its basic structural principles based on its light steel frame but has developed from its original closed system approach with limited aesthetic expression and flexibility to one which allows a wide freedom of expression whilst still maintaining the technical integrity resulting from nearly 30 years' development.

The system has been successfully used to construct over 3000 buildings. Its influence has also extended overseas to Hungary, Venezuela and Portugal and with derived systems in Germany, France, Switzerland, Italy and Spain. Most recently, CLASP has worked with Tarmac in joint venture to construct four hospitals in the earthquake zone of Mascara in Algeria at a cost of £46m.

Today, CLASP still shows the advantages which are typical of a well proven integrated light steel framing method. The use of a light standardized steel structure and brickwork detailing allowed the completion of projects within a time scale which would have been difficult by traditional means (Fig. 12.24). The city of Manchester, UK recently demonstrated its value when they were faced with the rapid completion of three neighbourhood centres.

BMW Headquarters, Bracknell, UK

Considerable advantage can be gained by treating the roof beams as structurally continuous. This reduces bending moments and deflections within the beams, allowing significantly smaller sections to be used. The disadvantage of such a system is the cost of achieving the continuity, but this has been largely overcome in a system pioneered by Peter Brett. This avoids the use of any rigid connection between the beams and supporting columns but instead uses relatively simple splice details to connect adjacent beam spans, leaving the column to provide vertical support only.

Peter Brett's BMW Headquarters [33] is probably the most celebrated example of this form of construction (Fig. 12.25). The warehouse consists of four 20 m (66 ft) spans of 406 × 178 × 54 UBs across the building and arranged at 2.5 m (8 ft) centres longitudinally. The beams are supported on the top flanges of 533 × 210 × 82 UBs which form spine beams spanning 10 m (33 ft) onto I-section columns. The construction details adopted, allowed structural continuity in both directions, minimizing bending effects in the beams, yet maintaining simple construction details. An interesting feature of the design is the use of just one column and two beam sizes and the success of the project is testified to by the short contract period on site.

Here, as at the Imperial War Museum extension, some use was made of site welding. This demonstrates that, where carefully integrated into the design and construction of a project, welding can be an economic, and in some respects a superior, solution for site connection.

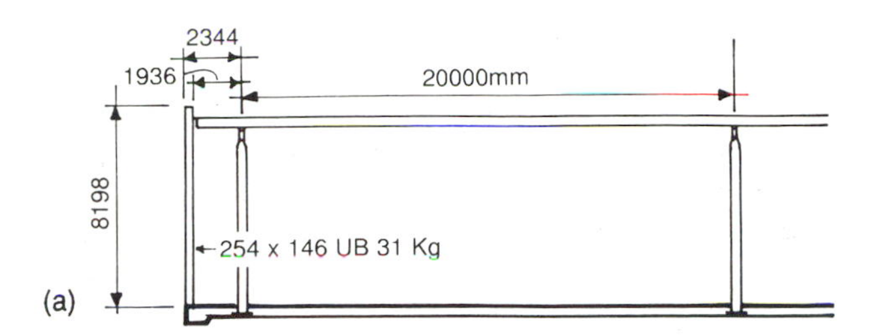

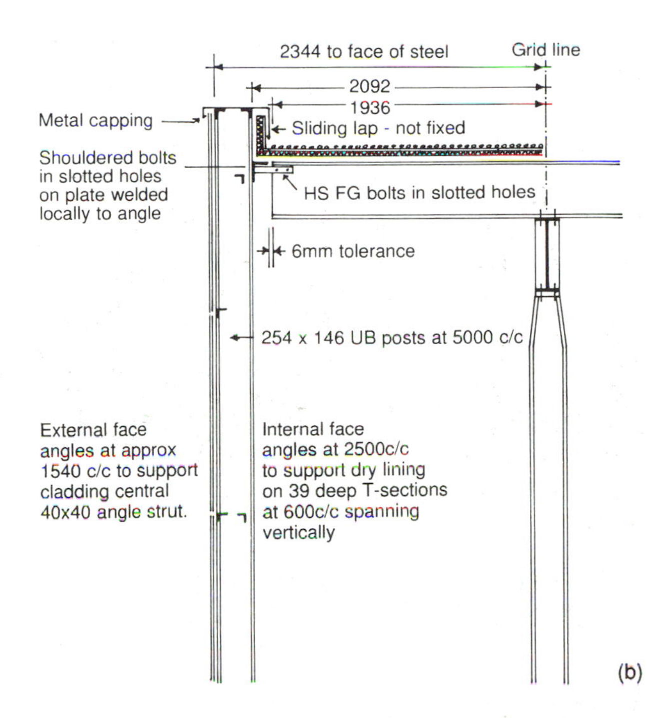

Fig. 12.25 *BMW Headquarters, Bracknell, UK (a) typical section; (b) structural detail (architects Nicholas Grimshaw and Partners: engineers Peter Brett Associates).*

The construction was undertaken on the basis of a design and build contract with Wiltshiers as the main contractor and Nicholas Grimshaw and Partners as architects. Despite a very short period for design and construction, interruptions in the supply of many primary building materials due to industrial disputes, and a cold, wet winter, the dry envelope solution and the large element of off-site fabrication enabled the building to be completed ahead of schedule.

After more than 10 years of use, which have seen many detailed changes to the functions within, the quality of the building has been proven many times over. With its relatively simple concept and form, it has demonstrated the value of a carefully designed and detailed solution appropriate to the client's requirements.

12.5 MULTI-SPAN STRUCTURES

In principle the support provided by the internal columns in multi-bay construction can be replaced by girders spanning along the length of the building.

National Exhibition Centre, Birmingham, UK

This is the system which was adopted at the National Exhibition Centre, Birmingham, UK, both in the original development [34–37] and in the subsequent phases. The exhibition halls required relatively column-free spaces with a headroom ranging from 12 to 23 m (40 to 75 ft). Cable suspended or domed roof structures were not considered because the proximity of Birmingham Airport meant that air safety control regulations limited the height of the exhibition buildings and yet it was essential to maximize exhibiting heights internally. For Halls 1 to 5, after comparative design studies, it was decided to adopt a flat roof form and to locate columns on a 30 m (100 ft) grid, with primary lattice trusses fabricated from rectangular hollow sections. These support a space frame roof, eliminating the need for a mass of secondary structure to support the services (Fig. 12.26). The form of construction allowed the greatest flexibility in the sequence of erection and avoided the need for major scaffolding. It also provided the maximum flexibility for the installation of plant and equipment, initially and during any subsequent changes. High-level rooflights, at about 4% of the roof area, and high level perimeter glazing, at between 15% and 20% of the perimeter area, provide a good level of natural light.

The columns are in the form of welded Vierendeel box sections consisting of four rectangular hollow sections. The primary trusses are also of box construction based on hollow sections, and the space frame roof is a Nodus two-layer system, the upper layer being on a 3.1 m (10 ft) grid to suit the roof decking. The primary trusses and columns form a portal frame effect, providing the necessary lateral rigidity without the need for cross-bracing. Although bracing could have been introduced into the perimeter wall, the client wished to maintain full flexibility, with the possibility of removing sections of walling to link into external exhibitions.

Hall 6 is somewhat smaller in scale with a height of 8.6 m (28 ft) and structural bays of 15 m (50 ft) for the two side spans and 20 m (66 ft) for the centre span. The structural form, although similar in concept to the other halls, is simpler; plane trusses spanning between columns form the primary structure which supports a grillage of hollow section purlins.

Subsequent development at the NEC [38,39] has adopted a similar design philosophy, with the 30 m (100 ft) column grid retained, although sloping roofs have been introduced in preference to the simple flat construction used on the earlier buildings (Fig. 12.27). The roof structure consists of plane primary trusses supporting triangular secondary trusses, creating a dominant linear form and facilitating the integration of service runs. The spacing of the triangular trusses is 2.75 m (9 ft), eliminating the need for purlins. Overall stability of the building is provided by raking props at the perimeter of each main grid line.

The NEC has proved a great success, the apparent simplicity of the structures allowing attention to be focused on the exhibits themselves. It has certainly attracted both exhibitors and visitors, who seem well pleased with the well proportioned halls and the interior environment.

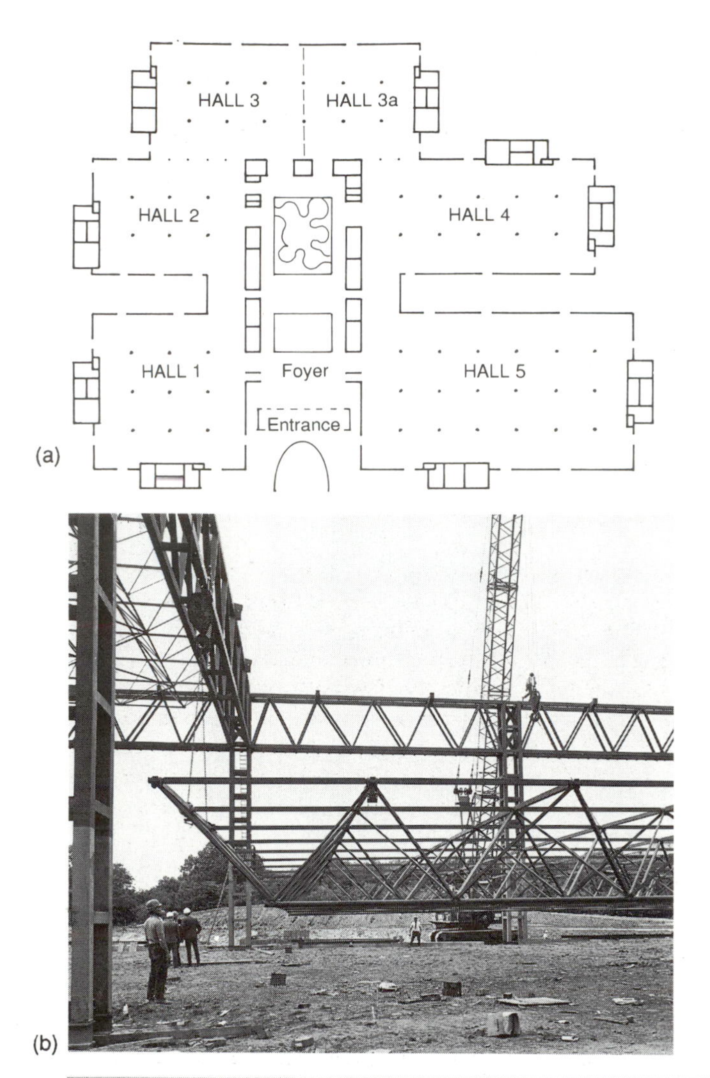

Fig. 12.26 *National Exhibition Centre, Birmingham, UK (a) typical plan arrangement; (b) erection (c) interior view; (d) aerial view (architects Edward D. Mills and Partners: engineer Ove Arup and Partners).*

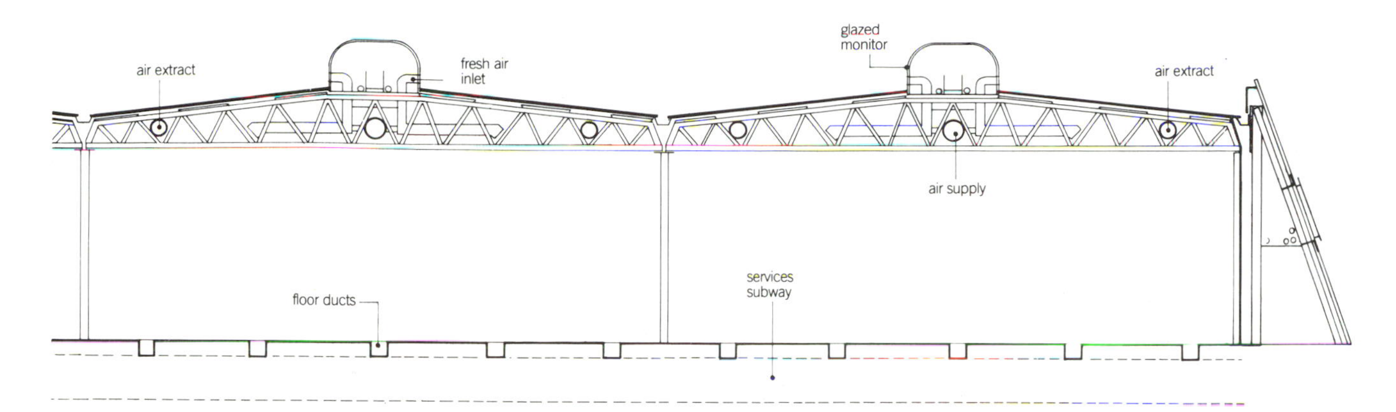

Fig. 12.27 *National Exhibition Centre (Phase II), Birmingham, UK – typical section (architect Seymour Harris Partnership: engineer Ove Arup and Partners).*

Chester-Le-Street, Durham, UK

Multi-span construction was also used by FaulknerBrowns at Chester-le-Street [40–42], where five 37 m (123 ft) span twin lattice girders are in turn supported near their centres by two single lattice girders (Fig. 12.28). All girders utilize RHS top chords with CHS bottom chords and bracings. The roof is a sandwich construction of long span profile which spans directly onto the trusses without purlins. The structure is enclosed by a well insulated curtain wall, and the result is a lightweight building, particularly appropriate to the poor ground conditions encountered on site.

One potential drawback of this system is the intrusion on headroom, although use can be made of the roof space to accommodate services, as at the NEC. In other cases, such as where planning restrictions impose limitations on building height, various systems have been developed to minimize this problem.

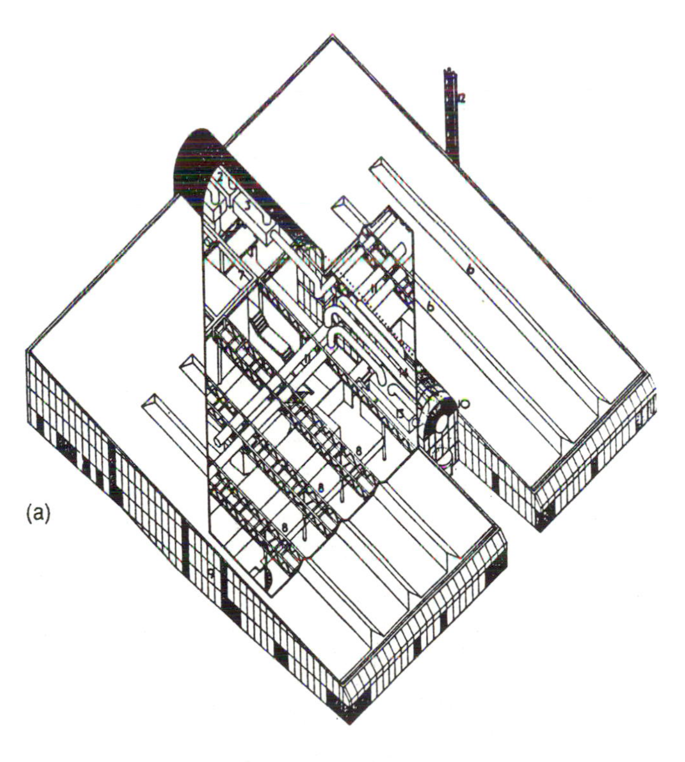

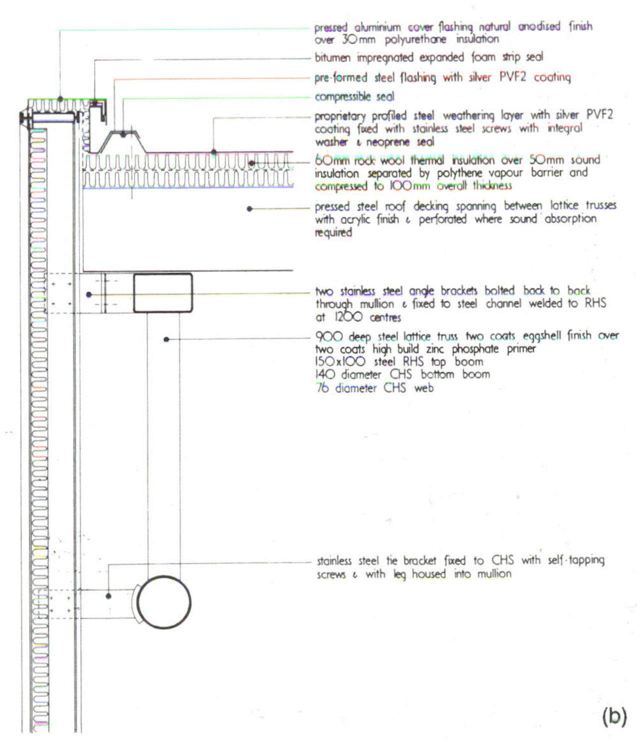

Fig. 12.28 *Chester-le-Street, County Durham, UK (a) axonometric view; (b) detail of roof edge (architects FaulknerBrowns: engineer Condall Johnson and Partners).*

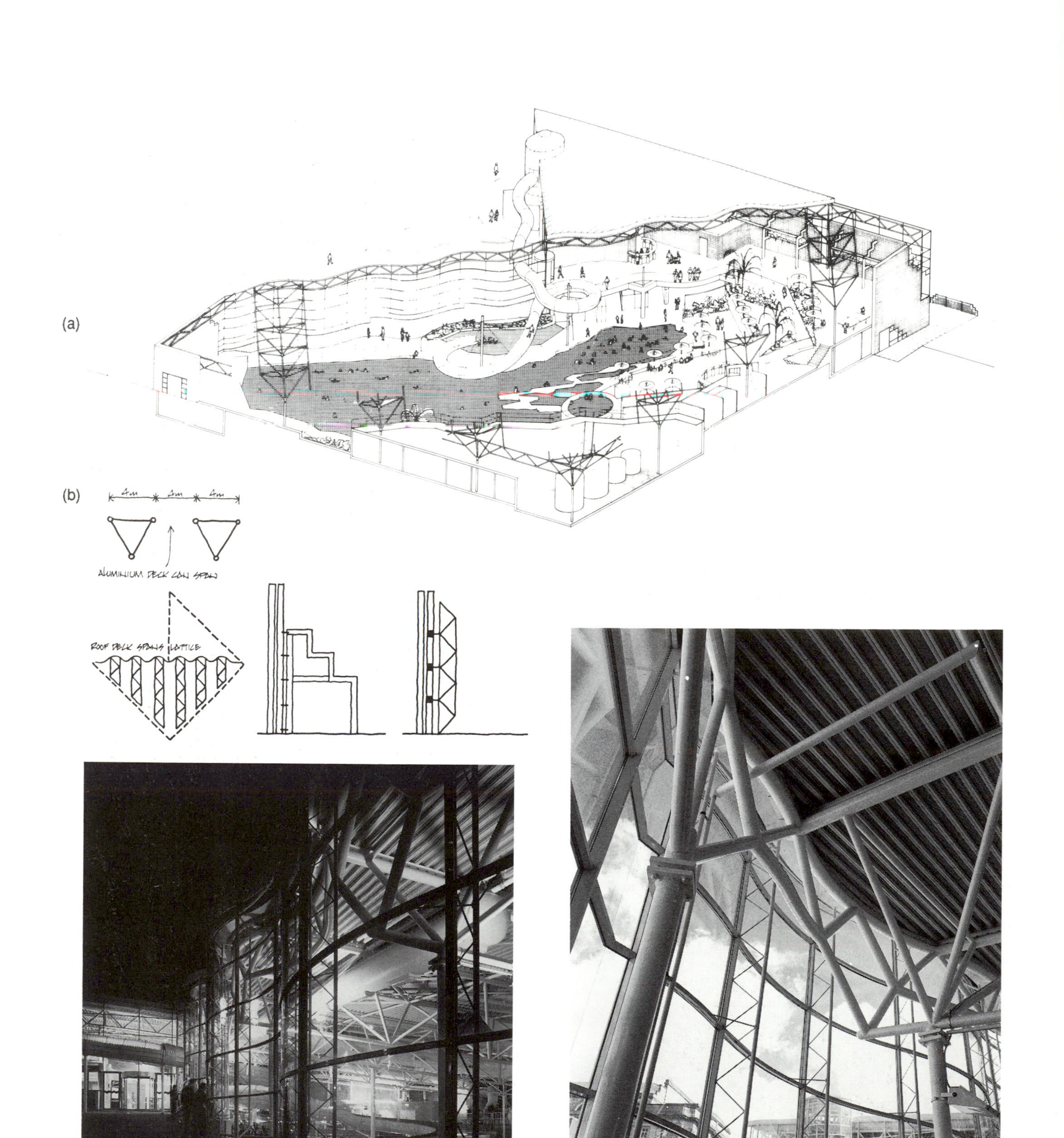

Fig. 12.29 *The Waves, Blackburn, UK (a) isometric; (b) principles of structure; (c) exterior view; (d) interior view (architects FaulknerBrowns: engineer F. J. Samuely and Partners).*

The Waves, Blackburn, UK

The Waves at Blackburn [43,44] is a leisure complex designed by FaulknerBrowns. The roof structure uses trusses of triangular cross-section and fabricated in high yield tubular steelwork (Fig. 12.29). These span up to 44 m (146 ft) diagonally across the pool hall and are supported on tubular columns, restrained laterally by a curved truss above a curving window – the serpentine wall. The main triangular roof trusses are 4 m (13 ft) wide and spaced at 8 m (26 ft) centres. The roof deck is a highly insulated structural aluminium system which spans the 4 m (13 ft) spacing of the main supports without secondary purlins. A triangular section rooflight 3 m (10 ft) wide runs across the pool, supported on steel trusses. Structural glazing is used for the rooflight, the panes simply resting against each other with a silicone joint at the apex. The exposed soffit, which is perforated for acoustic absorption, is therefore not only visually clean but also minimizes areas which might be particularly vulnerable to corrosion. Current paint specifications are now recognized as being capable of protecting steel from the aggressive conditions of swimming pool atmospheres. By exposing the steel, inspection and maintenance are made easier, potential condensation problems are reduced, and costs are saved by omitting false ceilings and pressurized voids. The use of steel on this project enabled early completion of the roof, allowing uninterrupted construction of the complex building works below. The result is an exciting building designed and constructed to a high standard and specification.

Cummins Engineering Works, Shotts, Lanarkshire, UK

The Cummins factory extension by Ahrends, Burton and Koralek (ABK) [45,46] makes use of the physical transparency of these structural forms to accommodate the services in an efficient manner, provide top light and to support an overhead crane. Principal trusses are triangular in section, spanning 15 m (50 ft) between main columns of circular hollow section and are external to the building enclosure (Fig. 12.30). Castellated beams are supported on the bottom chord of the trusses and at third span points by tension cables connected to the top chords of the trusses. Bracing in the direction of the main frames is provided in a conventional manner by securing to rigid reinforced concrete frames. However, in the direction of the secondary structure, bracing is provided by an arrangement of raked perimeter columns located at each frame position. This readily provides for future extension.

Sainsbury's, Camden Town, London, UK

The Sainsbury's store at Camden Town by Nicholas Grimshaw [47,49] is an unusual form of multi-span truss roof construction. The 43 m (143 ft) wide shopping hall is spanned by bowed roof trusses which are supported by T-shaped towers (refer to chapter 36 for details).

The design brief called for a clear span market hall, in scale with its surroundings and capable of being read by passers by. The area requirements for sales and other functions such as storage and preparation were met by providing first floor accommodation close to the supports. This achieved the required massing as well as improving structural efficiency.

The roof trusses forming the central span are located at 7.2 m (24 ft) centres. Their curved form facilitates drainage,

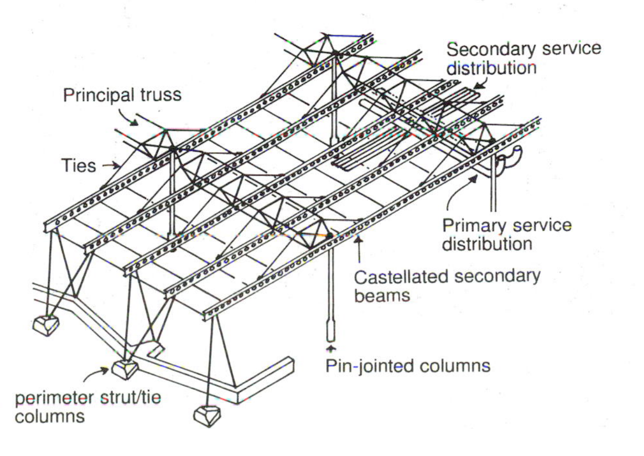

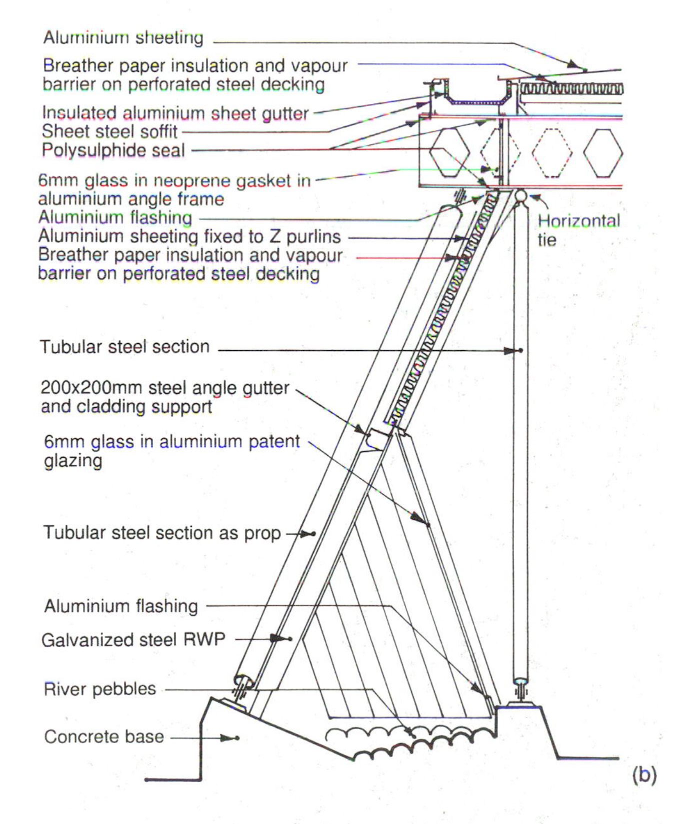

Fig. 12.30 *Cummins Engineering Works, Shotts, Lanarkshire, UK (a) structure; (b) detail (architects ABK).*

provides a smooth curving ceiling over the entire sales area, and enables simple expression on the external elevations, but the curvature was too shallow to enable any advantage to be taken of arching action. The truss was therefore designed as a moment resisting frame with universal column sections for the top and bottom chords and hollow sections for the bracing members.

The trusses are suspended from the ends of cantilevered plate girders using a pinned joint detail to allow relative movement between the two components. The detail is complicated by the need to accommodate the gutter for the main roof and the provision of a glazed strip to allow some sight of the roof from Camden Road. The cantilevers are in turn supported on tubular concrete-filled columns and tied down by groups of four 50 mm (2 in) diameter Macalloy bars anchored into the pile caps by post-tensioned rods via 75 mm (3 in) thick plates. Provision for accidental damage was made by protecting the tie downs with concrete bollards and introducing a secondary load path using storey-height trusses spanning across two bays to allow for the accidental removal of one set of tie downs.

By adopting the pinned support for the main roof, it was possible to treat the two-storey blocks as self-supporting fire-protected structures, allowing the main centre span roof to be unprotected. A weather-resisting epoxy-based intumescent material (ICI's Firec) was bonded onto the steelwork supporting the first floor, allowing full expression of the structural form and detail. Close co-operation between the design team and the steel contractor enabled this clear expression to be maintained throughout the structure.

Space frames

Space frames are the ultimate expression of such two-way spanning continuous systems, but suffer from problems associated with the cost of the specialized joints which are required. The spanning capability of space frames is demonstrated by the indoor athletics arena at Birmingham, UK. This consists of a three-tier Mero space frame fixed with tubular steel struts attached in groups to dedicated high strength central nodes in groups giving the appearance of a mass of bicycle spokes. The roof covers a main floor area of 130 m by 118 m (433 m), with 19 m (63 ft) clear headroom, and seating for 8000 spectators.

This is an interesting contrast to the nearby International Arena (originally named Hall 7) at the National Exhibition Centre [51–53], where space frames again formed the basis for the roof, but in this case an almost identical clear floor area was achieved with more modest structural depths by providing intermediate support in the form of cable stayed lattice box girders. The roof construction is very similar to that used for the other NEC halls described above, but the internal columns are replaced by tension supports in the form of raking circular hollow sections connected to the four-legged Vierendeel towers and anchored via outriggers to the ground (Fig. 12.31). Such forms of construction can

Fig. 12.31 *International Arena, Birmingham, UK (architects Edward Mills and Partners: engineer Ove Arup and Partners).*

be rather flexible and it was calculated that vertical deflections could be as high as 200 mm (8 in) at the tension support positions. Nevertheless, computer calculations demonstrated that the structure was capable of sustaining such deformations without detriment. Since the construction period was very tight and the fabrication time for the main structural trusses was longer than the simpler components, an unusual erection sequence was adopted. This involved pre-assembly of the space frames, complete with sprinkler and lighting services, at ground level before lifting into position onto temporary supports prior to installation of the primary structure.

The scale and style of the structure, and the speed of construction demonstrate what can be achieved in structural steelwork when well designed and accurately made.

12.6 CONCLUSION

This chapter has covered a wide range of case studies demonstrating the versatility of structural steelwork for roofing large spaces. Architects are enthusiastic about trusswork and often celebrate this aspect in atria or toplit interiors. Contemporary design employing welded tube often features in interiors (Fig. 12.31) as opposed to being lost within the ceiling space. Large-scale space frames offer the most stimulating visual quality, particularly where the forms are expressed both externally and internally; a seminal example is the Flower Market, Nine Elms, London, UK (Fig. 12.32). There is also considerable interest in the way steelwork is assembled by means of pin joints or special castings when the framing is exposed to view. Tom Schollar explores these details in chapter 21.

Fig. 12.32 *Space frame roof construction at the Flower Market, Nine Elms, London, UK 1970–75 (architects GMW: engineer Clarke Nicholls and Marcel).*

Fig. 12.33 *Model: Channel Tunnel Terminal, Waterloo Station, London 1992 (architects Nicholas Grimshaw and Partners: engineers Anthony Hunt/YRM).*

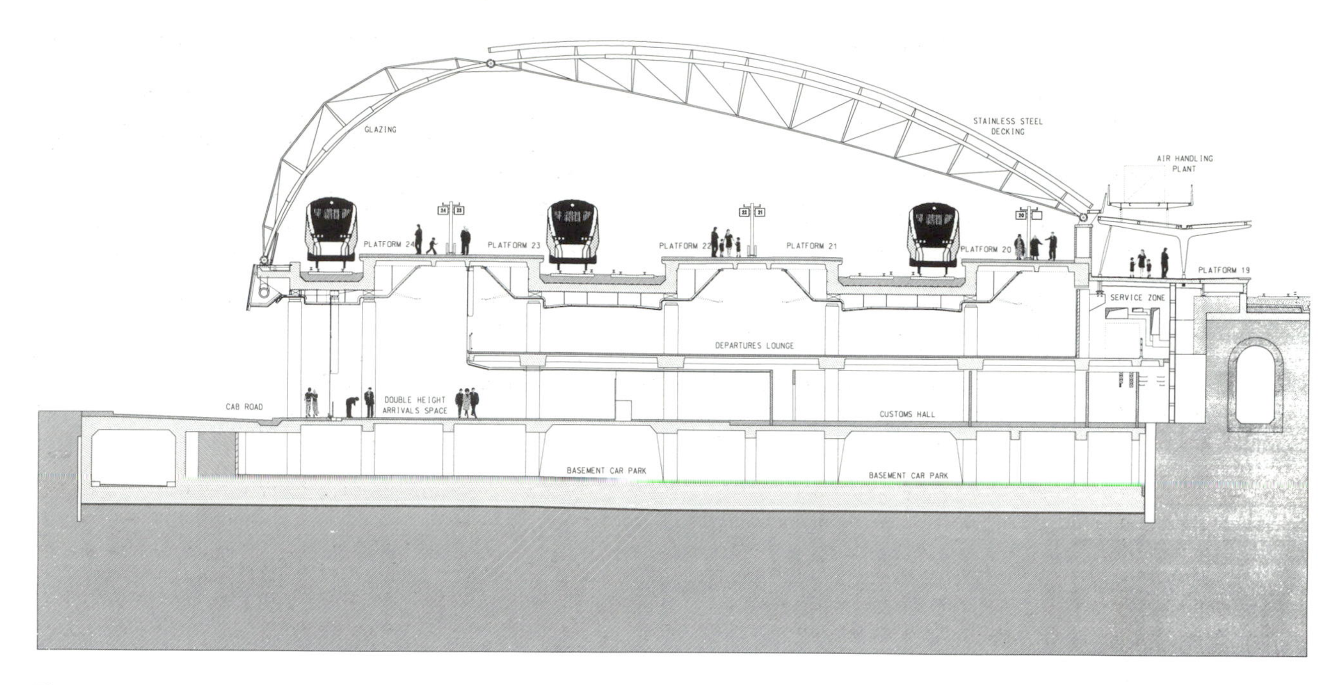

Fig. 12.34 *Channel Tunnel Terminal, Waterloo Station, London, UK.*

Finally there is the question of the framing layout and its relation to the footprint of the building. The most eloquent and subtle solution from the early 1990s must surely be the extension to Waterloo Station for the Channel Tunnel Terminal designed by Nicholas Grimshaw and Partners (Fig. 12.33). The smooth sinuous curves, which reflect the track layout below and extend over the increased length of the new trains to be received from the Channel Tunnel, fit gracefully against the Edwardian engineering of the older terminal. The appearance of the trusswork is enhanced by the use of tapering tubes. The cross-section (Fig. 12.34) reveals the graceful three-pin arch, with the 'centre pin' located to one side to create an asymmetrical geometry. The leaf-like form is necessary to accommodate train clearance requirements and to satisfy the constraints imposed by the raised viaduct. Passers by, as well as passengers, will be able to experience the drama of the new international trains as the entire western elevation is transparent. This inspirational design is equal in form and invention to the ideas of Paxton a century and a half ago.

REFERENCES AND TECHNICAL NOTES

1. Berry, J. and Pugh, R. Spectrum 7, Milton Keynes, *The Arup Journal*, Winter 1988/89 Vol. 23, No. 4., pp. 7–10.
2. Berry, J. and Ferraro, R. 'Low energy for industry: Spectrum 7 at Milton Keynes', *Architects' Journal*, 17 May 1989, Vol. 189, No. 20, pp. 73–77
3. Poole, D. 'Low energy factories: 4 Daylighting' *Architects' Journal*, 30 May 1990, pp. 63–65. Vol. 191, No. 22.
4. 'Case Study: high-tech roof deck', *Architect's Journal Focus*, January 1989, Vol. 3, No. 1, pp. 19–21.
5. Cunliffe, R. 'Building Study: The Bespak factory at Kings Lynn', *Architects' Journal*, 2 July 1980, Vol. 172, No. 27, pp. 17–32.
6. 'Case Study: the glass umbrella', *Architect's Journal Focus*, July 1989, Vol. 3, No. 7, pp. 19–23.
7. Ridley, T., Blackwood, D. and Carcas, J. 'The St Enoch Centre', *The Arup Journal*, Spring 1989, Vol. 24, No. 1, pp. 15–20.
8. 'Glasshouse in Glasgow', *Building Design Structures Supplement*, June 1989, pp. 26–29.
9. *New Civil Engineer*, 15 June 1989.
10. Redhead, D. 'Popular Pavilions', *RIBA Journal*, August 1989, Vol. 96, No. 8, pp. 65–68.
11. 'The Pavilions – Uxbridge Town Centre', *Steel Construction*, December 1990, Vol. 6, No. 6, pp. 22–23.
12. Structural Steel Design Awards 1990.
13. Ayiomamatis, A., Blunn, I., Butler, K. and Del Mese, G. 'The structure of the Imperial War Museum', *The Arup Journal*, Winter 1988/89, Vol. 23, No. 4, pp. 2–6.
14. 'The Imperial War Museum Extension', *Steel Construction*, December 1989, Vol. 5, No. 6, pp. 16–17. (Structural Steel Design Awards 1989.)
15. Kew: Structural Steel Design Awards 1986.
16. PSA at Kew.
17. *New Civil Engineer*, 29 March 1990.
18. Brookes, A. and Grech, C. (1990) *The Building Envelope*, Butterworth, London.
19. Hannay, P. 'Parking Business', *Architect's Journal*, 25 July 1990, Vol. 192, No. 4, pp. 30–41.

20. 'Stockley Park', *The Arup Journal*, Spring 1987, Vol. 22, No. 1, pp. 4–7.
21. Glover, M. 'The "other buildings" at Stockley Park', *The Arup Journal*, Spring 1990, Vol. 25, No. 1, pp. 38–42.
22. 'Case Study: research building, Stockley Park', *Architects' Journal Focus*, July 1988, Vol. 2, No. 7, pp. 24–27.
23. 'Hasboro Inc., Stockley Park', *The Arup Journal*, Summer 1989, Vol. 24, No. 2, pp. 22–23.
24. 'Case Study: Apple skin', *Architects' Journal Focus*, March 1990, Vol. 4, No. 3, pp. 17–19.
25. 'Case Study: Foster's frames', *Architects' Journal Focus*, May 1989, Vol. 3, No. 5, pp. 19–22.
26. Brookes, A. and Grech, C. (1990) *The Building Envelope*, Butterworth, London.
27. 'Stock in trade', *Architectural Record*, September 1989, Vol. 177, No. 9, pp. 80–83.
28. Zunz, G. J., Manning, M. W., Kaye, D. and Jofeh, C. G. H. 'Stansted Airport Terminal – the structure', *The Arup Journal*, Spring 1990, Vol. 25, No. 1, pp. 7–15.
29. Zunz, G. J., Manning, M. W. and Jofeh, C. G. H. 'The design of the structure for the new terminal building at Stansted Airport', *The Structural Engineer*, Vol. 66, No. 21, 1 November 1988, pp. 361–370.
30. Structural Steel Design Awards 1986.
31. Stonehouse, R. 'Building Study: soul of a new machine', *Architects' Journal*, 13 July 1983, Vol. 178, No. 28, pp. 39–58.
32. CLASP. For technical details, refer to CLASP International (Building Services) Ltd, Easthorpe House, Loughborough Road, Ruddington, Nottingham NG11 6LV. The architectural history of CLASP and other school buildings systems is portrayed in *Towards a Social Architecture* by Andrew Saint. Published by Yale University Press (1987).
33. *Framed in Steel 5*, British Steel.
34. Mills, E. (1976) The *National Exhibition Centre*, Crosby Lockwood Staples, London.
35. 'Building Study: National Exhibition Centre', *Architects' Journal*, 12 May 1976, Vol. 163, No. 19, pp. 931–946.
36. 'A National Showpiece', Building, 7 May 1976, Vol. 230, No. 19, pp. 96–108.
37. Haryott, R. 'The National Exhibition Centre', *The Arup Journal*, Sept 1975, Vol. 10, No. 5, pp. 19–23.
38. 'Case Study: taking the lid off the NEC', *Architects Journal Focus*, November 1989, Vol. 3, No. 10, pp. 32–38.
39. Structural Steel Design Awards 1981.
40. Cave, C. 'Building Study: Chester-le-Street Civic Offices, Part 1', *Architects' Journal*, 4 August 1982, Vol. 176, No. 31, pp. 31–46.
41. Carolin, P./Turnbull, B. & Taylor, N./Nelson, G. 'Construction Study: Chester-le-Street Civic Offices, Part 2', *Architects' Journal*, 11 August 1982, Vol. 176, No. 32, pp. 31–46.
42. Structural Steel Design Awards 1983.
43. Gravell, J./Barbrook, R. 'Building Study: Waves of leisure pleasure', *Architects' Journal*, 10 December 1986. Vol. 184, No. 50, pp. 31–48.
44. Wilcock, R. 'Case Study: Blackburn', *Architects' Journal Focus*, April 1987, Vol. 1, No. 1, pp. 21–27.
45. Gale, A./Owston, B./Kirkwood, R./Ahrends, P. 'Building Study: Cummins Engine Company, Shotts, Lanarkshire', *Architects' Journal*, 17 Feb. 1982, Vol. 175, No. 7, pp. 39–56.
46. Structural Steel Design Awards 1980.
47. Slade, R. E. 'The Sainsbury development, Camden', *The Structural Engineer*, Vol. 69, No. 18, 17 September 1991, pp. 317–326.
48. 'Urban encapsulation', *Architectural Record*, Sept. 1989, Vol. 177, No. 9, pp. 78–79.
49. Davey, P. 'Urban Grimshaw', *Architectural Review* 1989, Vol. 186, No. 1112, pp. 36–49.
50. Doyle, N. 'World class Birmingham', *New Builder*, 15 November 1990, pp. 20–21.
51. 'Building Study: Hall 7, Birmingham International Arena', *Architects' Journal*, 11 Feb. 1981, Vol. 173, No. 6, pp. 249–258.
52. Thilwind, J. 'Raising the roof at the NEC', *RDL Review*, Winter 1980/81, pp. 12–16.
53. Structural Steel Design Awards 1981.

Air handling services in relation to cables, lighting, pipework and structure.

13

Floor framing and services above and below floors

Tom Schollar and Anthony Gregson

13.1 INTRODUCTION

It is now customary for the services, like the floor framing itself, to be hidden either below the floor finishes or above a false ceiling, providing an aesthetic and practical solution. There is clearly a very close interaction between the design of the service runs and the floor framing system and this can have a major influence on the building economics. This chapter is principally concerned with the most economic or cost-effective solutions for integrating structure, services and finishes, although some unusual and unconventional methods are touched upon.

In modern buildings the choice of a floor framing system is influenced by a number of factors. These include the following, not necessarily listed in any order of priority:

(a) Floor grids, taking account of the site and the user requirements.

(b) Floor-to-floor heights which may be restricted, for example by planning regulations or the need to relate to aesthetics or height limitations of adjacent buildings.

(c) Cladding costs, which for sophisticated systems such as window walls may be as much as £600/m^2 (£56/ft^2) (1990 prices). The effect of envelope costs obliges designers to look critically at reduced floor-to-floor heights and this clearly has implications with regard to construction depth for structure and servicing (Table 13.1).

Types of services

Air handling ductwork is usually large in relation to the size of structural members, whereas pipework and electrics are usually small and can be broken down into individual services of smaller size (Fig. 13.1). The cost of services will frequently exceed the cost of the structure and it may well be advantageous to use a structural system that is not the cheapest in order to accommodate services and provide flexibility for change (Fig. 13.2).

Flexibility in use

Many owners express a desire for flexibility in the use of a building. This may determine the structural form where the

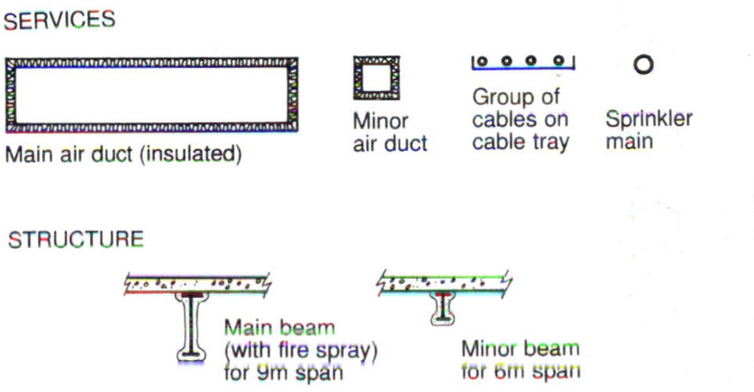

Fig. 13.1 *Air handling services in relation to cables, pipework and structure.*

Table 13.1 Floor-to-floor heights

	Facade cost £/m^2 (£/ft^2)	*Floor-to-floor ht m (ft)*	*Slab mm (in)*	*Services zone mm (ft)*	*Clear ht m (ft)*
Highest cost building £1000/m^2 (£93/ft^2)	800 (93)	4.5 (15)	150–300 (6–12)	1200–1350 (48–54)	3.0 (10)
Middle range £800/m^2 (£75/ft^2)	600 (55)	3.6 (12)	150–300 (6–12)	750–900 (30–36)	2.55 (8.5)
Lowest cost (typical of 1960s buildings) £600/m^2 (£55/ft^2)	400 (37)	3.0 (10)	150–300 (6–12)	300–450 (12–18)	2.4 (8)

From the above figures, facade costs will be found to vary from £1200 to £4500 per metre run (£366 to £1370/ft) i.e. for a 16 × 48 m (52 × 157 ft) floor plate, £200–750/m^2 (£18–70/ft^2), hence the pressure to reduce storey heights. Floor-to-floor heights of 3 m (10 ft) with a service zone of 300–450 mm (12–18 in) will not be sufficient for full servicing.

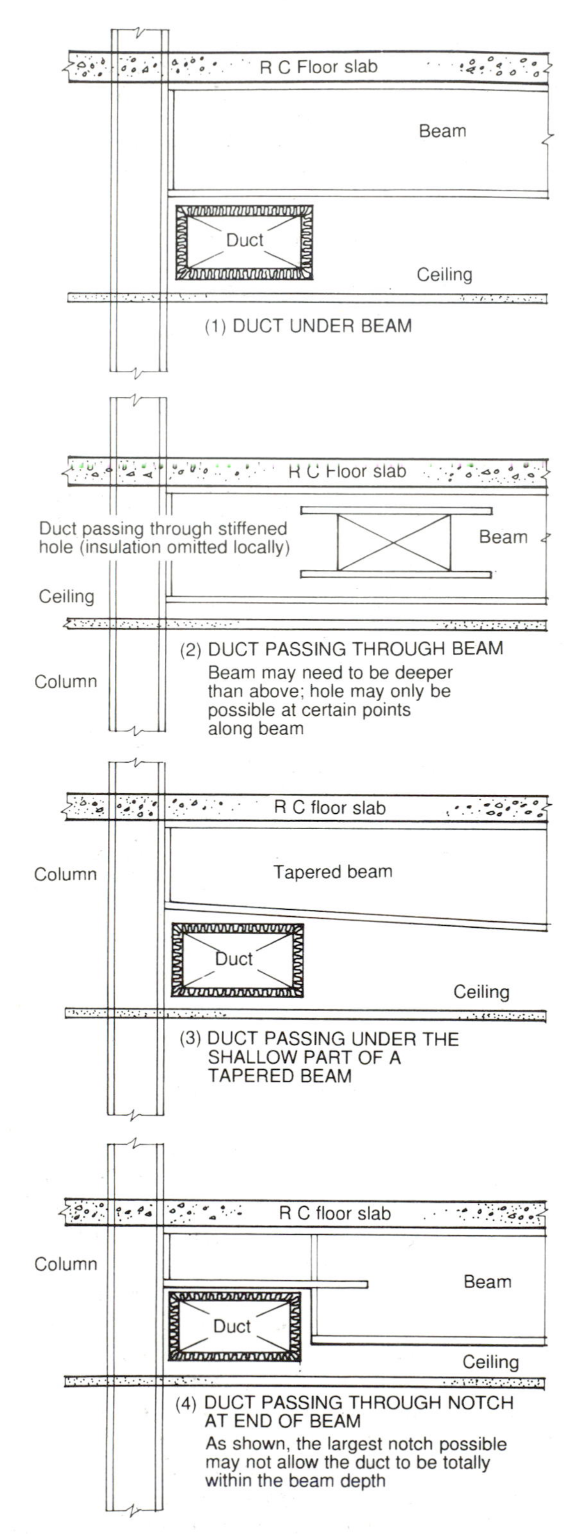

Fig. 13.2 *Complicated structure to accommodate services.*

owner is prepared to pay for such provision, since services and structure which are readily adaptable cost more in the first instance. Steel is relatively easy to adapt and can be readily trimmed for any flooring arrangement. However, strengthening steel columns to carry extra floors is comparable in complexity to modifying other materials.

Type of contract

The scale of the job determines the sophistication of services and structure. With small building works it is advisable to find methods which are within the capability of fabricators or specialists who are able to enter economic tenders for the work. With larger jobs (say £5 000 000 plus for the building cost) then it is possible to look towards more complex services and floor systems. Costs and time for fabrication and the lead-in time before erection occurs on site are other important factors.

13.2 STRUCTURAL FLOOR SYSTEMS

13.2.1 Timber

Timber floors are common only in domestic or semi-domestic applications. The structural floor in commercial properties usually serves as the fire separation between floors – a role for which timber is unsuitable. Noise transmission can also be a problem where a building is used by more than one tenant/occupier. (This was avoided in the 19th century by installing double floors). Load capacity can be high, as found in London's Docklands where a number of warehouses have been refurbished. Strengthening is normally easy to arrange, either with secondary steel beams or by installing spine beams and columns. The weight of wooden boards and joists can be lower than virtually any other system, and this may affect the choice in some applications. Timber floors can easily be taken up to accommodate services. For domestic floors the practical span limitation is 4.5 m (9 ft), and steel supporting beams are usually used if larger spans are required.

13.2.2 In situ reinforced concrete

Traditional solid in situ reinforced concrete floor slabs supported on downstand steel beams are no longer very common because of the high cost and inconvenience to the construction programme of temporary formwork and propping (approximately £20/m^2 at 1990 prices).

Alternative systems such as waffle and trough floors make more efficient use of material, whilst flat slab construction enables relatively straightforward construction but at the expense of using more material.

13.2.3 Precast concrete

This form of construction has been fairly common in recent years and there are a number of proprietary floor systems available. The units are made with plain or prestressed reinforcement and are formed in lightweight or normal concrete. Units may be manufactured with internal voids to reduce self weight, but deflections, vibrations and robustness must all be considered. Some suppliers have capacity to make up flooring units to special designs.

The cheapest assembly is to butt the precast units and to overlay with non-structural screed. Cracking through an unreinforced screed is unavoidable, ruling out in situ floor coverings. It is preferable to place an in situ reinforced concrete topping to act as a diaphragm. This will ensure more positive restraint from the floor slab system to the supporting beams, and make the floor capable of transmitting horizontal forces associated with building sway.

This topping can also be used to act compositely with the supporting steel beams, but this is not usually very effective because the thickness of in situ concrete is small – about 75 mm (3 in). Such floors are accordingly designed as non-composite, and are generally less economic than fully composite floors.

Economic spans for precast concrete vary according to the format chosen, an approximate guide being as follows (refer also to Fig. 13.3).

(1) Precast joists and block infill. These are usually suitable for domestic loading only, with spans up to around 6 m (20 ft).
(2) Prestressed planks with in situ reinforced concrete topping. These usually need propping while the topping gains strength, and the maximum span is similar to that for precast joists and block infill.
(3) Prestressed hollow-core units can span up to 12 m (40 ft).
(4) Prestressed double tee units can span up to at least 20 m (66 ft). These beams are commonly used for multi-storey car parks.

For all of these types of precast floor systems, the manufacturers publish load/span tables.

Adapting any form of precast work for services means subframing for slots at right angles to the span or making elements with recesses or slot holes (Fig. 13.4). Alternatively areas of in situ concrete can be specified at hole locations.

Practical sizes of precast units depend upon craneage and transportation. The usual limitation is 7.5 × 3.0 m (25 × 10 ft) and 7 metric tonnes weight, although double tee units are commonly much larger than this.

13.2.4 Composite steel deck floors

This form of floor construction, described in chapter 16, has

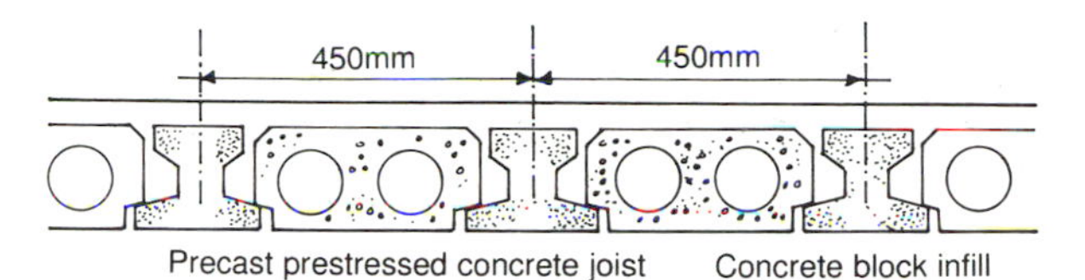

1. JOISTS AND BLOCK INFILL

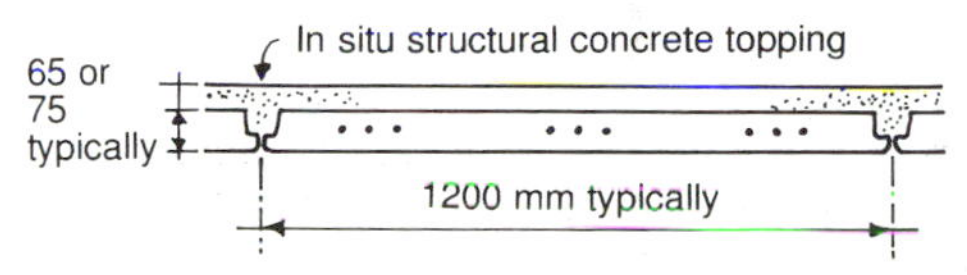

2. PRESTRESSED PLANK AND IN-SITU TOPPING

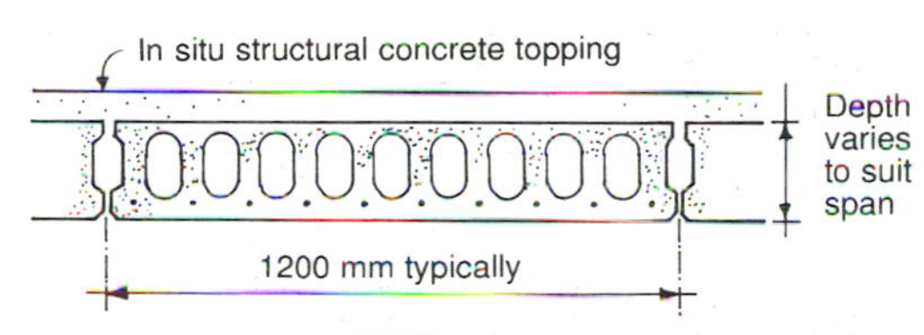

3. PRESTRESSED HOLLOW-CORE UNITS

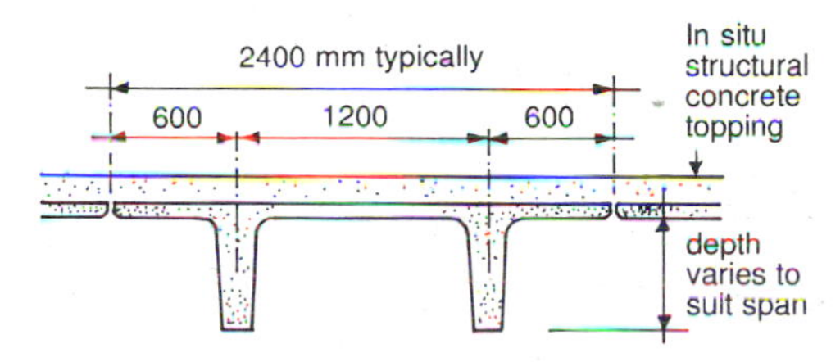

4. PRESTRESSED DOUBLE TEE UNITS

Fig. 13.3 *Types of precast concrete units.*

become popular largely because of its speed and ease of construction. To avoid propping, span limitations for commercial buildings are approximately 3.0–3.6 m (10–12 ft) depending upon loading conditions and decking type. At £20 per square metre (£2/ft^2) (1990 prices) metal decking compares favourably in terms of cost with other forms of flooring (Fig. 13.5). It is a less obvious choice if the slab soffit is exposed visually. This is particularly the case when used externally due to the shortened life of the galvanized protection. In addition, the top flanges of the supporting beams will be partially exposed and where these are unpainted to allow through-deck welding of studs, considerable corrosion risks exist.

Under most circumstances, additional fire protection measures are not necessary. However, where some protection is needed, cement fibre spray or intumescent coatings can be used where higher standards of appearance are not required such as on soffits over parking areas.

Some profiles have a dovetail shape which facilitates the

(a) SMALL OPENINGS - TIMBER FLOORS

The hole is limited to about 250-300mm (10-12in) wide by the timber joist spacing. There is no limit to the length of the hole.

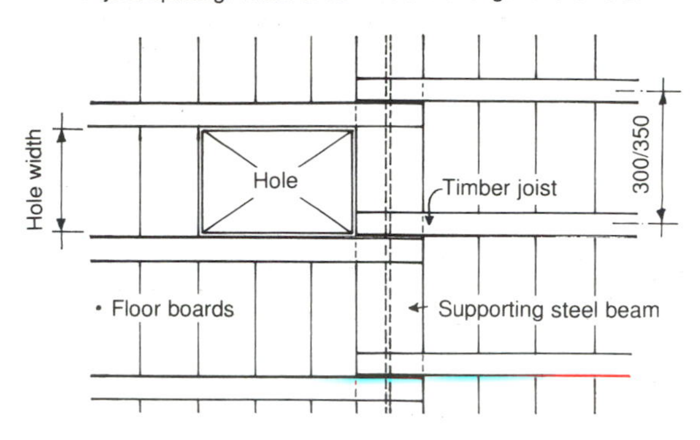

(b) SMALL OPENINGS - IN-SITU CONCRETE

Typically, for holes formed before the slab is cast, the width and length may be up to 2000mm (6ft8in)
For holes cut after the slab is cast, the width across the span will normally be limited to 500-750mm (20-30in)
The size of a possible hole is dependent on the number of bars removed/displaced, and whether the bars are fully stressed.

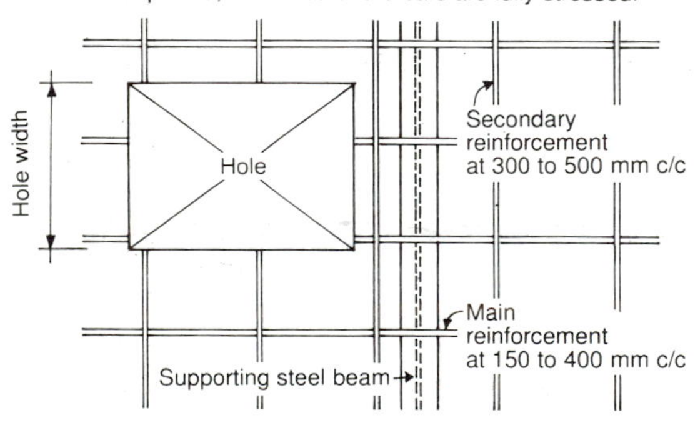

(c) SMALL OPENINGS - METAL DECK FLOORS

For holes made after the concrete topping is poured, the width may be up to 250-300mm (10-12in)
For holes formed before the topping is poured, using additional reinforcement at the sides of the hole, they may be up to 750mm (30in) wide.
In principle there is no length limit on the holes.

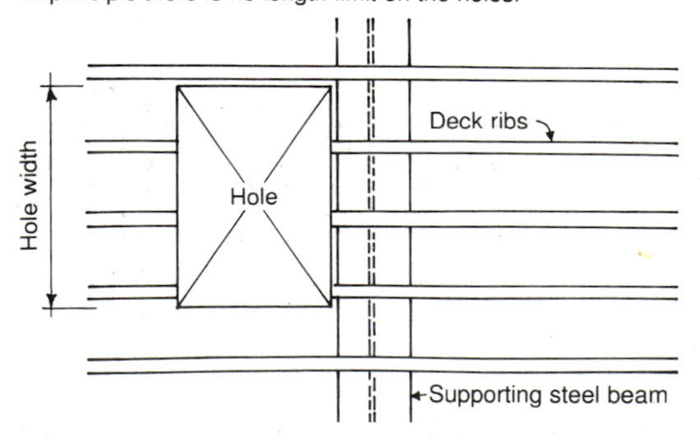

(d) SMALL OPENINGS - PRECAST FLOORS
Hollow-core (extruded) type

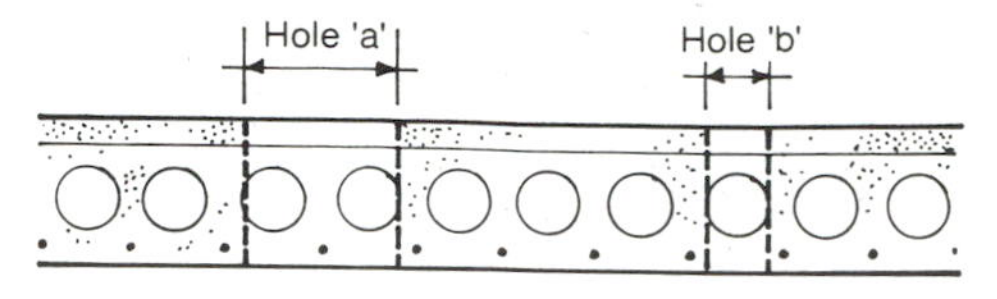

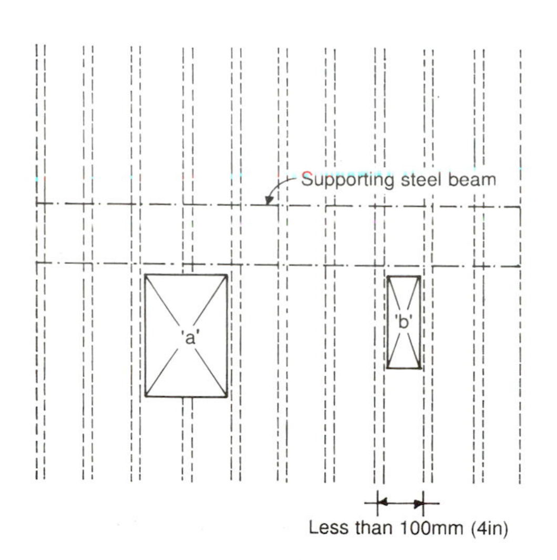

(e) SMALL OPENINGS - PRECAST FLOORS
Double Tee type

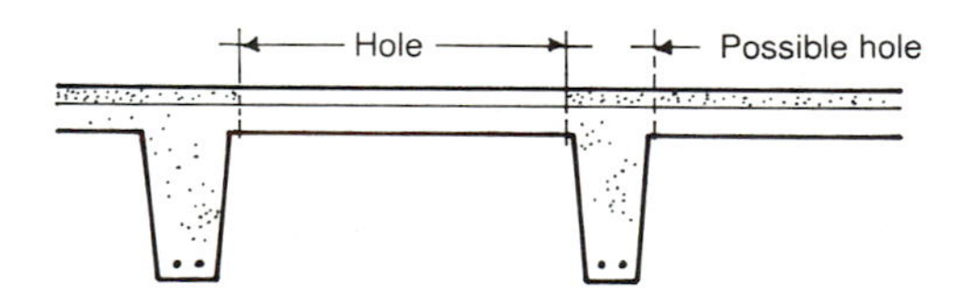

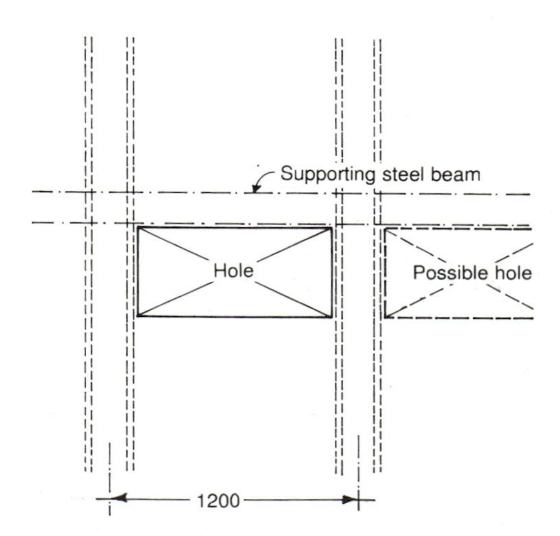

Fig. 13.4 *Accommodating vertical services within floor systems using precast units.*

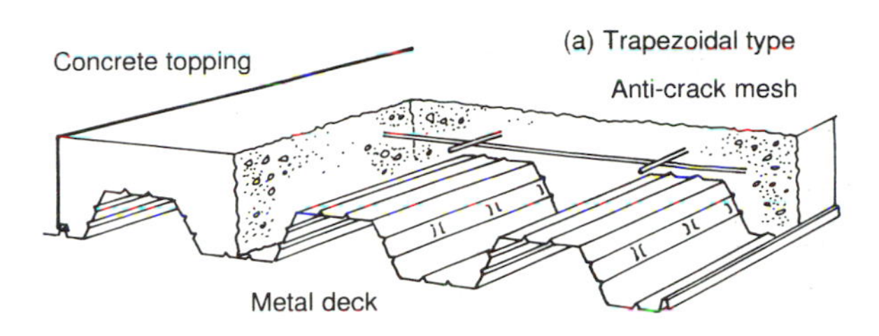

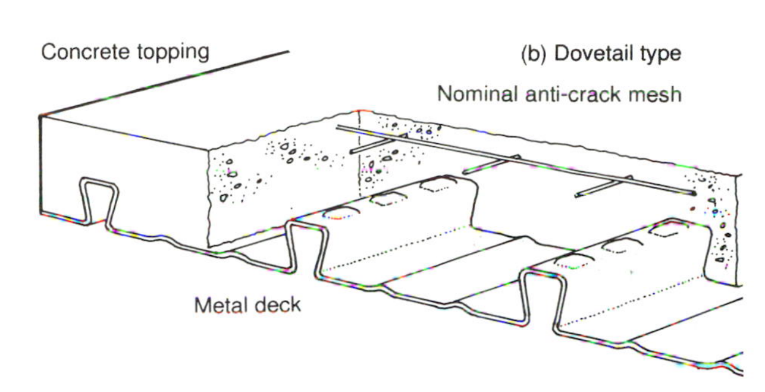

Fig. 13.5 *Two common types of metal decking (a) 'trapezoidal' type (b) 'dovetail' type.*

hanging of services. Small holes can be cut without difficulty but large openings will need subframing as for other flooring systems.

13.3 FLOOR BEAM SYSTEMS

Referring to Fig. 13.6, the most common floor systems are as follows:

(a) Composite beams – UBs UCs, plate girders (Fig. 13.6a).
(b) Composite beams – UBs, UCs, plate girders – with notches at ends or web openings (Figs 13.6b and c).
(c) Tapered beams (Fig. 13.6d).
(d) Trusses, composite or non-composite (Fig. 13.6e).
(e) Vierendeel and stub girder system (Fig. 13.6f).

Preferred dimensions for the spacing of columns are multiples of 1.2 and 1.5 m (4 ft and 5 ft) to suit economic modules for ceiling and floor tile layouts.

Practical minimum and maximum spans are 6 m (20 ft) and 18 m (60 ft). Although longer spans are possible, additional considerations arise, and these are outside the scope of this chapter.

Steel grades 43 (mild steel) and 50 (high yield steel) are most commonly used. Although grade 50 is slightly more expensive, the saving in weight which can be achieved usually makes it clearly more economic than grade 43. However, the elastic modulus is similar for all grades, so where deflection considerations are the principal design criterion, the higher grade material offers no advantage.

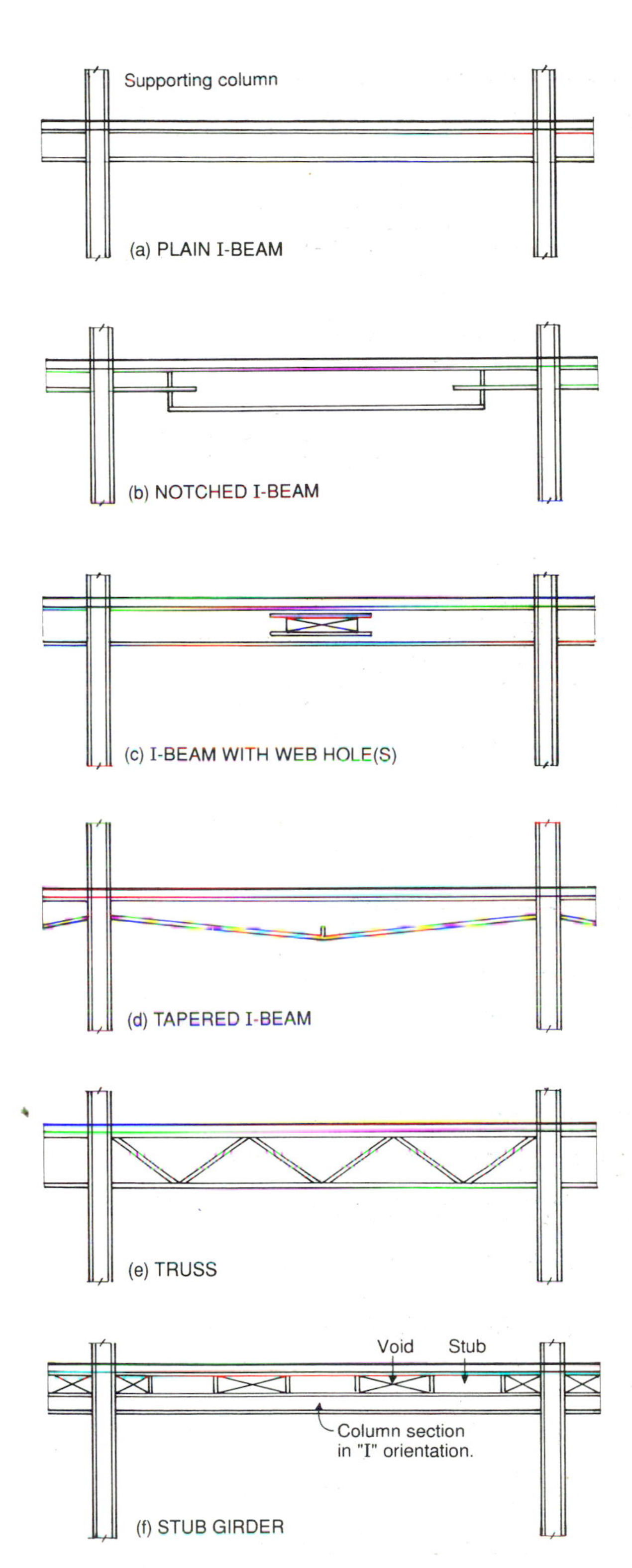

Fig. 13.6 *Basic floor beam systems. These may be at sufficiently close centres to avoid the need for secondary beams; alternatively they may be more widely spaced and support plain I-section secondary beams.*

13.4 PLANNING MODULES AND SERVICE GRIDS

The fundamental choice for any commercial building is between a 1.2 m (4 ft) and a 1.5 m (5 ft) grid. A 1.2 m (4 ft) grid is more convenient in the UK as there are more off-the-peg components available and it is consistent with the standard 600 × 600 mm (2 × 2 ft) raised floor tile and suspended ceiling systems.

The disadvantages include the mean space for corridors, the usual compromise being to provide 1.5 modules at 1.8 m (6 ft). There is the further disadvantage of close mullion spacings with higher cost for spandrel and window elements.

A 1.5 m (5 ft) grid is more usual in the USA and continental Europe, the larger scale dimension giving better proportioned offices and a visual improvement in terms of mullion spacing. In the UK higher costs are incurred, ceiling systems often require lots of cutting and floor tiles to suit these dimensions are also more expensive.

The choice is largely associated with the scale of the project. The larger contract can warrant specials in fitting out, whilst a smaller building (say under £4 million in the UK) needs to comply with standardized items on the 1.2 × 1.2 m (4 × 4 ft) module. A compromise solution might be to use a 1.2 m (4 ft) grid generally and provide a buffer zone at external walls to adjust to a wider scale of fenestration (Fig. 13.7). Zoning office areas into modular and non-modular plan patterns has considerable advantages, since the non-modular dimensions can absorb offsets with cores, service areas and window walls.

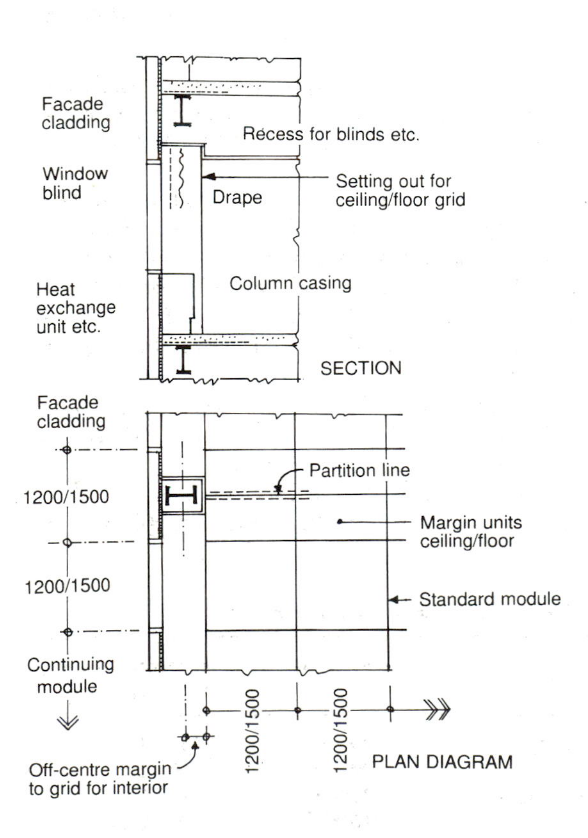

Fig. 13.7 *Compromise arrangement for grid at window zone.*

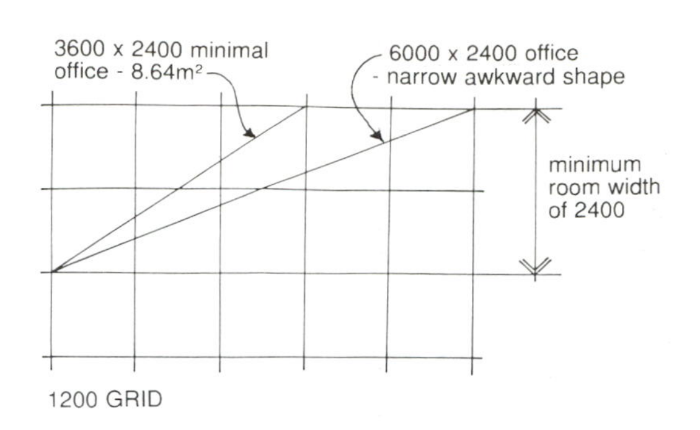

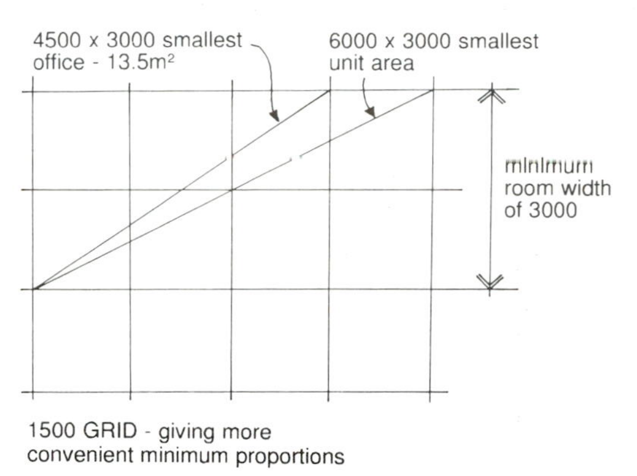

Fig. 13.8 *Comparison of office areas for two grids.*

The PSA Method of Building [1] refers to such a method: the grid should be separated by a 300 mm (1 ft) margin from external and spine walls (Fig. 13.7). The 300 mm (1 ft) banding could also be introduced as a tartan grid to form a column zone across the width of the block. Both the 1.2 and 1.5 m (4 and 5 ft) module can be divided into 300 mm (12 in) and 100 mm (4 in) increments to provide co-ordination for components, namely ceiling and floor tiles, mullion and partition.

Finally, a comparison between individual office sizes in the two grids reveals why the 1.5 m (5 ft) grid is so superior in terms of spatial planning of individual areas (Fig. 13.8).

Structural grids relate to the larger scale of column centres and should be multiples of the planning module. Both 7.2 m (24 ft) – 6 × 1.2 m (4 ft) and 7.5 m (25 ft) – 5 × 1.5 m (5 ft) are economic in terms of main beam and column sizing.

The geometry of services above and below the partition grid often means offsetting the service grid from the partition layout to enable access (Fig. 13.9).

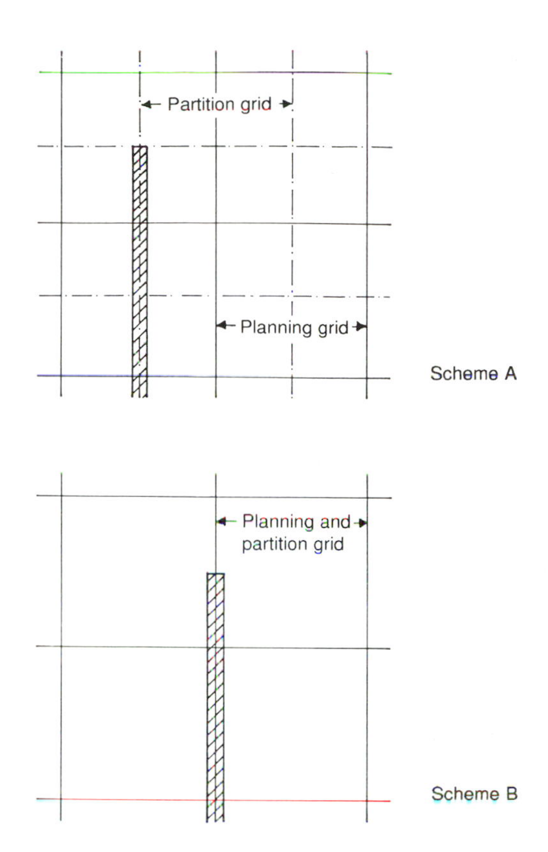

Fig. 13.9 *Relation between partitions and service grid.*

13.5 SECONDARY FLOOR SYSTEMS (FALSE OR RAISED FLOORS)

Secondary (modular access) flooring is raised above the structural slab and has been devised largely to meet the needs of the electronic office (Fig. 13.10). Access may be partial or total and the height can vary from 50 to 1000 mm (2 to 39 in). The support is based upon fully adjustable threaded steel pedestals, made specifically to meet various loading requirements such as office, computer, and heavy duty [1]. The floor void can accommodate electrical systems, telephone equipment and pipework, and may also act as a 'plenum' for the air conditioning system. Panels can be supplied incorporating grilles, air flow controls, electrical outlet boxes, telephone and computer points. Fire barriers must be installed at partition/passage lines to the requirements of the fire officer or for insurance purposes.

The first examples were constructed with timber battens and fireproof chipboard, and used only for the distribution of electrical wiring (Fig. 13.10a). Cheap installations are still of this form, the principal difficulty being the achievement of a level floor finish which will not flex excessively.

Floor trays are often metal framed with chipboard,

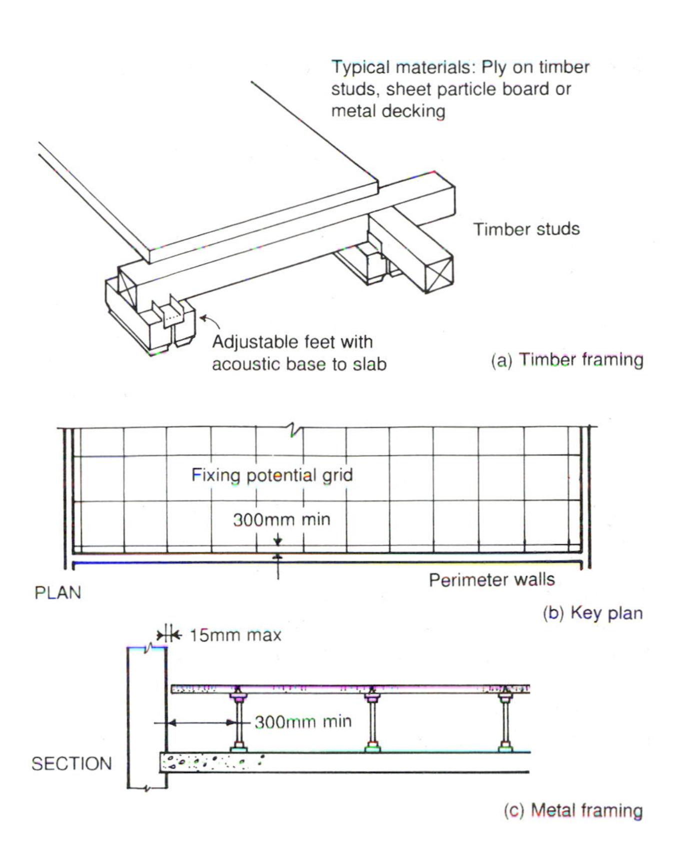

Fig. 13.10 *Typical standard secondary floor system. Close liaison will be required between the designers and the manufacturer to ensure that building services do not obstruct fixing points required for platform floor systems.*

composite board (for sound deadening) or plywood. The floor is typically finished with vinyl or carpet tiles. Standard pedestals are available in a range from 50 to 1000 mm (2 to 39 in) high (Fig. 13.11). Responsibility for erection, levelling and finishing rests with the manufacturer. The selection will be governed by partition and imposed loading, as shown in Table 13.2.

The floor slab must be finished to close tolerances since many pedestals are glued in place. Power floating the screed or slab is currently the favoured solution.

Raised floors are difficult to accommodate in refurbishment due to differences in floor level and to problems with

Table 13.2 Load classification for secondary floors

	Overall loads	*Concentrated point loads*
Heavy loading	12 kN/m^2 (240 lb/ft^2)	4.5 kN/25 mm^2 (1 kip/in^2)
Medium loading	8 kN/m^2 (160 lb/ft^2)	3.0 kN/25 mm^2 (0.7 kip/in^2)

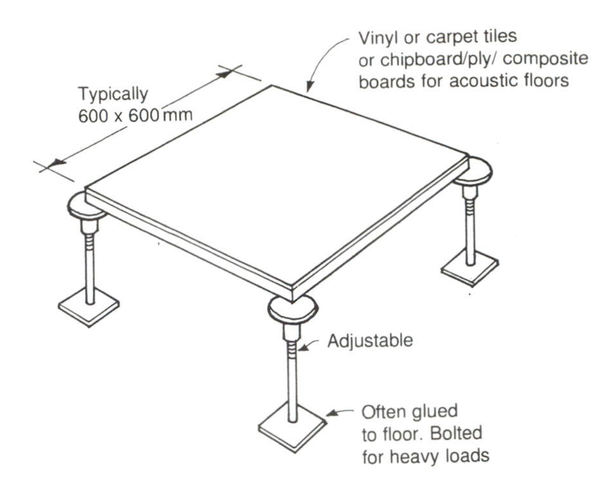

Fig. 13.11 *Metal pedestals and trays.*

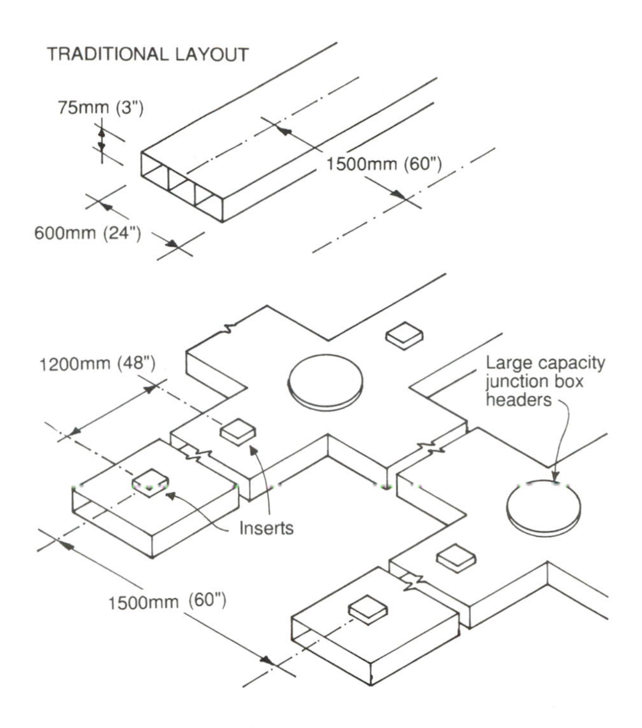

Fig. 13.12 *Floor duct systems.*

existing doors and sill levels. In addition, space-consuming ramps will be required at approaches to lift lobbies or stairs.

Design issues relating to raised floors in connection with fire and sound insulation are covered in sections 13.10 and 13.11 below. Electrical requirements relate to electrostatic properties, equipotential bonding and earthing, and installations should confirm to IEE wiring regulations and be tested at each particular site.

The floor system must not create dust or contaminants and this is particularly important where the void is used as a plenum for the air conditioning system. All materials must also be resistant to fungi, moulds and insects and resist infestation by vermin.

13.6 OTHER ACCESS SYSTEMS

In North America under-floor ducts are more popular than raised floor systems because of the possible savings in building height which may be as much as 600 mm (2 ft) per storey. This can make a substantial saving with a 90 storey block. Casting ducts within the screed or slab is also less expensive than for raised floors which may have a life cycle as short as five years. Because of their wide use in the USA there are many specialist companies experienced in connecting into duct systems to install equipment. In the UK no comparable service exists, and the work usually revolves around builders' work to make and change connections whilst the office struggles to continue business.

Duct systems in the UK are fabricated from aluminium or steel and run on a cellular basis (electrical, telephone and data) with or without service outlets (Fig. 13.13). Service outlets provide the user with convenient access – say at 1.2–1.5 m centres (4–5 ft) but make for problems with screeding. Leaving out the outlets means drilling through the screed each time a service connection is made.

Tolerances need to be considered between structure and metal duct systems, say 10 mm (3/8 in) to allow for bedding and fixing lugs.

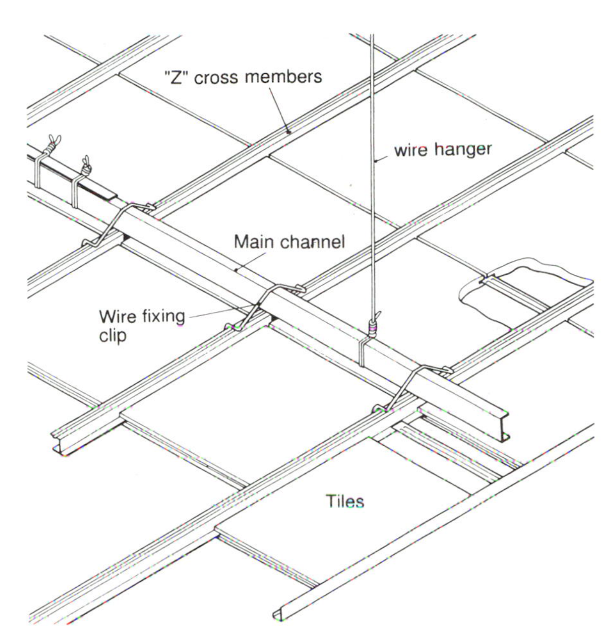

Frame and tile system using a concealed Z-section with mineral fibre tiles to create a relatively inaccessible ceiling.

Fig. 13.13 *Conventional frame and tile system (tile by the mile).*

13.7 SUSPENDED CEILINGS

Suspended ceilings provide an accessible zone for services. The reality is often a cosmetic exercise of 'tile by the mile' [2] which encloses largely inaccessible spaces and where ceiling modules bear little relation to partition runs or external walls. There are, however, several well integrated ceiling systems which provide good access for services with an orderly relationship to planning grids. The best designs contribute to good lighting, ventilation, acoustics and fire protection requirements.

Guidance on this considerable branch of sub-contracting is difficult to condense and the reader is advised in the UK to turn to organizations like the Suspended Ceiling Association [3] for detailed advice. It is, however, possible to categorize according to methods of construction and appearance (Figs 13.13 and 13.14) as Frame and Tile, Services integrated with Frame and Tile, Linear Strip and Open Louvre/Grid.

13.7.1 Typical standard ceiling

A 'typical' standard ceiling using steel components is of modular format with stove enamelled or embossed PVC finished steel tiles designed for clipping into a concealed

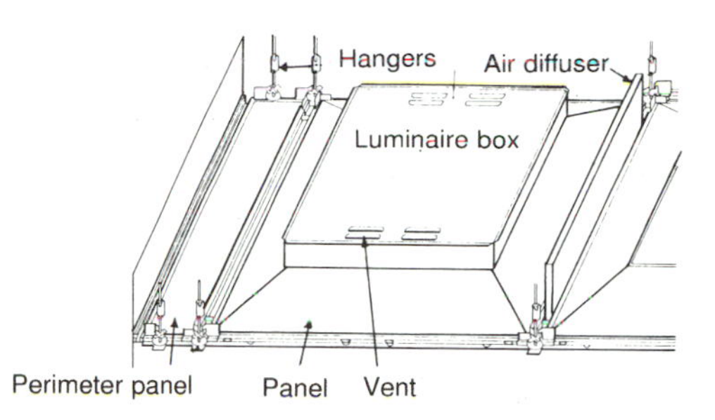

(a) Services integrated frame and tile sysyem, with coffered section and square fluorescent fittings. Air is supplied via the slotted exposed grid

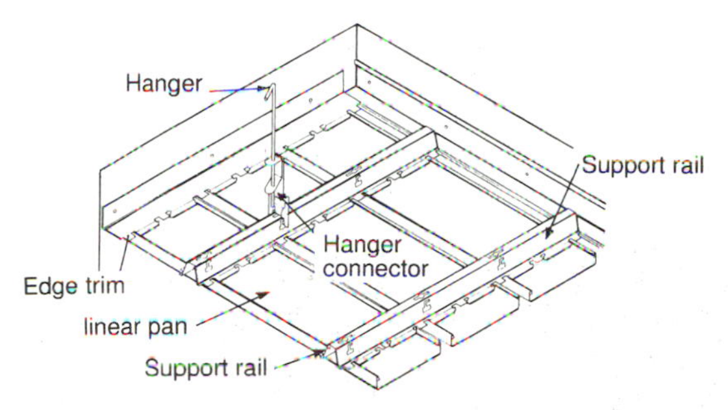

(b) Linear strip system with metal strips clipped to notched support rails.
Manufacturers use different methods of attachment

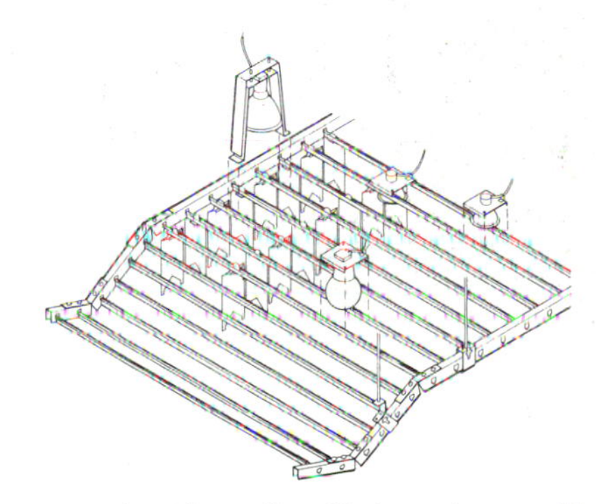

(c) An open Leaf-lite ceiling. Various shapes of leaves, of the same or different colours, can be clipped to the supporting rails

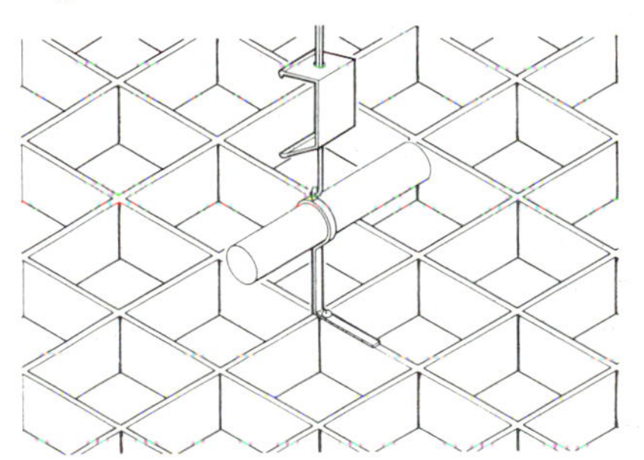

(d) An open grid ceiling system fixed to horizontal rods

Fig. 13.14 *Other categories of ceiling systems.*

grid. It will form butt jointed suspended, or directly fixed, ceilings (Fig. 13.13).

Dimensions: Tiles 300 mm (12 in) wide to 3000 mm (10 ft) in length, designed for clipping into a concealed grid at each end.

Profiles: These vary from channel forms, vee-shaped or open steel blade shaped grids.

Composition: 0.6/0.4 mm (24/16 thou) thick zinc coated mild steel, cold-rolled from stove enamelled paint finish metal strip.

Sizes: 85–300 mm (3½–12 in) on a 100 mm (4 in) module with lengths based on 300/600/900/1200/1500 (1/2/3/4/5 ft) or 150–3000 (6 in to 10 ft) maximum lengths.

Fire resistance: Steel tiles may be class 0 or class 1; the thermal resistance values vary with the choice of system.

Appearance: Generally based upon plain, perforated or embossed steel, with white semi-gloss the standard finish. Various colours are altered, over-spraying is often carried out with the final decoration. Dramatic effects are also possible with chromium plated finishes to give a mirror effect.

Accessibility: Ducts and pipes need brackets, insulation and space to allow labour to install them. The following gives approximate guidance on the space required in addition to the nominal size of a round pipe and an air duct:

40 mm (1⅝ in) thick insulation = 80 mm (3¼ in) diameter
30 mm (1¼ in) for fingers = 60 mm (2½ in)
Total addition = 140 mm (5¾ in)

Air ducts need 50 mm (2 in) thick insulation and flanges = 100 mm (4 in)
150 mm (6 in) top for installation = 150 mm (6 in)
Total addition = 250 mm (10 in)

13.7.2 Why a suspended ceiling?

Frank Lloyd Wright gave his view that 'Suspended Ceilings' were a death blow to modern architecture and many will question the cost or necessity for this additional layer of finish. There are possibly three situations where designers may dispense with suspended ceilings altogether and still provide full integration of services to the building. The first is where false floors are used extensively for services distribution, including air conditioning, and where direct lighting is used. It is usual to provide some form of acoustic treatment to the soffit of the slab and provide outlets for sprinkler heads.

Alternatively, suspended ceilings have been omitted in the so-called 'Hi-Tech' style of design, where the services are exposed on the soffit of the slab and expressed as sculptural forms (Terminal 4, Heathrow Airport).

Thirdly, some American buildings use double floors with the void accommodating the services. There is no suspended ceiling, the soffit of the slab becomes the ceiling finish. Service outlets are upward as in full false floor systems.

13.7.3 Relation of partitions to suspended ceilings

Partitioning is not a self-contained element in a building, because it is closely related both to suspended ceilings and raised floors with which it is integrated. There are two main approaches to the construction of partitions, those assembled on site and those that are factory assembled. The former include steel frame sheet panels which are delivered to site as elements and put together in situ. An outline of both systems is given in chapter 30.

Factory assembled systems include steel faced panel and storage wall types with some capability to take up tolerances with varying degrees of flexibility. Some manufacturers produce compatible systems for partitions and suspended ceilings as part of a factory assembled package (Figs 13.15 and 13.16).

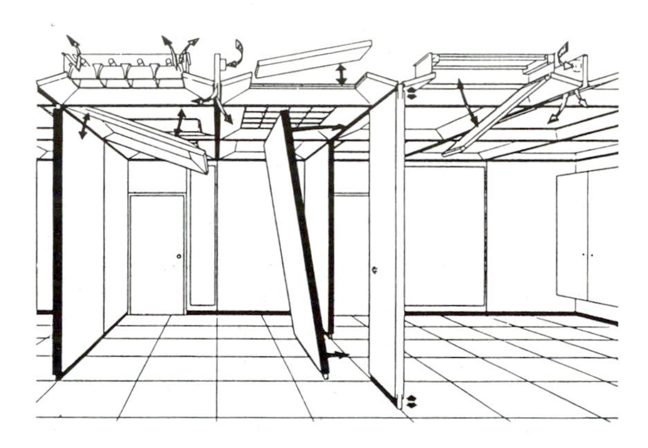

Fig. 13.15 *Typical modular approach for suspended ceiling, partition and raised floor.*

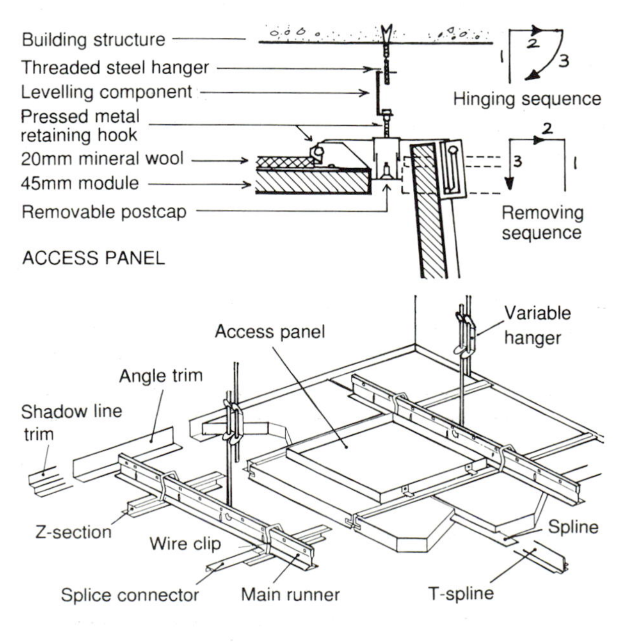

Fig. 13.16 *Access detailing to ceiling voids between partition zones.*

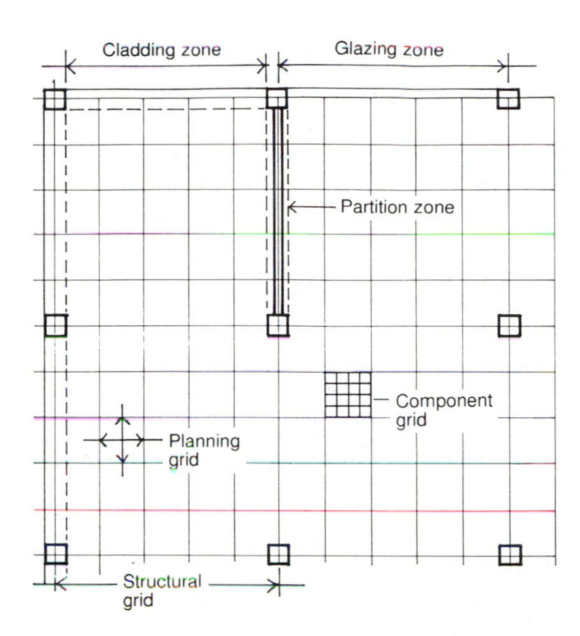

Fig. 13.17 *Planning (partition) and structural grids coincide.*

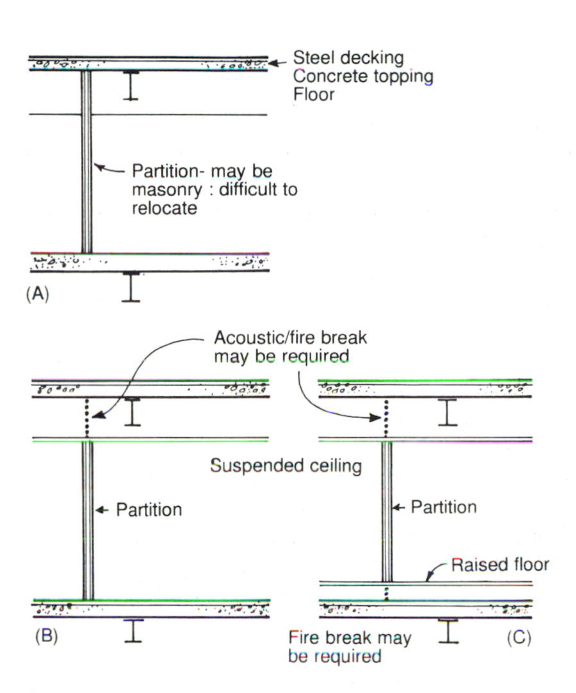

Fig. 13.18 *Partition layout offset from structural grid.*

It is often the case in practice that the floor and ceiling grids do not correspond with the main planning/structural grid (refer to Figs 13.7 and 13.9) to enable a continuous floor and/or ceiling panel system to be achieved. The ceiling/panel grid relates also to the window mullion system that may stop short of the main column zone. It will be seen that in scheme A in Fig. 13.9 one floor panel per bay is fixed by the partition location, whereas in scheme B both grids correspond. In the latter case two panels are fixed by the partition and the floor zone in that area is not available for service access. Refer also to Fig. 13.17 for partition zoning and grid lines.

There are three main constructional arrangements of partition (Fig. 13.18). In type A the partition is often built in masonry and is consequently difficult to relocate. Types B and C illustrate differing situations and relationships for industrialized partitioning with suspended ceilings and raised floors.

One might expect to find services dropping down inside the partition in 'B'. With 'C' there is the choice of either service route from the soffit or from the raised floor distribution system. Also in both 'B' and 'C' it is possible to fully integrate the ceiling with the partitioning system and include access to services, bay by bay as part of the ceiling design (Fig. 13.15).

13.8 SERVICES

The main services which need consideration are air distribution, air return, main cable distribution routes, and possibly sprinkler mains. Small cables, surface and foul water pipes (which normally run vertically) and hot water pipes are not usually troublesome, provided they do not run horizontally through beam flanges, or vertically through beams.

13.8.1 Horizontal services distribution and framing systems

The simplest and in many cases best way to accommodate services is to run them below the beams. This makes both initial fixing and subsequent alteration easy. It is also preferable for fast track jobs, where it may be impossible to co-ordinate a complex services layout with the structure at an early enough point in the programme to order the frame.

Ideally, the significant services will have a single main distribution direction, with secondary distribution at right

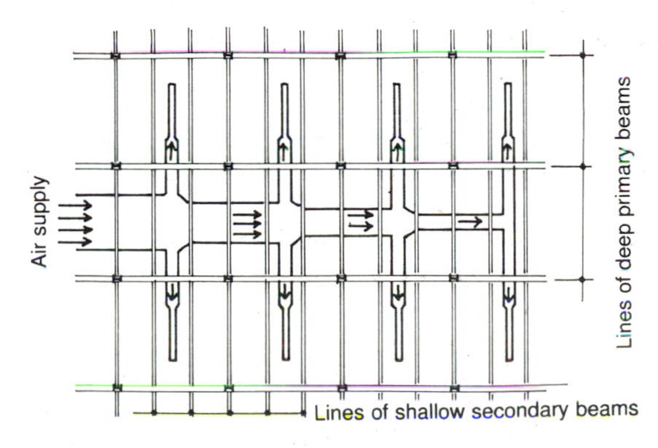

Fig. 13.19 *Floor plan showing relation of services to structural lines.*

Table 13.3 Beam sizes for the same loading and span using different design methods. Span = 7.5 m (24′ 7″), for office loading

	Secondary beams at 2500 crs	*Primary beams*
Composite UC		
gr50	203 × 203 UC 46	308 × 305 UC 97
gr43	210 × 205 UC 60	321 × 309 UC 137
gr50	260 × 260 UC 60	321 × 309 UC 137
Non-comp UC		
gr50	260 × 260 UC 89	321 × 309 UC 137
gr43	260 × 260 UC 89	340 × 314 UC 198
Composite UB		
gr50	349 × 126 UB 33	454 × 190 UB 67
gr43	353 × 126 UB 39	528 × 209 UB 82
Non-comp UB		
gr50	397 × 142 UB 39	528 × 209 UB 82
gr43	450 × 152 UB 52	537 × 210 UB 101

angles to it (Fig. 13.19). The structural arrangement can then follow this pattern, with the main (and deeper) beams running parallel with the main services, and the secondary (and shallower) beams running parallel with the secondary services distribution.

Beam depth is governed ultimately by span. It is possible to fabricate practically any shape of steel beam desired. The lack of beam stiffness will limit the use of very shallow long span beams unless additional plating or sections are added. Such procedures are not economic but can be countenanced at cross-over points for services. Refer to Table 13.3 for comparative designs and depths of members for the same span and loading.

Services can alternatively pass through holes in the webs of beams, or under a reduced depth at the end of a beam (Fig. 13.20). For small spans this may not be possible, because the beam will be too shallow for the size of service. If the air duct is 200 mm (8 in) deep, and perhaps 500 mm (20 in) long the beam must be roughly 600 mm (24 in) deep to have enough material above and beneath the hole for local bending (Fig. 13.21). Such a duct will not easily pass through a truss, unless the truss is quite deep. A stub girder may be a good solution. The duct could be replaced by a number of smaller circular ducts, e.g. 4 no. 350 mm (14 in) diameter, and these would more easily penetrate a truss. Un-ducted return air travels at slower velocities than ducted supply air, and often requires large voids to travel through: the air will normally have to pass beneath a beam, unless tapered beams, trusses or stub girders are used (Fig. 13.6d to f)

In a well ordered world, holes and hole cutting will be part of the initial design studies before steelwork is ordered. In reality, alterations will occur at the fabrication stage or on site. The following advice is offered concerning late changes of mind.

(a) Holes can be cut fairly easily in the fabrication shop.

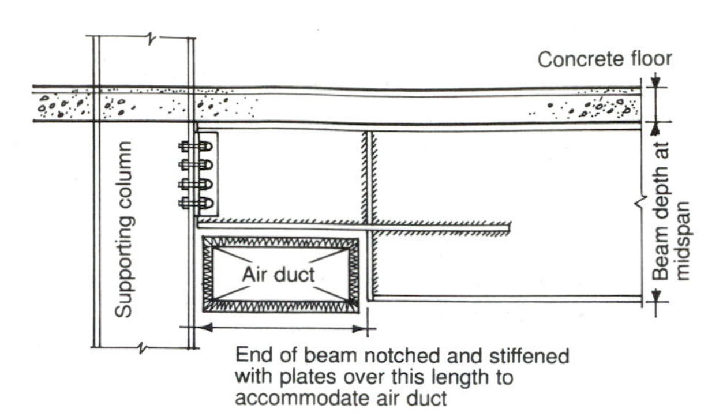

Fig. 13.20 *Beam notched at ends to accommodate services.*

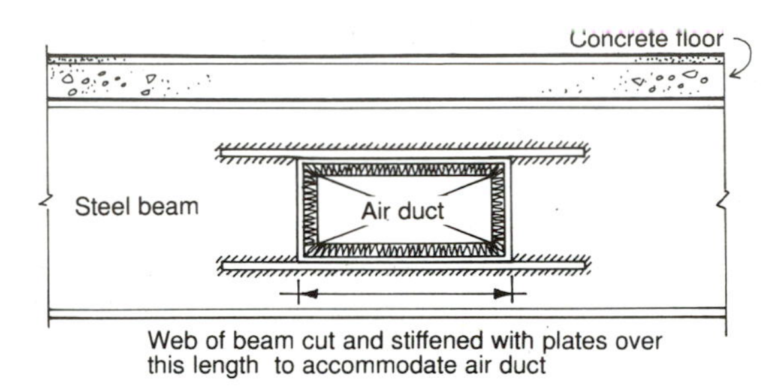

Fig. 13.21 *Hole for services in beam web towards mid-span.*

Within limits, stiffening plates can be added to replace the strength lost by hole cutting.

(b) Cutting of significant holes on site should be avoided due to the cost and disturbance caused.

(c) The best position for a hole depends upon how the beam has been designed. Non-composite beams can accept holes in their webs fairly easily if the hole is at mid-span. Near the support, where the shear is high the same size hole may require an unreasonable amount of stiffening.

(d) Composite beams use the web at mid-span in tension, so that the best places for holes are around quarter span. Using holes in composite beams is inherently more difficult than for non-composite beams, because the beam is physically smaller.

(e) Cutting a hole in a composite beam after casting the concrete is doubly difficult, due to the degree of shear connection between beam and slab that has to be increased locally at hole positions.

13.9 VERTICAL SERVICE DISTRIBUTION

The hierarchies of spaces for service distribution can be developed using the shape of a tree as a simile [4].

Services nearly always originate at a point and radiate out from there to serve the building. The routes which take the services to where they are needed require space which increases as the building gets large: ducts for air conditioning plants are often of a scale comparable with rooms. This leads naturally to a form for the services network in a building which can be thought of as a tree. There is a central trunk which disperses as large branches and finally small twigs reach out to the whole space. On the other hand, the size of floor structure can be constant throughout the building, if the column spacing does not vary. The size of columns and bracing members increases nearer to the ground, however. These two forms, services and structure have to accommodate one another.

The key problem is that the services distribution system changes in scale as it permeates the building. Large spaces are needed (usually vertically) which break down to small spaces (often horizontal). Structures do not usually change scale in this way. A successful approach is to accommodate services in a building by considering the problem at various levels in a hierarchical way.

Holes can be formed in floor systems (Fig. 13.22) by framing around the opening. Common locations are adjacent to vertical shafts such as lift wells and stairs, but locations will also be spread around the floor plans to ease horizontal distribution.

Upstand beams are sometimes used where ducts turn into a ceiling void due to radius and sizing requirements where a duct or cable runs from horizontal to vertical. With the usual column spacing, the upstand beams can be accommodated within a raised floor where such a feature exists, but if this is not possible, columns can be placed around the riser duct (Fig. 13.23). Riser ducts are often useful to the structural engineer as locations for vertical frame bracing. The risers are usually evenly spaced out and this is advantageous for bracing design. It is normal for the braced framing to be so positioned that it does not obstruct turning services at riser to ceiling or floor space connections (Fig. 13.24).

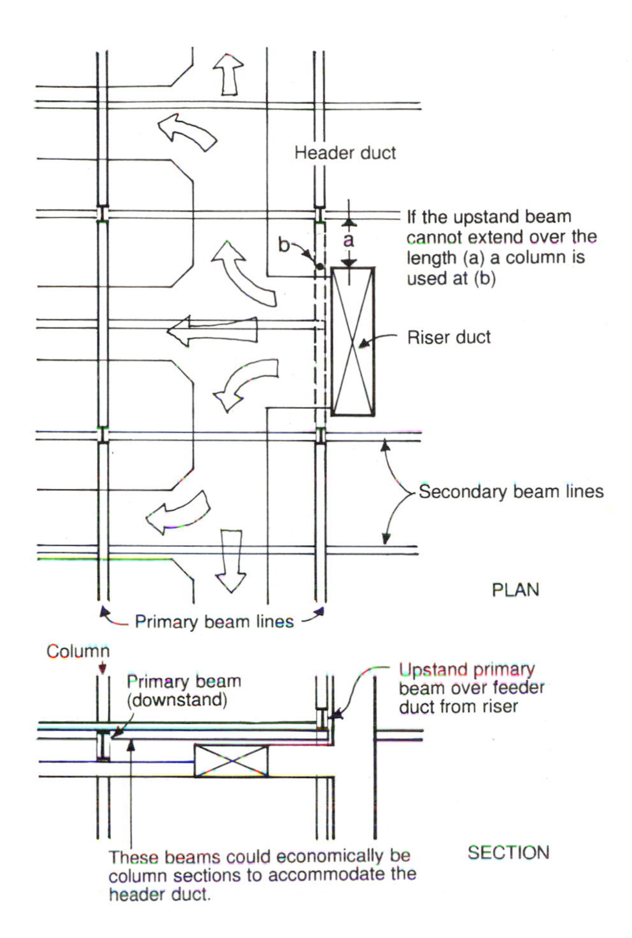

Fig. 13.23 *Upstand beams and periphery column framing for risers.*

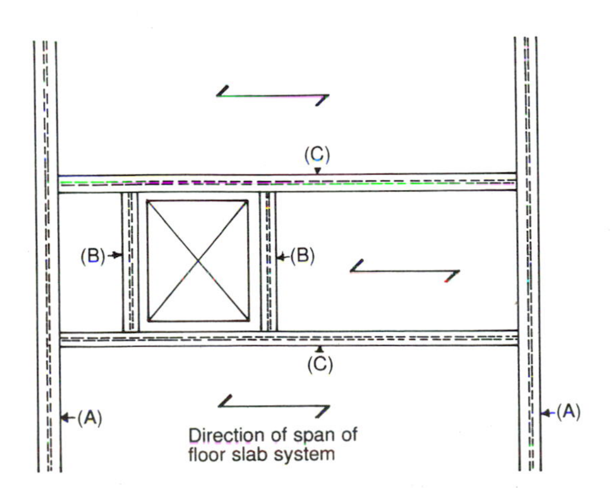

Fig. 13.22 *Trimming holes in floors for services. A = Main supporting steel beams. B = Trimming steel to support cut end of one-way floor system. C = Beams to carry loads back to main supporting beams.*

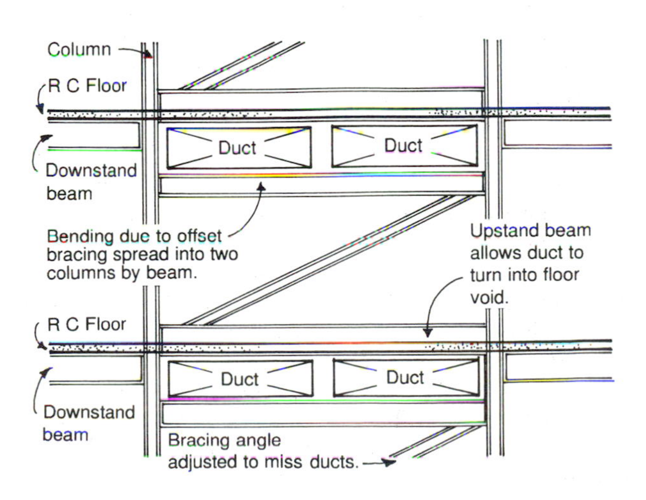

Fig. 13.24 *Elevation on braced frame, using riser duct location.*

13.10 FIREPROOFING

Compartment zones

The standard of fireproofing at floor-to-floor compartment zones depends upon the size of the building and the interpretation put upon the National Building Regulations by Fire Officers, as well as specific requirements of fire insurance advisers. Figure 13.25 illustrates varying details that will provide 1½, 2, 2½ and 3 h fire resistance using steel framing and various decking systems for suspended ceilings and raised floors. The compartment zones for office or working areas need to extend into voids such as ceiling and raised floors. The customary provision is a 'curtain' of fire resisting quilt, wired in place to ensure full performance under fire.

Vertical shafts

Vertical shafts for services constitute an equal hazard to uncontained horizontal voids. Duct enclosures will need to be fire-resisting, with fire dampers floor to floor in vertical air ducts and effective 'pugging' at the interface with structural floors (Fig. 13.25).

Ceiling areas

Exposed decking to the ceiling void can be upgraded by over-spraying and likewise suspended ceilings improved with overlay of mineral fibre quilt.

Raised access floors

The following design guidance is offered concerning fireproofing to raised access floors.

(a) The system is to meet the fire requirements of BS 5588: Part 3: British Code of Practice for Office Buildings [5]. When installed for housing electronic data processing equipment, it shall also comply with BS 6266: 1982: section 4.4 Fire protection for electronic processing systems [6].
(b) Spread of flame: within the cavity system a surface classification of 'class 1' (BS 476: Part 7) is to be achieved and an Index of Performance in accordance with BS 476 Part 6 [7].
(c) Panel cladding: panels constructed of combustible materials must be clad on the underside with non-combustible material with a defined melting point of 600°C (1100°F).

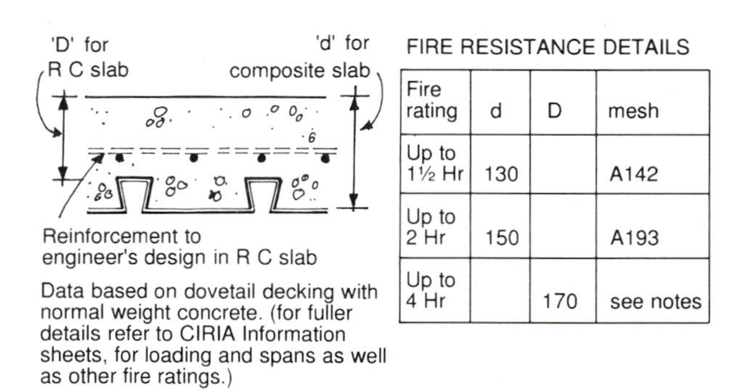

Fire rating	d	D	mesh
Up to 1½ Hr	130		A142
Up to 2 Hr	150		A193
Up to 4 Hr		170	see notes

(a)

(b)

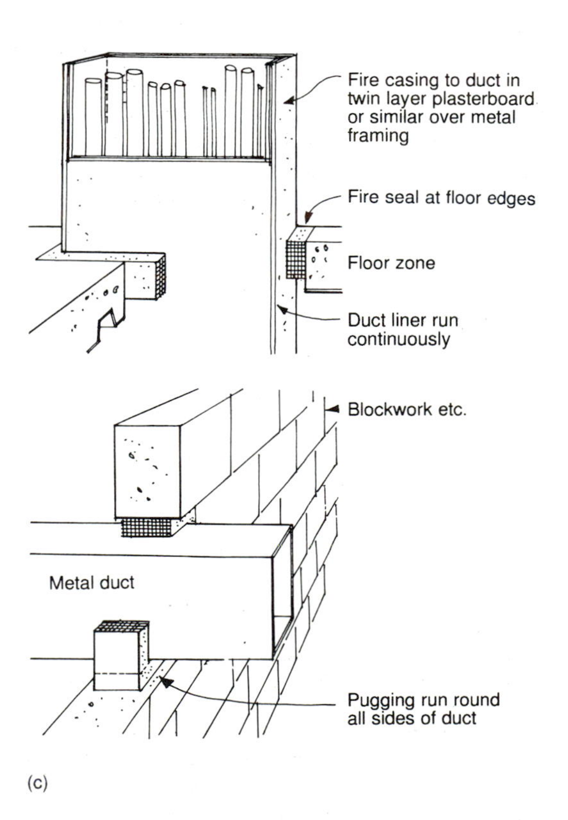

(c)

Fig. 13.25 *(a) Floor zone and fire resistance (1½, 2, 2½, and 3 h standard). (b) Fire curtains in ceiling and floor voids. (c) Fire casings to ducts and pugging.*

(d) Structural integrity: there are requirements for pedestals, stringers and other supports regarding non-combustability.
(e) Cavity barriers: these should be purpose made and their design and performance satisfy Fire Officer and Local Authority requirements. (Check how the design affects the layout and flexibility of services within the void.)
(f) Perimeter and bridging structure details. Check that the floor system, around columns and any bridging structures, including cut-out panels and perimeter supports, complies with relevant fire and safety requirements. The relationship with fire resistant partitions should be considered at this stage.

13.11 TRANSMISSION OF SOUND THROUGH RAISED FLOORS

It is useful to check whether any specific sound reductions will be required. Manufacturers should be requested to provide reports from a recognized sound laboratory giving an indication of the transmission of airborne sound. Sound insulation performance measurements are described in BS 5821:1984 [8] and the method of measurement prescribed in BS 2750:1980 [9]. Three categories may be considered; sound absorption (define absorption coefficients), impact sound insulation and airborne sound insulation, both recommended to be measured in dB between 125 and 2000 Hz. Cavity barriers are provided to improve sound insulation or isolation of floor to reduce impact noise.

There are two useful references, firstly *Platform Floors* by PSA Specialist Services, MOB PF2 PS (January 1990) [10]. Secondly there is the advisory service offered by the Building Performance Unit, School of Built Environment, Liverpool Polytechnic.

REFERENCES AND TECHNICAL NOTES

1. Property Services Agency (PSA) Method of Building Publications Useful titles:
   MOB 01: 707 (March 1982)
   Technical Guidance Platform Floors.
   MOB 09: 201 (December 1978)
   Technical Guidance Suspended Ceilings.
   MOB 08: 135 (February 1989)
   Partition with Integral Doorsets.
   Also updates which relate to specific product data, Robertson's Floors etc.
2. 'Tile by the Mile' a 'trade term' used to describe the standard suspended ceiling. Refer however to the beguiling illustrations prepared by Jacoby for Armstrong Tile Co. in the 1950s and 60s.
3. Refer to Suspended Ceiling Association, 29 High Street, Hemel Hempstead, UK (phone 0442–40313) – the most useful guides are 'good practice' booklets that help with detailing and specification work for all ceiling patterns. Advice is also available in current PSA manuals for ceiling construction.
4. Refer to writings by Max Fordham in the *Architecture Today*, May 1990.
5. BS 5588: 1983: Part 3 Code of Practice for Office Buildings (published in 8 parts). Fire precautions in the design, use and construction of buildings.
6. BS 6266: 1982 Section 4.4 Fire protection for electronic processing systems.
7. BS 476: Parts 6 and 7: Fire Tests on Building Materials and Structures.
8. BS 5821 Method of raising the sound insulation in building elements Part 1: 1984 Method for rating the airborne sound insulation in buildings and interior building elements. Part 2: 1984 Impact.
9. BS 2750:1980 Measurement of sound insulation in buildings and of building elements.
   Part 1 Recommendations for laboratories.
   Part 3 Laboratory measurement of airborne sound insulation of building elements.
   Part 4 Field measurement of airborne sound insulation between rooms.
   Part 6 Laboratory measurement of impact of sound insultation of floors.
   Part 7 Field measurement of impact of sound insulation of floors.
10. Property Services Agency (PSA) Method of Building Publications. *Platform Floors* MOB PF2 PS (January 1990).

Model of Whitefriars, Fleet Street, London, UK, constructed 1988–89, view from North-East (architect and engineer: YRM International).

14

Multi-storey frames

Bjorn Watson

14.1 INTRODUCTION

In this chapter the principles set out in chapters 11 and 12 are developed with reference to structural systems for multi-storey building frames. The structure is the key to the design of modern multi-storey buildings and the factors affecting the choice of the floor framing system with respect to gravity loads are outlined. Structural systems to resist wind and other lateral loads are introduced. These are developed more fully in chapter 15 which deals with high-rise buildings in which the lateral bracing system becomes a more critical element as the building height increases. The need for any framing system to be sufficiently robust to cope with accidental and unexpected loadings is dealt with, and practical advice on the choice of floor systems and vertical bracing systems is included.

Modern, steel framed buildings are designed on the principle of the structure as an independent loadbearing frame carrying both vertical and lateral loads down to the building foundations. This form of construction makes possible the creation of large column-free internal spaces which can be divided by interchangeable partitions and, by eliminating the external wall as a loadbearing element, allows the development of large window areas, curtain walling and cladding systems.

The term 'multi-storey building' encompasses a wide range of building forms made possible by the versatility and adaptability of structural steel. This chapter, however, concentrates on structural systems relating to modern commercial office developments which form the main-stream of this type of construction. In recent years, largely as a result of overcoming difficulties with fire protection and developing fast and efficient methods of construction, the development of steel framed buildings with composite metal deck floors has transformed the construction of office buildings in the UK. During this time, with the growth of increasingly sophisticated requirements for building services, the very efficiency of the design has led to the steady decline of the cost of the structure as a proportion of the overall cost of the building, yet the choice of the structural system remains the key factor in the design of a coherent and successful building.

14.2 FACTORS AFFECTING CHOICE OF STRUCTURAL SYSTEM

The basic elements of a multi-storey structure are floor slabs, beams, columns and bracing. The choice of a structural system is governed by what may be called the three Rs of building design: Rigidity, Robustness and Rapidity. The designer must first ensure that the structure is rigid enough to sustain the applied loads. The system chosen on this basis must be sufficiently robust to prevent the progressive collapse of the building (or a significant part of it) under accidental loading. Lastly, the structural system must facilitate the fast and economical construction of the project.

The design of steel framed buildings encompasses not only the structure, but also the building envelope, services and finishes. All these elements must be co-ordinated by a firm dimensional discipline which recognizes the modular nature of the predetermined grid layout. The current range of British Steel Universal profiles provides a wide choice of structural sections. Nominal sizes of beams and columns can be maintained constant for varying degrees of load by using different weights within the same serial size. This facilitates connection details, although the external cross-sectional dimensions vary according to the weight of particular section used.

14.2.1 Column layout

Structural steel floor systems consist of prefabricated standard components, and columns should ideally be laid out on a repetitive grid which establishes a standard structural bay (Fig. 14.1). Maximum repetition of the floor components reduces fabrication costs and erection time.

The function of the building will frequently determine the column layout. For example, financial dealing floors require clear, open spaces located on the lower floors, which would dictate a different structural solution to the rest of the building. Large, column-free areas at ground floor level may necessitate the use of a transfer structure at first floor to carry the upper floors on an economical column grid (Fig. 14.2). Such structural arrangements are considered in greater detail in chapter 17.

Planning requirements concerning 'rights of light' may dictate that upper floors are set back from the perimeter, resulting in stepped construction of the upper levels. This

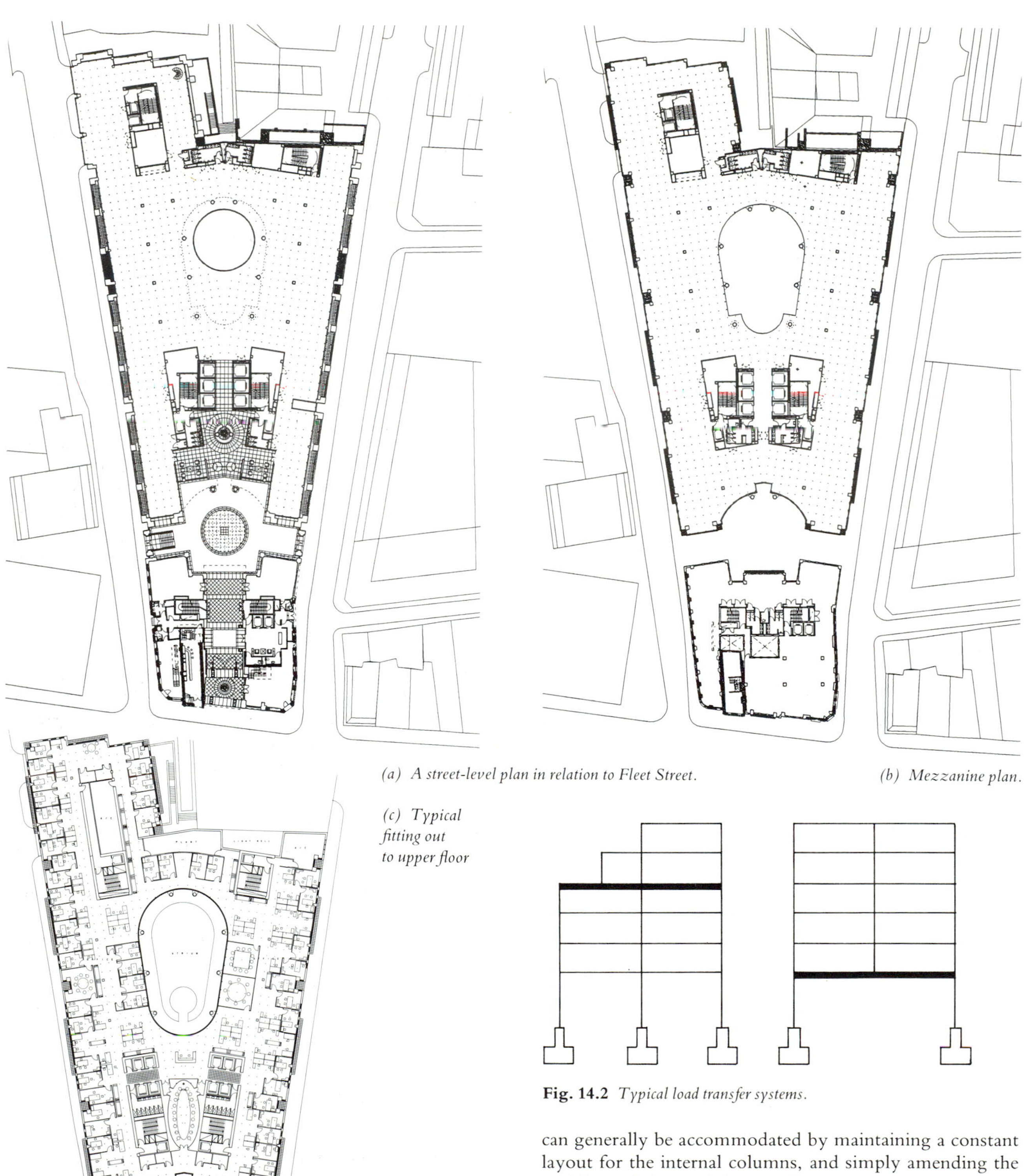

(a) A street-level plan in relation to Fleet Street.

(b) Mezzanine plan.

(c) Typical fitting out to upper floor

Fig. 14.2 *Typical load transfer systems.*

Fig. 14.1 *Typical layouts at ground and upper floors to multi-storey offices, Whitefriars, Fleet Street, London (architect and engineer: YRM International).*

can generally be accommodated by maintaining a constant layout for the internal columns, and simply amending the position of the periphery columns as necessary at the affected floor levels.

City centre development is seldom without restrictions of shape or site line. Splayed or curved plan forms or set back profiles are required to fit building lines or lighting angles. A classic example is the original BBC building in Portland Place, London, UK (1928–32, architect Val Myers). This encompasses a part oval site with severe light angle problems on the eastern facade. Another case was Norman Foster's proposal for the new BBC headquarters at the Langham Hotel site on the opposite side of the same street. Steelwork can be readily adapted for such non-rectangular plan layouts, taking advantage of the greater precision associated with steel fabrication compared with in situ concrete or masonry. Although it is more difficult to achieve a regular, repetitive grid in such cases, it often possible to confine irregularities to particular areas, for instance around the building perimeter.

14.2.2 Foundations

In inner city and difficult sites, the time and cost of constructing the foundations has a major effect on the viability of a project. The dead weight of a steel framed building can be between 60% and 75% of that for a comparable reinforced concrete building, depending on the floor construction, with a proportionate effect on the foundations. Further reductions in foundations and supporting structure can be achieved by using light construction such as composite metal deck floors and lightweight concrete.

Difficult ground conditions may dictate the column grid. Long spans may be required to bridge obstructions in the ground, and in exceptional circumstances transfer structures are used (chapter 17). Generally, widely spaced columns reduce the number of foundations and increase simplicity of construction in the ground (Fig. 14.3).

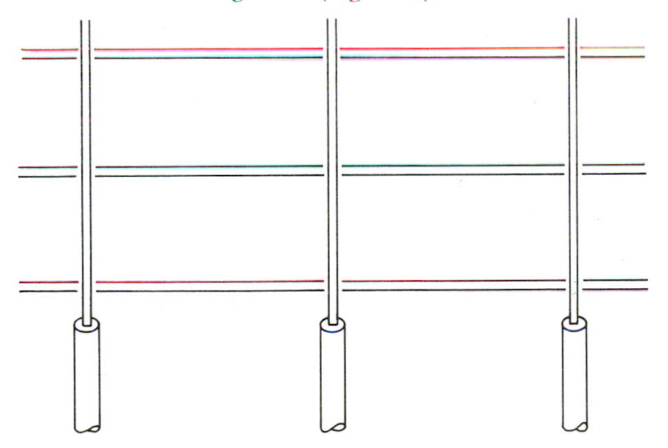

Fig. 14.3 *Widely spaced columns on large diameter bored piles.*

14.2.3 Integration of building services

The overall depth of the floor construction will depend on the type and distribution of the building services in the ceiling void. The integration of the services with the structure is an important factor in the choice of an economic structural floor system. The designer may choose to separate the structural and services zones, or accommodate the services by integrating them with the structure, allowing for the structural system to occupy the full depth of the floor construction.

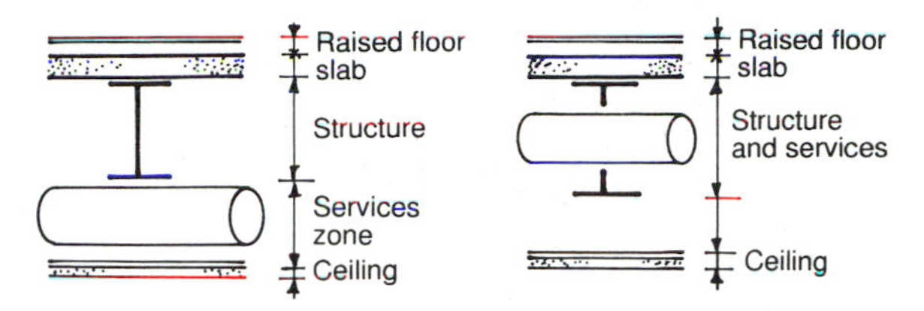

Fig. 14.4 *Building services and floor structure.*

Separation of zones usually confines the ducts, pipes and cables to a horizontal plane below the structure, resulting either in a relatively deep overall floor construction, or close column spacings. Integration of services with structure requires either deep, perforated structural components, or vertical zoning of the services and structure (Fig. 14.4). The size and frequency of holes for services will greatly influence the cost of structural floor systems and a highly disciplined approach to design will not only facilitate the construction, but shorten the contract programme and reduce costs.

14.2.4 External wall construction

The external skin of a multi-storey building is supported off the structural frame. In most high quality commercial buildings, the cost of external cladding systems greatly exceeds the cost of the structure. This influences the design and construction of the structural system in the following ways.

(a) The perimeter structure must provide a satisfactory platform to support the cladding system and be sufficiently rigid to limit deflections of the external wall.
(b) Reducing the floor zone may be more cost-effective than an overall increase in the area of cladding.
(c) Fixings to the structure should facilitate rapid erection of cladding panels.
(d) Reducing the weight of cladding at the expense of cladding costs will not necessarily lead to a lower overall construction cost.

14.3 STRUCTURAL PRINCIPLES

14.3.1 Floor loadings

The floor loadings to be supported by the structure have two components:

(a) The permanent or dead loading comprising the self-weight of the flooring and the supporting structure together with the weight of finishes, raised flooring, ceiling, air conditioning ducts and equipment.

(b) The superimposed loading which is the load that the floor is likely to sustain during its life and will depend on the use. Superimposed floor loading for various types of building is governed by BS 6399 [1], but the standard loading for office buildings required by developers and funding agencies is usually 4 kN/m^2 (80 lb/ft^2) where movable partitioning is used.

For normal office loadings, dead and superimposed loadings are roughly equal in proportion but higher superimposed load allowances will be necessary in areas of plant or to accommodate special requirements such as storage or heavy equipment. The optimum structural solution is to locate any heavier loadings close to columns or in areas where the floor spans are short.

14.3.2 Floor structures

The criterion for the choice of an economic structural system will not necessarily be to use the minimum weight of structural steel. Material costs represent only 30–40% of the total cost of structural steelwork. The remaining 60–70% is accounted for in the design, detailing, fabrication, erection and finishes for fire and corrosion protection. Hence a choice which needs a larger steel section to avoid, say, plate stiffeners around holes, or allows greater standardization, will reduce fabrication costs and may result in the most economic overall system.

The criteria determining the choice of a member size in a floor system vary with the span (Fig. 14.5). The absolute minimum size is limited by practical considerations such as fitting practical connections. As the span increases, the size will be determined by the bending strength of the member and, for longer spans, by the rigidity necessary to prevent

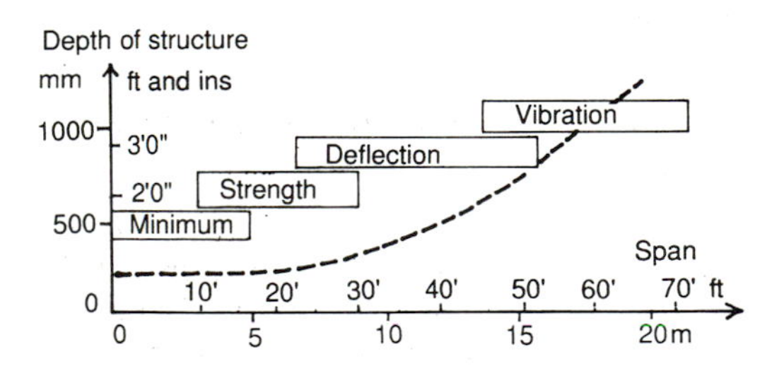

Fig. 14.5 *Structural criteria governing choice of floor beam.*

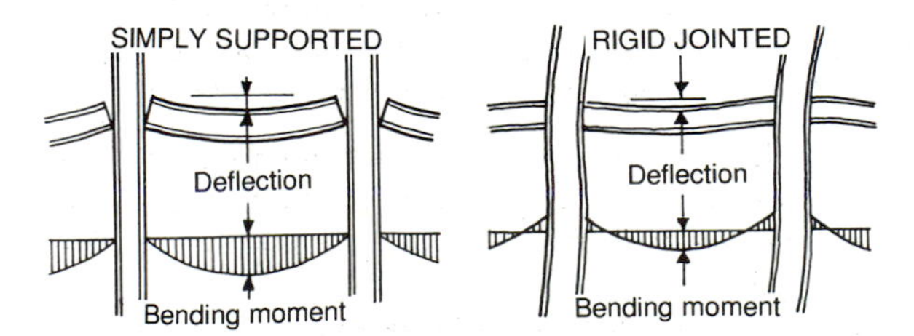

Fig. 14.6 *Floor framing.*

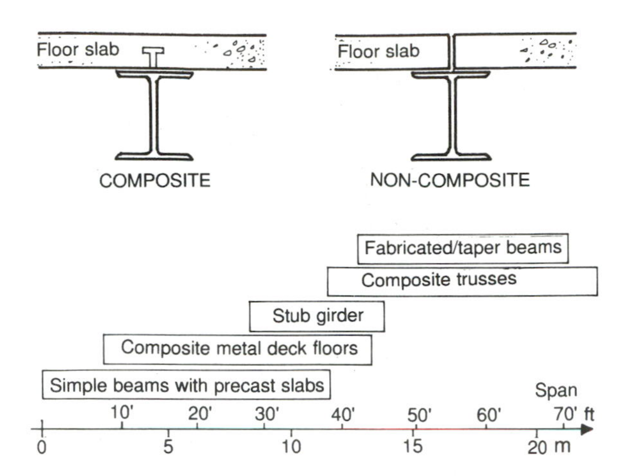

Fig. 14.7 *Composite and non-composite floor beam systems.*

excessive deflection under superimposed load or excessive sensitivity to induced vibrations.

For most multi-storey buildings, functional requirements will determine the column grid which will dictate spans where the limiting criteria will be rigidity rather than strength. Floor framing systems may be either simply supported or rigid at the supports (Fig. 14.6). Continuous construction is more efficient structurally, giving shallower floors, but requires heavier columns, increased complexity at junctions and connections with higher fabrication costs.

Floors may either act compositely with the supporting beam, or independently of it (Fig. 14.7). Composite action enables the floor slab to work with the beam, enhancing its strength and reducing deflection. Because composite action works by allowing the slab to act as the compression flange of the combined steel and concrete system, the advantage is greatest when the beam is sagging.

In practice, floors will be designed to limit sagging deflection under the superimposed loadings. The British Standard BS 5950 [2] governing the design of structural steelwork sets a limit on such deflections of span/200 generally and span/360 where there are brittle finishes. For very long spans, this limit is likely to be inadequate; for example, the sag allowed by the code on a 15 m (50 ft) span girder would be 42 mm (1⅝ in) and the designer may consider setting more stringent limits. Edge beams supporting cladding will be subject to more severe restrictions on deflection – say 10–15 mm (⅜–⅝ in). Deflections may be noticeable in the ceiling layout, and should be taken into account when determining the available cumulative effect of deflections in the individual members of a floor system, although the actual maximum displacement is in practice almost always less than those predicted by theoretical analysis. In some instances, vibrations of floor components may cause discomfort or affect sensitive equipment, and the designer should check the fundamental frequency of the

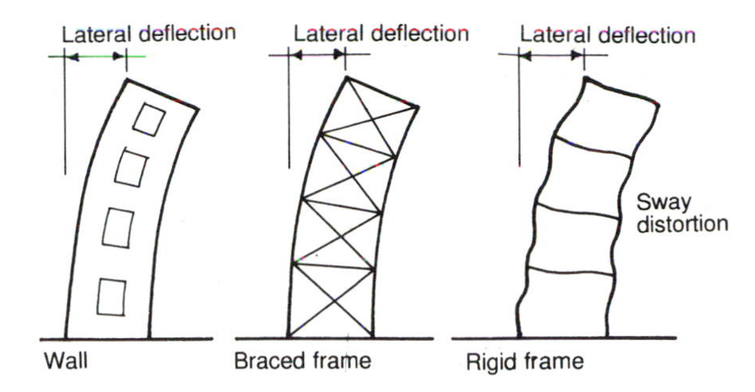

Fig. 14.8 *Lateral load bearing systems.*

floor system. The threshold of perceptible vibrations in buildings is difficult to define and present limits are rather arbitrary. There is some evidence that modern lightweight floors can be sensitive to dynamic loads which may have an effect on delicate equipment, but generally this is only a problem for very long spans or light floors.

14.3.3 Lateral rigidity

Steel buildings have to be rigid enough in the horizontal direction to resist wind and other lateral loads. In tall buildings, the means of providing sufficient lateral rigidity forms the dominant design consideration, and developments in this field have led to the construction of taller and taller buildings such as the John Hancock Building or the Sears Tower in Chicago (referred to in chapter 15).

Most multi-storey buildings are designed on the basis that wind forces acting on the external cladding are transmitted to the floors which form horizontal diaphragms, transferring the lateral load to rigid elements and then to the ground. These rigid elements are usually either lattice or rigid jointed frames, or reinforced concrete shear walls (Fig. 14.8).

Shear walls resist wind forces in bending by cantilever action and where they already exist, for instance to provide a fire protected service core, are an efficient method of carrying lateral loads. Lattice frames act as vertical steel trusses. Rigid jointed frames are less effective in providing lateral rigidity because of shear distortion in the vertical members. The British Standard BS 5950 sets a limit on lateral deflection of columns as height/300 but height/600 is a more reasonable figure for buildings where the external envelope consists of sensitive or brittle materials such as stone facings.

14.4 ROBUSTNESS

A series of incidents in the 1960s, culminating in the partial collapse of a system-built tower at Ronan Point, Hackney, London [3] in 1968, led to a fundamental reappraisal of the approach to structural stability in buildings. Traditional loadbearing masonry buildings have many in-built elements providing inherent stability which are lacking in modern steel framed buildings. Modern structures, refined to the degree where they can resist the horizontal and vertical design loadings with the required factor of safety, lack the ability to cope with the unexpected.

It is this concern with the safety of the occupants, and the need to limit the extent of any damage in the event of catastrophic or accidental loadings, that has led to the concept of robustness in building design. The Code of Practice in the UK, requires that any element in the structure that supports a major part of the building must either be designed for blast loading, or be capable of being supported by an alternative load path. In addition, there is a requirement for suitable ties to be incorporated in the horizontal direction in the floors and in the vertical direction through the columns. The designer should be aware of the consequences of the sudden removal of key elements of the structure and ensure that such an event does not lead to the progressive collapse of the building or a substantial part of it.

14.5 COMMON FLOOR SYSTEMS

The selection of a structural system for floor slab and beams, and provision for accommodating services is an important design consideration. In particular, overall depth of the floor zone can be a critical factor, with increased depths resulting in taller buildings, with consequently higher cladding costs, and possibly reductions in the number of storeys which can be provided. It is therefore worth exploring different arrangements of primary and secondary beams and floor slabs, in terms of both the depth of the floor zone and the weight of steelwork used.

14.5.1 Simple Universal Beams with composite metal deck slabs (Fig. 14.9)

The recent growth in the use of structural steelwork for multi-storey buildings has been largely the result of developments in the design and construction of structural floors consisting of simply supported Universal Beams acting compositely with a thin concrete slab supported on metal decking. In this system, the metal decking spans between secondary steel beams usually spaced at between 2.5 and 3 m (8 and 10 ft) centres. This is discussed more fully in chapter 16, but the advantages can be summarized as follows:

(a) Steel decking acts as a permanent shuttering which can eliminate the need for slab reinforcement and propping of the construction while the concrete develops strength.
(b) Composite action reduces the overall depth of structure. It provides up to 2 hours fire resistance without

Fig. 14.9 *Universal Beams with metal deck floor slabs.*

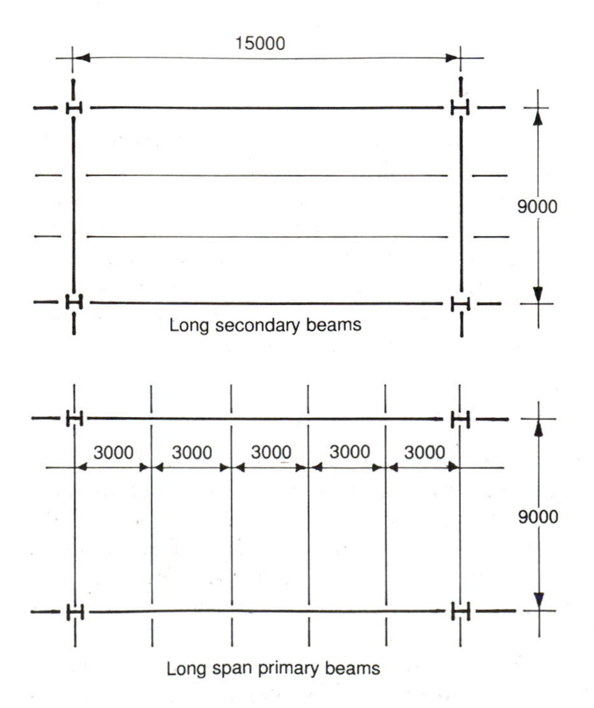

Fig. 14.10 *Alternative framing systems for floors.*

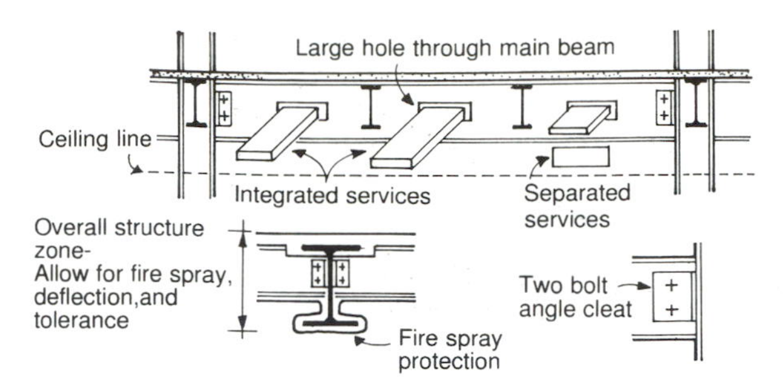

Fig. 14.11 *Integration of building services for beam systems.*

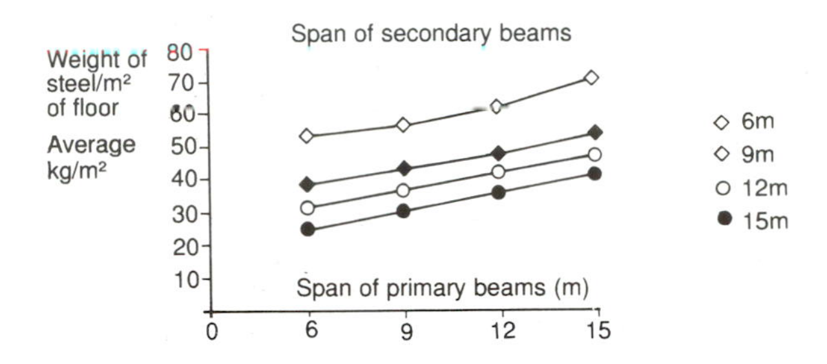

Fig. 14.12 *Weight of structural steel for composite floors.*

additional fire protection and 4 hours with added thickness or extra surface protection.

(c) It is a light, adaptable system that can be cut to awkward shapes and can easily be drilled or cut out for additional service requirements.

(d) Lightweight construction reduces frame loadings and foundation costs.

(e) It allows simple, rapid construction techniques.

Figure 14.10 illustrates alternative arrangements of primary and secondary beams for an optimum deck span of 3 m (10 ft), and a typical cross-section is illustrated in Fig. 14.11, showing alternative ways of integrating building services. The graph in Fig. 14.12, shows the effect of varying the arrangements of primary and secondary beams. The weight of steelwork per square metre for each arrangement is plotted against span of primary beam. This comparison has been based on a limiting criterion of span/360 for superimposed load deflection required by BS 5950 and incorporates an allowance for trimmers and connections.

The comparison highlights a number of interesting features relating to this type of floor system and floor grids in general. Long spanning secondary systems result in heavier floor steel than using long span primary beams. For example, a 9 m by 15 m (30 ft by 50 ft) structural bay with 15 m (50 ft) secondary beams uses 20% more steel than a 15 m by 9 m (50 ft by 30 ft) bay with 15 m (50 ft) primary beams. However, although the long span primary system is some 20% lighter than the equivalent long span secondary system, it involves as much as 40% more labour content in

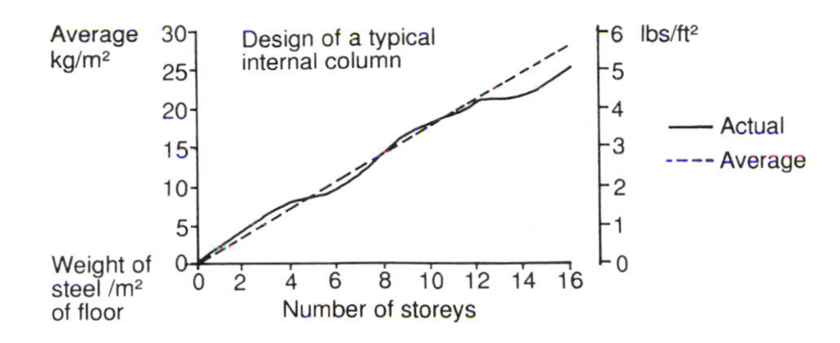

Fig. 14.13 *Weight of structural steel for columns.*

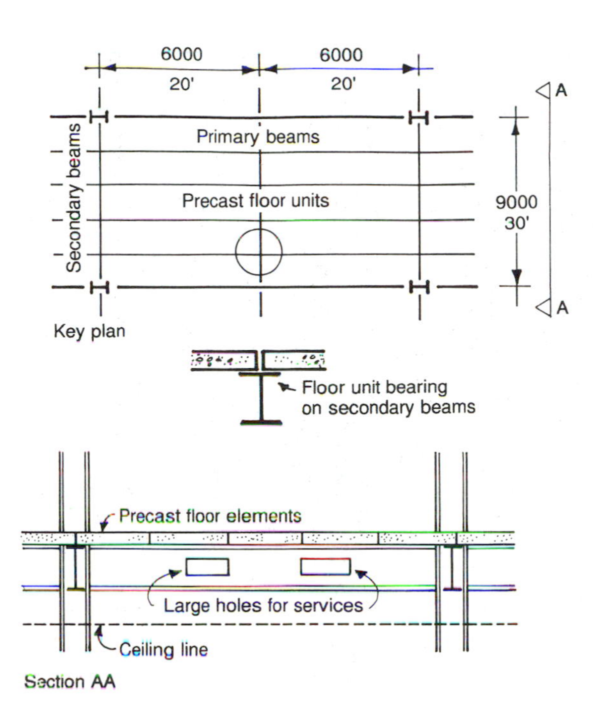

Fig. 14.14 *Typical floor layout for precast concrete floor.*

fabrication and erection. It is also evident that for the longer spans the effect of setting more stringent deflection criteria (say a flat limit of 25 mm (1 in) instead of span/360) is to increase the weight of steel required significantly (between 5% and 10%).

The graphs in Fig. 14.12 should be used with caution because they are based on idealized grids. Furthermore, although an allowance is made for items such as connections and trimmings around openings these are difficult to define. In practice, the irregularities encountered in a real building may have an overriding influence. The graphs also exclude the influence of the columns on the weight of the floor steel. Studies on composite floors have shown that, for practical column spacing, the average weight of column on a particular floor is largely independent of the span of the floor provided. The combined weight of steelwork in a building can then be determined by adding the weights of the columns and floors.

Figure 14.13 shows the weight per metre of typical columns, forming part of a 9 m by 6 m (30 ft by 20 ft) grid for a building with increasing height. To obtain an estimate of the overall tonnage of structural steel in a building, the weight per square metre for the floors can be added and multiplied by the gross floor area.

14.5.2 Universal Beams with precast concrete floors

Universal Beams supporting precast prestressed floor units have some advantages over other forms of construction. A typical floor layout is illustrated in Fig. 14.14, together with a typical cross-section.

Although a heavier form of construction than comparable composite metal deck floors, this system offers:

(a) Fewer floor beams since precast floor units can span up to 6–8 m (20–26 ft) without difficulty. No propping is required.
(b) Shallow floor construction can be obtained by supporting precast floor units on shelf angles.
(c) Fast construction because no time is needed for curing and the development of concrete strength.

On the other hand, the disadvantages are:

(a) Composite action cannot be readily achieved without a structural floor screed.
(b) Heavy floor units are difficult to erect in many locations and require use of a tower crane which may have implications on the construction programme.

14.5.3 Columns

Alternative cross-sectional forms for columns are relatively few. The wide flange H-section profile for columns gives unobstructed access to form beam connections to either flange or web. Additional column loads can be absorbed by plating flanges or by boxing in the section to form a plate column. Circular or rectangular hollow sections are another form that is efficient in load bearing capacity, although beam connections are more complicated to achieve.

14.5.4 Continuous construction

Structural frames may be designed as simple, rigid or semi-rigid depending upon the type of connections used. Simple bolted connections are assumed to transmit negligible bending moment across the joint and the beam is treated as simply supported. A variety of details are used and they are clearly the most popular form of connection for multi-storey steel frames.

With rigid joints the connection is 'monolithic' as with in situ reinforced concrete, and bending moments are transmitted across the joint. This is particularly popular in portal frame construction for single storey buildings. Multi-storey building frames can be developed by stacking portals one above the other, in which case there is no bending continuity from floor beams to the columns above. Alternatively, ladder frames with fully rigid joints between the beam and the column lengths both above and below may be used. Rigid joints not only give a better distribution of bending effects throughout the structure under gravity loading, but can also be used to provide the stiffening effect for wind bracing.

Semi-rigid construction describes beam-to-column connections where only a proportion of the bending moment is transmitted across the joint. Such joints are much simpler than rigid connections and fabrication is consequently much easier. However, the analysis is complex and wider application depends upon experimental evidence being more widely accepted.

It is not necessary to use one type of joint exclusively throughout a structure. For instance, buildings with double spine columns may use rigid joints on the internal connections and simple joints at the perimeter.

Although the use of rigid beam-to-column connections is a more efficient solution structurally, the increased cost of fabrication has tended to militate against their wider use. However, an economical form of construction can be obtained by supporting secondary beams on top of primary beams, arranged in pairs and attached on seatings to either side of the supporting column. Structural continuity of the beams, including provision for short cantilevers, can thus be achieved economically in both directions, and the secondary beams can be of composite construction. Fast erection programmes can be achieved as none of the beam sections have to fit precisely into exact dimensions. This system, pioneered by Peter Brett [4], is particularly suited to accommodate large service ducts without interference, particularly with short primary spans and a restricted floor zone.

14.6 ALTERNATIVE FLOOR FRAMING SYSTEMS

Although the framing systems described above represent the most common arrangements for multi-storey construction, trends towards longer spans and more extensive servicing, together with changes in economic factors have stimulated the development of alternative systems. Some of these are discussed in this section.

14.6.1 Composite steel floor trusses

Use of composite steel floor trusses as primary beams in the structural floor system permits much longer spans than would be possible with conventional Universal Beams (Fig. 14.15). The use of steel trusses for flooring systems is common for multi-storey buildings in the USA, but seldom used in the UK. Although they are considerably lighter than

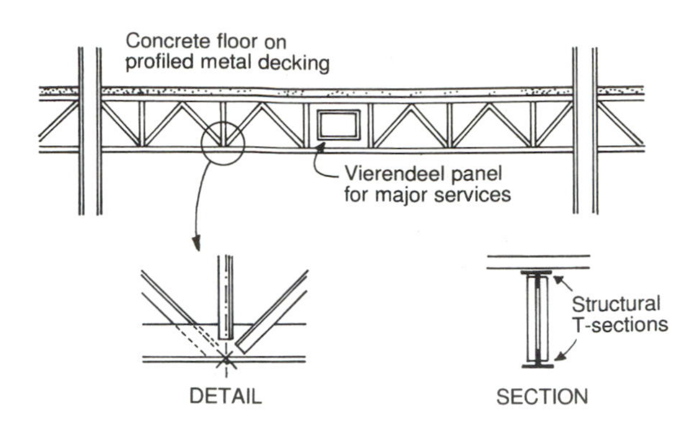

Fig. 14.15 *Typical composite truss details.*

the equivalent Universal Beam section, the cost of fabrication is very much greater, as is the cost of fire proofing the truss members. For maximum economy, trusses should be fabricated using simple welded lap joints. The openings between the diagonal members should be designed to accept service ducts, and if a larger opening is required, a Vierendeel panel can be incorporated at the centre of the span. Because a greater depth is required for floor trusses, the integration of the services is always within the structural zone.

14.6.2 Stub girder construction

Stub girders were developed in the USA in the 1970s as an alternative form of construction for intermediate range spans of between 10 and 14 m (33 and 47 ft). They have not been used significantly in the UK. Figure 14.16 shows a typical stub girder with a bottom chord consisting of a compact universal column section which supports the secondary beams at approximately 3 m (10 ft) centres. Between the secondary beams, a steel stub is welded onto the bottom chord to provide additional continuity and to support the floor slab. The whole system acts as a composite Vierendeel truss. A disadvantage of stub girders is that the

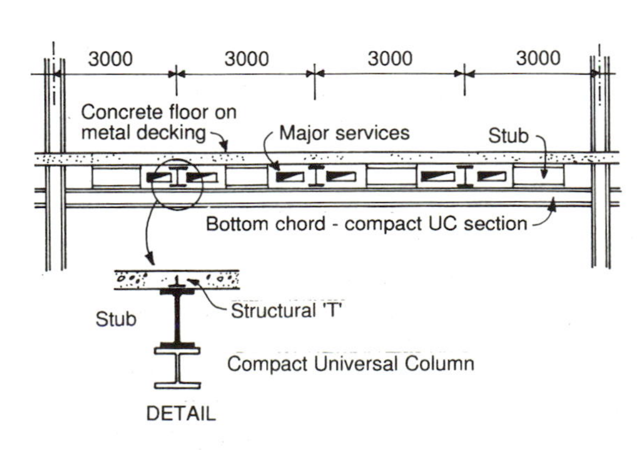

Fig. 14.16 *Typical stub girder details.*

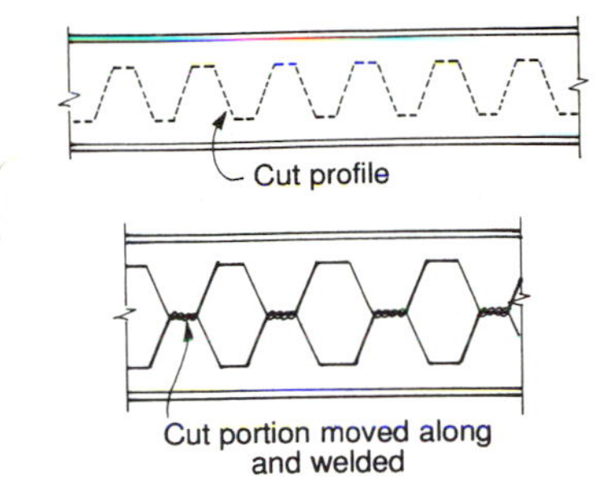

Fig. 14.17 *Typical castellated beam.*

construction needs to be propped while the concrete is poured and develops strength. However, an alternative stub girder scheme has developed using a T-section top chord, which eliminates the need for propped construction. Arguably, a deep Universal Beam with large openings provides a more cost-effective alternative to the stub girder because of the latter's high fabrication content, although making the secondary beams continuous in such a system would be difficult.

14.6.3 Castellated beam systems

Castellated beams have been used for many years to increase the bending capacity of the beam section and to provide limited openings for the services (Fig. 14.17). These openings are rarely of sufficient size for ducts to penetrate without significant modification, and fabrication costs are high. Also, limited shear capacity at each support prohibits their use for long spans and heavy loads.

These disadvantages prevent castellated beams from being used as primary floor members, and they are usually employed spanning between spandrel beams at relatively close centres.

Conventional universal beams span a maximum of about 15 m (50 ft). Recent advances in automatic and semi-automatic fabrication techniques have allowed the economic production of plate girders for longer span floors. It is possible to achieve economic construction well in excess of 15 m (50 ft), particularly if a non-symmetric plate girder is used.

14.6.4 Taper beams

Taper beams are similar to specially fabricated light plate girders, except that their depth varies from a maximum in mid-span to a minimum at supports, thus achieving a highly efficient structural configuration. For simply supported composite taper beams in buildings the integration of the services can be accommodated by incorporating the main ducts close to the columns. Small sized openings can also be

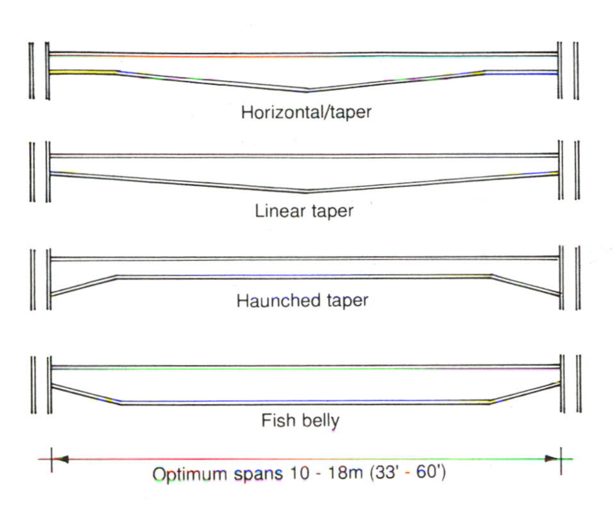

Fig. 14.18 *Taper beams – alternative profiles.*

incorporated within the web of the girder. Figure 14.18 shows alternative taper beam configurations which can be used to optimize the integration of the building services.

14.7 VERTICAL BRACING SYSTEMS

In addition to resisting gravity loads, the structure must incorporate some means of providing lateral stability. The same principles of providing rigidity in three non-parallel planes, discussed in chapter 11 for single storey buildings, still apply. This is normally achieved in the horizontal plane by using the in-plane stiffness of the floor slab, ensuring that it is of an appropriate form and that it is adequately attached to those parts of the structure providing the vertical bracing. This is very effectively achieved by using composite construction for the floor structure. The principal forms of vertical bracing for medium-rise construction are rigid frames, diagonal bracing forming lattice towers, and shear walls; each of these, which can be used in isolation or in combination, is described briefly below. The vertical bracing need not extend over a complete elevation or plane of the building. It is often sufficient to brace one or two bays and lean the rest of the structure against these. More sophisticated systems for high-rise buildings are dealt with in more detail in chapter 15.

14.7.1 Rigid frames

Rigid frames resist lateral forces through the stiffness provided by rigid joints between the horizontal floor components and vertical columns. The need to resist bending moments from wind loads increases the size of the column members and the complexity of the framing connections. For these reasons, rigid frames are only used when there is a particular functional reason for their use,

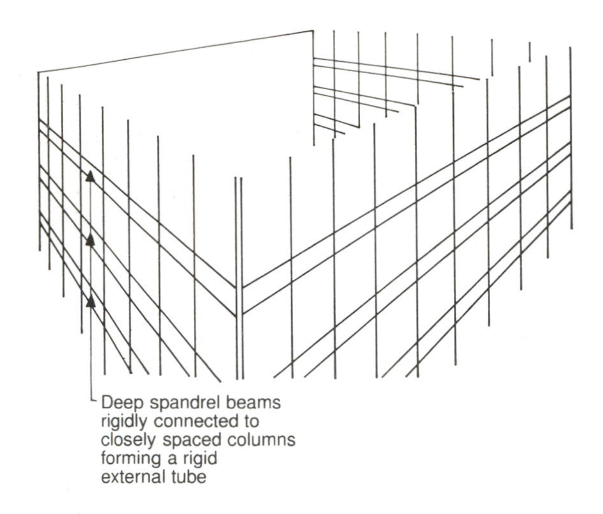

Fig. 14.19 *Facade frame.*

such as the need to provide unobstructed interior space with total adaptability. One possible exception to this general rule is the facade frame with a combination of closely spaced external columns and deep spandrel facade beams. Such a system is usually used for very tall buildings where the facade frame forms a rigid tube (Fig. 14.19).

It may not be necessary to use rigid frame construction throughout the building, although reducing its extent will increase flexibility. One technique which is sometimes adopted for low-rise buildings, for instance, is to use portal construction across the full width of the structure, but to make only the end bays rigid in the less critical longitudinal direction.

The advantages of the rigid frame are that: (a) open bays between all columns are created and (b) total internal adaptability is provided. However, the disadvantages are that: (a) they are almost always more expensive than other systems and (b) columns are larger than for simple connections. Generally, they are less stiff than other bracing systems and require large complex connections.

14.7.2 Lattice frames

Lattice frames act as vertical trusses which support the wind loads by cantilever action. The bracing members can be arranged in a variety of forms designed to carry solely tension, or alternatively tension and compression. When designed to take only tension, the bracing is made up of crossed diagonals. Depending on the wind direction, one diagonal will take all the tension while the other is assumed to remain inactive. Tensile bracing is smaller in cross-section than the equivalent strut and is usually made up of a back-to-back channel or angle sections. When designed to resist compression, the bracings become struts and the most common arrangement is the 'K' or 'V' brace (Fig. 14.20).

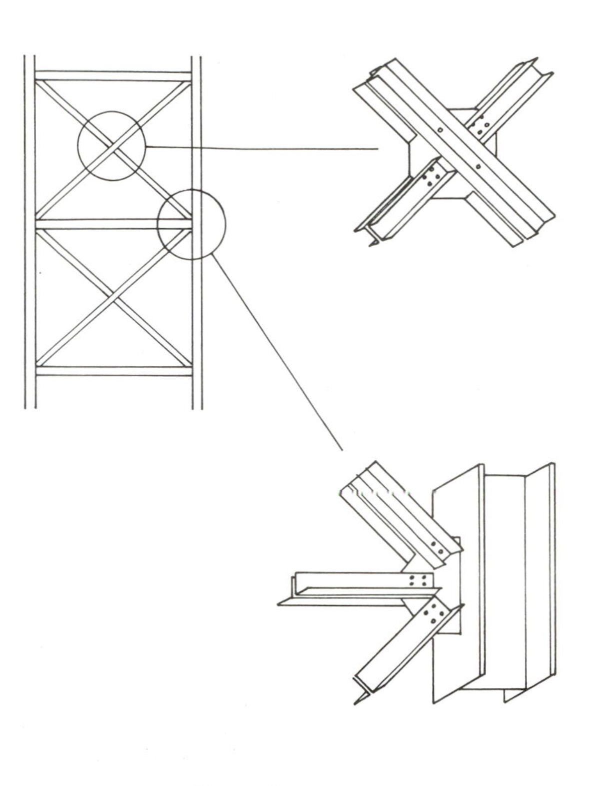

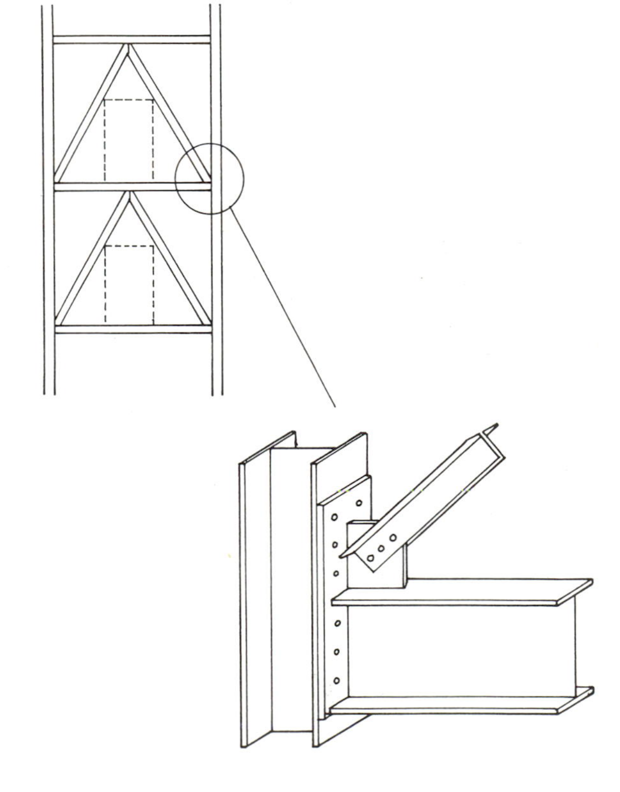

Fig. 14.20 *Typical cross bracing and 'K' bracing.*

The advantages of lattice frames are that: (a) lattice panels can be arranged to accommodate doors and openings for services, (b) bracing members can be concealed in partition walls and (c) they provide an efficient bracing system. The disadvantages are that: (a) diagonal members with fire proofing can take up considerable space and (b) adaptability is limited. Even if some other system of providing lateral stability is adopted, diagonal bracing is commonly used during erection to ensure that the structure is plumb and level until cladding is complete.

14.7.3 Shear walls and cores

Shear walls are normally constructed in in situ reinforced concrete, but precast concrete or brickwork can be used to infill frames creating an equivalent diaphragm effect if construction details are suitable (Fig. 14.21). They are more rigid than other forms of bracing, and there is a need for fewer of them. Shear cores are shear walls in box form which provide some torsional or twisting resistance as well as a highly effective bracing system. They are often incorporated as part of the fire protected shaft accommodating lifts, staircases and vertical distribution of services.

The provision of reinforced concrete or masonry shear walls may introduce an additional trade onto the construction site which can be a disadvantage with regard to the overall building programme. However, there are situations, for instance at boundary and party walls, where concrete or masonry walls are required for other purposes, and in such circumstances their contribution to the overall stability can be utilized. If shear cores are built before erection of the steel frame starts, perhaps using slipform construction, they provide a means of bracing tower cranes for subsequent erection and building work.

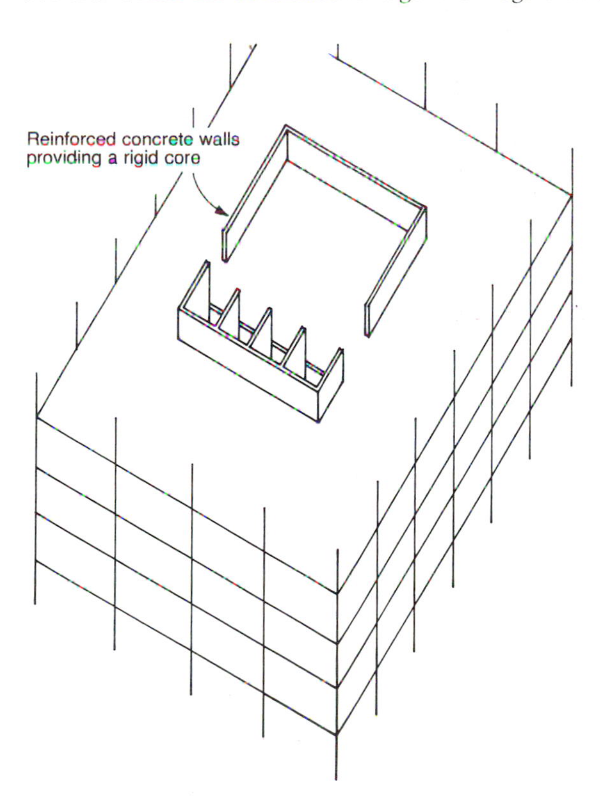

Fig. 14.21 *Building with shear wall core.*

The location of shear walls or cores is crucial, not only in the planning of buildings but also in providing overall stability. They are typically located at bay ends, corners or core enclosures. Cores should ideally be arranged symmetrically on plan and in such a way as to avoid torsional flexibility. Central cores may be adequate, but for more extensive plan forms two or more cores may be required. It is then helpful if these can be located towards the edges of the building. The requirements in terms of wall thickness, extent and arrangement will depend upon particular circumstances. As a general guide for infill panels, to provide an effective contribution to the stability of the frame they should have a thickness of at least 225 mm (9 in) with a maximum area of 25 m^2 (270 ft^2) and a maximum dimension of 7.5 m (25 ft) in any one direction. They should also be built into the main frame on all four edges of the infill bays.

The advantages of shear walling are that:

(a) Concrete walls tend to be thinner than other bracing systems and hence save space in congested areas such as service and lift cores,
(b) They are very rigid and highly effective,
(c) They act as fire compartment walls.

The disadvantages are that:

(a) They constitute a separate form of construction which may delay the contract programme,
(b) It is difficult to provide connections between steel and concrete to transfer the large forces generated.

14.8 CASE STUDY: WHITEFRIARS DEVELOPMENT, FLEET STREET, LONDON

This development in Fleet Street, architects YRM International, is a modern steel frame building in the City of London. The project consists of eight storeys of office accommodation with a central atrium and basement car parking as illustrated in Figs 14.1 and 14.22. The shape of the site and the need for set back floors at the upper levels (determined by planning constraints) dictated a complex structural form. The external elevation shown in Fig. 14.23 consisted of a sophisticated granite cladding system erected in storey height panels.

Fig. 14.22 *Whitefriars, Fleet Street – perspective view from South-East.*

(a)

(b)

14.8.1 Programme

It was important for the project to be completed as quickly as possible and the building was constructed very rapidly. The decision to proceed was taken immediately following planning approval and detailed design progressed at the same time as the existing News International building on the site was demolished. Alternative structural solutions in steel and concrete (Fig. 14.24) were developed, but the reinforced concrete scheme was abandoned because of the improved speed of construction offered by the steelwork.

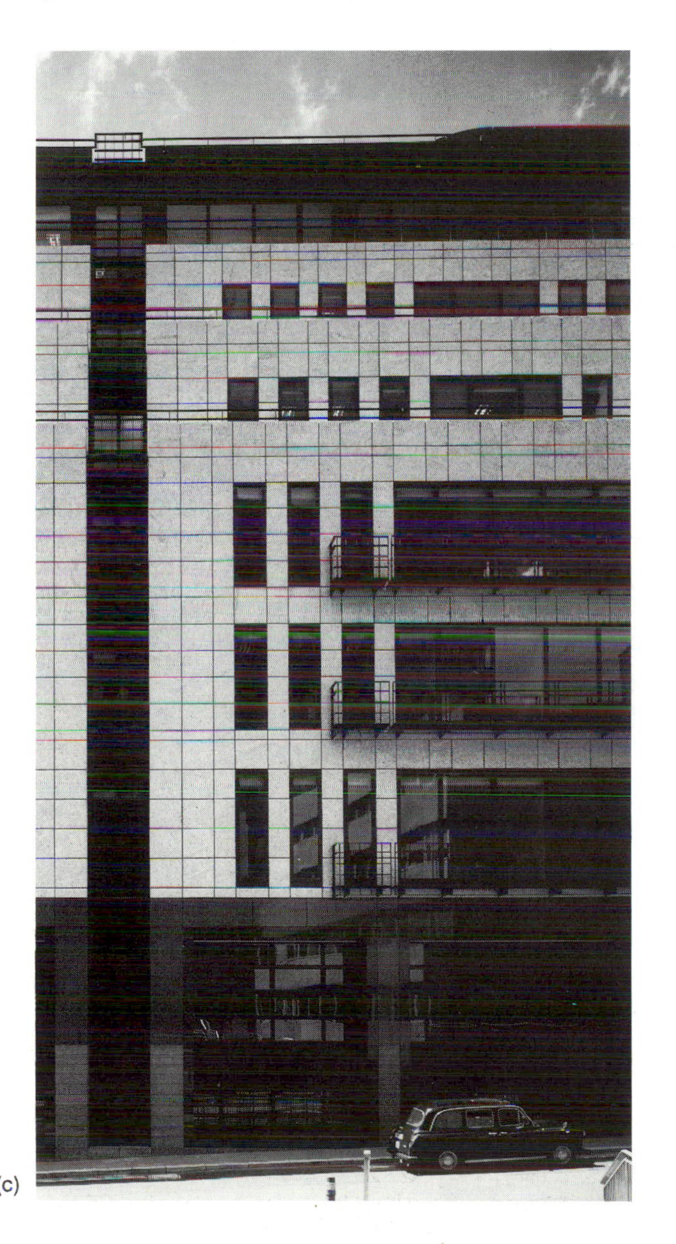

(c)

Fig. 14.23 *Whitefriars, Fleet Street (a) atrium; (b) entrance court towards Fleet Street; (c) main elevation to side street.*

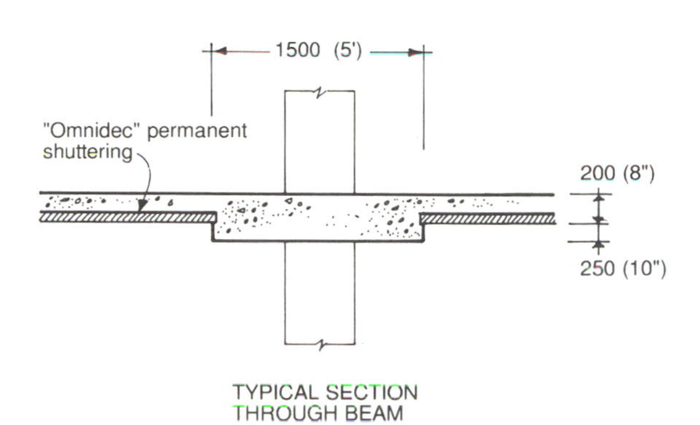

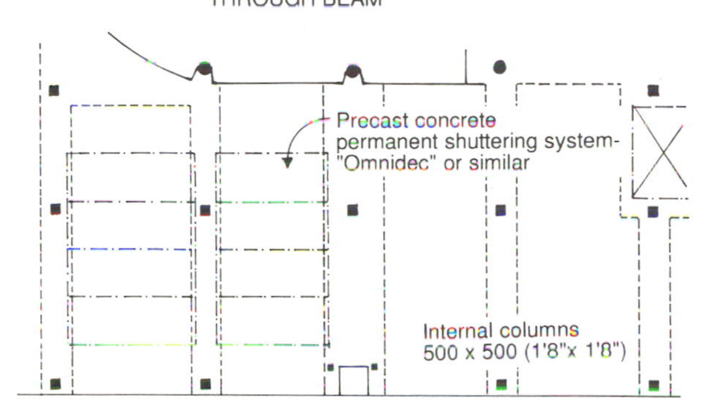

Fig. 14.24 *Whitefriars, Fleet Street – Part floor plan showing in situ frame with precast concrete floors (early study abandoned due to programme requirements).*

The structure was decided very early in the design process to enable the steelwork to be pre-ordered well in advance of the award of the steelwork contract. This reduced the lead-in time normally associated with steel to procure and fabricate the frame before erection can commence.

The steel was pre-ordered in September 1987 and a steelwork contractor appointed in October. Fabrication of the frame started in November on the basis of fabrication drawings prepared by the fabricator and approved by the design team. The first structural steel columns were erected in February and the frame was completed in July (with the exception of the atrium, which was a separate element); a total of 32 weeks for fabrication and erection of the structure.

14.8.2 Choice of structural system

The architectural concept incorporated long spans, set back floors at the upper levels and restricted floor depths. With these constraints and the need for the fastest possible construction programme, structural steel was chosen as the most suitable material for the frame construction. Steel also offered the advantage of a lighter and more adaptable structure, reducing the size of the foundations and allowing a floor system that was amenable to changes at a later stage. Although a concrete frame may well have resulted in a lower construction cost, it was estimated that steel would reduce the construction programme by 3–4 weeks with an overall saving to the contract of several hundred thousand pounds.

14.8.3 Design criteria

The floor zone make-up used in this study is as shown in Fig. 14.25 the main structural spans ranging from 7.5 to 18 m (25 to 60 ft). The live load deflection limitation was set at 25 mm (1 in) for internal beams and 15 mm (⅝ in) for perimeter beams. A greater restriction was imposed on the perimeter beams to suit the panel system of cladding adopted for the project.

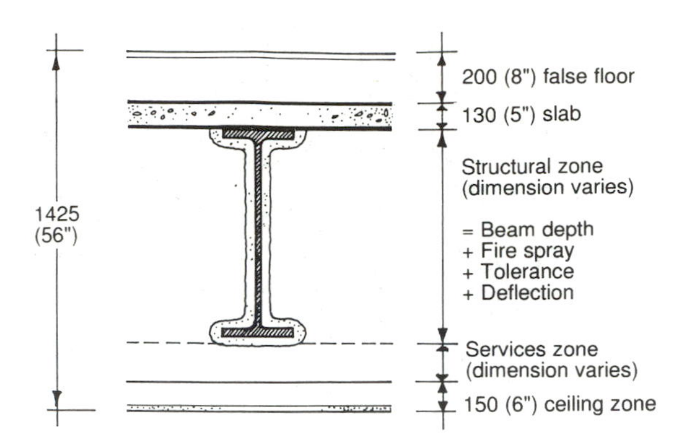

Fig. 14.25 *Whitefriars, Fleet Street – floor zone.*

14.8.4 Structural floor systems

Two alternative structural floor layouts were considered for a typical floor:

(a) Alternative 1: consisting of long span primary beams supporting short span secondary beams at 3 m (10 ft) centres.
(b) Alternative 2: consisting of short span primary beams supporting long span secondary beams at 3 m (10 ft) centres.

Both alternatives made use of a composite lightweight concrete slab on metal decking which eliminated the need for propping during construction.

Alternative 1, with long span primary beams, was the most efficient structure based on the weight of steel. Alternative 2 provided fewer restrictions to services, as the depth and size of the main structural members tends to be less than for alternative 1. On the basis of advice from the building services engineers, it was confirmed that alternative 1 could be used without serious restrictions being imposed on the mechanical and electrical services and this floor layout was adopted.

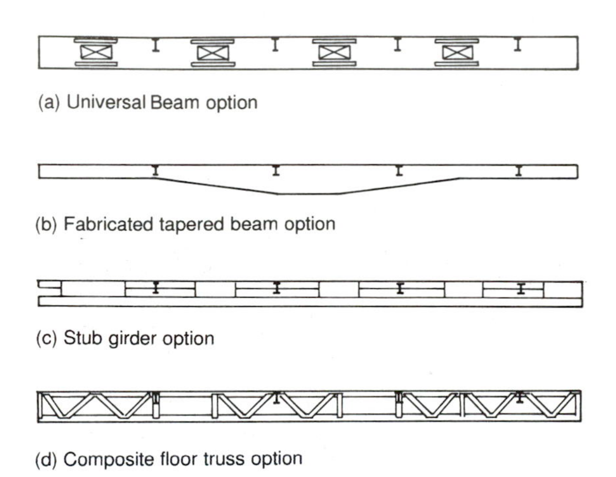

Fig. 14.26 *Whitefriars, Fleet Street – alternative floor framing elements.*

14.8.5 Main beam alternatives

Four different floor framing elements were considered for the primary beams (Fig. 14.26) as follows:

(a) Universal Beams with large holes for services.
(b) Fabricated tapered beams.
(c) Stub girders.
(d) Composite floor trusses.

A comparison of the weight of steelwork needed for each floor elements was carried out and the results are shown graphically in Fig. 14.27. The above floor framing elements were considered for the primary beams adjacent to the atrium. In other areas standard Universal Beam sections without major holes for services, which would be the most economical solution, could be readily adopted for primary beams.

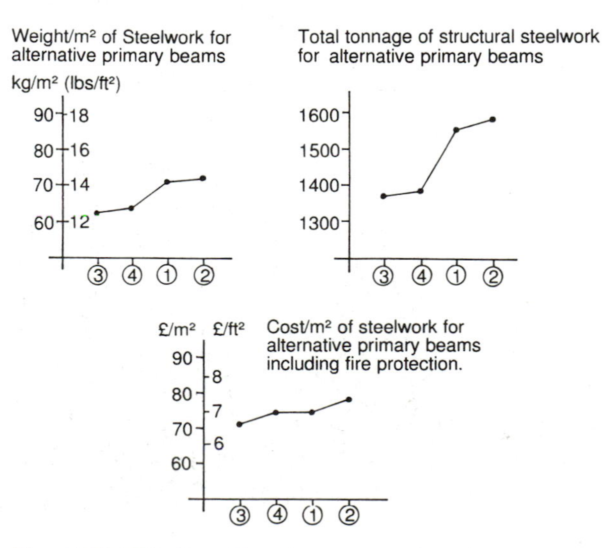

Fig. 14.27 *Whitefriars, Fleet Street – cost and weight comparisons for different floor systems.*

Fig 14.28 *Whitefriars, Fleet Street – composite beams generally adopted for floor framing.*

A rough comparison of the costs is also included in Fig. 14.27, based on recent advice from steelwork fabricators. These costs include the fabrication and erection of the structural steel frame and spray fire protection. They should be used for comparison purposes only.

14.8.6 Services/structure interaction

The inevitable interaction of the building services and structural zone on this project had an important bearing on the choice of floor beam system. From discussions with the building services engineers, it was decided that although Universal Beams with major holes cut into the web or stub girders would not place undesirable restrictions on major services routes, the composite truss with major framed openings was more favoured. In the event, a combination of both systems was chosen with composite trusses for long spans and Universal Beams for the more general condition (Figs 14.28 and 14.29).

Fig 14.29 *Whitefriars, Fleet Street – composite trusses adopted for long span conditions.*

Fig. 14.30 *Whitefriars, Fleet Street – the bracing system adopted for lateral stability.*

14.8.7 Lateral stability

The most efficient and economical form of providing lateral stability for this type of structure is by using either vertical bracing or shear walls. The former is achieved by using inclined structural steel members between each floor level; the latter by concrete walls constructed between substructure and roof levels. The vertical bracing alternative offered the simplest and quickest form of construction and was chosen on this project for that reason (Fig. 14.30).

14.8.8 Disproportionate collapse

For buildings over five storeys the UK Building Regulations require the structure to be so constructed that, in the event of an accident, the structure will not be damaged to an extent disproportionate to the cause of the accident. This is normally catered for by providing structural ties through the building, in accordance with the relevant Codes of Practice. However, at the set back floors this approach cannot be used. The two methods of conforming to the Building Regulations requirements at these floors are either to design beams supporting the columns as key elements (i.e. to resist a blast load) or to provide an alternative load path in order that the adjacent floors will remain intact on the loss of the member under consideration. The most economical structural solution is to provide alternative load paths, thus using the structure as designed to work in a different manner in the event of an accident. This eliminates the need for the heavy steel members which are required when beams are designed as key elements.

14.8.9 Column spacing

Reducing the long spans by the provision of additional internal columns facilitates the integration of services and reduces the cost of the structural frame, although this in turn eliminates the column-free office areas and inhibits space planning. It was estimated that if the main spans were halved by the introduction of internal columns this would result in a 10–15% reduction in the weight of the steel frame.

Following the exhaustive study described above, it was decided that long span floors could not be justified on cost grounds and a 7.5 by 9 m (25 by 30 ft) grid was chosen.

14.9 CONCLUSION

The design of multi-storey frames must accommodate a range of functional, performance and economic requirements. Having decided on the structural grid which meets the needs of the building, the designer must choose an economic structural floor system to satisfy all the design constraints. The choice depends on the span of the floor, the service requirements and any height restrictions. For spans up to 12–15 m (40–50 ft), simple Universal Beams with precast floors or composite metal deck floors are likely to be most economic. Above 15 m (50 ft) composite steel trusses or fabricated girders will be necessary. As the span increases, the depth and weight of the structural floor increases, and for spaces in excess of 15 m (50 ft) spans depth predominates because of the need to achieve adequate rigidity. Although lateral stability can often be easily achieved, provision for it must be made within the overall structural form at an early stage. For taller buildings, the importance of this aspect of structural design becomes increasingly important.

The discussion of these design factors is included to demonstrate the various options available to the structural designer and the process which should be followed in order to achieve a satisfactory solution.

REFERENCES AND TECHNICAL NOTES

1. BS 6399 Design loading for buildings: Part 1 (1984) Code of Practice for dead and imposed loads, Part 2 (1988) Code of Practice for imposed roof loads.
2. BS 5950 Structural use of steelwork in buildings: Part 1 (1985) Code of Practice for design in simple and continuous construction: hot-rolled sections.
3. *Ronan Point, London* (1968) Building Disasters and Failures by Geoff Scott (1976) Construction Press Ltd. Refer to Appendix 2 which gives extract of official report. report.
4. Peter Brett: refer to engineer's work on framing in the publication *Framed in Steel 5* by British Steel.

BIBLIOGRAPHY

Hart, F., Henn, W. and Sontag, H. (English edn., Godfrey, G. B. ed.) (1985) *Multi-storey Steel Framed Buildings*. Collins, London.

Copeland, B., Glover, M., Hart, A., Haryott, R. and Marshall, S., Designing for steel. *Architects' Journal*, 24 and 31 August 1983. Vol. 178, Nos. 34 and 35, pp. 41–57.

Computer-generated aerial view looking north over the Chicago loop created by SOM (architect and engineer Skidmore, Owings and Merrill (SOM)).

15

Tall structures

Hal Iyengar

15.1 INTRODUCTION

The birth of steel skyscraper buildings can be rightfully associated with the invention of passenger elevators which appeared in a practical form around the 1870s. Buildings prior to this date were generally limited to five to six storeys by the ability of a person to walk up. Early buildings of this type utilized masonry exterior loadbearing walls with cast iron interior columns. Wrought iron floor beams and girders, which were encased, supported shallow brick-vaulted floors. The exterior masonry wall provided not only the rigidity with respect to lateral wind loads, but also the support and fenestration for the exterior masonry facades.

Important engineering and planning principles pertaining to high-rise buildings were resolved in these initial applications. These included aspects such as structural fire protection, regular grid spacing of interior columns and planning with respect to service functions of lighting, heating and plumbing. Inclusion of hydraulic elevators for fast, vertical transportation made it possible to consider taller buildings in the eight to ten storey range. The inefficiency and the consequent massiveness of masonry walls as loadbearing elements had been recognized and they were gradually replaced by 'skeleton' or 'cage' buildings [1] in which iron columns and beams provided the full support to all floors and the roof. For the most part, in the latter half of the 19th century, the components were cast iron for columns, brackets for supporting beams, and lintels, whilst wrought iron was typically used for beams [2]. The tensile capacity of wrought iron was utilized in ties connecting the tops of columns and lateral beams rigidly connected to the columns by rivetting. This transformed the buildings into frames which could resist wind forces in addition to gravity forces. With the introduction of the Bessemer process to produce steel, the qualities of strength and toughness of the new material began to be appreciated and it was readily adopted for skeletal frames. These frames were still encased by heavy masonry walls which provided the necessary bracing for both wind loads and the destabilising effects of gravity loads.

By the end of the 19th century steel had replaced forged iron beams and cast iron columns due to its economic advantage, the new framing material proving to be 15% cheaper. In design terms, steelwork meant longer spans to the interior and less massive envelope walls. This led to large scale fenestration and articulation of the skeletal frame in the treatment of the elevation. The masonry walls became panel infill supported on the frame. A further advantage was the greater speed of building as the frame construction could proceed independently of the envelope. The older methods were far slower with the brickwork and framing advancing together floor by floor.

Exterior construction went straight up in the line of the exterior columns giving a systematic rhythm and arrangement for the exterior fenestration. The clarity and distinction of this form of frame construction found its expression in the Chicago School of Architecture [3] in the late 19th and 20th centuries and taller and taller buildings up to 20 storeys were built around the turn of the century.

Although the start of steel skeleton construction can be assigned to the Chicago School, its proliferation and extension to taller structures can be truly appreciated in New York, culminating in the construction of the Empire State Building around 1930.

It is worth studying the skyline of New York at the end of the 1920s, noting the clustering of a number of tall buildings. An outstanding example still is the 58 storey Woolworth Building (completed 1913) which rose to a height of 237 m (792 ft), the tallest design constructed up to that time. Banks of electric elevators, rising at 180 m (600 ft) per minute, were installed to cope with transportation. Steel construction still essentially consisted of the Vierendeel frame concept. This derived its essential lateral stiffness from smaller spans of 6–7.5 m (20–25 ft), deep frame girders, knee-braced or haunched joints, masonry enclosures and partitions, heavy exterior built-in masonry claddings and a solid reinforced concrete slab which also encased floor framings. The stiffening effect of all the secondary enclosures, though not counted in the calculations, was what made this type of building rigid enough to perform well under wind dynamics. Shedding of these built-in features has obviously transferred the stiffening responsibility to the steel components which had progressively to assume a larger role in lateral load resistance.

In the period between 1930 and 1950 multi-storey steel construction was constantly refined. Columns and beams were still encased in concrete for fire protection but reinforced concrete slabs replaced heavy brick vaults. The rectilinear form of the frame came to be considered as a Vierendeel framework either as a bridge structure for transfer loads or as a ladder frame to develop axial loads, together with moments and shear stresses resulting from the frame action in multi-storey structures.

In the period from 1950 to 1960, the same rectilinear frame vocabulary continued with bolted or welded rigid joints even for taller structures. Light discrete curtain wall claddings evolved and heavy masonry partitions were replaced by light drywall construction. Space planning demanded large open office areas, preferably free of columns, such architectural considerations leading to costly steelwork for frames rising to 30 storeys. The situation was compounded if setbacks occurred in the upper storeys where deep Vierendeel beams were needed to bridge interior volumes. Finally, the wide-spaced conventional frame was less reliable in terms of bracing and wind restraint when developed as slender slab or tower forms.

Prior to the 1930s, steel trusses had been developed for bridge construction. This led naturally to their use in buildings and in particular as trussed frames around building cores. This concept contributed substantially to wind load resistance as a replacement for masonry shear walls used in the 19th century.

A review of the structural system of the Empire State Building indicates slender but extensive internal trusses participating with the shear frames. The inclusion of vertical trusses was possible because of the organization of elevator banks, especially when more than one bank was needed, together with building fire stairs, toilets and utilities, which were all centralized in the building core. Such centralization provided many opportunities for vertical trusses to be placed behind the elevators.

In current design, planning and optimizing core elements is a significant aspect of co-ordinated architectural and structural design, the overall building efficiency depending on a compact, optimum core. Sizes of columns, beams and their spacings have an enormous impact on this integration. The extent to which the core can be utilized in evolving frameworks for wind resistance will also determine the extent of contribution needed from other framework systems in wind load resistance. In most instances, vertical shear frames can be combined with vertical trusses to provide for the total resistance of wind and gravity forces. This was the predominant form of steel construction through the mid-20th century and continues to be utilized for buildings up to 30 storeys.

In the 1960s alternative concepts were developed to provide a three-dimensional system efficiently to resist wind forces for high-rise structures in the range up to 110 storeys. These included truss-frame interacting systems (with belt and outrigger trusses), tubular and bundled tubular systems and mixed systems.

15.2 DEVELOPMENT OF LATERAL SYSTEMS

The total structural system is required to resist dead and live loads arising from weight and usage of the building (generally termed gravity loads) and the lateral forces attributable to either wind or earthquakes. The gravity loads are resisted by floor slabs, beams, girders and vertical elements, such as columns and walls. Deformations associated with gravity loads are beam deflections, column shortenings and lateral sway due to asymmetrical loads. Lateral loads produce shears and overturning moments which produce lateral sway. This needs to be limited and controlled to produce a usable stable building. As the height of the building increases, sway escalates as a fourth power of the height. Apart from strength, the predominant concern in the structural design of high-rise buildings is therefore providing enough stiffness to control lateral sway.

The assemblage of components such as columns, beams, diagonal bracings and shear walls which work together to resist lateral forces and sway can be called the 'lateral system'. As the building height increases, the demand for efficient composition of the lateral system becomes critical. Lateral forces are often viewed as a wind pressure applied to the wind sail area, but real wind forces are fluctuating and dynamic in nature. These characteristics produce overall dynamic oscillations, dependent on the dynamic property of the building frame. All ultra-tall structures need to be verified with respect to acceleration and change of acceleration levels due to dynamic behaviour in the higher zones, these steps being taken to avoid significant perception of wind movement or sway. Wind tunnel studies are often performed to verify dynamic performance.

Even though lateral systems resist gravity as well as wind loading, and must necessarily do so, for the purpose of comparison it is possible to focus on the lateral stiffness characteristics only. The evolution of lateral systems can be described in terms of the following arrangements:

Shear frame: Planar rectilinear arrangement of beams and columns with rigid joints.

Shear truss: Diagonalized bracing between columns in one or more directions in the form of vertical shear trusses with columns as chords.

Shear truss-frames: Systems involving both shear frame and shear trusses which interact with each other.

Shear truss-frame-outrigger and belt trusses: Systems where trusses in the core of the building are connected to fascia plane shear frames by floor-deep trusses – 'outriggers'. They may also involve a continuous band of trusses in the fascia frame at the level of outrigger trusses.

Framed tubes: Close spacing of columns on the exterior rigid frames forming a closed plan shape, equivalent to a vertical silo or tube with fenestration between columns and beams. The tube behaves like an overall cantilever fixed at the ground.

Truss tube: The same form as framed tubes with wider spacing of columns which are, in addition, tied across by a system of diagonals in each facade plane.

Bundled or modular tubes: Framed or trussed tubes grouped

together like cells to compose the overall building shape. The tube wall frames between cells are common to adjacent cells.

Superframe: Megaframe in the overall form of a Vierendeel frame where the in-plane depths of horizontal and vertical members are large and contain plane trusses which are several storeys deep or several bays wide.

Composite systems: Mixed reinforced concrete and structural steel systems involving concrete shear walls or concrete framed tubes combined with various structural steel framings.

15.3 THE SYSTEMS EVOLUTION

The high-rise systems developed after the 1960s fit a logical evolutionary pattern with one development leading to another and each new system a link in this process. It is essential to understand this process if one is involved in the design of high-rise steel buildings. The shear frame resists lateral loads primarily by bending of members. Its overall efficiency, and thus its economic feasibility, is controlled largely by bay spans and member depths. As the bay dimension and the number of storeys increased, disproportionately heavier members were required to control wind sway, thus limiting its economic viability. This system would be considered the weakest in its ability to resist wind forces and therefore placed at the beginning of system possibilities. At the other end of the spectrum, a pure cantilever which utilizes the entire three-dimensional form of the exterior can be recognized as the strongest and most rigid.

Having defined the spectrum of design it is possible to compare a series of system possibilities with varying degrees of efficiency relative to that of the 'pure cantilever' [4]. A systems chart (Fig. 15.1) was introduced in the mid 1960s to define a sequence of systems with particular height limitations for each [5].

The implication here is that the general economic effectiveness of a particular structural system can be reasonably expressed with respect to height. However, variations within a general range can occur due to the specific composition of a system. This set the stage for a 'systems approach' in the design of tall steel buildings, whereby the selection of an appropriate system was a significant design event. The process of optimization of the structure rested principally with the appropriate selection of a system, rather than minimizing member proportions. New systems were placed into the chart as they were developed.

Some general characteristics of the system evolution are worth noting. The systems need to have a high structural efficiency and minimum premium for height. The systems themselves must be applicable over a broad cross-section of structures and not just be a unique solution for a particular building. Figure 15.2 shows a systems chart generally conforming to this principle.

In the modern context, the shear frame building can be effective and efficient up to 20 storeys. The addition of the 'cantilever vertical truss' will greatly improve the efficiency, but the overall effectiveness depends on the depth and aspect ratio of the truss. Systems which involve both 'shear-frame and truss' can be efficient to about 40 storeys. Some systems have evolved which tie the core trusses to the exterior frame by 'outrigger trusses and belt trusses' on the exterior. In general, such systems can be effective up to 50 storeys. For taller structures, one needs to develop cantilever buildings, especially ones which utilize the exterior form of the building. 'framed tubes' placed on the exterior, with closely spaced columns all rigidly connected with beams, have a higher order of efficiency to resist lateral loads and have been used for this height range. The 'trussed tube' is a classic version of an exterior steel cantilever system and is highly efficient and obviously a candidate for 'supertall' buildings. 'Framed tube' elements can also be utilized as end channels or interior I forms. Similarly, 'Fascia Trusses' can be used at the ends or in the centre of the building mass. When used in parts, they represent partially complete tubes. Other systems for supertall buildings include the 'bundled tube' and the 'superframe'. Completed examples of these systems exist and it is well established that the system selection process was a key element of the structural design process. Similar system evolutions have also occurred in reinforced concrete systems and the current state includes mixed forms of reinforced concrete and structural steel elements (composite structures).

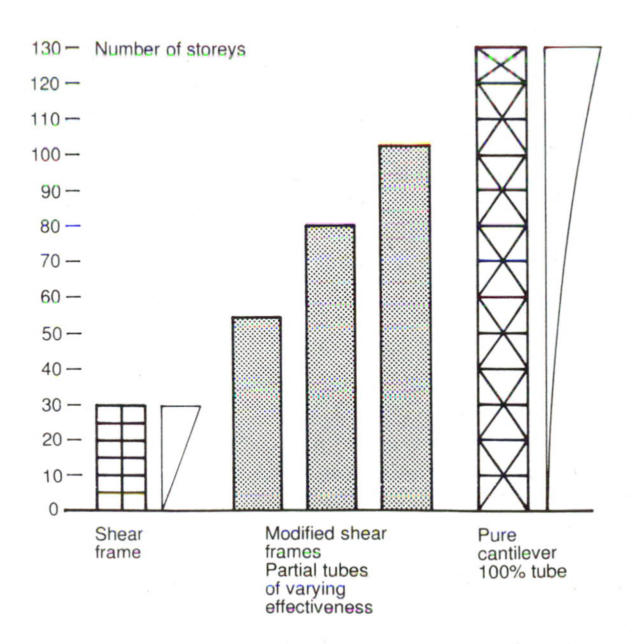

Fig. 15.1 *Systems chart.*

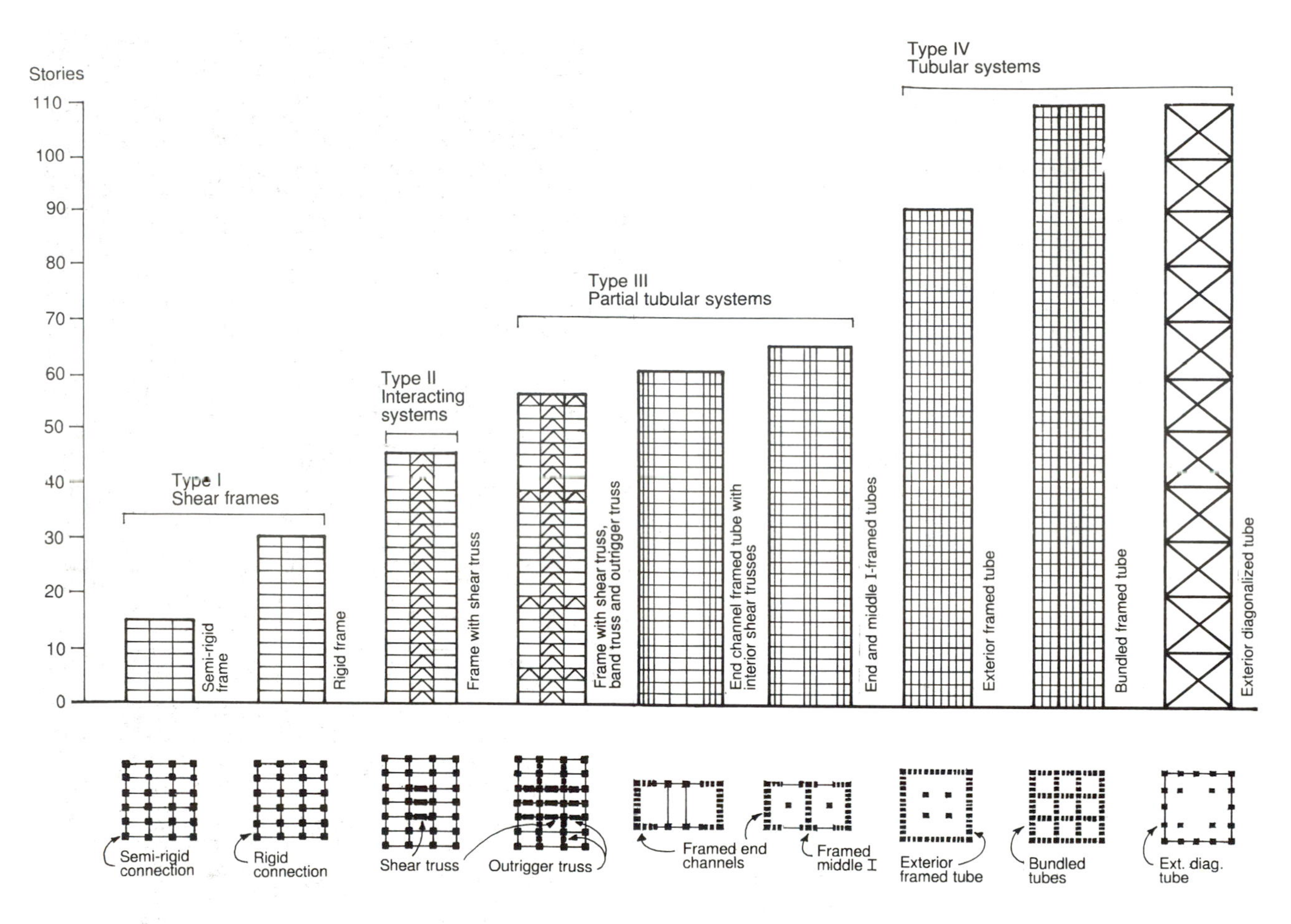

Fig. 15.2 *Comparison of structural systems.*

The majority of such building structures are in the low to medium rise category (up to 30 storeys) , supertall systems being rare and posing far more specialized problems. General advice is therefore concentrated on the former as detailed below.

15.4 THE 'SHEAR FRAME' SYSTEM

'Shear frames' or 'Vierendeel' frames, which are connected for moment resistance at joints, are placed in two orthogonal directions to resist the forces of wind in each direction. Each frame would be required to resist its proportion of the wind shear, which is determined on the basis of its relative stiffness compared to the total.

The efficiency toward lateral stiffness development is dependent on bay span, number of bays in the frame, number of frames and the available depth in floor framing for the frame girder. All these factors need to be considered in the planning of a frame building.

Bay dimensions in the range of 6–9 m (20–30 ft) are commonly used. In these shear frames, the predominant contribution to sway deflection under wind comes from the bending of beams and columns due to wind shear and, to a smaller extent, from column shortening or the cantilever component (Fig. 15.3). In general, about 80–90% of sway is due to bending of members. Therefore the design of these frames is controlled by individual member bending stiffnesses. The deeper the member, the more efficiently the bending stiffness can be developed. It should be noted that the bending stiffness requirement increases towards the bottom of the building, resulting in greater beam depths in the lower storeys.

When the frames are regularly spaced in both directions, a rectilinear column grid pattern is created which is suitable for isolated rectilinear forms and many frame concepts have been evolved on this basis. The architecture of these buildings has centred on bay or frame expressions. An outstanding example of this is a 20 storey structure built around 1960 (Fig. 15.4). Frames can be placed at angles or on an irregular basis to create various plan shapes to fill the area of an irregular site. Early frame structures planned around

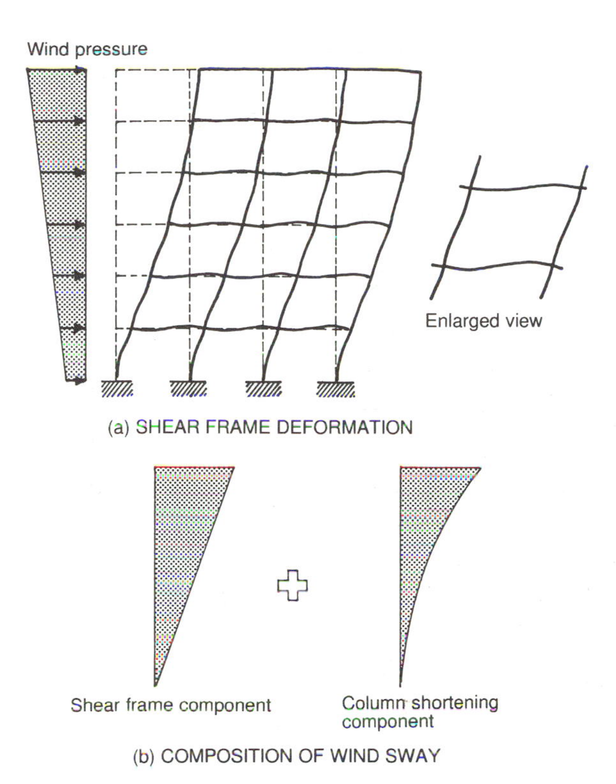

Fig. 15.3 *Plane shear frame behaviour.*

the turn of the century through the 1930s were generally irregular and often had varying bay dimensions dictated more by masonry enclosures on the exterior facades and interior columns. Since modern buildings have light claddings and thinner sprayed-on fire protection, regular grids dictated by modular spacings are generally utilized.

For taller structures beyond about 20 storeys, the depths of frame girder members on the building interior may interfere with the passage of service ducts, making it difficult to achieve constant floor-to-floor height. In these situations, one often resorts to frames only on the perimeter of the buildings where appropriate column spacings and member depths can be more freely organized. This, however, requires a more particular co-ordination with the exterior architecture of the facades. In some early structures, the column spacings on the exterior did provide the basis for the masonry bay and varieties of masonry infilled claddings. As these heavy masonry claddings were replaced by other materials, such as precast concrete, metal panels or stone veneer, the clear expression of the frame structure and the proportion of its members began to provide the architectural context for the facade. This is clearly expressed in the frame expression of the facade shown (Fig. 15.4).

In modern steel construction, pure frame buildings from a structural viewpoint are generally restricted to only a few storeys, since other more efficient forms are available. Such

Fig. 15.4 *Business Men's Assurance, Kansas City, Missouri (architect and engineer SOM). (Ezra Stoller © Esto.)*

forms typically include diagonals or trusses which may interfere with architectural and planning factors, particularly on restricted sites. In those cases Vierendeel forms may still be preferred as they give uncluttered rectangular spaces. The basic inefficiency in frame buildings, apart from steel quantities involved, is the need for moment-connected, rigid joints which are expensive to fabricate. The optimization of frames in a practical sense has centred on minimizing the number of such joints, minimization of site welding

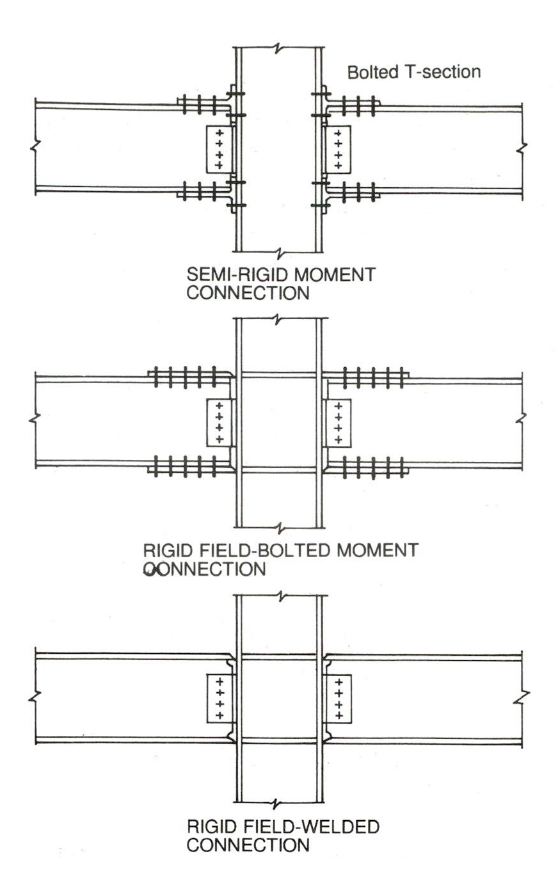

Fig. 15.5 *Typical moment connections between beams and columns.*

in lieu of site bolting and similar criteria. Various types of moment connections (Fig. 15.5) have been evolved over the years which are worth noting.

Early moment joints were semi-rigid types using T-sections or angles to make the connections with rivets. As the need for full rigidity increased, welded forms and a combination of welding and friction grip bolts were used. The cost of fabrication and erection labour has escalated considerably since World War II and as a result the economic effectiveness of forming rigid joint connections has been reduced. Consideration must therefore be given to shop welding in lieu of site welding, and the use of shorter spans – around 7.5 m (25 ft) – thus reducing the moments to be transmitted through connections and simplifying joints.

15.5 SHEAR TRUSS AND FRAME SYSTEMS

To increase the rigidity of frame moment connections, knee braces were added at the joints while still maintaining the rectilinear form. This later evolved into full bay, diagonal members connecting the floors, which would avoid or reduce bending in beam/column frame members. As elevators and cores were centralized, it became simpler to provide vertical trusses consisting of bracings connecting column chords. The restriction of not being able to pass through the truss was recognized in placing them in areas where they would not affect plan usability. Trusses were therefore generally placed in one direction only and behind elevators, while a shear frame provided wind resistance in the other direction. In some isolated instances, braces were provided in both directions, in which case particular co-ordination with respect to providing access into the core had to be considered. The behaviour of the 'shear truss-frame interacting system' is shown in Fig. 15.6.

From a structural standpoint, vertical trusses resist wind forces as a cantilever and are therefore more efficient than shear frames. However, the depth of the truss, which is dependent on the number of elevators in a row, limits the overall advantage of the system. K-forms, X-forms or single brace forms can be used (Fig. 15.7). The K-form is more common, since the bracings do not participate extensively in gravity load, and can thus be designed for wind axial forces without serious consideration of gravity load effects. In contrast, the design of X- and single diagonal brace forms may be dominated by gravity forces. The braces are generally double angle, T or channel shapes bolted to a central gusset plate on site (Fig. 15.7).

In buildings taller than about 15–20 storeys, multiple banks (low-, mid- and high-rise) of elevators may be needed which will allow for more trusses to be accommodated in

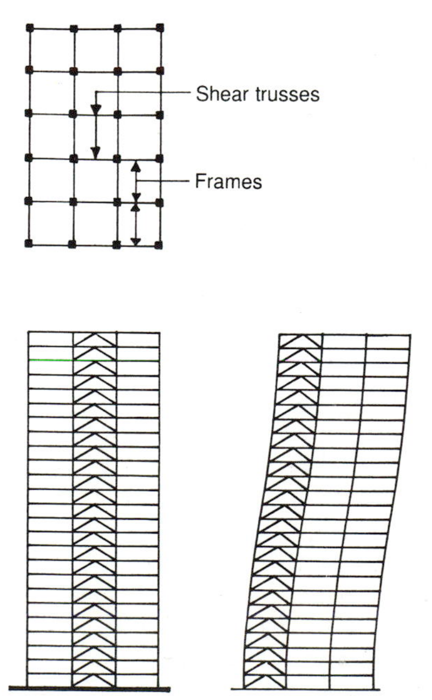

Fig. 15.6 *Shear truss-frame interacting system.*

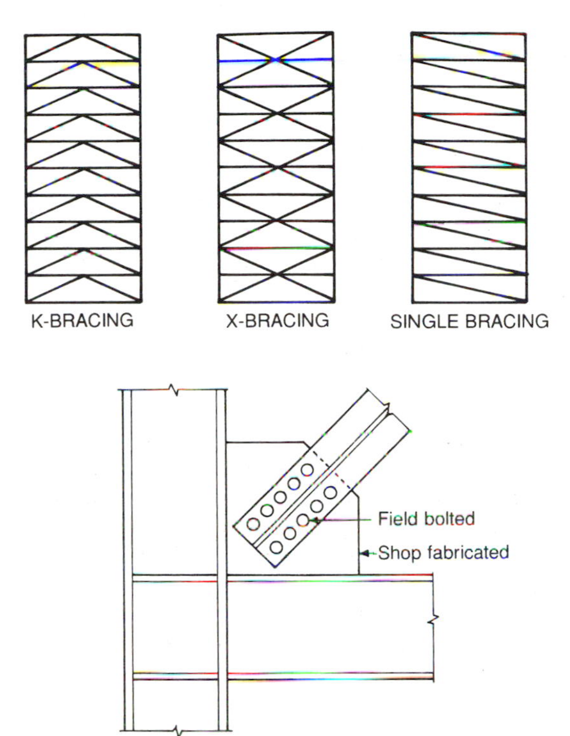

Fig. 15.7 *Truss diagonals.*

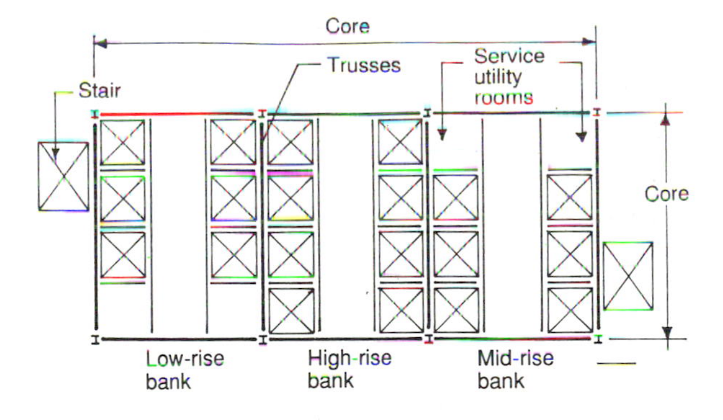

Fig. 15.8 *Building core (40 storey building).*

the core. The core for a recent 40 storey building illustrates the possibilities (Fig. 15.8).

A natural evolution of shear frames and vertical trusses is to combine both in the same system, so that together they will resist wind forces. These are termed shear-frame interacting systems. The linear wind sway of shear frames, when combined with the cantilever parabolic sway of the vertical trusses, produces desirable results in lateral sway efficiency. While the existence of this interaction had been recognized by engineers, it was not until the 1960s that such structures were designed truly accounting for the interaction. Most steel buildings in current design practice in the range up to 30–35 storeys would involve an interacting system of some kind. The usual combination involves core trusses and exterior frames.

The nature of the interaction can only truly be verified with the use of three-dimensional frame analysis programs, now widely available. The floor diaphragm, consisting of the floor slab which connects all frames, will act rigidly in plane to produce consistent lateral and rotational displacement. The deformation of each floor can then be appropriately represented by two lateral displacements and a rotation. The designer can thus allocate wind shears on the basis of relative frame stiffness. Various combinations of trusses and frames can then be evolved to meet the overall stiffness requirements. This has allowed for considerable flexibility in arranging structural components to respond to varieties of demands on shape, grid spacings and structuralist architectural expressions.

In terms of popular usage, the shear truss-frame interacting systems can be considered the basic workhorse system for structures up to about 40 storeys.

15.6 FRAMES WITH VERTICAL, BELT AND OUTRIGGER TRUSSES

The 'frame-vertical truss' systems are two-dimensional

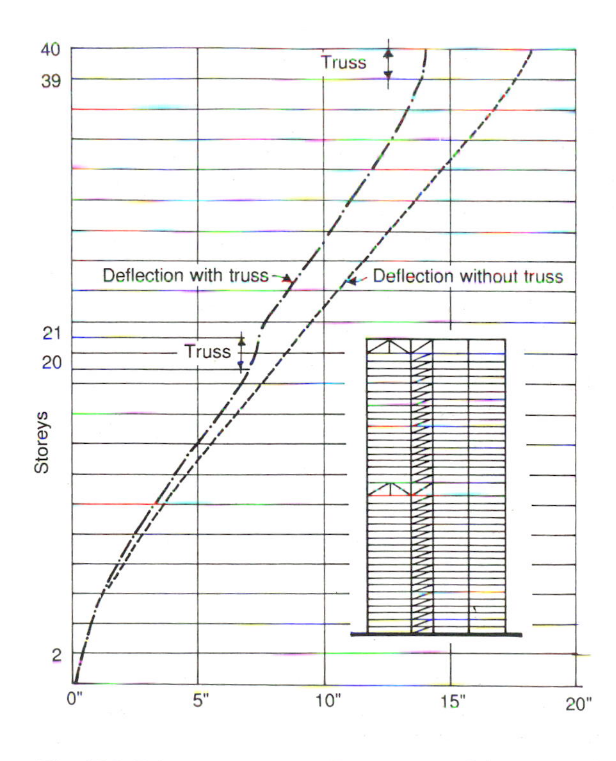

Fig. 15.9 *Belt truss arrangement, First Wisconsin Center, Milwaukee.*

planar frameworks which are arranged to function together to resist gravity and wind forces, with the floor slab diaphragm providing the lateral tie between them. The exterior fascia shear frames and the vertical trusses in the core can be tied together by a system of 'outrigger' and 'belt trusses' generally provided in plant room locations, where these trusses will not interfere with the interior space planning. Fig. 15.9 shows the arrangement of trusses. These horizontal trusses transform the plane frame system into a space frame system. One result of this tie is to induce participation of exterior columns in a cantilever mode and the system can thus be construed as a partial tubular system. The use of belt trusses in the facade planes further induces participation of exterior frames in the cantilever behaviour.

Fig. 15.10 shows an example for a 42 storey structure where the belt trusses and frames have provided the essence of exterior architecture. The building sway under wind can be seen to be significantly affected by the introduction of these trusses. A review of the deflection curve indicates two stiffening effects: one related to the stiffening as a result of belt trusses at plant levels and the other related to overall improvement in performance due to cantilever participation of exterior columns. Improvements in overall stiffness up to 25% can result as compared to the truss-frame system without such outrigger-belt trusses. The effectiveness of the system depends on the number of trussed levels and the depth of the truss at each level.

This system can be economically effective up to 45 storeys. Although this system can be moulded to a different shape, it is most effective for rectilinear prismatic shapes.

15.7 THE FRAMED TUBE [6]

If the facade shear frame is made stronger by closer spacing of columns and wider member proportions, and if such frames are continuous over corners, the overall frame is transformed into a cantilever-framed tube fixed at the ground (Fig. 15.11). The cantilever effectiveness depends on the proportion of the shear frame part of sway deflection. One basic objective is to reduce this component to less than 25% of the total sway so that predominant deformation is that of a cantilever. Because such frames are provided on all four faces of a tower form, one has a hollow tubular configuration and this punched silo form is most efficient in resisting wind forces. Fig. 15.11 also shows the distribution of column axial forces due to cantilever action. The closer the distribution is to that of a fully rigid box, the more efficient will be the system as a cantilever. Shear frame bending of columns and beams introduces 'shear lag' distribution of axial forces. This is a phenomenon which is significant in wide elements such as plated box girders and large tubes, and arises due to 'in-plane' flexibility. Minimization of shear lag is essential for an optimum cantilever tube.

The framed tube system was first introduced in the

Fig. 15.10 *First Wisconsin Center, Milwaukee – belt trusses (architect and engineer SOM). (Ezra Stoller © Esto.)*

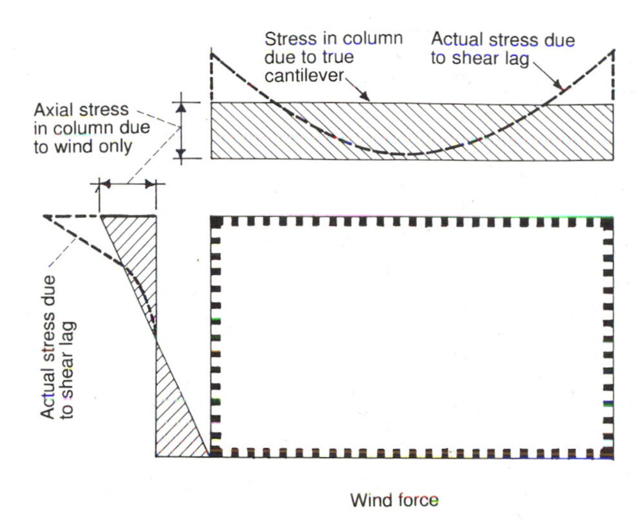

Fig. 15.11 *Framed tube efficiency.*

mid-1960s in reinforced concrete where the dense grid exterior structure can be readily formed, creating the appearance of a punched tube. This was then later adopted for steel tubular buildings. The system, while efficient structurally, had a decided effect on facade architecture which had hitherto been somewhat free from structural restraints. Tubular systems can therefore be termed 'structuralist', in the sense that the exterior frames are exposed, and many tall buildings in steel and concrete have adopted the structural expression of the tube.

Member proportions for framed tubes should be wide for both beams and columns, and joints need to be rigid. In concrete, the rigid joint is achieved by the monolithic nature of in situ concrete construction, whereas in structural steel the joints need to be welded for rigidity and the members built-up for larger widths, both of which have cost implications. The formation of a prefabricated framed tube 'tree' element (Fig. 15.12), where all welding can be done in the

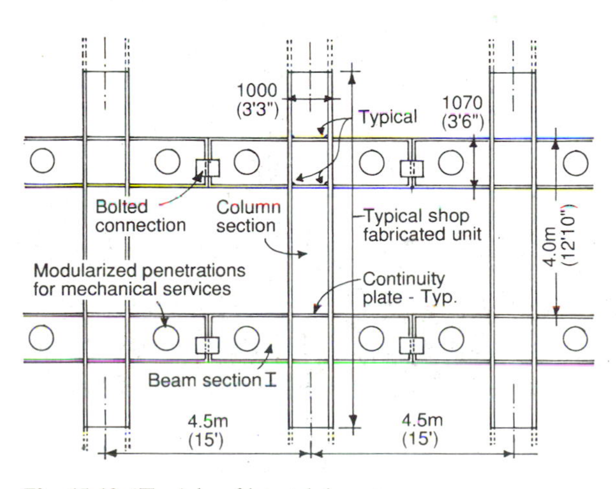

Fig. 15.12 *'Tree' shop fabricated element.*

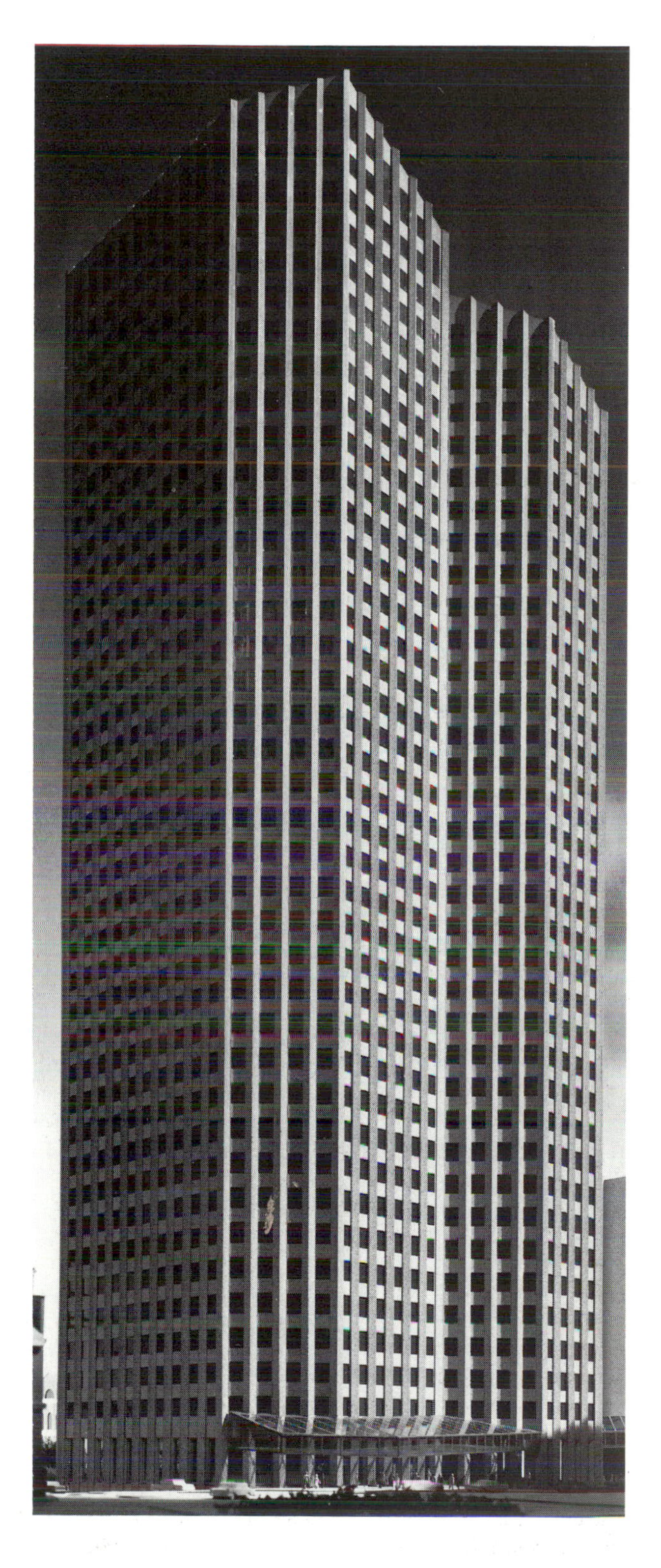

Fig. 15.13 *Sixty State Street, Boston, Massachusetts (architect and engineer SOM). (Ezra Stoller © Esto.)*

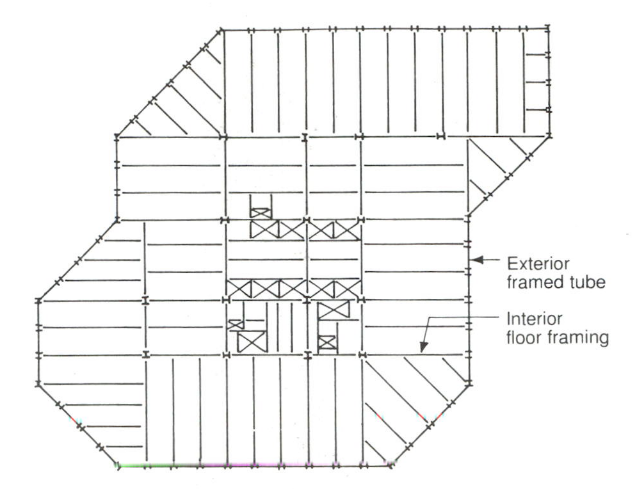

Fig. 15.14 *Sixty State Street, Boston, Massachusetts – framed tube.*

shop in a horizontal position, has made the steel frame tube more practical and efficient. The 'trees' are then erected by bolting at mid-span of the spandrel with minimum welds for column splices. Considerable speed of construction – of the order of three to four storeys a week – can result if 'trees' are used. A recent improvement in steel framed-tube construction in the 40–50 storey range utilizes 900, 825, 750 mm (36, 33, and 30 in) rolled beams as columns. The conventional 14W series columns (USA pattern) are not efficient as frame tube columns and deeper depths are required. The use of deeper beam shapes as columns makes built-up members unnecessary and this fact alone has made application of steel framed-tubes for medium height buildings in the 40–50 storey range economically viable.

Steel framed tube buildings involve column spacings of 3–4.5 m (10–15 ft) on the exterior which can be transferred into wider spacings, if required, at ground level to integrate street level activities. Tubular systems of this type have been extensively used for structures in the range of 30–110 storeys and an outstanding example is that of the World Trade Center in New York. Tubular systems are generally suitable for prismatic vertical profiles. For varying vertical profiles and buildings involving significant fascia offsets, the discontinuity of the tubular frame to fit the shape creates serious disadvantages. The system can however, be readily adapted to a variety of non- rectilinear plan forms.

An excellent example is the Sixty State Street Building (Figs 15.13 and 15.14) in Boston, a 45 storey office tower, configured to give the best fit on site and shaped to preserve sight lines from the existing high-rise buildings in the vicinity. The result was practically a 'free form' shape. The exterior framed tube uses columns at 3 m (10 ft) centres based on a 'tree' type erection unit. All interior framing is simply connected. The system uses a structural steel quantity of 18 pounds per square foot of gross floor area.

15.8 BUNDLED TUBE OR MODULAR TUBE SYSTEM [7]

The need for vertical modulation in a logical fashion has created a new type of tubular structure based on clustering or bundling of smaller size tubes, each of which can rise to different heights. This is typified by the bundled tube system of the Sears Tower in Chicago, composed of nine square plan modules 22.5 × 22.5 m (75 × 75 ft) lumped together (Fig. 15.15) to form the total system. These tubes rise to different heights and are terminated when they are no longer needed architecturally and structurally. The walls of the tube are formed by a set of closely spaced columns, at 4.5 m (15 ft) centres, and deep frame beams. The introduction of framed tube lines on the interior greatly reduces the influence of the shear lag effect which is present in exterior tubes of large peripheral dimensions. The essence of the system was not only to create a powerful structural system but also to create vertical modulation in a logical fashion. The development of a variety of floor sizes and shapes in the same building is considered a positive asset from a valuer's point of view.

The modularity and the conceptual basis of the 'bundled tube' have a broad application. The cells or tubes can be arranged in a variety of ways to create different massing; it can be applied to 30 storeys as well as ultra-tall structures. Furthermore, the shape of each tube itself can be changed to any other closed clustering shape, and examples exist of buildings using triangular and hexagonal units.

15.9 THE DIAGONALIZED TUBE [8]

The most efficient structure for cantilever behaviour is the one represented by an exterior 'diagonalized system'. This was first introduced in the John Hancock Center in Chicago, a multi-use, 100 storey structure (Figs 15.16 and 15.17).

The system is really a trussed tube with each fascia diagonal not only acting as a truss in its plane, but also interacting with the trusses on the perpendicular facades to effect the 'tube' action (Fig. 15.16). A principal advantage of the trussed tube is that it eliminates the need for closely spaced columns of a framed tube. In the John Hancock Center the column spacing on the broad face is 12 m (40 ft) and on the short face 7.5 m (25 ft). Another advantage of this tube is that the interior is freed from wind shear structures, the open plans giving the greatest flexibility in subdivision of space. Interior columns, as required, and simple floor framing complete the system. The 100 storey, 332 m (1107 ft) structure required only 29 lb/ft^2 of gross floor area of structural steel and the sizing of most components was dictated by gravity rather than wind stresses. This meant simpler fabrication and erection techniques, using shop fabrication for connections and conventional site bolting.

The clear discipline of the structure sets the basis for the

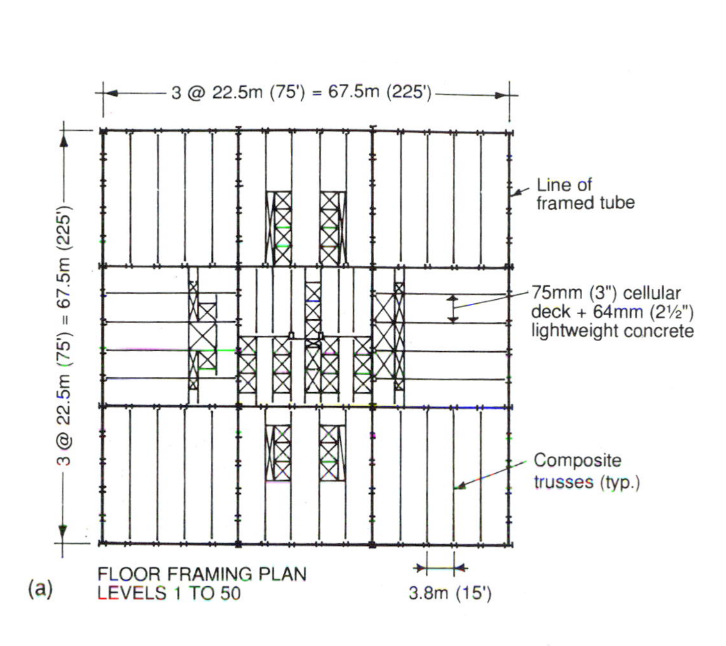

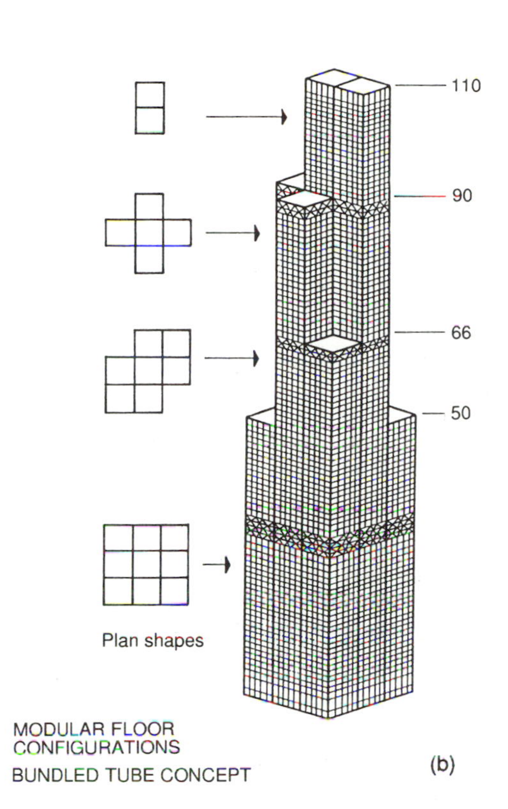

Fig. 15.15 *Bundled tube system, Sears Tower, Chicago. (a) Floor framing plan for levels 1–50. (b) Modular floor configurations.*

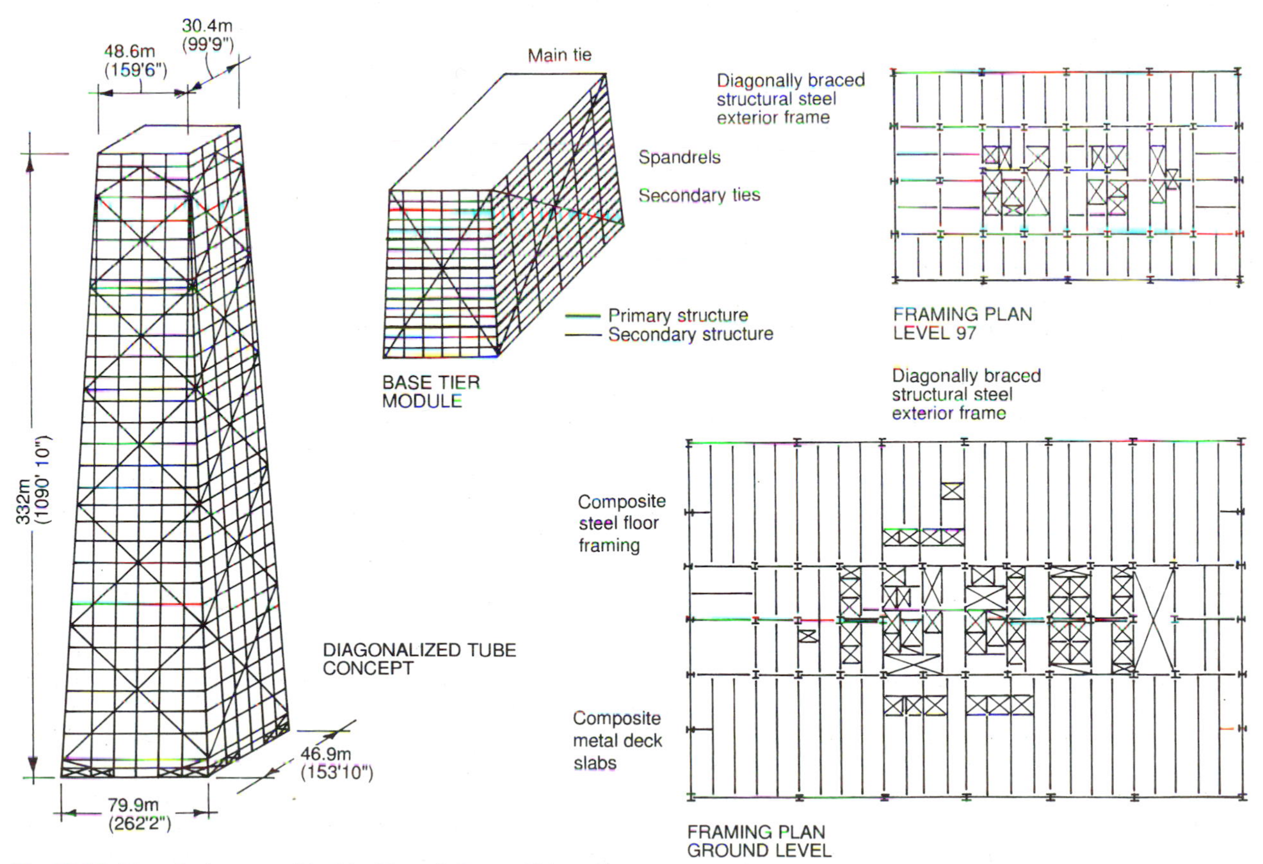

Fig. 15.16 *Trussed tube system, The John Hancock Center, Chicago (for other details, refer to Fig. 36.21).*

(a)

(b)

overall exterior architecture of the building, perhaps the finest tall building completed in the USA.

This system is most efficient for a single exterior closed form, especially the rectilinear shape, and as such, not readily usable where interior tube frame lines are present. In some special cases, the interior diagonals can be organized to suit specific office layouts. The principle of facade diagonals can be readily used for partial tubular concepts. For instance, in long rectangular buildings, the end frames along the short face only may be diagonalized, the long faces comprising framed-tube or shear frame construction. The end diagonalized frame may be a channel or 'C' shape in plan form to provide wind resistance in both directions. The diagonals can also vary from a broad 'X' form to smaller Xs thus transforming each facade into a diagrid braced form. There are many variations, each having its own impact on exterior architecture.

15.10 FORM AND STRUCTURAL SYSTEM

The ability to form and shape a high-rise building is strongly influenced by the structural system. This influence becomes

Fig. 15.17 *The John Hancock Center, Chicago, Illinois, USA 1969 – diagonalized trussed tube (a) exterior view; (b) detail view; (c) interior view (Ezra Stoller © Esto) (architect and engineer SOM).*

(c)

progressively significant as the height of the building increases.

Buildings up to about 20 storeys can be shaped without undue influence of the structure. In the range of 20–40 storeys, one must begin to identify a specific structural system, its composition and efficiency, and the flexibilities for shaping offered by the system. Structures which are 40–60 storeys tall will have more specific restrictions regarding asymmetry of profile and plan. The ability of the system to resist asymmetrical gravity loads and resultant torsions determines its effectiveness. Structures beyond 60 storeys are more decidedly affected by the structure. The primary structural concern is to develop sufficient lateral stiffness. Structures which utilize the building facade will be prime candidates to meet these structural needs, and this will affect the ability to shape the exterior. In addition, structures in this height range are affected by the aerodynamic character of the shape, as well as stiffness considerations dealing with human perception of wind motion which is measured in terms of the acceleration levels and change of accelerations. The dynamic properties of the structure, such as its natural period of vibration and mechanical damping, need to be evaluated with respect to the dynamic behaviour of the structure.

The systems selection process allows for considerable latitude in the choice of an appropriate system which is suited to a particular building. Recognition of the merits of different systems together with enhanced abilities to perform complex three-dimensional computerized structural analyses have made it possible to design varieties of symmetric and unsymmetric forms.

Vierendeel rigid frames generally conform to rectilinear shapes. Since these frames are provided in two orthogonal directions, buildings can be stepped back or offset along frame lines. Similarly, buildings can be stepped back in profile along frame lines. If the building volume is composed of three-dimensional rectilinear frames, varieties of plan and profile stepped forms can be created.

For non-rectilinear shapes, the frames are generally withdrawn to the interior of the building with secondary gravity framing provided to form the exterior shape.

Structural systems which utilize only the building core offer considerable flexibility of external shaping. These systems use core shear walls or vertical trusses in the core. They are obviously limited by the available dimensions of the conventionally designed core. However, considerable potential exists for unconventional core designs which will provide deep enough shear walls or core bracings so that all lateral resistance can be obtained in the core even in the 40–70 storey range. This obviously will provide considerable flexibility for exterior shaping.

Exterior tubular structures offer considerable potential for shaping buildings in plan because of their large torsional resistance. A variety of plan forms can therefore be created. The example of Sixty State Street (Fig. 15.14) illustrates the point. Tubular systems constitute an equivalent of an exterior bearing wall system and therefore frequently spaced out-of-plane vertical offsets are not easily accommodated. Some forms of gradual profile transitions can, however, be accommodated without affecting the structural integrity of the total system.

Bundled tube systems, just by their very composition, allow for vertical modulation along tubular lines. The modularity of the system allows for bundling of any number of cells or units required to meet the needs of space and profile.

Diagonally braced tubular systems are highly geometric and demand a great deal of discipline in shaping. They are generally suited to rectilinear prismatic or tapered forms.

15.11 SEISMIC DESIGN CONSIDERATIONS

Seismic design of tall buildings is influenced by the dynamic behaviour of the building due to ground motions of the earthquake and the strength and ductility of the structural system, which are indicators of the ability of the system to absorb energy and survive. The seismic criteria are superimposed on the conventional design for wind and gravity forces. In contrast to wind pressures which are externally applied, seismic motion generates internal forces due to vibration of the building. Performance under seismic conditions depends upon the building mass, its size and shape and its dynamic properties. The other principal factors to be studied are the physical character of the site, the seismic history, its stratigraphy and related geotechnical dynamic properties.

Ductility – that is the ability to sustain large deformations – is a primary property to be considered in determining an appropriate system for any high-rise building. This is influenced by the ductility of the members and joints, and the composition of the members. Clearly the material characteristics are very important in this context, and ductile materials such as steel are well suited where seismic resistance is required. Joint ductility is related to the ability of a joint to absorb large deformations.

Flexural systems in which bending of members is the primary action are more ductile than braced systems involving axially loaded members. Vierendeel frames are therefore most commonly employed in seismic regions. Varieties of dual framing systems which combine vertical trusses with ductile moment resisting frames must be designed for at least 25% of the imposed seismic forces. Other dual combinations may involve reinforced concrete walls and ductile moment-resisting frames. In general, seismic design codes imply that the less the ductility, the more the imposed lateral seismic force. Certain brittle systems may not be permissible for buildings taller than certain limiting heights.

Framed tube systems are special cases of ductile moment-resisting frames where the proportions of the beams and columns of the frame are adjusted to ensure the formation of plastic hinges in beams rather than columns so as to maintain the ductile behaviour of the system. Such framed tubes have been used for structures up to 60 storeys in regions of high seismic risk. Pure diagonally braced systems, even though highly efficient for wind resistance, suffer from the disadvantage of having insufficient ductility and therefore may not be permissible. Eccentric braced frames, where the diagonal member is made eccentric with respect to the joint so that the member axial force is transmitted by shear in the beam member, are efficient under seismic action. They develop the stiffness of the diagonally braced frame, but induce ductility at the joints. Concrete shear walls tend to be brittle and often need to be combined with another more ductile system.

Configuration irregularities create two basic kinds of problem. They are related to torsional response and stress concentrations in the system due to sudden changes in lateral stiffness. Both these conditions are undesirable, particularly where the design needs to provide for seismic action.

The primary impact of earthquake risks on architectural design relates to overall massing, shaping and profile changes. Abrupt changes in profile or volume are detrimental, as are building frames where major load transfer occurs. Frames involving diagonal structural components need to be carefully evaluated with respect to ductility and may well have serious limitations under seismic conditions. Finally, earthquakes also affect non-structural elements, particularly external cladding, which should be designed for lateral forces proportional to their mass.

15.12 THE DESIGN PROCESS

The structural systems used currently often borrow and combine elements from various previous systems, if they can be utilized efficiently to suit the needs of a specific project. Combinations may involve framed tubes of various shapes, vertical trusses, belt-trusses, tube-in-tubes, braced tubes and bundled tube systems. A variety of systems can be created in this way. In fact, the combination may involve reinforced concrete components for a variety of mixed steel/concrete systems, such as the composite tubular systems and the concrete core braced steel system. The composite tubular system combines an exterior reinforced concrete framed tube, with its closely spaced columns, and simple structural steel framing for the interior. The objective is to utilize the rigidity of concrete in resisting wind forces, with the ability of steelwork to span long distances creating a light interior structure. The absence of rigid connections on the interior eliminates the need for expensive welded steel connections and the elimination of reinforced concrete from interior framing results in a speed of construction comparable with that for an all steel structure. The exterior concrete can be moulded to any overall configuration of the building, and shaping of external members makes possible different architectural articulations.

In contrast, reinforced concrete can be employed to form a shear wall core to resist all wind forces, steelwork being used for the facades and interconnecting floor frames. This system is commonly used and is considered further in chapters 16 and 18.

15.13 CURRENT STATE OF THE ART

Future high-rise structures will involve a variety of forms and shapes and will demand considerable flexibility for creating exciting habitable and multiple use spaces. Simple and efficient solutions are possible provided that the 'rationale' of the structure is respected, the designer needing to conceive the frame as a three-dimensional arrangement resisting gravity and lateral forces. Computer-aided design has considerably advanced the speed in comparing engineering solutions. The challenge is to combine these advances with architectural development. Those specialists who combine architects and engineers within a single team have clear advantages over the traditional basis of separate professions working at arm's length. Computerized analysis has reduced the cost of engineering design and has clearly assisted in the promotion of more venturesome forms to comply with the greater variety and shaping demanded by designers. The real engineering challenge is the accommodation of a much wider range of building uses than dreamed of in the days of the UN Building, New York, where separate functions were housed in separate units. Today's mega blocks need 'transfer' structures and very sophisticated framing to encompass a range of volumes not dreamed of 40 years ago.

In the design process, the real event is the system selection process. While varieties of systems can be selected on the basis of structural efficiency, the real process involves a variety of disciplines including architects, clients, consulting engineers, contractors and service engineers. This process may start with conceptual, philosophical discussions by designers, soon to be evaluated on the basis of alternatives for the total building system. It should be recalled that what may be most efficient in a structural sense may not be effective as a total building solution. This is more the case in the present design process where flexibility and variety and to some extent, subjective aesthetic criteria on the part of planners, designers and clients, may dictate structural form and system. Under these terms each concept should be checked out with a variety of constructional systems using methods which take account of the availability of materials, building economics and above all constructability. In order to aid this process, the design leaders, both architect and engineer, need a wide knowledge of systems and an ability to appraise their efficiencies.

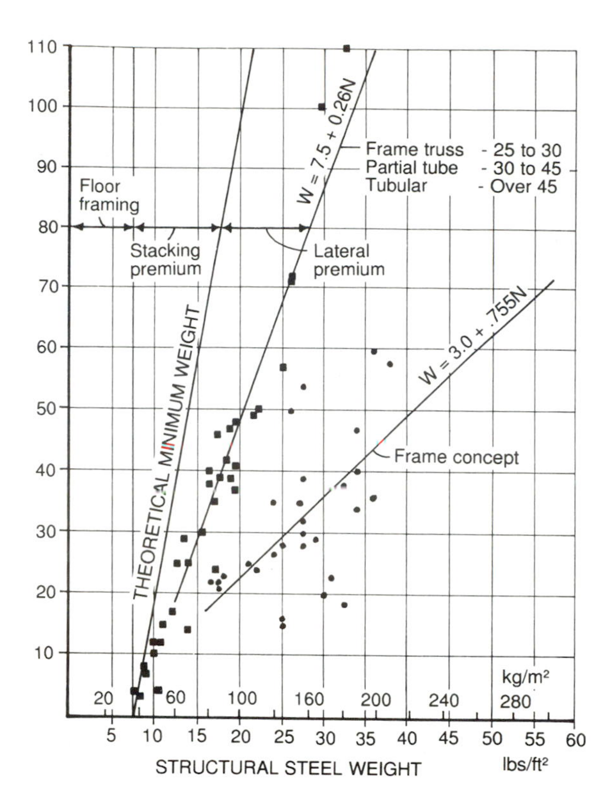

Fig. 15.18 *Systems weight chart.*

In steel framework the basic relationship between the amount of steel employed measured against the unit floor area is a crucial parameter [9, 10]. General details are shown in Fig. 15.18 in which the line depicting the theoretical minimum weight is for gravity loads only without the influence of lateral wind loads. This is composed of a constant floor framing component and an escalating stacking or column component. On this chart are plotted steel quantities for various existing steel systems up to 110 storeys. Two trend lines can be detected, one relating to shear frame buildings and the other which fits the system methodology already outlined. There is a wide divergence in detail when one considers the frame line; this is due to sensitivity to factors such as bay spans, numbers of bays and site geometry. By comparison, cantilever towers have much tighter parameters, since their geometric formulation is controlled to achieve effectiveness of the cantilever principle.

This chart not only aids a designer in the appropriate selection of a system, but also indicates generally the impact of system selection. Once systems are selected, each may be studied with respect to a second series of factors; these involve column spacings, floor spans, ability to fit a certain modulated profile, core layout and facade treatment. The first stages in structural design will use the 'experience base' in order to quantify the structural parameters and materials.

After selection of one or two systems, the design proceeds to a third stage. In each stage, the design is more refined and addresses more specific design criteria. As the stages progress, more input is required from the fabricators and erectors in the evaluation process.

Extensive computerization involving three-dimensional frames and a final depiction of steel members together with joint details and criteria is undertaken in the final design. This will usually result in a steel bid set of drawings, which, after successful completion of the bidding process, will be used to order steel and prepare construction and shop drawings.

An engineer's analytical abilities should extend to systematic appraisal and methodology by use of the latest computer aided process. However, all these qualities for analysis are no replacement for conceptual skills in arriving at an elegant structural design which typifies the true art of engineering high-rise buildings.

APPENDIX A. COMPARISON OF STEEL AND CONCRETE FRAMED BUILDINGS

(a) Steel frame

Summary of selected data *Building*	*Building height (ft)/ number of floors*	*Building width/ Building height (ratio)*	*Useable area/ gross area (%)*	*Dimensions of a typical framing bay*	*Typical beam depth/ span (ratio)*	*Mechanical equipment and shaft area/ gross floor area (%)*	*HVAC shaft area/ gross floor area (%)*	*Usable height/ Total floor height (%)*	*Glass area/ facade area (%)*	*Number of elevators/ number of floors (ratio)*
Seagram Building New York, USA	516/40	1/4.5	73	27′-9″ × 27′-9″	1/20.8	14.5	2.2	74	72	1/2.2
Knight of Columbus New Haven, USA	319/24	1/2.4	66	10′-0″ × 35′-10″	1/20.5	14.6	2.5	66	91	1/3.8
One Liberty Plaza New York, USA	728/56	1/4.5	74	46′-8″ × 47′-6″	1/21.1	13.8	2.3	68	41	1/1.4
Chase Manhattan New York, USA	813/61	1/6.9	76	29′-0″ × 33′-3″ & 42′-11″	1/18.5	13.2	3.0	70	58	1/1.4
Boston Company Boston, USA	536/41	1/3.8	78	9′-4″ × 42′-0″	1/24	10.2	2.0	71	46	1/2.1
Westcoast Transmission Vancouver, Canada	180/17	Core 1/6.0 Bldg 1/1.6	88	12′-0″ × 36′-0″	1/26.7	5.0	1.4	72	41	1/3.8
US Steel Pittsburgh, USA	841/64	1/3.7	72	13′-0″ × 48′-0″	1/22.3	12.6	3.3	72	24	1/1.2
Citicorp New York, USA	915/56	1/5.8	80	38′-0″ × 38′-0″	1/24.0	10.0	1.8	67	46	1/2.2
Averages/Steel Frame Building		1/4.7	76		1/22.2	11.7	2.3	70	52	1/2.3

(b) Concrete frame

Summary of selected data / Building	Building height (ft)/ number of floors	Building width/ Building height (ratio)	Usable area/ gross area (%)	Dimensions of a typical framing bay	Typical beam depth/ span (ratio)	Mechanical equipment and shaft area/ gross floor area (%)	HVAC shaft area/ gross floor area (%)	Usable height/ total floor height (%)	Glass area/ facade area (%)	Number of elevators/ number of floors (ratio)
CBS New York, USA	491/38	1/3.6	71	2′-6″ × 35′-0″	1/24.7	8.3	1.9	69	37	1/2.2
One Shell Plaza Houston, USA	685/50	1/4.9	03	6′-0″ × 37′-2″	1/18.6	5.3	1.2	69	39	1/2.1
Richards Medical Labs Philadelphia, USA	96/8	1/2.0	71	47′-4″ × 47′-4″	1/14.2	11.2	8.4	71	35	1/2.7
Hoffmann-La Roche Nutley, New Jersey, USA	113/8	1/0.87	73	41′-6″ × 41′-6″	1/20.8	5.3	3.0	71	71	1/2.7
Yale Art Gallery New Haven, USA	52/4½	1/.63	83	19′-9″ × 40′-0″	1/15.8	4.1	0.9	80	47	1/4
M.I.T. Earth Science Lab Cambridge, USA	275/21	1/5.0	74	9′-0″ × 48′-4″	1/13.8	9.3	3.0	70	23	1/6.3
American Life Willmington, Delaware, USA	283/23	1/4.3	73	6′-0″ × 72′-9″	1/23.4	10.8	2.8	71	22	1/7.0
Cornell Agronomy Lab Ithaca, USA	136/12	1/1.5	62	8′-6″ × 41′-2″	1/22.5	14.0	8.4	81	10	1/6.0
Averages/Concrete Frame Buildings		1/2.9	74		1/19.2	8.5	3.7	73	36	1/4.1
Averages/All Case Studies		1/3.8	75		1/20.7	10.1	3.0	71	44	1/3.2

REFERENCES AND TECHNICAL NOTES

1. Mujicha, F. (1929) *History of the Skyscraper*. Archaeology and Architecture Press. Property of the American Institute of Steel Construction.
2. Bethlehem Steel Corporation (1939) *Origin of the Skyscraper*. Report of the Committee Appointed by the Trustees of the Estate of Marshall Field for the Examination of the Structure of the Home Insurance Building by Ralph Fletcher Seymour.
3. Khan, F. (1967) Nature of high rise buildings. *Inland Architect*, July.
4. Iyengar, H. (1986) *Structural and Steel Systems*. Techniques and Aesthetics in the Design of Tall Buildings (Fazlur Khan Memorial Session), Institute for the Study of High-Rise Habitat.
5. Iyengar, H. (1972) *Preliminary Design and Optimisation of Steel Building Systems*. State of the Art Report No. 3, Technical Committee No. 14: Elastic Design, American Society of Civil Engineers – International Association for Bridge and Structural Engineering Joint Committee on Tall Buildings, August.
6. Iyengar, H. (1984) *Steel Systems for High-Rise Buildings*. International conference on Steel Structures, Singapore, March 7–19.

7. Iyengar, H. and Khan, F. (1973) *Structural Steel Design of Sears Tower*. Conference on Steel Developments, Australian Institute of Steel Construction, Newcastle, Australia, May 21–25.
8. Iyengar, H. (1973) *Structural Systems for Two Ultra High-Rise Structures* Australian and New Zealand Conference on Planning and Design of Tall Buildings, Sydney, Australia, August.
9. Halvorsen, R. (1988) *Efficiency and Design of Tall Buildings* presented to Structures Group, Metropolitan Section of American Society of Civil Engineers, Tall Building Seminar, January 25.
10. Picardi, A. (1972) *The Standard Oil* AISC Modern Steel Construction, first quarter.

FURTHER READING

Professional Handbook of Building Construction
Fundamentals of Building Construction Edward Allen (1985) published by John Wiley and Sons.

Design and Technology in Architecture David Guise (1991) published by Van Nostrand Rheinhold, New York.

Steel frame with decking stacked. No. 1 Finsbury Avenue 1985 (architect and engineer Arup Associates).

Concrete topping to decking units.

16

Composite floors and structures

Roger Plank and Anthony Gregson

16.1 INTRODUCTION

In current structural engineering practice, the term 'composite construction' has come to have the specific meaning of steel and concrete components (beams, decking and slabs) connected together in such a way that they behave as a single structural unit. In a more general sense composite construction can refer to the use of different materials within a structure to take advantage of their particular qualities, and these buildings can be referred to as 'composite structures'. In this chapter, both aspects will be considered.

16.2 COMPOSITE CONSTRUCTION FOR BEAMS AND SLABS

Different structural materials possess different characteristics. For instance, concrete and brickwork are relatively cheap bulk materials but have limited strength and are rather brittle, whilst steel is very strong and ductile. In order to maximize the respective benefits of these different materials, they are often used in combination. Perhaps the most common example is reinforced concrete in which the tensile strength and ductility are derived from the steel while the concrete provides the compressive strength. Reinforced masonry, although less common, acts in a similar way. Timber flitch beams and steel rods as ties in timber trusses are yet other examples. This combination of materials can be used in all types of structural elements, including slabs and beams.

One structural form which is very popular for beams has evolved from the conventional arrangement of a steel beam supporting a concrete slab. Under normal conditions these will behave independently. However, by ensuring that the two remain in intimate contact the slab can make a significant contribution to the bending strength of the beam. This arrangement is similar, in principle, to a reinforced concrete T-beam and is illustrated in Fig. 16.1. When the term 'composite construction' is used without qualification it generally refers to this form of structure.

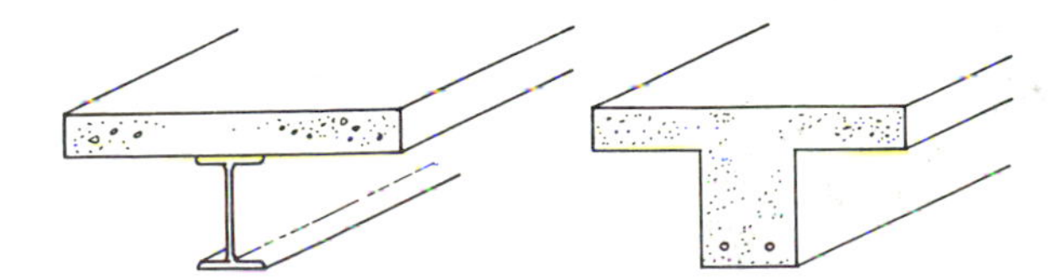

Fig. 16.1 *Composite beams compared with RC beam.*

As a result of the contribution of the slab to the bending strength of the composite beam, the steel section sizes used will be appreciably smaller. This provides direct economy in the tonnage of steelwork used, and may also give indirect economies due to a decrease in the construction depth of the floor. These advantages are obtained at the relatively small

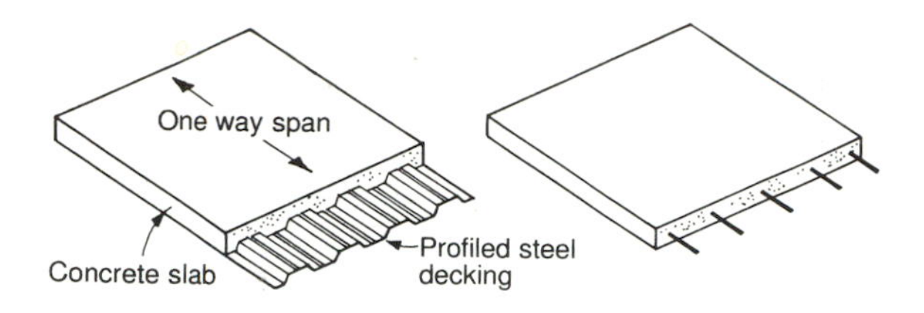

Fig. 16.2 *Composite floor compared with RC slab.*

cost of providing the connection between steel beam and concrete slab.

For slabs, the choice has traditionally been between precast units or some form of in situ construction. However, one form of composite floor has become very popular, offering the advantages of speed, safety and efficiency of construction. This consists of profiled steel sheeting with a concrete topping as shown in Fig. 16.2. The structural behaviour is similar in principle to that of a reinforced concrete slab, with the sheeting acting as the reinforcement. Profile heights are usually in the range 38–75 mm (1½–3 in) and slab thicknesses above the profile typically vary between 65 mm and 120 mm (2½ and 5 in) providing a maximum span of about 3.5 m (12 ft).

16.3 THE PRINCIPLES OF COMPOSITE ACTION

The principle of composite beam behaviour can be illustrated with reference to a pair of timber joists. If these are simply placed one on top of the other and loaded as a beam, there will be some relative movement between the two as shown in Fig. 16.3. Both joists will contribute independently to the bending strength which will simply be the sum of the strengths of the two joists. If each joist has a breadth b and depth d the bending strength of each can be quantified as:

$$bd^2/6$$

and hence the combined strength is simply double this quantity:

$$bd^2/3$$

If the joists are now connected together, say by spiking them at regular intervals or by gluing, the two will act together as a single unit with a depth of $2d$ as shown in Fig. 16.4.

The bending strength of the beam then becomes

$$b(2d)^2/6 = 2bd^2/3$$

representing a doubling of the previous strength of the unconnected joists.

In traditional construction of steel framed buildings the steel beam and concrete slab which it supports are not positively connected. The contribution of the slab to the strength of the beam is generally small and can be ignored. Consequently, the steel section alone is used to determine

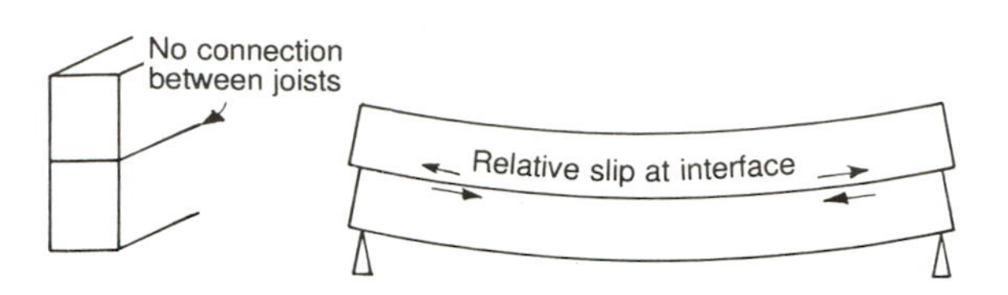

Fig. 16.3 *Independent behaviour of unconnected timber joists.*

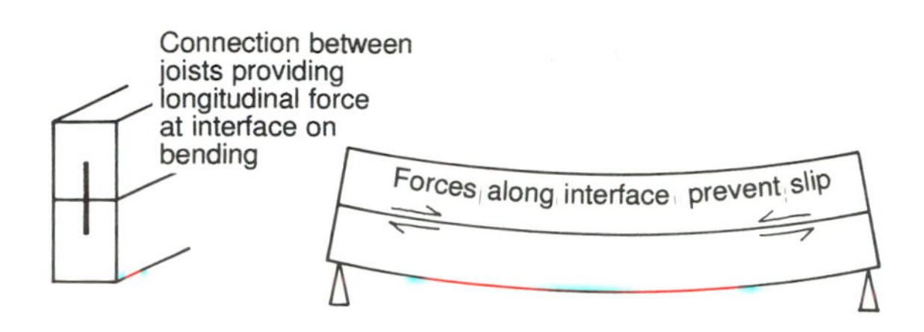

Fig. 16.4 *Connected timber joists acting as a single deep beam.*

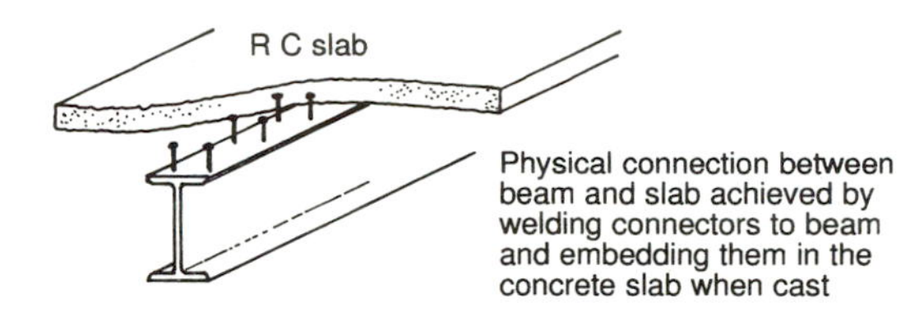

Fig. 16.5 *Connection between steel beam and concrete slab.*

the beam strength and stiffness. If the slab and steel beam are now connected as illustrated in Fig. 16.5, preventing any slip between the two, the strength will be increased as it was in the case of the timber joists.

Precisely how much better a composite beam is compared with the same beam used non-compositely depends upon the beam size and the slab details. However, it is likely that improvements of between 25% and 50% will be achieved. This means that composite beams are correspondingly lighter than non-composite beams for the same span and loading conditions.

16.3.1 Design principles

The philosophy of designing composite beams is to utilize the implicit strength of the concrete slab which is to be used for the floor. The form and thickness of this will have been determined by its functional requirements as a slab, taking account of the span between supporting beams and loadings. The sizing of the composite beam therefore starts with the thickness of the slab predetermined, and the process is to select a suitable steel cross-section (normally a universal beam) which, in conjunction with the slab, will satisfy the requirements of the beam in terms of strength and stiffness. The principal aspects of the behaviour of the composite beam which need to be considered in this respect are bending strength, the adequacy of the connection between the slab and beam, and its deflection performance.

16.3.2 Bending performance

The bending strength of a composite beam is dependent upon the strength and dimensions of the concrete slab and the steel beam. A reasonable estimate of the ultimate bending strength of the composite beam, M_u, is given by:

$$M_u = p_Y \cdot A_s(D + h_c)/2$$

where p_Y is the design strength of the steel beam,
A_s is the cross-sectional area of the steel beam,
D is depth of the steel beam, and
h_c is the thickness of the slab.

The total depth of the composite beam can be estimated by assuming a span:depth ratio of about 15. Thus

$$(D + h_c) = L/15$$

Given the thickness of the slab, it is then possible to select a universal beam section which satisfies both the above equations, providing a reasonable first estimate for the composite beam prior to a more rigorous calculation.

16.3.3 Connection between slab and beam

Composite action is clearly dependent upon the steel and concrete acting in concert. The connection between the two is normally achieved by headed studs, typically 19 mm (¾ in) in diameter, which are welded to the top flange of the beam and become bonded to the concrete. A typical detail is illustrated in Fig. 16.6. Note that studs may be arranged in pairs or singly (for beams with narrow flanges) at regular intervals along the length of the beam as shown.

The detailed design of the connection is clearly important. In particular, it is necessary that sufficient shear connectors are provided to prevent slippage along the interface, and the concrete is able to accommodate the high localized stresses transmitted by these connectors. These considerations will depend upon details such as the concrete strength, type of stud connector used and the slab thickness.

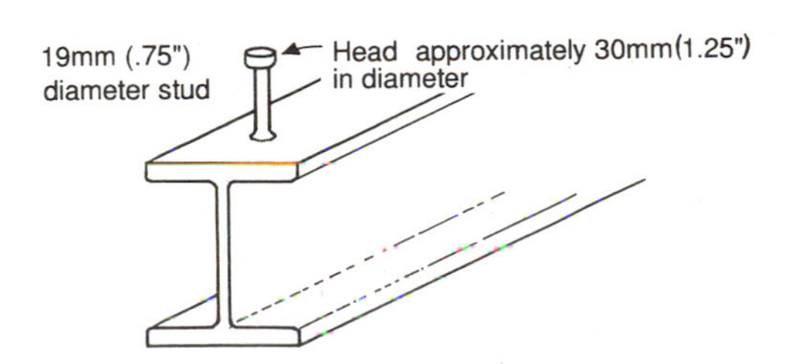

Fig. 16.6 *Typical stud connector.*

Fig. 16.7 *Principles of transformed sections.*

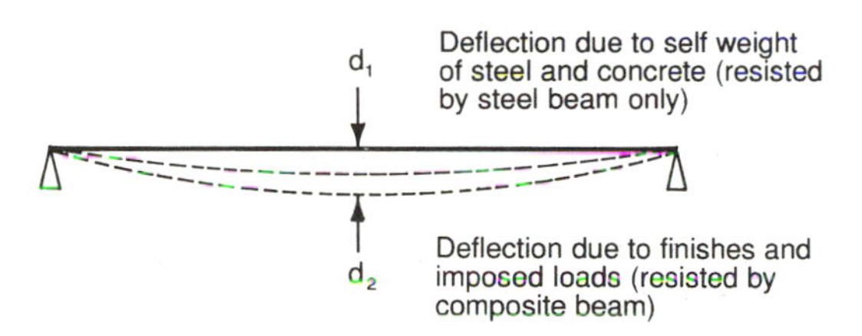

Fig. 16.8 *Accumulation of deflections on composite beams.*

16.3.4 Deflections of composite beams

Deflections of composite beams can be calculated using the principle of transformed sections. In this the concrete flange is replaced by an equivalent width of steel, in inverse proportion to the Young's Moduli for the two materials as shown in Fig. 16.7. This enables the second moment of area of the transformed section to be calculated. The deflection can then be determined as if the beam were composed entirely of steel.

As an alternative, satisfactory deflection performance can be ensured by limiting the ratio of the length of span of the beam to its overall depth.

Clearly, composite action is only achieved after the concrete has hardened. The deflection due to the self weight of the concrete and steel, d_1, is therefore sustained by the steel beam alone and should be calculated on the basis of the second moment of area of the steel section. Any finishes will normally be applied after composite action has been achieved, and the deflection due to these and imposed loads, d_2, should be determined on the basis of the transformed section. The total deflection sustained by the beam is then the sum of the two deflections, d_1 and d_2. This is shown in Fig. 16.8.

The use of temporary propping will reduce the total deflection although this can be a considerable inconvenience and result in less efficient construction.

16.4 ALTERNATIVE FORMS OF CONSTRUCTION

The behaviour of composite beams described above relates to simply supported beams and in situ solid concrete slabs. Where other forms are used this may be slightly modified, although the principles and advantages of composite action remain.

Precast concrete slabs can be used in composite construction, but there may be difficulties in effecting the connection between beam and slab, and in achieving continuity across individual slabs. Adequate containment for the connectors within the slab is normally achieved by leaving pockets or a continuous gap for the connectors as shown in Fig. 16.9. These are infilled with in situ concrete, providing a bond between the connectors and the precast units. Careful detailing is needed to ensure that this bond is achieved and that there is adequate bearing for the precast slab.

Structural continuity between adjacent precast units is necessary to accommodate the compressive force along the length of the composite beam. Since the units are laid individually, this can only be ensured by the use of an in situ topping and some types of unit, such as those with voids, may not be suitable.

The use of thin precast concrete decks with a relatively thick in situ concrete topping effectively overcomes both of these difficulties.

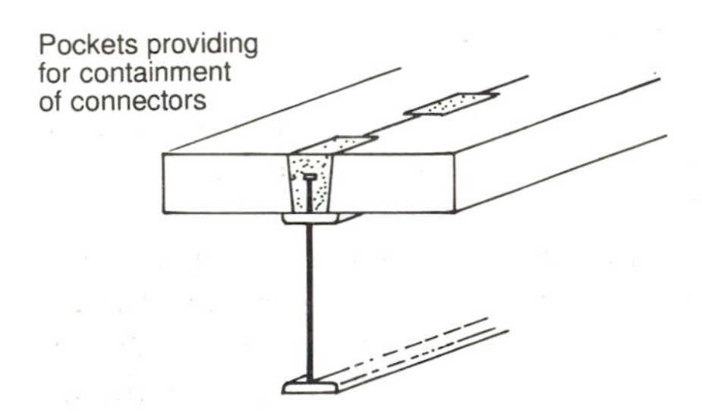

Fig. 16.9 *Using precast units in composite construction.*

Fig. 16.10 *Through-deck welding of stud connectors.*

Fig. 16.11 *Composite beam with composite floor.*

Composite floors, which are described below, are commonly used in conjunction with composite beams. Because of the need to lay the profiled steel sheets over the steel beams, the stud connectors cannot be fitted during fabrication. Instead, a system of 'through-deck welding' is normally adopted. This involves a semi-automatic welding procedure as shown in Fig. 16.10, which effectively fixes the stud and decking to the flange of the beam.

The design of the composite beam is largely unaffected, although it may be difficult to accommodate sufficient shear connectors. These can only be fitted where the profiled sheet is in contact with the steel beam, that is in the troughs of the profile as seen in Fig. 16.11. Where this applies, the interaction between the slab and steel beam is partial and the calculated bending strength of the composite beam must therefore be reduced.

16.5 COMPOSITE STEEL DECK FLOORS

Composite steel deck floors are one-way spanning slabs in which the compressive strength is provided by in situ concrete and the tensile strength derives from profiled steel sheeting. This also serves as the shuttering for the wet concrete during construction. This form of construction has become very popular and further details can be found in [1] and [2].

The sheeting is of thin gauge, typically 0.9 mm or 1.2 mm (35 or 48 thou) thick, and is therefore galvanized to provide corrosion protection. A number of companies manufacture

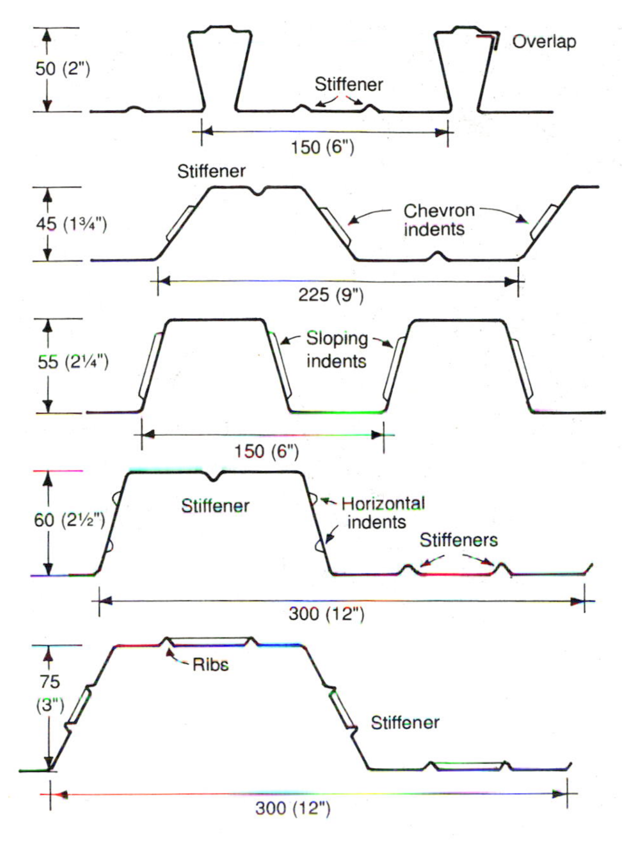

Fig. 16.12 *Typical sections for composite floor sheets.*

steel sheeting for this purpose and a range of profiles is therefore available. Some typical sections are shown in Fig. 16.12.

16.5.1 Designing composite floors

In designing composite floors it is necessary to ensure that strength and deflections both during construction (when the concrete is wet) and in service (when composite action has been achieved) are satisfactory. The following must therefore be checked:

(a) Bending strength of the steel sheeting to ensure that the weight of wet concrete can be supported during construction, before composite action has been developed;
(b) Flexural stiffness of the sheeting to prevent excessive deflections during construction;
(c) Tensile strength of the sheeting to provide the necessary reinforcement to the slab in its final composite form;
(d) Strength of the concrete in compression for which the floor is considered as an equivalent reinforced concrete slab;
(e) Stiffness of the composite slab to prevent excessive deflection under normal working loads;
(f) Bond between the concrete and the steel in order to achieve composite action.

Items (a) and (b) are concerned with the cross-sectional details of the sheeting, the strength and stiffness being derived from the profiling. The appropriate loading condition is the weight of wet concrete and an allowance for construction loads.

For items (c) to (f), normal loading conditions (dead and imposed) apply. The strength and stiffness of the slab are dependent on the overall depth of the composite floor, whilst the provision of ribs within the steel sheeting in the longitudinal direction ensures a good key with the concrete.

Because of the need to satisfy the various conditions outlined above, and the complexity of certain aspects of the behaviour of this structural form, the design of composite floors is normally based upon manufacturers' data. The critical parameters in this are span, thickness of concrete, imposed load intensity, and whether or not temporary props are used

The tabulated information takes account of all possible failure modes. Typically, the critical conditions are the bending strength of the steel during construction and deflections of the composite floor in service. There is thus a contradiction in the design – a thick topping of concrete provides an increase in stiffness of the composite slab, but also adds more load to the non-composite section during construction. The use of design tables, however, enables a simple selection to be made. Table 16.1 shows permissible spans for a typical 50 mm (2 in) deep profile.

Table 16.1 Permissible spans in metres (feet) according to BS 5950 for typical 50 mm (2 in) deep profile of thickness t and slab depth 100 mm (4 in)

Support condition	*Imposed loading kN/m² (lb/ft²)*					
	t = *0.9 mm*			t = *1.2 mm*		
	2.5 (50)	5.0 (100)	7.5 (150)	2.5 (50)	5.0 (100)	7.5 (150)
Single span (no props)	2.3 (46)	2.3 (46)	2.3 (46)	2.8 (56)	2.8 (56)	2.8 (56)
Multi-span (no props)	2.3 (46)	2.3 (46)	2.3 (46)	2.7 (54)	2.7 (54)	2.7 (54)
Single span (one prop)	4.5 (90)	3.9 (78)	3.3 (66)	5.1 (102)	4.1 (82)	3.6 (72)
Multi-span (+ props)	4.6 (92)	4.0 (80)	3.4 (68)	5.1 (102)	4.1 (82)	3.6 (72)

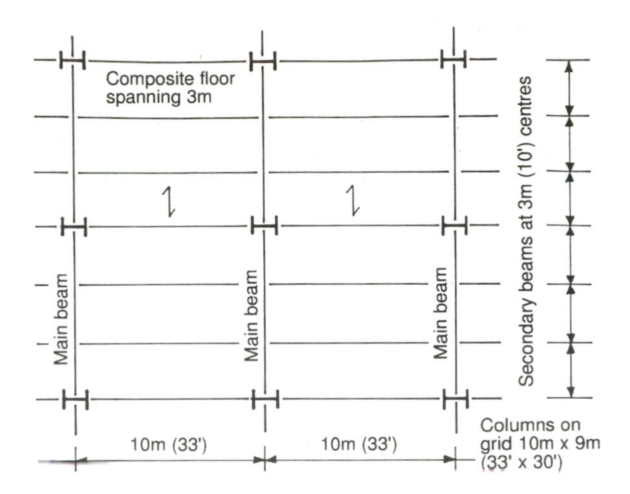

Fig. 16.13 *Typical arrangement of supporting structure.*

16.5.2 Supporting structure

Composite floors are invariably used in conjunction with steel beams for the supporting structure. Because of the problems of deflection and strength during construction, greatest efficiency is gained when the slabs span a relatively short distance. Typically this may be about 3 m, depending upon the particular profile and design conditions. This does not imply such a closely spaced grid of columns. Instead, a system of secondary beams is usually adopted. These may span up to 10 m (33 ft) or more, enabling large column-free spaces to be achieved. A typical arrangement is shown in Fig. 16.13.

The decking can be fixed to the supporting steel beams using shot-fired pins, self-tapping screws or welding. Lateral restraint to the steel framed structure can be achieved by ensuring that sufficient fixings are used. Where composite construction is required, shear studs are normally welded through the deck as described in section 16.4.

16.5.3 Lightweight concrete

In order to reduce loads both during construction and in service, use is often made of lightweight concrete. This may have a unit weight of as little as 15 kN/m^3 (95 lb/ft^2) compared with that for normal weight concrete of 24 kN/m^3 (150 lb/ft^2). However, use of very lightweight concrete can result in difficulties in fixing mesh reinforcement in the top of the slab, and typically an intermediate weight, say 19 kN/m^3 (120 lb/ft^2), will be used.

16.5.4 Secondary reinforcement

Where the slab crosses supports the bending moments and hence the bending stresses, become reversed. Under these circumstances the concrete becomes stressed in tension and it is therefore necessary to provide conventional reinforcement to accommodate this.

As concrete cures there is a natural tendency for it to shrink. To avoid cracks developing on the surface of the slab due to this shrinkage, anti-crack reinforcement, in the form of a relatively light mesh of steel bars, should be provided.

16.5.5 Fire rating

The composite floor must provide satisfactory performance in terms of stability, integrity and insulation in the event of fire. The last of these is simply dependent upon the thickness of the slab, whilst the integrity is generally ensured by the sheeting. This acts as a shield to the concrete and helps to contain and control spalling. The stability of the structure, that is its ability to avoid collapse during a fire, is often partly dependent upon conventional reinforcement in the slab. It may be that the nominal anti-crack reinforcement is adequate for this purpose, and for fire ratings up to 1 hour, the deck soffit can be unprotected provided that the loads, excluding the self-weight of the slab, do not exceed 6.7 kN/m^2 (135 lb/ft^2) and that the span is limited to about 3–3.6 m (10–12 ft). These loading conditions are normally sufficient for modern offices including computer installations. Heavier loading, such as for plant room floors, or more severe fire standards will require fire engineering calculations or additional protection. This can be achieved by increasing reinforcement and concrete topping. Alternatively, additional fire protection in the form of spray coating or intumescent paint can be applied to increase the fire rating up to 4 hours. Further details of the fire protection of composite deck floor slabs are given in [3].

16.5.6 Temporary propping

In order to increase the span of a composite floor, use can be made of temporary propping until composite action has been achieved. The steel sheeting is typically supported at its mid-span, thereby considerably reducing both bending stresses and deflections at this stage of construction. This does, however, eliminate one of the principal advantages of using composite floors, namely the speed of construction resulting from a free working space on lower floors. As a result, unpropped construction is normally used with closely spaced secondary beams and temporary propping is thus avoided.

16.5.7 Construction

The composite arrangement with profiled steel sheet fixed to steel I-beams overlaid with concrete topping enables extremely efficient construction. The profiled sheet not only performs the dual roles of reinforcement to the slab, coupled with permanent shuttering, but also eliminates the need for temporary propping. A typical construction sequence for a steel frame and composite deck flooring might be as follows:

(1) Erect steel frame
(2) Position and fix sheeting
(3) Fix supplementary reinforcement
(4) Cast concrete.

The steel decking is normally man-handled into place and requires no cranage other than to lift it in bundles onto each floor. Once the units have been placed, a working platform is provided which facilitates the remaining stages of construction and also allows work to continue on lower storeys in relative safety. There is, therefore, a considerable improvement in speed of construction compared with the traditional slab forms. A further implicit advantage of this system is that overall construction depth is reduced because of the relatively short spans used.

16.6 INTRODUCTION TO COMPOSITE BUILDING STRUCTURES

Construction in steelwork offers many advantages such as speed, strength and lightness. However, there are circumstances in which other materials may be more appropriate. Where bulk is required, such as for floor slabs or continuous walls, or when fire resistance requirements are particularly severe, concrete and masonry might typically be used. In some buildings it is possible that for certain parts of the structure steelwork is the preferred solution whilst for others concrete or masonry is favoured. In such cases it is quite acceptable to utilize a combination of structural forms. This should not be done without careful consideration of the economics of construction. For instance, in the case of a building with a brick facade this may reveal that a steel frame with non-loadbearing masonry cladding is more efficient than mixing loadbearing walls and a frame, with the associated complications in construction sequence.

In adopting a composite solution the basic framing principles are largely unaffected. However, great care must be exercised where different materials connect. Design of such details must take account of varying tolerances (tolerances for steelwork can be much finer than for other materials) and anticipated movements (concrete and masonry are subject to movement with time due to effects such as creep and shrinkage and changes of moisture content).

Some examples of composite structure types include reinforced concrete core or shear wall with steel frame, RC construction to podium with steel frame above, steel frame for lower storeys with RC cross-wall construction above, loadbearing masonry or reinforced concrete with steelwork for floor and roof structure, and bridge and suspended structures. These are discussed in the following sections.

16.7 RC CORE OR SHEAR WALLS AND STEEL FRAMES

This form of composite structure uses reinforced concrete walls to provide fire compartmentation and high in-plane stiffness to resist lateral loads. Steel provides framing for vertical loads with the potential for fast construction and long spans. The work to the RC walls is speeded by the use of slipforms. The concept, which stems from the USA, is described in chapter 15 (Tall buildings), with further details in *Design and Technology in Architecture* by David Guise [4].

The inclusion of a vertical core providing a fire-protected shaft for lifts, stairs and services is a common feature in many buildings. Advantage is often taken of this to accommodate the necessary stiffening to afford lateral stability to the complete building. Where a steel frame is used for the main structure, this can take the form of cross-bracing in the walls of the core, with the fire-protected shaft infilled with blockwork. Alternatively, slipformed reinforced concrete cores can be used. In this case its construction precedes the structural frame. The reinforced concrete tower can then be used to provide bracing for tower cranes used in the subsequent stages of the building. During construction of the core it is of course necessary to provide suitable fixing points for the steel beams. This can be done simply by leaving holes in the slipform.

The cores can be separated as towers, a seminal building

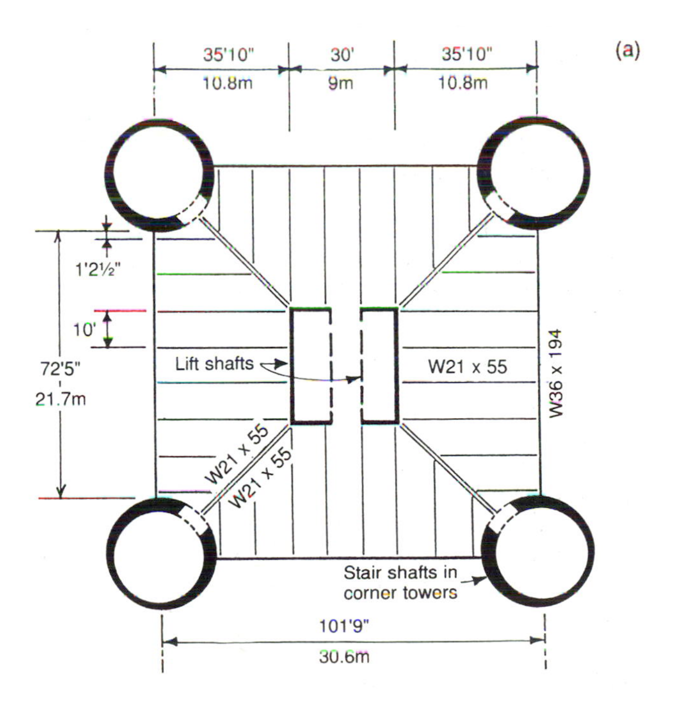

Fig. 16.14 *Knights of Columbus, New Haven Conn. USA, 1969 (architect Roche Dinkeloo) (a)* above *framing plan; (b)* over page *during construction.*

(b)

Fig. 16.14 contd.

of that form being Roche Dinkeloo's design for the Knights of Columbus, New Haven, USA, 1969 (Fig. 16.14).

16.8 RC CONSTRUCTION TO PODIUM WITH STEEL FRAME ABOVE

Reinforced concrete is frequently used for the construction of basement and sub-basement with possibly ground and first floor included to provide a platform or podium for a steel frame above. Early examples include pioneer structures by Le Corbusier and his partner Pierre Jeanneret, who was a qualified architect/engineer [5]. Amongst these are the Pavillon Suisse Paris (RC columns and deck with steel structure at first floor and above) (Figs 16.15 and 16.16), Maison Clarté, Geneva (RC basement and welded steel frame above), and the 'double house' at Weissenhof Stuttgart (steel frame with concrete floors and cross beams).

This subdivision of the structure is often reflected in the contractual arrangements whereby the foundation and groundwork's specialist is different from the main contractor responsible for the frame and shell of the building. Another advantage in this divided responsibility is the limitation of claims for delay spreading from the more uncertain aspect of building below ground to the critical and expensive finalizing stages.

This pattern has been generally adopted around the traffic interchange at Hammersmith, London in order to cope with difficult ground conditions and the problems of building piece by piece above a railway network. The most imaginative 'deck' scheme at Hammersmith, sadly not built, has the public square ringed by offices connected by a cable net roof, designed by Foster Associates (Fig. 16.17).

A rather different example of this form of composite structure was adopted for the Nat West Tower (Fig. 16.18), where the deep basement and podium work in reinforced concrete was let as a separate contract to the superstructure. The upper 52 storeys are carried by three large staggered reinforced concrete cantilever brackets of cellular section. The tower utilizes a 'cloverleaf' shaft of reinforced concrete surrounded by a periphery of steel beams and columns to form three fan-shaped towers. The complete structure is the tallest building in the City of London, standing 183 m (610 ft) above ground level, the visual impact of its height being emphasized by the vertical steel mullions. The office floors are steel framed with the outer ends of the universal beams spaced at 3 m centres (10 ft) with spans varying from 7 to 9 m (23 to 30 ft). The inner ends of the beams are supported on steel brackets attached to the reinforced concrete core walls. The floor construction is composite with 55 mm (2 in) trapezoidal steel decking overlaid by 120 mm (5 in) thickness in situ concrete slab with 22 mm (7/8 in) shear studs. Wind loads are absorbed by the curved core walls through the rigid action of the floor slabs on all three sides.

16.9 STEEL FRAME TO LOWER STOREYS, RC CROSS-WALL CONSTRUCTION ABOVE

This composite form is becoming more commonly used in the USA where open plan office or showroom premises are located below hotel or apartment buildings. Upper storeys use the partition walls in conjunction with the floor slabs to create a rigid cellular construction in in situ or precast concrete. The inclusion of major spaces in the lower floors

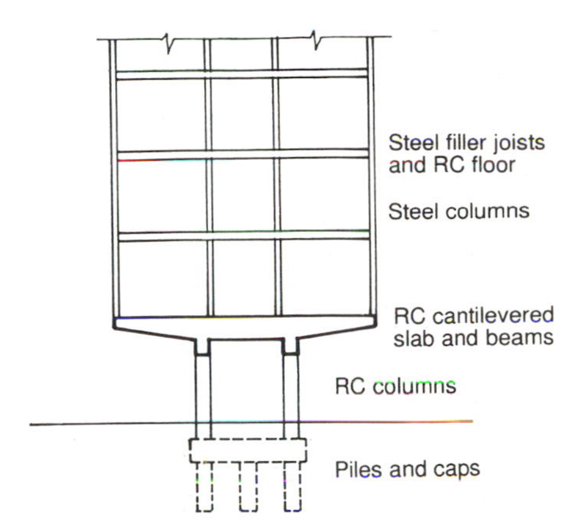

Fig. 16.15 *Pavillon Suisse Paris, 1930–32 (architect Le Corbusier and Pierre Jeanneret). Key section showing steel framing above RC podium.*

Fig. 16.16 *Pavillion Suisse Paris. External view in 1964.*

Fig. 16.17 *Hammersmith Development, London, UK, 1977 (architect: Foster Associates).*

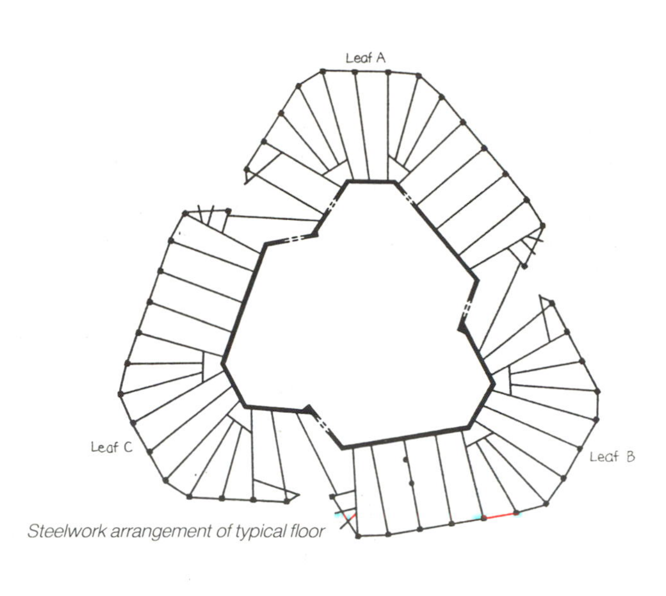

Steelwork arrangement of typical floor

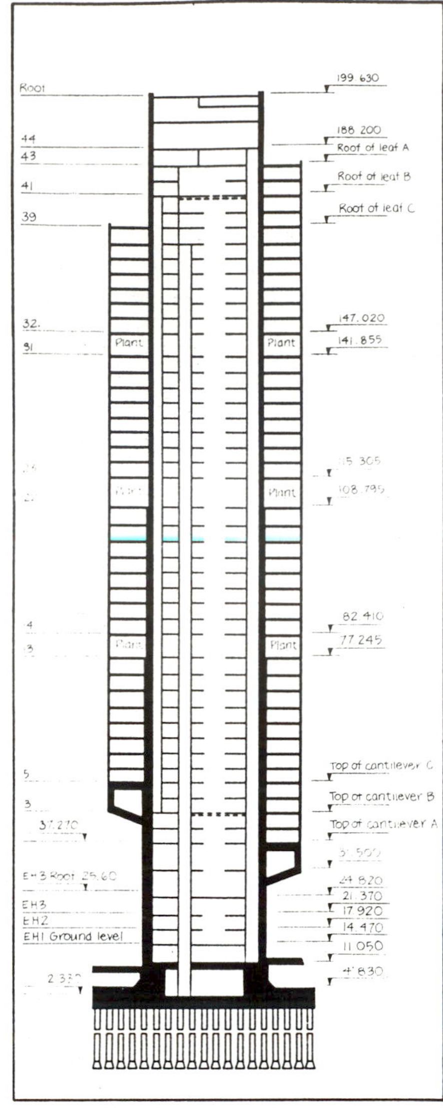

Section through tower block

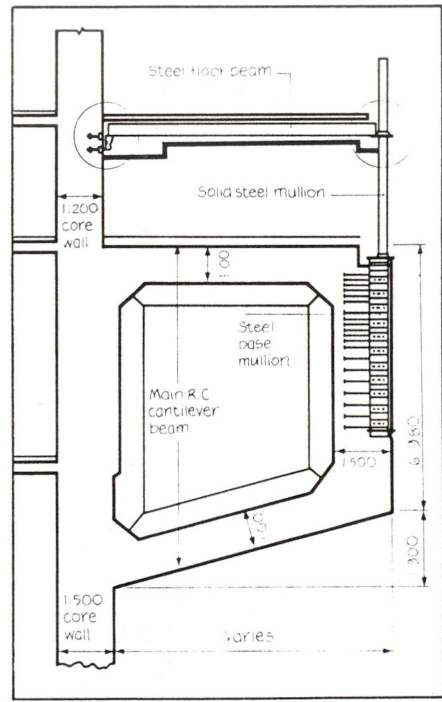

Typical section through main R.C. cantilever beam

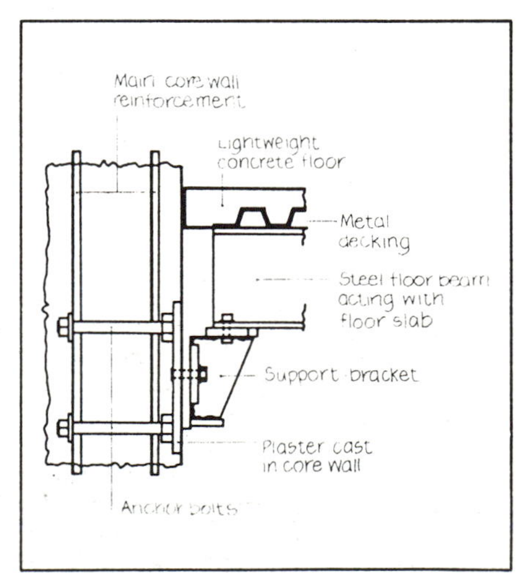

Connection of steel floor beam to main core wall

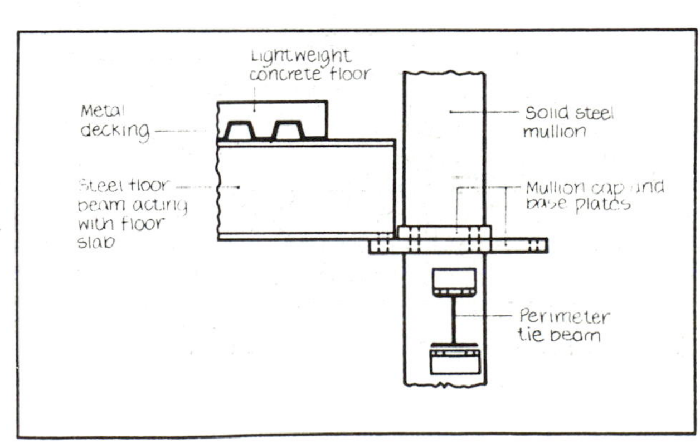

Connection of floor beam to perimeter mullion

Fig. 16.18 *Nat West Tower, City of London (architect R Seifert and Partners: engineer Pell Frischman and Partners).*

requires an open plan with longer spans and often steelwork is used to frame the podium storeys with a minimum number of columns.

Number 900 Michigan Avenue, Chicago (Fig. 16.19) is the most extreme example of this combination. It comprises high-rise flats, with a hotel rising from the 25th storey to the 66th floor, that element being concrete with in situ frame employing flat slab floors. Steel framing is utilized where non-cellular spaces are required for the office and retail zone (from street level to the 25th floor level). The reasons are linked to the changing grid that occurs between offices and the hotel/residential construction. The transfer structure occurs within the reinforced concrete walls and floor/beam system.

16.10 RC COLUMNS OR LOADBEARING MASONRY WITH STEELWORK

Loadbearing masonry, possibly with fin or diaphragm walls, is often used in association with a steel framed roof in single storey construction. This is a popular composite form for applications such as sports halls where high eaves levels and long roof spans are needed. The roof frame may be a simple arrangement of beams or trusses supporting the roofing material (for instance metal decking, precast concrete slabs, or woodwool units). Space frames might also be used, particularly where long clear spans are required. Alternatively, portal frame construction might be used for penthouse framing.

Multi-storey concrete buildings are often roofed with steel trusses to save weight and open up clear spans on the top storey. The multi-storey factory of Boots, Nottingham, UK (1932) is a well known example (Fig. 16.20). The pattern is also seen with many of the atria designs described in chapter 19.

Proprietary composite systems are available, particularly in the low- to medium-rise sector of the market, with precast concrete columns and steel framed roofing (Fig. 16.21). The precast elements can have up to 4 hours fire resistance, depending upon their cross-sectional area. The steel members are used to effect economies where there is little or no requirement for fire encasement.

Typical bay sizes are 6 m (20 ft) with spans approaching 45 m (150 ft) before a column is required. Where floors are introduced, they are normally formed with prestressed

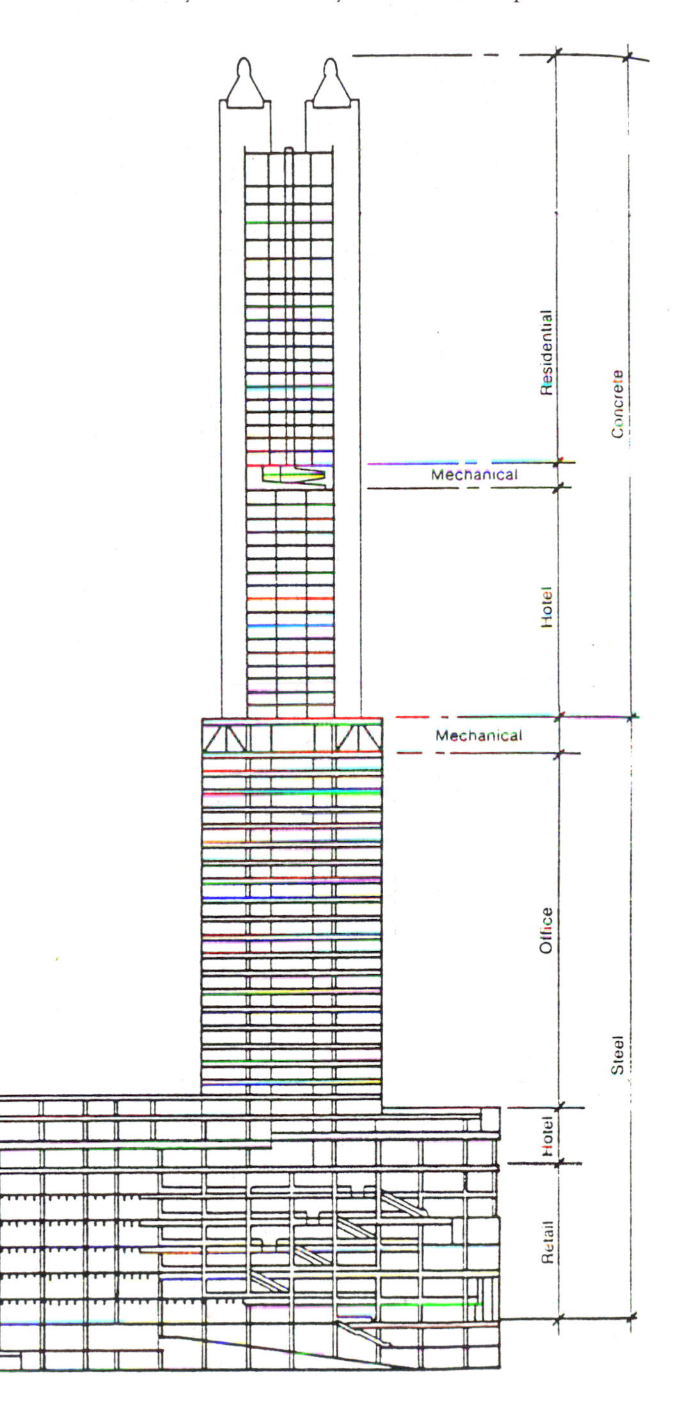

Fig. 16.19 *900 Michigan Avenue, Chicago 1992 (architect: Kohn, Petersen Fox).*

Fig. 16.20 *Boots Nottingham, UK – Steel trusses over manufacturing halls, 1932 (architect and engineer Sir Owen Williams).*

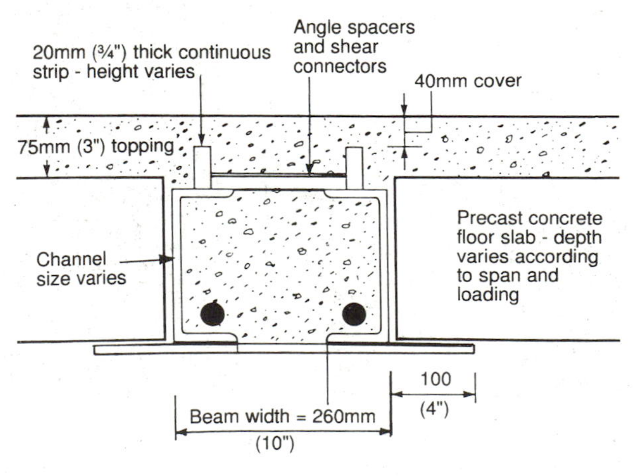

Fig. 16.21 *Proprietary systems for precast and steel framed buildings.*

concrete planks spanning around 7.5 m (25 ft). Shear walls are often required in addition to stair and lift core bracing. The steel roof beams are normally lattice girders or universal beams with a roof construction of steel decking and a choice of roof finishes. Refurbishment and renovation of buildings often involves new steelwork in association with existing masonry or concrete structures. One stunning example of this is the recently completed Imagination building in Store Street, London, UK, where lightweight steelwork has been used to great effect, both in the bridges connecting the two original buildings and the supporting structure for the roof.

16.11 SUSPENDED STRUCTURES

Although hanging or suspended structures were indicated by designers such as Mies van der Rohe (Glass Skyscraper, Berlin 1919), in reality, such concepts were not constructed until after World War II. The typical arrangement consisted of a reinforced concrete core with cantilever beams or structures at roof level. These supported suspenders at their edges.

The 1960s saw this imaginative solution capture the interest of designers in many parts of the world. Some early applications experienced technical problems in achieving adequate strength in the cantilever beams, the loads and spans being at the limit of the then attainable standards.

The Commercial Union tower (Fig. 16.22) in the City of London, arguably the most elegant example of a suspended structure in the UK, was completed in 1969 without any such problems. This proved the case that a suspended type of structure was the logical outcome of economic studies aimed at providing the maximum floor area. The use of structural steelwork proved its selection in lightness, speed of construction and overall economy, whether acting alone or compositely with concrete.

The building consists of a concrete service core measuring 22.89 × 15.2 m (75 × 50 ft) surrounded by a steel structure suspended from two cantilevered steel truss sections at the level of the plant floors. The upper plant room structure, containing the heating plant, supports 12 floors while the lower plant room, containing air conditioning equipment, supports 13 floors. The two systems are quite independent. This design was the outcome of a brief requiring maximum clear floor space and a minimum number of columns through the ground and basement floors The hangers, which are loaded purely in tension, vary in size from 230 × 2 mm (9 × 5/64 in) to 230 × 50 mm (9 × 2 in) and are contained entirely within alternate window mullions. The floor beams have a maximum span of 11.4 m (37 ft) and had to be designed to accommodate air conditioning ducts. The most economical solution was to employ 685 mm (27 in) deep high-yield steel-castellated beams with shear studs welded to the top to effect composite action with the 127 mm (5 in) lightweight concrete floor slabs. Both pre-

(a)

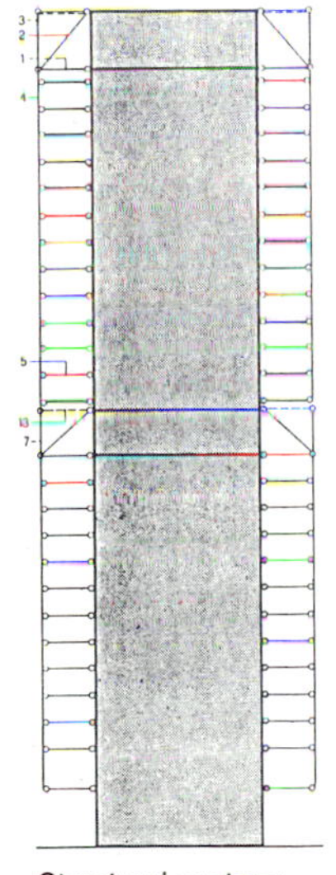

Structural system:
section through
core in longitudinal
direction

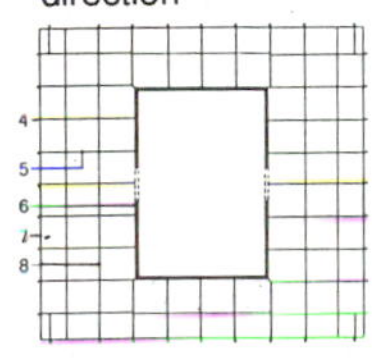

Beam arrangement
in a typical floor

(b)

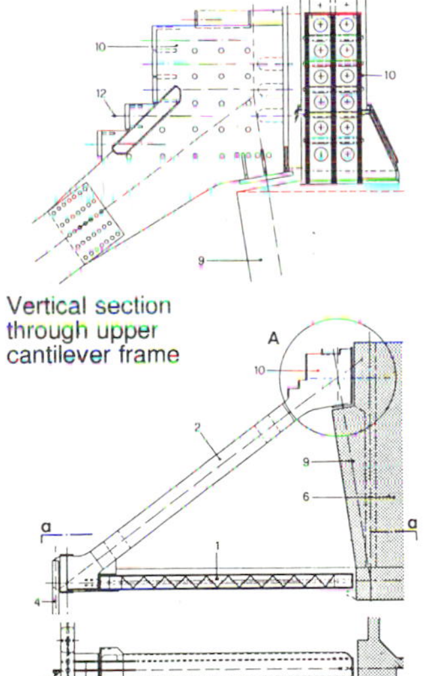

Vertical section
through upper
cantilever frame

1 Lattice strut
2 Diagonal tie
3 Lattice girder two storeys deep
4 Hanger, flats
5 Castellated beam
6 Concrete core
7 Longitudinal lattice grid chords
8 T-section longitudinal
9 Bearing bracket
10 Anchor block
11 Welded I-section
12 Centre lines of prestressing bars
13 Stabilizing girder

(c)

Fig. 16.22 *Commercial Union tower, City of London 1969 (a) elevation; (b) general arrangement; (c) constructive sequence (architect GMW Partnership: engineer Scott Wilson Kirkpatrick and Partners).*

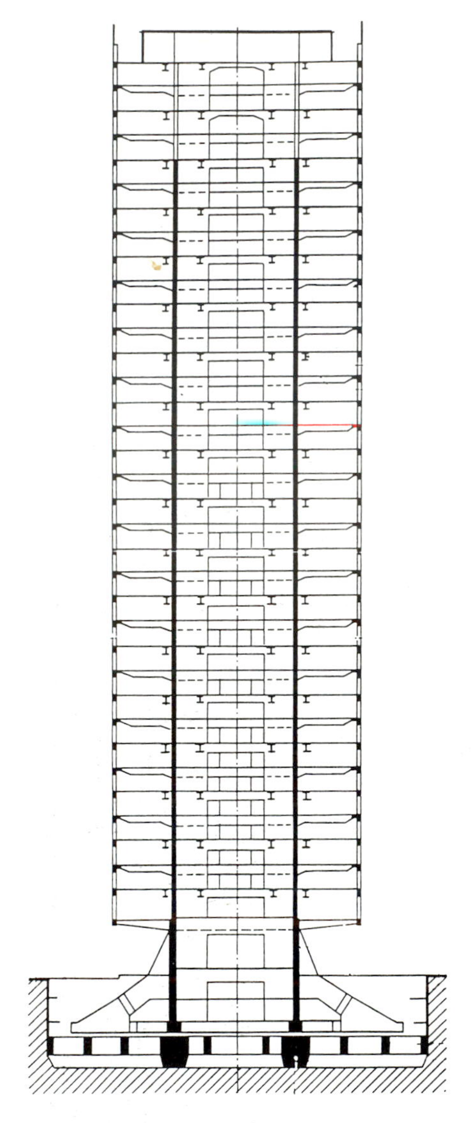

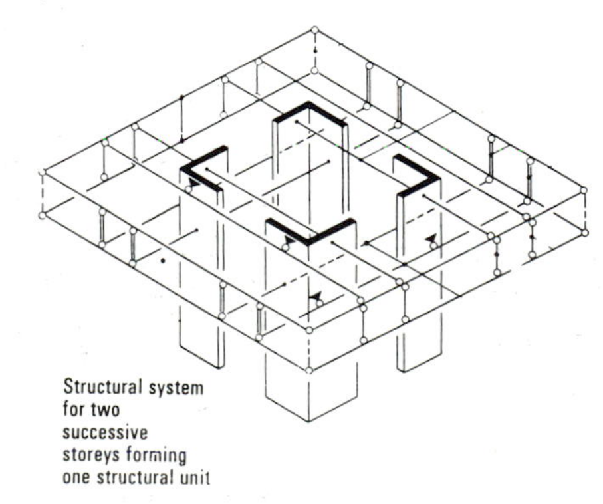

Fig. 16.23 *Tour du Midi, Brussels 1962–66 (architects R. Aerts and P. Ramon: engineer A. Lipsky).*

stressed concrete and steel were considered for the cantilever beams; steel was chosen as it did not require a special working platform at the top of the core. In addition, the erection of the floors could proceed without delays associated with concrete curing.

Fire breaks are provided by setting the perimeter beams in a 0.9 m (3 ft) downstand and in the event of failure of a hanger the load can be safely transmitted to the adjacent members. A total of 2500 tonnes of steelwork was used in the structure. The steelwork was erected in 24 weeks and in the later stages was being completed at the rate of one floor per day.

Suspended structures can take many forms other than that of concrete core, steel girders and steel plate hangers used on the Commercial Union building. The Standard Bank Centre, Johannesburg, is essentially of reinforced concrete construction. This 27 storey building is divided by three cantilever brackets (every ninth floor), each a full storey in height and located within a service floor. These brackets are cantilevered from the central building core. The external exposed hangers are of precast post-tensioned concrete and support the office floors.

The Tour du Midi, Brussels (Fig. 16.23), by contrast, is a structural steel solution. A central steel core supports four parallel girders and fascia beams at each floor level. The girders run east/west on even numbered floors and north/south on odd numbered floors so that the floors are supported in pairs independently of all the others. The north and south edges of the even numbered floors are suspended from the floor above by steel tubes. The load from the east and west edges is transferred to the floor below, but in this case the tubes are in compression rather than tension.

In the case of the Philips building in Eindhoven (Fig. 16.24) temporary columns were provided around the perimeter at ground floor level while the floors were built upwards. The steel hangers were used as the supporting structures until the triangular steel crown was completed at roof level. The temporary columns were then removed. This must have been a tense moment for the engineers and contractor.

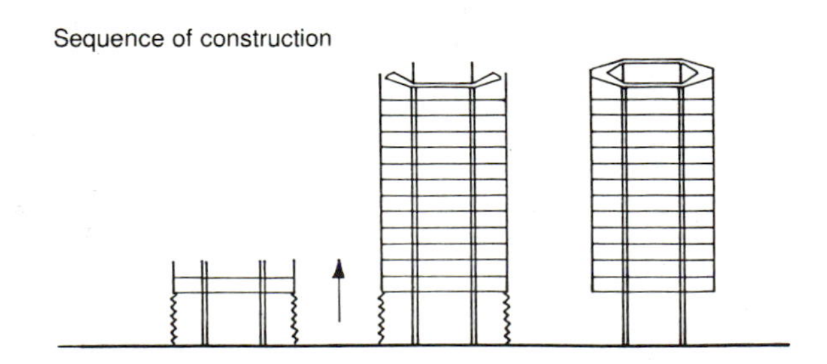

Fig. 16.24 *Philips Building, Eindhoven. Sequence of construction.*

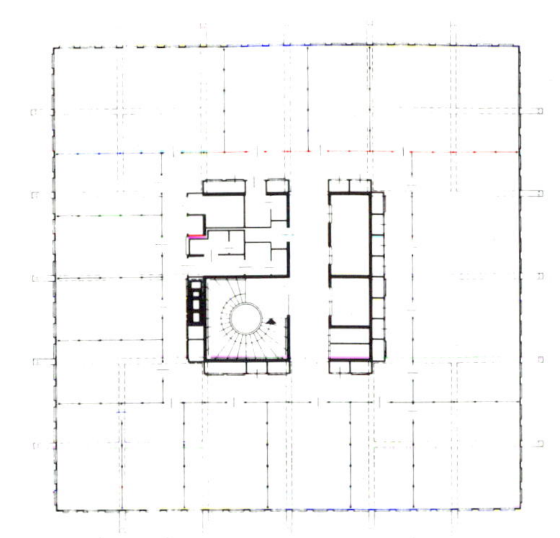

Typical floor

Arrangement of floor beams

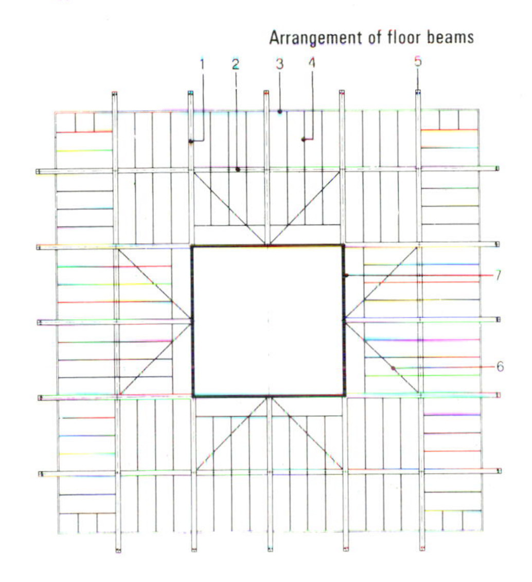

Plan of roof framework

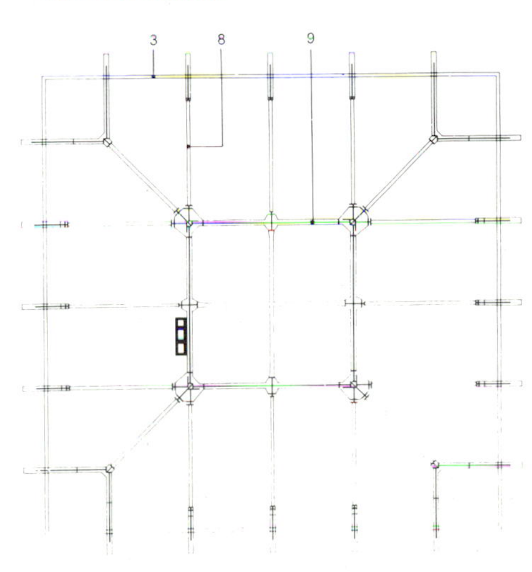

Structural system: section through the core

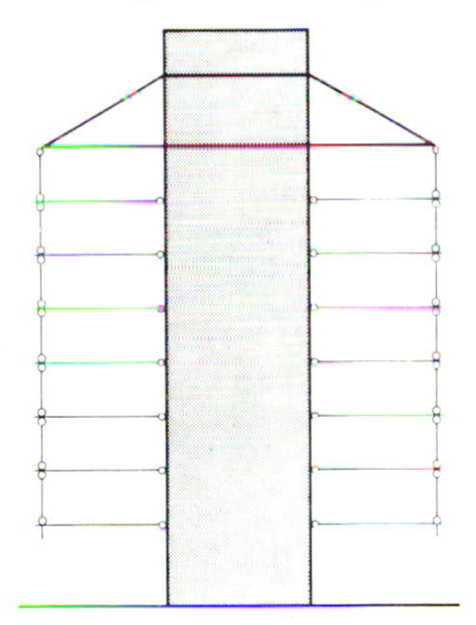

1 Main beam of welded I-section, 700 mm deep
2 Transverse beam, I 300
3 Pressed steel edge beam
4 Secondary beam, I 140
5 Hanger, two 45 mm dia bars
6 Horizontal wind-bracing
7 Concrete core
8 Diagonal tie, two 80 mm dia bars
9 Anchor frame

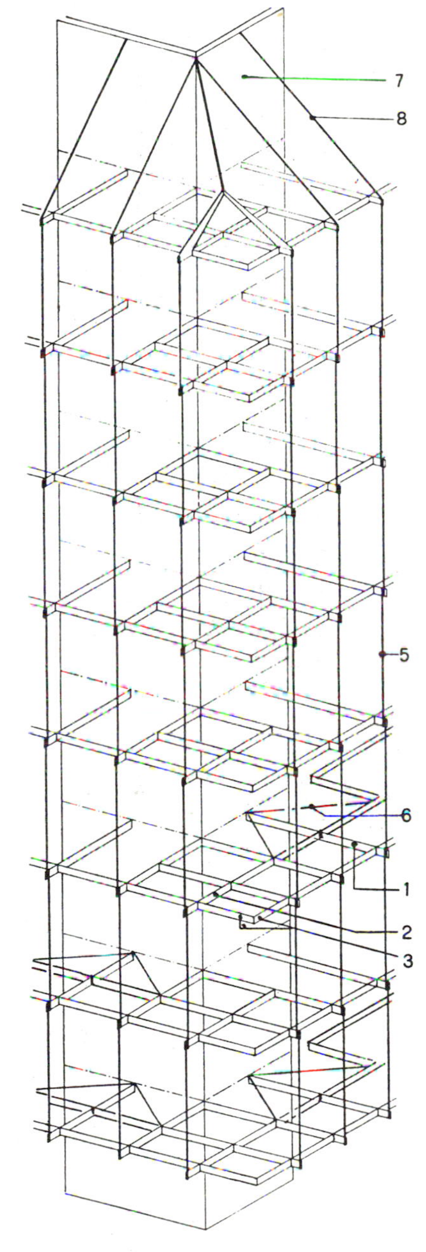

Suspension of upper floors

Fig. 16.25 *Siemens Corporation, Saint Denis, France 1969–70 (architect B. Zehrfuff: engineers J. Prouvé and L. Fruitet).*

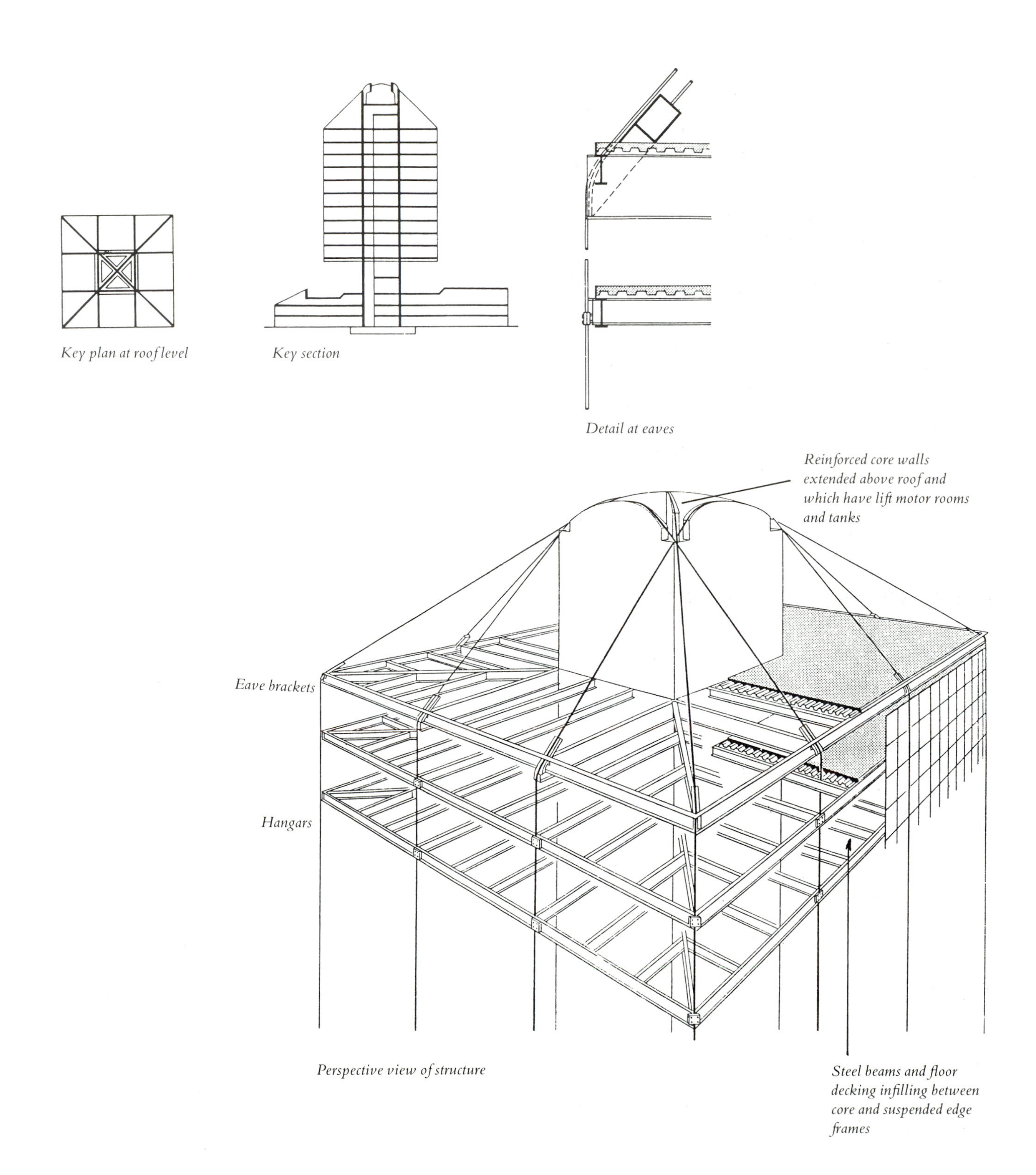

Fig. 16.26 *Westcoast Transmission Company, Vancouver 1969 (architect Rhone and Iredale).*

Other examples of suspended structures are the Siemens Corporation, Saint Denis, France (Fig. 16.25), Hearts of Oak Benefit Society, London, Overbeckhuis, Rotterdam, by Goldschmidt and Everbruggen (1965), and Westcoast Transmission Company, Vancouver, by Rhone and Iredale (1969) (Fig. 16.26).

One of the most elegant solutions for a composite concrete and steel structure was devised by Rhone and Iredale for the West Coast Transmission Company building in Vancouver, Canada. Here, the symmetrical concrete tower houses the lift and stair shaft, which are extended upwards for motor and tank housing, but are also shaped to allow the cable hangars to pass over saddles at the peak of the tower. The facades are framed by floor edge beams, which serve as trimming members for the flooring system of decking and secondary beams, as well as connectors for the cable hangars.

A recent visit to architects' offices in Chicago revealed that high-rise building structures were made the subject of three design options, namely concrete frame, steel frame and composite structural frames. The latter form is taking an increasing share of the market.

REFERENCES AND TECHNICAL NOTES

Composite construction

1. Gray, B.A., Mullet, D.L. and Walker, H.B. (1983) *Steel Framed Multi-storey Buildings. Design Recommendations for Composite Floors and Beams Using Steel Decks.* Section 1 Structural. SCI.
2. Copeland, B., Glover, M., Hart, A., Haryott, R. and Marshall, S. (1983) Designing for steel, *Architects' Journal*, 24 and 31 August 1983, Vol. 178, Nos. 34 and 35, pp. 41–57.
3. Newman, G.M. and Walker, H.B. (1983) *Steel Framed Multi-storey Buildings. Design Recommendations for Composite Floors and Beams Using Steel Decks.* Section 2 Fire resistance. SCI.

Composite structures

4. Guise, D. (1991) *Design and Technology in Architecture.* Van Nostrand Rheinhold, New York.
5. Walden, R. (ed.) (1977) *Essays on Le Corbusier.* MIT Press.

FURTHER READING

Johnson, R.P. (1975) *Composite Structures of Steel and Concrete.* Granada.

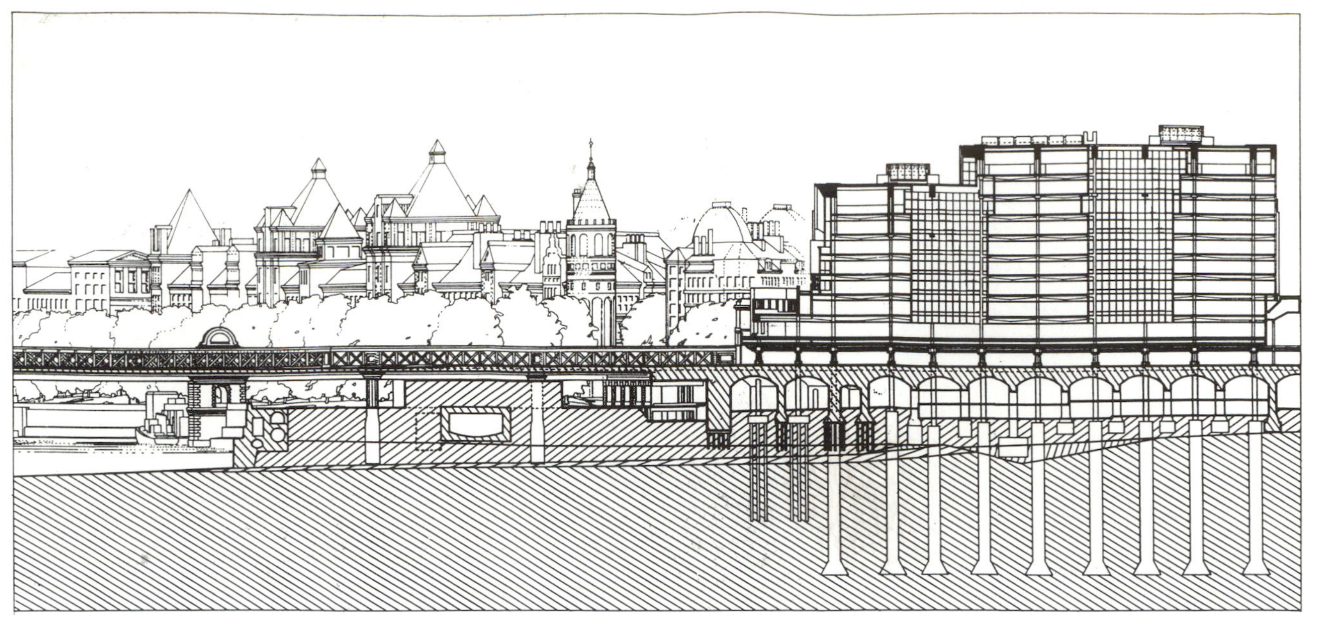

Embankment Place, Charing Cross, London, UK 1991, long section and cross-section (architect Terry Farrell and Co. Ltd: engineer Ove Arup and Partners).

17

Transfer structures

Bryn Bird

17.1 INTRODUCTION

Transfer structures take loads where they can conveniently be collected and transfer them to where they can conveniently be resisted. At one end of the spectrum, this can mean that a column line has to be interrupted to get round an obstruction or provide an opening. At the other end of the spectrum whole buildings might have only minimal areas of the site where foundations can be put down. A few typical problems are shown in Fig. 17.1.

In a building that needs a transfer structure, this will probably be the most challenging part of the design and will involve the whole design team. On site it will be on the critical path for both procurement and construction and will probably be the largest single piece of structure. In finished buildings they are often hidden. When seen, they are strong images in their own right. Good design teams will put them on the agenda early and will strive to avoid the need for one. However, avoiding transfer structures needs great confidence because introducing them late into a building design will be disastrous.

17.2 ALTERNATIVE FORMS

Transfer structures typically have high loads, low span to depth ratios and thick steel sections. These characteristics usually demand special calculations such as finite element analyses and special fabrication techniques. This need not be a deterrent, as the North Sea oil industry has expanded enormously the capabilities of heavy steel engineering.

To help visualize the forces involved consider a parabolic arch as shown in Fig. 17.2 in which the arch meets its point of support at about 45 degrees. Assuming the arch to be reasonably uniformly loaded, then it will be in compression with very little bending moment and therefore $R = W/2$, $H = R$ and $P = \sqrt{2}R = W/\sqrt{2}$.

These three large forces, each approximating to half the total weight of the building slice being considered, all meeting at a point are what make transfer structures so interesting for the engineer and architect. Transfer structures which are deeper will reduce the horizontal restraint H but involve more of the building, and those which are shallower will increase H and involve less of the building. It is within this area of debate that the right balance for the particular building has to be found. The devices used are

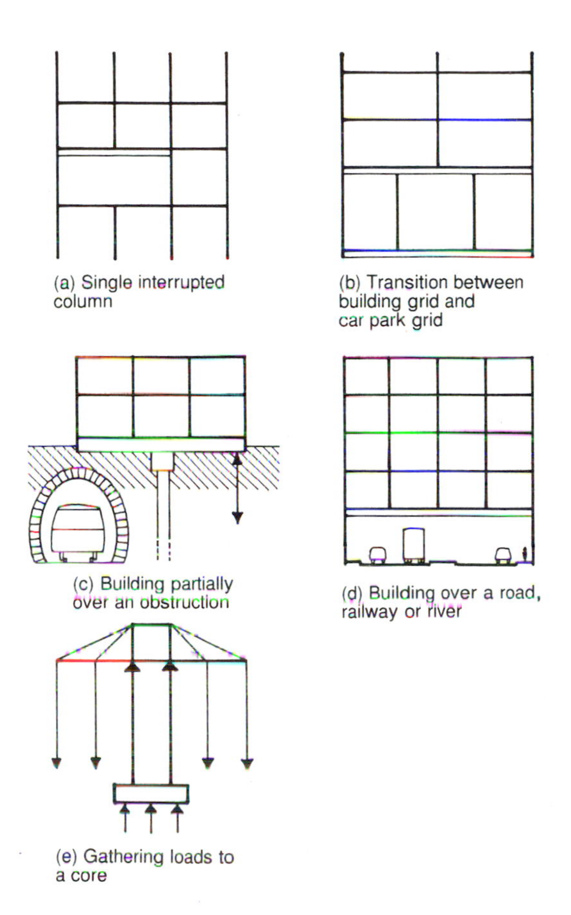

Fig. 17.1 *Typical 'transfer' designs.*

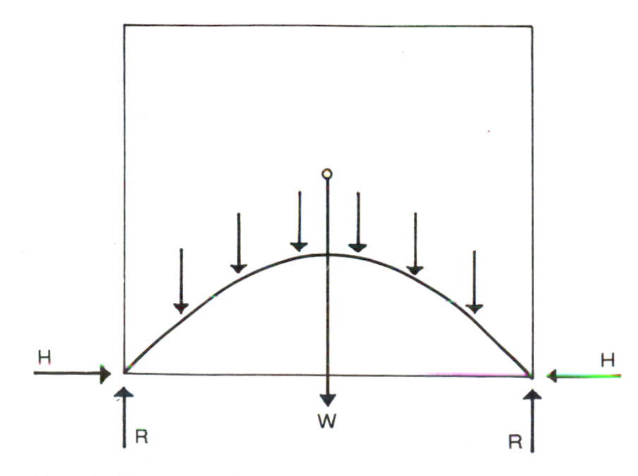

Fig. 17.2 *Diagram showing parabolic arch.*

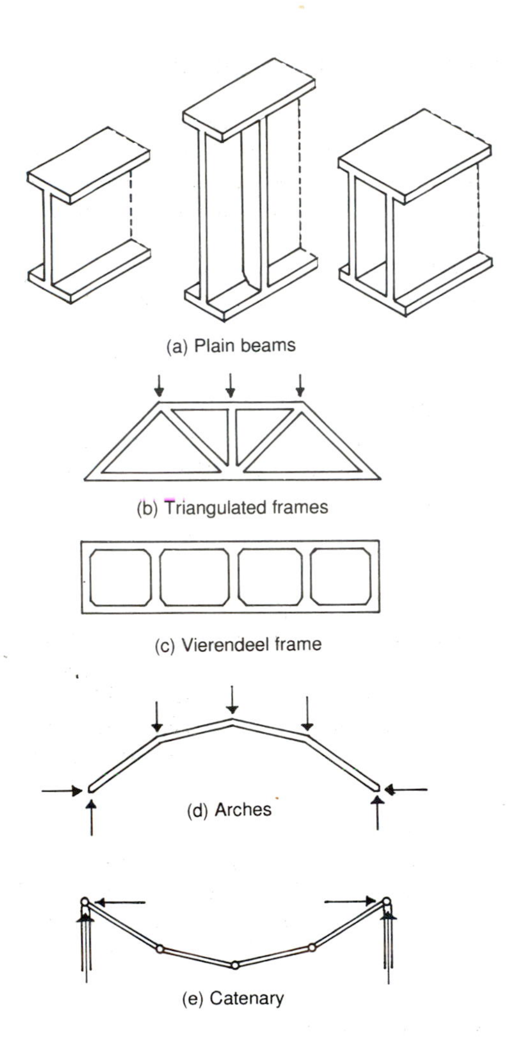

Fig. 17.3 *Alternative transfer devices.*

usually one of the following broad groups:

(a) Plain beams which will tend to have thick webs, deep webs or two webs (a box section) (Fig. 17.3a).
(b) Triangulated frames which will tend to have few triangles to reduce the number of connections (Fig. 17.3b).
(c) Vierendeel frames which will also tend to have few panels and will be thick and heavy but can still look attractive (Fig. 17.3c).
(d) Arches, which will be lighter than frames, can usually have simpler connections. They need complementary ties or abutments (Fig. 17.3d).
(e) Catenaries will be the most slender visually because they are in pure tension, but there must always be a complimentary compression member to accommodate somewhere (Fig. 17.3e).

Transfer structures have to compete for space with other elements of the building design and in particular services; indeed the need for a transfer structure sometimes arises from bridging services which have priority. In a visible transfer structure which achieves simple clarity of form it is worth stopping to reflect that time and effort have been spent in designing the services to go elsewhere. A hidden transfer structure will have all of the same problems but there will be less incentive to co-ordinate them. The basic problem is that transfer structures gather large forces, usually because there are few routes for them to the ground. The building services need routes to the ground too.

Steel often compares favourably with reinforced concrete and in transfer structures has some considerable advantages. In concrete the steel reinforcement does most of the work, and separate quantities will be provided for each of the analytical concepts of shear, tension and (if necessary) compression. With transfer structures, shear will often become critical first and even at the point where no more shear reinforcement can be added, steel will still be an order of magnitude stronger for the same cross-sectional area. Concrete thus soon becomes too big for the construction space available. Steel also has an advantage in quality control because it is straightforward to check before anything arrives on site. Densely reinforced concrete is difficult to place on site and relies on highly skilled workmen and inspectors with only indirect testing usually possible. There is also the need to wait for the cubes to be crushed.

17.3 DESIGN PRINCIPLES

The analysis of transfer structures usually concentrates on the joints. The overall analysis will tend to be straight forward at least to the first order of approximation because of the simplicity of the overall form. Considerations of deflection, interaction with the rest of the building and construction sequence will all engage the full analytical talent of the structural engineer in refining the design later on. Individual members of a transfer structure will tend to have low slenderness ratios, which means that even in compression members higher grades of steel can be used right up to their full strength capacity. Joints, however, interfere with the straight axial stress lines causing concentrations around bolts and welds. It is these stress concentrations which are difficult to visualize, and modern methods such as finite element analysis computer programs can prove very useful (Fig. 17.4).

Techniques for optimizing joints are important and it is worth looking at a few generalities. Welding is important because there is a temptation to think that 'full strength butt welds' will solve all the problems. Thicker sections, however, require multiple pass welds (see Fig. 17.5), each individual pass being small in relation to the parent metal and so the heat sink effect needs to be counteracted by

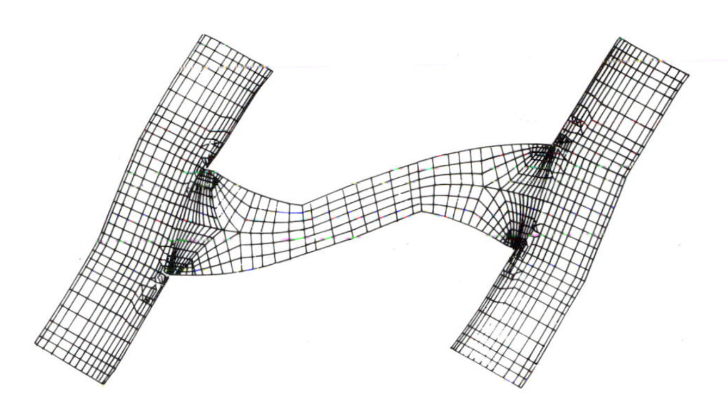

Fig. 17.4 *Stress pattern predicted by finite element analysis.*

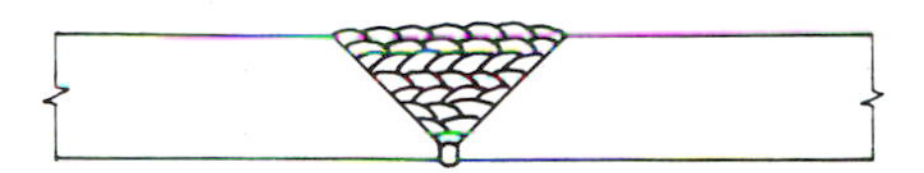

Fig. 17.5 *Multiple pass weld.*

preheating. Multiple pass welds also lock in stresses between the early passes and the later ones, needing a different form of heat treatment to achieve stress relaxation. This may work well for the specialist fabricator in his own yard and often with automatic welding equipment, but should be avoided for site joints wherever possible. Bolts or shear pins then become the answer, and it is important to use them to the best advantage. Bolts in double shear have twice the capacity of bolts in single shear (see Fig. 17.6). Larger bolts soon become difficult to handle and high grade shear pins take over (Fig. 17.7).

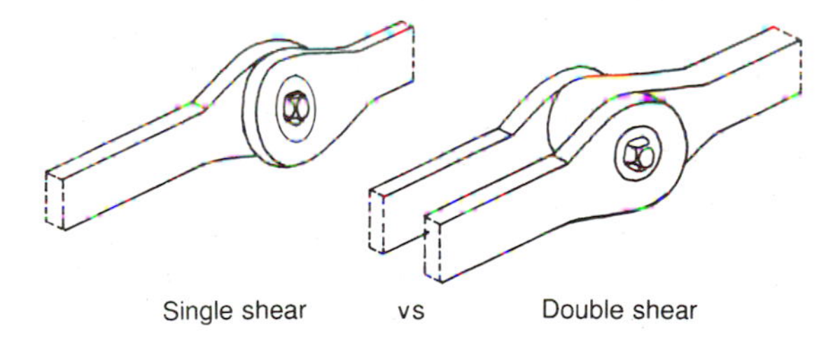

Fig. 17.6 *Single and double shear connection.*

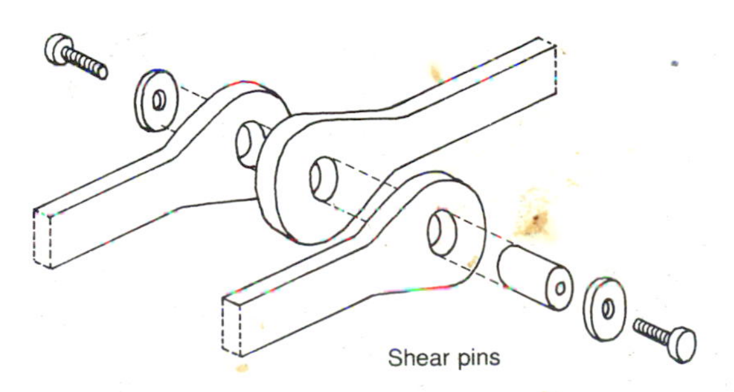

Fig. 17.7 *Shear pin connector.*

17.4 AVOIDING PROGRESSIVE COLLAPSE

In 1968, the partial collapse of Ronan Point, Hackney, London (see chapter 24, section 24.7.3) sharply focused the minds of engineers on the concept of disproportionate collapse. The concept is that failure of a single structural member should not be allowed to cause the progressive collapse of a disproportionate part of the building as a whole. Transfer structures, being key elements in any building, could easily do so. The techniques to overcome this problem fall into the following categories.

(a) Built in redundancy

By building in more members than are strictly necessary, various systems can be devised in which the removal of any one member merely results in redistribution of forces around the remaining members. This tends to be uneconomic in use of steel.

(b) Making each member blastproof

If a member will withstand a lateral pressure of 34.5 kN/m^2 (700 lb/ft^2) it is deemed to be able to survive an explosion. This is derived from the pressure required to cave in the cover of an electrical box found in the immediate vicinity of the Ronan Point explosion. That was an important piece of steel.

(c) Multiplicity of members

The principle here is that if a member is divided into say two components, each with a safety factor of two, then failure of one will result in the other surviving at a safety factor of one. Extra safety can be achieved by dividing into three or more components.

(d) Alternative structural systems

Suppose some incident caused a transfer structure to fail. If the remainder of the building were able to span, albeit deformed and at a reduced safety factor, then that would be acceptable.

17.5 EXAMPLES OF TRANSFER STRUCTURES

17.5.1 Simpson's, Piccadilly, London

Good examples of transfer structures are easy to find, especially as many of them are highly visible and recent. One example from the 1930s is both an inspiration and a cautionary tale. Simpson's, at No 26 Piccadilly, London, clearly wanted a distinctive modern building and engaged Joseph Emberton as the architect, and via a family connection with the Simpsons in Switzerland, Felix Samuely as the engineer. Samuely brought with him specialist knowledge of welding learned in Germany and Russia and fresh ideas on how to make economical structures. They devised a facade with a clear span above ground level and the structure was to

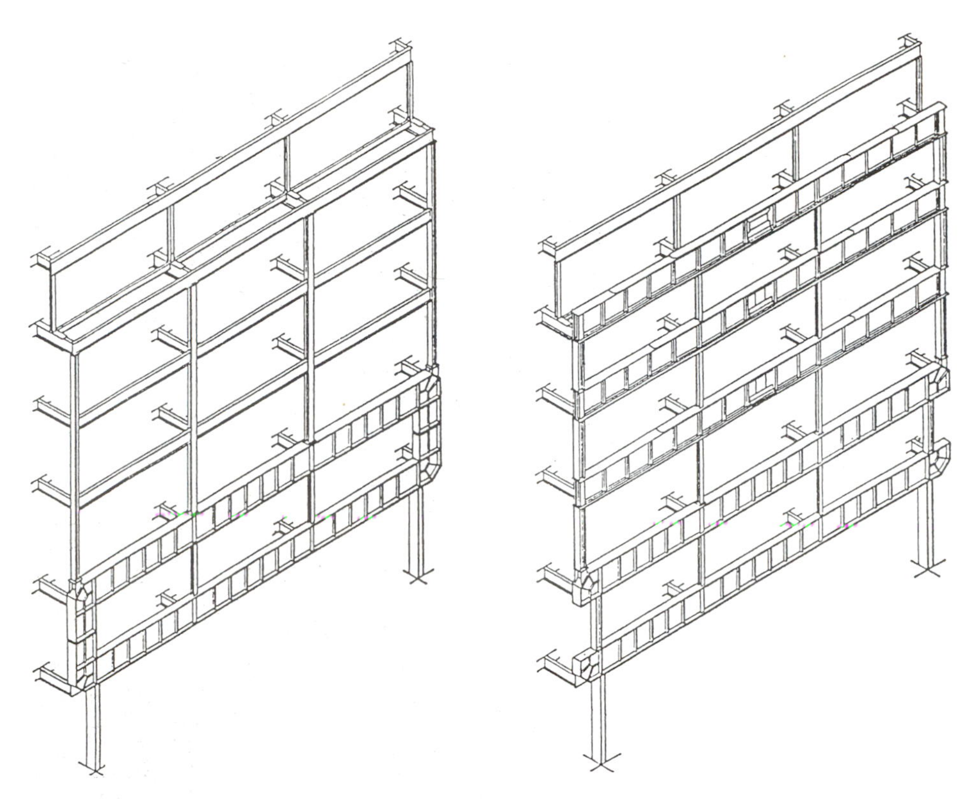

Fig. 17.8 *Before and after comparisons of Felix Samuely's Vierendeel frame.*

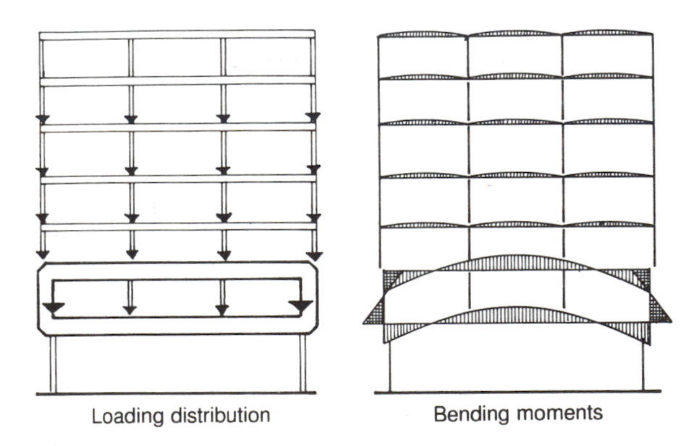

Fig. 17.9 *Samuely's original concept; Simpson's, Piccadilly, London, 1935 (architect Joseph Emberton: engineer Felix Samuely).*

be a welded Vierendeel frame. Welding was new in buildings, the first British welded steel building being the Bexhill Pavilion in 1935. Vierendeel frames were clearly unheard of in London and the London County Council District Surveyor dismissed the Vierendeel frame as the combination of the two new ideas was too much to swallow. Unfortunately this was after fabrication and during construction, so the whole facade structure had to be changed to simply supported beams at each level. The before and after comparison is shown in Fig. 17.8. The facade gives no hint of the trauma its designers suffered (Figs 17.9 and 17.10).

Fig. 17.10 *Completed elevation of Simpson's.*

17.5.2 First Exchange House, London

A recent arch solution is First Exchange House near Liverpool Street Station by Skidmore Owings and Merrill, architects and engineers. The problem was how to build over an active railway. The solution is arches integrated into the whole building frame. Other solutions were considered and among them were multiple chevrons and a catenary (Figs 17.11 and 17.12). The simple clarity of the arch speaks for itself. In comparison with the catenary, both the primary tension and compression routes are shorter. The multiple chevron would not have been good for the internal frames of the building.

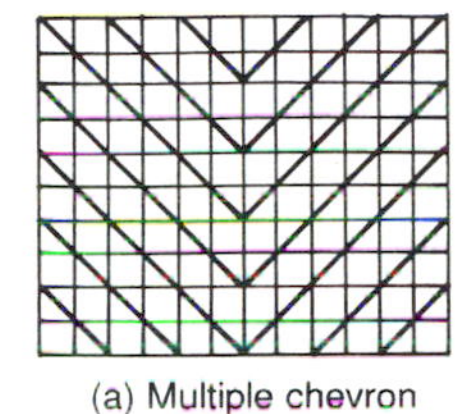

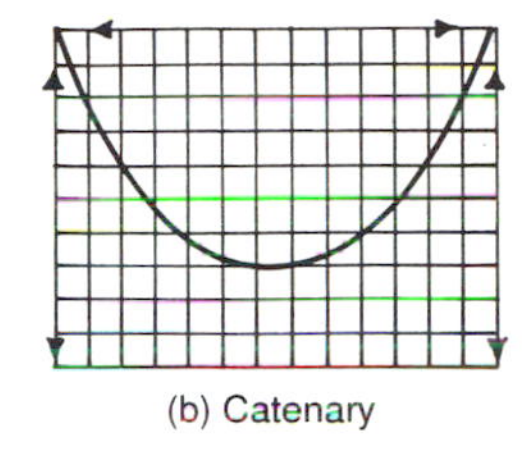

Fig. 17.11 *Alternative forms for bridging Liverpool Street Station, London, 1989 (architect and engineer: SOM).*

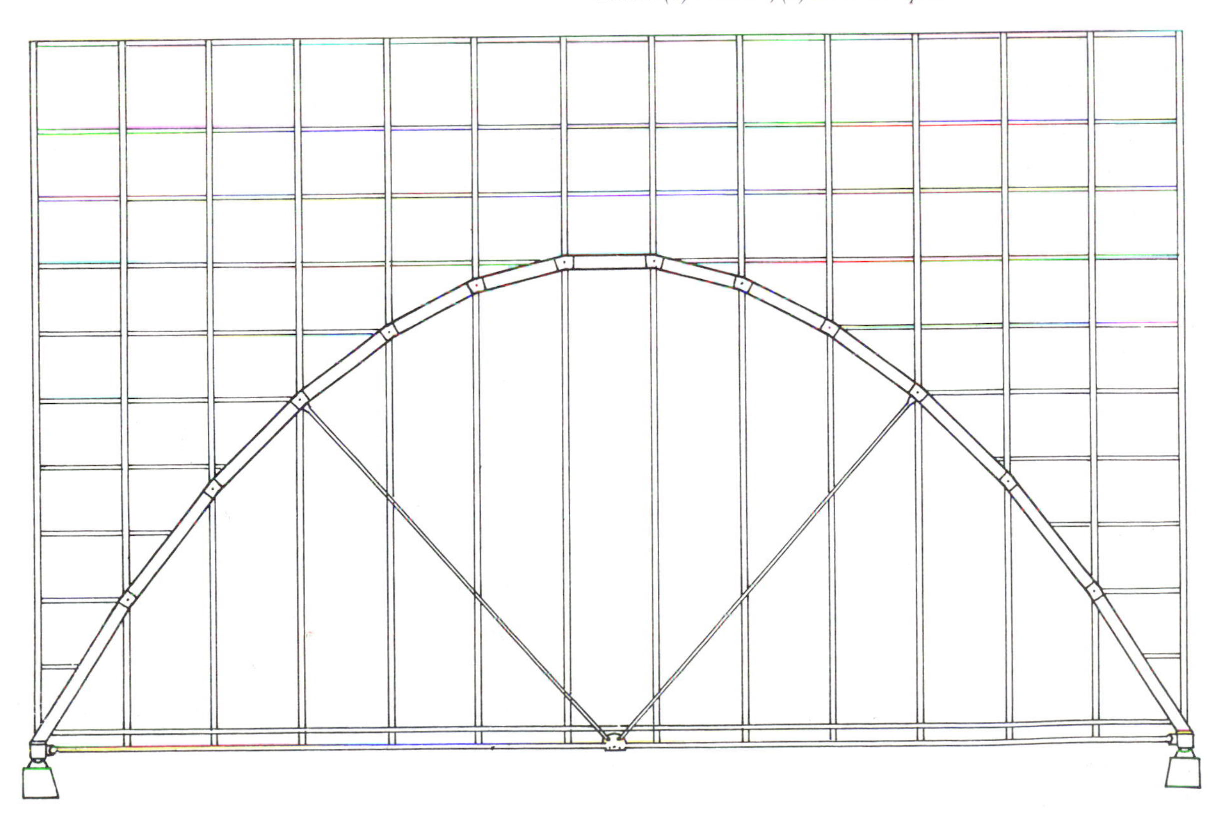

Fig. 17.12 *Final solution for First Exchange House, Liverpool Street, London (a) elevation; (b) structural layout.*

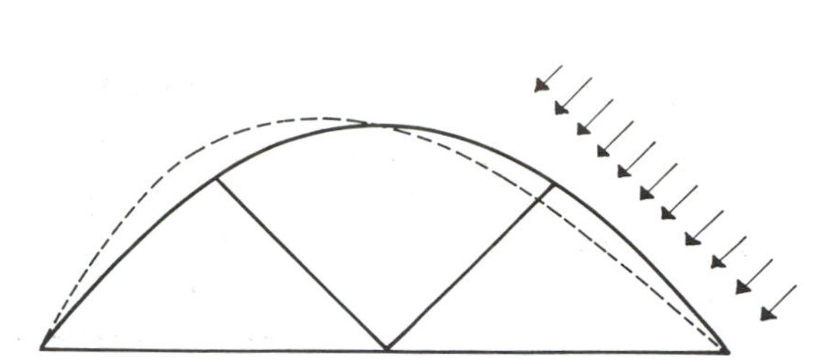

Fig. 17.13 *The diagonals help resist sideways thrust by preventing the arch moving to the dotted line.*

There are four arches, one on each main elevation (Fig. 17.12) and two internally. Above the arch, the columns are in compression, below the arch they are hangers. The arches themselves are twin fabricated channel sections in pure axial compression with some extra capacity to deal with extraneous bending moments. Grade 50 steel is used throughout. The arch ties are straight and hung beneath the building by the two diagonals. The tie force is made predictable and constant by allowing one end of the building to slide free, thus removing the problem of thermal stress. So the primary structural action is simple but the important secondary structural actions are more complex and interesting.

Wind, lateral stability and out of balance loads are dealt with primarily by moment connections in the whole of the two internal frames and those parts of the frame above the arch externally. This is helped by the two diagonal ties supporting the primary tie (Fig. 17.13).

Disproportionate collapse is dealt with by having a secondary tie which is also part of the lowest floor construction. It will act as a substitute primary tie at a safety factor of 1.05.

Fire engineering was used to enable the main elevation arches to remain unclad. The external envelope is 2 m (6 ft 6 in) from the exposed arches and is 1 hour fire rated but it was assumed that two floors could be engulfed and the cladding could fail in any one bay. The resulting heating of the arches was studied using evidence of real fires which tend to have slower starts then reach a flash-over point rising to a greater intensity than simulated fires in a furnace. The thick steel sections weighing just under 1 tonne/m, 2 m (6 ft 6 in) from the heat source and re-radiating to the outside were found to be adequate without protection. The result is a clarity of structure where the steel is seen in its true proportions.

17.5.3 Embankment Place, London

Embankment Place was designed by architect Terry Farrell and Co Ltd and engineer Ove Arup and Partners, and spans the platforms of Charing Cross Station. Here, the arches are at the top of the building and reveal their form in the roof line and the river elevation (Fig. 17.14). A transfer structure is needed because of the severe restrictions British Rail imposed on access to their platforms which had to be kept in operation at all times, and because columns were unacceptable through the Players Theatre which is accommodated in the arches under the platforms.

Having the arches at the top presented a number of advantages. The client wanted larger clear spans at the lower level which prevented the construction of a heavy transfer structure there. Hanging the floors from above meant the simple omission of some hangers and greater spans for only one floor. The arches were also found to have a resonant frequency of about 3 Hz which is the normal design frequency for vibration isolation, so by separating each floor from the main columns by rubber vibration isolation bearings the job of eliminating rumble from trains is completed.

The arches, as the largest and the slowest part of the structure to fabricate and test, could be erected last by building the general steel framework first off falsework over the station platforms. They were made in up to 12 separate segments by Redpath Offshore and Cleveland Bridge at Darlington and tested by Redpath Dorman Long at Glasgow.

The necessary ties for the arches are accommodated in the 12th floor and comprised groups of high strength alloy steel 'Macalloy' rods. These were prestressed at three separate stages as the loads were added.

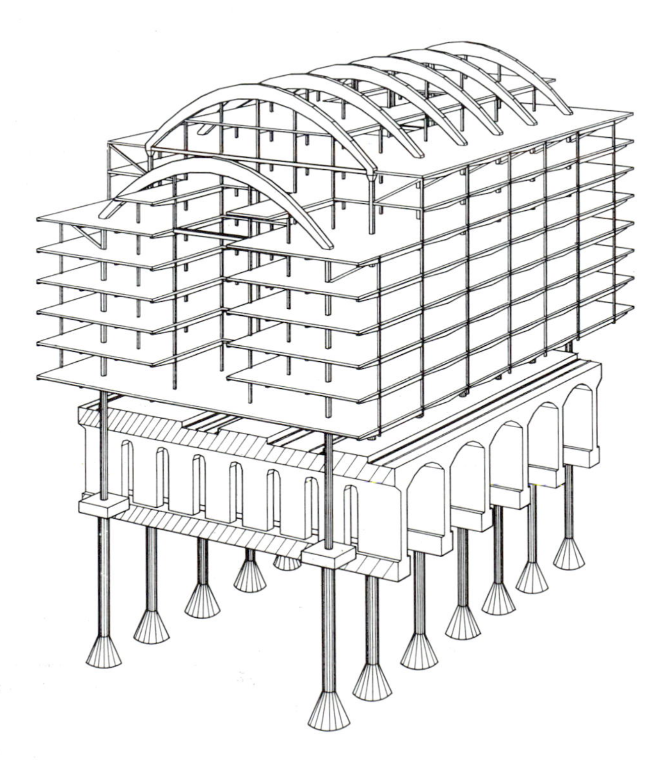

Fig. 17.14 *General arrangement of transfer structure at Embankment Place, Charing Cross, London 1991 (architect Terry Farrell and Co Ltd: engineer Ove Arup and Partners).*

17.5.4 Alban Gate, London

Another Terry Farrell/Ove Arup design is Alban Gate, a multi-storey office complex over London Wall where two forms of transfer structure were used. In the main east and west elevations there are arch transfer structures, circular in form to provide a symbolic gateway to the City of London. Between these are transfer structures of larger spans which allow clear sightlines at the junction with Wood Street. Various forms were tried (see Fig. 17.15), a two storey deep truss being the final solution (Fig. 17.16).

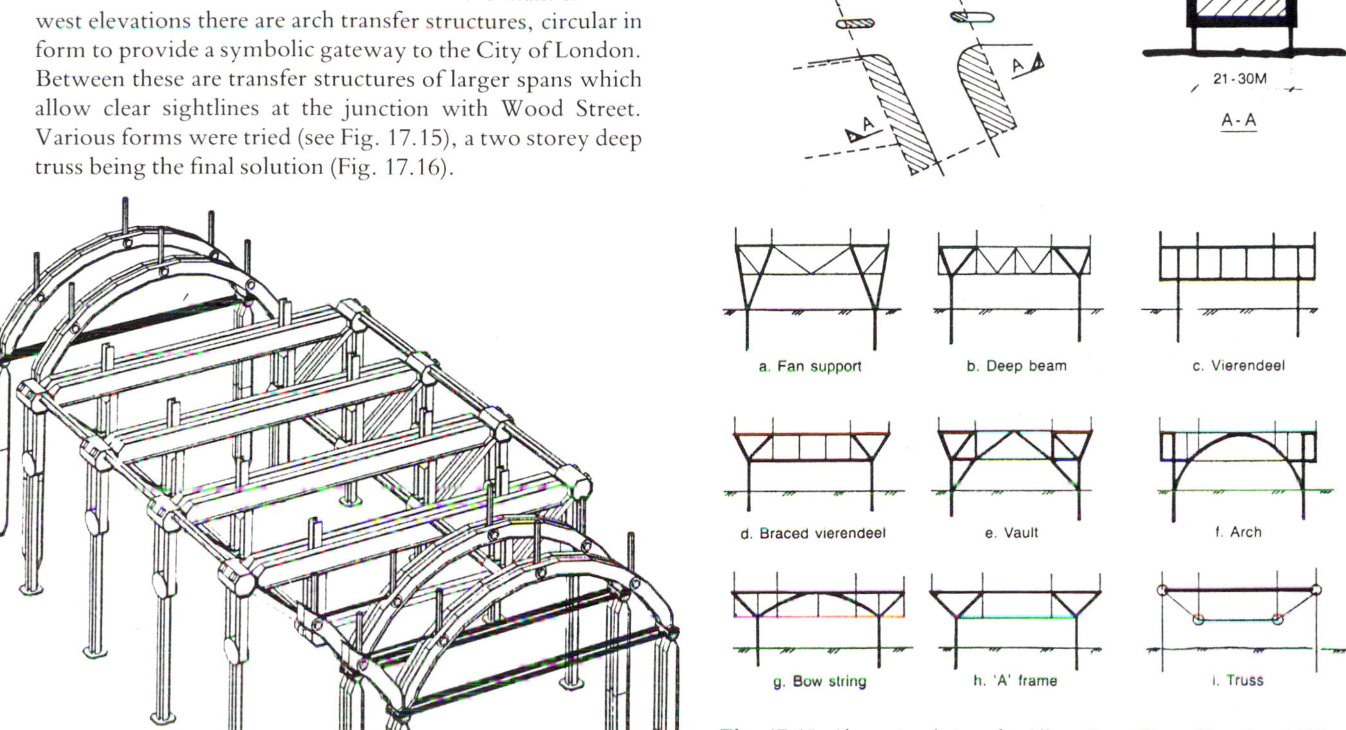

Fig. 17.15 *Alternative designs for Alban Gate, City of London, 1990 (architect Terry Farrell and Co Ltd: engineer Ove Arup and Partners).*

Fig. 17.16 *Alban Gate, City of London: final solution (a) isometric; (b) detail of central trusses.*

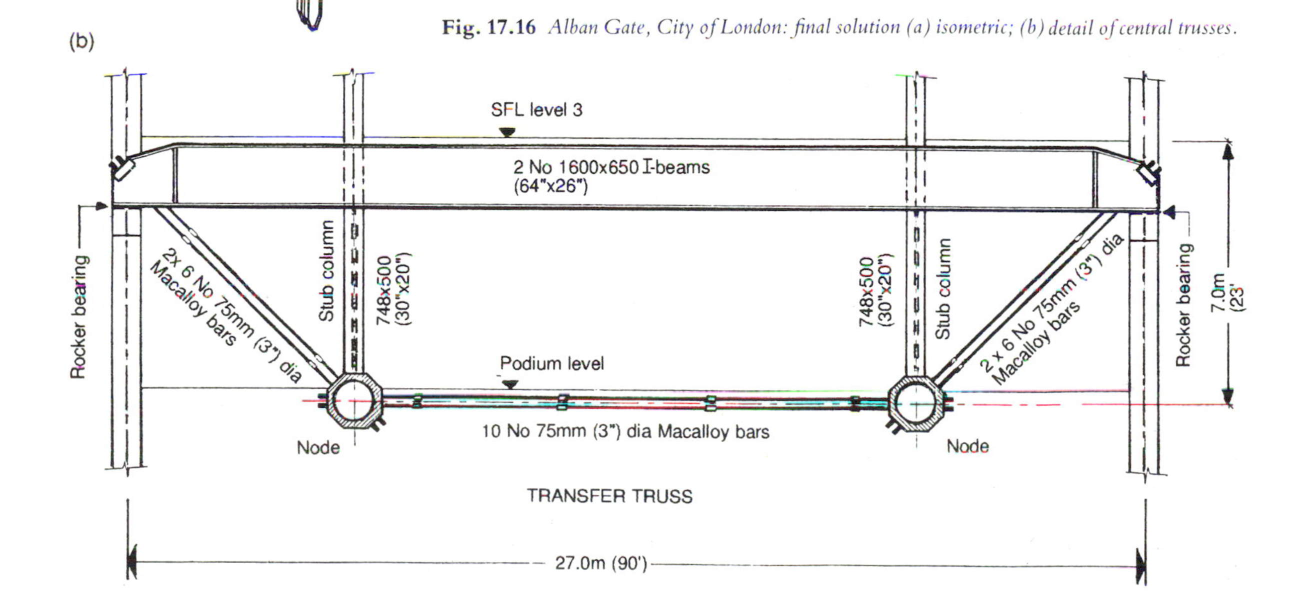

The tension members are Macalloy bars in two clusters of six for the diagonals between which crosses the horizontal cluster of ten bars. The two nodes take the anchorages for these bars and provide a bearing for the stub columns. The compression member is also a stiff steel beam dealing with any out of balance loads and thus allowing the middle bay to be clear and accommodate a mezzanine floor (not shown). The nodes, weighing 18 tonnes each, were cast in grade 50C steel by River Don castings of Sheffield and needed very little machining afterwards. Being squeezed and bent simultaneously required finite element methods to analyse the complex stresses.

Disproportionate collapse is dealt with by multiplicity of bars, it being considered acceptably improbable that all could fail at once. Fire protection is provided by sheaths of pre-formed intumescent 'Firec' by Nullifire with a tubular weathering sheath of anodized aluminium.

17.5.5 Ives Street, Chelsea, London

Plate girders are often useful when transfer structures need to be not seen and not heard. Take for example the terrace of high quality offices built over the London Underground District Line in Ives Street, Chelsea (Fig. 17.17). The architecture is traditional and the floor space precious. Plate girders, where the flanges were lost in the floors and the webs simply took the place of the inner skin of blockwork in a 11 inch (280 mm) cavity wall, provided the answer. Perforations were provided for windows and doors and here again finite element programs were used to analyse the complex stress patterns. In addition, the whole terrace was suspended on vibration isolation pads. The steelwork was fabricated by Redpath Dorman Long in Manchester. This simple device enabled a successful modest scale development on an otherwise impossible site.

Fig. 17.17 *Plate girder design, Ives Street, Chelsea, 1990 (architect Michael Brown and Associates: engineer Alan Baxter and Associates; designer in charge Bryn Bird).*

17.5.6 Hongkong and Shanghai Bank

To complete the examples, what better than the Hongkong and Shanghai Bank by Foster Associates, with engineer Ove Arup and Partners. It is much photographed and well written up, but still unavoidably spectacular as a form of transfer structure.

The idea was to build over the previously existing bank headquarters whilst it remained there in operation. The competition winning idea that rose to this challenge remained even after the brief was changed and the original bank no longer had to remain in place. Several ideas were considered along the way (Fig. 17.18) and the final transfer structure is shown in Fig. 17.19.

There are eight column clusters on four grids. Each transfer structure has two column attachments and provides three hangers. They occur at five different levels and suspend between five and nine floors each. The transfer structures also combine with the Vierendeel columns to provide the overall lateral resistance (see Fig. 17.20). Four simple members form each 'coat-hanger' truss by pin connections in double shear (Fig. 17.21). For further details refer to section 37.8.

17.6 CONCLUSION

Transfer structures are always powerful challenges to building designers. They draw out the full range of engineering skills. Architects can choose to express them or hide them but they cannot be ignored. They are invariably expensive but worth it. This use will increase as the need for double use of ground space increases and we build more over roads, railways and rivers. They demand thoroughness, and from this we derive satisfaction.

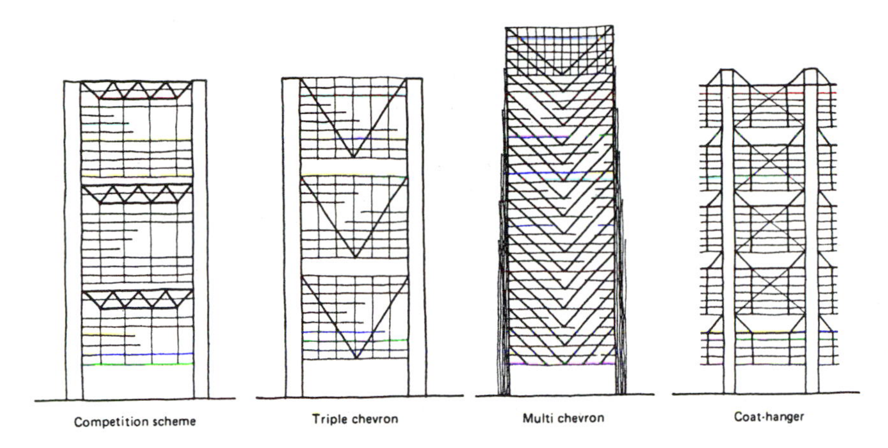

Fig. 17.18 *Alternative designs for Hongkong and Shanghai Bank 1986 (architect Foster Associates: engineer Ove Arup and Partners).*

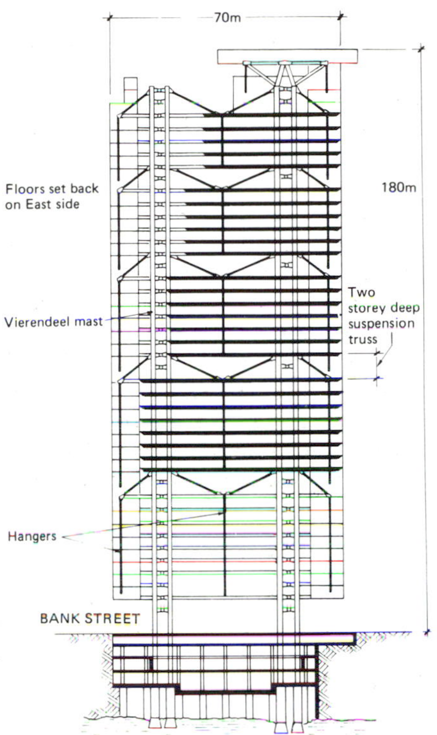

Fig. 17.19 *Hongkong and Shanghai Bank: final solution.*

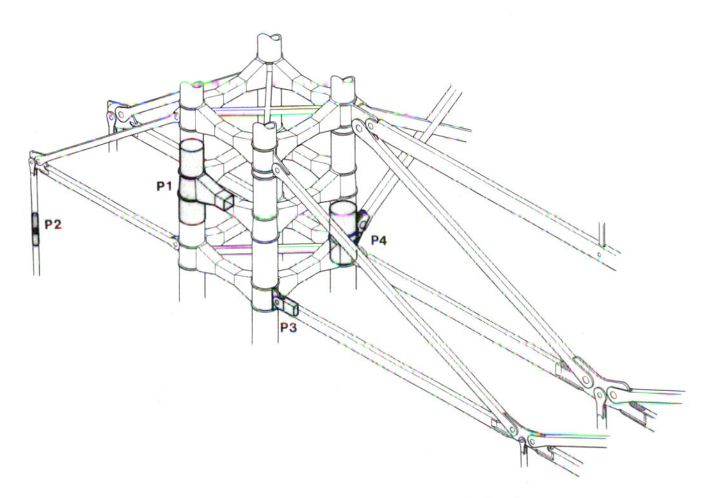

Fig. 17.20 *Hongkong and Shanghai Bank, Vierendeel columns.*

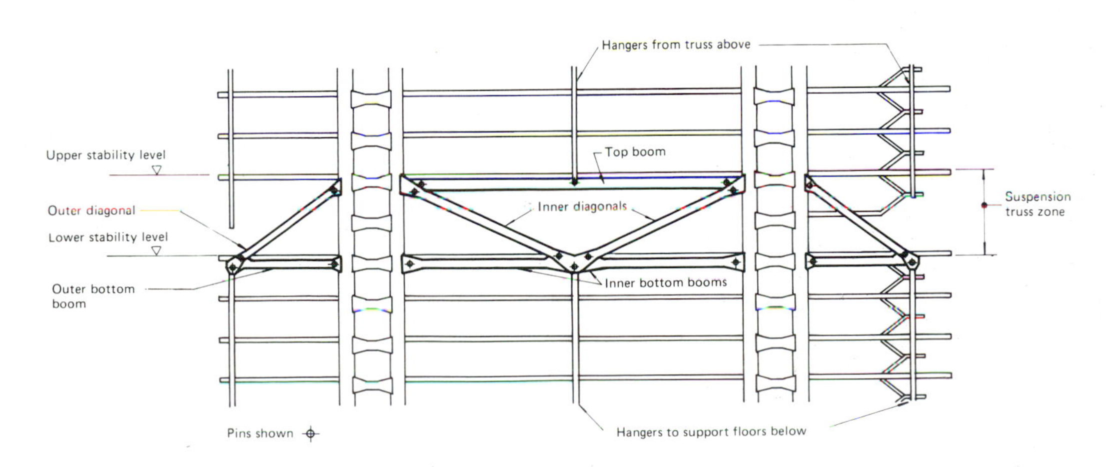

Fig. 17.21 *Hongkong and Shanghai Bank, coat-hanger truss.*

(a)

(b)

(c)

(d)

(e)

(a) Pile driving rig.
(b) Temporary sheet piling used to retain river banks during adjacent construction work.
(c) Sheet piles for bridge abutment.
(d) Driving sheet piles.
(e) Sheet piling for dockside work.

18

Foundation structures

Stefan Tietz

18.1 INTRODUCTION

For houses and small structures on level sites, building foundations can normally be simple; concrete pads and strip footings are frequently the cheapest and preferred solution. For larger buildings, especially if they have basements, more complex conditions have to be satisfied and foundations are frequently designed for a range of functions. Pile foundations, which minimize subsidence and avoid surcharging adjoining ground, are often used where ground is poor or loads are heavy; such piles can be in steel. Steel may also be used in foundations in the form of grillages, supporting more widely spread vertical loads closer to the surface.

For basements the surrounding ground and construction have to be retained; when building close to rivers or the sea temporary or permanent works may be necessary to keep out the water. Steelwork is used in such foundations in a variety of forms, the most common being sheet piling. Steelwork is also commonly used for temporary works in the form of shoring or propping, and trench sheeting may be used for shallow basements, trenches or steep earth banks.

18.2 SHEET PILING

The primary function of sheet piles is to support lateral loads for retaining earthworks, although they may also be subject to vertical loads, or for caisson construction in water or on very wet sites.

Sheet piling is normally driven into the ground before any major excavation. Soil is then excavated within the piled area, resulting in horizontal forces on piles due to the retained earth and any surcharge loads such as vehicles or adjoining buildings. These are most commonly resisted by the sheet piles acting as a cantilever, in which case the depth of drive must be sufficient to develop adequate bending restraint at the bottom of the excavation . Alternatively, the top of the pile may be anchored by horizontal or inclined ties.

Sheet piling is available in three grades of steel – mild steel, medium tensile and high yield - and can be alloyed with small amounts of copper to improve corrosion resistance.

18.2.1 Profiles

Sheet piling profiles need a good cutting edge in order that they can be readily driven into the subsoil, and an overall shape able to resist not only the permanent bending stresses but also the driving forces without excess distortion or damage. Trench sheeting is a much lighter form which is simply used for retaining shallow excavations for trenches, foundations or basements. Profiles are designed so that the edge of one sheet pile interlocks with the adjoining ones. The interlock, or clutch, has to provide a reasonably watertight final construction, yet allow sufficient freedom to drive adjoining piles.

The two main types of sheet piling are Frodingham and Larssen. The Frodingham pile is designed to be pitched in line, with the profile interlocking and is most appropriate for straight or near straight walls (Fig. 18.1). The Larssen pile (Fig. 18.2) is better able to deviate from a straight line and is therefore more suitable for circular or curved construction such as caissons or cofferdams. The back-to-back configuration generates greater bending resistance and is ideal for deeper excavations.

Suppliers' tables indicate a whole range of profiles, grades

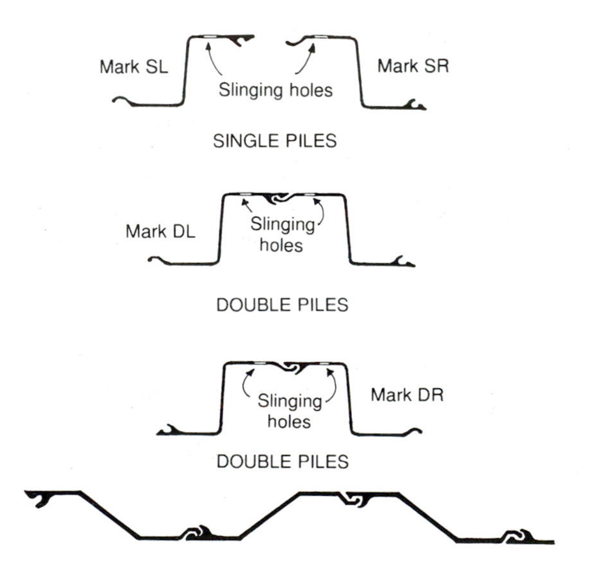

Fig. 18.1 *Frodingham pile profiles.*

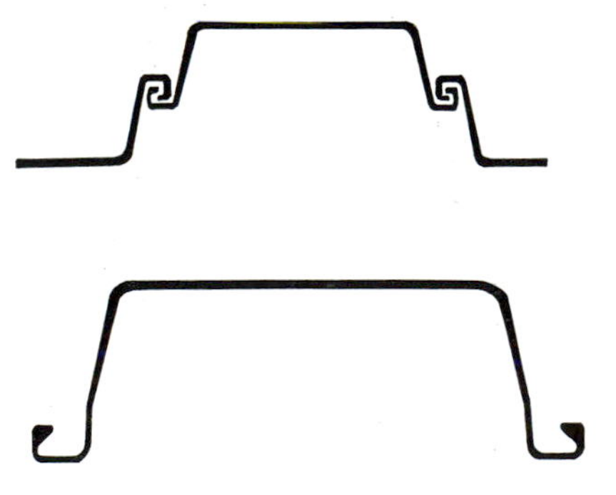

Fig. 18.2 *Larssen pile profile.*

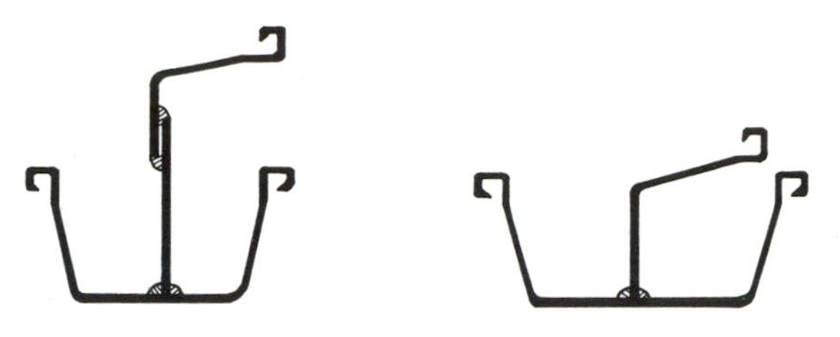

90° - Type 1b (welded) 1c opposite hand

90° - Type 3b (welded) 3c opposite hand

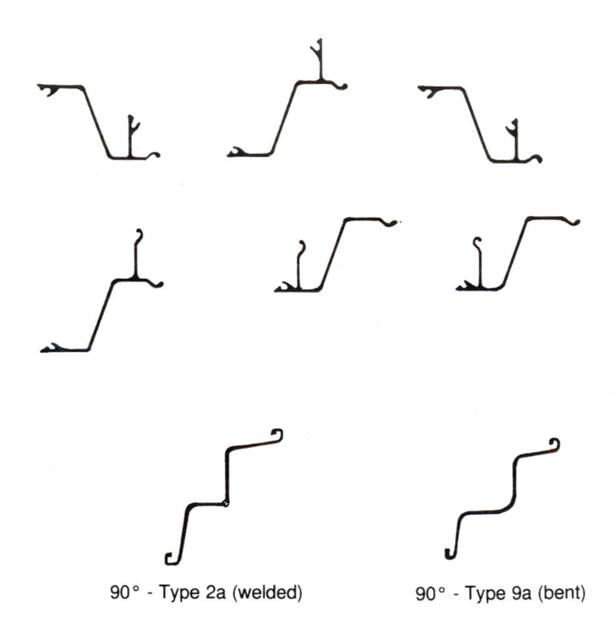

Fig. 18.3 *Frodingham and Larssen junction piles.*

and weights to suit the specific design. In addition, special sections can be assembled, normally built up by welding, to allow for corners, wall intersections and tapers in piled walls. Occasionally, such tapers also become unexpectedly necessary if adjoining piles break their clutch and one or more get out of line. Typical details are given in Fig. 18.3.

In general, the gauge of section depends upon the length to be driven and the bending moments to be resisted. For guidance refer to the *Piling Handbook*, published by British Steel [1].

Similar piling forms are used for both permanent and temporary works. In the latter case, the sheets are withdrawn and may be re-used. This is made simpler by the normal provision of anchor holes near the ends of the pile, which are also used for handling.

18.2.2 Jointing piles

Sections are normally supplied in lengths, up to maximum limits to suit particular requirements. However, there are practical problems on site of handling long piles, and there is also a considerable risk of long piles buckling when driving into hard ground. In these circumstances deeper profiles or shorter lengths are used. After the lowermost length has been driven home the pile can be lengthened by site welding.

18.2.3 Use of sheet piling in walls

The design of sheet piling is complex and engineering advice, including soil investigation and site surveys, is needed from the outset. The type of soil and subsoil, water table, and surcharge loads from surroundings areas are all important.

The pile design will depend heavily on the configuration of the site and the programme of works. Stresses on piling may be reduced by appropriate propping. This is particularly important where the total depth of an excavation is considerable, but where future floors or other forms of construction offer subsequent permanent propping action and thus reduce the free-standing height of the piles in their final installed form. The design of appropriate temporary works is therefore important to ensure that the piles are neither overstressed during the construction phase nor uneconomic in their permanent condition.

Good temporary works design must also ensure that temporary shoring does not unduly inhibit the activities of the contractor. For this reason, responsibility for the design of temporary works normally rests with the contractor. Good liaison with the designers of permanent sheet piled walls is, however, necessary to ensure that design assumptions in the wall design are understood and met.

18.2.4 Tied sheet piling

For long cantilever piles the stresses become excessive and tying is then often employed. Such ties run horizontally or at a slope into the soil behind the pile. At their free end, on the open face of the sheet pile, they are held by walings, often formed by pairs of channels or RSJs. Such ties may need to be long – probably many metres if the excavation is deep – as they must be anchored beyond the wedge of soil which is retained by the pile; this may be a limiting factor on restricted sites such as city centres (Fig. 18.4).

Anchors are commonly found behind old sea walls and some canal banks as permanent features of the wall design. As such they have to be retained and can inhibit the construction of later foundations and earthworks on the land traversed by the ties.

Methods by which the ties achieve their tying action depend upon the nature of the soil. In the simplest case of rock or stable, dense materials, friction between the tie and the ground it passes through is sufficient. The tie rod is normally grouted. Clearly friction is not sufficient by itself with more friable soils, loose sand or ground where substantial settlement is a factor. In such cases small diameter horizontal or raking piles may be driven instead, thereby achieving a larger surface area to resist tension. Alternatively, anchors can be driven into the ground some distance beyond the excavated area (Fig. 18.5). These provide a fixing for tie rods and act like pegs holding tent ropes. Sometimes a mixture of friction ties and other ground anchors is necessary in difficult ground. To avoid obstructions near ground level on adjoining sites in the same ownership (or where adjoining owners agree) ties can be raked.

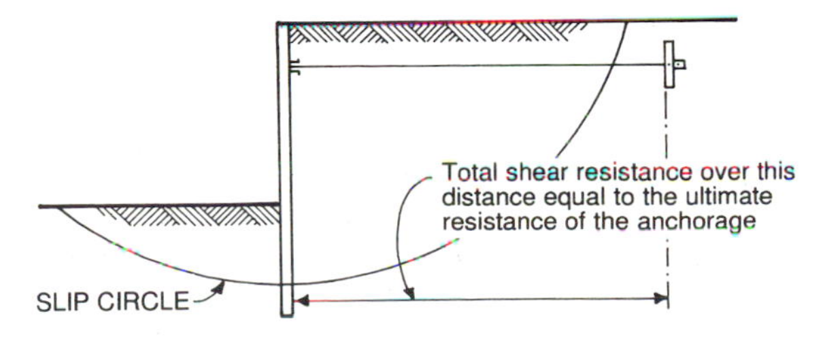

Fig. 18.4 *Location of anchorages in cohesive soils.*

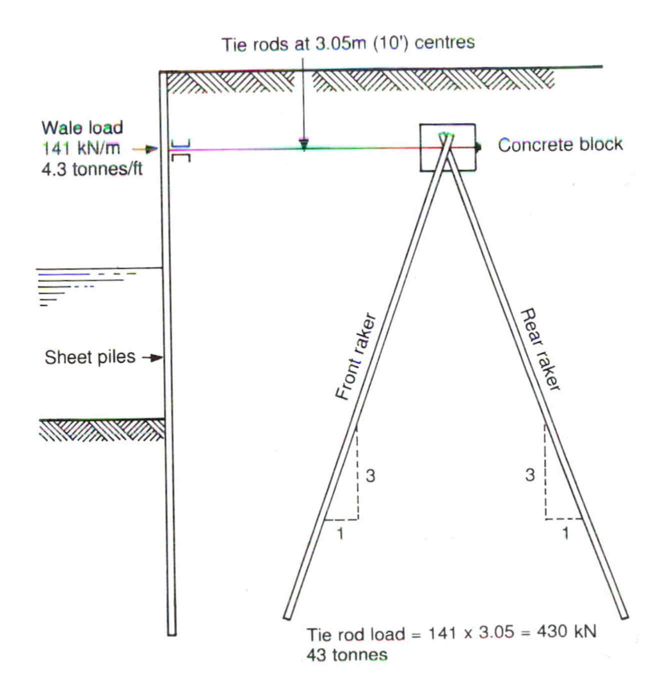

Fig. 18.5 *Typical raking pile anchors.*

If only the tops of sheet piles are to be anchored there may be other options such as a structurally designed pavement, tying the heads from the outside. When internal floors are incorporated, these fulfil that function as props but the temporary condition which exists before floors are in place then needs to be considered.

New construction built alongside deep excavations can occasionally be designed to provide the necessary restraint for ties. However, if such construction is on piles, these may need to be raked to accommodate the horizontal forces.

18.2.5 Walings and struts

Walings are horizontal beams used to restrain sheet piling and to ensure proper alignment of the wall. They typically take the form of structural steel sections but can be of timber or sometimes reinforced concrete (Fig. 18.6). For economy they are often designed to be strong in the horizontal plane, but weak in the vertical plane. Struts are then used to prop them.

In canal and dock construction the walings are given shock absorbing facings to reduce damage from shipping, the piling being frequently capped in concrete or steel to distribute loading from the dockside.

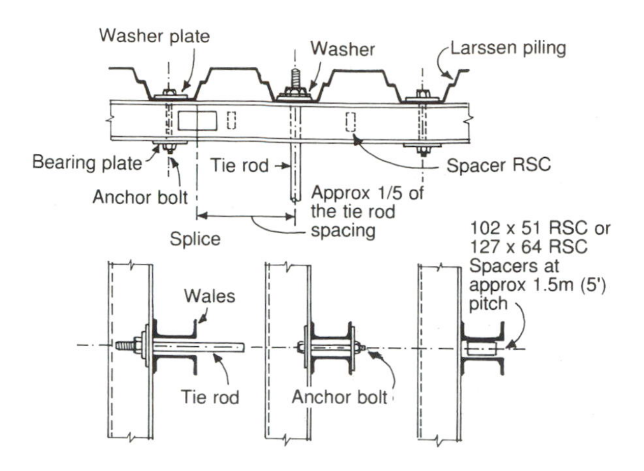

Fig. 18.6 *Typical walings: simple form and strutted.*

18.2.6 Cofferdams

Cofferdams are special applications of sheet piling, normally constructed to a circular or rectangular plan shape to form a shaft within which excavation can then take place (Fig. 18.7). Such works are particularly appropriate for deep foundations in water or wet ground.

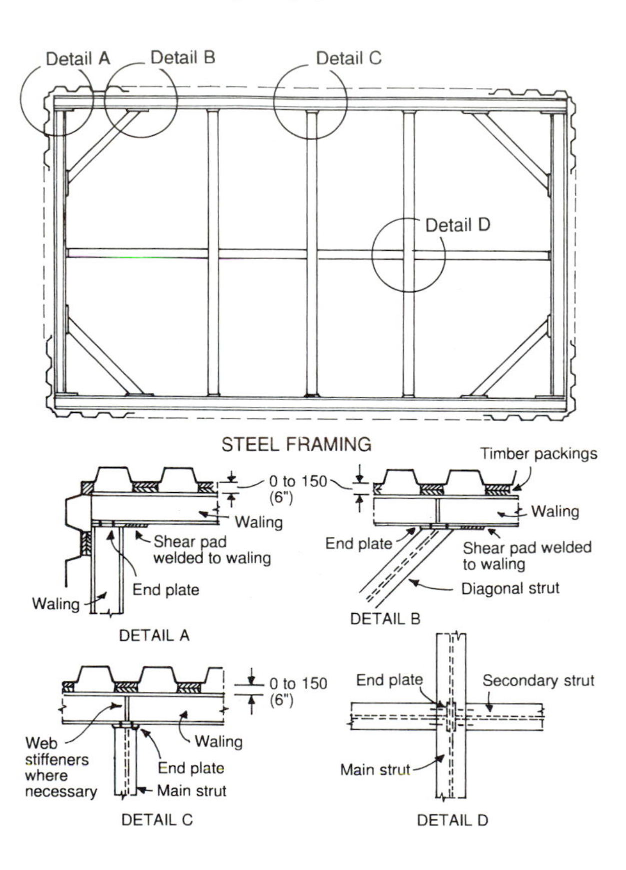

Fig. 18.7 *Cofferdam for deep basement.*

18.2.7 Driving of sheet piles

Sheet piles are first 'pitched', that is located and set to the correct angle, and then driven. Both operations may be carried out using special mobile frames. Alternatively cranes can be used to pitch the pile, with special grips being attached to the driving mechanism. Several piles are aligned and interlocked horizontally and then driven one after the other or sometimes two or three at a time. Good alignment is obviously important but not always easy to achieve, especially if there are localized underground obstructions. The height of driving rigs is considerable, having to rise some distance above the lengths of the undriven pile, standing vertically.

Traditionally piles were driven by a steam hammer which was raised to the top of a large rig and then dropped, either under its own weight or power assisted, onto a cap protecting the top of the pile against deformation. The weight and speed of impact of the hammer determined the driving characteristics and these, together with the type of soil, determined the amount of penetration achieved with each blow. Normally such hammers were heavier than the pile.

More recently, other kinds of piling rig have come into use. These include diesel driven and double acting air hammers, which rely on short hammer blows of high frequency, All of these piling methods are noisy on two counts – firstly, the power plant, but more intrusively the hammering of metal on metal. Restrictions regarding noise levels caused by piling operations may be stipulated in Building Regulation consents, and effectively restrict the form of piling which may be considered. 'Silent' rigs are now coming onto the market. In effect, these push the piles into place rather than relying on hammering. Other methods, which reduce noise levels, rely on vibration to shake the pile into the ground.

The first few sheet piles which are driven are critical. The interlock or clutch between piles will mean they will tend to follow the line of the first few piles. It is therefore particularly important that these are very accurately set out and are driven vertically. This may require quite rigid piling frames to ensure that the line is held during driving. For long piles, different hammers are occasionally used, a light one first to get the piles some reasonable distance into the ground and then the heavier one to complete the drive. The lighter hammer makes it easier to control pile driving at the stage where there is little to hold the pile in place, rather in the manner of a hammer driving nails, where the first few blows can readily cause the nail to go off line.

18.3 BEARING PILES

Bearing piles are designed to carry predominantly vertical loads. The piles may be arranged individually or, more commonly, in groups to facilitate load sharing (Fig. 18.8).

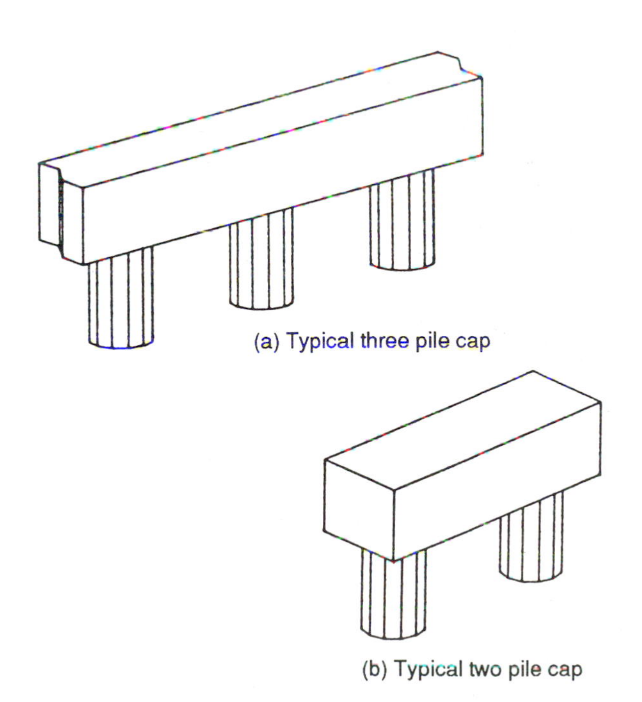

Fig. 18.8 *Multiple group of piles with extensive pile cap.*

The minimum practical distance between adjoining piles is determined by driving considerations and above all by soil characteristics, the aim being that each pile can develop adequate bearing without being weakened by its adjoining piles and their effect on the soil immediately surrounding them. The common spacing for friction piles is three diameters. Although there is no upper limit on spacing of piles in a single group, the stresses in pile caps increase as pile spacings increase.

Bearing piles may support their load in various ways:

(a) End bearing, provided by a hard stratum, perhaps rock, underlying softer strata;
(b) Friction between the perimeter of the pile and the soil;
(c) Partly end bearing and partly friction.

Pure friction piles are unusual since the strengths of most soils improve with depth so that there is normally some end bearing value to be obtained.

The amount of friction which may develop is proportional to the perimeter of the pile surface and depends on the kind of soil. 'H' shaped piles have a high perimeter related to their overall size and thus develop high friction resistance.

Piles are normally driven vertically but they can be raked in order to assist support of non-vertical loading; typical applications are dockside works where horizontal forces occur with ships berthing. There are also special cases where pile driving causes soil to adhere to the pile and act as an additional load rather than provide support for the pile. This is referred to as 'draw-down' and needs to be considered in pile design to avoid overload.

18.3.1 Pile driving

'H' piles are normally driven 'as rolled' in a similar way to sheet piles, but without a cap. A shoe can be fitted to the bottom of the pile where the pile must penetrate through hard ground or broken stone. Tubular profiles or welded channels are also used, but these have greater driving resistance and cutting shoes are normally used. Difficult ground conditions can cause unexpected misalignment during driving operations. In such cases further piles need to be added or, where this is impossible, piles may need to be withdrawn and redriven in a manner which allows penetration of the obstruction.

For driven piles, the exact depth of drive is normally determined by the number of blows which cause the pile to move an agreed distance, known as 'the set'. There are occasional exceptions, particularly with alluvial soils (estuary and river mud), where driving can go on for a very long time, whilst still causing considerable movement. If such piles are then left for a period of a few hours, it may be found that driving has become much harder; in fact the set has been achieved by recompaction of soil particles previously dispersed by the shock waves caused by piling operations.

For raking piles special rigs are necessary to maintain the pile in the correct line and angle while being driven.

Some types of concrete piling can be cast in situ to varying lengths which suit site conditions. In contrast, steel piles are normally designed to predetermined lengths. This requires good soil surveys to provide ground information and ensure that piles as delivered are sufficiently long to carry the load. Alternatively, it is necessary to preplan the provision of extensions, normally added by welding. Cutting back of long lengths would be wasteful and is avoided as far as possible.

Some steel sections are rolled specifically for use as piles [2], these profiles having web and flange thicknesses of the same weight in order to offer optimum conditions for piling work. Overall sizes are similar to universal columns; other sections are used with conventional heavier flanges where greater bending stresses have to be resisted on the main axis. Tubular and rectangular box section piles are also used, particularly where bending is expected about both axes. They are normally filled with concrete to reduce corrosion risks from within. The benefits of steel piles can be summarized as follows:

(a) Long lengths
Long pile lengths are possible. Lengths up to 26 m (85 ft) are available from the rolling mills, and longer piles may be achieved by site welding.

(b) Resistance to hard driving
Piles offer good resistance to hard driving through heavy ground.

(c) Good weight to strength ratio
Piles are relatively light, making handling easier.

(d) Less displacement
The displacement of soil when driving 'H' piles is less than that likely to occur when driving circular or rectangular piles. This will tend to reduce the risk of localized soil heave and could be significant when driving piles close to adjoining buildings.

18.3.2 Stress in piles

The analysis of stresses developed in piles is complex. Conditions during the driving stage are quite different from those under permanent loading, and where groups of piles are used, the distribution of loads between individual piles must be established. This depends on the stiffness of the pile cap and the precise location of loads. Another complicating factor is the inevitable deviation of piles from their intended alignment due to obstructions or irregular ground conditions. Slight imperfections are unavoidable but must be allowed for in the design. Single piles are commonly stabilized by ground beams linking foundations whilst piles in groups can offer mutual compensation.

18.3.3 Pile caps

The purpose of the pile cap is to transmit the loads, for instance from columns, to the pile group, distributing forces between individual piles. Since it is rarely practical to drive piles at a spacing of much less than three pile diameters, bending stresses in the pile cap are unavoidable and the analysis of caps for groups of five or more piles can be very complex.

Under normal circumstances the stress distribution in a pile cap is such that stresses occur in both plane directions. Pile caps were traditionally formed with a grillage of short steel beams and this form is still employed where speed is critical or where cantilever or transfer loads need to be allowed for on restricted sites. However, grillages have the disadvantage that the steel components are either at different levels or require complex connections to achieve two-way strength in a single plane. Reinforced concrete is therefore more commonly used in pile cap construction today.

The present mode of basement construction where asphalt tanking is omitted, raises the issue of steel protection within a wet concrete environment and with steel exposed to air. The deep basements to the new British Library have drainable cavities between structure and subfloors, or basement walls. In such conditions steelwork will need adequate cover and should perhaps be galvanized for additional protection.

18.4 TENSION PILES

Tension piles are more common in civil engineering than in building work. In rare cases, the innermost piles of cantilever foundations near site boundaries may be subject to uplift, but they can usually be arranged to coincide with other column positions to counteract this effect. Tent or cable supported structures may often create pull-out forces at foundation level and these require either dead load in the form of heavy foundations or adjoining structures, or tension piles. Where bearing piles are required to be tested, loading is often applied using hydraulic jacks reacting against a rigid framework, which itself must be anchored using tension piles.

Also for light buildings with basements or swimming pools in areas with a high water table, buoyancy may need to be resisted – often by the use of tension piles. [3]

Even in cohesive soils (clay), piles develop less adhesion (pile to ground) in tension than in compression and hence a larger number of tension piles will normally be required. They are therefore best avoided if other options exist.

18.5 EFFECTIVE LIFE AND CORROSION PROTECTION

The effective life of steel piling depends on the environment in which it is used. Rates of corrosion without protection will vary from about 0.03 to 0.15 mm (1 to 6 thou) per year according to circumstances. This compares with normal atmospheric corrosion of unpainted steel at an assumed rate of about 0.07 mm (3 thou) per year. The most severe conditions are in sea water, particularly in tidal zones where there is intermittent immersion. Corrosion risks are also high at ground level where the piles may be subject to cycles of wetting and drying, and in corrosive soil conditions. Under such circumstances tar paints may be used to extend the life of the pile. 'Oversizing', that is providing a greater thicknesses of steel and hence an adequate reserve of strength in the corroded state, or corrosion resistant steels can also be used to prolong pile life. At least risk are deep buried piles where oxygen supplies are restricted.

REFERENCES AND TECHNICAL NOTES

1. British Steel General Steels (1986) *Piling Handbook* – a most useful guidebook to the major suppliers with details of profiles and thicknesses.
2. BS 4: Structural steel sections: Part 1: 1980 Specification for hot rolled sections.
3. CIRIA (1989) Special publication 69: *The Engineering Implications of Rising Groundwater Levels in the Deep Aquifer Beneath London.*

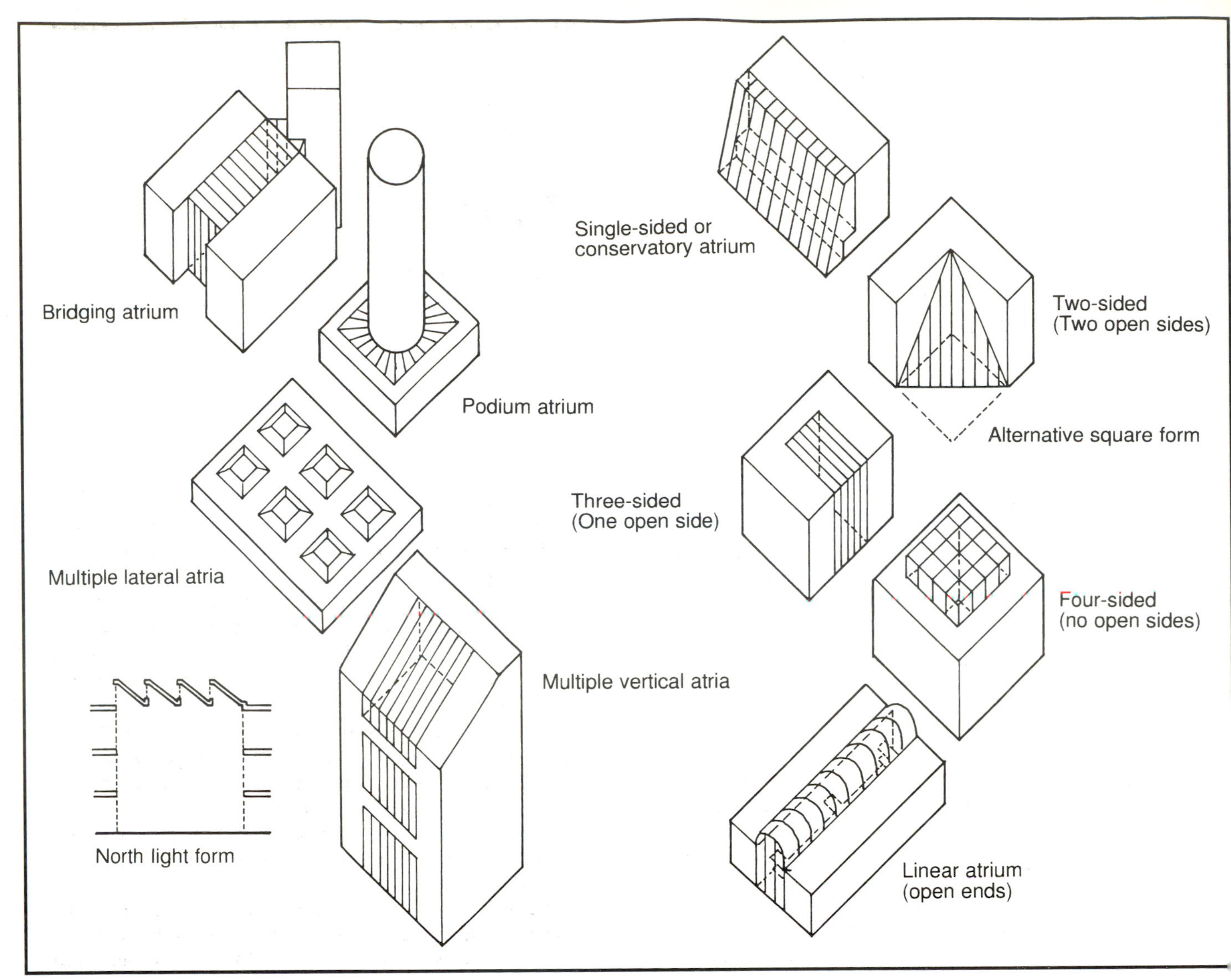

Fig. 19.1 *Basic forms of atria.*

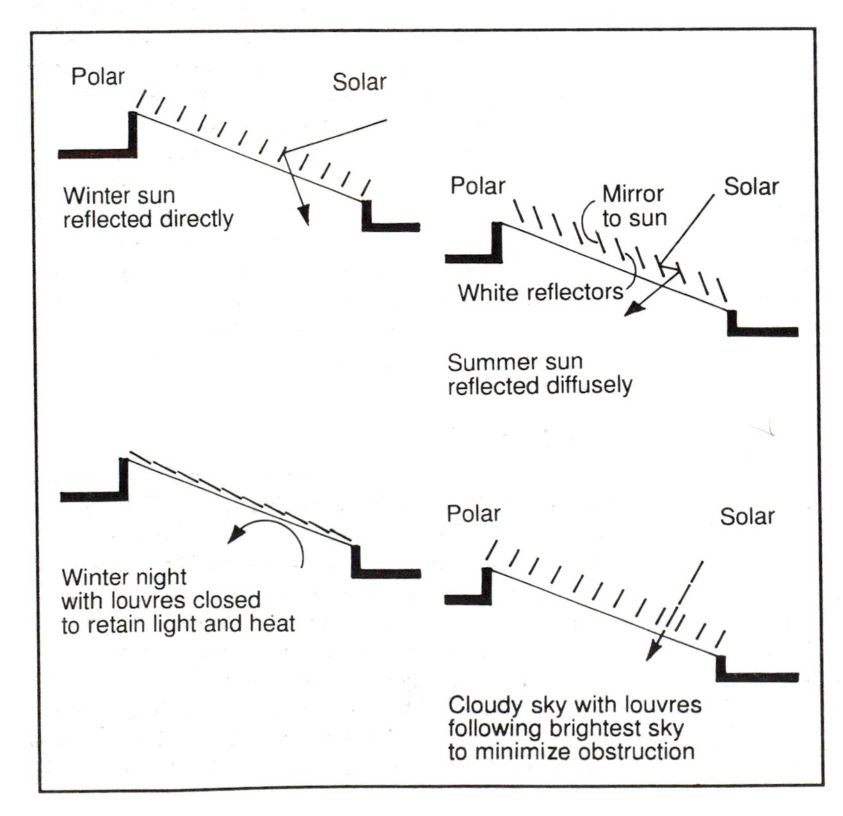

Fig. 19.2 *Convertible atria.*

19

Atria

Richard Saxon

19.1 INTRODUCTION

Atria are, by definition, voids between occupied blocks of building. Their enclosures, usually predominantly transparent or translucent, are technologies in themselves but interact strongly with the structure and treatment of the buildings surrounding them. The main building frame will probably derive economies from the use of an atrium, being lower and wider than it would otherwise have been. The atrium form encourages lower, site-covering buildings which will have more foundations but less wind load problems than a taller structure. This chapter concentrates on the design of structures carrying the roof, and walls if any, of the atrium space itself; for fuller references refer to *Atrium Buildings* by Richard Saxon (Butterworth Architecture) [1].

Steel is the structural medium in the great majority of atria. There are small numbers of atria with timber, concrete or aluminium frames but a discussion of atrium structures can usefully proceed on the basis that steel is the likely material.

19.2 DESIGN CRITERIA

Principal criteria governing the selection of the structural systems include the climatic role to be played by the envelope, the visual character sought and the practicalities of cleaning and maintenance. Two further detailed issues – fire resistance and thermal movement – also need careful consideration.

19.2.1 Climatic role

The role to be played by the atrium roof and outer walls as climate modifiers can be important to the choice of structure. Is the atrium to be fully climate controlled, or a freewheeling buffer space? Are the climatic location and building use ones which require a warming atrium (one which admits solar energy freely), a cooling atrium (an anti-solar shading structure) or a convertible atrium (one able to switch roles seasonally or daily)? A warming atrium will be oriented to collect sunlight, with its exact form related to latitude. Equator-facing glazed side walls and lantern lights would be expected, with roofs having a fully glazed surface in mild climates. Colder climates could need insulated lantern light sides, which additionally reflect low angle sun. Warm temperate climates could need sawtooth roofs designed to admit winter sun but reflect summer sun angles (Fig. 19.1).

A cooling atrium seeks to admit light without significant solar penetration. Polar facing sawtooth roofs and sidewalls might be needed, or solid roofs and fixed external shading features in tropical latitudes where all surfaces receive sun at some time.

Convertible atria have to use moveable features to change from admitting sun to rejecting it. Banks of operable louvres on solar facing slopes are the most common approach. These are ideally external to the roof or wall but are often placed internally to increase reliability, though at the cost of increased thermal stress in the structure and louvre system (Fig. 19.2).

The frame may be asked to carry air or water for climate control of the atrium space. Box columns and beams at the Bank of Canada in Ottawa (Fig. 19.38) carry air supplies to the cavity between two glass skins. In other buildings air may be blown across glass to remove condensation, or hot water carried to combat downdrafts by radiation. The structure may be asked to carry these services rather than obstructing views with a further set of members.

Natural ventilation, if provided, brings considerable stress as atria are natural chimneys with attendant stack pressure differentials. These must be accounted for in the design in order to keep doors and louvres operable.

Choice of glazing materials is also a way of providing admittance, insulation and shading, but assigning a climatic role to the envelope gives pointers to the shape and support needs which the selected system should possess.

19.2.2 Visual character

The atrium will probably be the part of the building with the strongest architectural character (Figs 19.3 and 19.4). The structure of the atrium is very likely to be the most visible and expressive structure in the whole building. Choice of structural approach will thus be strongly influenced by the character sought. The examples which illustrate this chapter indicate the enormous range of effects which can be achieved. Some designers choose a solid atrium wall with windows (Fig. 19.29), continuing the building's general frame, whilst others seek diaphanous fabric, with maximum uninterrupted transparency (Fig. 19.31). Most use the

Fig. 19.3 *Plaza of the Americas, Dallas, Texas, 1981.*

Fig. 19.4 *IBM Plaza, Mount Pleasant, New York, 1983 (architect Edward Larabee Barnes).*

rhythm of steel members to create scale and interest in themselves, usually in contrast to the expression of the surrounding building (Fig. 19.30). Frames can be light and close-centred or heavy and widely separated, shallow and sophisticated or heavy and industrial, with or without intermediate column support. Victorian forms can be selected to be consistent with historic character in the surrounding buildings or neighbourhood (Figs 19.8 and 19.15). Farm building shapes can be used in rural locations. Futuristic shapes are often found in resort or downtown buildings. Metaphor and allusion govern formal decisions on visible structure as much as in any other architectural element today.

19.2.3 Cleaning and maintenance

An industry is developing in cradle systems to give access to external and internal atrium surfaces. Some of these systems are very complicated and overcome extremely difficult access problems set by designers. Others are ugly intrusions which spoil the architect's concept. In contrast, other atria are dingy and unkempt because the access problem could not be solved economically. Incorporation of provision for feasible cleaning and maintenance gear into the design process is a powerful discipline (Fig. 19.18). Many roof and wall shapes are ruled out, but the final design retains its effect as the glass will be clean. Ease of cleaning favours extruded forms along which a gantry can run, rotational forms which can have a rotating gantry, and vertical planes serviceable from cradles. Tapering shapes are problematic, as are complex intersections. Where the structure allows integral catwalks this can make internal surfaces, lights and ventilation details accessible without gantries or cradles.

19.2.4 Fire protection

Roofs and external glazed walls are not regarded as elements of structure, in the sense that no occupied space is supported by them. They do not therefore require fire protection for life safety, which is the limit of regulation requirements. Insurers are concerned, however, by the cost of replacing such large and expensive features in the event of a major fire, even if occupied space is relatively well protected from damage. Roof structures in steel may need to be fire protected, with the choices including intumescent paint or sprinklers.

Smoke removal strategies for atrium buildings sometimes involve use of the atrium, with fans or natural ventilation openings in the roof. Volume is needed below the roof and above inhabited levels, especially if open to the atrium, to accommodate a smoke cloud being evacuated. This requires a lantern roof, with height to match the calculated smoke handling need.

BS 5588 Part 7 [2] for the first time provides consistent fire safety standards for atrium design. The guidance document recently issued by the LDSA on *Fire Safety in Atrium Buildings* [3] is also relevant.

The basic parameters of a fire safety plan are the height of the building, the extent to which the atrium enclosure separates it from the rest of the building and the function of the floor of the atrium. The LDSA guide includes typical building cross-sections with deemed-to-satisfy solutions incorporating a variety of safety measures. With increasing height of building, the stringency of the fire safety requirements increases. Safety precautions that may be employed include alternative methods of evacuating the building, the extent of fire resistance of the atrium walls and the use of sprinklers, heat vents and smoke controls.

In future it will be possible to design atrium buildings without safety standards being over specified as they have been in the past. Also, mixed-use buildings will no longer be regarded unfavourably as long as alarm and sprinkler systems are designed to be adequate for the most onerous of possible conditions.

19.2.5 Thermal movement

Atrium envelopes are light, with large and rapid thermal movements as the framework and glazing pick up solar heat. In atria without air circulation systems a temperature gradient of 1°C (1.8°F) for every metre of height is normal in the UK. Thus the top of a 20 m (66 ft) tall atrium may be 20°C (68°F) above ambient temperature. The whole roof must move successfully but the point of maximum danger is the joint between envelope and occupied building fabric where differential movements can be pronounced. This is especially complex where atrium roofs intersect occupied building walls. Heat under such roofs is a problem for comfort in immediately adjacent accommodation.

19.3 EXAMPLES OF ROOF FORMS

There is a wide range of different roof forms including level (planar, sawtooth, spaceframe), sloping forms, linear vaults (folded and arched forms), rotational forms (pyramids, lanterns and dormers), and complex forms (Vierendeel frames).

19.3.1 Level roof forms

These forms are sought when interior volume or exterior height is limited, and when intersection with other elements of the building makes other forms difficult to resolve. For most of the history of level glass roofs, the actual glass surface had to be pitched or vaulted in minor elements in order to drain. A recent development is the ability to lay near-level frameless glass roofs (Fig. 19.7).

When the roof is not to be primarily glass, as it rarely is in tropical latitudes, the temptation is to use conventional joist structures supporting decking. The Plaza of the Americas, Dallas, shows this low key form, with strips of rooflight cut across the decking. Visual banality is the risk (Fig. 19.3). Sawtooth roofs go back to the first glasshouses, and a good example is the garden atrium at the IBM Plaza in New York by Edward Larabee Barnes (Fig.19.4). The triangular volume provides the spanning depth required. External cleaning can usually be done from the gutters which are used as walkways. Internal cleaning can use rolling catwalks between the lower chords of each angled frame.

Spaceframes can easily provide the structure for level roofs. At the East Building of the National Gallery in Washington DC (Fig. 19.5) I.M. Pei has used a superscaled space structure of triangular pyramids in built-up steel members with cast steel connecting nodes. A great deal of sophistication has gone into the detailing to make it look simple. The whole roof is supported on nearly invisible projecting lugs at the edge nodes.

Fig. 19.5 *National Gallery, East Building, Washington DC, 1978 (architect I.M.Pei).*

Fig. 19.6 *Waverley Market Centre, Edinburgh, 1984 (architect BDP).*

Fig. 19.7 *J.P. Morgan Headquarters, London, 1991 (model) (architect BDP).*

Planar glazing makes a near flat (1–2% slope) roof glass possible as there is no projection to block run-off. The first example was BDP's Waverley Market, Edinburgh (Fig. 19.6) where steel joists at 1200 mm (4 ft) centres pick up glass sheet corners and also carry a secondary safety glass layer. A pre-engineered spaceframe supports the planar glass atrium roof at the Porsche showroom in Woking, UK. Each frame node supports a cluster of bolts picking up the corners of four double-glazed units. The BDP design for the J.P. Morgan Headquarters uses a box-section lattice to support adjustable pedestals carrying the corner bolt clusters and give a coffered ceiling appearance (Fig. 19.7).

Fig. 19.8 *Charles Englehardt Court, Metropolitan Museum, New York City, 1982 (architect Roche Dinkeloo).*

19.3.2 Sloping roof forms

Glass will drain itself in conventional framing or in patent glazing bar systems if held on a slope. Support at approximately 3 m (10 ft) centres maximum is needed and a variety of simple solutions is possible. Rolled steel sections give least obstruction but use most material. The roof at the Charles Englehardt Court, Metropolitan Museum, New York (Fig. 19.8), by Roche Dinkeloo is built that way. However, lattice members are most commonly used for the support grid. St Enoch Centre Glasgow, by GMW/Reiach and Hall demonstrates large scale sloped glazing support of this form. The most convincing use of a space frame for this task would seem to be at the Vancouver Law Courts by Arthur Erickson (Fig. 19.9). Steel trees spring off the underlying concrete frame to carry nodes in a suitable distributed manner. The presence of the sky is clearly felt through the gauze of members. Pennzoil Place, Houston, by Johnson Burgee (Fig. 19.10), shows a large span version of the space frame.

19.3.3 Linear vaults (folded and arched forms)

Pitched glass roofs over linear glazed spaces are common, though few use truss supports as they might if roof decking were to be supported, perhaps fearing the industrial aesthetic which could result. One exception is Helmut Jahn's Board of Trade extension in Chicago (Fig. 19.11). Roche Dinkeloo's John Deere office building (Fig. 19.12) uses the twice-folded gambrel roof forms of barn construction to roof the garden of this agricultural machinery giant, the steelwork being Cor-Ten. Greenhouse technology is used at the University of Trondheim by Henning Larsen (Fig. 19.13), in the form of lightweight latticed frames and the rolling sections which open the streets to the summer sun.

Arched roofs over galleria are an exceedingly popular

Fig. 19.9 *Law Court, Vancouver, BC 1981 (architect Arthur Erickson).*

Fig. 19.10 *Pennzoil Place, Houston, Texas, 1976 (architect Johnson Burgee).*

form, and have become almost a cliché in shopping malls. Arches can span a long way with an elegant light framework as they minimize bending stresses. There are several pre-engineered systems available using the glazing bar as the arch structure. On very wide spans special designs are needed. Eberhard Zeidler's Eaton Centre, Toronto (Fig. 19.14), shows a low-pitched, multi-centred lattice arch, with the upper chord rising to a point at the centre to avoid too low a glass pitch. The conservatory roofs of Francis Machin (Fig. 19.15) use reflex, ogee curves in polycarbonate to avoid the flat top and stiffen the plastic for its span between glazing bars.

Rolled steel joists or hollow sections can now be bent easily, and arched forms in rolled steel are appearing. The Palm House atrium of the Ealing Broadway Office Centre by BDP (Fig. 19.16) uses pressed, curved toughened glass to follow the arched forms. Hugh Martin's exuberent Princes Square centre in Glasgow uses curved pipe tubing.

Fig. 19.11 *Board of Trade, Chicago, Illinois, 1982 (architect Helmut Jahn).*

Fig. 19.12 *Deere West, Moline, Illinois, 1979 (architect Roche Dinkeloo).*

Fig. 19.15 *Machin conservatories, Francis Machin.*

Fig. 19.16 *Ealing Broadway Office Centre, London, 1984 (architect BDP).*

Fig. 19.13 *University of Trondheim, Norway, 1980 (architect Henning Larsen).*

Fig. 19.14 *Eaton Centre, Toronto, Canada, 1977 (architect Zeidler Roberts Partnership).*

Fig. 19.17 *Mile High Centre II, Denver, Colorado, 1983 (architect Johnson Burgee).*

Fig. 19.18 *Lloyds Building, London, 1984–6 (architect Richard Rogers and Partners: engineer Ove Arup and Partners).*

Fig. 19.19 *Lloyds Building, London, 1984–6 (architect Richard Rogers and Partners: engineer Ove Arup and Partners).*

Arched forms can rise to enormous scale, one such example being the Mile High Centre in Denver, Colorado where Johnson Burgee added a vast atrium to the existing Pei tower of the early 1960s (Fig. 19.17). However, the near level glass on the upper curved areas has been a problem, with packed snow turning to ice sliding off in avalanches.

Structure can be placed external to the glass surface, the most significant example being Lloyds of London (Figs 19.18 and 19.19) where both roof and vertical side walls are carried on space trusses giving a weightless effect internally.

Under this section it would be right to place the antiforms of the arch, namely the 'catenary'. Norman Foster has used this material saving form at the Hongkong Bank HQ (Fig. 19.20) as a glass ceiling, and at the Century Tower in Tokyo as a roof. At the Bank the glass plane is cut by escalators at the prescribed Feng Shui angle, creating extraordinary details at the junctions. (Feng Shui is Chinese geomancy, a mysticism linking the forces of good and evil to spatial arrangement.)

19.3.4 Rotational forms (pyramids, domes, lanterns)

Courtyard spaces with a vertical emphasis are complemented by a rising roof form, which offers other advantages such as the ability to catch sunlight and to provide a clear storey for the release of hot air and smoke. Regular forms over square or rectangular spaces facilitate the use of cleaning rigs and make for the simplest structures. Domes spanning up to 30 m (100 ft) can now be bought from catalogues, though individual designs, such as the arched frame at the Royals Centre in Southend-on-Sea (Fig. 19.21), are still competitive. Pyramids are naturally stable structures, and the frame chosen can be a simple one to provide support for glass framing, or a space structure picking up corner nodes. Pei's structure for the Louvre entrance atrium is a highly complex form, to support structural glazing. Another example is the half-pyramid which covers a food court at a shopping centre in Dallas by SOM. (Fig. 19.22).

Lantern light is a term used to cover all non-platonic tall

Fig. 19.20 *Hongkong and Shanghai Banking Corporation HQ, Hong Kong, 1986 (architect Foster Associates: engineer Ove Arup and Partners).*

Fig. 19.21 *Royals Centre, Southend-on-Sea, UK, 1988 (architect BDP).*

shapes. The Broadgate and Finsbury Avenue complexes by Arup Associates (Fig. 19.23) have a series of lantern topped octagonal atria, each with a ring beam near their summit to carry a cleaning gantry. The large lantern over the central space at Copley Place, Boston (Fig. 19.24), is of a similar form.

One of the most remarkable lantern lights in terms of shape and size is the one devised by Helmut Jahn for the State of Illinois Building, Chicago (Fig. 19.25) in which a vast circular drum is cut on the slope, with trusses used to carry each surface.

19.3.5 Vierendeel roof frames

Complex forms and plan arrangements are difficult to span economically with space frame or vaulted forms and the solution is often to use rigid 'Vierendeel' frames in both plan directions, as at the Scotia Bank Toronto (Fig. 19.26). An older example is Crystal Court Minneapolis by Johnson

Fig. 19.22 *Renaissance Centre, Dallas, Texas, 1987 (architects Skidmore, Owings and Merrill (SOM)).*

Fig. 19.23 *Broadgate (Phase 1 to 4), London, 1986–8 (architect Arup Associates).*

Fig. 19.24 *Copley Place, Boston, Massachusetts, 1984 (architect Architects Collaborative).*

Burgee (Fig. 19.27) where the roof comprises rigid cellular frames which are supported off the surrounding structures and carry pedestrian galleries on suspension rods.

19.3.6 Laylights

It was common practice in the 19th century to use two skins of glazing fixed externally and internally to industrial trusses. The inner glazing or 'laylight' concealed the structure and formed a light diffuser to the interior. Such designs often produced dramatic interiors, like Otto Wagner's Austrian Postal Savings Bank, Vienna (1904–6), or the opportunity for employing stained 'art glass' as ceiling decoration, an outstanding example being the domed space

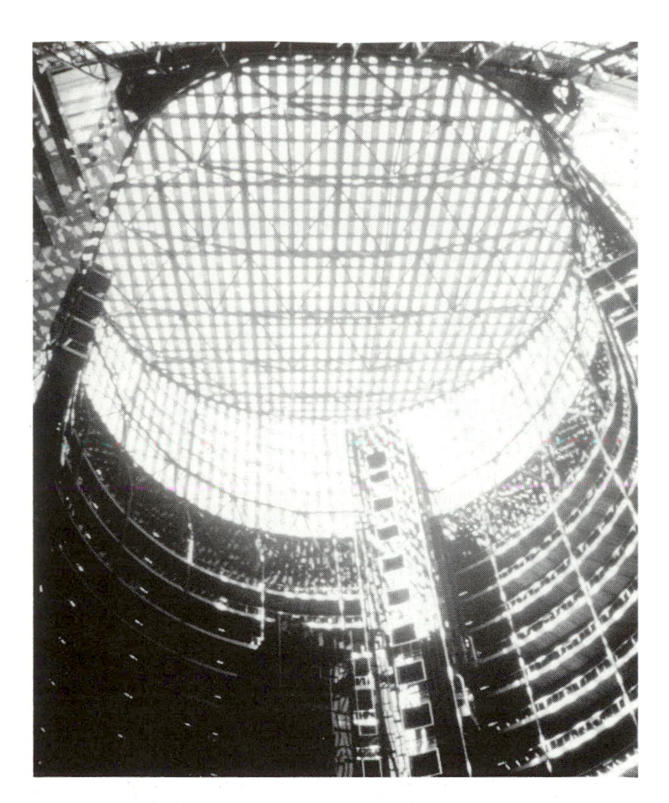

Fig. 19.25 *State of Illinois Building, Chicago, Illinois, 1986 (architect Helmut Jahn).*

Fig. 19.26 *Scotia Bank, Toronto, 1988 (architect WZMH).*

Fig. 19.27 *Crystal Court, IDS Centre, Minneapolis, Minnesota, 1972 (architect Johnson Burgee).*

Fig. 19.28 *Galeries Lafayette early 1900s, Paris.*

of Galeries Lafayette, the Paris department store (Fig. 19.28).

A few modern examples exist, the most elegant being the glasscrete vault inserted in a banking hall in Prague by Oldrick Tyl in 1930. Frank Lloyd Wright reverted to the Lafayette concept with the decorative laylight devised for the Guggenheim Museum in 1956.

19.4 WALLFORMS

Whilst the majority of atria have only roof glazing, a significant and growing number also have one or two sidewalls of glazing. In multiple-vertical or stacked atria, and in tropical latitudes, sidewall glazing is the only possible way of lighting. Views out of the atrium became possible and important to the design. Such walls may simply be continuations of the building frame and cladding or integrated into the planes used to accommodate wind or seismic bracing. Various forms are possible, including trussed walls supporting framed glass, planar glazed walls, lamella forms, and Vierendeel forms.

19.4.1 Walls as a continuation of building envelope

The Pan American Life Assurance building in New Orleans (Fig. 19.29) illustrates this form, often used by SOM. The two stacked atria are irregularly formed inside the envelope and this fact is disguised during daylight by the overriding frame and cladding treatment. The advantages are more than visual discipline; a high shade factor is achieved with little differential thermal movement in this hot climate.

19.4.2 Main building bracing as atrium wall structure

Diagonal bracing is an economic way to provide wind and seismic bracing but is usually unwelcome, running across inhabited window walls or, worse still, across interior space. Bracing in an atrium can be positively welcome as an expressive device, emphasizing the non-habitable nature of the volume. Examples include the Hennepin County Courthouse in Minneapolis by John Carl Warnecke (Fig. 19.30) and the Queens West Centre, Cardiff, UK, where diagonal lattice wall and roof frames are used.

19.4.3 Trussed walls supporting framed glass

Tall glass walls have considerable wind loads to resist, and rolled section framing set against the glass can get very bulky and expensive to span several storeys. Trussed mullions are now available with several curtain wall systems, for spans of three or more storeys; taller walls use trussed mullions, transoms or space structures. The Dallas Hyatt by Welton Becket (Fig. 19.31) has trussed mullions hanging from a bridge of bedrooms across the open side of

Fig. 19.29 *Pan American Life Assurance HQ, New Orleans, 1980 (architect Skidmore, Owings and Merill).*

Fig. 19.30 *Hennepin County Courthouse, Minneapolis, Minnesota, 1976 (architect John Carl Warnecke).*

the atrium. The Air and Space Museum in Washington, by HOK (Fig. 19.32), uses triangular space trusses linking mullion pairs. The Crystal Cathedral in Garden Grove, California, by Johnson Burgee (Fig. 19.33) uses a full space truss for walls and roof in this naturally climate-controlled glass building.

The sidelit atria at Arup Associates' Broadgate building have space trusses for transoms which provide cleaning access platforms and internal sunbreakers. Sunbreaker support is a logical role for trussed sidewalls in hot latitudes, as at the San Antonio Hyatt in Texas, by Ford Powell and Carson/TVS, where large angled shades sit on the sloping members (Fig. 19.34).

19.4.4 Planar glazed walls

The technology for suspended glass assemblies has made considerable advances and can provide frameless glass sidewalls up to five storeys tall. Planar glass can be carried on frames too and this is customary with walls over 15 m (50 ft)

Fig. 19.31 *Hyatt Reunion Hotel, Dallas, Texas, 1979 (architect Welton Beckett).*

Fig. 19.32 *Air and Space Museum, Washington DC, 1976 (architect HOK).*

Fig. 19.33 *'Crystal Cathedral', Garden Grove Community Church, California, 1980 (architect Johnson Burgee).*

high. The Spectrum Building, Denver by McOg Architects (Fig. 19.35) utilizes this method, with steel tubes spanning a void and carrying the glass sheets and stiffening fins unobtrusively. The Financial Times printing works in London designed by Nicholas Grimshaw (Fig. 19.36) uses external masts, projecting arms and tension cables to stiffen the glazed suspenders.

19.4.5 Lamella forms

The Roy Thomson Concert Hall in Toronto (Fig. 19.37) has an unusual form in which the foyer encompasses the circular auditorium block, the public spaces containing several levels of balconies and connecting stairs to the various levels of seating. The designer, Arthur Erickson, has wrapped the public space in a hyperboloid, that is a tapered curving skin similar to the lower part of a cooling tower. The structure is in the form of a lamella frame of steel tubes and the glass panes are 'flat' diamond shapes fixed by adhesive to each location strip. The circular form is used to advantage for cleaning, with rigs running between the head and foot beams.

19.4.6 Vierendeel wall frames

Wall skins, as well as roofs, can be framed on Vierendeel principles, the most famous being Felix Samuely's proposed structure to span the shop window facade to Simpson's, Piccadilly (1936), which is described in more detail in chapter 17. Vierendeel frames are used particularly where the wall forms are highly irregular. An example is the structure devised for the end walls of the atrium at the Royal Bank of Canada, Toronto, by designers WZMH (Fig. 19.38). All one can say is that the effect is totally overpowering and as such is a design curiosity.

Fig. 19.34 *Hyatt Hotel, San Antonio, Texas, 1981 (architects Ford Powell and Carson/TVS).*

Fig. 19.35 *Spectrum Building, Denver, Colorado, 1980 (architect McOg).*

Fig. 19.36 *Financial Times Printing Works, London, 1988 (architect Nicholas Grimshaw and Partners).*

Fig. 19.37 *Roy Thomson Hall, Toronto, 1982 (architect Arthur Erickson).*

Fig. 19.38 *Royal Bank of Canada, Toronto, 1975 (architect WZMH).*

Fig. 19.39 *Gateway House II, Basingstoke, 1983 (architect Arup Associates).*

Fig. 19.40 *State of Illinois Center, Chicago, Illinois, 1986 (architect Helmut Jahn).*

Fig. 19.41 *MacKenzie Health Sciences Centre, Edmonton, Alberta, 1983–6 (architect Eberhard Zeidler).*

19.5 OTHER STEEL STRUCTURES IN ATRIA

Atria are usually designed to be outside the fire safety area of a building, all escape routes, stairs and fire-fighting lifts being inside the occupied building. This means that exposed steelwork can be used for supporting galleries, lifts, escalators and stairs, subject only to the concerns of the insurers to minimize losses. Examples include Gateway House II at Basingstoke (Fig. 19.39), where Arup Associates have built an all-steel complex of walkways, lift towers and roof supports inside the atrium. The State of Illinois Building (Fig. 19.40) has steel perimeter walkways and linking stairs, and spectacular steel lift towers free-standing in space like siege engines. The MacKenzie Health Sciences building at the University in Edmonton, Alberta, by Eberhard Zeidler (Fig. 19.41) has steel lift and stair structures and trussed bridges crossing the atria. Major steel ventilation ducting also passes through the spaces, saving built volume and gaining service flexibility in a more practical way than with the external ducting at Lloyds. A smaller example of the same philosophy is Jahn's headquarters for Rust-oleum Paints, Chicago, which used a steel frame painted with intumescent finish, steel stairs and steel airhandling ducts (Fig. 19.42).

Current design with atria owes a great deal to modern developments with structural glazing. In combination with steel this offers increased technical possibilities. The latest concepts include responsive bracing which can accommodate building movement and there seems to be considerable scope for further development.

Fig. 19.42 *Rust-oleum Corporate Headquarters, Vernon Hills, Illinois 1978 (architect Murphy Jahn).*

REFERENCES AND TECHNICAL NOTES

1. Saxon, R. (1986) *Atrium Buildings*, Butterworth Architecture.
2. BS 5588 Part 7: Code of Practice for atrium buildings (1991).
3. London District Surveyor's Association (LDSA) Guide No 2 *Fire Safety in Atrium Buildings*

FURTHER READING

Greenhouses

Kohlmaier, G. and Von Sartory, B. (1981) *Houses of Glass, a Nineteenth Century Building Type* (translated by Harvey, J. C. from *Das Glashaus*). MIT Press.

Hix, J. (1974 and 1981) *The Glasshouse*, MIT Press.

Energy

Fitch, J.M. (1972) *American Building, the Environmental Forces that Shape It*, Houghton Mifflin.

Hawkes, D. and Owers, J. (eds) (1981) *The Architecture of Energy*, Construction Press.

Lundquist, G. (1980) *Camera Solaris*, Spanbergs Tryckener (Swedish).

Watson, D. (1982) The energy within the space within. *Progressive Architecture*, July.

Urban design

Geist, J.F. (1983) *Arcades: The History of a Building Type*, MIT Press.

Fire

Butcher, E.G. and Parnell, A.C. (1983) *Designing for Fire Safety*, Wiley.

Butcher, E.G. and Parnell, A.C. (1979) *Smoke Control*, E and FN Spon.

Interior plantscaping

Gaines, R.L. (1977) *Interior plantscaping – building designs for interior foliage plants*, Architectural Record Books, New York.

Economics

Portman, J. and Barnett, J. (1976) *The Architect as Developer*, McGraw Hill (also the best illustration of Portman designs up to 1976).

General

Andrews, J. and Taylor, J. (1982) *Architecture, a Performing Art*, Lutterworth Press (covers the varied atrium designs of John Andrews).

Fig. 20.1 *The Georges Pompidou Centre, Place de Beaubourg, Paris 1977 (architects Renzo Piano and Richard Rogers: engineer Ove Arup and Partners).*

20

Tensile structures

John Thornton and Ian Liddell

The term 'tension structures' encompasses a wide range of different forms, such as cable-stayed roofs, suspended structures, cable nets and membrane structures. This chapter describes many of these and explains the principles of their structural behaviour and design.

20.1 INTRODUCTION TO TENSION STRUCTURES

The term 'tension structure' can be taken to refer to structures in which members exclusively designed to carry tension are major elements in the overall structure. Most structural elements are able to carry bending forces as well as tension and compression, and are hence able to withstand reversals in the direction of loading. Tension elements are unique in that they can only carry tension. In compressive or bending elements the loading capacity is often reduced by buckling effects, while tension elements can work up to the full tensile stress of the material. Consequently, full advantage can be taken of high strength materials to create light, efficient and cost-effective long span structures. In buildings, such structures are generally associated with the support of roofs, often as a cable-stayed system. However, the Pompidou Centre (Fig. 20.1) and the Lord's Mound Stand (Fig. 20.2) for example, are also tension structures. Whole roof areas can themselves be in the form of tensile membranes, creating a different type of tension structure. The use of such membranes can be used to dramatic effect and can provide an economic solution, particularly for long span roofs.

To create useful spanning or space-enclosing structures the tension elements have to work in conjunction with compression elements. From an architectural point of view, the separation of the tension, compression and bending elements leads to a visual expression of the way the structure carries the loads, or at least one set of loads.

Tension structures come in a wide range of forms which can be broadly categorized as two-dimensional structures (suspension bridges, draped cables, cable-stayed beams or trusses and cable trusses), three-dimensional structures (bicycle wheels, cable truss systems and cable domes) and surface stressed structures (membranes, pneumatically stressed and prestressed surfaces).

All these forms of tension structure are related, not only in

Fig. 20.2 *The Mound Stand, Lord's Cricket Ground 1989 (architect Michael Hopkins and Partners: engineer Ove Arup and Partners).*

Fig. 20.3 *Brooklyn Suspension Bridge, New York 1867–8 (engineer John Roebling).*

the sense that they rely on elements which are designed to function only in tension, but also in that they both have their own internal structural logic, which is less forgiving than conventional beam and column structures to those who seek to impose stylistic decisions on the design.

20.2 HISTORICAL REVIEW

Pure tension members have been used in structures going back as far as recorded history. The designs have changed with materials and technologies and in response to social, technical and economic developments. The typical tension element is a strand of rope which usually consists of a number of filaments twisted together. Metal bars or chains are also used in certain circumstances. The earliest ropes were made of cellulose fibres, initially in the form of lianas or bamboo bundles and later in the form of twisted ropes of hemp or flax. These ropes were liable to stretch and would rot if left wet. Hence early tension structures, such as the early Chinese bridges, were temporary or were designed for continuous maintenance. Even now it is sensible to consider the needs of maintenance in the design. BD

With the development of wrought iron as a reliable tensile material, chains, initially of round bar and later made of linked flat bar for heavier loads, were developed for use as permanent tension elements for the construction of suspension bridges in the early 19th century by Captain Samuel Brown and designers such as Navier, Dufour and the Seguin brothers, and Chaley. Further developments were made by Thomas Telford who carried out a testing programme for flat bar chains for the design of the Menai Straits Bridge.

In 1831 Brunel used a single wrought iron round bar as a temporary crossing of the Avon Gorge and was hauled across it in a basket. This bar was made up out of lengths of iron hammer welded together presumably on site and one wonders how Brunel managed to assure himself of the reliability of the welds. The allowable stress in wrought iron chains was 88 N/mm^2 (13 ksi).

High tensile steel wire cables for suspension bridges were introduced by the European-educated John Roebling in the 1840s. His greatest work was the Brooklyn Bridge 1867–8 (Fig. 20.3). Improvements in the tensile capacity of the cable led to longer span bridges. The Japanese are now producing spans of 1600 m (5250 ft) using wire which at about 2000 N/mm^2 (290 ksi) has double the strengths of Roebling's. Currently, artificial fibres – particularly high modulus aramid fibre in parallel bundles – are being promoted for use in suspension bridges to gain even greater span from the reduced dead weight.

Tension structures have been used in buildings for a number of years, particularly for long span roofs where material efficiency keeps the dead weight down to a minimum. Victorian engineers created exciting and interesting buildings using the materials of cast and wrought iron. Many of these made use of tension rods and were articulated in a way that was to be echoed later, but Sir Henry Bessemer's process for making steel in large quantities marked the end for this type of structure.

The economics of using rolled steel sections with bolted, riveted and, later, welded joints, together with improved engineering understanding, meant that the steel frame and the welded truss became the norm. Some aspects of the Modern Movement in architecture also favoured the frame and, of course, for a long period there was great interest in exploiting the potential of reinforced concrete.

However, a number of architects and engineers became interested in structures which expressed how they worked in a more direct way. Tension structures have a diagrammatic quality and generate an aesthetic of detailing which satisfies this interest in legible, articulated structures.

In this respect, the Pompidou Centre can be seen as a key building in its detailing and the extensive use made of pure tension in primary and secondary structure. Most of the tension structures designed in the UK since then can be viewed in the context of a strand of development leading from that project.

There have also been considerable developments in tension, as distinct from cable supported, roofs. These roofs are usually cable trusses or networks with sheet metal cladding. More recently, stressed fabrics have been developed for structural and architectural purposes, and these materials have come to be used either as structures in themselves or as cladding for cable or steel frameworks.

20.3 REASONS FOR TENSION STRUCTURES

The reasons for the choice of a tension structure may be architectural or technical, although there is inevitably an overlapping of the two. External structure can make an industrial building more interesting and give it an architectural identity (Fig. 20.4); it reduces the visual bulk by minimizing the clad volume and avoids the blank anonymous appearance of many of these buildings. It minimizes the internal structure which can simplify the distribution of services.

If a building is to be extended, an external structure can be designed to reduce the disruption at the interface by making it possible to make the structural connections before opening the enclosure; furthermore, a two-directional square grid makes it possible for the building to take up any plan form without destroying the architectural unity.

Tension structures can be very light visually, since the bulk of the individual components is minimized and they have a diagrammatic quality which makes a dramatic statement from a distance. They present a strong image

Fig. 20.4 *Inmos Research Centre, Newport, Gwent 1982 (architect Richard Rogers Partnership: engineer Anthony Hunt Associates).*

which is appropriate for some projects and clients, while at a small scale the elements and details which form a tension structure provide interest and enrich the design. The aesthetics of the detailing of the tension system and the principle of suspension and tension can provide a motif which helps drive the whole design (Figs 20.5–20.6).

The reduction in component sizes can help transportation and erection. It can also be useful if heavy point loads are to be carried, since these may be connected to the suspension system at designated points without penalizing the whole structure. The effective structural depth available makes an efficient structure possible and the reduction in steel weight will offset the extra cost of some of the details.

A tension structure may also help solve problems related to a particular site. The Oxford Ice Rink, UK, is built on poor ground with a very low bearing capacity. The masts concentrate loads at two points and relieve loads elsewhere which means that expensive piled foundations are required in only two places (Figs. 20.7 and 20.8). The tension structure of the Lord's Mound Stand is a response to the particular problem imposed by the site with the existing seating and roadway and the need to minimize the obstruction to the spectators' view (Fig. 20.9).

Tension structures can offer overwhelming economic advantages on very long spans but otherwise they are simply one of a range of technical solutions, appropriate in some instances but not others. In common with all structural solutions they have advantages and disadvantages.

Although these comments apply strictly to cable stayed systems, similar advantages can be obtained with membrane structures.

20.4 GENERAL TECHNICAL CONSIDERATIONS

When engineering forms the basis of the architecture, as is the case with tension structures, the relationship between the engineer and the architect assumes a far greater importance than normal. Technical considerations must be given

Fig 20.5 *Bridge structure and mast props at Fleetguard, Quimper, Brittany 1960–61 (architect Richard Rogers Partnership: engineer Ove Arup and Partners).*

Fig. 20.6 *Fleetguard, Quimper, Brittany.*

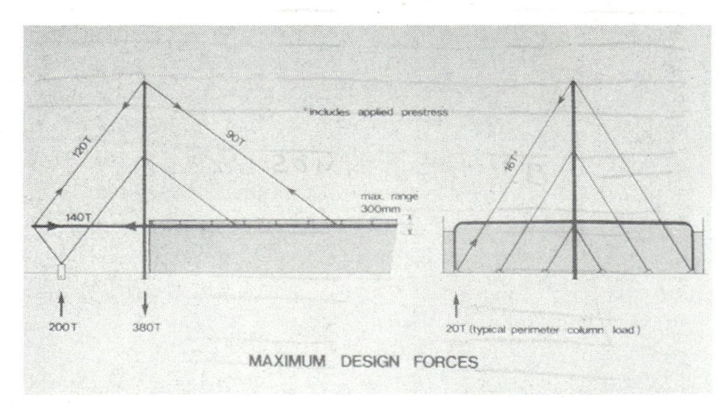

Figs 20.7 and 20.8 *Oxford Ice Rink and structural scheme, Oxford, UK (architect Nicholas Grimshaw and Partners: engineer Ove Arup and Partners).*

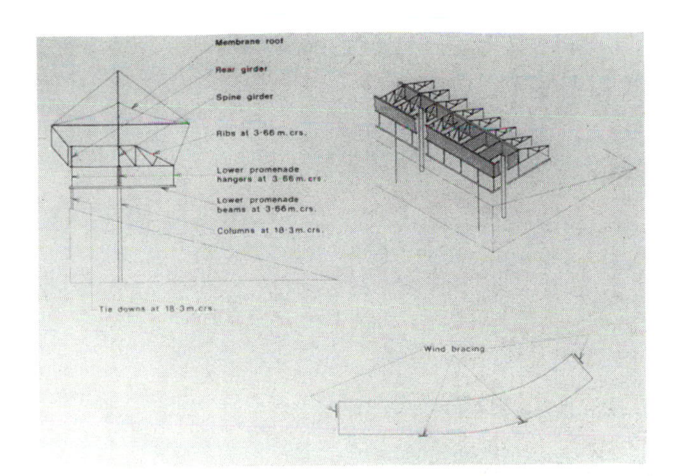

Fig. 20.9 *The Mound Stand, Lord's Cricket Ground 1989 (architects Michael Hopkins and Partners).*

due respect, otherwise there is a danger that the tension members simply become stylistic devices; without engineering rigour the design may sink into architectural whimsy. However, the engineer should, as always, be prepared to sacrifice some efficiency if this helps improve the design as a whole.

Some of the most successful designs have arisen from the solution of a particular technical problem; indeed, it can sometimes be difficult for a decision to proceed satisfactorily until the right problem has been found. So, the architect should be able to understand and differentiate between the architectural and technical reasons behind decisions. It is possible for engineers to make almost any structure work, within reason, but in so doing there is a danger that the plans will lack the intellectual rigour which seems to underlie the best designs.

The engineer in turn must contribute to the design at a conceptual level and not act simply to implement the architect's ideas without critical responses. The best designs arise from a dialogue between the architect and engineer; each with confidence in his own views and trust in the abilities of the other.

The following section describes aspects of structural behaviour that have a fundamental influence on the design of a tension structure. Some of them have a major influence on the overall form of the structure while others, although their effects may be less obvious, may nevertheless be of great concern to the engineer. It should be realized that many features of the design of tension structures, although they may appear stylistic to an architect, are functional.

The analysis of some of the structural behaviour can be difficult and, because the structures are unusual, it may take some time before all the problems have been found. The result of this is that it can take the engineer much longer to firm up the design than it would for a conventional building.

20.5 PRIMARY TECHNICAL CONSIDERATIONS FOR CABLE-STAYED SYSTEMS

Some examples illustrating different types of cable-stayed tension roofs include single bay (Fig. 20.10, National

Fig. 20.10 *National Exhibition Centre, Birmingham, UK 1979 (architect Edward D. Mills and Partners: engineer Ove Arup and Partners).*

Fig. 20.11 *Renault Swindon, UK 1983 (architect Foster Associates: engineer Ove Arup and Partners).*

Fig. 20.12 *Patscenter, Princeton, New Jersey, USA 1983 (architect Richard Rogers Partnership; engineer Ove Arup and Partners).*

Fig. 20.13 *Crystal Palace Athletics Stadium, London, UK 1956–64 (architect Sir Leslie Martin in collaboration with John Attenborough and Bryn Jones).*

Fig. 20.14 *Supermarket, St. Herblain, Nantes, France 1988 (architect Richard Rogers Partnership: engineer Ove Arup and Partners).*

Fig. 20.15 *Fleetguard factory, Quimper, Brittany 1960–61 (architect Richard Rogers Partnership: engineer Ove Arup and Partners).*

Exhibition Centre), multi-bay (Fig. 20.11, Renault), spine (Fig. 20.12, Patscenter), grandstand (Fig. 20.13, Crystal Palace), two-dimensional (Fig. 20.14, Saint Herblain), and three-dimensional (Fig. 20.15, Fleetguard).

20.5.1 Unbalanced load

In a single bay structure the effects of patch loading (uneven, and hence unbalanced, distribution of load), although they may be troublesome to analyse, will not cause a fundamental problem because the load path is the same as that which carries uniform load (Fig. 20.16). However, if the structure is multi-bay or spine, patch loading may put the adjacent bay into uplift. The beams under uplift receive no assistance from the suspension system and have to span between columns (Fig. 20.17). The increased flexibility of the larger span reduces the restraint to the column, and unless it is very stiff it sways and, in so doing, it allows the suspension points in the loaded span to settle. As a result, the benefits of reducing the span by suspension are decreased. In addition, the columns are put into bending; the forces can be large and cause an increase in section size and weight. Because the columns are double height, they represent a considerable percentage of the steel tonnage, so this penalty can be serious.

The system can be made to work by providing the appropriate stiffnesses. However, unless the patch loads are small, this is inefficient, and inconsistent with the principle behind this type of structure, since the columns are no longer mainly resisting compression nor are the beams spanning the minimum distance, which is that between suspension points.

A solution to this problem is to prevent the columns from deflecting enough to cause significant loss of support to the loaded span. There are three ways of achieving this: by

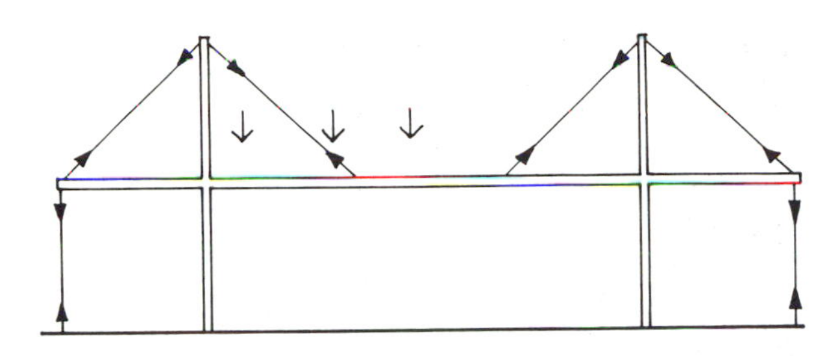

Fig. 20.16 *Patch loading on tension structures.*

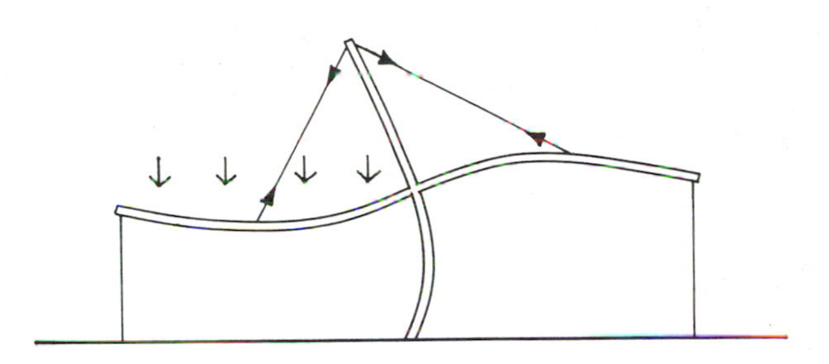

Fig. 20.17 *Uneven loading causing uplift.*

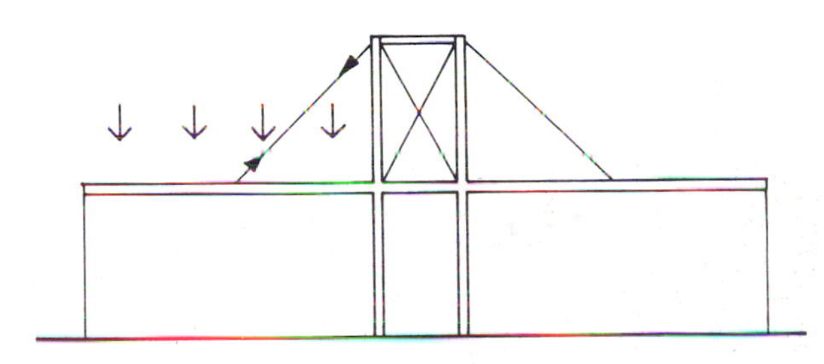

Fig. 20.18 *Stiff columns resisting the effects of unbalanced loading.*

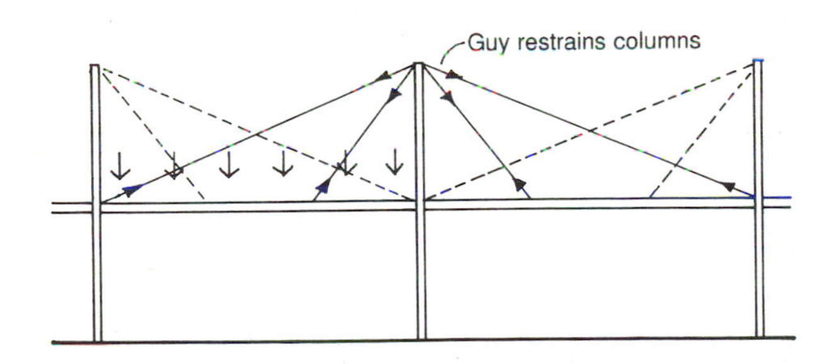

Fig. 20.19 *Use of guys to restrain columns.*

making the column structure stiff enough itself (Fig. 20.18), by guying the column directly (Fig. 20.19) or by devising a system that is efficient at resisting uplift and does not cause loss of column restraint (Fig. 20.20). The latter also solves the problem of wind uplift. In practice, designs may incorporate elements of more than one of these principles (Fig. 20.21).

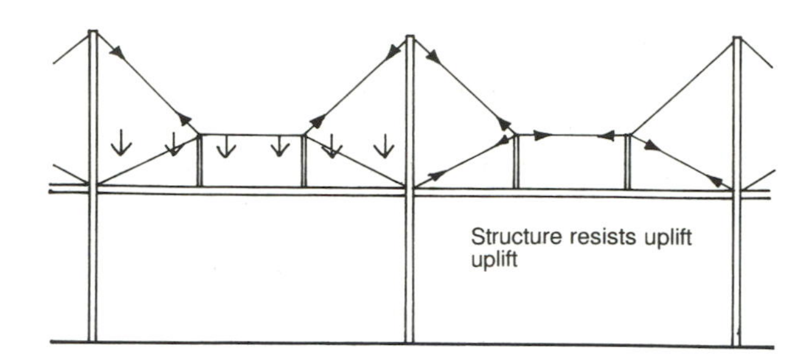

Fig. 20.20 *Systems efficient at resisting uplift.*

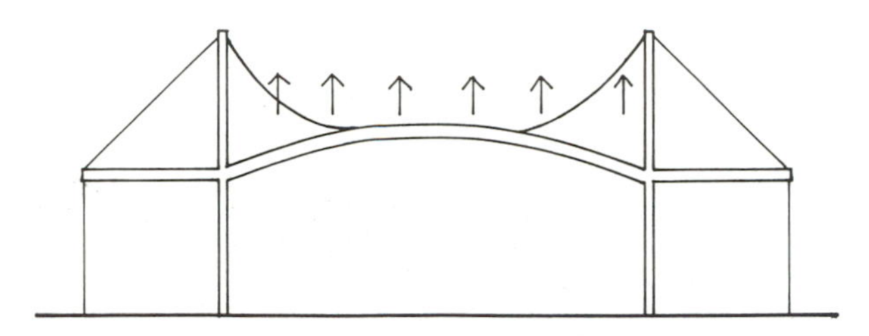

Fig. 20.22 *The effect of wind uplift.*

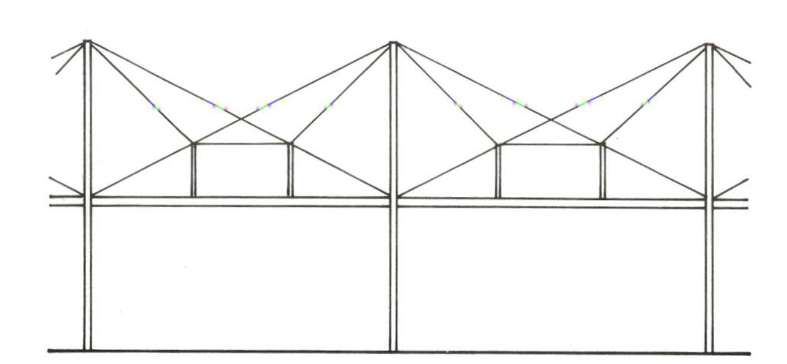

Fig. 20.21 *Combined systems to deal with unbalanced loading.*

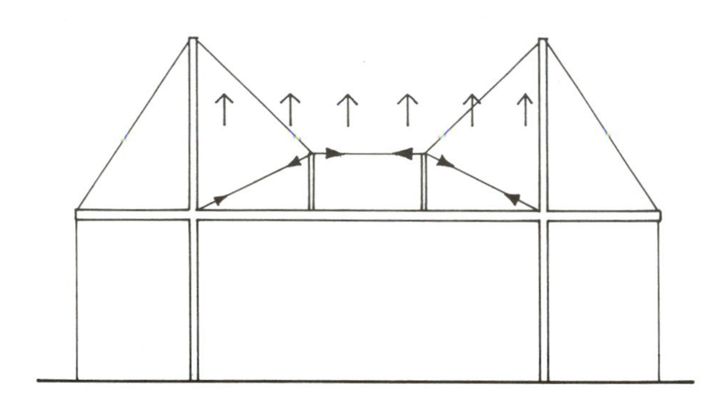

Fig. 20.23 *Tension structure to resist both upwards and downwards loads.*

20.5.2 Wind uplift

The wind in some areas can be sufficiently strong that the resultant uplift on a lightweight roof can be almost as great as the self weight. Whereas a conventional roof has the potential of equal strength against upwards and downwards load, a tension roof designed against downwards load may have very little strength against upwards load (Fig. 20.22). Wind uplift therefore needs to be considered as a primary design case.

The first approach to this problem is to ensure that the beams will span between the columns under uplift. In these circumstances deflection is likely to be the governing criterion since deflection is proportional to span^4 while bending is proportional to span squared (span^2). If the uplift forces are too large this becomes inefficient: it could be argued that this is the case if the upwards forces are determining the size of the beam rather than the downwards forces.

The second approach is to change the loads; it may be possible to decrease the wind loads by changing the profile of the edge of the roof; alternatively, the self-weight of the roof can be increased but this is hardly a respectable solution since it increases the loads for the primary load case.

The third approach is to arrange the tension structure so that it carries both upwards and downwards loads (Fig. 20.23).

The problems of unbalanced load and wind uplift are essentially the same and relate to the ability of the structure to absorb reversal of load. These problems can usually be solved by increasing the strength of individual members but this can be unsatisfactory in terms of economy and structural logic. The reason is that if the deflections of individual elements are mainly derived from the behaviour of the overall structure, increasing the strength, and hence stiffness, of these elements may simply attract more load to them. This is because in this case the deflections are not greatly reduced while the stiffer an element is the more load it attracts for a given deflection. The elegant solution is to arrange the structure so that these forces are carried in the overall structural behaviour rather than the member behaviour.

20.5.3 Horizontal stability

The structure must have resistance to horizontal loads which can be supplied by bracing or the frame action of the beams and columns. It is generally more economical in steel buildings to provide bracing, since this minimizes the sizes of members and simplifies connections. The language of tension structures is one which can easily accept cross-bracing or external props, as for example at Fleetguard (Fig. 20.24).

A tension structure which is designed to resist both upwards and downwards loads naturally has a stiff horizontal beam; it may then be possible, as in a conventional

Fig. 20.24 *Detail of external props and booms. Fleetguard factory, Quimper, Brittany.*

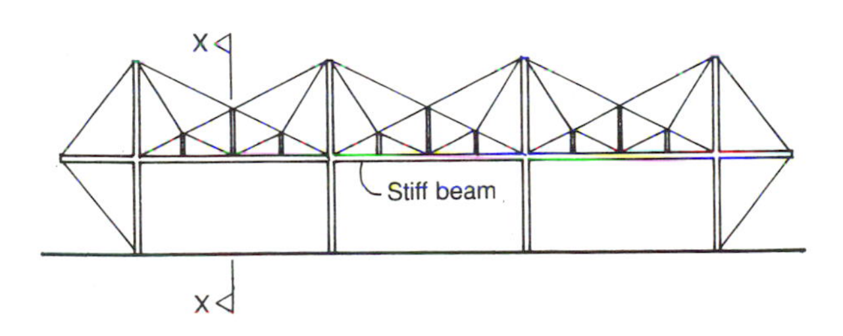

Fig. 20.25 *Ties to brace columns.*

structure, to omit the bracing if the columns are stiff enough. Care should be taken to check that this does not compromise the column weights. The tie-down, if it is angled, can help provide the necessary column stiffness (Fig. 20.25).

20.5.4 Non-linearity

The following is not intended to be a detailed explanation of a complicated subject, but rather a broad introduction to help understanding of some of the underlying issues in the structural analysis.

Tension structures are generally non-linear, i.e. the response of the structure to the applied loads is not constant. If the loads on a linear structure double, the stresses double; if the loads reverse, the stresses reverse. This is not the case with a non-linear structure.

The subject of non-linear structures is wide ranging and complex; at some levels it requires a degree of understanding and specialist analysis which not all engineers can bring to bear. In any field of activity the schemes proposed will usually be restricted to those which the participants feel are within their competence. With tension structures this means that unless the engineer is familiar with the problems of non-linearity it is likely that the designs proposed will be those which simply avoid those problems.

A tension structure may be arranged so that all the ties are under tension under one set of loads, say dead load. However, under a different set of loads, say wind uplift or unbalanced load, some of the ties may go slack. This means, in effect, that the structure is different (Fig. 20.26). From the engineer's point of view this means that it must be

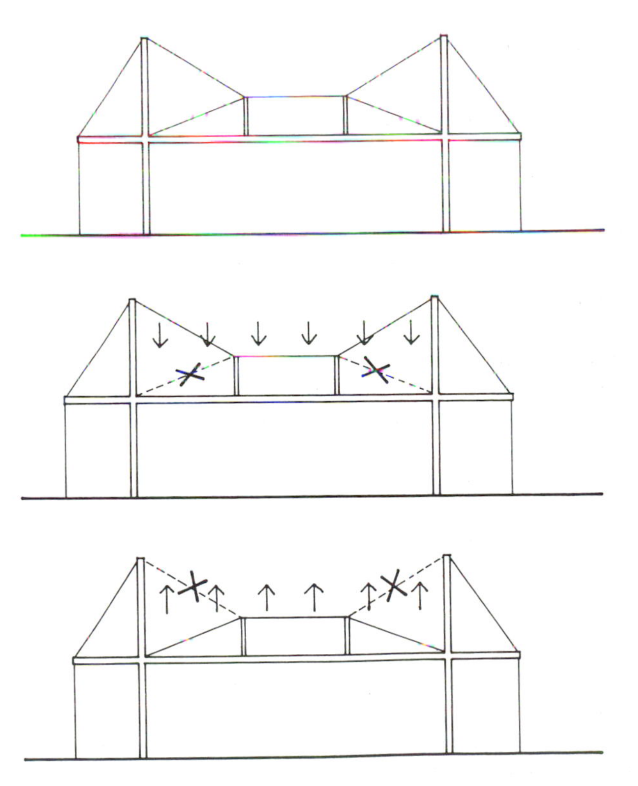

Fig. 20.26 *Differences in structural behaviour under different load conditions (on section line xx in fig. 20.25).*

re-analysed with the slack tie removed. Different ties may become inoperative under different patterns of load. This problem can be overcome by prestressing the ties so that they never lose tension, which has the incidental advantage that it may help the performance of the structure, since a prestressed tie acts as a strut for compression up to the amount of the prestress; this may stiffen the structure. However, the disadvantages are that it puts extra load into the structure and prestressing to a precise load can greatly complicate work on site.

The technique of analysing the structure conventionally then re-analysing after removing the ties which went into compression may be satisfactory for simple structures or preliminary analysis but it is inherently dangerous for the following reason. Take, for example, an analysis in which two ties were shown as taking compression in a conventional analysis. Using this technique those ties would be removed from the model and the analysis repeated. However, the reality of the situation might be that if only one of the ties were removed the other would remain in tension, which would not be revealed. A trick which avoids this is not to remove the ties from the model completely but to put them in as very thin members. The compression which they can take is too small to affect the analysis of the whole structure but it can be seen in the computer output whether they are taking compression or tension; if they are found to be taking tension they can be reintroduced at full size.

The proper procedure is to use a computer program which, in effect, constantly checks the distance between the ends of members and compares these with the original lengths in order to decide whether they are operative or not. This also deals with the following problem.

The geometric changes in conventional structures are not large enough to affect the distribution of forces in the structure, and most analysis techniques and computer programs operate on this basis. However, this is not the case in some structures. One example of this has been given above where geometric changes are sufficient to change the arrangement of a structure completely by one or more members becoming ineffective. Another example can be found in the behaviour of tie rods or cables. A tie which is not vertical will always have some sag in it which is proportional to its self-weight and the tension. The amount of sag decreases as the load on the tie increases. This 'pulling-out' of the sag is, in effect, an extension of the tie which must be added to the strain (stretch) of the tie itself. However, the situation is complicated by the fact that the strain in the tie is proportional to the curved length rather than the distance between the ends. The result is that the apparent modulus of elasticity (ratio of stress to strain) varies according to the load. Luckily this effect can usually be ignored.

Another example is where a mast and its stays fall in a single plane. Any disturbance out of the plane, due to say construction inaccuracy or wind, can cause the tension in the stays to induce bending in the mast as well as compression.

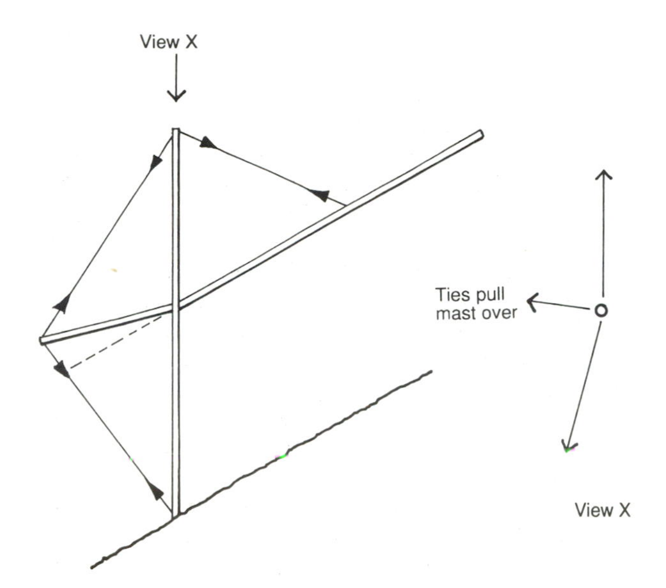

Fig. 20.27 *Effect of inclined tie-downs on the columns.*

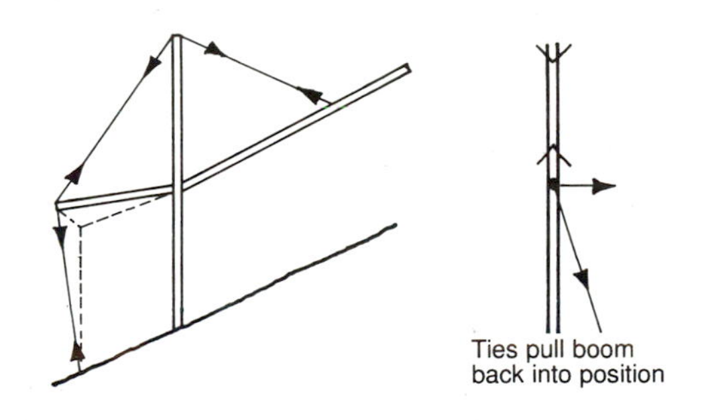

Fig. 20.28 *Vertical tie-downs.*

This bending causes a further deflection out of plane and so on (Fig. 20.27). On the Saint Herblain building the twin tie-downs to the booms were splayed to limit the amount of lateral displacement of the boom from construction error and wind force in order to restrict these effects. In contrast, the vertical tie-downs on Fleetguard combined with the fully restrained mast head allowed advantage to be taken of non-linear effects. Because the base of the tie-down is separated from the base of the mast, any tendency for the boom to move out of the plane described by the mast and the tie-down base is resisted by the cables, the resistance increasing with displacement (Fig. 20.28).

20.5.5 Stiffness

It is important that the geometry and member sizes of a suspension system should provide the necessary resistance to vertical deflection of the supported structure. It is possible to have a system which carries the self-weight of the roof but which is so 'soft' compared with the beams that as extra load, such as snow load, is added it is carried mainly by the beams.

It is sometimes thought that tension structures are more flexible than conventional structures but this is not necessarily the case. Steel structures are designed to deflection limits specified in codes of practice and as required by other elements of the construction. Tension structures can be made very stiff, depending on the geometry, because of the large effective structural depth of the tension system.

The problem of stiffness and deflection is actually more related to the length of span. For a given deflection/span ratio, the greater the span the greater the deflection; since tension roofs tend to have longer spans than conventional structures the deflections, and hence the detailing problems, may be greater. This is particularly so with multi-bay roofs since the spans, and hence the deflections around the perimeter, will be greater than for a typical conventional structure where the frames will tend to be more closely spaced. The problems of deflection of the roof relative to the cladding are, of course, eliminated if the wall is allowed to carry some of the weight of the roof but this 'impurity' runs counter to all the principles underlying the design of this type of structure.

20.6 SECONDARY TECHNICAL CONSIDERATIONS FOR CABLE-STAYED SYSTEMS

20.6.1 Rods versus cables

When looking for a pure tension member it is natural to think of using cables. They are used in many of the familiar types of tension structure and are very strong. They are also supplied with the various end fittings and adjusters which are needed. However, they do suffer from two disadvantages when used in tension roofs.

The need for the suspension system to have good vertical stiffness has already been explained. Unfortunately, cable has a low modulus of elasticity, which is to say it is stretchy; if full use is made of its strength, the strain in the ties will be three to four times greater than if a solid section were used. This has a corresponding effect on the overall vertical stiffness of the structure. This reduced stiffness is unimportant for the self-weight of the roof, since its effects can be allowed for by adjustment; but it is of concern for the imposed loads which can be more than twice the self-weight.

The second disadvantage concerns durability. Cables are supplied galvanized and packed with grease but there is a tendency for the grease to move down the cable, leaving interstices for water. The life of the galvanizing is limited and relates to the severity of exposure and the type of environment. Various treatments, coatings and sheathings can be used but none of them is entirely satisfactory.

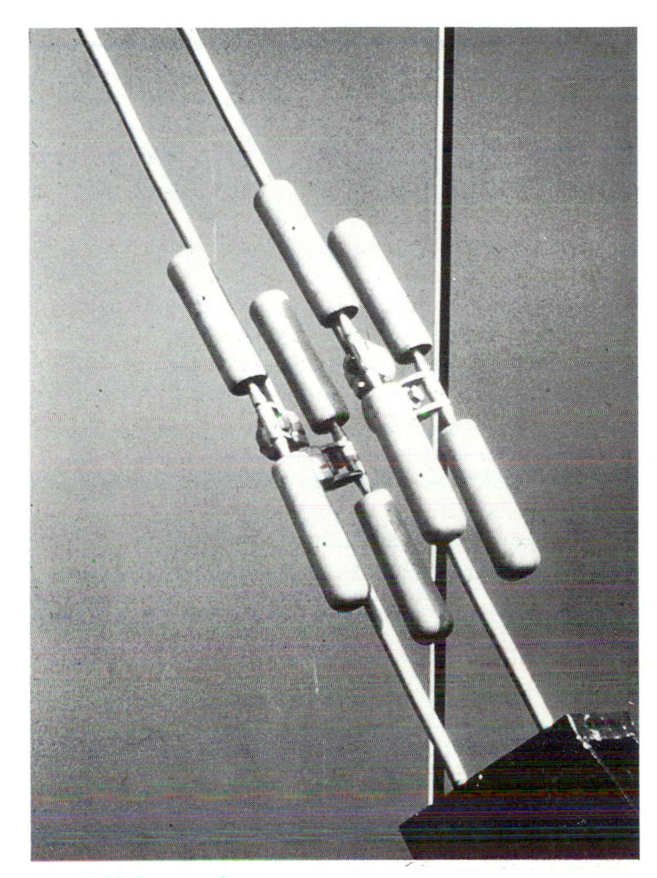

Fig. 20.29 *Dampers fixed to ties to minimize vibration. Oxford Ice Rink, Oxford, UK.*

In comparison, rods or tubes can be painted and maintained in the conventional way. They are also cheaper. So, although there is no technical reason why cables should not be used, they are unlikely to be as suitable as rods.

20.6.2 Wind on ties

A tie is liable to vibrate at a particular wind speed, which depends on the diameter of the tie, its length and the tension. This vibration takes place in the direction normal to the direction of the wind and is caused by vortex shedding. Dampers can be incorporated in the tie to eliminate this if necessary, as was done for the Oxford Ice Rink (Fig. 20.29).

There is more concern when twin ties are used; the ties can interact aerodynamically to cause vibration, which has occurred on a number of projects. A spacing of four diameters appears to be the worst.

20.6.3 Wind on masts

A similar problem of vibration due to the frequency of vortex shedding coinciding with the natural frequency of the mast can occur if the mast top is not restrained in both directions. Solutions are to choose a size of mast which will not suffer from this or to add aerodynamic devices at the top of the mast to prevent the rhythmic vortex shedding; these would be strakes or shrouds similar to those seen on steel chimneys. Another solution is to add proprietary dampers at the top.

20.6.4 Vertical versus inclined tie-downs

A feature which occurs in many tension structures is the tie-down passing over a boom. The question arises as to whether the tie-down should be vertical or whether it should return to the foot of the column (Fig. 20.30). If the tie-down is vertical it requires an anchorage foundation, which is an expense. If the ground-water level is close to the surface, the anchor may be partly submerged and thus larger to compensate for the loss in weight.

On the other hand, although an inclined tie-down imposes an extra compression in the boom the uplift force reacts against the column load and an anchor block is not required. The column load on the foundations is also reduced. Differential movement between the column and tie-down, which gives loss of support, is eliminated, which is particularly helpful on poor ground. The horizontal component of the tie force at ground level has to be resisted, either by the column foundation or by ties between the columns.

The inclined tie makes it easier to achieve stability by frame action as has been described before.

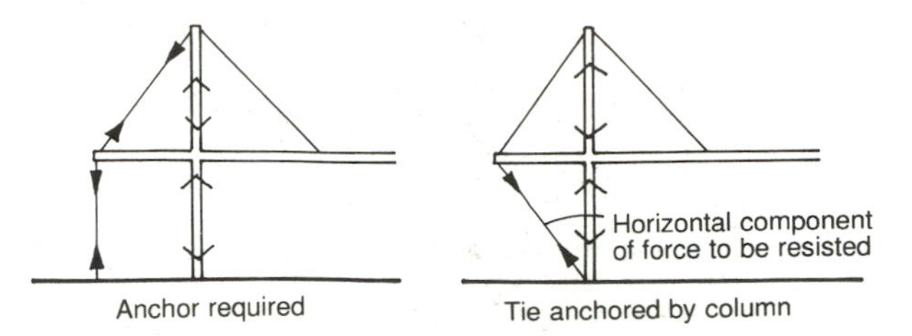

Fig. 20.30 *Vertical versus inclined tie-downs.*

Fig. 20.31 *Ductile iron forks at Renault, Swindon, UK.*

20.7 DETAILING FOR CABLE-STAYED SYSTEMS

20.7.1 Connections

It seems natural for the ties to be connected with pinned connections. There are engineering reasons also, since it gives angular tolerance and allows for rotation with the change in sag of the tie; it certainly simplifies site assembly.

The detail must be concentric, unless the loads are trivial and a bolt is used rather than a pin. This leads to a fork detail although splice plates have been used. It is generally easier to attach the fork to the rod in order to simplify the main fabrication.

Forks can be cast in ductile iron or steel (Fig. 20.31, Renault); they may be fabricated (Fig. 20.32, National Exhibition Centre) or they may be made from plate by flame-cutting and machining (Fig. 20.33, Fleetguard). Standard cast forks are available but are not necessarily as suitable as purpose designed castings. However, it takes time to develop and prove a satisfactory casting and this may not be available. Cast steel is more expensive and less accurate than cast iron but is stronger and can be welded, which cast iron cannot. With the cast iron forks on Renault, the rod was taken through the casting and secured with a nut which led to a bulkier detail than if they had been steel forks welded to the rods.

Castings offer the possibility of modelling at no extra cost. It may be necessary to limit the number of variations to avoid excessive pattern costs and, if the various members obviously carry widely different loads, this may be a problem architecturally.

Corrosion protection of the connection must be considered. This has been achieved by overpainting the connection, by sealing it or by using stainless steel pins. The latter only solves the problem of corrosion of the pin and neglects the plate and fork; there is also the problem of bimetallic corrosion between structural steel and stainless, although this can be overcome by the use of Tufnol isolating washers and bushes.

The best approach is to provide a recess at the junction between the fork and plate which can be pointed with an elastomeric sealant (Fig. 20.31, Renault). The ends of the pin should be sealed in the same way. The detailing for this can easily be provided in both castings and fabrications. However, although it increases the labour content of fabrications it only affects the pattern costs for castings.

It is consistent for all major connections to be pinned,

Fig. 20.32 *Fabricated forks at the National Exhibition Centre, Birmingham, UK (architects Edward D. Mills and Partners: engineers Ove Arup and Partners).*

Fig. 20.33 *Flame-cut and machined forks at Fleetguard factory, Quimper.*

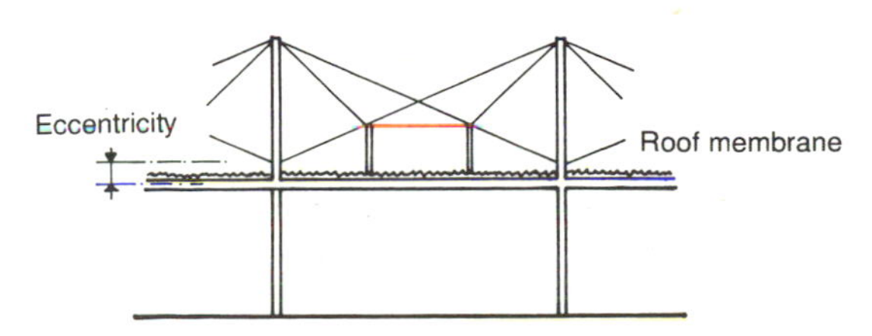

Fig. 20.34 *Eccentric connections to simplify waterproofing.*

since this makes it possible to design a family of details to suit various conditions. Apart from this and the architectural requirements for visual articulation, the pinned connection can improve the structural behaviour by allowing the beam and suspension system to deflect without this generating bending forces at the beam-to-column joints. It also simplifies erection.

20.7.2 Waterproofing

A suspended roof inevitably entails penetration of the waterproofing. However, inspection of a typical industrial building will show a number of penetrations for rainwater outlets, smoke vents, flues etc. Thus this is a change in the size rather than the nature of a problem and it has been found that leaks occur most often at rainwater outlets and parapets. It is relatively straightforward to design a waterproofing detail for a column or hanger penetration.

It is worth making conditions as simple as possible, and a number of things can be done in this respect. If, by accepting some eccentricity in the line of action of forces, connections can be moved outside the roof skin and penetrations avoided, this is worth doing; it can also help make the diagram of the structure more legible (Fig. 20.34, Fleetguard). Hangers should, if possible, pass through the skin normal to the surface. It is better not to take tie rods through the roof since it is difficult to dress the waterproofing around such small members. Also, it gives a visually 'blind' connection. It is worth providing a shroud for the waterproofing to tuck under (Fig. 20.35, Fleetguard).

It is sometimes thought that tension roofs create waterproofing problems because of greater movements. This is unlikely to be the case from the purely structural point of view, since deflections are limited by Codes of Practice and both tension and conventional roofs are likely to be designed

Fig. 20.35 *Use of shroud at Fleetguard factory, Quimper.*

close to these limits. Any difficulty is more likely to arise from a philosophical point.

In some projects, the walls are intended to support the perimeter of the roof and the tension system only assists the interior. On the other hand, if the roof is conceived as being entirely suspended from masts, it is inconsistent for it to be supported by the walls at the edges and a movement joint must be introduced between the wall and the roof. This may seem to be rather subtle but it is points such as these which distinguish between first and second-rate buildings.

20.7.3 Fabrication

Despite the complex appearance of tension roofs there is no reason why they need be difficult to fabricate, although there is always a danger in generalizing. The pinned connections themselves can be simple; the main problems are likely to occur in the places where a number of members meet. These problems will, to some extent, be unavoidable but during the scheme stage it is worth bearing in mind the consequences that decisions may have in fabrication time and cost. For example, a structure will have much simpler column/beam/tie connections if it is two- rather than three-dimensional.

20.7.4 Erection

Although the operations involved in the erection of a tension structure may be unusual they need not be difficult. Generally, there have been no great problems with erection, probably in part because unusual jobs tend to be thought about carefully in advance.

It is important for the erection process to be considered as part of the design and a procedure described to the tenderers. This should not be mandatory and is likely to be changed, but it helps give the tenderers confidence which should result in a more realistic price. It is also a good discipline for the designers.

20.7.5 Adjustment

The actual assembly of the components has tended to be straightforward and in large part this is a function of the type of architecture which favours repetition, large elements and pinned joints. The complications arise almost entirely in the subsequent adjustment of the structure. Unlike conventional structures, where sufficient adjustment for construction tolerance can be found within bolted connections, the large triangulated arrangements of these structures define the geometry very precisely and some form of adjustment must be provided to allow assembly and to ensure that the roof is at the correct level (Fig. 20.36). The adjustment is also used to control the distribution of forces within the system. It is wise to have as few adjustment points as possible so that the complexity of the operation is minimized.

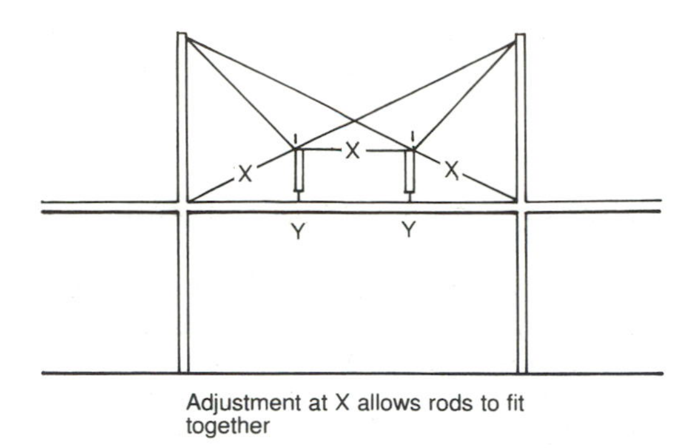

Adjustment at X allows rods to fit together

Adjustment at Y controls level of roof

Fig. 20.36 *Allowing for adjustment.*

20.7.6 Prestressing

It is obviously necessary to ensure that the ties are providing the correct degree of support to the beams, but the precision needed decreases as the ratio of imposed load to self weight increases. Different techniques have been used on the various projects.

The precision needed depends very much on the design of the structure. Both Fleetguard and Saint Herblain, for example, were designed so that the tension in the ties was not critical, in order to minimize erection time and cost. On the other hand Renault and Inmos both required careful control of the tension in the ties.

20.8 ECONOMIC FACTORS RELATED TO CABLE-STAYED STRUCTURES

It is unwise to generalize about costs, since these depend on both weight of steel and complexity; these in turn depend on the structural arrangement and the nature of the detailing. If cost comparisons are being made with conventional structures, then to be realistic, they should be equivalent architectural solutions since these too are unlikely to be the cheapest possible structures. Also, it is in the nature of buildings such as these that in the design of one element, much is included that is needed for others like cladding, glazing, services etc. In consequence it becomes difficult to establish the net structural cost.

It is better to consider the overall cost of a project rather than the structural cost alone, since the designers can choose how to allocate the budget to the best effect. It is worth noting that a number of projects have been for commercial developments where the client has seen them to be good value, but not necessarily in terms of building cost alone.

If a tension structure is to compare with other systems, it must use less steel in order to compensate for the unavoidable extra cost of some of the connections; the other components should also be simple. These goals are more likely to be achieved if the engineering aspects are understood and respected by the architect.

20.9 INTRODUCTION TO SUSPENSION FORMS

Suspension forms differ from cable-stayed systems in that their individual tension members are no longer straight. This is due to the action of forces which are not acting along the length of the member. Examples include the self-weight of membranes and the forces in the hangers of a suspension bridge. The design of such systems requires consideration of the curved form of the tension member, both in terms of the structural analysis and in developing the required shape.

20.10 ELEMENTARY CABLE MATHEMATICS

The load/extension relationship for a cable subject to tension, T, only is given by:

$$\text{Extension } e = Tl/AE$$

where l is the length of cable, A is the net cross-sectional area, and E is Young's Modulus.

A comparison of Young's Modulus and ultimate tensile strength (UTS) for different materials is given in Table 20.1.

The values for E shown in Table 20.1 apply after the construction stretch has been pulled out of wire rope by load cycling to 50% UTS. In wire rope the construction stretch can be as much as the stretch in the cable at maximum working load.

From considerations of equilibrium (Fig. 20.37), it can be shown that the tension, T, in a circular arc of radius R loaded radially with a load intensity P is given by:

$$T = P \times R$$

The radius is geometrically related to the span, s, and dip, d, as follows:

$$R = s^2/8d + d/2$$

For a catenary loaded vertically, the horizontal and

Table 20.1 Young's Modulus and ultimate tensile strength for different materials. *E* is Young's Modulus; *UTS* is the ultimate tensile strength

	E kN/mm² (ksi)	*UTS N/mm² (ksi)*
Solid steel bar	210 (30)	400–2000 (60–290)
Strand	150 (22)	2000 (290)
Wire rope	112 (16)	2000 (290)
Polyester fibres	7.5 (1.1)	910 (132)
Aramid fibres	112 (16)	2800 (400)

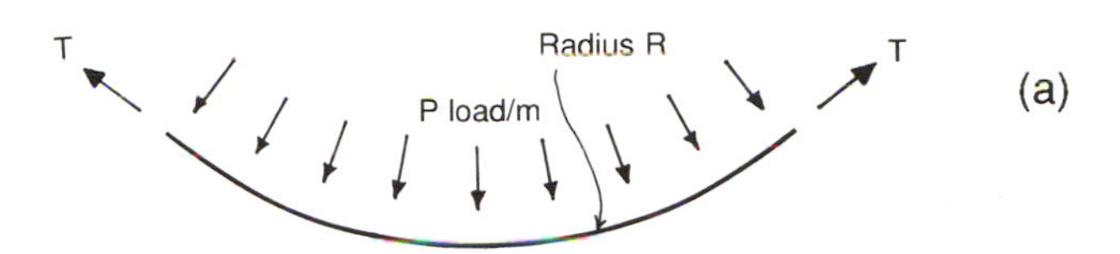

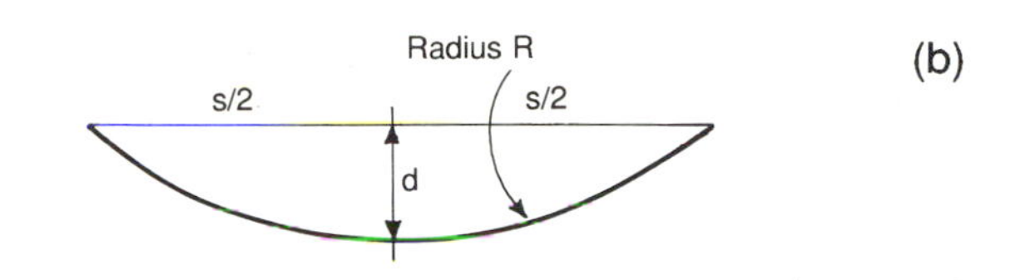

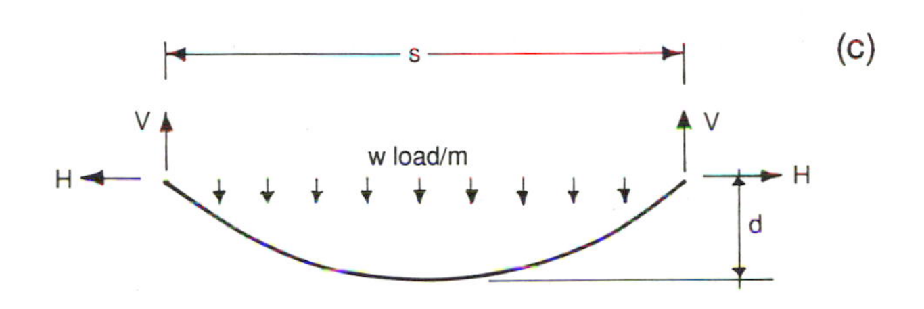

Fig. 20.37 *(a) A circular arc loaded radially. (b) Geometric relation between the radius, span and dip. (c) catenary loaded vertically.*

vertical force, H and V respectively, and maximum tension, T, are given by:

$$H = ws^2/8d$$
$$V = ws/2$$
$$T = \sqrt{(H^2 + V^2)}$$

With the above formulae, forces in cables can be estimated. For full and accurate analysis, it is necessary to use a non-linear computer analysis which takes into account the change of curvature caused by stretch. For well-curved cables, hand analysis is sufficiently accurate and gives a useful guide to the forces involved and the sizes of cables and fittings.

A special problem is the straight cable or flat fabric. To be straight, the cable must have an initial or prestress tension T_o and theoretically zero weight. In order to carry load, the cable must stretch and sag to a radius R.

If span $= s$, initial length $= L_o$, load $= w$/unit length, stiffness $= EA$, pre-tension $= T_o$, tension under load $= T$, then:

$$\text{Equilibrium equation } T = Rw \quad (1)$$

$$\text{New length } L = 2R\Theta = 2R \sin^{-1}(s/2R) \quad (2)$$

$$\text{Now, strain} = (L - L_o)/L = \frac{T - T_o}{EA} \quad (3)$$

Substituting (1) and (2) and rearranging:

$$\frac{L_o}{EA}(T - T_o) + L_o = \frac{2T}{w}\sin^{-1}\frac{ws}{2T} \quad (4)$$

This equation can be solved by trial and error. The central dip d can then be derived from equations above.

The important points to realize from these relationships are:

(a) The extension of a tie bar with low initial tension is considerably more than TL/AE since the dip of the bar must be pulled out.
(b) Straight cables or flat fabric can be used for load carrying but either the tensions will be very high or there will be large deflections.

20.11 STRUCTURAL FORM FOR TWO-DIMENSIONAL SUSPENSION STRUCTURES

20.11.1 Suspension bridge or draped cable

A suspension bridge (Fig. 20.38) is essentially a catenary cable prestressed by dead weight only. Early suspension bridges had flexible decks and suffered from large deflections and sometimes from unstable oscillation under wind.

Fig. 20.38 *The Severn suspension bridge, Bristol, UK 1966 (engineer: Freeman Fox and Partners).*

Fig. 20.39 *Dulles International Air Terminal, Washington, USA 1962 (architect Eero Saarinen: engineer Severud, Elstad and Kruegur).*

Fig. 20.40 *Burgo Paper Mill in Mantua, Italy 1960 (engineer Pier Luigi Nervi).*

Fig. 20.41 *Mecca Conference Centre, Saudi Arabia 1974 (architect Rolf Gutbrod: engineer Frei Otto).*

James Dredge, a bridge builder from Bath, UK, proposed a system of raking hangers to reduce deflections under live loads. The importance of the deck as a stiffening girder and of damping came much later.

The suspension cable is taken over support towers to ground anchors. The stiffened deck is supported primarily by vertical hangers. The system is ideally suited to resisting uniform down loads. The principle has been used for buildings mostly as draped cable structures. It is suitable for spans of 40–100 m (130–328 ft).

Examples include the Dulles International Air Terminal (Fig. 20.39), Burgo Paper Mill in Mantua, Italy (Fig. 20.40) and the Mecca Conference Centre (Fig. 20.41).

In the case of the Mecca Conference Centre, the dead load was similar to the wind uplift, stability being provided by some additional tie downs at the edges and high damping of the cladding.

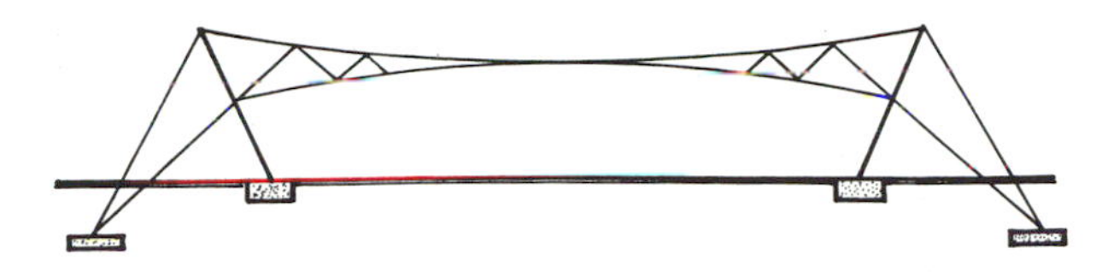

Fig. 20.42 *Hanging cable resists down loads and the hogging cable resists upload.*

Fig. 20.43 *Frankfurt Hangar 'Finsterwalder', Germany, 1960.*

20.11.2 Cable truss

The hanging cable resists down loads and the hogging cable resists upload (Fig. 20.42). If diagonal bracing is used, non-uniform load can be resisted without large deflections. An example of this type of structure is the Frankfurt Hangar 'Finsterwalder' (Fig. 20.43).

20.12 STRUCTURAL FORM FOR THREE-DIMENSIONAL STRUCTURES (TWO-WAY SPANNING)

20.12.1 Three-dimensional cable truss system (Fig. 20.44)

The classic form of this structure is the bicycle wheel roof. In this there is a circular ring beam which is braced against buckling by a radial cable system. The radial cables are separated into upper and lower cables by a central strut so that the centre is supported. This system is suitable for structures of 20–60 m (66–200 ft) diameter. Examples include the Palais de Sports, Tunis and an auditorium at Utica (Figs. 20.45 and 20.46). The dimensions are limited by the span of straight cables, see above. Larger spans can be achieved by introducing more rings of masts as at Madison Square Garden.

Le Ricolaus claimed, correctly, that a two-way or three-way double layer grid with struts on the interaction was more efficient than a radial bicycle wheel.

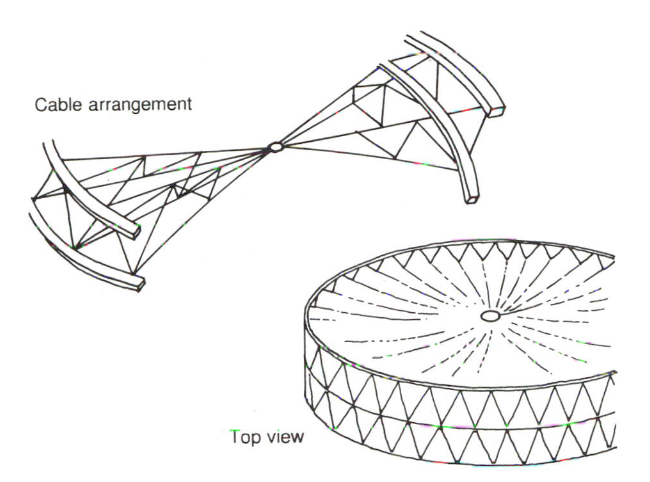

Fig. 20.44 *Three-dimensional cable truss system.*

Fig. 20.45 *Palais de Sports, Tunis, Tunisia.*

Fig. 20.46 *Auditorium at Utica, New York 1960 (engineer Lev Zetlin).*

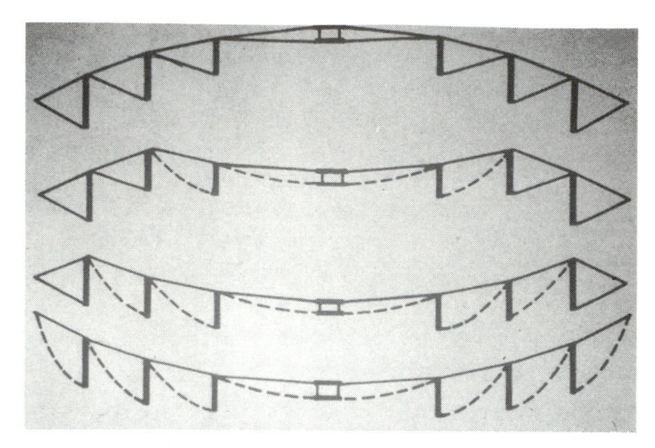

Fig. 20.47 *Cable dome, Seoul Olympics, South Korea 1987 (architect The Space Group of Korea: engineer David Geiger).*

Fig. 20.48 *Auditorium for the Seoul Olympics, South Korea (exterior).*

Fig. 20.49 *Auditorium for the Seoul Olympics, South Korea (interior).*

20.12.2 Cable dome

This system has recently been developed by David Geiger into a cable dome (Fig. 20.47). In this there are two or three rings of masts. The radial forces at the base of the masts are taken by circumferential cables. The masts are also cross cabled circumferentially to maintain their stability. The two auditoria for the Seoul Olympics shown in Figs 20.48 and 20.49 are recent examples of this type of structure.

20.13. SURFACE STRESSED STRUCTURES

In a surface stressed structure a membrane, which is a two-dimensional tension element, is stressed to form a load carrying structural component. The membrane can be either a coated woven fabric or a net of steel cables. The stress can be induced either by pressure acting on one side, in which case it is a pneumatic structure, or by tensioning the net system against the boundary, in which case it is prestressed.

Unlike frame structures or even the cable-supported structures described above, there is no cultural history of this form of construction leading to an established architectural language. Because of this, Otto in particular has drawn from analogies in nature such as soap bubbles, spider's webs and other organic structures to establish a language of his own [1].

20.13.1 Geometric properties of surfaces

A pneumatic structure adopts either single (cylindrical) curvature or double, positive gaussian, curvature. The description of 'positive gaussian' implies that the centres of the principal radii or curvature are on the same side. Another term for this is 'synclastic'.

Surfaces with negative gaussian or anticlastic curvature have the centres on different sides and a saddle surface results. These surfaces can be generated by a membrane prestressed to a continuous ring boundary which does not lie in a plane.

The lines of principal curvatures are where the greatest and least radii are found. They are at right angles to each other and there is no twist of the surface along these lines.

A geodesic or geodetic line along a surface is the line followed by a string stretched between two points. These lines have a number of useful properties. One is that the plane of curvature of the line is at right angles to the local plane of the surface. There is an infinite number of geodesic lines on a surface. Buckminster Fuller's use of the term 'geodesic' to describe his system of dome construction is a special case and is confusing to the subsequent discussions.

20.14 EQUILIBRIUM EQUATIONS

The surface stresses and curvatures must be in equilibrium with the applied pressure at all points. There is a simple equation relating these variables:

$$t_1/R_1 + t_2/R_2 = p$$

where t_1 and t_2 are tension per unit width in the warp and weft directions, R_1 and R_2 are the radii of curvature and p is the applied pressure.

For a cylindrical surface R_2 is infinite, hence

$$t/R = p$$

This is the same as the rope equation (2) above.

For an anticlastic surface R_1 is negative with respect to R_2. If the applied pressure is zero:

$$t_1/R_1 = t_2/R_2 = 0$$

or

$$t_1/R_1 = -t_2/R_2$$

20.15 FORM FINDING OF STRESSED SURFACES

A blown up paper bag is an example of a pneumatic structure. The bag forms a pneumatic shape but it is uncontrolled, does not fit any particular boundary and has severe wrinkles in some places and stress concentrations in others. Controlled form finding can be carried out by physical modelling, geometrical calculation or analysis based on equilibrium. These are discussed in more detail below.

20.15.1 Physical modelling

Physical modelling can be carried out using soap films (Fig. 20.50). These model a perfect membrane with equal surface tensions in all directions but are very difficult to measure. Another method is to use stretch fabric of one form or another, for instance ladies' tights, lycra fabric or heat shrinkable PVC foil. The last material can be used to make a fairly rigid model from which cutting pattern measurements can be taken using paper strips. From a reasonably scaled model the surface radii can be measured using equation (3) above or by using a radius curve. Then by using the equilibrium equations above, the surface stresses can be calculated. In the past a number of structures were built to calculations based on this method – the largest being the West German Pavilion at Montreal, architects Gutbrod and Otto.

An advantage of using physical modelling is that the members of the design group can understand the forms and surfaces and get an idea of the forces involved. This leads to an improved level of communication within the design group and hence to convergence on an elegant and efficient design solution [2].

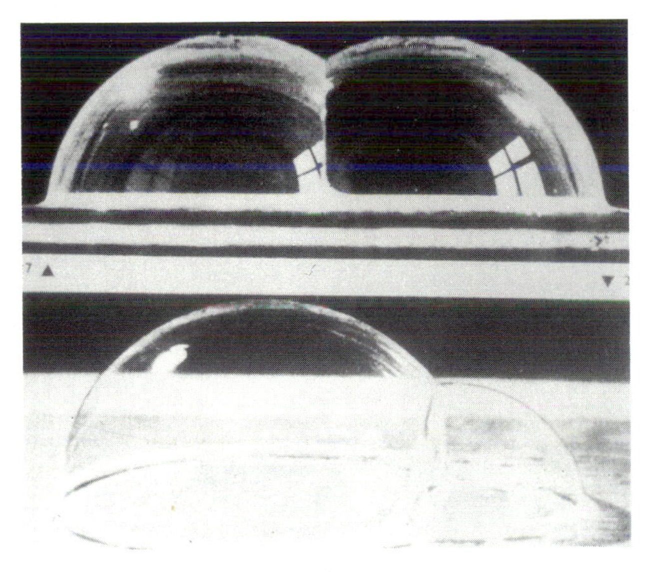

Fig. 20.50 *Physical modelling using soap films.*

20.15.2 Geometric calculation

For pneumatic forms, physical modelling is practically impossible. Air hall cutting patterns in the past were developed using a pragmatic geometric approach in which the angles at the corners of the gore line were matched up to obtain a sort of best fit. Usually this resulted in a lot of wrinkles in the corners.

Otto has demonstrated that a pneumatic form can be generated from a series of cones. This principle is used in a commercial computer program to generate cutting patterns for rectangular air halls.

20.15.3 Equilibrium calculations

Form finding calculations involving statical equilibrium are inevitably based on computer programs. In this method the surface is modelled as a pattern of elements, usually triangles. In the form finding mode the elements are set to have a constant predetermined stress no matter how much they change their size. This process is physically equivalent to soap film modelling except that a soap film can only have a constant uniform surface tension all over it while in the computer model the tensions can be varied. The same model can be used for load analysis and for establishing the cutting patterns and cable lengths etc. Examples of a computer analysis are shown in Fig. 20.51.

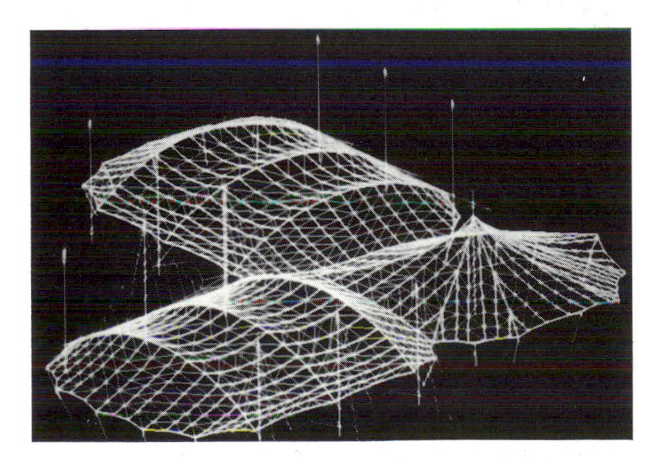

Fig. 20.51 *Example of computer analysis.*

A powerful program currently available is run by Minitec Ltd and they are co-operating with City University, London on research to enhance the program further. At present, data inputting and editing is carried out visually on screen and high quality graphic representations are available.

In this method the shape is controlled by specifying the warp and weft stresses in the various areas of fabric, thus necessitating a trial and error procedure to get the required form. However, with the increasing capacity and speed of computers and the development of user-friendly programs, the runs take less time and data can be varied quickly so that the required form can be readily developed. However, the operator must still understand the physical principles involved.

The program can handle pneumatic as well as tension structures. In the former case, it is necessary to control the shape with elastic strings along the seam lines as well as by varying the specified tension in the cloth.

These programs can also handle load analysis of the structure. For this, the constant stress triangular elements are replaced by elastic elements with specified load extension behaviour and loaded with gravity or pressure loads.

20.16 DETAILED CONSIDERATION OF STRUCTURAL FORM

20.16.1 Boundary elements

A highly stressed membrane must be attached to a boundary element which makes a closed ring. The significance of this can be demonstrated with a soap film which is initially formed in a circular wire ring. If the ring is opened, the film immediately ruptures. The boundary ring need not be flat and can be formed of cables. A uniform stress surface within such a boundary is known as a minimum surface. For instance, Fig. 20.52 shows a minimum surface bounded by four cables with two masts.

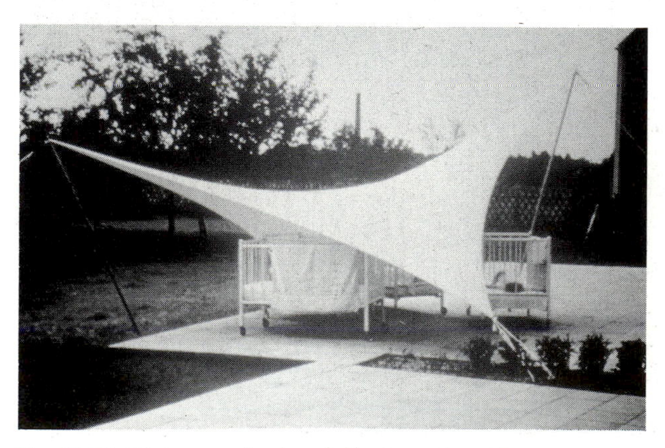

Fig. 20.52 *Minimum surface bounded by four cables with two masts.*

A minimum surface within a fixed boundary has the least possible surface area and the minimum strain energy. Hence it can be said to have maximum structural efficiency. It is possible to modify the surface by changing the ratio of stresses in the prestressed condition. To return to the previous example: if the surface tension in the direction between the high points is increased, the surface will rise in the centre. It may be desirable to do this for various reasons such as to improve the headroom within the building, to modify the visual appearance of the surface or to improve the performance under load.

20.16.2 Behaviour under load

If the above example is made from woven fabric or an orthogonal cable net, there are two sets of tendons at right angles to each other which ideally would follow the lines of principal curvature so that they then have opposing curvature. Prestress is required to stiffen the surface against deflection. If the surface is flat then prestress provides the only resistance to deflection. If it is well curved then the elastic properties of the membrane provide the resistance to deflection regardless of the level of prestress up to the point where yarns go slack in one direction, or where, under a local load, the curvature becomes synclastic. This effect becomes very important under snow loading.

Wind loading on such a surface consists of a random and varying set of surface pressures in which uplift generally dominates. The downward pressures are taken by the sagging set of tendons and the uplift pressures by the hogging tendons. The tension along any particular tendon remains sensibly constant, so local high pressures are taken by the surface deflecting. As a result, the radii of curvature change. The maximum tension in a particular hogging tendon is caused by the maximum averaged uplift pressure in the area of the tendon.

20.16.3 Snow loads

The same applies for down loads. Snow loading tends to slide down the steep slopes and remain on the flatter slopes. This results in high local patch loading on the horizontal areas. The high local load produces large local deflections. As discussed above, the local tensions are not particularly high; the increase in tension is spread over a large area of the structure with a corresponding strain in the fibres. This results in a large increase in strain energy in the structure which must be balanced by the decrease in potential energy, i.e. the local load × its deflection.

Large deflections cause problems with ponding if they are such that there is no longer any drainage away from the deflected pocket. Once this occurs, any additional rain or melt water will run into the pocket which will become larger and larger until the fabric tears or the supporting structure collapses. On a tensioned fabric structure, the problem of ponding can be avoided by ensuring that there are no flat, horizontal areas. On canopy structures which are used primarily in the summer, it is a sensible precaution to install drainage grommets in areas where ponding can occur.

Air supported structures also suffer from ponding if the local snow load exceeds the inflation pressure. Stadium structures with a primary net of cables are particularly sensitive to ponding since the snow tends to drift into the cable valleys. Means of preventing ponding need to be considered in the design stage.

20.17 BOUNDARY CONDITIONS

Each field of fabric must be bounded on all sides by boundary elements. These can be rigid elements such as beams, walls or arches, or flexible cable elements. It is difficult to form a useful space with a single hypar field, and hence a building will usually consist of a number of fields arranged together.

A membrane cannot be supported by a point. This is well demonstrated with a soap film which instantly bursts. Generally, at a mast point, there will be two ridge cables, sometimes three or four, which transfer the uniform stress in the fields to the concentrated load at the mast.

Examples of tents with masts and ridges include Baltimore Concert Tent, International Garden Festival, Liverpool Theatre Tent and Riyadh Stadium (Figs 20.53 to 20.55).

20.17.1 Conical forms

With conical (pseudo sphere) forms, there are often a large number of radial cables coming together at the mast. These usually lie freely under the fabric so the tension is constant and the fabric can slip over the cables. Some examples are La Verne College and Pink Floyd Umbrellas (Figs 20.56 to 20.57).

20.17.2 Ring supports

A single membrane can be supported by a large ring. Again, soap film modelling demonstrates the problem. If a film is created between an inner ring and an outer ring, the inner ring can be lifted to form a doubly curved surface. If the rings are moved further apart, it will be found that at a certain point, the film will always burst. This happens because the meridional radius of curvature becomes greater than the circumferential radius. At this point the conditions of equilibrium cannot be met so the film bursts.

With a real fabric, the meridional tension can be greater than the circumferential tension. Reinforcement can then be added by doubling the cloth or by broad-seaming so that the ring can be smaller than that which the soap film theory predicts. Even so, a relatively large ring is required. An

Fig. 20.53 *Baltimore Concert Tent, Baltimore, Maryland 1981 (architect FTL Associates: engineer Buro Happold).*

Fig. 20.54 *International Garden Festival Theatre Tent, Liverpool, UK, 1982 (architect William Gillespie and Partners: engineer Buro Happold).*

Fig. 20.55 *Riyadh Stadium, Saudi Arabia, 1985 (architects J. Fraser and J. Roberts: engineer Geiger and Berger, Jorg Schlaich).*

Fig. 20.56 *La Verne College, San Francisco, USA, 1973 (architect Shaver Partnership: engineer TY Lin International, Bob Campbell and Co.).*

example of this technique can be seen at the new Lord's Mound Stand.

20.17.3 Humped tents

These are a special system of building tents devised by Professor Frei Otto using woven fabric which is made up flat and without shaping along the seams. The fabric is supported on domed supports. Angle changing of the weave allows it to distort into a doubly-curved surface.

Humps can also be made as a linear arch supporting the fabric on a ridge line.

Examples include the BP Ceremony Tent at Dyce, Portobello Road Market Canopy, London and Yale Ice Rink by Severud, Elstad and Kruegur (Figs 20.58 to 20.60).

Fig. 20.57 *Pink Floyd Umbrellas, 1979 (architect Frei Otto; engineer Buro Happold).*

Fig. 20.58 *BP Ceremony Tent at Dyce, near Aberdeen 1975 (architect Design Research Unit: engineer Ove Arup and Partners).*

Fig. 20.59 *Portobello Road Market Canopy, London, UK (architect Franklin Stafford Partnership: engineer Buro Happold).*

Fig. 20.60 *Yale Ice Rink, New Haven, Connecticut 1958 (architect Eero Saarinen: engineer Severud, Elstad and Kreugur).*

20.17.4 Eye loops

Frei Otto devised a system of mast head supports using a loop picked up at one point which he used for the Montreal Pavilion. The system has occasionally been used subsequently by Larry Medlin and more recently by FTL Associates.

20.17.5 Moment-free arches

The chain analogy for predicting the line of thrust of an arch was first observed by Robert Hooke in 1640. It is possible to support a membrane by an arch which has no bending and is stabilized by the membrane. This form finding process can only be carried out using an equilibrium computer process. The arch is only moment-free under ideal prestress conditions. Under imposed loads, moments are generated and there are stability problems requiring bending stiffness. Frei Otto's entrance arch for the Cologne Bundersgartenschau demonstrates how slender the arch member can be. For larger structures, engineers have shied away from thin arches restrained by the membrane in preference for self-stabilizing trussed arches.

20.17.6 Surfaces supported by a compression ring

The classic example of this form of construction is the Raleigh Livestock Arena (Fig. 20.61) designed in 1953 by Macief Nowici with the engineer Fred N. Severud. The saddle surface roof is formed between two inclined parabolic arches covering an area of 92 × 97 m (300 × 320 ft). The surface is formed with cables varying from 13 mm to 32 mm (½ in to 1¼ in) diameter at 1.8 m (6 ft) spacing. The cladding is profiled steel covered with insulation and bitumen waterproofing.

Frei Otto designed a roof structure for a church at Bremen

Fig. 20.61 *Raleigh Livestock Arena, Virginia 1953 (architect Macief Nowici: engineer Severud, Elstad and Kruegur).*

Fig. 20.62 *Calgary Olympic Saddle Dome, Alberta, Canada, 1981 (architect Graham McCourt: engineer Jan Bobrowski/Buro Happold).*

(architect, Carsten Schrock) which consisted of a cable net spanning between laminated wood arches. Other examples include the Calgary Olympic Saddle Dome and Palazzo de la Sport, Milano (Figs 20.62 to 20.63).

This system has also been used for a roof at Dulwich College. In both this case and for the Calgary Olympic Saddle Dome, the structure was engineered by Jan Bobrowski. In these examples the cladding consists of reinforced concrete plates and the finished structure becomes a concrete shell.

Fig. 20.63 *Palazzo de la Sport, Milan, Italy, 1976.*

20.17.7 Air supported cable restrained roofs supported on a ring beam

Examples of this type of structural form include the mobile theatre in Boston (Fig. 20.64) and the US Pavilion at Expo '67, Osaka. For the latter the architects, Davis and Brody, as a cost-saving exercise, adopted a low profile cable-restrained air supported roof enclosed by an earth berm – an idea which had been promoted by the father of structural fabrics, Wally Bird. The generation of this concept was

Fig. 20.64 *Mobile theatre in Boston, Massachusetts, USA, 1959 (architects Karl Koch and Margaret Ross: engineer Paul Weidlinger/ Walter Bird).*

Fig. 20.65 *Silver Dome at Pontiac, Illinois, USA, 1975 (architect O'Dell, Hewlett and Luckenback: engineer Geiger/Berger).*

Fig. 20.66 *Minneapolis Metrodome, 1982 (architect Skidmore Owings and Merrill: engineer Geiger/Berger).*

wind flow. Positive pressures occur above rigid earth embankments, leaving the flexible roof subject only to uplift forces. To solve the problem of anchorage the engineer, David Geiger, proposed to use a moment-free compression ring. With the diagonal cable arrangement this ring became elliptical in form. The roof material was PVC coated glass fibre cloth laced to the cable net.

Bird and Geiger realized that this form of construction could be used for covering stadia. The development of teflon-coated glass fibre cloth which met the US fire requirements allowed these structures to go forward. The first was the Unidome. This was followed by the Silver Dome at Pontiac where the air supported roof was adopted after construction of the stadium had commenced (Fig. 20.65).

Subsequent developments were aimed at minimizing first costs, for instance by using larger panels of cloth, and performance in service was neglected. Most of these stadia in the northern half of the USA have experienced problems with snow drifting in the valleys causing local inversions which often lead to deflation of the roof. The cure is smaller panels, higher inflation pressure and more snow melt capacity – all of which increase the initial cost, but even so this form of construction is still the cheapest method of roofing very large areas.

Minneapolis Metrodome is another example of this form (Fig. 20.66).

20.18 CONSTRUCTION AND DETAILING

20.18.1 Cables

Wire rope cables are spun from high tensile wire. For structural work the cables should be multi-strand, typically 6 × 19 or 6 × 37 with independent wire rope core and galvanized Class A. Hoisting ropes with fibre core are usually ungalvanized and heavily greased, and are to be strictly avoided. For increased corrosion resistance, the largest diameter wire should be used and the cables can be filled with zinc powder in a slow-setting polyurethane varnish. This is done during the spinning process.

For greater corrosion resistance, heavier galvanizing, filled strand or locked coil strand can be used. These can also be fitted with a shrunk on polyurethane or polypropylene sleeve.

Stainless steel apparently offers total corrosion resistance but in some aggressive atmospheres, or if air is excluded, corrosion will occur and it can be more damaging than with carbon steel cables.

20.18.2 Terminations

The simplest and cheapest type of termination is a swaged talurit eye made round a thimble. This would connect into a clevis type connection or onto the pin of a shackle. If it is required that the shackle body is threaded onto the eye, then a reeving thimble must be used. Swaged end terminations are the neatest and most streamlined fittings.

Hot-poured zinc terminations still have to be used for very heavy cables, i.e. those with diameters greater than 50 mm (2 in). They are still occasionally used for smaller cables, but generally swaged fittings have taken over. Epoxy with steel balls as a filler can be used in place of zinc. This material offers an improvement in fatigue life at the termination.

20.18.3 Bull dog grips (U bolt grips)

These are used to make on-site connection. They are ugly and damage the rope. The ball type 'iron grip' is a better alternative.

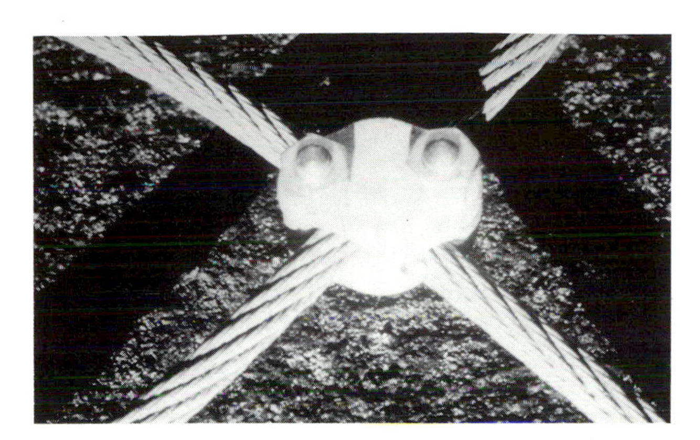

Fig. 20.67 *Three-part forged steel clamp.*

20.18.4 Cross clamps for cable net construction

The standard detail developed from the German Pavilion, Montreal from 1967 onwards is a three part forged steel clamp, of which the two outer parts are identical (Fig. 20.67). For a smaller structure the cost of dies for a forging may be too great. Consideration can then be given to using machined aluminium components. CNC (computer numerically controlled) milling machines can produce these very quickly.

If double cables are used, as at the Munich Olympic Stadium in 1972, then a swaged aluminium extrusion can be prefixed to each pair of cables which can then be connected by a single bolt.

20.18.5 Boundary cable clamps

For the attachment of net cables to edge cables, forged steel clamps are generally used. A bent plate clamp can be used as a low cost alternative. Machined aluminium clamps could also be used where only a limited number is required.

20.18.6 Durability of cables

The life of a cable is reduced by corrosion and fatigue. The fatigue life of cables subject only to tension has been studied by various researchers over the years and is normally represented in the form of an *S/N* graph. This relates the magnitude and number of occurrences of a stress level to cause failure of the material. On the basis of this it is wise to limit the maximum tension in a cable to 40% of the MBL (maximum breaking load) for long life structures. For temporary structures, i.e. a life up to 10 years, 50% is acceptable. Generally, the internal damping of clad cable-net structures or coated fabric structures is high so one would not expect a large number of cycles at high loads.

Corrosion of galvanized cables in a covered situation can be considered negligible. External cables should be strand or locked coil strand, galvanized and filled with zinc paste. In this condition a life of 50 years can be expected in normal environments.

Stainless steel is not 100% corrosion free. If it is enclosed so air does not circulate around it and the right corrosive agents are present, it will corrode very quickly and dangerously if it is under stress, so it should be used with caution.

The use of plastic sheaths is of doubtful value. If water and corrosive agents can enter, the resulting corrosion can be worse than if the cable is unprotected. Furthermore, it cannot be inspected. Generally in a cable nearing the end of its design life, wire breaks can be seen and the cable should then be changed. Cable fittings should be arranged to allow easy replacement.

20.18.7 Installation

The installation of cable net structures is illustrated in Fig. 20.68.

20.19 STRUCTURAL FABRICS AND FOILS

Woven fabrics have been used for protection against the weather since man developed the technology to spin and weave fibres into cloth. In these early times, the yarns would have been spun from natural fibres – cellulose fibres such as flax and cotton and animal fibres such as wool. The structures made from these fibres such as ropes, nets, tents and sails were relatively small scale and were used in situations where they could be easily taken down and repaired or replaced. This was just as well, since the fibres were subject to creep, rot and ultraviolet degradation.

The advent of synthetic fibres and of polymer coatings that resist degradation has led to the development of structural fabrics that offer greatly improved strength and stiffness properties with much longer lives. Industry now talks about permanent architectural fabric structures.

Engineering of fabric structures really began with the pressure airships around 1910 [3]. At that time a considerable amount of work was done on strength, creep and biaxial stress/strain behaviour for rubber-coated linen cloth by Haas and Ditzius [4]. In fact the only significant further developments were the investigations into the tearing of cloth in the 1960s which were stimulated by the use of parachutes for retarding space vehicles [5].

Acceptable levels of performance can now be obtained from fabric and film structures, but to achieve these, the structure must be correctly engineered with adequate levels of safety on the cloth. It must also be accurately manufactured from good quality materials with high levels of quality control. Minor damage during installation can be repaired, but the owner may not be too happy with the result. If damage does occur during a high wind, the whole section of fabric (which can be the whole structure) may be lost. This aspect should be taken into account when designing a structure for a particular application.

Fig. 20.68 *Installation of cable net structures.*

REFERENCES AND TECHNICAL NOTES

1. Otto, F. (1982) *Naturliche Knostruktionen*, DVA.
2. Happold, E., Liddell, I. and Dickson, M. (1976) Design towards convergence. *Architectural Design*, July.
3. Burgess, C.P. (1927) *Airship Design*, Ronald Press Co., New York.
4. Haas, R. and Dietzius, A. (1913) *Luftfart und Wissenshaft*, Julius Springer.
5. Hedgepeth, J.M. Stress Conception in Filamentary Structures, NASA TN D-882, May 1961.

FURTHER READING

Kerensky Memorial Conference on Tension Structures, Institution of Structural Enginers, June 1988.

AFSI Proceedings of a Conference on Architectural Fabric Structures, Orlando, Florida, 1984.

IL Publications from:

Institut fur Leichteflachentragwerke, Universitat Stuttgart, Pfaffenwaldring 14 7000, Stuttgart 80, Germany.

IL5 *Convertible Roofs*

IL8 *Nets in Nature and Technics*

IL15 *Air Hall Handbook*

Otto, F. (1973) *Tensile Structures*, Volumes 1 and 2, MIT Press.

Roland, C. and Otto, F. (1970) *Structures*, Longman.

Troitsky, M.S. (1977) *Cable Stayed Bridges – Theory and Design*, Crosby Lockwood Staples.

Makowski, Z.S. (1965) *Steel Space Structures*, Michael Joseph.

Bulson, P.S., Caldwall, J. B. and Severn, R. T. (eds) (1983) *Engineering Structures, Developments in the Twentieth Century*, a collection of essays to mark the 80th birthday of Sir Alfred Pugsley, University of Bristol Press.

Financial Times Print Works building under construction, London.

Part Four | # Steel Construction

Space frame node. Sama Bank, Riyadh, Saudi Arabia (engineer F.J. Samuely and Partners).

HSFG bolt (left) and black 8.8 bolt (right) reprinted by kind permission of Cooper and Turner, Sheffield.

21

Structural connections for steelwork

Tom Schollar

21.1 INTRODUCTION

This chapter seeks to explain the basic structural action of connections, the way stresses are distributed within a connection, and why different types of connection, for example welded or bolted, are used in different circumstances.

21.2 CLASSIFICATION OF CONNECTIONS

Connections can be classified in a number of ways – by the type and magnitude of load, the type of members connected and whether the connections are hidden or exposed.

21.2.1 Type and magnitude of load (compression, tension, shear, bending)

Loads can usually be carried in several ways. For example, compression loads in a connection could be carried by direct compression between members (Fig. 21.1a), by welding (Fig. 21.1b), or by using bolted splice plates (Fig. 21.1c).

If the section were in tension, however, welding or bolted splice plates would have to be used. If the tensile load were very large compared to the section capacity, the bolted connection might be unsuitable because the holes for the bolts weaken the section, and welding might therefore be the only option.

Connections for supporting beams (i.e. shear connections) will be quite different in form from tension and compression connections (Fig. 21.2). If the beam carries moment at the end, the connection will be different again, with the ability to carry the tensile force from the top flange and the compression force from the bottom flange as well as the shear force from the web of the beam (Fig. 21.3).

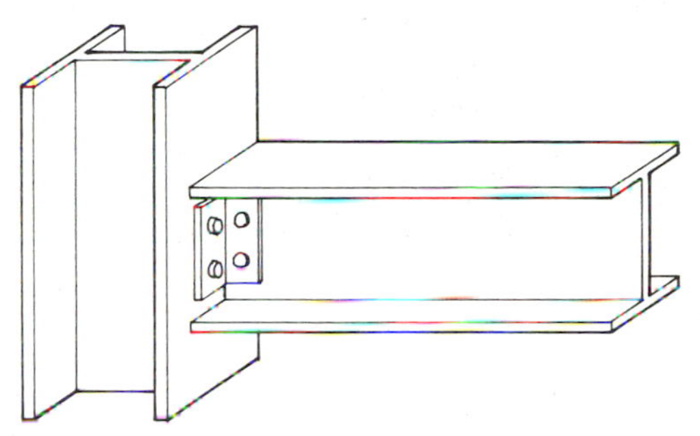

Fig. 21.2 *Typical beam to column connection.*

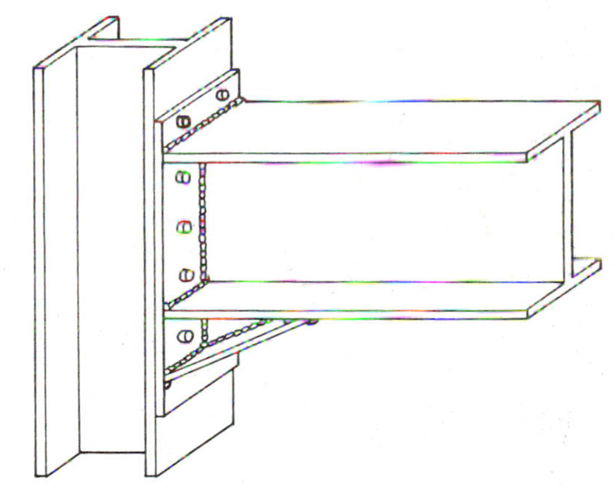

Fig. 21.3 *Typical moment connection.*

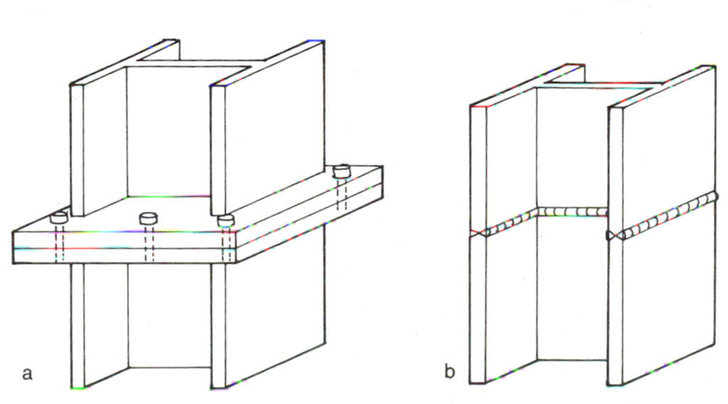

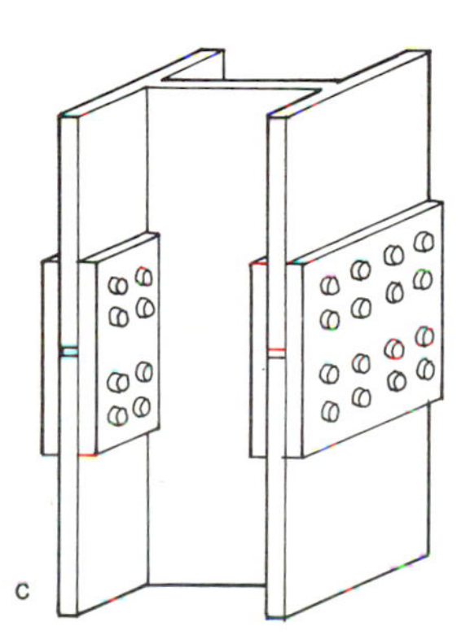

Fig. 21.1 *Direct compression in a column joint carried by (a) end plates; (b) on welds, and (c) on splice plates.*

Fig. 21.4 *Space frame members carrying large axial forces.*

The scale of the load and the size of the connecting members can be a significant limitation. Ultimately the number of bolts required, the length of the connection to accommodate these bolts and the thickness of the connecting plates can become impractical. If this happens, the engineer may have to reconsider the scale or form of the structure proposed (Fig. 21.4).

21.2.2 Member and material type

The designer must know the form and dimensions of members on either side of a connection so that a suitable detail can be designed. Connections between open cross-sections (I- and H-sections) are fundamentally different from those between tubular sections (circular and rectangular). This is inevitable because rectangular tubes have two webs and circular tubes have no flat planes for bolting.

Connections between steel and other materials need yet another different form of connection because the strength of concrete in compression (for example) is about one tenth that of steel.

21.2.3 Exposed connections

Exposed connections need to be considered from both aesthetic and practical points of view, and are usually developed by the architect and engineer working in close collaboration. In addition, externally exposed connections must be detailed to avoid corrosion by preventing the retention of water within the connection. The aesthetic aspect is further explored in the case studies in Part Six.

In times past lattice beams and truss work were assembled by rivet. The offsets and rivet pattern have an aesthetic related to standardized joint design and to the jigs created for drilling modules. Rail and road bridges in the first quarter of this century owe their visual delight to this discipline as do other notable structures such as the Blackpool Tower (Fig. 21.5). Truss work as seen at the Horticultural Hall, Islington reveals the art of assembly of chord to strut to tie which came as a natural expression of the forces to be resolved (Fig. 21.6). Direct heirs to this tradition can be seen in the trim detailing of many atrium structures such as that at Gateway II, Basingstoke (Fig. 21.7).

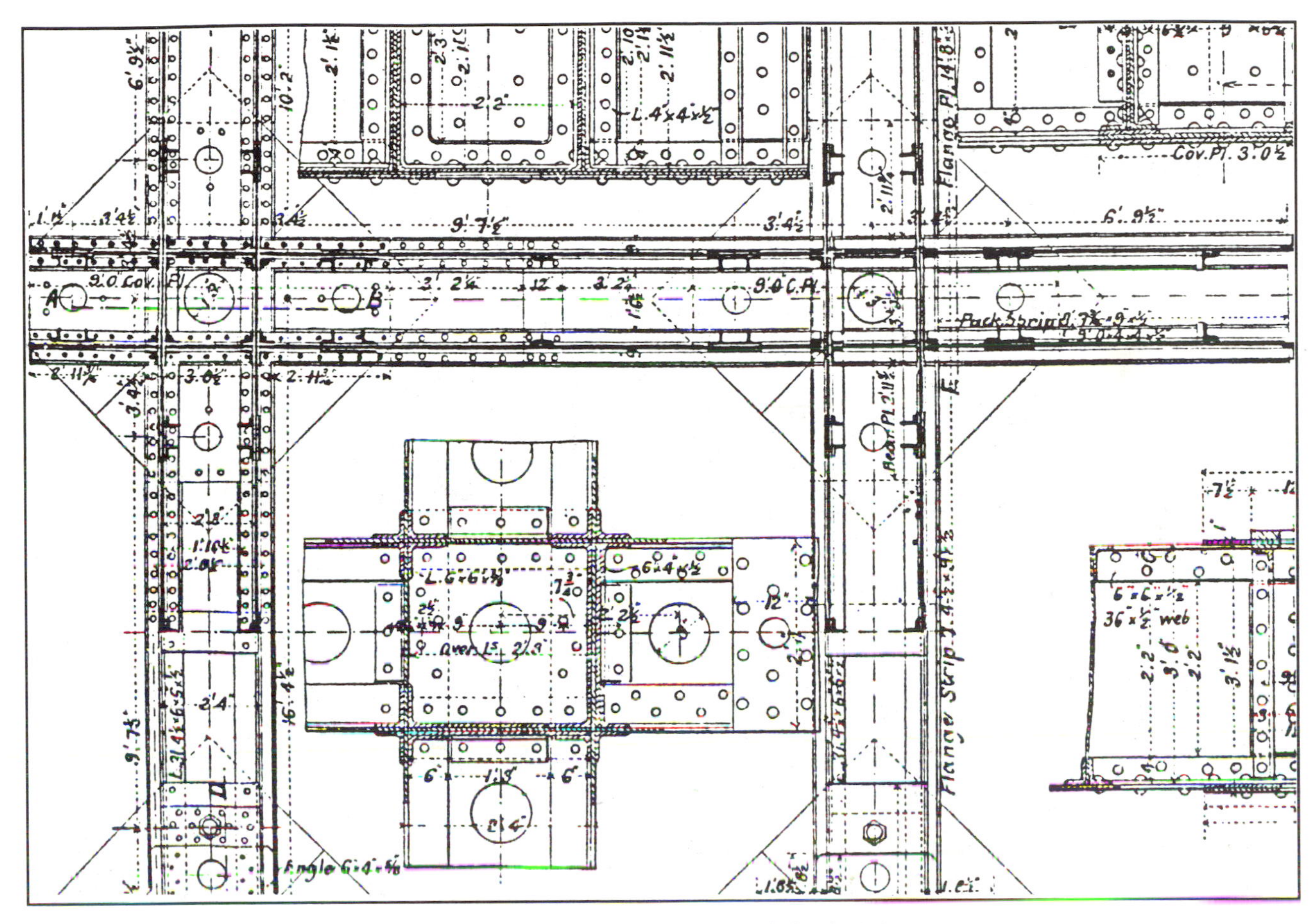

Fig. 21.5 *Typical riveted work in construction from early the 1900s (Blackpool Tower, Blackpool, UK).*

(a)

(b)

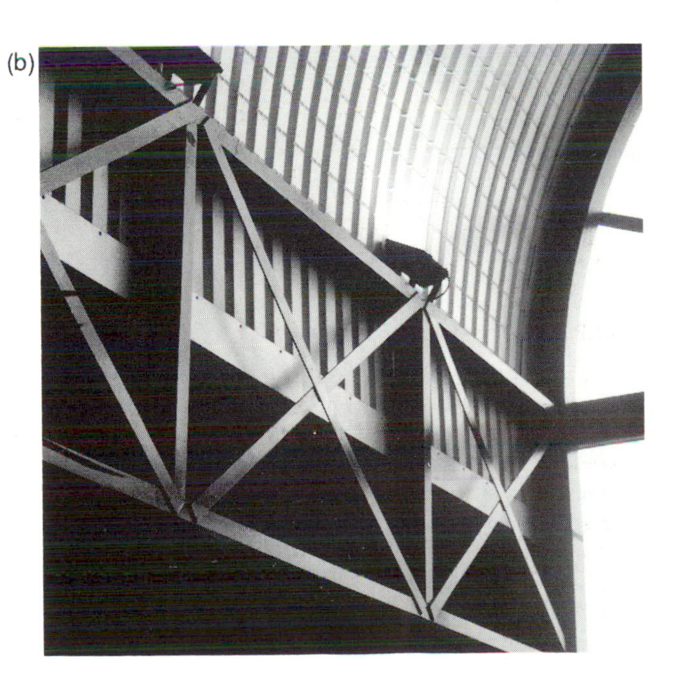

Fig. 21.6 *The Agricultural Hall, Islington, London, 1861–2. (a) Roof framing by Heaviside of Derby; (b) Compare with meaningless decorative strapwork of the 1980s.*

Fig. 21.7 *Atria trusses, Gateway II, Basingstoke, UK 1984. (architects and engineers: Arup Associates).*

21.2.4 Hidden connection

Connections which are not exposed are frequently designed by the engineer for economy, without consideration for appearance or sizing to a particular module. However, care must still be taken over the size and position of hidden connections. For instance, a column splice may need to be detailed so that it remains within a ceiling void, otherwise bolts and splice plates may dictate the size of the column cladding (Fig. 21.8), rather than the casing being related to the plain column section (Fig. 21.9). In the example shown in Fig. 21.8 at least 100 mm (4 in) is added to the clad size of the 305 x 305 column section due to the splice plate thickness of 20 mm (¾ in), and the bolt projection of a further 25 mm (1 in).

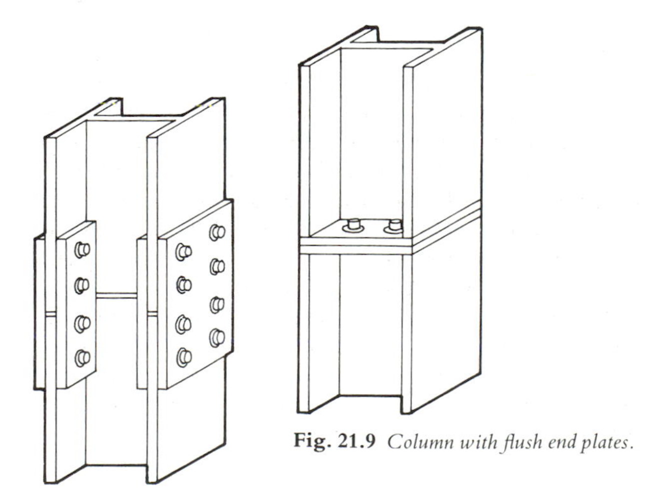

Fig. 21.9 *Column with flush end plates.*

Fig. 21.8 *Column with splice plates proud of the section.*

21.3 BOLTING VERSUS WELDING

It is generally cheaper to make a bolted joint than a welded one (particularly on site) so a designer will usually choose bolted work for both site and workshop with some shop welding where warranted by engineering design. Site welding is utilized where the full strength of a member must be used at a connection and where tolerance, geometry or aesthetics require welded connections (Figs 21.10 and 21.11). In externally exposed work, welding is often preferred to avoid rainwater penetrating behind splice plates on exposed steel (Fig. 21.12).

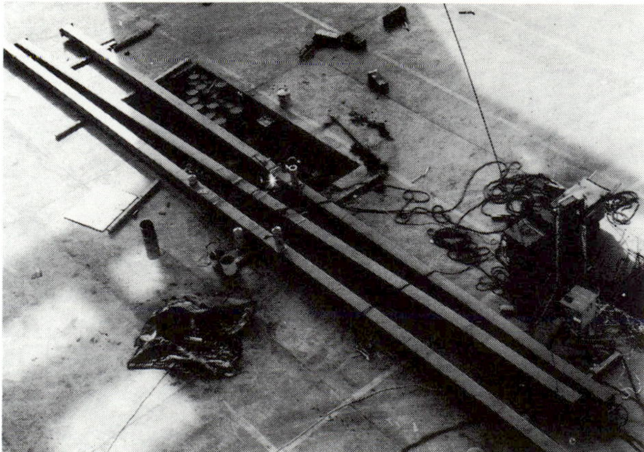

Figs 21.10 and 21.11 *Site welding of lift guide members.*

Fig. 21.12 *Bolted joint in exposed Cor-Ten roof truss.*

21.3.1 Bolting

Ordinary bolts act rather like pegs in holes, in tension or shear. They are available with shank diameters ranging from almost nothing – 6 mm (¼ in) – up to 36 mm (1½ in). Even larger sizes can be made to order. Two grades of steel are commonly used for such bolts and these are referred to as 4.6 and 8.8. The first digit relates to the ultimate strength of the material, whilst the second is the ratio of yield stress to ultimate strength. Thus the ultimate tensile strength of grade 4.6 and 8.8 bolts is 400 N/mm^2 (58 ksi) and 800 N/mm^2 (117 ksi) respectively, and the corresponding yield strengths are 0.6 and 0.8 of these figures. Simple grade 4.6 bolts without corrosion protection are commonly called 'black bolts'.

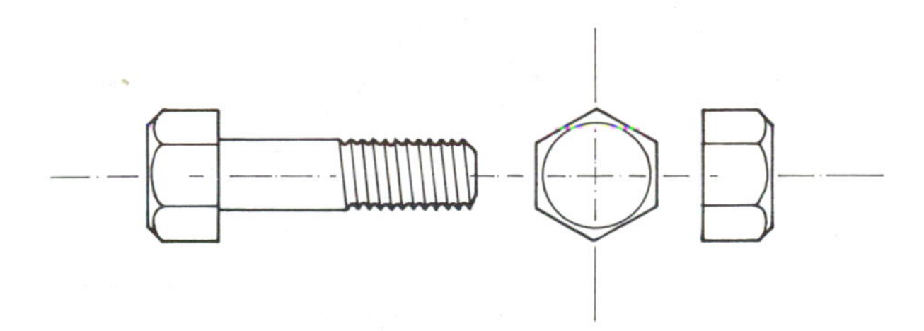

Fig. 21.13 *Hexagonal bolt.*

High strength friction grip bolts (HSFG bolts) work in a different way. They are made from a material very similar to grade 8.8 bolts but have different shaped heads and nuts (see lead-in figure and Fig. 21.13). After initial tightening the head is turned against the nut in a carefully controlled manner to put a large pretension into the bolt shank. This has the effect of clamping the plates between the head and nut together. The mating surfaces are called 'faying' surfaces and must be flat and unpainted so that there is no slip between them. The friction which develops at the interface transfers the shear between connecting elements.

Grade 8.8 bolts are more generally used on site than HSFG bolts because of the difficulties in ensuring that HSFG bolts are correctly tightened, and the complexity of masking the faying surfaces while corrosion protection is applied at the fabricator's works.

21.3.2 Historical review of welding

Arc welding dates from 1887 when the Russian Benardos used an electric arc for melting metals. In the following years first Zerener and then Slavianoff introduced different methods. In the USA acetylene was discovered in 1892 and used primarily for lighting purposes. In 1900 the first serviceable torch was constructed in England, and this was probably the true beginning of oxy-acetylene welding history.

In the early part of the 20th century electric welding in Britain was well ahead of progress abroad. Welded munition barges were used in the English Channel during the 1914–18 war and in 1921 the first all-welded ship, Fullagar, was launched. The same period saw the first welded frame structures erected near London.

During the 1930s welding began to supersede hot smithing and riveting for structural steelwork, with the design work of Felix Samuely and Hajnal-Konyi making significant contributions. One of the principal fabricators for early welded structures was Murex Industries Ltd.

World War II gave an immense impetus to welded steel both in building work and ship construction, and welding of plates and sections became widely established during the post-war period in Britain. This, together with the development of plastic analysis, transformed the design and fabrication of steelwork, culminating in the continuous welded frame used at the Hunstanton School in 1954 by architects Alison and Peter Smithson, and engineers Ove Arup and Partners (refer to Fig. 2.12 in Chapter 2).

As demand has grown for higher structural performance, welding technology has continued to progress and the section above gives only a general description of welding. More specific information can be obtained from *Structural Steelwork Fabrication* [1] by the BCSA.

21.3.3 General points on welding

Welding can save costs and reduce member sizes by dispensing with the need for brackets and plates at connections and by allowing the use of the whole cross-section of a member by eliminating holes for bolts.

The two basic types of weld are the fillet weld and the butt weld.

Fillet welds (Fig. 21.14) are normally used where the connection does not need to develop the full strength of the connected plates. They are relatively cheap because the edges of the plates do not have to be machined or shaped, the amount of weld metal placed is small, and inspection is easier than for butt welds.

Butt welding (Fig. 21.15) is used for highly stressed connections, and the plates are machined and chamfered so that the weld metal is placed across the whole plate thickness. To avoid stress-raising flaws at the root of the weld, the first weld runs are back-gouged before the second half of the weld is built up (Fig. 21.16). A major butt weld consists of many runs and is therefore relatively slow and expensive (Fig. 21.17). Partial penetration butt welds (Fig. 21.18) are used where an intermediate strength can be accepted. Partial penetration welds are not used for critical elements such as main tension members, however.

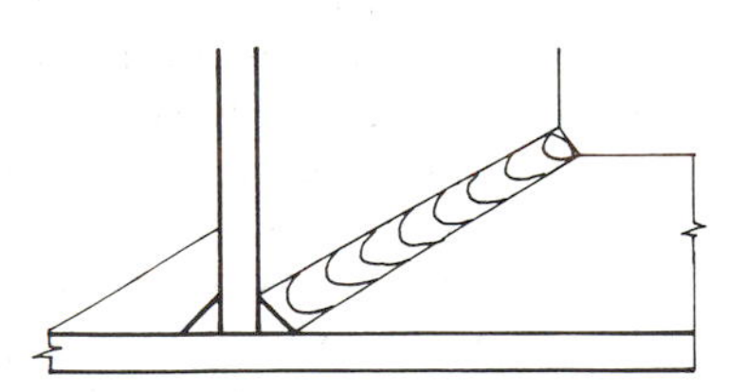

Fig. 21.14 *Fillet weld.*

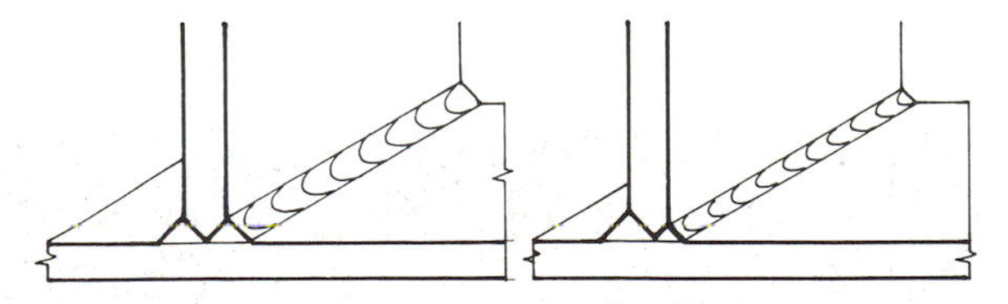

Fig. 21.15 *Full penetration butt weld.*

Fig. 21.17 *A multi-run butt weld.*

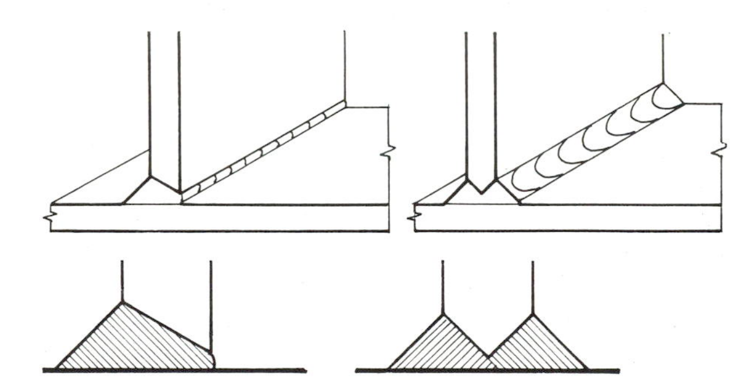

Fig. 21.18 *Partial penetration butt weld.*

21.3.4 Electric arc welding

The common characteristic of all welded joints is that the contact faces are united by fusion due to application of localized heat. Electric arc welding of steel uses an electric current to generate a temperature of about 3500 °C (6332° F) to melt the two surfaces to be joined. The electrode also melts providing filler metal to the weld. Atmospheric gases must be excluded from the weld zone, since these would otherwise interfere with the weld quality, and this can be achieved in a variety of ways. Welding may be carried out manually or semi-mechanically for long continuous weld deposits.

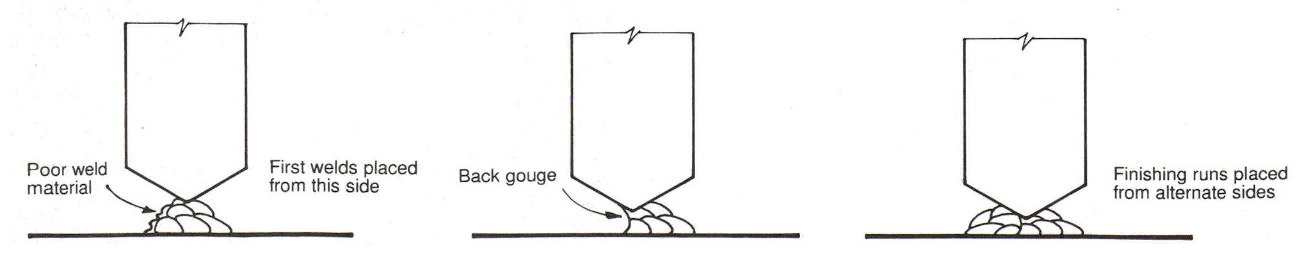

Fig. 21.16 *Build up of a major butt weld.*

The Manual Metal Arc (MMA) process uses a special steel filler rod covered with a flux which releases a shielding barrier of inert gas when fused. MMA welding is highly versatile but suffers from a disadvantage in that the flux also encases the weld in a layer of solidified slag which has to be chipped off. Productivity is also hampered by the need to constantly renew the electrode. To overcome such deficiencies, the Metal Inert Gas (MIG) process is now widely used. In this method, a continuous coil of bare filler wire is fed through a nozzle which also supplies a stream of inert gas such as carbon dioxide to shroud the arc from the atmosphere. In spite of higher capital and operating costs, deposition rates are faster, there is no slag to be removed and the incidence of defects is reduced. The equipment used for MMA and MIG welding is portable which allows it to be transferred easily to different work stations within the workshop, but MMA is almost always used on site.

21.3.5 Semi-automatic welding

For built up members using plate in the form of box or I-girders where long continuous runs of weld are necessary, semi-automatic welding plant of the 'submerged arc' type is used. The term is derived from the process whereby the weld arc is struck and maintained within a deposit of granular flux which partially fuses and provides the gas shield. This method also leaves a slag but it is easily removed (Fig. 21.19).

The weld produced is of very high quality with a smooth and uniform bead, making it highly suitable for heavy plate fabrication. Single or multiple weld runs can be laid down quickly, but because the plate components require special fixtures and manipulation equipment, this plant tends to be bulky and is confined to a specific area.

21.3.6 Weld defects

Cracks may occur due to contraction of the weld upon cooling either in the weld itself or in the parts being joined, although the use of correct welding procedures in BS 5135 [2] and appropriate electrodes will help ensure that the weld quality is sound and reliable.

However, examination in the form of non-destructive testing (NDT) may be specified to confirm the strength of key welds and whilst both X-ray and ultrasonic methods are capable of revealing internal flaws, dye penetrants or magnetic particle methods will suffice for visual examination. Weld examination is costly and should be conducted on a strictly selective basis.

The application of heat during the welding process causes expansion, which is followed by contraction on cooling. These movements are rarely distributed evenly and this can cause both locked-in stresses in a large or complex assembly and distortion in a member which is free to move. This will depend upon a number of factors but the effects can be substantially minimized by sound details and suitable welding procedures. In addition, the fabricator will also use presetting, prebending and preheating techniques to ensure that members are true and free from twisting. The locked-in stresses can be reduced by 'stress relief', which is a process of controlled heating and cooling of individual components in a furnace. However, this may not always be practical and for some designs the residual stresses may be a limiting factor. The welded fabrication shown in Fig. 21.20 has been painted with white contrast paint ready for magnetic particle inspection, and the black greased bolts are used to stop the thinner plates moving during stress relief of the assembly.

Another technical problem associated with welded connections is the development of transverse stresses in rolled plates. Due to the nature of the rolling process, rolled steels tend to have a layered structure, which gives the steel poorer

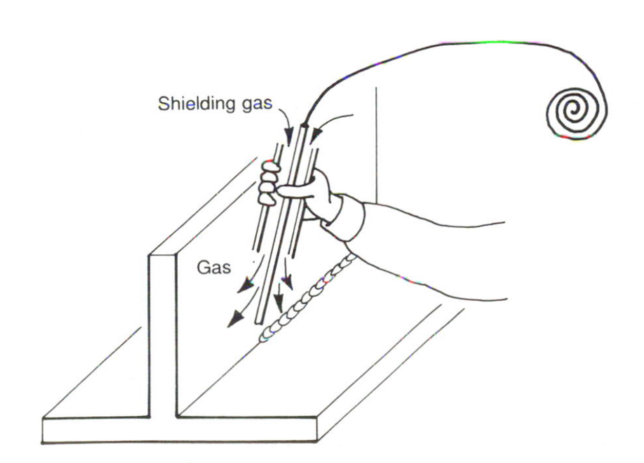

Fig. 21.19 *Submerged arc welding.*

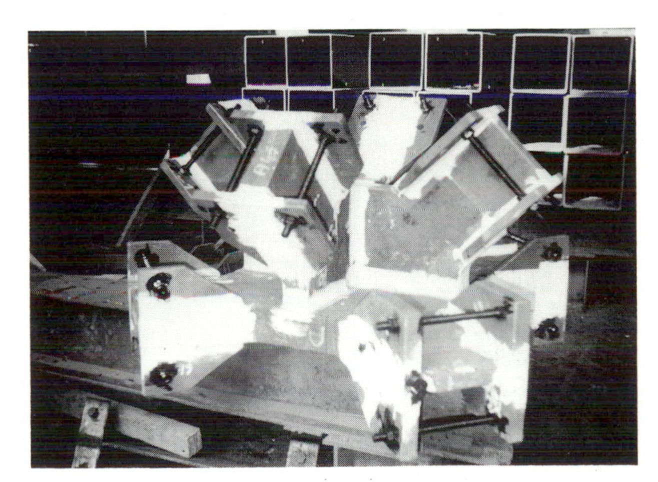

Fig. 21.20 *Welded node painted for inspection and braced for stress relief.*

Fig. 21.21 *Column splice using end bearing with flange location plates.*

properties through the thickness than along or across the plate. If these stresses are significant and cannot be avoided by design, special quality steels with good properties in the direction of the plate thickness (for example British Steel's 'Hyzed' steels) are available to special order. However, for normal building construction, normal grade steels are adequate in this respect.

21.4 ADVANTAGES AND DISADVANTAGES OF COMMONLY USED CONNECTIONS

In the following sections the 'pros and cons' of a number of connections are discussed, with simple diagrams to illustrate the points made.

21.4.1 Column section in compression

The simplest concept is a welded profile as shown in Fig. 21.1b, where stress is transferred directly from the column above, through the weld, to the column below. A connection like this would be made in the fabricator's shop.

An alternative (Fig. 21.1a) is to use shop-welded capping plates to each column length. These are bolted on site to locate the plates together. A considerable advantage is that different cross-sectional sizes can be accommodated. The end of the column must be accurately cut square to the shaft so that the upper column will be vertical when it sits on the lower column. Packing plates between the capping plates can be used to allow adjustment of levels. A variant is shown in Fig. 21.21.

Splice plates (Fig. 21.1c) are another common detail, which require no welding in the fabrication shop, and allow some directional tolerance during erection. Packing plates can be used where the column cross-sections are not the same size.

Looking at other aspects of these connections, the profile weld and capping plate (Fig. 21.1a and b) can be contained within the net column size, thus minimizing the size of the clad column. Splice plates (Fig. 21.1c) are unlikely to be acceptable for an exposed connection, and cannot be used for columns of circular hollow section.

Welded joints are very suitable for use in trusses which are fully fabricated in the shop, and for exposed work are much better than using splice plates which can trap water and hence cause corrosion.

21.4.2 Section in tension

In principle, the same connections (Figs 21.1a, b and c) could be used in tension as well as compression. However, the capping plate detail (Fig. 21.1a) is unlikely to be suitable because the tension forces would develop tension in the bolts and bending in the capping plates.

Splice plates (Fig. 21.1c) could be suitable, providing the member is not fully stressed in tension, otherwise the holes drilled for the bolts could make the net section too small.

21.4.3 Beam-to-beam or beam-to-column connection (Figs 21.22–21.25)

Beam-to-beam connections are possibly the commonest type of connection and the most straightforward to construct. Figure 21.22 shows bolted angle cleats which are ideal for rectangular grids. A popular variation of this is the welded end plate shown in Figs 21.23 and 21.24 which can be splayed to suit non-square joints. Shear loads are carried in the webs of I-beams, and both of these connections take the shear load directly from the web of the secondary beam and transfer it to the web of the supporting beam. An angle (seating cleat) is sometimes placed under the end of the supported beam (Fig. 21.25). In this case the load is transferred from the web through the bottom flange of this beam and into the web of the main beam through the angle.

The same principles are used in beam-to-column connections. Where the beam is connected to the web of the column the load is transferred almost concentrically. However, if

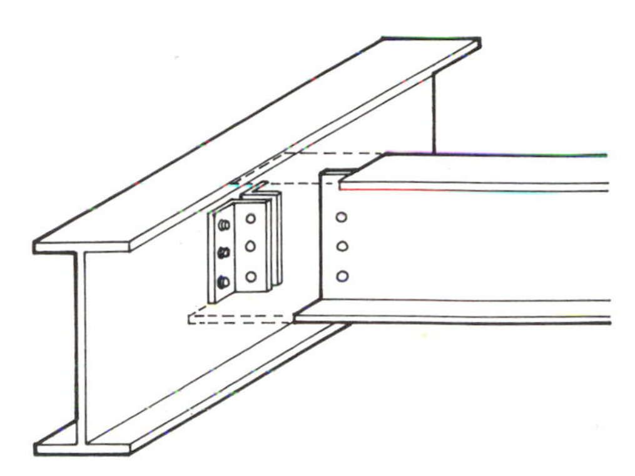

Fig. 21.22 *Beam-to-beam connection using web cleats.*

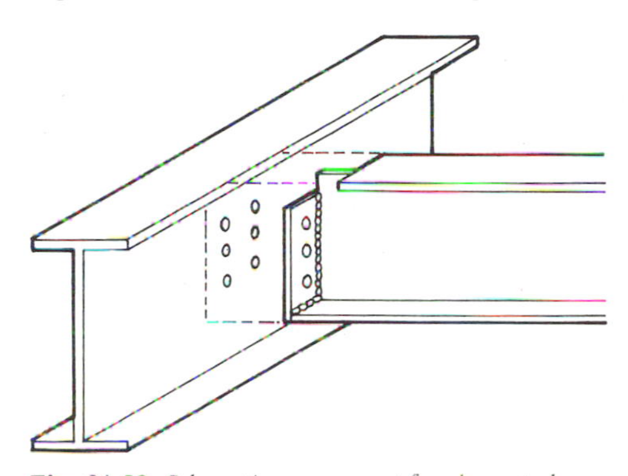

Fig. 21.23 *Schematic arrangement for a beam-to-beam connection using a welded end plate.*

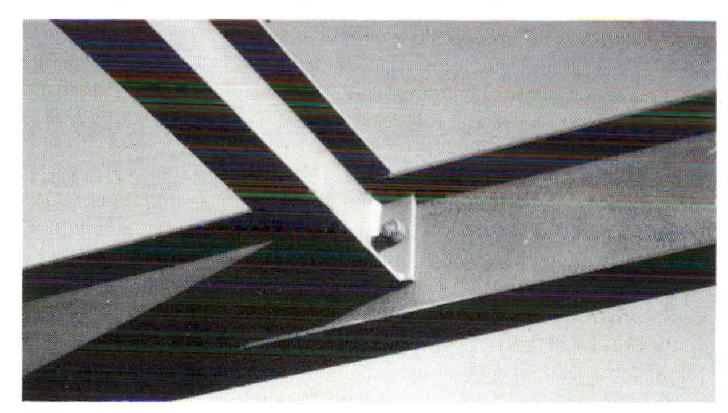

Fig. 21.24 *Typical connection with welded end plate (as in Fig. 21.23).*

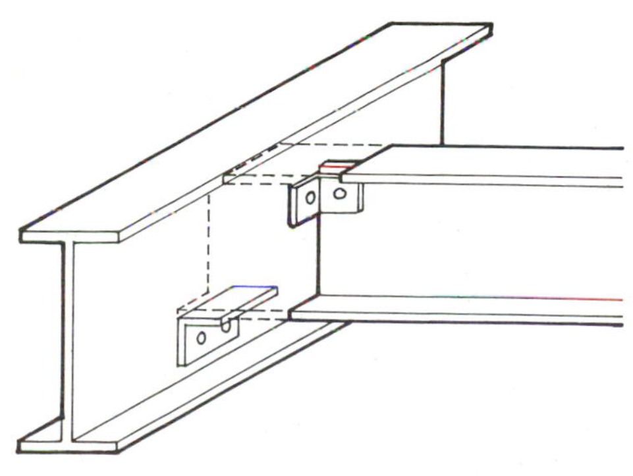

Fig. 21.25 *Beam-to-beam connection using seating and restraining cleats.*

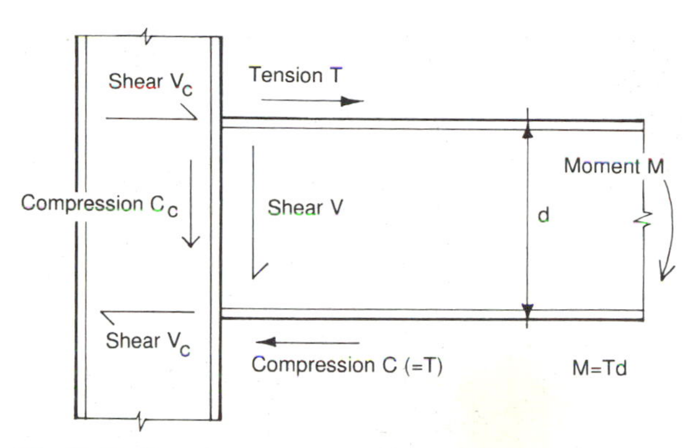

Fig. 21.26 *Forces in a moment connection.*

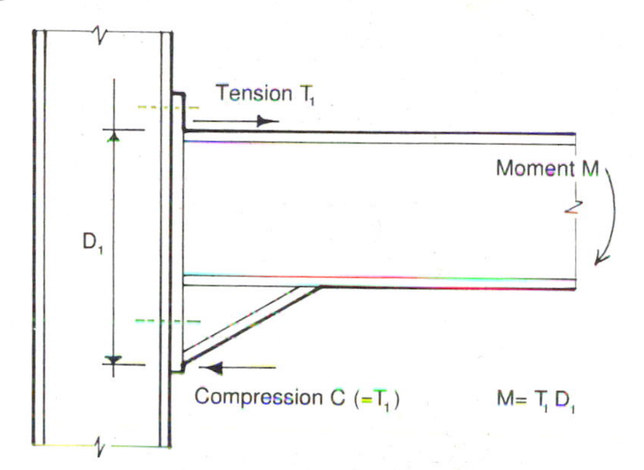

Fig. 21.27 *Schematic arrangement for a beam-to-column connection for moment connection using a haunch detail.*

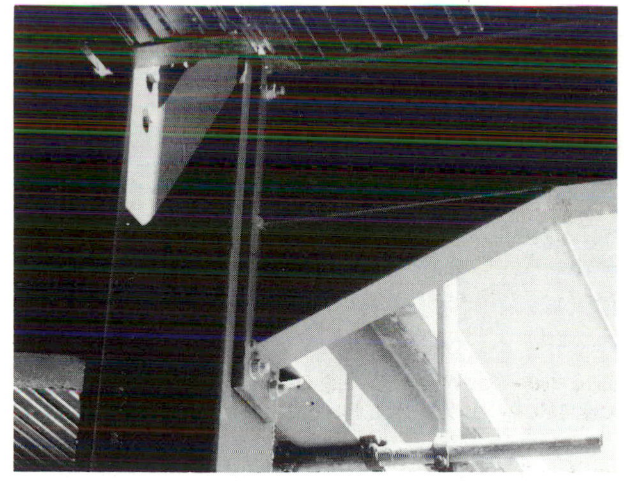

Fig. 21.28 *Beam-to-column connection for moment connection.*

the beam is connected to the column flange, the column is loaded with some eccentricity and this must be allowed for in the design of the column.

Beam-to-column moment connections are used in rigid construction such as portal frames. As shown in Fig. 21.26 the moment and shear actions at such a connection can be balanced by a pair of flange forces, tension in the top flange and compression in the bottom flange, with the shear staying in the web. Each of these forces must then be carried into the column, where they create shears in the web and compression in the flange. To reduce the magnitude of these forces, a haunch is often detailed at the end of the beam (ceiling space permitting). Figure 21.27 shows this diagrammatically, and Fig. 21.28 shows an actual connection.

21.4.4 Tension connections

Joints in direct tension are perhaps the easiest to understand, which probably explains their prominent place in 'High Tech' architecture (Fig. 21.29). There are many variations in form, depending on the scale of the forces and the size of the members. Generally, higher member stresses mean greater difficulty both in forming the connection and in keeping its size close to that of the member.

Wire ropes, which can carry the highest stresses, cannot be threaded or welded. For low loads the rope can be clamped, but for large loads the force is transferred by spreading the individual wires out in a conical shaped steel casting (Figs 21.30, 21.31, 21.32), and pouring molten zinc into the cone to socket the wires. The casting is attached to an anchorage or another length of rope by means of a pin or threaded coupler as shown in Fig. 21.33. The working

Fig. 21.30 *Wire rope being splayed out.*

Fig. 21.29 *Typical mast structure.*

Fig. 21.31 *Wire rope socket ready to have molten zinc poured in.*

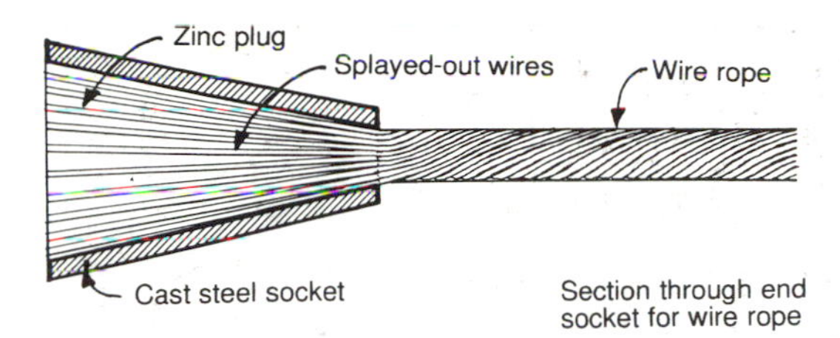

Fig. 21.32 *Diagram of splaying out of wire rope.*

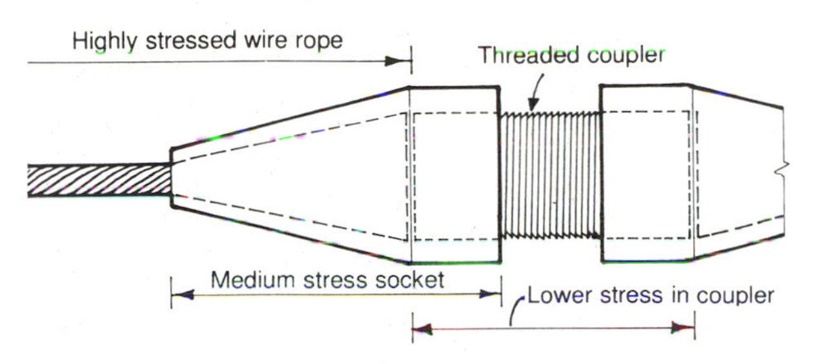

Fig. 21.33 *Threaded coupling for wire rope sockets.*

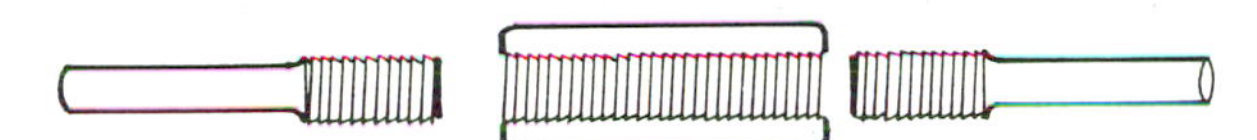

Fig. 21.34 *Threaded coupling for bars.*

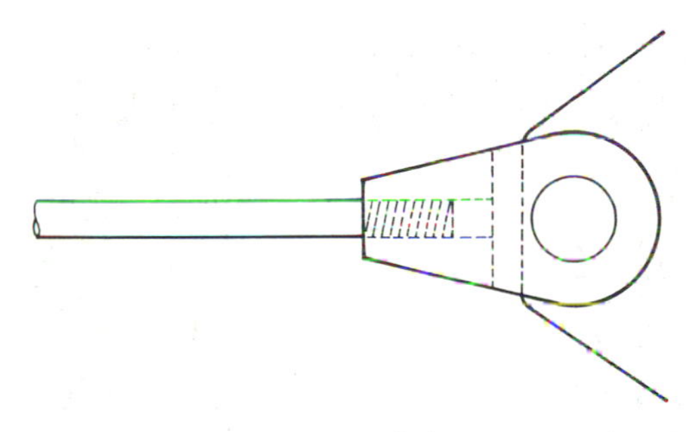

Fig. 21.35 *Pin joint connection for bar.*

stresses for couplers are lower than those for the rope itself, and consequently the coupling will be larger.

Although the working stresses are lower for a tension or tie bar, welding is often difficult or impossible and connections are formed by threading. The thread is not cut for the highest strength bars, but rolled onto the bar (Fig. 21.34) so that no sectional area is lost. The coupling as shown might be the simplest way to achieve a connection, but if such a joint is exposed a more expressive form may be required. In such cases a pin joint is often used (Fig. 21.35). Although these seem to cause great excitement, in engineering terms a pinned joint is simply an abstraction which allows the designer to control the distribution of forces in a structure. Mathematically, a pin joint is a region of low rotational or bending stiffness. Figures 21.36 to 21.38 illustrate three applications, the first showing a pin joint in the main tension

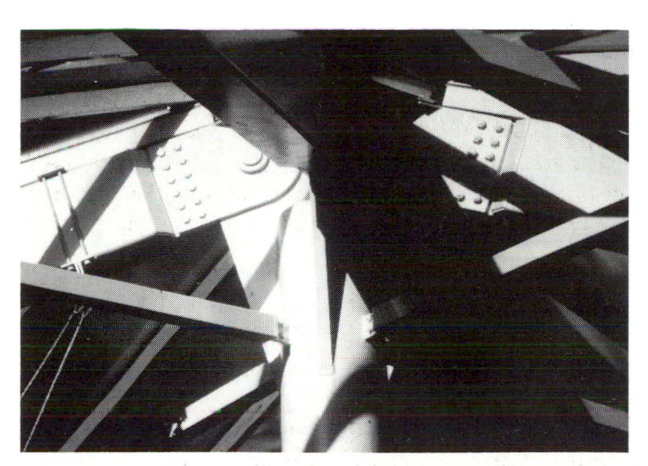

Fig. 21.36 *Pin joint in Windsor Leisure Pool roof, Windsor, UK.*

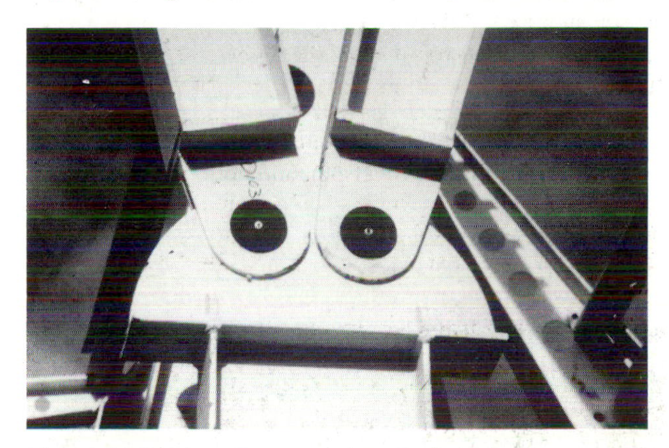

Fig. 21.37 *Pin joint in Doncaster Leisure Centre Mall, Doncaster, UK.*

Fig. 21.38 *Pin joint in Central Business Exchange Winter Garden, Milton Keynes, UK.*

Fig. 21.39 *Trusses at the Agricultural Hall, London, note enlarged washers at cross ties as in Fig. 21.6.*

hanger of a leisure pool roof where the pin is required to avoid secondary bending effects in the members. In the third example, the pin was made deliberately oversize to avoid it looking puny in the interior space. Making components larger in size is a common response when shaping couplings that form a significant feature in exposed roof frameworks, a situation not dissimilar to the exaggerated washers used at the Agricultural Hall (Fig. 21.39).

Tension structures are discussed in chapter 20 and further advice on the general arrangement of connections and couplings for wire ropes is included in chapter 4.

21.4.5 Joints in hollow sections

Joints in hollow sections are fundamentally different from those used in open wall sections (UBs, channels etc.),as tubes have few surfaces on which to fit splice plates and bolts.

A number of straight tube-to-tube joints are shown in Figs 21.40 to 21.44. The ugliest is the connection with end plates (Fig. 21.40). This is suitable for compression, but less good for tension because the end plates are stressed through their thickness and bending is set up in the end plate. If the loads are large many bolts and thick plates will also be required. The heavy welding needed for such thick end plates brings more problems, as the heat input for the single sided weld can cause bowing of the plate.

A fish plate connection can be made between tubes (Fig. 21.41) with enough bolts to transfer the load through the connecting plates. In practical terms the joint must be considered as pinned, making it unsuitable for use in the middle of a member in compression.

The joint in Fig. 21.42 is likely to work for any combination of applied loads, but it gives little scope for tolerance if erection and fabrication are not absolutely perfect. Figures 21.43 and 21.44 show the details of a very neat joint, particularly if the open side can be arranged away from view as shown in Fig. 21.45. However, as the number

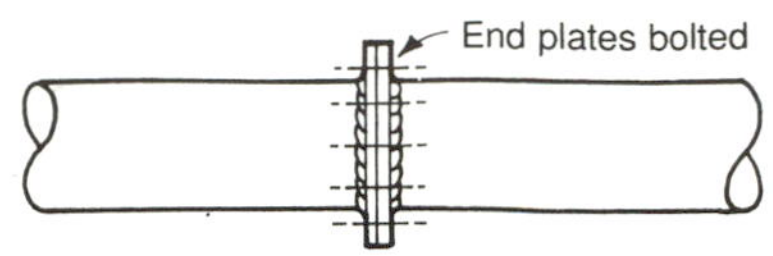

Fig. 21.40 *Tube-to-tube splice.*

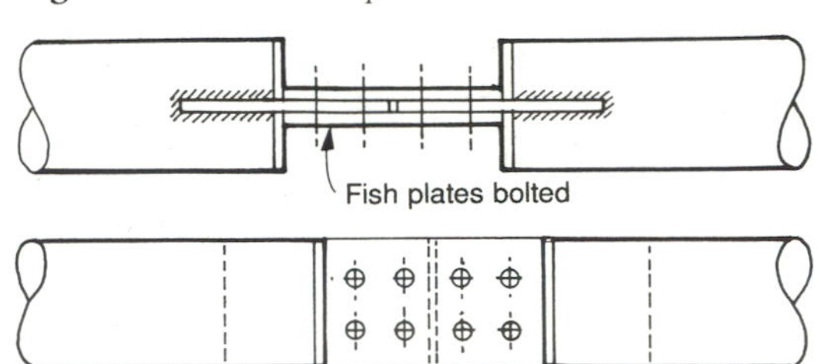

Fig. 21.41 *Tube-to-tube splice.*

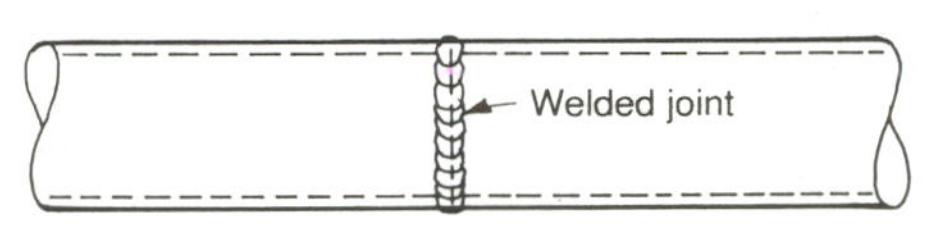

Fig. 21.42 *Tube-to-tube splice.*

of bolts which can be put inside the tube is limited, the connection is mathematically 'pinned', and the joint can be used for shear loads only. Figure 21.46 shows a joint which is suitable for light loads, in roof bracing members, for example.

Joints in tubular trusses are usually welded, because full profile welded joints not only look better (Fig. 21.47), but are also cheaper than creating elaborate bolted joints. It is usually cheaper to make truss connections if the chords are made from rectangular tubes, rather than circular. This is because the ends of the diagonals can be straight cut, rather than cut to the more complex intersection profile if circular chords are used. In either case the end of the diagonal may be cut in the same plane as the chords if a fillet weld is adequate. If a butt weld is needed the end of the diagonal must be properly prepared. A number of fabricators use profiling machines which automatically cut the diagonal to the correct line and end preparation for welding.

It is important that the truss geometry does not produce too small an intersection angle between members. The limit is about 30 degrees for rectangular hollow sections and 20 degrees for circular hollow sections, and below this value it is difficult to get the welding electrode in to make a weld.

21.5 FINISHES AND CORROSION PROTECTION

21.5.1 Grinding of welds

Structural welds are not usually ground down since the process adds unnecessary expense to the construction costs. Where required for aesthetic reasons, it is possible to grind butt welds flush with the adjacent plates, provided the weld is a straight butt, like that shown in Fig. 21.48. Other butt welds (called K-welds), as shown in Fig. 21.49, cannot be

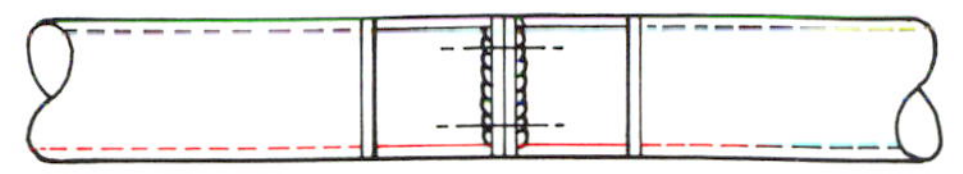

Fig. 21.43 *Tube-to-tube splice with end plate having cutaway.*

Fig. 21.44 *Assembly detail for Fig. 21.43.*

Fig. 21.45 *Open side to joint turned away from view.*

Fig. 21.46 *Lightly loaded tube end connection.*

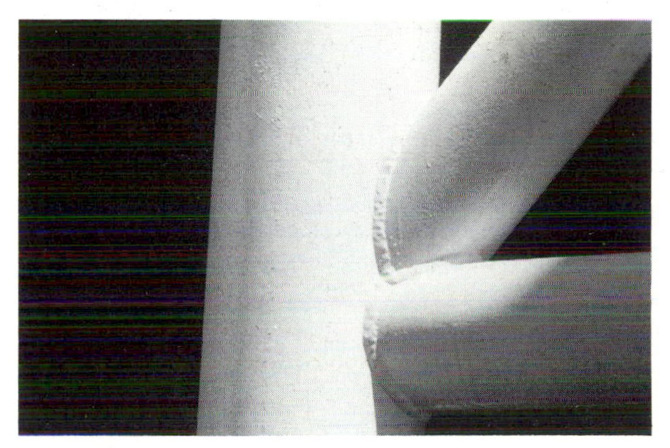

Fig. 21.47 *Welded joint in tubular truss.*

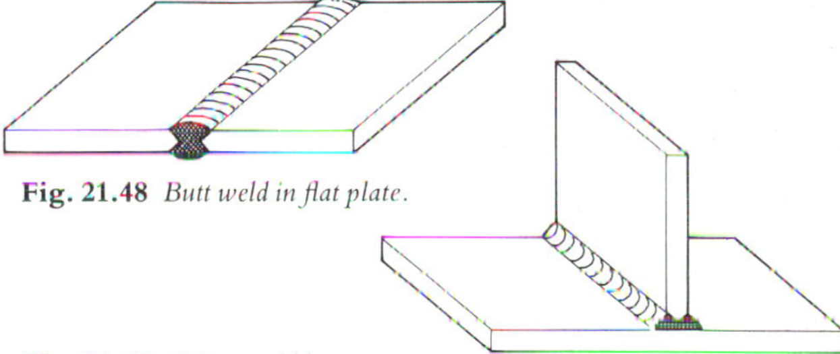

Fig. 21.48 *Butt weld in flat plate.*

Fig. 21.49 *K-butt weld between plates.*

ground because the fillet at the side of the weld acts as a reinforcement. Obviously grinding is not possible for fillet welds, because any grinding will cut away the connecting metal.

21.5.2 Bolt finishes and corrosion protection

All bolts, i.e. grade 4.6, grade 8.8 and HSFG bolts, are available in a variety of finishes as follows:

Black: With no corrosion protection, and either a black surface of mill scale, or a lightly rusted surface where the scale has come off.

Sheradized: A thin coating of zinc dust is deposited on the bolt. This gives limited corrosion protection until paints are applied. The zinc adheres well to the bolt. Galvanized bolts have reasonable thickness of zinc, but are somewhat difficult to paint on site.

Plated bolts: Zinc and cadmium plating are used, and have properties similar to galvanized bolts. The process is easier than galvanizing, but gives a more brittle coating.

Cor-Ten bolts: These are available to special order, and they have similar properties to other Cor-Ten material.

Stainless steel bolts are not usually used for the main structural frame. They might be used where components of the frame itself are of stainless steel, but not otherwise, because stainless steel can set up a galvanic cell when in contact with normal steel used for structural work. If stainless steel bolts have to be used in conjunction with a normal steel frame, separating washers (usually neoprene) must be used to keep the two materials apart.

REFERENCES AND TECHNICAL NOTES

1. Davies, B.J., and Crawley, E.J. (1980) *Structural Steelwork Fabrication*, Volume 1, BCSA.
2. BS 5135: 1984. Arc Welding of Carbon and Carbon Manganese Steels.

(a)

(b)

(c)

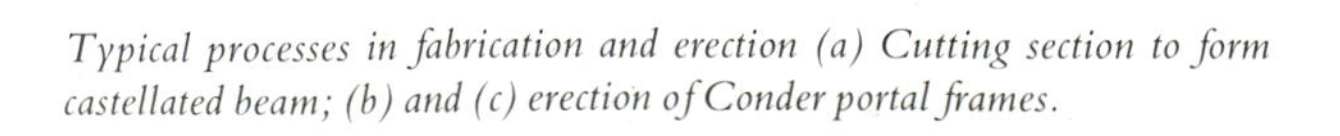

Typical processes in fabrication and erection (a) Cutting section to form castellated beam; (b) and (c) erection of Conder portal frames.

22

Fabrication and erection

R. Taggart

22.1 INTRODUCTION TO FABRICATION

The fabricator's role is to convert rolled steel sections into structural elements which can be readily assembled on site into a finished structure. This process can be broken down into various operational stages which are closely linked to form a flow network consisting of material stockyard, surface preparation, cutting, holing, assembly, painting, inspection, and despatch.

This network forms the basis for production control, which is time related to cost standards with output geared to meet the construction programme. This rarely coincides with the most effective use of all resources and the system has to be extremely flexible to respond to changes in demand whilst minimizing disruption and costly delays.

The introduction of semi-automated manufacturing equipment in the fabrication industry is now widespread and this continues to generate increased growth in productivity. However, the extent and nature of services can differ considerably from company to company depending upon scope and capacity; for this reason the layout of the sections preparation area in Fig. 22.1 is only a schematic outline to show the sequence from raw material to commencement of assembly.

22.2 PRINCIPLES OF FABRICATION

22.2.1 Material stockyard

Primarily, the stockyard acts as a raw material holding area to ensure that the correct material is available at the correct time to guarantee continuity of work. Only relatively small quantities of the commoner section sizes are held in open stock, most of the material being scheduled directly from the rolling mills about 12 weeks in advance and allocated to each contract as required. Smaller quantities and shorter delivery times are available from stockholders, but at a cost premium.

Material costs are minimized by placing bulk orders for at least 20 tonnes of any given size, weight and grade subject to immediate and anticipated demands. Because bundles of steel can be extremely heavy and cumbersome to handle, the stockyard has to be adequately serviced by suitable mechanical handling equipment for sections and plates using overhead or mobile cranes for rapid off-loading and stacking or conveyance to the workshops.

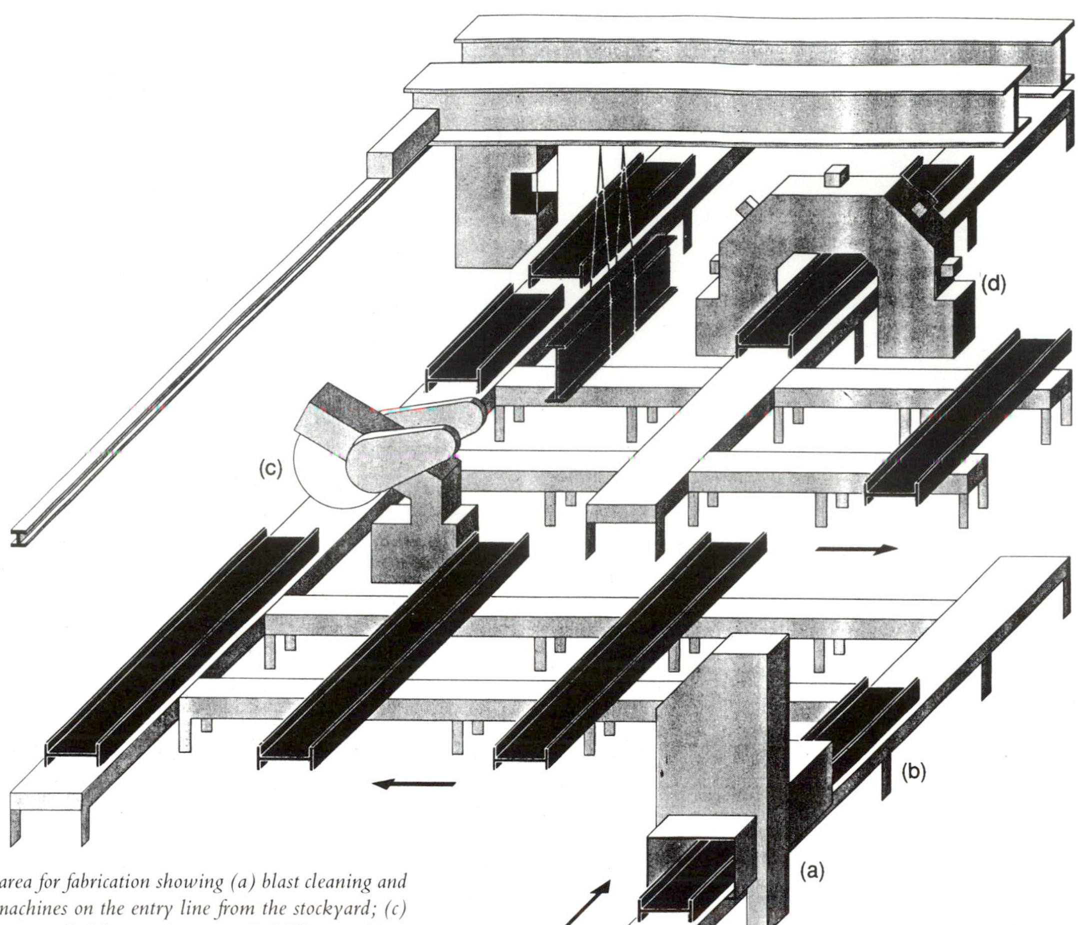

Fig. 22.1 *Preparation area for fabrication showing (a) blast cleaning and (b) automatic painting machines on the entry line from the stockyard; (c) cold saw; (d) numerically controlled three-axis automatic drilling machine. The machines are linked by conveyors and an overhead gantry crane transfers material. The assembly areas may be two or three times as large as the preparation area, and due to site limitations it may have to be in other buildings.*

22.2.2 Surface preparation

Upon delivery, the steel is usually covered with a layer of mill scale or superficial rust which should be removed as a preliminary step for subsequent painting. The only effective method of removal is by blast cleaning using abrasive particles which are projected onto the steel at high speed leaving the surface with a silvery grey uniform appearance.

Various levels of surface finish may be specified in terms of cleanliness and roughness, but for most general purposes SA 2½ in accordance with BS 7079: Part 1 – BS 7079: Part 1:1989 [1] will be satisfactory and economic. The subject of corrosion protection is discussed more fully in chapter 8.

The application of a prefabrication priming paint is not normally necessary provided the steel is kept dry and under cover since the fabrication cycle is of relatively short duration.

22.2.3 Cutting

Following surface preparation, cutting to length is the first task to be conducted and, for the heavier sections, a circular saw is the principal tool employed. The end may be bevel or square sawn and the larger saws can accommodate a 914 × 419 UB, the biggest section in the universal range.

Lighter angle sections are often sheared on a cropping machine which is not only much quicker but relieves demand on the saws. Cropping is particularly useful for substantial quantities of relatively short cut lengths such as small bracings or cleats.

Plates and similar flat products are not only more awkward to handle but require different cutting techniques. Accordingly, a different route is used where cutting to size is either conducted by shearing on a guillotine or by flame-cutting. The actual method depends upon a number of

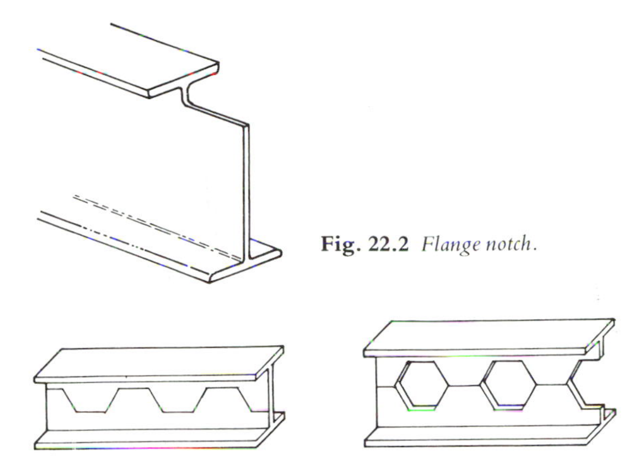

Fig. 22.2 *Flange notch.*

Fig. 22.3 *Castellated beam.*

factors but, as a broad distinction, shearing is confined to straight cuts whilst flame cutting is unrestricted and readily allows profiles or curved shapes.

The process of flame cutting, or more accurately 'oxygen fuel gas cutting' is used on a wide scale within the steelwork fabrication industry. Unlike mechanical methods which are limited to straight cuts, flame cutting is highly versatile.

The steel is heated locally by a pressurized mixture of oxygen and a combustible gas such as propane which pass through a ring of small holes in a cutting nozzle. The heat is focused on a very narrow band and the steel oxidizes (or burns) at 1500°C (2732°F) when a jet of high pressure oxygen is released through a separate hole in the centre of the nozzle to blast away the molten metal in globules.

Ease of handling and mobility of the equipment allows otherwise difficult tasks such as notching as in Fig. 22.2 to be accomplished manually, but in addition machine cutting is used extensively to cut plates of any thickness by mounting the cutting head on a portable powered trolley which runs along a special track allowing large plates to be reduced to manageable proportions very quickly. For example, a 25 mm (1 in) thick plate will be transversed at 1200 mm (4 ft) per minute. For profile cutting, the nozzles are mounted on horizontal arms attached to a travelling gantry either singly or in multiples, the pattern being directed by a control programme or traced from a template.

Perhaps the most widely publicized example of flame cutting is the castellated beam as in Fig. 22.3, an idea first credited to the Chicago Bridge Co. in 1910.

22.2.4 Holing

In most cases holes are formed by drilling, although punching, which is extremely rapid, is widely used for secondary members or thinner components such as gusset plates. On newer machines punching can also be combined with cropping.

Generally when considerable repetition can be established, holes are increasingly being drilled in groups on semi-automatic machines. These machines can operate on three separate axes which means that holes can be drilled through the web and both flanges of a universal section at the same time.

The traditional marking of cutting lines and hole positions by hand for linear elements has been largely superseded by computer-controlled measuring and sensing devices. These have been developed into fully integrated production lines, the latest of which combine material handling, sawing, drilling and transfer to the next workstation as a complete sequence.

22.2.5 Assembly

In tandem with the production of primary structural elements, components for fitting and assembly, such as brackets, gusset plates and stiffeners, also have to be manufactured separately. As this is often labour intensive, jigs and templates are used to ensure consistency and to save time, particularly where quantity production is involved.

As a general rule, shop connections tend to be welded in preference to bolting but, depending upon the nature of the structure, some shop bolting may be used if only for trial alignment and fitting. The choice between shop bolting and welding is generally one of cost and convenience related to the facilities offered by a particular fabricator.

22.2.6 Painting

Fabrication is usually completed by the application of a coat of priming paint. The key to the performance of any paint system is thorough preparation to remove initial mill scale and rust as already indicated, and final cleaning to remove contaminants such as grease or cutting fluids.

Paint coatings for structural steelwork should 'flash off' fairly rapidly to allow further handling and minimize congestion. Whilst brushing is suitable for touching up damage, large surfaces can only be covered economically by spraying. This can be carried out manually or automatically where the work is conveyed through an enclosed cabinet containing the spray nozzles which may also be supplemented by a drying kiln.

A wide range of paint specifications and specialist advice is available [2] for various environmental conditions and more detailed coverage of this important topic is given in chapter 8. However, for most structures contained within a cladding envelope, elaborate primer specifications are not necessary.

22.2.7 Inspection

Inspection needs to be carried out at each stage of fabrication to prevent compounding of possible errors, final inspection concentrating mainly upon overall dimensions, positions of brackets and holes for site bolts etc. Framed elements such as trusses or lattice girders tend to be self-checking by virtue of fit, a principle often utilized to prove the geometry of complex frameworks by trial assembly.

22.2.8 Despatch

Despatch operations involve a numerical check together with application of identification marks. Any loose fittings are wired or attached to the parent member and materials not needed for immediate despatch are stacked in the finished stockyard to await consignment.

The finished stockyard requires careful organization and pre-planning to control and distribute the flow of steelwork. In addition to the programmed erection sequence, due regard must be given to site limitations for off-loading and handling, and any restrictions regarding access times. Delivery routes must be planned carefully, with due consideration of physical limitations such as low bridges. Prior notice must be given to police authorities en route for loads wider than 2.9 m (10 ft).

22.2.9 Special operations

So far, the nature of operations, practices and type of equipment are those which would be employed by a general fabricator, but for work of a more specialized nature, purpose-designed machines are often required.

For the tubular welded joint illustrated in Fig. 22.4, cutting the ends of tubes to the exact profile would be a laborious and costly task by hand. By using a tube profile machine the tube is rotated at a steady speed whilst the end to be shaped is presented to a movable flame cutting head. The track followed, the head and its angle of inclination respond to tabulated data pre-set on a digital control system.

Pressing and forming by means of a brake press is useful for cold forming specific sections outside the normal hot rolled range. The principle is shown in Fig. 22.5 where the press tool exerts pressure on the material by forcing it into a

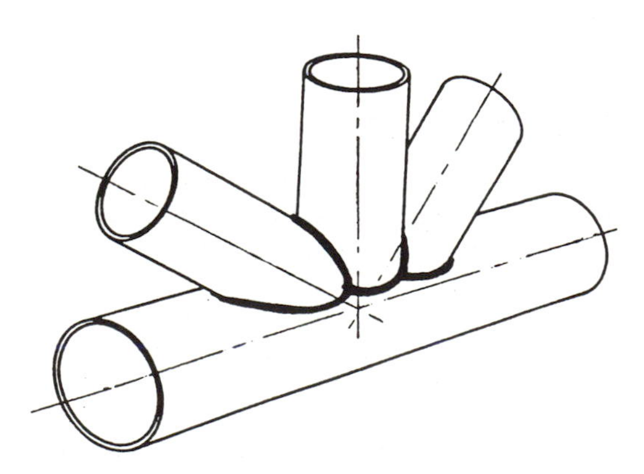

Fig. 22.4 *Tubular welded work.*

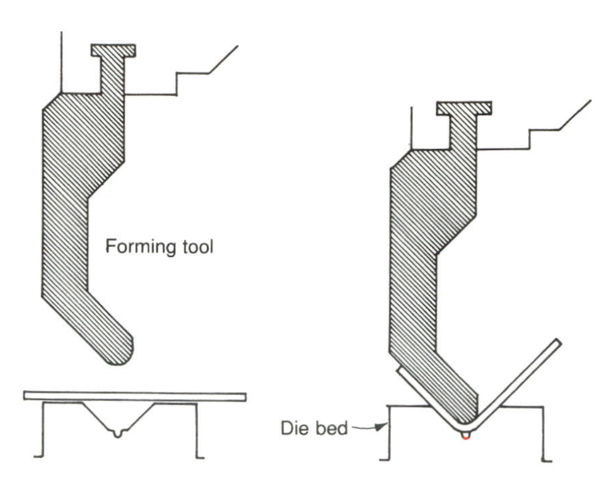

Fig. 22.5 *Cold pressing.*

die former. Different shapes may require different patterns of press tool and die and because pressures of up to 1000 tonnes may be required, press brakes are robustly built and occupy considerable floor space. Refer to chapter 5 on sheet and strip for particular uses. Cambering or curving of members is also a cold process conducted by rolling. Universal Beams and columns can be curved about either axis by passing the section through sets of rolls, the setting of which governs the final radius within precise limits. The minimum radius of curvature depends upon the cross-sectional profile, the axis of bending and the grade of steel. This is because the section tends to buckle locally on the compression face below the critical radius or in other cases thinning and possible cracking will occur on the tension face.

Specified curves are normally circular but may be parabolic or transition, that is with curvature about both principal axes. Cold rolling of this type has become highly specialized and demands special equipment and techniques. Consequently, work of this type is invariably entrusted to a specialist company. Specific examples are given in chapter 33.

22.3 ECONOMIC FACTORS CONCERNED WITH FABRICATION

By tradition, fabricated steelwork is often quoted on the basis of £/tonne and whilst this is an accepted arithmetic convenience, it can be completely misleading since true cost identity is obscured. In practice, the fabricator estimates costs by separating the various activities into categories such as cutting, drilling and welding; this enables man-hours to be allotted and valued to arrive at a total price.

Relying upon a combination of historical data and practical experience, the cost build-up bears little relationship to the weight of steel involved although cost references

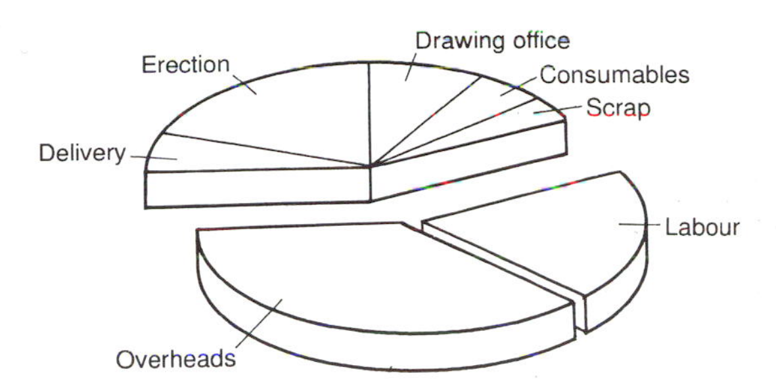

Fig. 22.6 *Fabricator's costs.*

in £/tonne can be a useful index for rapid comparison of different classes of work.

Figure 22.6 shows the average breakdown of the fabricator's costs for building structures in the light to medium category. This demonstrates that well over 50% of the fabrication cost (excluding material) is absorbed by direct labour (with attendant overhead allocation), and it is by minimizing labour costs that the greatest scope for economy is obtained [3]. Since the fabricator relies increasingly upon production engineering techniques to reduce time, this can only be achieved by better standardization with repetition of dimensions, geometry and member sizes where possible.

22.4 SELECTION OF A FABRICATOR

Since structural steelwork fabrication is a crucial early phase in a contract, a policy of selective invitations to tender is advisable to ensure a satisfactory response and avoid wasted effort. Clearly, the quoted price has a significant influence in evaluating a tender but the competitive effectiveness of this should not be judged in isolation. Where no previous history or relationship exists with the tenderer, consideration should also be given to the fabricator's expertise, resources, size/capacity and experience. Such factors will determine quality and performance and in turn will be related to the price of those services.

For speed, accuracy and reliability, steel is unrivalled as a construction material; nevertheless, discipline must be exercised to ensure thorough planning and organization from start to finish. Most importantly, this philosophy must be extended to the design and detail phases and a structure which is to be successfully constructed in steel must be conceived in steel.

22.5 INTRODUCTION TO ERECTION

The philosophy inherent in the prefabrication of steelwork is to save time by enabling the major structural elements to be delivered to site in a finished state ready for assembly. Because loads can be applied immediately to the assembled structure, following trades may also proceed without delay.

Whilst steelwork erection may be regarded as an extension of fabrication, erection is distinguished by two added features. Firstly, there is the dimension of height and the added time required for vertical movement of materials, equipment and labour. Secondly, work has to be conducted in the open with the risk of delays due to adverse weather conditions.

By its nature, site work tends to be costly and the primary aim of the programme should be to minimize costs by condensing the time scale as much as possible. This may require examination of a number of options at the design stage, otherwise the only course of action remaining may prove to be unduly expensive.

Clearly, the significance of the various issues will vary according to the type of building and any limitations which the site and its environment may impose. Even when structures possess marked similarities, different erection methods and procedures may need to be adopted and for this reason only general principles can be stated.

22.6 SITE PLANNING

Paradoxically, it is because of the rapid pace of steelwork erection that particular care and attention to detail is required during construction planning. The need for this becomes even more acute where steel erection has to be closely integrated with other trades, such as the installation of flooring units on a multi-storey building.

In other respects, however, construction planning is made easier because steel as a material ensures that erection is less susceptible to interruption due to frost or wet weather.

Nevertheless, site activity with its competition for resources is somewhat difficult to control and a disciplined and rational strategy has to be developed and pursued. As already indicated, this has to be individually tailored to suit each contract, and whilst this alone is not an automatic guarantee of success, the absence of such plans inevitably sponsors a series of problems which are often disproportionate to the cause.

22.7 SITE ORGANIZATION

A site with limited and restricted access may govern the maximum size and weight of the various steel members which can be delivered. Equally, narrow streets in a busy town centre may be the main drawback with limited space to manoeuvre. In some cases waiting time to off-load may be confined to specific periods. Matters of this kind must be investigated well in advance and decisions made accordingly.

Within the site, movement may be hampered by a variety of obstructions such as scaffolding, shoring, raised bases, excavation and so on which are fairly common. Service roads and off-loading areas need to be hard-cored and adequately drained to support heavy vehicles during the severest conditions of winter.

The steelwork has to be erected in the general sequence determined by the construction programme and each consignment of steel has to be closely regulated to a strict timetable. Whilst in some instances a few key components can be lifted directly from the vehicle into position, most of the material will need to be off-loaded and stacked temporarily until required. The area of the site allocated for this purpose has to be orderly and well managed, particularly where space is limited. To compensate for minor interruptions in delivery, for example due to traffic delays, a small buffer stock is usually held in reserve.

Space is also required for laying material out and for site assembly of frames or girders prior to hoisting into position.

22.8 SETTING OUT

Before commencement of erection, the plan position and level of the column bases should be verified by the erection contractor. This needs to be carried out as soon as possible to ensure that any errors can be corrected in good time, or at least alternative measures approved and introduced. Checks should include not only the centres of the foundation bolts relative to the grid lines, but the projection of the bolts above base level.

To compensate for minor discrepancies, a limited amount of deviation of the column from its true vertical and horizontal position is provided by the grout space and by leaving a movement pocket around each bolt during pouring of the concrete, as in Fig. 22.7. Normally this will allow latitude of about plus or minus 25 mm (1 in) in any direction.

The accuracy of setting out has often proved to be a source of contractual dispute. However, the tolerances recommended in BS 5950 : Part 2 [4] are both practical and realistic.

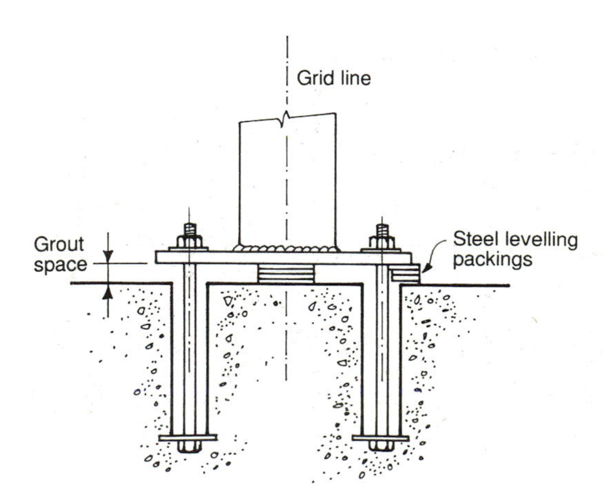

Fig. 22.7 *Column base detail.*

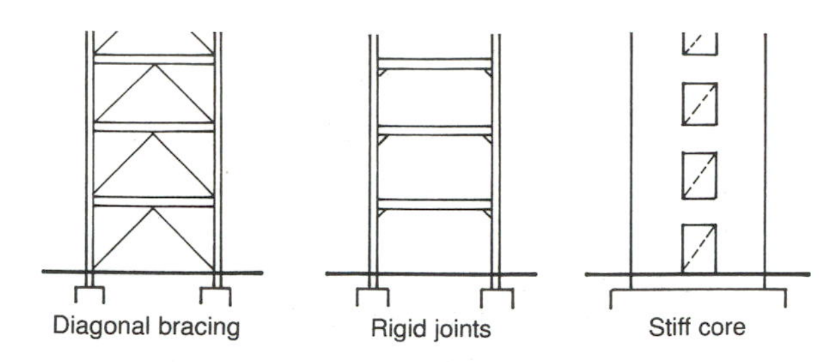

Fig. 22.8 *Stability.*

22.9 ERECTION OPERATIONS

Steel erection may appear to be a series of distinct operations but in reality these overlap and merge. Nevertheless, each stage of the work has to follow a methodical routine which consists of hoisting, temporary connections, plumbing, lining and levelling and, finally, permanent connections.

Because minor intolerances can accumulate during fabrication and setting out, it would be impractical to complete the entire structure before compensating for these by adjustment. The work is therefore subdivided into a number of phases which may be controlled by shape or simply an appropriate number of bays or storeys. For stability, each phase relies upon some form of restraint to create a local box effect and this may be achieved in various ways such as employment of diagonal bracing, rigid type joints or the stiff service cores present in some multi-storey buildings (see Fig. 22.8).

At this juncture, end connections and base anchorages have only been secured temporarily and after completion of plumbing, lining and levelling, all connections are made permanent by tightening up all nuts or inserting any bolts initially omitted to assist adjustment. This allows substantial areas to be released quickly for grouting, and following trades are able to proceed much earlier than would be possible otherwise.

22.10 ERECTION METHODS

As already outlined, the method of erection selected will depend upon the type of building and other related factors. Unless the site presents unusual difficulties, single storey buildings are quickly and easily erected. The majority of industrial buildings are portal frames and it is common practice to bolt-assemble the joints at ground level and then lift the complete frame upright using a mobile crane.

Ideally, erection should commence at an end which is

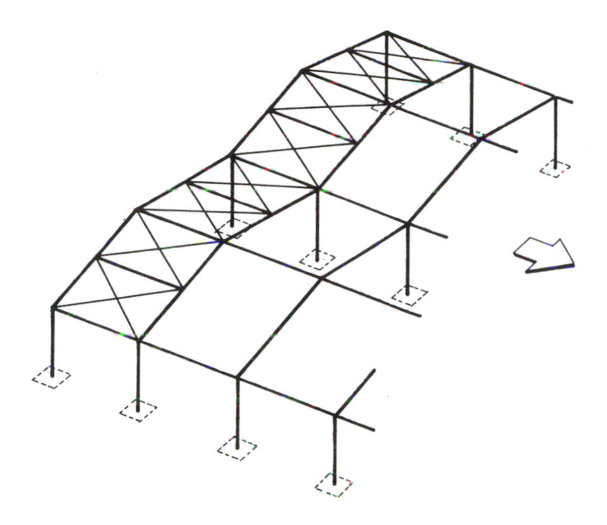

Fig. 22.9 *Erection stability.*

permanently braced, as in Fig. 22.9, but where this is not possible temporary bracings should be provided at regular intervals as a safeguard against damage or collapse.

Space frames are designed to span in two directions, and because of the number of connections required, it is much more economical to assemble the units at ground level where the joints are readily accessible and then hoist the framework complete. Two, possibly four, cranes may be needed depending on the size of the building, and work of this kind demands meticulous planning and co-ordination.

In most cases, multi-storey buildings are erected storey by storey because floors can be completed earlier, offering access, overhead safety and weather protection. Depending upon the site, a single tower crane may be the sole lifting facility, in which case its use will have to be shared between a number of sub-contractors, thereby limiting available 'hook' time for any given trade.

Since the position of a tower crane is fixed, as in Fig. 22.10, it is completely independent of any obstructions such as basements or ground slabs which could deny access to a mobile crane and this allows useful freedom in overall planning. However, the fixed location also means a fixed arc of lifting capacity where the load will be minimum at the greatest reach and this might entail providing site splices simply to keep the weight of the components within such limits.

Where the site is long and narrow and substantially enclosed by surrounding property, access may only be possible on a very limited scale. Situations of this kind are typical of building refurbishment with a retained frontage; due to the bottle-neck restrictions, the best solution may be to erect the steelwork bay by bay. Alternatively, this method and storey by storey erection can be combined to the best advantage where circumstances allow.

One of the major virtues of a mobile crane is its flexibility and independence which enables it to keep moving with the flow of the work. These cranes are generally fitted with a telescopic jib, allowing them to become operational very quickly, and the vehicle is stabilized during lifting by extended outriggers equipped with levelling jacks.

As illustrated in Fig. 22.11, beam and column elements may be pre-assembled into complete frames at ground level and lifted directly onto the foundations. This is much quicker and easier than bolting connections together in mid-air and reduces risk for erection crews and site inspectors.

Clearly, the mobile crane offers freedom of response and adaptability but creates specific demands for roads and level hardstanding on a site where such facilities may be limited.

It will be evident that the erection technique and means of

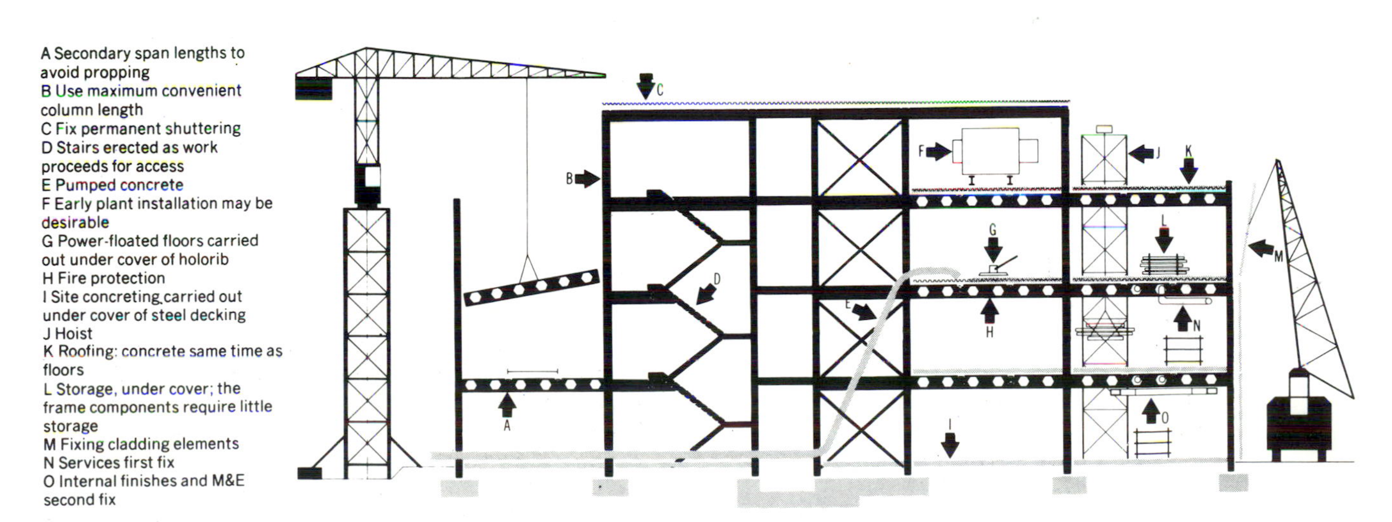

Fig. 22.10 *Erection methods.*

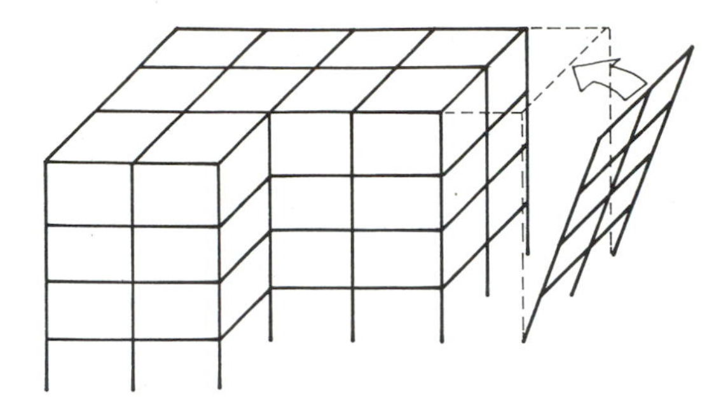

Fig. 22.11 *Pre-assembled frames.*

hoisting are closely related and that the method ultimately adopted will be influenced just as much by the suitability of the crane and its requirements as by the site conditions.

22.11 SPEED OF ERECTION

The rate of steelwork erection is subject to various factors, some of which are beyond the control of the building designer. Those which can be controlled and which will effect the pace of construction include the type of end connections, the extent of bolting or welding and the number of separate elements. All of these factors are deeply integrated and it is impossible to vary one without a corresponding effect on another. In addition, decisions at the design stage may have predetermined the size and weight of major elements and therefore the degree of site assembly required.

The actual hoisting of the members into place generally occupies about half the erection man-hours; the remainder of the time is spent on lining, levelling, plumbing and final bolting up, but for complicated connections or where access is restricted, extra time will be required, and this will have repercussions on the pace of the work.

By its nature, site welding is expensive and is highly dependent upon suitable weather conditions unless provision is made for purpose-made enclosures. Accordingly, site joints tend to be bolted which also means that only hand tools are required and this is a considerable advantage when working at heights. However, welding may be more convenient for alterations or remedial work.

As in the case of fabrication, particular benefit is gained by standardizing bolt sizes and grades as much as practicable. By eliminating (or at least reducing) the need for constant identification and selection, bolting up is simplified and the hazards to the erectors are minimized, especially in precarious positions.

Normally, connections are designed to suit grade 4.6 or 8.8 bolts. For ordinary structures, it should be noted that the use of high strength friction grip bolting has steadily declined in favour of grade 8.8 which are less costly but offer similar performance. Where HSFG bolts are specified then special tightening methods are required which may incur further costs because of the need for power tools, access staging and specific inspection procedures. More detailed information on the subject of bolting can be obtained from *Structural Fasteners and their Application* [5].

Whilst speed of construction is not the sole criterion of building costs, it is undoubtedly the most significant. This cost/time relationship was the basis of a research study by Constrado [6] which compared model construction timings for alternative designs in steel and concrete for three, seven and ten storey office buildings. These indicative figures were then used as the basis for cost evaluation and the study demonstrated that substantial cost benefits were realizable due to earlier completion by using steel framing.

22.12 SITE PAINTING

Despite the durability of modern paint treatments, it is unrealistic to assume that steelwork can be erected without some damage to the coating. This means that touching up will have to be carried out after the framework and the connections are complete, allowing bolts and nuts to be painted at the same time. Care must be taken to ensure that the paint applied is compatible with the original as recommended by the manufacturer and the surface of the steel should always be clean and dry.

The use of intumescent paints to provide fire resistance has grown dramatically in buildings and most of these now embody corrosion inhibition as well as a range of colours for appearance. There is a growing trend for these paint treatments to be shop applied and any damaged areas must be restored to the correct film thickness.

Galvanizing produces a very hard surface and serious transit or erection damage is rare, but if this has occurred the damage can be made good by the application of a proprietary zinc-rich paint. All bolts and nuts used on galvanized steelwork should also be galvanized to prevent bimetallic corrosion.

22.13 CONCLUSION

Steelwork erection normally occupies a relatively short period on the construction programme, but during this time considerable activity occurs which is instrumental to the performance of the contract as a whole.

The steel framework should not be seen in isolation but as an integral link in the construction chain where the time saved can have considerable impact in lowering overall costs.

So that the full benefits of steel may be realized, early consideration should be given to erection methods during design and detailing so that the need for belated changes and subsequent compromise can be substantially avoided.

REFERENCES AND TECHNICAL NOTES

1. BS 7079: Part 1: 1989 Preparation of steel substrates before application of paint and related products.
2. Corrosion Protection Guides for Steelwork in Exterior Environments, Building Interiors. Building Refurbishment and Perimeter Walls. British Steel General Steels, Teesside.
3. Taggart, R. (1986) Structural steelwork fabrication. *The Structural Engineer*, Volume 64A, No. 8, August.
4. BS 5950. Structural use of steelwork in building Part 2 1985: Specification for materials, fabrication and erection; hot rolled sections.
5. Boston, R.M. and Pask, J.W. (1978) *Structural Fasteners and their Application*, BCSA.
6. Constrado. *Steel Framed Multi-Storey Buildings. The Economics of Construction in the UK.* Second Edition (1985). An excellent reference and essential background reading.

FURTHER READING

Davies B.J. and Crawley, E.J. (1980) *Structural Steelwork Fabrication*, Volume 1, BCSA.

Minster Court, City of London, 1991 (architects GMW).

23

Tolerances and movements in building frames

Julian Ryder-Richardson
(with contributions from Michael McEvoy)

23.1 INTRODUCTION

This is an emotive topic that has given rise to many disputes between designers and specifiers on the one hand and fabricators and sub-contractors on the other.

The extent of tolerances required between building components varies from project to project. This chapter is of necessity a general discussion of the subject; any overall prescription would be invalidated by the pecularities of a specific building site.

The lack of correlation between British Standards has been the cause of confusion. BS 5606 (dealing with general building tolerances) was first published in 1978 and has recently been revised. The earlier edition was capable of widely differing interpretations. Dimensional standards were so loosely defined that as a basis for accepting or rejecting work on site BS 5606:1978 proved of little use. Tolerances could be added component by component, reflecting the methods of masonry construction where the mortar joint is the variable dimension between nominal and working sizes. Concrete, particularly precast concrete, was treated in a similar way, leading to sizeable permitted deviations relative to steel framing, which is a rather more precise form of assembly. The structural steelwork tolerances described in BS 5950 were unrelated to BS 5606, so the integration of building tolerances for cladding, floors and steel frame was difficult to achieve. Not surprisingly, architects have tended to avoid reference to BS 5606 and to write specification clauses of their own.

23.1.1 BS 5606: 1990

The new edition has been re-written to make the document easier to use. As well as changes of style, some significant alterations have been made although the general terminology remains the same.

23.1.2 Characteristic accuracy

All building construction and to a lesser extent manufacturing processes are inaccurate. The 1978 British Standard was the first attempt to establish the relative accuracy of different trades and materials on site. The dimensional data were gleaned from a survey carried out for the BRE in the 1970s. This sought to establish that, within a defined statistical range, the sample inaccuracies they had measured could be assumed to be characteristic of building operations generally, thus the notion of 'characteristic accuracy'. The tolerances allowed did, however, encompass a wide range of situations. They were based on the assumption that in 369 out of 370 cases the permissible degree of inaccuracy would be representative of general site practice. These not very stringent standards could consequently be met by 'traditional' techniques without the need for any 'special measures' such as quality control, dimensional checking leading to possible remedial action, or the use of more accurate construction techniques, all of which were described as 'likely to incur greater costs'.

In BS 5606:1990 the permitted deviations have been reduced and the likelihood of them according with normal building practice has also been reduced to 21 cases out of 22. Whereas the 1978 BS was widely considered too favourable

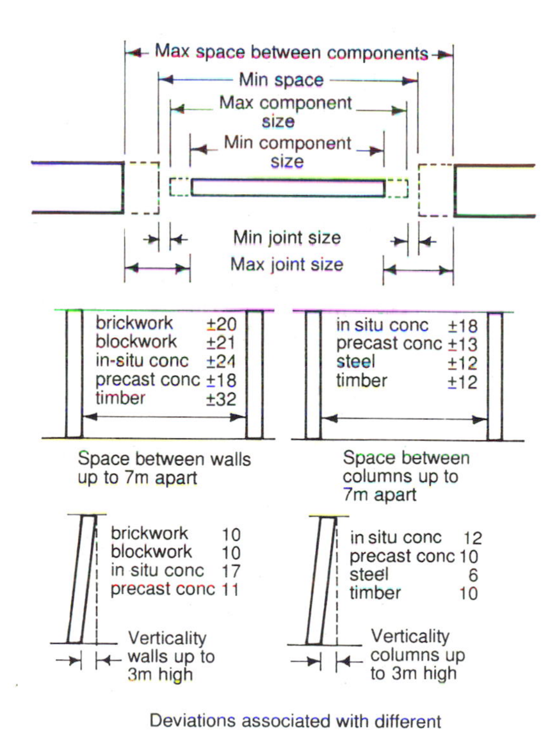

Fig. 23.1 *Variation in joint sizes as a result of tolerances in construction and manufacture of components (from BS 5606: 1990 Guide to Accuracy in Building).*

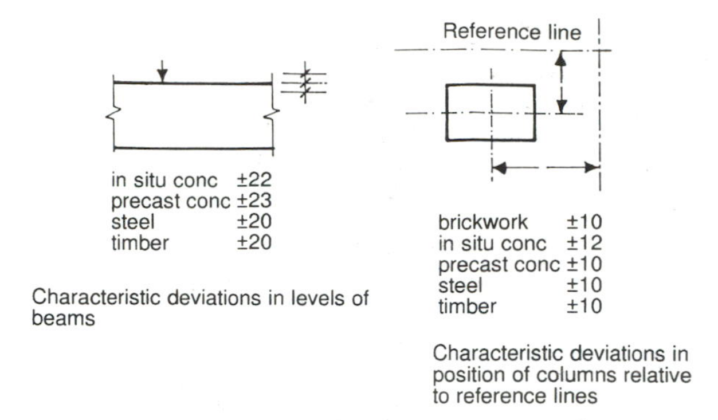

Fig. 23.2 *Characteristic deviations in structural frame components (from BS 5606: 1990 Guide to Accuracy in Building).*

to constructors as opposed to clients, the new standard intended to be applicable to all forms of construction, including the most sophisticated, is not so biased (Fig. 23.1).

As previously, the BS defines two distinct causes of inaccuracy in building (Fig. 23.2):

Induced deviations that are the result of errors in setting out and assembly, that is reasons intrinsic to the process of building.

Inherent deviations due to the nature of materials or site conditions, for example thermal expansion or contraction and consolidation of foundations.

A further survey has been carried out by the BRE and incorporated into the 1990 edition. This quantifies anticipated inaccuracies in factory-made components including welded steel fabrications and drilled holes for fixings. These values assume 'normal manufacturing techniques, the use of conventional materials of the required quality, current standards of workmanship and the appropriate level of dimensional quality control'. An incomplete list of steelwork tolerances is included. Requirements for dimensional accuracy are, however, contained in other British Standards, so for example, figures from BS 5950 Part 2:1985 *Structural Use of Steelwork in Buildings*[1] can be incorporated into calculations. The method of determining the tolerance required between elements of construction at particular points within a building has also been simplified. Under BS 5606: 1978, tolerances were allowed to accumulate to unreasonable dimensions. Now, the locations of elements of structure are to be related to reference lines and levels ('characteristic accuracy' in setting-out also having been surveyed). The tolerances anticipated for secondary components are to be related to adjacent parts of the structure.

In the past it was necessary to specify that more accurate construction techniques should be used if the 'characteristic accuracy' was considered insufficient. In the 1978 Standard the actions to be taken if permitted deviations were exceeded were described as rejection, rectification or 'stand-by' design (for example using different gaskets when gap sizes are exceeded). To achieve the tighter tolerances anticipated by the new BS, a rigorous system of monitoring will be required and the method of measurement will need to be clearly specified. If it seems unlikely that such a system can be imposed in practice, it may be advisable to accept inaccuracies and design accordingly. However, as the old code pointed out, there are other requirements to be considered, namely:

(a) Aesthetics – the visual quality of the building.
(b) Structural – different (and sometimes closer) tolerances are required for structural reasons; reference should be made to BS 5950. Concrete construction begs the question 'how inaccurate will it be?' Whereas when building in steel, which has the advantage of greater predictability, the question asked is 'how accurate can it be?'
(c) Legal – a particularly accurate relationship to site boundaries may be necessary or the maximum height of the building may be a requirement of statutory approvals. In the latter case the tolerance allowed in the camber of beams, for example, may become a significant issue.
(d) Practical – it may be more cost-effective to require greater structural accuracy enabling fitting out, or cladding with prefabricated, non-structural components – a choice between altering the structure or modifying the design of components.

To this list, in the light of recent practice, must be added the requirements of fast-track construction. Building at speed is inherently inaccurate but casing-out the frame allowing generous clearances for the structure may significantly reduce a building's lettable area. The simplicity of detailing often advocated for 'fast-track' may be at odds with other determinants of the design. All these factors must be considered by the designer and a decision made whether to accept the range of deviations normally achievable in construction (as per BS 5606,) or whether to specify tighter limits together with the actions required in case of non-compliance. Accepting the latter course will entail:

(1) Increased costs of structural components. Accurate building may only add a small percentage to the total building cost but the additional time required may not be possible within a fast-track building programme.
(2) Supervision to check that the specified limits have been actually achieved.

23.1.3 BS 5950

The tolerances specified in BS 5950 and other design codes are the values assumed in structural design formulae and when establishing design recommendations.

They are of a different nature to those in BS 5606 and exceptions to them cannot normally be countenanced.

Theoretically, some forms of inaccuracy in steelwork, such as steel beams that become bent during rolling, could be checked for curvature but this is rarely done in building structures, except perhaps when deciding whether accidental damage needs remedial action.

The fact that BS 5950 accepts a particular dimension is of little or no relevance to the problem of fitting-out with non-structural components let alone aesthetic or legal considerations.

23.2 DIMENSIONAL STRATEGIES

23.2.1 Basic frame dimensions

The basic plan module of a frame structure is obviously based upon column centre lines generating the beam grid subdivided by the layout of secondary beams. Sectional dimensions are taken from finished floor levels with downward offsets to the top flanges of floor beams (Fig. 23.3.) The basic setting out of the frame defines the principal and critical dimensions [2].

Compared to curtain walling or marble veneer, a steel structural frame is a relatively inaccurate assembly (refer to Fig. 23.2), though in general far more precise than a reinforced concrete frame or masonry construction. The tolerances that BS 5950 allows are noted in brackets on Fig. 23.3. Accumulating errors are not permitted but nevertheless the three-dimensional effect on a 10 storey tower with a plan size 18.0 × 18.0 m (59 × 59 ft) can amount to the discrepancies shown in Fig. 23.4. This is probably best understood in axonometric.

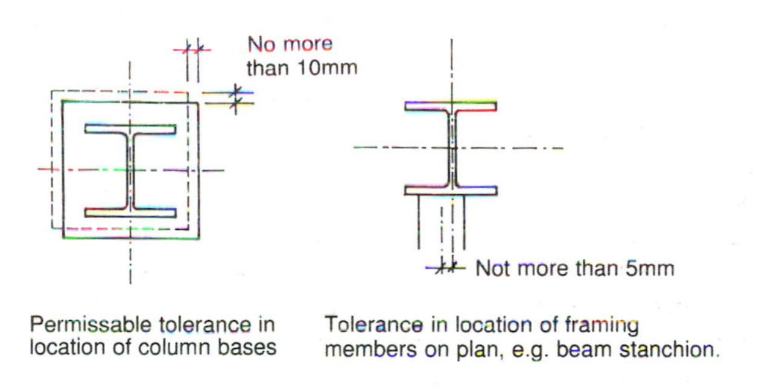

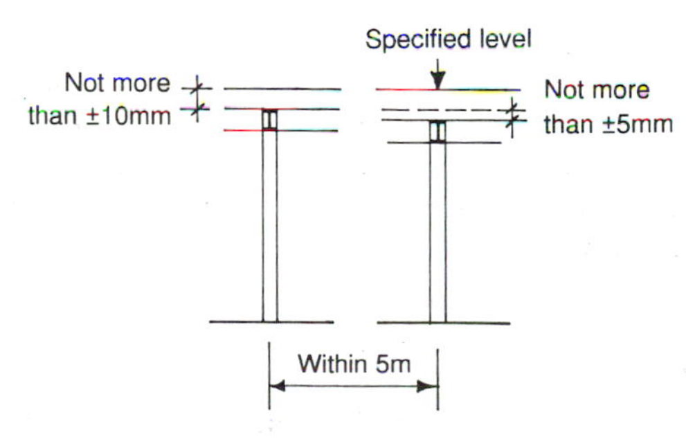

Fig. 23.3 *Steelwork erection tolerances (from BS 5950: Part 2: 1985 Structural Use of Steelwork in Building).*

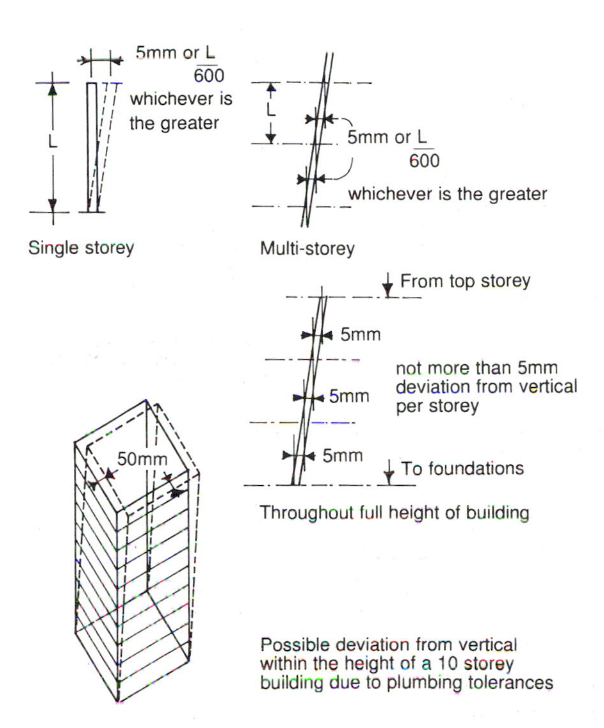

Fig. 23.4 *Permissible tolerances for plumbing and alignment of columns (from BS 5950: Part 2 1985 Structural Use of Steelwork in Building).*

Tolerance problems in steel are compounded by the fact that sections are hot-rolled. This results in uneven surfaces due to varying furnace temperatures and rolling inaccuracies. In terms of straightness, a typical 305 × 305 mm (1 × 1 ft) universal standard beam or column of 6.0 m (19 ft 8 in) length has a permitted rolling tolerance of plus or minus 6.24 mm (¼ in) (refer to BS 4 Part 1: 1980). Lack of surface alignment can be particularly noticeable where exposed steelwork is placed in close proximity to more highly finished materials such as armoured plate glass or polished marble. Some designers cite the precision obtained by Mies van der Rohe in the Barcelona Pavilion but his rolled steel sections had 'clip-on' profiles of chromium plated brass to create a true alignment (Fig. 23.5).

Inaccurate construction is often evident in the commercial world of office construction; the following tale from a partner of EPR Architects concerns a new building in London's Victoria Street. The lease of the building had been purchased and the letting agents set about measuring the actual floor areas against the architect's plans. The 150 m (490 ft) long building was found to be 20 mm (¾ in) in error, and the length was checked three times since the surveyor had never before encountered such accuracy. On being

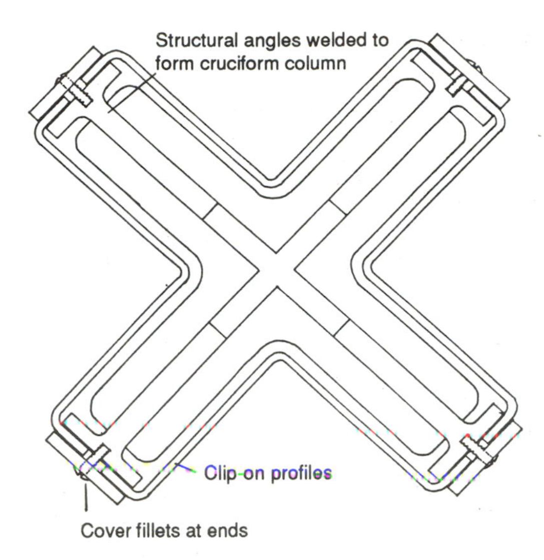

Fig. 23.5 *Clip-on profiles to achieve alignment for rolled sections, Barcelona Pavilion 1929 (architect Mies van der Rohe). Refer to chapter 10 Fig. 10.6 for plan.*

questioned, the agents explained that errors of 300 mm were common in London buildings with a length of 100 m or more.

23.2.2 National Structural Steelwork Specification for Building Construction

This BCSA publication, dating from March 1989, is aimed at specifiers and brings together data from BS 5950 Part 2 and other advice relevant to steel fabrication and erection. The most useful references are the diagrams given on accuracy standards for erected steel (Fig. 23.6).

The expression 'relatively inaccurate assembly' has been used already; the accompanying diagrams show that columns and beams can be out of line by 5 mm (3/16 in) and floor beams can be out of level plus or minus 10 mm (3/8 in).

23.2.3 Deflections

The deflections characteristic of steel structures are particularly noticeable on longer spans. Deflection increases to the power of 4 as span distance is enlarged. Bending moment only increases to the power of 2, so it is deflection that becomes the principal determinant for steel sizing when spans are greater than 9 m (29 ft 6 in). Over short spans heavier sections are used to counter this problem or beams are fabricated with a reverse camber sufficient to accommodate the anticipated loadings on the completed structure. The extent of deflection as well as the rolling, fabrication and erection tolerances of the steelwork are particularly important when establishing zones for services and the level of suspended ceilings.

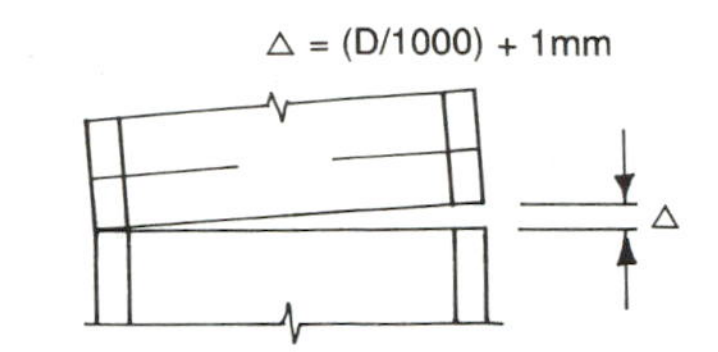

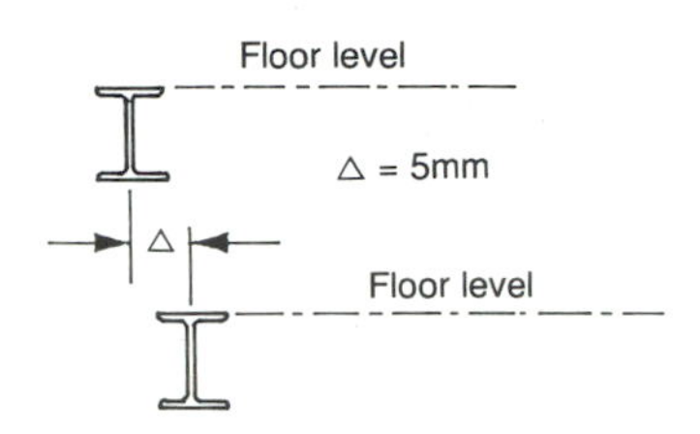

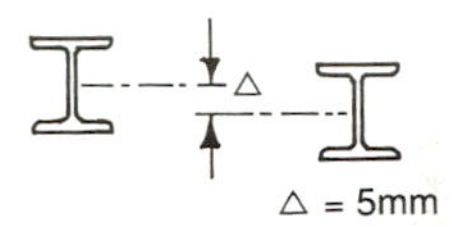

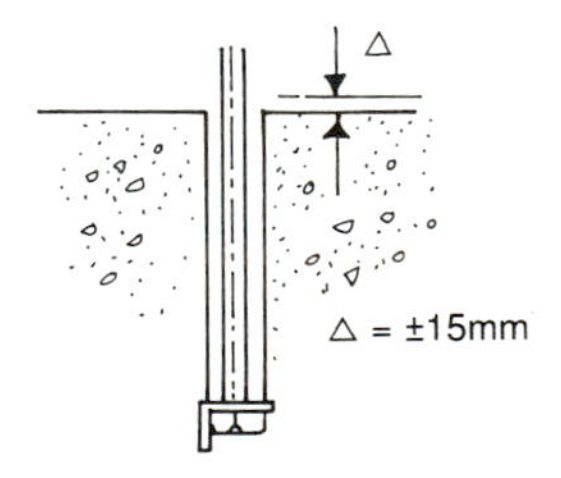

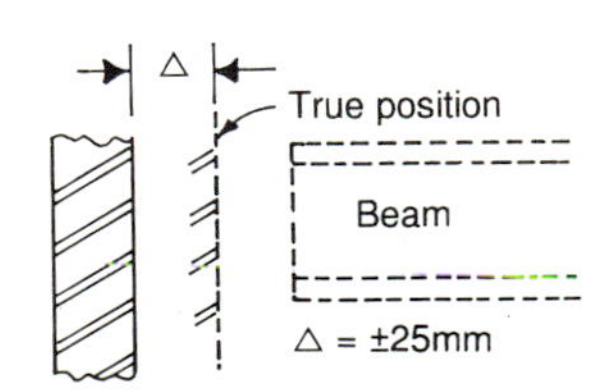

Fig. 23.6 *Accuracy of erected steelwork (from the National Structural Steelwork Specification for Building Construction, BSCA, March 1989: section 9 BCSA references in brackets).*

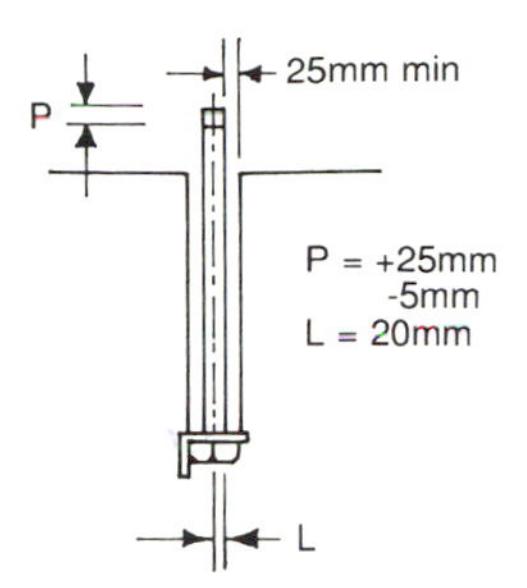

Permitted deviation of foundation bolts or groups of bolts when designed for adjustment in terms of level, location and min movement in pocket

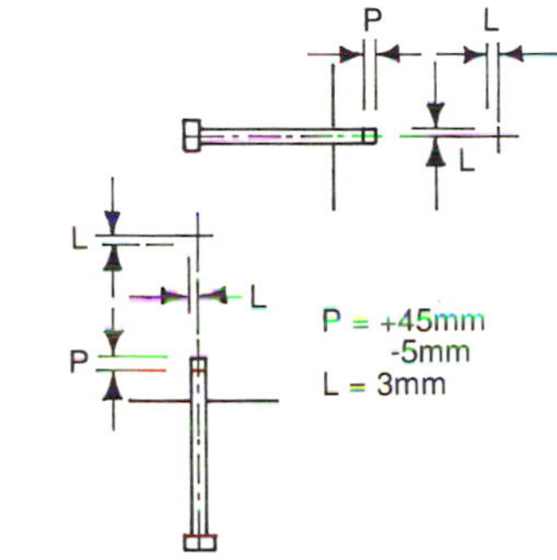

Permitted deviation of foundation bolts or groups of bolts when not designed for adjustment in terms of level, location and protrusion

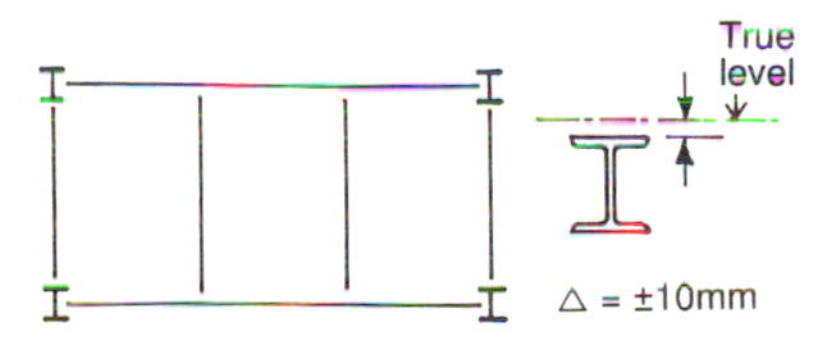

Permitted deviation in level of floor beams from required level at a supporting stanchion

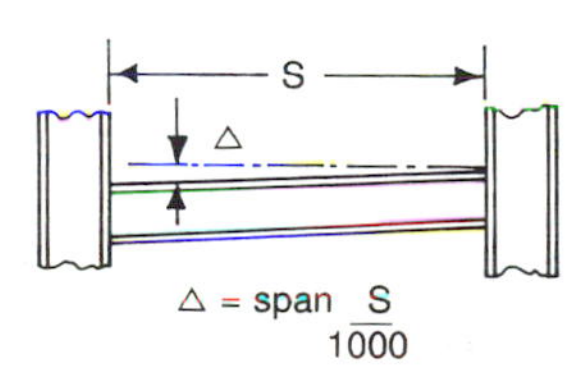

Permitted deviation in level of floor beams from one end to the other of the same beam

Permitted deviation in overall plan (Δ) dimensions - length or width:

If the true overall dimension = L

Then L ≤ 30m, Δ = 20mm
Then L ≥ 30m, Δ = 20mm+ 0.25 (L-30)mm
where L is in m

23.2.4 Cladding assemblies

A cladding system is a three-dimensional assemblage of relatively accurate components attached at its edges (Fig. 23.7) to the structural frame of the building (Fig. 23.8). This relationship can be defined by its three axes, centre to centre, horizontally (usually between column centres), bottom to top edge (usually based on repeated floor-to-floor heights), and thickness (with vertical tolerances on one or both faces). Complications arise at fixing locations to the main frame, and bolting methods have to allow for adjustment in all three directions to overcome discrepancies within the steel frame.

The adoption of a zoning system for cladding provides a discipline for facade construction. A notional plane is established at the point of fixing to the main frame. Offset from this can be established a dimension to the inner wall lining and the visually critical dimension to the outer wall face. Lack of straightness of vertical mullions or lack of alignment between polished stone and glazed panels causes an unsatisfactory rippling effect.

Controlling tolerances can be defined relative to the

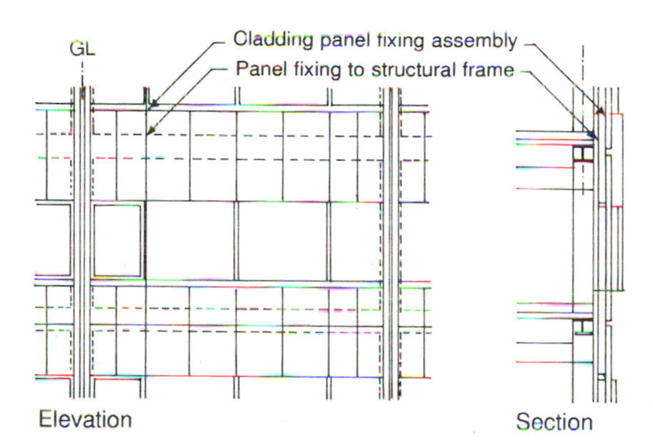

Fig. 23.7 *Diagram of typical cladding assembly.*

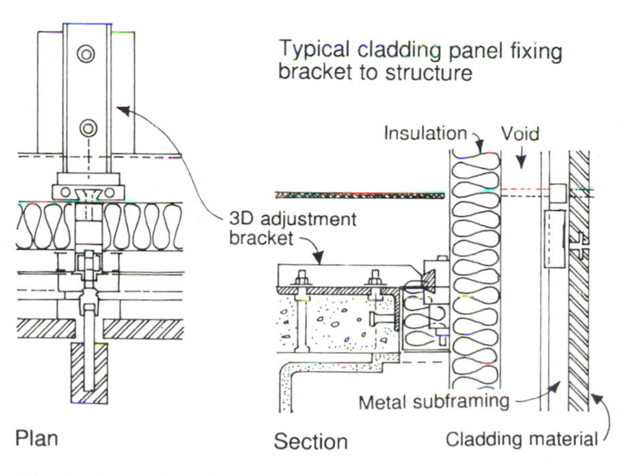

Fig. 23.8 *Relation of assembly to frame.*

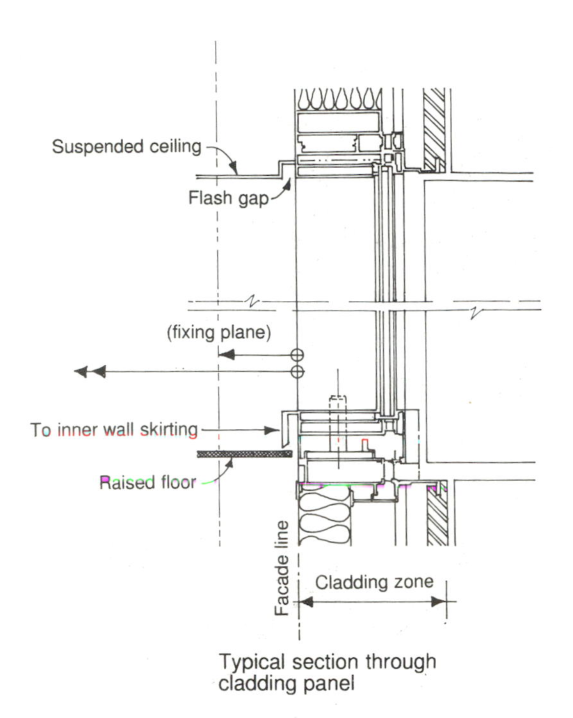

Fig. 23.9 *Planar faces at frame/wall line and different tolerances that might be used.*

facade line, fixing plane and inner wall. The last of these may also be the edge of cill, lining face or last grid line for the raised floor and suspended ceiling system (Fig 23.9). The facade line is all important, whereas the floor/ceiling grid could have a joint of perhaps 20 mm (¾ in) beyond the gridline, covered by the skirting or with a recessed 'flash gap' detail.

23.2.5 Sway and thermal gain

The problem of sway is explained in chapters 14 and 15 (multi-storey and tall buildings). These movements within the structure have to be accommodated within the design of cladding joints, otherwise panels at the upper storeys can become distorted 'out of square' [3]. Other inherent deviations can result from solar gain which can also warp facades. Even the generally moderate weather conditions in the UK can cause substantial thermal movements on south and south west elevations. Increases in height and length can induce stresses at fixing positions which in turn overstress glazing or panels [4]. The tolerances to be allowed for sway and thermal gain are the responsibility of engineering consultants. The problems encountered at the Hancock Tower, Boston and the Hearts of Oak Headquarters, London, show just how complicated these matters can become.

23.2.6 Ceiling and floor planes

Planning layouts are explained in chapter 13. The principal problem when fitting out buildings is the extreme accuracy required of raised floor and suspended ceiling constructions. In effect a three-dimensional grid is required, enabling partitions to form enclosed offices on 1200 mm (4 ft), 1500 mm (5 ft) or whatever module is appropriate to both the ceiling and floor components. The wise designer will obviously isolate these modular volumes from walls and windows so that services within spandrel panels can pass lengthwise without intruding into the enclosed office spaces. Internal columns may be contained within cores or occur in circulation areas with lower ceilings (Fig. 23.10).

Levelling of the finished ceiling and floor is critical. Setting-out and its limitations have to be taken into account when establishing parameters for floor alignment in terms of deflection and tolerances. Present day raised-floor components are easier to adjust to uneven surfaces but the pace of fitting out contracts presents particular problems. Also the fact that commercial interiors have a brief life of no more than 10 years requires the basic shell (floor zone above and structure below,) to be constructed to a reasonable degree of accuracy to suit a range of fitting-out alternatives.

Although floor screeding is now less widespread with the increasingly common use of raised floors, the NBS tolerances are as follows:

Power floated concrete	Plus or minus 10 mm (⅜ in)
Slabs for bonded screeds	Plus or minus 15 mm (19/32 in)
Slabs for overlaying with unbonded screeds (floating floors)	Plus or minus 20 mm (¾ in)

BS 5606:1978 [5] permitted deviations in the level of structural slabs from zero to 100 mm (4 in) in level when using a 50 mm (2 in) screed!

23.3 LOOSE-FIT INTERFACE

The use of buffer zones between elements has already been mentioned in relation to the perimeter detail of ceilings (refer to Fig. 23.10). The notion of a simple 'loose-fit' connection between accurate and inaccurate construction can be extended to the full range of building details. The factory-made and therefore more precise components should be fabricated with sufficient leeway to avoid the range of dimensional innacuracies that may be expected of work done solely on site.

Fast-track construction requires far more generous tolerances. This is particularly because relatively exact components such as curtain walling may have to be designed before the details of the structure have been finalized.

One example is the construction of Minster Court,

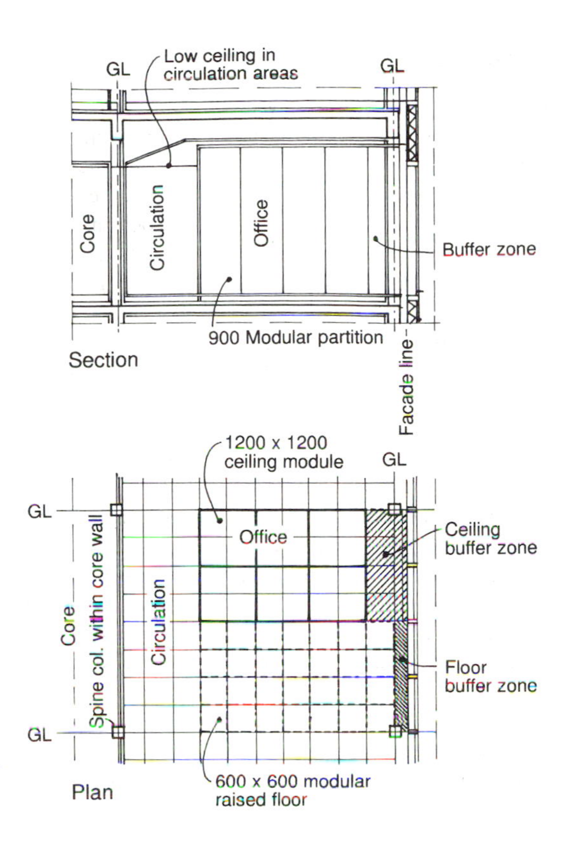

Fig. 23.10 *Office modules versus envelope. A plan and section showing typical modules with raised floor, false ceiling and partition system in conjunction with wall/window zone and core, also the buffer zone ceiling to wall.*

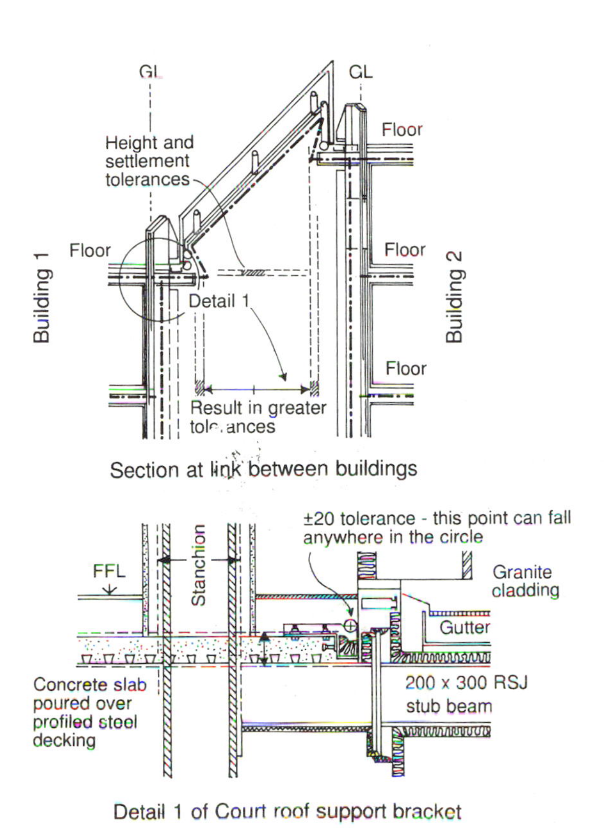

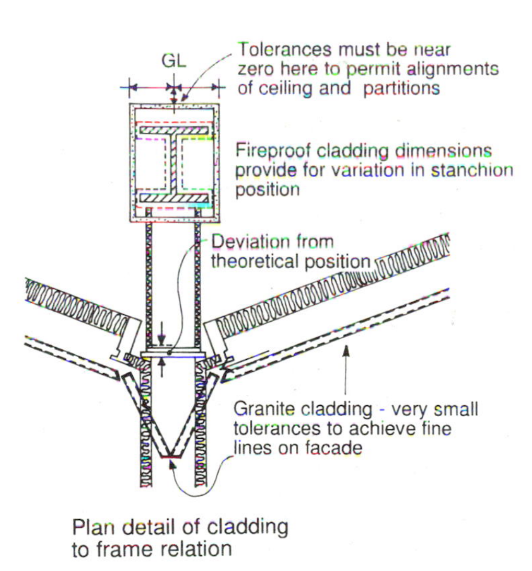

Fig. 23.11 *Detail of Minster Court, Mincing Lane, London 1991 (architects GMW).*

Mincing Lane, London (Fig. 23.11 and 23.12), where columns or floor slabs were permitted only within a limited zone defined by a margin of space measured away from the main structural grid (columnar or floor-to-floor). The tolerances obtained by this method can be adjusted according to the relative importance of location and are easier to control on site. Laser technology now provides an excellent way of establishing 'face-to-face alignment' as compared with 'centre line setting-out.'

A particular problem of tolerances was posed at Minster Court by the configuration of the buildings. The scheme consists of three separate blocks connected by a central steel-framed glass roof. The fast-track programme did not allow time for site measurement of the distance between fixing brackets so the prefabricated steel roof had to be made to accommodate the tolerance in length between the completed buildings. The alternative approach of using longer cantilever brackets to absorb these tolerances would have required heavier structure throughout the height of the three structures. Difficulties of this sort, due to a condensed sequence of construction, have become particularly marked in recent years with the increasing speed expected of building contracts.

23.4 NATIONAL BUILDING SPECIFICATION AND BS 5606: 1990

The NBS has kept abreast of developments in setting-out techniques and it is worth looking at some aspects of the National specification and BS 5606: 1990 in greater detail.

The basis for the Standard is contained in three tables. Tables 1 and 2 describe induced deviations. Measured levels of accuracy for site work have been surveyed and statistically converted to isolate a middle range corresponding to an achievable standard of construction. The BS survey has also been expanded to now define 'characteristic accuracies' for manufactured components.

Many designers found the permissible deviations in the 1978 BS unacceptable. Part 9 of BS 5606: 1990 is helpful in determining the critical dimensions described in section 23.3. It advises on practical measures to guard against the visual effects of inaccurate dimensions and requirements for the location of fixings. Further advice is given by the NBS on designing for the sequence of trades, suggesting that each successive operation can conceal or compensate for previous deviations (the 'cover fillet' or 'gap' philosophy once more).

23.4.1 NBS and setting out

Accuracy of instruments is essential. This should be stipulated in the preliminary clauses of the specification (which should also outline the degree of precision required in setting-out.) The accuracy of plumb dimensions and levels needs clear reference to critical locations described both in the specification and shown on the contract drawings [6].

These crucial dimensions and tolerances have implications for the building's finishes. Further references to them will be needed in the specification when describing envelope walls (for example dimensioning to the face of mullions or of stone veneer), or when relating finished levels to floor finishes and suspended ceilings and face dimensions for column casings, fenestration, wall linings, lift and stair shafts. Prefabricated items such as kitchen units or lavatory pods are other components where fit is critical.

23.5 SAMPLE SPECIFICATION

The following sample specification of setting out and tolerances is offered merely as a guide. On most projects it will be necessary to compile a list of the crucial dimensions and tolerances to be specified.

Particularly on inner city sites there will be critical dimensions defined by light angles, the permitted size of building and the limits of the site itself. Within these constraints some components may have specific problems of fit. Continuous runs of windows or light fittings may for example, have to be made not to exceed a specified size.

Set out: Establish and maintain lines and levels in each part of the works, using the most accurate system of setting-out, to which all adjacent works shall be related. The co-ordinating dimensions are those of the structural grid of . . . metres on plan and . . . metres vertically.

Tolerances: The design of the building has been based on levels of accuracy which can be achieved in practice and the setting-out of components has been related in all cases to the structural grid. Due allowance has been made in the design for necessary tolerances to permit fit and jointing of components. Where components are to be manufactured in accordance with British Standards then the design of assemblies takes account of the tolerances in manufacture and assembly of such components defined in the relevant British Standard. In the case of non-standard components other than structural elements then the drawings take into account the degree of tolerance that can be accepted and which is defined in the specification for that work.

Set out structural members from the grid and construct such that any point on the structure in relation to the nearest grid and any two points on the structure as built shall agree with the required dimension whether shown or calculable from the drawings within the degree of accuracy indicated in Table 1.

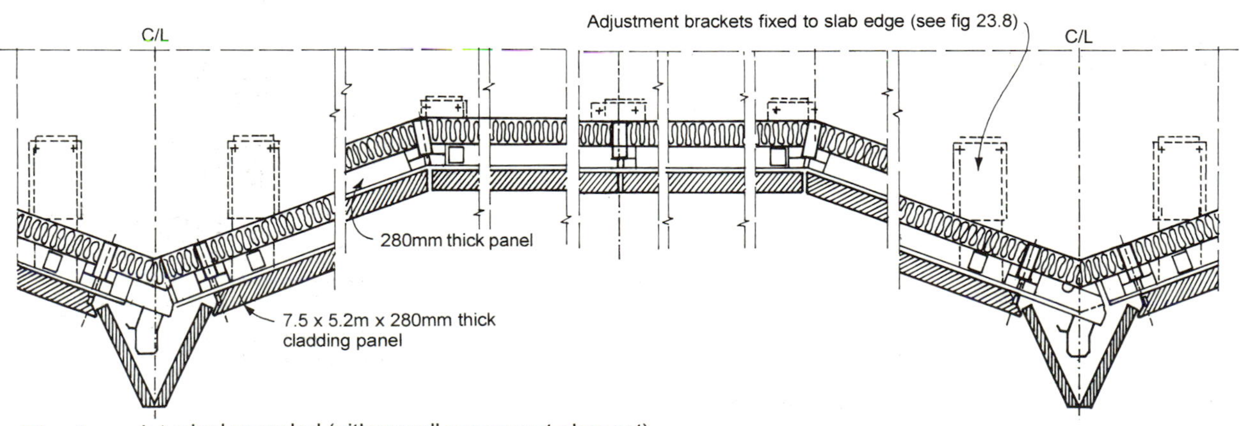

Plan through typical spandrel (either wall or parapet element)

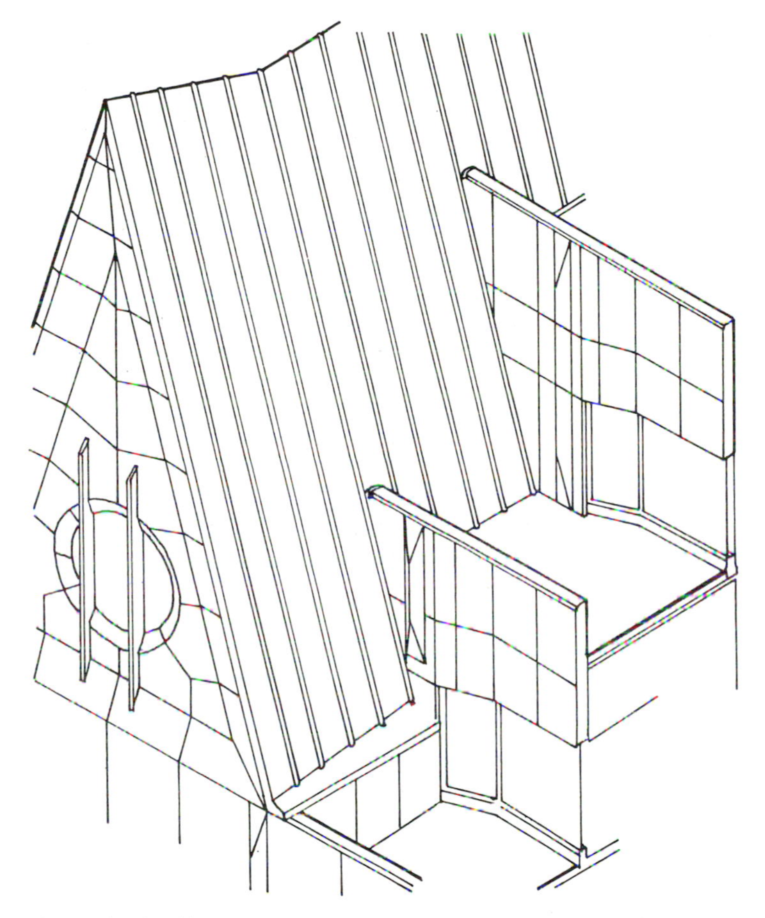

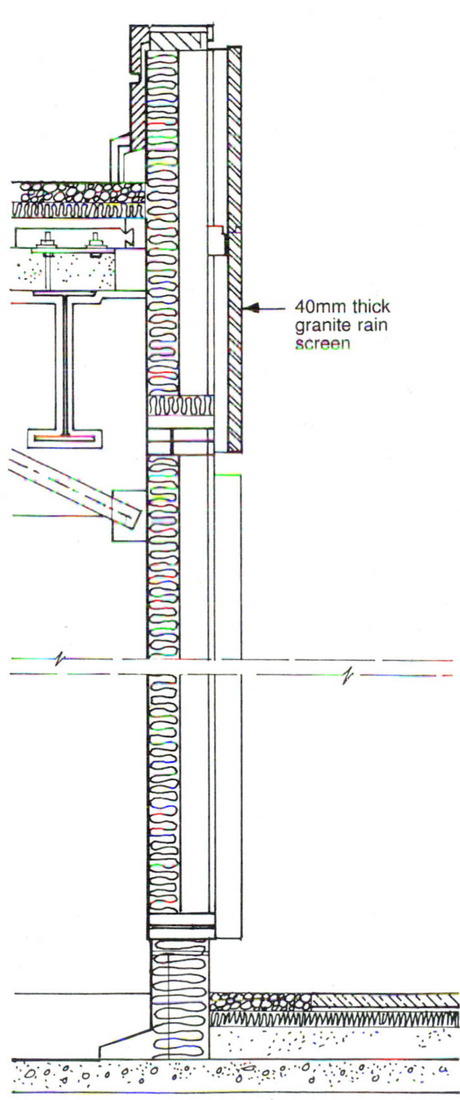

Fig. 23.12 *Minster Court: detail in relation to fast-track construction.*

Appearance to fit:

(1) Arrange the setting out, erection, juxtaposition of components and application of finishes (working within the practical limits of the design and the specification) to ensure that there is satisfactory fit at junctions and that the finished work has a well aligned, true and regular appearance.
(2) Wherever satisfactory accuracy, fit and/or appearance of the work are likely to be critical or difficult to achieve, obtain approval of proposals or of the appearance of the relevant aspects of the partially finished work as early as possible.

Deviations which fall outside those specified or defined will not be acceptable. They will not be cumulative.

Records: Keep records in an approved form of the dimensions of all work as constructed. These records shall be available for inspection at any time and shall be submitted immediately after completion of each section as directed.

Permanent bench marks: Construct on or near site permanent non-ferrous metal bench marks and setting out points which are to be set in concrete, all as and when directed by the architect.

Survey of completed works: Survey the structure floor-by-floor for correctness of the position, levels, dimensions, and alignment of all parts of the works as soon as possible and advise the architect of the result in writing within three days of completion of each survey.

23.6 CONSTRUCTION MANAGEMENT

New forms of contract have been introduced in recent years to reduce the length of building programmes by making an early start on site. This requires that major aspects of the design are based on assumptions. The elevations may be fully developed before the steelwork has been designed: the foundations will need to be finalized before major decisions about the superstructure.

Sub-contract packages are tendered separately, implying the need for tolerance between different packages. This becomes particularly crucial where several packages meet at the same point. Speed of construction and the changing balance of responsibilities between the contractor and consultants often make it impossible for unsatisfactory work to be done again. Also the increasing use of performance specifications and detailed design by specialist sub-contractors makes imperative a predetermined strategy for the degree of constructional accuracy to be allowed for each package and the accommodation of tolerances between them.

23.7 CONCLUSION

In the final analysis, achieving a satisfactory degree of accuracy on site requires more attention and additional time for checking and supervision. Specific information has to be included in the designer's drawings and specification. Clearly, high standards cost more money than slipshod ones.

From the end of World War II, levels of performance anticipated by British Standards have principally been those of mass housing. The 1978 edition of the British Standard for *Accuracy in Building* proved unsatisfactory in practice. The latest revision which is a significant improvement upon its predecessor has yet to be tested. Clients will often suggest that elaboration is not needed and that 'builder orientated' documents like the NHBC Handbooks are adequate. It should be realized, however, that high-quality commercial buildings cost £1080–1620 per m^2 (£100–150 per ft^2) as compared with £350 per m^2 (£32.5 per ft^2) for speculative housing under the NHBC [7]. A significant factor is the high rental value of offices particularly in Central London: at around £645 per m^2 (£60 per ft^2) every square metre of space has an effect on the development equation. The use of specifications requiring insufficient standards of accuracy can cost for example 75 mm (3 in) in external wall thickness to overcome coarse tolerances. In the case of a 10 storey tower £60,000 would be lost in rental income per year [8].

The more sophisticated forms of construction now in widespread use (such as high-performance rain screen facades), are thinner than conventional masonry skins and faster to erect than precast panels. The accurate fit required of these components needs greater accuracy in frame erection than was previously the case (Fig. 23.12).

Fast-track construction and new forms of contract have made design to accommodate tolerances a crucial issue requiring consideration at the early stages of a project. This is because the process of design is governed far more by the building process than by the logical design sequence to which designers have worked in the past. All design issues therefore need to be brought forward together and the tolerances of fit need to be decided far earlier than they would otherwise be. Assumptions have to be made based on standards recognized in the industry, but modified by experience of the practically achievable.

REFERENCES AND TECHNICAL NOTES

1. BS 5950: Part 2: 1985 *Structural use of steelwork in buildings* gives detailed recommended permissible deviations.
2. 'Critical Dimension' – this term needs to be used with discretion: for main grids, floor-to-floor heights, relationship to the site boundaries and where tightest tolerances are required.
3. Hancock Tower, Boston
   This famous failure due to building sway is fully documented in *Glass Age*, Vol. 20, No. 3, August 1977, pp 25–6.
4. Hearts of Oak HQ, Euston Road. This was a suspended facade, the S and SW glazing could not adapt to the 'sag' in summer time.
5. British Standards. BS 5606:1978 has now been superseded by BS 5606:1990 *Guide to Accuracy in Building*.
6. National Building Spec, Clause 360 The previous clause in the NBS was well prepared, and states the following: *Critical dimensions*: The following are critical; set out and construct the works to ensure compliance with the stated permissible deviations, then follow the dimensions, location and permitted deviation in each case.
7. The National House Building Council (NHBC) of the UK. The NHBC has taken over the role of government agencies such as the Department of Environment (DoE) in laying down standards for house construction.
8. The rental equation. The 10 storey tower is assumed to be 20 m (65 ft 8 in) square, with 360 m^2 (3874 ft^2) lettable per floor: a 75 mm (3 in) intrusion into this space due to tolerances results in the loss of 4 m^2 (43 ft^2) per floor, a yearly loss over ten storeys of £60,000 assuming a rental of £1000 per m^2 (£93 per ft^2).

Fig. 24.1 *Ghirardelli Square, San Francisco, 1962–67 (architects Wurster Bernardt and Emmons, with Lawrence Halprin). A seminal example of the reuse of old buildings.*

24

Insertion and strengthening of frames and upgrading facades

Peter Wright and Alan Blanc

24.1 INTRODUCTION

There has been increasing interest in the reuse and refurbishment of existing buildings. Despite the complications of construction, it is often cheaper to refurbish substantial buildings from the last century instead of demolishing them and rebuilding. The financial advantages are afforded by tax incentives in North America or VAT savings in Europe. In Europe the recession which followed the oil crisis of 1972/3 saw a slump in new construction and developers turned to refurbishment as a cheaper and quicker way of achieving a building programme. In London the saving of Covent Garden has as much to do with these economic factors as changes in planning taste towards conserving city centres.

The trend towards conservation has been popular with the public and has led planning authorities to schedule an increased number of buildings – and indeed, whole areas – for conservation. The most notorious London example is Peter Palumbo's difficulty in obtaining consent for a modern building on the Mappin and Webb site (opposite Mansion House). The London region of English Heritage and pressure groups have continuously sought the rehabilitation of the 19th century island site rather than accepting new designs by Mies van der Rohe or James Stirling. Another London victim of the conservation movement is Spence and Webster's Parliament Office Building, cancelled despite a successful competition award. The early phases of refurbishment work are already complete in repairing and remodelling to the old frontages. Selective demolition has occurred in the rear yards with new buildings hidden by the old towards Whitehall. The final stage will, however, be more complex since the main steel beams spanning the Metropolitan Underground lines have to be removed due to lack of strength. The ultimate solution will involve a vast basement construction which embraces both the Metropolitan and extended Jubilee Underground lines. The box form of the sub-basement will support offices built around a courtyard.

A further move towards conservation and rehabilitation has been the declaration of enterprise zones in Britain where cash incentives of rate-free periods and 10% grants have been offered to encourage redevelopment of the depressed inner city areas. Similar policies in the form of tax incentives are used in North America to bring derelict areas back into use.

One of the seminal examples from the early 1960s is Ghirardelli Square, San Francisco, where a collection of derelict factories were remodelled and strengthened to form a new shopping mall. Steel and concrete were employed to make the masonry and timber framing earthquake resistant. The refurbishment started in 1962 and has inspired the successful renewal of two kilometres of quayside (Fig. 24.1).

24.2 LOAD ASSESSMENT

A significant task with refurbishment work is the need for careful appraisal of dead loads in the existing building. The removal of superfluous weight from the structure will reduce loading on walls and, more significantly, on the foundations. Obvious elements to remove are chimney stacks, and non-loadbearing partitions. Conservationists can perhaps be assuaged by providing reproduction glass reinforced polyester (GRP) for lightweight replacement of chimneys and other features that weigh a fraction of the original. A typical case study is the reconstruction at parapet level of St Paul's House, Leeds (Fig. 24.2). Any savings in load will counter the effect of additional structures or increased loading due to change of occupancy. Purists will argue that GRP is artificial but the completion of the fan vaulting at the Anglican Cathedral of Liverpool was achieved with GRP and is a perfect match to the older parts of the building. Any savings in load will counter the effect of additional structures or increased loading due to change of occupancy.

The extra load must be considered carefully in relation to the maximum allowable bearing pressures below the existing foundations. This often rules out roof-top extensions or parking bays at basement or ground level. Structural alterations should seek to spread load rather than cause point loading on foundations to avoid differential settlement. This is particularly important in old masonry 'box' construction. Underpinning is sometimes the only solution, as illustrated with needle piles at Hays Galleria, London (refer to Fig. 24.20).

Settlement cracks and signs of movement in existing buildings must be carefully recorded. Current techniques of photometry enable elevations to be printed to 1:50 scale with every crack or defect photographically recorded (Fig. 24.3). Old settlement, for instance, due to lack of alignment, may never be cured but underpinning can be used to secure existing foundations to accommodate extra loading and to prevent further movement.

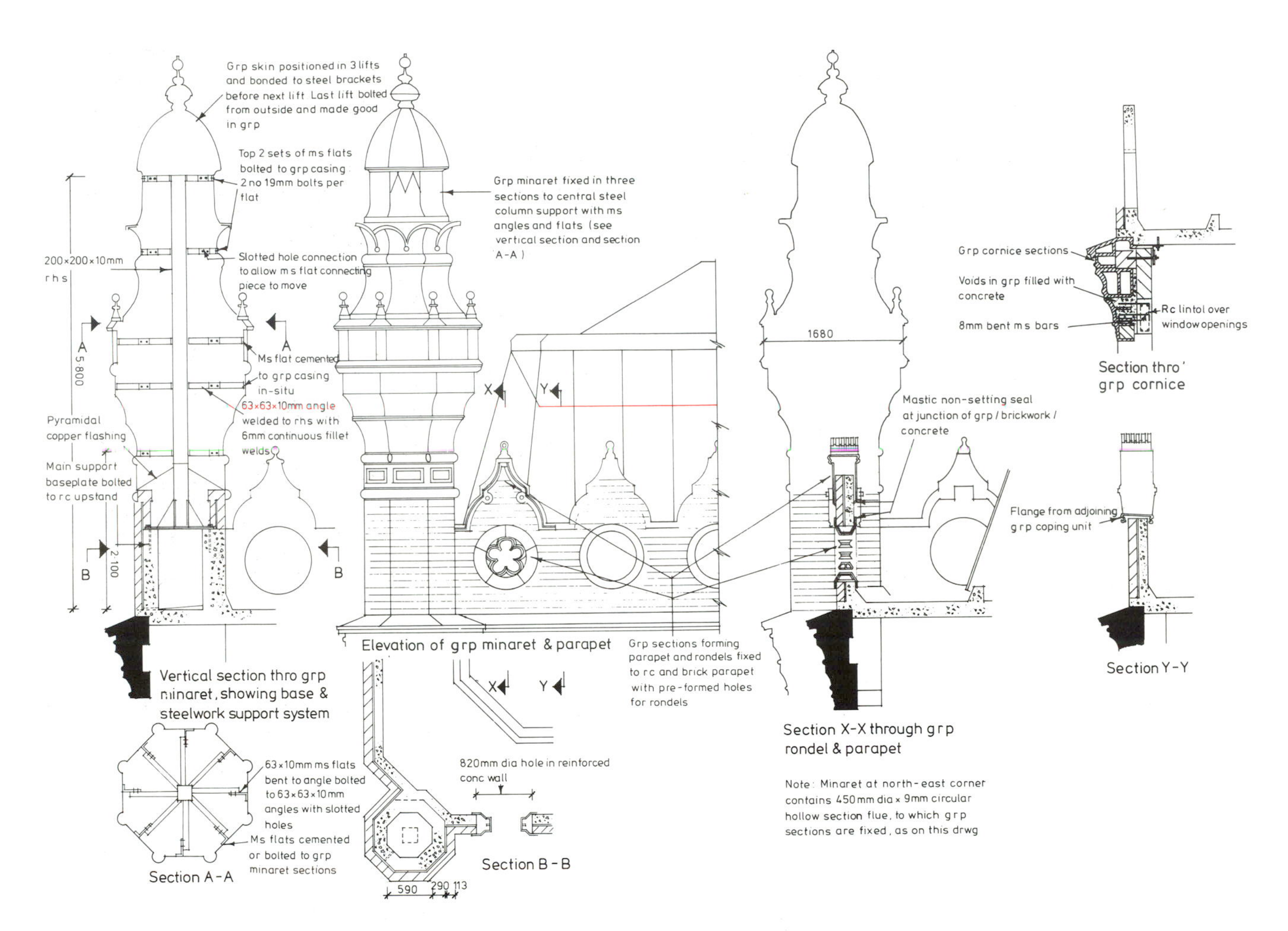

Fig. 24.2 *Detail of GRP finials on steel supports at St Paul's House, Leeds (architects Booth Shaw and Partners: engineers Alistair McCowan and Partners).*

Fig. 24.3 *Photogrammetry used by Historic Buildings Division of Greater London Council for repairs of Fowlers Market, Covent Garden, London.*

24.3 UPGRADING LOADBEARING STRUCTURES

Refurbishment of loadbearing structures may simply involve strengthening floors, or more extensively removing some of the walls and replacing their loadbearing function with an alternative structural system. Steel members can be used to strengthen existing unframed structures, typically by providing reinforcement to floor joists, beams or walls. Because of difficulties in assessing both the strength of existing elements and determining the proportion of load carried by the new and old components, the new steelwork is usually designed to carry the full load. Clearly the section must be detailed to ensure that the reinforcement can be physically added on site!

Where walls are carrying only vertical loads, they can often simply be replaced with steel beams supported on walls or piers. However, in some older buildings, horizontal stability was provided by massive cores of loadbearing brickwork.

The conversion of 1 and 3 Baxter's Place, Edinburgh into modern offices provides a good example of how restrictive core walls can be removed. At Baxter's Place all internal walls and floors were replaced by a steel frame giving open offices to comply with current requirements. The envelope walls had to be braced by flying shores until the new framing had been installed; this extended upwards to support mansard extensions, to avoid loading the existing masonry envelope (Figs 24.4 and 24.5).

24.4 STRENGTHENING IRON AND STEEL FRAMED BUILDINGS

Chapter 1 describes the development of framed buildings in the 19th century, from the earliest examples of masonry box with a framed spine of cast iron columns and wrought iron beams. Fully framed buildings also used both cast iron and wrought iron, and it was not until the end of the last century that mild steel took over as a framing material (Figs 24.6 and 24.7). It should be remembered that wrought iron was still used in the first decade of this century for built up sections in lattice girders and trusses and often intermingled with rolled steel sections. Work for the London Underground Railways up to 1914 is typical.

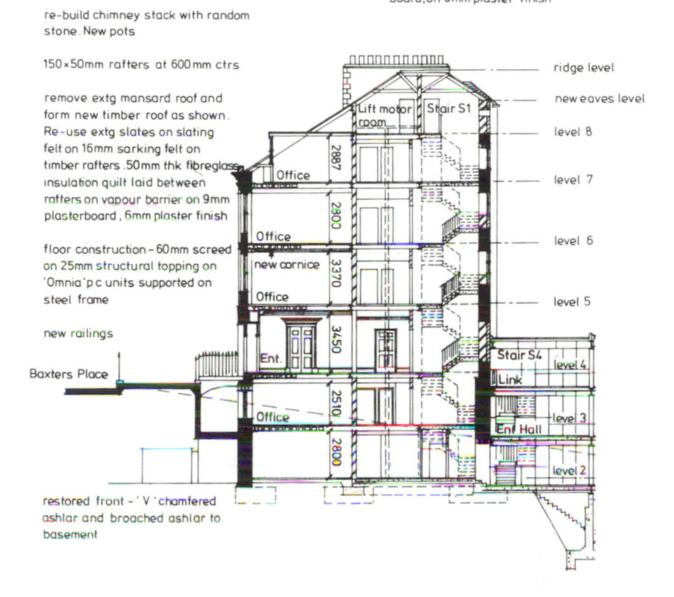

Fig. 24.4 *Section through Baxter's Place, Edinburgh (architects Robert Hurd and Partners: engineers Laing Properties).*

Fig. 24.5 *Front elevation of 1 and 3 Baxter's Place after refurbishment.*

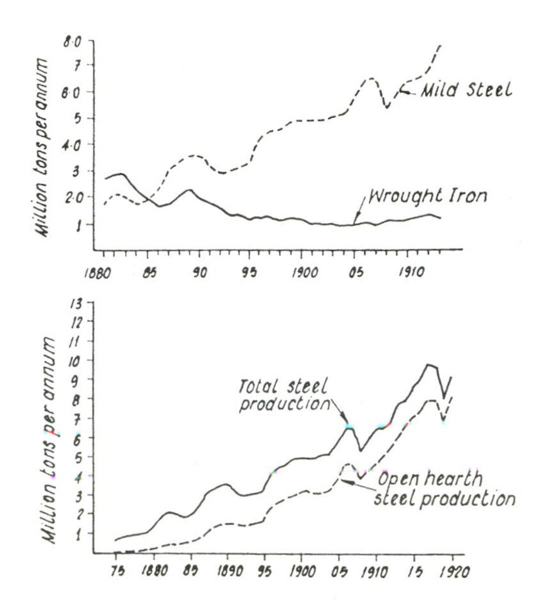

Fig. 24.6 *Graph showing transition from dominance of wrought iron to dominance of steel in Britain.*

24.4.1 Materials

The first priority with any modification to existing framed buildings involving cast iron, wrought iron or steel is to identify the materials used and ascertain their physical and chemical properties. Visual examination is an essential first step (Fig. 24.8). The following guidance is taken from Michael Bussell's article in the *Architects' Journal* [1].

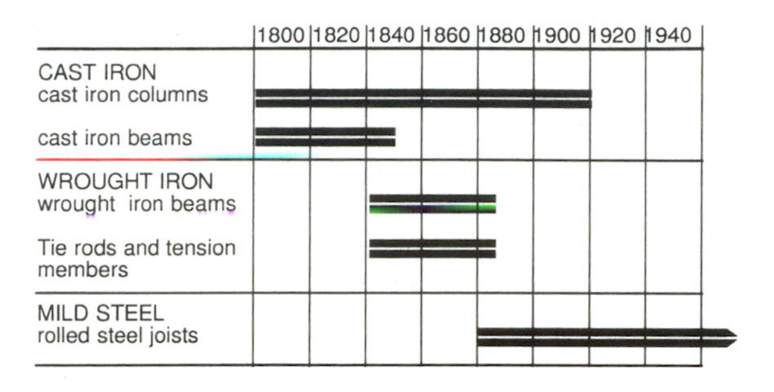

Fig. 24.7 *Time chart regarding sections utilized.*

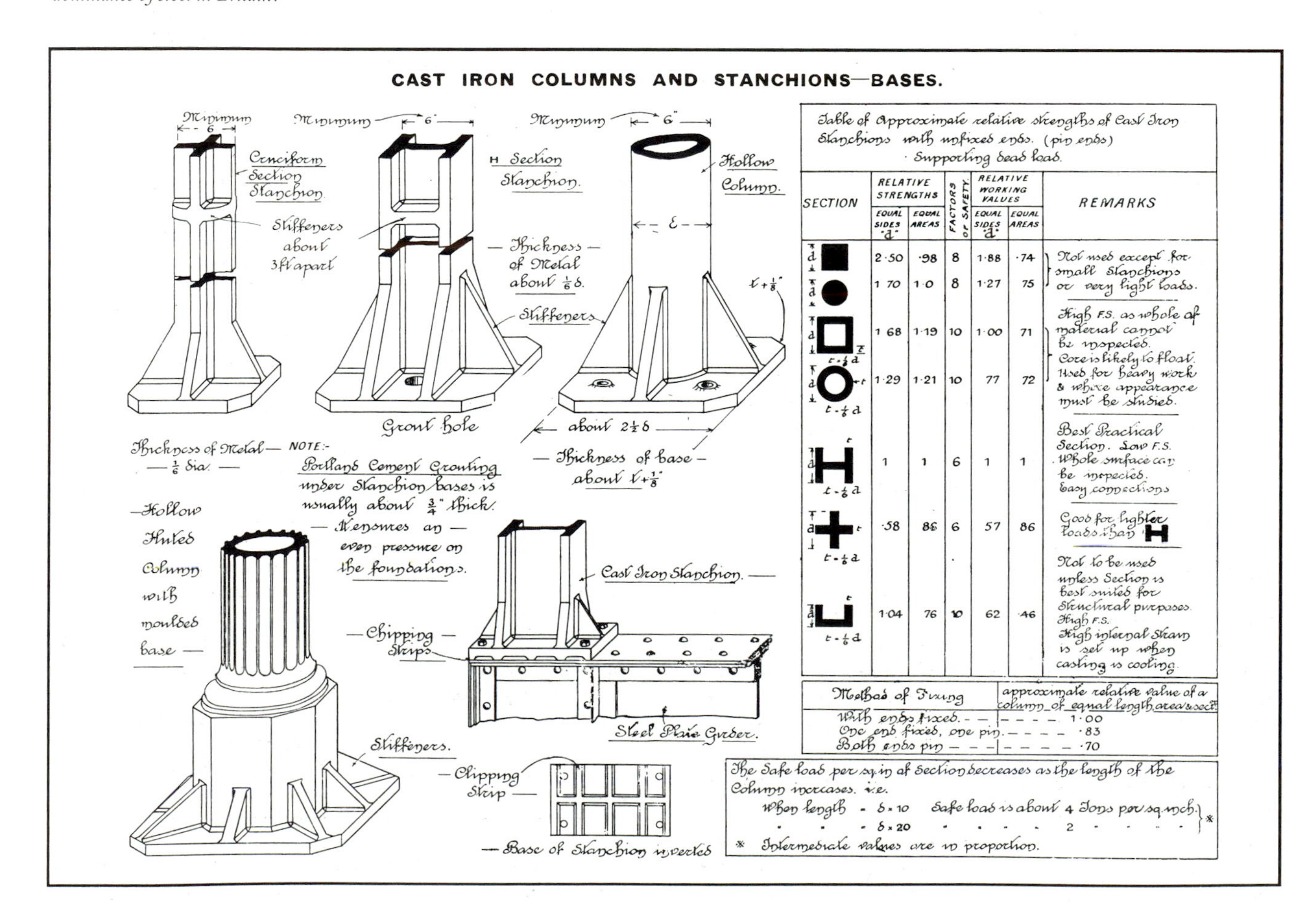
CAST IRON COLUMNS AND STANCHIONS—BASES.

Table of Approximate relative strengths of Cast Iron Stanchions with unfixed ends. (pin ends) · Supporting dead load.

SECTION	RELATIVE STRENGTHS		FACTORS OF SAFETY.	RELATIVE WORKING VALUES		REMARKS
	EQUAL SIDES "d"	EQUAL AREAS		EQUAL SIDES "d"	EQUAL AREAS	
■ (solid square)	2·50	·98	8	1·88	·74	Not used except for small Stanchions or very light loads.
● (solid round)	1 70	1·0	8	1·27	75	
□ (hollow square), t = 1/6 d	1 68	1·19	10	1·00	71	High F.S. as whole of material cannot be inspected. Core is likely to float. Used for heavy work & where appearance must be studied.
○ (hollow round), t = 1/6 d	1·29	1·21	10	77	72	
H, t = 1/6 d	1	1	6	1	1	Best Practical Section. Low F.S. Whole surface can be inspected. Easy connections
+ (cruciform), t = 1/6 d	·58	86	6	57	86	Good for lighter loads than H
⊔ (channel), t = 1/6 d	1·04	76	10	62	·46	Not to be used unless Section is best suited for Structural purposes. High F.S. High internal Strain is set up when casting is cooling.

Method of Fixing	approximate relative value of a column of equal length, area & sect.
With ends fixed.	1·00
One end fixed, one pin.	·83
Both ends pin	·70

The Safe load per sq. in of Section decreases as the length of the Column increases. i.e.
When length = 5 × 10 Safe load is about 4 Tons per sq. inch. *
When length = 5 × 20 Safe load is about 2 *
* Intermediate values are in proportion.

Fig. 24.8 *Late 19th century construction manual for cast iron components.*

(a) Features of cast iron

Internal corners rounded.
Bottom (tension) flange often larger than top (compression) flange in beams.
Thick 'coarse' sections.
Beam often 'fish bellied' in elevation and plan.
Connections usually simple bearing or bolted.
Columns often ornately detailed with flowing mouldings – Doric/Corinthian capitals common.
Circular columns usually hollow, not always concentrically moulded.

(b) Features of wrought iron

Beams and columns frequently built up from plates and angles rivetted together.
Rolled sections only in small sizes.
Sections regular and more crisply edged than most cast iron.
Large sections often built up from several beams and many flange plates.

(c) Features of mild steel

Large sections rolled.
Dimensions, if measurable, may allow section to be identified from tables (old or current).
Connections in early steel were rivetted, but were later more commonly bolted or welded.
The makers name is often to be found stamped on the web.

For work prior to 1910, tests may be necessary to distinguish wrought iron from steel; remember that material strength *cannot* be assessed by visual means.

Early steel sections were available in a much wider range of sizes than today, the individual steel makers deciding the sections to be rolled [2]. The first attempt to control this multiplicity was BS 4 which introduced British Standard Sections. In 1921 this was modified for Beams and Pillars (nomenclature changes as well as technology) then termed NBSB (New British Standard Beams) and NBSHB (New British Standard Heavy Beams and Pillars). Universal Beams and Columns were finally introduced in 1964, with metric units replacing imperial in 1972.

24.4.2 Strengthening methods

Steelwork and wrought iron can be strengthened by the addition of angles, plates or sections using bolts or site welding (Fig. 24.9). For structural purposes, cast iron cannot be welded and needs special consideration, such as filling hollow columns with reinforced concrete, as was done at the Tate Gallery, Liverpool. Another alternative is to use new, independent construction to carry all imposed loads, leaving weaker elements to be simply self-supporting. This was the solution at New Concordia, Southwark, London where new concrete floors were inserted to take the imposed loading, the timber floors (with joists and boarding) being left intact to form the ceilings.

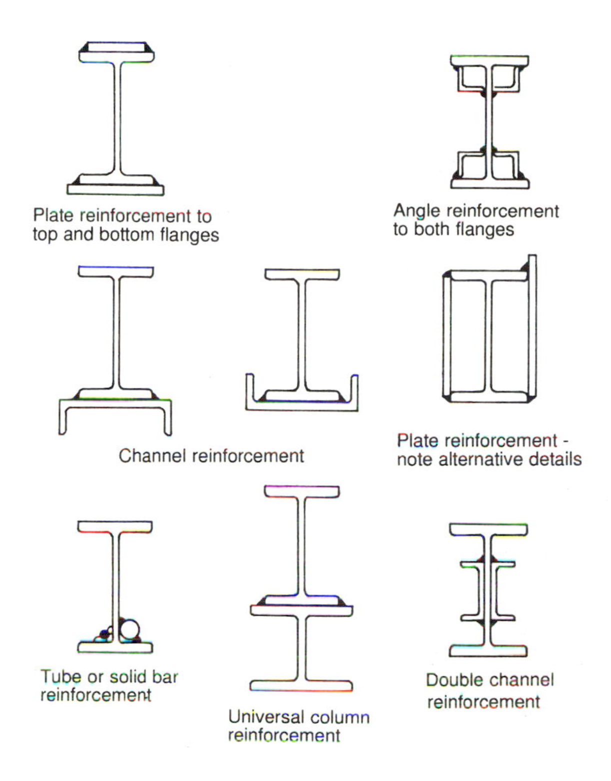

Fig. 24.9 *Various methods of strengthening sections.*

Table 24.1 Recommended welding techniques for various structural materials

Material	*Welding techniques*
Cast iron	Cannot be welded (except for non-structural fixings where very high nickel electrodes are used). Cast iron welding primarily involves decorative work, brackets, frets and railings, although the latter will probably require wrought iron framing for horizontal rails and standards to satisfy current codes (refer to chapter on Staircases).
Wrought iron	Low hydrogen electrodes are used (dry to manufacturer's recommendations at approx. 350°C).
Mild steel (low carbon content min 2% and high sulphur content)	Low hydrogen electrodes are used. Preheating needed for sections greater than 25 mm.
Mild steel (high carbon content) generally from 1910–30 period	As above but preheating for all structural welds.

Weldability needs to be assessed in terms of the recommendations in Table 24.1. For general details of steel welding refer to chapters 21 and 22.

24.5 NEW BUILDING FRAMES BEHIND EXISTING FACADES

Conservation policies commonly involve preservation orders on specific facades and interior features, necessitating their retention as part of the construction programme. The saving of facades may also lead to higher plot ratios than would result from demolition and a new design, and planning consent may be more readily obtained.

It is most unusual for a retained facade without floors and spine construction to be self-supporting. A system of support must therefore be devised both as temporary works and for the permanent construction after rehabilitation. In an ideal situation the temporary and permanent works would be the same, but such arrangements are not always possible due to cramped site conditions or programme requirements which demand clear space for construction of the interior.

If an existing steel frame is to be replaced then it may be sufficient to strengthen the existing facade frame by the

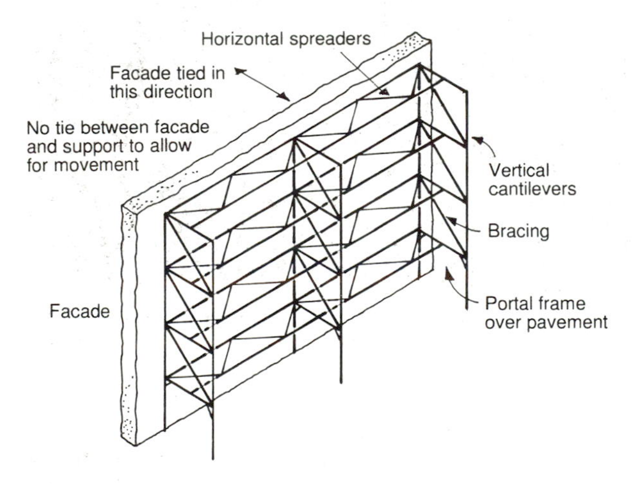

Fig. 24.10 *Typical arrangement of temporary support to facade.*

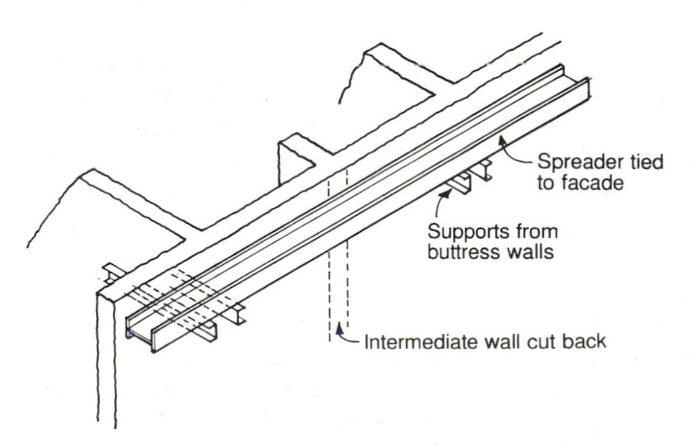

Fig. 24.11 *Use of existing buttress walls connected by horizontal spreader.*

Fig. 24.12 *Retention of old steel framing with shores to existing facade, Bentalls store, Kingston-upon-Thames, London, 1992 (architects and engineers: Building Design Partnership).*

Fig. 24.13 *Use of existing party walls. Coutts Bank, London, 1979 (architects Frederick Gibberd and Partners).*

introduction of temporary bracing (Fig. 24.10) or, less efficiently, by stiffening the connections (Fig. 24.11). However, if the existing frame cannot be suitably strengthened, a new permanent temporary facade retention system might be used. This is a new frame which will support the facade during the demolition of the interior and then, with minimal modification, form part of the new structure (Fig. 24.12).

In the case of the Bentalls store development, the main facade was listed grade II and had to be conserved including the details of the bronze shop fronts. The 1920s construction was steel framed with the old steelwork connected to new concrete framing of the store, a case of composite construction due to the complex geometry where new meets existing work.

The retention of masonry facades is more problematical

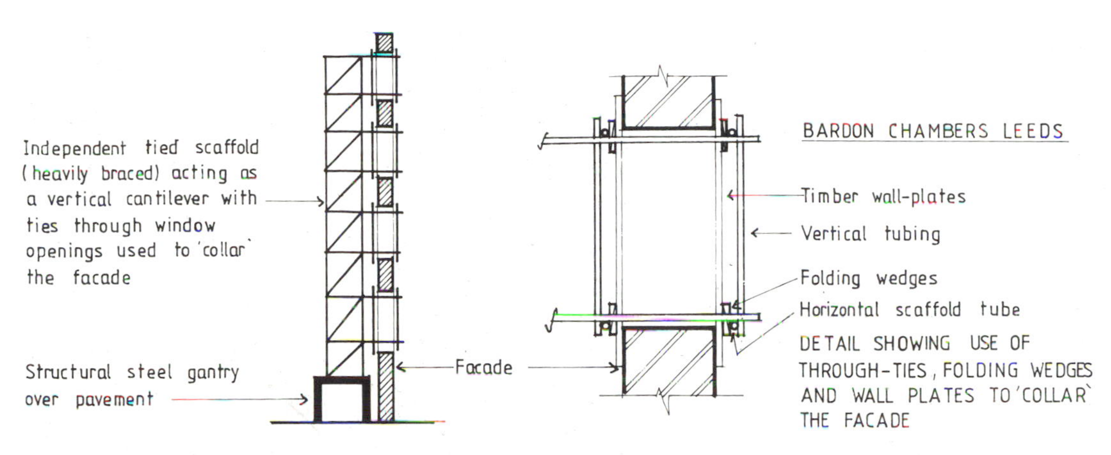

Fig. 24.14 *Wholly external temporary support system.*

Fig. 24.15 *Hammersmith Road Development completed renovation, London, 1991 (architects Carl Fisher and Partners).*

Fig. 24.16 *Retention of front facade only of early 19th century terrace (architects Carl Fisher and Partners). Front elevation (preserved): scaffold supports were placed on pavement.*

and temporary restraint, in the form of vertical cantilevers and horizontal spreaders, is usually necessary. These vertical cantilevers can be either existing masonry walls as at the Coutts Bank (Fig. 24.13), or else scaffold towers, lightweight steel sections or UB/UC sections. Old structures in poor condition may need to be secured for some time until suitable reuse can be found [3].

The support may be placed inside, which may be restrictive, or outside the site, in which case access must be provided for pedestrian traffic. This may involve a heavy portal frame at ground level, as illustrated in Fig. 24.14 and where a braced scaffold tower acts as a vertical cantilever with ties through each window opening to anchor or 'collar' the facade.

Where pavement access is not a problem, it is customary to provide scaffold supports on a double line with bracing down to ground level. The example at the Hammersmith Road Development is typical in London where 18th or early 19th century facades are being retained (Figs 24.15 and 24.16). The scaffold members are constructed from standardized perforated sections.

A more famous example is the conservation of Thomas Archer's house front at Hammersmith Station and where the facade of Butterwick House had been previously vandalized when converted to a tramway depot in the late 19th century. In this example, the fragile work that survives from the 1720s is cradled by a custom-made structural frame until such time as the masonry envelope of Butterwick

Fig. 24.17 *Condition of Thomas Archer's House at Hammersmith, London, 1992 before work started in 1989.*

House is restored to its original form (Figs 24.17, 24.18 and 24.19).

Flying shores are normally associated with restraining party walls of adjacent buildings. Such techniques could be utilized to restrain rear and front facades by bridging over streets and yards onto buildings outside the site. Consent is difficult to obtain, hence raking shores or skeletal supports bridging the pavement zone around the site.

Old masonry structures need to be carefully tested where connected to new framing. These tests involve the assessment of brick, stonework and mortar strengths in order that loadbearing properties can be determined. Such methods were employed in the retention of the Hays Dock facades dating from the mid–19th century in the redevelopment scheme known as London Bridge City. The project involves new build alongside refurbishment of historic warehouses. The latter were completed between 1856 and 1861 by engineers W. Snooke and H. Stock using 450 mm (1 ft 6 in) envelope walls with the floors supported on cast iron spine columns. A serious fire led to the wooden joisted floors being replaced in the 1860s by wrought beams carrying jack arches on every other floor.

Refurbishing to modern standards meant stripping out the cast iron columns and the mixture of floor construction with replacement comprising a new steelwork frame supporting composite floors. The old masonry envelope was found to be very robust due to the buttressing and to the curving geometry. It was not supported when the old floor framing was cut away and in the final structure provided horizontal stability and vertical support to the new flooring system (Figs 24.20, 24.21a and b). The former dock has been roofed over as a galleria with contemporary tubular framing that matches the Italianate elegance of Hays Dock.

The final case study is the story of the improvements to the Royal Exchange, London and based upon the report by

Figs 24.18 and 24.19 *Thomas Archer's House: present condition, custom made cradle supports and proposed restoration (architects EPR Partnership).*

R. D. Reith [4]. In essence the enlargements to the 150 year old building have been made to rationalize the interior spaces without altering the parapet or pediment line externally. A total of 1300 m^2 (about 13,000 ft^2) of highly serviced floor space has been arranged at the new third and fourth

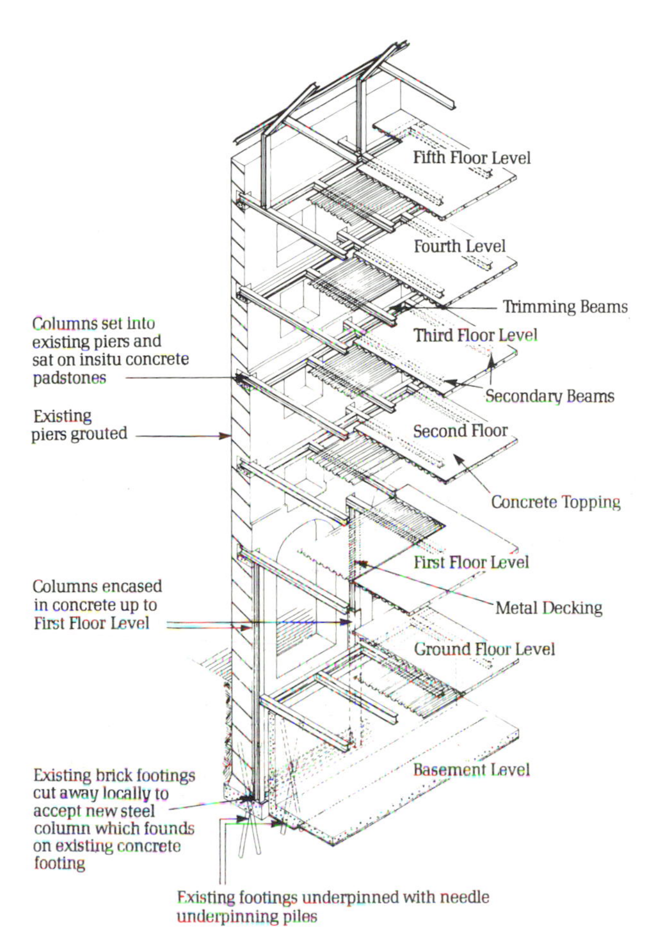

Fig. 24.20 *Hays Galleria, Southwark, London – structural arrangement.*

floors behind the attic storey whilst the main trading floor has been protected by a new aluminium and glass atrium roof. The mid-Victorian building has been considerably modified over the years: the open courtyard of Sir William Tite was roofed over by Charles Barry in 1884 and subsequently an additional mezzanine floor added to the central space. The loading from these previous alterations coupled with the need for additional floors presented serious problems with overstressing to some areas of the existing brickwork and masonry. Existing floors were removed to relieve loading and replaced by steel decking and screed that formed the newer and lighter construction (refer to Figs 24.22a and b).

The operation was considerably complicated by the continued use of the ground floor by the London International Financial Futures Exchange, which meant that a temporary roof had first to be fitted as protection. Finally a 'crash deck' had to be formed to give both a working platform and a resistant surface from falling debris and materials. Opening up of the existing masonry was needed

(a)

(b)

Figs 24.21a and b *Reuse of brick envelope walls tied to new steel frame. Hays Galleria, Southwark, London, 1986 (architects Michael Twigg Brown and Partners: engineers The Waterman Partnership). Sectional detail (a) airview; (b) interior of Galleria.*

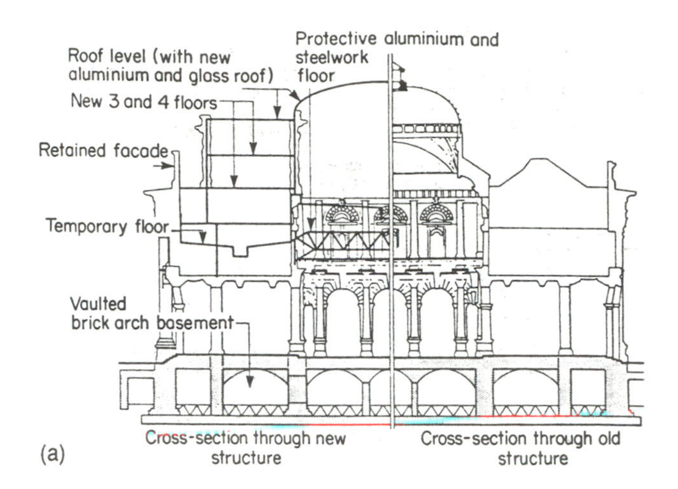

to establish precise loading limits. Investigation of the vaulted brick arched basement found adequate strength in the lime concrete raft but overstressing existed in the brick piers: these were strengthened by 200 mm (8 in) concrete 'corsets' and that in turn supported precast arches to sustain increased loading on the old vaults.

Fig. 24.22a and b *Improvements to the Royal Exchange, London, 1991 (architects Fitzroy Robinson Partnership: engineers Oscar Faber Consulting Engineers Ltd) (a) sectional detail; (b) airview of construction.*

(b)

24.6 LIFT WELLS AND STAIRCASE CORES

Refurbishment of older buildings often means improving the vertical circulation in terms of fire escapes as well as lift access for general convenience as well as fulfilling current requirements for disabled persons. In larger retail premises the upgrading could also introduce the provision of escalators.

Installing new lifts and stair shafts in masonry buildings is often made easier by the construction of freestanding braced shafts framed together from cold formed sections or small structural components (tubes or channels). Drylining is used inside and out to provide the requisite fire protection. Refer to chapter 30, section 2 for technical details.

A lift motor at ground or basement floor based upon hydraulic drive will reduce the structural load and save the complication of a roof motor room. Many lift suppliers offer to supply and fit the mechanical installation complete with the steel structure involved. Partially framed buildings often have restricted masonry cores around stairs and lift shafts. The thickness and weight of such construction makes enlargement or lift modernization both complicated and expensive. Replacing masonry cores by steel framing can help to rationalize the space needed and assist in replanning the circulation with inner lobbies to comply with current fire codes. In fully framed structures, the problem is easier and can be resolved by subframing the floor bays to take care of vertical shafts. A larger scale rearrangement applies with the installation of escalators and where often the floor bays and spanning layout are changed to suit the extensive slots needed for escalator construction.

24.7 STRENGTHENING WORK

24.7.1 Domes

There are many examples in the history of masonry domes where steel chains have been used to control outward thrust above the springing line of the vault. The following notes have been prepared in consultation with Sir Bernard Feilden concerning the various measures taken to stabilize the dome of St Paul's Cathedral.

The raised dome of St Paul's comprises three elements. One is the structural core of brickwork which is the main structural feature and which in turn supports the timbering for the lead covering. The inner dome visible from the interior is also brickwork, the two leaves of masonry joining at the head of the tapered drum above the 'Whispering Gallery' and secured in Wren's time by an external chain of wrought iron.

Three other chains were added by Wren to the upper half of the structural cone to prevent spreading under wind load.

All went well for 200 years until the Central Line underground railway was constructed to the north-east of

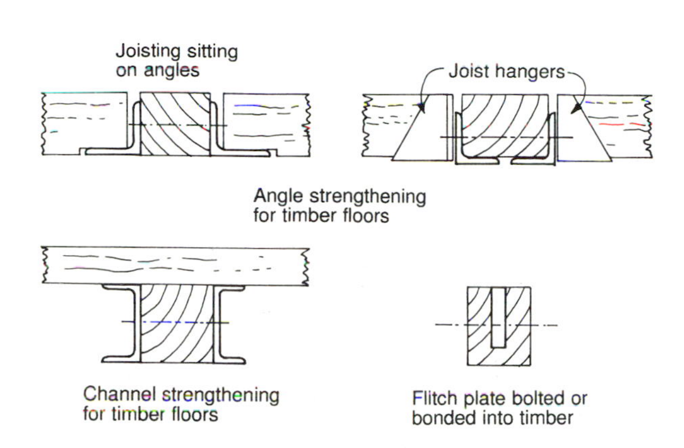

Fig. 24.23 *Typical strengthening methods.*

the Cathedral c. 1912. Settlement then followed to the north trancept and that lead to cracking and a programme of repair under firstly Sir Aston Webb and then Sir Ralph Nott, also as it happened, chief engineer to the Central Line. A pair of stainless chains encased in concrete was added at the crucial line where the twin domes join the drum [5]. There is no evidence that the latest chains have stretched and it could be said that Wren's original precautions have stood the test of time.

24.7.2 Remedial work to timber frames

Strengthening timber frames with nailed ply, or reinforcing joints with spiked plates are commonplace techniques today, a review of current metal fixings being given in chapter 29. Restoring ageing timber roofs is still often a matter of combining plates and tie rods to reinforce tension members or to reinstate bearings at truss and beam ends (Fig. 24.23). A typical example is the repair work to the roof and joists of Trinity College Library, Cambridge (Fig. 24.24). The chapel trusses had to be further reinforced by steel lattice girders assembled in the length of the roof void to strengthen the purlins (not shown in figure).

24.7.3 Remedial work to reinforced concrete structures

The first step in any remedial work to reinforced concrete structures is to ascertain the cause of the problem. This may be adverse chemical reaction within the concrete itself, between the concrete and reinforcement or environmental attack on any of the constituent materials – cement, aggregate or steel reinforcement. Alternatively, the cause of the problem may be structural distress due to overloading of the member or displaced and/or missing reinforcement.

In cases of internal chemical breakdown, specialist advice must be sought, and the Concrete Repair Association, a trade association incorporating specialist sub-contractors,

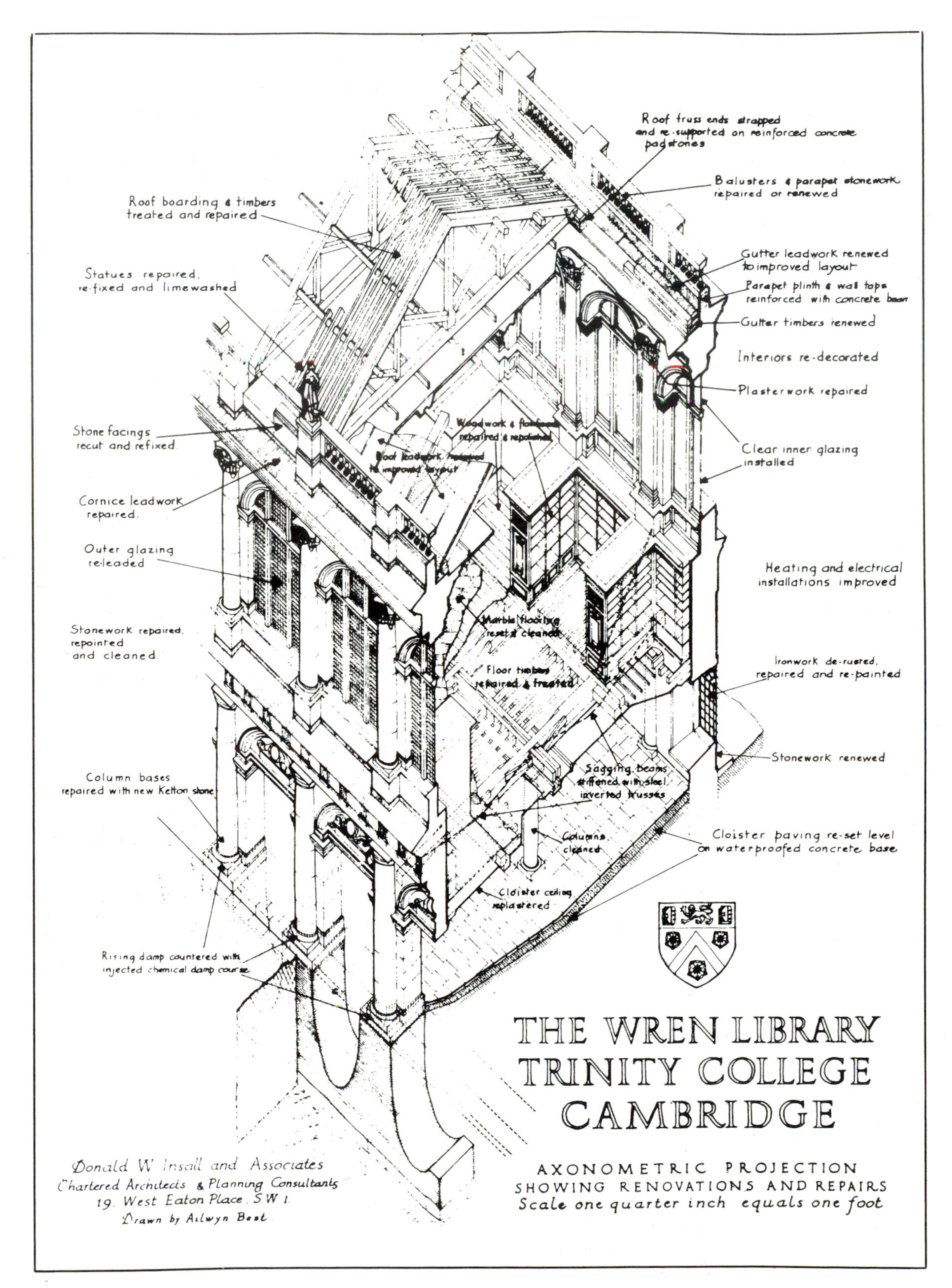

Fig. 24.24 *Repairs to Trinity College, Cambridge, 1974 (architects Donald W. Insall and Associates: engineers John Mason and Partners).*

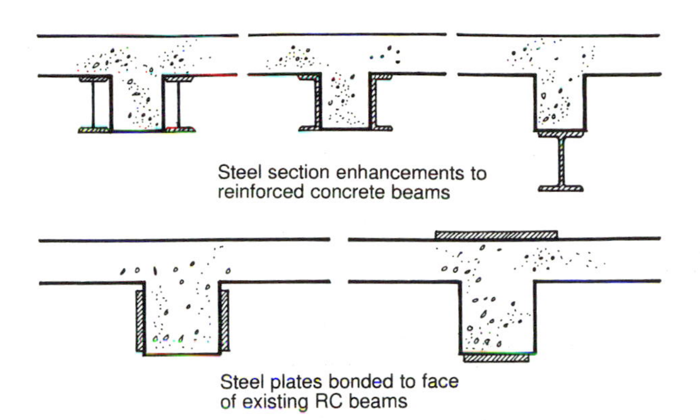

Fig. 24.25 *Methods of bonding steel to concrete beams.*

consultants, testing laboratories etc. may be able to help.

Appropriate remedial action to counter environmental attack depends on the results of a chemical analysis of the concrete. If it can be shown that the problem is caused by inadequate cover to the reinforcement – either physically insufficient cover, or the concrete is porous – allowing the agents of corrosion to attack the steel reinforcement, then the remedy is quite straightforward: any loose concrete must be replaced and a suitable treatment applied to the whole of the exterior surfaces to prevent further attack.

On the other hand, if it is only the concrete which has been attacked and the steel has not been affected or has some corrosion protection such as epoxy coating, galvanizing or stainless steel, then it may be sufficient to make good followed by treatment with a neutralizing agent and a suitable paint finish.

In cases of structural distress or the need to improve load carrying capacity, reinstatement of individual members may be necessary. However, in many cases strengthening can be achieved, either by fixing steel sections adjacent to the reinforced concrete members, or by gluing plates onto the sides or the bottom of the member. Figure 24.25 indicates typical arrangements that can be considered.

The following general advice is given on bonding steel plates to RC work:

(a) Grit/shot blasting is required to both steel and concrete surfaces.
(b) Thickness of binding agent to be as thin as possible.
(c) Stainless steel could be considered where corrosive conditions exist.
(d) Bolting may be needed at plate ends to prevent lifting.
(e) Insufficient data are available at present where concrete profile is inadequate for shear.
(f) Self load of very heavy plating is counter productive.

Another area which has required attention is the upgrading of precast concrete buildings following the Ronan Point disaster in 1968 [6]. This typically involves strengthening precast connections to 'box frame' elements by bolting through angle cleats at weak edges to prevent progressive collapse under accidental loading conditions. A large number of similar system-built high-rise buildings constructed to meet the acute housing shortage of the 1960s have had to be treated. Most of the systems used in the 1960s no longer exist, so it is very difficult to obtain working drawings. The quality of workmanship also left a lot to be desired, and a detailed site investigation is therefore essential.

Considerable doubts have been raised about the viability of bolted angle repairs and the final cost of the remedial work has been estimated at £180 million excluding any allowance for the wholesale demolition that has occurred.

REFERENCES AND TECHNICAL NOTES

1. The use of redundant buildings, *Architects' Journal*, 29 March 1979.
2. Bates, W. (1984) *Historical Structural Steel Handbook*, BCSA publication No. 11/84.
3. *Structural Renovation of Traditional Buildings*, CIRIA Report 111 (1986).
4. Reith, R.D. *Steel Construction Today* December 1990.
5. Sir Mervyn McCartney's drawings of the Dome Repairs, published by the Architectural Press in the 1930s.
6. *Ronan Point London 1968* Building Disasters and Failures by G. Scott (1976) Construction Press Ltd. (Refer to Appendix 2 which gives a extract from the official report.)

FURTHER READING

Highfield, D. (1991) *The Construction of New Buildings Behind Historic Facades*, E & FN Spon.

Cantacuzino, S. (1975) *New Uses for Old Buildings*, Architectural Press.

Reference should also be made to a series of articles by Sam Webb in *Architectural Design* (Jan and August 1969), also *New Civil Engineer* (7th June and 5th and 12th July 1984) and *Building Design* (January 1973) entitled 'Missing the point'.

Details of cladding to St Enoch Square, Glasgow (architects GMW and Reiach and Hall).

Part Five | Secondary Steel Elements

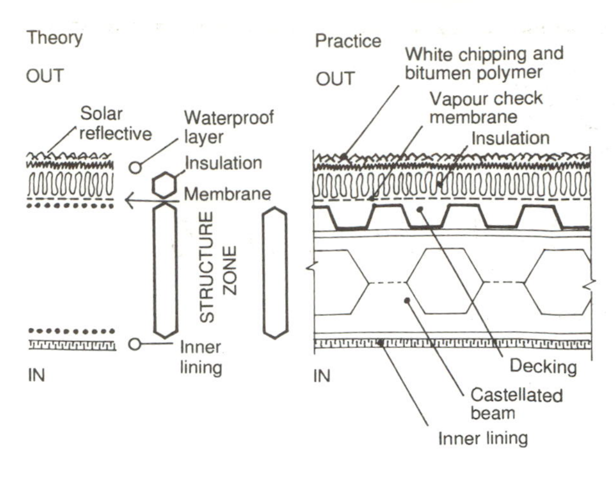

Fig. 25.1 *Zoning: protected frame (roof).*

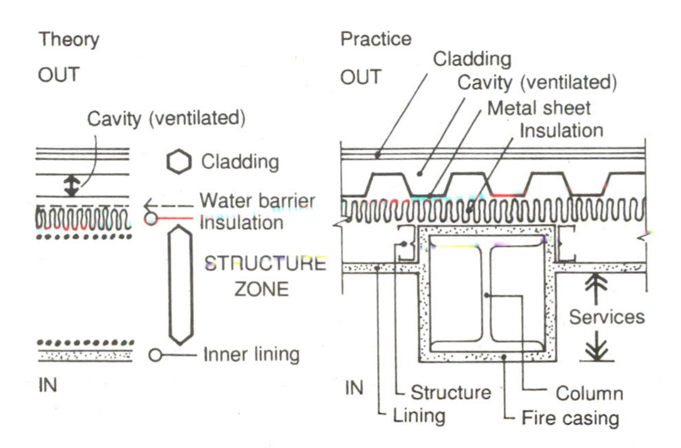

Fig. 25.2 *Zoning: protected frame (wall).*

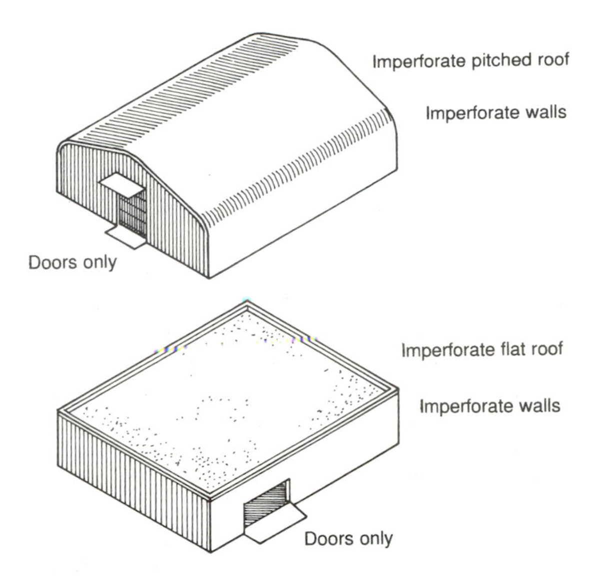

Figs 25.3 and 25.4 *Typical windowless storage buildings.*

25

Principles of cladding

Alan Blanc

25.1 INTRODUCTION

The following Part explores the wider role of steel in the creation of architecture. The discussion proceeds from strategic decisions about the relationship between structure and enclosure to the principles of modern cladding. The final chapters are devoted to consideration of those individual building components commonly made from metal (and steel in particular).

What follows has been distilled from lectures given at the Polytechnic of Central London and North London Polytechnic in the early 1980s. Illustrated notes highlighted basic principles whilst more detailed information and a range of alternative solutions were presented in the form of case studies. The updated material included here has the same intention, that is to enable designers to appraise and select possible approaches rather than seeking copy book answers (the way in which construction textbooks were used in times past). For that reason, nominal sizes are given which will need to be checked by calculation to anticipate the performance of components. Engineering advice will be particularly necessary when establishing the strength of elements in terms of wind resistance.

This opening chapter is concerned with the choice of location for a building's enclosure relative to its structure, that is the 'zones' from external to internal that may be occupied by these elements, how these choices modify details and in general terms the performance required of building envelopes.

An important consideration throughout is that insulation standards in the UK have been increased, altering much of what was standard construction. It is assumed that readers are familiar with methods for calculating the thermal performance of cladding [1]. Requirements for insulation (which are still only a half of what is necessary in Scandinavia), are now:

Walls (domestic and commercial)	0.45 W/m K
Roofs (commercial)	0.45 W/m K
Roofs (domestic)	0.25 W/m K

For further reading, the *Architects' Journal*, the *Architectural Review* and American, French and German magazines where case studies are included are useful sources, as are the general references for the drawing office included at the end of this chapter.

The use of architects' drawings as a reference should never be overlooked. It is worthwhile collecting examples of how others put things together, making a file perhaps called 'Little Things that Matter' [2]. For purposes of comparison, information on work done in Europe or North America is particularly valuable. Architects' detail sheets are published from time to time in the *Architects' Journal* and in times past the *Architect and Building News*. These redrawn details are often incomplete and may be suspect unless one has the chance of seeing the building itself.

Increasingly nowadays, specialist detailing is being sublet on the North American pattern. The architect establishes performance criteria and required shapes and sections, the subcontractor then produces shop drawings referenced back to the original documents. This is not the way that Aalto, Jacobsen or Prouvé detailed their buildings but it is fast becoming the norm.

25.2 ALTERNATIVE RELATIONSHIPS OF FRAME AND ENCLOSURE

25.2.1 Internal frame

This familiar method of construction (Figs 25.1 and 25.2) used for building single storey steel-framed sheds, for example, positions the structural frame internal to the weatherproof enclosure and insulation. The structure may then be either expressed internally or hidden within the internal finished surfaces. In this position, the frame is totally protected from the weather and easily insulated from the possibility of fire and extremes of ambient temperature. Continuity of external enclosure lessens the likelihood of external noise being transmitted into the building through the structure. Similarly, the weatherproofing and insulation form an uninterrupted environmental shield of uniform thermal resistance which minimizes the risk of cold bridging and condensation.

Industrial buildings are often constructed as windowless boxes (Figs 25.3 and 25.4), not only to avoid reliance upon the vagaries of climate for internal daylighting and ventilation (as opposed to the relative consistency of artificial servicing), but also to avoid the problems that result from penetrating the building's environmental enclosure. Windows inevitably form local areas of weakness in a building's thermal performance. Although still unusual in industrial applications, the problem is significantly reduced

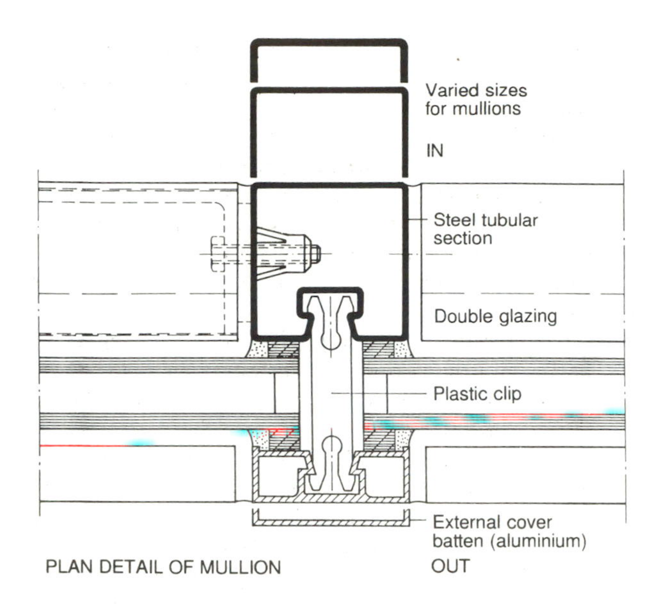

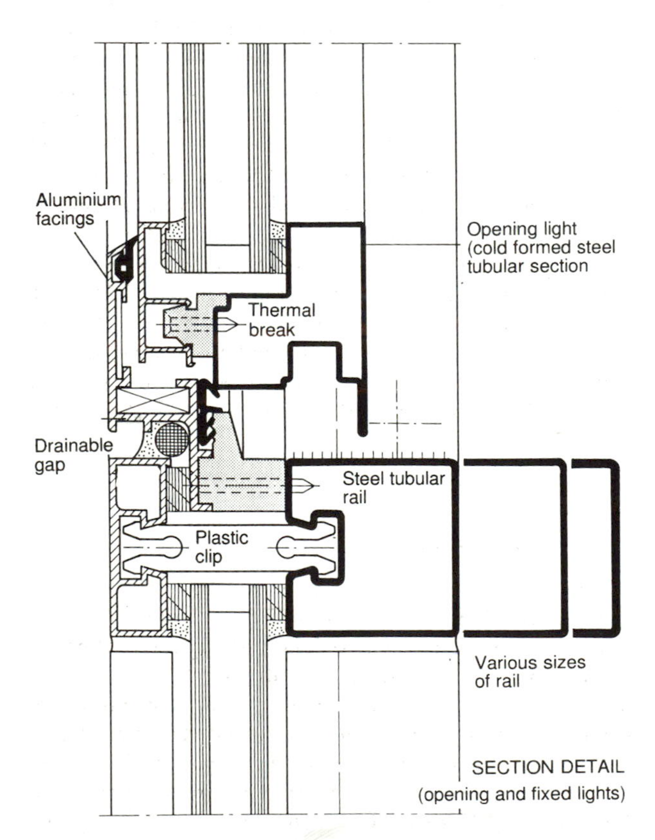

Figs 25.5 and 25.6 *Typical thermal breaks in glazed walls (Swiss 'Jansen' facade system). Printed by kind permission of Jansen AG.*

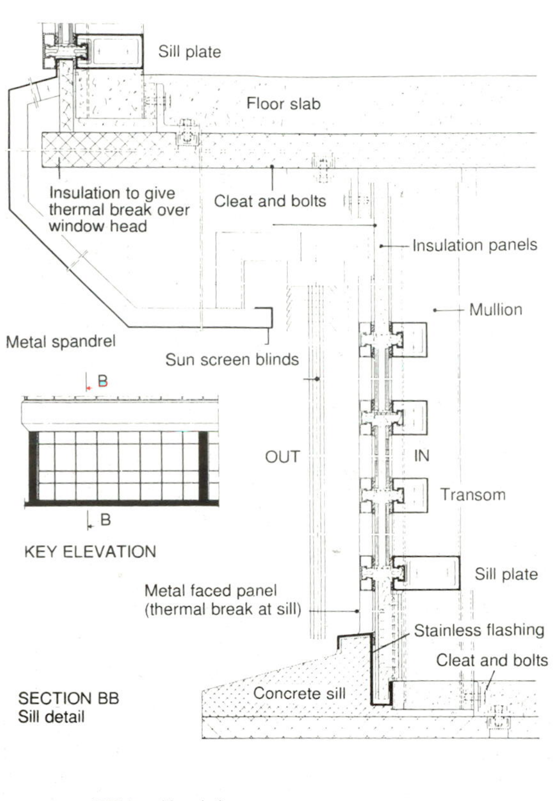

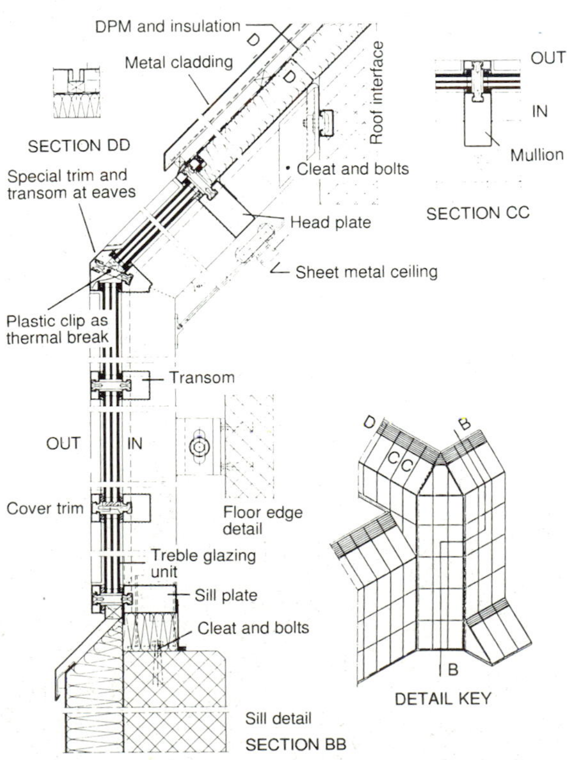

Figs 25.7 and 25.8 *Window to wall interface (Swiss 'Jansen' facade system). Printed by kind permission of Jansen AG.*

Fig. 25.9 *Broadgate phases 1–4, London, 1988 (architect Arup Associates).*

Fig. 25.10 *Portland Public Services Building, Oregon, 1983 (architect Michael Graves).*

frames (Figs 25.5 and 25.6), also thermal insulation between internal and external surfaces where they meet at the edges of windows (Figs 25.7 and 25.8). The illustrations are of a Swiss cladding system designed to present an external surface of consistent thermal performance, thermally broken throughout to eliminate totally continuity of metal parts from inside to outside. Increasingly, facade design is tending towards multi-layered construction with high performance glass skins protected by a layer of screen or sunshade.

The grid of metal sections typical of curtain walling is also associated with the growing use of rain-screen cladding – traditional materials such as ceramic tiles or stone slabs are mechanically fixed off a metal framework, itself attached back to the structure. The final gridded appearance either expresses the underlying structure (Fig. 25.9: Broadgate phases 1–4), or presents an unarticulated decorative surface (Fig. 24.10, Portland Public Services Building).

British Steel and the Brick Development Association's joint publication *Brick Cladding for Steel Framed Buildings* [3] suggests a similar layering, the outer leaf of brickwork being supported on steel shelf angles and providing the weatherproof element of the construction (Figs 25.11 and 25.12). The wet outer skin is isolated by the use of conventional cavity wall details. One might question the logic of supporting a half brick skin off a steel frame and the complexities this entails (refer to chapter 26 for alternative methods of construction).

Some contemporary technologies, such as composite panels with weather-lapped interlocking joints, can be used for both wall and roof construction allowing continuity in the relationship between structure and enclosure (Figs 25.3 and 25.4). Similarly, glazed atria may be detailed to isolate skin, insulation and structure on vertical and sloping planes (Figs 25.13).

25.2.2 Exposed frame

Alternatively, the frame may be exposed externally, either encased or left unclad but containing the volume of the building within it (Fig. 25.14). The cladding and roofing are supported off the secondary structure, which, being smaller in size, places a lesser constraint on the distribution of services than does an internal primary structure. For a similar floor area, a building with an external frame will occupy a larger overall site area than if the frame was internal (Fig. 25.15). This form of construction is consequently best suited to unconfined 'green-field' locations, or city centre sites that front onto public spaces (e.g. the Pompidou Centre in Paris).

The external structure may define a zone also occupied by floor level balcony/walkways that provide ready access for window cleaning and maintenance. They may also be designed to sunshade the facade and to generally lessen its

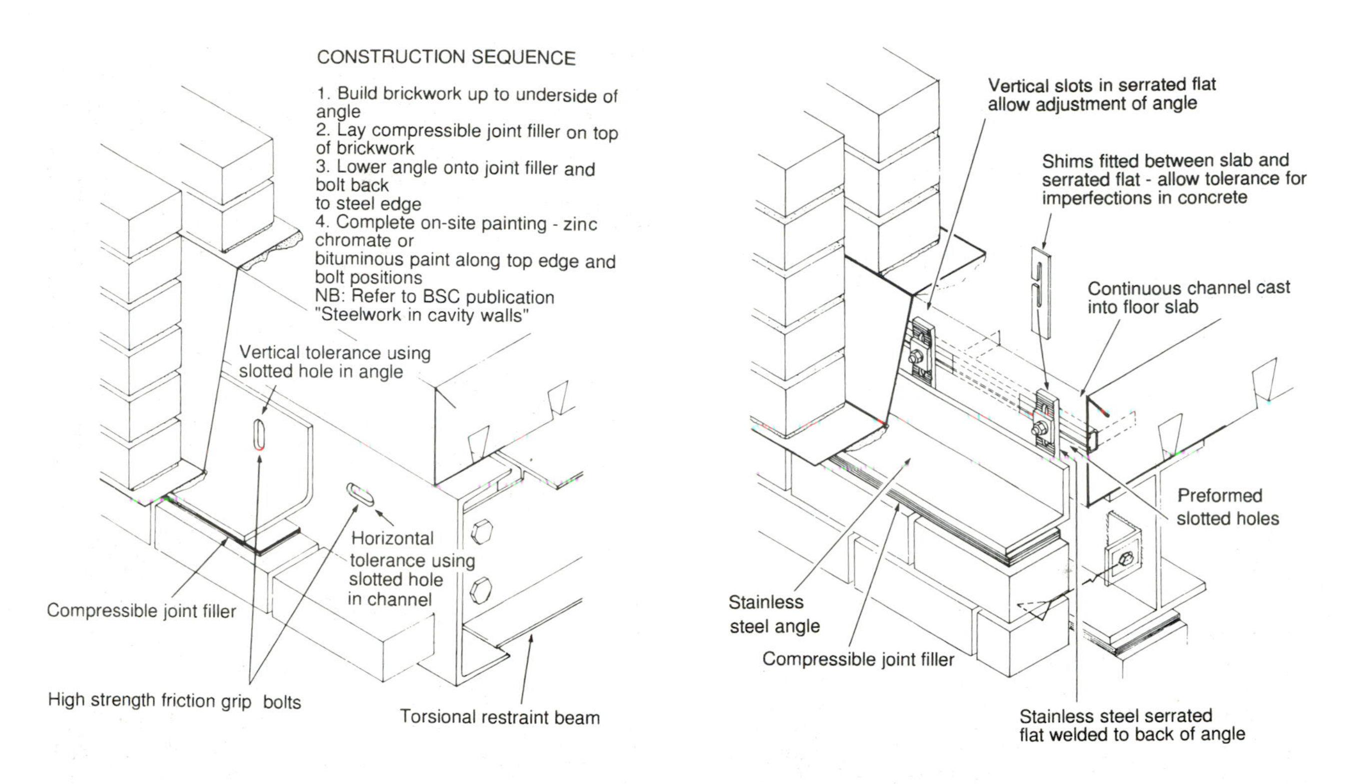

Figs 25.11 and 25.12 *Shelf angles used to tie brick skin to steel frame. Printed by kind permission of BDA.*

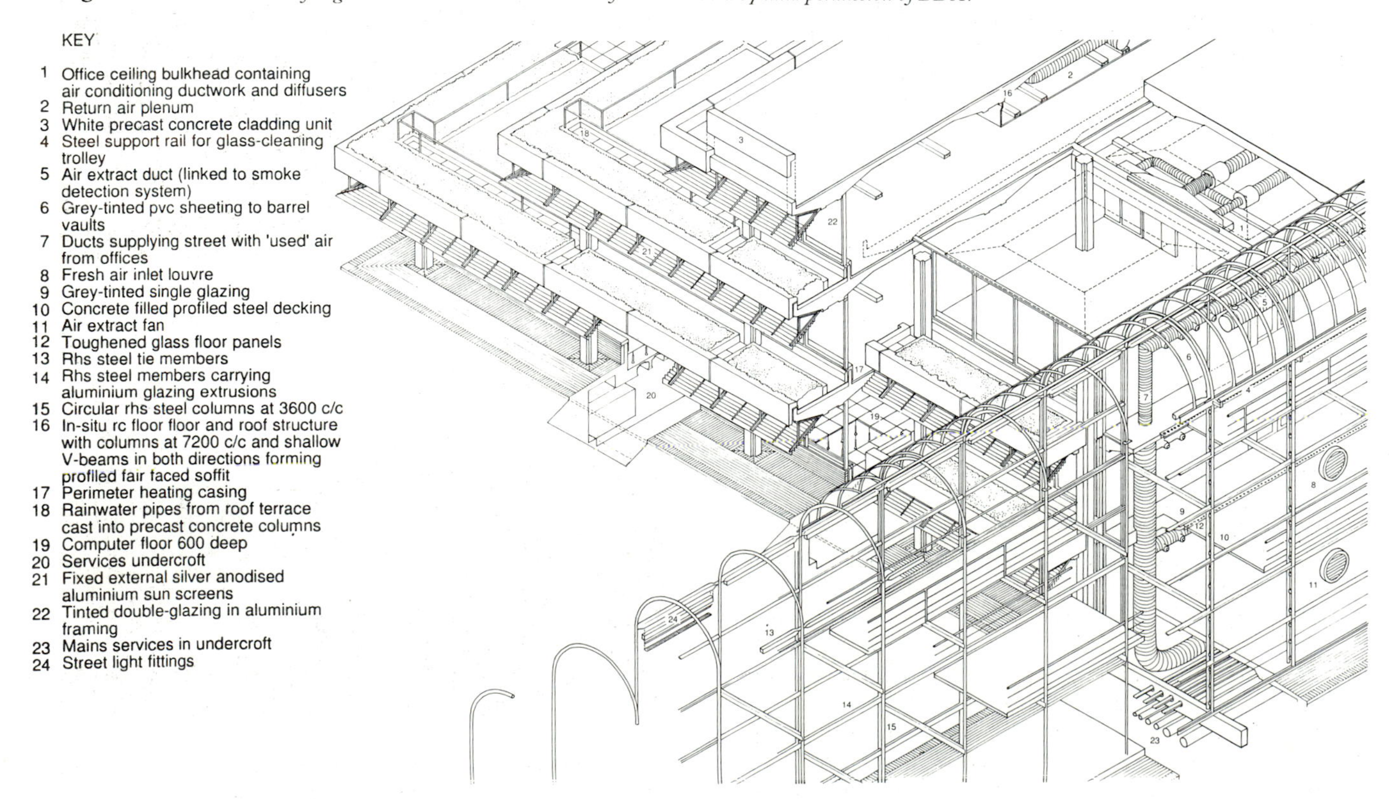

Fig 25.13 *Atria detailing. IBM, Portsmouth, Hampshire, UK, 1982 (architects and engineers Arup Associates).*

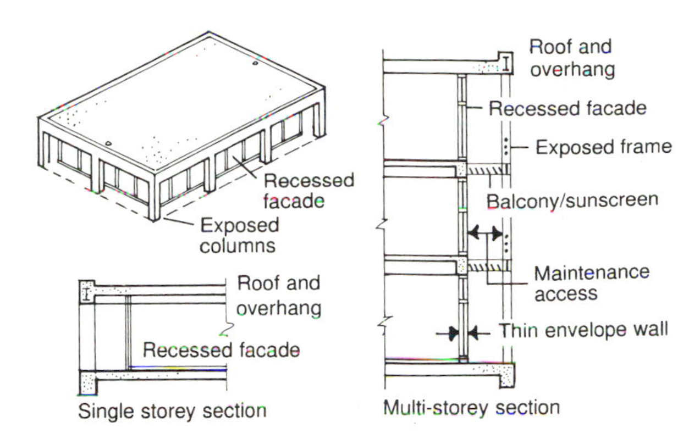

Fig. 25.14 *Exposed frame principles.*

Fig. 25.15 *Boots HQ, Nottingham, UK, 1968 (architects SOM and YRM).*

Figs 25.16 and 25.17 *Contrast in framing principles No. 1 Finsbury Avenue, London, 1985 (architects and engineers Arup Associates) versus the latest phase at Broadgate 1990 (architects and engineers SOM).*

weather exposure by reducing the volume of water running down the face of the building. The requirement for weather resistance may as a consequence be of only domestic proportions. Clearly tall buildings (over 30 m in height) are subject to higher wind speeds and design standards for water exclusion are correspondingly more stringent. Low-rise construction incorporating a three-dimensional facade of structure and walkway sunscreens offers architectural possibilities in terms of elevational modelling (Fig. 25.16) that are absent from the sheer facade treatment so often favoured for the cladding of contemporary buildings (Fig. 25.17).

Exposed steel frames present a number of technical difficulties particularly where beams puncture the waterproof, thermal and acoustic layers of the building envelope. Fire protection of external structural steelwork can be achieved in a variety of ways. Part of the external envelope of the building can be of fire-resistant construction so as to fire-shield external columns and beams. Tubular elements, usually columns (or a diagonal lattice as at Bush Lane House,

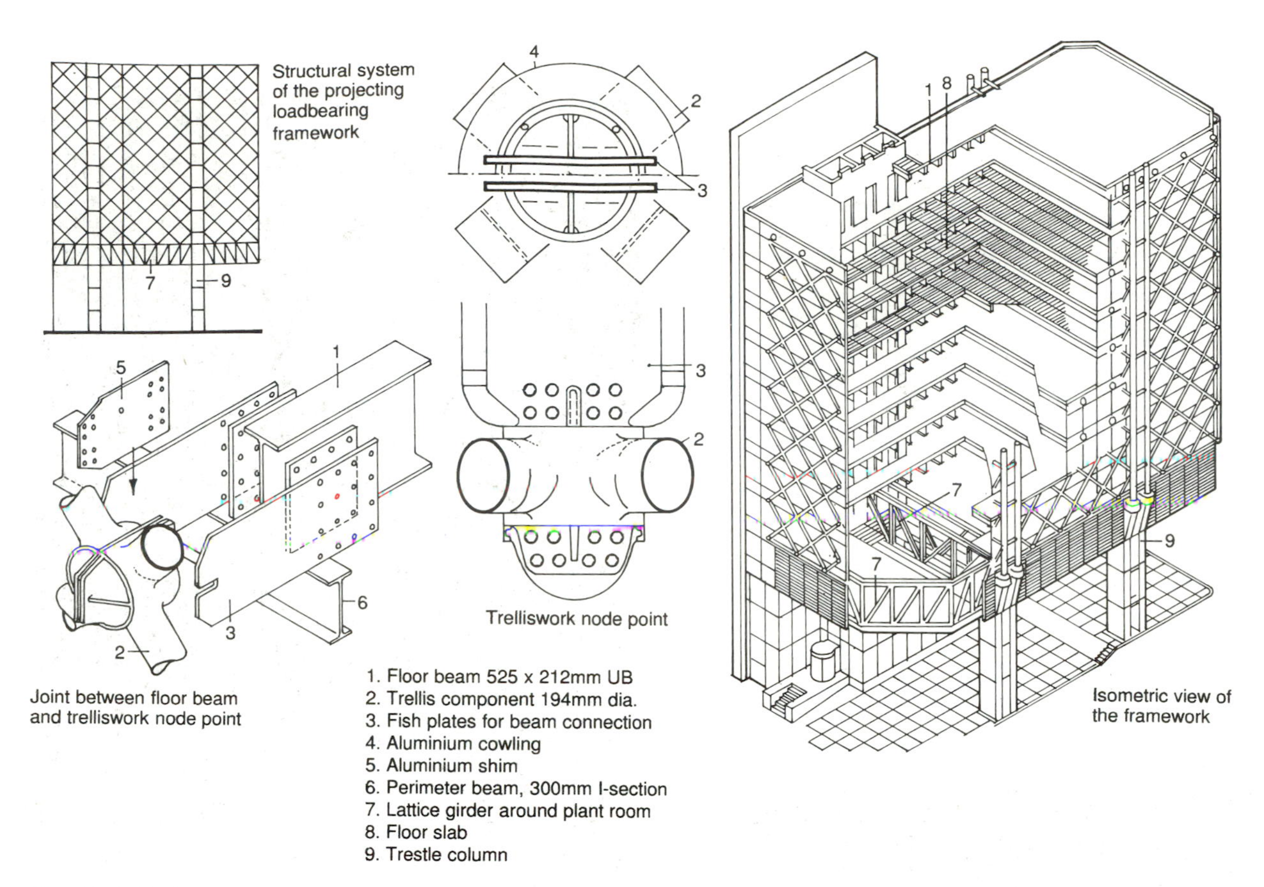

Fig. 25.18 *Bush Lane House, London, 1976 water-filled stainless steel tubular lattice (architects and engineers: Arup Associates).*

Fig. 25.19 *Pompidou Centre, Paris, 1977 (architects Piano and Rogers: engineers Ove Arup and Partners).*

London: Fig. 25.18), may be filled with water and as a result kept cool should fire break out. Another possibility is a system employing dry encasement to shield areas of exposed steel, according to the distance between the structure and the facade and its orientation relative to the building (see Fig. 25.19: frame elements at the Pompidou Centre).

Alternatively, a dry encasement system may cope with both corrosion protection and fire resistance (Fig. 25.20: Alcoa Building, San Francisco). Recent developments in intumescent paint technology now allow external painted steelwork to have up to four hours' fire resistance (extensively used at Nicholas Grimshaw's Sainsbury's store, Camden Town, London Fig. 25.21).

25.2.3 Mixed construction

There are many instances where exposed and protected structure both occur within a single building, for example the umbrella frames designed by Foster Associates for the Renault Centre in Swindon, UK. The umbrellas penetrate the roof, standing partly above and partly below it, and local environmental control is achieved by heaters that reduce the likelihood of condensation (Fig. 25.22).

Much now historic architecture from the 'heroic period' of modernism was undermined by building failures, Mies

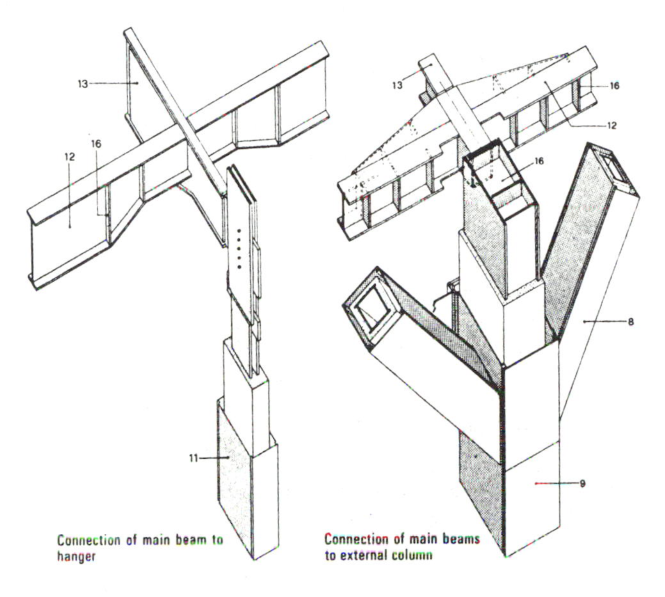

8, 9 and 11 casings in aluminium, 12 edge beams, 13 main beams, 16 stiffening plates.

Fig. 25.20 *Alcoa Building, San Francisco, 1968 (architect SOM).*

van der Rohe's IIT campus, Chicago for example (Fig. 25.23). Despite a climate that ranges in temperature from 30°C in summer to –15°C in winter, solid brick wall panels were bedded in mastic against naked rolled steel sections. This resulted in extreme thermal movement, chronic overheating and floods of condensation in winter. Van der Rohe was eventually sacked for his intransigence in technical matters; the textbook for IIT construction technology should be regarded as a primer for disaster [4].

Fig. 25.21 *Sainsbury's at Camden, 1989 (architects Nicholas Grimshaw and Partners: engineers Kenchington Little and Partners).*

Fig. 25.22 *Renault Centre, Swindon, 1984 (architects Foster Associates: engineers Ove Arup and Partners).*

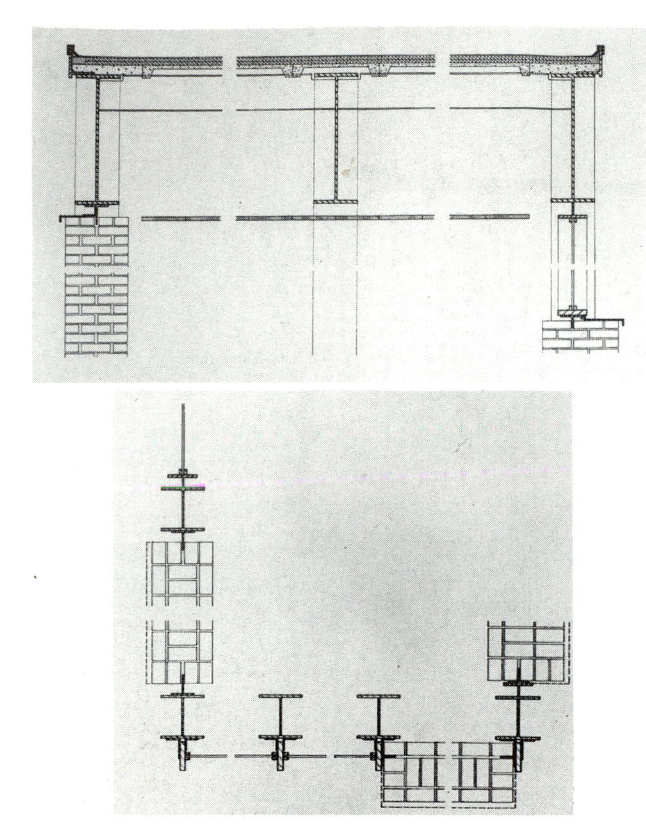

Fig. 25.23 *Mies van der Rohe.* Illinois Institute of Technology Library and Administration Building, *1944–1945. Chicago, Illinois. Structural details. Sections. Ink on illustration board, 30 × 40″ (76.1 × 101.5 cm). Mies van der Rohe Archive, The Museum of Modern Art, New York. Gift of the architect.*

Steelwork is probably the best material for a frame structure that is to penetrate the outer building envelope; the alternatives are difficult to detail at the meeting of wet and dry – timber rots [5], and concrete is liable to become saturated with interstitial condensation [1]. The conduction of heat and sound through steel structures is the major problem to be addressed when detailing the junction between frame and environmental enclosure.

By way of illustration, consider a house designed by one of Britain's most famous architects for his parents. The experimental design dates from the early 1960s and was intended as a prototype for mass production. Elegant portal frames are exposed just within the fully glazed gable end walls. The house is open plan so that each morning, at the corner steel stanchions, the warm and humid air of the previous evening has condensed into pools of water that are mopped up with the accompanying remark – 'This is the cost of genius'. Other than in the tropics where there may be little difference between internal and external temperatures, structure that coincides with or crosses the outer walls of the building is likely to be subject to the design problems outlined above.

25.3 CLADDING MATERIALS

The range of available materials is bewildering. The following advice is offered in the form of a Designer's Checklist for use when choosing a weatherproof cladding. An outline schedule of the principal techniques concludes this chapter. A distinction between lightweight and heavyweight methods is made in sections 25.4.2 and 25.4.3: reference should be made to chapter 26 for a more detailed discussion.

25.3.1 Lightweight weatherproof versus weather shedding

(a) First concept: the upturned boat

An ideal weatherproof specification for both roofs and walls may be difficult to achieve. A continuous envelope is in theory possible using plastic coatings such as bitumen polymer or synthetic rubber. On steeply sloping or vertical surfaces these materials creep, making it difficult to maintain an adequate bond (Fig. 25.24).

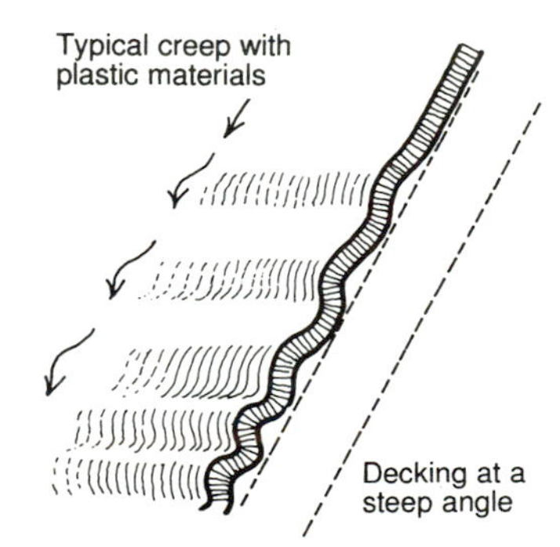

Fig. 25.24 *Creep with elastic coatings.*

(b) Second concept: the shed roof

Alternatively, different specifications might be used for wall and roof construction. Materials in watertight layers are ideal for flat roofing. Careful detailed design is necessary at junctions with the eaves or parapet which have greater exposure to weather than the wall below. At these points the possibility of water entering the building requires damp-proof courses or other 'second lines of defence' designed to shed water back to the outside. The differing performance requirements of roofs and walls are in part a function of the differing extent of rainwater flowing over them. Roofs are totally exposed from any direction whereas the degree to which a facade is vulnerable depends upon its orientation, if protection is provided by roof overhangs or if the elevation is broken up storey by storey with balconies or screens (Fig. 25.25). In these alternative ways, walls can be sheltered from the full severity of the weather, a function traditionally performed by a building's roof, its eaves forming an umbrella over the walls.

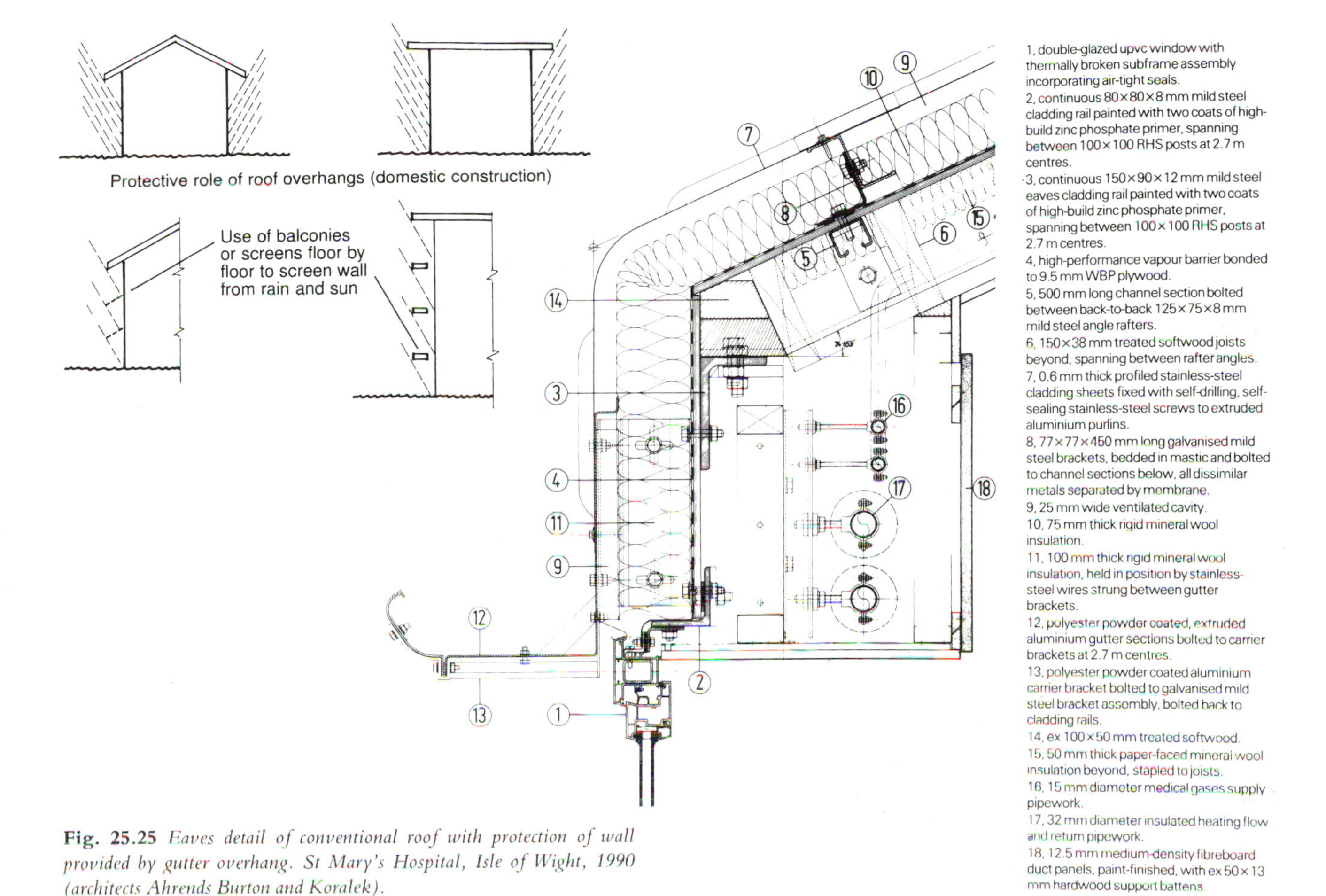

Fig. 25.25 *Eaves detail of conventional roof with protection of wall provided by gutter overhang. St Mary's Hospital, Isle of Wight, 1990 (architects Ahrends Burton and Koralek).*

(c) Third concept: wrap around panels

A wide range of cladding components are available for use on both walls and roofs, for example, silicone bonded glass (although still only in its infancy for roofing purposes), patent glazing, composite metal panels and some forms of rain screen panel. The designer can then, using the same material, make the transition from horizontal to vertical plane, an alternative strategy to conventional roofing (Fig. 25.25).

This technology relies upon mastics, sealants and gaskets which, mainly due to ultraviolet degradation, have an anticipated life shorter than would be required of the building as a whole. The original design must envisage the method by which these elements will be replaced with the minimum of disruption to the building's users. Roof repairs may necessitate installation of a temporary roof above the building whereas wall repairs may simply require internal screens and external polythene whilst the work is in progress.

The conventional method, the 'shed roof', will be much cheaper to maintain unless the building envelope is to be expendable after around 20 years or if it is intended to be upgraded (just as building services or interiors are stripped out and changed at intervals). At the present time buildings from the 1950s and 1960s are being totally reclad [6]. The cost of a sophisticated 'rain-screen' facade is now as much as 40% of the building total, and this may deter owners from writing off such an expensive item when the building has reached only a third of its expected life.

Impervious facades are more easily detailed for use on the vertical plane and have fewer inherent waterproofing problems than when sloping. Panels may be jointed mechanically with compressible neoprene gaskets that entail a 'precise fit' rather than short life and relatively imprecise mastics. The system should incorporate drainage cavities designed to anticipate localized failures.

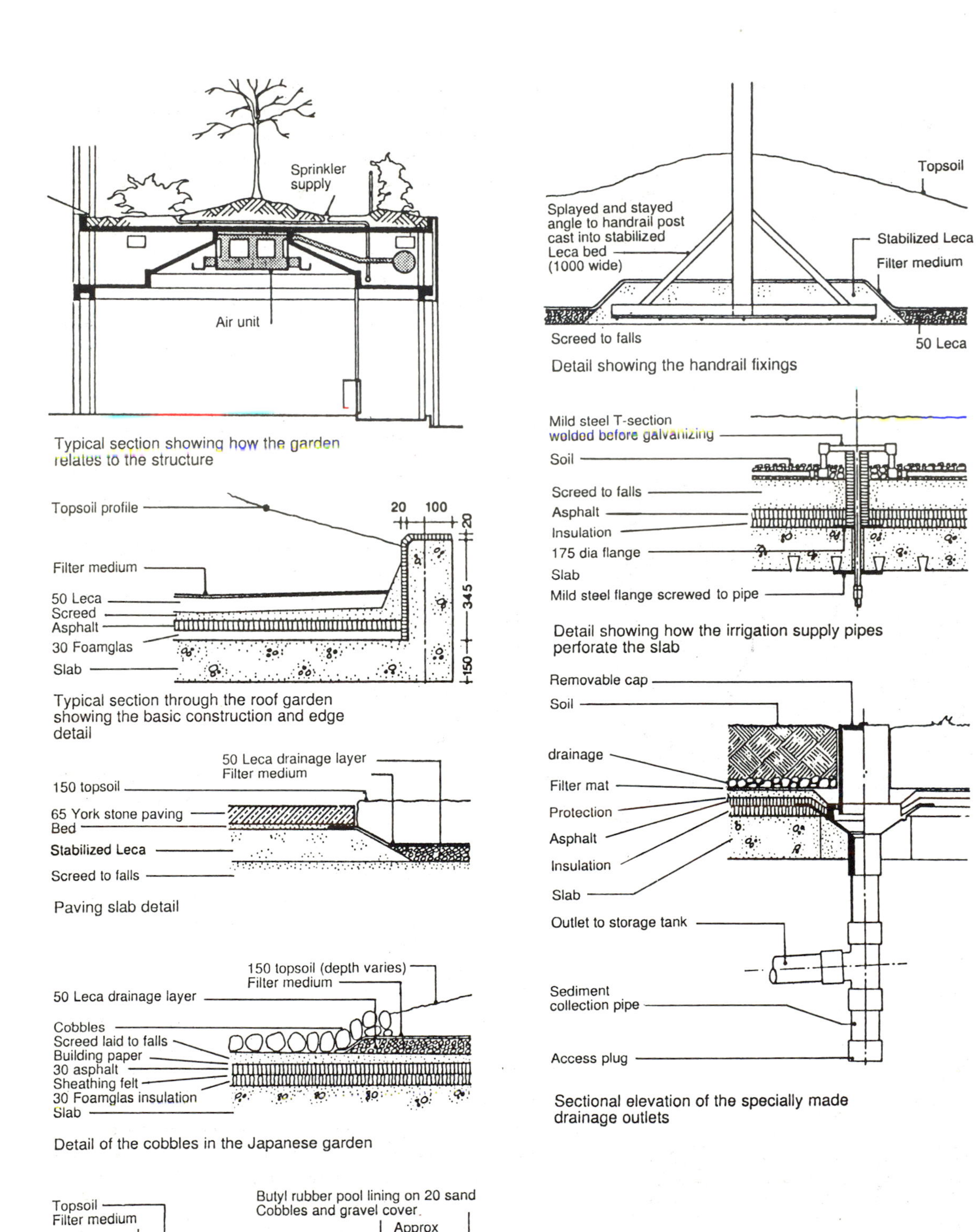

Fig. 25.26 *Ecological roof: Wiggins Teape, Basingstoke, 1980, phase 2 (architects and engineers: Arup Associates).*

25.3.2 Heavyweight and weather absorbing

(a) First concept: ecological roof

As an alternative to lightweight construction, there is now much interest in combining the advantages of framed structure with the environmental benefits of carefully disposed thermal mass. The 'ecological' or 'green' roof, now commonplace in Continental Europe, is usually an upturned tray comprising waterproof, insulating and drainage layers and a sufficient thickness of soil to serve as a thermal and rainwater reservoir (Fig. 25.26).

Because the deadweight of frozen soil is equivalent to that of concrete, commercially available systems employ mixtures of peat and sand to reduce the loads imposed upon the supporting structure (Figs 25.27 and 25.28).

Fig. 25.27 *Swiss installation with minimal peat/sand roof covering.*

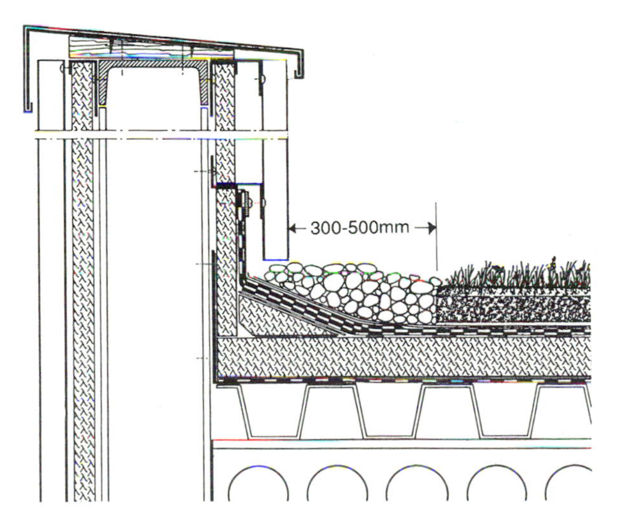

Fig. 25.28 *Proprietary material used over metal decking (Erisco Bauder System). Printed by kind permission of Erisco Bauder plc.*

(b) Second concept: thermal storage walls

A related notion has guided the design of Richard Horden's Office Building at Stag Place in London. At the rear of the all-glass atrium is to be a heavy masonry wall, utilizing the dry thermal capacity of heavyweight construction so as to reduce the building's energy consumption (Fig. 25.29 and 25.30). Another version of this idea is to be found at Grays Inn, where office extensions have been built with an internal steel frame totally isolated from the enclosing minimally-glazed, brick-box envelope. This ensures a good standard of acoustic as well as thermal insulation and permits the owner to remodel the interior spaces without having to alter the exterior facade (Fig. 25.31).

25.3.3 Stresses caused by movement

The difficulty of reconciling the movement of a building's structure with the design of its elevations has led to some spectacular failures. One of the most infamous, the Hancock Tower in Boston, swayed so much that fixings were loosened and window panes sent crashing to the ground. The Hearts of Oak Headquarters in London's Euston Road has projecting facades suspended from steel hangers: differential thermal expansion as the sun moved around the building caused sufficient cracked glazing as to eventually require its complete refenestration.

The causes of movement within buildings can be summarized as follows:

Sway. This elastic movement may be compared to the oscillation of a pendulum, sway can also be rotational. The total movement out of the vertical may be 1/500 of the height. Over a single floor-to-floor height of 4 m, this may amount to a deflection of 8 mm.

Edge beam deflection. Building Codes permit 1/350 of the span, for example 20 mm for an edge beam spanning 7 m.

Settlement. The differential settlement of tall buildings, over 18 storeys, can often be 20 mm.

Thermal expansion. Thermal movement most severely affects the external faces of south, east and west elevations.

Chemical expansion. Some materials, most notably clay brickwork and limestone, expand over time as a result of chemical reaction with atmospheric moisture.

When detailing the elements of a facade, the category of movement which is of greatest concern is structural movement; failure to make allowance for it will result in the cracking, fracture or loosening of components. The scale of movement can be extreme (earthquakes) or three-dimensional like a vortex (wind induced sway in towers, Fig. 25.32) or non-reversible (shrinkage of concrete elements or expansion of clay brick and mortar construction [3]. Engineering input is needed when designing all forms of cladding that are to withstand structural movements, particularly when employing the most sophisticated of current methods – a 'cladding truss' – to brace the facade.

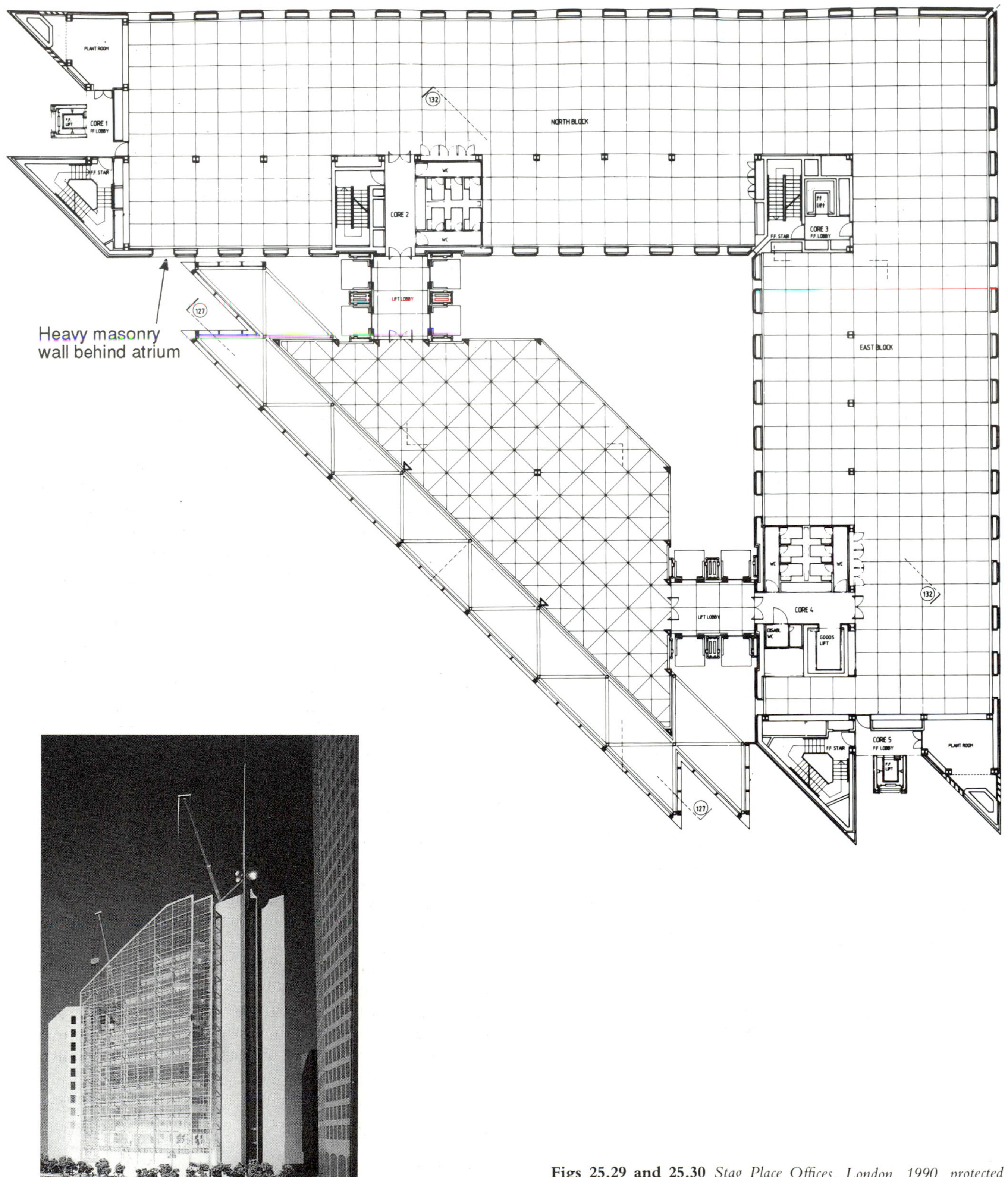

Figs 25.29 and 25.30 *Stag Place Offices, London, 1990, protected masonry wall used for thermal storage (architect Richard Horden).*

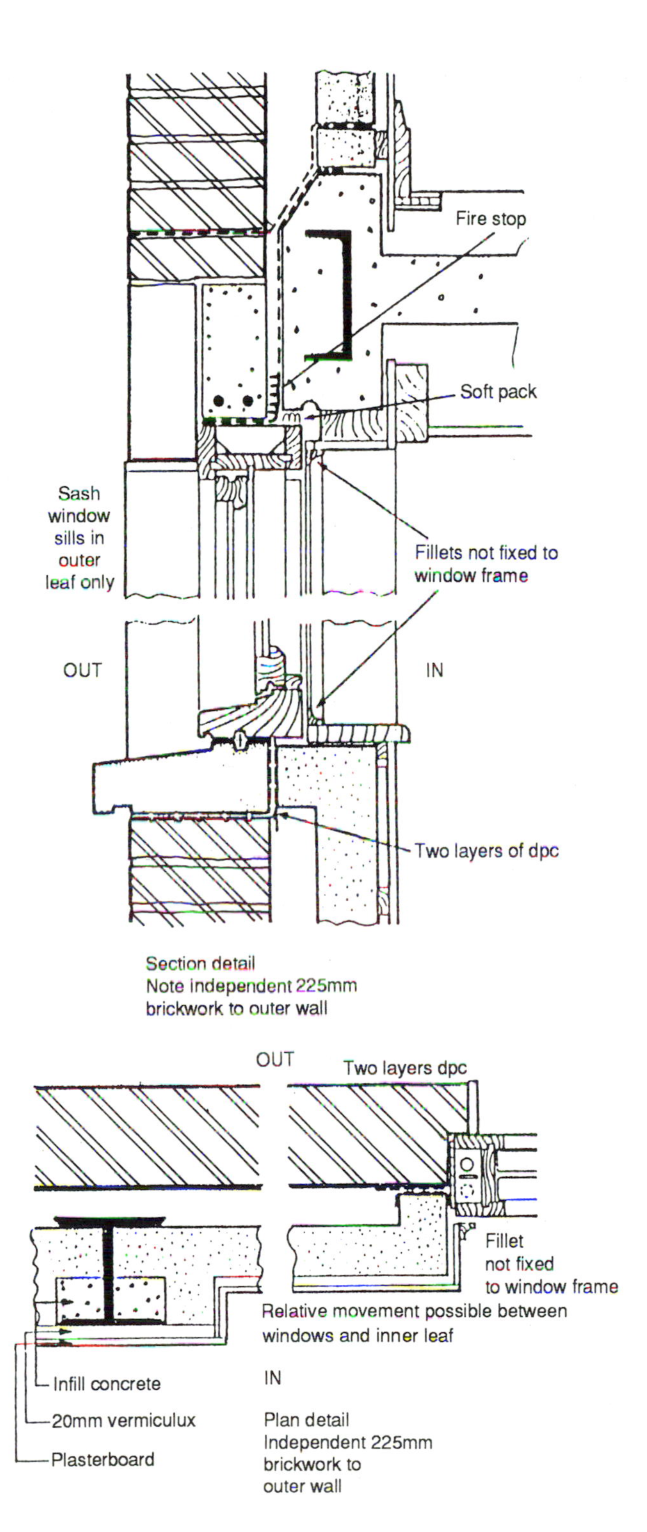

Fig. 25.31 *Extension to Grays Inn Chambers, London (architect Troupe, Steel and Scott).*

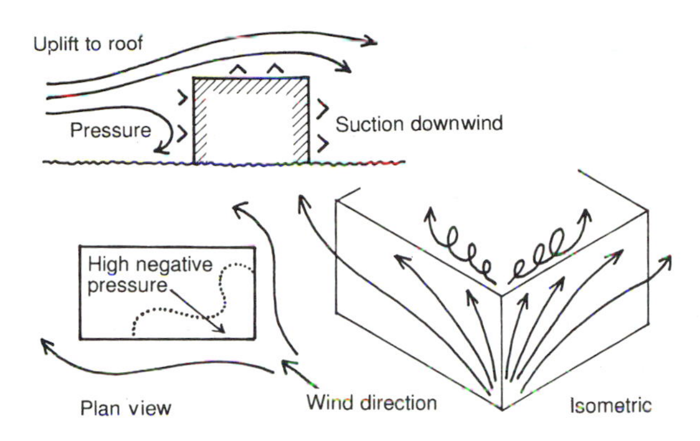

Fig. 25.32 *Vortex movements.*

(See the forthcoming textbook *Steel Trusses in Building Envelopes*, to be published by the Steel Construction Institute).

The likely effects of thermal movement are more difficult to assess, depending as they do upon the extent of exposure or overshadowing and the colour of surface materials (dark tones being absorbent and lighter ones reflective). The tables in *Principles of Modern Buildings* (Vol. 1, p 184) give proportional figures, obviously the selection of materials with comparable coefficients of thermal expansion will minimize the likelihood of differential movement (see Further Reading).

Buildings do not face only in one direction, however, and movement of the sun causes each elevation to be stressed in turn although the south to south-westerly aspect of a frame will generally be at a higher temperature than the rest.

Metal brackets with slotted holes may eventually corrode, giving a 'friction hold' instead of the 'sliding fix' that was intended. The present quest for perfectly aligned profiled cladding may prove an impossible goal to achieve over the long term. The weatherbeaten appearance of ageing aircraft (like the 1940s Dakotas that are still flying) gives a more realistic impression of the future appearance of 'Hi-Tech' metal panels than does the frontispiece of glossy brochures.

Essentially thermal movement cannot be resisted: thin panels will buckle and deform under thermal stress, ribbing or curving the surface of a panel masks deformation but never prevents it. The extent of thermal movements may require the use of mastic sealants between cladding components to prevent joints from opening in winter. Although sealants subject to movement stress fail faster than others (the most vulnerable being those directly exposed to solar radiation), unanticipated contraction can cause gasketted joints to completely disassemble.

25.3.4 Compatibility

Traditionalists like Charles Holden addressed this problem in a remarkable way. At the Senate House, Russell Square,

Fig. 25.33 *Senate House, London 1936 (architect Charles Holden: engineer Travers Morgan).*

London dating from 1936 [7], the bookstack has a steel frame supporting the imposed loads, whilst the external walls are self-supporting and made from ashlar (Portland stone facing backed with Cattybrook engineering bricks). Five hundred years life was required of the envelope, whilst the steel frame may be replaced at an earlier date if warranted by corrosion or fire damage (Fig. 25.33). Holden selected his materials according to the compatibility of the particular brick and stone (which have similar characteristics of moisture and thermal movement), contrasting with the resiliance of steelwork and its differing movements. This approach is unusual, but it suggests that because steel is not only a suitable material for the frame of a building but also steel fixings are the usual attachments for lightweight cladding, almost fully compatible construction can now be achieved.

A recent technical advance is spring loading of the subframe so that facade elements can respond to movement and help dampen it (alleviating the oscillations that loosened the glass of the Hancock Tower, Boston, and more recently damaged the Hancock Tower, Chicago).

A usual criterion for compatibility is the performance of differing materials in the presence or progressive absence of moisture, (refer to *Principles of Modern Building*, Vol. 1, p. 187 onwards), for example the gradual expansion of brick/stone or shrinkage of concrete. Another significant problem is corrosion when dissimilar materials are adjacent in the presence of water. This can occur for example when rainwater washes off the surface of limestone or marble onto sandstone causing it to erode.

Bimetallic corrosion is one of the most serious problems facing the designer of metal cladding systems [8]. In an ideal world, like metals should only be used with like. Simplistically this would mean that a duralumin framed greenhouse would be 'dural' throughout. The reality, however, is that ironmongery is often plastic coated steel, and steel holding plates are stainless or coated steel (for strength) but isolated by washers to prevent bimetallic contact. This consideration profoundly affects the sophisticated detailing of metal cladding. The completed assembly may include stainless steel or powder coated aluminium weather-shielding components, coupled to galvanized internal framing (with plastic sheathed bolts and washers), itself attached to the painted steel structure. Detailing has to ensure that moisture is kept within 'single metal' contact. Site precautions have to be carefully supervised to avoid the inadvertent use of incorrect fixing screws or bare metal edges (not touched up with paint) that may in future jeopardize the metalwork's protection from corrosion.

25.3.5 Fire resistance

The standard of fire resistance required of an elevation is dictated by its location (distance from a boundary), building use and building size. The principles affecting selection of cladding are surface spread of flame and the ability of the total construction (floor, frame and spandrel) to prevent fire spreading from one floor to the next. Steel, whether painted, galvanized or stainless, is frequently used for securing cladding back to the structure because of its proven strength and its incombustibility (but the fire protection of all steel components has to be carefully considered).

25.3.6 Maintenance

Replacement costs for facade cladding have already been mentioned. A day-to-day aspect of maintenance is routine external cleaning, as much a problem for traditional as for non-traditional materials. The cleaning of Portland stone-faced elevations in London is a familiar aspect of city life; the Festival Hall for example is cleaned every 10 years and the Shell Centre every 20 years. The terrazzo clad Dorchester Hotel is washed on a regular five-year basis but the smooth, shiny, metallic facings of today are best cleaned at the same time as the windows. No material, however smooth, is self-cleaning; the modern urban cocktail of pollutants contains diesel fumes, dust and the gases and by-products of petrol combustion. Particularly problematic are sites in the vicinity of airports where kerosene is dumped by planes coming in to land. As an illustration, after a fall of snow in Richmond Park, white rapidly turns to grey/brown in great swathes.

Materials in an urban environment that are not regularly cleaned become coated with a glutinous oil-based dirt. This can only be shifted with a water spray and perhaps detergent if surfaces are to stay bright and clean (for example glass, metals and plastic), or true to their original colour (polished stone, terrazzo or tile).

Some local authorities ask established window cleaning firms to confirm that a proposed building can be cleaned safely. It is good practice for designers to obtain a written report on cleaning techniques to be used and the type of equipment required before a scheme is finalized. The limitations of track layout for suspended gondolas can be a constraint upon a building's shape and affect the initial cost of its cleaning installation. In practice there are three methods of facade cleaning: firstly, operatives working from permanent balconies or gantries, floor by floor, using harnesses attached to track (as used at the New Zealand Government Building, Haymarket, London); secondly, gondolas (with or without operatives) that travel down vertical tracks contained within window mullions (Vickers Tower, Millbank, London); or thirdly, cranes with mobile gondolas for complex, curved and sloping surfaces (Lloyds Building, London).

Traditionalists will point out that brickwork needs little maintenance. Experience of pre-war London brick buildings suggests that after about 50 years, repointing becomes necessary, requiring full scaffolding unless the building originally incorporated anchor bolts for track and cradles. The tower blocks of the Ronan Point era have proved massively expensive to maintain, as they have to be scaffolded top to bottom to reseal mastic joints or repair concrete panels. Of course this was not a consideration when the initial construction budgets were fixed.

25.4 GUIDE TO DRY LIGHTWEIGHT CLADDING

Refer to chapters 26, 27 and 31 for details, the following schedules outlining materials and listing their main applications.

Type	*Material*	*Application*
Corrugated and trapezoidal metal sheet	Steel (coated) Stainless steel Aluminium (coated)	Walls and roofing
Insulated forms of above, termed composite panels	Ditto with foamed cores – polyurethane or polyisocyanurate	Ditto, can incorporate built-in windows or roof lights
Laid up panels	Steel (coated) Stainless steel Aluminium (coated) Copper with cores of wood fibre cement/cement glass fibre	Walls and roofing
Glass	Usually double/triple glazed with thermally broken framing (steel/stainless steel/aluminium/plastic subframes)	Vertical walling some suitable for pitched application
Acrylic/polycarbonate	Ditto	Commonly used in barrel vault or pyramid form for roofing
Bonded glass	Toughened with silicone joints and steel/stainless clips and struts/suspenders	Vertical walling and roofing
Patent glazing	Steel or aluminium T-shaped bars with glazing (single or multiple)	Vertical walling and roofing
Rain-screen facades (a new term for facade systems that may incorporate a range of materials fixed to a metal frame). Also used for upgrading old facades	Materials as described above and also ceramic tiles, stone veneer slabs	Vertical walling and roofing

25.5 HEAVYWEIGHT (PRECAST OR 'TRADITIONAL') CLADDING

Precast cladding

Precast assemblies	Precast concrete with factory applied finishes and veneers (tile, stone or brick). Also available factory glazed and in plain plank form for industrial cladding	Walls

Heavyweight 'traditional' construction

Brick veneer	Brick usually in half brick veneer carried on shelf angles – often used in conjunction with a lightweight blockwork inner skin	Walls

Brick-box	One brick (or thicker) masonry box to provide environmental screen to building (external to frame)	Walls
Factory built brickwork	Jigged and reinforced brick panels (supported on shelf angles). Inner leaf blockwork or other materials	Walls
Ashlar	Traditional masonry-wall usually 225 mm (9 in) or 340 mm (13 in) thick comprising solid stone and brick backing (commonly used technology – pre-1939)	Walls
In situ reinforced concrete	Used for fire encasement and infill, aerated concrete being used for panels (wall and roof) to lighten dead loads. Inner leaf – blockwork or other materials	Walls and roofs. Needs over-cladding to meet performance requirements (rain and thermal resistance)

25.6 CONCLUSION

This chapter has sought to identify the variety of approaches that can be adopted when designing contemporary cladding systems, and also the considerations of building science that govern the relationship of building enclosure and building structure.

Some of these notions date from lunch time conversations back in 1952 when Walter Segal began studies for a small modular factory [9]. Plans, sections, detailed construction and elevational ideas were developed simultaneously on small squares of paper, forming a basis for dialogue with clients or anyone else interested in the art of construction. The dialogue continued until all matters were settled.

The Segal concept of a 'flow and return' in ideas is possible with small study groups but writing the script beforehand makes the process into a monologue. My request is that you do answer back, try other theories, test them out, develop alternative details – in essence, work from first principles rather than trusting in recipes.

REFERENCES AND TECHNICAL NOTES

1. Interstitial condensation. Refer to *Condensation in Dwellings*, Part 1, Ministry of Public Building and Works: *A Design Guide* London, HMSO (1970); Part 2, Department of the Environment: *Remedial Measures* London, HMSO (1971).
2. *Little Things that Matter: to Those That Build*, a delightful textbook by Edwin Gunn on traditional construction of the 1920s. Published by the Architectural Press, 1925.
3. Refer to Bradshaw, Buckton and Tonge (1986) *Brick Cladding for Steel Framed Buildings*, joint publication by the Brick Development Association and British Steel.
4. The IIT Archives . . . a reprint of the course technology as devised by Mies van der Rohe and others, titled *Mies van der Rohe, Architect as Educator*, edited by Kevin P. Harrington, University of Chicago Press (1989).
5. House at Halland 1938 by Serge Chermayeff. The Jarrah frame rotted where passing from inside to open air below the first floor roof and had to be partly replaced after 25 years.
6. Refurbished Frames. Typical examples from the late 1980s include Alexander Fleming House (Erno Goldfinger 1962/66) which may be totally reclad in metal interlocking panels.
7. Refer to *A Qualitive Study of Some Buildings in the London Area*, HMSO Special Report No. 33 (1964) by Hope Bagenal and others, chapter 11. The whole book is worth studying as it involves London buildings that were about 30–50 years old.
8. Refer to *Corrosion and its Prevention at Bimetallic Contacts*, Admiralty, War Office and Ministry of Aviation Inter-Service Metallurgical Research Council, HMSO (1963). A most useful guide drawn up by the Air Force and Navy from experience with aircraft frames and boat hulls.
9. The Premier Pickle Factory Refer to *Architects' Journal*, 2.10.58, pp 493/500 and 25.8.65, p. 432 and 1.9.65, p. 494, also *Architect's Working Details*, Architectural Press, editor Colin Boyne, Vol. 7, 1960, pp 34/35 and pages 94/95. This choice of a simple factory envelope with glazed monitor lights is chosen as it illustrates the way technology rapidly dates, the building at the time was an elegant solution to the constructional problems but today it would *not comply* with the structural or thermal requirements of the Building Regulations. This shows the difficulty in using ideas 30 years old and out of their original context.

FURTHER READING

For further reading, the *Architects' Journal*, the *Architectural Review* and American, French and German magazines where case studies are included are useful sources, as are the following:

Building Regulations

The Building Regulation Explained and Illustrated, by Vincent Powell Smith and M. J. Billington, Collins 9th edition (1992).

Principles of Building

Principles of Element Design (1977) by Peter Rich, George Godwin Ltd.

Principles of Modern Building, Vols 1 and 2, HMSO (1959).

Materials for Building, Vols 1–4, 1972–76 by Lyall Addleson, Iliffe Books.

National Regulations and Construction (standardized details published by Norwegian Institute of Architects).

Zoning Principles, Delft University.

The Building Envelope by Alan J. Brookes and Chris Grech, Butterworth Architecture 1990.

The Art of Construction Series in the *Architects' Journal* (1980s).

Focus supplement to the *Architects' Journal* on topics such as cladding, glazing and sealants.

Wall Technology, CIRIA Special Publication 87. Seven volume set (1993).

Curtain Wall Connections to Steel Frames by Ray Ogden, The SCI (1992).

Standard & Guide to Good Practice for Curtain Walling. Published by the Centre for Window and Cladding Technology (1993).

Constructional studies

Some of the following books may be out of date and need to be carefully checked against current regulations:

Multi Storey Buildings in Steel by Hart Henn and Sontag, Granada.

Buildings for Industry, Vols 1 and 2, by Henn, Iliffe.

Steel in the Australian Context by Alan Ogg, published by Royal Australian Institute of Architects.

Connections: studies in building assembly by Alan J. Brookes and Chris Grech, published by Butterworth Architecture.

Flat Roofing Design and Good Practice by Arup Research and Development, published by the British Flat Roofing Council and CIRIA.

Manuals

The Steel Construction Institute publishes a range of manuals on framed construction.

British Steel publish general booklets on products such as metal cladding as well as brochures that feature specific projects such as Broadgate, BMW's HQ, and Gateway House.

The British Steel and Brick Development Association's book called *Brick Cladding for Steel Framed Buildings* is an essential reference for the combined use of brick and steel. Published 1986 see [3] above.

New cladding to offices, Gower Street, London 1990 (architect John Winter).

John Winter's explanation of his design.
In the early 1950s a four-storey warehouse building was constructed on this bombed site. Its narrow frontage concealed a very large three-storey space at the rear used for many years as Simmonds second-hand office furniture storage. The street front was constructed of precast concrete. Originally the east side of Gower Street was a fine terrace of early Victorian houses, but most disappeared and the site to the south of 180/182 has recently been rebuilt as a reinforced concrete framed pastiche.

The brief was to remove the 1950s cladding and replace it with a more attractive and energy efficient skin. Flank walls and structural frame were retained and a new metal and glass curtain wall was designed. The first floor was cut back to provide a generous entrance and to imply that this is the frontage to a large building, not just another house in the street.

26

Lightweight and heavyweight cladding

Alan Blanc

26.1 INTRODUCTION

In this chapter the theory of cladding outlined in chapter 25 is explored further, followed by a description of the range of available cladding systems from lightweight to heavyweight, including those principally made from steel. The term 'lightweight' will be used to describe corrugated and formed metal, composite and 'laid-up' panels and glazing, whereas 'heavyweight' includes precast and in situ concrete, brickwork and ashlar. Methods of lightweight construction have been the subject of considerable development in recent years. Often they are composite in nature, relying on the combined characteristics of several different materials.

The high strength to weight ratio of steel makes it an obvious choice for both cladding and cladding fixings. Steel also has the advantage of being relatively fire resistant compared with other metals. A temperature of 550°C (960°F) was the traditional limiting temperature at which steel lost approximately half its strength, the equivalent figure for aluminium for example, is only 200°C (330°F).

Reference should also be made to earlier chapters dealing with related topics – chapter 1: historical background, chapter 5: sheet and strip steel, including an outline of the technology of corrugated and formed steel and their application to cladding, chapter 6: stainless and related steels and chapter 32: metal windows. Throughout this chapter construction details are used to evaluate alternative approaches whilst highlighting constructional difficulties that might result in building failures.

26.2 A GUIDE TO LIGHTWEIGHT CLADDING

26.2.1 Profiled sheet

The Building Regulations require roof and wall cladding and fixings to comply with BS CP3 chapter V: Part 2 and BS 6399: Part 1: 1984[1]. One of these stipulations, the necessity for cladding to withstand imposed loads up to 0.75 kN/m^2 is a major determinant of the profile of panels, the centres of fixings and the design of the fixings themselves; manufacturers publish this data for their particular systems. Wind loads can often, however, exceed all imposed loads and be considerably in excess of 0.75 kN/m^2 especially near the edges of roofs and walls. At these locations the strength of fastenings is of particular importance and the number of fixings may have to be locally increased. In addition, the necessity to withstand concentrated point loads, especially resulting from maintenance access to roofs, establishes a minimum thickness for much profiled steel sheet. It may also determine the profile of sheet to be used because sheets with wide pans are more susceptible to damage than those with corrugations at closer centres.

It is usual for a consulting engineer to design the supporting structure and establish that it and the cladding will withstand anticipated loads and wind pressure. Figure 26.1 shows typical details for fixing wall and roof panels of profiled steel sheet. Conventional purlins and sheeting rails are made from cold-formed steel sections or rolled angles and channels spaced by 'rule of thumb' as shown in Table 26.1.

Ideally, each sheet should be lapped over the next at the ends and sides without any cutting to shape or to make openings. This is simply not feasible if a building is to have doors and windows and so manufacturers publish standard details for these junctions. Sheets can be precisely cut in the factory, making for a good fit on site, but it is still commonplace to site-trim edges with relative inaccuracy and the risk of future corrosion (if the bare metal is left unpainted or without other protection). The design of cover flashings and cover pieces is of paramount importance in terms of appearance and eventual weathering. Cladding details need to be much concerned with the sections of these components and the method of fabrication (Fig. 26.2). Composite panels are a more sophisticated product and are much superior in terms of edge finish and fit (see below and Fig. 26.6).

It is usual for corrugations to run down the roof slope, with lapped joints at the head and sides. Thick sheet materials such as fibre cement, heavy duty plastic and fibre cement/steel sandwich panels have the top left and bottom

Table 26.1

	Roof purlin centres (m)	*Wall rail centres (m)*
Normal profiled sheet	1.600–2.500 (5 ft 3 in–8 ft 2 in)	1.600–3.300 (5 ft 3 in–10 ft 10 in)
Deep profiles	3.500–6.000 (11 ft 6 in–19 ft 8 in)	4.500–7.000 (14 ft 9 in–23 ft 10 in)

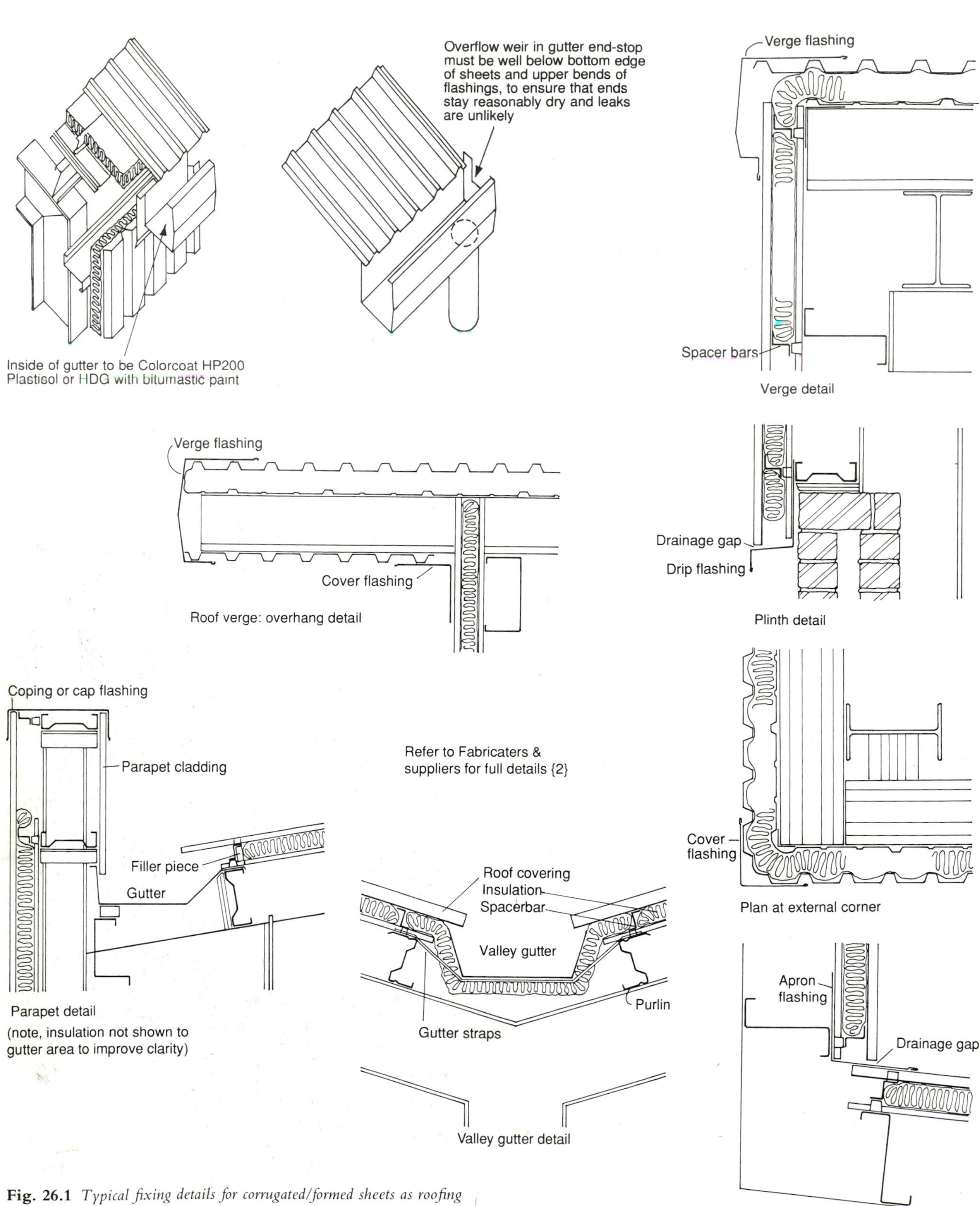

Fig. 26.1 *Typical fixing details for corrugated/formed sheets as roofing and walling. Redrawn from illustrations supplied by British Steel Strip Division.*

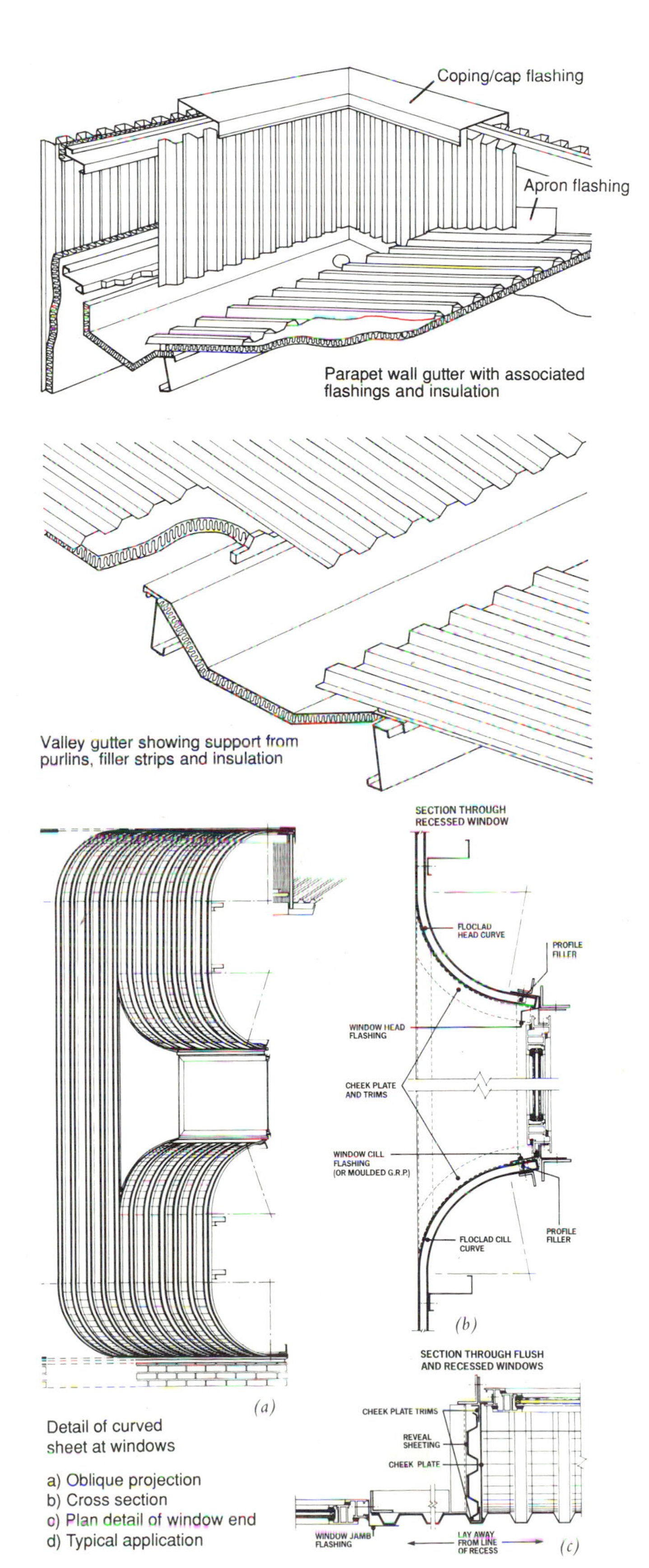

Parapet wall gutter with associated flashings and insulation

Valley gutter showing support from purlins, filler strips and insulation

Detail of curved sheet at windows

a) Oblique projection
b) Cross section
c) Plan detail of window end
d) Typical application

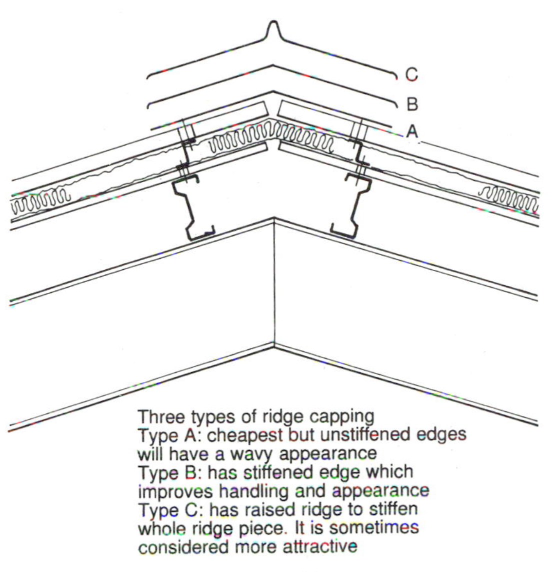

Three types of ridge capping
Type A: cheapest but unstiffened edges will have a wavy appearance
Type B: has stiffened edge which improves handling and appearance
Type C: has raised ridge to stiffen whole ridge piece. It is sometimes considered more attractive

Typical application of double curved sheets for cladding

(d)

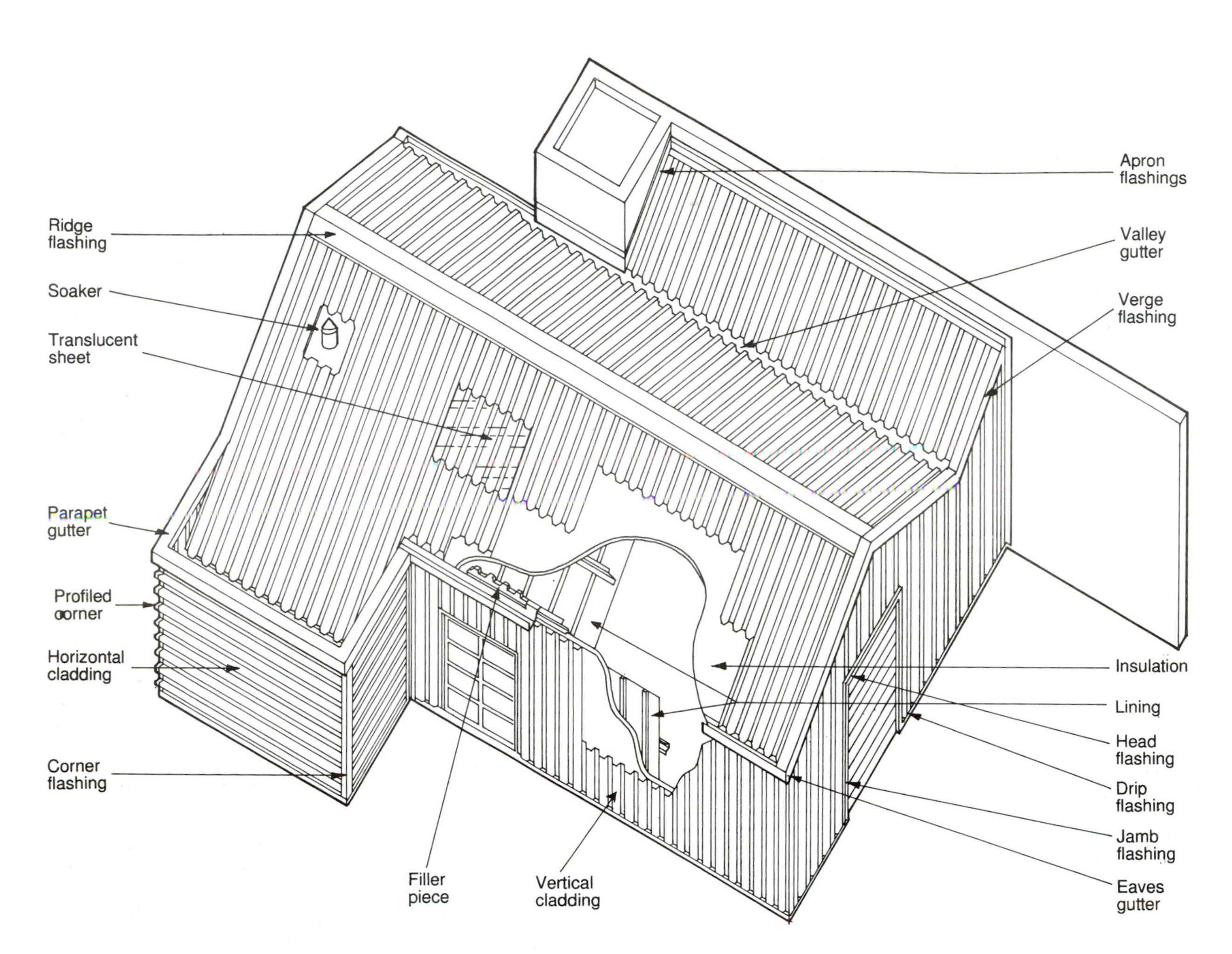

Fig. 26.2 *Typical uses of profiled steel in building construction, showing areas requiring attention at design stage. Location axonometric for cover flashings. Redrawn from illustrations supplied by British Steel Strip Division.*

right hand corners cut off to a 45 degree angle so that only two sheets at a time overlap, although four sheets coincide at corners. Wall cladding can be fixed either vertically or horizontally. If horizontal, joints can be made satisfactorily by overlapping upper sheets over lower but the end laps between sheets forming a vertical joint are vulnerable to water penetration and need to be sealed by a ribbon of mastic pressed between the two surfaces. Horizontal cladding, traditional in farm building, was a design feature of the award winning COSIRA Factories by Broome and Conder; it is now widely used for industrial buildings (Fig. 26.3).

Window sills and cover flashings at junctions and corners need to be generously dimensioned if they are to provide effective weathering against driven rain and snow (Fig. 26.1).

Steel sheeting is resistant to spread of flame but has poor fire resistance. If an elevation is adjacent to a site boundary, the building regulations effectively limit the use of profiled sheet or require that it has a fireproof lining of mineral wool, fibre cement board or masonry. Most manufacturers now make composite fire-proof panels for this purpose.

Where car parking or a road is adjacent to a facade clad with corrugated sheets down to ground level, it is wise to protect the building by a guard rail or bollards or to avoid using metal that is liable to be damaged. In the past it has been very common to construct a brickwork plinth 1200 mm (4 ft) high as protection against vehicles. Alternatively, a taller plinth 2400 mm (8 ft) in height will establish a zone containing all windows and doors in traditional masonry construction above which the elevation can be made from uninterrupted profiled sheet (Fig. 26.4).

It should always be remembered that single sheet roofing, whatever the material (fibre cement, plastic or profiled metal), is relatively unsophisticated and may leak draughts of air in windy weather. The limitations of this simple if draughty technology are best accepted rather than trying to modify it by complex detailing. Nowadays, as a consequence, not very much single skin roofing is used without

Fig. 26.3 *Horizontal cladding at factory units, Temple Meads, Bristol (architect Richard Hemingway). Printed by kind permission of British Steel Strip Division.*

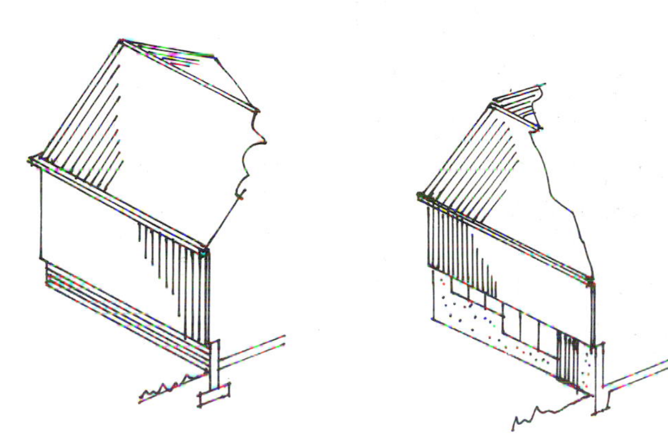

Fig. 26.4 *Plinth details.*

an inner metal liner and insulation, either below or above the purlins. There is, however, a substantial risk associated even with this more sophisticated method. Radiation of heat to the night sky can cause condensation to form on the inner face of the outer sheet, saturating the insulation and corroding fixings. This problem can be alleviated by fixing a breather membrane above the insulation (so as to drain condensation into a gutter at the eaves), and extracting at source any humidity produced inside the building.

26.2.2 Insulated forms of corrugated and profiled sheet (termed 'composite' panels)

At its simplest, profiled steel sheet is merely a latterday version of corrugated iron. Insulation is held in place below the roof by lining boards, a labour intensive method with the inherent risk of cold-bridging at purlins and fixings. To counter these disadvantages, the factory pre-assembly of sheeting, insulation and liner into 'composite' panels was developed. This product acquires much of its strength from the bonding of the rigid insulation to the inner and outer steel sheets. As a result, foam-cored panels are roughly 30% stronger than profiled sheeting (if it is simply fixed to purlins or rails with independent insulation).

The maximum manufactured size of rolled strip is 1200 mm (4 ft), and this is consequently the maximum width for flat panels, but if they are to be pressed into box sections the dimension is limited to approximately 1000 mm (3 ft 3 in). The length can be up to 12 m (39 ft 6 in) but considerations of site handling and transport are liable to reduce sizes to around 6–7.5 m (20 ft to 24 ft 6 in). The ability to withstand loads in excess of 0.75 kN/m^2 determines the strength of wall and roof panels and necessitates supports at centres between 2.0 m and 6.0 m (6 ft 6 in and 20 ft) depending upon the gauge of sheet metal, its profile and the finished thickness of the panel.

A continuous production line is used to bond the insulating foam between the inner and outer sheets, explaining why such long panels can be made. The foam is either polyisocyanurate or polyurethane both of which emit poisonous fumes if burnt. It is usual for the panels to be made up from pre-finished steel sheet. The long edges can be produced tongued and grooved so panels can be mechanically joined, or alternatively they can be locked together with secret fixing brackets (Fig. 26.5). Wall panels can be jig cut to make round-edged openings for doors and windows, details that are made waterproof by the use of neoprene gaskets.

For windowless industrial buildings simple composite panels are manufactured with a single profiled metal sheet bonded to board insulation. Because these incorporate voids on the cold side of the insulation, condensation problems may be experienced (as discussed above).

Commonly used for long span roofing are deeply profiled trough-shaped planks with standing seams that snap together. The resulting joint is waterproof down to pitches as low as 2.5 degrees (Fig. 26.6). Reference should be made to chapter 5 for advice on weathering.

Standards for factory made insulated panels are not described by a Code of Practice. Panels are tested in the same way as windows; test rigs are calibrated to measure performance at different degrees of exposure. The crucial junctions are between panels and particularly at fourway joints that are made with neoprene gaskets welded together to form a grid of what is in effect, secret gutters. These hidden crevices require inspection and cleaning from time to time and mastic joints need resealing, so this form of cladding is not maintenance free and needs more sophisticated care than traditional profiled roofing.

Contemporary methods using deeply profiled sections and site-folded metal sheets enable the advantages of standing seam roofing, previously confined to copper and zinc, also to be extended to coated steel or stainless steel.

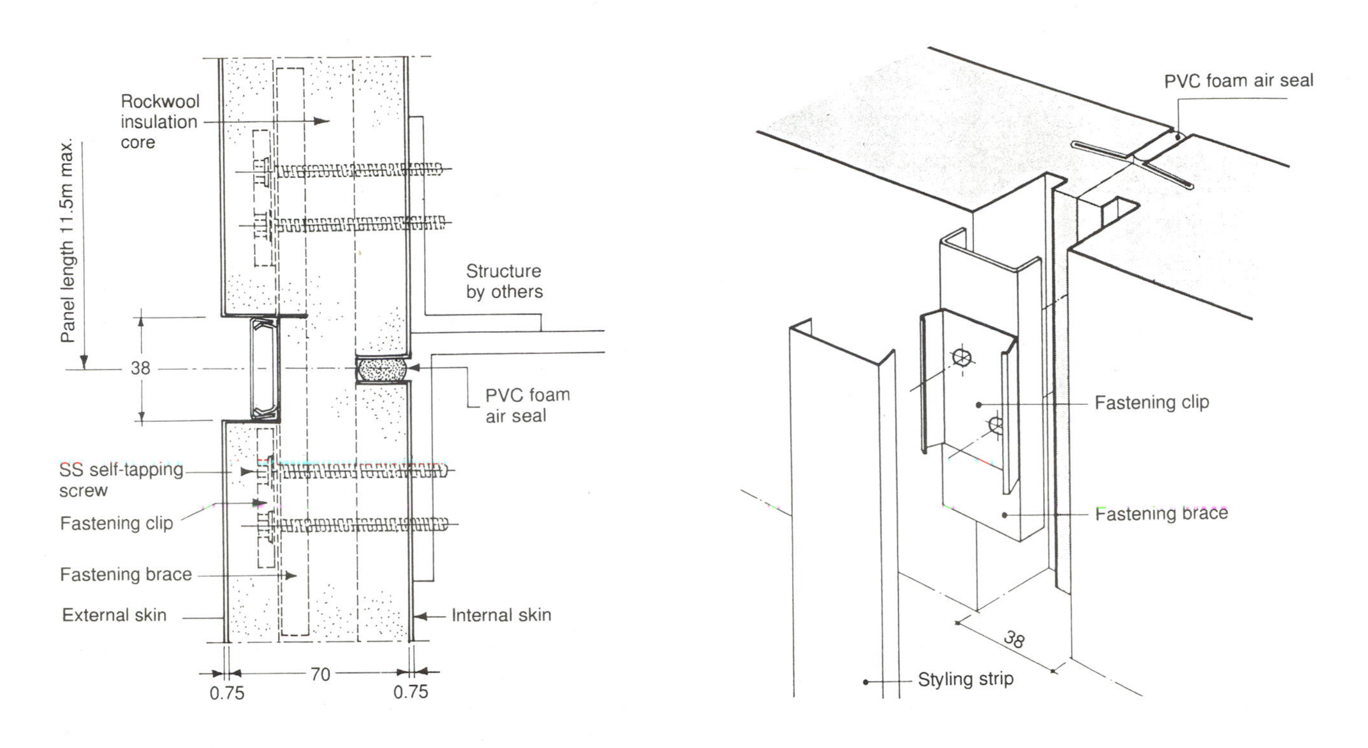

Fig. 26.5 *Composite panels, edge details and fixing. Printed by kind permission of Damplaat Ltd.*

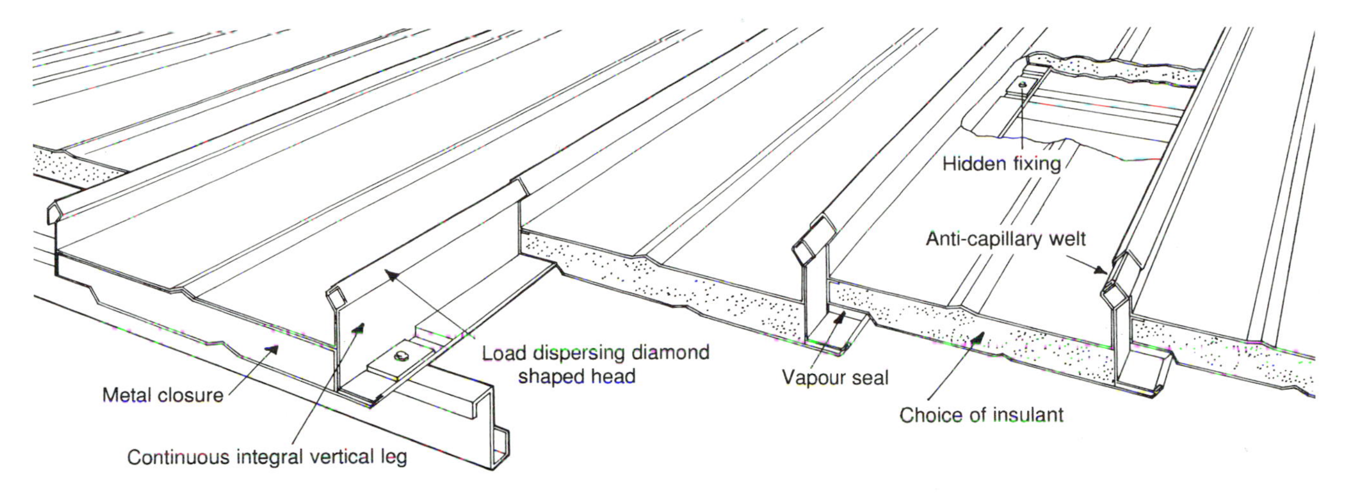

Fig. 26.6 *Standing seam roofing panels. Redrawn from illustraions supplied by Grozier Building Systems.*

European equipment (French and Swedish at the time of writing), is available for site-welding stainless roofing into continuous lengths up to 15 m (49 ft 3 in) for factory-profiled work, 32 m (105 ft) if folded on site, to make roofs with virtually no slope. These insulated standing seam roofs of bonded or composite construction provide an 'umbrella' covering that avoids the use of bitumen or synthetic polymers and their related problems of loss of bond and fatigue failure due to thermal movement.

The secret fixings now available do not require metal panels to be cut or drilled, the places at which conventionally fixed corrugated/profile sheet usually starts to corrode. The earlier ways of fixing insulated roofing panels either compress the insulation, reducing its performance, or distort the metal, leading to leaks at fixing holes. This mode of failure resulted in the re-roofing of the well-known housing scheme at Byker in Newcastle, UK. In that particular case, webbed distance pieces have been used to counter the problem but much coated steel roofing still remains fixed through the furrows of the sheets with raw metal at the drilled holes.

26.2.3 Laid-up panels

The manufacturing process used to make 'laid-up' panels differs from the continuous assembly line production of 'composite' panels. 'Laid-up' panels are bench fabricated and their various layers are usually glued together. Their production dates from the first attempts to factory pre-assemble roof cladding and insulation. The decking materials used were compressed straw, which proved to be a disaster (as described in chapter 28), or woodwool slabs (cement-wood fibre). The early types were copper-faced with upturned edges for bending on site into conventional standing seams. The use of woodwool slabs generated the basic module of 600 mm (2 ft) width by 3–4.5 m (9 ft 10 in to 14 ft 9 in) length.

Current production methods are more sophisticated, and panels can now be made into curved shapes with inset louvres and windows with a variety of core materials and slotted fixings at seams. One system includes laid-up

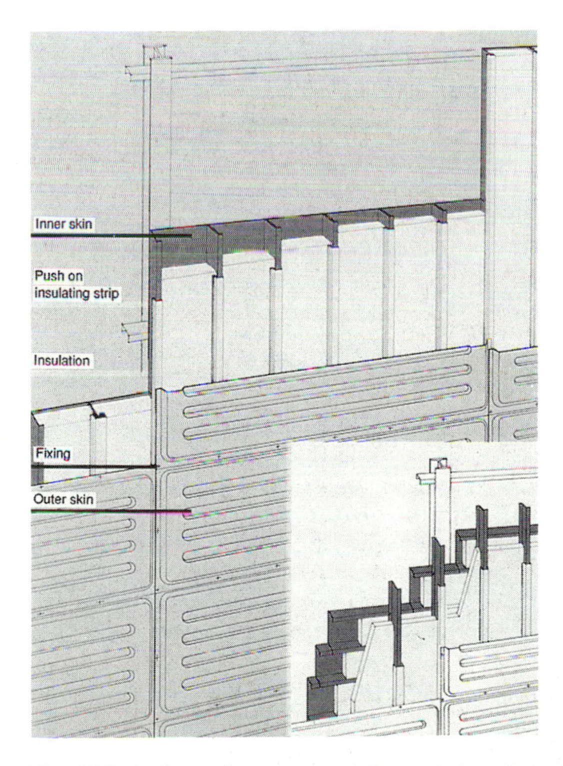

Fig. 26.7 *Roof or wall panels using laid-up technique. Printed by kind permission of Riedinger. Right-hand insert shows multiple layers of insulation.*

'planks' that can be hinged to construct horizontal and vertical sliding doors or fixed to make wall panels.

The method of assembly can resemble 'composite' panels with tongued and grooved joints and hidden brackets fixed at the seams (Fig. 26.7). It is also possible to include 'laid-up' panels within curtain walling using the same fixing methods as for glazing such as beads or compression flanges. To facilitate this, the edges of panels can be made to the same thickness as insulated glazing units. The most significant European developments in this technology have been made in Switzerland and Germany where window walling systems have been devised including fully interchangeable panels and windows (refer to Figs 25.5, 25.6, 25.7 and 25.8 in chapter 25).

A wide variety of metallic facing materials may be used such as colour-coated steel, Cor-Ten, lead or zinc-coated steel, vitreous-enamelled or stainless steel, anodized, mill-finished or colour-coated aluminium and sheet copper, lead or zinc. In addition non-metallic panels are available faced with glass, glass-fibre reinforced cement (GRC), fibre cement or glass reinforced plastic (GRP). The core material can be foam-based insulation but it is more usual to use fire-proof boards such as compressed mineral fibre or fibre cement or a combination according to the fire resistance required.

The criteria for strength set out in BS CP3 [1] apply as for other cladding components. For most systems the preferred size of panel is 1.2 m by 4.5 m (4 ft to 14 ft 10 in), although it is possible to manufacture lengths up to 6 m (19 ft 9 in).

Larger lengths entail a considerable premium in handling costs, both within the works and on site. Aluminium and steel (carbon and stainless) faced panels are made from cold-rolled coil which, as for profiled sheet, limits the width for flat panels to 1.2 m (4 ft).

Panels up to 2.0 m (6 ft 6 in) wide can be made from fibre cement, GRC and GRP but there are penalties to be paid. Fibre cement is brittle and needs to be protected from impact damage. GRP has only a limited life if not maintained (around 20 years), and needs an additional coating if it is to have a flame retardant surface.

The finished size of metal panels is dependent not only on the sheet sizes that are available but also on the method of fabrication and the machines that are used. In the UK for example, 'tray' type panels are made by folding the edges of sheets in a break press and then welding the corners; with currently available presses the maximum size is 4 m by 1.5 m (13 ft by 5 ft). Alternatively, metal-forming or stamping presses can be used to make three-dimensional profiles, the maximum size available from UK manufacturers is generally 1.8 m by 1.2 m (6 ft by 4 ft) but much larger (5.7 by 2.2 m, 18 ft 8 in by 7 ft 2 in) panels are available from Switzerland. In addition, laid-up panels can be made by some manufacturers on very large presses (often several panels are made at one pressing); the maximum panel size is then 7.0 m by 2.5 m (23 ft by 8 ft 2 in).

If sheet metal is bonded to a rigid backing material, panels can be made with enhanced resistance to impact that are useful for the construction of canopies, roof edges and spandrels that are able to withstand maintenance gondolas and ladders. Typical steel-based panels of this type are made from lead-coated steel or stainless steel, with a backing sheet of fibre cement board. Stiffness is imparted to aluminium panels by profiling their surface or gluing a rigid core of plastic between the sheets of metal (for example 'Alucobond' and similar materials).

26.2.4 Conclusion

The Modern Movement in architecture is identified with the finish of machine-made components, particularly with the precision possible when detailing in metal. Designers whose work particularly displays this enthusiasm tend to be very concerned about the 'skin' of their buildings. A brief look at the award winning schemes included in chapter 37 reveals that interest.

Many of the technical developments underlying the aesthetic were originated by Jean Prouvé (1901–1989). Trained as a blacksmith, for many years he was proprietor of a metal furniture factory in Nantes. He collaborated with architects such as Beaudouin and Lods, Le Corbusier and Oscar Niemeyer on designs for cladding, many in cold-formed steel. The Maison du Peuple at Clichy, Paris (Fig. 26.8) is the most famous: pressed steel components are used

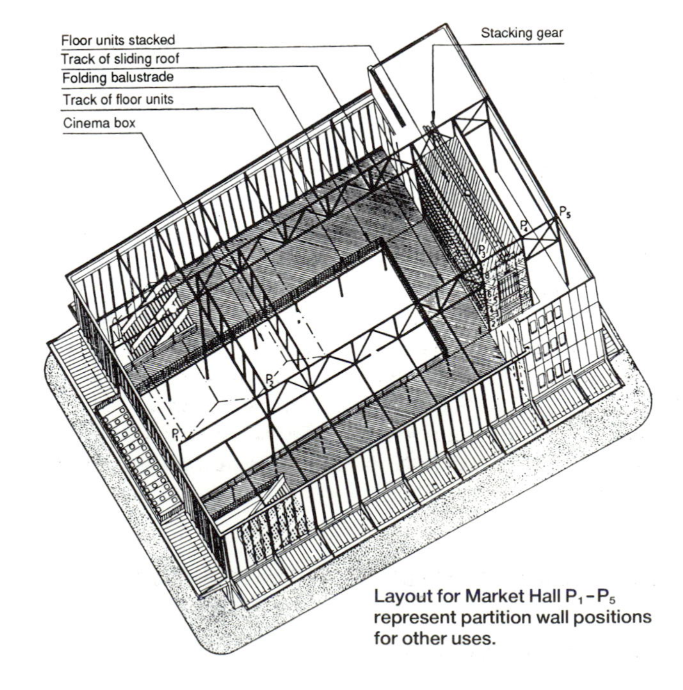

Fig. 26.8 *Maison du Peuple, Clichy, Paris 1939. Metal detailing and framing by Jean Prouvé.*

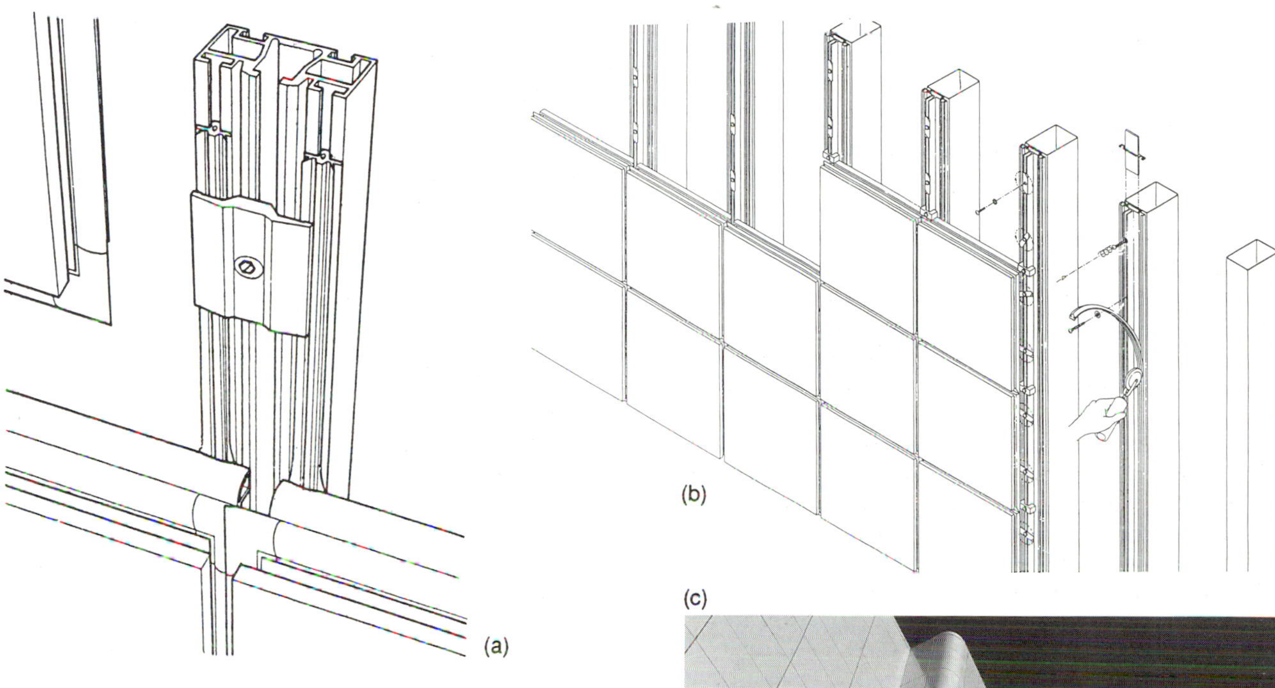

Fig. 26.9 *Insulated panels fixed to carrier system over steel mullions. (a) Panels meeting on the rear carrier with continuous tubular primary EPDM gasket forming the main weather seal. The vertical air seal mounted on the carrier is compressed by the back of the panel. The horizontal rear air seals are mounted on the panel. (b) Insulated panels fixed using clamping plates to aluminium rear carriers which in turn are fixed back onto steel mullions aligned, plumbed and shimmed to a flat plane. Panels are interchangeable with windows, doors and louvres. System details a and b designed by Alan Brookes Associates and printed with their kind permission. (c) Application of prototype system at St Enoch Square, Glasgow (not designed by Alan Brookes Associates).*

throughout the building for windows, flooring, partitions and staircases.

Lightweight panel cladding has become associated with the 'vernacular' of steel framed buildings in Australia. ([3], see also the Australian designs in chapter 36). The rather different climate of Northern Europe has required the evolution of 'rain-screened' elevations. These composite building envelopes incorporate a screen of glass or metal, a drainable and ventilated cavity, a moisture barrier and fire and thermal insulation in front of the structural frame. An example designed by Alan Brookes Associates is given in Fig. 26.9.

26.3 A GUIDE TO HEAVYWEIGHT CLADDING

26.3.1 Precast cladding

It is said that reinforced concrete was invented in the mid-19th century when a gardener at Versailles began making concrete flowerpots with wire reinforcement. The first large-scale precasting of concrete (as opposed to on-site construction of concrete), was developed by the US Army for building barracks following the Spanish/American War, modular walls and foundations were cast using the 'tilt form' process. The same method was used by Rudolph Schindler and Irving Gill for the construction of wall panels for houses (employing second hand steel shutters bought as Army Surplus, [4]). American technology was sufficiently advanced by the mid-1920s to be exported to the Weimar Republic for the large-scale housing schemes initiated by Ernst May. Precasting was used at Neue Frankfurt for floor and wall components of both low rise and multi-storey housing [5].

European patents for reinforced concrete and particularly precast concrete were most numerous in France. The best known designers were the architect/engineer offices of Auguste Perret and Beaudouin and Lods. The latter's most publicized work was the prefabricated housing at Cité de la Muette in Drancy, a scheme of steel framed slab and tower blocks clad with vertical planks of precast concrete. The framing employed the Mopin system of construction, in which multi-storey frames were put together on the ground and then hoisted to be fixed when vertical (Fig. 26.10). The Mopin system was in fact a complete failure, and both the flats at Drancy and a later project at Quarry Hill in Leeds have been demolished. Inadequate concrete cover (25 mm – 1 in or less) over ungalvanized reinforcement led to corrosion and spalling of the panels. Eventually moisture penetrated to the unprotected steel frame which also began to rust, and after a life of 35 years or so the buildings were demolished.

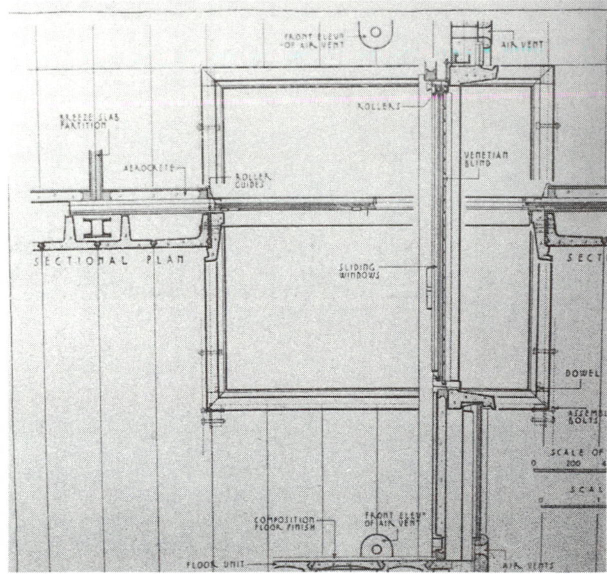

Fig. 26.10 *Cité de la Muette 1934 (architects Beaudouin and Lods. Mopin system of steel framing with precast cladding. Top figure shows steel frames and cladding partly erected.*

Nowadays it is appreciated that precast concrete cladding must effectively resist water penetration and cladding fixings made of ferrous metal have to be properly protected from corrosion. It is current practice, in both North America and Europe, to always use galvanized reinforcement and stainless steel bolts.

Despite the failures, pre-war precast concrete has in some cases performed satisfactorily. A significant example in London is the terrazzo facing to the Dorchester Hotel. Its designer, Sir Owen Williams, allowed sufficient cover to ensure that bar corrosion did not occur. It helps that the Dorchester is cleaned every few years from top to bottom (removing atmospheric deposits that might prove corrosive) and that the slabs are frequently repointed so weathering is reduced to a minimum (Fig. 26.11).

The problem posed by inadequate cover to unprotected steel was still not understood at the time of the Hertfordshire Schools Programme (1945–51) in the UK. Most of the buildings have now had to be reclad as a result of the deterioration of the original thin precast panels but for their replacements galvanized steel reinforcement was used.

Fig. 26.11 *Cladding to Dorchester Hotel, London 1930. Terrazzo faced slabs (engineer Sir Owen Williams). Printed by kind permission of Dorchester Hotel.*

26.3.2 Current North American and European practice

Canada and the USA receive many visitors seeking to discover how they achieve such high speed construction, particularly when building 'high-rise' and skyscrapers. A prevalent North American type is a steel frame structure clad with high quality precast panels. Publications such as *Architecture* (the AIA Journal) or *Progressive Architecture* provide well indexed background information on their methods of working with precast concrete. Typically, large pieces of facade are factory prefabricated. In part this is because of a shortage of bricklayers and masons for on-site construction of brick or stone cladding. Also in their harsh winter climate it is rarely practical to work to a tight schedule off high scaffolding. There is severe cold and heavy snow for three or four months of the year in cities like Chicago, Montreal, New York or Toronto.

A typical cladding detail (Fig. 26.12) shows the quality and skill of their precasting. It also illustrates the way in

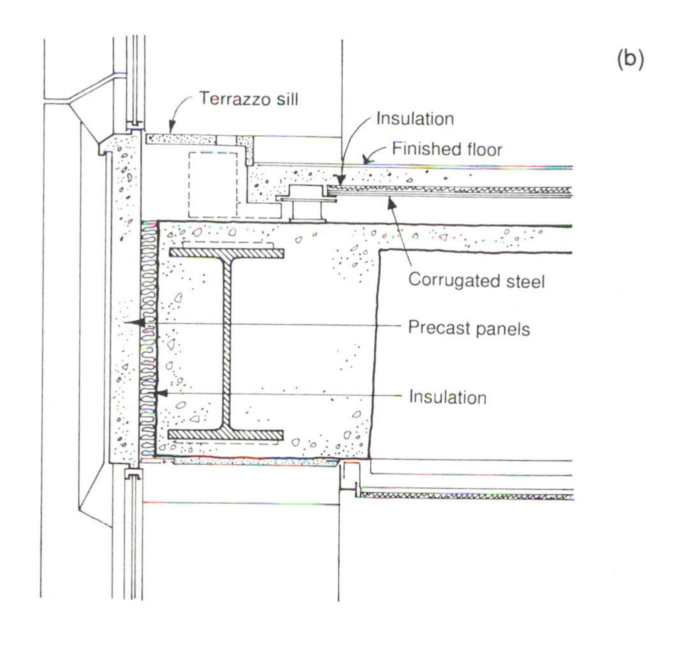

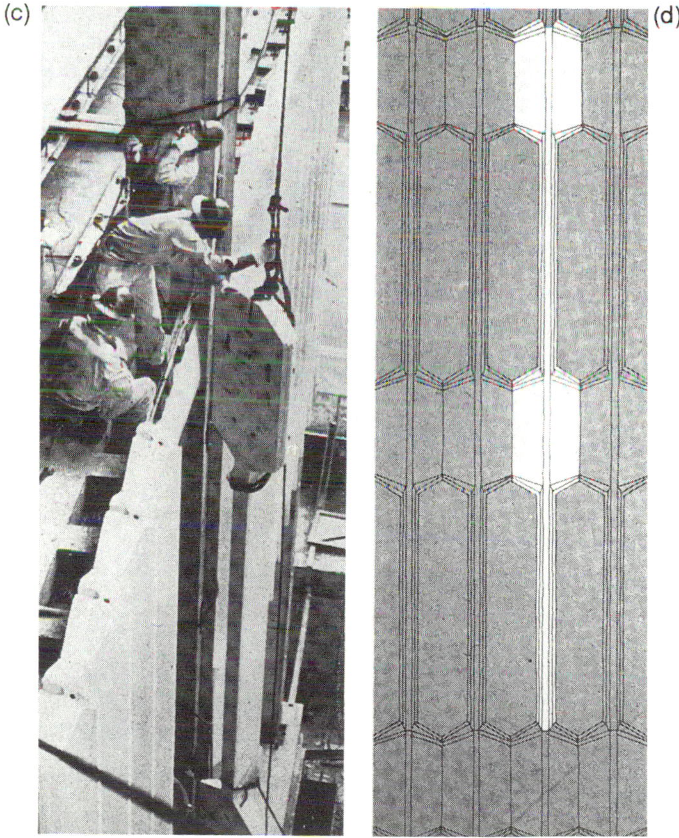

Fig. 26.12 *Typical North American precast panels. Michigan consolidated Gas Building, Detroit 1964 (architect Minoru Yamasaki). (a) External view of cladding; (b) detail at floor junction; (c) hoisting units; (d) elevational detail.*

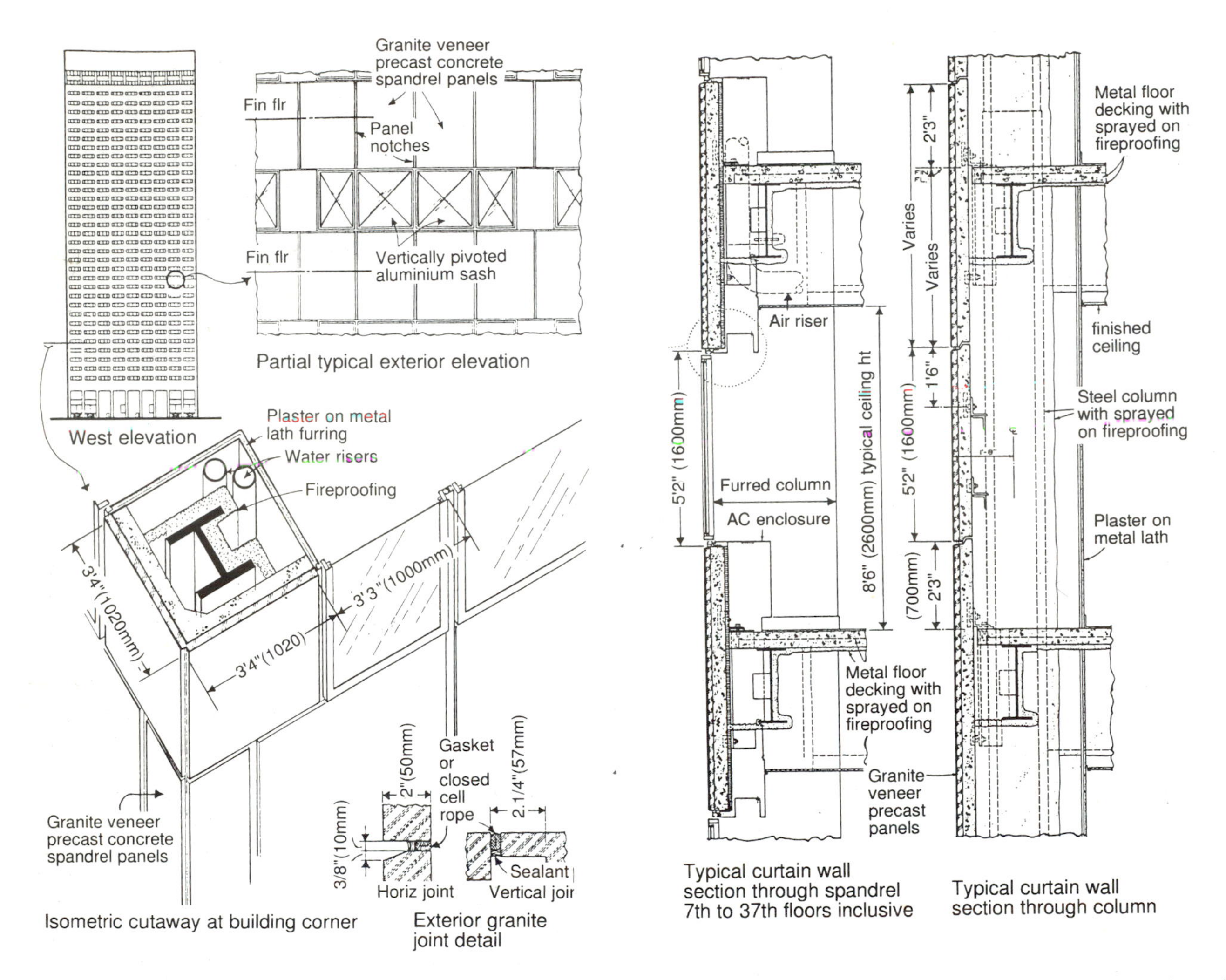

Fig. 26.13 *Typical North American stone faced precast work. New England Merchants National Bank, Boston, Massachusetts (architect Edward Larrabee Barnes).*

which panels can be modelled, windows accommodated and effective self-draining joints made at the edges of the units. Moulds used in the factory are either ply or steel, designed for precise jigging of the cage reinforcement. The accuracy that is achieved enables the steel fixing lugs, that attach the panel to the structure, to be precisely located. The usual surface finish is essentially artificial stone, made by mixing coloured cement with durable aggregates, either granite or quartz and sometimes sandstone. The aim is to achieve a dense surface that is then lightly textured by acid-washing or grit-blasting. This is in marked contrast to the 'naturbeton' favoured in Europe, the surface of which tends to crack, allowing water penetration and the risk of corrosion 40 or 50 mm deep into the cladding panels.

It is typical North American practice for buildings to be regularly cleaned so that corrosive salts from acid rain do not become encrusted on the facade. Regular maintenance also includes examination of the joints between panels and, if necessary, the replacement of mastic. This is important considering that exposed mastic has an estimated life of only 20 years.

The brick, brick tile, ceramic tile or stone-faced precast panel is another prefabricated form of cladding produced in North American factories. Brick and tile veneered panels are fixed mechanically with stainless steel angles spaced at 900–1200 mm (3–4 ft) intervals. Large ceramic tiles (up to 500 × 500 mm – 1 ft 8 in × 1 ft 8 in) and stone slabs, are laid face down in the bottom of the mould, and dovetailed cleats glued to the back of the veneer are cast into the concrete which is then poured on top. So that shrinkage of the concrete does not stress the veneer, plastic foil is used to separate them. Mastic joints between the ceramic tiles or slabs of stone absorb overall shrinkage (Fig. 26.13).

Reservations could be expressed about this form of

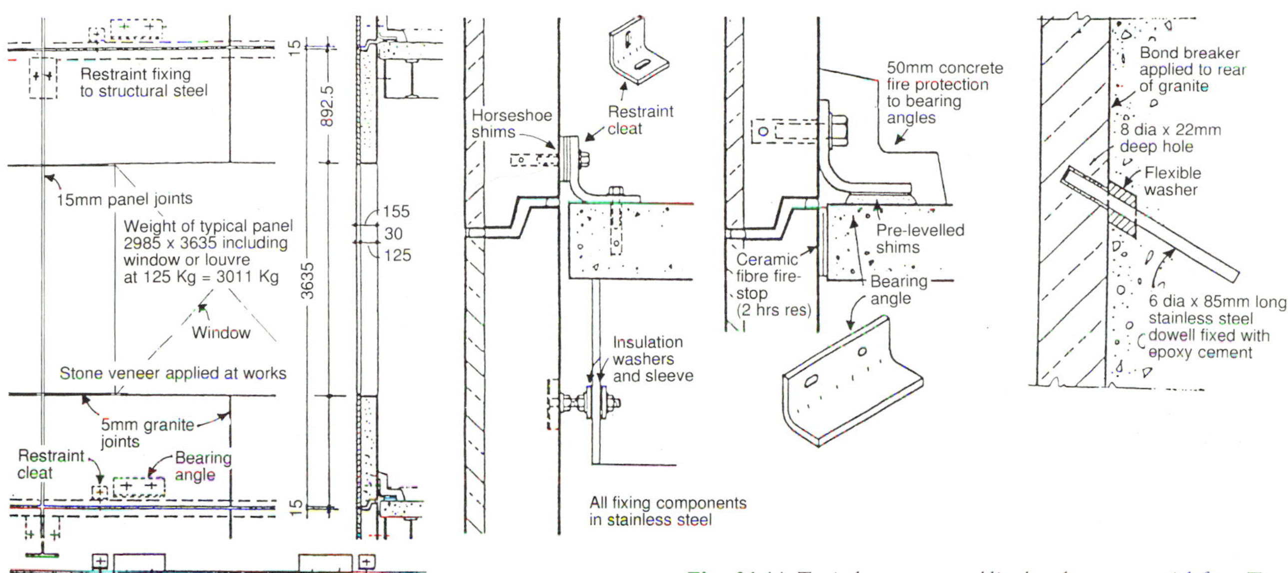

Fig. 26.14 *Typical precast assemblies based upon material from Trent Concrete Structures (details of glazing and insulation not shown). Redrawn from illustrations supplied by Trent Concrete Structures.*

construction. It is not easy to physically test the bond between veneer and glued metal or between cast in situ cleats and the surrounding concrete. Also the cleats are normally stainless steel and could be in contact with galvanized steel reinforcement within the panel resulting in bimetallic corrosion.

This type of construction is now being adopted in Britain, and recent examples of work by Trent Concrete Structures are illustrated in Fig. 26.14.

In the period following the Second World War, experiments were conducted in Scandinavia into the technology of aerated concrete. These lightweight concretes have considerable potential for precast panel construction, since they weigh 50% less than structural concrete. The same precautions are required if the corrosion of reinforcement is to be avoided but the material has successfully been in use for some time (Fig. 26.15). Factory made vertical or horizontal 'planks' for industrial cladding are now available up to 10 m (33 ft) in length and 1200–1800 mm (4–6 ft) in width. Lightweight concrete has the advantage of high thermal insulation provided that it is kept dry. Adverse weathering of the outer face of aerated concrete can only be prevented by coating with a durable paint that has to be well maintained. Consequently, this is a very significant factor if aerated concrete is selected, unless it is to be overclad with impervious materials such as cement-fibre sheet or metal panels. Lightweight concrete was a major component of many prefabricated housing systems. The idea of 'rain-screen' cladding, now achieving widespread acceptance, originated in methods for upgrading the lightweight concrete walls of houses that had become saturated either by weather penetration or interstitial condensation [6].

The obvious advantage of precast concrete, whether lightweight or not, is that it provides a fireproof envelope to a building and with appropriate detailing can insulate from fire those parts of the steel frame that are adjacent to the external wall. Another advantage of concrete is its thermal mass, particularly for roof and wall panels. A further asset is the ease with which factory assembled concrete panels can incorporate a whole range of external finishes with insulation on the inner face. On the other hand, all concrete products suffer from the disadvantage of drying shrinkage. The resulting stresses have to be anticipated if a concrete panel is joined to a rigid frame and at its junction with any external veneer, otherwise brickwork tiles and slab veneers will come loose, a problem that has plagued many post-war European buildings [7].

The limitations of lifting and transportation to site in the UK determine the maximum size and weight of panels, and the customary limits are as follows:

Semi-vertical delivery on a low loader:	4.2 m ht × 3.0 m width (13 ft 9 in × 9 ft 10 in)
Flat delivery:	9.0 m ht or width × 3.0 m ht or width (29 ft 2 in × 9 ft 10 in)
Weight:	Up to 10 tonnes but 7 tonne weight is the average preferred for handling.

Hope Bagenal [8] once said that concrete is a most useful basic material, providing that it is always overclad: his conservative opinion is always worth bearing in mind.

Vertical sections (parapet)

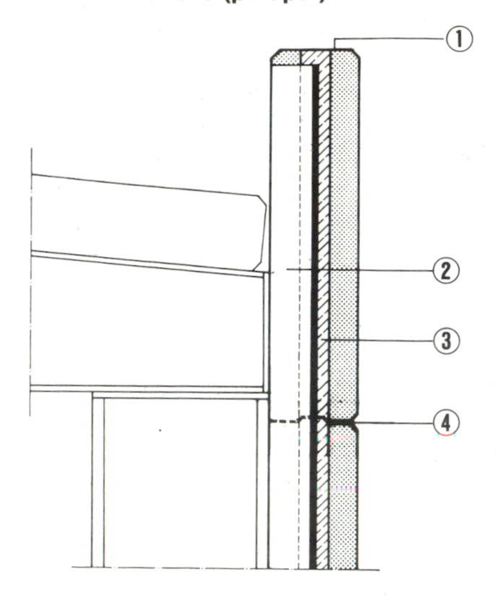

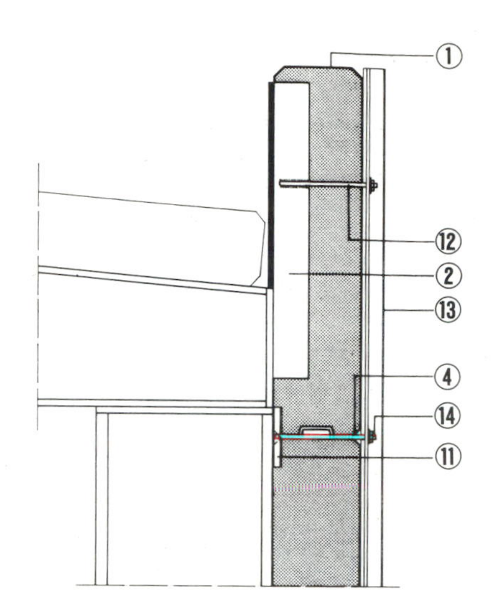

Horizontal sections (parapet)

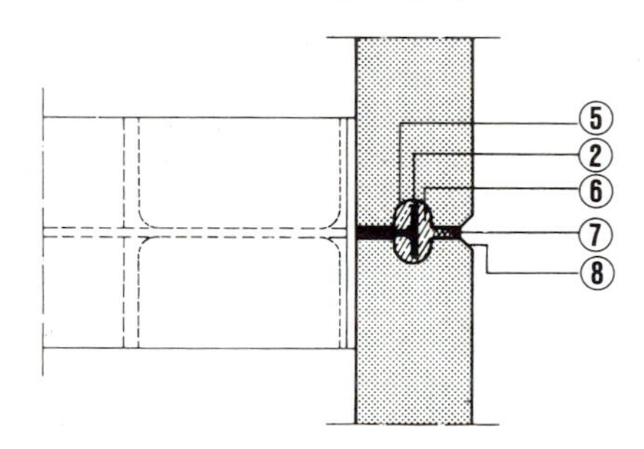

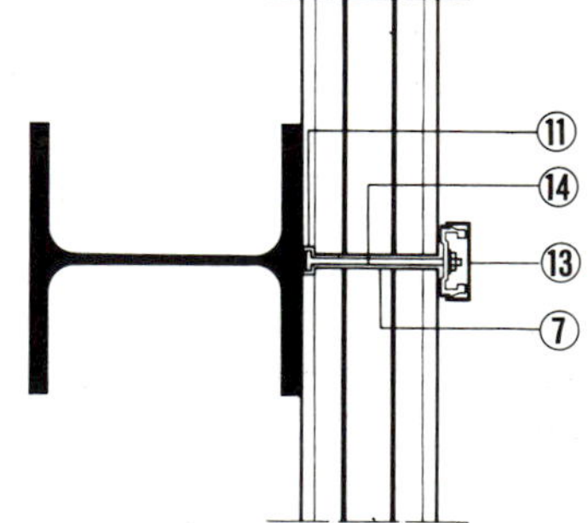

All metal fixing material which is not inserted in cement mortar must be rust protected or of stainless steel

Horizontal sections

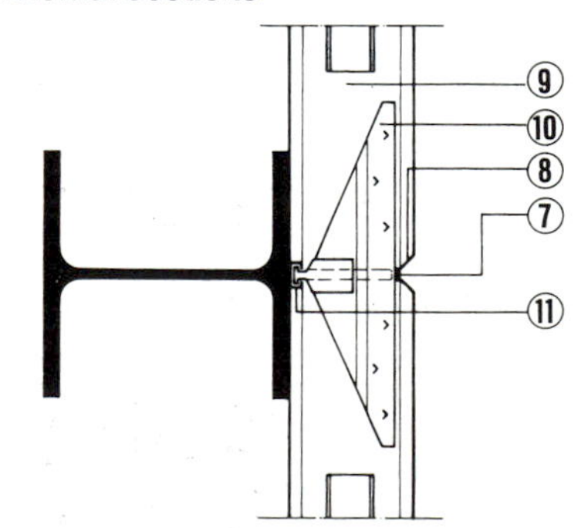

1. cover plate to be fixed
2. T-section welded on steel structure
3. deepened splined joint filled with cement mortar
4. horizontal joint filled with plastic mortar
5. deepened splined joint
6. cement mortar
7. vertical joint (about 10 mm) filled with mineral wool and sealed with elasto-plastic or elastic sealing compound
8. chamfered on site
9. YTONG tongue cut on site
10. fixing plate of stainless steel
11. welded channel
12. threaded bolt (stainless steel)
13. aluminium cover plate
14. T-headed bolt

Fig. 26.15 *Lightweight aerated precast concrete. Printed by kind permission of Thermalite plc.*

26.3.3 Brick veneer

Great Britain is blessed with a well organized brick making industry which energetically markets its wide range of products. The Brick Development Association's 'Brick is Beautiful' campaign has captured popular taste, which partly explains why brick veneer is so popular in commercial and domestic construction. Organizations linked to property investment in Britain, that is the insurance companies and advisors to the construction industry, from time to time issue a list of their preferred materials accompanied by a blacklist of products that they dislike. So far clay brick has never fallen foul of these edicts and, partly as a consequence, our city centres are being rebuilt with brick-clad office blocks and shopping centres.

The increasing number of brick-clad steel buildings has led the Brick Development Association and British Steel to publish a useful two-part volume on the topic [9]. *Brick Cladding to Steel Framed Buildings* is intended to span between the academic and practical worlds. It has been prepared with an engineering bias by design teams representing the brick and steel industry and from a distinguished firm of consulting engineers. Architects may dislike this intervention, but the harsh reality of the revised Building Regulations, certification and 'claims' have resulted in engineering input becoming central to cladding decisions. 'Fast track' methods require building designers to make fast judgements, so future textbooks may be similar to this one in having two parts, one explanatory and one illustrative.

26.3.4 Brick veneer versus brickbox

The basic message of these two volumes is clear enough. Our contemporary thin panelled brick cladding differs considerably from the massiveness of the first brick and steel frame buildings constructed at the turn of the century. Examples are the 1200 mm (4 ft) solid masonry envelopes of the steel framed British Museum extension (1914), or the three and four brick thicknesses used to construct Selfridges, London a few years before. By comparison, modern brickwork, often being only one half brick in thickness, is lightweight and brittle. The gradual expansion, which is characteristic of brick combined with mortar, has now to be considered in relation to the thermal movements of steelwork. Technological change eventually affects every text on one's bookshelf; the dog-eared 'classics' within an arm's length of my board are Fitzmaurice's *Principles of Modern Building*, volume I (1938 Edition) and Hope Bagenal's post-war writings [8]. Both embody the notion based on pre-war jobs that well-fired bricks present no difficulties as a result of moisture expansion. Comforting phrases like 'no special precautions necessary' abound, the figure stated is as low as 0.001%, that is moisture movement of 2 mm for a 20 m height wall. Fitzmaurice does explain however, that the basis for his findings was only a 15 year research period and that longer time was needed for valid judgements to be made. Failures due the moisture movement of cladding had been reported in the USA in the late 1930s but were not investigated by Fitzmaurice.

Half a century later, the specialists are more knowledgeable and cautious. Code of Practice BS 5628: Part 3 [10] recommends that for purposes of movement joint design (both moisture and thermal) a rule of thumb of 1 mm per metre run for unrestrained and lightly restrained walls should be assumed. That largely explains why modern masonry cladding is so well seamed in mastic. Nowadays we allow for a typical range of moisture movement of somewhat less than 0.02%, a 20-fold increase from the 1930s! Fitzmaurice's over-optimistic conclusions were based on research that had the defect of using bricks without mortar, soaked and dried over a 15 year period in a laboratory: the test material for BS 5628 was a mortar bonded brick wall.

This history shows that construction research needs to build upon past experience and not simply be oriented to the current preferences of the market. Recent publications tend to leave unanswered the question posed by history, namely whether the current proclivity for supporting half bricks on shelf angles may in fact be an illogical way of building (Fig. 26.16). It may be advantageous in terms of future durability if masonry is independent of the structure, for example (9 in) 225 mm self-supporting walls designed to be merely tied

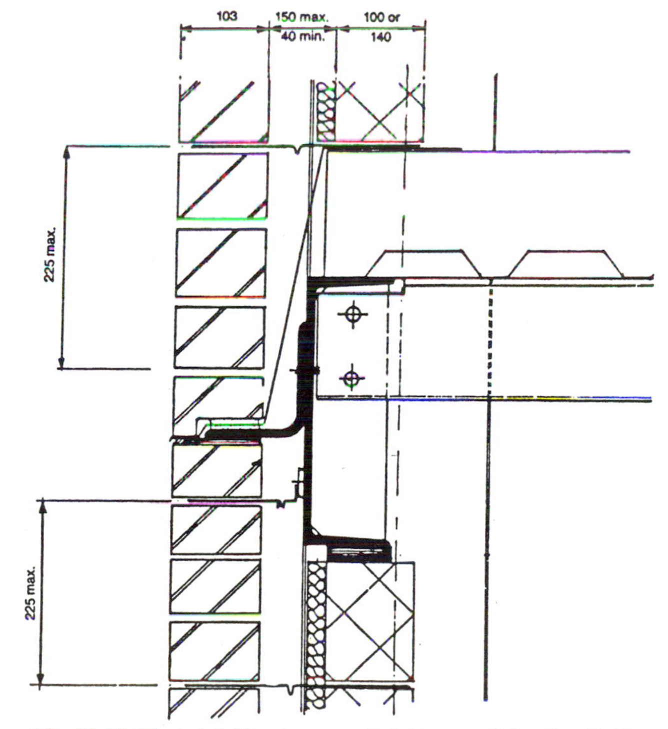

Fig. 26.16 *Typical shelf angle support for brick veneer (taken from* Brick Cladding to Steel Framed Buildings*). Printed by kind permission of BDA.*

back to the frame which supports the floors and roof. This has been successfully tried before, by Charles Holden for the construction of the Senate House (London's tallest pre-war structure), which has a massive loadbearing masonry envelope independent of the steel-framed book stack.

A similar, but more refined solution has been chosen for the latest additions to Grays Inn, London (Fig. 26.17). For these lawyers' offices, a steel frame is employed to support the highly serviced interior space, the facades are of one brick thickness, free-standing and designed to be complementary with their 18th century setting. The reasons for the separation of skin and structure are environmental as well as contextual. The use of thicker walls give enhanced sound and thermal insulation compared with conventional cavity construction, whilst the internal frame can be changed and modified to suit requirements 100 or 200 years in the future (refer back for illustration in Fig. 25.31).

British Steel research on steel framed buildings 80 or 90 years old has shown that corrosion caused by contact between masonry and steelwork is limited to points of contact between the metal and the wet brickwork or ashlar. It has also been found that a cavity of 40 mm (1⅝ in) is sufficient to separate the outer leaf of a brick cavity from primed steelwork. There is, however, the difficulty of connecting shelf angles back to the main frame (refer again to Fig. 26.16). Shelf angles should be galvanized or stainless steel but cold bridging across these connections may cause condensation on the main frame and points of corrosion if the steel frame is only protected by primer. Rusting steel in direct contact with masonry presents particular problems because corrosion increases the volume of the metal by two or three times. A rusting shelf angle, for example, would effectively increase the bed joint between it and the brickwork it supports enough to crack and dislodge the cladding.

26.3.5 Factory-built brickwork

Reinforced brickwork was invented in the 1920s by embedding bitumen-coated steel mesh within the horizontal joints of a brick wall. Although this technique enabled brick spandrel beams or cross walls to be built in a factory and then site assembled like precast concrete, it was more commonly used for on-site construction. The remarkable six storey flats designed by Hugo Haring at Siemensstadt North (1929–31) were made of reinforced brickwork throughout (Fig. 26.18).

Experiments continued after World War II in France and Holland and the method became established as a competitor to precast panels for the construction of housing. Bitumen coated steel eventually corrodes if it is in contact with wet mortar (Haring's flats had to be extensively repaired). The brick reinforcement used nowadays is galvanized or stainless steel mesh (Fig. 26.19).

The advantages of brick laying under factory conditions are a controlled environment and that jigs used in the

Fig. 26.17 *Separate brick envelope to steel frame. The Atkin Building, Grays Inn, London, 1987 (architects Troupe Steel and Scott). External view and detail. See 25.31 for technical detail.*

Fig. 26.18 *Reinforced brickwork at Siemensstadt North Berlin 1929–31 (architect Hugo Haring).*

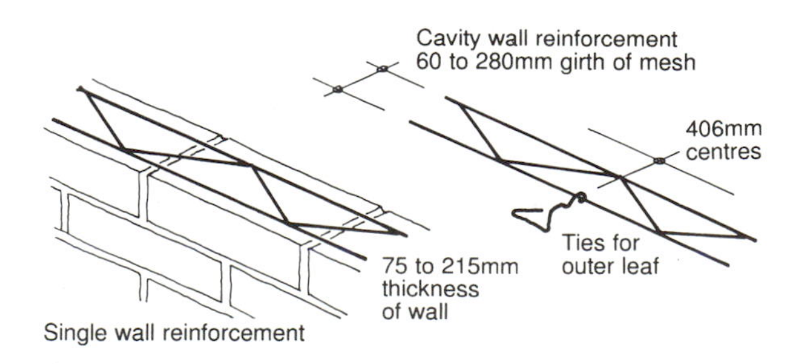

Fig. 26.19 *Stainless steel reinforcement.*

Fig. 26.20 *Factory-made brick-faced spandrel unit.*

workshop can ensure better accuracy (Fig. 26.20). The limits imposed by transportation are similar to those for precast panels (7.5 m by 3.0 m – 24 ft 6 in by 10 ft 10 in – and a weight limit of 7.0 metric tonnes). The use of factory brickwork in the UK is often in combination with precast concrete as a fully bonded facing restrained by stainless anchors and ties. A common application is in the fabrication of moulded spandrel units with stepped corbels and offsets at the head and sill of windows.

This form of construction in the UK has spawned a style of architecture perhaps derived from British breweries and waterworks. Figure 26.21 shows the remarkable brickwork designed by Hugo Filippi (engineer) and Julian Leathart (architect) for the London Brick Company in 1936 and built at Olympia; a structure that realized the potential of the material and method without any stylistic preconceptions.

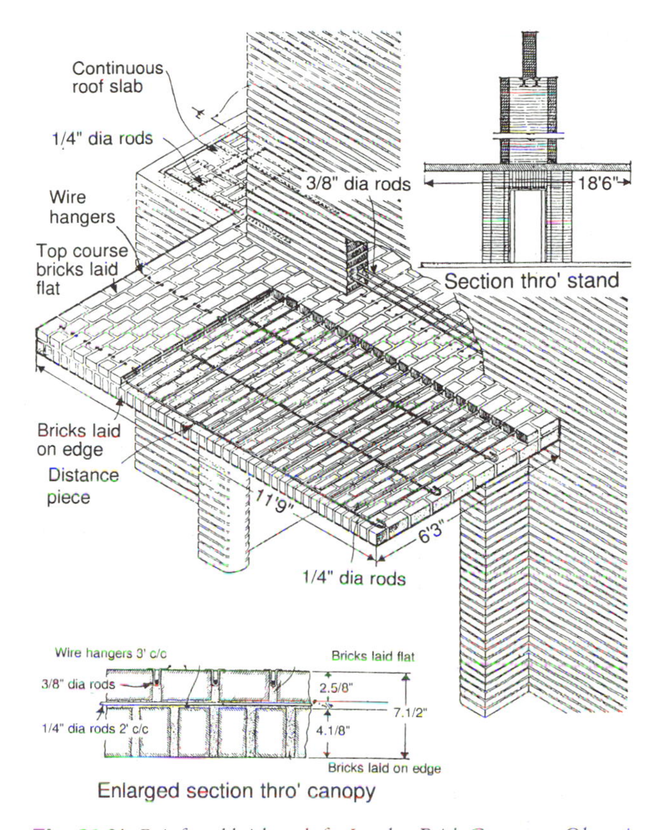

Fig. 26.21 *Reinforced brickwork for London Brick Company, Olympia 1936.*

26.3.6 Ashlar

Ashlar, a form of construction that dates back to Roman times, is a method by which bonded stone blocks are toothed into a solid backing (of blockwork, brickwork or mass concrete). The Roman technique for making stone-faced walls was rediscovered during the Renaissance. Early skyscrapers in Chicago (refer to chapter 1) were built with ashlar walls to give wind restraint to the spine framework of cast iron columns and wrought iron beams.

Late 19th century architects trained in the Beaux Arts tradition combined this ancient technology with the novelty of steelwork (with its unrivalled potential for the enclosure of vast interior spaces), by wrapping their neo-classical facades around steel structures. The perimeter of the frame, being contiguous with the outer walls, permitted the facade to be detailed at a large scale without the cost of massive load bearing walls and columns. Good examples of this 'dressing up' are the Ritz Hotel, London's first steel framed building dating from 1903/6 (designed by Mewès and Davis see Fig. 2.4 in chapter 2), or Selfridges dating from 1907–9 by the Chicago architects Daniel H. Burnham and Co (Fig. 26.22). In both these cases the steel frame supported the floors and roof, leaving the elevation free to follow its own logic. This lack of correlation between interior and exterior and total absence of structural honesty was abhorrent to early modernists. Frederick Gibberd had no doubts about this falsity: in his book *The Architecture of England*[11] he described an illustration of the Edwardian buildings in the the Strand with the caption 'Although the new materials and structural systems are used, they are disguised by ornamental facades which have every appearance of carrying the weight of the building'.

Holden's Senate House, London was of ashlar construction. Increasingly nowadays there are projects where civic design or contextual considerations require the appearance of solid stone, whatever the cost. Current examples in London are Robert Venturi's framed extension to the National Gallery, and Skidmore Owings and Merrill's proposed alterations at County Hall.

The cost of ashlar has led to the development of a whole technology for cladding with a thin stone veneer which is now the most usual specification. Stone slabs used in this way can be of greatly reduced thickness, typically 25 mm (1 in) for marble and slate, 40 mm (1⅝ in) for granite, and

Fig. 26.22 *Selfridges, London 1907–9 (architect Daniel Burnham and Co. Printed by kind permission of Selfridges Ltd).*

Fig. 26.23 *Hennebique propaganda photograph.*

50 mm (2 in) for limestone and sandstone. This lack of substance reveals itself at quoins and window jambs. Fixing is by stainless steel cramps or bolting back to a supporting wall or a steel lattice if designed as a 'rain-screen' facade. A further description of these alternatives to solid ashlar is given in chapter 27.

26.3.7 In situ reinforced concrete

The archives of the French concrete pioneer Hennebique reveal how his researches into reinforced concrete had the central intent of proving that ferro-concrete (the Hennebique term) was a totally fire-resisting form of construction. His firm's publicity constantly stressed that the rival method, uncased frames of cast or wrought iron, would succumb to fire (Fig. 26.23).

The adoption in the UK of frame structures in both in situ reinforced concrete and steel happened in the first years of this century, the first commercial reinforced concrete frame in London being the structure of the Building Centre in Store Street dating from 1904.

Fire precautions led to the requirement for steel frames to be encased with in situ concrete. Building Regulation thicknesses are 50 mm (2 in) concrete cover to achieve (for structural steelwork), a 4 hour fire resistance and 25 mm (1 in) for 2, 1 and ½ hour. This method was the convention in the UK up to the early 1970s. The excessive weight of concrete casing led American engineers to seek alternatives for the construction of skyscrapers. By the 1920s a sprayed coating of cement and asbestos fibre (called 'limpet spray') and asbestos board linings were being employed in the USA. The use in Britain since the 1970s of lightweight and speedy methods of fire encasement is one of the main reasons why steel construction has captured a greatly increased share of the market.

Also of growing importance has been the composite construction of in situ reinforced concrete and steelwork, utilizing their combined qualities to best effect (for a detailed exposition refer to chapter 16). Heavy industrial plant installations are a typical example. The machine floor of a power station needs a strong supporting structure with a high level of fire resistance, both characteristic of concrete. By comparison, the upper long span structure of the machine hall roof can be exposed steel with light cladding.

Typical vertical composite constructions are multi-storey reinforced concrete lift cores which are commonly built in advance of the steel frame which is attached to them, or a reinforced concrete envelope wind bracing a steel spine structure. The latter type is common in North America, especially if the elevations are to combine in situ and precast concrete. Two storey lifts of shuttering are temporarily propped by the steel spine which ultimately forms the load bearing frame (supporting floor loads, wind loads being resisted by the walls, as further described in 'Tall structures', chapter 15).

26.4 CONCLUSION

This chapter on light and heavyweight cladding has drawn many strands together. Building methods can no longer be simply categorized under headings such as roof construction or wall construction when similar or interchangeable components might be used for either. Building envelopes now need to perform as a responsive skin despite increasingly wide ranging requirements. The most impressive technical advances have been made in the design of glazing and window wall assemblies. This is to be expected given that the proportion of the building budget allocated to this element has been increasing, to in some cases equal one third of the whole building cost. This emphasis upon sophisticated 'skin' in turn changes expectations of the skeleton because precise engineering design is needed to fit one with the other. The emphasis of this chapter has naturally been on 'stick construction', the related design requirements of steel

Fig. 26.24 *Indigestible designs.*

for structure and in components for cladding. The alternative tradition of 'mud and stone' (quoting Derek Sugden) has not been forgotten, however, concrete and masonry cladding having also been discussed.

The choice of materials has never been greater, a rich diet that perhaps explains the preponderance of indigestible designs (Fig. 26.24).

REFERENCES AND TECHNICAL NOTES

1. British standards, refer to BS CP3 Chapter V Part 2: 1972 Wind loads. Remember that 'S' factor should never be taken as less than one. If the actual load is greater than the design loads from BS 6399 Part 1: 1984, then the actual load should be used.
2. References to fabricators and suppliers
   Colorcoat in Building (a guide to architectural practice). Published by British Steel Strip Products, April 1990.
   Single Storey Framed Buildings (a design manual for students). Jointly published by British Steel and the Conder Group PLC March 1988.
   Special Issues of the *Architects' Journal*:
   Products in Practice: Cladding 25 Feb 1987 by Dr Alan Brookes.
   Element Design Guide: Profiled Metal Sheet, by Barry Josey, 30 July 1986.
3. *Architecture in Steel in the Australian Context*, by Alan Ogg, published by RAIA.
4. US Army Shutters for Tilt Form Construction. The origins of this method were discovered by Prof. Catherine Bicknell (Washington State University) when researching the early work of Irving Gill (1870–1936), particularly the Klauber House, San Diego 1907.
5. Neue Frankfurt. Reference to American involvement with the concrete technology at Neue Frankfurt was confirmed by Dr F. Kramer (a member of the Ernst May team) on the editor's visit to Romerstadt in 1979.
6. Interstitial condensation
   Condensation in Buildings, Part 1. *A Design Guide*, HMSO 1970. *Architect's Journal*, 19.5.71, p 1149 onwards: Condensation in buildings.
7. Failures
   Structural Failure in Residential Buildings, Volumes 1, 2 and 3, published by Granada, editor Erich Schild).
8. Hope Bagenal born 1888. Acoustic consultant for, among others, Royal Festival Hall, London. Publications include *Practical Acoustics and Planning against Noise* and *Theory and Elements of Architecture*. He was also involved in publications of the Building Research Station and the post-war Building Studies.
9. *Brick Cladding to Steel Framed Buildings*, published jointly by the Brick Development Association and British Steel in September 1986.
10. BS 5628 Code of Practice for Use of Masonry Part 3: 1985 materials components, design and workmanship.
11. Gibberd, F. (1938) *The Architecture of England*, The Architectural Press.

FURTHER READING

Books on failures

My library shelves have a whole section dedicated to this area of growth within the building industry, the following titles have been selected as the most useful references, the balance of my material being cuttings from magazines and newspapers.

BRE Digests: These are carefully written and presented but tend to be published a long time after the event.

Structural Failure in Residential Buildings, Volumes 1–3 inclusive, published by Granada (Editor Erich Schild). Totally thorough and a frightening exposure of building failures in Germany since the 1950s.

A Qualitative Study of Some Buildings in the London Area, HMSO Special Report No. 33. A most excellent book that reviews famous buildings with a lot of wisdom from the late Hope Bagenal.

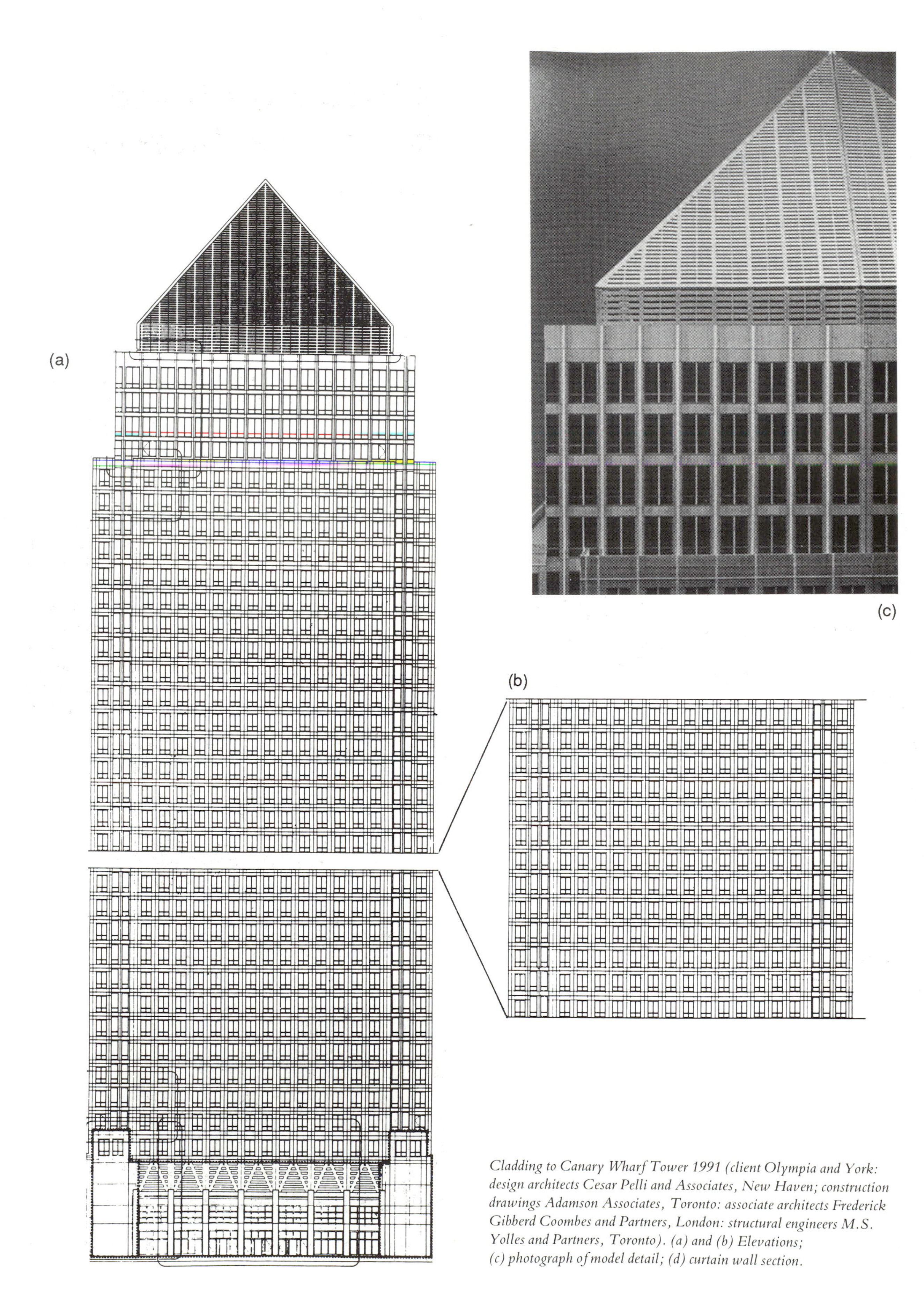

Cladding to Canary Wharf Tower 1991 (client Olympia and York: design architects Cesar Pelli and Associates, New Haven; construction drawings Adamson Associates, Toronto: associate architects Frederick Gibberd Coombes and Partners, London: structural engineers M.S. Yolles and Partners, Toronto). (a) and (b) Elevations; (c) photograph of model detail; (d) curtain wall section.

27

Window walls and rain-screen facades

Alan Blanc

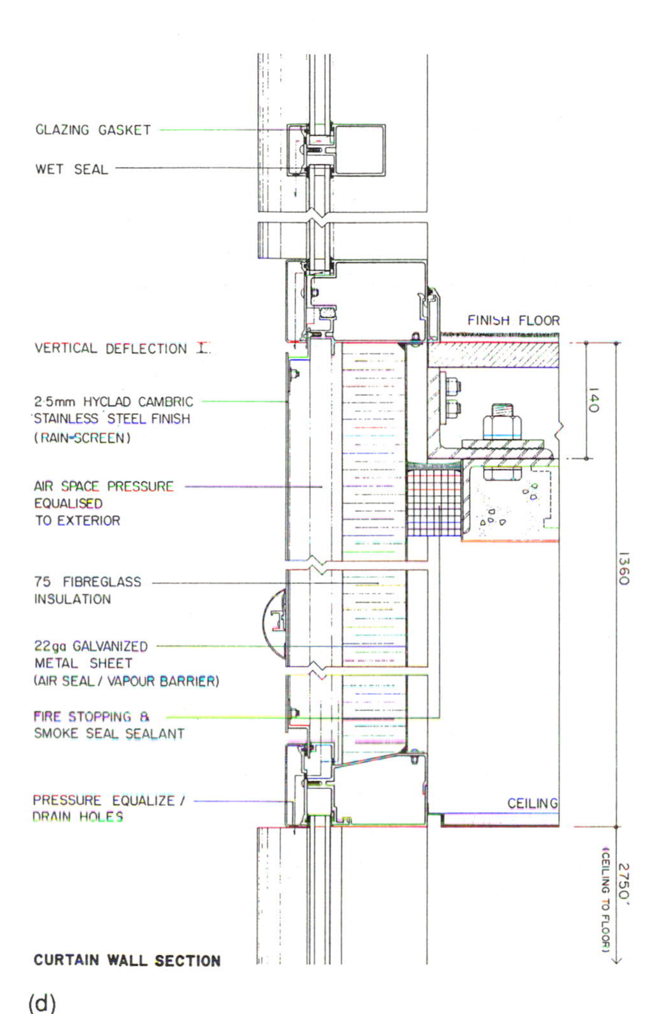

(d)

27.1 INTRODUCTION

Chapter 31 traces the historical development of metal windows and patent glazing and the emergence of the 'window wall' – a curtain of glass and glazing bars. By the 1940s the term 'curtain walling' was commonly used when describing contemporary cladding technology in the United States.

Dating from 1948, the Equitable Building, Portland, Oregon (designed by Pietro Belluschi, Fig. 27.1 and [1]) is an early North American example. Aluminium 'stick' frames were superimposed onto the structure in a grid pattern, forming a facade that was then clad with glass and aluminium panels. The wall plane had a total thickness of 100 mm (4 in). The new technology was promoted as a 'space saver' since infilling the structural frame with conventional masonry amounted in thickness to 400 mm (1 ft 4 in) or 450 mm (1 ft 6 in). The construction of early curtain walling falls into two types. The commonest pattern

Fig. 27.1 *Curtain wall at the Equitable Building, Portland, Oregon, 1948 (architect Pietro Belluschi).*

Fig. 27.2 *New Cavendish Street Offices, London, 1955 (architects GMW).*

employed tubular sections, either extruded aluminium or steel, forming vertical 'sticks' spanning floor-to-floor and fixed to the edge of each slab. The glass and panels were carried on mullions and transoms, waterproofing of the junction between them relying upon sleeved joints and mastic. The alternative and superior technique involved a skeletal frame of flat bars or tubular sections, onto which was fixed a profiled metal cap. This method incorporated self-draining cavities, making it the precursor to today's 'rain-screen' facades. (see *Walls off the Peg* by Michael Brawne in the *Architectural Review*, Sept 1957 for a more complete history of the 'curtain wall').

Significant examples of both techniques are to be seen in London:

(a) Daily Mirror Building, Holborn (Sir Owen Williams and others)

Dating from 1957–60 the aluminium curtain walling was made from simple tubular sections; after 25 years the metal surfaces became badly corroded and were painted over. The building is now due to be demolished.

(b) New Cavendish Street Offices (GMW)

There were two interesting early curtain wall facades in New Cavendish Street (Electrin House and the offices opposite), both designed by GMW in the mid 1950s. The assembly (Fig. 27.2) included galvanized steel opening lights and anodized cover strips to the mullion and transom grid. It is due to be renovated, to a new design by GMW, so as to upgrade the standard of insulation.

(c) Vickers Tower, Millbank, 1961–2 (Ronald Ward and Partners) refer also Fig. 6.10

Incorporating stainless steel capping sections (by the Morris Singer Foundry) superimposed over galvanized steel sub-framing, this curtain wall is still in service after 25 years and without major problems. The system depends upon effective cover laps rather than the use of mastic. (See Fig. 6.10.)

27.2 DESIGN TRENDS TODAY

In times past, the shortcomings of British curtain walling were not simply due to corrosion and leaks but also the lack of solar control. The hot summer of 1976 resulted in many London 'curtain wall' offices being evacuated when interior temperatures soared above 100°F.

The response from an environmental viewpoint has been threefold. Firstly, the National Building Regulations now require a building's window to wall area to be reduced to 35% (unless the designer can compensate by specifying other parts of the construction to be of improved thermal performance). This 'trading off' encourages an increase in the insulation of walls and windows, to the standard that can be achieved by a conventional masonry 'hole in the wall' elevation (Fig. 27.3).

Secondly, British insulation standards were raised in 1986 to 0.6 $W/m^2 K$ for walls, and raised again in 1990 to 0.45 W/m^2K.

Thirdly, energy saving has been promoted by government. The BRE for example, have constructed, as a demonstration, offices with built-in solar protective external blinds and louvres to reduce cooling loads [2].

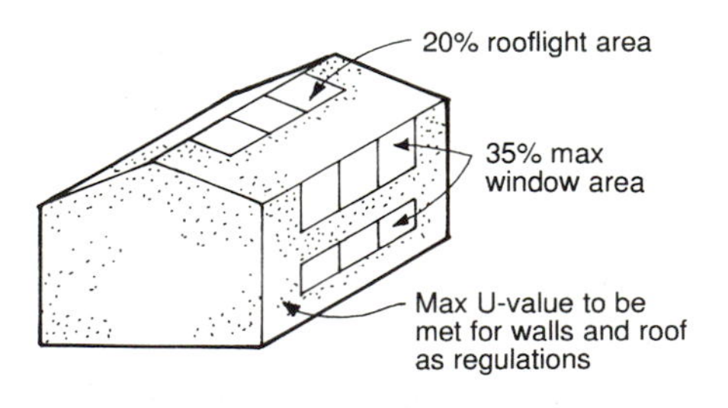

"Deemed to Satisfy" approach

Calculations for all areas made

Window elements calculated

Calculated design: Total exposed surfaces to meet 0.6W/m²K

Fig. 27.3 *'Trading off' approach within the UK Building Regulations.*

27.3 RESPONSE TO ENERGY SAVING IN FACADE CONSTRUCTION

The response from designers and the building industry to changing regulations as well as greater concern with energy saving is detailed below.

27.3.1 Window areas and insulation

Double or triple glazing is now commonplace, as are thermally broken framing systems. Multi-ply glass, used by some continental curtain walling manufacturers, allows substantially improved thermal performance.

Coated glasses are being developed that change from clear to tinted with the application of an electric current switched by environmental sensors. Building envelopes will become fully responsive to changing climatic conditions. It will then be possible for the whole facade to be of consistent thermal performance and limitation of window size will no longer be a prerequisite of energy efficiency.

27.3.2 Increased insulation standards

Wall panels can readily be made to achieve these higher standards, whereas each increase is more difficult to accommodate within the confines of traditional masonry construction.

27.3.3 Built-in energy saving

It is now common practice to look at the total energy equation for a building (ground slabs, roofing and walling) and for elevation design to take into account orientation and solar protection measures.

27.4 BASIC FORMS OF WINDOW WALL

27.4.1 Stick system

This term (from the USA) describes a system of vertical metal studs that are fixed floor edge to floor edge, bottom to top of the facade (Fig. 27.4). Between them are individual transom members to help support glass and spandrel panels. Vertical movement is allowed by the use of sleeve joints at the junction with floors. The whole assembly requires a large number of site fixings. Two-piece brackets with slotted holes (to absorb lack of alignment in the frame) attach the curtain walling to the structure. The system may include track for cradle gear, which can be devised to assist

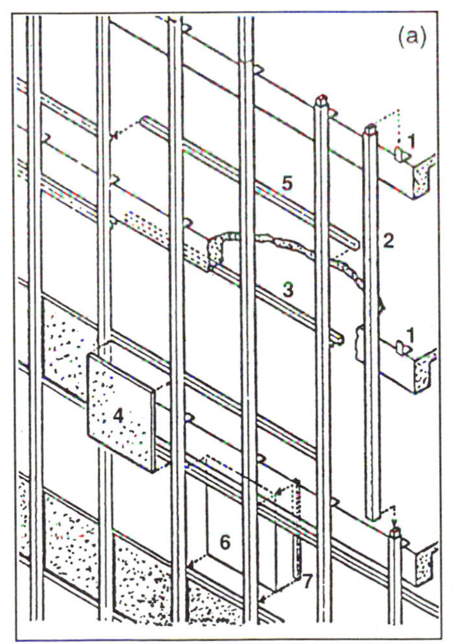

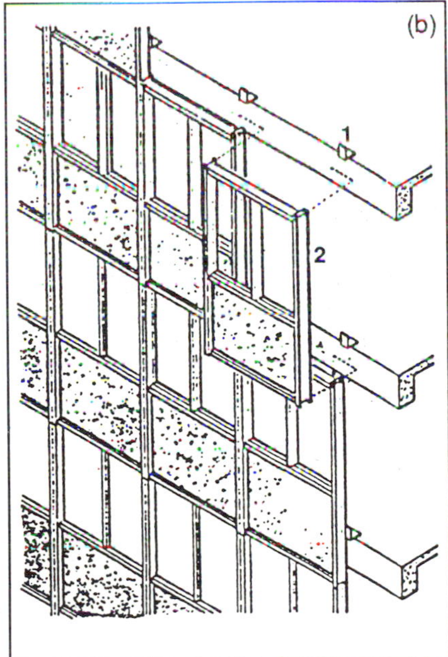

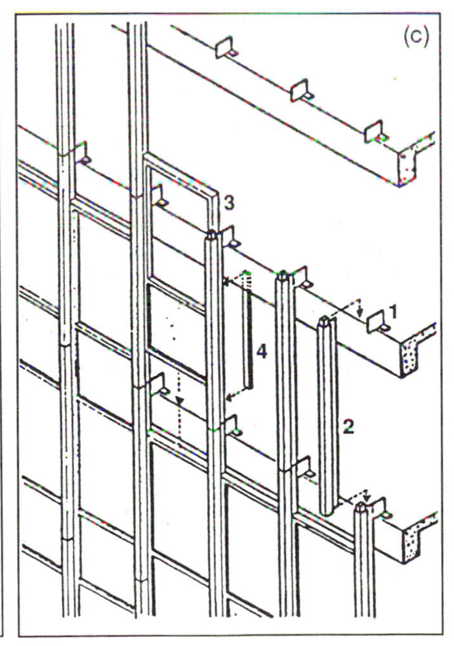

Fig. 27.4 *Stick frame in curtain walling. Reprinted by kind permission of Architectural Forum. (a) Stick system. 1: Anchors. 2: Mullion. 3: Horizontal rail (gutter section at window head). 4: Spandrel panel (may be installed from inside building). 5: Horizontal rail (window sill section). 6: Vision glass (installed from inside building). 7: Interior mullion trim. (b) Unit system. 1: Anchor. 2: Pre-assembled framed unit. (c) Unit-and-mullion system. 1: Anchors. 2: Mullion (either one- or two-storey lengths) 3: Pre-assembled unit lowered into place behind mullion from floor above. 4: Interior mullion trim.*

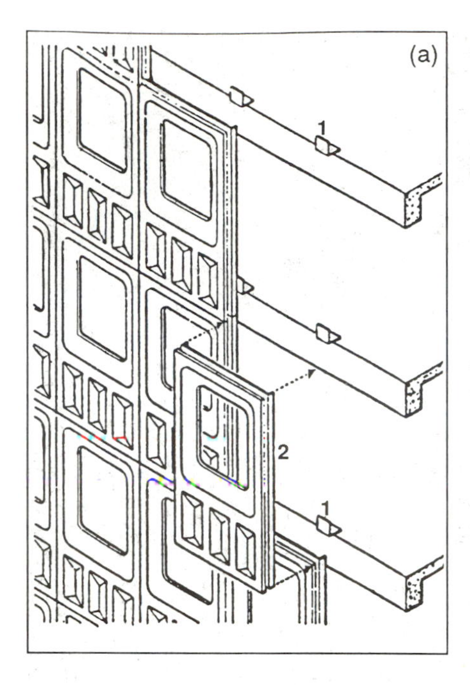

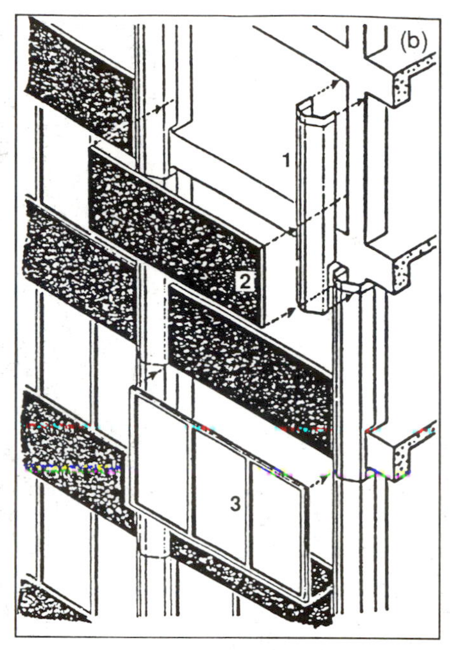

Fig. 27.5 *Spandrel systems. Reprinted by kind permission of Architectural Forum. (a) Panel system. 1: Anchor. 2: Panel. (b) Column cover and spandrel system. 1: Column cover section. 2: Spandrel panel. 3: Glazing infill.*

during construction, avoiding the necessity for external scaffolding. The average overall thickness is 200–220 mm (8–9 in) including thermal breaks, insulation and a fire barrier at floor level.

A more sophisticated version (called the 'unit system'), employs pre-manufactured panels that are simply abutted side by side without independent mullions.

27.4.2 Spandrel system

The characteristic of this method is the horizontal format of alternating spandrel panels and windows. The window frames, continuous from column to column, may come from the factory pre-glazed (Fig. 27.5); the window fixings are made at sill and head. The zone between one range of windows and the next, at the column grid, is infilled by a panel of masonry or precast concrete or some other material (perhaps to match the spandrel panel). The wall thickness is around 230–250 mm (9–10 in) greater than that of a stick system due to the extra strength required for transportation. Lengths up to 9 m (29 ft 6 in) are possible but a principal consideration is the limitation imposed by break-press sizes (up to 7.5 m – 24 ft 6 in) for ancillary sheet metal work, sills or head flashings, that need to be in one piece and leakproof, between abutments or fixings.

27.4.3 Structural glass (glass blocks and lenses)

This term was coined by Pilkington's to describe a number of structural concepts for glass in building enclosures. The original construction method employed toughened glass hollow blocks or lenses which were cemented together with reinforced joints or cast with reinforced concrete ribs to form translucent walling. The most famous example is the 'Maison de Verre' (1927–32) by Pierre Chareau and Bernard Bijvoet (Fig. 27.7).

The use of reinforced concrete ribs also enabled floor slabs and vaults to be constructed with glass blocks and lenses. Steel or wrought iron trays permitted this material to be used for mundane tasks such as pavement lights or for more sophisticated applications such as treads for steel staircases. The glass block and steel framed floor of Wagner's Post Office Savings Bank Vienna (1903–6) was designed to illuminate the basement sorting office (refer to chapter 1). Another version of steel tray and glass construction is used to light the eight storey stair well, top to bottom at the Immeuble 'Clarté', Geneva by Le Corbusier (1930–32) (refer to chapter 33).

Glass block construction in masonry form (with wire reinforced mortar joints) or framed in reinforced concrete or steel makes an excellent interior material. Its opalescent quality brings light and sparkle to internal spaces (Fig. 27.8). The performance of 'glasscrete' externally is disappointing. The temperature range from winter to summer causes considerable differential movement of glass and framing and internal stresses that can finally crack toughened blocks or lenses.

An example dating from 1930, a glass block vaulted

banking hall in Prague, Czechoslovakia, has been preserved by overcladding with conventional patent glazing. Glass block panels no larger than 2.4 × 2.4 m (8 × 8 ft), are deemed to be ½ hour fire resistant under the Inner London Building Acts and are useful for the construction of stair enclosures.

27.4.4 Other structural glasses (toughened/bonded glass)

The weakness of glass in bending and compression can be reduced by annealing (heating and cooling), to form toughened glass which has high compression prestress at its

Fig. 27.7 *Maison de Verre, Paris 1927–32 (architects Pierre Chareau and Bernard Bijvoet).*

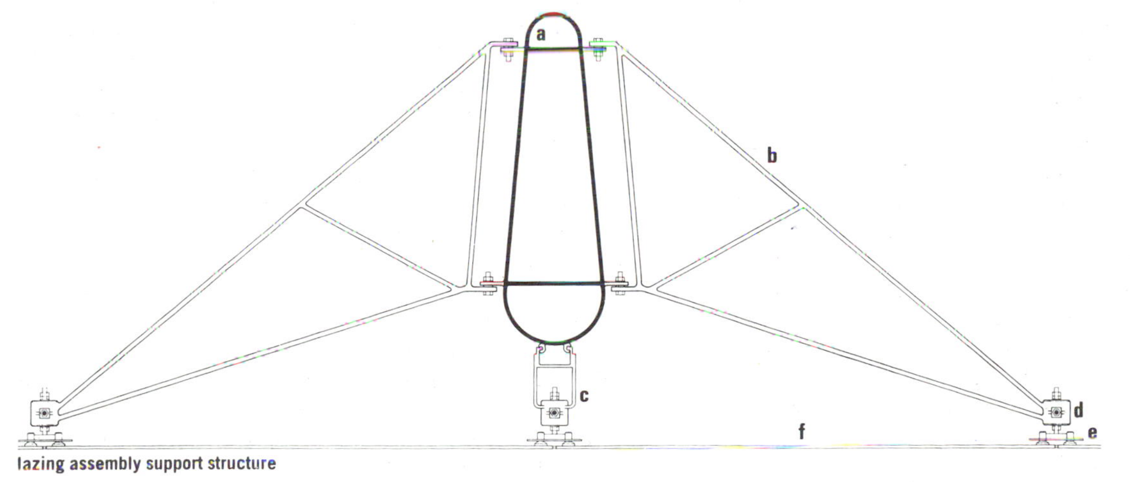

Fig. 27.6 *Planar glazing. Financial Times Works, London, 1989 (architects Nicholas Grimshaw and Partners). a: Fabricated steel aerofoil column. b: Wind restraint glazing arm. c: Sliding connection to column and suspension rod. d: Suspension rod. e: Glass fixing assembly. f: Toughened glass panel.*

Fig. 27.8 *Entries to the Science and Technology Museum, Parc de la Villette, Paris 1988 (designer Rice, Francis and Ritchie).*

surfaces with a balancing tension stress at its centre. As a result, toughened glass has better loadbearing qualities and higher impact resistance. The annealing process is used to toughen glass blocks, trough sheets (patent name Profilit) and float glass (patent name Armourplate).

Toughened glass sheets may be joined by connecting plates or tees attached to vertical stiffening webs of toughened glass. Glass walls of this kind, suspended to benefit from the relative strength in tension of glass [3], can be constructed up to 20 m (65 ft) in height (Fig. 27.8). A key consideration in the choice of glass size is that toughened glass has a minimum 1:7 proportion of length to width.

'Planar' glazing (the system of suspended structural glazing developed by Pilkingtons), utilizes the strength of 3 or 5 ply glass or toughened glass. The connection pane to pane is made with silicon adhesive, and the assembly is restrained against the wind by metal framing bolted to the inner face of the glass.

The interior framing can be constructed as a lattice to brace the window wall. A most elegant solution is the stainless steel truss designed by Rice, Francis and Ritchie for the Science and Technology Museum, Parc de la Villette, Paris (Fig. 27.9).

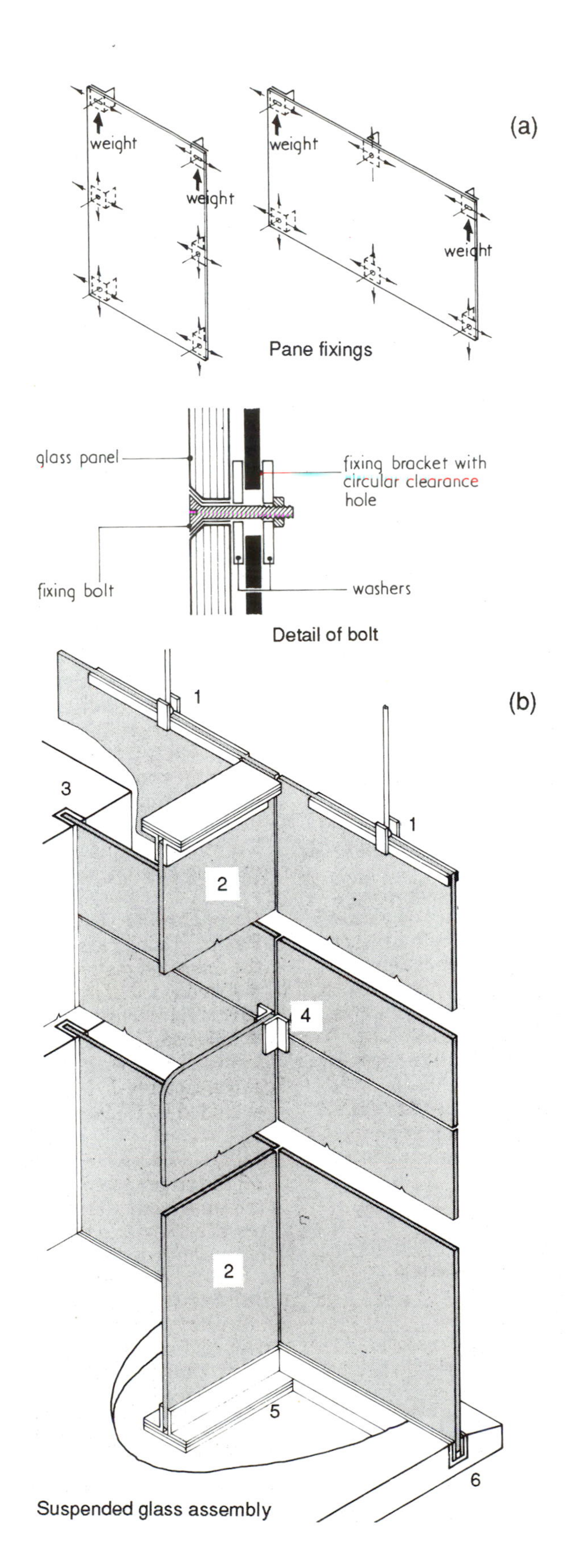

Fig. 27.9 *Armourplate assemblies. Reprinted by kind permission of Pilkington Glass Ltd. (a) Each pane is suspended and restrained by bolts countersunk into the glass and fixed through washers into the supporting structure behind. Fixings that carry the weight of the glass are slotted, allowing lateral movement only. (b) Basic components of a suspended glass assembly. 1: Glass hangs from its top edge by an adjustable suspension system which allows for irregularities and deflections in the substructure. 2: Glass stabilizer fins provide lateral resistance to wind load. 3: Side channel allows movement in the plane of the glass but resists lateral movement. 4: Metal patch fittings are used to connect panes and to join panes to fins. 5: The bottom of a fin may be clamped to prevent rotation or it may be held in a shoe that allows vertical movements while restraining lateral ones. 6: The base channel must allow vertical movement of the glass without bottoming. If the range of movement is large, neoprene gaskets are used.*

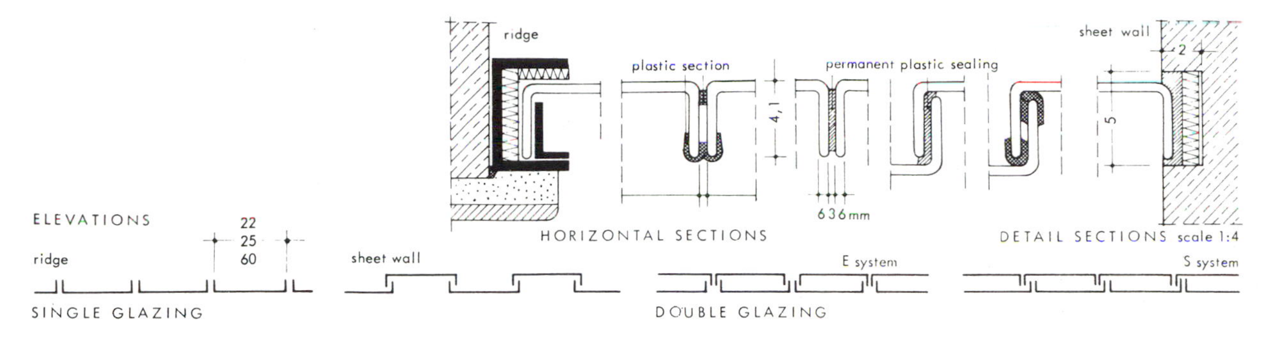

Fig. 27.10 *'Profilit', typical details.*

'Profilit' glazing consists of U-section glass planks placed side by side (Fig. 27.10); the flanges allow the glass, without any framing, to span between supporting and tie members (angle or channel) at the top and bottom of each panel. Attempts have been made to use 'Profilit' as a glazed roofing material but without much success.

A material more often used today is multi-ply glass. A variety of requirements (e.g. security and solar) can be accommodated within the layers of glass and film that make up the laminated 'sandwich'. Three or five layers of glass are used to balance the stresses around the central core. The films are adhesive and selected for their solar reflective qualities. The glass layers can be 'float plate' or toughened, their thickness varying, ply by ply, to improve sound deadening over a range of frequencies. The most effective sound insulation is, however, achieved by double glazing with a 100 mm minimum air space between panes.

Fig. 27.11 *'Pyran' fire-resisting bonded glass. Reprinted by kind permission of Pilkington Glass Ltd.*

27.4.5 Fire resisting glazing

The fire resistance of bonded glass can be increased by making the last face (towards the fire risk) 'georgian wired', though as a consequence the maximum size of a pane will be 1.6 m^2.

An optically clear alternative is edge bonded glass (patent names Pyran etc., Fig. 27.11) that embody intumescent material within the cavity. Such glass panes can be toughened and designed to provide 2 hours fire resistance if fixed with solid steel beads and steel framing. Aluminium is not permitted to have any structural role and if used in detailing has to be considered as sacrificial.

27.5 CASE STUDIES

Three case studies have been selected to illustrate the construction of window walls from glass and steel.

Compared with aluminium, bronze, plastic or timber, steel, or for that matter cast and wrought iron, have advantageous fire resisting capabilities when used as glass framing materials. The National Building Regulations and the surviving Inner London Byelaws (under Section 20 – for large buildings) include 'deemed to satisfy' conditions for 6 mm Georgian wire glass in combination with steel frames, using solid steel or other fire-resistant beads. Aluminium, bronze or timber are not permitted except in a sacrificial way. Fire resistance is not only a requirement of glazed fire compartment walls within buildings but also at critical junctions in envelope walls, particularly at floors. Reference should be made to the requirements of BS 476 [4].

The increasing use of performance specifications is changing the attitude of designers towards 'deemed to satisfy' conditions. Because steel (carbon, Cor-Ten or stainless) has greater strength at higher temperatures than other metals, it is still the most frequently selected material for cladding fixings and for structural elements within window walls.

27.5.1 Patera system (1982)

This system [5], a universal 'umbrella' for light industrial, office and storage buildings, has been patented by the designer Michael Hopkins and his client Nigel Dale. Its flexibility permits a Patera building to be relocated, reassembled and reused. Services are external to the environmental envelope so they can be modified and upgraded without disrupting the internal functions of the building. The wall and ceiling panels are modular and comprise either steel composite panels or steel framed window units; a universal connector allows panels to be clipped onto or removed from the steel umbrella frame (Fig. 27.12).

The insulation standards of the original system are those of the 1986 National Building Regulations which have now been superseded.

The cladding and structural principles derived by Dale and Hopkins are of particular interest, an instructive example for the design of small industrial buildings. Steel was selected for both skin and structure because of the high strength required for each component and to limit bimetallic corrosion risks at the large number of exposed points of contact.

27.5.2 Jansen VISS system

Jansen, a Swiss company, have been marketing cold formed and tubular components for 60 years, and their patented profiles are used for door and window fabrication. The necessity for compliance with European codes for wall insulation has led to the development of rooflight and window systems made from structural tubular studs (a 'warm' frame) with 'clip on' thermally broken glazing. Unlike the Patera system, where the frame is on the 'cold weather' side, Jansen have employed the opposite concept.

The Jansen VISS System is a structural window wall that resists wind loads and also helps carry floor loads, in effect a 'balloon' frame in tubular steel sections (Fig. 27.13, also refer back to details in Figs 25.5 to 25.8).

27.5.3 BMW headquarters

For the BMW headquarters, Nicholas Grimshaw and Partners designed custom-made window wall panels: the production programme was sufficiently large to warrant fabrication of a 'one-off' system specific to this project.

The BMW buildings are steel framed office and warehouse blocks with internal structure (i.e. on the 'warm' side of the envelope, see Fig. 27.14). The cladding is totally external to the frame, forming a window-less shell around the warehouses, and an adaptable skin to the offices. The connecting lugs and peripheral members are made from steel sections, panel materials are GRP, glazing or pressed aluminium.

The construction, which is extremely lightweight and simple, demonstrates the way in which the functional

(a)

(b)

Fig. 27.12 *Patera system. (a) General view of offices for British Telecom, Canary Wharf, London. (b) Detail of facade and framing system. (c) Assembly of roof components. (d) Assembly of wall components. Printed by kind permission of Michael Hopkins and Partners and Mark Whitby (engineer responsible with Anthony Hunt).*

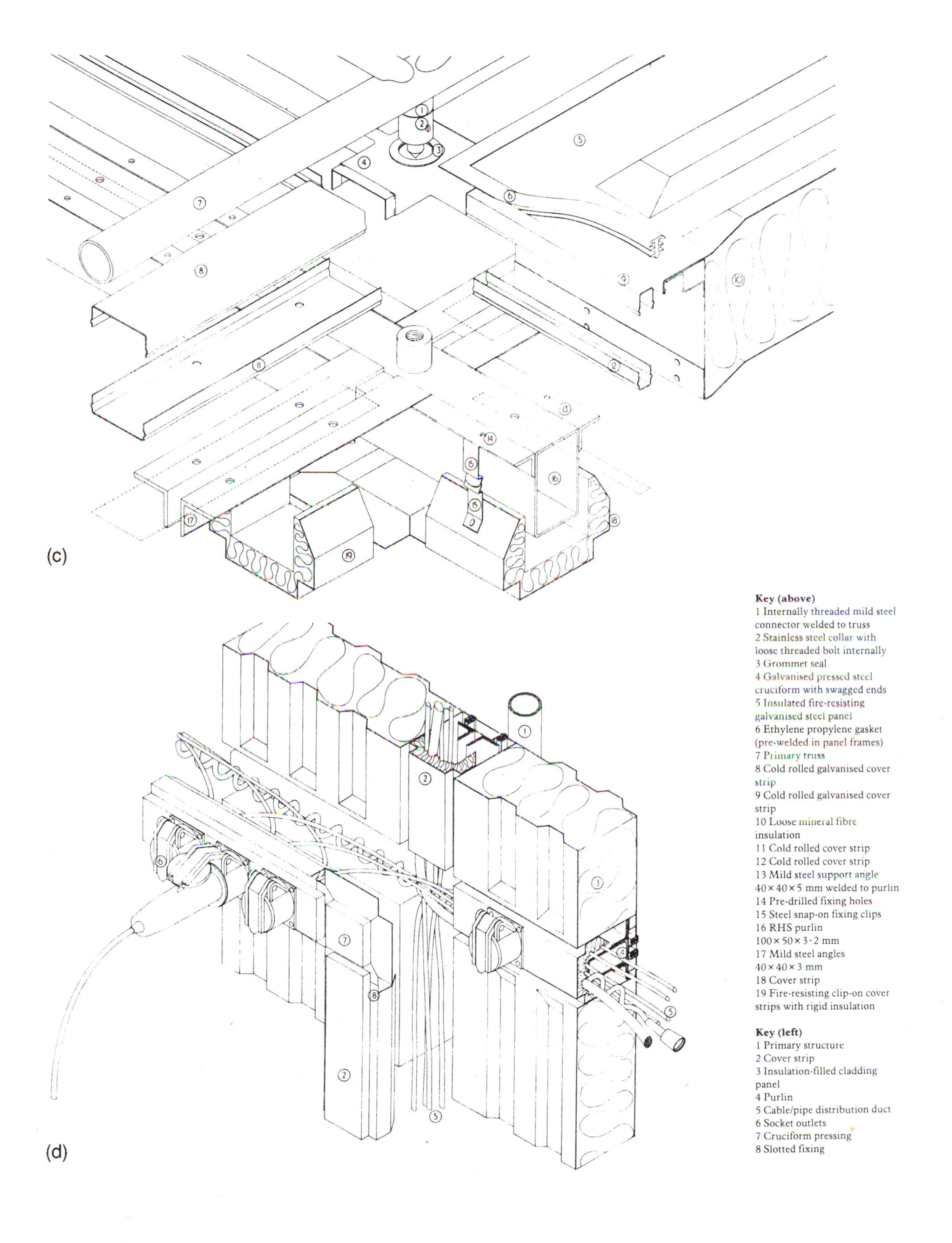

(c)

(d)

Key (above)

1 Internally threaded mild steel connector welded to truss
2 Stainless steel collar with loose threaded bolt internally
3 Grommet seal
4 Galvanised pressed steel cruciform with swagged ends
5 Insulated fire-resisting galvanised steel panel
6 Ethylene propylene gasket (pre-welded in panel frames)
7 Primary truss
8 Cold rolled galvanised cover strip
9 Cold rolled galvanised cover strip
10 Loose mineral fibre insulation
11 Cold rolled cover strip
12 Cold rolled cover strip
13 Mild steel support angle 40 × 40 × 5 mm welded to purlin
14 Pre-drilled fixing holes
15 Steel snap-on fixing clips
16 RHS purlin 100 × 50 × 3·2 mm
17 Mild steel angles 40 × 40 × 3 mm
18 Cover strip
19 Fire-resisting clip-on cover strips with rigid insulation

Key (left)

1 Primary structure
2 Cover strip
3 Insulation-filled cladding panel
4 Purlin
5 Cable/pipe distribution duct
6 Socket outlets
7 Cruciform pressing
8 Slotted fixing

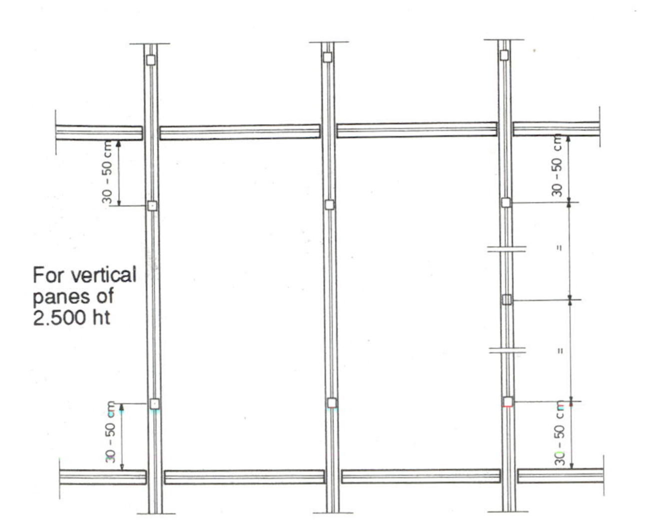

Framing method with vertical proportion

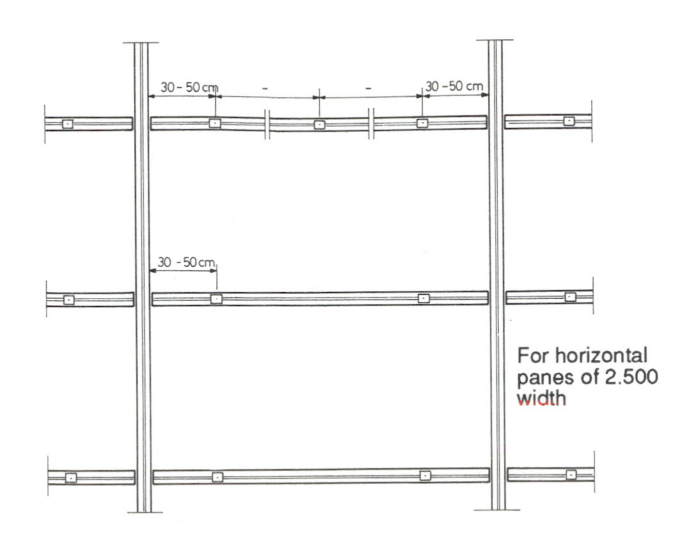

Framing method with horizontal proportion

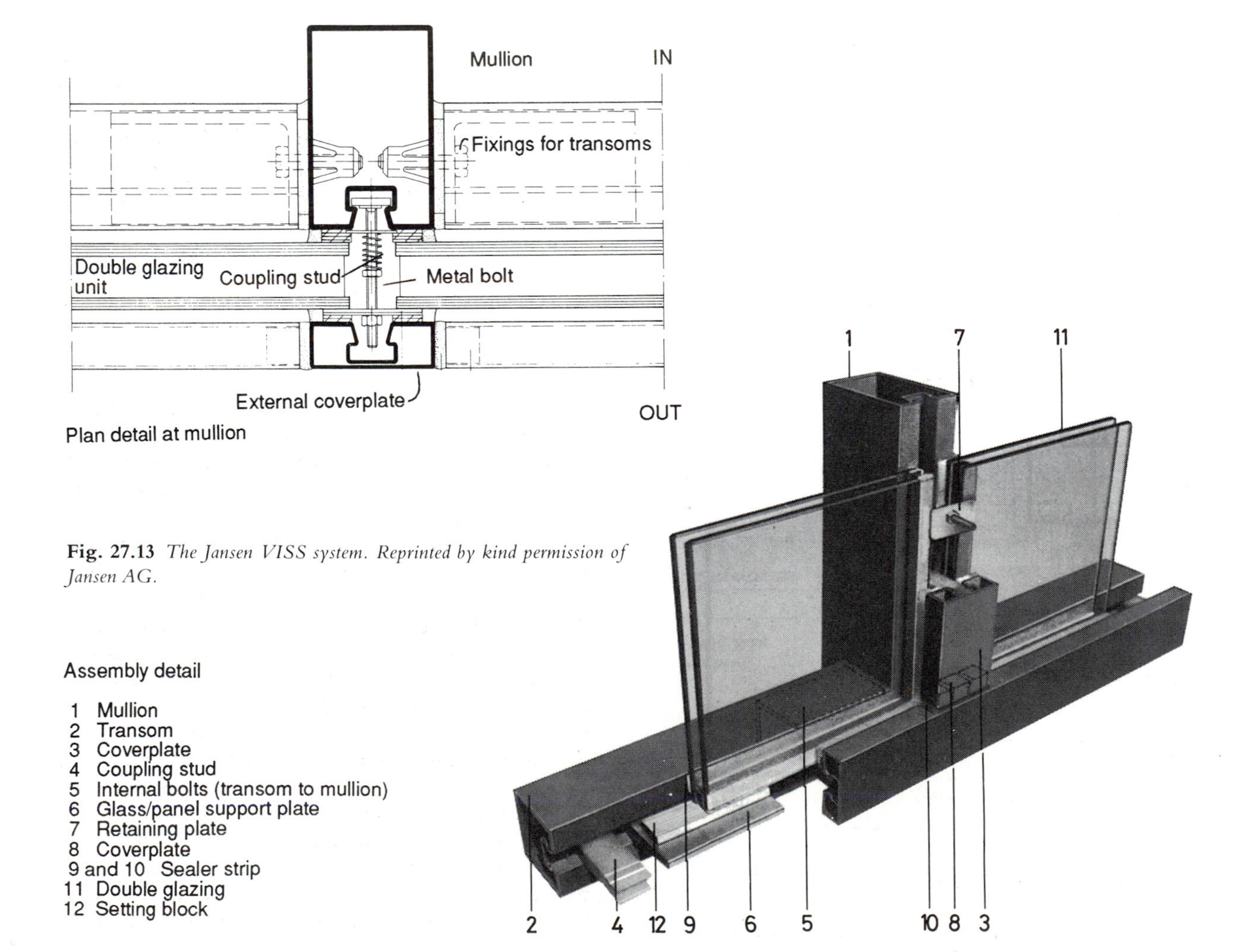

Fig. 27.13 *The Jansen VISS system. Reprinted by kind permission of Jansen AG.*

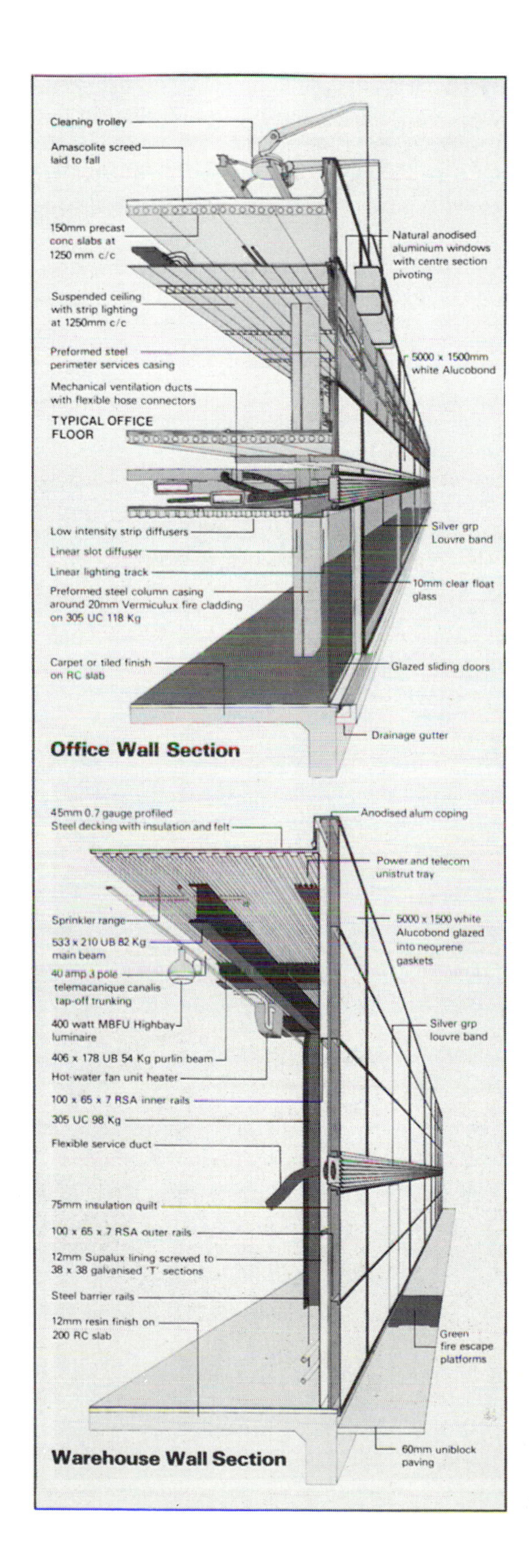

Fig. 27.14 *BMW Headquarters, Bracknell, Berks, 1979 (architects Nicholas Grimshaw and Partners: engineers Peter Brett Associates). Refer also to fig. 12.25 for frame details.*

requirements of building enclosure can be zoned in section, resulting in an elegant solution to the cladding of steel structures. Once again, the insulation standards to which this scheme was designed pre-date the 1986 revision of the Building Regulations, details would have to be reconsidered for a future project or if British Codes are increased to meet European standards after 1992.

27.6 RAIN-SCREEN FACADES

27.6.1 Principles

There are several methods by which water can breach the outer envelope of a building, for example by gravity as rain runs down its face, the kinetic energy of raindrops hitting its surface or capillarity between layers of the construction. The largest volume leaks are, however, caused by differences in air pressure, internal/external to the building enclosure. As a result, air and accompanying rainwater are drawn inside through any imperfect joints in the outer envelope.

The distinction between layers or zones of construction performing different tasks, i.e. waterproofing, insulation and structural support is common to all 'rain-screen' systems, whether made from ferrous or non-ferrous components. The rain-screen is a 'weather coat' at the outer skin of the building, shedding most water but allowing any rain that penetrates the surface to be led to a point where it can be discharged back to the outside. The ultimate defence, the airtight construction separating internal and external air pressures, may be achieved by the use of gaskets or mastic behind the rain-screen and thereby protected from solar radiation. Clearly this sophisticated layering needs to be assembled in such a way that cavities can be inspected and relatively short life components such as mastic or plastic can be replaced.

Typically, a rain-screen facade will have an outer skin of impervious material supported by a metal subframe, designed to incorporate drainage ways to collect and discharge leaks whilst maintaining separation from the inner insulated and airtight layers of the wall.

27.6.2 Rehabilitation

Rain-screen cladding is used not only for new building but also as method of rehabilitating buildings, particularly those constructed in the 1950s and 1960s and now suffering from weather penetration and poor insulation. Over-cladding is now widespread, usually by the use of insulated panels and windows that are fixed to a studwork of cold formed profiles attached to the original facade (Fig. 27.15). The design of these systems draws upon pioneering experience of rain-screen cladding in mainland Europe and in North America. Over-cladding older buildings has not proved trouble free, and concrete frames may present continuing difficulties due to shrinkage or sway. In the case of tall structures (18 storey and over) sway can cause loosening of fixings and joints (see chapter 25).

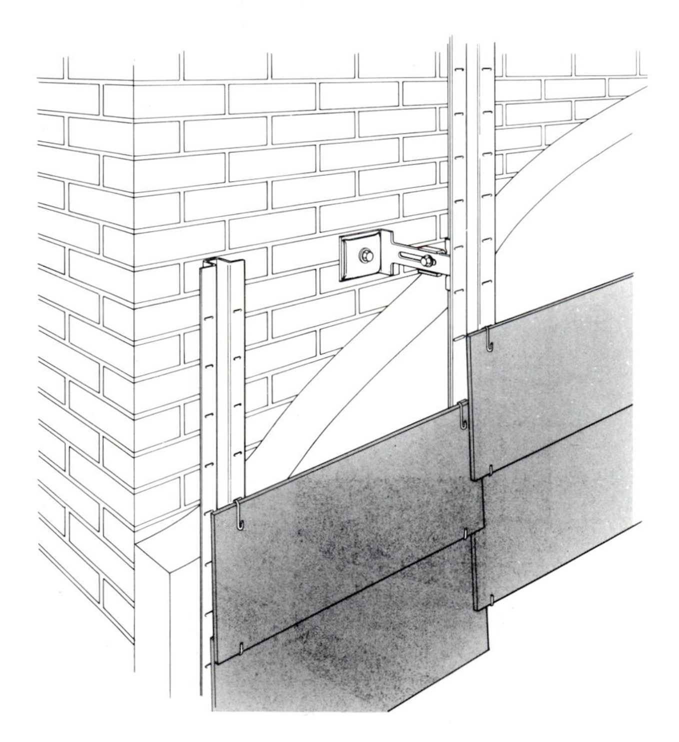

Fig. 27.15 *Eternit in rain-screen facade. This forms a ventilated rainscreen of decorative panels, supported on a galvanized steel framework, and provides an adjustable void for ventilation and insulation. The decorative cladding panels are hook fixed onto the galvanized steel vertical profiles, which are fixed at a predetermined distance from the supporting structure to allow for ventilation and the designed thickness of the insulation. Galvanized steel support brackets are used. Reprinted with kind permission of Eternit UK Ltd.*

27.7 RECENT DEVELOPMENTS – THE DESIGN OF TRUSSED ELEVATIONAL UNITS

The history of post-war building reveals a hit and miss attitude to building science. For example, building failures resulting from the shrinkage of in situ and precast concrete frames led to the idea of the 'soft-joint', imparting head restraint to storey-height panels whilst allowing further shrinkage of the concrete frame (Fig. 27.16).

Window wall manufacturers rely upon slot hole fixings that in theory take up tolerances, also grooved face plates that form a 'slip plane' in the event of shrinkage or sway. Rigid planar elements such as glass or stone veneer will not tolerate the resulting distortion, hence the frequency of failure.

Such problems are commonplace (see *Structural Failure in Residential Buildings*, a catalogue of mistakes from the 1960s, written by Erich Schild *et al.*, Granada, 1979).

Consulting engineers have investigated techniques that can isolate individual elements, panes of glass or slabs of granite, from movement stresses. One current solution is the use of large-scale trussed elevational units that span from column to column. Most simply, the concept could be compared to 'plate mail' – two top 'hinge' points allowing the cladding to sway without distortion occurring. A more complex method is to weld the trussed unit in place which can contribute rigidity to the structural frame. It is possible to foresee, in the 21st century, responsive facades with cables and power jacks slackening or tightening the trusses and withstanding varying stresses, as and when they occur.

At present, steel trussed elevations are most familiar for the cladding of steel framed buildings (the details that follow are based on material supplied by Christopher McCarthy (of Battle and McCarthy) and Sean Billings).

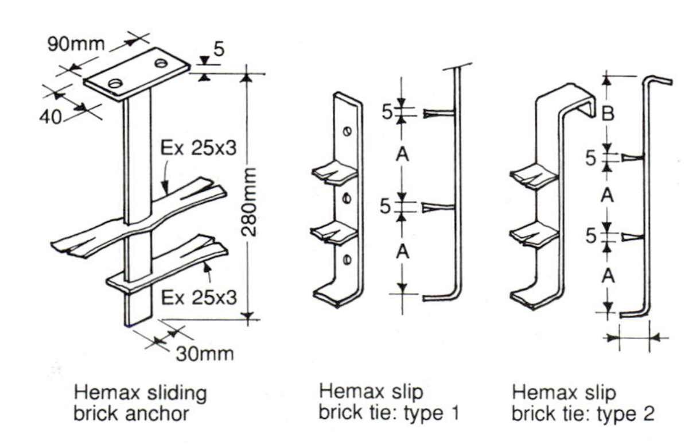

Fig. 27.16 *Slip joints.*

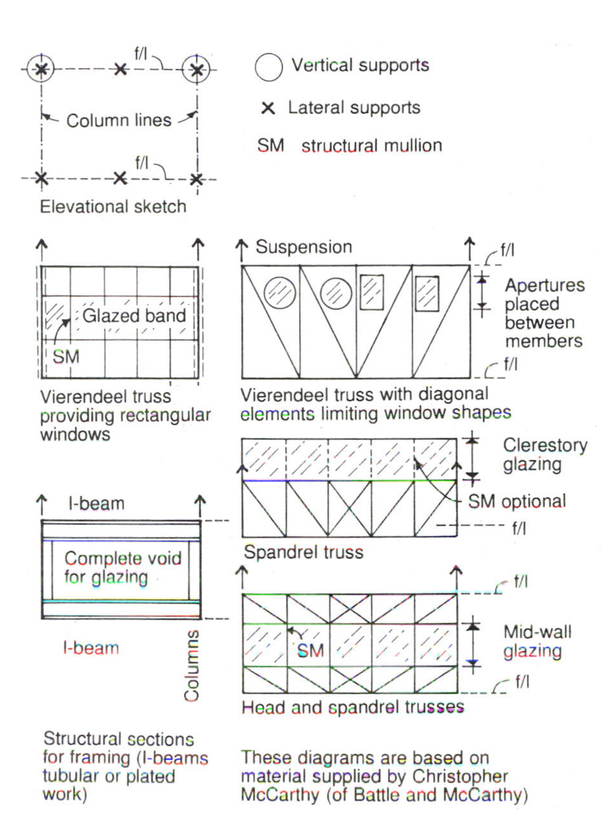

Fig. 27.17 *Elevational trusses and details.*

27.7.1 Manufacturing methods

The fabrication of steelwork resembles conventional truss construction; structural sections (angles, universal beams, tubes and channels) are welded to include two pairs of fixing lugs (Fig. 27.17). The truss is then transferred to the cladding shop where the finished facing and windows are applied, using cement fibre board as insulant and fire liner between the facing material and frame. The core is filled with mineral wool which doubles as a cavity fire stop at the crucial junction of floor and spandrel. The inner finishes are usually fire liner board plus decoration or facing panels including integrated electrical, heating and mechanical services. The total thickness is around 300 mm (12 in).

27.7.2 Limitations

Weight and maximum sizes for transportion are the main design limitations and in particular clear heights at bridges. The usual means of delivery is by road trailer with the panels sloping against a vertical rack. Consequently a maximum delivery has a dead load of 10 tonnes and is 4.5 m (15 ft) in height and 12 m (40 ft) in length. Delivery by rail allows a longer component length of 21 m (69 ft) but a reduced

Fig. 27.18 *The Portland Public Services Building, Portland, Oregon, 1983 (architect Michael Graves). Cladding carried on trussed elements to facade.*

height of 2.4 m (8 ft), perhaps requiring trussed panels to be joined on site and resulting in a banded pattern on elevation.

There are no limitations in plan or section since the framing steel can be fabricated to any geometry. The cladding can resemble a rain-screen facade with glass, metal or stone veneer used as the finishing material (Figs. 27.18–20). The methods of assembly vary considerably with specialist fabricators.

27.7.3 External facing

The cladding system can be described in section as a series of zones; from the outside these are weather face, insulation, structure and inner face. As in any construction concealing inaccessible steel structure, the correct placement of vapour barriers is of prime importance. The outer skin can be designed as a rain-screen facade, with a drainage cavity isolated from the the insulated steel framing. It is important that each component of the facade is mechanically fixed to withstand handling during construction and also wind loads once it is permanently fixed in place.

Facing materials must be readily cleaned, durable and fire resistant, for example bonded glass, ceramic 'plates', granite veneer or metal panels perhaps with powder coated aluminium or stainless steel for visible trim and window surrounds. Typical examples currently in London are Alban Gate, London Wall and the Embankment Place at Charing Cross (by Terry Farrell and Partners, Architects with Ove Arup and Partners, Consulting Engineers).

27.7.4 Examples from the USA

Building Codes in the USA allow wall trusses to be constructed from cold formed galvanized steel. American facades are consequently lighter in weight than their European equivalent. Relatively lightweight facings such as thin ceramic plates or glazed artificial stone are most often employed. A celebrated example of the use of these materials is the Portland Public Services Building, Oregon designed by Michael Graves (Fig. 27.18). The technical details of similar construction are given in Figs 27.19 and 27.20. Each ceramic plate has projecting discs for bolt attachment.

27.9 CONCLUSION

Steel trussed facades are an example of the continuing industrialization of the building process. It continues the development of curtain wall technology from the 1940s and 1950s. The contemporary scale of building operations requires large components that are completely constructed in the factory and ready for site assembly.

The use of trusses enables the contractor to erect wall cladding without scaffolding and only shortly behind completion of the frame. The range of facing materials and elevational forms is not diminished by these means but increased.

As always, the art of construction is the outcome of taste and technology. Or put another way, it is a matter of selection of materials, their proportions and the method of their combination. The final phases of Broadgate reveal the advantages and disadvantages of the new freedom in facade construction . . . deja vu!

To understand this viewpoint, refer back to Fig. 25.17 and compare with Figs. 27.21a,b,c and d which conclude this chapter.

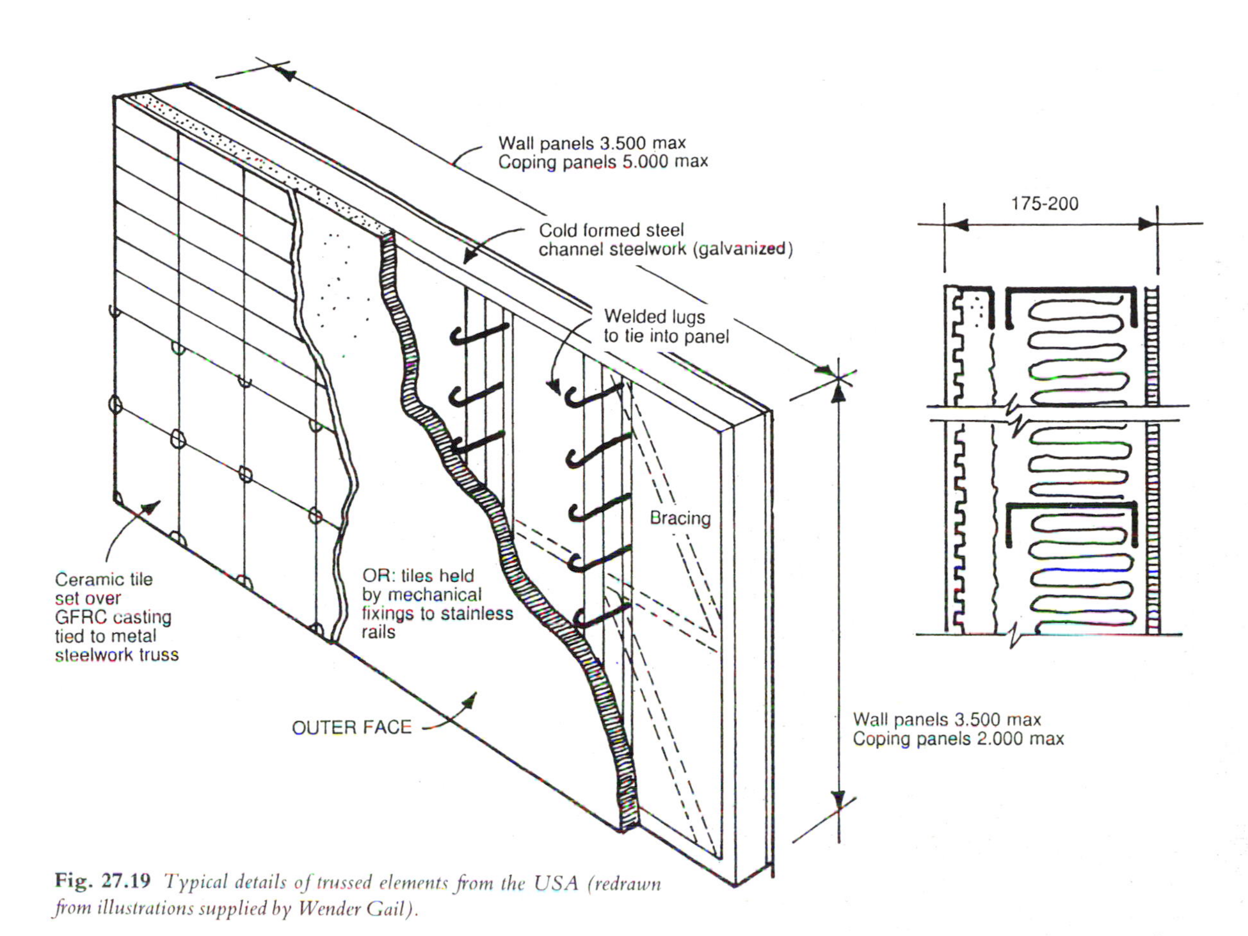

Fig. 27.19 *Typical details of trussed elements from the USA (redrawn from illustrations supplied by Wender Gail).*

Fig. 27.20 *Metal subframe for cladding. Reprinted by kind permission of Harris and Edgar Ltd. Prefabricated subframes can be constructed by using jointing plates or welding. Frames may be up to two storeys in height, but with large frames, thermal movement must be allowed for. It may be possible to pre-clad an assembly on site prior to lifting it into position. The frame can also be used to carry the internal lining of the building and services can be carried in the cavity.*

(a)

(b)

(c)

(d)

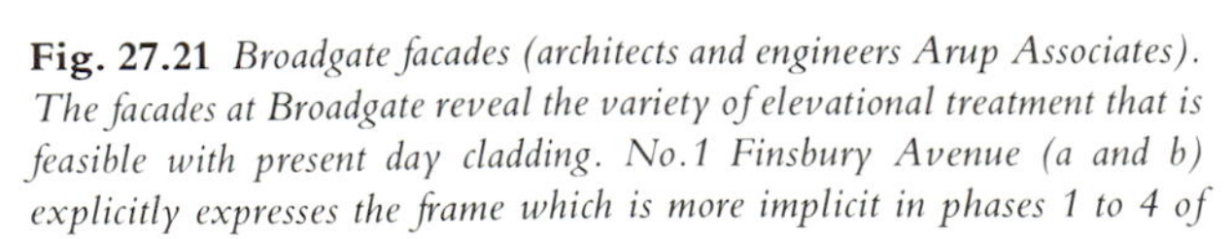

Fig. 27.21 *Broadgate facades (architects and engineers Arup Associates). The facades at Broadgate reveal the variety of elevational treatment that is feasible with present day cladding. No.1 Finsbury Avenue (a and b) explicitly expresses the frame which is more implicit in phases 1 to 4 of Broadgate (c and d). The final phases, by SOM (refer back Fig. 25.17), revert to pattern making and pastiche. Much the same may be said of Canary Wharf.*

REFERENCES AND TECHNICAL NOTES

1. The Equitable Building, Portland, Oregon (1948) *Architectural Review*, Aug 1950.
2. Energy saving offices. Refer to publications by the BRE: John, R.W., Willis, S.T.P. and Selvidge, A.C. (1990) *Electric Heating in Highly Insulated Buildings: Experience from the BRE Low Energy Office*.
   John, R.W. and Selvidge, A.C. (1988) *The BRE Low Energy Office: A Longer Term Perspective*. BRE Information Paper No. 4.
3. Refer to current publications by Pilkington Glass Ltd on planar glazing and on bonded and toughened glass.
   Safety Glass Laminates, Pilkington's Architectural Division, 8/89.
   Armourplate Toughened Glass, Pilkington's Architectural Divison, 7/89.
   The Pilkington Planar System, Pilkington's Architectural Division, 8/91.
4. *BS 476 Fire Test on Building Materials and Structures*.
5. Patera System. For full details refer to Architects' Journal (September 1982).

FURTHER READING

Wall Technology, CIRIA Special Publication. Seven volume set (1993).

Curtain Wall Corrections to Steel Frames by Ray Ogden, the SCI (1992).

Standard Guide to Good Practice for Curtain Walling, published by the Centre for Window and Cladding Technology (1993).

The Building Envelope, Alan Brookes and Chris Grech, Butterworth Architecture (1990).

Connections, Alan Brookes and Chris Grech, Butterworth Architecture (1992).

Fig. 28.1 *Decking and lattice roof framing for West Sussex School 1936 (architect C.G. Stillman). Compare with school construction of the 1990s in bottom left-hand view (chapter 37 case study, 11).*

28

Decking and built up roofing

Alan Blanc

28.1 BACKGROUND

In the 19th century, floor and roof decks were constructed by casting concrete over various types of permanent form-work supported between the bottom flanges of wrought iron beams. Using corrugated iron shuttering, vaults became a prevalent form later to be superseded by dovetail sheets of trapezoidal section spanning horizontally over the top flanges of steel beams.

Modern techniques were developed in the first quarter of this century. In Europe in the 1920s, experiments were made combining flat and profiled sheets of asbestos cement as well as galvanized steel. A composite slab of concrete cast over lightweight decking is now a method commonly used in steel framed construction (for details refer to chapter 16.) Profiled sheets are used in a whole range of self-finished roofing and walling components as described in chapter 26. Steel decking is also employed as the substrate for bitumen felt 'built-up'roofing. An early example was an industrialized school building system for West Sussex designed by C.G.Stillman in 1936; its roof decking was supported by steel trusses spanning 24 ft (7.3 m) at 8 ft 3 in (2.5 m) centres ([1] and Fig. 28.1). Wartime factories were constructed in a similar way.

When continuous runs of steel decking are fixed to achieve composite action with the roof beams, high shear strength under applied loads and improved wind resistance can be attained. The advantages of this form of 'diagrid' construction are described in chapter 12. A related and elegant form of long span roof is a curved lamella shell of decking fixed to diagonal beams (cold formed, lattice or rolled; refer to chapter 11 for further discussion of the structural role of decking in roof frames).

During the inter-war period there was much research into lightweight structural decking. One of the first new inventions was the woodwool slab ([2] and Fig. 28.2). A combination of wood shavings and cement, woodwool slabs are rot-resistant and dimensionally stable provided that they are kept dry. When the edges are reinforced with galvanized steel channels, slabs of 600 mm (2 ft) or 750 mm (2 ft 6 in) width can span up to 4.5 m (15 ft) or 6 m (20 ft). Another product of that period was Gypsum plank, a reinforced form of plaster of Paris eventually found to be too hygroscopic for roofing purposes.

At the same time the technology of concrete decking was revolutionized by the introduction of prestressed reinforcement, aerated mixes and high alumina concretes. As a result precast slabs became lighter and thinner; for example, a prestressed plank spanning 6.0 m (20 ft) with a thickness of only 75–100 mm (3 ft 4 in). High alumina cement degrades in damp conditions and is no longer used structurally. A relatively recent innovation, glass fibre reinforced cement, might have potential as a material for decking but so far has been used only for wall panels and permanent shuttering to in situ waffle or ribbed slabs.

One of the strangest cul-de-sacs in the development of roofing technology was a product made from chopped straw glued between two sheets of building paper. The first patents were taken out in France, and in the 1940s the process was sold to a Swedish company which exported the suspect concept to the UK. Because straw is even more hygroscopic than plaster of Paris, the roofing readily sagged, tearing the waterproofing. A heavy storm shortly

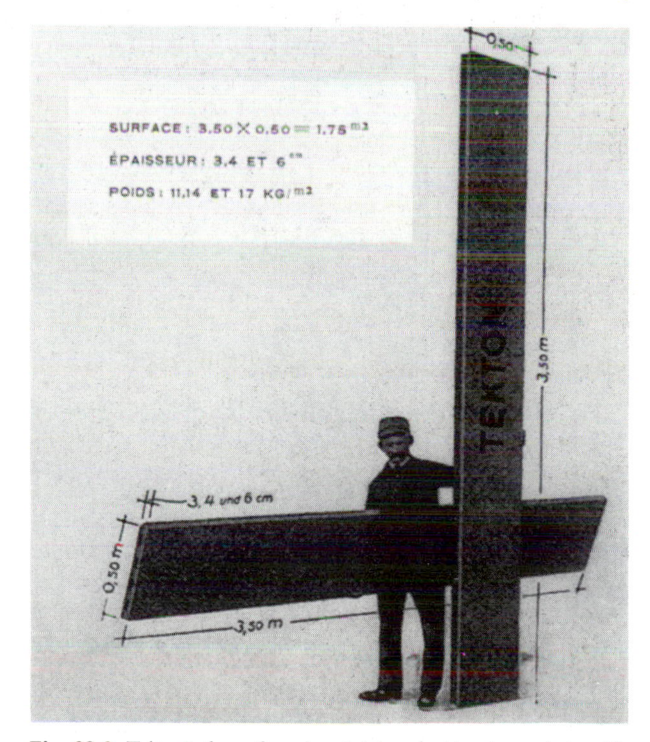

Fig. 28.2 *Tekton'a form of woodwool slab as used in a house designed by Richard Döcker, Weissenhof, Stuttgart 1927. A technical advertisement taken from the original publication of Weissenhof in L'architecture Vivart en Allemagre 1928.*

before the opening of the Festival of Britain totally collapsed the Royal Retiring Rooms that were roofed in the material [3]. Flaxboard and chipboard are subject to similar problems; roof decking has to withstand moisture and thermal movements otherwise its waterproofing will be endangered.

Warning also needs to be given about the possibility of fire spread through the horizontal voids sandwiched within roofs constructed from corrugated decking. One of the most extensive fires on record occurred when the 150,000 m^2 General Motors Plant at Livonia, Michigan burnt down in August 1953. The fire started in the paint shop and ignited a drip pan 12 m long and then the wood block floor. The heat was sufficient to distort the frame and roof decking so that flames leap-frogged from the interior to the bitumen roof and back again until the whole structure was destroyed. The buildings only had 20% sprinkler coverage and no effective fire breaks through the roof at compartment walls. British Codes anticipate this eventuality, but the recent fire at a Salisbury shopping centre showed the need for careful site control to ensure that fire barriers are properly installed.

The most useful general reference to decking and roof covering is *Flat Roofing: A Guide to Good Practice* [4], published by Tarmac in 1982 and distributed by RIBA Publications. Their details are repeated in the specification manuals of most major flat roofing contractors. Another source [5] for up-to-date information on specialist firms and new materials is the Flat Roofing Contractors' Advisory Board and Metal Roof Deck Association Design Code, which contains informative engineering data (especially concerning roof loads to be accommodated during construction).

28.2 ROOF DECKING AND FIXING: STRUCTURAL CONSIDERATIONS

Roof structures have to be designed to comply with the appropriate codes of practice [6], which describe the fixings to be made between decking and structure, insulation and decking and bonding of the weather-coat to the insulation.

Obviously the extent to which a site is exposed will influence the specification of roofing materials with anticipated wind resistances of 2.4, 3.0 and 3.6 kN/m^2. Fixings through the deck can be clips, hook bolts or direct bolting, in order of strength. Mechanical fixings for the connection of insulation to metal decking are usually self-tapping screws with 70 mm (2¾ in) washers and an average 'pull-up' strength per fixing of 0.4 kN. Regarding the wisdom of membranes being penetrated by fixings, two schools of thought exist. One approach is to avoid the problem by using sandwich membranes with plate washer fixings placed below the membrane, the other entails

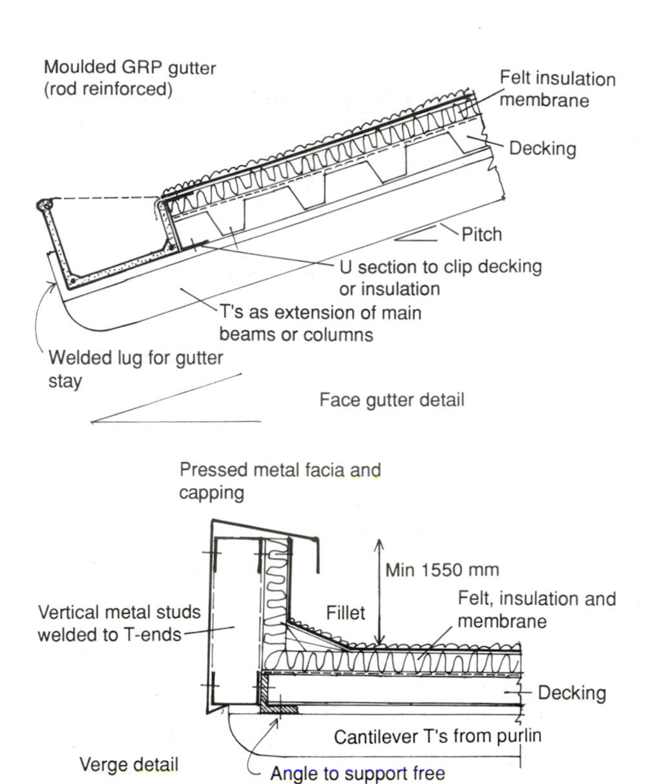

Fig. 28.3 *Typical eaves and verge overhang details for decking.*

individual patches being made at each penetration (requiring considerable skill).

Openings made through decking may require additional structural framing, similarly at overhangs and verges (Fig. 28.3). Short cantilevers are possible but engineering advice will be needed if there are potential problems due to wind uplift [7].

28.3 DESIGN FOR THERMAL INSULATION, MOVEMENT AND THE CONTROL OF CONDENSATION

Most steel deck roofing can be termed a 'warm roof' because the insulation is usually above deck level and the decking and supporting steelwork are maintained at the ambient temperature of the building (Fig. 28.4).

Interstitial condensation above the steel decking can cause corrosion that first becomes visible at fixing holes. The textbook *Flat Roofing: A Guide to Good Practice* provides sample calculations, advice on ventilation and correct assembly of the roof's components so as to avoid condensation. Condensation risks exist under many circumstances, for example if the building is not continuously heated, also local to openings in the building such as the interior of glass canopies and porches. At roof perforations, around roof

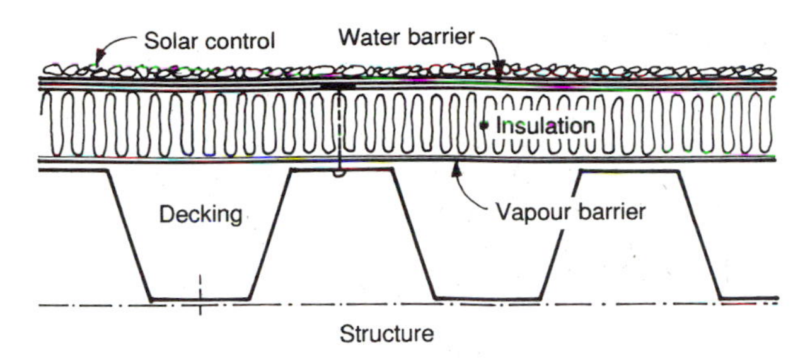

Fig. 28.4 *Warm roof concept.*

lights and clerestory windows, local heating may need to be incorporated to combat the likelihood of condensation.

As a general rule, thermal movement joints are needed in structures at approximately 30 m (100 ft) intervals, the responsibility for that decision resting with the consulting engineer. The seasonal temperature range in the UK can be as much as 40°C. Facades are often shaded or oblique to the sun; roofs are subject to its full force and are consequently subject to greater thermal movement. Flat roof membranes can be protected by roof landscaping whether by earth or water but both of these when frozen are equal in weight to concrete [8]. Lightweight roofing depends upon a top layer of felt with a metal reflective surface, paint or white stone chippings for solar protection. In Switzerland, experimental landscaping using a lightweight mixture of peat and sand, only 75 mm (3 in) in thickness, has sustained the growth of tolerant plant species. 75 mm of frozen saturated soil is still equal in weight to 75 mm of concrete paving slab, a roof loading not compatible with spans that are economic for many decking systems (refer to 'ecological roofs' in chapter 25, section 25.3.2).

28.4 RAINWATER DISPOSAL

A cold-formed steel upstand forming a kerb at the roof edge (similar to the verge in Fig. 28.3), or either side of an expansion joint, a common detail for 'built-up' roofs on metal decking, makes each roof into a self-contained 'tray' for the purposes of rainwater disposal. Roofing codes suggest a minimum height of 150 mm (6 in) for kerb upstands but an increase to 200 mm (8 in) or 250 mm (10 in) may be necessary to contain driving rain or snow if the roof is very exposed to the elements (Fig. 28.5).

Blocked rainwater outlets, resulting in an accumulation of water within the upstand edges, can cause total collapse of the roof once the weight of water becomes too great for the structure [9]. To avoid this potential disaster, it is essential either to provide adequate overflows, or on roofs with multiple outlets to increase the outlet sizes or double their number as a safety measure. The basic principles for rainwater disposal are outlined in Fig. 28.6.

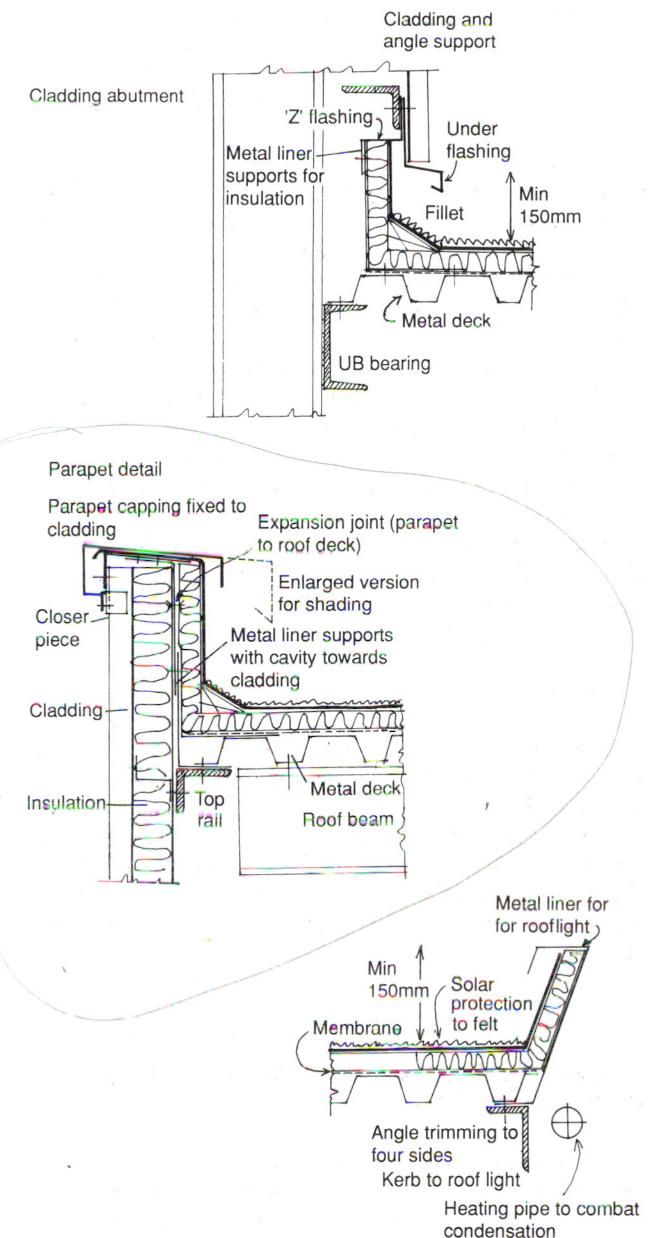

Fig. 28.5 *Typical kerb details.*

The pros and cons of the varying methods can be summarized as follows:

1. A central outlet is in many ways ideal, as any deflection of the roof structure over time will increase the fall on the roof towards the centre and help direct water to the outlet. A location on plan that is column-free may, however, make for difficulty in accommodating rain-water pipes within the building.
2. Tilted roof. Roof slopes should notionally be a minimum of 1 in 40.

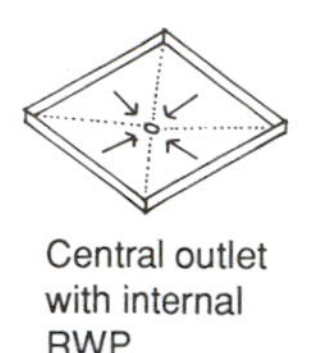

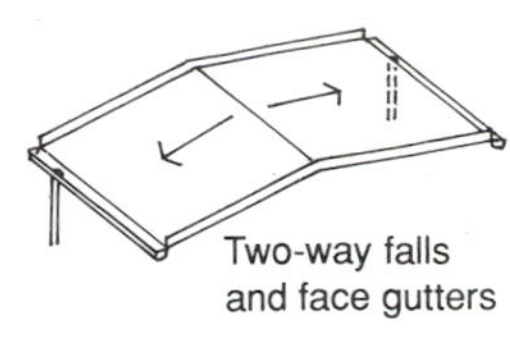

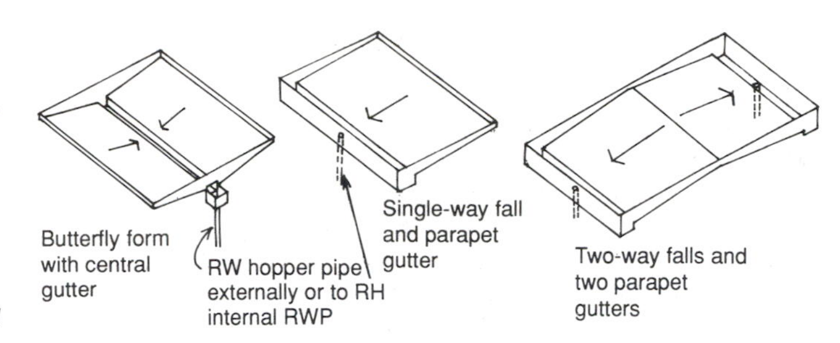

Fig. 28.6 *Basic principles for rainwater disposal. Note: falls exaggerated for clarity.*

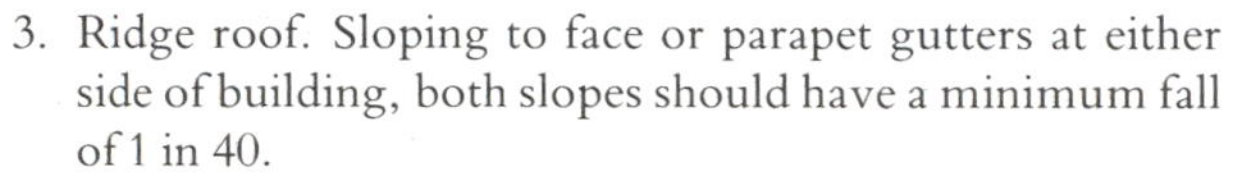

3. Ridge roof. Sloping to face or parapet gutters at either side of building, both slopes should have a minimum fall of 1 in 40.
4. Butterfly roof. A single valley gutter may either discharge to outlets at internal columns or hopper heads and external rain water pipes at each end.
5. Face gutters are the cheapest solution to rainwater disposal and have the advantage that any excessive accumulation of water is likely to be external to the building rather than flooding its roof.
6. Parapet and valley gutters must have an overflow or standby rainwater pipes to avoid a backup of water finding its way into the building should an outlet become blocked.

Roofing contractors are inclined to recommend 1 in 80 as the minimum falls for built-up roofs. Deflection and building tolerances may drastically reduce the actual slope so that reverse falls and ponding can occur. It is preferable either to design to 1 in 40 or to calculate finished levels based on a fall of 1 in 80 with the addition of 25 mm (1 in) or more to give a margin of safety. The relationship between roof area and the provision of rainwater outlets is given in BS 6367: 1983 [10]. An excellent guide is provided in *Flat Roofing: A Guide to Good Practice* [4] published by Tarmac plc. Overflows or standby pipes (Fig. 28.7) are useful devices to prevent flooding of roofs in storms.

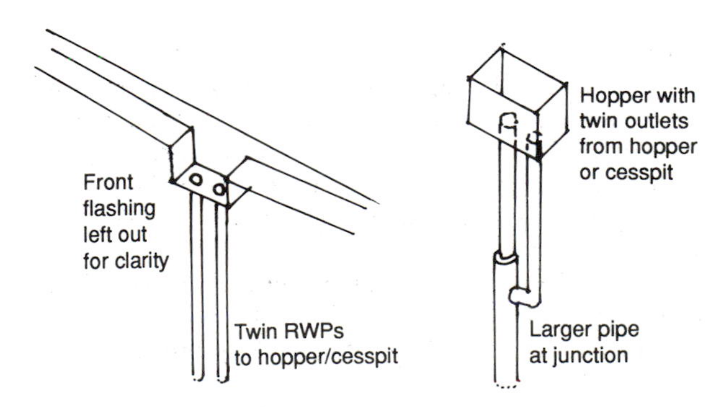

Fig. 28.7 *Overflows and standby pipes.*

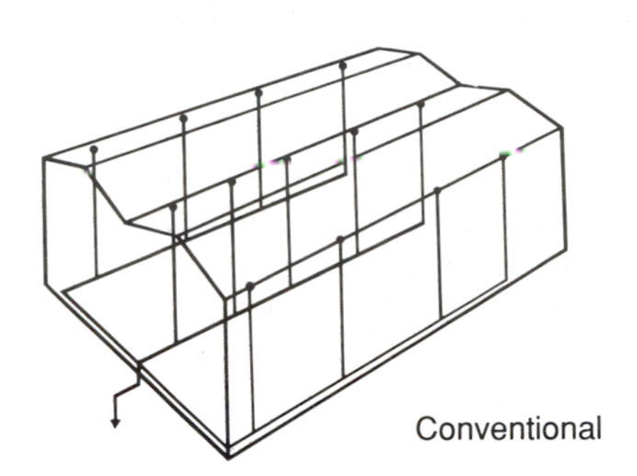

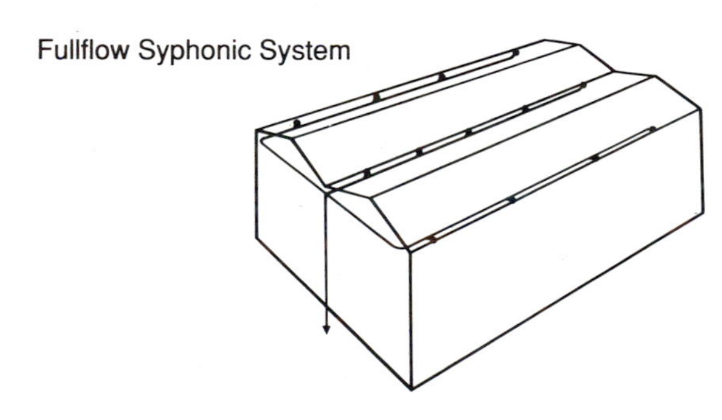

Fig. 28.8 *Rainwater systems. Fullflow syphonic system.*

28.4.1 Rainwater outlets

The shape and size of a rainwater outlet and the form of its junction with the downpipe greatly affects the speed of water flow and the efficiency of rainwater disposal. The crudest type of connection is when the pipe is taken directly to the flat roof surface and water falls over the vertical edge as if over a weir. Its efficiency can be improved by tapering the outlet, a pattern favoured by most manufacturers of rainwater goods. The advantage of increasing the depth of water adjacent to the rainwater pipe is that in heavy rainfall 'orifice flow' can then take place (as it does when water is discharging from a washbasin). A sump also helps orifice flow but needs to have sufficient cross-section to give a large enough head of water above the outlet pipe. The use of enlarged pipes directly below the roof is a further refinement to speed rainwater (Fig. 28.8).

28.4.2 Integral gutter versus channel/face gutter

Arguments can be advanced for either of these solutions; the decision depends upon the roof geometry and the desired eaves profile.

A gutter, integral with the roof covering and decking, has the thermal advantage that the roofing system is not interrupted, although the performance required of the waterproof membrane is increased, as the volume of water flowing in the gutter is greater than across the roof generally. Single and multiple ply roofing is laid with laps parallel to the slope to prevent ponding at the seams. Such an arrangement does, however, lead to the risk of ponding in integral felted gutters since the roofing laps at right angles to the water flow (Fig. 28.9).

Channel or face gutters can be waterproofed without the use of sheet roofing materials. GRP or welded steel is fabricated in single lengths for parapet or valley gutters. This solution requires the base of the gutter to be below the plane of the decking (Fig. 28.10). The roofing contractor's responsibility usually stops at the edge of the gutter. Traditional detailing appropriately allows movement between decking and one piece (GRP/welded aluminium/steel) gutters (Fig. 28.3). There is a risk of leaks along that crucial junction under snow and storm conditions, explaining the relative popularity of integral gutters within the plane of the decking.

Channel shaped gutters require frequent maintenance and should be made deep enough (300–400 mm, 1 ft–1 ft 4 in) and of sufficient strength to withstand foot traffic.

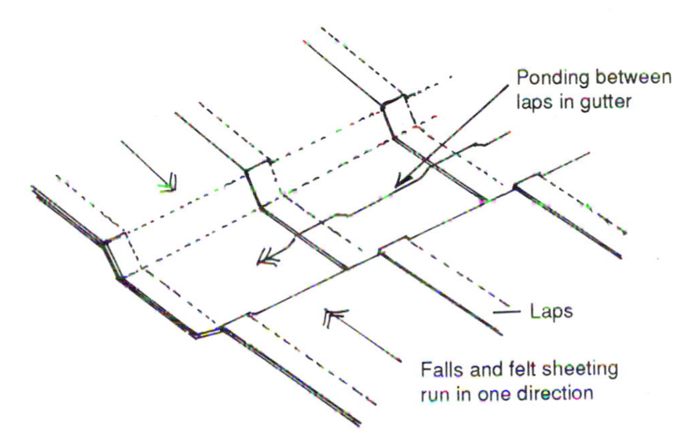

Fig. 28.9 *Relation between flow and laps.*

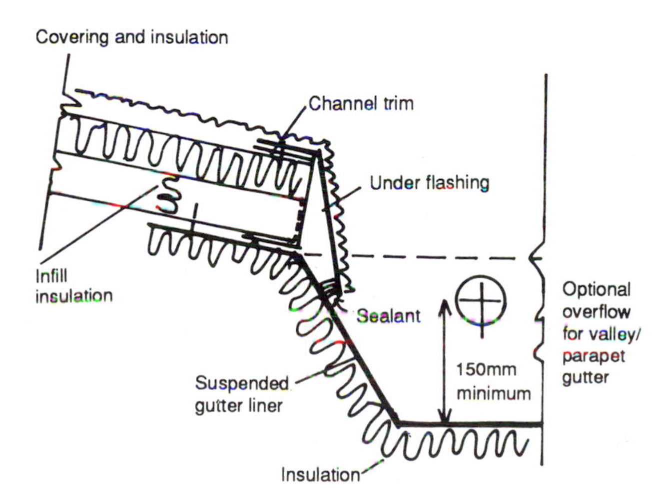

Fig. 28.10 *Channel gutter interupting deck.*

Table 28.1 Types of covering materials [10]

Form	*Classification*	*Type*
Multi-layer	BS 747 1977 (1986)	Class 1: fibre Class 3: glass fibre Class 4: sheathing felt Class 5: polyester base
	Bituminous Roofing Council (BRC)	Group 3: HSPB polymer modified bitumen SBS or APP Group 4: Calendered polymeric Metal foil surfaced felts
	Unclassified	Non-calendered polymeric isotropic
Single-ply	Unclassified	Metal foil finished, self-adhesive Sand faced, self adhesive ECB: Ethylene co-polymerized bitumen PVC: Polyvinylchloride CPE: Chloropolyethylene CSM (CSPE) Chlorosulphonated polyethylene PIB: Polyisobutylene Butyl rubber EPDM: Ethylene Propylene diene terpolymer Silicone
Liquid coatings	Unclassified	Neoprene/Hypalon Silicone Co-polymer Polyurethane Tar-extended polyurethene Pitch epoxide Bitumen emulsion (reinforced) Asphaltic liquid
	BS 988/1162	Asphalt
	Unclassified	Sprayed reinforced asphalt

28.4.3 Covering materials

The weatherproof layer or layers have to be secured against the possibility of wind uplift and turbulence, usually by partial bonding with bitumen poured over a perforated felt underlay. Alternatively, pressure clips can be used to provide a tear-proof mechanical fixing.

The types of membrane materials that are available are listed in Table 28.1. Guarantees of 12–20 years may be obtained from some contractors. It is important to ensure that one specialist takes responsibility for the installation of decking, insulation and covering so that the division of responsibility is clearly established.

28.4.4 Non-metallic decking

The advantage of woodwool slabs or lightweight precast roofing is its fire resistance and improved sound insulation as compared with metal deck. To vapour seal the porous soffit of woodwool slab or aerated concrete effectively is difficult to achieve. Consequently, it is necessary to include vents for the discharge of water vapour within the decking. These work well in roofs with relatively small bays, for example sloping monitor or saw tooth roofs. Large flat areas are more difficult; relief ventilators may obstruct movement of the roof membrane causing it to tear and creating a maintenance problem. Panels on a 600 or 750 module (2 ft or 2 ft 6 in) are, however, ideal for small buildings, particularly where the dimensions of rooflights and roof panels can be co-ordinated within a modular pattern (Fig. 28.11).

REFERENCES AND TECHNICAL NOTES

1. West Sussex Schools 1936–39
   For general background on pre- and post-war prefabricated schools refer to *Towards a Social Architecture*, by Andrew Saint (published Yale University Press 1987).
2. Woodwool slabs
   'Heraklith' was one of the original makes and was used at the 1927 Weissenhof in Stuttgart; also by Walter Segal for the construction of his first framed houses at Ascona in 1932 (for further details refer to *Architects' Journal*, 4 May 1988).
3. Compressed straw (editor's note)
   Concerning the collapsed Royal Retiring Rooms at the Festival site, the site agent, upon viewing the mess, remarked that it 'looked like a donkey's dinner' – the material had started sprouting green shoots.
4. *Flat Roofing: A Guide to Good Practice*, published by Tarmac in 1982 and distributed by RIBA Publications.
5. Flat Roofing Contractors' Advisory Board and the Metal Roof Deck Association: Maxwelton House, 41/43 Boltro Road, Haywards Heath, West Sussex RH16 1BJ, UK. Tel: 44 (0)444 440027.
6. Codes of Practice for Decking and Roofing. Refer to the following:
   BS 6399 Part 1: 1984 *Code of Practice for Dead and Imposed Loads.*
   CP3 Chapter V: Part 2: 1972 *Wind Loads.*
   BS 648: 1964, Table 1 *Schedule of Weights of Building Materials.*
7. Uplift at overhangs
   Monopitch roofs with overhangs on the rising face are particularly at risk. Lightweight decking is vulnerable.

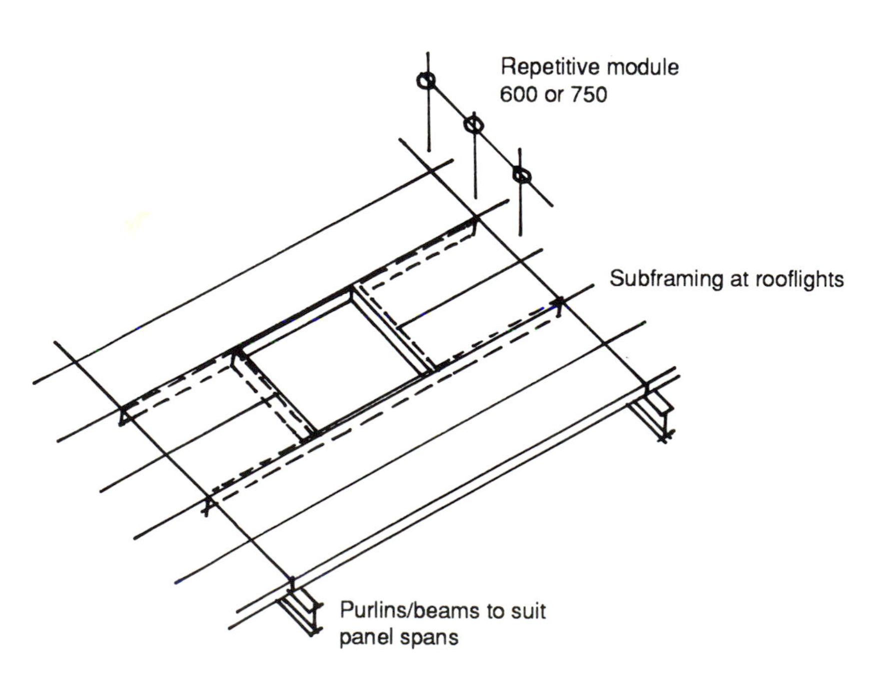

Fig. 28.11 *Typical panel module (woodwool slabs with trimming at roof lights).*

A notorious case occurred at Hatfield New Town in 1957, when corrugated aluminium roofs fixed to rafters took off as if 'hinged lids' during 93 mph winds (see *Architects' Journal*, 1st February 1978, 'Wind pressure on buildings'.

8. The weight of ice or frozen soil/sand mixes are as follows:
ice: 913 kg/m^3
Saturated soil/sand: 1922 kg/m^3
aerated concrete: 961 kg/m^3
stone aggregate concrete: up to 2240 kg/m^3.
9. Dead weight of rainwater (editor's note)
The following account was given by a roofing contractor: A high performance roof failed abruptly, flooding the building below shortly before it was due to be officially opened. The roof was of typical tray construction with a single rainwater outlet pipe that was blocked by a dead bird. Trapped rainwater accumulated up to the level of the kerb, in turn causing the partial collapse of the roof due to the dead load of standing water.
10. BS 6367: 1983 Code of Practice for Drainage of Roofs and Paved Areas.

FURTHER READING

For a review of decking and roof coverings refer to:
Architects' Journal, Products in Use. Roofing Two (25 April 1984). For DOE/PSA advice refer to *Flat Roof: Technical Guide*, 2nd Edition 1981 by the PSA.

Length × diameter range (mm)	*Form*	*Application*
15 × 1·4 to 150 × 6·0		**Round wire nail** (sometimes known as French nail). Used for general purpose carpentry mainly in unseen situations. Pilot holes may be necessary to avoid splitting timber. In steel or copper
25 × 2·6 to 150 × 7·1 × 5·0		**Lost head nails:** can be punched below the surface and filled—can be obtained with round or oval section of shank, and with alternative brad heads in most sizes. Ovals are less likely to split wood. Round section nails are sometimes used for flooring instead of cut floor brads. Not suitable for thin or soft wood. Steel, copper or aluminium
20 × 2·0 to 100 × 5·0		**Annular nail:** ringed shank provides considerably increased resistance to withdrawal. Used in non-ferrous form for boats and external joinery
200 × 2·0 to 100 × 5·0		**Helically threaded nail:** for roofing, especially corrugated sheet. Thread gives some increased resistance to withdrawal
38 × 2·0 to 75 × 3·2		**Cut floor brads:** made from flat steel sheet, used to fix floor boarding, flat point cuts wood fibres without wedge action and does not usually split timber. Also in aluminium
50 × 2·6 to 200 × 6·0		**Cut clasp nail:** made from flat steel sheet, used frequently for heavy carpentry and fixings to masonry—difficult to extract
45 × 3·0 to 100 × 5·6		**Duplex head nail:** (double head shutter nail). For temporary fixing; easy to withdraw
20 × 2·5 to 100 × 3·5		**Masonry nail:** hardened steel pin to penetrate and hold in masonry and concrete
20 × 2·65 to 100 × 4·5		**Clout nails** (slate nails). Used for roofing, roof felt, fencing, etc. Steel, copper or aluminium
13 × 3·0 to 30 × 3·0		**Extra large head clout** (felt nails), smaller sizes (max 30 mm) for felt fixing
6		**Clout head tile peg:** steel or aluminium clout with alternative sharp or 'dumped' point. For roofing
		Purlin nails: relatively thin (3·7 mm) copper nails
10 × 0·8 to 75 × 2·65		**Panel pins:** small head, fine gauge and easily punched home and filled. For fixing plywood and other joinery. In steel or aluminium
20 × 1·4		**Hardboard panel pins** (hardboard pins). Obtainable in round or square section shank, both types having diamond profile head which is hidden in the hardboard when driven home
19 × 1·8 to 40 × 2·0		**Lath nail:** traditionally for fixing plaster and similar laths to softwood. Flat, fairly small head
		Cut lath nail: sharp long point for fixing laths. Wedge action may split wood but head holds both sides
30 × 2·6 to 75 × 2·6		**Plasterboard nails** (jagged shank): countersunk head and indented shank to assist retention
		Gimp pin: small pin with relatively large head
		Cedar shake nail: a copper or aluminium pin for fixing cedar cladding
		Tack: for fixing fabric to wood or carpets to flooring
		Sprig: headless tack for fixing glass into wood frames
		Escutcheon pins: brass convex head pin for fixing escutcheon plates
20 to 65 × 3		**Plastic-topped nail** with annular grooved zinc-plated shank for fixing wood, plastic or plasterboard. White or coloured top
50 × 5 to 75 × 5·6		**Nails for corrugated sheet roofing:** round nails, nipple head nails and spring head nails (with washer)—all galvanised steel and aluminium with convex heads
Steel 75 × 8 to 150 × 8		**Pipe nails** (chisel point nail). Used to fix rainwater goods into masonry. Steel or aluminium
15 × 1·6 to 50 × 50 (many other sizes available for machine fixing)		**Staple;** usually made from galvanised steel wire. Two available point designs (presser and diamond). Tenterhook is a staple with one leg longer than the other allowing easier fixing

Fig. 29.1 *Various forms of common nail. Reprinted with kind permission of* The Architects' Journal.

29

Fastenings

Alan Blanc

Designers often speak of the 'nuts and bolts' approach to construction. This is perhaps an expression from the 'Meccano' age but it seems pertinent in a volume dedicated to building in steel to provide a chapter on nails and screws and other fastenings. These small components have in the past enabled the construction of some of the world's largest structures. The nailed timber trusses that housed the US Navy Airships spanned up to 72 m (240 ft) covering spaces that were only eclipsed in volume by the steel framed rocket launch sheds at Cape Kennedy completed in 1964.

The following components will be discussed: nails, screws, rivets, other light fastenings, masonry fixings and other fittings.

29.1 NAILS

Although they are claimed to have been a Chinese invention, the Romans are credited with the earliest manufacture of forged nails. Hand forging, the hammering of a square cut nail into annular form with an enlarged head (Fig. 29.1) produces nails remarkably close in shape to many that are nowadays manufactured by machine. The antique methods of 300 BC were still in use until the 1600s saw the development of drawn wire nails with hand-finished points and heads, a process that was continued as a craft industry around Birmingham until the early years of this century. Current production methods for cut and wire nails are totally mechanized, and the materials used range from steel sheet (for cut nails) and steel wire (wire grade and high strength nails) to stainless steels and non-ferrous metals (copper and duralumin).

Ferrous metals are finished 'bright', that is polished by cleaning in rotating bins, or coated with plastic, shellac (japanned) or molten zinc. There are also a number of 'electro-plated' finishes such as brass, cadmium, copper, nickel, tin or zinc.

The basic types are shown in Fig. 29.1; for further details refer to BS 1202: 1974 Specification for Nails and to makers' catalogues and timber engineering leaflets [1]. The references at the end of this chapter describe the usual applications of each type (for recommended fixing centres refer to suppliers of sheet materials).

29.2 SCREWS

29.2.1 Manufacture

Screws are drawn from wire, and their materials and finishes are similar to those described for nails. BS 1210: 1963 Specification for Wood Screws gives information on slot head screws and some patterns of recessed head [2]. BS 5268 Structural use of Timber: Parts 2–7 specifies centres for fixings but these should be checked against potentially more up-to-date information available from manufacturers of sheet materials.

29.2.2 Finishes

Most finishes on steel screws are decorative rather than protective. Stainless or non-ferrous types should be used for external locations where good durability is required without the necessity for regular repainting. Here is a summary of the available finishes:

1. Stainless steel	The best choice for hostile environments.
2. Fluoroplastic	A relatively new addition to the range (PTFE) of 'overcoatings', an alternative to zinc or cadmium plating but with better resistance to corrosion. Fluoroplastic coatings resist bimetallic corrosion where ferrous fixings are used to join other metals.
3. Sheradized or bright zinc plate	Both will survive 10 or more years without painting.
4. Electro-brassed	A shiny yellow copy of brass, used internally for fixing reproduction brass ironmongery.
5. Blued	Blued steel has a dark oxide coating with a temporarily protective lubricating oil finish. Not suitable for external use and has to be painted internally.
6. Japanned or Berlin	A cheap black enamel finish only suitable for internal use. Commonly associated with 'Tudorbethan' taste. Today there is a large range of decorative finishes to steel fixings,

Name	*Applications*	*Materials*	*Sizes*
Countersunk	General joinery not visible on the finished item, and wherever a flush surface is required.	Steel Brass	6 mm × 0 sg to 152 mm × 18 sg 6 mm × 0 sg to 102 mm × 20 sg
Raised countersunk	Protects surface from screwdriver damage, used where screw visible on finished item of quality.	Steel Brass	9·5 mm × 2 sg to 51 mm × 12 sg 9·5 mm × 2 sg to 64 mm × 12 sg
Round head	For materials too thin to countersink, eg sheet metal.	Steel Brass	6 mm × 0 sg to 89 mm × 12 sg 6 mm × 1 sg to 76 mm × 14 sg
Capped or domed	Bright metal or coloured plastic tops may be screwed into the head of special countersunk screws fixing mirrors, window frames, etc.		19 mm × 8 sg to 51 mm × 10 sg (domed screw sizes)
Coach screw	Coach screws are used to locate heavy timber sections. They are hammered in and tightened with a spanner on the square head.	Steel Zinc-plated	25 × 6·4 mm to 152 × 12·7 mm 38 × 6·4 mm to 127 × 9·6 mm
Cups	Use with countersunk to protect surface specially where frequent screw removal is necessary.		

Fig. 29.2 *Screw heads. Reprinted with kind permission of* The Architects' Journal.

	bronze coloured and plated (nickel, cadmium). Cadmium is toxic and should not be used in food preparation areas. Chromium plated screws are commonly used in motor car manufacture; they need frequent cleaning to stay bright.
7. Bright steel	Rusts if moisture is present.

29.2.3 Basic forms

Screws can be classified by function and by head type. Refer to Figs 29.2 and 29.3 for a description of the types of shank and screwhead. The major development in recent years has been the introduction of self-drive and self-tapping screws with special heads for use with power tools. Also now available are case-hardened wire grade or stainless screws that perform as if made from high-tensile steel.

29.2.4 Bolts and machine screws

These are threaded fasteners which engage either a matching pre-tapped threaded hole or a nut. The term 'bolt' tends to be applied to fasteners over 6 mm diameter which have a thread that does not extend right to the head. Refer to Fig. 29.4 for types of bolt head and captive nut; the design of bolted structural connections is discussed in chapter 21. There are also special forms of fastening for cladding and other related roles (Fig. 29.5).

29.2.5 Resistance to vibration

Under ideal conditions a bolt/nut combination or a set-screw should not fail if tightened to the correct tension. They do, however, tend to work loose due to sustained vibration, shock loads or changes in temperature. Traditional locking devices include tabwashers and wire and split pins but now there are also deformed and tapered threads, nuts with nylon bushes and thread-locking compounds that will give a secure fastening.

29.2.6 Resistance to vandalism

This problem requires the investment of as much effort by the builder as is exerted by the vandal. The ultimate deterrent would be a totally shear-headed screw leaving no choice other than drilling out the fixings should a

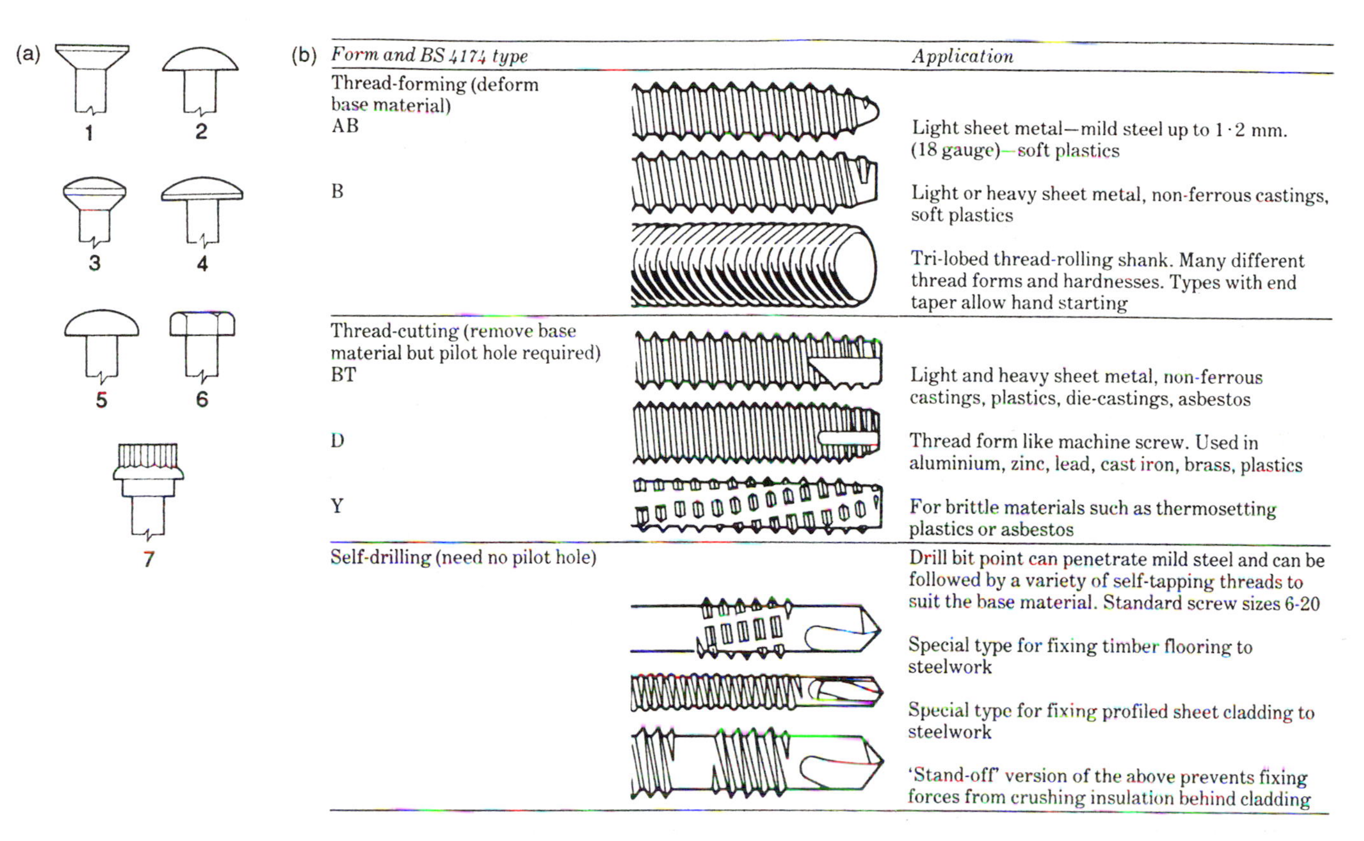

Form and BS 4174 type	Application
Thread-forming (deform base material) AB	Light sheet metal—mild steel up to 1·2 mm. (18 gauge)—soft plastics
B	Light or heavy sheet metal, non-ferrous castings, soft plastics
	Tri-lobed thread-rolling shank. Many different thread forms and hardnesses. Types with end taper allow hand starting
Thread-cutting (remove base material but pilot hole required) BT	Light and heavy sheet metal, non-ferrous castings, plastics, die-castings, asbestos
D	Thread form like machine screw. Used in aluminium, zinc, lead, cast iron, brass, plastics
Y	For brittle materials such as thermosetting plastics or asbestos
Self-drilling (need no pilot hole)	Drill bit point can penetrate mild steel and can be followed by a variety of self-tapping threads to suit the base material. Standard screw sizes 6-20
	Special type for fixing timber flooring to steelwork
	Special type for fixing profiled sheet cladding to steelwork
	'Stand-off' version of the above prevents fixing forces from crushing insulation behind cladding

Fig. 29.3 *Self-tapping heads and machine screws. (a) Head types available for self-tapping screws. 1: Countersunk. 2: Round or mushroom. 3: Raised countersunk. 4: Flange. 5: Pan. 6: Hex. 7: 12-sided. (b) BS4174: 1972 and other self-tapping, self-drilling screws. Reprinted with kind permission of* The Architects' Journal.

Fig. 29.4 *(a) Machine screw and bolt-head types. 1: Mushroom. 2: Round. 3: Fillister. 4: Raised countersunk. 5: Cheese. 6: Countersunk. 7: Pan. 8: Socket: 9: Binder pan. 10: Large slotted. (b) Captive nut inserted into predrilled hole and clenched with a special tool. This type receives machine screws. Reprinted with kind permission of* The Architects' Journal.

component need replacing (Fig. 29.6). A cautionary tale needs to be told concerning the space frame roof of the Ape House at London Zoo where, despite the nodes having been torsion bolted, the orangutans started to dismantle their new home, an exercise only defeated when every recess had been plugged with 'aerolite' glue. The strength of conventional fixings can in fact be improved by glueing: another tamper-proof measure is the use of inset screw heads that require tightening with custom-made screw drivers.

29.3 RIVETS

Lightweight rivets are used for jointing stressed sheet metalwork and other thin sheet materials (cement fibre sheet, fibre and hard-boards, GRP plastics and plywood). For structural rivets refer to chapter 21.

29.4 OTHER LIGHT FASTENINGS

A large range of light fastenings has been developed for quick-assembly furniture; they are also designed to be easily disconnected (for details contact the Furniture Industry

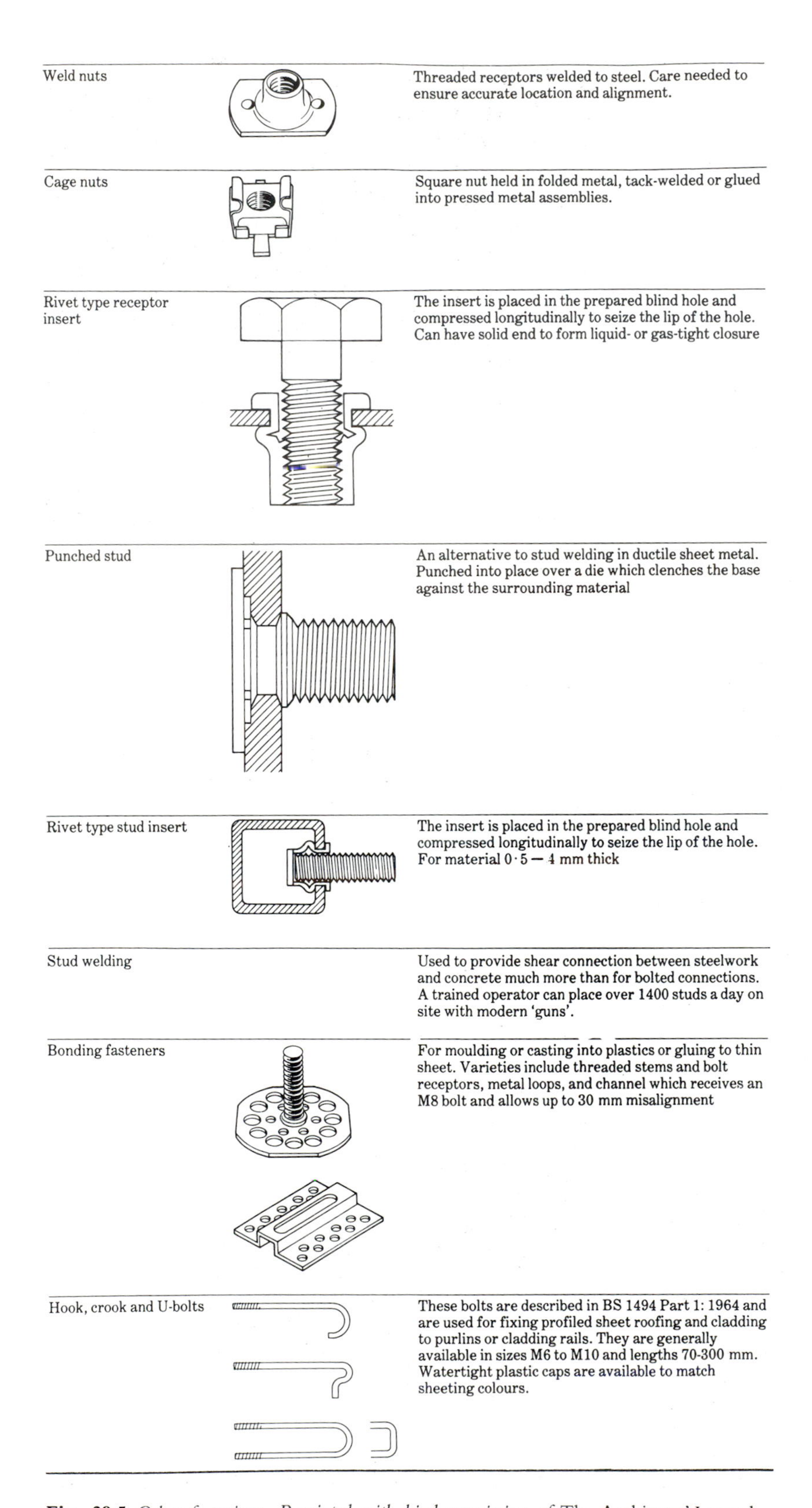

Weld nuts	Threaded receptors welded to steel. Care needed to ensure accurate location and alignment.
Cage nuts	Square nut held in folded metal, tack-welded or glued into pressed metal assemblies.
Rivet type receptor insert	The insert is placed in the prepared blind hole and compressed longitudinally to seize the lip of the hole. Can have solid end to form liquid- or gas-tight closure
Punched stud	An alternative to stud welding in ductile sheet metal. Punched into place over a die which clenches the base against the surrounding material
Rivet type stud insert	The insert is placed in the prepared blind hole and compressed longitudinally to seize the lip of the hole. For material 0·5 — 4 mm thick
Stud welding	Used to provide shear connection between steelwork and concrete much more than for bolted connections. A trained operator can place over 1400 studs a day on site with modern 'guns'.
Bonding fasteners	For moulding or casting into plastics or gluing to thin sheet. Varieties include threaded stems and bolt receptors, metal loops, and channel which receives an M8 bolt and allows up to 30 mm misalignment
Hook, crook and U-bolts	These bolts are described in BS 1494 Part 1: 1964 and are used for fixing profiled sheet roofing and cladding to purlins or cladding rails. They are generally available in sizes M6 to M10 and lengths 70-300 mm. Watertight plastic caps are available to match sheeting colours.

Fig. 29.5 *Other fastenings. Reprinted with kind permission of* The Architects' Journal.

1. One-way slot screw which cannot be unscrewed. **2.** The Vandlgard nut is tightened until the hexagonal head shears off leaving a smooth conical head that cannot be unscrewed. **3.** A special version of the Torx driving tool with a central hole is needed to turn this Resis Torx fastener (Linread). **4.** The Torx driving head of the AudiTorx bolt shears off when it is tightened to a smooth head which cannot be undone.

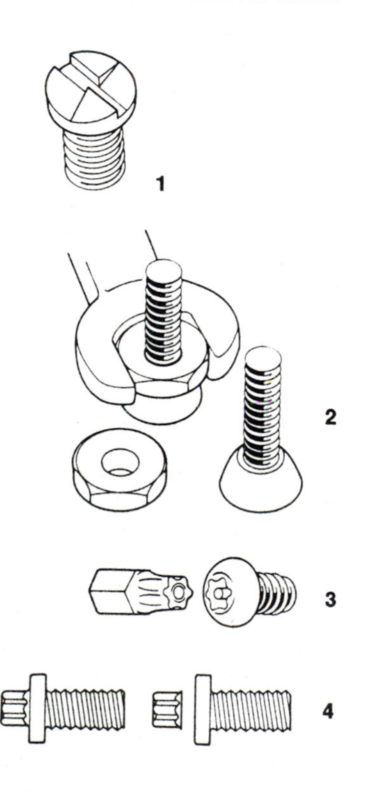

Fig. 29.6 *Examples of anti-vandal screws.*

Research Association – FIRA). Structural carpentry increasingly relies upon galvanized steel strip made into anchors, connectors and joist hangers (a technology that is comprehensively described in the Timber Research and Development Association's publications).

29.5 HEAVY MASONRY FIXINGS

29.5.1 Historical review

The building of metal cramps and dowels into masonry work is a form of construction that goes back to the bronze age. The stones at Delphi (Fig. 29.7, c. 400 BC) still display mortices for anchoring bronze dovetailed cramps (that at a later date were removed and melted down to make bullets).

At the beginning of this century, designers of pioneer steel framed buildings enveloped the structure with massive traditional ashlar walls (a composite construction of stone facing blocks toothed into brickwork). Window openings were larger than previously and various forms of anchor and tie bar were invented to carry stone veneer and cornice blocks back to the hidden framework of RSJs (Fig. 29.8). The metals used for these structural fixings were bronze (gun metal grade) or plain steel, both of which have given rise to considerable problems.

The strengths of bronze alloys are not reliable due to the difficulty of achieving consistency in casting. As a result, it is now usual to test bronze components under load and also to X-ray them for casting defects. The time-honoured practice of embedding wrought iron in external stonework has caused widespread damage to the monuments of antiquity. The process of ferrous corrosion, resulting in the progressive expansion of layers of rust, dislodged the massive cladding of the Colosseum and split the lintel blocks above the Erechtheion. In both cases the original copper-based cramps had been replaced by iron, which corroded and failed.

29.5.2 Stainless steel fixings [3]

Nowadays, bronze is reserved for internal work. Structural fixings for cladding are usually made from stainless steel, as shown in Fig. 29.9, they are defined as either 'loadbearing' or 'restraint' fixings. The loadbearing type is used to support the base of the panel or facing slab and has a corbel plate bolted back to the structure. The traditional method using grouted fixings is still used for internal thin facing veneers. External cladding has to resist wind forces and extremes of exposure. Mechanical fixings have the advantage that they are of consistent and established strength, enabling calculations to be made and each anchor to be tested. The number and spacing of bolts varies according to the background (Table 29.1).

Fig. 29.7 *Mortices for bronze cramps, Delphi (c. 400 BC).*

Table 29.1 Stainless steel fixings

Background	*Fixing method*
Concrete/masonry	Expanding or resin anchors or cast-in bolts or bolted to inserts within cast-in dovetail slots
Masonry	Expanding or resin anchors
Steelwork	Direct bolting

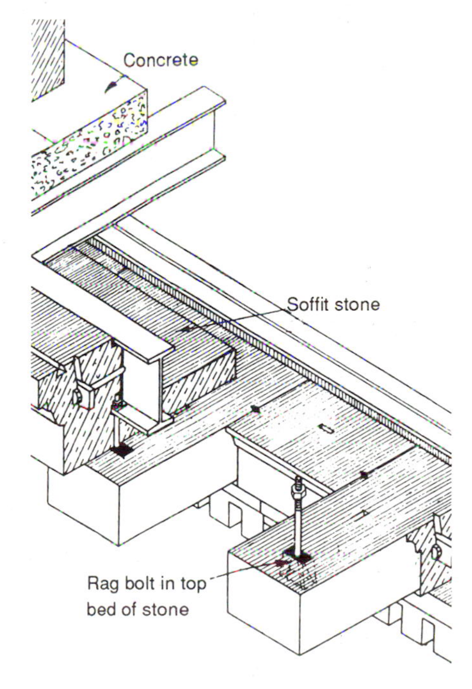

Fig. 29.8 *Stone veneer and cornice blocks tied back to frame (c. 1900s). Reprinted by kind permission of Harris and Edgar Ltd.*

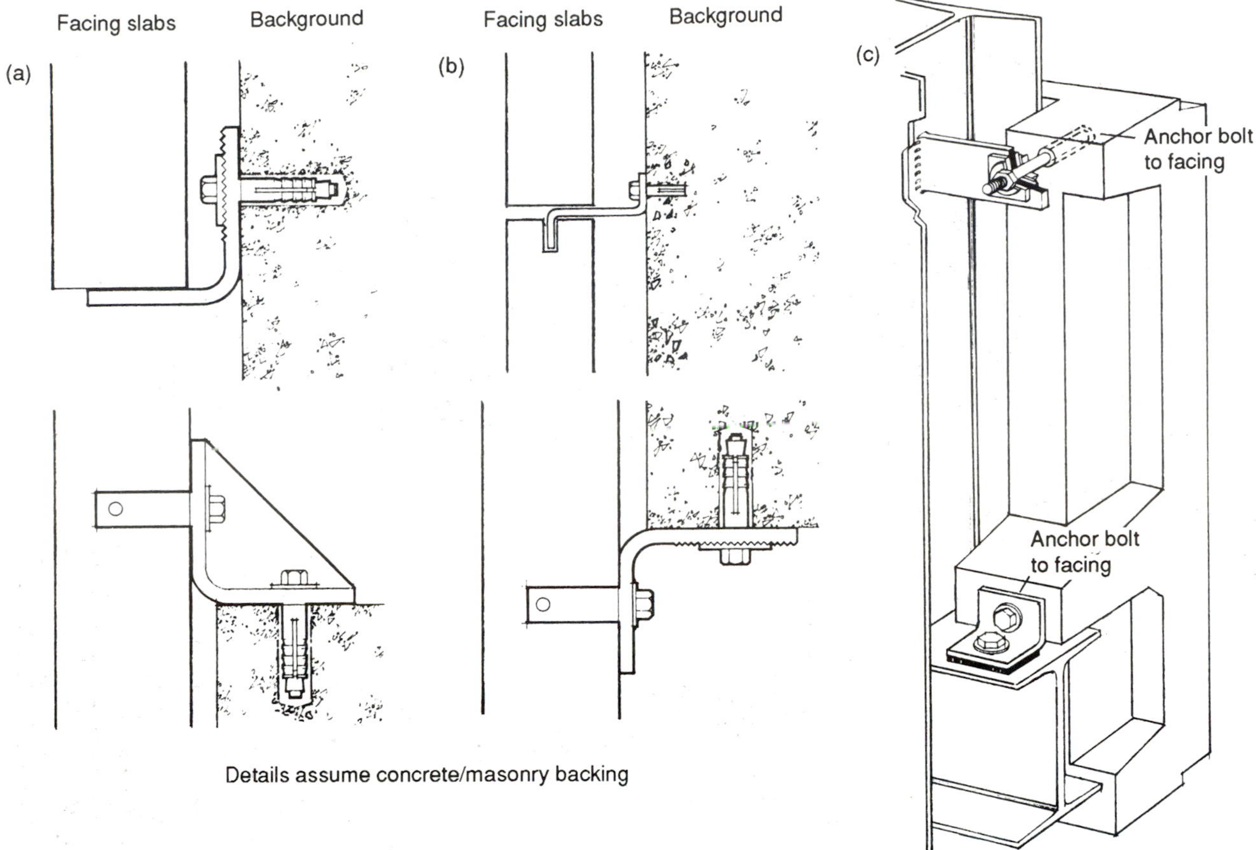

Fig. 29.9 *Principles of fixing cladding. (a) Loadbearing fixings. These are designed to carry the weight of the cladding and transfer it back to the structure. For materials such as stone, brick or glass reinforced cement, the fixings will almost invariably be positioned underneath the cladding and supporting it. For materials such as precast concrete, metal or glass reinforced plastic, the fixing may be positioned higher, with the cladding unit suspended or partially suspended. (b) Restraint fixings. These are designed to tie the cladding to the structure of the building. Under normal conditions, the fixing will not be permanently stressed, or at least should only have to sustain minimal permanent stress. When the fixing is subject to cyclic stresses caused by the applied loads, these stresses may become tension or compression depending on the direction of the loads. In a stressed condition, the load on the fixing may be positive as well as negative where the cladding is subject, for example, to wind loading. Reprinted by kind permission of Harris and Edgar Ltd.*

Each panel or slab is supported on two bearing corbels with a restraint tie (usually paired) at the top edge. A whole series of specialized fittings is available with anchor channels and slot hole fixings to accommodate three-dimensional tolerances. A further variety of types is manufactured for use with the entire range of cladding materials including brickwork veneer and precast slabs.

29.5.3 Channel grid systems

These have been developed for use with thin precast, metal or stone veneers, and they provide support from a continuous background grid of stainless steel channels bolted back to the structure. Aspects of this technology are further described in chapter 27, section 30.5. A variety of toggle fixings are also manufactured for attaching thin linings to walls which are inaccessible from the rear, making conventional bolting impossible.

29.6 OTHER FITTINGS

By a process of architectural lateral thinking, steel framing used to carry pipework has been adapted to make support channels for external cladding. It is worthwhile studying proprietary bracket systems to discover alternative ways of using them. Many industrial railings and shelf supports, consisting of a kit of steel components with bolted or keyed connectors (Fig. 29.10), can be modified for the construction of building enclosures and lightweight framed structures.

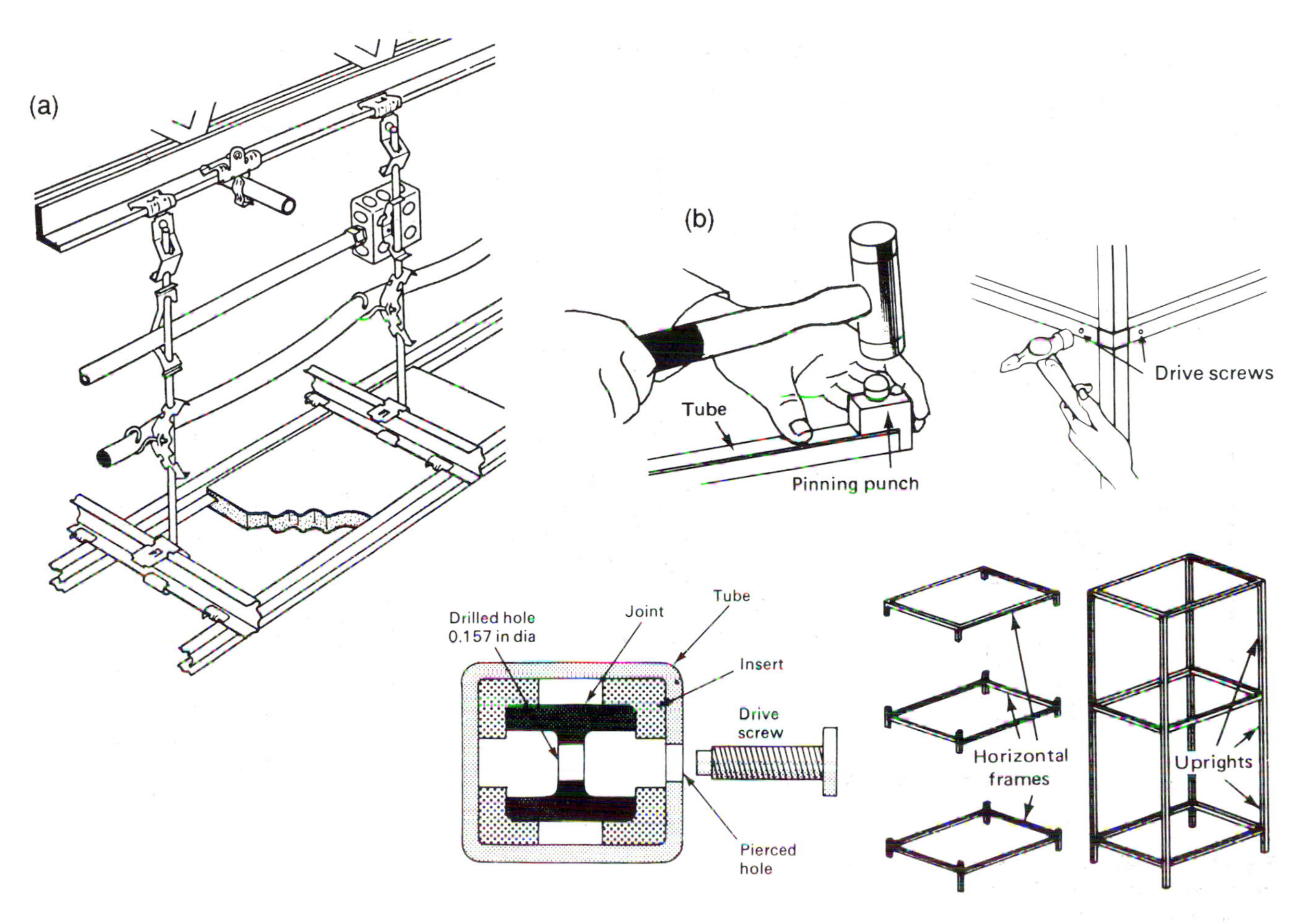

Fig. 29.10 *Other support systems. Reprinted by kind permission of Dexion Ltd. (a) Use of strap fastenings for servcices; (b) 'Apron' tuke for framing.*

REFERENCES AND TECHNICAL NOTES

1. General references: *Fixings and Adhesives*, Supplement to *Architects' Journal* for July 1983. Also current publications on fasteners by TRADA: *Mechanical Fasteners for Structural Timberwork* (1985) and current manufacturer's catalogues (see below).
   Engineer's schedules: Virginia Polytechnic and State University Wood-Research and Wood Construction Laboratory.
2. General references: Supplement to *Architects' Journal* for July 1983 and current catalogues.
3. Stainless steel fixings: refer to advice and catalogues obtainable from leading manufacturers, e.g.
   Abbey Building Supplies, 213 Stourbridge Road, Halesowen, West Midlands B63 3QY, UK.
   Tel: 44 (0)21 550 7674.
   Halfen Ltd, Griffin Lane, Aylesbury, Buckinghamshire HP19 3BP, UK. Tel: 44 (0)296 20141.
   Harris and Edgar Ltd, Progress Works, 222 Purley Way, Croydon, Surrey CR9 4JH, UK.
   Tel: 44 (0)81 686 4891.

Fig. 30.1 *(Upper) Construction photograph. (Lower) The Lovell House, Los Angeles 1929. View taken 1986 (architect Richard Neutra).*

30

Metal studwork and lath

Alan Blanc

30.1 INTRODUCTION

The history of metal studwork and lath dates back to the first quarter of this century when cold-formed sheet steel began to be used for roofing components and decking. At the same time cold-formed steel profiles and pressed sections were developed to serve as cladding rails, purlins and trim. One of the earliest applications was at Hollywood, USA and Boreham Wood, UK where render on metal lath and studwork was the method adopted for the basic fireproof construction of film studios.

The equable warm climate of Los Angeles encouraged architects to use lightweight framing in general building. The most famous 'steel' design of that period was the Lovell House of 1929, designed by Richard Neutra, the frame of which was completed in a mere 40 working hours (Fig. 30.1). Many of Neutra's houses at that time employed metal studwork, clad with metal lath and render or interlocking metal panels (which were a precursor of those used today). The Lovell House has worn extremely well due to the careful detailing of overhangs, sills and copings, galvanized steel was used for window frames and trim [1].

Prefabricated building with metal studwork was well established in the United States by 1933 [2], when a number of 'off the peg' houses were exhibited at The Century of Progress Exposition in Chicago. The method was similar to 'platform framing'; floor and wall panels were made up in the factory for delivery and assembly on site. It was, however, as lengths of rail and stud that the material sold most readily, rather than as pre-assembled dry partitions. Light steelwork and plasterboard casing, as anticipated by the Lovell House, became a common mode of construction in the States before the Second World War. Insurance companies preferred it compared with timber-framed building, particularly for commercial or public work.

Steel stud construction is a familiar method in the UK today, largely due to the expertise of the British gypsum industry who market a range of metal-framed ceiling, lining and partition systems for use with plaster and plasterboard. Canadian experience in recent years suggests that steel studwork may have a potentially greater role for house building; this might also be the case in the United Kingdom.

30.2 PARTITIONS

30.2.1 Stud/sheet systems

The framing of metal stud partitions is made from 0.55 mm thick cold-rolled steel sections (to BS 2994: 1976 (1987) Metal Studs), with a hot-dipped zinc coating, that are site cut and fixed between channel head and sole plates (Fig. 30.2). The standard studs are supplied in lengths from 2.40 to 3.60 m (8–12 ft) although a wider section 4.2 m (14 ft) long is available which can be further extended by clipping studs together to form partitions up to three or more storeys. The width of section varies from 48 to 148 mm to suit different partition thicknesses. Cross noggings secure fixings at the

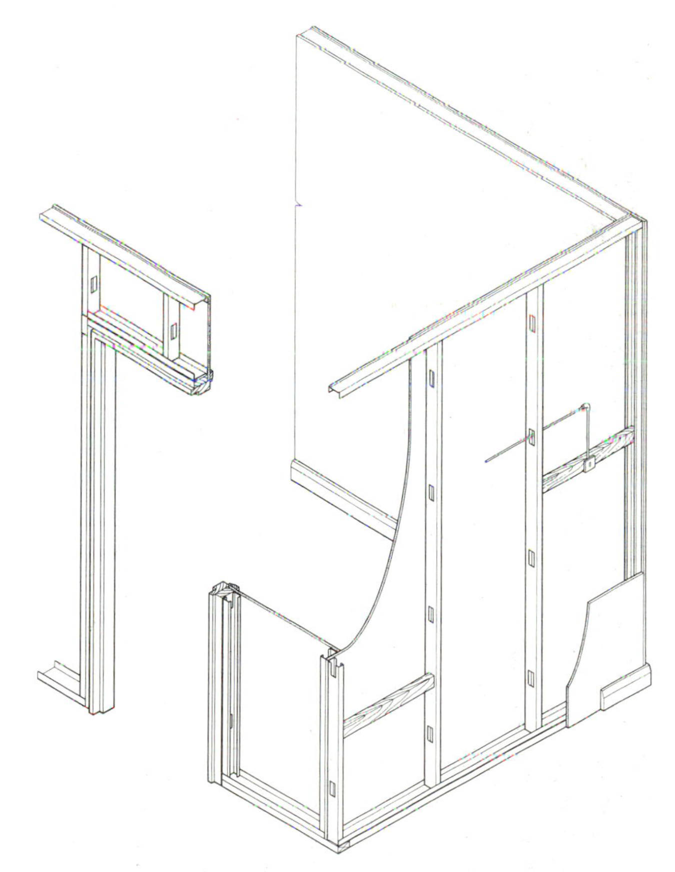

Fig. 30.2 *Gyproc metal stud components. Reprinted by kind permission of British Gypsum.*

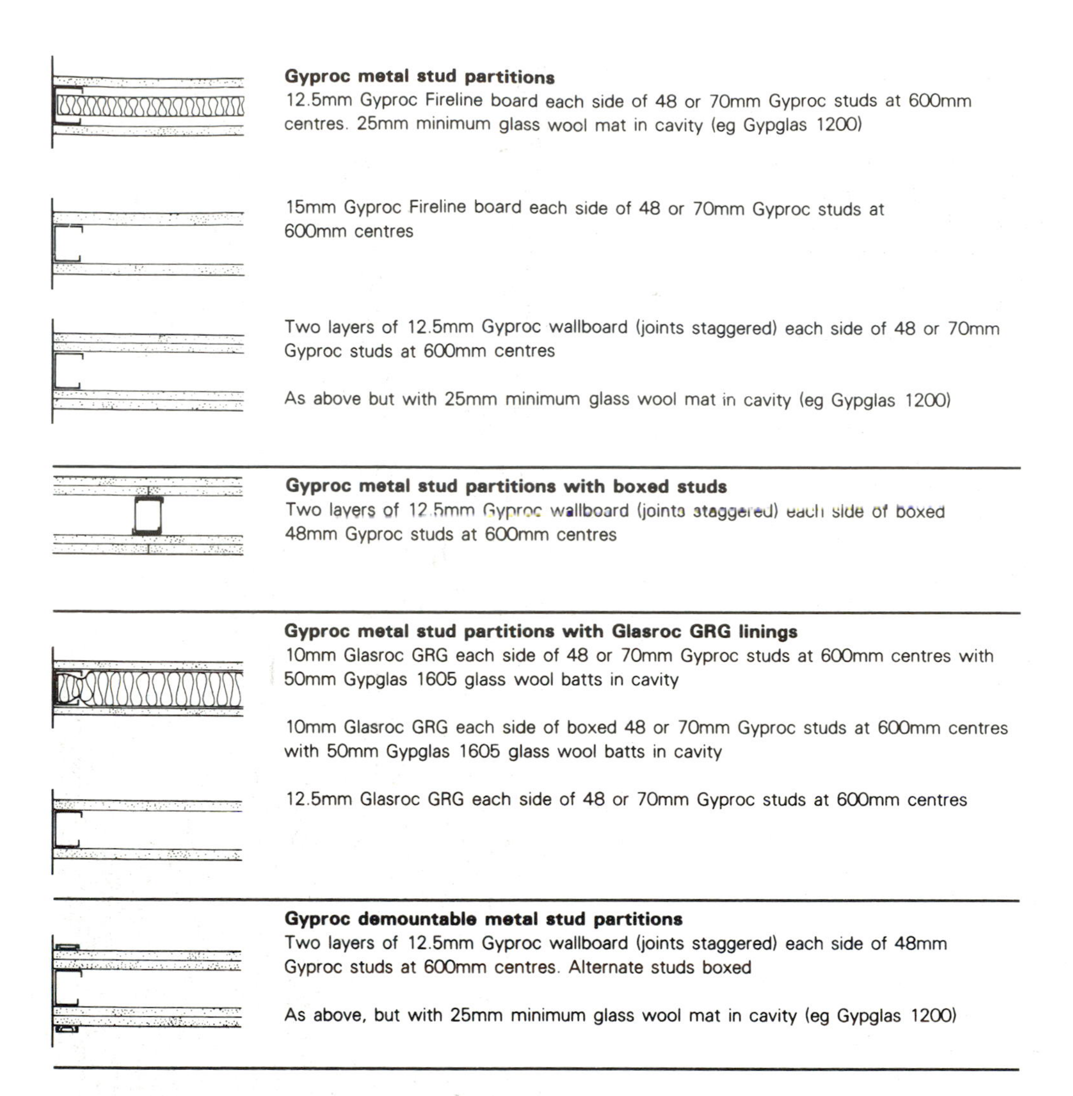

Gypproc metal stud partitions

12.5mm Gyproc Fireline board each side of 48 or 70mm Gyproc studs at 600mm centres. 25mm minimum glass wool mat in cavity (eg Gypglas 1200)

15mm Gyproc Fireline board each side of 48 or 70mm Gyproc studs at 600mm centres

Two layers of 12.5mm Gyproc wallboard (joints staggered) each side of 48 or 70mm Gyproc studs at 600mm centres

As above but with 25mm minimum glass wool mat in cavity (eg Gypglas 1200)

Gyproc metal stud partitions with boxed studs

Two layers of 12.5mm Gyproc wallboard (joints staggered) each side of boxed 48mm Gyproc studs at 600mm centres

Gyproc metal stud partitions with Glasroc GRG linings

10mm Glasroc GRG each side of 48 or 70mm Gyproc studs at 600mm centres with 50mm Gypglas 1605 glass wool batts in cavity

10mm Glasroc GRG each side of boxed 48 or 70mm Gyproc studs at 600mm centres with 50mm Gypglas 1605 glass wool batts in cavity

12.5mm Glasroc GRG each side of 48 or 70mm Gyproc studs at 600mm centres

Gyproc demountable metal stud partitions

Two layers of 12.5mm Gyproc wallboard (joints staggered) each side of 48mm Gyproc studs at 600mm centres. Alternate studs boxed

As above, but with 25mm minimum glass wool mat in cavity (eg Gypglas 1200)

Fig. 30.3 *Fire proofing to obtain one hour fire resistance from either side. Reprinted by kind permission of British Gypsum.*

Detail	Construction	Nominal* overall partition thickness (mm)	Maximum height (mm)	Approximate weight (kg/m²)	Fire resistance** (hours)	Sound insulation** 100-3150Hz R_w(dB)***
	two 12.5mm Gyproc wallboards each side 48mm studs alternate studs boxed	100	3000	43	1	47
	as above with 25mm minimum Gypglas 1200 in cavity	100	3000	43	1	51

* Suject to tolerances on associated materials

** The fire resistance and sound insulation performances are based on imperforate partitions. The fire resistances are the result of tests to BS 476:Part 8:1972, or assesments based upon those tests. The sound insulation performances are the result of laboratory tests to BS 2750:1980

*** The R_W figures are calculated in accordance with BS 5821:1984

Fig. 30.4 *Sound insulation detail. Reprinted by kind permission of British Gypsum.*

end and middle of the boards used to case the studwork, and help construct fire closures in the height of voids within partitions.

Fire resistance is provided by a plasterboard lining in combination with its mechanical fixing back to the steel studwork. A range of fire proofing methods is shown in Fig. 30.3 [3]. The extent of sound insulation provided by hollow partitioning depends on its weight and if structural discontinuity can be introduced into the framing, Fig. 30.4. shows how up to 51 dB reduction in sound transmission can be achieved.

The method can be adapted for special structures, lift shafts for example (Fig. 30.5), and enclosures within buildings such as kiosks or similar units in airports and shopping malls. Ceilings, either self-supporting or suspended, can be made from cold-formed joists or light channel sections. Marks and Spencer have used all types of steel studwork extensively in the fitting out of their stores because of the relative speed of dry construction in the finishing stages of a project. Metal-framed partitions can be disassembled and reused, unlike block or brick that are demolished and discarded as rubble.

30.2.2 Panel systems

The technology of steel panel partitioning dates back to the construction of the Chrysler Building in New York (1928–30), where the first fully demountable and flexible partitions were installed (which are still in service today [4]). The basic forms of demountable partition can be described as frame/sheet, frame/panel or panel/panel.

Frame/sheet systems are those most commonly used for off-site fabrication. The framing consists of I and U shaped steel sections with an overlapping trim of aluminium or plastic (that makes no contribution to any requirement for fire resistance). They are easily demounted and rearranged and can incorporate glazing and sound deadening insulation sufficient to achieve a reduction in sound transmission of 25–30 dB. A typical example is shown in Fig. 30.6. An industrial version also exists which can be used to construct partitions of up to 11 m in height.

Frame and inset panel types can be largely self-supporting so the frame can be smaller than that of a stud system, a well-designed example is shown in Fig. 30.7.

Panel-to-panel partitioning is the most interesting of the three types from a design point of view. In principle they consist of structurally self-sufficient panels that are butted together. A leading French manufacturer uniquely achieved the integration of ceiling, floor and partition components seen at, for example, IBM at Greenford (architects – Foster Associates, Fig. 30.8). Today, a wide range of UK specialists offer ranges that give equal flexibility in partition design.

These partition systems have in common the capability of considerable fire resistance (½, 1 and 2 hours), as a result of the mechanical bonding of the cold-formed steel frame and the fire-resistant sheets forming the outer facing (plasterboard or cement fibre board), and further enhanced if the core is packed with insulating quilt. There are other types that include steel components in some form, for example sliding/folding partitions with overhead channel track and 'jack-up screens' that have adjustable anchor bolts at the top and bottom. The method of assembly resembles curtain

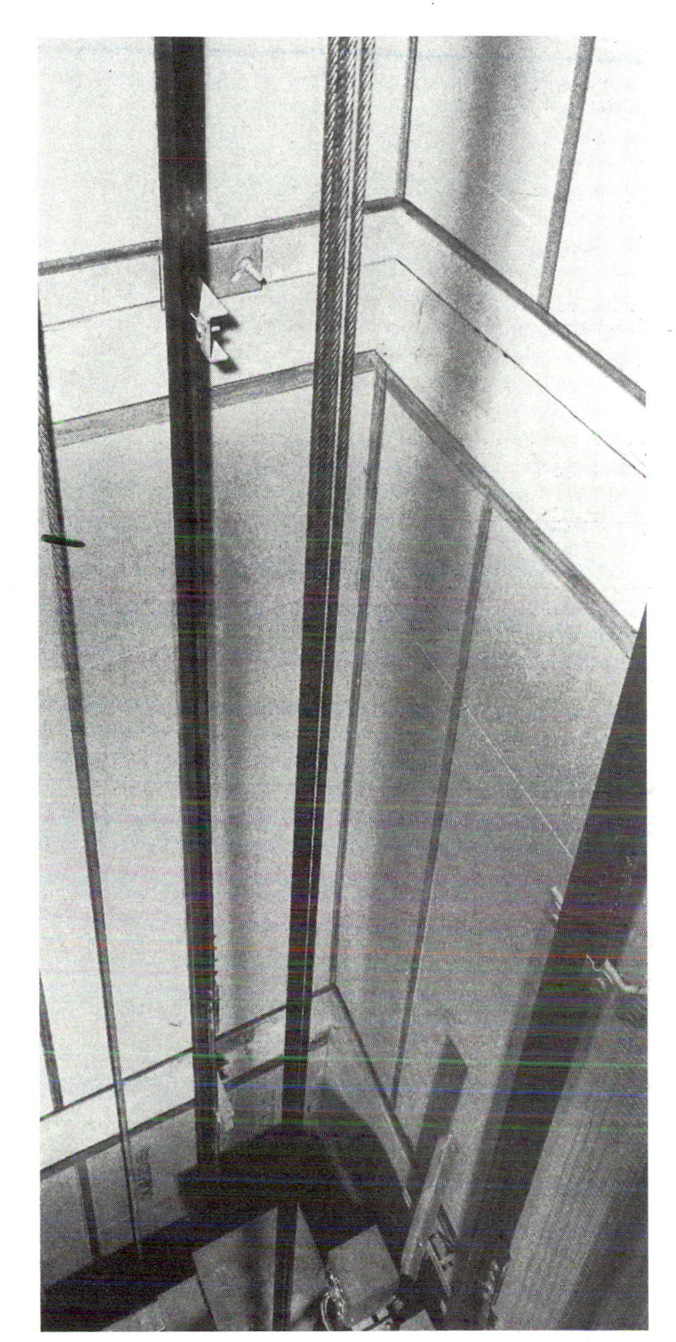

Fig. 30.5 *Lift shaft construction. Reprinted by kind permission of British Gypsum.*

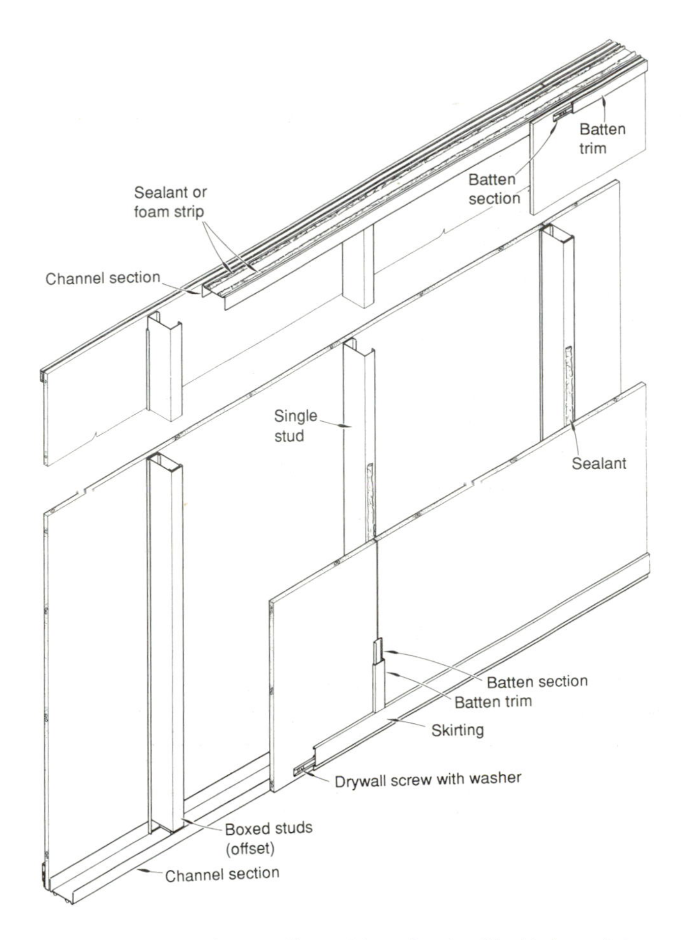

Fig. 30.6 *Gyproc demountable partitions. Reprinted by kind permission of British Gypsum.*

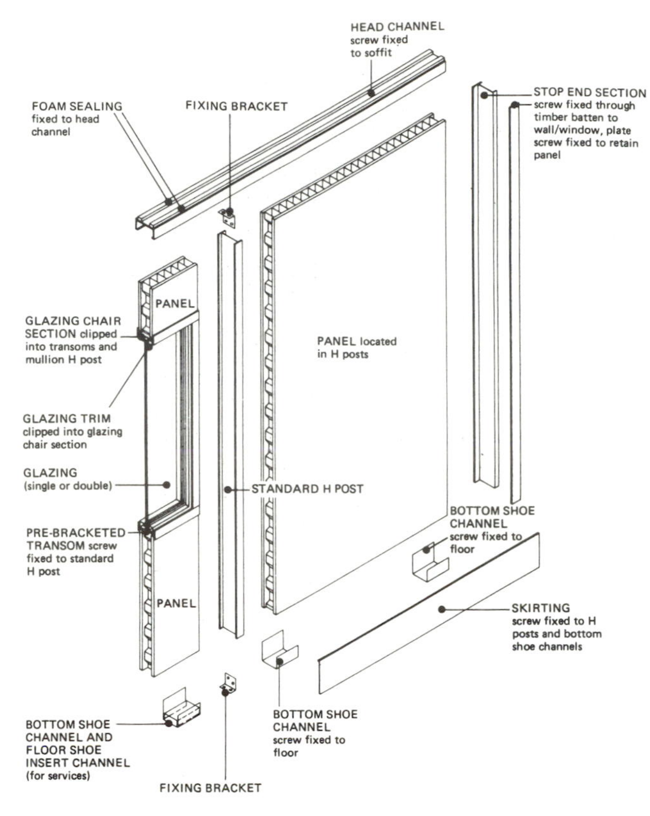

Fig. 30.7 *Permlock Slimcost system.*

walling, special profiles to receive doors and glass are attached to standard frame sections. It is possible using these ranges of fittings to devise a partition system for a particular contract against a performance specification, and to achieve sizes beyond the 1.2 m (4 ft) range offered 'off-the-shelf.'

30.3 EXTERNAL STUDWORK

Compared to that used internally, steel stud framing for external construction is more robustly constructed to cope with the loads imposed by floors, roofs and wind pressure: typical profiles are shown in Fig. 30.9. The general method, vertical members being cut to span between channels at head and sill, is similar to that described for internal partitions. Thermal insulation is fixed external to the frame. An effective moisture barrier is needed between the insulation and its cladding and a barrier to water vapour is necessary internally to prevent condensation from forming on the surface of the metal studs.

Metal studwork is commonly used for the lightweight external framing of penthouses and for the construction of shop fronts. In the United States its use is widespread for commercial and domestic work up to a height of three storeys.

Fig. 30.8 *Clestra Hauserman system for ceiling, floor and partition components at IBM Greenford (architects Foster Associates). Reprinted by kind permission of Clestra Hauserman.*

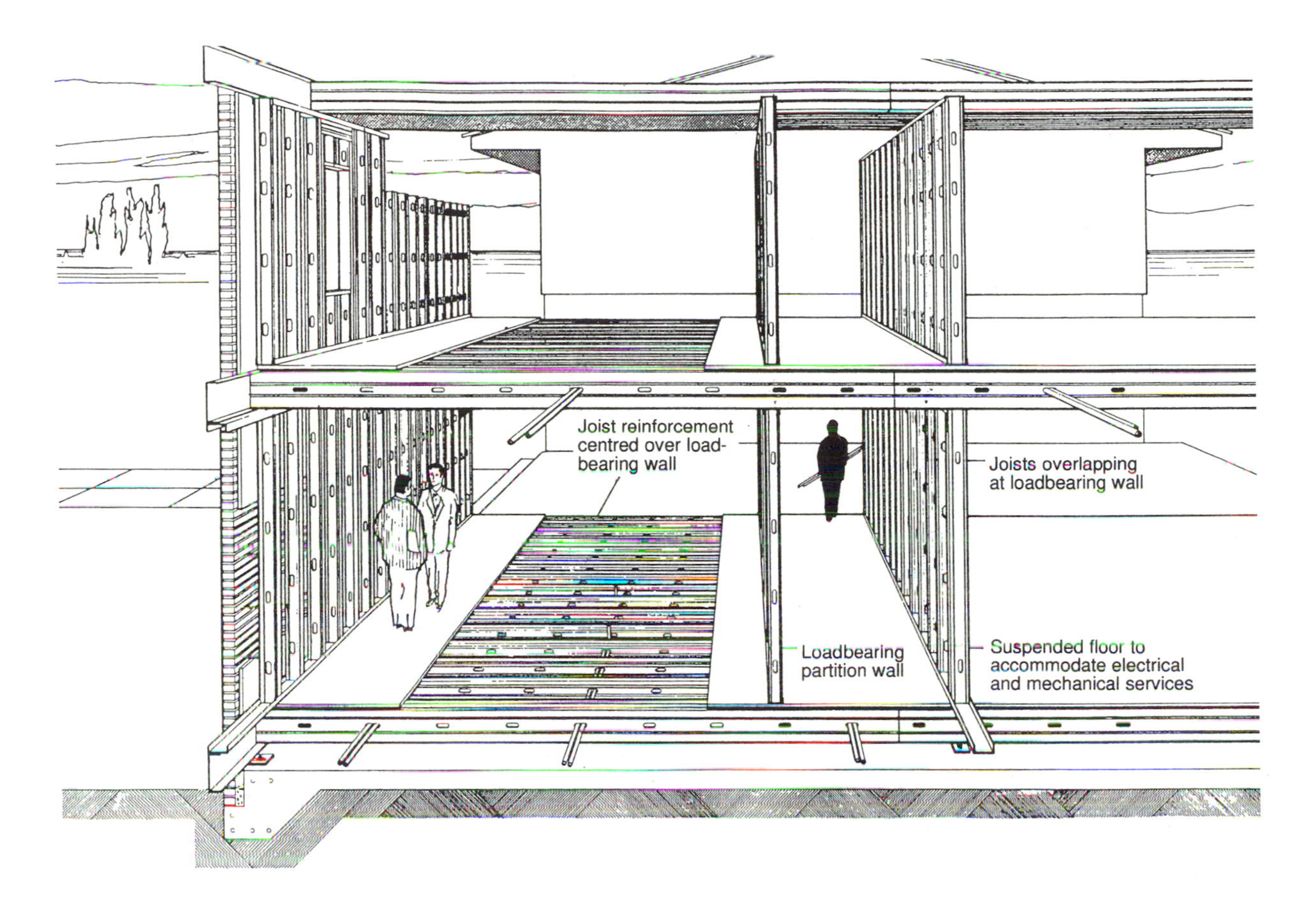

Fig. 30.9 *Typical studwork for external and structural walls. Reprinted by kind permission of Steel Framing Systems Ltd.*

30.4 METAL FRAMED HOUSING

The introduction to this chapter describes the role of steel in the development of North American prefabrication but there were also considerable achievements by others in this field and not just limited to the 'Nissen Huts' of World War I [6]. After 1918 the Lloyd George Government instituted a programme of prefabrication. A surprising number of houses were built with a structure of steel frame or alternatively steel panels using technology in part derived from the ship building industry. The number of houses completed was as follows: Dorman Long (Dorlon Co. Light Steel Frame), 10 000, Weir Atholl and Lowieson (steel angle and plate over timber), 2700, Dennis Wild System (standard RSJ frame), 9000 built, Thorncliffe System by Newton Chambers with cast iron flange panels, about 600, Telford House by Braithwaites with load bearing steel trays, 174. Many still survive from that era of 'Homes Fit for Heroes', some are even listed buildings or have been transported to open air museums!

In the aftermath of World War II 'Guns into Ploughshares' again became a theme for house construction; in this period the total volume of industrialized one and two storey houses produced was well over half that achieved by traditional means. Technical aspects of the programme were carefully monitored in the 1940s by Government agencies. Manuals such as the House Construction Reports published as Post-War Building Studies are well worth reading to assess the technical endeavour entailed in attempting to construct 300 000 houses per year. In the event a figure of 184 230 was attained in 1948 before cutbacks caused by rearmament and the Cold War put steel into a restricted category.

One of the most popular short-term 'prefabs' was the Arcon House developed by an architect/engineering team in association with Taylor Woodrow. This had a light steel frame clad with insulated panels of asbestos cement including steel windows, efficient heating and a fully fitted kitchen. The original order was for 40 000 prefabs at a cost of £1000 apiece. Their advanced concept was somewhat compromised by the Ministry's insistence upon conventional footings instead of a 'skid chassis' but despite this interference, they are an obvious predecessor of the 'Portakabin', one of the current generation of mobile buildings.

Permanent steel-framed housing was promoted by the

Fig. 30.10 *Gibberd's 'Waistcoat and Trouser' design for British Iron and Steel Federation House (type B) 1946 (detailer Gerhart Rosenberg).*

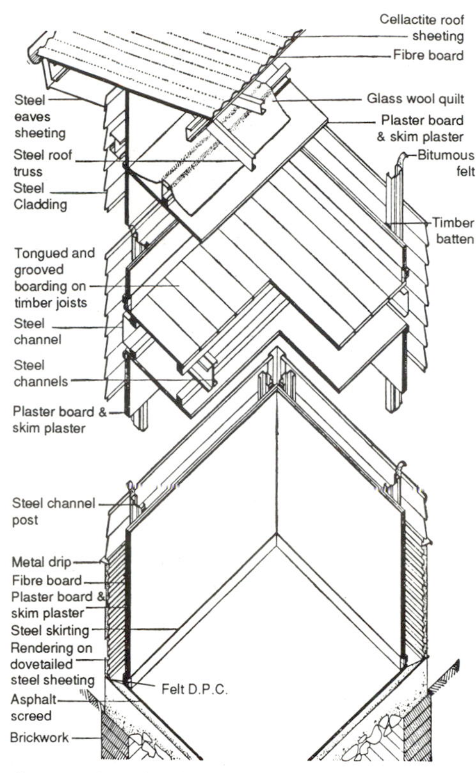

Fig. 30.11 *British Iron and Steel Federation House (type B) construction at axonometric (from Post-War Building Studies House Construction Second Report [7]).*

Fig. 30.12 *Gibberd's Howard House, detailing team Powell and Moya, promoter John Howard and Co.*

British Iron and Steel Federation through collaboration with the late Sir Frederick Gibberd. His design, a light steel frame of either hot-rolled 100 × 50 mm (4 in × 2 in) channels or cold-rolled sections on a 1050 mm (3 ft 6 in) module, could be clad in a variety of ways. Gibberd referred to the solution as 'Waistcoat and Trousers', with differing 'Waistcoats' fitting various sorts of 'Trousers': in reality this meant corrugated metal cladding to the first floor with either brick or other traditional materials at the ground storey (Fig. 30.10). The job detailer for the familiar BISF Mark 1 and 2 (Fig. 30.11) was an emigré architect Gerhardt Rosenberg; meanwhile Powell and Moya (then young assistants straight from college) were also in the Gibberd office, developing the more adventurous Howard House (Fig. 30.12). Over 36 000 of these sturdy steel framed buildings were constructed, many still exist but now have a new envelope made from other materials. (Figs 30.10, 30.11 and 30.12 reproduced with the permission of the Controller of Her Majesty's Stationery Office.)

This remodelling has made some 'prefabs' unrecognizable but it should be borne in mind that as people personalize their homes, components such as roof cladding or windows are likely to be replaced after 30 or so years, superficial characteristics such as paint colour or other finishes may change with each changing owner! After an intermission of some 40 years, 'steel frame' is once again emerging as a viable method for house building [5], in direct competition with timber-framed construction that until recently secured a quarter of the market.

One final story ought to be told concerning a surveyor who was called upon to investigate a thin-walled 'two-cell' bungalow of strange proportions near Byfleet in Surrey, UK. Discreet drilling revealed the body frames of two single-decker buses (placed side by side), behind the stockbroker's Tudor of pebbledash and half timber selling for £150 000 in that part of the Thames Valley. Which goes to show that for housing to endure, it is the structure that matters whether it be bus, prefab, or Southern Californian Hi-Tech.

30.5 METAL LATHING

Metal lath is made by stretching perforated steel sheet to make a twisted diagonal mesh. It may be strengthened by crimping a 'V' fold into the sheet and can then be made into a structural panel if coated on both sides with sand and cement. By pouring a concrete topping over the mesh a composite floor slab can be constructed spanning up to 3 or 3.3 m (10 or 11 ft).

Metal lath has the advantage of being able to be bent to shape, and as a result it has been employed to make vaulted permanent formwork between steel beams for concrete filler joist floors. It is more commonly used nowadays to form an uninterrupted background for plastering or rendering, a ceiling for example.

Continuous jointless surfaces may be required for fire resistance, or to achieve smooth decorative paintwork, or to give a robust surface instead of tiling that may be subject to damage, or plasterboard that is vulnerable to moisture penetration. The choice of lath is crucial. A background of expanded metal provides the best guarantee of stability but it is critical to make the correct choice of metal and type of plaster if corrosion is to be avoided. Dovetailed or keyed patterns have greater strength, heavier grade galvanizing gives good on-site protection. The correct application of cement and sand render onto a ceiling mesh forces the finish into the lath so that the rear face is totally encased in mortar. The fixings used are bitumen-coated galvanized steel or stainless steel. The structural forms of lath will span 1.8 m (6 ft) between supports. This technique has been put to large-scale use for the refurbishment of London's Underground stations, where stainless steel channels have been fixed clear of the old station walls to support arches made from lath finished in render and tiles (Figs 30.13 and 30.14).

Fig. 30.13 *Galvanized Riblath over steel firrings. Reprinted by kind permission of Gail Ceramics.*

Fig. 30.14 *Tiled finish to Piccadilly Tube Station, London, over rendering and galvanized Riblath. Reprinted by kind permission of Gail Ceramics.*

30.5.1 Fire

Encasement of steelwork with plaster or render on metal lath is an effective method of fire insulation. Here are some sample specifications, a reduced specification is used to obtain 1 hour or ½ hour fire resistance.

Typically to obtain a 2 hour fire rating for a steel beam, it should be encased with expanded metal attached to 25 × 3 mm (1 × ⅛ in) flat or 6 mm (¼ in) mild steel rod stirrups at 350 mm (1 ft 2 in) centres. These should be fixed either by clipping or welding to the steelwork or bolt anchoring to the concrete soffit. A 13 mm (½ in) thickness of vermiculite-gypsum plaster is required with angle beads to form arrises. To achieve a 4 hour fire rating, the same specification is used but the thickness of plaster is increased to 32 mm (1¼ in), angle beads are fixed after completion of the render coat. Lightweight flat expanded meshes can also be obtained galvanized and are suitable for the encasement of small beams and service ducts.

30.5.2 Condensation

There is an inherent risk of condensation forming on metal-reinforced rendering and care should be taken in humid spaces to ensure that paintwork is very well maintained. It is also important that mastic is used to seal around conduit or pipes so as to form a continuous vapour barrier. A number of failures have occurred where the cheaper black japanned meshes and aluminium expanded metal have corroded. Particularly problematic is the highly corrosive reaction that takes place between gypsum plaster and unprotected steel.

30.5.3 Technical innovations

Pier Luigi Nervi, the celebrated Italian engineer, made considerable innovations in the use of mesh reinforced concrete (termed: ferro-cement). By spraying render onto both faces of steel fabric, he made it possible to manufacture thin concrete shells off-site, which were used as permanent shuttering for his famous shell concrete domes. Another technique using spray concrete is the construction of fire-resistant service ducts from metal mesh wrapped around a framework of angles which is then sprayed from both sides. The finish is textured to mask the slight unevenness of the sprayed surface. Notable in this regard are any of Arthur Rank's surviving cinemas, the Odeon in Leicester Square being a prime example of the decorative possibilities of jointless ceiling construction.

Fast-track building often involves the spray-coating of intumescent finishes directly onto a structural steel frame.

Fig. 30.15 *Flats in steel framing with stud and profiled cladding at Dijon 1988 (architects Eric Dubosc and Marc Landowski).*

Fig. 30.16 *Steel framed houses using standardized framing and 'Cor-Ten' cladding at Charleroi, Belgium 1980 (architect Paul Petit).*

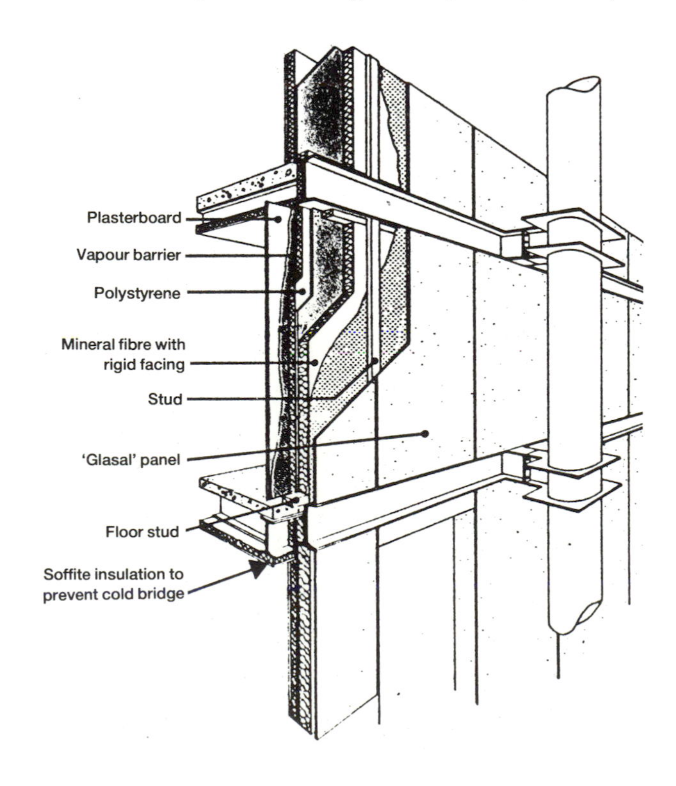

There are, however, areas of buildings such as garages, porches or overhangs where these finishes can suffer from damp and where a sealed false ceiling will be needed. Expanded metal and painted render provides better protection from atmospheric moisture than board materials, which are generally hygroscopic.

Another use of ribbed expanded metal in fast track building, is as floor decking that can span up to 4.8 m (16 ft). A structural screed topping is applied and the soffit is rendered to fireproof the construction if it is eventually to be concealed within a ceiling, or rendered and then set (finished in gypsum plaster) if the soffit is to be visible.

30.6 CONCLUSION

Domestic construction in steel is an Australian tradition dating from the 19th century. The houses of Glenn Murcutt, illustrated in chapter 5 (Fig. 5.2) and also in chapter 36 case study 36.2.2, are typical of many modern designs in Australia. On mainland Europe there is also a more adventurous attitude to domestic building methods, and more importantly, to architectural expression sympathetic to metal construction. The designs by Dubosc and Landowski (Fig. 30.15) are confident examples of the design of steel frames with profiled cladding. Paul Petit's work (Fig. 30.16) also honestly expresses the steel frame without recourse to the concealment by a brick envelope, as is usual in the UK. What a pity that British house builders are so timid in their approach to industrialized building.

REFERENCES AND TECHNICAL NOTES

1. Early Neutra Houses, Los Angeles.
   The accompanying photograph and the views expressed in the text follow the editor' s tour of Neutra's houses in August 1986, the appearance of the Lovell House and others at Silver Lake revealed that over the years few repairs to the buildings have been necessary.
   The Neutra experimental house at Silver Lake (1933) was of metal stud construction. It burnt down in an electrical fire in the 1970s. The present building is a faithful reconstruction.
   For details of early Neutra Houses refer to *Richard Neutra, Buildings and Projects*, edited by Willy Boessger, Vol.I. 1923–50. Published by Ginsberger, Zurich 1951.
2. Century of Progress Exposition Chicago 1933.
   Fifteen modern houses were exhibited, including steel houses by General Houses, Armco and Stran-Steel, the most exotic was called the 'House of Tomorrow made with phenoloid board and steelwork', designed by George Keck. From *The Dream of the Factory Made House*, by Gilbert Herbert, MIT Press (1984).
3. *The White Book*. This is the standard reference to the products marketed by British Gypsum Ltd, Head Office, East Leake, Loughborough, Leicestershire LE12 6HX, UK. Tel: 44 (0)602 844844.
   The general details in section 31.2 are drawn from that source. Also applicable are British Standards with which *The White Book* complies:
   BS 8212: 1988 Code of Practice for Drylining and Partitioning.
   BS 8000: Part 8: 1989 Code of Practice for Plasterboard Partitions and Drylining (Workmanship).
   BS 1230: 1985 Part 1, *Gypsum Plasterboard*.
4. The Chrysler partitions.
   Confirmation was obtained from Myron Wander of the Steel Institute of New York.
5. Steel framed prefabs in the UK. Refer to framing designs by PMF Ltd using the latest technology – computer-aided calculations and fabrication jigs; also work by Steel Framing Systems Ltd, Cathedral House, 5 Beacon Street, Lichfield, Staffordshire WS13 7AA, UK. Tel: 44 (0)543 250100 and Ayrshire Metal Products plc, 11 Church Street, Irvine, Ayrshire KA12 8PH, UK. Tel: 44 (0)294 74171.
   Another departure is the work by British Rail Workshops, Derby who produce steel framed bathroom and service modules for domestic and office buildings.
6. The Nissen Hut. Invented by the Canadian military engineer Lieutenant Colonel P.N.Nissen in 1916. The sophistication of its design is fully described in Pawley, M. (1990) *Theory and Design in the Second Machine Age*, Blackwell, Oxford.

For further reading refer to *Specification* (Architectural Press), the *Architects' Journal Focus* for October 1987 and to manufacturers catalogues.

Fig. 31.1 *Medieval windows. Typical horizontal wrought iron ties to leaded work, built into stone mullions.*

Fig. 31.2 *Renaissance windows. Hawksmoor's standard window grids for Limehouse, St Annes, London 1712–30.*

Fig. 31.3 *Wrought iron glazing bars at Claydon House, Buckinghamshire, UK (late 18th century).*

31

Metal windows and louvres, sills and lintels

Alan Blanc

31.1 HISTORICAL REVIEW

Iron has been used for making windows since the Middle Ages. Medieval stained glass was subdivided by wrought iron bars that tied the leaded lights back to the enclosing tracery made of stone [1]. This composite construction is in effect iron-reinforced masonry, the slender stonework being in compression, the transverse ironwork supporting the glass and resisting wind loads (Fig. 31.1).

Large renaissance church windows were often framed with a grid of stout wrought iron bars carrying the glazing and lacing together the masonry on either side of the window openings. The Commissioners' 50 new churches that were planned following the 1710 Act were of standardized construction. The window grids had the same framing whether the architect was Gibbs, Hawksmoor or James (Fig. 31.2).

The gradual refinement of the Georgian sash window resulted in the reduction of hardwood glazing bars down to sizes as slender as 15 × 45 mm (⅝ × 1¾ in). Window makers then turned to the use of shaped wrought iron bars to achieve slenderness without sacrificing strength. The sashes at Claydon House for example are divided by forged iron astragals set within hardwood sashes (Fig. 31.3). Another use of blacksmith's work in the 18th and 19th century was for the insertion of discrete 'night ventilators' within the sight line of traditional windows. Figure 31.4 shows an example from Edinburgh where this detail was particularly popular, avoiding as it did the draught caused by opening the whole sash. By the time of the Adam Brothers (coincidentally John Adam was a partner in the Carron Iron Foundry), cast iron frets were used in fixed fanlights, both north and south of the border.

The cast iron frames (both fixed and opening sashes), made for mills in the late 18th century (Fig. 31.5), were the first mass-produced metal windows. A contemporary domestic version was available, divided by cast iron bars into diamond or square-shaped panes (Fig. 31.6). Specialist

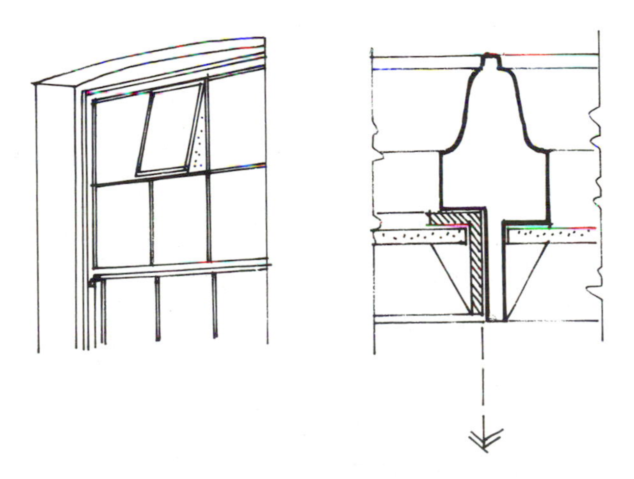

Fig. 31.4 *Night ventilator. Right-hand sketch shows metal ventilator frame against sash bar.*

Fig. 31.5 *Early pattern of cast iron industrial light, Kings Mill, Shelford, Cambridge (studio of Sir Leslie Martin).*

Fig. 31.6 *Domestic version of cast iron sashes.*

foundries still produce replicas in this style [2]. Modern techniques for welding cast iron also make it possible to repair old windows.

A revolutionary process developed in the 19th century enabled wrought iron glazing bars to be rolled into continuous lengths that could be used to make totally glazed roofs. The first application was for the construction of conservatories, most notably the Palm House at Kew dating from 1844 (Fig. 31.7). Also by metal forging, bulbous T-bars were fabricated with compression and tension chords which were joined with fish plates (like rail track)to make extended pieces of consistent section. This technology allowed the lightweight roofing of fully-glazed halls, most particularly London's main line railway stations: for example the roof at King's Cross constructed in 1852 using Hartleys 45 × 75 × 10 mm (1¾ × 3 × ⅜ in) rolled iron bar. Also characteristic of this time was the glass-roofed street or 'galleria' the most celebrated examples of which are to be found in Milan and Naples (Fig. 31.8). Side-wall glazing was a natural development of this method, eventually leading to the 20th century ability to make completely glass buildings.

By the late 19th century industrial metal windows in Europe were manufactured from I- and T-shaped bars, brazed and fixed together in trellis framing. Rolled mild steel had superseded the use of forged iron by the early 1900s. Domestic windows using the now characteristic hot rolled Z-section were first made in the United Kingdom by Crittall's in 1904 at Braintree, Essex. This was a result of W.F. Crittall's purchase of the patent for 'Fenestra' steel windows from the Karl Zucker company of Dusseldorf. In this system the casements were dimensioned on a module of

Fig. 31.7 *Palm House, Kew 1844–8 (architect Decimus Burton: engineer Richard Turner).*

Fig. 31.8 *Galleria Principe, Naples.*

500 mm, hence the 1 ft 8 in range that became the accepted standard in the UK.

Steel windows retain a significant share of the window market. Steel's fire-resisting qualities result in the inclusion of mild steel cores and structural components into modern curtain walling, patent glazing and rain-screen facades. Finishes for steel now include galvanizing, electrostatically applied powder paints and over-cladding with aluminium, bronze, plastic or stainless steel. A 19th century invention, lead-coated ferrous metal, is still used for industrial glazing.

31.2 METAL WINDOWS, SECTIONS AND SIZES

31.2.1 Sections and sizes

W.F. Crittall was educated at an art school and had a lifelong interest in design that encompassed the geometry of components, the pattern of window elevations and publicity material. From the first 1904 cottage casements a range was developed based upon a standard 54 degree angle, a proportion that was very popular with Lutyens (Fig. 31.9 [3]).

The modular frames permitted standard glass sizes to be used provided that sashes had subframes. The original manufacturing process for machine welding Z-sections is still used 70 years later (Fig. 31.10). The window sections are made by passing 50 × 50 × 1200 mm (2 × 2 in × 4 ft) steel rods through rolling mills that convert each piece into 21 m of sash profile (Fig. 31.10).

The size of frame depends on the weight of section used. A lightweight bar for the original range was made from 1920 to 1954. A modified section made for the 2 ft range (600 mm) was itself repeatedly updated, for example weather-stripping was introduced in 1962. In 1972 the windows were metrically co-ordinated on a 100 mm (4 in) module by consultant designer Frederick MacManus.

More robust profiles have always been milled; called 'universal sections', they are available in light, medium and heavy weight. Devised for purpose-made windows and particularly for sashes wider than 600 mm (2 ft), the sections allow the 'sight line' of both fixed and opening lights to be constant (Fig. 31.11). The fundamental difference between standard windows for housing to BS 6510 [5] and purpose-made windows is one of 'sight line'. The universal section's 'box' profile allows casements, French doors, pivoting windows, both side and top hung, to be made with a constant glass to metal 'sight line'. The ingenuity of the section is explained in Fig. 31.12. The frames are stronger

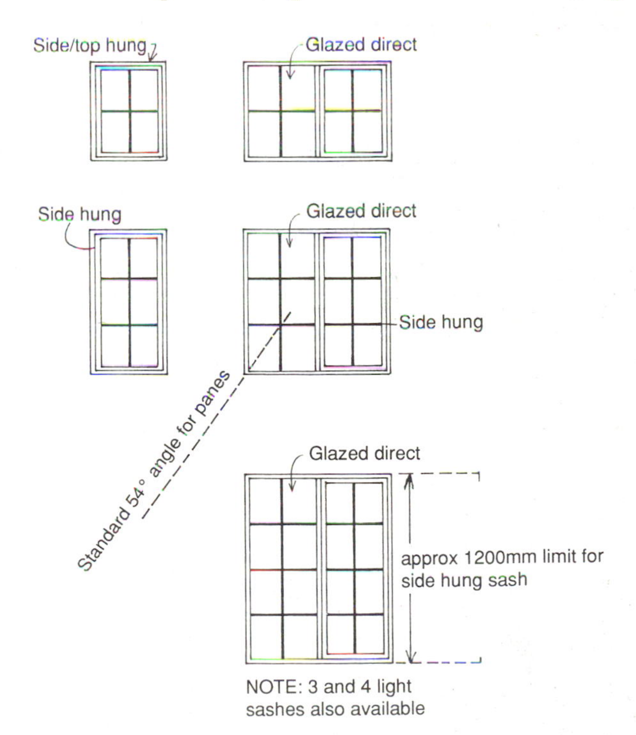

Fig. 31.9 *Lutyens style casements. The early standardized cottage casements used for housing shortly after World War I.*

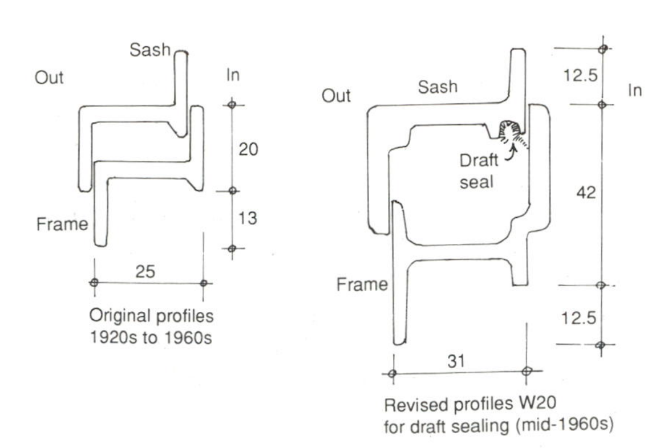

Fig. 31.10 *Typical 'Z' sections.*

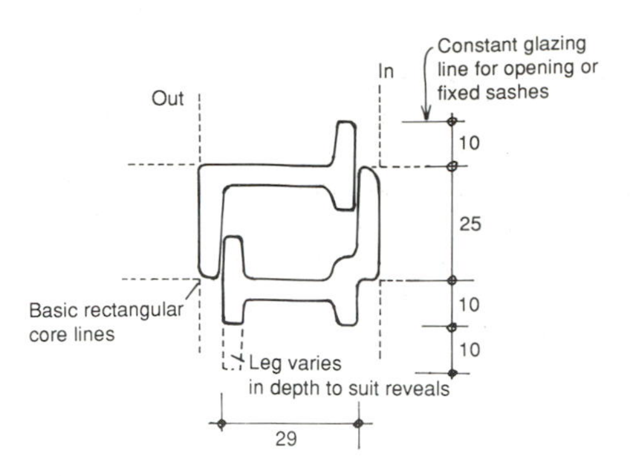

Fig. 31.12 *Basic geometry for universal sections.*

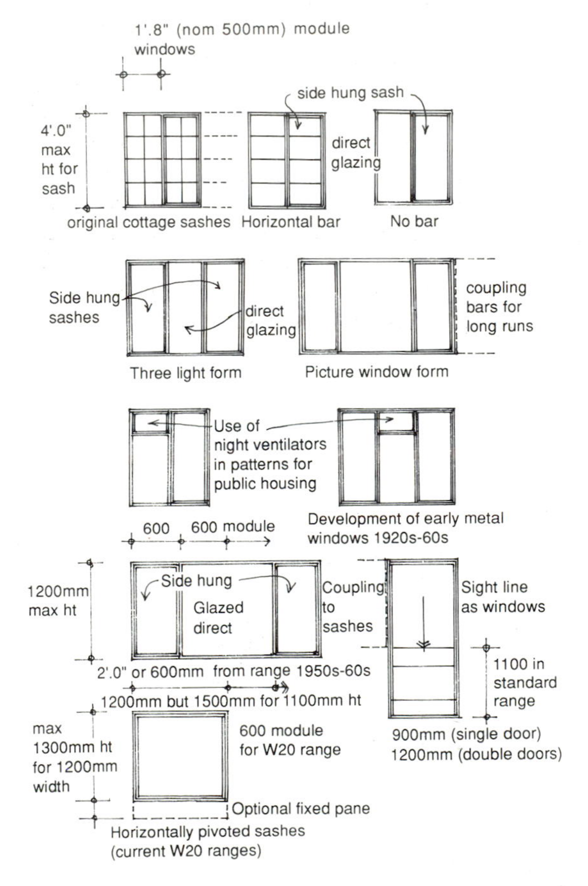

Fig. 31.11 *Typical window ranges related to standard bar section.*

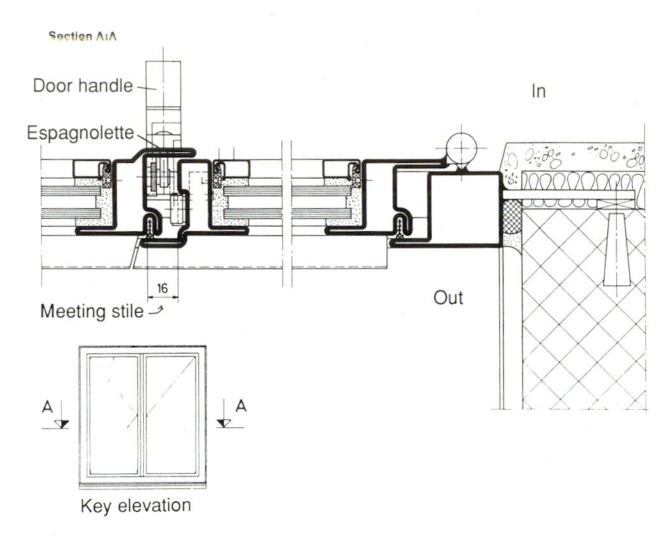

Fig. 31.13 *Cold-formed sections (Jansen system). Reprinted by kind permission of Jansen AG.*

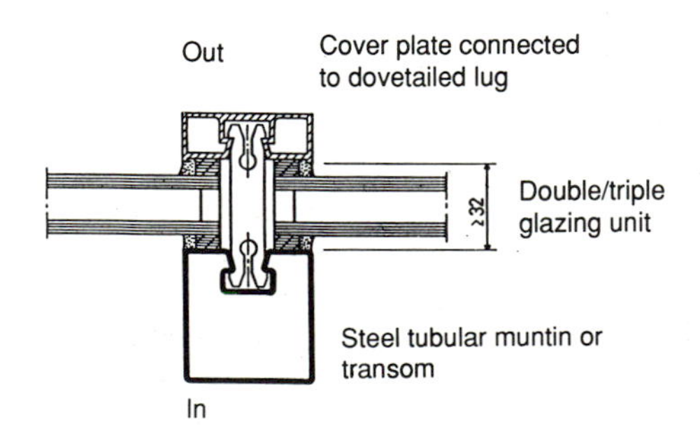

Fig. 31.14 *High performance windows (Jansen-VISS) based upon tubular steel cores. Reprinted by kind permission of Jansen AG.*

because the greater cross-section of metal gives greater strength in torque than does the simple Z-section frame. Universal sections are used throughout the world, in countries where steel is not produced, fabrication can be carried out locally, the basic rolled sections being imported.

In many places the advantages of metal windows over timber are that they need relatively little maintenance and there is no risk from fungal attack or twisting due to moisture movement. In Israel, timber windows may not be used for government projects, partly due to a shortage of appropriate durable timber, but also because of a lack of expertise in maintaining and painting woodwork [4]. A lesson might be learnt in the UK from their example.

Cold-formed and tubular sections are also manufactured for window frames and opening lights by folding 2 mm (1/16 in) gauge sheet into a number of interlocking shapes (Fig. 31.13). The Swiss 'Jansen' system is the best known, the basic lengths are sold to fabricators for cutting and jig-welding to individual designs. Jansen's other patents include tubular steel cores for high-performance, 'thermally broken' window walls (Fig. 31.14), a topic addressed in greater detail in chapter 26 under 'light cladding'.

31.2.2 Finishes

Protection of the earliest steel windows depended mainly upon red oxide primer and paint, while galvanizing was reserved for bathrooms and kitchens. Those that were only primed have proved an endless maintenance problem because of their propensity to rust. After the Second World War specifications [5] were improved, galvanizing has become standard practice and commercial and domestic windows are also being over-painted. Today factory-coating is commonplace. Industrial windows are often left just galvanized for 10–15 years before being painted, though now many factory-applied finish coatings are also available.

A relatively new technology, electrostatically applied polyester powder paint [6], can be used on prepared steel. Some ranges of low cost metal windows are now finished in this way but damage during installation or by vandalism places these window coatings at risk (although they can be re-touched on site). The Steel Window Association give the following guidance as to the anticipated life of steel windows, depending upon their exposure (Fact Sheets available from PO Box 143, Tring House, Tring, Herts HP23 5PS):

Specification a	Galvanized steel windows (if left unpainted)	15–30 years
Specification b	As above but site painted once every 7–10 years	40–60 years
Specification c	Powder coating over galvanized steel	40–60 years (though site painting will be needed after 20–25 years)
Specification d	Lead 'terne' coated on steel	60 years (though this can be extended by site painting)

Because steel finishes are likely to become abraded at moving parts such as catches and hinges, the areas of these components having metal to metal contact are likely to be made of bronze, plastic or stainless steel.

31.2.3 Glazing

A window frame's depth of rebate for glazing varies according to the steel section used, the simplest method is a metal clip hidden behind a putty fillet (suitable given a wind stress limitation of 1500 N/m^2). Other methods include solid steel beads (for fire resistance and security) or aluminium channels sometimes with curved clips covering the corners (Fig. 31.15). Plastic setting blocks can also be used, similar to those for glazing in timber, two are fixed at each bearing point, and BS 6262: 1982 Glazing for Buildings describes the correct locations.

The lightweight sections that are still available need to be extended to receive double glazing. The frames now made under BS 6510 are far superior, and their depth permits either double-glazed or heavy duty laminated panes to be installed. European standards of thermal resistance require steel frames either to be thermally broken (as described in Fig. 31.14), or to incorporate secondary interior glazing.

Glass sizes and thicknesses are limited by the exposure of the site, itself a function of geographic location, altitude and height of the window above the ground. It must be remembered that the old BS window ranges for housing [8], were specifically limited to the maximum available size of 32 oz. drawn sheet glass. Consequently the maximum height and width was 1200 mm (4 ft). Float glass may be used in much larger sizes but it is necessary to check its anticipated performance relative to its thickness when refurbishing older windows, since the depth of rebate in light frame sections places limitations on the dimensions of the replacement glass (as described in Fig. 31.15).

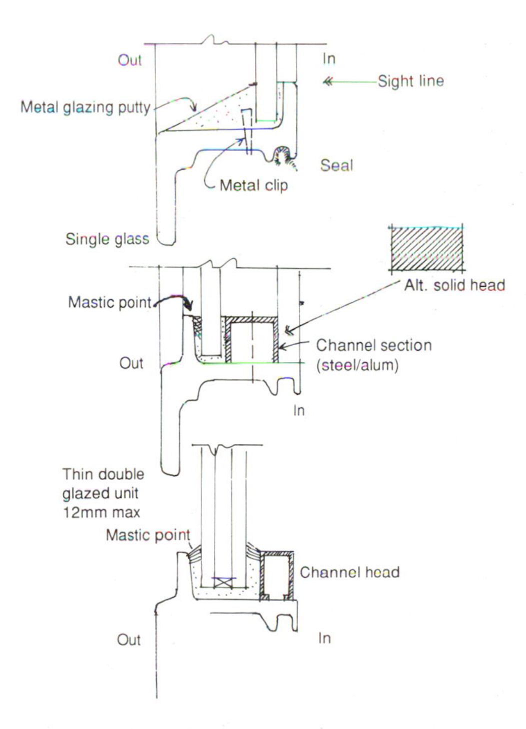

Fig. 31.15 *Glazing methods for metal windows.*

Table 31.1 Limiting sizes for steel frames

Nominal overall thickness	*Each pane of glass*	*Size limitation*
11–18 mm (7/16–11/16 in)	3 mm (1/8 in)	1270 (4 ft 2 in) square or up to 1270 × 1780 (4 ft 2 in × 5 ft 10 in)
13–30 mm (1/2–1 3/16 in) 18 mm (11/16 in) is about the maximum glass thickness that can be used in BS 6510 sections	4 mm (5/32 in)	1300 (4 ft 3 in) square or up to 2130/2400 (7 to 8 ft) wide × 1300 (4 ft 3 in) ht

Square pane sizes for economical double glazing are still fairly limited in size, as shown in Table 31.1 (metric sizes given reflect current British practice).

Sealed units can in fact be made up to 5 m wide × 3.18 m height (16 ft 6 in × 10 ft 6 in) with 12 mm (1/2 in) glass in each pane and an overall thickness of 36 mm (7/16 in), well beyond the scope of BS 6510 sections. Under these circumstances the designer has to adopt a custom-made, high performance form of assembly (refer again to Figs 31.13 or 31.14).

31.2.4 Fixing methods

Frames may either be built-in as the jambs are constructed or inserted at a later stage. The fixing lugs which are bolted to the inside of the frame are either straight or splayed for building-in or L-shaped straps for fixing to the face of the

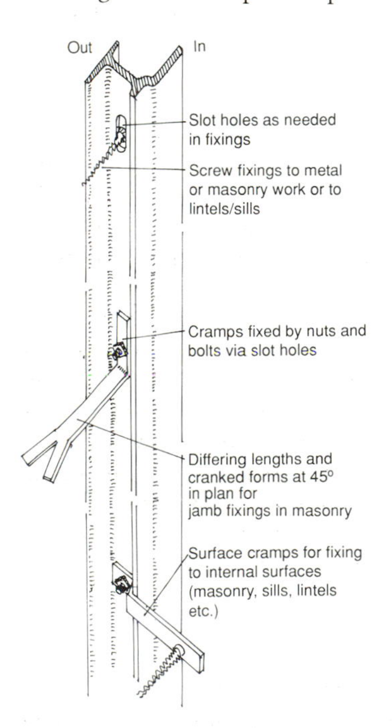

Fig. 31.16 *Fixing metal windows. Various methods.*

Fig. 31.17 *Wood subframing with steel opening lights.*

internal reveals [5]. It is also possible to plug and screw the frames to the jambs when they are to be fixed after the opening has been constructed (Fig. 31.16). A tolerance of 3 mm (1/8 in) should be allowed between all the four edges of the window and the structure, the gap being sealed with a bead of mastic. The weather resistance of metal windows will be improved by setting them back at least 75 mm (3 in) from the outer face [7]. Traditionally in Scotland windows are recessed to form reveals of approximately 110 mm (4 3/8 in) that are later rendered, long-legged sections are still made to suit this detail.

In the past it was common for steel windows to have timber subframes, and consequently fixed lights and panels had wooden frames, steel being used for the opening lights

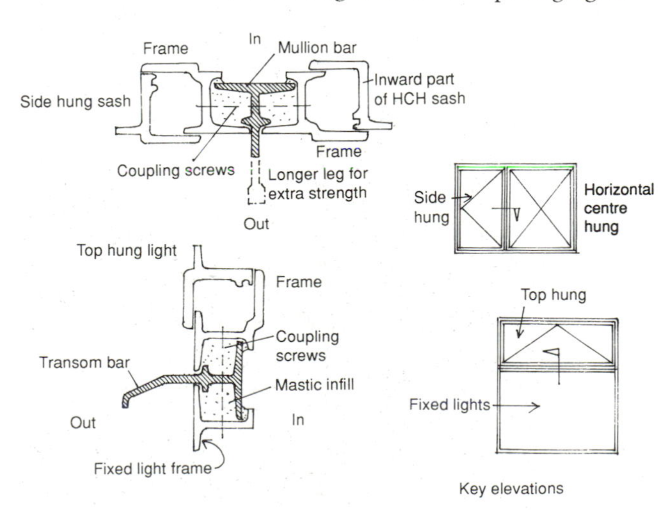

Fig. 31.18 *Coupling steel windows.*

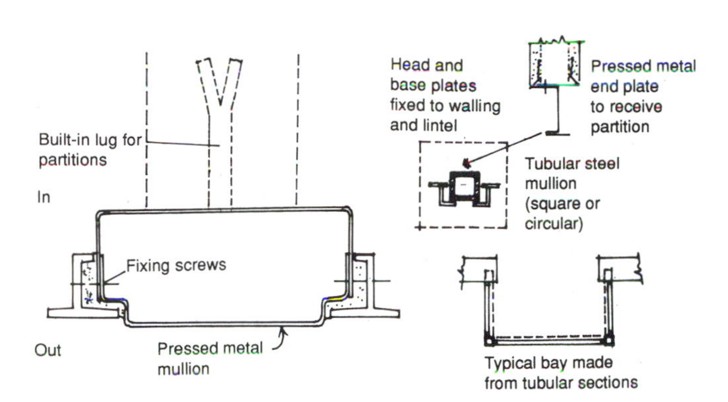

Fig. 31.19 *Tubular steel subframing.*

where greater strength is needed. This composite assembly is still very popular in Holland (Fig. 31.17). In the United Kingdom, standard subframes are scarcely available although they are still covered by BS 1285: 1980 Specification for Wood Surrounds for Steel Windows and Doors. It is more common nowadays for subframes and sills to be made of cellular core plastic that is self-coloured and does not require future repainting. Similarly pressed metal subframes are described in BS 1285 but are also being superseded by the use of plastic (UVPC).

31.2.5 Coupling frames

The maximum size of jig-welded frames is limited by restrictions of work bench space and transportation to 4.5 × 4.5 m (14 ft 9 in × 14 ft 9 in). For larger openings frames can be coupled together on site, both horizontally and vertically, to form continuous ranges of windows. The coupling bars are T-shaped or project to weather-proof horizontal junctions between lights (Fig. 31.18). Steel tubes (either circular or square) can also be used to make subframes for casements and to form structural mullions or corner columns for bay windows. The ends of these tubes should have plates welded across them for fixing at the sill or pad-stone and bolting or welding to connect with the lintel or roof slab (Fig. 31.19). Early types of curtain walling utilized a similar form of construction, a typical example being the Bauhaus at Dessau (1925–26), recently reconstructed with replica sashes, flat bar couplings and tubular supports (Fig. 31.20 and [9]).

Fig. 31.20 *Restored 1926 Bauhaus windows, Dessau, Germany, 1982.*

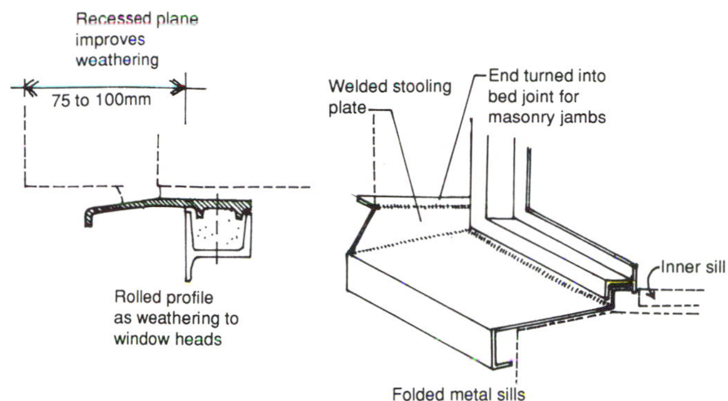

Fig. 31.21 *Periphery details (sills and heads).*

31.2.6 Peripheral details

Coupling pieces are also used to weather the fenestration at head and sill and elongated sections are available to form wide sill flashings. British and North American details typically butt lengths of sill together and seal the joint with mastic. European details are superior, for example cills have stools welded at each end to prevent water from running over and staining the wall below (Fig. 31.21). Galvanized or lead-coated steel should be used at these exposed locations but if the back face is to be in direct contact with wet masonry, extra protection is required. This is because the alkalinity of fresh concrete, limestone or mortar reacts chemically with zinc and lead so the materials should be isolated from one another, by the use of bitumen paint where components are bedded in mortar and by mastic to seal the junction between masonry and metal.

31.2.7 Ironmongery

The usual types of cock spur and stay resemble the ironmongery of timber windows. Hinges are face mounted and stand proud for easy cleaning. Espagnolette bolts are

Fig. 31.22 *Immeuble 'Clarté', Geneva 1930/32 (architects Le Corbusier and Pierre Jeanneret).*

most commonly face-fixed but can be accommodated within the largest sized tubular sections (reference should again be made to Fig. 31.13).

Narrow margin locks are made for incorporation within steel french windows. Normal locks require a hollow crossbar within the frame made up from welded plate, a method that dates back to the 1920s when the use of horizontal bars within metal frames was a familiar design motif (Fig. 31.11). Fittings need to be compatible in strength with steel windows plastic catches and components tend to suffer from fatigue.

31.2.8 Aesthetics

The Modern House in England [10] lists 52 outstanding houses from the main stream of modernism: steel windows were used in 43 of them. Modernists were greatly attracted by the clean lines typical of steel casements as is well illustrated by this quotation from Raymond McGrath: 'The development of the standardized metal-frame window has had an enormous effect on architecture, generally to its advantage. . .'. He went on to explain the fact that metal fenestration resembles 'Tudor' windows that can be extended horizon-

Fig. 31.23 *Workshop windows to AEG Turbine Works, Berlin 1909 (architect Peter Behrens) contrasted with lower picture showing the Fagus Works 1913 (architects Gropius and Meyer).*

tally and vertically and cites Le Corbusier's Immeuble 'Clarté' at Geneva as a prime example (Fig. 31.22 and [1]).

Double-glazed steel windows were used to form the extensive fenestration of the building. The structure was a welded steel frame to which the window system was itself welded! Corbusian technology was always a hit and miss

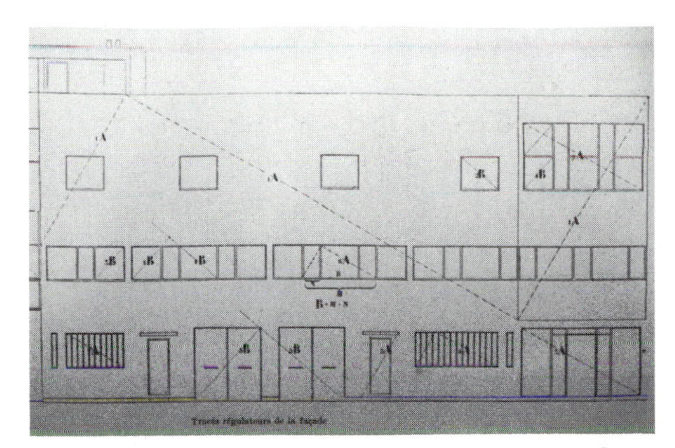

Fig. 31.24 *Elevation of Maison La Roche-Jeanneret, Paris 1923 (architects Le Corbusier and Pierre Jeanneret). Alphabetic references refer to his modular proportional system.*

Fig. 31.25 *Silver End, Essex 1927–28. Horizontal bar windows for the Crittall commission, designed by T.S. Tait with Frederick MacManus.*

Fig. 31.26 *Miramonte, Kingston, London (1936–37). Sliders and coupled sashes (maker Williams and Williams: architect Max Fry).*

affair. Replacement windows for the Immeuble 'Clarté' have to take into account the thermal movements that were ignored in the original design, resulting in much broken glass. The idea of a facade made as a steel grillage, vertical bars dividing the window-wall into a series of equal panes, is characteristic of many pioneer factory designs (for example the AEG Turbine Hall of 1909 and the Fagus Works of 1913 [11] and Fig. 31.23).

The method of fabrication was derived from French and German industrial buildings of the late 19th century that were lit by window-walls made from brazed and interlocked metal bars. Claude Monet's studio windows at Giverny (Fig. 31.23) were of the same type as were the glazed walls of Le Corbusier's houses for Lipchitz, Ozenfant and Roche-Jeanneret (Fig. 31.24).

The emergence of modern architecture in Britain was aided by the window manufacturers. Firstly, the Crittall family commissioned a garden suburb, called 'Silver Street', to house their workers at Braintree. The first phase used industrialized construction of modular blockwork and standard metal windows, with a character similar to the early Le Corbusier designs for a suburb at Chaux des Fonds (c. 1914). The architect of the early experiments at Silver Street was H.B. Quennell, the later buildings were designed in 1927–28 by T.S. Tait working with Frederick MacManus. They omitted the vertical bar in their Lutyens-style casements, making horizontally divided windows much in keeping with the taste of that time. The most significant of their houses was Le Chateau at Silver End (Fig. 31.25).

'No Bar' windows were introduced soon after in line with developments on the continent. Col. J. Fox Williams (of Williams and Williams, window makers) provided prototype details for leading architects such as Max Fry [12] and Connell, Ward and Lucas. The trend towards the use of sliding and sliding/folding windows and doors was an aspect of the architectural pursuit of transparency, uniting space as a continuum inside and outside of the building, Fry's 'Miramonte' for example, that had continuous sliding windows and tubular steel columns supporting the first floor concrete slab. The detailed development of glazing sections and track carried out experimentally by Williams and Williams was a step towards the production of standard steel sliding windows (Fig. 31.26).

The concertina window is a type also characteristic of architecture in the 1930s, and the most celebrated windows of this kind were installed at The London Gliding Club, Dunstable, to close a gap 24 m (80 ft) in width (Fig. 31.27).

Fig. 31.27 *The London Gliding Club, Dunstable 1934–5. Longest run of sliding folding sashes (maker Williams and Williams: architect Christopher Nicholson).*

Fig. 31.28 *Public housing at Loddon, Norfolk by Taylor and Green 1952. Standard windows 'doubled up' for living room. Similar concept for BSIF Housing by Frederick Gibberd, designer Gerhard Rosenberg (refer back to Fig. 30.10).*

The most famous export order was completed by Hope's who supplied the windows for Frank Lloyd Wright's Falling Water. Included were steel shelves welded onto the horizontal glazing bars and painted mid-brown to simulate redwood.

Post-war housing and prefabs made extensive use of the standard ranges of metal windows, their size limitations being overcome by 'doubling up' the windows in living rooms (Fig. 31.28).

The steel components available nowadays for windows and environmental enclosures generally, have far greater flexibility than before. Wide variations are possible in the form and shape of window-walls, a notable example in this regard being the fenestration of the Electricity, Gas and Water Offices, Cologne (1981) (Fig. 31.29, [13]). The lightness and transparency of this final example shows that the spirit of Modernism still endures.

31.3 PATENT GLAZING

32.3.1 Historical review

Patent glazing can be defined as a form of puttyless glazing, usually a combination of glass or plastic (single or multiple glass, toughened glass or plastic) and metal (galvanized or lead-coated steel, aluminium or bronze).

Early experiments by Paxton for the Great Conservatory at Chatsworth (1837–49) and the Crystal Palace (1851) used grooved wooden battens as glazing bars, the rebate made sufficiently deep for the glass to be replaced without dismantling the roof. Each pane was held in place by a zinc clip and was sealed into the grooves with putty. The framework of bars formed a ridge and furrow profile that discharged into wooden gutter beams. Paxton's detail proved to be a disaster. The 250 miles of sash bar at the Crystal Palace [14] was the source of endless difficulties. Demolition finally cured the problem at Chatsworth, whilst the Crystal Palace roof was eventually replaced in 1899 using Mellowes Limited's system of patent glazing (Fig. 31.30).

The removal of duty on glass in 1845 encouraged the British enthusiasm for conservatories. Meanwhile, the French were interested in developing fire-resistant roof

Fig. 31.29 *Electricity, gas and water offices, Cologne, 1981 (architects Kraemer Sieverts and Partners).*

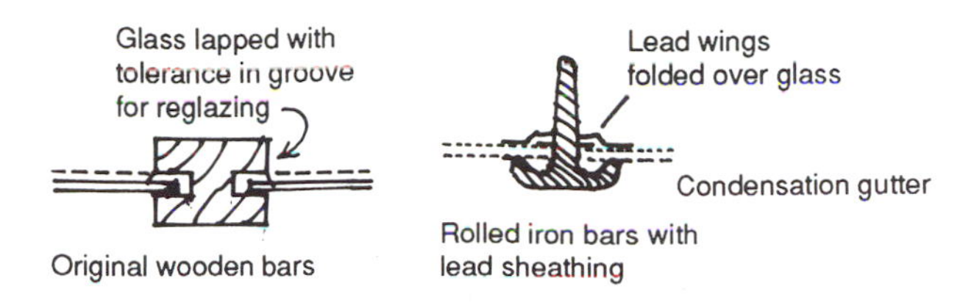

Fig. 31.30 *Crystal Palace rebuilt at Sydenham. Mellowes patent glazing (1899) replaced Paxton's wooden bars of ridge and farrow pattern.*

construction. The earliest glass arcade with iron glazing bars is said to have been the Galerie d'Orleans at Le Palais Royal of 1828–30 [15]. Its bars were T-shaped and can be seen in a restored form at the Hothouse of the Jardin des Plantes built in 1833–34 (Fig. 31.31). The major engineering advances in Britain were the result of the innovative construction of the Palm House at Kew Gardens (1844–48). The design by Decimus Burton and Richard Turner employed wrought iron T-bars joined together with fish-plate connectors. The original bars having been weakened by corrosion were finally replaced in 1988 by stainless steel replicas, white

Fig. 31.31 *Hothouse Jardin des Plantes, Paris (1833–34) reconstructed 1907.*

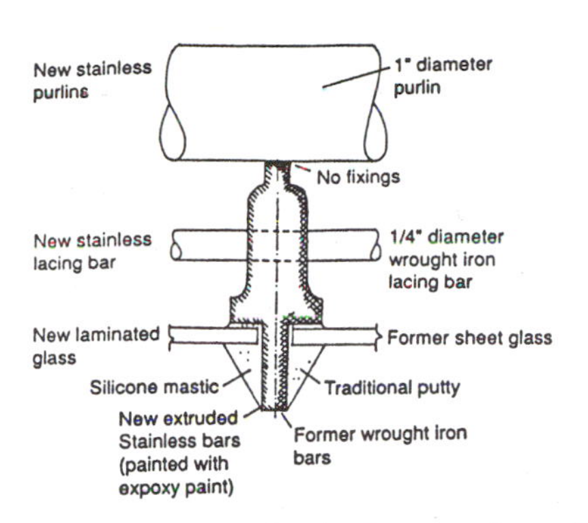

Fig. 31.32 *Original and replacement glazing bars at the Palm House, Kew.*

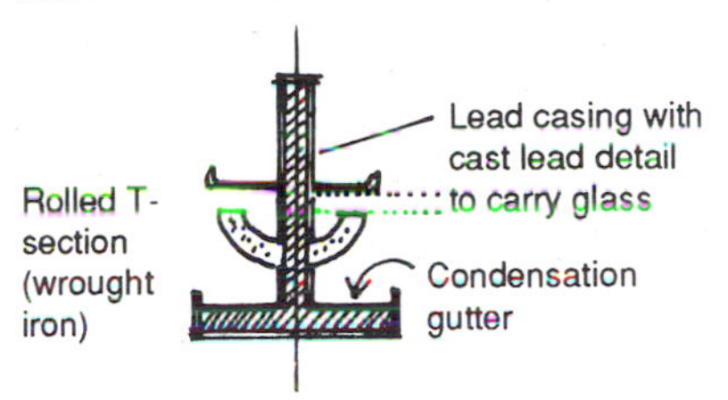

Fig. 31.33 *Typical 19th century glazing bar.*

plastic coated to copy the original colour (Fig. 31.32).

By the end of the 19th century, the glass-roofed shed had become a highly developed form of construction. By the early 1900s, the use of rolled wrought iron for glazing bars had been superseded by rolled steel. Figure 31.33 shows the type of zinc or lead-coated bar section that was available and the way in which condensation gutters were incorporated. The bars were consistently spaced to accommodate a 2 ft width pane of glass, a module that has continued to the present day as the standard dimension for patent glazing.

31.3.2 Current technology

Figure 31.34 illustrates the steel bars that are available now. They are finished either hot-dip galvanized or sheathed in extruded lead or plastic, or stainless steel bars may be used (as they were at Kew). One hour fire-resistant patent glazing is manufactured, and depending on the thermal performance required, the glass itself can be installed in single, double or treble thickness. Double glazing usually has a

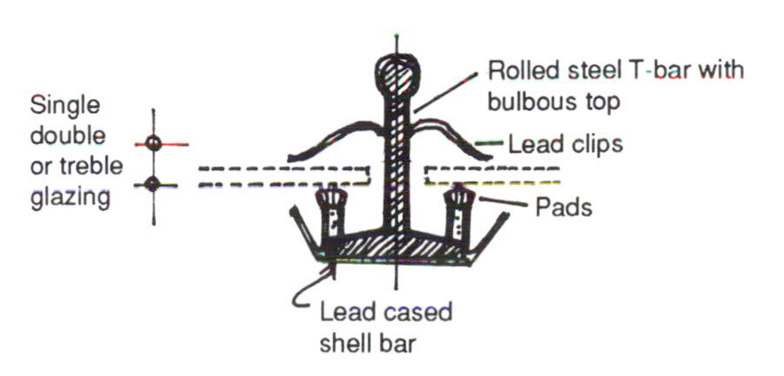

Fig. 31.34 *Current steel glazing bars.*

sheet of wired glass to the inside with 6 mm (¼ in) cast or laminated glass forming the outer leaf. The bars have a maximum span of around 3.3 m and are spaced 610 mm (2 ft) centre to centre so as to allow the standard 600 mm (1 ft 11½ in) width of glass (the development of laminated glass now permits a wider bar spacing of 900 mm (3 ft). Aluminium glazing bars are extruded instead of rolled but the lesser strength of aluminium means that bars have to be 30% larger in size [16].

The Patent Glazing Contractor's Association advise that roofs should slope at a minimum angle of 30 degrees to avoid condensation dripping from the glass, also that mastic should be used to seal the junction of glass and framing if a pitch less than 15 degree is intended. The well publicized failure of the glass roof at the History Faculty Library, Cambridge (1966 68) has highlighted the difficulty of making complicated shapes in patent glazing and relying upon the use of mastic. With age mastic loses its flexibility, giving rise to enormous maintenance problems. Inspiration may be drawn from standard horticultural greenhouses which are designed for high standards of performance; condensation dripping onto growing plants is totally unacceptable. Internal climate and shading often seems to be better considered for plants than it is for humans; a notable example of sophisticated environmental control is the award-winning Princess of Wales Conservatory at Kew (refer to chapter 37).

31.3.3 Building forms

Industrial greenhouses are usually of a consistent 30 degree pitch. Other typical cross-sections for glazed roofs are barrel-shaped, haystack-shaped, lean-to, monitor, north light or pyramid (Fig. 31.35). There is no overall size limitation, the logic imposed by the maximum length of bar and glass dictates the location of the vertical steps that form weather-tight junctions in the slope of the roof (Fig. 31.36).

Patent glazing can be laid to as low a slope as 5 degrees but the weather-proofing will be highly dependent upon mastic. Also the width of the roof is then limited to 3.3 m (10 ft 10 in) because the overlapping joints usual for patent glazing cannot be adequately sealed when the roof is so close to being flat.

The thermal coefficients of glass and steel are roughly equal, resulting in the possibility that a 3.3 m (10 ft 10 in) length of patent glazing may expand up to 1.5 mm ($^1/_{16}$ in) under the climatic conditions usual in Britain [17]. Aluminium and plastic expand to an greater extent than this, resulting in problems for large glazed roofs made from these materials unless they are divided by movement joints.

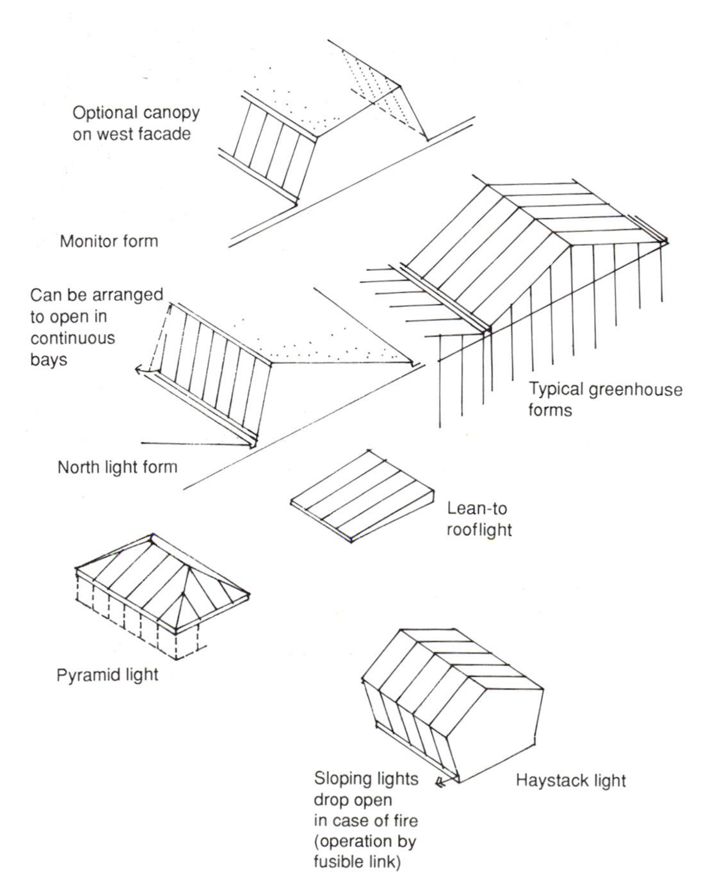

Fig. 31.35 *Typical building forms in patent glazing.*

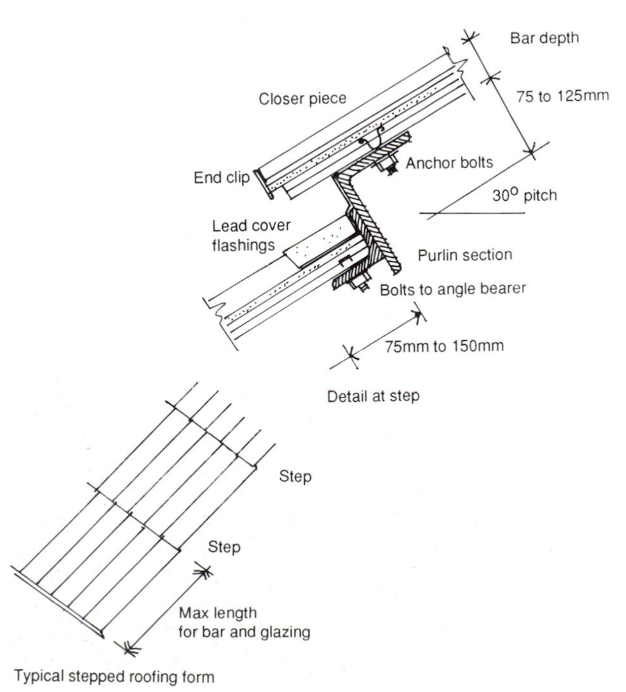

Fig. 31.36 *Weather stepped falls.*

31.3.4 Building details

Traditional patent glazing details for head, jambs, laps, opening lights and rails can be taken straight from manufacturers' literature as long as the designer obeys traditional limitations of pitch, shape and size.

31.3.5 Opening lights

Subframes can be fixed within patent glazing to allow the installation of opening lights either in groups or as continuous runs and mechanically operated by remote winding gear. Haystack lights have top hung side vents that drop open to allow smoke to escape in the event of fire (refer back to Fig. 31.35).

31.3.6 Side-wall glazing

Industrial glazing can be made either with continuous vertical bars and lapped glass, or alternatively sloping steps

Fig. 31.37 *Fawley Power Station, Hampshire, UK with side-wall glazing 1950s (architects Farmer and Darke).*

Fig. 31.38 *Boots Factory, Nottingham, 1930–2 (architect and engineer Sir Owen Williams).*

between panes permitting whole areas of the facade to have multiple opening lights or ventilators (Fig. 31.37). Many electrical and manufacturing plants have lightweight glazing so that in case of explosion there is minimum containment of the blast. Under these circumstances polycarbonate is used instead of glass to reduce the possibility of injury by flying splinters. Fully glazed factories such as Van Nelle in Rotterdam (1927–30) or Boots' Factory, Nottingham (1930–32) have side-wall glazing with steel T-bars and clips (Fig. 31.38 and [18]).

The further history, describing how this simple type of construction was developed into the sophisticated complexity of curtain walling, is the subject of chapter 27.

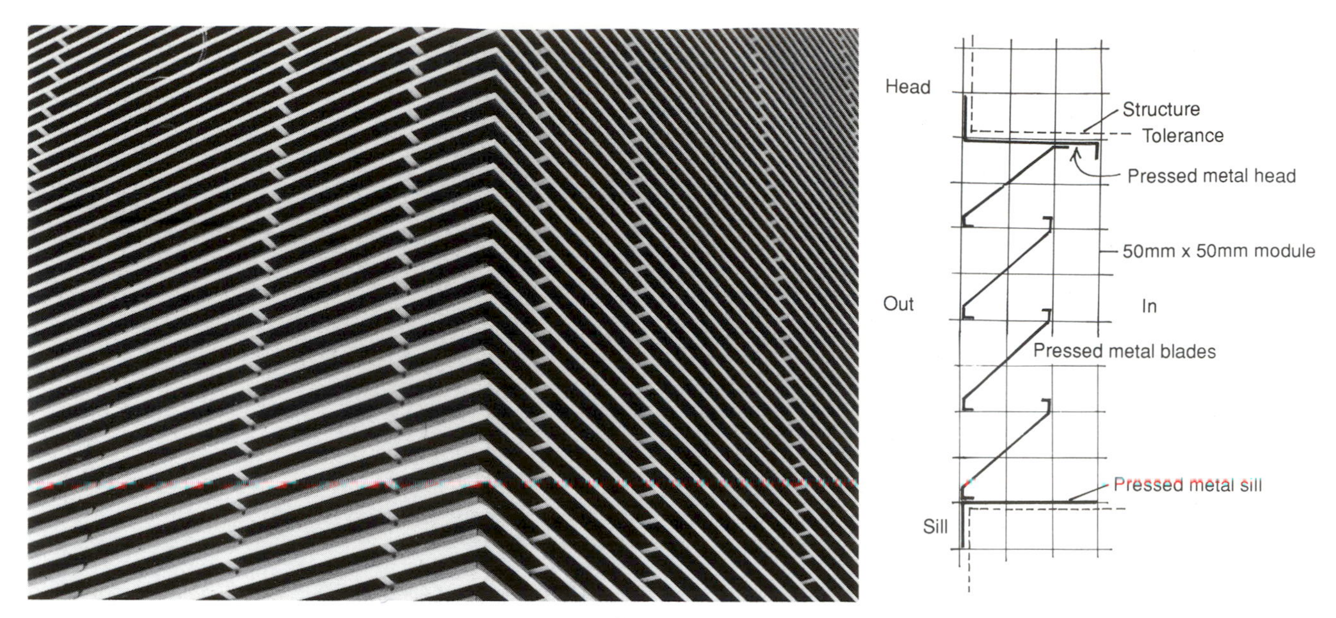

Fig. 31.39 *Unit louvres, including doors and traps.*

Fig. 31.40 *Smoke ventilation. Detailed view at top of atria and foundry roof.*

31.4 LOUVRES

31.4.1 Louvre patterns

The basic shapes of steel louvre for industrial and plant room ventilation combine the least obstruction of air flow with the best weather-proofing. Bird and insect mesh are usually fixed at the inside face. Louvre panels can be made into whole elevations, including doors and escape hatches (Fig. 31.39).

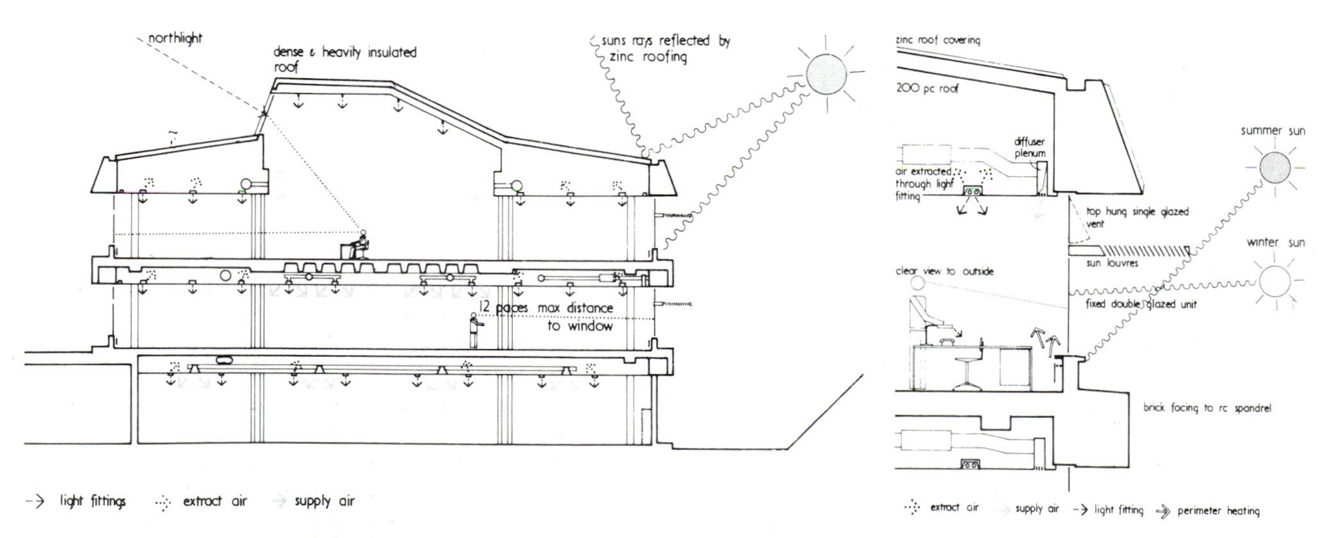

Fig. 31.41 *Solar screening, Hereford and Worcester District Council Offices 1973–5 (architect RMJM: designer Hugh Morris).*

31.4.2 Smoke ventilators

Adjustable louvre blades, mechanically operated, are used for smoke ventilation in atria (refer to chapter 19) and in foundries. The control mechanism is triggered by a thermocouple or a smoke alarm (Fig. 31.40).

31.4.3 Solar screening

The most effective location for brise-soleil is external to the facade and separated from the actual window glass. Louvres set close by windows will act as 'radiators' and continue to radiate warmth after the sun has departed. Horizontal or sloping screens infilled with louvres provide an ideal solution providing that they are adequately designed to shed rainwater. The way in which steel framed louvres can provide effective screening is illustrated by the design of the Hereford and Worcester District Council Offices (Fig. 31.41).

31.4.4 Air bricks and window ventilators

Ventilation where it was least expected has been the unfortunate legacy left by Florence Nightingale and the late lamented London County Council. Our inheritance from those days expired on April 1st, 1986 [19]; until then all bathrooms in inner London were built with a permanently open slot or ventilating brick, amounting to at least 20 in^2 (12 500 mm^2). In domestic construction properly adjustable ventilation is advantageous, however, especially to combat condensation in bathrooms and kitchens. High-level vents help air movement, and metal window louvres can be adequately secured (Fig. 31.42). Heat exchange units or conventional radiators are often combined with a controllable fresh air supply. Figure 31.43 shows a continental detail for a pressed metal sill incorporating 'hit and miss' air bricks.

There are many residential locations, such as access balconies or ground floor rooms, where fresh air supply is required without the loss of security implied by 'opening' windows. Metal louvres and sill vents made in 16 or 18 gauge steel, cold-formed and galvanized, provide a convenient method of ventilation. Under recent changes to the regulations, small winter ventilation slots are built into all windows that are to be installed in dwellings.

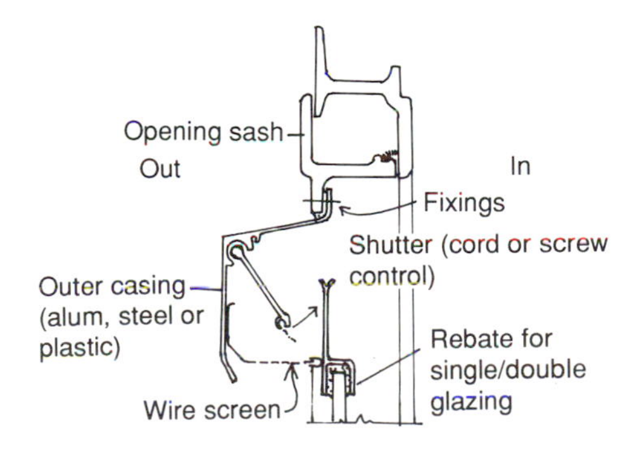

Fig. 31.42 *Metal window louvre.*

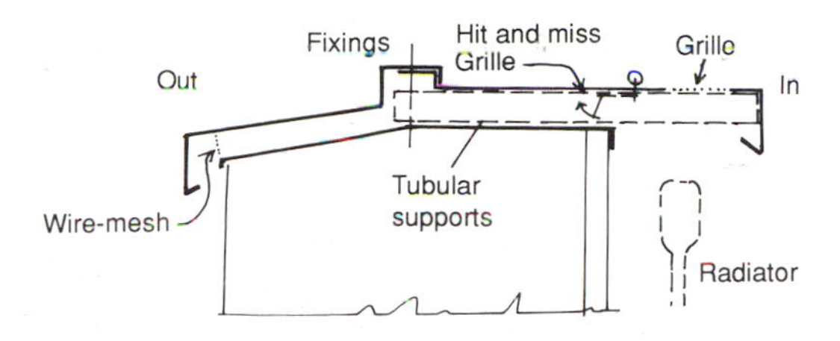

Fig. 31.43 *Pressed metal sill and air brick.*

31.5 SILLS AND LINTELS

31.5.1 Sills and flashings

Since the turn of the century, steel sections have been rolled specifically for the purpose of coupling steel windows and in the case of sills and transoms forming a projection to throw rainwater clear of the wall below. Window manufacturers in the 1920s started making wider pressed metal internal and external steel sills (Fig. 31.44). Their fabrication is now standardized by BS 6510: 1984, 14 swg steel sheet is used, galvanizing is customary and depending on the size of press, the maximum length is between 3 and 4.5 m (10–15 ft). To make longer continuous lengths, pieces have to be joined by internal sleeves sealed with mastic.

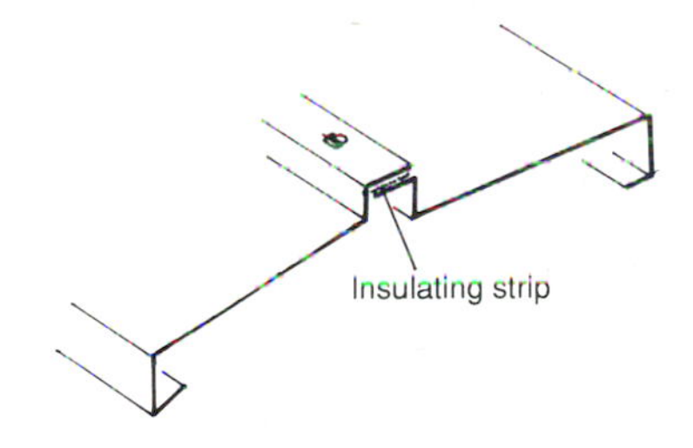

Fig. 31.44 *Pressed steel sills (internal and external).*

Industrialized cladding with profiled sheet requires special forms to weather door and window openings. The detailing resembles BS 6510: 1984 (Specification for Steel Windows, Sills, Window Boards and Doors), but extended to suit cladding requirements. Welded corners will give weather-tight construction but the gauge of metal has to be increased to 12 SWG in order that welding does not distort the profile. Long production runs imply that special profiles can be economic and where the advantage of factory applied finishes can be utilized (enamel or powder coating).

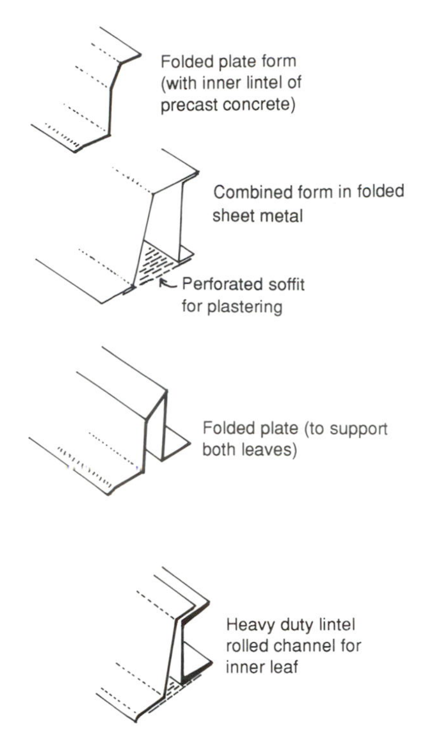

Fig. 31.45 *Cavity lintels (review of various forms).*

31.5.2 Lintels

Cold-formed steel lintels were first introduced by Dorman Long in 1954; they were made as a 'tray' fitting over an internal precast beam. This pattern has now been superseded by composite pressings that support both the inner and outer leaves of the wall. Variations on this basic type are made, for example incorporating steel beams for long span construction (Fig. 31.45). The steel sheet that is pressed to make these lintels is from 2 to 5 mm ($\frac{1}{16}$–$\frac{3}{16}$ in) in thickness and is either galvanized or stainless steel. A number of precautions should be borne in mind. Firstly, in situations that are likely to be particularly wet or alkaline, galvanized steel should well coated with bituminous paint, particularly on embedded and hidden surfaces, or preferably a stainless steel lintel should be used. Secondly, the strength of lintel required should be clearly established, some district surveyors in London still do not regard the thinnest gauges of steel lintel as adequate. The NHBC has recently recommended that a separate DPC should be used to cloak and protect galvanized lintels in highly exposed situations: stainless steel lintels were introduced in response to these concerns. The recent changes in thermal insulation standards (Part 1 of the National Building Regulations) will require cavity lintels either to be thermally broken or else to count the lintel area into the non-insulated part of the wall. A variety of new components, such as insulated cavity closers, have been introduced to eliminate cold-bridging around windows and doors.

The particular design of lintel that has become one of the most widely used in the UK today was an offshoot of a system of prefabricated housing designed by architect Alex Gordon in the 1960s. A simple pressed steel combined flashing and window head was devised to have a universal application, and prototype houses were built, but the system was not further developed. As a result the patent to the lintel design was sold and its manufacturers have since flourished.

REFERENCES AND TECHNICAL NOTES

1. The Structure of gothic windows
   Refer to RIBA Journal Jan 18 1936, thesis by Gerhart Rosenberg, also page 94 of *Glass In Architecture and Decoration*, by Raymond McGrath and A.C. Frost, Architectural Press (1937).
2. Cast iron windows
   Refer to *History of Cast Iron in Architecture*, by J.E. Gloag and D.P. Bridgewater, George Allen and Unwin (1948). For current day production refer to Building Centre.
3. 54 degrees proportion (editor's note)
   The roof slope of 54 degrees, popular with Lutyens, is the result of drawing a line across the points of intersection of brickwork joints in Flemish bond. This means that the intersection of the roof and wall can be made without cutting bricks other than at the natural rake of the brickwork.
4. Metal windows in Israel (editor's note)
   The views expressed follow conversations with Professor Alfred Mansfield.
5. BS 6510: 1984 Specification for Steel Windows, Sills, Window boards and Doors.
   Refer to the *Specifier's Guide to Steel Windows*, published by: The Steel Window Association, PO Box 143, Tring House, Tring, Herts HP23 5PS, UK. Tel: 44 (0)442 890768 and to the Steel Window Association for finishes and for other Specifications (Agricultural, Industrial etc).
6. Syntha-Pulvin
   For polyester coatings and their composition refer to chapter 5 – Sheet and Strip.
7. Writings by Col. J. Fox Williams
   The former director of Williams and Williams wrote a series of excellent guides on metal windows in *Specification* published by the Architectural Press during the 1950s and 1960s including wide ranging advice on the topic.
8. BS ranges
   BS 6510: 1984 is today the key document, older British Standards having been withdrawn, or the products withdrawn. The historic BS codes were 990 for housing work, 2503 for agricultural windows and 1787 for industrial lights.
9. Bauhaus, Dessau
   Refer to the article on the building's reconstruction by

Alan Blanc, *Building Design*, July 9th 1982. The design was commissioned from Gropius and Adolph Meyer. The drawings are signed by Karl Fieger and the site architect was Ernst Neufert.

10. *The Modern House in England*
    A review of interwar Modernist houses by F.R.S. Yorke, published in two editions, 1937 and 1944.
    Also of considerable historical interest is *Glass in Architecture and Decoration and Redecoration*, by Raymond McGrath and A.C. Frost, Architectural Press, London, 1937 and 1961 (new edition).
11. Pioneer factories
    Refer to Dennis Sharp's historical review in chapter 2, particularly Behren's AEG Turbine Hall and to Gropius' and Adolf Meyer's Fagus Works.
12. Prototype designs by Williams and Williams
    The notes on prototype designs follow the editor's conversations with Max Fry after visiting Miramonte, Kingston in 1980, this house features in the *Architectural Review*, Nov. 1937.
13. Designs by Kraemer, Sieverts and Partner
    Refer to the *Architects' Journal*, 3 November 1982.
14. Paxton's leaking roofs at the Crystal Palace. 'On the last day of the Hyde Park Exhibition rain came through the roof like water through a cullender, and we know that there are hundreds of leaks in the roofs every wet day at Sydenham' (from *The Builder*, 1856)
15. Galerie d'Orleans, designers Percier and Fontaine (1828–30)
    Refer to *Iron in the Soil, Architectural Review*, July 1988.
16. Aluminium bars at Kew Gardens (editor's note)
    It is worth studying the comparative size of glazing bars in the new Palm House (slender plastic clad stainless steel) and the mill finished aluminium bars of the Australia House (c. 1960). The latter are clumsy in profile and are now dark grey in colour as a result of corrosion.
17. Thermal movement of glass and steel
    Refer to *Principles of Modern Building*, Vols 1 and 2, 1961. Linear coefficient of thermal expansion per °C ($\times 10^{-6}$): glass 8–9, steel 11–13, aluminium 25, lead 29.
18. Boots Nottingham
    The New Architecture, Alfred Roth. *Les Editions d'Architecture* (1947) gives a full technical explanation of side wall glazing.
19. Air bricks and the late London County Council
    The 'School Board' pattern of cast iron ventilator developed in the late 19th century still set the standard for the amount of open air ventilation insisted upon by the Greater London Council 90 years later, namely 20 in^2.

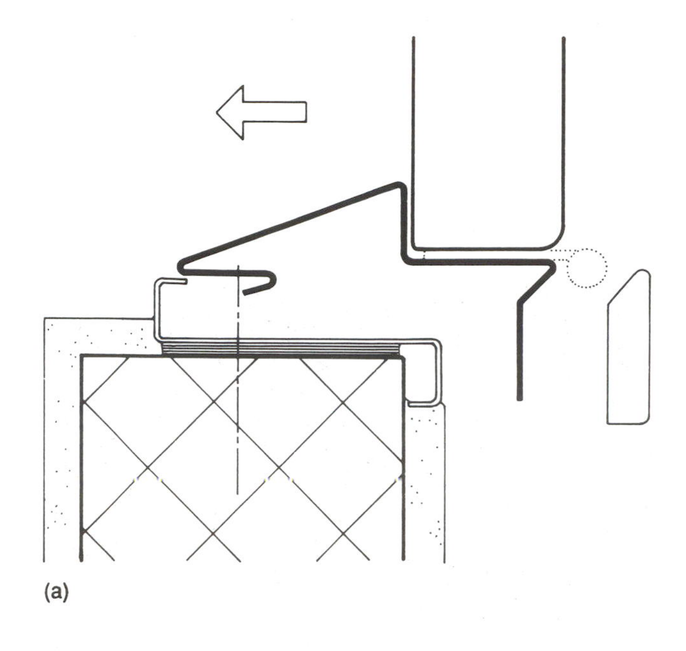
(a)

(b)

Recently designed metal door frame sets (a) metal liner and subframe with clip-on architraves; (b) view of door frame and door; (c) detail of clip-on architraves; (d) hinge relationship (manufacturers G & S Allgood: designer Alan Tye Design).

(c)

(d)

32

Metal door frames, screens and security

Alan Blanc

32.1 BACKGROUND

Metal faced doors have been made since the end of the Stone Age; the main gate of Mycenae had bronze-faced pivoted doors, with solid rebated jambs. The original hollow cast bronze doors at the Pantheon (AD 124) are still in working order (Fig. 32.1) and their pivot mechanism resembles that at Mycenae.

The compromise between the conflicting requirements of defence and attack provides the rationale for the design of steel doors and their related security systems. The most impressive result of these combined considerations can be seen in bank vaults but even dwellings can, if in New York or Tel Aviv, have some of the most heavily defended entranceways one is ever likely to encounter. British technology follows the North American pattern, surveillance techniques being reckoned as important as armour plate.

Fire security provides another role for steel-cored doors and screens. Nowadays, this construction combined with heat absorbing glass allows transparency to return once again to staircase enclosures and interior volumes to spatially interconnect (Fig. 32.2). This is a far cry from the

Fig. 32.1 *Hollow cast bronze doors at the Pantheon AD 124.*

Fig. 32.2 *Glazed rotunda and doors, Redhill Station, Surrey, UK 1992 (architects Troughton and McAslam). By permission of Solaglas Architectural Systems.*

solidity of the first steel partitions ever installed, at the Chrysler Building, New York 1928–30 [1], which still function as fire screens.

32.2 SECURITY AGAINST INTRUDERS

32.2.1 Specialist advice

Unless the needs of electronic surveillance are considered from the beginning of a project, the security provided by armour plated bank vault construction will be valueless. There are many specialist firms [2] who provide a whole range of services from ironmongery advice to total design for security management (systems that require an independent low voltage supply to serve automated controls and sensors). A parallel development has taken place in the design of modern fire alarm systems (refer to chapter 9) and energy management controls. Safety from exterior attack is another aspect of the 'Fort Knox' approach to building, and most police departments in Britain now offer advice on building design if the surrounding environment is hostile.

The integrity of any security system is dependent upon the honesty of its designers. One ill-famed Parisian architect turned from the international practice of architecture to a career in bank robbery [3] whilst using his previous knowledge of the buildings' plans.

32.2.2 Entry doors

The first line of defence is at the entrance. The design of doors and screens depends on whether they are to be relatively welcoming or alternatively highly protected. Embassies often rely on external screens of military proportions (Fig. 32.3). An alternative approach is to allow access to a lobby before a secure doorway is reached, and revolving doors are a popular solution since they can be locked open or shut and controlled to permit only one person at a time to enter. High turnstiles have the same characteristic (Fig. 32.4).

Banking halls are public places but access is restricted beyond defined boundaries, and degrees of security are established by a system of controlled lobbies and check points, each protected against armed attack. Standard bank doors are manufactured to resist shot guns and high velocity rifles, their construction comprising steel jambs and stops and including armour plate within the framing of the doors themselves (Fig. 32.5).

A sign frequently found mounted at the entrance to houses in Los Angeles reads 'Armed Response', the actual doorway is often made from moulded steel (Fig. 32.6). Entry doors that are hidden from view warrant extra care in detailing. Reinforcement of the framing may be necessary, particularly around the locks, in order to resist prolonged interference.

The following points are offered as advice.

1. A secure entrance door should have only one leaf opening outwards and without fanlights or sidelights.
2. It should be hung from 1½ pairs of steel hinges and including a pair of hinge dogs.
3. The frame should be fabricated from tubular steel built into the wall; stops should be made from steel and welded into the frame.
4. Use steel construction throughout or at least reinforce the door with 3 mm steel plate and without any glazing (other than than a spy hole!).

Fig. 32.3 and 32.4 *Revolving doors. Secure form of door with monitor controls (metal detectors, etc.) and turnstiles (stainless steel).*

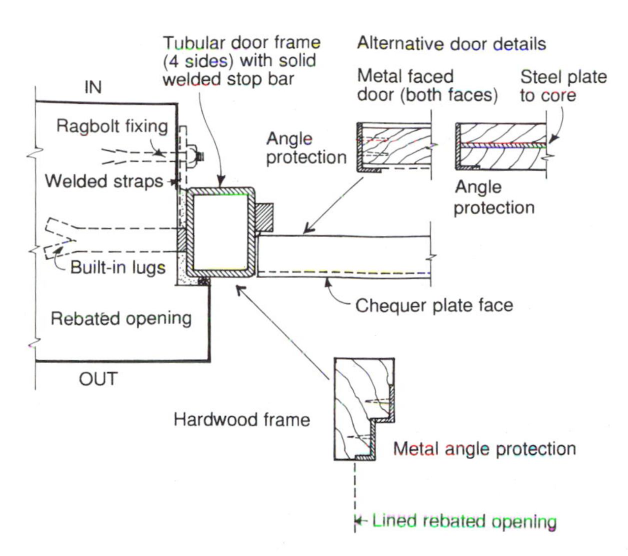

Fig. 32.5 *Armoured door.*

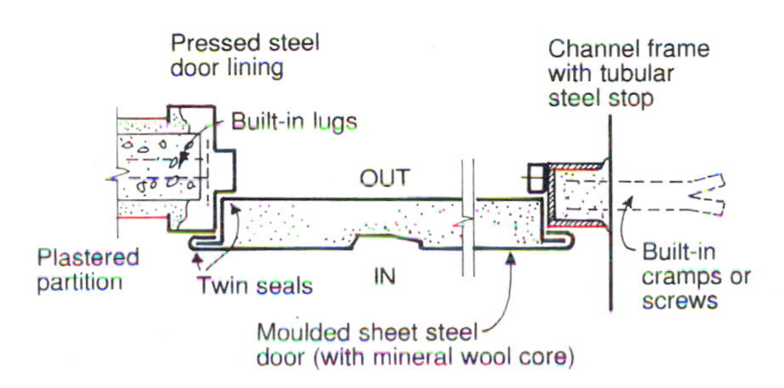

Fig. 32.6 *Moulded steel door.*

5. Build the letter box into a wall rather than the door.
6. Incorporate two locks, one with 200 mm steel face plate.
7. Include a multiple steel bar lock (an espagnolette for instance, top and bottom and side to side) or fit a pair of steel 200 mm face bolts.

32.2.3 Vault construction

Strongroom doors are amongst the most perfectly crafted examples of steel forging and machining. Figure 32.7 gives some idea of the outstanding workmanship required. The vault beyond the doors has to be constructed to an equivalent standard of security. Films like 'Rififi' are illustrative of the lengths taken to break into vaults both by tunnelling or by attack with an electric arc or thermal lance. The concrete structure has therefore to be of extra strength, a suitable specification being two parts of cement with two parts sharp sand, one part of 6 mm (1/4 in) granite chippings and five parts of 18 mm (3/4 in) granite aggregate. Many patent methods of vault construction use both precast and in situ concrete; hollow blocks are threaded through by bars in both directions and then filled with concrete. High tensile reinforcement of twisted plate pattern is used to make penetration a very noisy and slow operation. Alarms now incorporate acoustic or vibration sensors to give warning of intruders. Modern vaults have of course been broken into but 'inside information' is usually required, in other words where thieves follow in the footsteps of the ill-famed Parisian (refer back to 32.2.1).

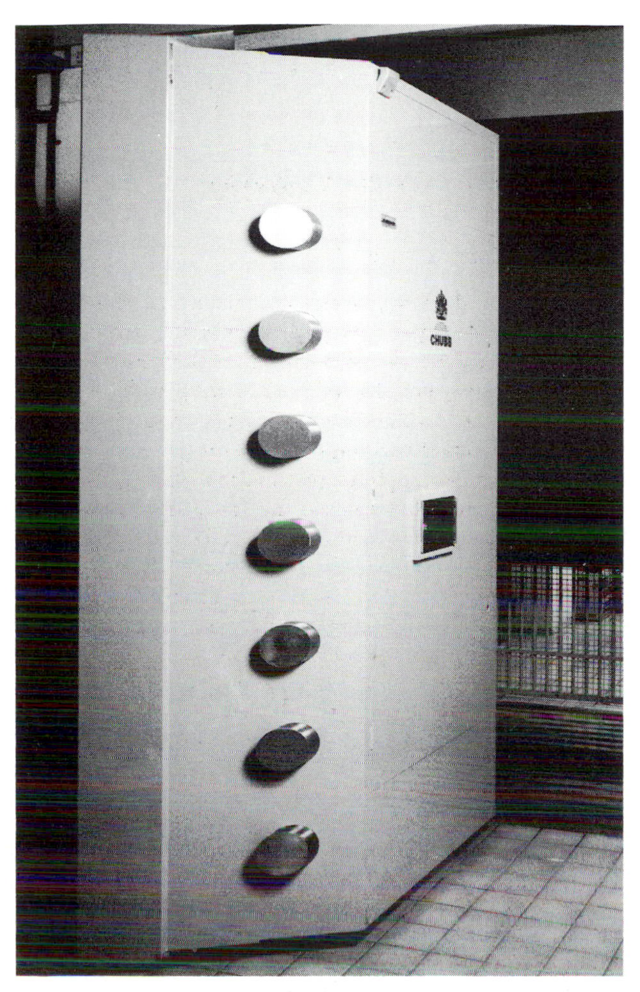

Fig. 32.7 *Strongroom doors, typical assemblies.*

32.3 SECURITY AGAINST FIRE

32.3.1 Historical review

The former London County Council and Greater London Council Byelaws defined acceptable methods of construction for fire-proof glazing, and their 'deemed to satisfy standards' have guided the detailing of London's buildings over the past 100 years. Long accepted ways of building resulted in a familiar family of details, for example 6 mm Georgian wired glass fixed in angle frames with solid steel beads limited by a maximum glass area of 12 ft^2 (1.2 m^2). Another type (still used for lift gates) is copper light glazing, an assembly of small panes limited in area to 4 ft^2 (0.4 m^2). These rules long governed the design of ½ and 1 hour glazing for the enclosure of fire compartments.

The essential difference when interpreting the current National Building Regulations is that fire resistance is now a matter of achieving a performance standard under test, rather than simply adopting a text book answer. Their requirements are described in terms of extent of insulation and the integrity to be achieved when tested.

32.3.2 Definitions

Table 32.1 describes definitions that are current in the United Kingdom. Those in the right hand column are those used in the draft BS code DD171: 1987 [5].

A further 'S' category has been added for doors to which edge seals have been added to provide smoke resistance.

Table 32.1 From BS476 part 8, paragraph 1.
(Note 30/20 means 30 minutes stability and 20 minutes integrity)

		New designation 1987
30/20	1/2 hour Fire Check (FC)	FD 20
30/30	1/2 hour Fire Resisting (FR)	FD 30
60/45	1 hour FC	FD 45
60/60	1 hour FR	FD 60
90/90	1 1/2 hour FR	FD 90
120/120	2 hour FR	FD 120
180/180	3 hour FR	FD 180
240/240	4 hour FR	FD 240

32.3.3 Role of steel framing

A steel frame of cold-formed, tubular or structural sections is usually required to support fire resisting glazing in doors and screens, particularly when ratings of 1, 1½ or 2 hours are required. A structural steel core is often sheathed with aluminium, bronze or hardwood, the casing being purely decorative and contributing nothing to the fire resistance. Typical examples of components with steel cores are shown in Fig. 32.10, including fire-resisting glass that permits a long period to elapse for heat transfer from one face to the other [4].

A similar design achieving a fire-resistance of up to 2 hours is feasible with more complex cold-formed steel sections. A further example is the fire screen glazing (Fig. 32.9) within the atrium of the Hongkong and Shanghai Bank (by Foster Associates).

In the plan of deep section buildings there are many places where vision is needed both for entry and escape in the event of emergency and for day-to-day use. Fire screens can now be made from glass and steel components of sufficient thermal resistance to permit a degree of spatial transparency that would have been undreamt of in times past.

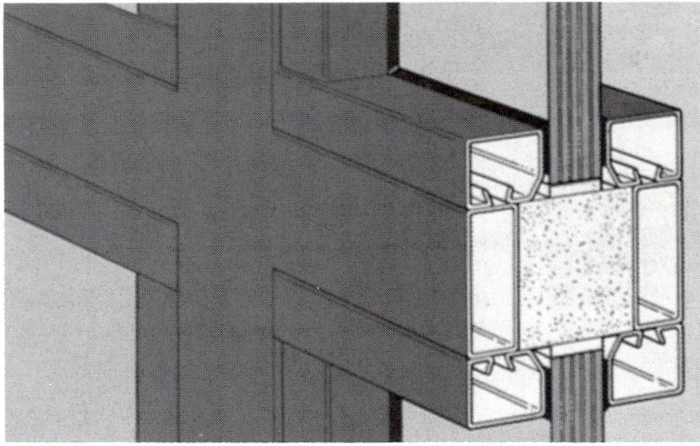

Fig. 32.8 *Steel cored doors and screens. Typical assemblies with Fyrespan system. Details and photos of workshop for Porsche by Dewhurst Haslam (1 hour standard). By permission of Solaglass Architectural Systems.*

32.3.4 Fire shutters

These industrial doors (available with a fire-rating of 1, ½, 2, 3 and 4 hours) are installed at openings in compartment walls, multi-use spaces, shops and warehouses: the shutter is electrically activated or released by a fusible link. The usual types are roller shutters, either guillotine or sliding doors (Fig. 32.10). They are fabricated from steel angles bolted to the concrete or masonry surround; the shutter itself is made with a compound core of 10–20 mm (⅜–¾ in) thick cement fibre sheet sandwiched between 12 swg steel bound at the edges with structural steel plate.

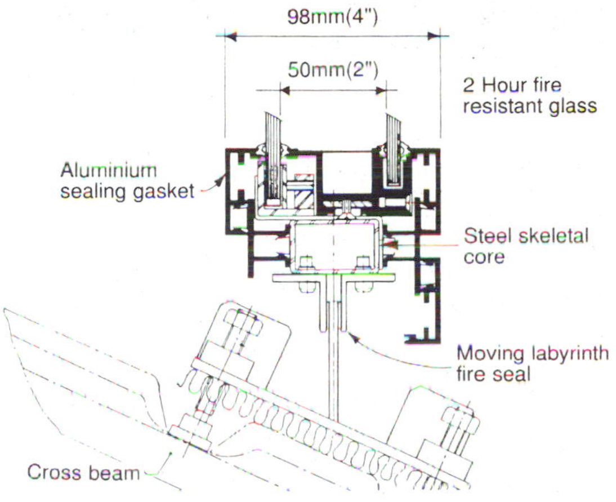

Fig. 32.9 *Plan detail of 120 minutes fire screen at Hongkong and Shanghai Bank (architects Foster Associates). Redrawn from illustrations supplied by Solaglass Architectural Systems.*

32.3.5 Pressed steel door linings and fire doors

Conventional doors within standard partitions can also benefit from choice of a steel door and lining. BS 1245 and 459 [6] set down standards for steel linings as developed for post-war housing though in fact dating back to the 1930s, when pressed steel door trim was commonly used.

Current developments include pre-hung door sets, also solid industrial doors that will achieve a 4 hour fire resistance. The appearance of these factory-finished components is far superior to industrial shutters. In fact the latest ranges of imported steel fire doors meet the visual standards associated with lift gates and architraves (another familiar form of steel construction. Refer to lead-in pictures for a new range of pre-hung door sets with revised profiles for pressed metal frames and architraves.

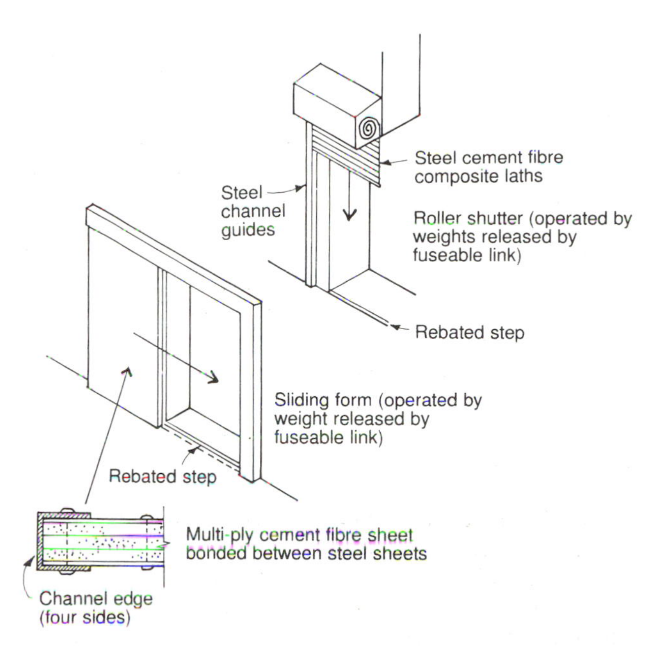

Fig. 32.10 *Four hour standard fire shutter.*

REFERENCES AND TECHNICAL NOTES

1. Metal and steel partitions
   Refer to the *Architects' Journal* article of 3rd November, 1982 by Alan Blanc, the Chrysler Building's original spray-coated steel doors and partitions were still in evidence in January 1989.
2. Chubb's assistance
   The notes in 32.2.1 are based upon advice by Kevin Fiske of Chubb, a firm familiar to the Editor by virtue of their collaboration on projects for Barclays Bank. Similar advice is available from safe and vault suppliers and from the major banks. See also the *Architects' Journal* ('Focus' issues of Feb. 88 and Jan. 84).
3. Architect turned bank robber
   This infamous fellow was involved with the design of the steel-framed French Pavilion at the Bruxelles Exhibition (1958) that partly collapsed after completion; he died in a shoot out with Parisian Police in the early 1980s.
4. Fire insulating glass
   The principle involves laminated glass three or five layers thick with intumescent cores that slow conductive and radiant heat transfer from one face to another. An important example is Pilkingtons 'Pyrostop'; another proprietary name is 'Pyran', manufactured by Schott Glass Ltd, Drummond Road, Astonfields Industrial Estate, Stafford ST16 3EL, UK. Tel: 44 (0)785 46131.
5. BS DD171: 1987 Guide to Specifying Performance Requirements for Hinged or Pivoted Doors (including test methods).
6. BS 1245 and 459: 1975 (1986) Specification for Metal Door Frames (steel).

Staircase engineering. Design of stair balustrade and treads, Joseph Store, Fulham Road, London (architect Eva Jiricna: engineers Whitby and Bird, detailer Matthew Wells).

33

Staircases and balustrades

Alan Blanc

33.1 DESIGN CODES

33.1.1 British legislation

This is not the appropriate place to summarize the various legalities [1] that govern the design of staircases: suffice to say that the views of Fire Officers are still of paramount importance. Their advice should be sought to establish underlying principles rather than copying details from other buildings or examples from textbooks or for instance the case studies at the end of this chapter. The intention behind these detailed case studies is inspirational and intended to be a pointer rather than a set of instructions.

The 1985 revision of the Building Regulations effectively relaxed the rules governing the design of staircases and allowed them to be of greater visual interest. As a result of developments in the technology of fire-resistant glazing (as defined by BS 476: 1987, in particular Parts 20 to 23), stair shafts can again be transparent and form part of a building's spatial experience. An invitation to 'promenade in space' as suggested by Le Corbusier [2]. One has yet to see designers taking full advantage of the opportunities offered, compared with for example Charles Garnier's dramatic staircase at the Paris Opera House (Fig. 33.1), or Gunnar Asplund's masterpiece for the Courthouse extension at Gothenburg (case study 33.4.3). Both of these, incidentally, employed framed construction to achieve their spatial effects.

The codes relating to spiral stairs [3] now allow them to function as accommodation stairs in commercial buildings, though they are still not allowed by Fire Officers to form part of principal escape routes. There is also a greater potential for the use of fixed and hinged ladders, half steps, or minimal spirals (Fig. 33.2), where they are to be for maintenance or other occasional purposes. In addition the 'Safety at Work' regulations and the Shops, Offices and Railways Act also need to be consulted when designing for maintenance access, particularly regarding the provision of guard rails and hand holds.

33.1.2 Co-ordination

The process leading to the detailed design of common public or service stairs should start with a set of plans clearly showing how means of escape and fireman's access are to be achieved. These should be read in conjunction with a specification, agreed with the Fire Officer, describing the anticipated construction and sizes of components. Any changes in the use of the building either during construction or after completion greatly complicate matters. One of the sillier rules still mandatory in Britain distinguishes between different catagories of stair (Table 33.1) requiring three different ratios of tread to rise. In a multi-use complex these could occur side by side. The wise designer adopts the most generous stipulated proportion (180 × 280 mm) as a common formula, to satisfy any eventuality and to standardize stair components.

Fig. 33.1 *Paris Opera House, foyer and stair spaces, with wrought iron beam supports 1860–1875 (architect Charles Garnier).*

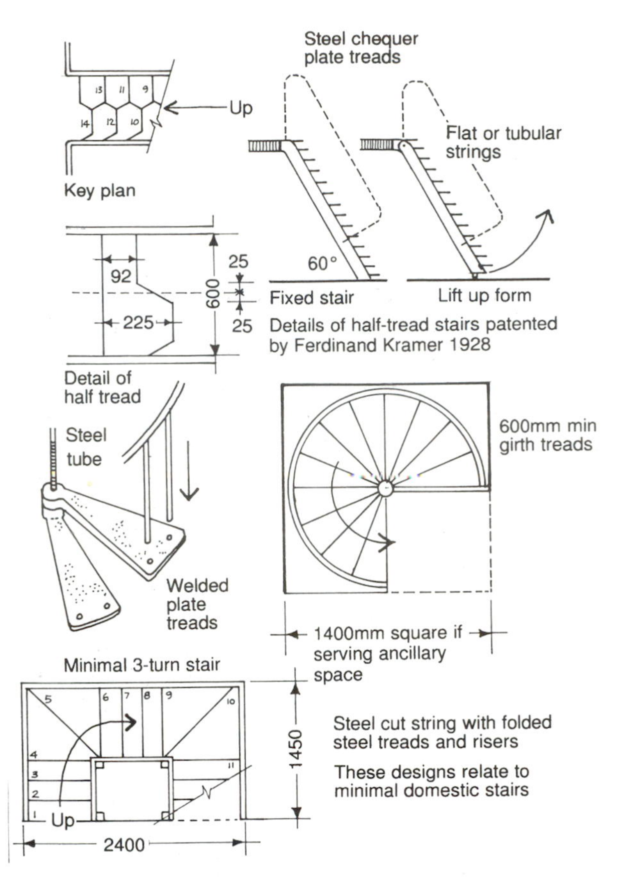

Fig. 33.2 *Minimal stairs (fixed and hinged half steps and minimal spirals).*

Table 33.1 Building Regulations Approved Document K1, rise and going

	Rise (max)	*Going (min)*
1. Private stair*	220 mm	220 mm
2. Common stair	190 mm	240 mm
3. Stairway in:		
a. Institutional building (unless it will only be used by staff)	180 mm	280 mm
b. An assembly building and serving an area used for assembly purposes unless the area is less than 100 m^2		
4. Stairway not described in 1, 2 and 3 above	190 mm	250 mm

* The 'pitch' rule of maximum slope (for private stairs) of 42° rules out 220 × 220 proportion and modifies this to 220 msc × 244 going.

Private stair: Any rise between 155 and 220 mm with any going between 245 and 260 mm. Any rise between 165 and 200 mm used with any going between 220 and 305 mm.
Common stair: Any rise between 155 and 190 mm used with any going between 240 and 320 mm.

However, 180 × 280 mm does not match 150 × 300 mm for comfort and one would be hard pressed to find that easy going quality of stair, commonly used by Wren, in any of today's public buildings. It is obvious that our regulation writers can be little involved with the ordinary world of construction. None of the preferred riser dimensions in the British rule book correspond with the courses of traditional brickwork [4] nor the preferred metric module of 100 mm, sensible considerations usual in Canada or the Common Market (where metrication is taken seriously).

British architects also have to contend with the regulation 100 mm building inspector's ball, the symbolic sphere that must not be able to pass through gaps in balustrades or open risers. The current rules further require that balustrading is not to be easily climbed if children are expected to be amongst the building's occupants. As a result, balustrading in this country is commonly made of close rod, mesh,

Fig. 33.3 *Stairs at State Library, Berlin 1978 (architect Hans Scharoun).*

toughened glass or solid panels. The resulting opacity precludes the visual qualities of which staircases are capable, though it does at least succeed in camouflaging the variety of handrail heights ranging from 900 mm (to the pitch), to 1000 mm or 1100 mm (above landings), that is another curiosity of the current regulations.

Hans Scharoun seemed to be mercifully free from such pettifogging restrictions when designing the staircases that grace, rather than destroy, the interiors of the State Library and Philharmonie in Berlin (Fig. 33.3).

33.2 FABRICATION

33.2.1 Framed stairs

Throughout most of this century, steel stair construction has consisted of steel channel framing to strings and landings with reinforced concrete infill. At the turn of the century, it would have been more usual to use 'filler joists', brick arches spanning the flights and across the landings and finished in concrete, a method that one still sees in Spain (Fig. 33.4).

Fig. 33.4 *Traditional steel and filler joist stairs.*

The disadvantage of these methods is one of construction programme. The stair is likely to be required for builder's access and so either temporary stairs have to be constructed or else the finished stair is built floor by floor as the concrete work is advanced.

33.2.2 Folded sheet stairs

Off-site fabrication of folded sheet or welded plate has been commonplace in the United States since steel framing was first used in the building of skyscrapers. Standardized folded sheet treads and risers with welded strings are now the usual components. Those readily available (Fig. 33.5) are suitable for the fabrication of dog-leg, straight and three-quarter turn as well as helical stairs. The principal advantage of prefabricated steel staircases is that they can be installed as the frame is erected, giving immediate builder's access to each floor level for decking out (of particular importance in fast track construction).

Granolithic, terrazzo or tile finishes to the concrete infilling the treads makes for fire-resistance, in combination with render or plaster onto metal lath for the soffit and perhaps the balustrading as well, if it is required to be solid. The treads can be designed to receive a variety of finishes,

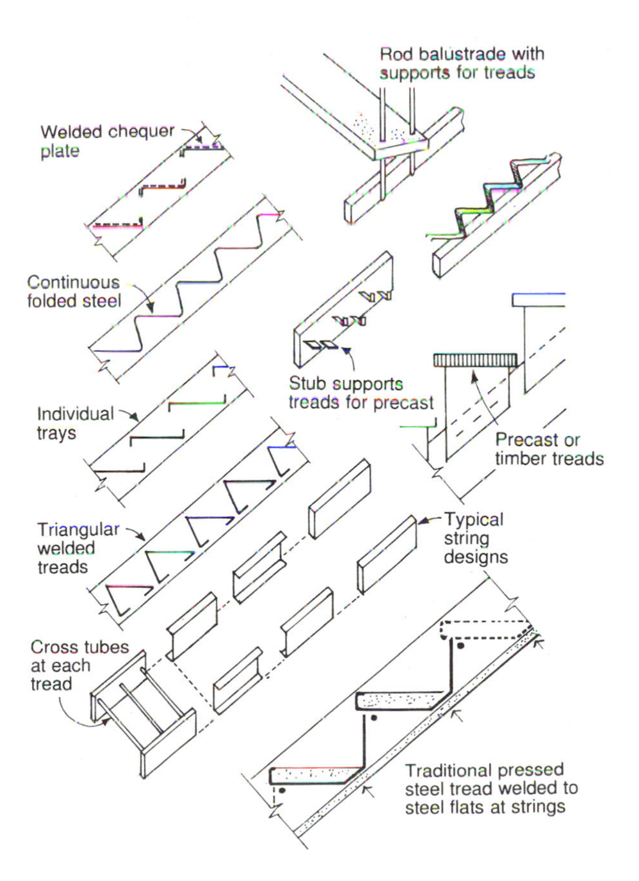

Fig. 33.5 *Standardized sheet steel stairs.*

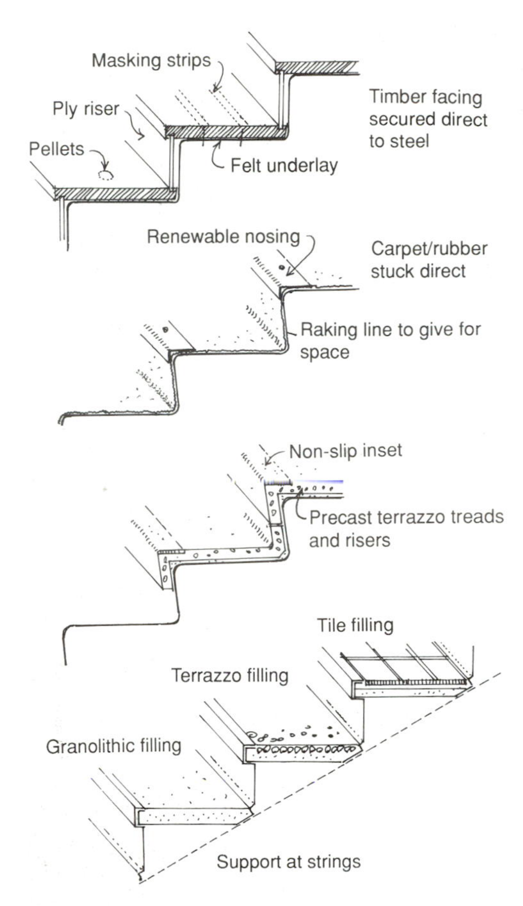

Fig. 33.6 *Various finishes to steel stairs.*

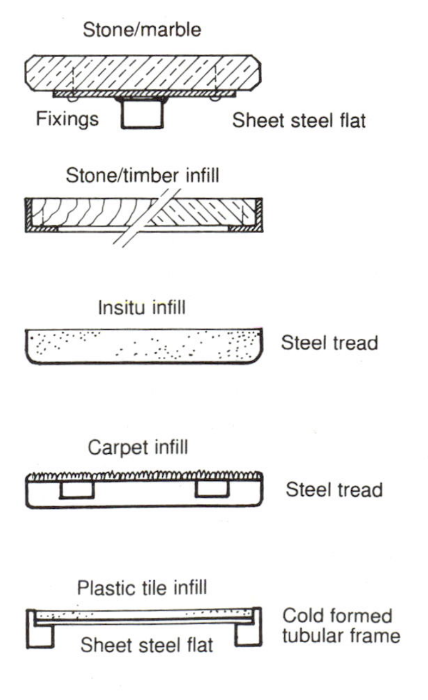

Fig. 33.7 *Individual tread detailing.*

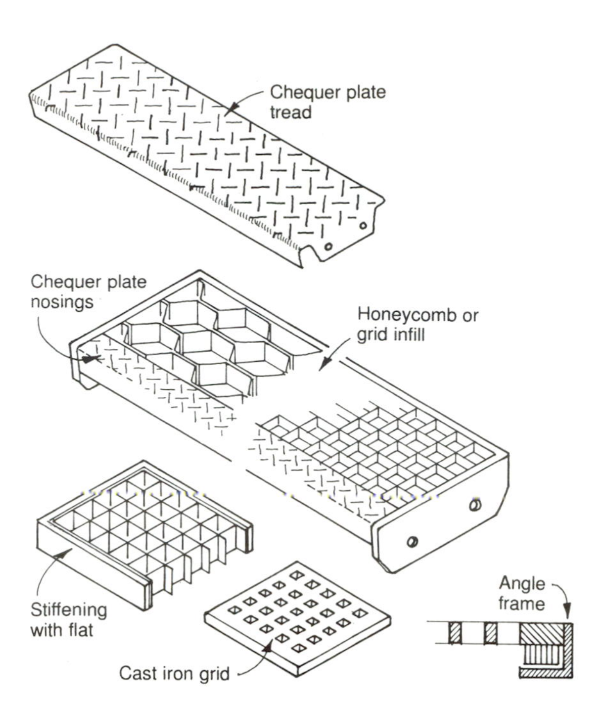

Fig. 33.8 *Steel chequer plate and open grid treads.*

depending upon the fire-resistance required and the location, which means that carpet or sheet vinyl or timber are feasible for accommodation stairs (Fig. 33.6), as are open treads that can be supported on brackets (Figs 33.7 and 33.8).

More elaborate finishes can be achieved by replacing the builder's access stairs with factory-assembled components that are bolted into place close to completion of the building. Arne Jacobsen's detailing at Rödovre (case study 33.4.1). cannot be considered practical other than as a piece of furnishing, installed at the last moment.

Welded sheet in combination with steel tubes can result in the most elegant designs for stairs with perforated strings and treads, as achieved for example by the team at the Federation du Bâtiment in Paris, whose spiral staircase is sculpture and not simply construction (case study 33.4.2).

33.2.3 Spiral stairs

Helical (cylindrical) and spiral (tapering) stairs are attractive to designers because of their sculptural possibilities but a comprehensive list of restrictions on their use is contained in BS 5395. These effectively limit tapered or winding stairs to form a cylindrical shape, with an overall minimum diameter of 1820 mm unless the flight serves only a single room or is for maintenance purposes (Table 33.2). Fire officers are often hesitant to permit tapered steps for escape purposes, so the attractions of cylindrical and helical staircases are still largely confined to domestic situations or accommodation

Fig. 33.9 *Electricity showroom, Regent Street, London 1938 (right) (architect Gropius and Fry), compared with Sainsbury Centre (above), Norwich 1977 (architect Foster Associates).*

Table 33.2 Spiral sizes in Britain (BS 5395): stairs, ladders and walkways

Category	*Application*	*Diameter*
A	Small private	1400
B	Private	1800
C	Small semi-public	2100
D	Semi-public	2300
E	Public	2550

stairs providing secondary access in commercial or public buildings.

There is, however, sufficient market potential for a number of manufacturers to offer a design and fabrication service that assists the lazier detailer. Also with the advent of computer aided drawing there are now specialists [5] producing packages of plans and details that reduce the amount of information required from the architect. The case studies in this chapter have principally been chosen from where designs tend to be more individual than the off-the-peg approach favoured. A notable exception is Norman Foster's investigation of helical geometry. The elegance of his solution matches that of the pre-war staircase by Gropius

and Fry at the Electricity Showroom in London's Regent Street (Fig. 33.9).

33.2.4 External escape stairs

Protection against corrosion is an important factor in the selection of components. Consequently treads are either steel (chequer plate or open grid) or fretted cast iron (Fig. 33.8) with a zinc coating, by electro- or hot-dip galvanizing. The structure is assembled from rolled or tubular steel sections so that the protective zinc coating can be satisfactorily applied after fabrication, without the risk of the hot-dip process causing distortion. An alternative is a protective lead coating, although this is not used where skin contact occurs unless it is painted over. The most significant use of lead-coated structural steelwork is in the construction of steel pylons and ring ladders for the electricity industry.

The design principles for layout and lighting are matters to be agreed with the Fire Officer. Amongst their basic concerns are that windows overlooking stairs need to be resistant to fire breaking out from the inside; also that a consistent clockwise or anti-clockwise pattern of circulation should be adopted from top to bottom with landings that are

Fig. 33.10 *North American fire escape stairs.*

Fig. 33.11 *Caging to fire escape. Reprinted with kind permission of Welland Grating (UK) Ltd.*

Fig. 33.12 *Typical area steps in London.*

unobstructed by outward opening doors. The dimensional requirements for risers, treads and balustrade heights are the same as for internal stairs.

External stairs always entail a loss of security, explaining the hinged bottom section of fire escapes that overhang streets in North American cities (Fig. 33.10). In Europe the usual solution is to cage or glaze-in the lowest flight (Fig. 33.11) with doors operated by panic bolts.

There are many instances where external steel staircases are lighter and more sympathetic than concrete or masonry, particularly in central London where Georgian and Victorian terraces typically are approached by a 'bridge' from

Fig. 33.13 *Bridge approach at Cité de Refuge, Paris 1933 (architects Le Corbusier and Pierre Jeanneret).*

the street sometimes with steps leading down to the basement (Fig. 33.12). This mode of entry was used at the Cité de Refuge by Le Corbusier with great effect (Fig. 33.13), where the infill to the steel framed deck is glass block and tile. An open metal grid at entrances has the practical advantage of being a ready-made foot wiper (even more so in countries where ice and snow are plentiful. Figure 33.14 illustrates an example from Scandinavia of a steel deck and porch). A useful standard item available in Northern

Fig. 33.14 *Steel open grid deck at entry in Oslo, used for cleaning off ice and snow.*

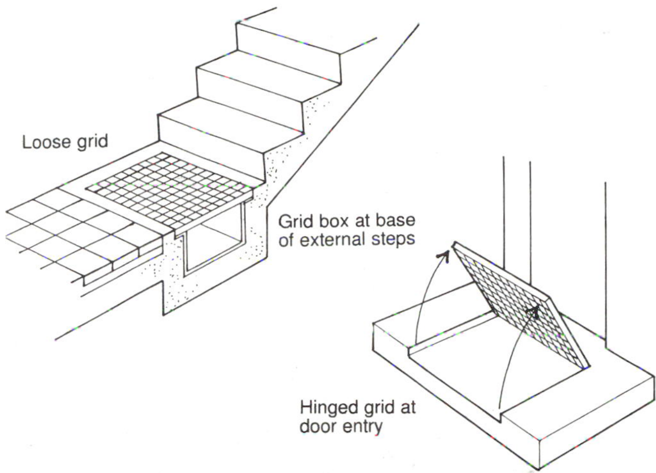

Fig. 33.15 *Standard grit box and grid.*

Europe, to be found outside everyones' front door (Fig. 33.15), is a sunken tray, with grid and grit box.

Fire escape stairs tend to be an afterthought but the catwalks and ladderways designed by Richard Rogers' practice for the skyline of Lloyds has elevated their construction into an art form.

33.2.5 Ramps

The length and pitch as well as provision of guardrails on ramps in the UK is controlled by BS 5395 Part 1. The method of fabrication tends to be similar to external escape stairs, typically a steel channel or tubular frame supporting a chequer plate or open grid walkway. Standard guard rails can be chosen from catalogues, while guidance on balustrading types and their specification is given in section 33.3.2. The alteration of existing buildings often requires old steps to be adapted to current requirements for disabled access. Simple wheelchair ramps are available that can be moved into place as and when required. Snow and ice can make both stairs and ramps slippery and dangerous, a problem overcome by building an electric heating element into screed finished with quartz granules (as used for roadworks), non-slip tiles or embossed rubber sheet. Non-slip floors are often made from open-grid steel grating but the choice of type has to be made carefully if it is to be effective. At the Princess of Wales Conservatory, Kew, in order to satisfy the 'Safety at Work' regulations, the floor grating was turned over to expose its rougher face.

33.3 COMPONENTS AND FINISHES

33.3.1 Treads and risers

In times past, concrete or filler joist stairs might be finished on site in a wide variety of materials. Increasingly, the

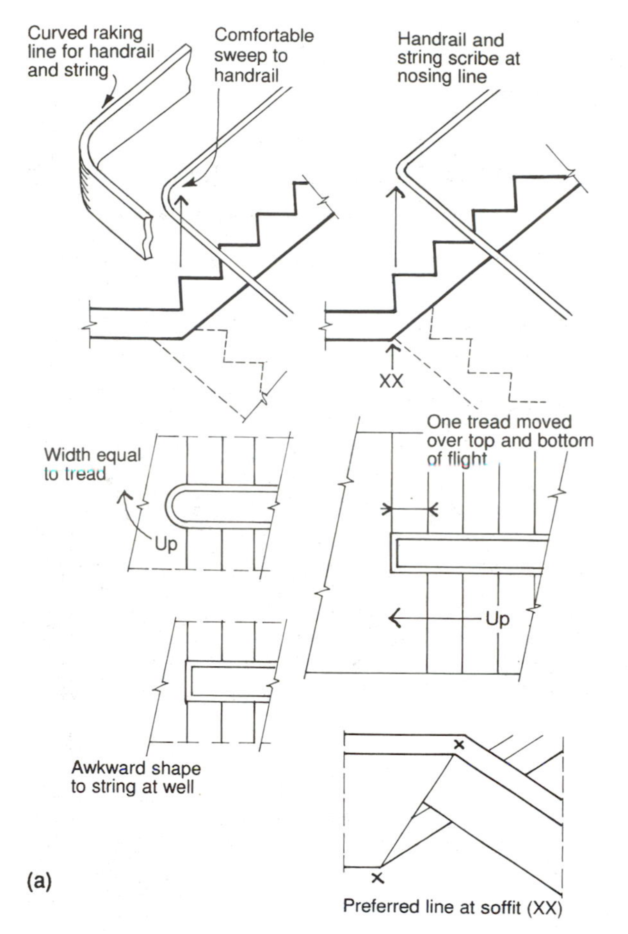

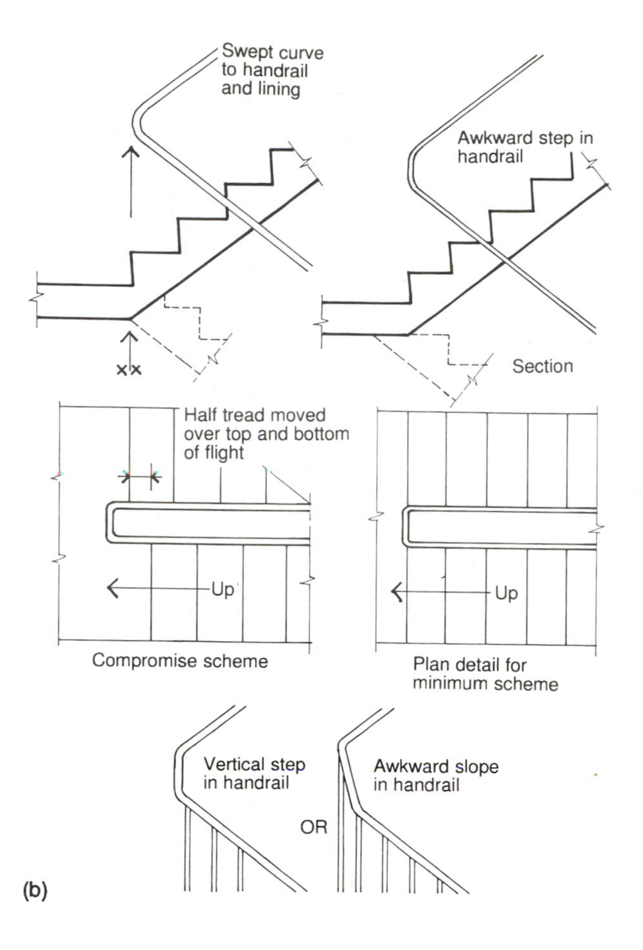

Fig. 33.16 *Minimal string and handrail relationships showing awkward slope in handrail.*

present trend is towards components and finishes being factory made.

As a consequence, treads and risers are now likely to be constructed from precast terrazzo or tile-clad concrete fixed onto the folded steelwork or steel 'trays' forming the stair structure. Alternatively, carpet, sheet rubber, vinyl or timber planks may be glued directly onto the metal. With the exception of the examples by Asplund and Salvisberg, the outstanding examples forming the case studies at the end of this chapter comprise elements fabricated off site which have been delivered and assembled like built-in furniture.

Stairs constructed from steel plate usually have straight uncut strings forming the main structural element. At the ends of the flight the string can be designed to extended beyond the last nosing which makes the detailing at the intersection with the landing much simpler. This geometric arrangement also allows better tolerances for assembly (Fig. 33.16a) and facilitates sweeping handrails that glide round corners rather than erratically changing direction (Fig. 33.16b).

33.3.2 Balustrades

BS 6180: 1982 [6] describes the structural strength required of balustrades, which in the case of private or common stairs have to resist a horizontal force of 0.36 kN per metre length or for all the remaining categories, 0.74 kN. This fairly stringent regulation is a major determinant of how the balustrade, handrail and the fixing back to the structure are to be detailed. Steel is often used as part of the assembly, at least as the structural core. In which case, because steel also has better fire resistance than other materials such as aluminium, bronze or hardwood, they may be used as the final finish but will only be 'sacrificial' for purposes of fire and serve no structural function.

The glass used for balustrades has to be laminated or toughened glass or glass blocks, 6 mm (¼ in) wired plate is no longer permitted for this purpose. Figure 33.17 shows some methods of making and assembling balustrading. The structural stability required by the Code of Practice either needs engineering input at the design stage or for the problem to be presented to the manufacturer as a performance specification. The same precautions apply when selecting proprietary or stainless tubing or designing structural glass balustrading (Fig. 33.18).

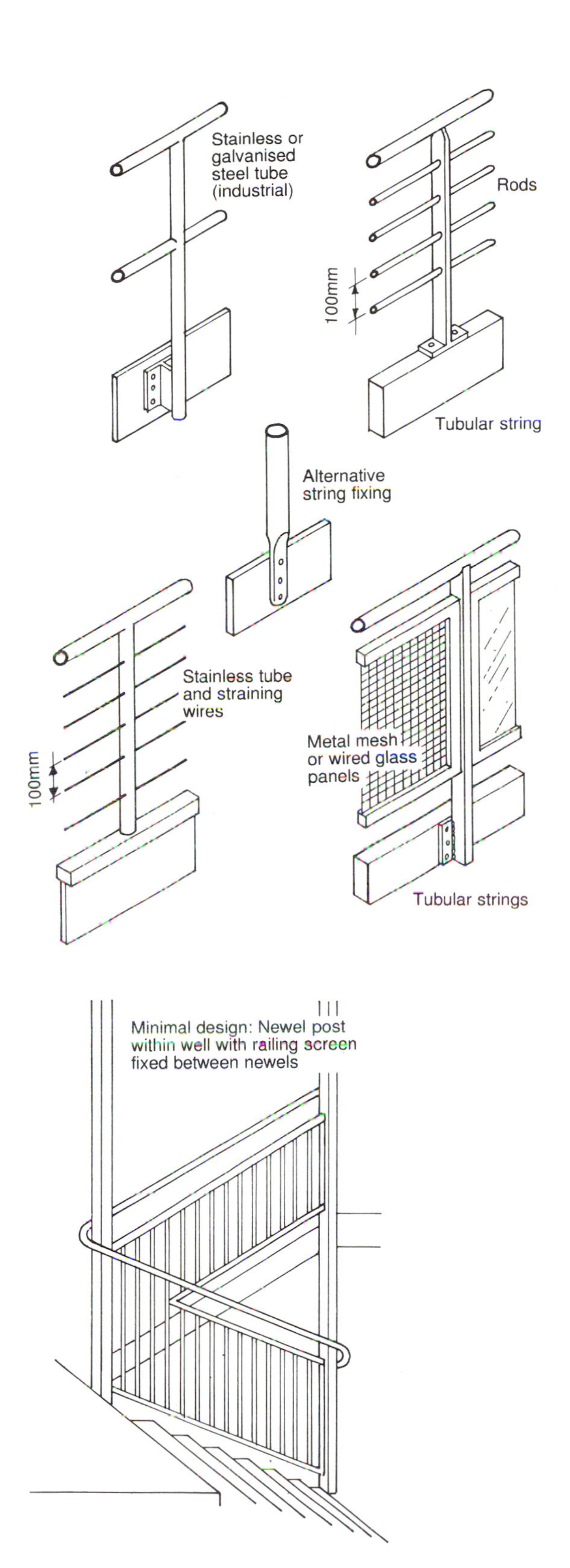

Fig. 33.17 *Steel railing assemblies.*

Fig. 33.18 *Stainless and glass assemblies. (a) Glass and steel framing to stair panels. RAC Offices Milan (1960s); (b) Steel and curved polycarbonate 'Galleri Centre' Svenborg, Denmark (1980s)*

Fig. 33.19 *Suspended steel stairs. Rödovre Town Hall 1950s (architect Arne Jacobsen) (a) key section (b) plan (c) perspective (d) section D (e) section E (f) detail F (g) section C and detail A.*

33.4 CASE STUDIES

33.4.1 Suspended stairs: Rödovre Town Hall (1955)

Architect: Arne Jacobsen (Fig. 33.19)

This superbly crafted piece of metalwork employs 24 mm rods to suspend the weight of the dogleg stairs and cantilevered landings. The string was cut from 50 mm plate to a uniform 100 mm on elevation, following the shape of the risers and treads and masking the ends of the trays that form the treads and landings. The stair is at the rear of the main entry hall and is seen outlined against the principal window that is a full three storeys in height. The skeletal structure, the stepped strings, open treads and elemental handrails present the most elegant and minimal silhouette.

(a) Key section

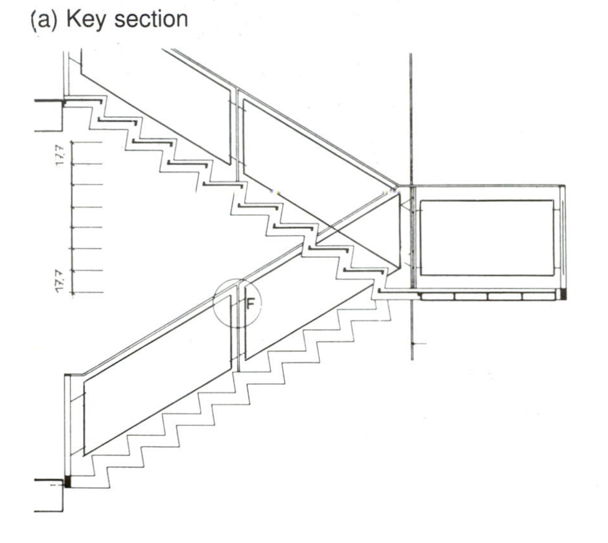

(b) Plan

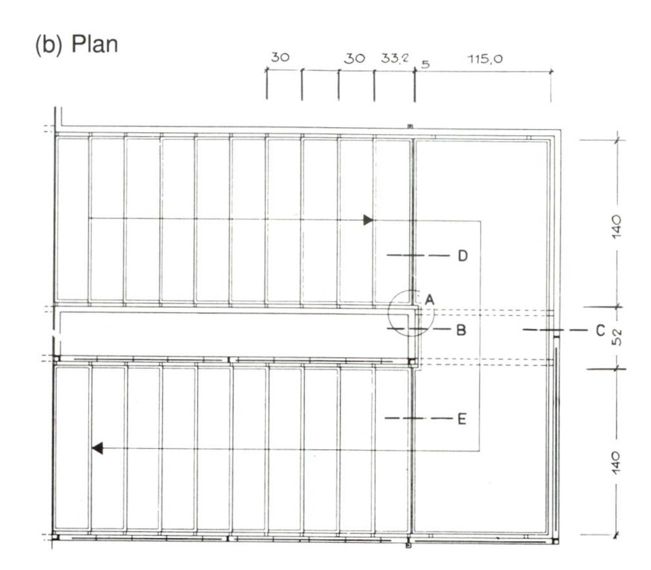

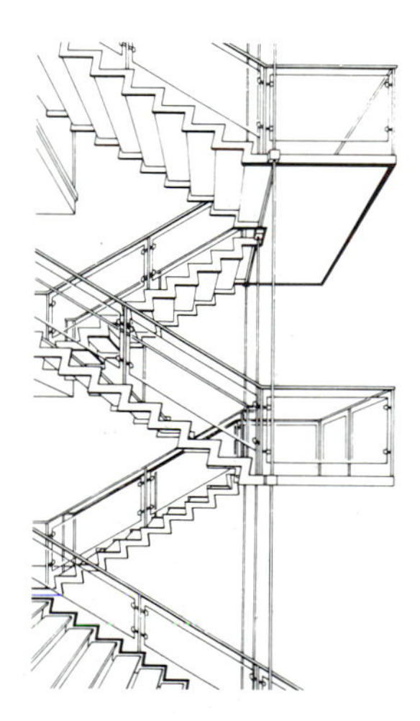

(c) Perspective

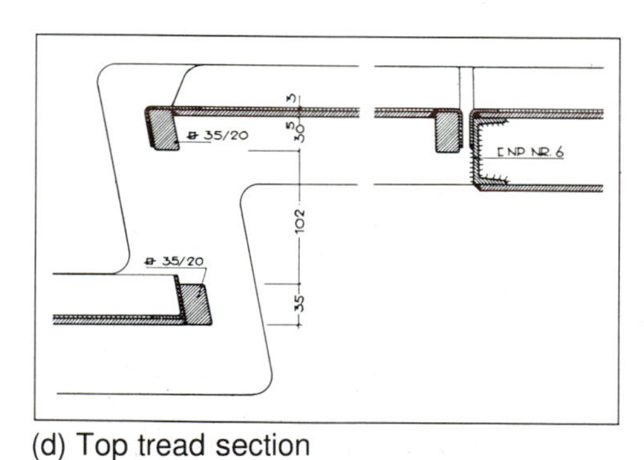

(d) Top tread section

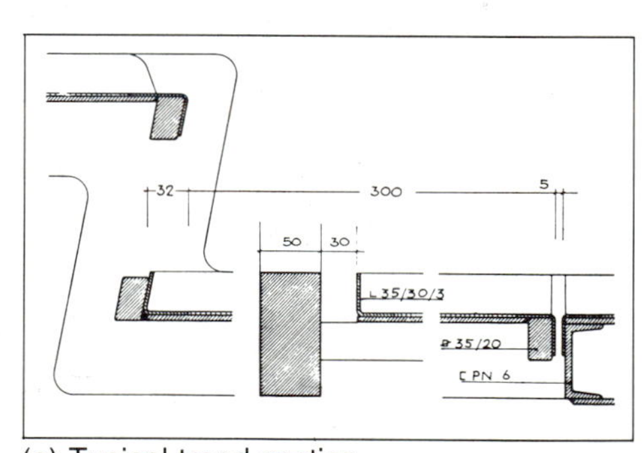

(e) Typical tread section

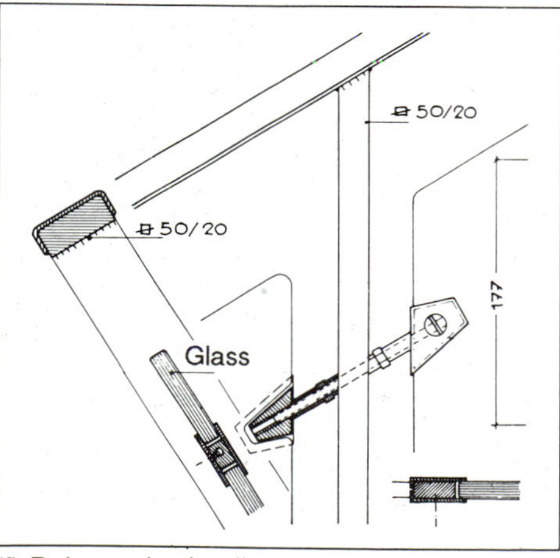

(f) Balustrade detail

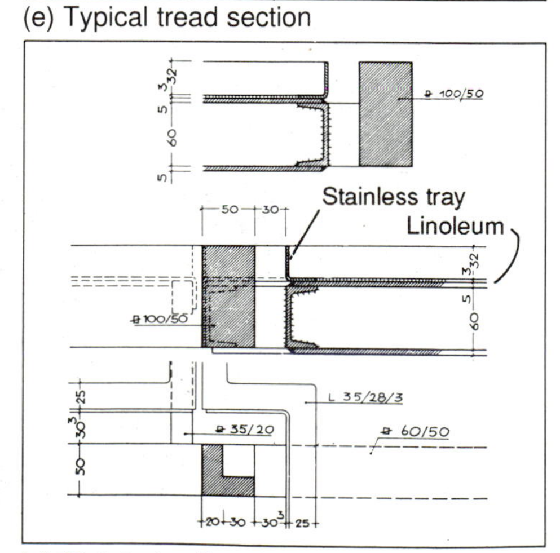

(g) Stair to landing detail

Fig. 33.20 *(a) and (b) Steel spiral stairs. Fédération du Bâtiment, Paris 1960s (architects Daniel Badani, Michael Foliasson, Abro Kanjian, Pierre Roux-Dorlut).*

33.4.2 Spiral stairs: Fédération du Bâtiment, Paris (1960s)

Architects: Danil Badani, Michael Foliasson, Abro Kanjian, Pierre Roux-Dorlut (Fig. 33.20)

This example shows the sculptural quality that can be achieved using welded plate to make spiral tubes and hollow trapezoidal forms for treads. Safety regulations differ in France, and there is no necessity for infill between the handrail and the stair flight. A greater concern with safety in use would require filling the gaps and modifying the form to follow a central circular well. An example offered for comparison is at the History Museum in Hanover designed by Prof. Dieter Oesterlen (Fig. 33.21). The string is bent 12 mm plate to which are bolted standards also made from steel plate supporting the acrylic and hardwood balustrade and the handrail which has a steel core.

Fig. 33.21 *Steel spiral stairs with tubular strings and metal tray treads. Historisches Museum, Hanover 1960s (architect Dieter Oesterlen).*

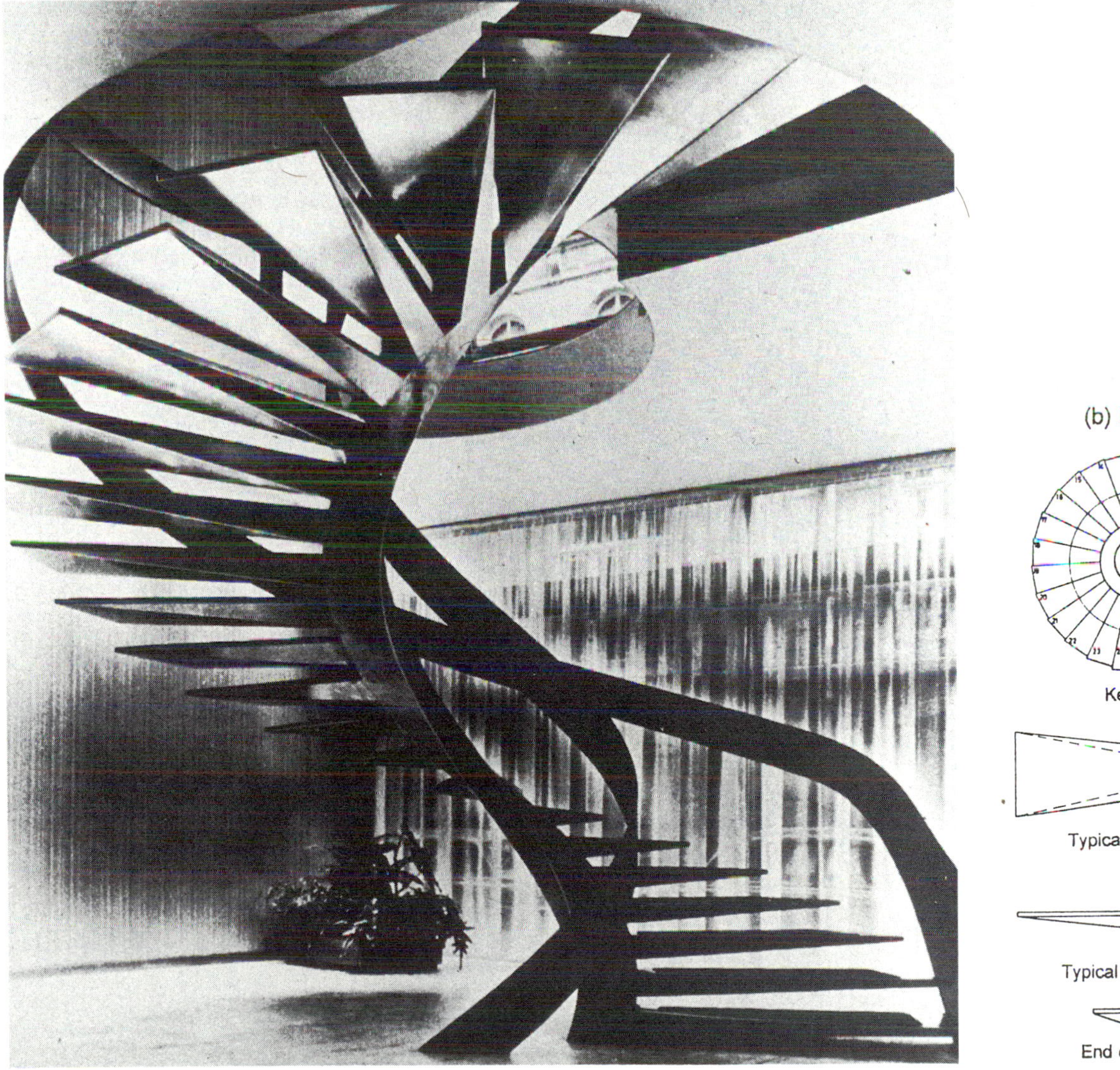

(a) General view

(b) Details

33.4.3 Straight flight: Gothenburg Court House (1937)

Architect: Gunnar Asplund (Fig. 33.22)

This impressive formal stair is the judges' approach to the first floor courts at Asplund's Gothenburg masterpiece, completed in 1937. The visual effect is heightened by the placement of the staircase near a fully glazed facade and eccentric to the open well containing the main circulation to the 'piano nobile'. Bridges are suspended within the steel framed foyer by small steel rolled section hangers carrying the channel strings. The steel components are fire protected by either fibrous or traditional plaster applied over wire reinforcement, the visible rounded shapes being symbolic of the encased steel sections. The stair pitch of 110 mm × 360 mm is one of the easiest to negotiate. The delight of Asplund's detailing is in the structural refinement of the tapered beams and floor edges, as well as its having accommodated commonsense practicalities by the use of closely spaced balustrading and a generous overrun at the landing to allow comfortable wreathing of the handrail.

Fig. 33.22 *Concrete-cased steel stairs. Courthouse, Gothenburg 1937 (architect Gunnar Asplund).*

Printed by kind permission of Julius Hoffman Verlag.

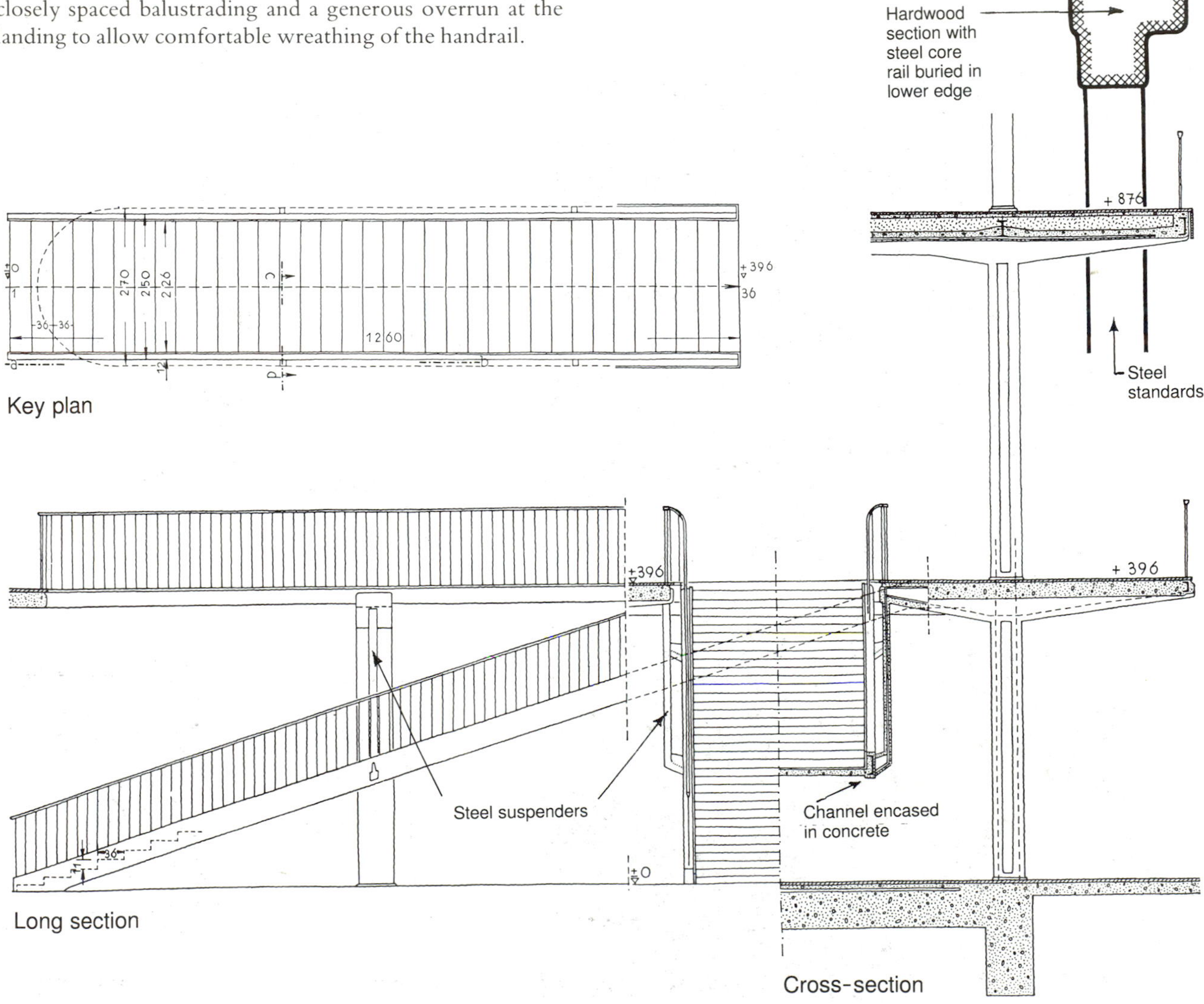

Fig. 33.23 *Technical High School, Basel 1931 (architect Otto Salvisburg). Printed by kind permission of Julius Hoffman Verlag.*

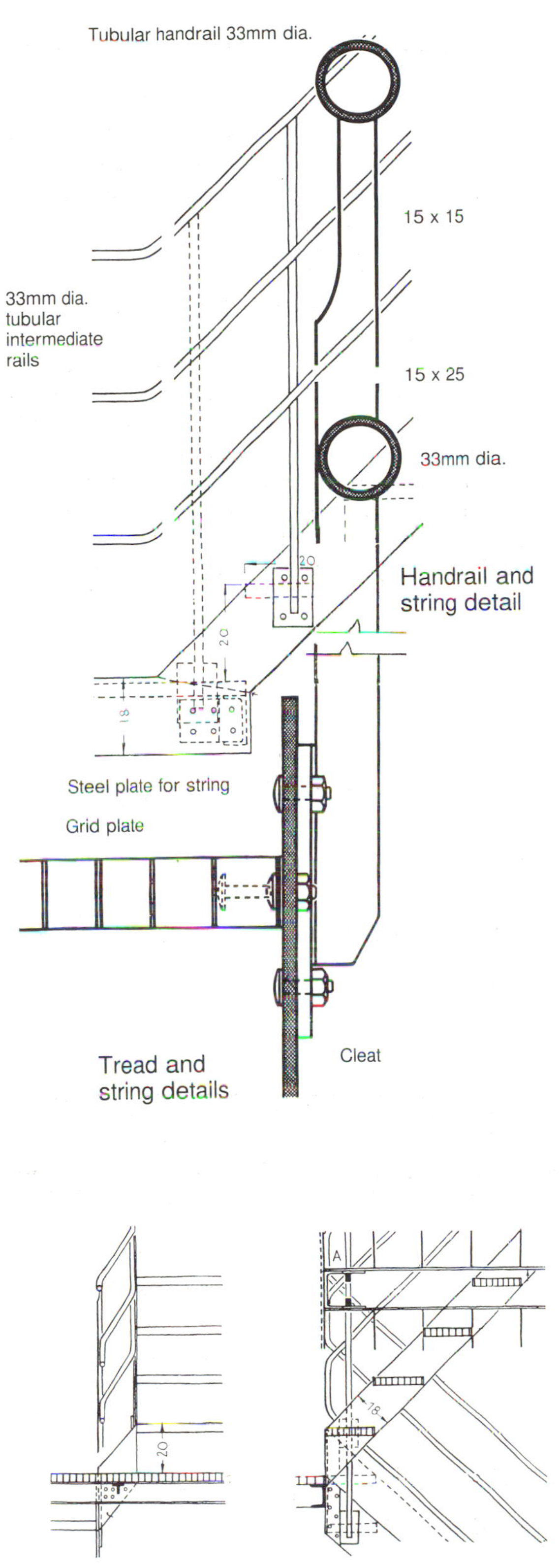

33.4.4 Three-quarter turn stair: Technical High School, Basel (1931)

Architect: Otto Salvisberg (Fig. 33.23)

Salvisberg had a greater flair for flow and line in stair detailing than did his contemporary Erich Mendelsohn as is illustrated by this example. The geometry of the treads makes each flight of equal pitch although the inside strings are made from continuous bent plate. A smooth swept line is also imparted to the handrailing, horizontal rails and strings. The construction is conventional, 12.5 mm (½ in) plate strings are welded to shaped 105 × 105 mm (4⅛ × 4⅛ in) Tees and tubular handrails, while the treads are folded plate (requiring expensive hand finishing of the tapered ends).

33.4.5 External access: Lloyds headquarters, London (1987)

Architect: Richard Rogers Partnership
Engineer: Ove Arup and Partners (Fig. 33.24)

These spiral stairs selected from the Lloyds Building are part of the filigree of elegant metalwork which completes the roofline. Refer also to chapter 35, Figs 35.13 and 14 for the general context. The stair layout is cut back to form quarter landings at the upper floors; the space for the flight is maximized by mounting the circular handrailing and supports external to the sheet steel string. The simple geometry of the three-quarter drum set against the balcony is reinforced by the mesh infill which provides a welcome transparency. The ensemble could be described as sculpture in the sky.

Fig. 33.24 *Steel gantries and extended stairs featuring on the roofscape of Lloyds headquarters, London 1987 (architect Richard Rogers and Partnership: engineer Ove Arup and Partners).*

(a) General view

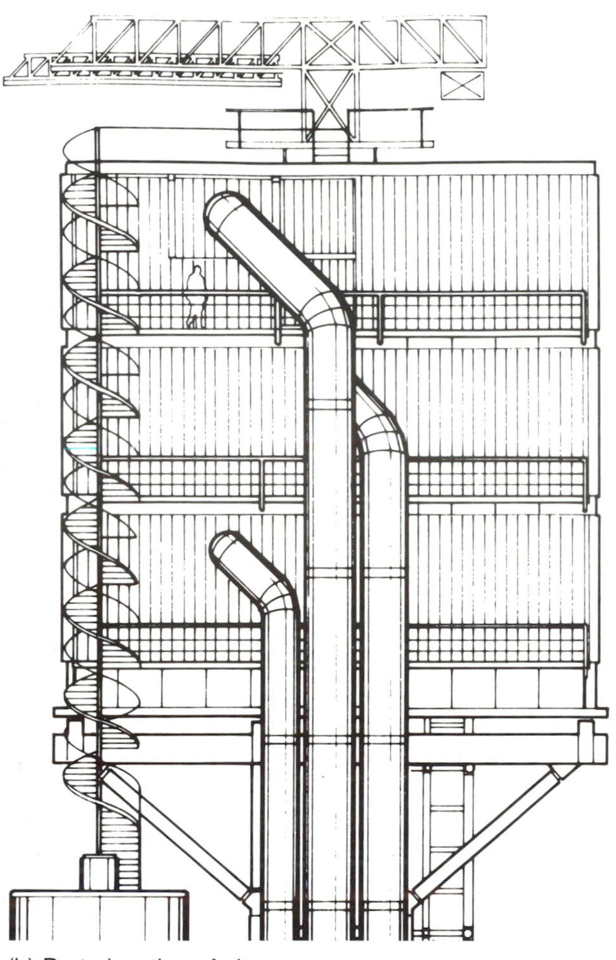

(b) Part elevation of plant room (with spiral stair to left hand)

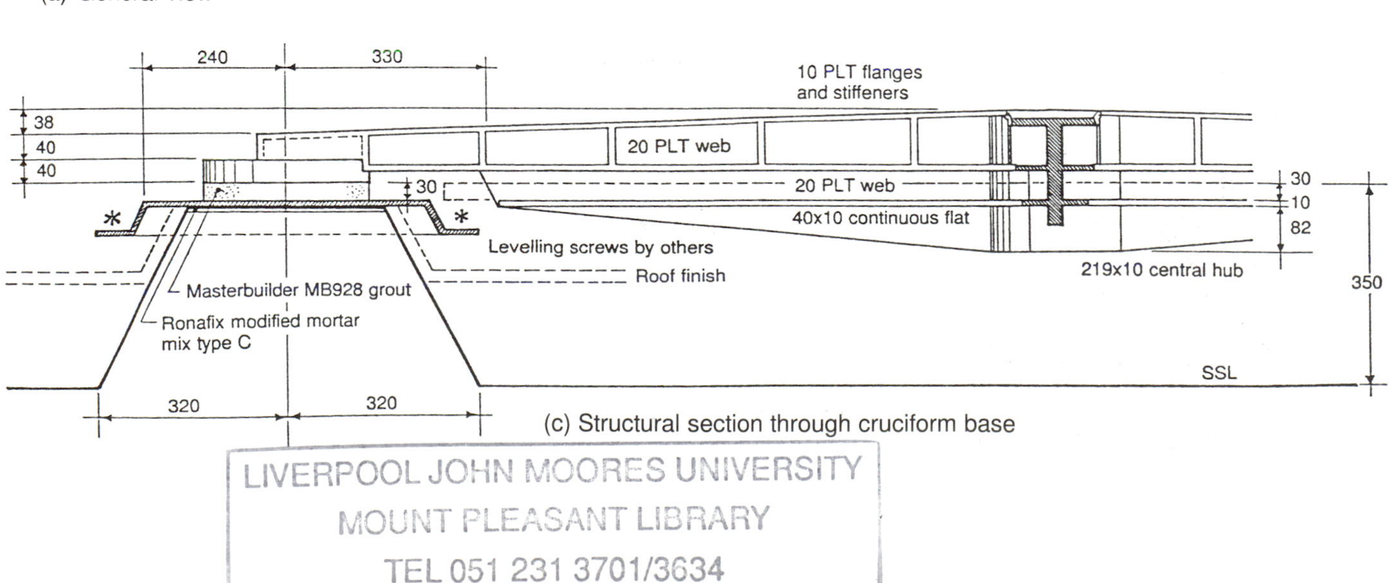

(c) Structural section through cruciform base

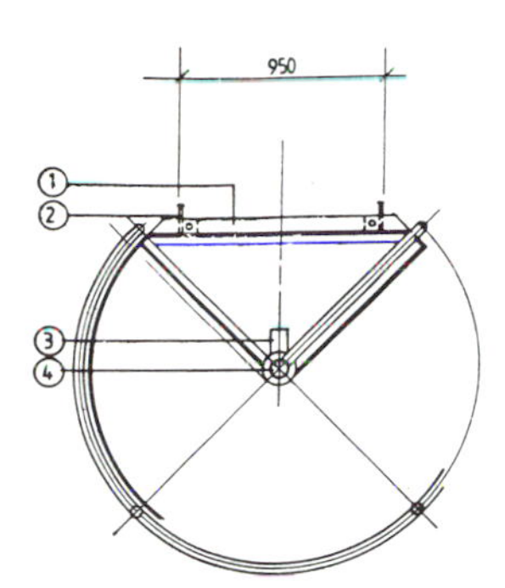

Plan at level 13.4

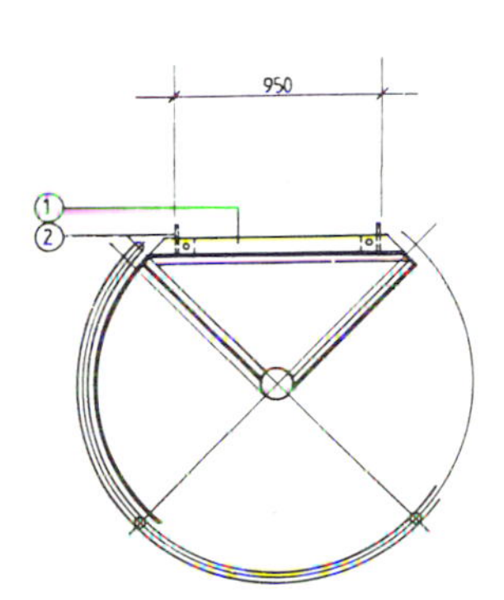

Plan at level 13.3

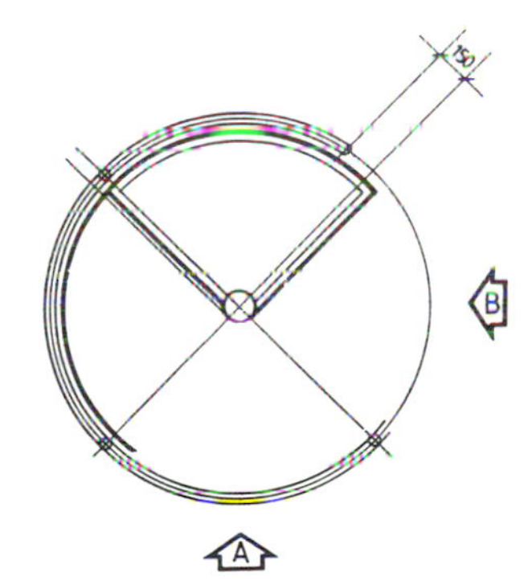

Plan at level 13.2

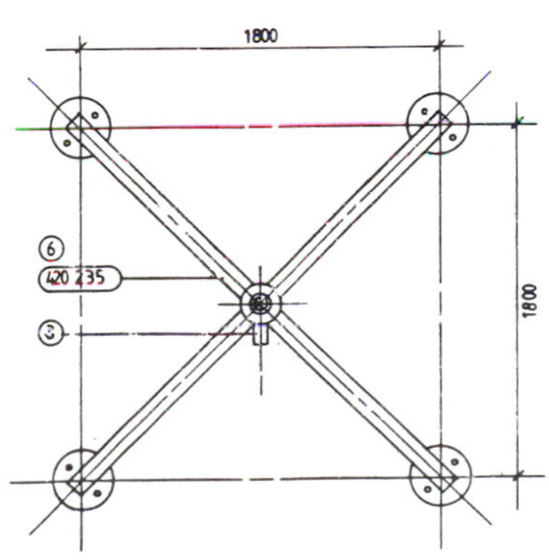

Plan at support structure

d) Key plans at each level

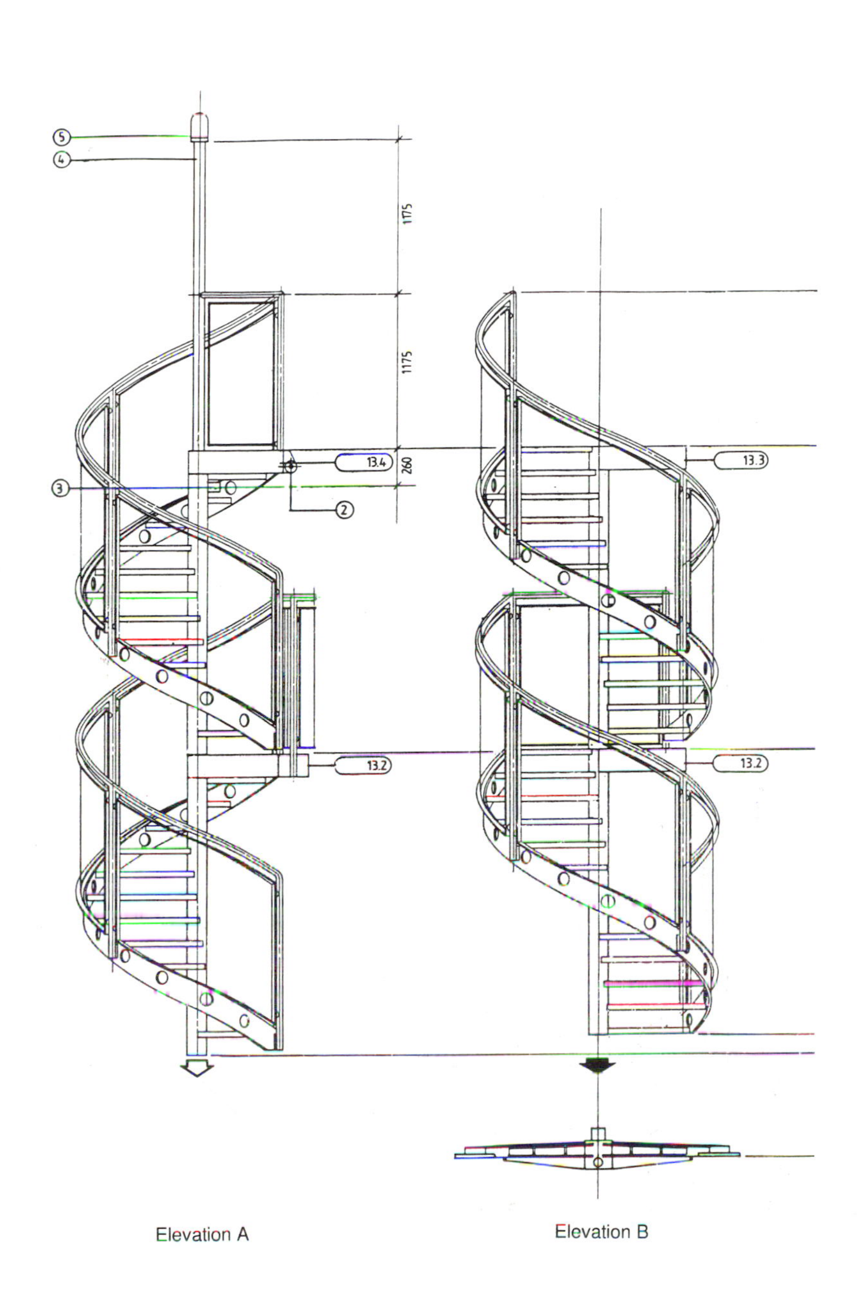

Elevation A

Elevation B

(e) Elevational details

Key:

1. Landing edge
2. Fixing cleat
3. Support lug
4. Central column
5. Terminal cap

33.4.6 Accommodation stairs: Joseph Store, Sloane Street, London (1989)

Architect: Eva Jiricna
Engineer: Matthew Wells of Whitby and Bird (Fig. 33.25)

The sculptural effect of the Jiricna staircases is closer to furniture, with the engineering honed to the absolute minimum. The example from the Joseph store in Sloane Street, London, is typical, where the triple flight feature is the centrepiece of the interior. The lightness of this eye-catcher is enhanced by glass treads and balustrading, whilst the structure is an assembly of stainless steel rods and connectors that provide a spider's web of supporting members. The art of constructing stairs with this skill is a combination of architectural and engineering design, hence shared credit to Eva Jiricna and Matthew Wells, the latter a rare designer, both architect and engineer, now a partner with Barton and Wells.

Fig. 33.25 *Detail views of steel rod and glass stairs at the Joseph Store, Chelsea, London 1989 (architect Eva Jericna: engineer Mathew Wells of Whitby and Bird).*

(a) General view of glass treads.

(b) View of under framing with steel rod bracing.

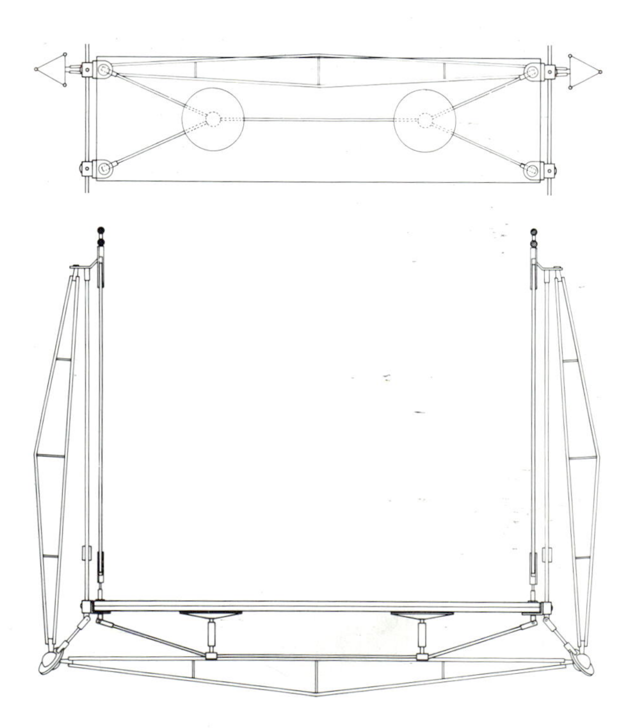

(c) and (d) Plan and section through typical tread.

REFERENCES AND TECHNICAL NOTES

1. The Building Regulations in England and Wales that came into force 1.6.92 (including Section Kl) are amply described in the 9th edition of M.J. Billington and Vincent Powell-Smith's guide *The Building Regulations Explained and Illustrated*, Blackwell Scientific Publications (1992), the Scottish regulations and those for N. Ireland being regrettably more complicated, need direct reference to the actual Building Acts.

   The former LCC/ILEA area of London still retains particular by-laws (as from 6.1.86. under Section 21 of the LBA (Amendment) for buildings of considerable height or volume. These requirements are more stringent than the National Building Regulations vis-a-vis fireproofing, means of escape and staircase design.
2. A promenade in space or "Architectural Promenade", a term coined by Le Corbusier in *Oeuvre Complète 1910–29*. For further references turn to pages 148–154 in Russell Walden's *The Open Hand*, MIT Press (1977).
3. For helical and spiral stairs refer to BS 5395 Part 2: 1984 Code of Practice for the Design of Helical and Spiral Stairs.
4. In times past vertical brick modules and stair risers were totally integrated, the 150 mm riser equating with two 75 courses or the steeper 187.5 riser having to be used in flights of even number (8/10 or 14/16/18 etc) to give a relationship of two steps per five 75 mm courses (namely 375 mm = 2 × 187.5).
5. Computer aided design; reference may be made to: Albion Design of Cambridge, Unit F Sawston Industrial Estate, Babraham Road, Sawston, Cambridge CB2 4LH, UK. Tel: 44 (0)223 836 128.

   Cornish Stairways Ltd, Kernick Industrial Estate, 3 Jennings Road, Penryn, Cornwall TR10 9DQ, UK. Tel: 44 (0)326 74662.

   Crescent of Cambridge Ltd, Edison Road, St Ives, Cambridge PE17 4LF, UK. Tel: 44 (0)480 301522.
6. BS 6180: 1982 Protective Barriers in and about buildings.

FURTHER READING

Proprietary railings and screens; refer to catalogues of leading suppliers of steel components in the UK, namely: Edwin Clarke Stairways, Coultham Street, Lincoln LN5 8HQ, UK. Tel: 44 (0)522 530912.

Harris Architectural Metalwork, Progress House, 21 Progress Way, Croydon, Surrey CRO 4XD, UK. Tel: 44 (0)81 680 3364.

Hewi (UK) Ltd, Scimitar Close, Gillingham Business Park, Gillingham, Kent ME8 0RN, UK. Tel: 44 (0)634 377688.

Norton Engineering Alloys Co. Ltd, Norton Grove Industrial Estate, Norton, Malton, N. Yorks YO17 9HQ, UK. Tel: 44 (0)653 695721.

Starkie J. Gardner Ltd, Lady Lane Industrial Estate, Hadleigh, Ipswich, Suffolk IP7 6DG, UK. Tel: 44 (0)473 822525.

Stewarts and Hastings Ltd, The Priory, Syresham Gardens, Haywards Heath, W. Sussex RH16 3LB, UK. Tel: 44 (0)944 417505.

1863 cast iron hopper head contrasted with 1990 stainless steel hopper designed by Arup Associates.

34

Gutters, downpipes and overflows

Alan Blanc

34.1 GUTTERS

34.1.1 Sizing of gutters and overflows

Reference should be made to the rainwater disposal guide in chapter 28. A critical design consideration for parapet and valley gutters is the necessity for an overflow to be incorporated at a lower level than any possible point of entry for water between layers of the construction. Otherwise, if downpipes were to become partly or totally blocked, melting snow or storm water would find its way into the building (the critical junction for metal gutters being where the roofing laps the guttering). There are various solutions to this problem; firstly and simply, to provide an overflow pipe emitting from the gutter or weir outlet (Fig. 34.1), at a slightly higher level than the outlet itself, or alternatively, to increase the number of rainwater pipes. Poor maintenance can, however, still lead to grit, leaves and snow blocking every pipe. The provision of overflows is the best solution as each potentially blocked outlet can be designed to have an overflow to relieve it.

The same consideration applies to face gutters or hopper heads (Fig. 34.2), though overflowing water at these locations will only soak the exterior walling at first, rather than immediately flood the interior.

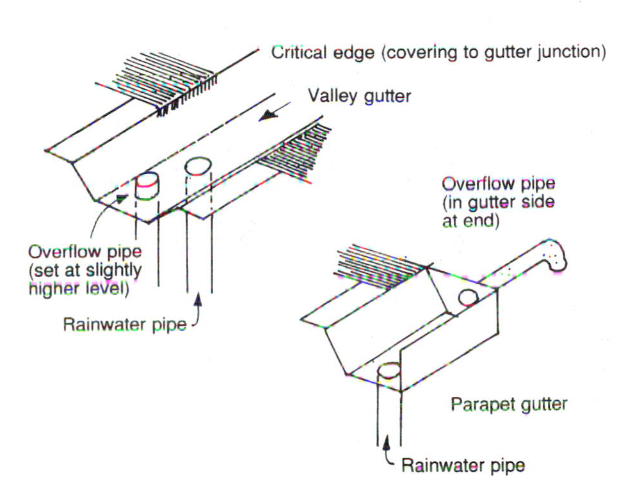

Fig. 34.1 *Gutter overflows (parapet/valley).*

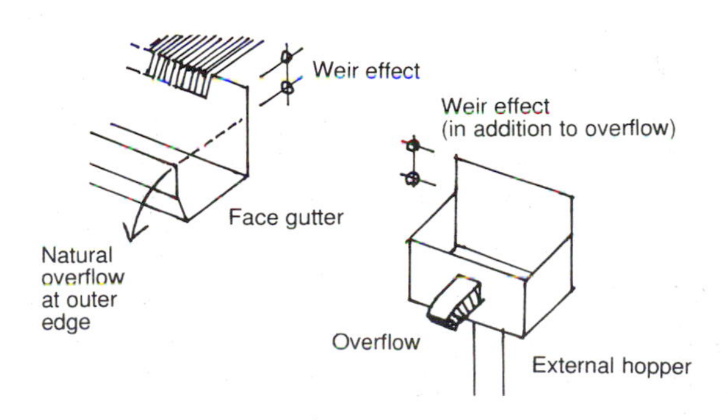

Fig. 34.2 *Gutter and hopper overflows.*

34.1.2 Materials

(a) Cast iron

This traditional material is still available in medium, heavy and extra heavy grades with a few specialist firms able to match obsolete patterns [1] for use in building conservation. The advantage of iron over steel is its greater resistance to corrosion. Cast iron can be made into gutter profiles that have greater strength and capacity than those available in folded aluminium or plastic and which are of infinitely greater architectural interest, particularly those with beaded edges or full cyma-reversa curves (Fig. 34.3 illustrates a few of the sections still manufactured in 1800 mm lengths).

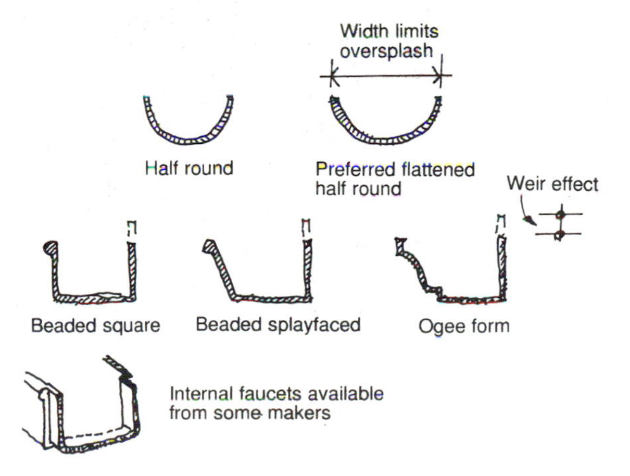

Fig. 34.3 *Traditional iron face gutters.*

Fig. 34.4 *Gutters at Tobacco Dock, London Docklands 1988 (architects Terry Farrell and Co.)*

Figure 34.4 illustrates the gutter detailing Tobacco Dock, London where special bracket profiles were made.

Cast iron gutters are made with both external and internal faucets: the latter impart a clean outer line but with an increased risk of ponding. In times past, cast iron was protected by the use of bituminous finishes such as 'Dr Angus Smith's Solution'. Today galvanizing and paint treatment is the usual specification. Should bitumenizing be considered, it is preferable for the inside of gutters and pipes to be factory treated. This will eliminate bare surfaces that may be subject to bimetallic corrosion if other metals are in proximity.

(b) Steel

Cold formed coated steel sheet has largely replaced cast iron for parapet and valley gutters, and the shapes that are available have been developed to run level and to suit proprietary metal roofing (Fig. 34.5). Steel gutters are

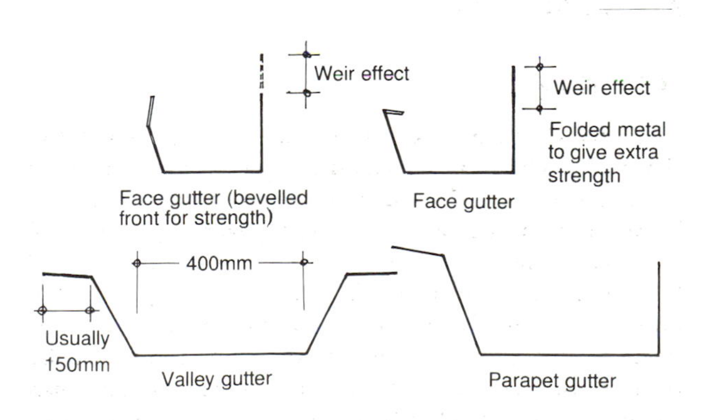

Fig. 34.5 *Steel sheet gutters.*

typically manufactured in lengths of 3 m (10 ft) with external or internal faucets and bolted connections. Galvanizing is the usual specification, possibly overpainted with bitumen for additional protection. A wide variety of factory-applied paint finishes is also available, and they can be selected to match coatings on adjacent steel roofing sheets. Some gutter fabricators are again offering vitreous enamel, a finish worth considering where appearance is of particular importance. Steel has a larger coefficient of thermal expansion than cast iron, and as a result mastic joints between steel components need more maintenance. Eventually this problem may involve a bitumastic overcoating to the whole gutter: a reference to the *Yellow Pages* telephone directory under the heading 'Roofing Services' reveals the large number of businesses coping with this perennial problem. A better solution is to fabricate guttering from welded steel plate with its base made to slope and then finished with high performance roofing felt (which has sufficient ductility and girth to cope with flood conditions).

(c) Stainless steel

In recent years a technique has been developed for site installation of machine folded metal roofing, including the introduction of profiling tools that will roll out continuous lengths of stainless steel coping and valley guttering. These components may be used as a liner in repair work or as a part of the total roofing system, whether in stainless steel or other materials.

Refer to chapter 5 for selection of grades of stainless steel and their anticipated life. A significant consideration when using the method described above for 'internal' guttering is that continuity obviates the necessity for mastic joint sealant or a waterproof overlay. The tough surface of the metal is resistant to vandalism and roof workers' footwear. Stainless alloys cause corrosion when in wet contact with plain steels and react similarly if in contact with zinc galvanizing. Detailing of the weather surfaces around stainless steel gutters should avoid unprotected raw steel or galvanized fastenings that might lead to corrosive run off or rust staining.

In refurbishment work old steel gutters will therefore need bitumenizing before being overclad.

(d) Other metals and finishes

To avoid bimetallic corrosion, materials for face or internal guttering are chosen for their compatibility with any metal selected for the rest of the roof cladding. Zinc or lead coated steel sheets are milled for related gutter work.

Non-ferrous roofing using aluminium alloys/copper/zinc sheeting is best served by the specification of matching metals or by gutters lined with a neutral material such as GRP or heavy duty polymer. Detailing that mixes metals in the presence of water has to be avoided if corrosion risks are to be eliminated (for further reading refer to HMSO publication (1963) *Corrosion and the Prevention of Bimetallic Contact* [2])

34.1.3 Composite details

(a) Glass reinforced polyester (GRP)

GRP is primarily used for gutter refurbishment, the iron or steel internal gutter being used as a former and support for a plastic liner. The relative rates of thermal expansion for GRP and steel are sufficiently close to enable continuous lengths up to 15 m to be formed. The life expectancy of the polyester resin is the critical consideration, 20 years being the likely maximum before recoating is needed.

(b) Lined gutters

Face-fixed gutters on mainland Europe incorporate liners, independent of the building envelope, to deal with levels of snowfall greater than is usual in the UK. European skill in sheet metalwork is employed in a typical detail (Fig. 34.6) for a zinc box gutter, supported by a light galvanized steel structural framework, adapted for eaves overhang, soffit fixing and members strong enough to support snow guards or temporary outrigging for maintenance purposes. By comparison, uPVC or folded aluminium lined gutters are flimsy and not able to support ladders.

34.1.4 Access and cleaning

Parapet and valley gutters need sufficient 'footspace' for maintenance access, a minimum width of 400 mm at roof level, and body width if the parapet has vertical sides. Face gutters need to be strong enough for 'ladder rests': three storeys is the limiting dimension for ladder work, trestles being used for greater heights. The present fashion for pitched roof high-rise implies excessive gutter maintenance costs unless boxed gutters are inset within roof slopes, requiring footspace and a bracket arrangement for guard

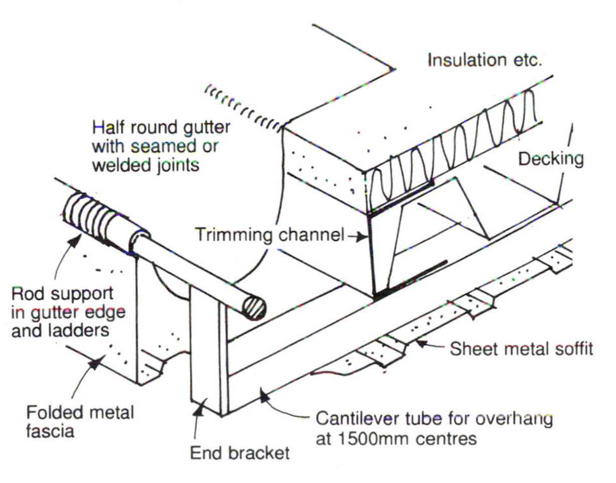

Fig. 34.6 *Continental sheet metal work.*

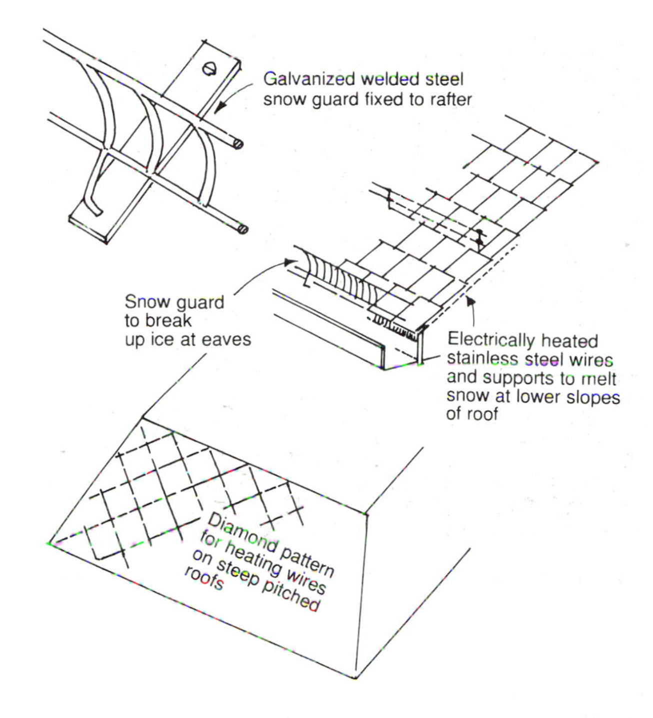

Fig. 34.7 *Snow guards and heating wires.*

rails to fulfil safety at work regulations. European and Canadian details (Fig. 34.7) invariably incorporate snow guards and electrical trace heating (so that a dangerous weight of ice does not accumulate) on roofslopes that overhang public thoroughfares. London architects are slow to learn these fundamental details, a classic failure being the steep metal mansard at the Guards Barracks, Knightsbridge, London where on one cold winter's night a few hundredweight of frozen snow dropped down 16 storeys and crushed the colonel's mini.

34.2 DOWNPIPES

34.2.1 Sizing

Reference should be made to the rainwater disposal guide in chapter 28. The critical junction of a rainwater system is the entry to the downpipe which should taper to avoid turbulence: flask shaped outlets are now available for internal gutters [3]. Another recent development is the use of sealed horizontal pipe runs below flat roofs so that pipes run full bore and increase the rate of flow through syphonage effect. As a result, the diameter of pipework can be substantially reduced whereas in a conventional system pipes smaller than 75 mm diameter readily block and should never be used. Discharge from gritted areas will need at least 100 mm pipes with access points at bends; landscape roof drainage where cementicious or sand deposits may occur should be 150 mm diameter with bucket gullies or cesspits to catch the debris.

34.2.2 Materials

(a) Cast iron

Pipes are still made in medium, heavy and extra heavy duty circular socketed pattern (still termed LCC in the UK), the material being eared or plain [3,4]. Plain pipe is more useful since it can be properly aligned and have sufficient backspace to enable the back of the pipe to be painted easily where adjacent to a wall. The fixing brackets are two-piece collars as for other service pipes (Fig. 34.8). A combined drainage system still exists in inner London where heavy duty cast iron is obligatory and can be used to ventilate sanitary systems. Materials and methods for finishing and painting are as described for gutters (section 34.1.1).

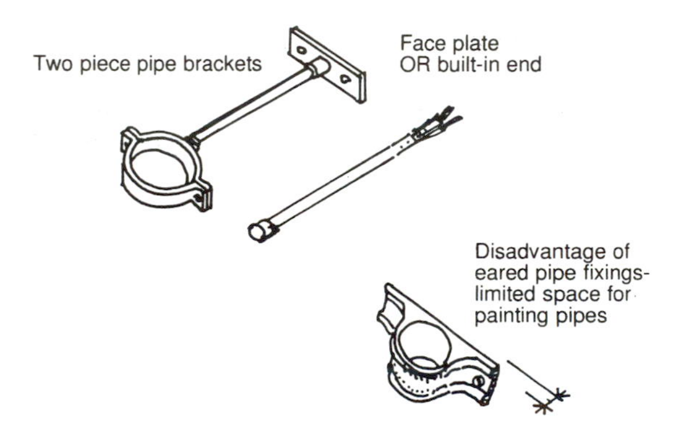

Fig. 34.8 *Cast iron pipe fixing.*

Fig. 34.9 *Ugly rainwater pipes at Richmond town centre (1980s).*

(b) Steel

Galvanized seamed or spun pipes are usual and are circular or rectangular in shape. Coupling is by means of screwed or welded joints. Welding has the advantage that cranked or straight unbroken lengths can be formed and then fixed, at welded lugs, back to the structure. Any galvanizing should be carried out after fabrication because the protective coating is destroyed by welding.

(c) Stainless steel

Anywhere that stainless steel or guttering or roofing is specified, care should be taken that run-off from stainless finishes does not degrade zinc coatings or steel further along the rainwater drainage system. Joints are made mechanically or by welding [5].

(d) Other metals

Section 34.1.2 discusses the arguments in favour of one metal only being specified in a rainwater system. Plastic pipe, if used below roof outlet level, eliminates the likelihood of bimetallic corrosion but has the disadvantages of lack of fire resistance and strength. In many cases matching the material of the roof will be a principal consideration. Aluminium, copper, lead or zinc are often considered but theft of expensive metals may effectively reduce the range of choice (unless there are overriding conservation requirements).

(e) Aesthetics

There seems little reason to disfigure elevations with ribbons of ugly pipework when a mundane matter like rainwater can be disposed of by internal plumbing. The disfiguring of Leningrad or for that matter the newest parts of Richmond town centre, UK (Fig. 34.9) seems a totally unnecessary display of the plumber's art. Salvisburg's steel framed sheds for Roche at Welwyn Garden City, UK (Fig. 34.10) show that pre-war designers could come to terms with services and structure. Their neat and practical de-

Fig. 34.10 *Neat gutters and rainwater pipes for Roche at Welwyn Garden City, UK 1939 (architect: Otto Salvisberg).*

Fig. 34.11 *Direct discharge off lead coated steel sheet onto pebble margin of roof garden at Lloyds HQ Chatham 1980 (architect Arup Associates).*

tailing of gutter and pipe in light steelwork remains an inspiration.

The alternative to 'pipery' is to avoid the problem altogether and, taking a leaf from Japanese tradition, allow overhanging roofs to drip onto a pebble margin (Fig. 34.11) or direct water by chain to gully, planter or pool. None of these ideas are permitted, however, under the Building Regulations for roof drainage outside the confines of the site. Ice and icicles will create problems, not necessarily solved by heated outlets in very cold spells.

REFERENCES AND TECHNICAL NOTES

1. The current British Standards for cast iron drainage above ground are: BS 460: 1964 Specification for Cast Iron Rainwater Goods, and BS 416: 1990, Part 1 Specification for Spigot and Socket Systems and Part 2 Specification for Socketless Systems.
2. HMSO publication (1963) *Corrosion and the Prevention of Bimetallic Contact.*
3. The current British Standard for galvanized pressed steel guttering is: BS1091:1963 Specification for Pressed Steel Gutters, Rainwater Pipes, Fittings and Accessories.
4. Insulated outlets that are also available with an integral heating element are manufactured by Harmer Holdings Ltd.
5. Reference should be made to BM Stainless Steel Drains Ltd., who make an extensive range of stainless pipe and accessories to BS 5572:1978.

FURTHER READING

Old copies of the Ellerby's catalogue form an invaluable reference for all types of traditional cast iron guttering and hoppers.

Fig. 35.1 *Craftwork in cast iron, wrought iron and steel.*

(a) Late medieval helmet revealing quality of hand forged work.

(b) Cast iron bollard, Albert Docks, Liverpool (1850s), demonstrating durability.

(c) Gatehead at St Fagin's Castle, Cardiff, Wales (mixture of cast and wrought iron from the 18th century.

(d) Gate guards in wrought iron, Blenheim Palace, typical of inventive quality in smith's work.

(e) The tortuous quality in wrought work. Window handles at Neuschwanstein with forked tail turned on itself.

(f) Spider's web in mild steel at Portmerion, Wales (designer Clough Williams-Ellis), constructed cheaply with flat bar sections.

35

Decorative iron and steel

Alan Blanc

35.1 INTRODUCTION

This concluding chapter in the story of secondary iron and steel elements needs a preface. These few words will help explain my life-long enthusiasm for the art of metalwork and hence an interest in the nuts and bolts of construction. The truth of the matter is one of family background.

The English branch were blacksmiths for a century, whilst by contrast, the French paternal branch was engaged in jewellery and goldsmith work dating back to the earliest records, made in 1789, the year of the French Revolution. My earliest intent was to become a jeweller, but that changed to illustration and then finally to architecture. One hundred years ago, I would have been a metalworker, at a goldsmith's bench or blacksmith's forge.

Exploiting the potential of metals entails, in my view, identifying with the skills of fabrication. It is a matter of design ideas and the method of execution being understood simultaneously. The very process of drawing involves tactile sensations in the fingers, whilst head and hands are required when anticipating construction to a larger scale. These interpretive skills are the essence of hand-working iron and steel and can be experienced in smith's work whether iron age or present day.

The historical and technical introduction (chapters 2 and 3) described the differences between cast iron, wrought iron and the varieties of steel. It suffices at this stage to show eight key examples from this range of ferrous metals (Fig. 35.1) illustrating a spectrum of craft work from times past.

(g) 1991 replica of Victor Horta design made by Pillow and Son Ltd in mild steel. This remarkable piece of work was made following a study of photographs from the Horta museum.

(h) Modern work with replacement gates at Layer Marney Towers, Colchester. Fine blacksmith's work with varied spaces and interesting variety in profiles.

Fig. 35.2 *Cast steel lettering at the Tate Gallery, Liverpool 1987 (designers Pentagram).*

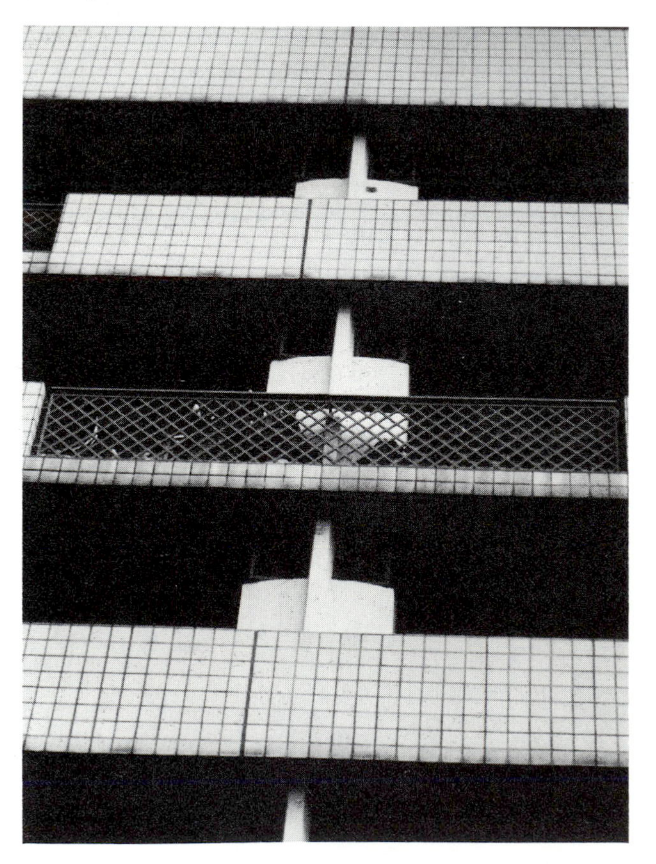

Fig. 35.3 *Railing grids at Spa Green, Roseberry Avenue, London 1951 (architect Lubetkin and Tecton).*

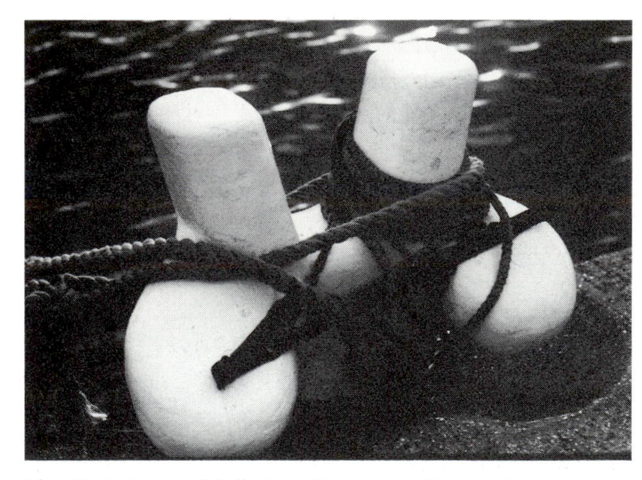

Fig. 35.4 *Cast steel bollards at Fred Olsens Quay, Milwall, London 1971.*

35.2 MODERN CAST IRON

Contemporary designs in cast iron include historic reproductions for street furniture, bollards, gratings, lighting columns, litter bins and tree guards, also specialist items such as ironmongery and spear heads for steel railings. Progressive ideas are less common but the attractions of robustness and texture have for instance led graphic artists to use cast letters, as can be seen at the Tate Gallery, Liverpool (Fig. 35.2). The Lubetkin and Tecton flats at Spa Green, Roseberry Avenue, have cast iron railings of modern design

Fig. 35.5 *Cast iron balusters at Herstmonceux 1958 (architect Brian O'Rourke).*

Fig. 35.6 *New manhole covers, City of Budapest.*

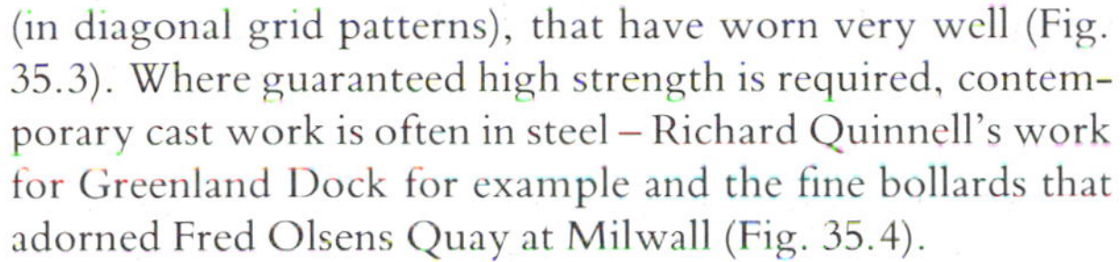

(in diagonal grid patterns), that have worn very well (Fig. 35.3). Where guaranteed high strength is required, contemporary cast work is often in steel – Richard Quinnell's work for Greenland Dock for example and the fine bollards that adorned Fred Olsens Quay at Milwall (Fig. 35.4).

A more conventional design with reeded standards was devised by Brian O'Rourke for the Royal Observatory at Herstmonceux (Fig. 35.5).

Mundane objects like manhole covers need more delightful embellishments than just studs and the maker's name, and the new patterns from the City of Budapest are highly decorative and non-slip (Fig. 35.6).

35.3 FORGED STEEL AS AN ART FORM COMPARED WITH WROUGHT IRON

The arresting tactile character of wrought iron elevates its fabrication into a form of art. It is interesting to observe how a design requiring curlicues in relatively awkward turns can become graceful and modulated when a skilled hand takes over (Fig. 35.7). This example illustrates the thesis that the spaces between wrought iron work are as important visually as the particular shapes given to the component parts.

The current revival in the blacksmith's art stems from the concern of designers with personal expression to building detail at points of contact such as entry doors, screens and stairs (Fig. 35.8). There is also the continuing thread of the arts and crafts tradition in contemporary architecture, seeking to employ construction as the significant expression of the design (Fig. 35.9). The architectural practices whose detailing springs to mind are Aldington Craig and Collinge, Arup Associates and Edward Cullinan.

All the examples illustrated have a structural role but their

Fig. 35.7 *Awkward drawn design and delightful execution.*

Fig. 35.8 *Stairs, with personal expression at contact points. Alan Dawson's balustrade at the main stairs, Princes Square, Glasgow 1988 (made by Shepley Dawson, Architectural Engineering Ltd).*

connections and assembly reveal a pattern and proportion equal to the finest historic wrought iron. These fabrications are largely mild steel with some special forged elements, and the point of illustrating these particular examples is to show how well considered detail can advance the art of steel construction.

35.3.1 Lemsford Mill

The new work at Lemsford Mill, Welwyn, Hertfordshire included renovation of the structure and the provision of new bridges and stairs; steel tubes and forged steel brackets form the principal members. The engineering input was to approximate lengths and sizes of connection whilst the architectural details precisely outlined junctions and profiles (Fig. 35.10). The end result is a magnificent piece of detailing in the functional tradition. The project was given the RIBA's Regional Award in 1988. The materials used were galvanized and painted plate and tubular steel. Paul Collinge was the designer with engineering advice by John Austin of Structures and Services Partnership and the fabricators were Tubular Structures and Glazzards (Dudley).

Fig. 35.9 *Bridge at Lemsford Mill, Welwyn, Hertfordshire (1986) (Designer Paul Collinge of Aldington Craig and Collinge).*

Fig. 35.10 *Other details at Lemsford Mill.*

Fig. 35.11 *Atria trusses, Broadgate (phases 1–4) 1982–88 (architect Arup Associates).*

35.3.2 Atrium roof framing at Broadgate (phases 1–4)

The various blocks gathered around Broadgate Square, London are distinguished by differing design details within each of their atria, a device that creates a sense of identity at each entrance hall. The rooflights complete the picture, the design of the steel trusses varying with the geometry of the location. Derek Sugden has already explained in his introduction that steel trusswork was a fundamental aspect of his training as an engineer. This design displays that taste for the simple fit of angle, flat and tee, which in Sugden's words feel and look right in complex three-dimensional assemblies. The engineering of the atria roof trusses (Fig. 35.11) is to the highest standard and reflects an enthusiasm for elegant fabrication and the skills of the detailing team and of the fabricators.

35.3.3 Docklands tradition

The redevelopment of old warehouses has brought back the tradition of balconies or access platforms that are strapped with steel sections to the facade (Fig. 35.12). This feature has

Fig. 35.12 *Typical balconies in docklands.*

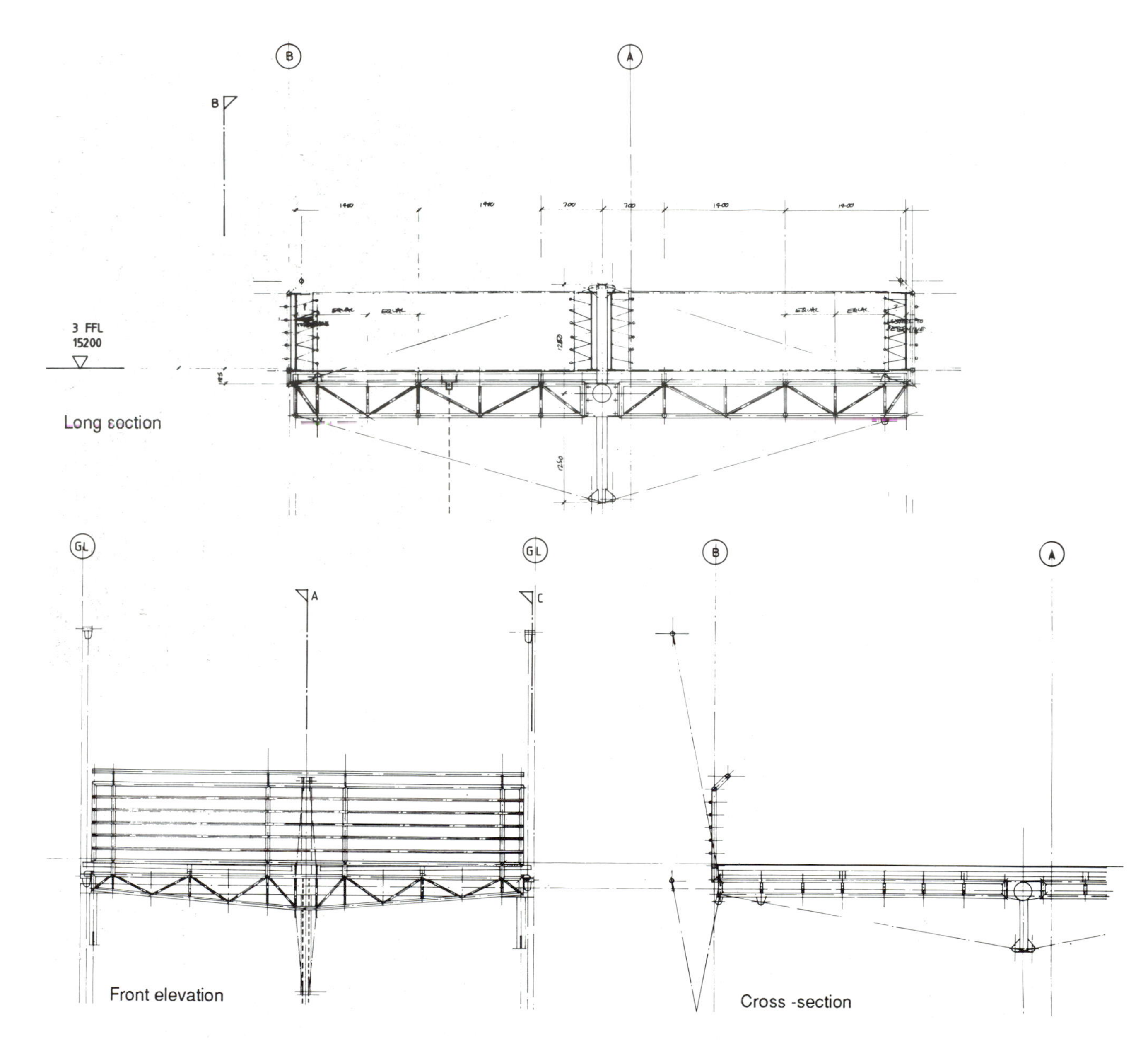

Fig. 35.13 *Detailed drawings for balconies at Hammersmith Development (architect Richard Rogers Partnership).*

also been adopted by the designers in the upgrading of social housing where balconies can be introduced to enhance south facing rooms.

35.3.4 Richard Rogers Partnership

Finally, there is another mode of detailing found in larger offices when a particular designer is dedicated to a certain aspect of detail. The closing case study is the work of the Richard Rogers Partnership similar to the ensemble of gangways and ladders that form a crisp filigree at the roofline of Lloyds (refer back to Fig. 33.24). Another example of these combined skills in the art of steel construction is the ship-shape balcony work to the new flats adjoining the partnership offices at Hammersmith (Figs 35.13 and 14).

35.4 ARTIST BLACKSMITHS

There are also individual designers such as Arno Jobst, Izzy Metzstein and John Outram whose work is closely linked to the new generation of artist blacksmiths who specialize in components rather than structures.

Fig. 35.14 *Balconies at Hammersmith Development 1989 (architect Richard Rogers Partnership).*

Fig. 35.15 *Railing and gate screens, Crown Reach, Vauxhall 1982 (architect Lacey and Jobst, artist blacksmith James Horrobin in association with the workshops of Richard Quinnell).*

Fig. 35.16 *Gates for Oriel House, Connaught Place, London 1984 (artist blacksmith James Horrobin in association with the workshops of Richard Quinnell).*

35.4.1 James Horrobin

This creative designer has worked with a range of architects in the production of gates and railings. The Crown Reach development (architects Lacey and Jobst) is distinguished by splendid metalwork screens between the building blocks (Fig. 35.15). The steel sections have been forged and shaped then finished with graphite paint. Another example from Horrobin's workshop are gates for Oriel House, Connaught Place, London (Fig. 35.16). Both these commissions were carried out in association with Richard Quinnell.

35.4.2 Robinson College, Cambridge

The most recent college built at Cambridge has some remarkable craftsmanship, particularly the door hinges and face metalwork designed for primary entrances and gates (Fig. 35.17). The artistry is due to the combined work of architect Izzy Metzstein and artist blacksmith Mrs J. Steiger. They are constructed from forged steel protected by galvanizing and paint.

Fig. 35.17 *Robinson College, Cambridge (architect Coia, McMillan and Metzstein, and artist blacksmith Mrs J. Steiger).*

35.4.3 John Outram

The materials used at the Isle of Dogs pumping station are standard tubular steel sections combined with flat bars. The design is redolent of the main elevation with the rondels and curves reflecting the forms of the pumping station (Fig. 35.18).

35.4.4 Richard Quinnell

Richard Quinnell has played a central role in reviving the art of blacksmithing by involving architects and designers to expand the creative aspect of the work. A typical example is the Swan Gates for St Hugh's College, Oxford, made to the designs by Lawrence Whistler, with detail work in execution by Alan Puddick (Fig. 35.19).

35.5 MATERIALS, TECHNIQUES, EQUIPMENT AND FINISHES

The following notes are taken from Richard Quinnell's foreword to the 1987 Building Centre Exhibition of nearly 100 pieces of work from members of the British Artist Blacksmiths Association [1]. Many illustrations in the preceding text come from this source.

Fig. 35.18 *Gates and screen to pumping station, Isle of Dogs, London 1988 (architect John Outram).*

Blacksmiths' work today still involves heating, hammering and forging ferrous metals, though the material is more likely to be steel than wrought iron, the last puddling furnace in Britain having been closed. If purists insist upon genuine wrought iron, then imported material must be obtained from France or Germany. Re-rolled wrought iron scrap is available but is expensive and of unreliable quality. A competent blacksmith can do anything with mild steel that can be done with wrought iron, including the most complex forge-welds. The two materials are indistinguishable in appearance and in performance for all practical purposes. Mixing mild steel and wrought iron is feasible provided that bare metal is protected from face to face contact in a wet environment. The ideal form of protection is galvanizing after fabrication, or zinc coating before fabrication if external bolted connections are to be made between differing ferrous metals.

Mild steel is available hot-rolled (termed 'black') in a wide range of round, square, rectangular, angle, tee, and half-round sections, usually in 6 m (20 ft) lengths, also heavy rolled structural angles, tees, channels, H- and I- beams. It is also produced in precision cold-drawn (termed 'bright') form in rounds, squares, rectangles, angles and hexagons. Tubes are also available (round, square and rectangular) in 'black' or 'bright' grades together with sheet and plate from paper thin to 100 mm (4 in) thick and more. Other forgeable metals used by artist/blacksmiths include stainless steels, copper, brass, forging bronzes, aluminium alloys and titanium.

The essential tools of the artist/blacksmith remain the coke or coal-fired forge, the anvil, hammer, tongs, and vice, chisels for cutting, punches for piercing or indenting, saws and files. To this basic armoury have been added machines for grinding, drilling, sawing, and turning. More recently gas heating and electric welding equipment, and most importantly, the power forging hammer have facilitated the increase in scale that characterizes the work of many modern

Fig. 35.19 *Swan Gates, St Hugh's College, Oxford (1980s), designed by Laurence Whistler, made by Richard Quinnell workshops.*

smiths. Nowadays, workshops are usually equipped with heavy lifting gear such as overhead cranes and fork-lift trucks, and smiths are exploring the possibilities offered by powerful hydraulic presses and profiling equipment that can be used to cut intricate shapes in heavy steel plate.

Forging exploits that property of wrought iron and steel, of softening when red-hot and thus being able to be shaped by bending, hitting or squeezing, rather like very stiff Plasticine. The metal becomes hard and springy again when it cools and the heating, forging, and cooling process can be repeated again and again without harm to the metal. The basic processes of blacksmithing are: drawing-down (thinning); jumping-up (thickening); bending; splitting; punching; twisting; and welding (joining by hammering together at high temperature). All decorative forgework is made in one of these ways, to which can be added the non-forging techniques of fusion-welding, removal of metal by machining or grinding, and cutting by burning.

All ferrous metals except stainless steels rust very rapidly in moist air and in the case of mild steel this can destroy outdoor work within its maker's lifetime if it is not protected. Outdoor pieces are therefore almost always finished with a high quality paint system including anti-corrosion primer and undercoats. Paint finishes often now contain graphite or mica, or may be brightly coloured. Metallic automobile paints are also used. Most smiths protect their work further by first coating it with metallic zinc, either by the hot-dip or flame-spray metallizing processes. Cor-Ten steel is unusual in that it develops a surface coat of rust and then stops corroding. The higher grades of stainless steel can usually be exposed without any protective coating. Indoor work can be simply burnished, lacquered and waxed to show the full texture of the forged surface.

Other finishes include patination by the burning-on of copper alloys, chemical treatments to produce coloured surfaces, electroplating, polishing, and gilding with gold leaf.

REFERENCE

1. British Artist Blacksmiths Association. For details of membership contact: Peter King, Rosebank Plaxtol, Sevenoaks, Kent, UK. Telephone: (44) (0)732 810729.

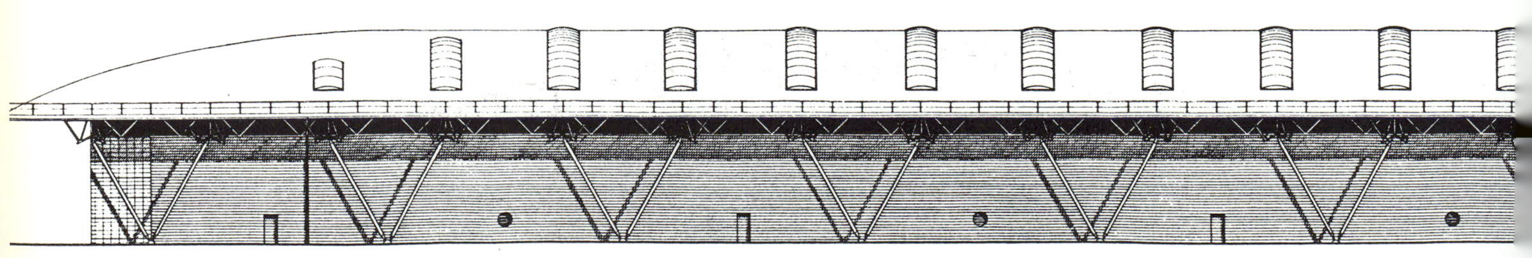

Stratford Market Depot, proposed Jubilee line extension, London Underground (architect Chris Wilkinson Associates: engineer Acer Consultants).

Part Six

Outstanding Contemporary Steel Architecture

IBM Headquarters, Bedfont Lake, London 1992 (architect Michael Hopkins and Partners: engineer Buro Happold).

36

The last 25 years

Dennis Sharp

36.1 PREAMBLE

This survey of outstanding world designs over the past 25 years demonstrates the use of steel in many forms. It looks at steel supported structures, at steel panelled structures and at constructions which use steel as a predominantly flexible and lightweight material. It looks at the many and various ways of designing excellent buildings in steel: at the Australian architect Glenn Murcutt's artists' studio house in North Sydney which employs corrugated sheeting, to the prefabricated and elemental type of construction employed by Richard Horden for his own house in Poole, Dorset, a structure that uses a limited range of steel tensile supports.

These examples of the application of steel are therefore universal, showing a wide range of ideas employed by some of the most inventive architects over the past three decades. In some cases where speed and economy of construction have been regarded as the criteria, the results have often proved spectacularly successful, producing a rational simplicity in design not seen for many years. This use of steel has emphasized the part this kind of technologically based architecture has played in the continuity of Modern Movement ideas, many of which were set on exploring the opportunities provided by the use of metal structures (e.g. the houses by Gropius and Muche).

Some of the more recent buildings have been constructed by efficient technical means and clearly display their simple structural lines as a means of architectural expression. Thus they have enriched the form potential of recent architecture without recourse either to historicism or the now outmoded fashion of what was referred to as Post-Modernism. Indeed in some cases the enrichment of the external expression of a basic steel shell – curved or straight – by decorative embellishments has rekindled a desire for craftsmanship, decoration and that most notable of traditions that was summed up in Le Corbusier's memorable phrase about the the 'Engineer's Aesthetic'.

In recent developments the lead has been given very largely by British firms of architects and engineers, although significant contributions to the genre have also come from Germany and France and as far afield as Japan and Australia.

A broad survey such as this can only touch upon a few selected examples, but in making a choice I have tried to provide as wide a range of examples as possible, innovation and variety, excellent design and cogent composition were the critical touchstones in my selection.

36.2 RESIDENTIAL BUILDINGS

36.2.1 Architect's own house, Highgate, London, 1968

Architects: John Winter and Associates
Structural engineer: Herbert Heller

This original house by a leading British architect, John Winter, acknowledges a life-long interest in the work of the architect Mies van der Rohe. However, it moves on, in terms of the use of materials, from the simple trabeated I-section architecture of Mies, although it retains the simplicity and directness of the Miesian aesthetic. Winter's house was one of the first examples in the UK of the use of Cor-Ten steel for domestic architecture. Basically a three-storey house, it is sited on a small wooded site adjacent to Highgate Cemetery.

The subdivision floor by floor reflects family needs. The ground floor relates to the gardens and the communal activities: cooking, dining, and entertaining. The first floor is a quiet buffer zone of bedrooms and bathrooms. The piano nobile is the second floor, with superb views in all directions and with ample quiet space for relaxation or work.

The construction comprises a welded frame in three 6.0 × 3.6 bays with 150 × 150 universal columns and relatively shallow 250 × 100 beams. The floors are in situ concrete achieving composite action between the steel and the RC by means of welded channels incorporated within the slabs. This device allowed beams of similar depth to be web for both wall and main beams.

The Cor-Ten sheathing is also welded and isolated from the main frame by 50 mm insulation. The double-glazed fixed windows or wall panels are set just behind the cladding with ventilation obtaining by pivoted insulated panels. The welding was performed by a sub-contractor of Ford of Dagenham, then on strike, who took considerable pains. The strike was lengthy and as a consequence the welds were eventually finished with emery paper. Skill has paid off, the Cor-Ten has a superb even patina some 24 years later.

Fig. 36.1 *(a) Floor plans; (b) detail view; (c) general view.*

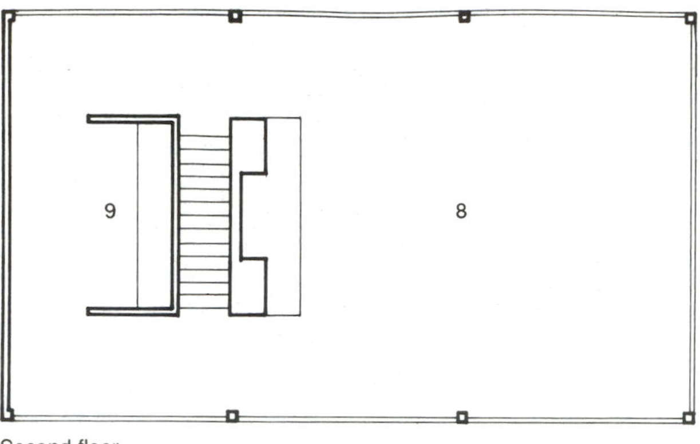

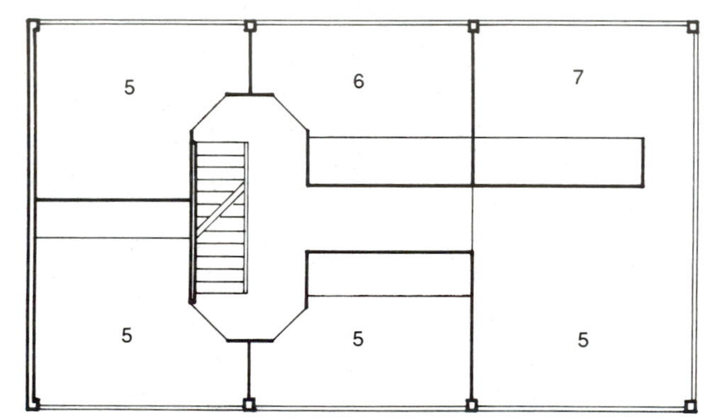

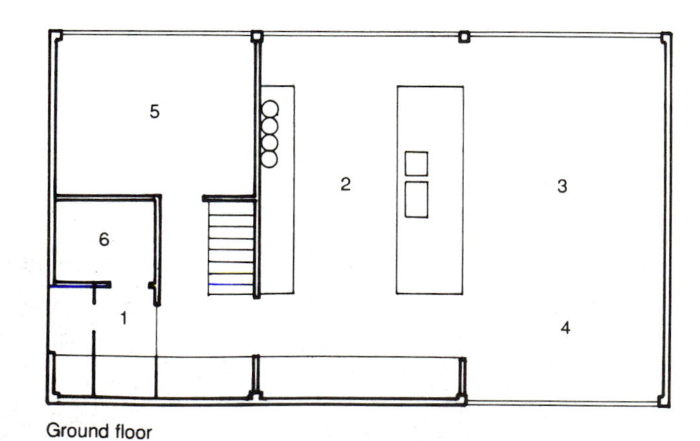

(b)

(c)

36.2.2 Artists' house, The Ball/Eastway House, Glenorie, Sydney, Australia, 1983 (1982–83)

Architect: Glenn Murcutt
Engineer: James Taylor of James Taylor and Associates, Mosman, Sydney, Australia

Situated in the bush countryside north of Sydney this artists' house is used for permanent living. The two artists for whom it was designed have built their own separate studios in the grounds. Today, with the ever-increasing expansion of Sydney, many new houses and roads have been developed nearby although the sense of isolation and uniqueness is little diminished. The house is situated on a rugged rock-strewn site amidst the local vegetation. It is a long, low, single-storey column and beam platform house, entirely constructed in and framed in steel, with a corrugated iron curved roof carried by cold-formed purlins secured to arched portals. Externally, the steel floor beams continue to support traditional duckboarded decking on hardwood joists.

Fig. 36.2 *(a) Isometric view (courtesy Alan Ogg:* Architecture in Steel; *(b) ground floor plan; (c) view from roadway; (d) interior.*

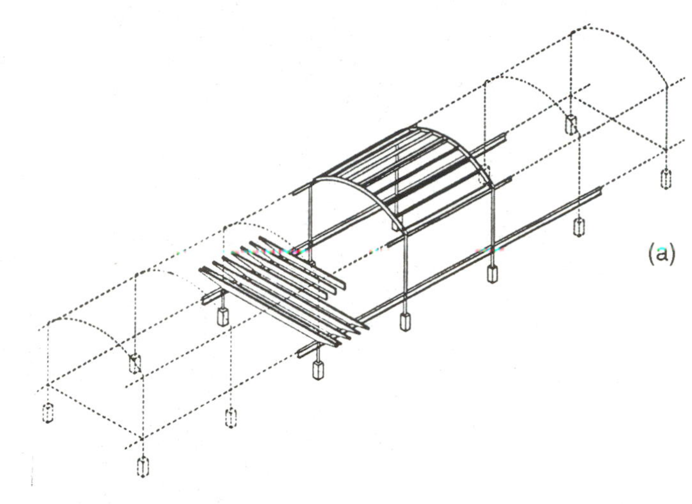

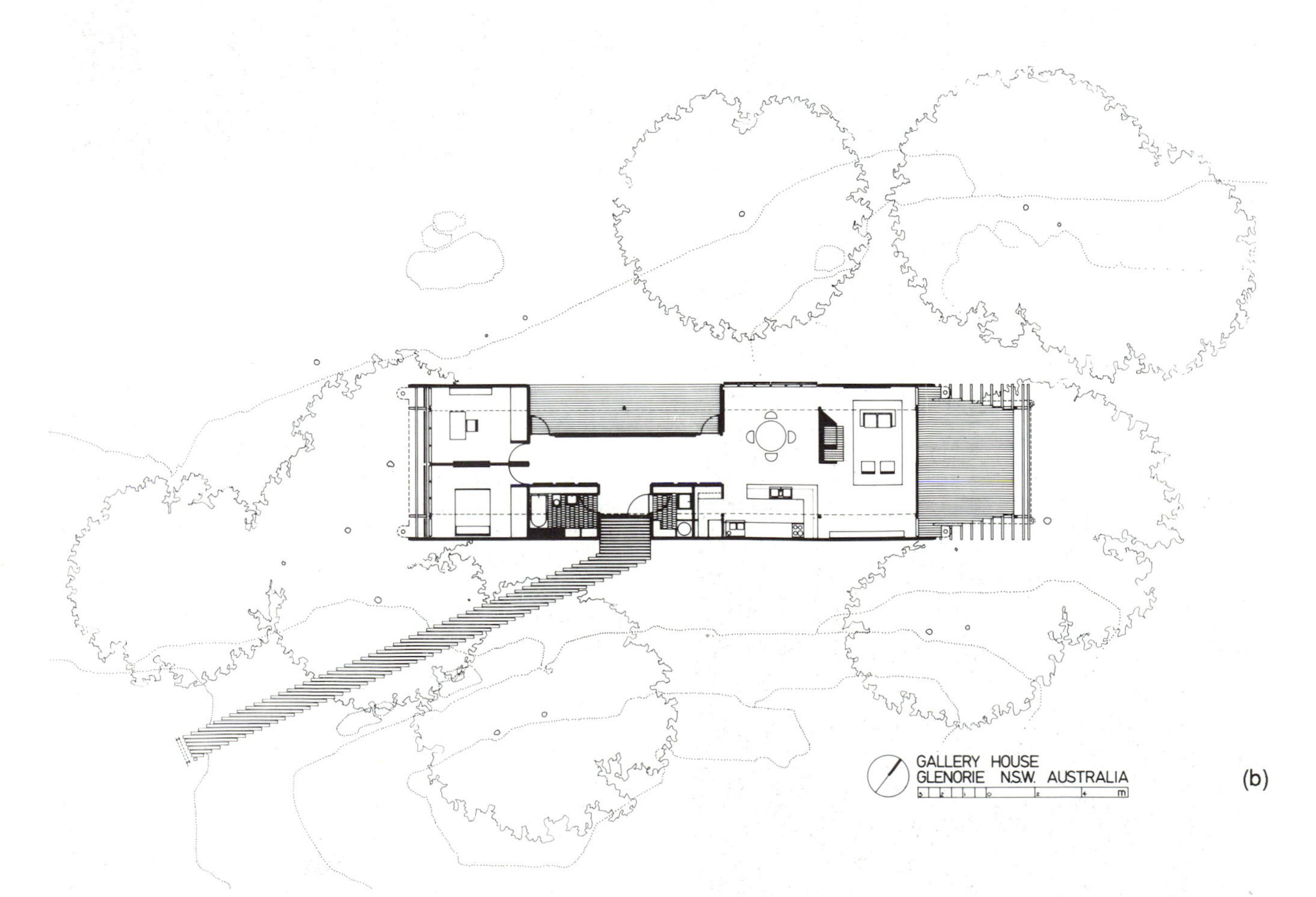

(c)

(d)

It sits poised above the undulating ground level on its six pairs of I-section columns protected from bush fires by complete coverage from an external sprinkler system. The envelope to roof and walls is formed in corrugated sheets to give further protection from fire spread. Solar insulation is provided by 100 mm rockwool and plasterboard internally and windows are protected by extensive roof overhangs and external adjustable metal Venetian blinds.

The house was designed, according to the architect, to provide the minimum of interference with nature and the existing site.

A small open-sided platform bridge runs from the car parking enclosure to the house itself, another precarious reminder of the vulnerability of living in the countryside. Adjacent to the house are two commercial farmyard Dutch barns purchased straight out of a catalogue but ingeniously converted into spacious and waterproof artists' studios. The aesthetic of farmyard type buildings adopted here is part of the local vernacular and has been carefully assimilated by Murcutt in this innovative and influential domestic scheme.

Fig. 36.3 *(a) Street level plan; (b) cross section; (c) garden elevation; (d) interior of first floor.*

36.2.3 Architect's own house, Downshire Hill, London (1975–76)

Architect: Michael and Patty Hopkins
Engineer: Anthony Hunt Associates

Built by the architects for themselves and their three children this two-storey, steel and glass house in Hampstead has a short 12 m frontage to an elegant London street. Designed in 1975 it was a bold, and indeed controversial, attempt to create an up to date version of the Modern Movement glass house. Within it, light is everywhere, reflected through the perimeter windows creating a truly three-dimensional four-square crystalline enclosure. Its two floors are freely planned and it is approached by a steel footbridge. In a sense, it is a transposition of the antecedent case study steel houses designed by people like Charles and Ray Eames on the west coast of the United States some 30 years earlier, but in some ways it is very different. It recognizes the currency of the energy question and is a house with a remarkably fast thermal response. It also takes into account – particularly in this area of London – the need to create a well crafted artefact. It is heated by gas-fired warm air and the whole heat consumption during the winter period has proved extremely economic. The glass walls on the street and garden sides are backed by aluminium reflective slats which are used to control heat gain. In the winter period special 'duvet' quilts were to be press buttoned to some areas of glazing in cold spells but they have not proved necessary.

The house is based on a grid of 4 × 2 m, enabling the steel structural sections to be kept small (tubular columns 63.5 × 63.5 mm) but large enough to eliminate a secondary structure. Perimeter columns are placed at 2 m. Before construction a number of different plan arrangements were developed with partitions along the lines of the structural grid. However, the house is dominated by its generous large spaces and transparent appearance.

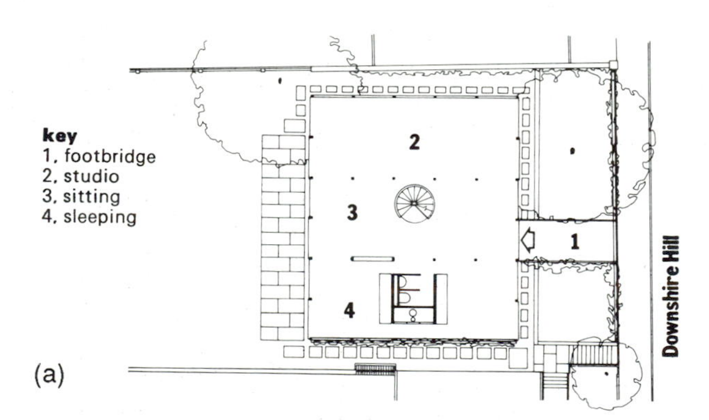

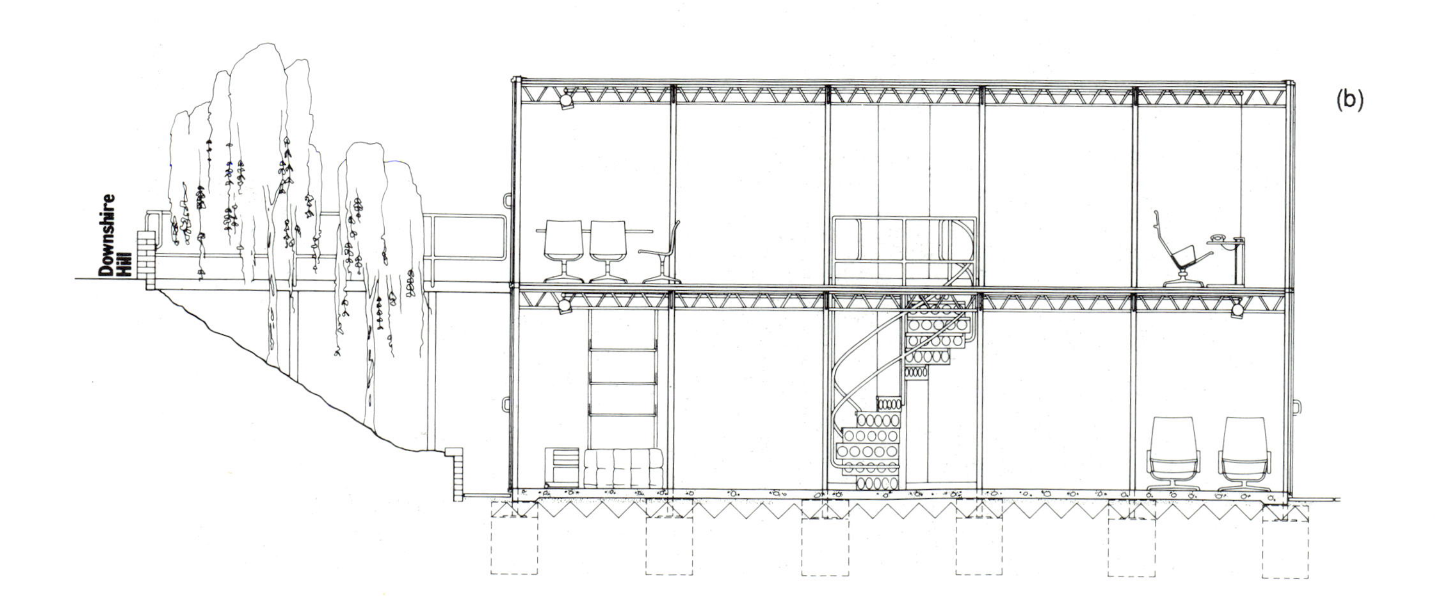

(c)

(d)

Fig. 36.4 *(a) Interior; (b) elevation; (c) general view; (d) detail of exterior.*

36.3 EDUCATION BUILDINGS

36.3.1 Queen's Inclosure Middle School, Cowplain, Hampshire (1990)

Architect: C. Stansfield-Smith, Hampshire County Architect
D. J. Morris and A. Upton, Project Architects
Engineer: R. J. Wilkinson and Partners
Contractor: Wates Construction (South) Ltd

Perhaps not the most spectacular or original of the long line of Hampshire school designs that have emerged since Colin Stansfield-Smith became County Architect, but certainly the best known, having won the BBC Design Award in 1990. It also received a RIBA National Award in 1990 and the President's Gold Medal in 1991.

The Inclosure School's uncompromisingly modern aesthetic relies on the simplest of structural statements – two shallow curved barrel roofs that are separated by a central top-lit spine. These two vaulted roofs serve as sun reflectors which direct the sun's rays back through simple horizontal projecting brise soleil or sun scoop blinds on the north side; on the south side the process is reversed. The barrels also define the major areas devoted to open teaching with an area subdivided only by white painted blockwork partitions. The simple steel tubular structure is unobtrusive but performs its structural purpose in an elegant and inventive manner.

Set on the edge of dense woodland, the tall windows offer magnificent views. The building is seen as a contrast to surrounding nature and as a simple unobtrusive low profiled structure that effectively uses the surrounding Queen's Inclosure Woodland as a backdrop. It does, of course in reverse, offer marvellous views out for the children and teachers. It has also been designed in such a way that it can be easily extended as the school itself grows.

(a)

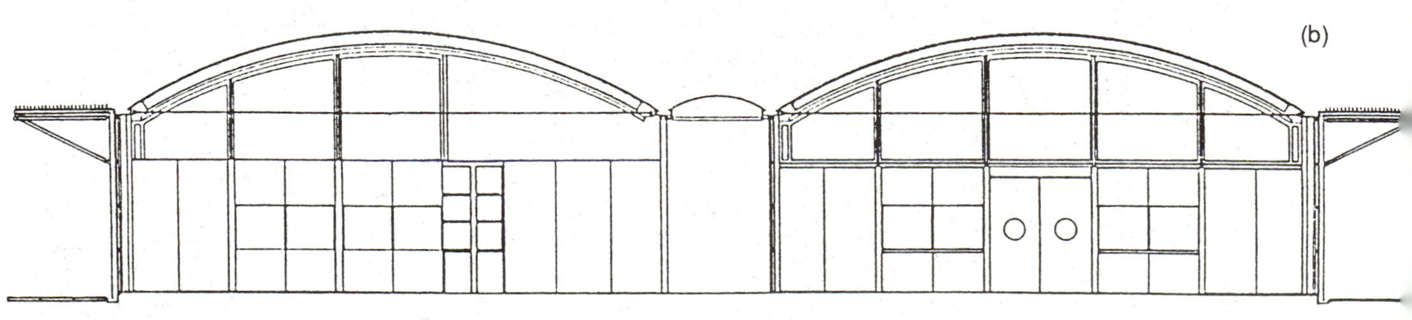

(b)

(c)

(d)

Fig. 36.5 *(a) Ground floor plan; (b) interior; (c) general view; (d) detail of elevation.*

36.3.2 Hysolar Research Building, Stuttgart University (1987)

Architect: Günter Behnisch and Partners

In keeping with its programme, a solar research institute within a technological university, this steel-framed building really does give the appearance of a laboratory, perhaps even an experiment. This it certainly is, with its oversailing solar collectors, separated elements and glazed walls, all of which is so typical of Behnisch's design interest in the unity of diversity. In his work disparate elements are brought together in a seemingly haphazard arrangement but one which really has a strict underlying logic and purposeful functional intention.

It is in a sense analogous to Jazz form in music which appears freely improvised but is controlled by arrangement, expertise and artistry. In this case we have an experimental building housing experiments and expressing itself through a conspicuously experimental architectural style. Its idiosyncrasies are not easily justifiable, with sloping mullions to the external glazing, horizontal windows and metal catwalks cutting through the volume of the building. However, its animated character is undoubtedly exciting, its planned chaos, is an expression of faith and an inspirational piece of building research in itself.

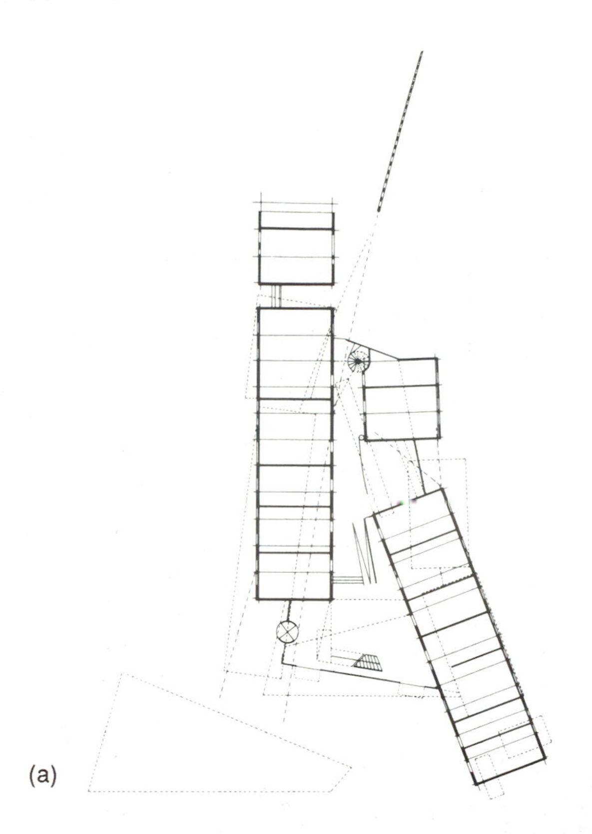
(a)

(b)

(c)

(d)

Fig. 36.6 *(a) General view; (b) plan; (c) the building as an integration of related systems.*

36.3.3 The Sainsbury Centre for Visual Arts, University of East Anglia, Norwich (1977)

Architect: Foster Associates
Consulting engineer: Anthony Hunt Associates

This great metal barn situated in the tranquil rural surroundings of Lasdun's University of East Anglia (1964–70) is elegantly detailed with huge glazed end walls and panelled side walls and roof. It is a single, huge volume enclosed by a 2.5 m deep exposed tubular steel space frame. Technically, the walls and roof form continuous trusses and all the service elements are housed within this double outer wall zone. It is fully air conditioned.

One of the key buildings of the international Hi-Tech movement of the 1970s, it provides a stark contrast, with its metal cladding, to the multi-layered concrete architecture of Sir Denys Lasdun's University. Inside it is a highly tuned and well engineered shed designed to house art, its study and research. It was entirely sponsored by private funds. It is a building of classic simplicity built at half the cost of conventional gallery construction.

At the Sainsbury Centre Foster further developed his ideas on the flexibility of components. At the time his architecture was moving towards simplicity of component connections; thus the three types of panel – solid, grille and glazed – used on the exterior of the building were all interchangeable simply by the manipulation of six bolts. Any part of the walls or roofs of the buildings can be changed in only a few minutes from glazing to solid panel, or vice versa.

The Sainsbury Centre received the R.S. Reynolds International Award of the AIA in 1979, the Structural Steel and Finniston Award in 1978 and a national RIBA Award also in 1978.

(a)

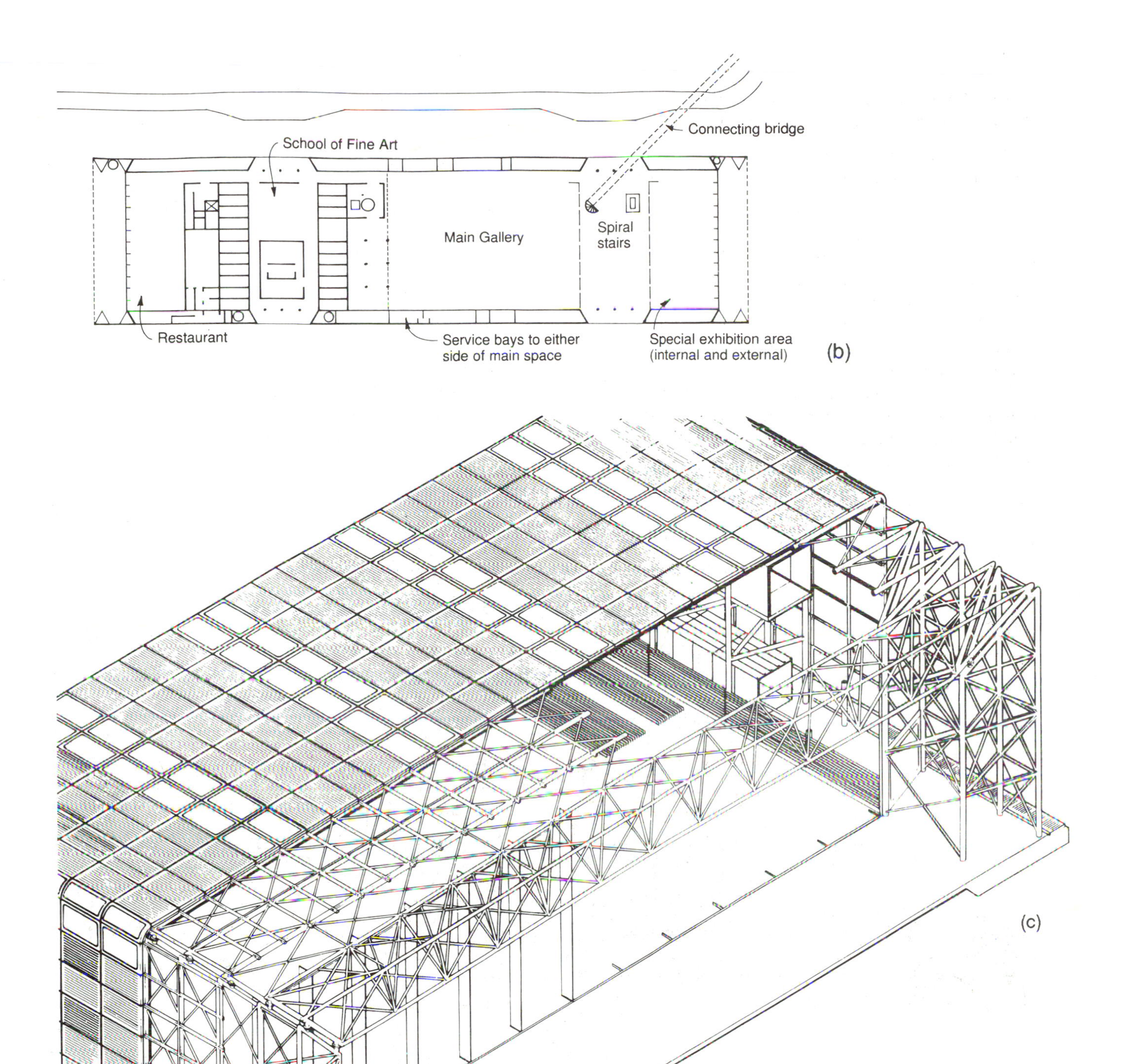
Connecting bridge
School of Fine Art
Main Gallery
Spiral
stairs
Restaurant
Service bays to either
side of main space
Special exhibition area
(internal and external)

(b)

(c)

36.4 CIVIC AND CULTURAL BUILDINGS

36.4.1 State of Illinois Center, Chicago, USA (1979–85)

Architect: Helmut Jahn and Partners (formerly Murphy and Jahn)

The State of Illinois Center, Chicago, houses 56 State Agencies with 4600 employees. It was opened in May 1985. The State Governor's office is situated on the 16th floor. It is quite unlike any other building in the downtown business district of Chicago. On two sides it follows the gridiron pattern of the great American city, but its huge conical container form on the other two sides, characterized by the sweeping curved facade, directs attention towards its fully glazed atrium interior. It is an extraordinary building which has not been without its problems from a sun/heat penetration point of view. The main entrance to the building is through the lower doors of the curved facade which lead from a rather restricted open plaza which is given emphasis by the sloping sides of the glass building. Certainly, it is one of the least successful elements in the whole ensemble. However, what works so well from an architectural and monumental aspect is the skylit atrium which has been carefully chosen as a building form in opposition to the plethora of rectangular cubic setback Chicago building volumes. The setbacks provided by the canted facade divide the building into three tiers with floor areas of 77 000–48 000 sq ft and each tier is vertically striped in silver and opaque blue panels some 2 ft 6 in wide. Like an Anthroposophical drawing, the shade of blue becomes progressively lighter the higher it goes up the building.

Fig. 36.7 *(a) Plan at street level; (b) view of skylit atrium; (c) Illinois Center in the context of the gridiron pattern of Chicago; (d) atrium interior with free-standing elevator towers.*

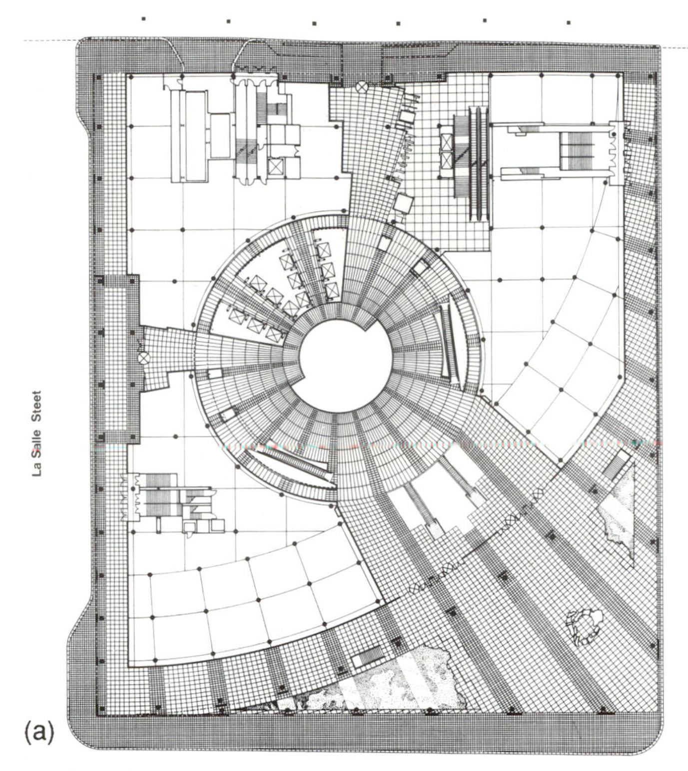

(a)

The construction of the building was carried out with a simple structural steel framework resting on normal Chicago-type caisson foundations with a composite metal deck and concrete floor system.

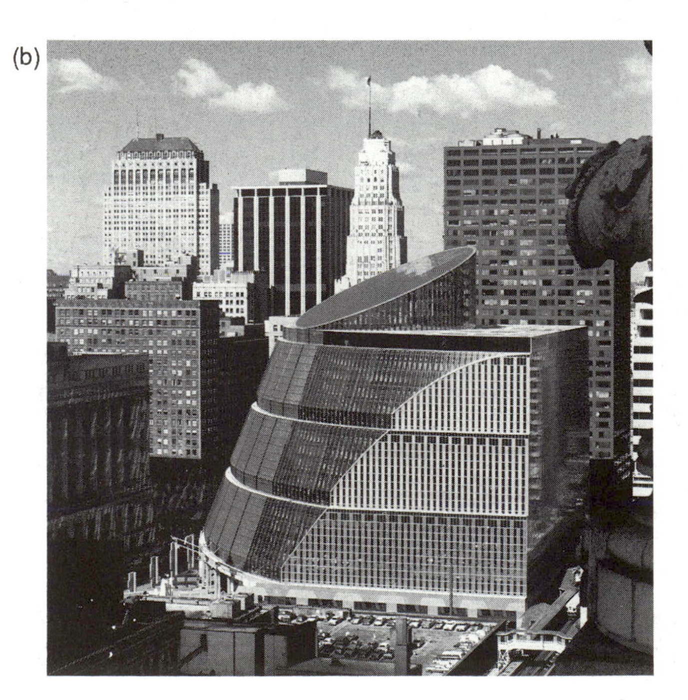
(b)

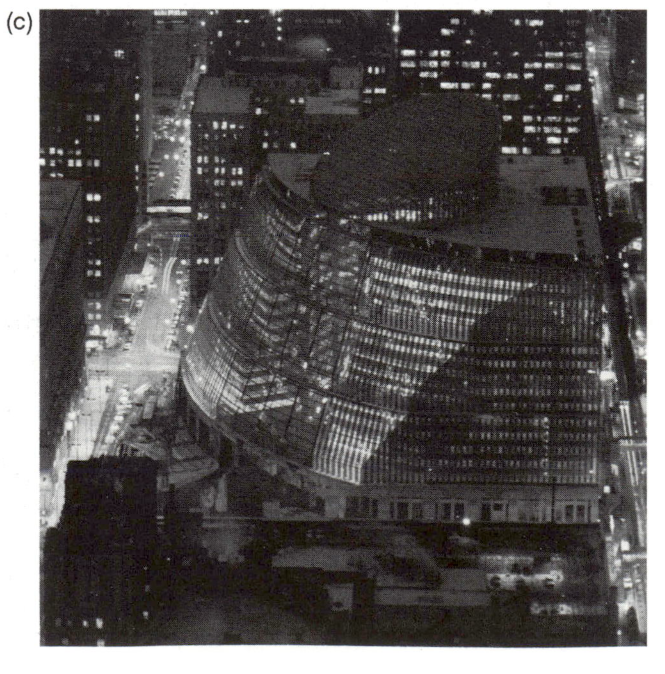
(c)

(d)

Fig. 36.8 *(a) Isometric view from NW; (b) elevation to public square; (c) aerial view;*

36.4.2 The Georges Pompidou Centre, Place de Beaubourg, Paris (1977)

Architects: Renzo Piano and Richard Rogers
Engineer: Ove Arup and Partners

The most important international competition building of postwar Europe, the Pompidou Centre in Paris has exceeded all expectations in becoming the most discussed, most liked and most visited cultural complex in the world. When first completed it was considered one of the wonders of the modern world with its exposed fretwork of clearly expressed structure and services and its great diagonal circulation escalators, as well as its brightly coloured facades and open planning. It has been referred to as a built piece of *Archigram* architectural design deriving from the British avant-garde rather than the French (at a time when Paris was still largely under the shadow of Le Corbusier). That it has been totally subsumed into Parisian popular culture and life would seem to justify the faith the two designers had in its technology not as fiction but as buildable fact. Perhaps not as well detailed as either Piano or Rogers's later work, it was nevertheless a well built structure largely in structural steelwork supplied by Krupps, with Pont-a-Maison making the large cast tubes. Practically, the design achieved a new standard in open space flexibility. The structural and services functions were expressed in the perimeter walls of the building and the inside could be freely subdivided to provide for a multitude of institutional and public uses.

The Pompidou Centre was designed to reflect change and to encourage changes to take place in a building which allows people the freedom to 'do their own thing'. It was conceived as a giant Meccano set rather than a formal group of enclosures. The basic concept is one of extreme simplicity and comprises a series of clear span volumes stacked one above the other supported on 2.5 m deep trusses. The sizes are gargantuan with trusses of 45 m length at 12.8 m centres. These in turn are carried by a tubular colonnade along both long facades. The scale of the building explains the remark by Sir Ove Arup that the challenge of the Pompidou Centre was equal to the difficulties surmounted at Sydney Opera House. The concept which came from Peter Rice, an engineer with Arup's, attracted the enthusiastic support of Piano and Rogers. The bending stresses imposed upon each column are countered by 'Gerberettes', a pin-jointed cantilever bracket which receives each truss whilst its free end is held downwards by slender steel rods fixed to ground anchors. This balancing arrangement gives a 7.6 m extension to the exterior volume, thereby providing space for services on the eastern facade whilst the western frontage is reserved for public access via escalators, lifts and walkways. Longitudinal stability is provided through the steel floor

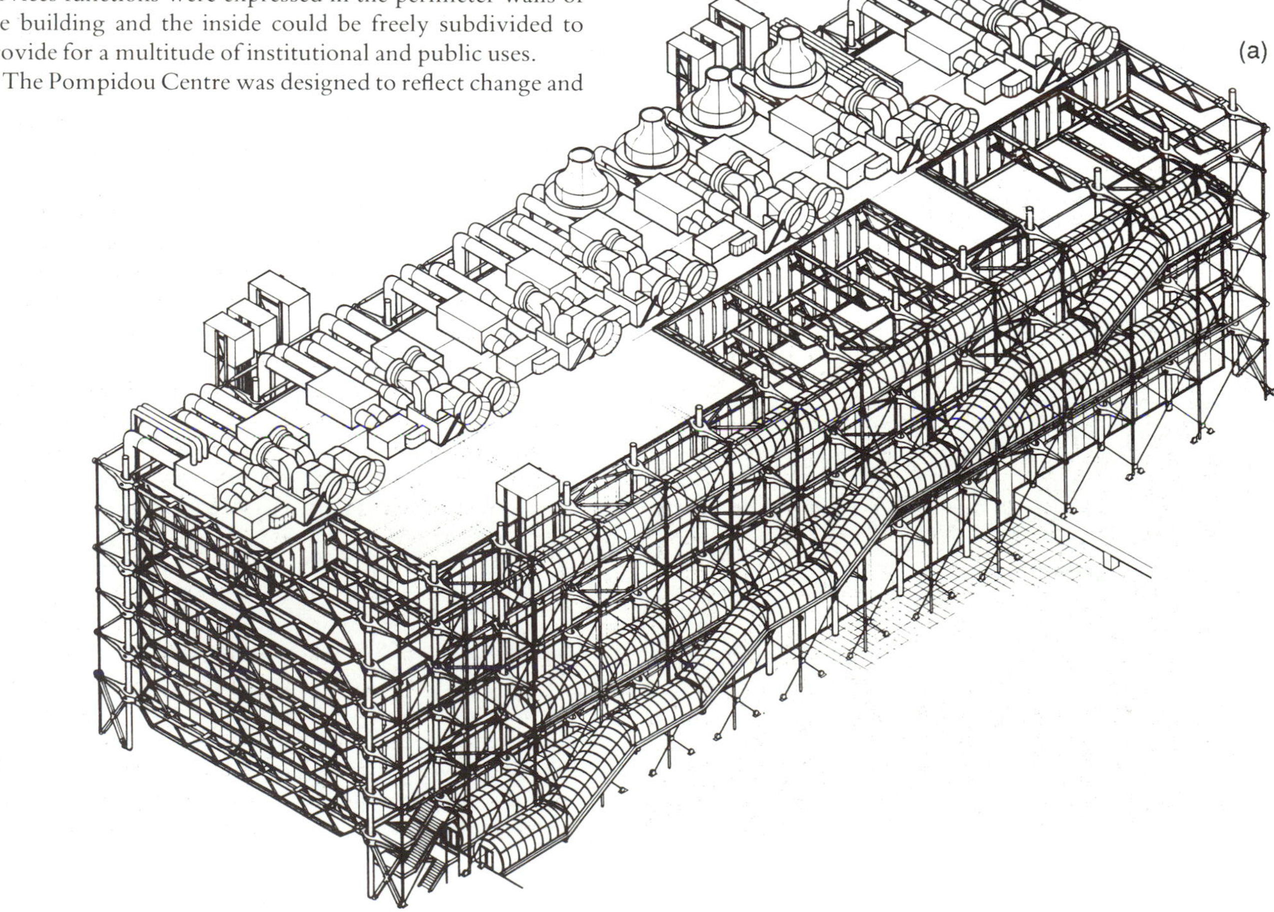

(b)

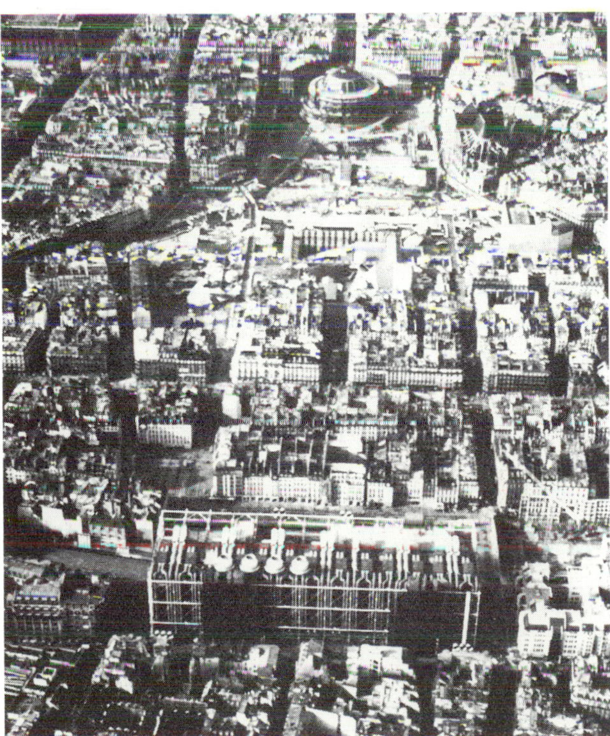

(c)

beams, acting in concert with the tubular columns and in conjunction with concrete floor slabs and internal bracing. Externally, Vierendeel portal frames encompass the end walls with a diagrid of 62 mm rods forming continuous bracing along the extreme edge of the main facades. A special feature of the construction is the use of machined components for connections as in mechanical engineering; there were also many parts that were threaded together. All this work required much tighter tolerances than those normally needed in structural engineering. Site welding was limited to end-to-end connections of the 850 mm diameter columns, no mean task since the metal thickness was around 85 mm. The Gerberettes were probably the most difficult component to fabricate. The casting weighed more than 17 tonnes had to be formed and machined to very fine limits. The total weight of steel erected in 12 months amounted to 13 000 tonnes with an additional 750 tonnes to provide temporary bracing. The fortunate width of Parisian boulevards meant that the trusses could be taken at night from the station at La Villette down to Rue Sebastopol for the daytime process of erection (two bays at a time to attain a balanced structure at each stage of the erection process).

The externally exposed steelwork has been subjected to extensive treatment to ensure maximum protection: sand-blasting (some column work was cold chiselled), zinc spraying, primer, micaceous iron oxide in two coats, then epoxy resin paint finished with polyurethane. Recoating has taken place 15 years later.

The rectangular plan of the Pompidou Centre is divided into 13 bays of 12.8 m width each supported by a standard frame of beams spanning onto the Gerberettes which rest on the columns and are restrained by the ties. Each frame supports six floors and is simply connected to the next one. Through this ingenious methodology a neat, repetitive facade emerged which acts as a perfect foil to the newly created square for the public.

Fig. 36.8 *(contd)*
(d) isometric showing general arrangement of the repeated structural bay; (e) elevation; (f) typical upper floor plan; (g) section through primary circulation zone. (d), (e), (g) courtesy Alan Ogg: Architecture in Steel.

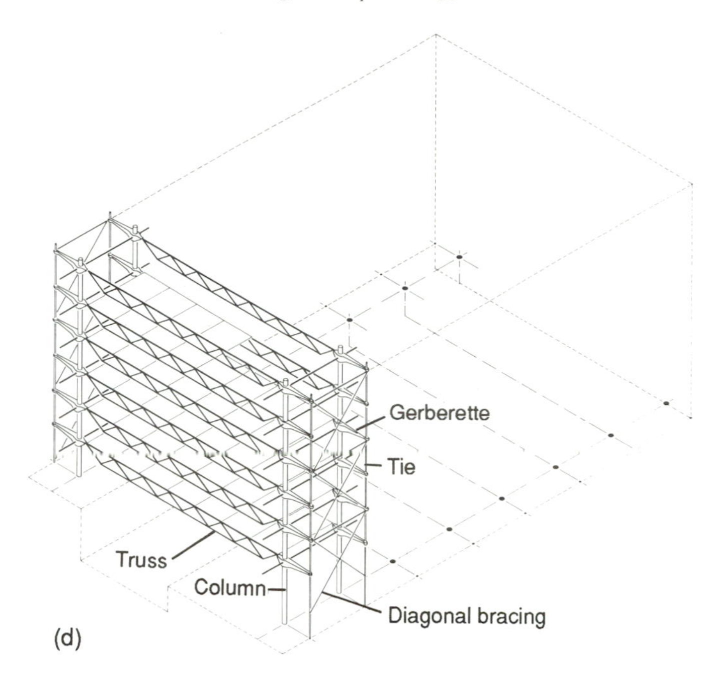

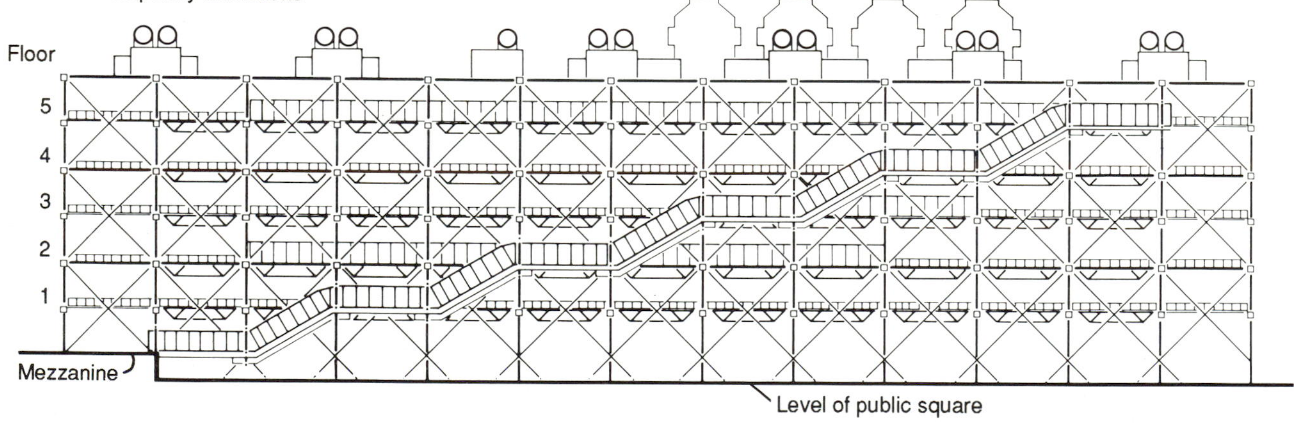

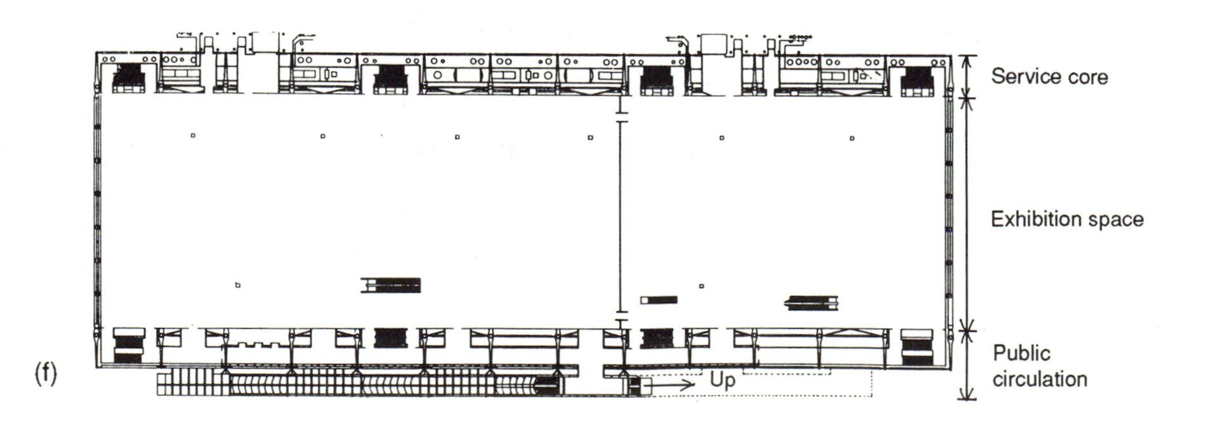

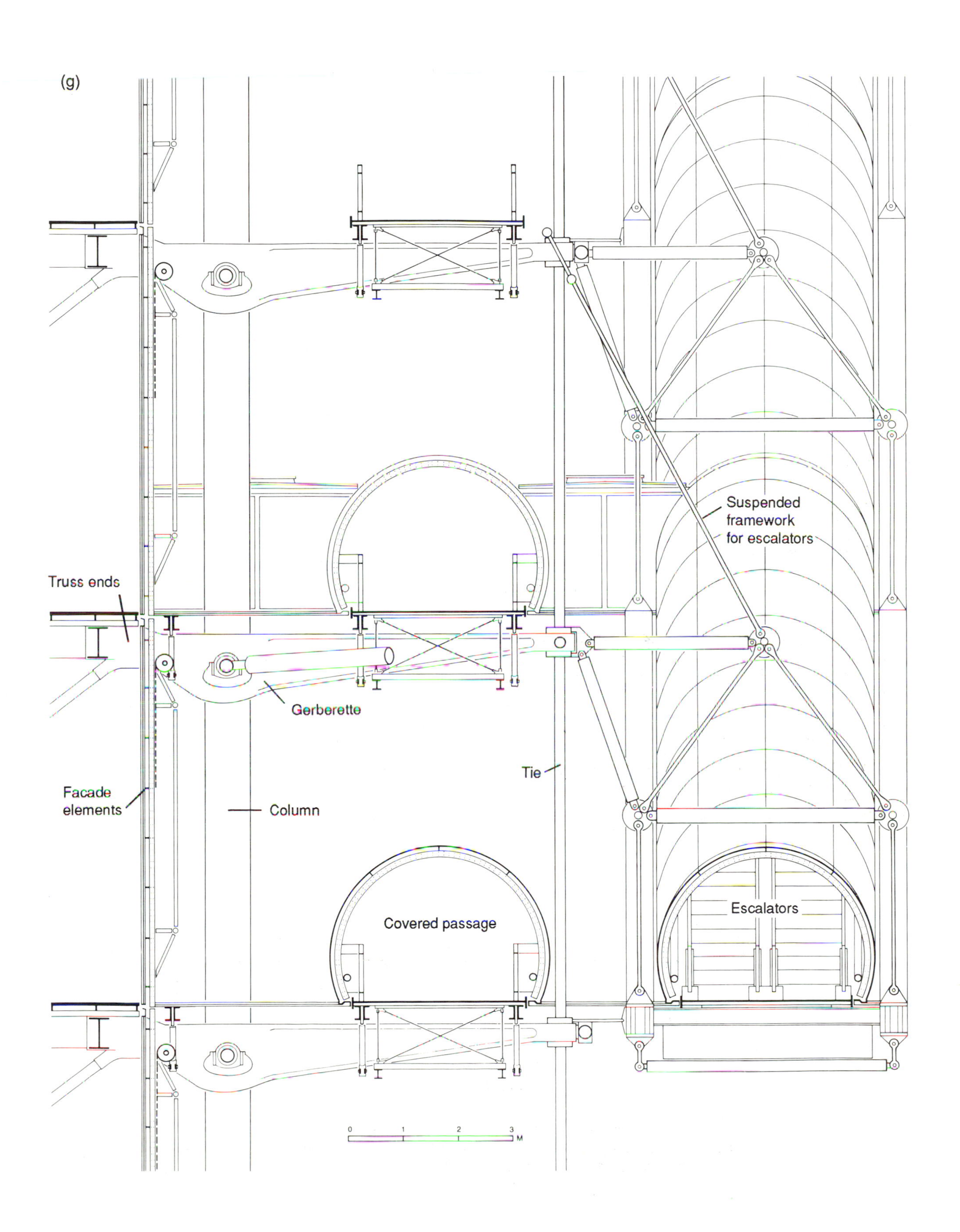
(g)
Suspended framework for escalators
Truss ends
Gerberette
Tie
Facade elements
Column
Covered passage
Escalators
0
1
2
3
M

Fig. 36.9 *(a) Detail of modular facade below roof canopy; (b) general view; (c) signeage; (d) enamelled steel door with painting by Le Corbusier.*

36.4.3 Centre Le Corbusier, Zurich, Switzerland (1967)

Architects: Le Corbusier and Heidi Weber
Cladding engineer: Jean Prouvé

The last of the great architect's buildings originally designed to accommodate an ambitious exhibition on mankind now houses a collection of Le Corbusier's own work. Designed a decade after the Ronchamp chapel, it was also a radical departure from his normal work. It is steel framed; one of the few examples (others include a 1937 pavilion at the Paris Exhibition of that year and the Philips Pavilion – designed in conjunction with Xenakis – Brussels Expo, 1958) of the use of the material in Le Corbusier's extensive *oeuvre*. It was also designed in collaboration: a unique gesture in an architect whose individuality was always carefully guarded. The pavilion is, as in so much of Le Corbusier's work, a microcosm of a larger symbolic world; a world within a world, a form within a form. Under the great folded steel roof rests a smaller core pavilion constructed from steel curtain wall panels proportioned according to the 'Modulor' principles and inset with either brightly coloured enamelled steel sheets or glass. These panels are structurally self-supporting, as are the steel enclosing asymmetrical umbrella roofs that are carried to the ground by huge hollow rectangular columns welded from steel plate. The references to the classical portico are quite clear in the shaping of this roof. The roofs achieve more than an architectural stylistic reference, for practically they protect the terrace that sits above the exhibition halls from inclement weather.

The masterpiece is distinguished by fine Swiss workmanship, the donation of the Centre Le Corbusier to the City of Zurich by Heidi Weber ensuring that this elegant pavilion will be properly maintained in perpetuity.

(a)

(c)

(b)

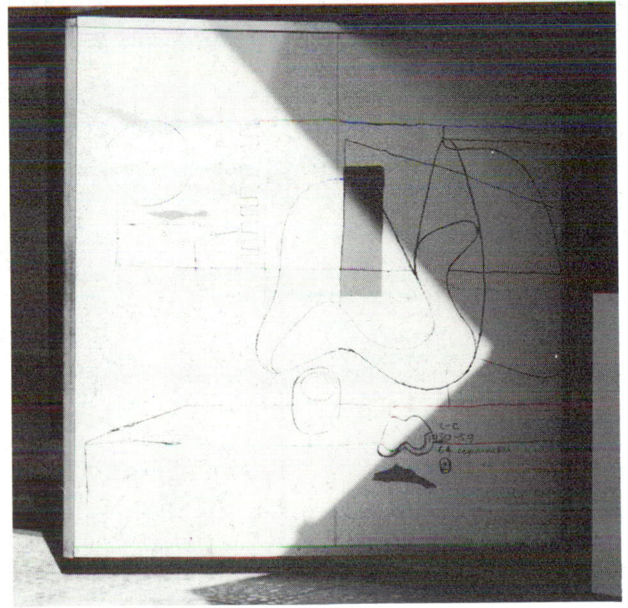

(d)

Fig. 36.10 *(a) Central space, Eisenstadt; (b) general view, Eisenstadt; (c) rooflight, Eisenstadt; (d) earth station, Aflenz.*

36.4.4 Austria ORF Radio Stations: Salzburg, Aflenz, Innsbruck, Eisenstadt and Graz (1968–81)

Architect and engineer: Gustav Peichl

One of Austria's most exciting post-war architects, Prof. Gustav Peichl, has gained international attention with his various projects for ORF, the Austrian TV and radio company. Since the late 1960s when he began designing ORF studios he has built six notable examples as well as an extension to the central broadcasting studios in Vienna. His radio station Aflenz (1976–79) was a conservationist project and built in a prohibited area in the countryside. Peichl's solution was to construct an underground building with the large metal radio antenna being the only visible object in this landscape. However, all the other famous ORF studios including the examples in Salzburg, Innsbruck, Graz and Eisenstadt were designed in a machine-like manner. They embody flexibility, functional efficiency and create a modern 20th century technological aesthetic.

(a)

(b)

(c)

(d)

Fig. 36.11 *(a) Site plan; (b) concourse plan; (c) long section; (d) entrance facade; (e) concourse; (f) canopy; (g) station level.*

36.4.5 London Airport, Stansted, Essex (1991)

Architect: Foster Associates
Structural engineering: Ove Arup and Partners and BAA Consultancy

Foster's Stansted is a radical departure in airport design. Built on the site of the former Stansted Aerodrome, it provides London with its third major airport created by a Government decision in 1979. The new terminal has so far taken 10 years to construct. It consists of three main building elements: the huge steel and glass single-storey terminal concourse building, which is connected to a new underground British Rail station, and the airside satellite departure and arrival buildings, of which there will be four on completion.

The airport concept is based on the simple idea that passengers should see the whole activity of the runway from the terminal and be quickly conveyed by rail links to departure points in the satellites. All the buildings are extendable and the capacity of the airport will be increased from 8 million persons per annum to a maximum of 15 million persons per annum as required.

Foster Associates have made a definite decision about the relative permanent and impermanent aspects of the scheme, the external envelope is relatively permanent while the elements within it are all treated as 'temporary' structures. Thus, the shops, food courts, luggage areas, toilets, etc. are constructed as 'demountable' cabins and are all serviced from a duct below the main floor.

The rural setting in which the buildings exist is unusual and the architects have succeeded in fitting the massive terminal structure – which in section seems to reflect the proportions of the Baths of Caracalla – elegantly and lightly amongst the Essex trees. The compact way in which the single-storey terminus fits into the landscape also belies its enormous size. It measures 198 × 198 m across the roof which form a continuous rigid structure without movement joints. Thermal movement and wind loading is taken up by flexing the steel members themselves. The drainage of this vast roof area is by a syphonic drainage system, without falls.

The floor of the concourse is an entirely separate reinforced concrete frame structure. The key element within the concourse is the modular structural 'tree'. There are 36 of these steel trees each measuring 3.5 m × 3.5 m × 17 m high. They were manufactured off site and set into prepared foundation pods. The steel erectors attached the branches to

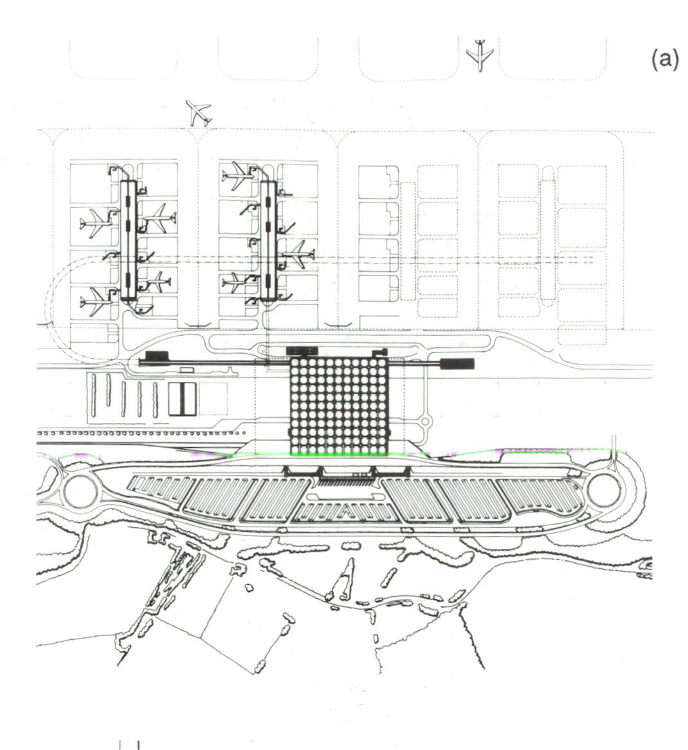

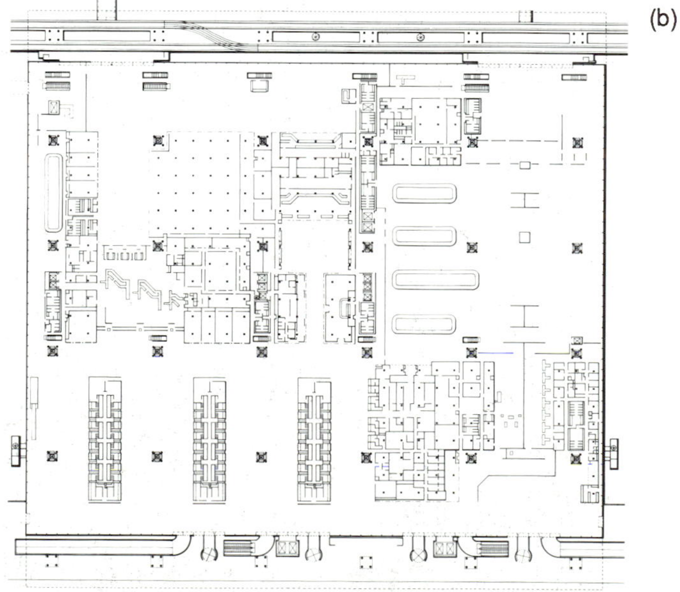

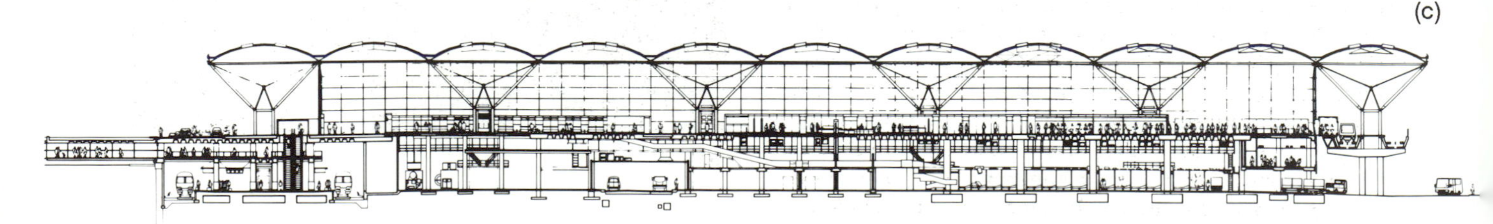

(d)

(e)

(f)

(g)

the base structure by four grid line beams and eight tension rods. These tree pavilions incorporate all the services within the roof support structure. At the top of each is an intricate rooflight that allows natural light to flood through the whole space. The same basic modular design is followed for the canopies on two sides of the building and the articulation of the architecture is based on this unit of construction, creating a wonderful unity and clarity of design intention.

36.4.6 Royal Exchange Theatre, Cotton Exchange, Manchester (1976)

Architect: Levitt Bernstein Associates
Engineer: Ove Arup and Partners

Erected within the historic Cotton Exchange building in Central Manchester, the Exchange looks more like a stranded alien space module than a theatre. At the cost of £1m in the mid-1970s it seemed an expensive piece of hardware, but its cost and its purpose in this venerable old building have proved most worthwhile and it has housed some memorable performances by a company that has achieved an international reputation.

The theatre, a suspended steel structure, is a magical experience in itself. With its seven sided centralized auditorium it is basically a theatre in the round, with only limited facilities for flying scenery.

It can house audiences of up to 750 seated on its three levels, the upper two of which are suspended from the roof trusses by steel rods.

Having solved the major acoustical problems of the vast existing cathedral-like space by totally enclosing the new auditorium, it was found that the existing floor was not strong enough to support 750 people at one time. Alternative means of support had to be devised, from which the chief characteristics of the structure developed. Two giant welded tubular trusses spanning 30 m and nearly 5 m deep were fixed to the four great piers that hold up the Exchange's dome; similar secondary beams span between the main trusses, completing a square on plan. Within the square seven radial steel roof trusses define the seven sided space of the auditorium itself. The main square framework of trusses also supports the two levels of galleries which are hung from the roof on inch thick steel rods.

(a)

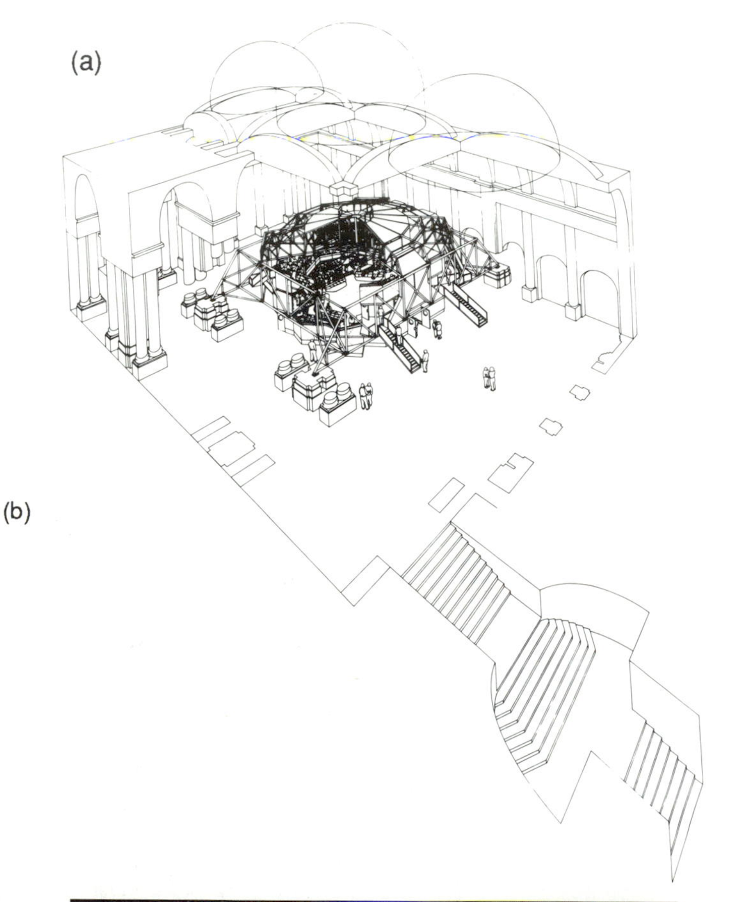

(b)

(c)

Fig. 36.12 *(a) Structural concept; (b) theatre frame within context of existing building; (c) auditorium.*

Fig. 36.13 *(a) Plan; (b) elevation.*

36.4.7 Darling Harbour Exhibition Centre, Sydney, Australia (1985–89)

Architect: Cox, Richardson and Taylor
Engineer: Ove Arup and Partners

This 25 000 m^2 exhibition centre provides flexible space within five main halls designed to be used either separately or jointly. Each hall can be closed off from its neighbour by the mechanically operated sliding walls which are suspended from stacked gantries in the narrow service zones between halls.

The main public and circulation space allows separate or combined access to the five halls and is concentrated on a mezzanine level which extends the length of the eastern facade. Loading bays and ancillary facilities for exhibitors are located along the western side of the building.

Each hall is separately air conditioned with supply air delivered by exposed overhead ducts suspended from the prismatic trusses. Other services such as water drainage, electricity, compressed air and telephone are distributed within the floor slab located on a 6 m two-way grid.

The cable stayed structure is identical over each hall and achieves a clear span enclosure of 87 × 60 m in plan, with a clear height of 15 m. Fully welded primary prismatic trusses span the long dimension of each hall are suspended from the mast heads by solid mild steel rods which vary in diameter from 50 mm to 90 mm. All structural connections are pin-jointed using stainless steel pins. The primary and secondary trusses are exposed internally and support a steel roof deck set with falls to rainwater gutters located above each truss. Walls are either fully glazed or of sandwich panel construction. The 32 m long masts were delivered in one piece. The structural details are influenced by those of the Inmos building by Richard Rogers.

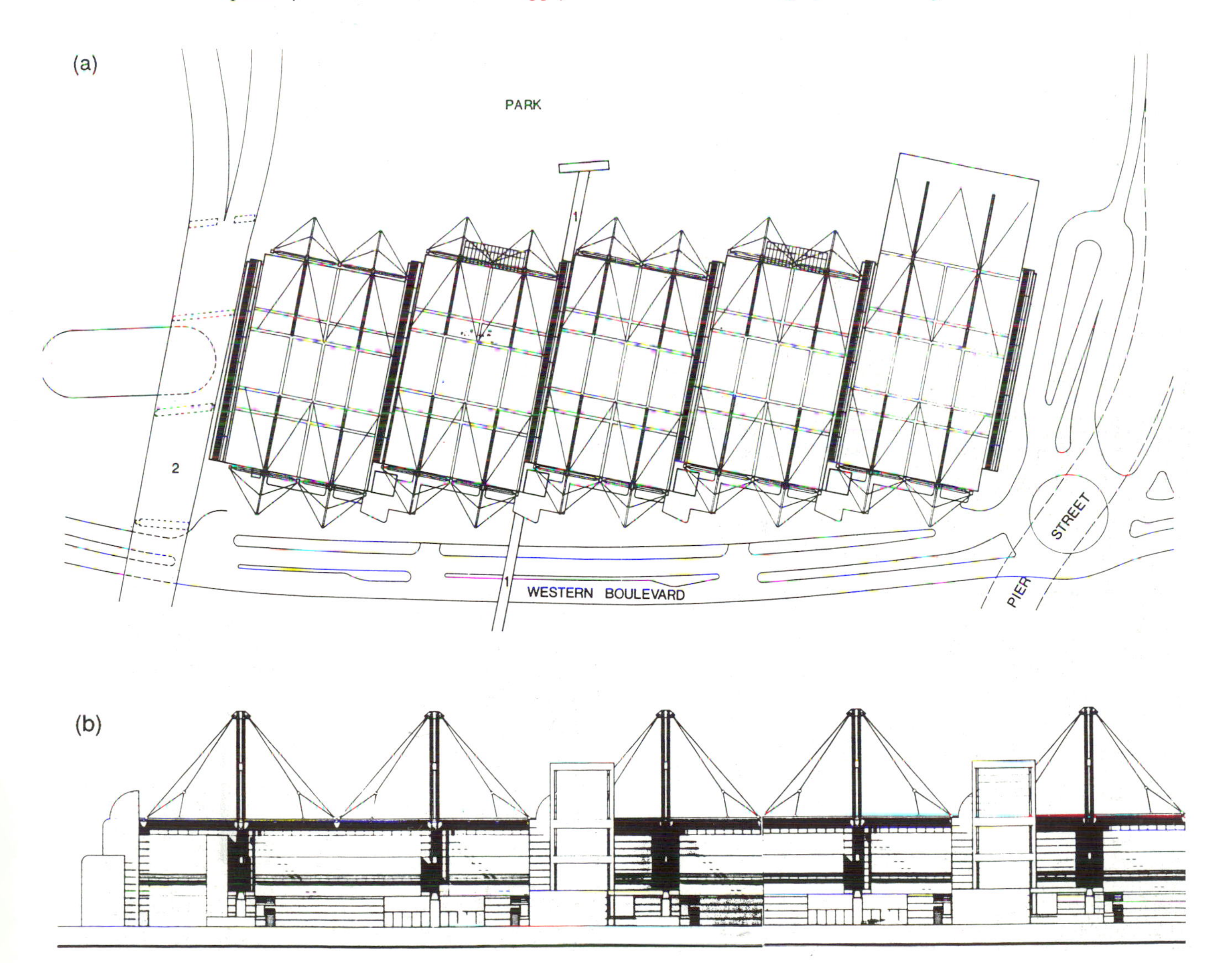

Fig. 36.14 *(a) Plan and section; (b) view from grounds; (c) the stand in use; (d) lift tower (to LH) formed with steel plate; (e) layered facade.*

36.4.8 The Mound Stand, Lord's Cricket Ground, London (1989)

Architect: Michael Hopkins and Partners
Engineer: Ove Arup and Partners

In this remarkable building the opposing factions of Modernism and the Conservationists have succumbed to the ingenuity and sensitivity displayed by the Hopkins team in the art of good construction. The structure is neatly layered with the ground floor formed in traditional brickwork, Frank Verity's well proportioned arcade being extended four fold. The upper terraces appear as ships' decks, lightly suspended from masts with lattice trusses hidden away in the mid-level service floor. There are slender tubular suspenders to carry the promenade level of the dining rooms and private boxes that float above the public terraces. The shipshape image is extended roofwards to a range of sail-like canopies that spring from each mast, the undulating form follows those of the traditional marquee. The structure is honestly expressed with visible plate girders and plate work to the end walls and to the lift enclosures.

It is very much a 'summary' design that captures the spirit of the cricket ground and its origins on the village green. In a very short time it has become a very popular modern building.

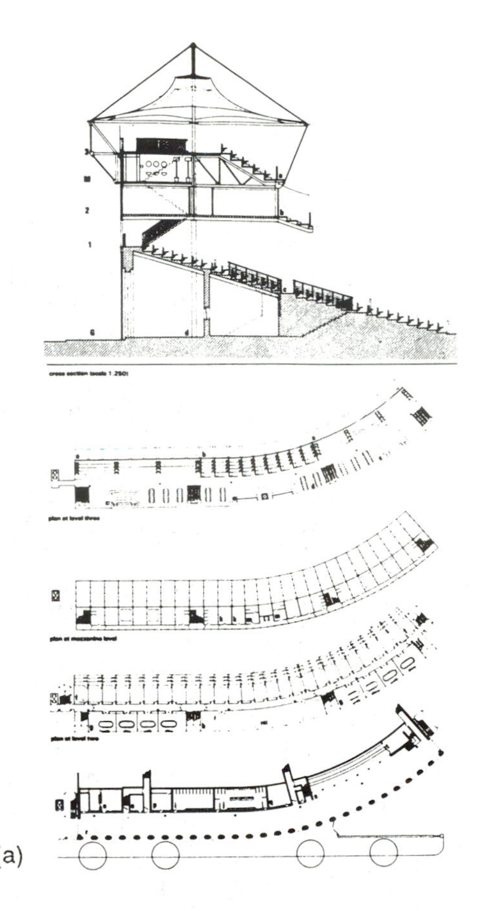

(a)

(b)

(c)

(d)

(e)

36.4.9 Sydney Football Stadium, Sydney, Australia (1986–88)

Architect: Cox, Richardson and Taylor
Engineer: Ove Arup and Partners

The Sydney Football Stadium was opened in 1988 on a site adjacent to the famous Sydney Cricket Ground. Designed to hold approximately 40 000 spectators, its great free-flowing and undulating metal roof offers weather protection for about 65% of the maximum crowd. The most vulnerable areas are at the rear of the stand, which has a cobweb of structural supports which anchor the ribbon of roof to the rear wall of the stand; these offer a modicum of protection to the adjacent spectators.

The grandstand seating, angled at 30 degrees, is supported on a three and four storey concrete sub-structure in which are housed the various ground facilities including restaurant, bars, toilets and clubrooms. Adjacent to the pitch and below these structures a concrete terraced slab of seating has been dug into the earth, the last row of which comes right up to the elegant grass playing surface. There are no barriers between the spectators and their sport.

The huge cantilevered steel roof is supported by a series of steel trusses which transfer vertical loads downwards to the perimeter universal steel columns. Steel-to-steel connections were used throughout the project for simplicity of construction, although they have now been concrete encased for fireproofing purposes. The ribbon roof itself is continuous and sweeps up over the east and west enclosure stand, dipping down over the lower terraces to the north and south of the ground.

Fig. 36.15 *(a) Site plan; (b) typical structural bay; (c) elevation of structure; (d) general view.*

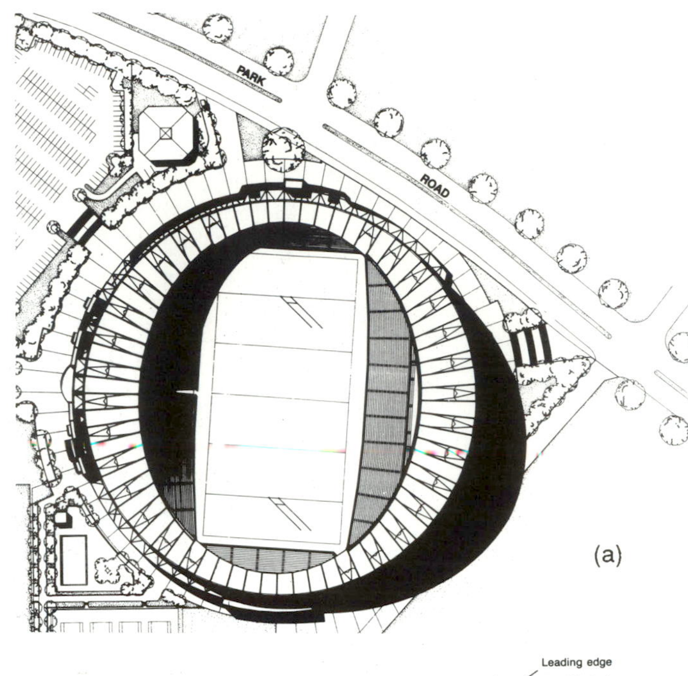

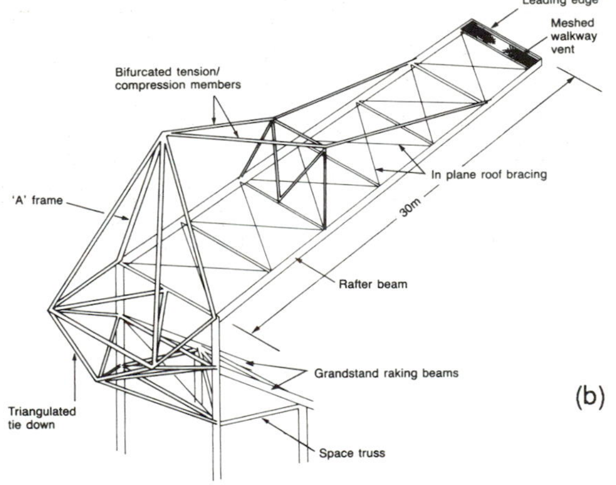

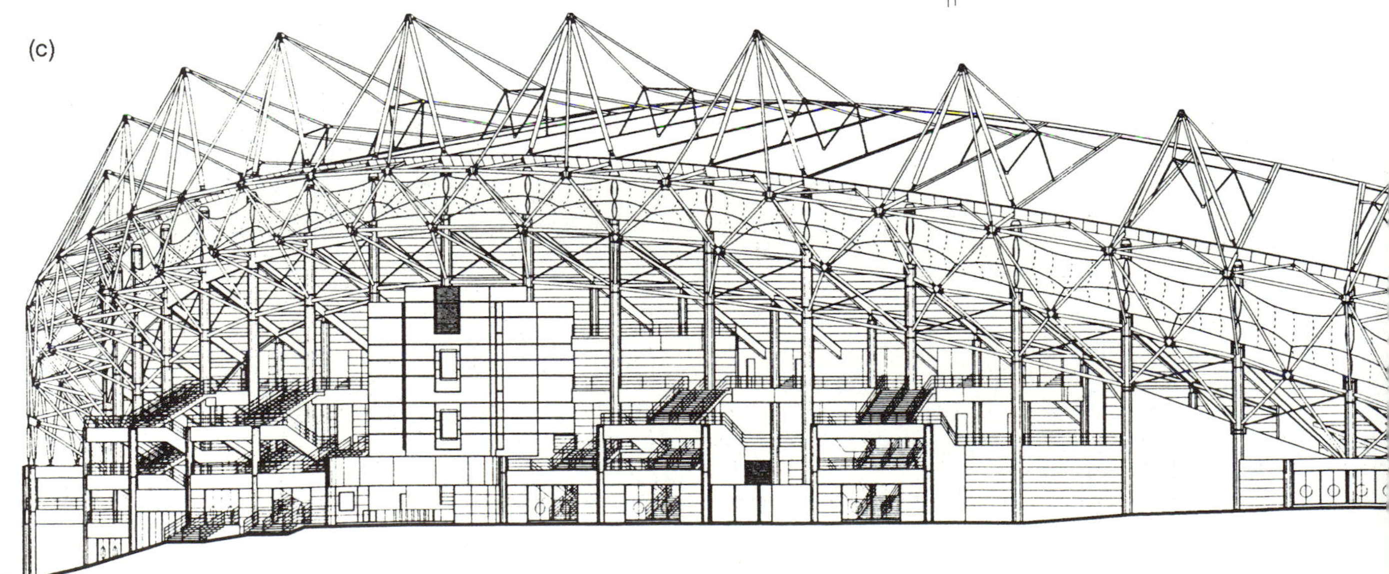

(d)

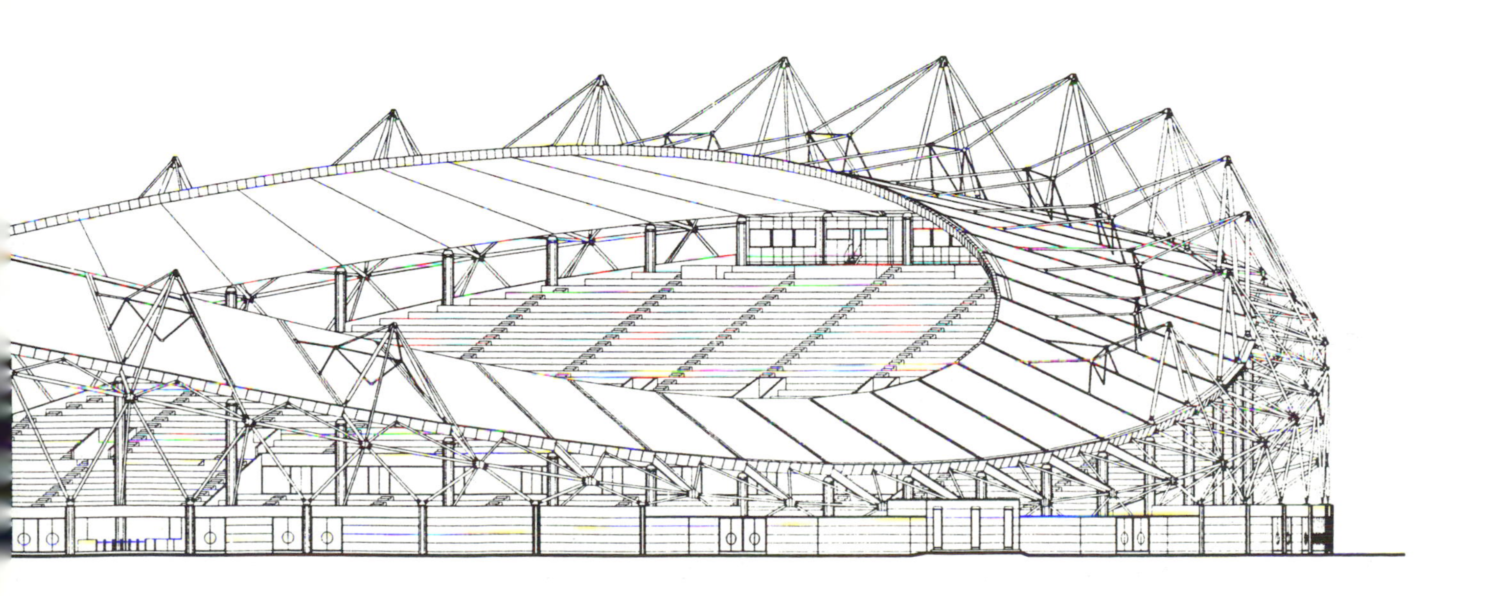

Fig. 36.16 *(a) View to West from Sully Pavilion; (b) North-South section; (c) ground level plan; (d) spiral stair with Pavilion Richelieu seen through pyramid.*

36.4.10 Grand Louvre Pyramid, Paris (1990)

Architect: Pei, Cobb, Freed and Partners

Of all the Grands Projets in Paris in recent years, none has created such a stir as the Pyramids in the courtyard of the famous Louvre Museum. Spectacular in concept and form, it provides a startling reminder of the ability of modern architects to invigorate and re-circulate traditional architectural forms. In a way, nothing is more static than the heavy pyramid shape familiar in its most solid form as for example the Pyramid of Cheops at Giza (144 metres high). Pei's audacious scheme depended on the creation of a visual impact in steel and glass comparable in some ways to other modern and spectacular structures such as the Eiffel Tower and Poelzig's Water Tower at Posen. The main Pyramid (barely 25 m high) is a complex inter-linked steel structure sheathed in reflective glass. In fact it is a doorway. It provides a long-overdue entrance portico to the main galleries within the Louvre. As one descends into the interior entrance foyer the dramatic nature of the intervention becomes apparent. The main pyramid is countered by two smaller pyramids which provide further light and ventilation to the subterranean spaces. The staircase and the cylindrical liftdrum that rises and falls within the compass of the spiral stairs provides a superb counterfoil to the surrounding design.

(a)

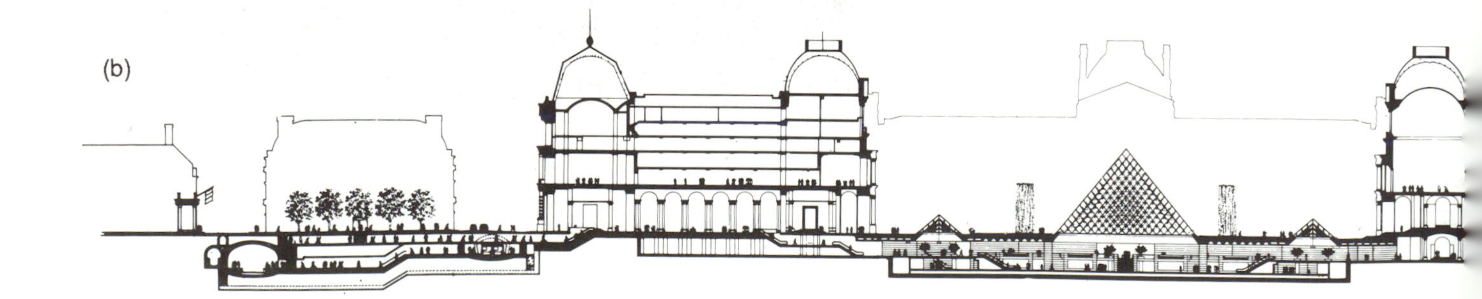
(b)

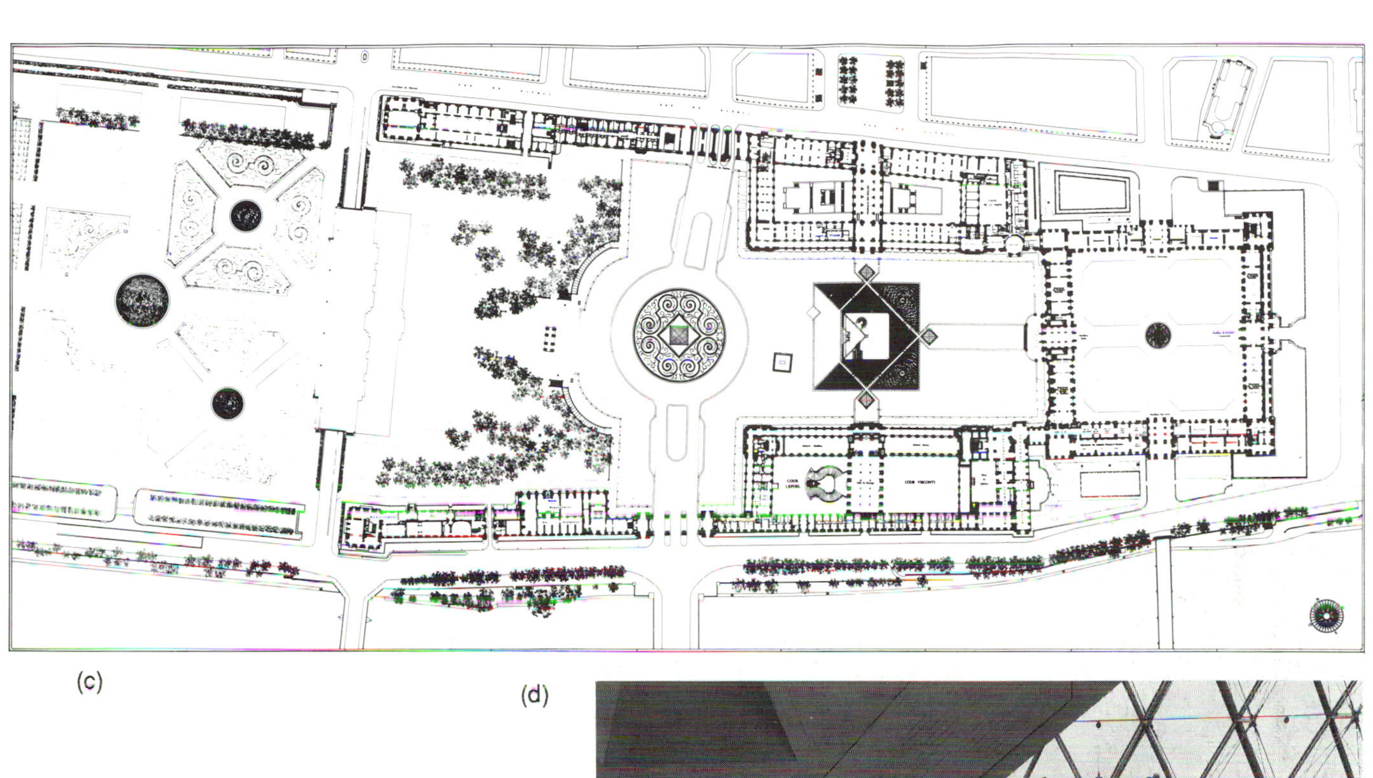

(c)

(d)

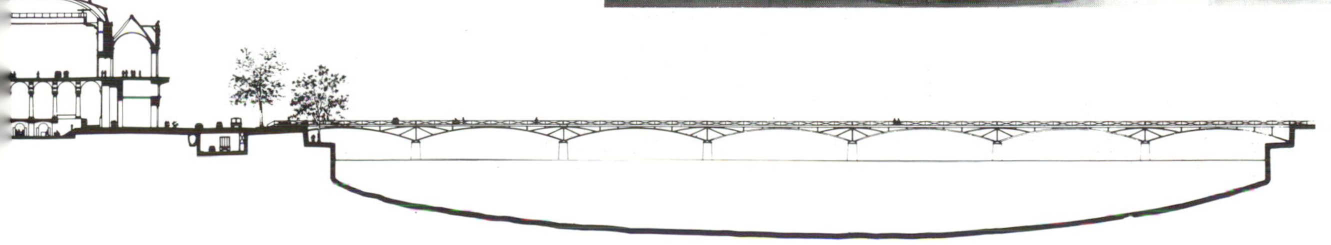

Fig. 36.17 *(a) High altar; (b) setting within parking lot; (c) external form; (d) balcony.*

36.4.11 Garden Grove Community Church, California, USA (1980)

Architects: Philip Johnson and John Burgee

The American architect Philip Johnson often boasts that he is basically an eclectic. Indeed the references he uses in his buildings related to certain stylistic moments in 20th century architectural developments. He is not averse to taking up 19th century references too.

'The Crystal Cathedral' as it is known in California is a 'TV temple' for the evangelical wing of the Reform Church but its basic concept owes more to the weird and bizarre elements of the glass architectural designs of German Expressionist circles in the early 1920s. During that period there was a great interest in religious cults and in the symbolism to be derived from multi-faceted crystal forms. Philip Johnson's building is less a 'garden' church than a church glasshouse which clearly has its roots in the original German ideas for a *Glas Architektur*. However, it is done with modern sophisticated techniques and materials, a huge space frame of a complex nature, its steel frame clad in solar responsive glazing. Cascades of seats fall down the raking stadium tiers. It is said that the acoustics work well and that for any performance in this cathedral there is an entry charge on some occasions of $10–12. Just like a night at the pictures.

(a)

(b)

(c)

(d)

36.4.12 'Follies', Parc de la Villette, Paris, France (1989)

Architect: Bernard Tschumi

The various steel structures situated in the new Parc de le Villette, Paris, are the result of a competition won by the architect Bernard Tschumi whose original design was for 42 'Follies' located on an invisible grid laid across the 55 hectare, 19th century abattoir site to the north of Paris. The first 15 hectares were opened in the autumn, 1987. The framework devised for these pavilions derives very much from Jacques Derrida's Deconstructivist ideas. The 'Follies', or pavilions, have no specific function and Tschumi is quoted as saying that the whole project had a specific aim: 'to prove that it was possible to construct a complex architectural organisation without resorting to traditional rules of composition, hierarchy or order', and that 'each Folly is a result of the intersection between spaces, movements and events'. Much of this non-hierarchical approach can be appreciated by simply walking around the park, the various levels of the walkways, and admiring (or otherwise) the individually constructed bright red pavilions. It is a salutary and rewarding experience.

Fig. 36.18 *(a) Covered walk; (b) gazebo; (c) cafe and canal-side elevated walkway; (d) poles and vines; (e) perspective of concept.*

(a)

(b)

(c)

(d)

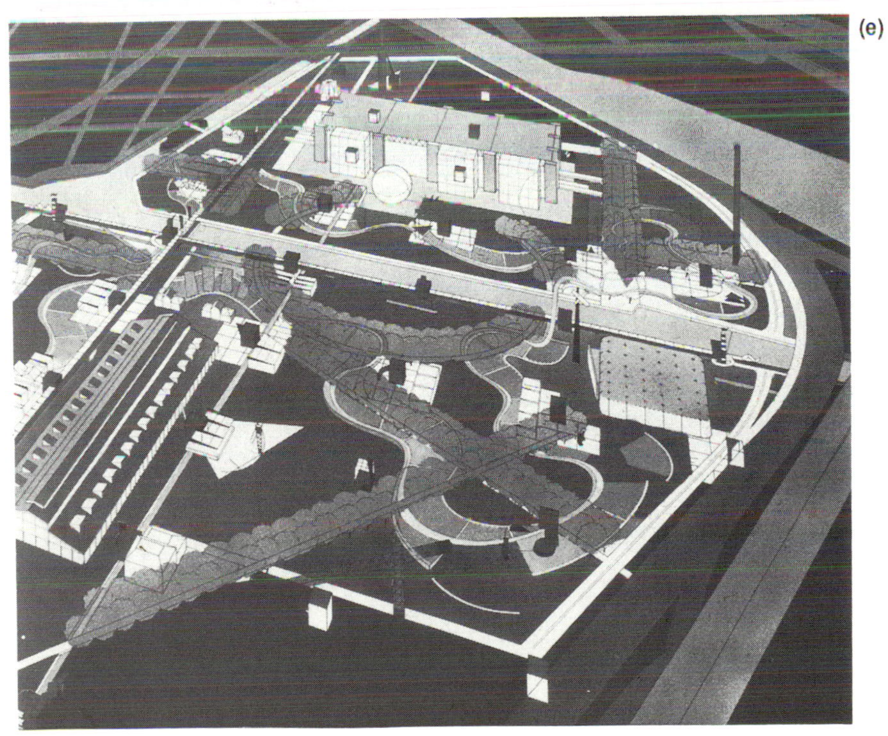

(e)

Fig. 36.19 *(a) Cross-section; (b) ship-like pavilion within park; (c) plan; (d) axonometric; (e) interior with browsing bench to face track form.*

36.4.13 Bookshop for the Venice Biennale (1991)

Architect: James Stirling, Michael Wilford and Associates with Tom Muirhead
Engineer: Feronanco Andolfo

The concluding design is perhaps a seminal work of the 1990s and represents a return to the mainstream of modernism by Stirling and Wilford. The associate architect Thomas Muirhead writes as follows concerning the new direction taken, and in particular the relation to marine architecture. . . . 'The architecture of the little Bookshop (which as it happens, is almost exactly the same size as a "vaporetto") certainly owes a good deal to this outrageous but refeshing aspect of the contemporary Venetian scene'. He continues in similar vein with references to Joseph Emberton, Eric Mendelsohn and to recent work by Gustav Peichl.

The Electra art bookshop is a permanent pavilion in the park used for the Venice Biennale and is placed within a tree-lined avenue. The browsing bench runs in race track form round the corridor plan with cash desk and services at the gable end. Solar screening is achieved by generous overhangs clad externally in patinated copper. The steelwork detailing by Feronanco Andolfo maintains the upper deck quality of marine architecture. A refreshingly modern work of architecture.

(a)

(b)

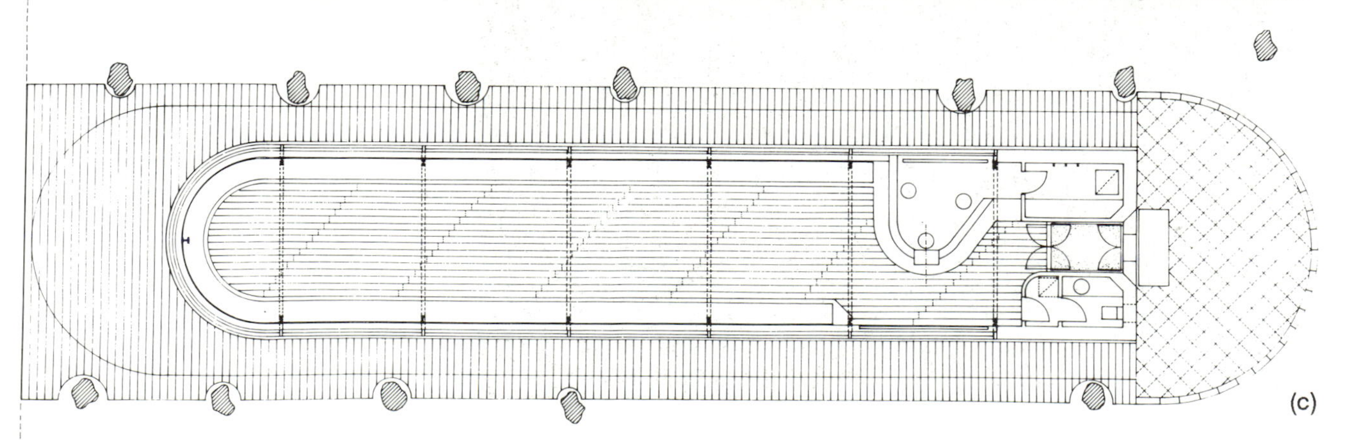

(c)

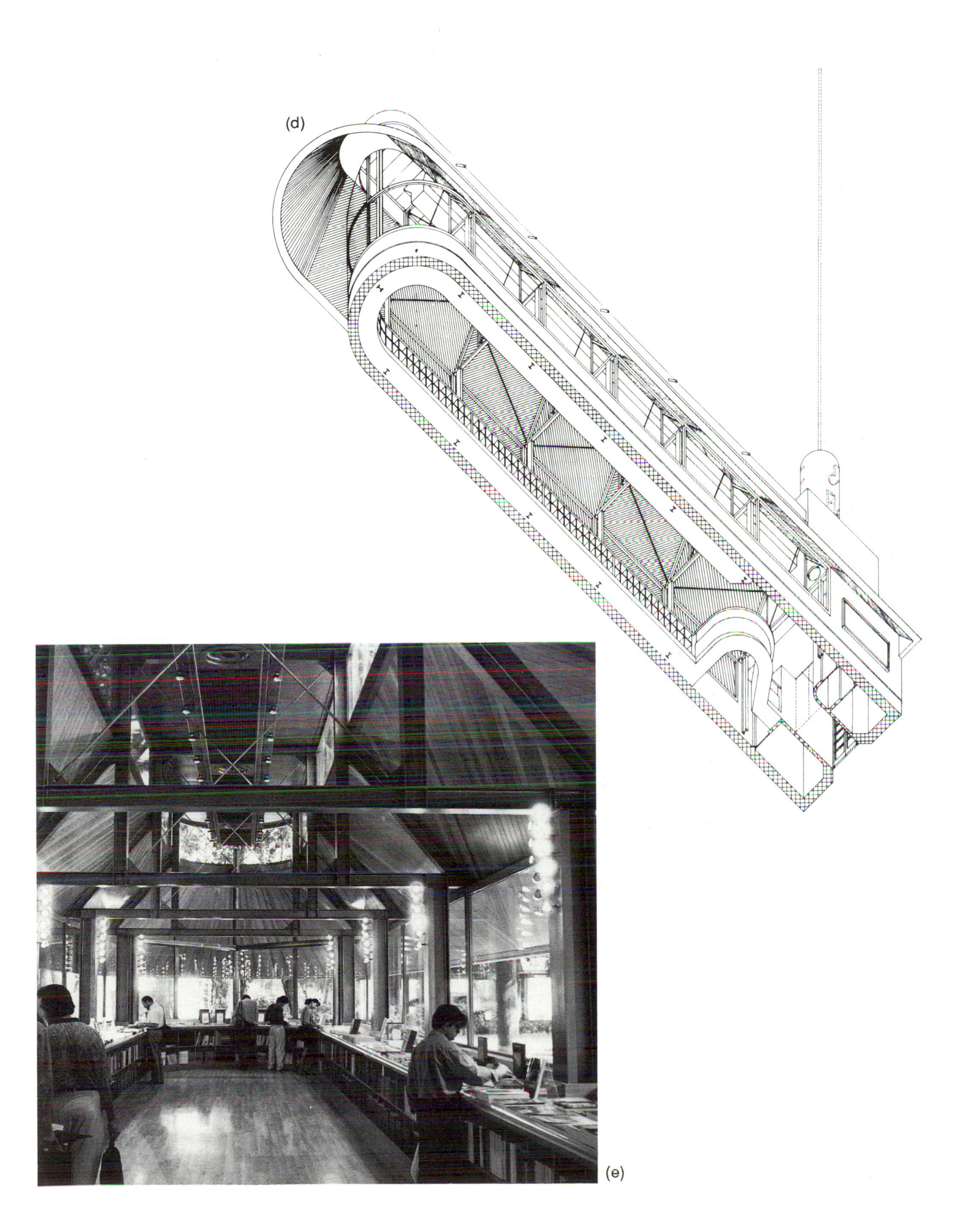
(d)

(e)

Fig. 36.20 *(a) Side view; (b) general view; (c) section and plan.*

36.4.14 Sculpture Pavilion, Arnhem, Holland (1986)

Architect: Benthem Crouwel
Engineer: ABT Arnhem

The structural potentials of toughened glass and stainless steel connectors are realized here to the full. This glazed promenade both embraces the exhibits and reflects the green surroundings. The scale of panes and module of lattice beams overhead bring a dimension to the sculpture, reminiscent of another Dutch masterpiece, the Rietveld Sculpture Pavilion in nearby Otterloo. That structure depends upon blockwork, joists and the sub-division of metal framed windows, whilst the contemporary version at Arnhem strips the enclosure to the vestigial simplicity of a perfect display case.

The tragedy with this work of art is that the exhibition was temporary and no longer exists except in photographs.

(a)

(b)

Section showing stepped footings below ground

Plan with lines of footings dotted

(c)

36.5 COMMERCIAL BUILDINGS

36.5.1 The John Hancock Center, Chicago, Illinois, USA (1969)

Architect and Engineer: Skidmore Owings and Merrill

Known to Chicagoans as 'Big John', this 1105 ft high block was one of the most notable monoliths of the 1960s. By any standard it is an amazing building, held together by giant steel braces which provide it with a dynamic appearance but one which is disturbed by the breaks these create in the vertical and horizontal floor treatment. The criss-cross facades also taper towards the low clouds that usually shroud the upper storeys of this 100 level block of apartments and offices. However, like other Chicago buildings in the area it is economic in its use of site area, occupying only 40% of its original site. Constantly swaying in the winds off Lake Michigan, the occupiers of the top apartments have commented on the sensation they enjoy of living on top of the world.

The sophistication of the structure, defined as a 'diagonalized truss', is fully discussed in chapter 15 by the leading SOM engineer, Hal Iyengar.

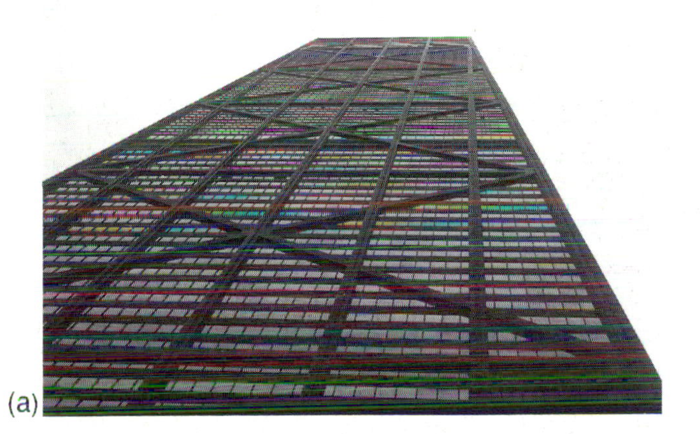

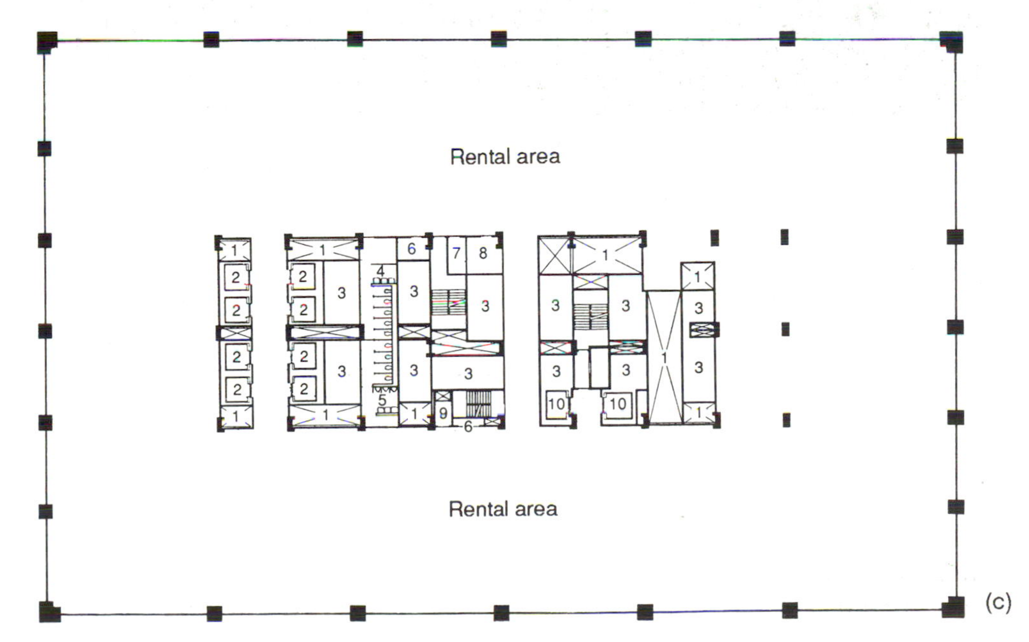

Fig. 36.21 *(a) Perspective view of tower; (b) the tower in the context of Chicago; (c) standard floor plan (13th–16th and 18th–23rd floors).*

Fig. 36.22 *(a) Isometric; (b) flats overlooking canal; (c) covered entry to store; (d) main facade to store; (e) ground floor plan.*

36.5.2 Sainsbury's Superstore, Camden Town, London (1989)

Architect: Nicholas Grimshaw and Partners
Structural engineer: Kenchington Little and Partners

An ambitious scheme, Grimshaw's Sainsbury's Store was designed to give a new architectural dimension to shopping in London. A giant hangar of a store, it is meticulously detailed and cleverly planned. It provides bold, urban street facades and around an internal parking court are workshops, stores and access to the new housing. The underground car park is connected directly to the store by a moving pedestrian ramp that has a surface enabling shopping trolleys to be safely handled up or down. The store is situated on an important traffic node in north London. The buildings have been designed to respect the scale and grain of the area, which is predominantly speculative Georgian intermixed with less distinguished Victorian and interwar structures. Set on a triangle of land, formerly occupied by the old ABC Bakery, the new buildings are bounded on two sides by the endlessly busy Camden and Kentish Town roads and on the third side by a calm stretch of the majestic Grand Union Canal. The scheme includes a spectacular three-storey steel faced block of 12 canal-side house units, a generous 300 vehicle car park, workshop units and to Camden Road the great 'market shed' of a superstore. Although unlit from above, the great shallow barrel vaulted store roof provides an impressive space some 5 m high at its centre narrowing down to 2.75 at the springing. The roof spans 40 m with support on each side from cantilevered girder/beams.

The main structure is based on a 7.2 m grid composed of seven elements including the main circular steel columns, and cantilevered beams, which extend to the steel cable tie rods. These are anchored to the piled foundations through the basement below. The exposed structural steelwork has a proprietary, rigid, epoxy-based fire protection system applied to all visible surfaces. The protective balustrades are in matt finished stainless steel. The shop front is in toughened glass with silicone joints.

The canal-side housing is constructed from a mixture of steel and aluminium. The double height living rooms have a solar louvre system and are approached by a private covered pathway set beneath the main metal facade. Access is also provided from the garage side, although for obvious reasons no windows overlook the superstore yard.

It has been said that the standard box-like format for the store has little relation to the structural gymnastics displayed externally, but each element fulfils a separate aim.

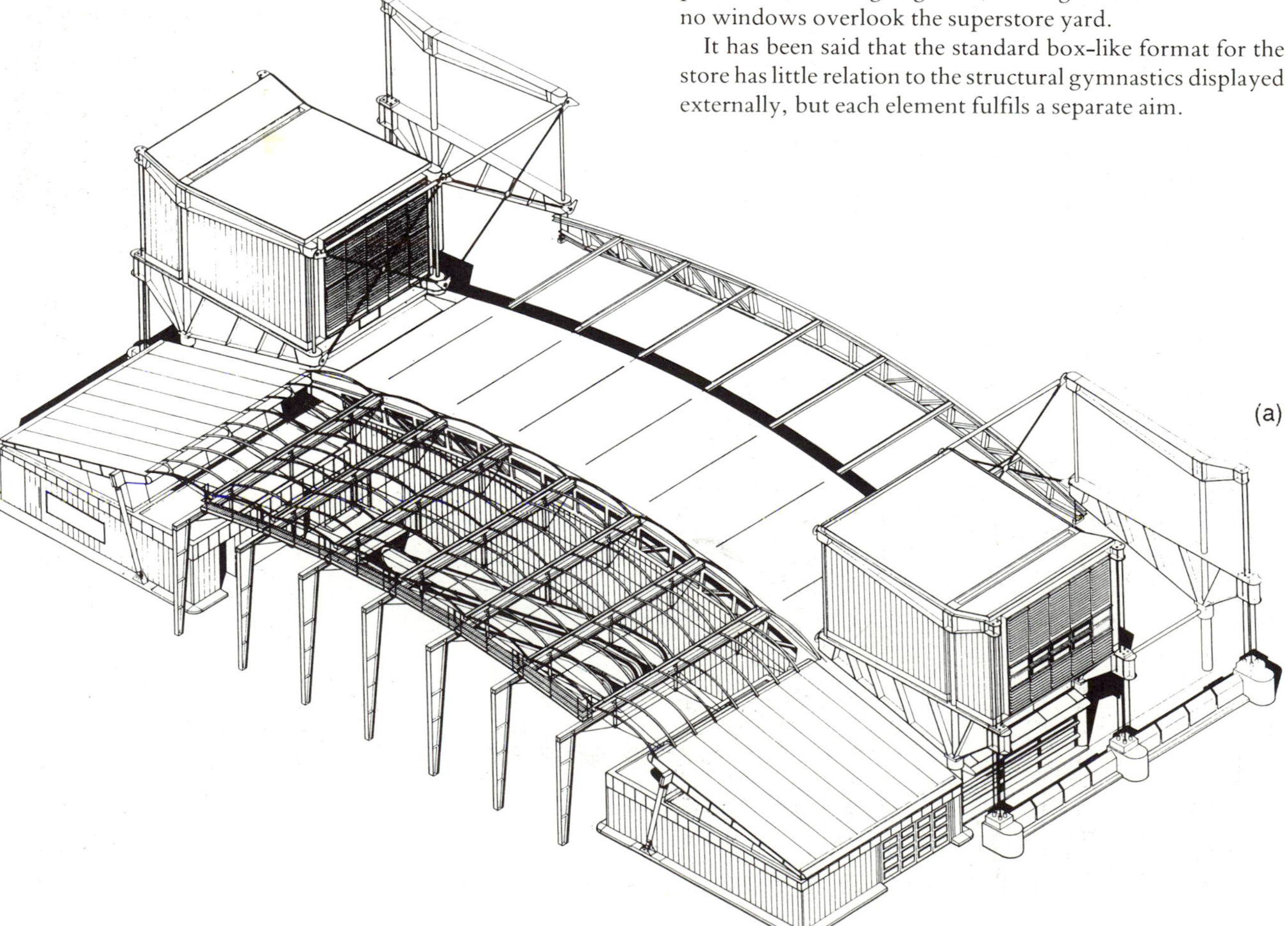

(b)

(c)

(d)

(e)

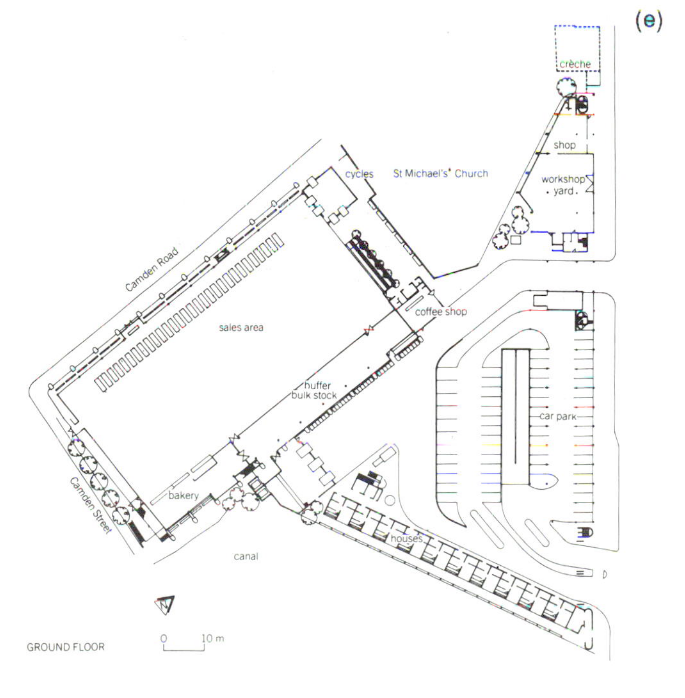
crèche
shop
workshop yard
St Michael's Church
cycles
Camden Road
sales area
coffee shop
huffer
bulk stock
car park
bakery
Camden Street
houses
canal
GROUND FLOOR
0
10 m

36.5.3 Stockley Park, Heathrow, London (1991)

Master planners: Arup Associates Architects + Engineers + Quantity Surveyors
Architects: Arup Associates Architects + Engineers + Quantity Surveyors, Geoffrey Darke Associates, Foster Associates, Eric Parry Associates, Ian Ritchie Architects, Skidmore Owings and Merrill Inc, Troughton McAslan Ltd
Civil engineer: Ove Arup and Partners
Landscape architect: Ede Griffiths Partnership
Landscape consultant: Charles Funke Associates
Reclamation consultant: Grontmij NV, Holland
Golf course architect: Robert Trent-Jones Inc
Construction manager: Schal International Ltd
Project manager: Stanhope Properties plc

Stockley Park is a spectacular example of a recently developed planning concept: the Business Park. It is ideally located at a node on a global communications network – five minutes from Heathrow and adjacent to motorway connections to London and the rest of Britain via the M25. The project is the brainchild of developer Stuart Lipton. A derelict 350 acre gravel extraction site filled with 12 m deep landfill with all the attendant pollution problems of methane and leachate has been transformed into Britain's foremost Business Park.

In 1984, 3.5 million m^3 of rubbish was moved to the north of the site and gravel and clay extracted from limited areas of the site to create a platform for the 100 acre business park. Speed was of utmost importance. Arup Associates were commissioned in March 1984. Inspiration came from the Syntex Labs Inc. in Stamford Park, Palo Alto and Rohm Corporation near San Jose – low-rise buildings with pitch roofs set in superbly landscaped parkland. Pleasant places for people to work in creatively was the basic theme. Landscaping, parking and good access to road and air networks were essential elements of the brief.

Stanhope Properties plc, with Arups and DEGW carried out initial research to establish the development brief. The business park would occupy 100 acres and the remaining 250 acres would be available for an 18-hole golf-course, playing fields, and public open space.

The concept can be compared to the vision of 'rus in urbe' devised by Nash and Repton for Regents Park in the 1820s. Stockley Park exhibits many parallels, with balancing lakes to facilitate drainage, the excavated material enabling the terrain to be moulded and shaped for major tree planting.

The 'white pavilions' appear through the greenery or across the water and give the illusion that the whole business park is an extension of the green belt, rather than reclamation of a refuse tip. The 'seed' building by Arup Associates set the standard of design with a high-quality, low-key approach. The pavilion type offices express the frame grid with slated roofs. Variety is given by the differing forms used by other architects within the discipline of steel, aluminium, glass or white cladding.

The structures are steel framed, based upon modest spans, the structural principles being outlined by Dr Roger Plank in chapter 12. The architectural language reveals how

Fig. 36.23 *(a) The concept of 'rus in urbe'; (b) typical 'seed buildings' designed by Arup Associates; (c) design by Geoffrey Darke Associates; (d) design by Foster Associates; (e) design by Troughton and McAslan; (f) site planning and context.*

(a)

(b)

differing designers have interpreted the brief. This commonality of purpose has ensured that a model estate has been developed with new commercial buildings which, very largely, represent the state of the art in British architecture today. In addition to the 12 buildings designed by Arup Associates, other practices involved include those of Sir Norman Foster, Troughton McAslan, Ian Ritchie and Geoffrey Darke. All of the buildings designed by these architects employ steel in their construction: they have all contributed exciting variations on the organic theme set out in Arup Associates' Master Plan.

Nearly all employ sunscreens to protect their glazed facades. The building by Troughton McAslan, occupied by Apple Computers, has a series of fabric canopies to the south elevation. Ian Ritchie Architects' 80 000 ft^2 pavilion is dominated by a huge horizontal sunscreen shading a setback metal and glass facade.

In conclusion, Stockley Park demonstrates that Modernism is thriving and that a total environment can be created equal to the urbanism of Nash and Repton without falling back on the pastiche of Bankers' Georgian.

(c)

(d)

(e)

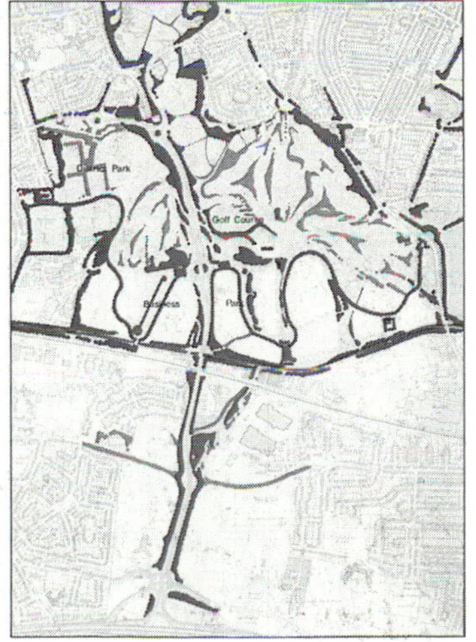
(f)

36.5.4 Grosvenor Place Development, Sydney, Australia (1982)

Architect: Harry Seidler and Partners

This huge development is located at the northern end of Sydney. It occupies a site that enjoys fantastic panoramic views towards the harbours and over Lang Park. It consists of a 46-storey office tower block made up of opposing quadrant shaped floors (2000 m^2 each) in order to maximize the opportunities afforded by these five views. The simple geometrical measurement allows the 14.6 m deep column free construction to use identical steel floor beams and granite-faced facade elements. The main core is of slip formed concrete.

Energy-saving technology is used to generate power from roof-mounted solar collectors and provide economic night-time electricity. Energy is stored in a huge ice bank in the basement for daytime peak demand air conditioning.

The tower is surrounded by public plazas both open and glass covered. In the high entrance lobby are three large wall-relief paintings by Frank Stella.

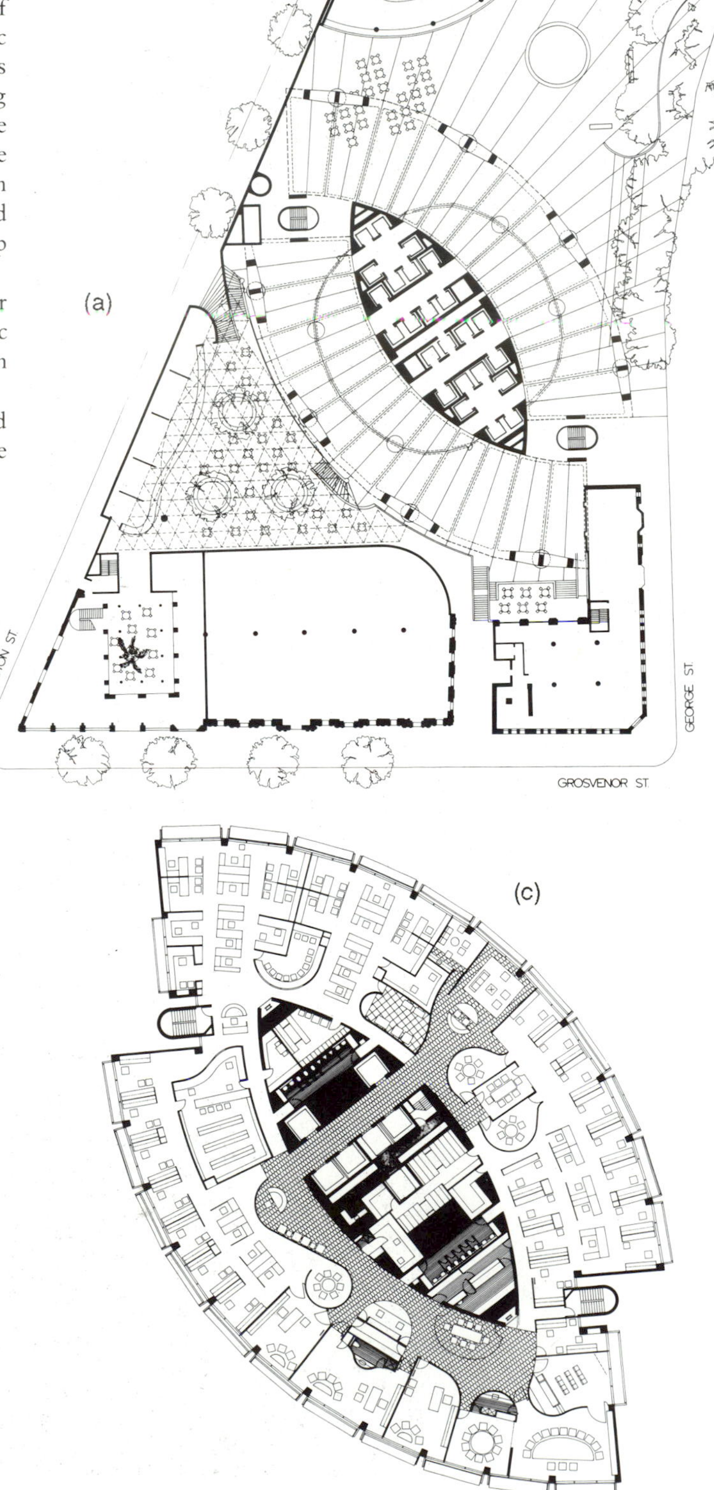

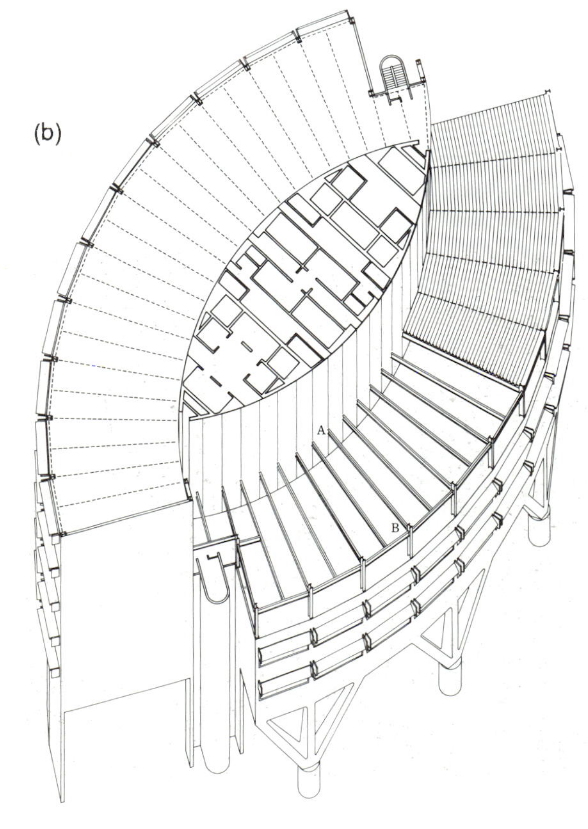

Fig. 36.24 *(a) Upper plaza plan; (b) isometric showing general arrangement of structural frame (courtesy Alan Ogg:* Architecture in Steel*); (c) 44th floor plan; (d) tower and fountain plaza; (e) main lobby with three murals by Frank Stella; (f) main entrance.*

(d)

(e)

(f)

Fig. 36.25 *(a) Plan; (b) detail of section showing services; (c) section; (d) Detail view of facade bracing and bridge connection; (e) Elevation of end wall and facade bracing.*

36.5.5 B and B Italia Offices, Novedrate, Como, Italy (1973)

Architects: Renzo Piano – Studio Piano and Rogers
Design team: F. Marano, C. Brullmann, G. Fascioli, A. Sacco, S. Cereda
Services consultant: Amman Impianti, Milan

This simple rectangular box of offices is entirely covered by a dramatic tubular steel space frame, a technical design device that appears to derive from Ezra Ehrenkrantz's SCSD school prototype of the mid-1960s. This space frame deck supports a secondary roof/ceiling structure in steel that also acts as a services housing duct. Furthermore, this space frame also acts as an environmental filter which is designed to reduce the solar heat-load on the 25 000 ft^2 of offices beneath.

The main structure is made up of 20 portal frames in welded steel tube spanning some 30 m with an additional portal of 50 m span which links the new building to an existing office block. The office interior is entirely column free and the building itself is capable of responding to change and growth internally and externally.

The project was one of the last collaborations in the Piano/Rogers Studio and Richard Rogers' later work appears to have used this building as a prototype for such schemes as the Inmos Factory in Gwent. Its importance as a prototype for economic and highly tuned technical design was underlined by the eminent architectural historian Dr Reyner Banham who, writing of the B and B Offices in Como, said: 'There is nothing to be seen in, or on, this building beyond what is necessary as architecture'.

The principles adopted for the space frame ventilation are based on the traditional attic or roof space system for allowing free circulation of natural air in this space between the roof surface and the ceiling.

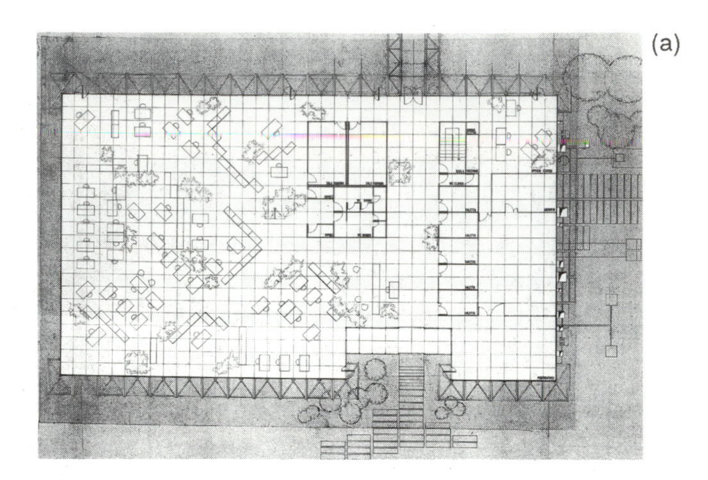
(a)

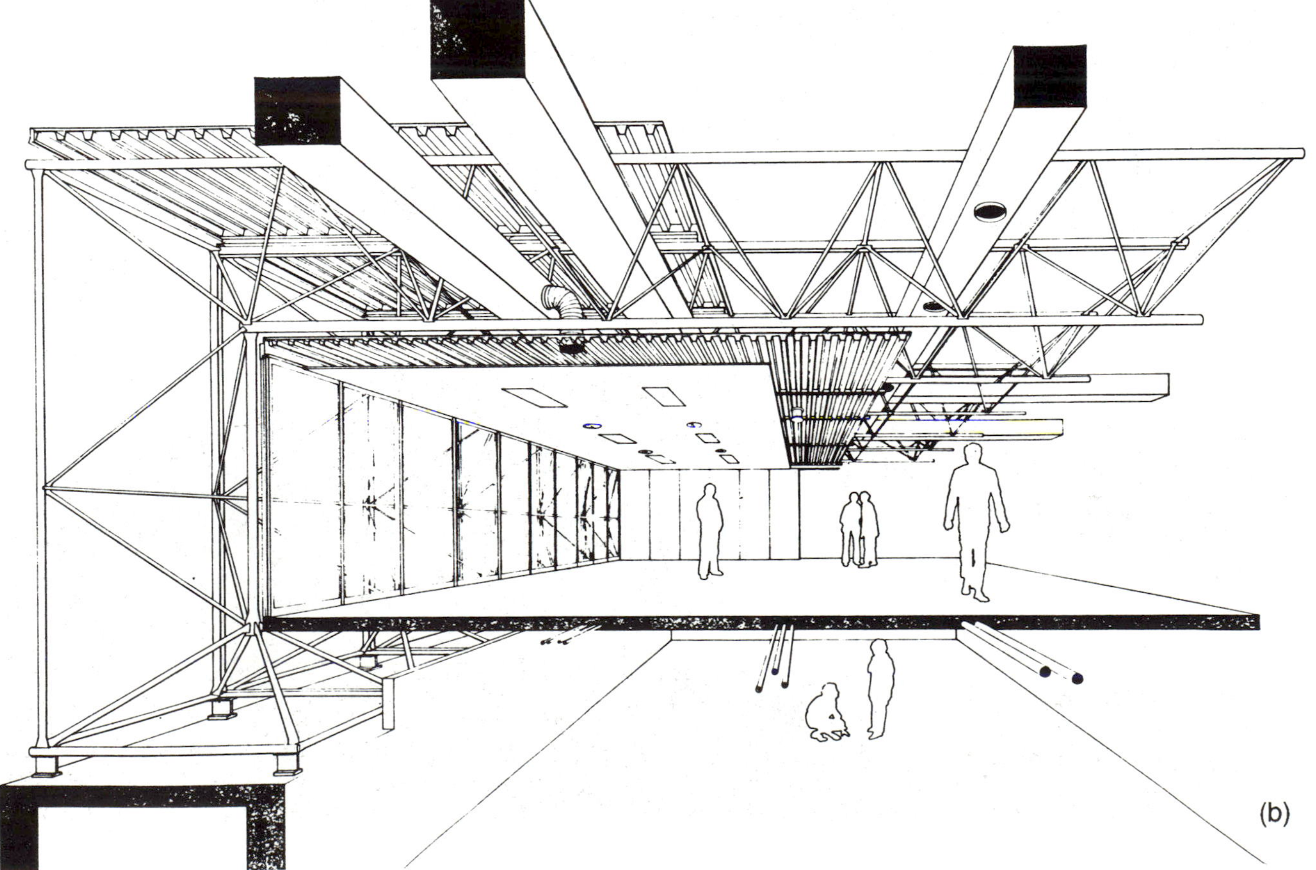
(b)

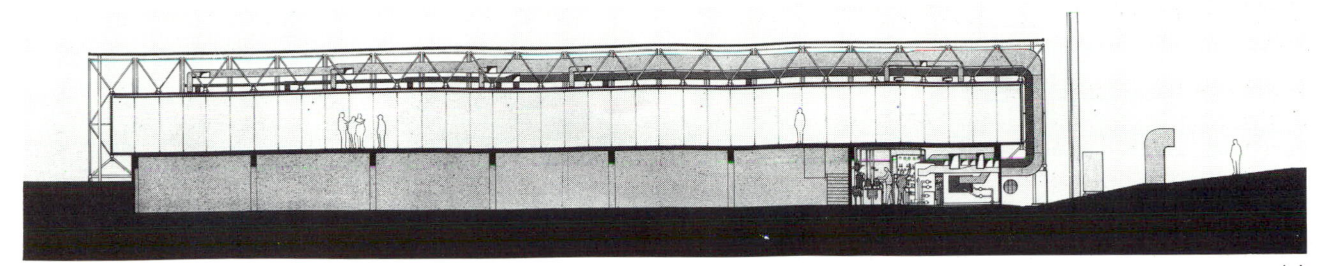

(c)

(d)

(e)

Fig. 36.26 *(a) Roof house (left) and penthouse (right) plans; (b) isometric of structure; (c) exterior view; (d) interior view.*

36.5.6 Rooftop extension to the Richard Rogers Partnership Office, Hammersmith, London (1990)

Architects: Lifschutz Davidson + the Richard Rogers Partnership
Engineer: Ove Arup and Partners

The original industrial buildings that predate the Richard Rogers Partnership conversion, had permission for a rooftop extension. The growth of the practice required the planning permit to be re-activated to provide partners' and other accommodation. The existing warehouse structure comprises a steel framed structure with reinforced concrete floors. A steel curved truss cage and platform floor was the least weighty solution, ensuring that the old foundations did not need to be underpinned. The selected structure was made off site with prefinishing to the metalwork to minimize scaffolding and working time. The atelier is a north lit studio space but with the gable end fully glazed to encompass the river views. Heat control is ensured by solar sensored blinds that unfurl like yacht sails to each segment of the arched end wall. The air conditioning plant is an extension of the existing services and carried by the lift structure at the flank of the building.

The extension forms a superb eye-catcher at this reach of the Thames. It is also an interesting example of one distinguished practice commissioning another to complete its offices.

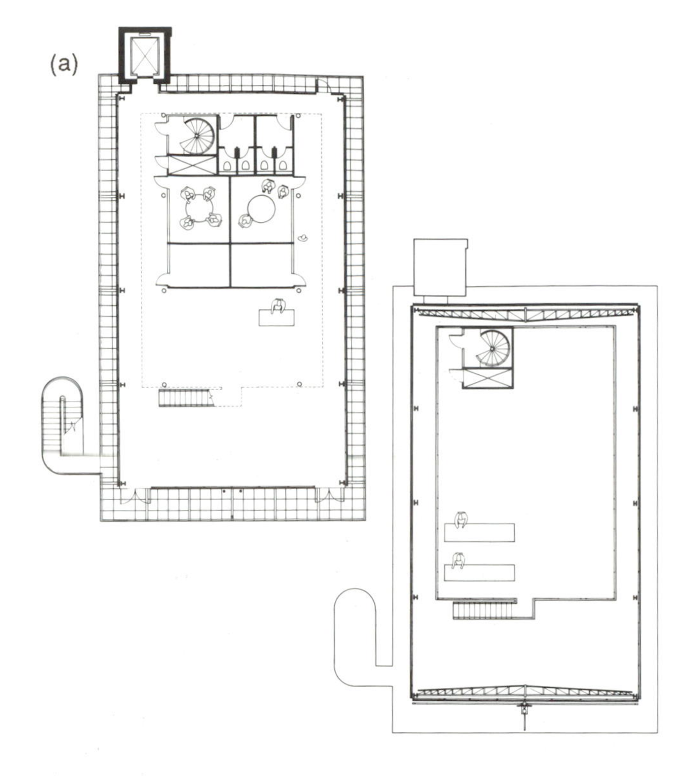

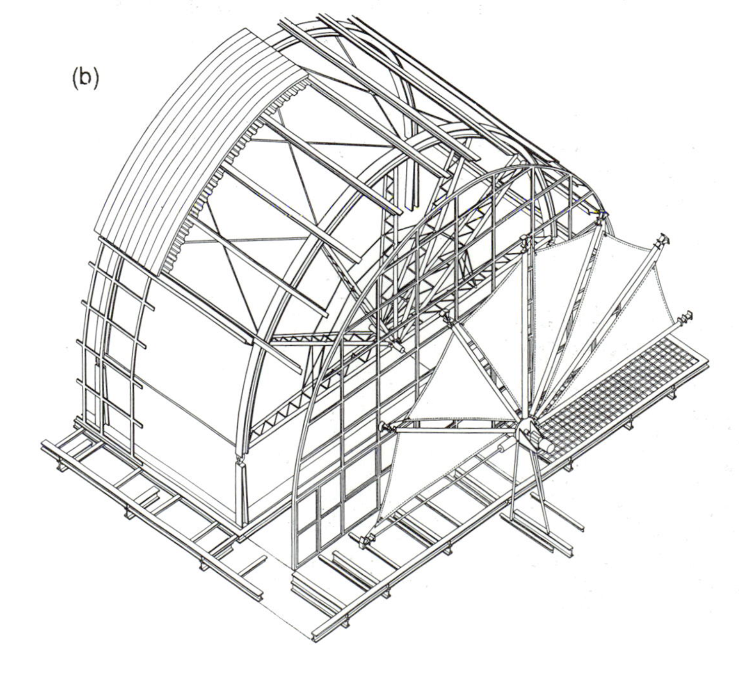

36.5.7 Central Shopping Centre, Milton Keynes, Buckinghamshire, UK (1978)

Chief architect and planner: Derek Walker
Design architect: Stuart Mosscrop and Christopher Woodward
Engineer: F. J. Samuely and Partners

This huge, rectangular enclosed shopping centre is the neatest, largest and still one of the most imaginative and best controlled shopping centres in Britain. It covers some 130 000 m^2. It has not lost any of its magic since it opened in 1978 as one of the main strategic elements in the development plan for the new city of Milton Keynes. It is a scheme that solved not only new constructional and architectural problems and successfully provided for the access of pedestrians, vehicular traffic, with car parks set out around the centre. The spacious open air car parks are under constant supervision and over 2000 car spaces were originally designated as part of the 12 hectare development.

The Centre's structural steel system is simplicity itself with bays of 12 × 6 m and 6 × 6 m and a variety of column sizes dependent on positions. The sizing of columns also allows for vertical expansion to three storeys in places.

The first and second floors are in ribbed precast concrete slabs with structural in situ topping. The division walls are blockwork throughout. The roofs are of lightweight corrugated metal decking spanning 3 m on steel purlins and beams. The external curtain walling is ambitious, with large glazed walls. Above the first floor these are in stock steel section, angles and tees directly glazed with 6 mm heat-resistant mirror self cleaning glass set into the legs of the sections with structural neoprene gaskets. The tall windows to the arcade areas use similar sections and all the steelwork of the curtain walls and all the other exposed stanchions are painted.

Fig. 36.27 *(a) Courtyard; (b) cross-vista between malls; (c) key section; (d) location plan.*

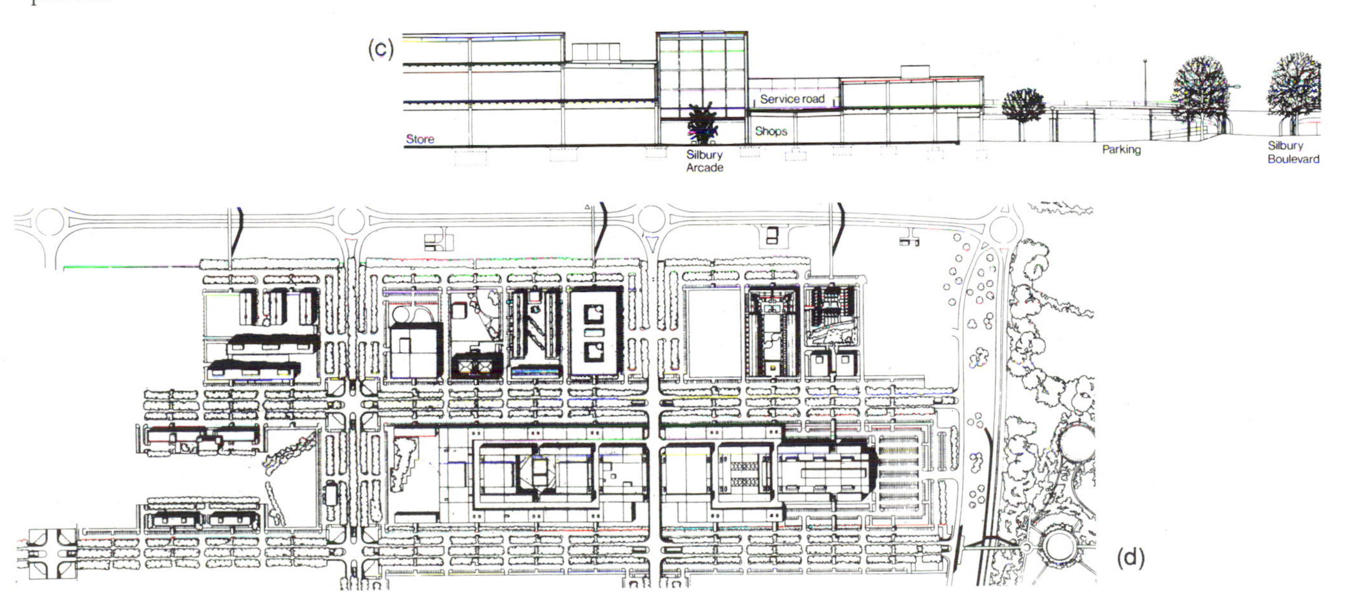

Fig. 36.28 *(a) Detail at night; (b) main elevation; (c) detail of stair towers.*

36.5.8 Financial Times Print Works, Docklands, London (1988)

Architect: Nicholas Grimshaw and Partners
Structural engineer: J. Robinson and Son Ltd

The *Financial Times* print works was completed in 1988, the year of its centenary. One of the more important enterprises to be relocated out of Fleet Street and in the London Docklands Enterprise Zone, it is a spectacularly fine building.

Sir Owen Williams revealed the newspaper printing process behind the glazed walls of his *Daily Express* buildings in London and Manchester in the 1930s, Nicholas Grimshaw and Partners adopted a similar approach to their new building in Docklands. It is a pavilion-structure with a single height Press Hall and three storeys of offices and composing rooms behind. The roadside facade is dominated by four 'lozenge' shaped curved entrance and staircase towers.

The main facades incorporate a modular cladding system of aluminium panels which are fixed back to main steel structural supports. The planar system of glazing, supplied by Pilkingtons, is similar to that developed by Foster Associates for the Willis Faber Dumas building at Ipswich (1971–75), although there is a difference in that each pane of glass is independently restrained. The gridded panes of glass dominate the facade in a similar fashion to the way 'Vitrolite' and glass panels used by Owen Williams in his Fleet Street building. The glazing is hung on aerofoil profile columns which in turn are fastened to circular hollow half sections welded to flat steel connection plates. The outrigger columns (at 6 m centres) carry the weight of the glazing which is suspended by tensioned rods located behind each column and at the ends of the outriggers. These connect the so-called 'dinner plates' and are tied to the triangulated plate assembly at the top and the bottom of each column. The architect refers to the fact that the 'overall lateral stability of the building is provided by paired I-section columns with tubular cross brace connections which span above the heads of the columns, forming a perforated "entablature" . . .' just below the parapet level.

(a)

(b)

(c)

Roof structure to extension of Waterloo Station, London 1993 (architect Nicholas Grimshaw and Partners: engineer Anthony Hunt, YRM).

37

Structural Steel Design Awards

Alan Blanc

37.1 INTRODUCTION

British Steel and the British Constructional Steelwork Association have been involved with Award schemes for many years. These Awards draw attention to the best steel buildings and structures in the United Kingdom and form a body of work that has been drawn upon in the preparation of this book.

1980 has been taken as the commencement date for inclusion, but space prevents the inclusion of every Award, since many are already covered in other chapters. Those included have been selected to highlight the application of structure in architectural design. The following list is a summary of this pre-selection:

Chapter 12 – Multiple bay single storey buildings
Cummins Engine Factory (1980)
Birmingham International Arena and National Exhibition Centre (1981 and 1989)
Bespak plc, Kings Lynn (1981)
Civic Centre, Chester-le-Street (1983)
Princess of Wales Conservatory (1986)
Kiln Farm 7 Special Units, Milton Keynes (1986)
Imperial War Museum Extension (1989)
The Pavilions, Uxbridge (1990)

Chapter 17 – Transfer structures
Embankment Place (1991)

Chapter 20 – Tensile structures
Inmos Lab, Newport, Gwent (1982)

There are also technical references in chapter 20 to the Renault Centre and to the Schlumberger Research Centre that received a Commendation in 1988.

Bridge design warrants another book, since Awards are given in most years. Readers will have to be content with the Humber Bridge, perhaps the most splendid suspension bridge in the world: it is certainly the longest span.

Making judgement in advance for Awards for the Mid-1990s is not feasible, but there are some noteworthy steel framed designs completed or under way:
Croydon Station (Alan Brookes and Partners)
IBM at Bedfont Lakes (Michael Hopkins and Partners)
The extended terminal at Waterloo (Nicholas Grimshaw and Partners)
The Jubilee Line Maintenance Depot (Chris Wilkinson)

The following pages provide a balanced, illustrated sample of the recent Award projects, and feature key examples in the advancement of building design. The format is arranged in chronological order with brief notes on the principles involved as well as references to the projects where published in journals or elsewhere.

37.2 DRAUGHT BEER DEPARTMENT FOR GREENE KING AND SONS LTD, BURY ST EDMUNDS (1980)

Architect: Michael Hopkins and Partners
Engineer: Anthony Hunt Associates
Steelwork: Tubeworkers Ltd

The citation in the Design Award is quoted in full:

> This building, designed specifically to house a relatively heavy production process, is an excellent example of the art of combining good clean structural design and careful planning with attractive architecture. The use of structural steel is obvious and is enhanced by the use of white finishes and glazed loading dock doors at each end. These factors, together with the effective use of steel cladding, well insulated, create an excellent working environment.

The elegant refinement of plan and structure is clearly expressed in this industrial shed, the basic 6 m planning grid provides a common module for roof and wall cladding, including the glazed roller door ends. The tubular column grid is based upon a spine system giving structural bays of 12 × 18 m with a grid of warren lattice trusses to carry the roof deck and to provide lateral restraint end to end. Cantilevers provide a protective canopy to the loading dock. The access ways either side of the working area have extended beams propped on the cladding posts.

The whole working platform is raised on a concrete sub-structure to lift the floor above flood level. The cladding is carefully detailed using standard industrial building components, with profiled steel insulated decking. The cladding panels are used both externally and internally with insulation sandwiched between the sheets.

The aesthetic is one of utmost simplicity and where no element is superfluous in the architectural expression.

Reference

1. Publication in the *Architectural Review*, March 1981, pp 146–149.

Fig. 37.2 *(a) plan and section; (b) interior view; (c) general view.*

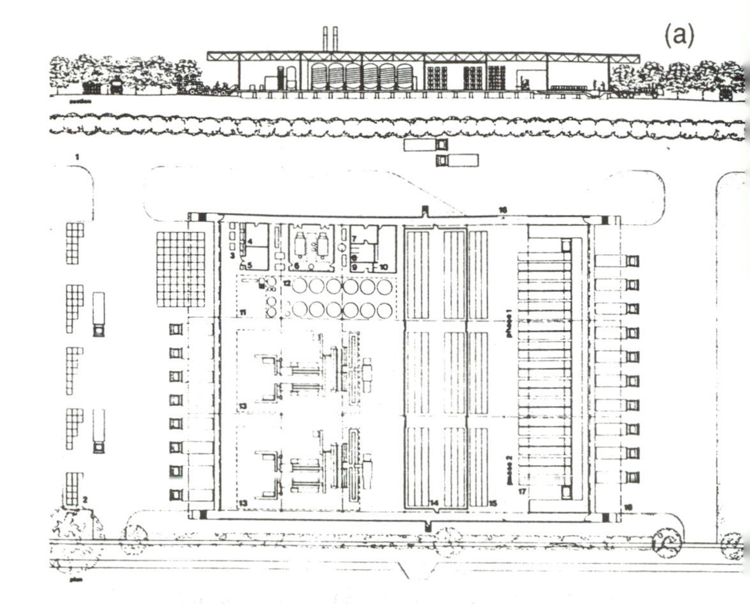
(a)

(b)

(c)

Fig. 37.3 *(a) View of Humber Bridge from North Bank; (b) under construction; (c) section through deck; (d) elevation.*

37.3 THE HUMBER BRIDGE (1982)

Consulting Architect: R.E.M. Slater
Engineer: Freeman Fox and Partners
Steelwork: British Bridge Builders Ltd

One of the most breathtaking structures amongst the 1980s Awards. The statistics of the world's longest bridge are as follows:

Clear span: 1410 m
Total length: 2220 m
Height of RC towers: 162.5 m
Weight of suspended steelwork: 17000 tonnes

These figures do not convey the visual surprise greeting one from the estuary or approach roads. The first impression is the gossamer lightness of the deck and suspending cables that span virtually a mile across the river. Closer examination reveals a consistency of detailing that makes the Humber Bridge one of the finest achievements in British engineering. There are many aspects of advanced bridge design where it is possible to postulate that tomorrow's technology is already in place. The leap forward in design work achieved by Bernard Wex and his team culminated at Humberside in a structure that creates a stimulating visual entity. The innovative box girder has been refined in profile to perfect the performance of the road decks that span the Severn and Bosporus.

Reference

1. Publication in *The Structural Engineer*.

(a)

(b)

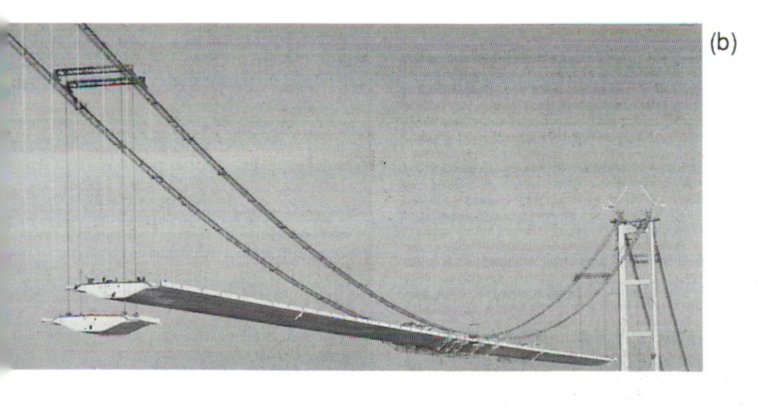

(c)

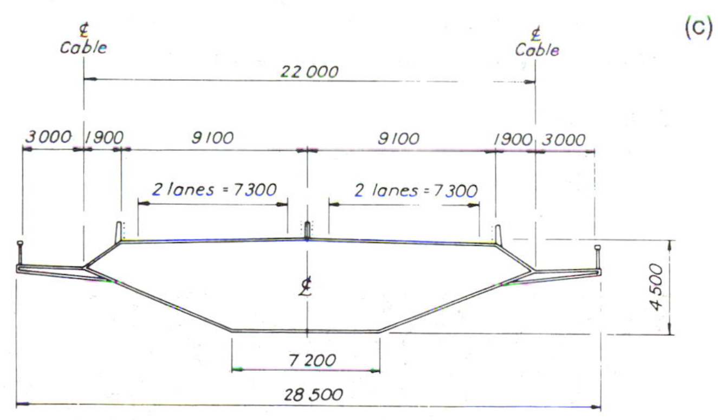

(d)

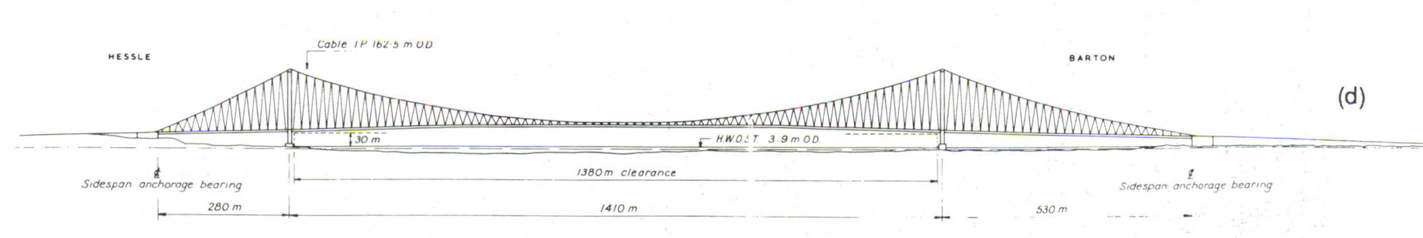

37.4 THAMES BARRIER RISING SECTOR GATES FOR THE GREATER LONDON COUNCIL (1983)

Architect: Greater London Council, Architects Department
Engineer: Rendel Palmer and Tritton
Steelwork: Davy Cleveland Barrier Consortium

The Thames Barrier is one of the most significant works of civil engineering to be completed by the former Greater London Council. Raising the defences for London and providing a tidal barrier has enabled riparian development of Thameside to be fully achieved without the restrictions that formerly limited building use due to flood risk below high tide level. The crowning achievements of the barrier are the steel rising sector gates, 10 in number, the main navigational channel having four spans of 61 m between trunnion supports. The remainder are 31.5 m spans.

The visible elements are the stainless steel clad engine housing designed by GLC architects and sited fore and aft of each abutment. The gates themselves normally rest on the river bed, they can be raised partially or to full height in case of flood surge. Full reversal is also feasible for maintenance work above tidal level. The gates are of cellular construction that permits the free flow of water in raising and lowering operations. Construction involved fabrication at Teeside with plate girder units clad in plate to form off site units with a maximum weight of 1400 tonnes. They were floated to site by North Sea barges for erection by floating cranes. The steel generally used was grade 43D in order to cope with exposure to freezing air conditions.

Reference

1. *The Structural Engineer*, Volume 62A, No. 4, April 1984.

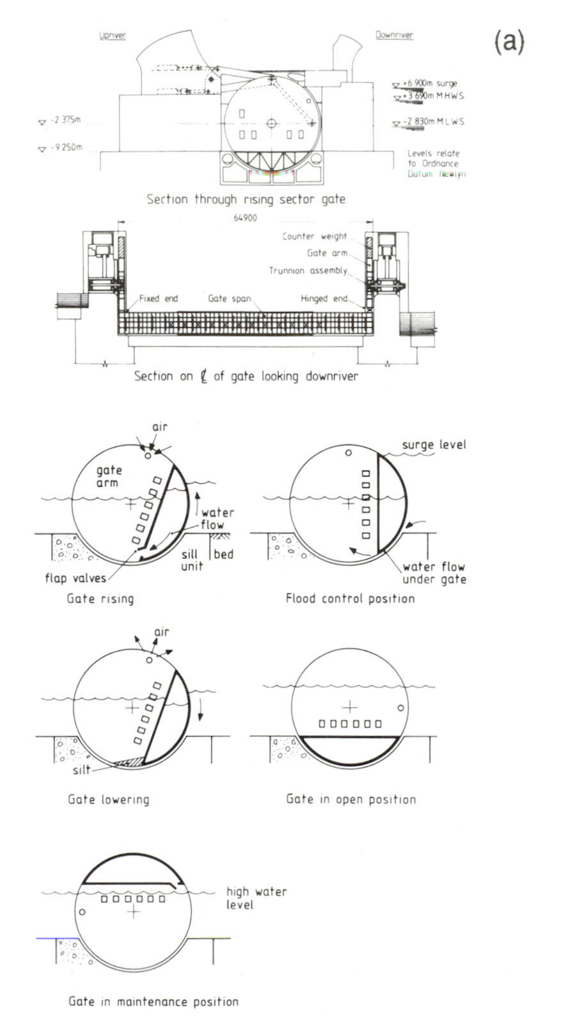

Fig. 37.4 *(a) Basic concept of the gate operation; (b) aerial view; (c) downstream view of Barrier.*

37.5 LIVERPOOL INTERNATIONAL GARDEN FESTIVAL EXHIBITION BUILDING (1984)

Architect: Arup Associates
Engineer: Arup Associates
Steelwork: Tubeworkers Ltd

This building was the centrepiece of the Liverpool Garden Festival, the first of its kind to be held in Britain. It had to perform two separate functions, firstly, its role as an exhibition hall covering 7500 m^2, secondly to provide in the long term a covered sports centre seating 3000 spectators.

An important consideration was that it should make a form sympathetic to the contours of the relandscaped area. Space requirements were combined with the structural efficiency of the curvilinear form resulting in minimum material content and a favourable ratio between external surface area and plan area.

The structural frame is made up from two primary elements:

(a) A two layer barrel vault structure of 60 m span and 78 m length, comprising braced arched frames of 3 pin configuration at 3 m centres. The upper and lower booms are connected by longitudinal members. The lower longitudinal member connects through to the domes providing the path for axial forces, and supports services and acoustic panels in selected areas. The upper longitudinal member acts as a purlin for the polycarbonate sheet cladding. The intermediate arch frames are connected by braced frames which, with the on-grid frame, transfer their reactions to bipod frames at 6 m centres.

(b) Half domes of 62 m span at each end of the vault. These are of segmental ribbed single layer construction with circumferential rings at 3 m centres connected through via the longitudinal lower vault members.

The out-of-plane forces at the junction of the dome and vault are resisted by the end three arched frames which are braced together with both in- and out-of-plane bracing. In order to minimize member sizes at the top of the dome use is made of an architectural feature, the oculus, which is a continuation of the ventilation structure. This is framed to give a braced girder semi-circular in plan, triangular in section which, cantilevered from the last three braced vault frames, picks up the braced in-plane ends of the dome ribs. The steel sections used are a combination of joists, universal beams and tubes. The height to the underside of the dome is 13.8 m, giving a total enclosed volume of 72 200 m^3.

(a)

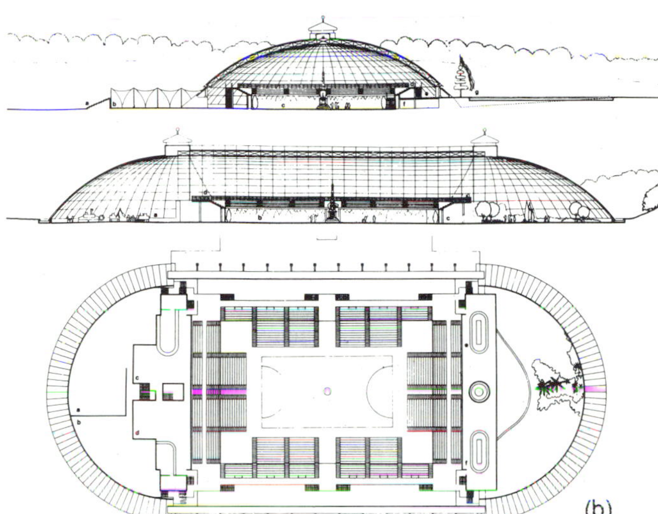

(b)

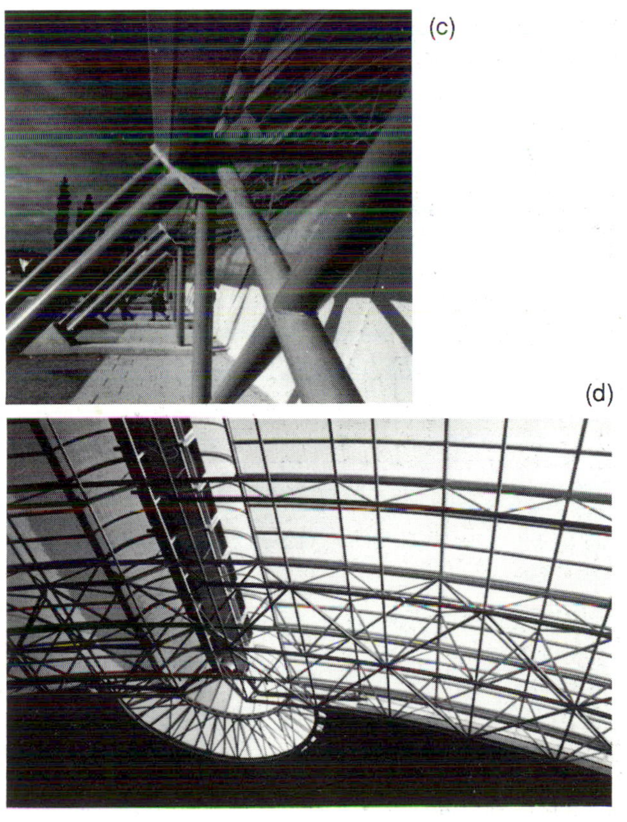

(c) (d)

Fig. 37.5 *(a) General view of building in the context of the site; (b) cross-section, long section and plan; (c) detail view of truss supports; (d) interior showing roof trusses.*

Fig. 37.6 *(a) Aerial view of building; (b) part section; (c) main façade; (d) plan arrangement; (e) elevation from buttercup field; (f) interior view; (g) structural principles; (h) general view.*

37.6 THE RENAULT CENTRE, SWINDON (1984)

Architects: Foster Associates
Structural engineers: Ove Arup and Partners
Steelwork: Tubeworkers Ltd

The structural characteristics of mast structures are discussed by John Thornton in chapter 20. The Renault Centre is a superb example providing the client with large clear span volumes that can be extended. In effect, the plan grid is 24 m^2. The facade system is off-centre by 2 m to avoid junctions between cladding and mast structures.

A series of I-beam mullions line the periphery at 4 m intervals bracing glazed or panel infilling. The wall framing is ground-supported and enables alterations to the building envelope without affecting integrity of the main structure.

The roof comprises arched steel beams supported from the top of prestressed circular hollow steel masts at quarter points. The remainder of the roof consists of arched beams on the diagonals of the column grid with steel purlins at 4 m centres. In essence, the structural system is an unbraced continuous portal frame. Despite many penetrations for structure and services in the final roof covering, it consists of one continuous solvent-welded reinforced PVC membrane joined to downpipes within the tubular masts.

The Renault Centre is a 'flagship' for the company in Britain, the yellow 'house colour' providing a cheerful identity to the exposed frame elements within and without the ensemble. The concept of top-lit umbrellas provides a universal quality to the spaces whether these are reserved for warehousing, sales or staff facilities. The porte-cochere and exhibition hall reveal the imaginative spatial use of a really elegant structure.

(a)

References

1. *Architectural Review*, July 1983, pp 15–37.
2. *Norman Foster Buildings and Projects*, Vol. 2, 1971–88, publisher Watermark.

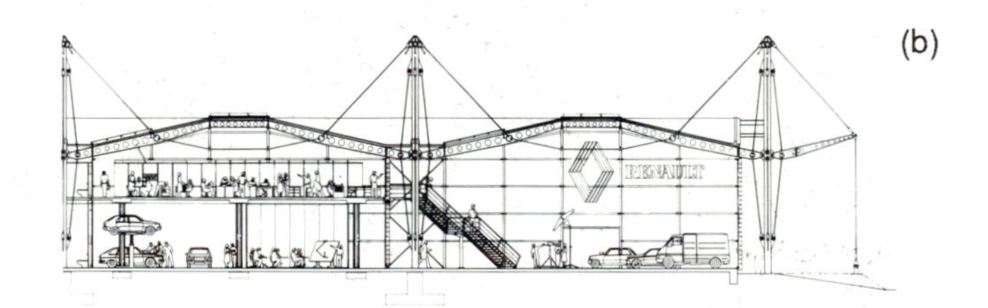

(b)

(c)

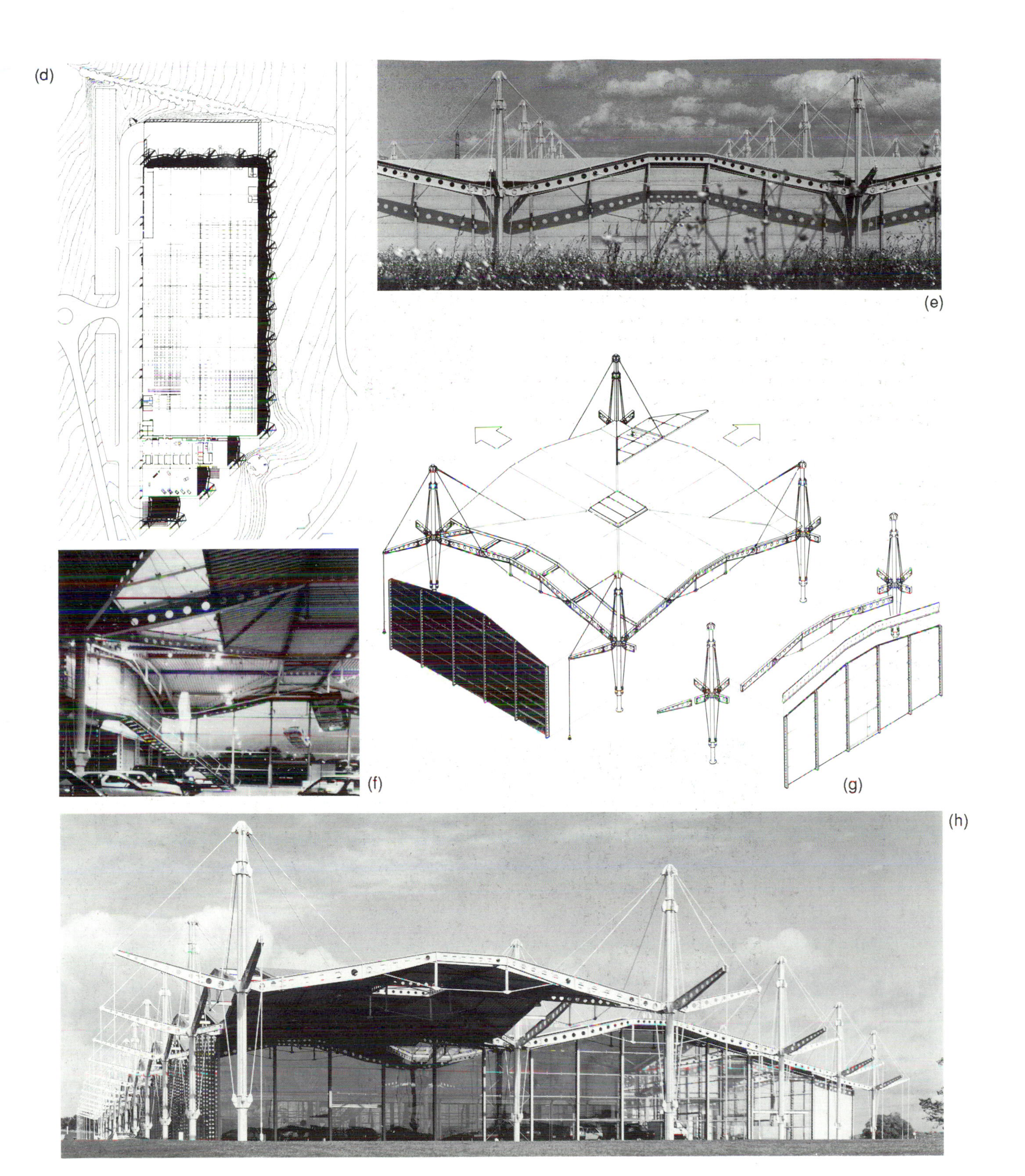
(d)
(e)
(f)
(g)
(h)

Fig. 37.7 *(a) Elevation; (b) detail of facade; (c) rooflight; (d) East-West section; (e) ground floor plan.*

37.7 NO. 1 FINSBURY AVENUE, LONDON, FOR ROSEHAUGH GREYCOAT ESTATES LTD (1985)

Architect: Arup Associates
Engineer: Arup Associates
Steelwork: Graham Wood Structural Ltd

The scheme is the first of a three-phase development that forms the western extremity of Broadgate Square all by the same developer and design team. The early phases of Broadgate are distinguished by a finely tuned architectural expression of the structure. No.1 Finsbury Avenue has the additional advantage of the simplest plan form which enables the layout and section to provide well proportioned spaces without splays and cut off lines. The total office area is 25 000 m^2. The race track plan encompasses a central atrium with a pair of cores for lifts and services in the cross wings. Secondary stairs and firemen's access break the long elevations to Wilson Street and Finsbury Avenue. The light angles ensure set backs in the upper storeys that reduce the bulk of the design and ensure that the main building facades at back of pavement are in scale with the older surroundings of Liverpool Street Station.

The framing grid has a basic dimension of 6 m, expanded to 7.5 or 9 m where longer bays are required with 13.5 m for some roof areas. The secondary beam bay is 3 m to suit the metal deck flooring designed as a composite structure with lightweight concrete topping. The vertical dimensions are current to requirements with 3.650 m floor-to-floor allowing 1.050 m service depth between raised floors and suspended ceilings. The average depth of office is around 14 m and of prime value relating to fenestration on both sides, whether atrium or facade glazing.

The facades have been developed as a tracery of solar screens with balconies or shading devices coupled with planting areas to soften the austere palette of bronze anodizing and bronze tinted glazing. The superb detailing and well crafted metalwork make the elevations of No. 1 Finsbury Avenue into the best piece of London 'streetscape' created in the 1980s. The same skills applied to the public atrium have made this into the most handsome of interior spaces.

Reference

1. Detail *Zeitschriff fur Architektur + Baudetail 26 Serie* 1986.4.

(a)

(b)

(c)

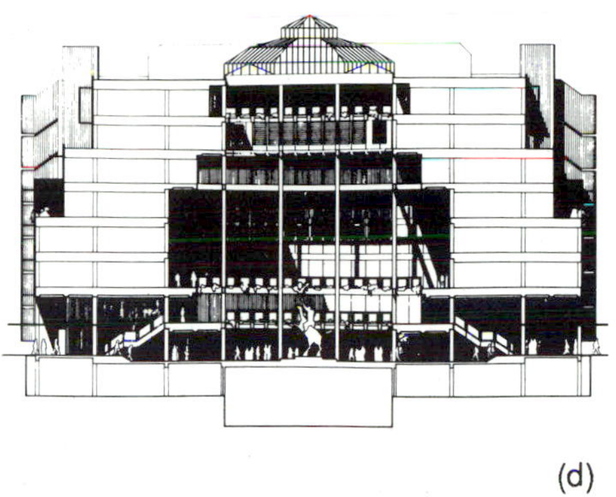

(d)

(e)

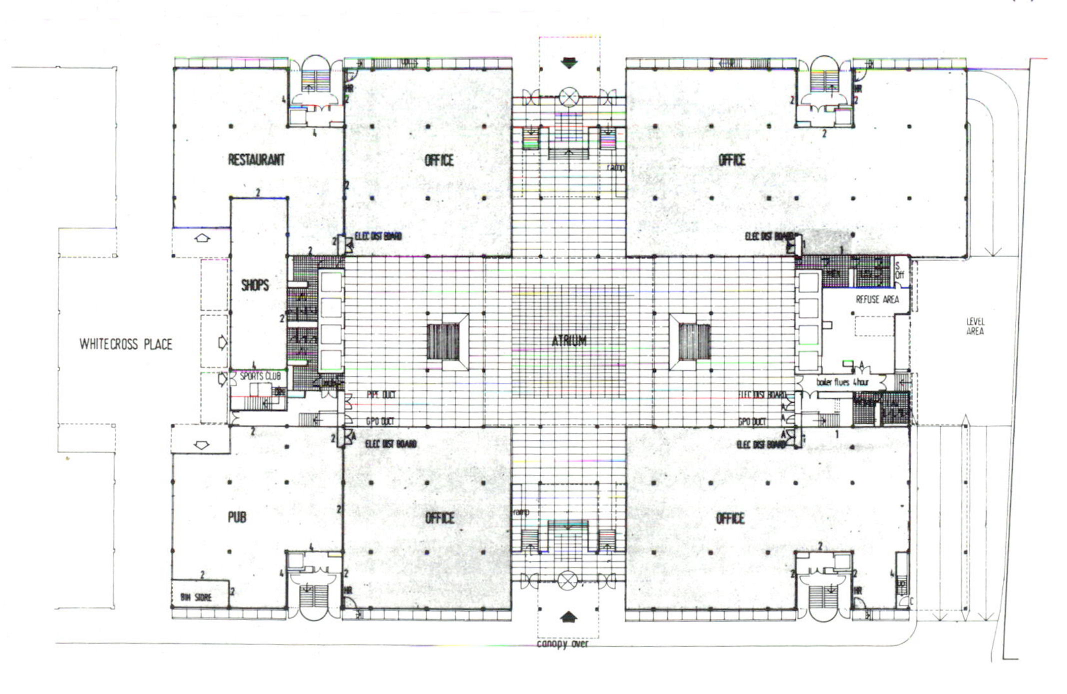
RESTAURANT
OFFICE
OFFICE
SHOPS
WHITECROSS PLACE
SPORTS CLUB
ATRIUM
REFUSE AREA
LEVEL AREA
ELEC DIST BOARD
PIPE DUCT
GPO DUCT
boiler flues 4hour
PUB
BIN STORE
OFFICE
OFFICE
ramp
canopy over

Fig. 37.8 *(a) General view; (b) looking up atrium through the glass underbelly; (c) North–South cross-section; (d) upper floor plans;*

(a)

(b)

37.8 NEW HQ FOR HONGKONG AND SHANGHAI BANKING CORPORATION (1986)

Architect: Foster Associates
Engineer: Ove Arup and Partners
Steelwork: British Steel Corporation/Dorman Long Joint Venture

The Hongkong and Shanghai Banking Corporation's new headquarters building is one of the tallest examples of a suspension structure office tower. It stands 180 m above ground, with four basement levels. There are 47 floors in all totalling 100 000 m^2. The bank's unique structural system gives a completely open floor plan. At ground level the public plaza which passes beneath the tower is interrupted by just eight steel masts that carry the entire superstructure down to bedrock. Each mast is made of a cluster of four circular steel tube columns connected by rectangular haunched beams at floor intervals. These cross beams have the effect of turning the masts into vertical Vierendeel structures of considerable stiffness. The fabricated tubes have diameters reduced from 1.400 to 800 mm from base to top of building, with the wall thickness varying from 100 mm down to 25 mm.

The building forms a rectangle in plan approximately 54 × 70 m, the longer dimension being East-West. The two lines of masts are at 16.2 m centres on the North-South axis with primary floor beams spanning East-West for 33.6 m below the main working areas. Cantilever ends of 10.8 m are provided to accommodate stairs, service modules and lift lobbies. Details of the transfer trusses are given in chapter 17.

Vertically, the structure is divided into five zones by double-height suspension trusses supported by the masts. Every floor is made from in situ concrete carried by a secondary steel structure suspended by tubes from the node points of the nearest truss framework above. Longitudinal stability is provided on the short North-South axis by two-storey X-shaped braces spanning between the main trusses and three storeys deep for the open atrium. The foundations in the bedrock and superstructure are so designed that the building can be increased in area by 30%.

The Bank required a minimum lifespan for the structure of 50 years, so an anti-corrosion treatment was specially formulated. This consisted of a special sprayed mixture of polymer modified cement, sand and stainless steel fibre to a protective thickness of 12 mm, a considerable weight saving over a comparable concrete encasement of 50 mm.

Fire protection for the masts and trusses is provided by ceramic fibre blanket fixed to a stainless steel mesh. The external encasement is fluoropolymer coated 5 mm aluminium sheathing fabricated by Cupples Products, the USA-based specialist who was responsible for all the external cladding and glazing.

The most advanced computer-aided techniques were used coupled with exhaustive testing in the design of the structure

(e) perspective section of typical one bay office floor; (f) plan of banking hall level; (g) view of atrium showing sunscoop lighting all levels.

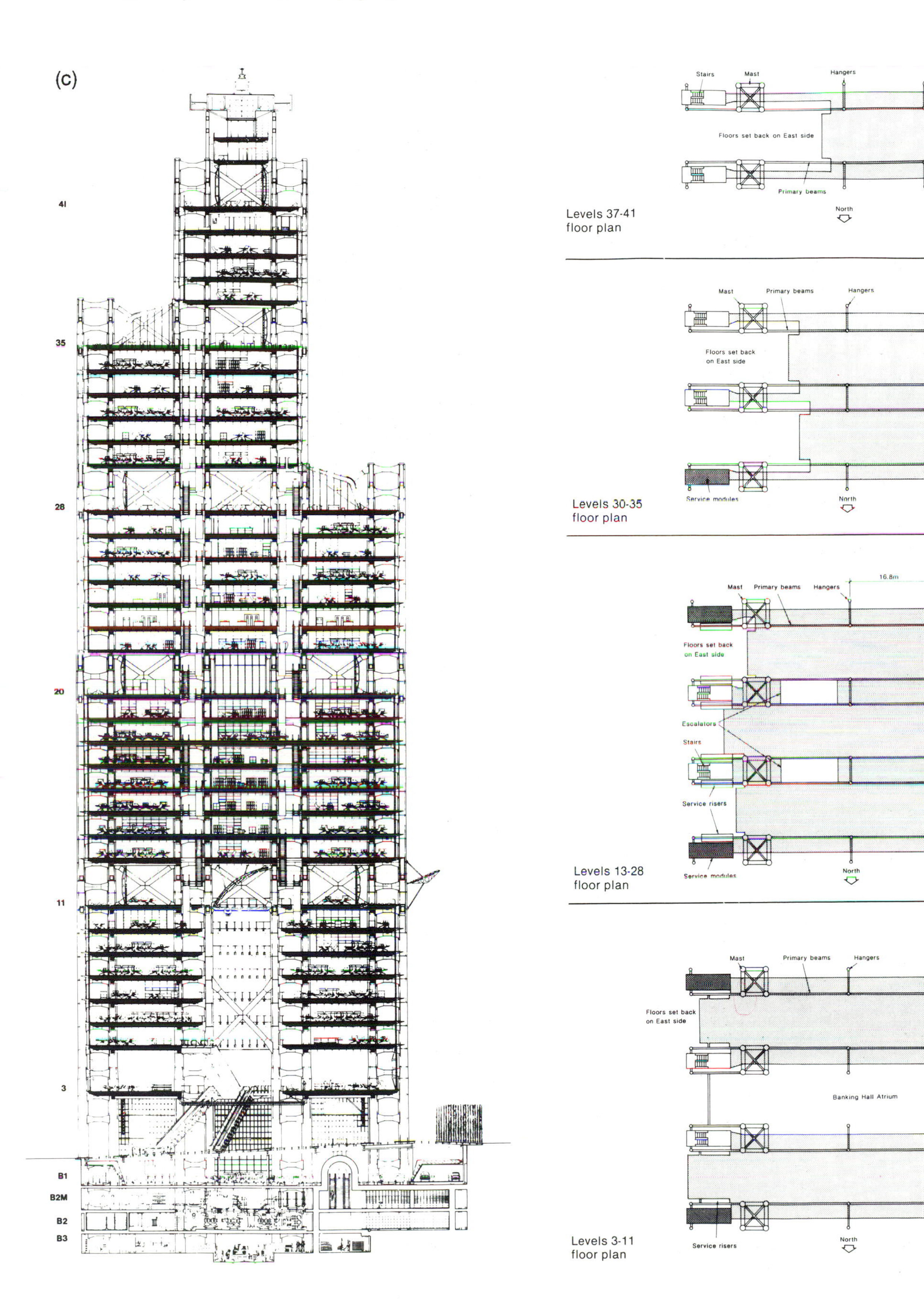

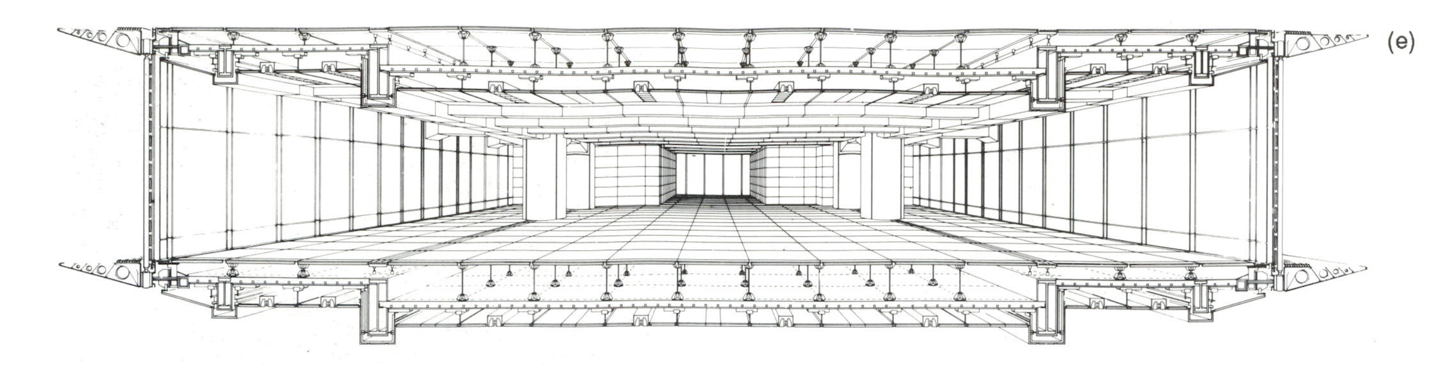
(e)

and cladding. Wind loading, in an area which regularly experiences typhoons, was of particular importance to the structural design. It was necessary to obtain exact information on wind behaviour to predict the size and nature of any conceivable combination of wind loads. For this purpose the University of Western Ontario carried out wind tunnel tests utilizing a 1:500 scale model, including all structure present and projected, round the new building, and another model at 1:2500 scale analysing wind regimes throughout the territory. Based on this data, the structure has been calculated to deflect to a maximum of 300 mm under the statutory equivalent station wind load.

The architectural solution is unlike the cosmetic treatment of skyscrapers favoured in the United States, where a veil of mirror glass or a skin of patterned materials is drawn across the frame. Foster's language is a direct expression of the structure, the complex forms relating to the complexity of the design brief. Light angles and planning codes required set backs, hence the breakdown of the main volumes into three differing heights. The internal arrangement of the bank led to the varied floor layouts, the suspended structure permitting complete flexibility in using the central space between the structural masts. Fire security has been met by double storey lobbies that split the vertical circulation into five lobby areas, escalator access being the preferred route in the office modules between floors. There is a consistent quality of excellence in the differing zones of the building, whether director's suite, banking area or public spaces. There is no diminution of experience at street level, nor aggrandizment into 'Bankers Georgian' that disfigures the Lloyds building. The armature and skin of the architecture is clearly articulated with finely made details at every interface, the finest example of the 'state of the art' constructed in the 1980s.

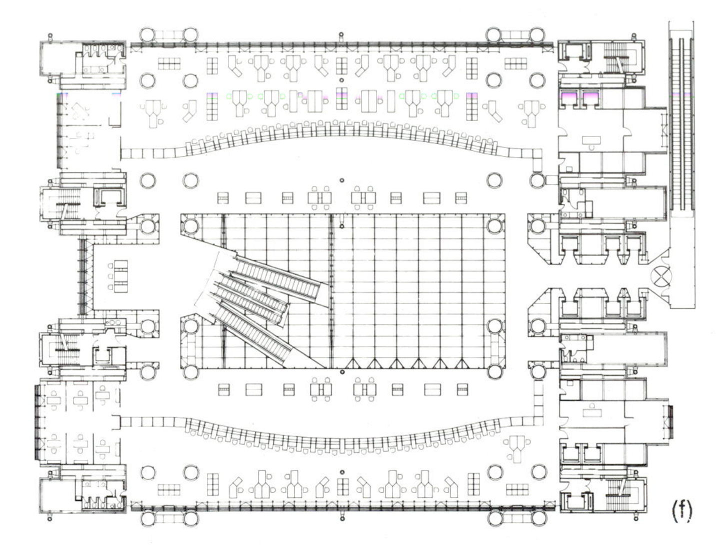
(f)

(g)

References

1. Norman Foster: Foster Associates Volume 3, *Buildings and Projects* 1978–1985, pp 112–255, published by Watermark.
2. *The Architectural Review*, April 1986.

37.9 PRINCESS OF WALES CONSERVATORY, KEW GARDENS (1986)

Architect: Property Services Agency
Engineer: Department of Environment
Project architect: Gordon Wilson
Steelwork: Blight and White Ltd

Portal framing principles are explained in chapter 12, and are here used to meet the clients' requirements of minimal shading and easy access for maintenance. The conservatory replaces a range of greenhouses built over the past 150 years, a whole spectrum of tropical and semi-tropical plants is now accommodated under one roof. The collection is housed in various climatic zones, differing volumes accommodate the various types. Tanking systems used for pools meant that monolithic reinforced concrete retaining walls, fenders and slabs were formed for the basements and ground structures. Steelwork was reserved for portal roof elements and entry porches. The climate within the glass houses is extremely hostile with hot, humidair, condensation and mist sprays to simulate tropical rain forests. Cleaning down also occurs on a regular basis with high pressure water sprays. The steel detailing has avoided bolted connections in exposed situations, site welding ensuring continuity without crevices. Base plates and portal feet are cast within 100 mm of concrete to provide protection at vulnerable points. The steelwork protection system is paint based, allowing for grit blasting, flame spraying with chlorinated rubber paint (175 microns).The gutters are all demountable and independent of the structure. The pattern of varied pitched roof volumes provides a perfect, uncluttered setting for the outstanding plants of this Kew collection. The subtle grading of the site whereby the larger volumes are stepped down into the ground gives the least intrusion into the landscape setting of Kew Gardens. The design demonstrates the true simplicity that can be achieved in well detailed structural steelwork.

Fig. 37.9 *(a) View from the grounds; (b) interior view; (c) exterior view; (d) plan.*

(a)

(b)

(c)

(d)

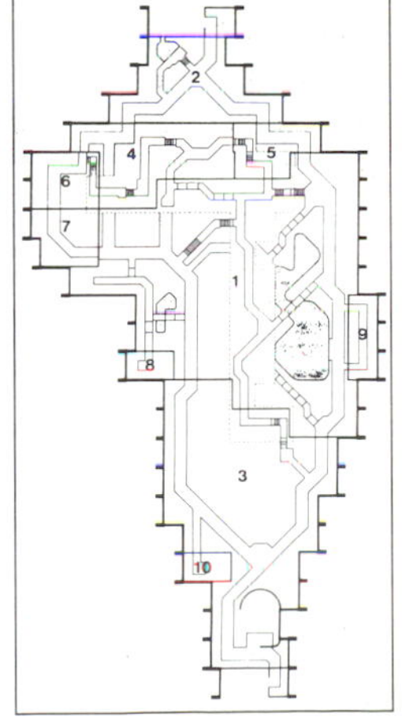

Left, plan showing 1 display zone, 2 ferns, 3 ferns, 4 orchids, 5 orchids, 6 carnivorous plants, 7 tropical zone, 8 cloud forest, 9 arid zone, 10 plant resources.

Fig. 37.10 *(a) Aerial view; (b) main building and loading dock.*

37.10 WESTERN RIVERSIDE SOLID WASTE TRANSFER STATION, LONDON (1987)

Architect: Chamberlain, Powell, Bon and Woods
Engineer: Mott, Hay and Anderson
Steelwork: Robert Watson and Co. (Steelwork) Ltd, Bristol

Steelwork Awards are often for simple straightforward building frames. The Waste Transfer Station is typical of this category and comprises a large clear storey lit plant room with external steelwork for gantries and the dockside cranes. The building use may be mundane but the exposed steelwork imparts a dignity to the fundamental elements of the building and to the craneways. The same functional tradition saw the development of 19th century engineering with the Sheerness Boat Store, referred to in chapter 1. The riverside qualities have been well captured by the designers with brickwork enclosures at dock and streetside facades coupled to reinforced concrete decks and quayside construction. The steelwork has a fine scale with the pitched roof clad in coated steel giving a dramatic form to the skyline. The colour and character of materials are well contrasted in a vigorous composition of steel, brickwork and reinforced concrete.

(a)

(b)

Fig. 37.11 *(a) Gable elevation; (b) section and plan, the toned area on plan indicates rubber flooring; (c) central circulation route; (d) environmental design section.*

37.11 FLEET VELMEAD INFANTS SCHOOL FOR HAMPSHIRE COUNTY COUNCIL (1988)

Architect: Michael Hopkins and Partners Ltd
Engineer: Buro Happold
Steelwork: Tubeworkers Ltd

The deep plan form follows that developed for other Hampshire schools with the accommodation planned either side of a central corridor. Corridor is a misnomer since the spine is linked to the teaching spaces on either side which gives a very spacious quality to the whole interior. The 'barn' roof, rising from 3.2 to 5 m, is supported by twin columns along the spine with a clear run of barrel rooflights end to end of the major volume.

(a)

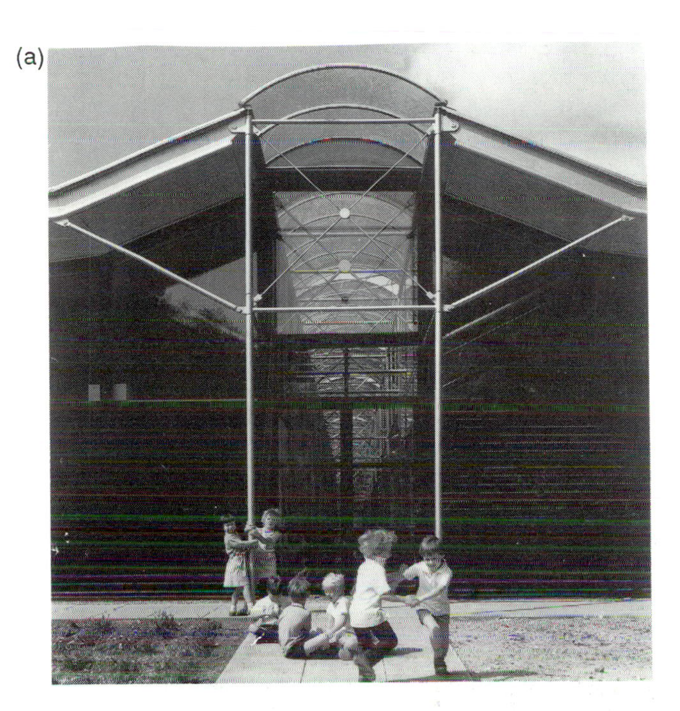

(b)

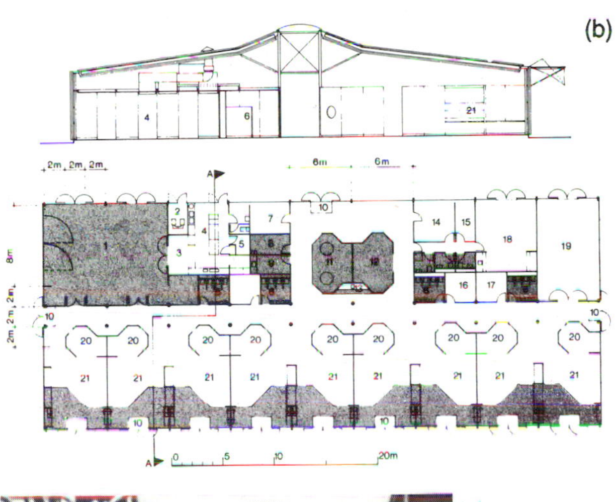

The single storey exposed frame comprises tubular elements fabricated with plated webs for wall columns or with welded Tees to form the main roof beams (cranked at the propping point). The wall columns are of dumbell shape made from two 76 mm diameter CHS, the inner line of tubes doubling as rainwater pipes. The head tie is made by a welded structural channel that in turn forms a gutter profile fitted with an insulated GRP liner. Lateral stability is provided by the braced mast structure to the spine linked by props to the cranked main beams. The principal frame dimensions accommodate the basic teaching module of 6 × 10 m.

The architectural expression follows the philosophy clearly developed in the Hopkins House from the 1970s: firstly, the honest expression of the structure, inside and out; secondly, the absolute refinement of the structure as the principal contributor to architectural form. Finally there is the transparency to weld together the interior spaces and to relate inside and outside.

(c)

(d)

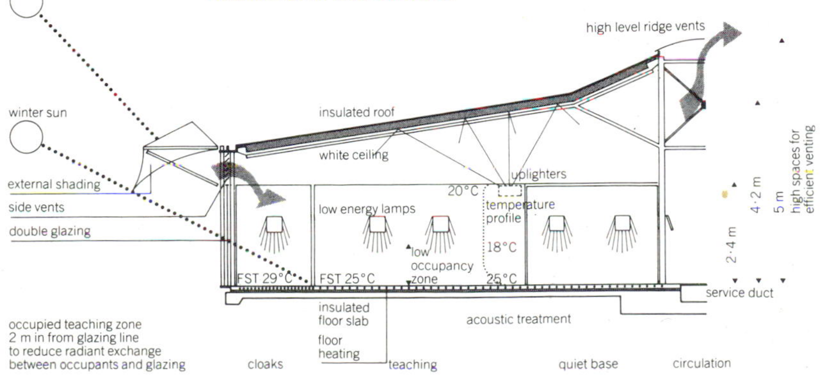

Fig. 37.12 *(a) Model of phases 1–4; (b) phase III under construction; (c) detail of glazing; (d) sculpture; (e) Broadgate Arena; (f) Broadgate Arena, detail of terraces; (g) Broadgate Arena, detail of facades.*

37.12 BROADGATE (PHASES 1–4), LONDON FOR ROSEHAUGH STANHOPE DEVELOPMENTS PLC IN PARTNERSHIP WITH BRITISH RAIL PROPERTY BOARD (1988)

Architect: Arup Associates
Engineer: Arup Associates
Steelwork: Redpath Dorman Long Ltd

The development at Broadgate, which is the largest commercial development undertaken in Europe with a total construction involving 500 000 m^2 on a 26 acre site, illustrates the 'advantages of steel'. The developers, Rosehaugh Stanhope, appointed Arup Associates for the first 150 000 m^2 built. Fast-track construction is integral to the building process at Broadgate, the initial management contract being with Bovis Construction. The planning history concerning Broadgate is typical of our time, with something like 15 years for the gestation period, whilst various proposals and public appeals were prepared. The actual lead-in time to construction and site work was by contrast extremely short, phases 1–4 being two years from inception to handover. The economic pressures for speed were largely due to the bank rate and post-inflation economics.

The key advantage of steel framing at Broadgate has been the use of off site prefabrication for not only frame but also facade elements, providing speed and quality assurance in building production. It is worth dwelling on this as it represents the largest application of a new concept whereby prefabricated steel framing for envelope and structure enable the highest speed of assembly to be obtained. Similar techniques have been used since World War II for high-rise buildings in North America and increasingly in Europe, where rain-screen facades are commonplace. Broadgate simply follows this trend. The inflation in land prices around the Liverpool Street area has seen prices rising 200–300% in recent years with labour rates up 50% in 1986–87. These pressing economic factors are the reason for the emphasis on offsite work and for the virtual elimination of wet trades.

A significant trend in the current work of Arup Associates is the development of rain-screen facades constructed over steel frames. These also incorporate much of the heating and ventilation facilities and are craned into position complete with cladding and fenestration, current techniques allowing for a composite veneer of glass, granite and metal cladding. The present taste for a pattern, symbolic of framing but not directly expressing the frame versus the panel, can be seen in the later phases (5–14) by Skidmore, Owings and Merrill. The total construction period has been five years from 1985 until 1990, the accommodation eventually providing an environment for 41 000 office workers. It has led to the creation of a virtual town within the city with its own public spaces and squares. Broadgate has been criticized as oversized but in reality it is simply reflective of the scale of contemporary urban regeneration where 19th century efforts in the railway age are remodelled for the 21st century. The Great Eastern Railway, in its time, tore apart the eastern approaches to the City, adding pollution and congestion for good measure.

(a)

(b)

In contrast, Broadgate provides a traffic-free island and a newly made Broadgate Arena, the first public space created in London for pleasure since Sir Hugh Casson's 'Fairways', the outdoor dance floor constructed on the South Bank, in 1951. The surrounding buildings were the steel-framed centrepiece of that exhibition, which, despite the Korean War, took only two years to complete – the same time as spent on site for Broadgate phases 1–4.

(c)

(d)

(e)

(f)

(g)

Fig. 37.13 *(a) View of doors to runway; (b) view from runway; (c) aerial view; (d) plan; (e) aerial view; (f) detail view of roof trusses; (g) general view of building and ancillary accommodation.*

37.13 STANSTED MAINTENANCE FACILITY FOR FFV AEROTECH LTD (1989)

Architect: Faulks Perry Culley and Rech
Engineer: Burks Green and Partners and Sir Frederick Snow and Partners
Steelwork: Hunt Steel and Cladding Ltd

The diamond-shaped hangar developed from the brief's spatial requirements accommodates a pair of B747 Jumbo jets at one time. The dual triangular working areas lead to a non-rectangular form which saves roughly 20% in volume compared with the usual oblong shed. The engineering solution provided one of the largest column-free spaces constructed in Europe, 170 × 98 m with a clear height of 23 m. The back up zone comprises a covered service road cum fire separation area, while the remaining buildings to the 'landside' periphery are two ranges of workshops, each 75 × 30 m and a central office block.

The hangar roof was originally designed to have 6 m depth trusses. Considerable savings were made by Burks Green and Partners by adjusting the design of the cubic space frame for the roofing to provide two directional trusses on the Vierendeel principle. Each module was jig welded and made to cruciform profile 2.0 × 3.5 with a 4 m depth. Connections were made by splice plates on site without further welding. A pre-camber was arranged in the setting out to ensure a 1 m fall to the outer edges of the roof surfaces. The Vierendeel does not require diagonal bracing, this permitting the 4 m depth of roof deck to fully accommodate services in both directions. This vast structure is supported by sets of corner columns designed as cantilevers from a fixed base, each cluster is 3 m^2 with 356 × 406 UC sections. The remainder of the structure is conventional steelwork for offices and workshops.

Considerable care was taken to reduce the visual impact of the building mass. The colours were selected to reduce the contrast between the building and the sky, allowing it to visually 'recede' into the background when viewed from middle and in particular long distances. The horizontal banding of white, silver and grey enhances the horizontality. The main cladding comprises coated profiled steel sheet with sophisticated composite panels employed for the office facades.

Environmental considerations within the hanger space led to artificial lighting to provide 800 lux at floor level, the white quartz tipping to the floor ensuring reflected light into the underwing areas. Heating operates on a recycling principle so that rising heat and sources from lighting fixtures are blown downward within high velocity ducts, for distribution at a 6 m height above floor level.

The Vierendeel space frame has provided the most effective enclosure to a well considered working environment and containing an engineering tradition that produced the innovative Cardington and Brabazon hangars of times past.

(a)

(b)

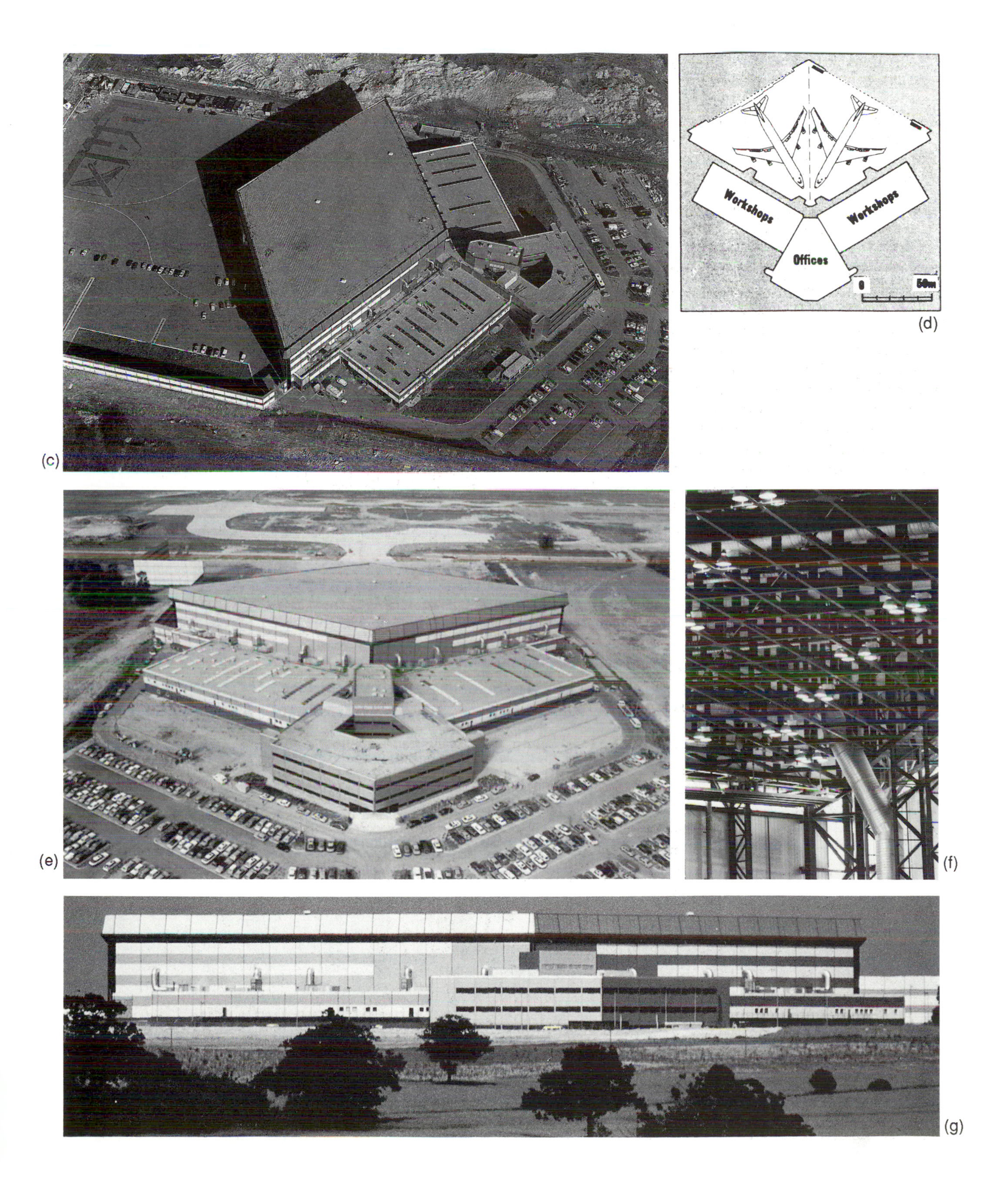

(c) (d) (e) (f) (g)

Fig. 38.1 *The future is today. Interior, showing 'cycle truss' to roof of David Mellor's factory at Hathersage, Derbyshire (architects Michael Hopkins and Partners: engineers Whitby and Bird).*

38

Futures

Mark Whitby and Alan Blanc

38.1 INTRODUCTION

The 20th century has witnessed changes brought about by engineering inventions and scientific investigations that are as fundamental as those of the industrial revolution. Just as the mass production of iron, the generation of power from steam engines and the creation of machine tools transformed society in the 19th century, the mass production of steel, the application of various forms of power, the investigation of radioactivity and the development of medicine have fashioned the 20th century.

Inspired by the French military's concern about the weakness of cast iron guns during the Crimean War, Bessemer pioneered the process for mass producing steel. Before 1856, it had only been produced in batches of up to 40 kg, but the Bessemer process radically reduced the cost of steel and made it possible to make castings over 5000 kg. The process rapidly revolutionized the style and manufacture of armaments which completely changed the conduct of war. However it was not until 1890 that the first all-steel bridge was built although a steel ship had been constructed as early as 1863.

38.2 20TH CENTURY DEVELOPMENTS

In the 20th century successive generations have fashioned applications from steel, electricity and radioactivity – developing the internal combustion engine, jet and space travel, electric light, radio, the computer, atomic power and so on.

Britain's first production motor cars were manufactured by Lanchester in 1901, who as early as 1892 had proposed manufacturing a lightweight internal combustion engine for flying machines. French and American engineers pioneered flight, but the British developed designs which led to the supercharged Rolls Royce Merlin engine of the Second World War. These developments led directly to the successful production of jet engines, whose application made possible Whittle's dream of high level flight and the jet air liner as it is known today.

To Lanchester, who died in 1946, such progress must have been quite extraordinary, with the organizations involved becoming quite beyond the control of a single man and his factory. These 20th century achievements are the result of considerable teamwork – operations where individuals have worked together in teams for a common ambition with remarkable success. However, such success brings with it the need to maintain very complicated systems. For example, in the case of the jet aeroplane, infrastructure of support ranges from satellite navigation systems and airports to engine maintenance and ticket sales.

38.3 TRENDS INTO THE 21ST CENTURY

This century has witnessed proposals to build huge structures, mile high buildings, covered cities in Alberta, wonderworlds for amusement, and cities literally floating at sea – each the ultimate in technology. But whilst the last mentioned must have serious application in the creation of new territory, all are now questioned both for their extravagance and unnecessary complexity.

These elaborate uses of technology cannot be justified as we move into the 21st century. This new age may well witness as significant a change as both of the preceding centuries, with the desire for progress being tempered by an evaluation of the risks and a greater respect for the individual. The main restriction on development will be the global consideration of the environment and use of energy, the impact of such proposals on the community, and a realization of our inability to manage our own creations. An integrated, whole life design approach considering all of these issues will be necessary, with an energy and environment audit taking account of materials, manufacture, construction, building usage, servicing, maintenance and finally demolition and recycling. This will require a fundamental review of recent design strategies and may result in some novel solutions, whilst others may revert to less advanced methods of construction.

38.4 THE INFLUENCE OF COMPUTERS

Computers as agents for change are probably in the same league as the technologies that were developing at the end of the 19th century. Many of these steps forward depended upon new materials or new methods of production. For instance, the change from the forging of wrought iron to the mass production of steel affected the art of building within two decades. That trend led to steel construction and reinforced concrete dominating framing methods for buildings in the 20th century.

A more oblique comparison can be made in the field of warfare. Computer science has revolutionized artillery and naval weaponry in the 1990s, as did the material sciences developed by the Krupps armaments empire in the period 1870–1890, combining steel and high explosive.

The continuing development of computer applications for the design of structures will make for significant savings, particularly where modes of failure are analysed or energy consumption modelled. Factors of safety can be established within a structure, and the sizing of the member will reflect this. For elements where failure may not lead to a progressive collapse, it will become possible and therefore justifiable to apply lower factors of safety than those applied to a member whose collapse could jeopardize the stability of the total structure.

Furthermore, designers will be able to adopt a more holistic approach to buildings, choosing solutions which will be based on considerations of a broader nature – choosing for instance structural materials for their ability to meet thermal requirements – concrete for buildings requiring a stable environment, steel for buildings subject to intermittent use.

Similarly, design for fire resistance will become very much more refined. Computer models will enable a more rational explanation of the consequences of design decisions, such that designs can, particularly with steel, be less inhibited by rules which are sometimes arbitrary as applied at present.

38.5 DESIGN LEGISLATION

Engineering and architecture are currently governed by rules which relate to environmental, spatial and structural criteria. These rules, however, can limit the design to such a degree that interest in creative solutions is stifled. It should be possible to relax codes of practice and evaluate the context and behaviour of a building in a more creative manner, with the consequence that, driven by a need for honesty and economy, more buildings will express their structure. Iron or steel loadbearing facades will become practical, and as a result, buildings will become more honest, echoing the values of some Victorian buildings which will serve as a precedent.

With the power of the computer, the designer will be able to fulfil the apparent dream of all the building professionals by becoming akin to his ancestral counterpart. Unlike the aeroplane pilot who was created as a result of technology and who is now almost redundant as a result of it, the new age professional who has been dominated by the technology, will at last be freed by it.

In Europe the decade of the 1980s has seen a remarkable development in building technology. There is little doubt that British engineers have led the field in structural steelwork and will continue to do so through the 1990s.

38.6 STEEL ARCHITECTURE FOR THE NEXT EPOCH

Mark Whitby's optimism for the future of steel engineering stems from the advent of the computer age and the way these facilities can maximize skills and minimize the amount of material used in a structure. It is demonstrated in the design work of his consultancy, Whitby and Bird, where refinement whittles down the elements to the minimum possible size (Figs 38.1 and 38.2). The welcome forecast that building codes will be adjusted to the increasing ability to make accurate complex calculations implies the lightest possible structures in the future. This conjures up a mental picture of gossamer threads in the sky (Fig. 38.3).

38.7 THE NEW REVOLUTION

The revolution in computer skills is equal to the leap forward in metal engineering techniques that occurred in the later 18th and early 19th centuries, illustrated by Dennis Sharp in chapter 1. Readers will have noted that the established architectural aesthetics of the last century hardly recognized the qualities revealed by the pioneer engineers, Brunel, Stephenson or Telford. Dennis Sharp rightly affirms that it was the Modern Movement which championed the virtues of 19th century engineering. In other words, the architectural attributes were not fully discerned until the following epoch. It would be surprising if the present rapid evolution in design technology were fully assimilated by the majority of architects except in superficial aspects such as the pattern making that is the hallmark of Post-Modernism. This and the other decorative 'isms' that cloud the millenium tempt one to coin a phrase for the fin de siècle that envelopes us. Let us call it the 'ismatic' phase that embraces every variety of decadent revival (Fig. 38.4). When questioned as to the future, Walter Segal replied that nothing much will happen that is new in design, until the 'grandiloquent' has disappeared from view.

38.8 MECHANIZATION TAKES COMMAND

The present superfluity of architectural styles is reflective of consumerism, the overpowering need for self expression prevails whilst economic forces drive building production towards repetitive forms. This premise that 'mechanization takes command' is the advanced edge of our construction industry in the UK and in much of the developed world. The economics of mechanization are at the root of Modern Architecture and is one reason why this much abused style

Fig. 38.2 (b) Tropical Bird Aviary, London Zoo (architect John S. Bonnington Partnership: engineer Whitby and Bird).

Fig. 38.3 *Mile wide cable structure for Shale Oil Field in northern Alberta (engineer Buro Happold and Frei Otto).*

Fig. 38.4 *The 1991 proposal for Paternoster Square, London. An 'ismatic' phase for the fin de siècle.*

has a virile ability to adapt or outlive the 'ismatic'. Either way factory made elements will be part of the future building scene, with steel being as significant in the 21st century as in the 20th.

38.9 THE FUTURE OF THE PAST

Reverting to historic vision, the past and future are intrinsically linked on both the aesthetic and technical fronts, but not from a conservationists viewpoint. Bodies such as The Civic Trust, who devised the slogan 'The Future of the Past' overlook the possibility of the leap into the unknown. Today's innate conservatism would have stalled the innovations of Brunelleschi, Brunel and Frei Otto. A future tied to the architecture of the immediate past would have similarly precluded Haussmann's Paris or Nash's London. A competition in London Docklands in the late 1980s where the 'modern' solution was put aside for the 'decadent', led Martin Pawley to write that we were witnessing a revival of Teutonic ideas from the late 1930s, namely 'blood and hearth' for housing, 'neo-classic' for public building and 'Hi-Tech' for industry. A tour of Docklands from the light railway confirms this dismal view.

Steel framing certainly represents a significant part of the new Docklands, whatever the architectural style, leading a visiting Dutch architect to be most complimentary on the elegance of the new frames and especially the tower cranes (Fig. 38.5)! He complained strongly however that the cladding appeared to be a serious crime (Fig. 38.5). The vaguely Edwardian imagery given to Canary Wharf will surely strike the next generation as a chronic lack of faith in modern materials.

38.10 OPTIMISM FOR THE FUTURE

There are optimistic signs of revolt by young architects against the boredom of historicism, judging by recent student awards. It is also significant that Britain's advanced engineers are joining with progressive designers in achieving competition successes outside Britain (Fig. 38.5).

Visually the offices at Marseilles resemble the Wellsian vision of the 'Shape of Things to Come', perhaps a welcome sign that the 21st century beckons. To many Modernists 'the future is today' and there is sufficient healthy evidence in the past half century to reveal that Modern Architecture, (in Dennis Sharp's terms) still thrives and will continue to blossom afresh with each generation.

An economic and political forecast as to which materials will dominate the market is impossible to tell. There is however, one certainty that any advanced building technology will utilize steel technology in some form or another.

Fig. 38.5 *Frames at Canary Wharf, London Docklands.*

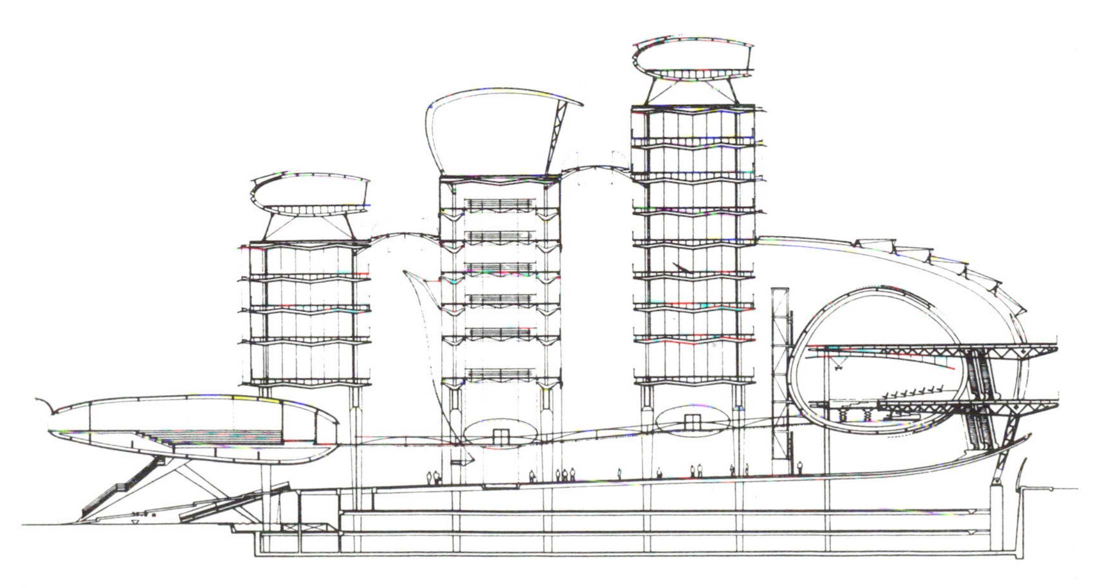

Fig. 38.6 *Offices at Marseilles. The 'Shape of Things to Come' (architect Alsop and Stormer: engineers Ove Arup and Partners).*

Appendix A

Relevant codes, standards and general publications

USA

ANSI/AWS D.1. 1990. Structural Welding Code – Steel
American Welding Society, 1990

ANSI/ASCE 7–88 (previously ANSI A58.1– 1982)
Minimum Design Loads for Buildings and Other Structures.
American Society for Civil Engineers, 1988.

National Fire Protection Association (NFPA) Fire Codes

ASTM Section I Iron and Steel Products (issued annually in 7 volumes) American Society for Testing and Materials

Manual of Steel Construction: Load and Resistant Factor Design.
American Institute of Steel Construction (AISC) 1986

Specification for Structural Steel Buildings: Load and Resistant Factor Design.
American Institute of Steel Construction (AISC) 1986

Code of Standard Practice for Steel Buildings and Bridges
American Institute of Steel Construction (ASIC) 1875

Steel Structures Painting Manual (2 volumes)
Steel Structures Painting Council.

CANADA

CAN/CSA S16.1–M89
Steel Structures for Buildings: Limit States Design
Canadian Standards Association, 1989

CAN/CSA.20–M87
General Requirements for Rolled or Welded Structural Quality Steel
Canadian Standards Association, 1987

CANM/CSA G40.21–M87
Structural Quality Steel
Canadian Standards Association, 1987

Handbook of Steel Construction: 4th edn
Canadian Institute of Steel Construction.

AUSTRALIA

AS 4100 – 1990
Steel Structures
Standards Australia, 1990

AS 1170-2: 1989
Loading Code – Minimum Design Loads on Structures
Part 2: Wind loads
Standards Association of Australia: 1989.

See also publications from the Australian Institute of Steel Construction.

INTERNATIONAL ORGANIZATION FOR STANDARDIZATION (ISO)

ISO 630: 1980
Structural Steels.

ISO 657 (published in various parts)
Hot Rolled Steel Sections.

ISO 8501-1: 1988
Preparation of Steel Substrates before Application of Paints and Related Products.

Appendix B

Advisory Services for the Steel Construction Industry

UNITED KINGDOM

The Steel Construction Institute
Silkwood Park
Ascot
Berkshire SL5 7QN
Telephone: 0344 23345
Fax: 0344 22944

Office also at:
Unit 820, Birchwood Boulevard
Birchwood, Warrington
Cheshire WA3 7QZ
Telephone: 0925 838655
Fax: 0925 838676

European Office:
B03040 Huldenberg
52 De Limburg
Stirumlaan
Belgium
Telephone: Int + 32 2 687 8532
Fax: Int + 32 2 687 7094

British Steel plc Sections
British Steel General Steels
Commercial Office – Sections
PO Box 24, Recar
Cleveland TS10 5Q L
Telephone: 0642 474111
Fax: 0642 489466

Plates
British Steel General Steels
Commercial Office – Plates
PO Box 30, Motherwell
Lanarkshire ML1 1AA
Telephone: 0698 66233
Fax: 0698 62020

Steel Piling Products
British Steel General Steels
Piling Technical Services
PO Box 1, Scunthorpe
South Humberside DN16 1BP
Telephone: 0724 280280
Fax: 0724 282040

Underground Roadway Supports
British Steel General Steels
Underground Roadway Supports Technical Services
PO Box 1, Scunthorpe
South Humberside DN16 1BP
Telephone: 0724 280280
Fax: 0724 282040

Tubes
British Steel General Steels
Welded Tubes
PO Box 101, Corby
Northamptonshire NN17 1UA
Telephone: 0536 402121
Fax: 0536 404005

Strip Products
British Steel Strip Products
PO Box 10, Newport
Gwent NP9 0XN
Telephone: 0633 290022
Fax: 0633 272933

Stainless Steel
Avesta Sheffield Ltd
PO Box 161, Shepcote Lane
Sheffield S9 1TR
Telephone: 0742 443311
Fax: 0742 448280
also: 0742 443311 Ext 4127

Regional Structural Advisory Service London and South East
42–44 Grosvenor Gardens
London SW1W 0EB
Telephone: 071 235 1212
Fax: 071 259 9066

West Midlands and North West
Midland House
New Road, Halesowen
West Midlands B63 3HY
Telephone: 021 585 5522
Fax: 021 585 5241

South West and South Wales
Tower House
Fairfax Street
Bristol BS1 3BZ
Telephone: 0272 290461
Fax: 0272 252157

North West
The Genesis Centre
Science Park South
Garrett Field, Birchwood
Warrington WA3 7BH
Telephone: 0925 822838
Telex: 627038
Fax: 0925 838769

Scotland and Northern Lakes
PO Box 30, Motherwell
Lanarkshire ML1 1AA
Telephone: 0698 66233
Fax: 0698 62020

Ireland (and Eire)
Leeson Court
88 Lower Leeson Street
Dublin 2
Telephone: Int + 3531 616773/616761
Fax: Int + 3531 616773 Ext 216

Hot line
(A 'hot line' service is operated to help customers if the local engineer is unavailable, the number for Sections is 0642 474242 and Fax 0642 489466; the number for Tubes is 0536 404120.)

The British Construction Steelwork Association Ltd
4 Whitehall Court
Westminster
London SW1A 2ES
Telephone: 071 839 8566
Fax: 071 976 1634

OVERSEAS

Australia

Australian Institute of Steel Construction (AISC)
BP House, 100 Alfred Street
PO Box 434
Milsons Point, NSW2061
(Steel Fabricators Association)
Att: Mr A. Firkins
Telephone: Int + 61-2/9296666
Fax: Int + 61-2/9555406

Austria

Österreichischer Stahlbau Verband (ÖSTV)
Larochegasse 28
A – 1130 Wien
(Steel Fabricators Association & Steel Industry Information Centre)
Att: Dipl Ing H Massiczek
Telephone: Int + 43/222/826170
Tlx: 134-827 wbw a
Fax: Int + 43/222/2244333

Belgium

Fabrimental, Groupe 5
rue des Drapiers 21
B - 1050 Bruxelles
(Steel Fabricators Association)
Att: Mr M. Dewez
Telephone: Int + 32-2/5102311
Tlx: 21078 b
Fax: 32-2/5102301

Centre Belgo-Luxembourgeois D'Information De L'Acier (CBLIA)
Rue Montoyer 47
1040 Bruxelles
(Steel Industry Information Centre)
Att: Mr P Brochgraeve
Telephone: Int + 32 2 509 1411
Fax: Int + 32 2 509 1400

Brazil

Brazilian Association of Steel Construction
CEP 01452
Sao Paulo sp
(Steel Fabricators Association)
Telephone: Int + 55 11 212 3699
Tlx: 11.32514 abcm br

Instituto Brasileiro de Siderurgia
Rua Araujo Porto Alegre, 36
7 Andar – Rio de Janeiro - RJ
CEP 20030
Att: M. Moacelio de Aguiar Mandes
Telephone: Int + 55 21 210 3255
Fax: Int + 55 21 22725

Canada

Canadian Institute of Steel Construction (CISC)
Suite 300
201 Consumers Road
Willowdale
Ontario
(Steel Fabricators Association)
Att: Mr H. A. Krentz
Telephone: Int + 416-4914552
Tlx: 6-986547
Fax: Int + 416-4916461

Denmark

Dansk Stalinstitut
Overgade 21-2
DK – 5000 Odense C
(Steel Fabricators Association and Steel Industry Information Centre)
Att: Mr B. Nielsen
Telephone: Int + 45-66/130888
Fax: Int + 45-65/918789

Finland

Federation of Finnish Metal & Engineering Industries
Eteläranta 10
SF – 00130 Helsinki 13
Att: Dipl Ing P Kaunisto
Telephone: Int + 358-0/19231
Tlx: 124997 fimet sf
Fax: Int + 358-0/6244462

Federation of Finnish Metal, Engineering & Electro-Technical Industries
Fredrikinkatu 51–53
00100 Helsinki
Att: Mr Jukka Mantayala
Telephone: Int + 358 0 68081
Fax: Int + 358 0 6808288

The Finnish Constructional Steelwork Association (FCSA)
PO Box 623
Fredrikinkatu 51–53 B
SF – 00101 Helsinki
(Steel Fabricators Association & Steel Industry Information Centre)
Att: Mr P. Sandberg
Telephone: Int + 358 0 6948630
Fax: Int + 358 0 6948577

France

Syndicat de la Construction Metallique de France
20 rue Jean Jaurès
F – 92807 Puteaux Cedex
(Steel Fabricators Association)
Att: Mr H. Libert
Telephone: Int + 33-1/47746615
Fax: Int + 33-1/40900860

Centre Technique Industriel de la Construction Metallique (CTICM)
Domaine de St Paul
(Steel Research Association)
78470 St Rémy lès Chevreuse
Att: Mr M. Parmantier
Telephone: Int + 33 1 30852000
Fax: Int + 33 1 30527538

Office Technique pour l'Utilisation de l'Acier (OTUA)
19 Le Parvis
Immeuble Elysees La Defense
Cedex 35
92072 Paris La Defense 4
(Steel Industry Information Centre)
Att: Mr H. Bommart
Telephone: Int + 33 1 4767 8775
Tlx: 611672 SISYNDI
Fax: Int + 33 1 4767 8577

Germany

Deutscher Stahlbauverband (DSTV)
Ebertplatz 1
D – 5000 Koln 1
(Steel Fabricators Association)
Att: Dr Ing K. Kunert
Telephone: Int + 49-221/77310
Fax: Int + 49-221/7731121

Stahl-Informations-Zentrum (SIZ)
Breite Strasse 69
Postfach 16 11
Dusseldorf
(formerly Berantungstelle für Stahlverwendung)

(Steel Industry
Information Centre)
Telephone: Int + 49 211 829369
Tlx: 8582286 D
Fax: Int + 49 211 82931

Studiengesellschaft für Anwendungstechnik von Eisen & Stahl
Kasernenstrasse 36
Postfach 1611
4000 Dusseldorf 1
(Steel Industry Information Centre)
Att: Dr Ing Ekkehard Schulz
Telephone: Int + 49 211 829 318
Tlx: 211713
Fax: Int + 49 211 829 231

Italy

Associazione Fra I Cost. In Acciaio Italiani (ACAI)
Viale Abruzzi 66
I – 20131 Milan
(Steel Fabricators Association)
Att: Dr Ing G. Vannacci
Telephone: Int + 39-2/ 29513143-29513175
Fax: Int + 39-2/221324

Federacciai
Piazza Velasca 8
20122 Milan
(formerly ASSIDER SIDERSERVIZI)
(Steel Industry Information Centre)
Att: Dr G. De Martino
Telephone: Int + 39 2 860 351
Fax: Int + 39 2 72022206

Associanzione Svilluppo Strutture Acciaio (ASSA)
20133 Milano
via Molino Delle Armi 4
Att: Dr Ing Angelo de Prisco
Telephone: Int + 392 7601 5287/298
Fax: Int + 392 7601 52965

Japan

Society of Steel Construction of Japan (JSSC)
848 Shin Tokyo Building
3-3-1 Marunouchi
Chiyoda-ku
J – Tokyo 100
(Steelmakers Organization)
Att: Mr A. Miki
Telephone: Int + 813-212-0875
Fax: Int + 813-212-0878

Iron and Steel Institute of Japan
Keidanren Kaiden, 3rd Floor
9–4 Otemachi I-chome
Chiyoda - Ku
J – Tokyo 100
(Steelmakers Organisation)
Att: Mr Yashuhiro Yagi
Telephone: Int + 813 279 6021
Tlx: 02228153 isijtkj
Fax: Int + 813 245 1355

Kozai Club
Tekko Kaikan Building
3–2–10 Nihonbashi-Kayabacho
Chuo-ku
Tokyo
(Steel Designers Society)
Telephone: Int + 813 3669 4811
Tlx: 02523607
Fax: Int + 813 3667 0245

Luxembourg

Service Recherches et promotion
Techn. Struct. Arbed Recherches
rue de Luxembourg 66 BP 141
L – 4221 Esch/Alzette
Att: Ing Dipl J B Schleich
Telephone: Int + 352-55512130
Tlx: 2167 arech lu
Fax: Int + 352-547964

Netherlands

Branchegroep Staalbouw
Bredewater 20
Postbus 190
NL – 2700 AD
Zoetermeer
(Steel Fabrications Association)
Att: Ing W. Van Der Bilt
Telephone: Int + 31-79/ 219221
Tlx: 32157 fme nl
Fax: Int + 31-79/531365

Stahlbouw-Kunding Gennotschap
Groothandelsgedouw A-4
Postbus 29076
3001 GB Rotterdam
(Steel Designers Society)
Att: Ing R. L. Schipholt
Telephone: Int + 31 10 4110433
Tlx: 26458 staal nl
Fax: Int + 31 10 4121221

Centrum Staal
Groothandelsgebouw A-4
Postbus 29076
3001 GB Rotterdam
(Steel Industry Information Centre)
Att: Ir C. L. Bijl
Telephone: Int + 31 10 4110433
Tlx: 26458 staal nl
Fax: Int + 31 10 4121221

New Zealand

New Zealand Heavy Engineering Research Association
Gladding Place
Manukau City
PO Box 76–134
Auckland
(Steel Fabricators Association & Steel Research Association)
Att: Dr W. L. Richards
Telephone: Int + 64 9 262 2885
Tlx: NZ60334 heranz
Fax: Int + 64 9 262 2756

Norway

Staalkonstruksjonsgruppen i N.V.S.
Postboks 7072-Homansbyen
N – 0306 OSLO 3
(Steel Fabricators Association)
Att: Dr Ing B. Aasen
Telephone: Int + 47-2/ 465820
Tlx: 76625
Fax: Int + 47-2/461838

Singapore

Singapore Structural Steel Society
150 Orchard Road
7–14 Orchard Plaza
Singapore 0923
(Steel Designers Society)
Att: Mr Cheung Lap Yuen
Telephone: Int + 65 5612288
Tlx: RS 35377
Fax: Int + 65 2650951

South Africa

South African Institute of Steel Construction
6th Floor, Swiss House
86 Main Street
Johannesburg 2001
South Africa
(Steel Fabricators Association)
Att: Mr K. O. Horngren
Telephone: Int + 27 11 838 1665
Tlx: 4/86759 SA
Fax: Int + 27 11 834 4301

Sweden

Swedish Institute of Steel Construction (SBI)
Drottning Kristinas väg 48
S – 11428 Stockholm
(Steel Fabricators Association)
Att: Mr Johan Hedin
Telephone: Int + 46-8/24980
Tlx: 12442 fotex s steel
Fax: Int + 46-8/248782

Switzerland

Schweizerishce Zentralstelle fur Stahlbau (SZS)
Seefeldstrasse 25
Postfach 388
CH – 8034 Zurich
(Steel Fabricators Association & Steel Industry Information Centre)
Att: Mr U. Wyss
Telephone: Int + 41-1/2618980
Fax: Int + 41-1/2620962

Turkey

Istanbul Teknik Universitesi
Insaat Fakultesi
80626 Ayazaga
Istanbul
Att: Professor Dr T. S. Arda
Telephone: Int + 90-1/1763814
Tlx: 28186 itü tr
Fax: Int + 90-1/1766587 tr

USA

American Institute of Steel Construction (AISC)
One East Wacker Drive
Suite 3100
Chicago, Ill 60601–2001
(Steel Fabricators Association)
Att: Mr G. Haaijer
Telephone: Int + 1-312/6702400
Tlx: 9103506816
Fax: Int + 1-312/6705403

American Iron and Steel Institute (AISI)
1135 15th Street
Washington, DC 20005–2701
(Steelmakers Organization)
Telephone: Int + 202 452 7184
Fax: Int + 202 463 6573

Iron and Steel Society Inc.
410 Commonwealth Drive
Warrendale
PA 15086
Telephone: Int + 412 776 9460
Tlx: 6503113507
Fax: Int + 412 776 0430

INTERNATIONAL ORGANIZATIONS

European Convention for Constructional Steelwork (ECCS)
32–36 avenue des Ombrages Bte 20
B-1200 Brussels
Belgium
(Steel Fabricators Association)
Att: Mr J. van Neste
Telephone: Int + 32 2 762 0429
Fax: Int + 32 2 762 0935

Eurofer
Square de Meeus 5, Bte 9
1040 Brussels
Belgium
(Steelmakers Organisation)
Telephone: Int + 32 2 512 1580
Tlx: 621 12 eurfer b
Fax: Int + 32 2 512 0146

International Association for Bridge and Structural Engineering (IABSE)
ETH-Hönggerberg
CH 8093 Zurich
Switzerland
Att: Mr A. Gourlay
Telephone: Int + 41 1-377 26 47
Fax: Int + 41 1-371 21 31

International Iron and Steel Institute (IISI)
Rue Colonel Bourg 120
B-1140 Brussels
Belgium
Att: Brian T. Loton
Telephone: Int + 32 2 735 9075
Tlx: 22639
Fax: Int + 32 2 735 8012

Comité International pour le Développement et l'Etude de la Construction Tubulaire (CIDECT)
81 Rue de Belles Feuilles
Paris 16
France
(International Research Organisation for Developing the Use of Hollow Sections in Steel Construction)
Att: Mr J. van Neste
Telephone: Int + 31 1 267 80 80
Tlx: Int + 27002 F

Index of buildings

Page numbers appearing in **bold** refer to figures.

Index of architects and engineers

Page numbers appearing in **bold** refer to figures.

Subject index

Page numbers appearing in **bold** refer to figures and page numbers appearing in *italic* refer to tables.